# Lecture Notes in Computer Science 12935

More information about this subseries at http://www.springer.com/series/7409

Carmelo Ardito · Rosa Lanzilotti ·
Alessio Malizia · Helen Petrie ·
Antonio Piccinno · Giuseppe Desolda ·
Kori Inkpen (Eds.)

# Human-Computer Interaction – INTERACT 2021

18th IFIP TC 13 International Conference
Bari, Italy, August 30 – September 3, 2021
Proceedings, Part IV

 Springer

*Editors*
Carmelo Ardito 🆔
Department of Electrical and Information
Engineering
Polytechnic University of Bari
Bari, Italy

Alessio Malizia 🆔
Computer Science Department
University of Pisa
Pisa, Italy

University of Hertfordshire
Hatfield, United Kingdom

Antonio Piccinno 🆔
Computer Science Department
University of Bari Aldo Moro
Bari, Italy

Kori Inkpen 🆔
Microsoft Research
Redmond, WA, USA

Rosa Lanzilotti 🆔
Computer Science Department
University of Bari Aldo Moro
Bari, Italy

Helen Petrie 🆔
Department of Computer Science
University of York
York, UK

Giuseppe Desolda 🆔
Computer Science Department
University of Bari Aldo Moro
Bari, Italy

ISSN 0302-9743      ISSN 1611-3349  (electronic)
Lecture Notes in Computer Science
ISBN 978-3-030-85609-0      ISBN 978-3-030-85610-6  (eBook)
https://doi.org/10.1007/978-3-030-85610-6

LNCS Sublibrary: SL3 – Information Systems and Applications, incl. Internet/Web, and HCI

This Springer imprint is published by the registered company Springer Nature Switzerland AG
The registered company address is: Gewerbestrasse 11, 6330 Cham, Switzerland

# Welcome

It is our great pleasure to welcome you to the 18th IFIP TC13 International Conference on Human-Computer Interaction, INTERACT 2021, one of the most important conferences in the area of Human-Computer Interaction at a world-wide level. INTERACT 2021 was held in Bari (Italy) from August 30 – September 3, 2021, in cooperation with ACM and under the patronage of the University of Bari Aldo Moro. This is the second time that INTERACT was held in Italy, after the edition in Rome in September 2005. The Villa Romanazzi Carducci Hotel, which hosted INTERACT 2021, provided the right context for welcoming the participants, thanks to its liberty-period villa immersed in a beautiful park. Due to the COVID-19 pandemic, INTERACT 2021 was held in hybrid mode to allow attendees who could not travel to participate in the conference.

INTERACT is held every two years and is well appreciated by the international community, attracting experts with a broad range of backgrounds, coming from all over the world and sharing a common interest in HCI, to make technology effective and useful for all people in their daily life. The theme of INTERACT 2021, "Sense, Feel, Design," highlighted the new interaction design challenges. Technology is today more and more widespread, pervasive and blended in the world we live in. On one side, devices that sense humans' activities have the potential to provide an enriched interaction. On the other side, the user experience can be further enhanced by exploiting multisensorial technologies. The traditional human senses of vision and hearing and senses of touch, smell, taste, and emotions can be taken into account when designing for future interactions. The hot topic of this edition was Human-Centered Artificial Intelligence, which implies considering who AI systems are built for and evaluating how well these systems support people's goals and activities. There was also considerable attention paid to the usable security theme. Not surprisingly, the COVID-19 pandemic and social distancing have also turned the attention of HCI researchers towards the difficulties in performing user-centered design activities and the modified social aspects of interaction.

With this, we welcome you all to INTERACT 2021. Several people worked hard to make this conference as pleasurable as possible, and we hope you will truly enjoy it.

Paolo Buono
Catherine Plaisant

# Preface

The 18th IFIP TC13 International Conference on Human-Computer Interaction, INTERACT 2021 (Bari, August 30 – September 3, 2021) attracted a relevant collection of submissions on different topics.

Excellent research is the heart of a good conference. Like its predecessors, INTERACT 2021 aimed to foster high-quality research. As a multidisciplinary field, HCI requires interaction and discussion among diverse people with different interests and backgrounds. The beginners and the experienced theoreticians and practitioners, and people from various disciplines and different countries gathered, both in-person and virtually, to learn from each other and contribute to each other's growth.

We were especially honoured to welcome our invited speakers: Marianna Obrist (University College London), Ben Shneiderman (University of Maryland), Luca Viganò (King's College London), Geraldine Fitzpatrick (TU Wien) and Philippe Palanque (University Toulouse 3 "Paul Sabatier").

Marianna Obrist's talk focused on the multisensory world people live in and discussed the role touch, taste and smell can play in the future of computing. Ben Shneiderman envisioned a new synthesis of emerging disciplines in which AI-based intelligent algorithms are combined with human-centered design thinking. Luca Viganò used a cybersecurity show and tell approach to illustrate how to use films and other artworks to explain cybersecurity notions. Geraldine Fitzpatrick focused on skills required to use technologies as enablers for good technical design work. Philippe Palanque discussed the cases of system faults due to human errors and presented multiple examples of faults affecting socio-technical systems.

A total of 680 submissions, distributed in 2 peer-reviewed tracks, 4 curated tracks, and 3 juried tracks, were received. Of these, the following contributions were accepted:

- 105 Full Papers (peer-reviewed)
- 72 Short Papers (peer-reviewed)
- 36 Posters (juried)
- 5 Interactive Demos (curated)
- 9 Industrial Experiences (curated)
- 3 Panels (curated)
- 1 Course (curated)
- 11 Workshops (juried)
- 13 Doctoral Consortium (juried)

The acceptance rate for contributions received in the peer-reviewed tracks was 29% for full papers and 30% for short papers. In the spirit of inclusiveness of INTERACT, and IFIP in general, a substantial number of promising but borderline full papers, which had not received a direct acceptance decision, were screened for shepherding.

Interestingly, many of these papers eventually turned out to be excellent quality papers and were included in the final set of full papers. In addition to full papers and short papers, the present proceedings feature's contributions accepted in the shape of posters, interactive demonstrations, industrial experiences, panels, courses, and descriptions of accepted workshops.

Subcommittees managed the reviewing process of the full papers. Each subcommittee had a chair and a set of associated chairs who were in charge of coordinating the reviewing process with the help of expert reviewers. Two new sub-committees were introduced in this edition: "Human-AI Interaction" and "HCI in the Pandemic". Hereafter we list the sub-committees of INTERACT 2021:

- Accessibility and assistive technologies
- Design for business and safety-critical interactive systems
- Design of interactive entertainment systems
- HCI education and curriculum
- HCI in the pandemic
- Human-AI interaction
- Information visualization
- Interactive systems technologies and engineering
- Methodologies for HCI
- Social and ubiquitous interaction
- Understanding users and human behaviour

The final decision on acceptance or rejection of full papers was taken in a Programme Committee meeting held virtually, due to the COVID-19 pandemic, in March 2021. The technical program chairs, the full papers chairs, the subcommittee chairs, and the associate chairs participated in this meeting. The meeting discussed a consistent set of criteria to deal with inevitable differences among many reviewers. The corresponding track chairs and reviewers made the final decisions on other tracks, often after electronic meetings and discussions.

We would like to express our strong gratitude to all the people whose passionate and strenuous work ensured the quality of the INTERACT 2021 program: the 12 sub-committees chairs, 88 associated chairs, 34 track chairs, and 543 reviewers; the Keynote & Invited Talks Chair Maria Francesca Costabile; the Posters Chairs Maristella Matera, Kent Norman, Anna Spagnolli; the Interactive Demos Chairs Barbara Rita Barricelli and Nuno Jardim Nunes; the Workshops Chairs Marta Kristín Larusdottir and Davide Spano; the Courses Chairs Nikolaos Avouris and Carmen Santoro; the Panels Chairs Effie Lai-Chong Law and Massimo Zancanaro; the Doctoral Consortium Chairs Daniela Fogli, David Lamas and John Stasko; the Industrial Experiences Chair Danilo Caivano; the Online Experience Chairs Fabrizio Balducci and Miguel Ceriani; the Advisors Fernando Loizides and Marco Winckler; the Student Volunteers Chairs Vita Santa Barletta and Grazia Ragone; the Publicity Chairs Ganesh D. Bhutkar and Veronica Rossano; the Local Organisation Chair Simona Sarti.

We would like to thank all the authors, who chose INTERACT 2021 as the venue to publish their research and enthusiastically shared their results with the INTERACT community. Last, but not least, we are also grateful to the sponsors for their financial support.

Carmelo Ardito
Rosa Lanzilotti
Alessio Malizia
Helen Petrie
Antonio Piccinno
Giuseppe Desolda
Kori Inkpen

# IFIP TC13 – http://ifip-tc13.org/

Established in 1989, the Technical Committee on Human–Computer Interaction (IFIP TC 13) of the International Federation for Information Processing (IFIP) is an international committee of 34 member national societies and 10 Working Groups, representing specialists of the various disciplines contributing to the field of human–computer interaction. This includes (among others) human factors, ergonomics, cognitive science, and multiple areas of computer science and design.

IFIP TC 13 aims to develop the science, technology and societal aspects of human–computer interaction (HCI) by

- encouraging empirical, applied and theoretical research
- promoting the use of knowledge and methods from both human sciences and computer sciences in design, development, evaluation and exploitation of computing systems
- promoting the production of new knowledge in the area of interactive computing systems engineering
- promoting better understanding of the relation between formal design methods and system usability, user experience, accessibility and acceptability
- developing guidelines, models and methods by which designers may provide better human-oriented computing systems
- and, cooperating with other groups, inside and outside IFIP, to promote user-orientation and humanization in system design.

Thus, TC 13 seeks to improve interactions between people and computing systems, to encourage the growth of HCI research and its practice in industry and to disseminate these benefits worldwide.

The main orientation is to place the users at the center of the development process. Areas of study include:

- the problems people face when interacting with computing devices;
- the impact of technology deployment on people in individual and organizational contexts;
- the determinants of utility, usability, acceptability, accessibility, privacy, and user experience ...;
- the appropriate allocation of tasks between computing systems and users especially in the case of automation;
- engineering user interfaces, interactions and interactive computing systems;
- modelling the user, their tasks and the interactive system to aid better system design; and harmonizing the computing system to user characteristics and needs.

While the scope is thus set wide, with a tendency toward general principles rather than particular systems, it is recognized that progress will only be achieved through both general studies to advance theoretical understandings and specific studies on practical issues (e.g., interface design standards, software system resilience, documentation, training material, appropriateness of alternative interaction technologies, guidelines, integrating computing systems to match user needs and organizational practices, etc.).

In 2015, TC13 approved the creation of a Steering Committee (SC) for the INTERACT conference series. The SC is now in place, chaired by Anirudha Joshi and is responsible for:

- promoting and maintaining the INTERACT conference as the premiere venue for researchers and practitioners interested in the topics of the conference (this requires a refinement of the topics above);
- ensuring the highest quality for the contents of the event;
- setting up the bidding process to handle the future INTERACT conferences (decision is made at TC 13 level);
- providing advice to the current and future chairs and organizers of the INTERACT conference;
- providing data, tools, and documents about previous conferences to the future conference organizers;
- selecting the reviewing system to be used throughout the conference (as this affects the entire set of reviewers, authors and committee members);
- resolving general issues involved with the INTERACT conference;
- capitalizing on history (good and bad practices).

In 1999, TC 13 initiated a special IFIP Award, the Brian Shackel Award, for the most outstanding contribution in the form of a refereed paper submitted to and delivered at each INTERACT. The award draws attention to the need for a comprehensive human-centered approach in the design and use of information technology in which the human and social implications have been taken into account. In 2007, IFIP TC 13 launched an Accessibility Award to recognize an outstanding contribution in HCI with international impact dedicated to the field of accessibility for disabled users. In 2013, IFIP TC 13 launched the Interaction Design for International Development (IDID) Award that recognizes the most outstanding contribution to the application of interactive systems for social and economic development of people in developing countries. Since the process to decide the award takes place after papers are sent to the publisher for publication, the awards are not identified in the proceedings. Since 2019 a special agreement has been made with the *International Journal of Behaviour & Information Technology* (published by Taylor & Francis) with Panos Markopoulos as editor in chief. In this agreement, authors of BIT whose papers are within the field of HCI are offered the opportunity to present their work at the INTERACT conference. Reciprocally, a selection of papers submitted and accepted for presentation at INTERACT are offered the opportunity to extend their contribution to be published in BIT.

IFIP TC 13 also recognizes pioneers in the area of HCI. An IFIP TC 13 pioneer is one who, through active participation in IFIP Technical Committees or related IFIP groups, has made outstanding contributions to the educational, theoretical, technical, commercial, or professional aspects of analysis, design, construction, evaluation, and use of interactive systems. IFIP TC 13 pioneers are appointed annually and awards are handed over at the INTERACT conference.

IFIP TC 13 stimulates working events and activities through its Working Groups (WGs). Working Groups consist of HCI experts from multiple countries, who seek to expand knowledge and find solutions to HCI issues and concerns within a specific domain. The list of Working Groups and their domains is given below.

WG13.1 (Education in HCI and HCI Curricula) aims to improve HCI education at all levels of higher education, coordinate and unite efforts to develop HCI curricula and promote HCI teaching.

WG13.2 (Methodology for User-Centred System Design) aims to foster research, dissemination of information and good practice in the methodical application of HCI to software engineering.

WG13.3 (HCI, Disability and Aging) aims to make HCI designers aware of the needs of people with disabilities and encourage development of information systems and tools permitting adaptation of interfaces to specific users.

WG13.4 (also WG2.7) (User Interface Engineering) investigates the nature, concepts and construction of user interfaces for software systems, using a framework for reasoning about interactive systems and an engineering model for developing UIs.

WG 13.5 (Resilience, Reliability, Safety and Human Error in System Development) seeks a framework for studying human factors relating to systems failure, develops leading edge techniques in hazard analysis and safety engineering of computer-based systems, and guides international accreditation activities for safety-critical systems.

WG13.6 (Human-Work Interaction Design) aims at establishing relationships between extensive empirical work-domain studies and HCI design. It will promote the use of knowledge, concepts, methods and techniques that enable user studies to procure a better apprehension of the complex interplay between individual, social and organizational contexts and thereby a better understanding of how and why people work in the ways that they do.

WG13.7 (Human–Computer Interaction and Visualization) aims to establish a study and research program that will combine both scientific work and practical applications in the fields of human–computer interaction and visualization. It will integrate several additional aspects of further research areas, such as scientific visualization, data mining, information design, computer graphics, cognition sciences, perception theory, or psychology, into this approach.

WG13.8 (Interaction Design and International Development) is currently working to reformulate their aims and scope.

WG13.9 (Interaction Design and Children) aims to support practitioners, regulators and researchers to develop the study of interaction design and children across international contexts.

WG13.10 (Human-Centred Technology for Sustainability) aims to promote research, design, development, evaluation, and deployment of human-centered technology to encourage sustainable use of resources in various domains.

New Working Groups are formed as areas of significance in HCI arise. Further information is available at the IFIP TC13 website: http://ifip-tc13.org/.

# IFIP TC13 Members

## Officers

**Chairperson**

Philippe Palanque, France

**Vice-chair for Awards**

Paula Kotze, South Africa

**Vice-chair for Communications**

Helen Petrie, UK

**Vice-chair for Growth and Reach out INTERACT Steering Committee Chair**

Jan Gulliksen, Sweden

**Vice-chair for Working Groups**

Simone D. J. Barbosa, Brazil

**Vice-chair for Development and Equity**

Julio Abascal, Spain

**Treasurer**

Virpi Roto, Finland

**Secretary**

Marco Winckler, France

**INTERACT Steering Committee Chair**

Anirudha Joshi, India

## Country Representatives

**Australia**
Henry B. L. Duh
Australian Computer Society

**Austria**
Geraldine Fitzpatrick
Austrian Computer Society

**Belgium**
Bruno Dumas
IMEC – Interuniversity
Micro-Electronics Center

**Brazil**
Lara S. G. Piccolo
Brazilian Computer Society (SBC)

**Bulgaria**
Stoyan Georgiev Dentchev
Bulgarian Academy of Sciences

**Croatia**
Andrina Granic
Croatian Information Technology
Association (CITA)

**Cyprus**
Panayiotis Zaphiris
Cyprus Computer Society

**Czech Republic**
Zdeněk Míkovec
Czech Society for Cybernetics
and Informatics

**Finland**
Virpi Roto
Finnish Information Processing
Association

**France**
Philippe Palanque and Marco Winckler
Société informatique de France (SIF)

**Germany**
Tom Gross
Gesellschaft fur Informatik e.V.

**Ireland**
Liam J. Bannon
Irish Computer Society

**Italy**
Fabio Paternò
Italian Computer Society

**Japan**
Yoshifumi Kitamura
Information Processing Society of Japan

**Netherlands**
Regina Bernhaupt
Nederlands Genootschap
voor Informatica

**New Zealand**
Mark Apperley
New Zealand Computer Society

**Norway**
Frode Eika Sandnes
Norwegian Computer Society

**Poland**
Marcin Sikorski
Poland Academy of Sciences

**Portugal**
Pedro Campos
Associacão Portuguesa para o
Desenvolvimento da Sociedade da
Informação (APDSI)

**Serbia**
Aleksandar Jevremovic
Informatics Association of Serbia

**Singapore**
Shengdong Zhao
Singapore Computer Society

**Slovakia**
Wanda Benešová
The Slovak Society for Computer
Science

**Slovenia**
Matjaž Debevc
The Slovenian Computer Society
INFORMATIKA

**Sri Lanka**
Thilina Halloluwa
The Computer Society of Sri Lanka

**South Africa**
Janet L. Wesson & Paula Kotze
The Computer Society of South Africa

**Sweden**
Jan Gulliksen
Swedish Interdisciplinary Society for
Human-Computer Interaction
Swedish Computer Society

**Switzerland**
Denis Lalanne
Swiss Federation for Information
Processing

**Tunisia**
Mona Laroussi
Ecole Supérieure des Communications de
Tunis (SUP'COM)

**United Kingdom**
José Abdelnour Nocera
British Computer Society (BCS)

**United Arab Emirates**
Ahmed Seffah
UAE Computer Society

**ACM**

Gerrit van der Veer
Association for Computing
Machinery

**CLEI**

Jaime Sánchez
Centro Latinoamericano de Estudios en
Informatica

## Expert Members

Julio Abascal, Spain
Carmelo Ardito, Italy
Nikolaos Avouris, Greece
Kaveh Bazargan, Iran
Ivan Burmistrov, Russia
Torkil Torkil Clemmensen, Denmark
Peter Forbrig, Germany
Dorian Gorgan, Romania

Anirudha Joshi, India
David Lamas, Estonia
Marta Kristin Larusdottir, Iceland
Zhengjie Liu, China
Fernando Loizides, UK/Cyprus
Ochieng Daniel "Dan" Orwa, Kenya
Eunice Sari, Australia/Indonesia

## Working Group Chairpersons

**WG 13.1 (Education in HCI
and HCI Curricula)**

Konrad Baumann, Austria

**WG 13.2 (Methodologies
for User-Centered System Design)**

Regina Bernhaupt, Netherlands

**WG 13.3 (HCI, Disability and Aging)**

Helen Petrie, UK

**WG 13.4/2.7 (User Interface
Engineering)**

José Creissac Campos, Portugal

**WG 13.5 (Human Error, Resilience,
Reliability, Safety and System
Development)**

Chris Johnson, UK

**WG13.6 (Human-Work
Interaction Design)**

Barbara Rita Barricelli, Italy

**WG13.7 (HCI and Visualization)**

Peter Dannenmann, Germany

**WG 13.8 (Interaction Design
and International Development)**

José Adbelnour Nocera, UK

**WG 13.9 (Interaction Design
and Children)**

Janet Read, UK

**WG 13.10 (Human-Centred
Technology for Sustainability)**

Masood Masoodian, Finland

# Conference Organizing Committee

**General Conference Co-chairs**

Paolo Buono, Italy
Catherine Plaisant, USA and France

**Advisors**

Fernando Loizides, UK
Marco Winckler, France

**Technical Program Co-chairs**

Carmelo Ardito, Italy
Rosa Lanzilotti, Italy
Alessio Malizia, UK and Italy

**Keynote and Invited Talks Chair**

Maria Francesca Costabile, Italy

**Full Papers Co-chairs**

Helen Petrie, UK
Antonio Piccinno, Italy

**Short Papers Co-chairs**

Giuseppe Desolda, Italy
Kori Inkpen, USA

**Posters Co-chairs**

Maristella Matera, Italy
Kent Norman, USA
Anna Spagnolli, Italy

**Interactive Demos Co-chairs**

Barbara Rita Barricelli, Italy
Nuno Jardim Nunes, Portugal

**Panels Co-chairs**

Effie Lai-Chong Law, UK
Massimo Zancanaro, Italy

**Courses Co-chairs**

Carmen Santoro, Italy
Nikolaos Avouris, Greece

**Industrial Experiences Chair**

Danilo Caivano, Italy

**Workshops Co-chairs**

Marta Kristín Larusdottir, Iceland
Davide Spano, Italy

**Doctoral Consortium Co-chairs**

Daniela Fogli, Italy
David Lamas, Estonia
John Stasko, USA

**Online Experience Co-chairs**

Fabrizio Balducci, Italy
Miguel Ceriani, Italy

**Student Volunteers Co-chairs**

Vita Santa Barletta, Italy
Grazia Ragone, UK

**Publicity Co-chairs**

Ganesh D. Bhutkar, India
Veronica Rossano, Italy

**Local Organisation Chair**

Simona Sarti, Consulta Umbria, Italy

## Programme Committee

### Sub-committee Chairs

Nikolaos Avouris, Greece
Regina Bernhaupt, Netherlands
Carla Dal Sasso Freitas, Brazil
Jan Gulliksen, Sweden
Paula Kotzé, South Africa
Effie Lai-Chong Law, UK

Philippe Palanque, France
Fabio Paternò, Italy
Thomas Pederson, Sweden
Albrecht Schmidt, Germany
Frank Steinicke, Germany
Gerhard Weber, Germany

### Associated Chairs

José Abdelnour Nocera, UK
Raian Ali, Qatar
Florian Alt, Germany
Katrina Attwood, UK
Simone Barbosa, Brazil
Cristian Bogdan, Sweden
Paolo Bottoni, Italy
Judy Bowen, New Zealand
Daniel Buschek, Germany
Pedro Campos, Portugal
José Creissac Campos, Portugal
Luca Chittaro, Italy
Sandy Claes, Belgium
Christopher Clarke, UK
Torkil Clemmensen, Denmark
Vanessa Cobus, Germany
Ashley Colley, Finland
Aurora Constantin, UK
Lynne Coventry, UK
Yngve Dahl, Norway
Maria De Marsico, Italy
Luigi De Russis, Italy
Paloma Diaz, Spain
Monica Divitini, Norway
Mateusz Dolata, Switzerland
Bruno Dumas, Belgium
Sophie Dupuy-Chessa, France
Dan Fitton, UK
Peter Forbrig, Germany
Sandnes Frode Eika, Norway
Vivian Genaro Motti, USA
Rosella Gennari, Italy

Jens Gerken, Germany
Mareike Glöss, Sweden
Dorian Gorgan, Romania
Tom Gross, Germany
Uwe Gruenefeld, Germany
Julie Haney, USA
Ebba Þóra Hvannberg, Iceland
Netta Iivari, Finland
Nanna Inie, Denmark
Anna Sigríður Islind, Iceland
Anirudha Joshi, India
Bridget Kane, Sweden
Anne Marie Kanstrup, Denmark
Mohamed Khamis, UK
Kibum Kim, Korea
Marion Koelle, Germany
Kati Kuusinen, Denmark
Matthias Laschke, Germany
Fernando Loizides, UK
Andrés Lucero, Finland
Jo Lumsden, UK
Charlotte Magnusson, Sweden
Andrea Marrella, Italy
Célia Martinie, France
Timothy Merritt, Denmark
Zdeněk Míkovec, Czech Republic
Luciana Nedel, Brazil
Laurence Nigay, France
Valentina Nisi, Portugal
Raquel O. Prates, Brazil
Rakesh Patibanda, Australia
Simon Perrault, Singapore

Lara Piccolo, UK
Aparecido Fabiano Pinatti de Carvalho, Germany
Janet Read, UK
Karen Renaud, UK
Antonio Rizzo, Italy
Sayan Sarcar, Japan
Valentin Schwind, Germany
Gavin Sim, UK
Fotios Spyridonis, UK
Jan Stage, Denmark
Simone Stumpf, UK
Luis Teixeira, Portugal

Jakob Tholander, Sweden
Daniela Trevisan, Brazil
Stefano Valtolina, Italy
Jan Van den Bergh, Belgium
Nervo Verdezoto, UK
Chi Vi, UK
Giuliana Vitiello, Italy
Sarah Völkel, Germany
Marco Winckler, France
Dhaval Vyas, Australia
Janet Wesson, South Africa
Paweł W. Woźniak, Netherlands

## Reviewers

Bruno A. Chagas, Brazil
Yasmeen Abdrabou, Germany
Maher Abujelala, USA
Jiban Adhikary, USA
Kashif Ahmad, Qatar
Muneeb Ahmad, UK
Naveed Ahmed, United Arab Emirates
Aino Ahtinen, Finland
Wolfgang Aigner, Austria
Deepak Akkil, Finland
Aftab Alam, Republic of Korea
Soraia Meneses Alarcão, Portugal
Pedro Albuquerque Santos, Portugal
Günter Alce, Sweden
Iñigo Aldalur, Spain
Alaa Alkhafaji, Iraq
Aishat Aloba, USA
Yosuef Alotaibi, UK
Taghreed Alshehri, UK
Ragaad Al-Tarawneh, USA
Alejandro Alvarez-Marin, Chile
Lucas Anastasiou, UK
Ulf Andersson, Sweden
Joseph Aneke, Italy
Mark Apperley, New Zealand
Renan Aranha, Brazil
Pierre-Emmanuel Arduin, France
Stephanie Arevalo Arboleda, Germany
Jan Argasiński, Poland

Patricia Arias-Cabarcos, Germany
Alexander Arntz, Germany
Jonas Auda, Germany
Andreas Auinger, Austria
Iuliia Avgustis, Finland
Cédric Bach, France
Miroslav Bachinski, Germany
Victor Bacu, Romania
Jan Balata, Czech Republic
Teresa Baldassarre, Italy
Fabrizio Balducci, Italy
Vijayanand Banahatti, India
Karolina Baras, Portugal
Simone Barbosa, Brazil
Vita Santa Barletta, Italy
Silvio Barra, Italy
Barbara Rita Barricelli, Italy
Ralph Barthel, UK
Thomas Baudel, France
Christine Bauer, Netherlands
Fatma Ben Mesmia, Canada
Marit Bentvelzen, Netherlands
François Bérard, France
Melanie Berger, Netherlands
Gerd Berget, Norway
Sergi Bermúdez i Badia, Portugal
Dario Bertero, UK
Guilherme Bertolaccini, Brazil
Lonni Besançon, Australia

Laura-Bianca Bilius, Romania
Kerstin Blumenstein, Austria
Andreas Bollin, Austria
Judith Borghouts, UK
Nis Bornoe, Denmark
Gabriela Bosetti, UK
Hollie Bostock, Portugal
Paolo Bottoni, Italy
Magdalena Boucher, Austria
Amina Bouraoui, Tunisia
Elodie Bouzekri, France
Judy Bowen, New Zealand
Efe Bozkir, Germany
Danielle Bragg, USA
Diogo Branco, Portugal
Dawn Branley-Bell, UK
Stephen Brewster, UK
Giada Brianza, UK
Barry Brown, Sweden
Nick Bryan-Kinns, UK
Andreas Bucher, Switzerland
Elizabeth Buie, UK
Alexandru Bundea, Germany
Paolo Buono, Italy
Michael Burch, Switzerland
Matthew Butler, Australia
Fabio Buttussi, Italy
Andreas Butz, Germany
Maria Claudia Buzzi, Italy
Marina Buzzi, Italy
Zoya Bylinskii, USA
Diogo Cabral, Portugal
Åsa Cajander, Sweden
Francisco Maria Calisto, Portugal
Hector Caltenco, Sweden
José Creissac Campos, Portugal
Heloisa Candello, Brazil
Alberto Cannavò, Italy
Bruno Cardoso, Belgium
Jorge Cardoso, Portugal
Géry Casiez, France
Fabio Cassano, Italy
Brendan Cassidy, UK
Alejandro Catala, Spain

Miguel Ceriani, UK
Daniel Cermak-Sassenrath, Denmark
Vanessa Cesário, Portugal
Fred Charles, UK
Debaleena Chattopadhyay, USA
Alex Chen, Singapore
Thomas Chen, USA
Yuan Chen, Canada
Chola Chhetri, USA
Katherine Chiluiza, Ecuador
Nick Chozos, UK
Michael Chromik, Germany
Christopher Clarke, UK
Bárbara Cleto, Portugal
Antonio Coelho, Portugal
Ashley Colley, Finland
Nelly Condori-Fernandez, Spain
Marios Constantinides, UK
Cléber Corrêa, Brazil
Vinicius Costa de Souza, Brazil
Joëlle Coutaz, France
Céline Coutrix, France
Chris Creed, UK
Carlos Cunha, Portugal
Kamila Rios da Hora Rodrigues, Brazil
Damon Daylamani-Zad, UK
Sergio de Cesare, UK
Marco de Gemmis, Italy
Teis De Greve, Belgium
Victor Adriel de Jesus Oliveira, Austria
Helmut Degen, USA
Donald Degraen, Germany
William Delamare, France
Giuseppe Desolda, Italy
Henrik Detjen, Germany
Marianna Di Gregorio, Italy
Ines Di Loreto, France
Daniel Diethei, Germany
Tilman Dingler, Australia
Anke Dittmar, Germany
Monica Divitini, Norway
Janki Dodiya, Germany
Julia Dominiak, Poland
Ralf Dörner, Germany

Julie Doyle, Ireland
Philip Doyle, Ireland
Fiona Draxler, Germany
Emanuel Felipe Duarte, Brazil
Rui Duarte, Portugal
Bruno Dumas, Belgium
Mark Dunlop, UK
Sophie Dupuy-Chessa, France
Jason Dykes, UK
Chloe Eghtebas, Germany
Kevin El Haddad, Belgium
Don Samitha Elvitigala, New Zealand
Augusto Esteves, Portugal
Siri Fagernes, Norway
Katherine Fennedy, Singapore
Marta Ferreira, Portugal
Francesco Ferrise, Italy
Lauren Stacey Ferro, Italy
Christos Fidas, Greece
Daniel Finnegan, UK
Daniela Fogli, Italy
Manuel J. Fonseca, Portugal
Peter Forbrig, Germany
Rita Francese, Italy
André Freire, Brazil
Karin Fröhlich, Finland
Susanne Furman, USA
Henrique Galvan Debarba, Denmark
Sandra Gama, Portugal
Dilrukshi Gamage, Japan
Jérémie Garcia, France
Jose Garcia Estrada, Norway
David Geerts, Belgium
Denise Y. Geiskkovitch, Canada
Stefan Geisler, Germany
Mirko Gelsomini, Italy
Çağlar Genç, Finland
Rosella Gennari, Italy
Nina Gerber, Germany
Moojan Ghafurian, Canada
Maliheh Ghajargar, Sweden
Sabiha Ghellal, Germany
Debjyoti Ghosh, Germany
Michail Giannakos, Norway

Terje Gjøsæter, Norway
Marc Gonzalez Capdevila, Brazil
Julien Gori, Finland
Laurent Grisoni, France
Tor-Morten Gronli, Norway
Sebastian Günther, Germany
Li Guo, UK
Srishti Gupta, USA
Francisco Gutiérrez, Belgium
José Eder Guzman Mendoza, Mexico
Jonna Häkkilä, Finland
Lilit Hakobyan, UK
Thilina Halloluwa, Sri Lanka
Perttu Hämäläinen, Finland
Lane Harrison, USA
Michael Harrison, UK
Hanna Hasselqvist, Sweden
Tomi Heimonen, USA
Florian Heinrich, Germany
Florian Heller, Belgium
Karey Helms, Sweden
Nathalie Henry Riche, USA
Diana Hernandez-Bocanegra, Germany
Danula Hettiachchi, Australia
Wilko Heuten, Germany
Annika Hinze, New Zealand
Linda Hirsch, Germany
Sarah Hodge, UK
Sven Hoffmann, Germany
Catherine Holloway, UK
Leona Holloway, Australia
Lars Erik Holmquist, UK
Anca-Simona Horvath, Denmark
Simo Hosio, Finland
Sebastian Hubenschmid, Germany
Helena Vallo Hult, Sweden
Shah Rukh Humayoun, USA
Ebba Þóra Hvannberg, Iceland
Alon Ilsar, Australia
Md Athar Imtiaz, New Zealand
Oana Inel, Netherlands
Francisco Iniesto, UK
Andri Ioannou, Cyprus
Chyng-Yang Jang, USA

Gokul Jayakrishnan, India
Stine Johansen, Denmark
Tero Jokela, Finland
Rui José, Portugal
Anirudha Joshi, India
Manjiri Joshi, India
Jana Jost, Germany
Patrick Jost, Norway
Annika Kaltenhauser, Germany
Jin Kang, Canada
Younah Kang, Republic of Korea
Jari Kangas, Finland
Petko Karadechev, Denmark
Armağan Karahanoğlu, Netherlands
Sukran Karaosmanoglu, Germany
Alexander Kempton, Norway
Rajiv Khadka, USA
Jayden Khakurel, Finland
Pramod Khambete, India
Neeta Khanuja, Portugal
Young-Ho Kim, USA
Reuben Kirkham, Australia
Ilan Kirsh, Israel
Maria Kjærup, Denmark
Kevin Koban, Austria
Frederik Kobbelgaard, Denmark
Martin Kocur, Germany
Marius Koller, Germany
Christophe Kolski, France
Takanori Komatsu, Japan
Jemma König, New Zealand
Monika Kornacka, Poland
Thomas Kosch, Germany
Panayiotis Koutsabasis, Greece
Lucie Kruse, Germany
Przemysław Kucharski, Poland
Johannes Kunkel, Germany
Bineeth Kuriakose, Norway
Anelia Kurteva, Austria
Marc Kurz, Austria
Florian Lang, Germany
Rosa Lanzilotti, Italy
Lars Bo Larsen, Denmark
Marta Larusdottir, Iceland

Effie Law, UK
Luis Leiva, Luxembourg
Barbara Leporini, Italy
Pascal Lessel, Germany
Hongyu Li, USA
Yuan Liang, USA
Yu-Tzu Lin, Denmark
Markus Löchtefeld, Denmark
Angela Locoro, Italy
Benedikt Loepp, Germany
Domenico Lofù, Italy
Fernando Loizides, UK
Arminda Lopes, Portugal
Feiyu Lu, USA
Jo Lumsden, UK
Anders Lundström, Sweden
Kris Luyten, Belgium
Granit Luzhnica, Austria
Marc Macé, France
Anderson Maciel, Brazil
Cristiano Maciel, Brazil
Miroslav Macík, Czech Republic
Scott MacKenzie, Canada
Hanuma Teja Maddali, USA
Rui Madeira, Portugal
Alexander Maedche, Germany
Charlotte Magnusson, Sweden
Jyotirmaya Mahapatra, India
Vanessa Maike, USA
Maitreyee Maitreyee, Sweden
Ville Mäkelä, Germany
Sylvain Malacria, France
Sugandh Malhotra, India
Ivo Malý, Czech Republic
Marco Manca, Italy
Muhanad Manshad, USA
Isabel Manssour, Brazil
Panos Markopoulos, Netherlands
Karola Marky, Germany
Andrea Marrella, Italy
Andreas Martin, Switzerland
Célia Martinie, France
Nuno Martins, Portugal
Maristella Matera, Italy

Florian Mathis, UK
Andrii Matviienko, Germany
Peter Mayer, Germany
Sven Mayer, Germany
Mark McGill, UK
Donald McMillan, Sweden
Lukas Mecke, Germany
Elisa Mekler, Finland
Alessandra Melonio, Italy
Eleonora Mencarini, Italy
Maria Menendez Blanco, Italy
Aline Menin, France
Arjun Menon, Sweden
Nazmus Sakib Miazi, USA
Zdeněk Míkovec, Czech Republic
Tim Mittermeier, Germany
Emmanuel Mkpojiogu, Nigeria
Jonas Moll, Sweden
Alberto Monge Roffarello, Italy
Troels Mønsted, Denmark
Diego Morra, Italy
Jaime Munoz Arteaga, Mexico
Sachith Muthukumarana, New Zealand
Vasiliki Mylonopoulou, Sweden
Frank Nack, Netherlands
Mohammad Naiseh, UK
Vania Neris, Brazil
Robin Neuhaus, Germany
Thao Ngo, Germany
Binh Vinh Duc Nguyen, Belgium
Vickie Nguyen, USA
James Nicholson, UK
Peter Axel Nielsen, Denmark
Jasmin Niess, Germany
Evangelos Niforatos, Netherlands
Kent Norman, USA
Fatima Nunes, Brazil
Carli Ochs, Switzerland
Joseph O'Hagan, UK
Takashi Ohta, Japan
Jonas Oppenlaender, Finland
Michael Ortega, France
Changkun Ou, Germany
Yun Suen Pai, New Zealand

Dominika Palivcová, Czech Republic
Viktoria Pammer-Schindler, Austria
Eleftherios Papachristos, Denmark
Sofia Papavlasopoulou, Norway
Leonado Parra, Colombia
Max Pascher, Germany
Ankit Patel, Portugal
Fabio Paternò, Italy
Maria Angela Pellegrino, Italy
Anthony Perritano, USA
Johanna Persson, Sweden
Ken Pfeuffer, Germany
Bastian Pfleging, Netherlands
Vung Pham, USA
Jayesh Pillai, India
Catherine Plaisant, USA
Henning Pohl, Denmark
Margit Pohl, Austria
Alessandro Pollini, Italy
Dorin-Mircea Popovici, Romania
Thiago Porcino, Brazil
Dominic Potts, UK
Sarah Prange, Germany
Marco Procaccini, Italy
Arnaud Prouzeau, France
Parinya Punpongsanon, Japan
Sónia Rafael, Portugal
Jessica Rahman, Australia
Mikko Rajanen, Finland
Nimmi Rangaswamy, India
Alberto Raposo, Brazil
George Raptis, Greece
Hanae Rateau, Canada
Sebastian Rauh, Germany
Hirak Ray, USA
Traian Rebedea, Romania
Yosra Rekik, France
Elizabeth Rendon-Velez, Colombia
Malte Ressin, UK
Tera Reynolds, USA
Miguel Ribeiro, Portugal
Maria Rigou, Greece
Sirpa Riihiaho, Finland
Michele Risi, Italy

Paul van Schauk, UK
Koen van Turnhout, Netherlands
Jean Vanderdonckt, Belgium
Eduardo Veas, Austria
Katia Vega, USA
Kellie Vella, Australia
Leena Ventä-Olkkonen, Finland
Nadine Vigouroux, France
Gabriela Villalobos-Zúñiga, Switzerland
Aku Visuri, Finland
Giuliana Vitiello, Italy
Pierpaolo Vittorini, Italy
Julius von Willich, Germany
Steven Vos, Netherlands
Nadine Wagener, Germany
Lun Wang, Italy
Ruijie Wang, Italy
Gerhard Weber, Germany
Thomas Weber, Germany
Rina Wehbe, Canada
Florian Weidner, Germany
Alexandra Weilenmann, Sweden
Sebastian Weiß, Germany

Yannick Weiss, Germany
Robin Welsch, Germany
Janet Wesson, South Africa
Benjamin Weyers, Germany
Stephanie Wilson, UK
Marco Winckler, France
Philipp Wintersberger, Austria
Katrin Wolf, Germany
Kim Wölfel, Germany
Julia Woodward, USA
Matthias Wunsch, Austria
Haijun Xia, USA
Asim Evren Yantac, Turkey
Enes Yigitbas, Germany
Yongjae Yoo, Canada
Johannes Zagermann, Germany
Massimo Zancanaro, Italy
André Zenner, Germany
Jingjie Zheng, Canada
Suwen Zhu, USA
Ying Zhu, USA
Jürgen Ziegler, Germany

## Partners and Sponsors

**Partners**

International Federation for Information Processing

In-cooperation with ACM

In-cooperation with SIGCHI

**Sponsors**

**EULOGIC**

**eusoft**
more than a lims

**Experis**™
ManpowerGroup

exprivia

**openwork**
Just solutions

**ORA ZERO**
GROUP

**sincon**
ICT SOLUTIONS

# Contents – Part IV

## Interaction Techniques

Auditory-Centered Vocal Feedback System Using Solmization for Training
Absolute Pitch Without GUI. . . . . . . . . . . . . . . . . . . . . . . . . . . . . . . . . . . .  3
   *Nozomu Yoshida, Kosaku Namikawa, Yusuke Koroyasu,*
   *Yoshiki Nagatani, and Yoichi Ochiai*

Dealing with Input Mode Confusion During Dual-Language
Keyboard Use. . . . . . . . . . . . . . . . . . . . . . . . . . . . . . . . . . . . . . . . . . .  20
   *Paraskevas Petsanas, Christos Sintoris, and Nikolaos Avouris*

Empirical Evaluation of Moving Target Selection in Virtual Reality
Using Egocentric Metaphors. . . . . . . . . . . . . . . . . . . . . . . . . . . . . . . . . .  29
   *Yuan Chen, Junwei Sun, Qiang Xu, Edward Lank, Pourang Irani,*
   *and Wei Li*

HyperBrush: Exploring the Influence of Flexural Stiffness on the
Performance and Preference for Bendable Stylus Interfaces . . . . . . . . . . . .  51
   *Alfrancis Guerrero, Thomas Pietrzak, and Audrey Girouard*

Leveraging CD Gain for Precise Barehand Video Timeline Browsing
on Smart Displays. . . . . . . . . . . . . . . . . . . . . . . . . . . . . . . . . . . . . . . . .  72
   *Futian Zhang, Sachi Mizobuchi, Wei Zhou, Taslim Arefin Khan, Wei Li,*
   *and Edward Lank*

Seasons: Exploring the Dynamic Thermochromic Smart Textile
Applications for Intangible Cultural Heritage Revitalization . . . . . . . . . . . .  92
   *Qi Wang, Ying Ye, Martijn ten Bhömer, Mengqi Jiang, and Xiaohua Sun*

Time-Penalty Impact on Effective Index of Difficulty and Throughputs
in Pointing Tasks . . . . . . . . . . . . . . . . . . . . . . . . . . . . . . . . . . . . . . . . . .  100
   *Shota Yamanaka, Keisuke Yokota, and Takanori Komatsu*

Towards Multi-device Digital Self-control Tools. . . . . . . . . . . . . . . . . . . .  122
   *Alberto Monge Roffarello and Luigi De Russis*

Typing on Midair Virtual Keyboards: Exploring Visual Designs
and Interaction Styles . . . . . . . . . . . . . . . . . . . . . . . . . . . . . . . . . . . . . . .  132
   *Jiban Adhikary and Keith Vertanen*

## Interaction with Conversational Agents

"Please Connect Me to a Specialist": Scrutinising 'Recipient Design'
in Interaction with an Artificial Conversational Agent . . . . . . . . . . . . . . . . .     155
    Iuliia Avgustis, Aleksandr Shirokov, and Netta Iivari

An Interactive Paradigm for the End-User Development of Chatbots
for Data Exploration . . . . . . . . . . . . . . . . . . . . . . . . . . . . . . . . . . . . . . .     177
    Ludovica Piro, Giuseppe Desolda, Maristella Matera, Rosa Lanzilotti,
    Sara Mosca, and Emanuele Pucci

ReflectPal: Exploring Self-Reflection on Collaborative Activities Using
Voice Assistants . . . . . . . . . . . . . . . . . . . . . . . . . . . . . . . . . . . . . . . . . .     187
    Eleftherios Papachristos, Dorte P. Meldgaard, Iben R. Thomsen,
    and Mikael B. Skov

## Interaction with Mobile Devices

Exploring How a Digitized Program Can Support Parents to Improve Their
Children's Nutritional Habits . . . . . . . . . . . . . . . . . . . . . . . . . . . . . . . . .     211
    Diogo Branco, Ana C. Pires, Hugo Simão, Ana Gomes, Ana Pereira,
    Joana Sousa, Luísa Barros, and Tiago Guerreiro

MAWA: A Browser Extension for Mobile Web Augmentation . . . . . . . . . . .     221
    Iñigo Aldalur, Alain Perez, and Felix Larrinaga

NotificationManager: Personal Boundary Management on Mobile Devices . . .     243
    Tom Gross and Anna-Lena Mueller

The Role of Mobile and Virtual Reality Applications to Support
Well-Being: An Expert View and Systematic App Review . . . . . . . . . . . . . .     262
    Nadine Wagener, Tu Dinh Duong, Johannes Schöning, Yvonne Rogers,
    and Jasmin Niess

## Methods for User Studies

BRIDGE: Administering Small Anonymous Longitudinal HCI Studies with
Snowball-Type Sampling . . . . . . . . . . . . . . . . . . . . . . . . . . . . . . . . . . . .     287
    Frode Eika Sandnes

Detecting and Explaining Usability Issues of Consumer
Electronic Products . . . . . . . . . . . . . . . . . . . . . . . . . . . . . . . . . . . . . . . .     298
    Dario Benvenuti, Emanuele Buda, Francesca Fraioli, Andrea Marrella,
    and Tiziana Catarci

Introducing Asynchronous Remote Usability Testing in Practice: An Action
Research Project . . . . . . . . . . . . . . . . . . . . . . . . . . . . . . . . . . . . . . 320
    *Jonna Helene Holm Pedersen, Malene Sørensen, Jan Stage,*
    *and Rune Thaarup Høegh*

Investigating User Perceptions Towards Wearable Mobile
Electromyography . . . . . . . . . . . . . . . . . . . . . . . . . . . . . . . . . . . . . 339
    *Sarah Prange, Sven Mayer, Maria-Lena Bittl, Mariam Hassib,*
    *and Florian Alt*

Words, Worlds and Freedom – Insights from School Students in Indonesia
and UK . . . . . . . . . . . . . . . . . . . . . . . . . . . . . . . . . . . . . . . . . . . . 361
    *Janet C. Read, Eunice Sari, I. Scott Mackenzie,*
    *and Josh (Adi) Tedjasaputra*

**Personalization and Recommender Systems**

Automated Adaptations for Improving the Accessibility of Public
E-Services Based on Annotations . . . . . . . . . . . . . . . . . . . . . . . . . . . 373
    *Aritz Sala, Myriam Arrue, J. Eduardo Pérez, and Sandra M. Espín-Tello*

Identifying Group-Specific Mental Models of Recommender Systems:
A Novel Quantitative Approach . . . . . . . . . . . . . . . . . . . . . . . . . . . . 383
    *Johannes Kunkel, Thao Ngo, Jürgen Ziegler, and Nicole Krämer*

Should I Add Recommendations to My Warning System? The RCRAFT
Framework Can Answer This and Other Questions About Supporting the
Assessment of Automation Designs . . . . . . . . . . . . . . . . . . . . . . . . . . 405
    *Elodie Bouzekri, Célia Martinie, Philippe Palanque, Katrina Atwood,*
    *and Christine Gris*

**Social Networks and Social Media**

Improving the Debate: Interface Elements that Enhance Civility
and Relevance in Online News Comments . . . . . . . . . . . . . . . . . . . . . 433
    *Emilie Bossens, Elias Storms, and David Geerts*

Quantifying the Effects of Age-Related Stereotypes on Online
Social Conformity . . . . . . . . . . . . . . . . . . . . . . . . . . . . . . . . . . . . . 451
    *Senuri Wijenayake, Jolan Hu, Vassilis Kostakos, and Jorge Goncalves*

Us Vs. Them – Understanding the Impact of Homophily in Political
Discussions on Twitter. . . . . . . . . . . . . . . . . . . . . . . . . . . . . . . . . . . 476
    *Danula Hettiachchi, Tanay Arora, and Jorge Goncalves*

## Tangible Interaction

A Lens-Based Extension of Raycasting for Accurate Selection in Dense
3D Environments . . . . . . . . . . . . . . . . . . . . . . . . . . . . . .    501
   *Carole Plasson, Dominique Cunin, Yann Laurillau, and Laurence Nigay*

Designing a Tangible Device for Re-Framing Unproductivity . . . . . . . . . . .    525
   *Judith Sirera and Eduardo Velloso*

Designing for Inaccessible People and Places . . . . . . . . . . . . . . . . . . . .    546
   *Judy Bowen and Annika Hinze*

Effect of Attention Saturating and Cognitive Load on Tactile Texture
Recognition for Mobile Surface . . . . . . . . . . . . . . . . . . . . . . . . . . .    557
   *Adnane Guettaf, Yosra Rekik, and Laurent Grisoni*

Endless Knob with Programmable Resistive Force Feedback . . . . . . . . . . . .    580
   *Yuri De Pra, Federico Fontana, and Stefano Papetti*

*GrouPen*: A Tangible User Interface to Support Remote
Collaborative Learning. . . . . . . . . . . . . . . . . . . . . . . . . . . . . . . .    590
   *Yanhong Li, Yu Sun, Tianyang Lu,*
   *and Thomas WeberHeinrich Hußmann*

TactCube: Designing Mobile Interactions with Ambient Intelligence . . . . . . .    599
   *Pietro Battistoni, Marianna Di Gregorio, Marco Romano,*
   *Monica Sebillo, and Giuliana Vitiello*

The Hubs: Design Insights for Walking Meeting Technology . . . . . . . . . . . .    610
   *Ida Damen, Steven Vos, and Carine Lallemand*

Touch, See and Talk: Tangibles for Engaging Learners into Graph
Algorithmic Thinking . . . . . . . . . . . . . . . . . . . . . . . . . . . . . . . .    630
   *Andrea Bonani, Andreas Bollin, and Rosella Gennari*

## Usable Security

An Empirical Study of Picture Password Composition on Smartwatches . . . .    655
   *Marios Belk, Christos Fidas, Eleni Katsi, Argyris Constantinides,*
   *and Andreas Pitsillides*

Communicating Privacy: User Priorities for Privacy Requirements in Home
Energy Applications . . . . . . . . . . . . . . . . . . . . . . . . . . . . . . . . .    665
   *Lisa Diamond and Peter Fröhlich*

Designing Parental Monitoring and Control Technology:
A Systematic Review . . . . . . . . . . . . . . . . . . . . . . . . . . . . . . . . . . . 676
  Zainab Iftikhar, Qutaiba Rohan ul Haq, Osama Younus, Taha Sardar,
  Hammad Arif, Mobin Javed, and Suleman Shahid

Integrating Dark Patterns into the 4Cs of Online Risk in the Context
of Young People and Mobile Gaming Apps . . . . . . . . . . . . . . . . . . . . . . 701
  Dan Fitton, Beth T. Bell, and Janet C. Read

Passphrases Beat Thermal Attacks: Evaluating Text Input Characteristics
Against Thermal Attacks on Laptops and Smartphones . . . . . . . . . . . . . . 712
  Yasmeen Abdrabou, Reem Hatem, Yomna Abdelrahman, Amr Elmougy,
  and Mohamed Khamis

Understanding Insider Attacks in Personalized Picture Password Schemes . . . 722
  Argyris Constantinides, Marios Belk, Christos Fidas,
  and Andreas Pitsillides

Visuals Triumph in a Curious Case of Privacy Policy . . . . . . . . . . . . . . . . 732
  Shree Nivas, C. J. Gokul, Vijayanand Banahatti, and Sachin Lodha

Correction to: TactCube: Designing Mobile Interactions
with Ambient Intelligence . . . . . . . . . . . . . . . . . . . . . . . . . . . . . . . . . C1
  Pietro Battistoni, Marianna Di Gregorio, Marco Romano,
  Monica Sebillo, and Giuliana Vitiello

**Author Index** . . . . . . . . . . . . . . . . . . . . . . . . . . . . . . . . . . . . . . . . 743

# Interaction Techniques

# Auditory-Centered Vocal Feedback System Using Solmization for Training Absolute Pitch Without GUI

Nozomu Yoshida[1]([envelope]), Kosaku Namikawa[1], Yusuke Koroyasu[1],
Yoshiki Nagatani[2], and Yoichi Ochiai[1,2]

[1] University of Tsukuba, Tsukuba 305–8577, Japan
{nozo,namikawa,koroyu,wizard}@digitalnature.slis.tsukuba.ac.jp
[2] Pixie Dust Technologies, inc., Tokyo 101-0061, Japan
yoshiki.nagatani@pixiedusttech.com
https://digitalnature.slis.tsukuba.ac.jp
https://pixiedusttech.com

**Abstract.** This study proposes an auditory-centered training system using solmization to artificially acquire and train absolute pitch by providing vocal feedback of musical notes through a musician's voice. Most current training systems and applications for absolute pitch acquisition have focused on providing visual feedback. However, many people having perfect pitch describe that they hear music as words rather than envisioning visual notes. Therefore, we propose a training system that does not require a graphical user interface. In an experiment with 10 participants, our system's training with vocal feedback improved six non-potential absolute pitch users' absolute pitch by approximately 25%, although extant system with visual feedback didn't make an improvement.

**Keywords:** Auditory feedback · Learning method · Pitch training

## 1 Introduction

This study proposes a auditory-centered training system using solmization to artificially acquire and train absolute pitch by providing vocal feedback of musical notes by musician's voice. Absolute pitch is the ability to name or produce a note of a given musical tone without an external reference tone [24]. People with this ability are rare, and its prevalence in the general population in North America and Europe is estimated to be less than 10,000 people [2,20,24]. Absolute pitch is not an essential skill; however, having absolute pitch can sometimes be beneficial, especially for professional musicians. For example, it is difficult to detect minor pitch errors by determining pitch relations in atonal music [5].

**Electronic supplementary material** The online version of this chapter (https://doi.org/10.1007/978-3-030-85610-6_1) contains supplementary material, which is available to authorized users.

© IFIP International Federation for Information Processing 2021
Published by Springer Nature Switzerland AG 2021
C. Ardito et al. (Eds.): INTERACT 2021, LNCS 12935, pp. 3–19, 2021.
https://doi.org/10.1007/978-3-030-85610-6_1

Additionally, a composer with absolute pitch can sometimes work efficiently with one note at a time, compared to a composer without absolute pitch who has to work in two-note increments [15].

Most current absolute pitch training systems provide musical note names and pitches via the graphical display as visual feedback. Here, visual feedback refers to the feedback of information via the user's vision. However, most individuals having absolute pitch state that they hear music as words rather than envisioning it as notes [12,17]. Therefore, the proposed method adopts a musical note-singing method called solmization; a method of singing while calling out each sound by its note name (e.g., *do, re, mi*). Solmization provides singers with vocal feedback of notes in the form of words, facilitating pitch training. Here, vocal feedback refers to the feedback of information via the user's hearing by speech. Furthermore, our proposed system does not require a Graphical User Interface (GUI), in contrast to traditional training systems, such as tuners and the visualized guide melody of Karaoke.

Our contributions are as follows. First, we constructed a system that allows users to recognize note names aurally via solmization. Second, we compared our vocal feedback system with existing visual feedback systems and identified which type is more effective.

## 2    Related Work

### 2.1    Pitch Training

Various training methods have been developed to improve the musical sense of pitch [9,10,16,21,23]. Solfege, which applies solmization at the scale of C, uses the *sol-fa* syllables to name or represent the tones of a melody or scale. It refers to training that involves writing down the music heard by ear onto a score and singing the melody while looking at it. Additionally, musical-instrument and singing instruction can be regarded as sound training that requires a teacher. It is known that paying attention to the pitch of both voice and instrument improves the vocal and aural senses.

Karaoke provides a visualized training tool for similar purposes. For example, the Live Dam Stadium DX-G[1] is an analytical scoring system for Karaoke, and it feeds back the singer's pitch in real-time as a visualized melody. There are several such pitch-training applications. In the work of [13], a self-training mobile application was built that improved the sense of pitch as the user sang into an interactive user interface. Additionally, [6] provided a singing and pitch-training application for children with cochlear implants. With the Ear Training Myu-Tre[2] and OtoAte[3] applications, users train their absolute pitch by listening to a specific pitch and guessing the note. The C-major scale (i.e., CDEFGAB) is displayed on the screen to assist the user visually. The Pitch[4] application provides information on note names and pitches of 3–7 scales, and by guessing the presented

---

[1] https://www.clubdam.com/app/dam/seimitsusaiten/, Accessed on Jan 18, 2021.
[2] https://apps.apple.com/jp/app/id1015269208, Accessed on Jan 18, 2021.
[3] https://apps.apple.com/jp/app/id763325064, Accessed on Jan 18, 2021.
[4] https://apps.apple.com/jp/app/id942373213, Accessed on Jan 18, 2021.

notes, users train their relative pitch. This tool requires a GUI. The Singing Assessment and Development [11,26] tool was a pioneer project that incorporated real-time visual feedback into educational software for singing. It provided a pedagogical tool for assessing and developing the singing voices of UK primary school children using real-time visual feedback technology. The ALBERT tool [22] provides acoustic output while monitoring laryngeal action. Thus, the system provides a greater diversity of feedback displays and parameters, such as F0, larynx closed quotient, spectral ratio, sound-pressure level (amplitude), shimmer, and jitter. The SING and SEE [3] tools distinguished three parameters (i.e., pitch, vowel identification, and timbre). Although SING and SEE focused on maximizing visual feedback, the VOXed project [25] involved psychologists, vocalists, singing instructors, and students to investigate the usefulness of direct feedback using commercially available visual feedback software. MiruSinger [18] proposed a method of automatically assessing a user's singing ability by providing visual feedback of musical information without using musical notation.

## 2.2 HCI Study Using Auditory Feedback

Kuber et al. demonstrated the potential for non-visual speech-based audio and haptic feedback systems in the design of accessible memory games to aid visually impaired users who would otherwise remain excluded from most mainstream gaming applications [14]. They recommended that speech-based feedback be presented in conjunction with haptic cues when developing a non-visual game. Stina et al. proposed a running-technique training system that combined real-time visual and audio feedback [19]. In their proposed system, the visual feedback displayed acceleration, and the audio feedback conveyed the runner's rhythm using beeps. This study suggested that, if the users were in a situation where the screen could not be seen, the audio feedback would provide suitable feedback. Therefore, when inducing user movement, voice feedback may be suitable if the amount of data transmitted is succinct, such as that of rhythm or note names. Guardati et al. proposed a method to assist with writing rehabilitation [8]. The system was designed for human-in-the-loop operations, and it could analyze handwriting in real-time while providing vocal feedback to guide the patient during exercise. The advantage of the proposed method is that it could be easily used at home without a trainer. Christiansen et al. investigated in-vehicle input and output techniques to compare their effects on driving behavior and attention, finding that using audio resulted in significantly fewer eye glances but longer task completion times with inferior primary driving task performance compared with visual cues [4]. Gaver et al. proposed Auditory Icon, an alternative approach to the use of sound in computer interfaces that emphasized the role of sound in conveying information about the world to the listener [7]. By combining auditory and visual feedback, all information could be accessed more efficiently. For example, when an error occurred on a computer, a beeping sound in addition to a warning screen display would instantly inform the user of the situation.

## 2.3   Vocal Feedback as Cybernetics

Cybernetics is a research field that attempts to study the structure of control and communication/information transmission in a wide range of mechanical, biological, and social organizations from basically the same methodological perspective [27]. The core concept of the discipline is circular causality or feedback, i.e., where the outcomes of actions are taken as inputs for further action [1]. The vocal feedback system also includes the concept of Cybernetics in terms of performing a feedback loop. The user communicates with the vocal feedback system by actions (such as one's voice or UI operation), receives feedback by listening to the system output, and performs self-regulation after referring to it.

## 2.4   Position of This Study

The research question for this study is "can absolute pitch be trained by a vocal feedback system?" Extant pitch-training methods provide visual feedback containing the note information. However, individuals with absolute pitch describe their experience as audible instead of visual. Furthermore, previous studies indicate that auditory feedback is useful for providing simple information. Therefore, we construct a system that allows users to aurally recognize note names. Then, we compare the auditory feedback system with the extant method to identify which one is more effective.

# 3   Implementation

## 3.1   Design Principles

Figure 1 shows the design of our proposed system. It consists of five modules.

**Random Test Generator:** A module that determines the correct pitch. The fundamental tone is 60 (C4, 261.6 Hz), and it randomly selects the correct pitch from the C-major scale range at one octave from the fundamental tone.

**User Input:** A module in which the user inputs a note number via a slider. The slider's pitch change rate per width is random for each quiz to prevent the user from memorizing the note according to slider position.

**Oscillator:** A module that sounds input and correct pitches. The triangular-wave oscillator reproduces the pitch corresponding to the input. The user interface has a fundamental tone button, an input tone button, and correct tone button, but they are not played simultaneously to prevent delivering hints for guessing.

**Vocal Feedback:** A module that outputs vocal feedback corresponding to the input pitch. From the input sounds, the microtonal music is rounded off to the nearest semitone unit. The sound source material used for vocal feedback is sampled from a vocalist who had mastered vocal music.

**Display:** A module that returns the user's input pitch in text form. The displayed pitch entered with the slide bar is rounded off to the nearest semitone unit.

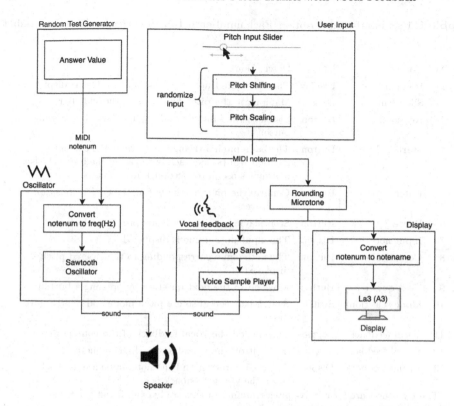

**Fig. 1.** Design of absolute pitch trainer consisting of five modules: random test generator, user input, oscillator, vocal feedback, and display. In our system, the note name is given auditory feedback in real-time, unlike the existing software learning method that visually feeds back the note name.

## 3.2   User Interface

Figure 2 provides a screenshot of the interface, and Table 1 describes each button of the display interface. The interface provides a random pitch test for training, and it is used as the proposed system for absolute pitch training in an experiment. In addition to the vocal feedback feature, our application has a visual feedback feature for comparative experiments, as shown in Nos. 12 and 13 in Table 1. The visual feedback feature displays staff notation with note names. In the proposed vocal feedback system, GUI-free pitch training is possible. However, because the experiment requires the user to provide the pitch input using a slide bar, a GUI was adopted. The only difference between vocal and visual feedback is the type of note-name fed back, and the other specifications are the same.

**Table 1.** User interface description. Each number in Table 1 corresponds to the number in Fig. 2.

| No | Name | UI type | Description |
|---|---|---|---|
| 1 | Random test | Display | The designated note name as random test is displayed |
| 2 | Slide bar | Drag | Manipulate the pitch by dragging the slide bar |
| 3 | Keynote[a] | Button | Listen to the fundamental triangle wave by pressing a button |
| 4 | Start | Button | The bar's pitch's triangular wave at the current position will be fed back by pressing the button. Also, it resumes oscillator feedback from Pause |
| 5 | Enter | Button | Confirm the pitch of the bar at the current position as an answer |
| 6 | Pause | Button | Stop playing the oscillator by pressing a button |
| 7 | Input note | Display | The input note name is displayed |
| 8 | Correct pitch | Button | The note name corresponding to the entered pitch is displayed |
| 9 | Next question | Button | Move on to the next question by pressing a button |
| 10 | Mode selection[a] | Switch | Switch between absolute pitch mode and relative pitch mode |
| 11 | Vocal feedback | Toggle | Turn on/off the vocal feedback of the note name |
| 12 | Visual feedback | Toggle | Turn on/off the visual feedback of the note name |
| 13 | Visual feedback | Display | The staff notation and the note name are fed back when the visual feedback is on |

[a] These features are for relative pitch training. In this study experiment, we focused only on absolute pitch, so we did not use them.

## 4  Experiment

We anticipated that the vocal feedback of the note name presented by the proposed system would be more effective in improving the absolute pitch than the visual feedback of the existing system. Thus, we conducted an experiment to determine the same. The experiment consisted of a preliminary test and a main test. Additionally, a pre-questionnaire was conducted to determine attributes, such as the participants' musical experience prior to the experiment. A post-survey was also conducted to evaluate the experiment process and the usability of the system. The experiment was conducted with the approval of our institution's ethics review committee.

### 4.1  Participants

We recruited 10 men with no reported physical or mental disability ranging in age from 20 to 24 years old as participants (M: 22; SD: 1.3). We accepted participants regardless of their musical experience. All participants have never received singing instruction or music theory instruction, though four people (P2, P8, P9, P10) had experience playing the piano or electric piano, and three people (P2, P8, P10) had ever taken the piano lesson.

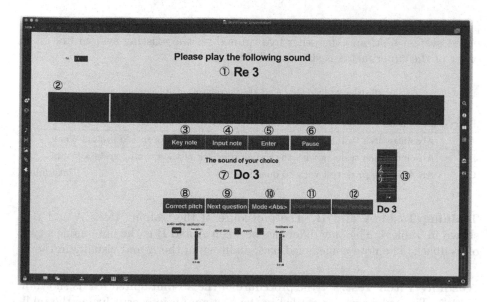

**Fig. 2.** User interfaces for training and learning absolute pitch. Each number in Fig. 2 corresponds to the number in Table 1. There are two types of training modes: the auditory feedback mode (proposed system) and the visual feedback mode (existing system). There is also a test mode for absolute pitch test, which excludes the training mode's feedback function.

## 4.2 Preliminary Test

Using an existing pitch-training application (Ear Training Myu-Tre), the participants attempted the absolute pitch quiz 10 times and recorded their scores. The contents of the test was as follows. First, for each trial, one of the seven C-major scale notes was given as a piano note sound: $Do$/C, $Re$/D, $Mi$/E, $Fa$/F, $Sol$/G, $La$/A, and $Si$/B. Next, the participants attempted to identify the note name at the same pitch as the given piano note sound. The score was recorded as "correct" or "incorrect," but the pitch distance between the correct pitch and the input pitch was not recorded.

## 4.3 Main Test

We conducted the main test to verify the hypothesis: vocal feedback of the note name by the proposed system is more effective in improving the absolute pitch than the visual feedback of the note name by the existing system-based counterpart. For the convenience of explanation, we defined the training provided by the proposed system as A. The training provided by the existing system is B. The absolute pitch test, C, is shown in Table 2. In this experiment, the participants were trained in absolute pitch using both systems (A and B). Additionally, we quantified the improvement of the absolute pitch tests conducted before and after the training. They took test C before and after training A and B. To reduce possible bias caused by the training order, five participants trained on the proposed system first, and the other five trained on the existing system first. The order of the experiments is shown in Table 3.

**Table 2.** Definition of the experimental process

| Process | Definition | Time |
|---------|-----------|------|
| A | Absolute pitch training with the vocal feedback of the proposed system | 5 min |
| B | Absolute pitch training with the visual feedback of the existing system | 5 min |
| C | An Absolute pitch test with 10 questions | Until finish |

**Training Task: A and B.** The procedure of the training tasks A and B is shown in Table 4. The only difference between A and B is the note name's type of feedback; The note name is fed back auditory in the A and visually in the B.

**Absolute Pitch Test: C.** the procedure of the absolute pitch test is shown in Table 5. Two values were recorded in the system: an integer value as the midi-note number of the correct note name and a real value as the midi-note number of the input note name. Therefore, it could measure the distance between the correct and input pitches. For example, when the correct pitch was C4 (midi-note #60) and the input pitch was C#4 (midi-note #61). A distance of 1.0 was recorded as an error. Both the correct and input pitches could be octaves, and the distance was calculated by the difference between the input pitch and the nearest correct pitch.

## 5   Result

### 5.1   Preliminary Test

For grouping purposes, in the preliminary test, the four people who recorded perfect scores were defined as "potential absolute pitch," and the other six were defined as "non-potential absolute pitch." The scores from the preliminary test for potential and non-potential absolute pitch are shown in the second columns of Tables 6 and 7, respectively. All potential absolute pitches had experience playing the piano or electric piano, and three (P2, P8, P10) had ever taken the piano lesson for several years between 4 and 13 years old. All non-potential absolute pitches had neither experience playing the instruments nor lessons of any musical instruments (except for the class in the school).

**Table 3.** Experiment pattern

| Pattern | # of Participants | Order |
|---------|-------------------|-------|
| 1 | 5 | C A C Interval C B C |
| 2 | 5 | C B C Interval C A C |

**Table 4.** Procedure of training task: A, B

| Step | Description |
|---|---|
| 1 | A randomly specified note name is displayed; participants imagine the pitch and note name |
| 2 | Operate the slide bar to approach the pitch you imagined while listening to the oscillator sound |
| 3 | Stop the bar at the position where the specified note name is auditory (A) or visually (B) fed back, and press the enter button. At that time, be sure that the pitch name and pitch are associated and memorized |
| 4 | Listen to the correct pitch. At that time, be sure that the floor name and pitch are associated and memorized |
| 5 | Click the "next question button" to move to the next question |
| 6 | Repeat a series of steps 1–5 for 5 min |

**Table 5.** Procedure of absolute pitch test: C

| Step | Description |
|---|---|
| 1 | A randomly specified note name is displayed; participants imagine the pitch of that note name |
| 2 | Operate the slide bar to approach the pitch you imagined while listening to the oscillator sound |
| 3 | Stop the bar at the position that is thought to be correct and press the enter button |
| 4 | The note name corresponding to the input pitch is displayed, and the real value of the midi note number is recorded in the system |
| 5 | Click "the next question button" to move to the next question |
| 6 | Repeat a series of steps 1–5 10 times |

## 5.2   Main Test

The results were divided into two categories: potential and non-potential absolute pitch. The average error is the average difference between the midi number of the correct pitch and that of the input pitch from the 10 questions of test C (c.f. Sect. 4.3). The improvement value refers to the difference between the average error before and after training. The improvement rate refers to the value obtained by dividing the average error before training by that after training.

**Potential Absolute Pitch.** Table 6 shows the results of the experiment of potential absolute pitch. Generally, neither the proposed nor the existing system showed significant improvement. The average improvement value was slightly negative (−0.09), and the average improvement rate was positive (+11%) in the proposed system. The average improvement value was slightly negative (−0.07), and the average improvement rate was almost 0 in the existing system (Fig. 3).

**Table 6.** Result of potential absolute pitch (PS: Pretest Score, BT: Before Training, AT: After Training, IV: Improvement Value, IR: Improvement Rate).

| | | Proposed system | | | | Existing system | | | |
| | | Average error | | Improvement | | Average error | | Improvement | |
| ID | PS | BT | AT | IV | IR | BT | AT | IV | IR |
| 2 | 10 | 0.29 | 0.16 | 0.13 | +82% | 0.23 | 0.21 | 0.02 | +12% |
| 8 | 10 | 0.34 | 0.49 | −0.16 | −32% | 0.50 | 0.52 | −0.02 | −4% |
| 9 | 10 | 0.41 | 0.39 | 0.02 | +4% | 0.33 | 0.32 | 0.01 | +2% |
| 10 | 10 | 2.97 | 3.30 | −0.33 | −10% | 2.87 | 3.16 | −0.30 | −9% |
| Ave | 10 | 1.00 | 1.09 | −0.09 | +11% | 0.98 | 1.05 | −0.07 | +0% |

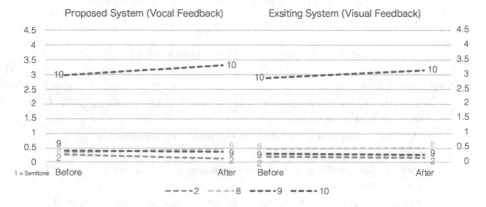

**Fig. 3.** Average error transition of potential absolute pitch.

**Non-potential Absolute Pitch.** Table 7 shows the result of non-potential absolute pitch. Generally, the proposed system showed some improvement, whereas the existing system did not. In the proposed system, both the average improvement value and the average improvement rate were positive (0.65 and +25%, respectively). In particular, P4 had an improvement value of 1.40, implying that the absolute pitch accuracy improved by more than a semitone. In contrast, in the existing system, both the average improvement value and the average improvement rate were negative (−0.49 and −12%, respectively). The existing system did not show any improvement, except for one person on P7 (Fig. 4).

**Statistical Hypothesis Testing.** We conducted a Wilcoxon signed-rank test at a significance level of 5% to compare the average error before and after training in the proposed/existing system. The null hypothesis stated that there would be no difference in the average error before and after training with the proposed/existing system, and the alternative hypothesis stated that there would

**Table 7.** Result of non-potential absolute pitch (PS: Pretest Score, BT: Before Training, AT: After Training, IV: Improvement Value, IR: Improvement Rate).

| | | Proposed system | | | | Existing system | | | |
| | | Average error | | Improvement | | Average error | | Improvement | |
| ID | PS | BT | AT | IV | IR | BT | AT | IV | IR |
|---|---|---|---|---|---|---|---|---|---|
| 1 | 6 | 1.91 | 1.88 | 0.02 | +1% | 1.66 | 2.20 | −0.54 | −25% |
| 3 | 4 | 3.47 | 3.04 | 0.43 | +14% | 1.91 | 3.53 | −1.63 | −46% |
| 4 | 4 | 4.15 | 2.76 | 1.40 | +51% | 2.74 | 3.76 | −1.02 | −27% |
| 5 | 2 | 4.17 | 3.30 | 0.87 | +26% | 2.35 | 3.41 | −1.07 | −31% |
| 6 | 5 | 3.11 | 2.47 | 0.64 | +26% | 2.47 | 2.45 | 0.02 | +1% |
| 7 | 5 | 2.28 | 1.73 | 0.56 | +32% | 3.58 | 2.27 | 1.31 | +58% |
| Ave | 4.33 | 3.18 | 2.53 | 0.65 | +25% | 2.45 | 2.94 | −0.49 | −12% |

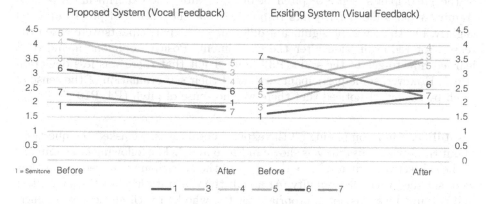

**Fig. 4.** Average error transition of non-potential absolute pitch.

be a difference in the average error before and after training with the proposed/existing system.

– Potential absolute pitch with the proposed system: We confirmed that there was no significant difference (N = 4, p-value = 0.625, Z = −0.730).
– Potential absolute pitch with the existing system: We confirmed that there was no significant difference (N=4, p-value = 0.875, Z = −0.365).
– Non-Potential absolute pitch with the proposed system: We confirmed a significant difference (N = 6, p-value = 0.0313, Z = 2.20).
– Non-Potential absolute pitch with the existing system: We confirmed that there was no significant difference (N = 6, p-value = 0.438, Z = −0.943).

In summary, it showed significance only when people with non-potential absolute pitch trained with the proposed system. No significance was shown when the non-potential absolute pitch trained with the existing system or when the potential absolute pitch trained with either the proposed system or the existing system.

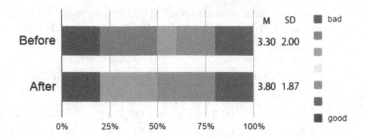

**Fig. 5.** Self-evaluation of the pitch of the participants

## 5.3   User Study

**Self-evaluation of the Pitch.** Figure 5 shows the results of the self-evaluation of the participants' sense of pitch before and after the experiment. After the training task, some participants responded that their sense of pitch improved slightly, but there was no significant difference. The participants were asked the reason for the evaluation after the experiment. Positive opinions included "I learned how to get to the scale (P3)" and "I felt that there was less deviation (P6)". However, some participants reviewed their self-evaluation of the sense of pitch by saying, "I noticed that there was no sense of pitch (P4, P10)."

**Usability.** After completing all the experimental tasks, we asked the questions about the system's usability as shown in Fig. 6 and 7. The following is a summary of the subjective feedback. More than 50% of the participants answered that they were satisfied with the usability. Although the difficulty level of the sound test and training task was not appropriate for P8, who had with musical experience, 70% of the participants in the experiment answered that it was appropriate. 90% said they were less tired overall, and the degree of fatigue was only 50% for the eyes and 30% for the ears. Additionally, we asked whether the existing system or the proposed system could be used for long-term sound training (e.g., 1 h/day for a month). 80% said that they would like to use the proposed system. When asked about improvements, they mentioned some related to the user interface and feedback system. One of the user interface improvements was to change the button layout. Regarding vocal feedback, it was recommended that the voice of the vocal feedback should be selectable. There was also a desire for multiple choices of feedback voice and for shortening the long word, "sharp".

**User Interview.** Fig. 8 displays the impressions of the users of the proposed system. 90% of the respondents displayed a lack of confidence regarding listening to music and singing with others. Most said that the proposed system did not affect their motivation for music activities: "music is fun even if you do not know the scale (P4)," and "music is naturally fun (P9)." However, more than 50% said that they became more aware of pitch (Third question in Fig. 8) and more than

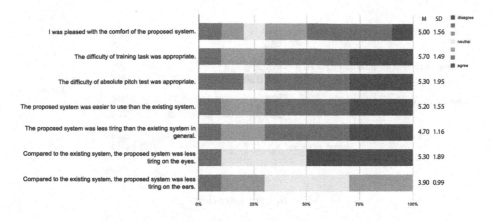

**Fig. 6.** Questionnaire about Usability

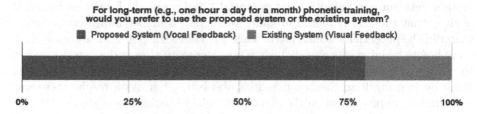

**Fig. 7.** Questionnaire about Usability2

80% said they thought the proposed system is a great way to improve their pitch (Fourth question in Fig. 8).

## 6    Discussion

For the "potential absolute pitch" participants, as discussed in Sect. 5.2, neither the proposed system nor the existing one showed significant training effect. One possible reason is that the error recorded in test C before training for potential absolute pitch participants was initially small. Thus, it was difficult to show improvement. However, as a result of the discussion in Sect. 5.2, in the case of non-potential absolute pitch participants, the average improvement rate was 25% higher than before training and 37% higher with the existing system. In addition, Wilcoxon signed-rank test comparing the average errors before and after the proposed system's training confirmed a significant difference (Sect. 5.2). Thus, the proposed system may show beneficial results regarding the absolute pitch training of non-potential absolute pitch participants.

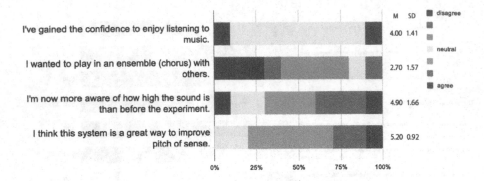

**Fig. 8.** User interview

Figure 9 shows the distribution of pitch improvement values in the proposed system between non-potential and potential absolute pitch. From this figure, it is clear that the non-potential absolute pitch had a higher improvement value than did the potential absolute pitch. This is because the potential absolute pitch score before training was already high. Thus, the score after training was unlikely to change. Therefore, as shown in Sect. 5.2, we investigated the improvement value by limiting it to the non-potential absolute pitch. As a result, there was a significant improvement in the absolute pitch. Thus, it is considered that the proposed system has certain advantages over the existing system.

## 7   Future Work

### 7.1   Relative Pitch Training

In this study, the experiment was designed to train absolute pitch. However, initially, it could also train relative pitch. When training the relative pitch, the idea of movable *Do* is applied. For example, with the voice that feeds back the pitch name of *Si*/B when *La*/A is used as the fundamental tone, the pitch remains *Si*/B, but the pitch name becomes *Re*/D. Because it is possible to test the relative pitch using this principle, future verification is needed.

### 7.2   Non-GUI Application

In this research experiment, a GUI-based slide bar was used as the system input to unify the experimental conditions. However, by limiting the system input system to auditory system only, ubiquitous sound training becomes possible, as opposed to the GUI-based system.

**Voice Input.** In the training task, by inputting the user's voice into the system input, it is possible to perform sound training by vocalization. Therefore, the users can train their pitch sense by simply wearing earphones with a microphone. Additionally, users can improve their ability to utter their voice at the height of the pitch they imagined. As a case study, users could walk around outside while training their pitch sense and vocalization.

**Improvement Value of proposed method**

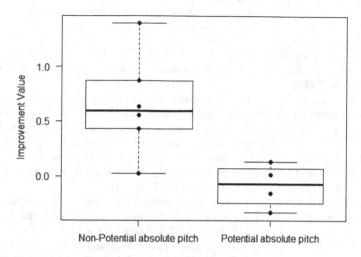

**Fig. 9.** Distribution of pitch improvement values in the proposed system

**Gesture Input.** By using a pressure sensor-type slide bar attached to the hand as a system input, the users can perform a training task by indicating pitch by gesturing the sliding of the finger. As a case study, users can employ gesturing when in crowds or when it would otherwise be difficult to sing.

## 8   Conclusion

This study proposes a novel auditory-centered training system using solmization to artificially acquire and train absolute pitch by providing vocal feedback to a musician's musical notes. Our contributions are as follows. First, we constructed a system that allows users to recognize note names aurally via solmization. Second, we compared our vocal feedback system with existing visual feedback systems and identified which type is more effective. In an experiment with 10 participants, our system's training improved six non-potential absolute pitch users' absolute pitch by approximately 25%. We also proposed GUI-free pitch training by vocalization or reflecting pitch with finger motion, which is beneficial in situations where it is difficult to hear or speak. Future verification is needed on relative pitch training and GUI-free application with vocal feedback.

## References

1. Ashby, W.R.: An Introduction to Cybernetics. Chapman & Hall Ltd., Boca Raton (1961)
2. Bachem, A.: Absolute pitch. Physcol. Bull. **161**(1948), 1180–1185 (1948)
3. Callaghan, J., Thorpe, W., van Doorn, J.: The science of singing and seeing, pp. 15–18 (2004)

4. Christiansen, L.H., Frederiksen, N.Y., Jensen, B.S., Ranch, A., Skov, M.B., Thiru-ravichandran, N.: Don't look at me, i'm talking to you: investigating input and output modalities for in-vehicle systems. In: Campos, P., Graham, N., Jorge, J., Nunes, N., Palanque, P., Winckler, M. (eds.) INTERACT 2011. LNCS, vol. 6947, pp. 675–691. Springer, Heidelberg (2011). https://doi.org/10.1007/978-3-642-23771-3_49

5. Crutchfield, W.: There may be more to music than meets a typical ear. The New York Times (1990)

6. Duan, Z., Gupta, C., Percival, G., Grunberg, D., Wang, Y.: SECCIMA: singing and ear training for children with cochlear implants via a mobile application (2017)

7. Gaver, W.W.: Auditory icons: using sound in computer interfaces. Hum. Comput. Interact. 2(2), 167–177 (1986). https://doi.org/10.1207/s15327051hci0202_3

8. Guardati, L., Casamassima, F., Farella, E., Benini, L.: Paper, pen and ink: an innovative system and software framework to assist writing rehabilitation. Presented at the (2015). https://doi.org/10.7873/DATE.2015.0453

9. Hoppe, D., Sadakata, M., Desain, P.: Development of real-time visual feedback assistance in singing training: a review. J. Comput. Assist. Learn. 22(4), 308–316 (2006). https://doi.org/10.1111/j.1365-2729.2006.00178.x

10. Howard, D.M.: Technology for real-time visual feedback in singing lessons. Res. Stud. Music Educ. 24(1), 40–57 (2005). https://doi.org/10.1177/1321103X050240010401

11. Howard, D.M., Welch, G.F.: Microcomputer-based singing ability assessment and development. Appl. Acoust. 27(2), 89–102 (1989). https://doi.org/10.1016/0003-682X(89)90002-9

12. Itoh, K., Suwazono, S., Arao, H., Miyazaki, K., Nakada, T.: Electrophysiological correlates of absolute pitch and relative pitch. Cerebral cortex (New York, N.Y. : 1991) 15, 760–769 (2005). https://doi.org/10.1093/cercor/bhh177

13. Kin Wah Edward, L., Anderson, H., Hamzeen, H., Lui, S.: Implementation and evaluation of real-time interactive user interface design in self-learning singing pitch training apps (2014). https://doi.org/10.13140/RG.2.1.1757

14. Kuber, R., Tretter, M., Murphy, E.: Developing and evaluating a non-visual memory game. In: Campos, P., Graham, N., Jorge, J., Nunes, N., Palanque, P., Winckler, M. (eds.) INTERACT 2011. LNCS, vol. 6947, pp. 541–553. Springer, Heidelberg (2011). https://doi.org/10.1007/978-3-642-23771-3_41

15. Langfeld, H.S.: Psychological monographs. Psychological Review. Publication (1932)

16. Leong, S., Cheng, L.: Effects of real-time visual feedback on pre-service teachers' singing. J. Comput. Assist. Learn. 30(3), 285–296 (2014). https://doi.org/10.1111/jcal.12046

17. Matsuda, M., Igarashi, H., Itoh, K.: Auditory t-complex reveals reduced neural activities in the right auditory cortex in musicians with absolute pitch. Front. Neurosci. 13, 809 (2019)

18. Nakano, T., Goto, M., Hiraga, Y.: MiruSinger: a singing skill visualization interface using real-time feedback and music CD recordings as referential data. In: Ninth IEEE International Symposium on Multimedia Workshops (ISMW 2007), pp. 75–76 (2007). https://doi.org/10.1109/ISM.Workshops.2007.19

19. Nylander, S., Jacobsson, M., Tholander, J.: Runright - real-time visual and audio feedback on running (2014). https://doi.org/10.1145/2559206.2574806

20. Profita, J., Bidder, T.G.: Perfect pitch. Am. J. Med. Genet. 29(4), 763–771 (1988). https://doi.org/10.1002/ajmg.1320290405

21. Richardson, P., Kim, Y.: Beyond fun and games: a framework for quantifying music skill developments from video game play. J. New Music Res. **40**(4), 277–291 (2011). https://doi.org/10.1080/09298215.2011.565350
22. Rossiter, D., Howard, D.: Albert: a real-time visual feedback computer tool for professional vocal development. J. Voice Official J. Voice Found. **10**(4), 321–336 (1996). http://europepmc.org/abstract/MED/8943135
23. Shiraishi, M., Ogasawara, K., Kitahara, T.: HamoKara: a system that enables amateur singers to practice backing vocals for karaoke. J. Inf. Process. **27**, 683–692 (2019). https://doi.org/10.2197/ipsjjip.27.683
24. Takeuchi, A.H., Hulse, S.H.: Absolute pitch. Psychol. Bull. **113**(2), 345–361 (1993). https://doi.org/10.1037/0033-2909.113.2.345
25. Welch, G., Himonides, E., Howard, D., Brereton, J.: VOXed: Technology as a meaningful teaching aid in the singing studio, pp. 166–167 (2004)
26. Welch, G., Howard, D., C, R.: The SINGAD (singing assessment and development) system: A classroom-based pilot study with poor pitch singers. Canad. J. Music Educ. Res. Edn. (1988)
27. Wiener, N.: Cybernetics: or Control and Communication in the Animal and the Machine, 2nd edn. MIT Press, Cambridge (1948)

# Dealing with Input Mode Confusion During Dual-Language Keyboard Use

Paraskevas Petsanas, Christos Sintoris$^{(\boxtimes)}$ ⓘ, and Nikolaos Avouris ⓘ

Interactive Technologies Laboratory, University of Patras, 26500 Patras, Greece
{sintoris,avouris}@upatras.gr
https://hci.ece.upatras.gr

**Abstract.** Dual-language or multiple-language keyboards are widely used in many parts of the world, where users need to type in more than one scripts. During use of such keyboards, 'input mode errors' often occur when the user types in one language mode while the keyboard layout is set to a different one. These errors, along with frequent switching between input modes, are a source of confusion and distraction. In this paper we report on a study of this condition among Greek-speaking dual language keyboard users and describe a tool for automatically detecting this kind of errors and dealing with them in the case of an English-Greek keyboard. We also investigate the effects of this input mode error correction tool on a group of typical users during a study that lasted several days.

**Keywords:** Text input · Input mode · Keyboard interaction

## 1 Introduction

Multilingual text entry is prevalent among users who write in non-roman alphabets, such as the alphabets used by Greek [1], Arabic [2,4], Cyrillic [8], and other writing systems, such as those used in Asian countries [3,7,14]. When using the keyboard for text entry, these users frequently alternate between the available language modes by using a key stroke sequence or by using the mouse to select the input mode. A review of relevant literature shows that this is an acknowledged problem among users of multiple keyboard layouts [3,5,7,14], although we are not aware of any studies that report on the extend of this condition.

Input mode errors might occur when users perform tasks that require frequent mode switching, for example when writing non-English texts that require English terms, or when working on multiple concurrent tasks that require application-switching, for example typing an answer in an email composer while the primary task is programming in a code editor. Input mode errors have an adverse effect on user experience [14] since, in order to correct an error, the user has to become aware of it, erase the input, switch input mode and finally retype.

© IFIP International Federation for Information Processing 2021
Published by Springer Nature Switzerland AG 2021
C. Ardito et al. (Eds.): INTERACT 2021, LNCS 12935, pp. 20–28, 2021.
https://doi.org/10.1007/978-3-030-85610-6_2

This paper focuses on a study of the occurrence of input mode errors among Greek speaking users. We propose a method for detecting the errors and subsequently a method for auto-correcting such errors without switching input mode.

## 2    Related Work

A number of software utilities have been developed to mitigate input mode errors that occur while typing (Keyboard Ninja [11], Key Switcher [10], LangOver [12], PuntoSwitcher [15], LayoutFix [13]). Most of them work properly with English and other languages, mostly Russian, but none of them is optimized for Greek, i.e. all have either problems with character encoding when switching between Greek and English, do not support Greek accented characters, or do not support automatic mode switching, i.e. to correct the input mode error, the user has first to select a text portion and then invoke the tool.

Solutions and mechanisms for alleviating the effects of input mode errors have been explored by researchers. Most recently, Lee et al. [14] proposed three methods for tackling input mode errors, offering, in some cases, on-the-fly correction, while others [3,5] proposed methods for automatic correction of input mode errors. The auto-replace method presented here resembles most closely the auto-switch method proposed in [14]. The cognitive process related to switching between different scripts and the technology that may cause a breakdown of interaction [18] during typing needs to be further studied in the lab and in the wild, in the case of various linguistic contexts. The study and the prototype presented next aim towards this direction.

## 3    Approach

A novel key-monitor prototype was designed and made available for the purpose of the reported study to a number of Greek-speaking users. The key-monitor's purpose was to detect and log input mode errors while running in the background and to automatically correct such errors. The key-monitor logs the following events: (a) word typed using input mode $L$, where $L$ denotes the currently selected input language, (b) input mode switch, (c) change of active window, (d) type I input mode error, i.e. the user typing in the wrong input mode, (e) type II input mode error, i.e. the user becoming aware of the input mode error before finishing typing a word and correcting it, (f) input mode error after input mode switch, and (g) input mode error after window change. In order for these events to be detected and logged, it is necessary for the key-monitor to recognize individually typed tokens (words) and to detect mode errors.

### 3.1    Token Identification

A 'word typed' event is recognized when at least one typed alphabetical character is followed by a *delimiting* character. Delimiting characters are the space character, the return character, and any punctuation mark or special character such as commas, exclamation marks, parentheses, the @ sign etc. Upon such a sequence, a 'word typed' event is logged, along with the input mode used, i.e. Greek or English input mode. Certain keystrokes cause the key-monitor to stop the recognition process for the current word and start anew, such as when the user presses a keyboard arrow, the tab button and the home/end or pageup/pagedown buttons. Finally, compound keystrokes, such as Ctrl+a, are ignored.

Having identified a newly typed word, the next task of the key-monitor is to classify it in one of the two languages, Greek or English.

## 3.2   Language Identification

After a token has been identified, the language identification task is launched, to determine whether the user used the correct input mode to type the word. The language identification task aims to classify a recognized token into one of three categories, (a) current input language $L$, (b) alternative input language $L*$, or (c) inconclusive. Language identification relies on the basic dictionary lookup [9] method. Spell-checking dictionaries containing Greek and English words were constructed using publicly available lists of Greek[1] and English[2] words. The dictionaries are incorporated in the key-monitor apparatus in the form of an embedded database. Alternative methods were considered but discarded either due to insufficient implementation for both languages, as, for example, Greek stemmers have a very low performance, or due to overly complicated setup. On the other hand, spell-checking dictionaries were considered sufficient for the task.

**Fig. 1.** The standard Greek layout in comparison to the US English one [17]. Greek and Roman letters occupy the same keys. A shortcut alternates between input modes.

The language identification task is aware of (a) the active input mode, (b) the application window currently in focus, and (c) the three most recent language identifications. Otherwise, no knowledge of the user-level context or tasks is assumed, i.e. the key-monitor is not aware if the user casually chats or browses,

---

[1] https://www.elspell.gr/.
[2] https://github.com/dwyl/english-words.

is involved in a programing task or composes a formal document. The word identified by the token identification task is first looked up in the $L$ dictionary, i.e. the one corresponding to the current input mode. It is then looked up in the alternative $L*$ dictionary. For the alternative dictionary it is necessary to transliterate the word, since English and Greek are written using different alphabets. Transliteration follows the character mapping of the standard keyboard layouts for the Greek and English keyboard layouts. For example, the English letter 'u' and the Greek letter '$\theta$' share the same key on a standard keyboard, i.e. transliteration occurs between characters that occupy the same key (Fig. 1). If the word is found in either one of the $L$ or $L*$ dictionaries, or in neither of them, it is classified accordingly. Some words can be found in both dictionaries, since they have the same key profile, such as the English 'to' and Greek '$\tau$o'. For these words, the three most recent identifications are taken into account and the decision is based on a weighted average of the previous three mode identifications of the words that were typed.

**Mode Errors.** When a word is identified as belonging to the alternative, $L*$, mode, an input mode error is registered. Input mode errors are considered to occur when the user intends to write in mode $L$ and the keyboard is set to the alternative mode $L*$. The key-monitor registers two types of mode errors.

– A *type I mode error* occurs when a full word is typed in input mode $L$ and the key-monitor classifies it as belonging in the alternative mode $L*$.
– A *type II mode error* is registered when the user, before finishing typing a full word, notices the wrong input mode and backtracks to correct the error, i.e. before finishing the token in mode $L$, the user deletes the typed characters and retypes in $L*$ the same or more characters.

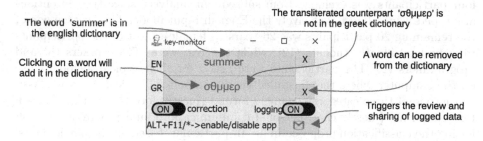

**Fig. 2.** Overview of the interface of the key-monitor prototype, as was made available to the participants in phase B. The key-monitor runs in the background and registers all keyboard input. In this instance, the user has just typed the word 'summer', which was found in the English dictionary, as indicated by the green color. The transliteration of the word in Greek was not found in the Greek one, as indicated by the red color. The user can add or remove words in the dictionary through the interface. (Color figure online)

### 3.3   Automatic Replacement

Upon registering a mode error of type I, the key-monitor (Fig. 2) automatically replaces the typed word (typed in input mode $L$) with the transliterated word (in input mode $L*$). The input mode remains the same.

## 4   Evaluation Study

The purpose of the study was to identify and understand the typing behaviour of dual input mode users, especially regarding the occurrence of mode errors, to evaluate the effectiveness of the auto-replace method and to determine whether it can improve the users' typing experience.

### 4.1   Participants

To assess the occurrence of input mode errors and evaluate the auto-replace method we conducted a field study involving 24 Greek language users. The study was split in two phases. In phase A, lasting 7 days, keyboard events were silently logged by the key-monitor. In phase B, an updated version of the key-monitor was distributed, which intervened following the auto-replace method described in Sect. 3.3 in order to assist the users when input mode errors were detected. However, in order to account for any novelty effects, phase B lasted 3 days longer than phase A and we took into account typing data for the last 70% of the typing logs.

Participants were recruited through personal and academic contacts. Most used two modes for input for writing Greek and English text, except for four of the participants, who almost exclusively typed Greek text using the Roman alphabet, a practice known widely as Greeklish [1,16]. The data related to these four participants was excluded from subsequent analysis, since they intentionally typed using almost exclusively the English input mode. The average age of the remaining 20 participants was 26 years (8 female). Most of the participants were undergraduate students (12), while the rest were office workers (6) and programmers (2). The participants were asked for their typical keyboard use on the computer where they installed the key-monitor. Typical use was classified in one of three categories, namely formal (mostly formal Greek or English text), informal (mostly chat, personal communication), and programming, following the classification proposed in [6]. In particular, based on the participants' answers in the post-study interview, 14 declared that they mostly type informal text, 1 used the keyboard for both formal and informal typing, 2 used it for programming and formal text while 3 were not available for the interview.

In total, all 24 users provided us with logged data for both phases of the study and all but 3 participated in the semi-structured interview after the study.

## 4.2   Procedure

Informed consent was obtained by all participants. To assure the participants that no private or sensitive data would be exposed, since they would be justified in mistrusting running a key-logging application on their workplace or personal computer, it was stressed that before sharing the collected data, each participant would have the opportunity to review the data and to decline sharing them.

Two versions of the key-monitor prototype were made available to all study participants. In phase A the key-monitor was capable only of detecting and logging input mode errors. The participants were asked to start the key-monitor and leave it running in the background while they conduct their usual activities for 7 days. After reviewing the logged data, every participant chose to submit it for analysis. In phase B, the version of the key-monitor with enabled auto-replace functionality was made available to the participants and they were asked to use it for 10 days (Fig. 2). Similarly to phase A, the event logging continued and at the end all participants, after reviewing the logged data, agreed to share it with no exceptions. In both phases the participants could enable and disable logging at will, as they could do with the auto-replace functionality in phase B.

Finally, individual semi-structured interviews were conducted at the end of phase B, in order to gather insights on user experience.

## 5   Results

**Phase A.** Phase A data show that the participants did encounter problems relating to input mode confusion in their everyday typing. Input mode error rate was computed per participant. On average, the participants made almost 4 times more type I mode errors than they made type II mode errors. In particular, 78.6% of the cases the users didn't notice an input mode error and typed a complete word in the wrong input mode while in the remaining 21.4% of the input mode errors, the users noticed it and backtracked to correct it (type II input mode error). This is in contrast to the results reported by Lee et al. [14] in the evaluation of their auto-switch method for Korean-English users, where they found that in 75.2% of the cases the users noticed and corrected a mode error before completing a word. This difference might be even greater, since the key-logger used in the present study does not take into account words that the user finished typing and then backtracked to rewrite in the alternative layout. The alternative, i.e. that the key-logger is overly sensitive in registering type I mode errors is not plausible, as it is evident in the results of phase B and the participant feedback in the post study interviews. The tools used in the two studies have differences, e.g. in the Korean-English study, input mode prediction is triggered by the space key, which limits the number of times it is triggered and thus it might under-count type I errors. Although differences relating to cultural issues might also explain part of the divergence, nevertheless the observation warrants further study.

The rate of mode errors when the users omit switching to the Greek input mode is the same as when they omit switching to the English input mode, on average 49.5% vs. 50.5%. On average, 10% of the input mode errors occur directly after a mode switch and 9% directly after a window change. These results are again in contrast to [14], where it is reported that in 78.3% of the cases the mode errors occurred immediately after an application switch. Overall it is evident that mode errors pose a non negligible problem in the everyday experience of dual mode Greek-English keyboard users.

**Table 1.** Mean and standard deviations of the total number of words the participants wrote, the number of mode switches, the number of mode errors per total words and the mode switch rate (Eq. 1). A consequence of the strategy for detecting mode errors is that in phase B, type I input mode errors are note being counted. Since they are automatically detected and corrected, users take advantage of this and continue typing in the wrong input mode.

| | | Phase A | Phase B |
|---|---|---|---|
| Total words | Mean | 1695.6 | 1899.7 |
| | SD | 1373.3 | 1800.7 |
| Total mode switches | Mean | 135.2 | 131.4 |
| | SD | 119.9 | 125.8 |
| Type I mode error rate | Mean | 7.37 | – |
| | SD | 3.38 | – |
| Type II mode error rate | Mean | 26.1 | 17.3 |
| | SD | 23.8 | 18.6 |
| Mode switch rate | Mean | 15.7 | 19.1 |
| | SD | 15.1 | 11.7 |

**Phase B.** In phase B, with the auto-replace functionality enabled, the overall typing behavior of the participants was improved while using the key-monitor. To quantify this we use the *mode switch rate* (Eq. 1), which measures the amount of words a user types between two consecutive mode switches,

$$\text{MSR}_\phi = \frac{\text{TW}_\phi}{\text{MS}_\phi} \tag{1}$$

where $\text{TW}_\phi$ is the count of total words written in phase $\phi$ of the study and $\text{MS}_\phi$ is the count of mode switches in phase $\phi$.

On average, the words typed between two consecutive mode switches show a slight increase in phase B, from 15.7 words to 19.1. Twelve of the participants show an increase in $MSR_b$ while two show a high decrease. One of them was not available for post-study interview, while the other reported that during phase A he was writing a long text, a task which rarely required input mode switches.

To further investigate the potential improvement of the auto-replace method, we first identified outliers by calculating the interquartile range (IQR) for the improvement in the mode switch rate, $MSR_{improved}$, where $MSR_{improved} = MSR_B\text{-}MSR_A$, which lead to the exclusion of the data of three participants as outliers. Subsequently, we performed a one-tailed Mann-Whitney test on $MSR$ scores for the two phases, which yielded a statistic $W$ of 267 with $p=0.006$.

**Semi-structured Interviews.** The semi-structured interviews confirm the results of the analysis. Most of the participants found the prototype very useful and stated that it optimized their typing experience, both in dealing with mode errors when they forgot to switch the input mode and in their overall typing efficiency. Two participants mentioned that the auto-replace functionality distracted them from their work, so they occasionally disabled the auto-replace functionality. Both stated that they would prefer the key-monitor to indicate a mode error, more emphatically than it did, without correcting it, e.g. by underlining the corresponding word similarly to spelling correction in word processors. On the other hand, eight of the participants confirmed that they adapted their behaviour in phase B and switched input modes less often. Furthermore, concerning the accuracy of the auto-replace functionality, nine participants stated that they felt that most of the time the key-monitor interfered correctly. Finally, two users mentioned that they used the key-monitor as a 'typing assistant', in order to achieve a better typing experience, i.e. they often omitted switching input modes, a behaviour which lead to their exclusion from the analysis of phase B as outliers, but which is nevertheless indicative of the prototype's usefulness.

## 6  Discussion

This study focused on occurrence of input mode errors of users of dual language keyboard (Greek-English). It should be observed that the demographic involved in this study (mostly university students and young professionals) during their everyday typing activity quite often have to switch between the two language modes half way through a text, so, as it was evident during phase A of the study, a high number of type I and type II input mode errors were observed. The introduction of the key-monitor prototype has improved both user experience and performance, as the mode switch rate improved significantly after introduction of the developed prototype. Although the results of this study are encouraging, nevertheless a number of limitations need to be taken into account. Firstly, the sample of participants is small and no claims can be made regarding its representativeness, both regarding the participant profiles and the nature of the typing tasks performed in both phases. On the other hand, this study investigates the typing behaviour and the effect of input mode errors of dual-language Greek-English users in their normal conditions of work, without interfering with their everyday activity. Furthermore, the improvements of the auto-replace method are evident both in the quantitative analysis and in the testimonies of the participants themselves. Next steps include improvements in the input mode error detection and the auto-replace method, by investigating the adequacy of alternative methods for language identification [9] and testing, both with a larger sample for a longer period and in controlled settings.

# References

1. Androutsopoulos, J.: 'Greeklish': transliteration practice and discourse in the context of computer-mediated digraphia. In: Standard Languages and Language Standards – Greek, Past and Present, pp. 249–278, Routledge (2016). https://doi.org/10.4324/9781315610580-20
2. Bianchi, R.: 3arabizi, Greeklish, and SMSki: the hybrid making of language in the age of the internet and mobile technology. Tasmeem **2015**, 1 (2015)
3. Chawannakul, C., Prasitjutrakul, S.: Keyboard layout mismatch error detection and correction system utility. In: The 8th Electrical Engineering/ Electronics, Computer, Telecommunications and Information Technology (ECTI) Association of Thailand - Conference 2011, pp. 488–491 (2011). https://doi.org/10.1109/ECTICON.2011.5947881
4. Darwish, K.: Arabizi detection and conversion to Arabic. arXiv:1306.6755 [cs] (2013)
5. Ehara, Y., Tanaka-Ishii, K.: Multilingual text entry using automatic language detection. In: Proceedings of the Third International Joint Conference on Natural Language Processing: Volume-I (2008). https://www.aclweb.org/anthology/I08-1058
6. Feit, A.M., Nancel, M., John, M., Karrenbauer, A., Weir, D., Oulasvirta, A.: AZERTY amélioré: computational design on a national scale. Commun. ACM. **64**, 48–58 (2021). https://doi.org/10/gjp75k
7. Ikegami, Y., Sakurai, Y., Tsuruta, S.: Modeless Japanese input method using multiple character sequence features. In: 2012 Eighth International Conference on Signal Image Technology and Internet Based Systems, pp. 613–618 (2012). https://doi.org/10.1109/SITIS.2012.93
8. Ivković, D.: Cyber-Latinica: a comparative analysis of latinization in internet slavic. Language@Internet **12** (2015)
9. Jauhiainen, T., Lui, M., Zampieri, M., Baldwin, T., Lindén, K.: Automatic language identification in texts: a survey. J. Artif. Intell. Res. **65**, 675–782 (2019). https://doi.org/10.1613/jair.1.11675
10. Key switcher. http://www.keyswitcher.com/. Accessed 16 Dec 2020
11. Keyboard Ninja. http://www.keyboard-ninja.com/Download.aspx. Accessed 16 Dec 2020
12. LangOver. http://langover.com/. Accessed 16 Dec 2020
13. LayoutFix. https://layoutfix.soft112.com. Accessed 16 Dec 2020
14. Lee, S., Lee, J., Lee, G.: Diagnosing and coping with mode errors in Korean-English dual-language keyboard. In: Proceedings of the 2019 CHI Conference on Human Factors in Computing Systems, pp. 1–12. Association for Computing Machinery, New York, NY, USA (2019). https://doi.org/10/gf3q8n
15. PuntoSwitcher. https://yandex.ru/soft/punto. Accessed 16 Dec 2020
16. Tseliga, T.: "It's All Greeklish to Me!" In: The Multilingual Internet: Language, Culture, and Communication Online. Oxford University Press (2007)
17. Wikimedia. https://commons.wikimedia.org/wiki/File:KB_Greek.svg. Accessed 16 Dec 2020
18. Winograd, T., Flores, F.: Understanding Computers and Cognition: A New Foundation for Design. Addison-Wesley Longman Publishing Co. Inc., Boston (1987)

# Empirical Evaluation of Moving Target Selection in Virtual Reality Using Egocentric Metaphors

Yuan Chen[1,2(✉)], Junwei Sun[2], Qiang Xu[2], Edward Lank[1], Pourang Irani[3], and Wei Li[2]

[1] University of Waterloo, Waterloo, ON, Canada
{y2238che,lank}@uwaterloo.ca
[2] Huawei Technologies, Markham, ON, Canada
{junwei.sun,qiang.xu1,wei.li.crc}@huawei.com
[3] University of Manitoba, Winnipeg, MB, Canada
irani@cs.umanitoba.ca

**Abstract.** Virtual hand or pointer metaphors are among the key approaches for target selection in immersive environments. However, targeting moving objects is complicated by factors including target speed, direction, and depth, such that a basic implementation of these techniques might fail to optimize user performance. We present results of two empirical studies comparing characteristics of virtual hand and pointer metaphors for moving target acquisition. Through a first study, we examine the impact of depth on users' performance when targets move beyond and within arms' reach. We find that movement in depth has a great impact on both metaphors. In a follow-up study, we design a reach-bounded Go-Go (rbGo-Go) technique to address challenges of virtual hand and compare it to Ray-Casting. We find that target width and speed are significant determinants of user performance and we highlight the pros and cons for each of the techniques in the given context. Our results inform the UI design for immersive selection of moving targets.

## 1 Introduction

Selection of moving targets is a common interaction in video games and when inspecting surveillance videos [21]. Moving target acquisition is challenging as it requires users to predict the speed and trajectory of objects. Furthermore, if the object is moving in depth, i.e. towards or away from users, users may also need to accurately predict its depth. In addition, acquiring moving targets in virtual

---

Y. Chen—The work was done when the author was an intern at Huawei Canada.

---

**Electronic supplementary material** The online version of this chapter (https://doi.org/10.1007/978-3-030-85610-6_3) contains supplementary material, which is available to authorized users.

© IFIP International Federation for Information Processing 2021
Published by Springer Nature Switzerland AG 2021
C. Ardito et al. (Eds.): INTERACT 2021, LNCS 12935, pp. 29–50, 2021.
https://doi.org/10.1007/978-3-030-85610-6_3

environments lacks the feedback when commonly interacting with the movement of physical objects, such as catching a baseball.

With the introduction of high-performance headsets and controllers, immersive experiences in augmented reality (AR) and virtual reality (VR) are increasingly available to consumers. Pursuing immersion has always been an end-goal in AR/VR research, and interacting with moving targets – in games [53], training environments [10], and virtual worlds (e.g. Second Life) – is an important component of this goal [10,53].

Despite extensive research in target selection techniques [7,31,39,43] and the common occurrence of moving target interaction, we identify two issues with existing work. First, the majority of target selection work in 3D environments focuses on static objects, which does not directly translate to an understanding of moving target acquisition. Second, when looking specifically at AR/VR environments, techniques for pointing and selection remain clustered across two primary metaphors—the virtual hand and the virtual pointer – which have different characteristics. Poupyrev et al. [42] identified characteristics of these two metaphors for static object selection and re-positioning tasks, however we know very little about their performance in a moving target selection task.

In this paper, we empirically explore the performance of these two common selection metaphors (virtual hand and virtual pointer) when acquiring moving targets in VR. Our work consists of two studies to evaluate these selection metaphors. In the first study, participants were asked to use a 1-to-1 mapped controller with a virtual hand and with Ray-Casting to select a moving target which appeared in a limited volume within arms' reach and at a distance. We found that depth had a significant impact on both metaphors. Given that a 1-to-1 mapping limits the reachable space when using the virtual hand, in the second study we designed a technique, called reach-bounded Go-Go (rbGo-Go), an extension of the Go-Go [43] technique, to capture distant targets. We compared rbGo-Go with Ray-Casting and found that Ray-Casting was more efficient than rbGo-Go, but had similar accuracy. We found that target speed and width were dominant factors in users' performance. Our results lead us to believe that both Ray-Casting and rbGo-Go are viable alternatives with advantages and disadvantages for distant moving target selection in VR/AR contexts. We discuss these complementary advantages and disadvantages to provide guidance for designers of experiences that incorporate moving target selection in virtual environments.

In summary, the contributions in this paper include:

- Two empirical studies to evaluate the performance of virtual hand and pointer metaphors and establish baselines to capture moving targets in VR.
- A summary of technique characteristics and design considerations for both virtual hand and pointer metaphors to acquire moving targets in VR.

## 2    Related Work

### 2.1    Virtual Hand and Virtual Pointer

Poupyrev et al. [42] identified a class of manipulations labeled as egocentric manipulations of objects in virtual environments. They further divided this class of egocentric manipulations into two categories: virtual hand and virtual pointer. The virtual hand metaphor [38] and Ray-Casting [7] (a virtual pointer technique) are the most popular 3D pointing techniques within virtual environments.

Many variants of ray-casting and virtual hand techniques have been proposed for interacting with 3D objects in virtual environments (VE) [5]. Considering first, Ray-Casting, many techniques explore variants for depth-aware pointing, such as manually adjusting the length or depth of a ray [11,19], creating a curved ray [39,44] and allowing bimanual interaction between rays [52] to increase targeting precision. In dense environments, techniques such as SQUAD [31], Expand [13] and Disambiguation Canvas [16] use iterative refinement by rearranging or filtering content to support Ray-Casting selection. More recently, the RayCursor technique [7] incorporates a set of pointing facilitation augmentations including the 1€ filter [14], a bubble cursor mechanism [18] and visual feedback to achieve better performance on small and distant targets. Finally, Ray-Casting from a user's eyes [4] has been shown to have some performance advantages in both sparse and cluttered environments, and a similar technique – cursor control using head – has also been adopted in existing AR headsets, for example the Microsoft HoloLens.

In contrast to Ray-Casting, where a ray points to a target, the virtual hand metaphor allows users to directly interact with objects using their bare hands or controllers [6]. One challenge with virtual hand techniques is the acquisition of distant targets; to address this, the Go-Go technique [43] enables users to grab targets beyond arms' reach with a non-linear mapping function; close interactions leverage basic virtual hand input mapped to a controller, but, as the user reaches further than a threshold from their body, a control-display (CD) gain function magnifies the movement of the hand beyond the threshold. Although Go-Go is functional for distant targeting, it does not perform as well as Ray-Casting based techniques for object positioning [42,46]. Another body of work within the category of virtual hand metaphors for distant reaching focuses on maintaining body ownership while enabling users to reach distant targets [48].

## 2.2   Moving Targets Acquisition Models

Acquiring moving targets is challenging to model. When acquiring a moving target, users may use different strategies (pursuit, head-on, receding, and perpendicular) to intercept a moving object [47]. Li et al. [34] argued that different model clues (vision, haptic and audio and their combinations), motion direction, and speed could affect users' performance in VR. Fitts's Law [17] is the most commonly used approach to study new acquisition techniques in a spatial acquisition task. It links movement time (MT) to the concept of the index of difficulty (ID): $MT = a + bID$ where $ID = log_2(\frac{2D}{W})$. However, Fitts' Law was initially proposed to model stationary target selection in 1D. While it has been extended to 2D pointing tasks [2], it is clear that extensions to Fitts' Law are needed to account for, at minimum, target speed (i.e. faster targets should be harder to acquire). With this goal in mind, Jagacinski et al. [26] extended Fitts' Law and proposed an empirical model to predict movement time as a function of initial amplitude

(A), target speed (V) and target width (W): $MT = c + dA + e(V + l)(\frac{1}{W} - 1)$. Hoffmann [22] later examined three extensions to Fitts' Law which all indicated that the difficulty to select a moving target is correlated with the target speed.

In addition to modeling the movement time, previous work also focuses on predicting the endpoint distribution and the error rate of target selection. One of the benefits to studying endpoint distribution is that it allows replacement of nominal target width with the target's effective width [55], where ideally 96% of the endpoints land within a target following a Gaussian distribution that corresponds to the target width (W) perceived by the user, i.e., $W = \sqrt{2\pi e}\sigma$ [36]. This 4% error rate assumption by Fitts' Law provides insights into adjusting $W$ and $W_e$, and, based on this, Wobbrock et al. [50] derive an error model implicitly implied by Fitts' Law with three task parameters: target width, distance and movement time. They extend the error model to 2D [51] and Bi et al. also propose the FFitts' Law [9] to model the endpoint distribution of finger input on a touchscreen given the challenges of *fat finger* input. For moving targets, Lee and Oulasvirta [32] propose a statistical model to predict the error rate by considering moving target selection as a temporal pointing task where users intend to select a target within a limited time window. Several other researchers propose Ternary-Gaussian models to describe the endpoint distribution of moving targets in 1D [24], 2D [25], and with crossing-based movement [23]. Focusing specifically on VR and AR environments, Yu et al. [54] recently designed an empirical model *EDModel* to describe the distribution of pointing selection tasks in VR environments. These endpoint distribution and error rate models imply that the target width and effective target width of the selection task have more impact on the error rate of selecting moving targets than the distance.

## 2.3   Moving Targets Acquisition Techniques

Based on the above mentioned models, many researchers have investigated approaches to efficiently and accurately completing a stationary selection task; these facilitation techniques can be characterized into two broad categories: (1) decreasing movement distance from the cursor to the target [8], (2) increasing the effective width with larger cursor width [28,45], target width [37] or activation area [18,45]. Adopting these techniques, Hassan et al. [21] propose Comet and Target Ghost to capture moving targets in 1D and 2D space. With Comet, targets are expanded with a long tail such that the activation area is increased while Target Ghost ignores targets' speed and creates static proxies to the targets. Similarly, the Hold [3] technique temporarily pauses the content of the display to enable a static target selection. Aside from these approaches, Hook [40] adopts a vote-score heuristics designed to select a moving target in a dense and occluded environment while Khamis et al. [29] propose an eye-pursuit technique to select moving targets in a VR environment. These techniques are designed on top of basic interaction techniques, e.g. mouse cursor, Ray-Casting and eye-tracking.

Interestingly, although myriad techniques based on virtual hand and virtual pointer have been proposed for selection in virtual environments, evaluation of the performance of these two metaphors [42] has typically focused on static selection tasks. The lack of empirical understanding of the basic performance of these established techniques to acquire moving targets in virtual environments still exists and we are aware of no prior work that has explored these two metaphors in the context of moving targets in AR/VR.

# 3    Study Set-Up

In this section, we describe our virtual pointer, virtual hand, and configuration parameters for our moving target selection task.

## 3.1    Virtual Pointer

Ray-Casting is the most common technique built on top of the virtual pointer metaphor. For our virtual pointer selection technique, Ray-Casting is implemented using a constant control display (C/D) gain to map a controller orientation onto a ray direction. A maximum 10-m white line shooting from a virtual controller indicates the ray direction. When a ray intersects with an object, the white line's length is then the distance from the controller to the object and a cursor appears to indicate the hit position. We do not enable cursor manipulation and acceleration along the ray because this would shift users' attention when acquiring a moving target, possibly increasing the selection time. Approaches which can improve Ray-Casting's efficiency and stability, such as increasing the effective width [18] of a target or smoothing of the ray [14] are not implemented because these approaches will benefit Ray-Casting over the virtual hand, which violates our initial motivation towards the understanding of virtual hand in comparison to the pointer in moving target selection. A press down&up gesture on the corresponding trigger of the VR controller selects a target intersecting the ray. We call this technique **Ray-Casting** in our experimental condition.

## 3.2    Virtual Hand

Using bare hands or a controller to hit/select a target is the most basic form of virtual hand. The basic virtual hand metaphor allows users to acquire objects within arms' reach. While this constraint mimics the real world, researchers have also recognized that, at times, users may wish to acquire and interact with targets beyond arms' reach. As a result, modifications to the virtual hand metaphor to support more distant target acquisition exist [33,43,48].

The variant we initially explore, is a teleporting technique where the virtual hand is located at a distance from the user. The virtual hand remains directly mapped via a constant CD gain onto the controller movement. This teleporting technique permits distant targeting while preserving the virtual hand metaphor. We call this technique **Controller-mapped virtual hand** or **Controller** for our experimental condition.

### 3.3    Randomize Movement Direction with Bounded Space

As targets are moving, and, because users find it difficult to select targets outside the field-of-view in the virtual environment [15], we designed a bounded space which is anchored to the virtual environment and contains all moving targets in front of the user. This allows us to analyse the effects from target speed, width and technique without visual search and out-of-field-of-view confounds. The bounded space is designed based on empirical analysis of the reachable workspace within arm's length [30, 41] so we can use a linear 1-to-1 mapping between the physical and virtual hand to interact with targets within the bounded space. The bounded space is 60 cm (depth) × 120 cm (height) × 120 cm (width) in size; thus enabling users to reach each side of the bounded space. To aid depth estimation and avoid visual distraction, the wall nearest to a user's chest is invisible while other walls are semi-transparent.

Alongside objects' movement range, another important factor that affects users' performance is movement direction. Prior work [47] has suggested that the direction of motion relative to the cursor can result in different targeting strategies. Instead of controlling the target motion directly, we added a bounce feature on each wall of the bounded space so that whenever a target hits a wall, it will reflect and bounce away. Therefore, target motion direction is randomized and users can leverage different strategies to capture a moving target.

### 3.4    Pilot Study to Guide Moving Target Speed

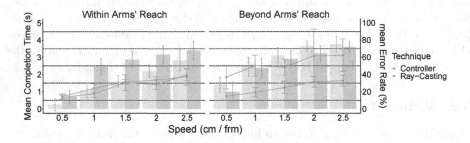

**Fig. 1.** Mean selection time (plotted in line) and accuracy (in bar), with 95% confidence intervals, of Controller and Ray-Casting to acquire moving targets within/beyond arms' reach at different speeds. The frame rate is 72 fps.

Higher motion speed implies longer selection time and higher error rate [22, 26, 32]. Without pre-assuming the acceptable minimum and maximum speed values in the experiments, we conducted informal pilot test with 4 adults for feedback on speed with regard to selection accuracy and completion time. As the goal of our pilot study was to guide speed values, we did not vary target width. The task in the pilot study is a simple selection task where participants were expected to select the only sphere moving within and beyond arms' reach across different speeds: min = 0.5 cm/frm, max = 2.5 cm/frm, step = 0.5 cm/frm.

We used 3 Block × 2 Position × 2 Technique × 5 Speed × 10 trials in this study. Examining Fig. 1, the error rate reached 50% at 1.0 cm/frm for distant moving target selection using the virtual hand and participants reported it was too easy to select targets nearby at 0.5 cm/frm, so we selected speed values of (0.75 cm/frm, 1.00 cm/frm, 1.25 cm/frm) for target movement.

## 4    Initial Study

Given speed values from our pilot study, our initial experiment's goal was to explore if virtual hand (**Controller**) and virtual pointer (**Ray-Casting**) have different performance when selecting moving targets with different speeds and at different positions (Fig. 2).

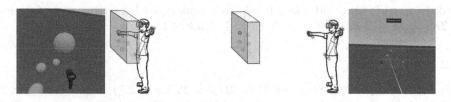

**Fig. 2.** Within (left) and beyond (right) arms' design: Given a user's head position, near space's center is generated at 0.3 m in front of and 0.4 m below the head position. Far space's center is 2 m beyond that of near space. These configuration values were consistent across participants.

### 4.1    Apparatus and Implementation

The system was implemented in Godot v3.2.2 stable and deployed on an standalone Oculus Quest at 72 fps. No other hardware resources were required.

### 4.2    Experimental Design

A repeated-measure within-subject design was used. The independent variables (IVs) were *Technique* (Controller, Ray-Casting),*Position* (Within, Beyond), *Speed* (0.75 cm/frm, 1.00 cm/frm, 1.25 cm/frm), and *Block* (1-4). As *Position* might affect perceived width for moving targets and to handle the confounding problem, target width was fixed to 10 cm.

Participants were instructed to capture a set of moving targets during the experiment. Spheres (targets) were generated, moving and bouncing back and forth in the bounded space. *Position* was either within arms reach or out of reach. *Technique* by *Position* generates four combinations and the order of the combination was counterbalanced across participants using a Latin square [49].

Each participant performed 4 blocks of trials. To start each block and control the initial position, each participant was instructed to select a static white sphere ("dummy" target) positioned in front of the participant in the virtual space.

Within each block, 15 selections were made for each of the 3 target motion speeds, presented in random order in each block, given the *Technique* and *Position* condition being analyzed. For each trial, six spheres, including 5 white spheres (distractors) and 1 blue sphere (goal target) were generated within the bounded space with the same *Speed* but moving in random direction. When Controller overlapped with a sphere or Ray-Casting intersected a sphere, the sphere was highlighted orange and the participant pressed the index-finger button of the corresponding controller to capture it. The experimental system moved to the next trial when the goal target was correctly selected. When a target was missed or a distractor was selected, the goal target did not disappear. Once correctly selected, the current goal target vanished and the next goal target would generate at a distance (20 cm, 30 cm, 40 cm in random order) from the selection position of the *Technique*, i.e. the Controller's position or the hit position of Ray-Casting. When each participant finished a block, the static "dummy" target was displayed and the participant could take a break. In summary, each participant performed 2 *Technique* × 2 *Position* × 3 *Speed* × 4 *Block* × 15 trials = 720 trials.

### 4.3  Participants

We recruited 8 participants (ages 21 to 30 ($\mu = 25.3, \sigma = 2.7$), 5 male, 3 female, 2 left-handed), of which 2 were experienced VR users. Participants were recruited by word-of-mouth in our organization. The experiment lasted for 40 min.

### 4.4  Procedure

Participants were welcomed to the study and were instructed to stand in a open area. They first read the study instructions and verbal consent was obtained. Before the study, they were asked to answer a questionnaire about demographic information (gender, age), handedness, and daily and weekly usage of VR devices to characterize the demographics of our participant sample. Participants were warned about potential motion sickness induced from VR, and were allowed to have a 30 s break between each block. If they felt uncomfortable at any time during the study, the study immediately stopped. Before participants wore the Oculus Quest and controllers, both the headset and controllers were sanitized with alcoholic wipes. Prior to the study, a training session was provided so participants practiced and became familiar with the provided techniques and environment. Participants were instructed to avoid continually hitting the select button. When participants finished a block, they could take a break; when they finished a *Technique* and *Position* condition, they were allowed to take off the headset and have a 3 min break and, at the same time, they were instructed to complete a raw NASA TLX [20] questionnaire grading their experience.

### 4.5  Results

The goal of our experiment is the contrast of virtual hand and virtual pointer metaphors for moving target selection. We acknowledge that various extensions based on Fitts's Law and endpoint prediction models have been proposed to analyze moving target selection experiments. However, in our study, the complexity of 3D targeting in the immersive environment, unpredictable movement direction caused by reflection in the bounded space, and distracting moving objects introduce confounds in analysis. Therefore, in the following sections, we analyze our results in two dimensions: (1) objective measures: selection time and error rate, and (2) subjective measures: TLX loads and user feedback. The selection time refers to the time elapsed between selections. Selection failure is counted as an error and the error rate refers to the percentage of erroneous trials among 15 trials.

We removed outliers by eliminating any non-erroneous trials whose selection time was more than three standard deviations from the mean, yielding 5684 trials (98.68%) in total for analysis. We conducted a multi-way repeated-measure ANOVA ($\alpha = 0.05$) for selection time and error rate respectively on three IVs: *Technique*, *Position*, and *Speed*. When sphericity was violated using Mauchly's test, we applied Greenhouse-Geisser corrections to the DoFs. The post-hoc tests were conducted using pairwise t-tests with Bonferroni corrections when significant effects were found. Effect sizes are reported as partial eta squared ($\eta_p^2$) values.

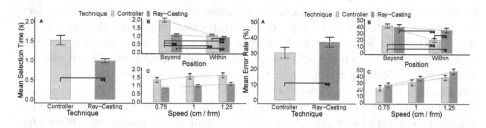

**Fig. 3.** Mean selection time (left) and mean error rate (right) for (A) *Technique*; (B) *Technique* by *Position*; (C) *Technique* by *Speed*. Error bars are shown with 95% confidence intervals. The statistic significance evaluated by pairwise t-test are marked with + (++ = p < 0.01 and + = p < 0.05).

**Selection Time.** A Box-Cox transformation ($\lambda = -0.5$) was applied to non-normal residuals of the selection time. Although we found a significant effect of *Block* ($F_{3,21} = 3.61$, p < 0.05, $\eta_p^2 = 0.03$), the pairwise t-test did not report any significance between each pair of block. Therefore, all 4 blocks were kept for the analysis.

The subsequent analysis revealed a significant effect of *Technique* ($F_{1,7} = 58.02$, p < 0.001, $\eta_p^2 = 0.45$) on selection time. The pairwise t-test showed that Controller (mean = 1.52 s) was significantly slower than Ray-Casting (0.99 s, p < 0.001). We found a significant effect of *Position* ($F_{1,7} = 51.40$, p < 0.001, $\eta_p^2 = 0.44$) on the selection time and a significant interaction effect between *Technique* and *Position* ($F_{1,7} = 44.85$, p < 0.001, $\eta_p^2 = 0.20$). Participants spent significantly (p < 0.001) more time selecting moving targets at a distance (1.52 s) than within arms' reach (0.99 s). The selection time increased significantly (p < 0.001) with Controller when targets appeared beyond arms' reach (1.97 s) than within arms' reach (1.06 s). Similarly, when using Ray-Casting, the selection time increased significantly (p < 0.001) when targets appeared far away from (1.07 s) than near participants (0.92 s). We also found a significant effect of *Speed* ($F_{2,14} = 44.74$, p < 0.001, $\eta_p^2 = 0.21$). Selecting targets moving at 0.75 cm/frm (1.10 s) was significantly (p < 0.005) faster than those moving at 1.00 cm/frm (1.29 s) and 1.25 cm/frm (1.37 s). We only found a significant interaction effect between *Speed* and *Position* ($F_{2,14} = 3.90$, p < 0.05, $\eta_p^2 < 0.01$) but not with *Technique*. To potentially avoid a type-I error, we consider the interaction effect trivial given the effect size.

**Accuracy.** We did not find any significant effect of *Block* on error rate. Analysis reveals a significant effect of *Technique* ($F_{1,7} = 7.56$, p < 0.05, $\eta_p^2 = 0.10$) on the error rate. Controller (mean = 30.40%) caused significantly less erroneous selections than Ray-Casting (37.25%, p < 0.001). We also found a significant effect of *Position* ($F_{1,7} = 205.61$, p < 0.001, $\eta_p^2 = 0.29$) on error rate; selecting moving targets that appeared at a distance (40.57%) caused significantly more errors than within arms' reach (27.09%, p < 0.001). We found a significant interaction effect between *Technique* and *Position* ($F_{1,7} = 17.28$, p < 0.005, $\eta_p^2 = 0.15$). With Controller, participants made significantly more erroneous selection when selecting targets at a distance (41.45%) than within arms' reach (19.35%, p < 0.001). Ray-Casting was less impacted by distance; i.e., errors at a distance (39.68%) and within arms' reach (34.83%) were similar. We found a significant effect of *Speed* ($F_{2,14} = 52.99$, p < 0.001, $\eta_p^2 = 0.35$) on the error rate but we did not found any significant interaction effect between *Speed* and other IVs on the error rate. Unsurprisingly, selecting targets moving at 0.75 cm/frm (24.57%) caused significantly (p < 0.001) lower erroneous selection than those moving at 1.00 cm/frm (33.77%) and 1.25 cm/frm (43.14%).

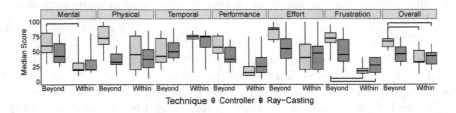

**Fig. 4.** Box plots for perceived task loads of the TLX questionnaire. The statistical significant differences are marked as connecting lines.

**Task Loads Analysis and User Feedback.** Results from Fig. 4 showed differences for perceived task loads between techniques beyond and within arms' reach. A Friedman test showed significant effect of *Technique* × *Position* on *Mental*, *Effort*, *Frustration* and *Overall*: $\chi^2_{Mental}(3) = 21.83$, p < 0.001, $\chi^2_{Effort}(3) = 11.95$,

$p < 0.01$, $\chi^2_{Frustration}(3) = 20.01$, $p < 0.001$, $\chi^2_{Overall}(3) = 15.83$, $p < 0.005$. The pairwise Wilcoxon test reported that using Controller to acquire moving targets beyond arms' reach caused significantly higher mental demand ($p = 0.05$), higher frustration ($p < 0.05$), and required significantly ($p < 0.05$) higher overall loads than using Ray-Casting or Controller to select moving targets within arms' reach. To explore more fully *Position*, we found a significant effect of *Position* on all attributes except *Physical, Temporal*, and *Performance*: $\chi^2_{Mental}(1) = 8, p < 0.005$, $\chi^2_{Effort}(1) = 6, p < 0.05, \chi^2_{Frustration}(1) = 8, p < 0.005, \chi^2_{Overall}(1) = 8, p < 0.005$. We only found a significant effect of *Technique* on *Mental*: $\chi^2_{Mental}(1) = 4.5$, $p < 0.05$.

All participants reported that it was hard to use Controller to select moving targets at a distance because it was difficult to estimate the depth of both targets and virtual controllers when in motion. The results above also indicated that *Position* increased both *Mental* and *Effort* loads. With the teleportation of the Controller, some participants felt that large body movement seemed to cause relatively smaller Controller movement due to perspective. Some also reported that visually smaller target width and hand tremor caused unexpected movement, especially when aiming at targets at a distance.

## 4.6  Discussion

When selecting moving targets, Controller is slower but more accurate than Ray-Casting. Figure 3 and user feedback reveal that *Position* impacts both Controller and Ray-Casting; more specifically, depth affects perceived visual size. For Ray-Casting, due to perspective, a distant moving target has visually smaller width, which causes difficulties for aiming. For Controller, in addition to targeting visually smaller targets, participants also must estimate depth, adding mental demand to selection, as shown in Fig. 4. *Speed* is a dominant factor affecting users' selection time and accuracy. Interpreting these graphical results in light of statistical analysis, these results argue that selection time and error rate is correlated to target speed.

## 5  Reach-Bound Go-Go

Examining the results above, we note that the virtual hand metaphor had significant accuracy advantage when selecting near targets (19.35%) versus at a distance (41.45%), and the teleportation of virtual hand resulted in high workload scores. This, then, leads to the question of whether we can enhance the virtual hand for more elegant distant targeting.

The technique we leverage to support enhanced distant targeting using the virtual hand metaphor is a variant of the *Go-Go* technique [43]. Earlier, we noted that the *Go-Go* technique leverages a non-linear mapping function to enable reaching beyond arms' length. The *Go-Go* technique maps virtual hand position to physical hand position up to a certain distance from the user. Beyond this range, the distance of the virtual hand is magnified by a multiplier (Fig. 5).

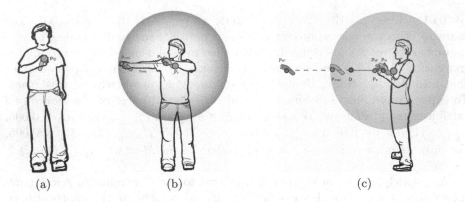

**Fig. 5.** rbGo-Go: (a)&(b) body posture calibration: $P_C$ is recorded as the center position of a user's chest. $r_{Max}$ is measured as the larger length between two arms' length. $P_S$ is a shoulder position, and $P_{Max}$ is the user's maximum reachable position. $P_S$ and $P_{Max}$ are recorded when a user stretch arms. (c) Motor space is divided into a linear mapping and non-linear mapping components by a tuned parameter $D$.

We call our modification to the *Go-Go* technique reach-bounded Go-Go interaction. Specifically, we restrict the movement space of (*Go-Go*), augment it with the body posture calibration as in [48], and simplify its configuration so that *rbGo-Go* can be used without the need for body tracking.

From [48], the amplified position of the virtual hand is defined as $P_{H*} = P_C + f(r) * (P_H - P_C)$ where $P_H$ is the physical hand position while holding a controller, $P_C$ is the neural point which is defined as the center position of the chest. In *rbGo-Go*, as in [48], we use an amplification function, but the non-linear piece-wise amplification function $f(r)$ is a variant of Go-Go, taking the amplification slope and offset into consideration, as follows:

$$f(r) = \begin{cases} 1.0 & 0 \leq r \leq D \\ (\frac{L_{Max}-r_{Max}}{r_{Max}*(1-D)^2}) * (r - D)^2 + 1.0 & D < r \leq 1 \end{cases}$$

Here $L_{Max}$ is the maximum length of the reachable space (e.g. bounded space in our experiment), $r_{Max}$ is the maximum arm length, and $D$ is the threshold that divides the physical and virtual hand mapping into direct mapped and non-linear parts. The value of D is $\frac{2}{3}$ based on the empirical experience from [43] but can be tuned in different scenarios. $r$ is the physical offset defined as the ratio of the distance between $P_H$ to $P_C$ and $P_{Max}$ to $P_C$: $r = \frac{|P_H-P_C|}{|P_{Max}-P_C|}$.

## 6   Follow-Up Study

Weaknesses in distant targeting for virtual hand resulted in *rbGo-Go*, but one open question is whether *rbGo-Go* enhances virtual hand interaction for moving targets. To test this, we increased the size of the bounded space (300 cm (depth) × 120 cm (height) × 120 cm (width)) to allow targets to move in a more general space and conducted a follow-up study evaluating *rbGo-Go* against Ray-Casting (Fig. 6).

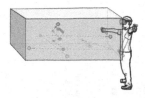

**Fig. 6.** The size-increased bounded space with possible target motion direction.

## 6.1   Experimental Design

A repeated-measure within-subject design was used. The independent variables (IVs) *Technique* (rbGo-Go, Ray-Casting), *Speed* (0.75 cm/frm, 1.00 cm/frm, and 1.25 cm/frm), *Width* (6 cm, 10 cm) and *Block* (1-4).

Each participant performed 4 blocks of trials and was instructed to select a static white sphere ("dummy" target) to start a block and control the initial position. Given the *Technique*, within each block, for each of the 3 target motion speeds in random order, 15 selections were made for each of the 2 target widths, also presented in random order. Six spheres, with only 1 blue sphere (goal target) were generated within the bounded space with the same *Speed* and same *Width* but moving in random direction. The experimental system moved to the next trial when the goal target was correctly selected. When a goal target was missed or a distractor was selected, the goal target did not disappear. Once correctly selected, the current goal target vanished and the next goal target would generate at a distance (40 cm, 80 cm, 120 cm in random order) from the virtual controller' position of rbGo-Go or hit position of Ray-Casting. When each participant finished a block, the static "dummy" target showed up and the participant could take breaks before selecting the "dummy" target. In summary, each participant performed 2 *Technique* × 3 *Speed* × 2 *Width* × 15 trials × 4 *Block* = 720 trials.

## 6.2   Procedure

The only difference in procedure for this study from our initial study was that participants were asked to calibrate the neutral point, shoulder position, and arms' length to generate the required parameters for *rbGo-Go*. During the experiment, participants were asked to limit changes in body posture to ensure stable chest position.

## 6.3   Participants

10 participants were recruited by word-of-mouth in our organization (ages 20 to 28 ($\mu = 23.8, \sigma = 2.7$), 6 male, 4 female, 1 left-handed), 3 experienced VR users. Given the Covid-19 pandemic, 6 participants from the initial study also took this study. A training session, including posture calibration and technique practice, took about 10 min, and the experiment lasted for 35 min.

## 6.4   Results

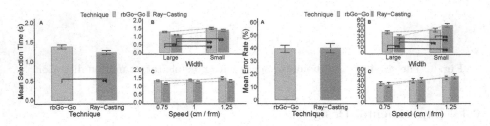

**Fig. 7.** Mean selection time (left) and mean error rate (right) for (A) *Technique*; (B) *Technique* by *Width*; (C) *Technique* by *Speed*. Error bars are shown with 95% confidence intervals. The statistic significances evaluated by pairwise t-test are marked with + (++ = p < 0.01 and + = p < 0.05).

**Selection Time.** After removing outliers (<1%), our data contained 7134 trials across 10 participants, a Box-Cox transformation ($\lambda = -0.38$) was applied to non-normal residuals of the selection time. We found a significant effect of *Block* ($F_{3,27} = 9.05$, p < 0.001, $\eta_p^2 = 0.11$). Pairwise t-test reported that Block 1 (mean = 1.44 s) took significantly longer (p < 0.001) than Block 3 (1.27 s) and Block 4 (1.27 s). Therefore, Block 1 was removed in the following analysis.

We found a significant effect of *Technique* ($F_{1,9} = 20.05$, p < 0.005, $\eta_p^2 = 0.13$) on the selection time. rbGo-Go (1.38 s) was significantly slower than Ray-Casting (1.23 s). We found a significant effect of *Speed* ($F_{1,9} = 23.22$, p < 0.001, $\eta_p^2 = 0.07$). Selecting targets moving at 0.75 cm/frm (1.24 s) was significantly faster than at 1.25 cm/frm (1.28 s, p < 0.005). We did not find a significant interaction effect between *Speed* and other IVs. We found a significant effect of *Width* ($F_{1,9} = 151.39$, p < 0.001, $\eta_p^2 = 0.29$). Selecting targets with large width (1.17 s) was significantly faster than small width (1.43 s, p < 0.001). We found a significant interaction effect between *Technique* and *Width* ($F_{1,9} = 8.35$, p < 0.05, $\eta_p^2 = 0.02$) on selection time. Considering large versus small widths, Ray-Casting's improved performance over rbGo-Go was primarily for large targets. While Ray-Casting was on average faster for both large and small targets, the corrected post-hoc difference was not statistically significant when considering only small targets.

**Accuracy.** In the absence of failing the normality assumption, we treat the residual of error rate as normal for analysis. Without Block 1, we did not find significance of *Block* on the error rate.

We did not find a significant effect of *Technique* on the error rate between rbGo-Go (mean = 39.34%) and Ray-Casting (39.90%). We found a significant effect of *Speed* ($F_{2,18} = 52.74$, p < 0.001, $\eta_p^2 = 0.24$). Selecting targets moving at 0.75 cm/frm (32.53%, p < 0.001) caused significantly less erroneous selection than the other two speeds. Also, selecting targets moving at 1.00 cm/frm (40.05%)

caused significantly less erroneous selection than at 1.25 cm/frm (46.28%, p < 0.001). We did not find any significant interaction effect between *Speed* and other IVs. We found a significant effect of *Width* ($F_{1,9} = 52.80$, p < 0.001, $\eta_p^2 = 0.30$). Selecting targets with large width (33.01%) caused significantly less erroneous selection than small width (46.23%, p < 0.001). We found a significant interaction effect between *Width* and *Technique* ($F_{1,9} = 99.97$, p < 0.001, $\eta_p^2 = 0.15$). Ray-Casting caused significantly higher error rate on small targets (50.72%) than large targets (29.07%, p < 0.001). However, rbGo-Go caused a similar error rate on targets with large width (36.94%) and small width (41.75%) (Fig. 8).

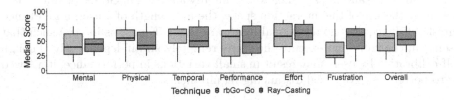

**Fig. 8.** Box plots for perceived task loads of the TLX questionnaire.

**Task Loads Analysis and User Feedback.** A Friedman test did not report any significance effect of *Technique* on any perceived task loads. In other words, rbGo-Go has similar loads for all attributes as Ray-Casting, while noticeably, rbGo-Go had lower much median score on *Frustration* than Ray-Casting.

Since rbGo-Go is a non-linear mapping between the real and virtual hands, participants found it hard to control this technique during early use, especially for targets moving at high speed. However, as they practiced, they (P0, P5, & P7-9) felt more confident and found it easier to select targets with small width and at distance, which was consistent with the learning effect we found in the selection time analysis. Target width was considered as an important factor affecting participants' performance (P6: *If not considering the technique, target width plays a very important role ... targets with small width at a distance are hard*). This was obvious for Ray-Casting, as several participants commented that it was hard to select targets with small width, and they perceived more hand jitter. Some participants (P6, P8) also reported that, using Ray-Casting, they found it harder to select targets moving up&down and left&right, compared with those moving towards and away from them, where rbGo-Go had the opposite feedback as depth estimation on targets was necessary.

## 6.5   Discussion

Similar to the former study, Ray-Casting was more efficient than rbGo-Go, but participants had a similar and high error rate. Graphically examining the results of Fig. 7, the selection time and error rate was positively related to *Speed* while negatively correlated to *Width*, as per Jagacinski et al.'s model [26] of moving target selection.

rbGo-Go, by design (virtual hand), has a larger selection area because the spatial extents of the hand are larger than those of a line (Ray-Casting). This contributed to improved accuracy for rbGo-Go despite difficulty controlling the non-linear mapping. On the other hand, Ray-Casting, or broadly virtual pointer, had a narrow ray such that selecting a small target became challenging. As participants noted, using Ray-Casting to select targets moving left&right and up&down was challenging because, to capture these targets, a narrow ray needed to translate a larger distance, during which a mis-selection could easily occur.

rbGo-Go simplifies the tuning process required by Go-Go. For rbGo-Go, the amplification parameter, $k$, which was manually adjusted in Go-Go, is now determined by the size of the interaction space, the arm length of a user, and a tuned threshold. It requires no additional hardware (e.g. a Kinect as in [48]) such that users can configure and execute the study remotely and independently. Though self-calibration by users may result in small variations in performance, it allowed us to better preserve social distancing requirements.

## 7  General Discussion

Considering both experiments, similar to results in 1D and 2D [22,26,32] targeting, *Speed* has a strong influence on the performance of virtual hand and virtual pointer metaphors. Specifically, higher motion speed causes longer selection time and higher error rate. Therefore, it is reasonable to design techniques that reduce motion speed, such as the Hook [3] and Target Ghost [21]. In terms of *Width*, interestingly, we observe an impact on these two metaphors in the moving target selection task similar to that observed in Poupyrev et al.'s static target selection study [42]: Compared with Ray-Casting, rbGo-Go is comparably fast and more accurate when selecting small objects. Additionally, compared with moving target selection tasks in 1D [24] and 2D [25], object depth will also impact users' perceived width. This problem is a speciality in 3D and more complicated when targets move in any direction. Since in our study, the impact of depth on target width is identical for both *Techniques*, we believe that this confound is controlled across conditions. Investigating this issue and exploring strategies to address it is another way to study these two metaphors.

One might be tempted to dismiss virtual hand as an interactive metaphor for moving target selection unless interaction is restricted to arms' length. After all, it is slower in both experiments, and only has an error rate advantage at close distances in the initial study. Furthermore, it is tempting to conclude that rbGo-Go serves no purpose due to its increased error rate compared to naive virtual hand. However, we would caution against such a simple interpretation.

First, virtual hand and virtual pointer are different pointing metaphors. Virtual hand asks a user to control all three, sweep, elevation, and depth, to fully target a unique, 3D location in space. Virtual pointer, in contrast, is an intersection-based technique where users can point at targets in a depth agnostic way. In many instances, virtual pointer is feasible. However, there may be moving target tasks where the goal location may not be identifiable by the system: as one example, imagine a virtual drawing application where a user selects an initial position and then draws a smooth trajectory along a desired path through the immersive environment. Interactions like this are not immediately possible via virtual pointer; they require some augmentation to control depth [7,19]. *rbGo-Go*, in contrast, can facilitate these tasks without enhancement.

Second, to allow virtual hand to target increased volumes, our *rbGo-Go* technique increases the range of movement of the virtual hand metaphor when the user reaches beyond a specific distance from themselves, $D$, but preserves behavior for distances less than $D$. For proximal targeting, users continue to benefit from the 1-to-1 direct mapping. As users reach beyond $D$, mapping smaller physical depth movements of the user onto larger depth transitions for the virtual hand metaphor means that, for *rbGo-Go*, targets are smaller in depth in motor space. The fact that error rate converged on Ray-Casting but with the added ability to specifically select depth supports the utility of a technique like rbGo-Go as an alternative to virtual pointer techniques, particularly in cases where depth must be controlled during targeting.

Recall that, compared with Ray-Casting, rbGo-Go is comparably fast and is more accurate when selecting small objects. Therefore, we would argue that rbGo-Go and Ray-Casting play off against each other in terms of advantages, i.e., that it is most important to understand the relative pros and cons of each metaphor in moving target acquisition. To summarize, there exist potential benefits to each metaphor in the context of moving target selection, as follows:

- Virtual hand: (1) Lower error rate for proximal moving target selection. (2) Higher immutability of error rate across different target widths. (3) Depth control.
- Virtual pointer: (1) Generally faster. (2) Consistent (though relatively high) error rate. (3) Existing rich facilitation techniques [7,14,18,35] for efficiency and stabilization.

Overall, we would argue that these advantages in moving target selection are useful data points for designers who wish to incorporate an ability to select moving targets into their virtual environment applications.

## 7.1   Future Work

**Facilitation Techniques.** One aspect we have not evaluated concerns facilitation techniques which could aid target acquisition. For virtual hand, depth cues (such as motion parallax [27], and visual guidance [7]) may simplify depth estimation of both targets and hands. For virtual pointer (Ray-Casting), increasing the effective size [18] and activation area [21] of targets, or the selection area of a ray (volume ray) [35] are promising approaches, although dynamic and elastic width caused by unpredictable motion may be a concern. Additionally, weakening the speed effect, e.g. transforming a dynamic selection task to a static selection task [3,21], and stabilizing control with filtering [14] are possible solutions to address hand jitter's and speed's impact on targeting, two common challenges for both metaphors.

**Factors Beyond Speed and Width.** Alongside target speed and width, there are other factors that could influence metaphor choices when considering the use of virtual hand and pointer metaphors in 3D VR/AR environments for the capture moving targets. As one example, the performance of these metaphors for crossing-based selection tasks [1], where users select targets by crossing a target's boundary instead of pointing inside its perimeter, is an open question. This crossing paradigm has its unique values as it can adapt to these two metaphors more naturally (e.g. avoiding the Heisenberg effect) and can also improve user performance in particular scenarios, for example the Saber Beat game. In addition, the use of these two metaphors in real-world VR/AR applications will raise questions about how various feedback techniques could affect users' immersive experience while selecting moving targets. For example, haptic feedback [12] on a virtual hand may enhance users' experience, and improved visual feedback on the ray during Ray-Casting [7] may improve users' environmental awareness.

## 8   Conclusion

Alongside our introduction of *rbGo-Go*, a variant of the *Go-Go* technique, we provide two empirical studies to compare virtual hand (Controller/*rbGo-Go*) and virtual pointer (Ray-Casting) metaphors in the context of moving target selection in virtual environments. Using a classic virtual hand metaphor (both proximal to the user and at distance), we find that virtual hand has a lower error rate in proximity to the user but slower selection time. Given the advantages and disadvantages of the basic virtual hand metaphor, we evaluate *rbGo-Go*, our modified version of the *Go-Go* technique. We find, again, that *rbGo-Go* is slower than Ray-Casting, but note advantages of the technique both in terms of small target precision and in terms of an ability to support target agnostic depth selection. We argue that the complementary advantages of the technique provide useful guidelines for designers of virtual environments when introducing interactions to support moving target acquisition.

**Acknowledgements.** We would like to thank Shino Che Yan for her help in creating Figs. 2, 5, and 6, Da-Yuan Huang for valuable feedback, participants for their help in this difficult time, and reviewers for valuable suggestions. This research received ethics clearance from the Office of Research Ethics, University of Waterloo. This research was funded by a grant from Waterloo-Huawei Joint Innovation Laboratory.

# References

1. Accot, J., Zhai, S.: Beyond Fitts' law: models for trajectory-based HCI tasks. In: CHI 1997 Extended Abstracts on Human Factors in Computing Systems, CHI EA 1997, p. 250. Association for Computing Machinery, New York (1997). https://doi.org/10.1145/1120212.1120376
2. Accot, J., Zhai, S.: Refining Fitts' law models for bivariate pointing. In: Proceedings of the SIGCHI Conference on Human Factors in Computing Systems, CHI 2003, pp. 193–200. Association for Computing Machinery, New York (2003). https://doi.org/10.1145/642611.642646
3. Al Hajri, A., Fels, S., Miller, G., Ilich, M.: Moving target selection in 2D graphical user interfaces, pp. 141–161 (2011). https://doi.org/10.1007/978-3-642-23771-3_12
4. Argelaguet, F., Andujar, C.: Efficient 3D pointing selection in cluttered virtual environments. IEEE Comput. Graphics Appl. **29**(6), 34–43 (2009)
5. Argelaguet, F., Andujar, C.: A survey of 3D object selection techniques for virtual environments. Comput. Graph. **37**(3), 121–136 (2013)
6. Arora, R., Kazi, R.H., Kaufman, D.M., Li, W., Singh, K.: Magicalhands: mid-air hand gestures for animating in VR. In: Proceedings of the 32nd Annual ACM Symposium on User Interface Software and Technology, UIST 2019, pp. 463–477. Association for Computing Machinery, New York (2019). https://doi.org/10.1145/3332165.3347942
7. Baloup, M., Pietrzak, T., Casiez, G.: Raycursor: a 3D pointing facilitation technique based on raycasting. In: Proceedings of the 2019 CHI Conference on Human Factors in Computing Systems, CHI 2019, pp. 1–12. Association for Computing Machinery, New York (2019). https://doi.org/10.1145/3290605.3300331
8. Baudisch, P., et al.: Drag-and-pop and drag-and-pick: techniques for accessing remote screen content on touch- and pen-operated systems (2003)
9. Bi, X., Li, Y., Zhai, S.: Ffitts law: modeling finger touch with Fitts' law. In: Proceedings of the SIGCHI Conference on Human Factors in Computing Systems, CHI 2013, pp. 1363–1372. Association for Computing Machinery, New York (2013). https://doi.org/10.1145/2470654.2466180
10. Bideau, B., Kulpa, R., Vignais, N., Brault, S., Multon, F., Craig, C.: Using virtual reality to analyze sports performance. IEEE Comput. Graphics Appl. **30**, 14–21 (2010). https://doi.org/10.1109/MCG.2009.134
11. Bowman, D.A., Hodges, L.F.: An evaluation of techniques for grabbing and manipulating remote objects in immersive virtual environments. In: Proceedings of the 1997 Symposium on Interactive 3D Graphics, pp. 35–ff (1997)
12. Buchmann, V., Violich, S., Billinghurst, M., Cockburn, A.: Fingartips: gesture based direct manipulation in augmented reality. In: Proceedings of the 2nd International Conference on Computer Graphics and Interactive Techniques in Australasia and South East Asia, GRAPHITE 2004, pp. 212–221. Association for Computing Machinery, New York (2004). https://doi.org/10.1145/988834.988871
13. Cashion, J., Wingrave, C., Laviola, J.J.: Dense and dynamic 3D selection for game-based virtual environments. IEEE Trans. Visual. Comput. Graphics 634–642 (2012)
14. Casiez, G., Roussel, N., Vogel, D.: 1€filter: a simple speed-based low-pass filter for noisy input in interactive systems. In: Proceedings of the SIGCHI Conference on Human Factors in Computing Systems, CHI 2012, pp. 2527–2530. Association for Computing Machinery, New York (2012). https://doi.org/10.1145/2207676.2208639

15. Chen, Y., Katsuragawa, K., Lank, E.: Understanding viewport- and world-based pointing with everyday smart devices in immersive augmented reality. In: Proceedings of the 2020 CHI Conference on Human Factors in Computing Systems, CHI 2020, pp. 1–13. Association for Computing Machinery, New York (2020). https://doi.org/10.1145/3313831.3376592

16. Debarba, H.G., Grandi, J.G., Maciel, A., Nedel, L., Boulic, R.: Disambiguation canvas: a precise selection technique for virtual environments. In: Kotzé, P., Marsden, G., Lindgaard, G., Wesson, J., Winckler, M. (eds.) INTERACT 2013. LNCS, vol. 8119, pp. 388–405. Springer, Heidelberg (2013). https://doi.org/10.1007/978-3-642-40477-1_24

17. Fitts, P.M.: The information capacity of the human motor system in controlling the amplitude of movement. J. Exp. Psychol. **47**(6), 381–91 (1954)

18. Grossman, T., Balakrishnan, R.: The bubble cursor: enhancing target acquisition by dynamic resizing of the cursor's activation area. In: Proceedings of the SIGCHI Conference on Human Factors in Computing Systems, CHI 2005, pp. 281–290. Association for Computing Machinery, New York (2005). https://doi.org/10.1145/1054972.1055012

19. Grossman, T., Balakrishnan, R.: The design and evaluation of selection techniques for 3D volumetric displays. In: Proceedings of the 19th Annual ACM Symposium on User Interface Software and Technology, UIST 2006, pp. 3–12. Association for Computing Machinery, New York (2006). https://doi.org/10.1145/1166253.1166257

20. Hart, S.G.: Nasa-task load index (NASA-TLX); 20 years later. In: Proceedings of the Human Factors and Ergonomics Society Annual Meeting, vol. 50, no. 9, pp. 904–908 (2006). https://doi.org/10.1177/154193120605000909

21. Hasan, K., Grossman, T., Irani, P.: Comet and target ghost: techniques for selecting moving targets. In: Proceedings of the SIGCHI Conference on Human Factors in Computing Systems, CHI 2011, pp. 839–848. Association for Computing Machinery, New York (2011). https://doi.org/10.1145/1978942.1979065

22. Hoffmann, E.R.: Capture of moving targets: a modification of Fitts' law. Ergonomics **34**(2), 211–220 (1991). https://doi.org/10.1080/00140139108967307

23. Huang, J., et al.: Modeling the endpoint uncertainty in crossing-based moving target selection. In: Proceedings of the 2020 CHI Conference on Human Factors in Computing Systems, CHI 2020, pp. 1–12. Association for Computing Machinery, New York (2020). https://doi.org/10.1145/3313831.3376336

24. Huang, J., Tian, F., Fan, X., Zhang, X.L., Zhai, S.: Understanding the uncertainty in 1D unidirectional moving target selection. In: Proceedings of the 2018 CHI Conference on Human Factors in Computing Systems, CHI 2018, pp. 1–12. Association for Computing Machinery, New York (2018). https://doi.org/10.1145/3173574.3173811

25. Huang, J., Tian, F., Li, N., Fan, X.: Modeling the uncertainty in 2D moving target selection. In: Proceedings of the 32nd Annual ACM Symposium on User Interface Software and Technology, UIST 2019, pp. 1031–1043. Association for Computing Machinery, New York (2019). https://doi.org/10.1145/3332165.3347880

26. Jagacinski, R.J., Repperger, D.W., Ward, S.L., Moran, M.S.: A test of Fitts' law with moving targets. Hum. Factors **22**(2), 225–233 (1980)

27. Jones, A., Swan, J.E., Singh, G., Kolstad, E.: The effects of virtual reality, augmented reality, and motion parallax on egocentric depth perception. In: 2008 IEEE Virtual Reality Conference, pp. 267–268 (2008)

28. Kabbash, P., Buxton, W.A.S.: The "prince" technique: Fitts' law and selection using area cursors. In: Proceedings of the SIGCHI Conference on Human Factors in Computing Systems, CHI 1995, pp. 273–279. ACM Press/Addison-Wesley Publishing Co., USA (1995). https://doi.org/10.1145/223904.223939

29. Khamis, M., Oechsner, C., Alt, F., Bulling, A.: Vrpursuits: interaction in virtual reality using smooth pursuit eye movements. In: Proceedings of the 2018 International Conference on Advanced Visual Interfaces, AVI 2018. Association for Computing Machinery, New York (2018). https://doi.org/10.1145/3206505.3206522

30. Klopcar, N., Lenarcic, J.: Kinematic model for determination of human arm reachable workspace. Meccanica **40**, 203–219 (2005)

31. Kopper, R., Bacim, F., Bowman, D.A.: Rapid and accurate 3D selection by progressive refinement. In: 2011 IEEE Symposium on 3D User Interfaces (3DUI), pp. 67–74 (2011)

32. Lee, B., Oulasvirta, A.: Modelling error rates in temporal pointing. In: Proceedings of the 2016 CHI Conference on Human Factors in Computing Systems, CHI 2016, pp. 1857–1868. Association for Computing Machinery, New York (2016). https://doi.org/10.1145/2858036.2858143

33. Li, J., Cho, I., Wartell, Z.: Evaluation of cursor offset on 3D selection in VR. In: Proceedings of the Symposium on Spatial User Interaction, pp. 120–129. Association for Computing Machinery, New York (2018). https://doi.org/10.1145/3267782.3267797

34. Li, Y., Wu, D., Huang, J., Tian, F., Wang, H., Dai, G.: Influence of multi-modality on moving target selection in virtual reality. Virtual Reality Intell. Hardware **1**(3), 303–315 (2019). https://doi.org/10.3724/SP.J.2096-5796.2019.0013

35. Lu, Y., Yu, C., Shi, Y.: Investigating bubble mechanism for ray-casting to improve 3D target acquisition in virtual reality. In: 2020 IEEE Conference on Virtual Reality and 3D User Interfaces (VR), pp. 35–43. IEEE Computer Society, Los Alamitos (2020). https://doi.org/10.1109/VR46266.2020.00021

36. MacKenzie, I.S.: Fitts' law as a research and design tool in human-computer interaction. Hum.-Comput. Interact. **7**(1), 91–139 (1992). https://doi.org/10.1207/s15327051hci0701_3

37. McGuffin, M., Balakrishnan, R.: Acquisition of expanding targets. In: Proceedings of the SIGCHI Conference on Human Factors in Computing Systems, CHI 2002, pp. 57–64. Association for Computing Machinery, New York (2002). https://doi.org/10.1145/503376.503388

38. Mine, M., Brooks, F., Jr., Sequin, C.: Moving objects in space: exploiting proprioception in virtual-environment interaction (1997). https://doi.org/10.1145/258734.258747

39. Olwal, A., Feiner, S.: The flexible pointer: an interaction technique for selection in augmented and virtual reality (2003)

40. Ortega, M.: Hook: heuristics for selecting 3D moving objects in dense target environments. In: 2013 IEEE Symposium on 3D User Interfaces (3DUI). IEEE, March 2013. https://doi.org/10.1109/3dui.2013.6550208

41. Pheasant, S., Haslegrave, C.: Bodyspace: Anthropometry, Ergonomics and the Design of Work (2018). https://doi.org/10.1201/9781315375212

42. Poupyrev, I., Ichikawa, T., Weghorst, S., Billinghurst, M.: Egocentric object manipulation in virtual environments: empirical evaluation of interaction techniques. In: Computer Graphics Forum, vol. 17, no. 3, pp. 41–52 (1998). https://doi.org/10.1111/1467-8659.00252

43. Poupyrev, I., Billinghurst, M., Weghorst, S., Ichikawa, T.: The go-go interaction technique: non-linear mapping for direct manipulation in VR. In: Proceedings of the 9th Annual ACM Symposium on User Interface Software and Technology, UIST 1996, pp. 79–80. Association for Computing Machinery, New York (1996). https://doi.org/10.1145/237091.237102

44. Steinicke, F., Ropinski, T., Hinrichs, K.: Object selection in virtual environments using an improved virtual pointer metaphor. In: Wojciechowski, K., Smolka, B., Palus, H., Kozera, R., Skarbek, W., Noakes, L. (eds.) Computer Vision and Graphics, pp. 320–326. Springer, Dordrecht (2006). https://doi.org/10.1007/1-4020-4179-9_46

45. Su, X., Au, O.K.C., Lau, R.W.: The implicit fan cursor: a velocity dependent area cursor. In: Proceedings of the SIGCHI Conference on Human Factors in Computing Systems, CHI 2014, pp. 753–762. Association for Computing Machinery, New York (2014). https://doi.org/10.1145/2556288.2557095

46. Sun, J., Stuerzlinger, W.: Extended sliding in virtual reality. In: 25th ACM Symposium on Virtual Reality Software and Technology, VRST 2019. Association for Computing Machinery, New York (2019). https://doi.org/10.1145/3359996.3364251

47. Tresilian, J.: Hitting a moving target: perception and action in the timing of rapid interceptions. Percept. Psychophys. **67**, 129–149 (2005). https://doi.org/10.3758/BF03195017

48. Wentzel, J., d'Eon, G., Vogel, D.: Improving virtual reality ergonomics through reach-bounded non-linear input amplification. In: Proceedings of the 2020 CHI Conference on Human Factors in Computing Systems, CHI 2020, pp. 1–12. Association for Computing Machinery, New York (2020). https://doi.org/10.1145/3313831.3376687

49. Williams, E.: Experimental designs balanced for the estimation of residual effects of treatments (1949). https://doi.org/10.1071/CH9490149

50. Wobbrock, J.O., Cutrell, E., Harada, S., MacKenzie, I.S.: An error model for pointing based on Fitts' law. In: Proceedings of the SIGCHI Conference on Human Factors in Computing Systems, CHI 2008, pp. 1613–1622. Association for Computing Machinery, New York (2008). https://doi.org/10.1145/1357054.1357306

51. Wobbrock, J.O., Jansen, A., Shinohara, K.: Modeling and predicting pointing errors in two dimensions. In: Proceedings of the SIGCHI Conference on Human Factors in Computing Systems, CHI 2011, pp. 1653–1656. Association for Computing Machinery, New York (2011). https://doi.org/10.1145/1978942.1979183

52. Wyss, H.P., Blach, R., Bues, M.: isith - intersection-based spatial interaction for two hands. In: 3D User Interfaces (3DUI 2006), pp. 59–61 (2006)

53. Yoon, J.W., Jang, S.H., Cho, S.B.: Enhanced user immersive experience with a virtual reality based FPS game interface. In: Proceedings of the 2010 IEEE Conference on Computational Intelligence and Games, pp. 69–74 (2010). https://doi.org/10.1109/ITW.2010.5593369

54. Yu, D., Liang, H.N., Lu, X., Fan, K., Ens, B.: Modeling endpoint distribution of pointing selection tasks in virtual reality environments. ACM Trans. Graph. **38**(6) (2019). https://doi.org/10.1145/3355089.3356544

55. Zhai, S., Kong, J., Ren, X.: Speed–accuracy tradeoff in Fitts' law tasks–on the equivalency of actual and nominal pointing precision. Int. J. Hum.-Comput. Stud. **61**(6), 823–856 (2004). https://doi.org/10.1016/j.ijhcs.2004.09.007. Fitts' law 50 years later: applications and contributions from human-computer interaction

# HyperBrush: Exploring the Influence of Flexural Stiffness on the Performance and Preference for Bendable Stylus Interfaces

Alfrancis Guerrero[1], Thomas Pietrzak[1,2] (iD), and Audrey Girouard[1(✉)] (iD)

[1] Carleton University, Ottawa, ON, Canada
AlfrancisGuerrero@cmail.carleton.ca, audrey.girouard@carleton.ca
[2] University of Lille, Lille, France
thomas.pietrzak@univ-lille.fr

**Abstract.** Flexible sensing styluses deliver additional degrees of input for pen-based interaction, yet no research has looked into the integration with creative digital applications as well as the influence of flexural stiffness. We present Hyper-Brush, a modular flexible stylus with interchangeable flexible components for digital drawing applications. We compare our HyperBrush to rigid pressure styluses in three studies, for brushstroke manipulation, for menu selection and for creative digital drawing tasks. HyperBrush yields comparable results with a commercial pressure pen. We concluded that different flexibilities could pose their own unique advantages analogous to an artist's assortment of paintbrushes.

**Keywords:** Deformable devices · Pen-based interfaces · Digital styluses · Creative supporting tools

## 1 Introduction

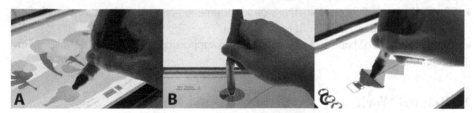

**Fig. 1.** The flexible stylus HyperBrush is being bent while touching the screen, used for creative drawing (A), menu selection (B) and brushstroke width targeting task (C).

---

**Electronic supplementary material** The online version of this chapter (https://doi.org/10.1007/978-3-030-85610-6_4) contains supplementary material, which is available to authorized users.

© IFIP International Federation for Information Processing 2021
Published by Springer Nature Switzerland AG 2021
C. Ardito et al. (Eds.): INTERACT 2021, LNCS 12935, pp. 51–71, 2021.
https://doi.org/10.1007/978-3-030-85610-6_4

Pen-based interfaces have been used for various digital applications such as sketching, drawing, writing, and 3D modelling [9, 19, 21, 34, 48]. Research prototypes and consumer electronic products can feature additional degrees of freedom to provide a larger input vocabulary, and have exhibited positive results: tip pressure [34, 36], tilting in a direction [43], rolling with the fingers [6], or tapping the barrel [19, 40]. One can use these extra degrees of freedom to create variable brushstroke sizes [3, 15], manipulating the orientation and positioning of models, selecting items [18], and operating menus [4, 51]. The initial goal behind having additional inputs is to increase productivity, efficiency, and promote creativity [3]. Such research has attempted to simulate the experience of using non-digital tools such as the pencil [12] or paintbrush [3, 15]. While these inputs can be of great benefit to stylus-based applications, there are still some limitations posed to each. For example, pen pressure input can be difficult to control while decreasing in pressure opposed to increasing in pressure [36, 52].

We present HyperBrush, a flexible digital stylus capable of sensing bend input to be functioned as additional degrees of freedom for pen-based interfaces (Fig. 1). We designed HyperBrush with interchangeable flexible components that differ in flexural stiffness. Our HyperBrush measures two degrees of bend input: absolute bend—the amount of bend being applied—and rotational bend—the azimuth angle relative to the barrel of the stylus. Fellion et al. first introduced the concept of a flexible stylus with their FlexStylus device [15]. Their study explored stationary brushstroke width manipulation with bend input, which concluded in comparable performances to pressure input. This result paved the way for a new area of research on flexible styluses. It motivated us to further this field by evaluating the usability of bend input during simultaneous movement of the stylus. We also assessed the performance of our bend input technique on a menu selection task. We focused on measuring the effects of various flexural stiffnesses within both experiments. Finally, we investigated HyperBrush with regards to creativity, an ultimate goal. Our contributions are:

- C1: Design and fabrication of a modular flexible digital stylus with bend input capabilities.
- C2: Evaluation of flexural stiffness on bend input during menu selection.
- C3: Evaluation of flexural stiffness on simultaneous control of bend and positional input during brushstroke width manipulation.
- C4: Comparison of bend and pressure input on supporting creativity in digital drawing applications.

## 2 Related Work

Our research was built on different areas of stylus interfaces, grip techniques, and deformable devices. We explored prior work that has evaluated popular stylus-based input techniques such as pressure, tilt, rotation. We discussed research on pen gripping techniques that suggested contextually relevant tools and mode switching. Lastly, we examined different pen-based menu stylus, menu techniques, and deformable based interfaces.

## 2.1 Pen Input Techniques

Previous research explored various forms of auxiliary input such as pressure [10, 15, 34, 36], tilt [19, 43, 47], rolling [6, 19, 20], and bend [15] that are beyond tracking the X-Y position of the pen tip on the screen [6, 49]. These additional inputs enable pen modes, selections, or tools without having to distract the users' attention away from the focus on the pen tip's position [49].

**Pressure.** Ramos et al. explored a multitude of widget designs that coupled pressure with change of position, scale, or angle [34]. Pressure Marks introduced pen strokes coupled with pressure for selection and action tasks simultaneously [36]. Early research has looked at the concept of changing digital brushstroke width with varying pressure; Fellion et al. compared pressure with bend accuracy [10, 15]. Research has also found that it was difficult for users to perform tasks that required a decrease in pressure levels as it compromised completion time or accuracy [9, 36].

**Tilt.** As opposed to pen pressure and rolling, where visualizing the change in their variability can be difficult, the tilt angle of the pen can be easily indicated by observing the physical angle of the pens barrel relative to the surface of the screen [47]. Vertical tilt angle and the azimuth angle of the pen, was found to be suitable techniques for radial menu interaction [19, 43, 47]. Xiangshi et al. also promoted that tilt can also be used to modify the width of a brush stroke from being a "hard" to "soft" brush [47].

**Roll.** Researchers have applied pen rolls, i.e., rolling along the barrels axis, for applications such as zooming, scrolling, rotation of objects and menu selection tasks [6, 19, 20]. While being a beneficial technique, researchers have found that it can be difficult to avoid unintentional rolling and is restricted to transverse of items to go from point A to B, which can lead to higher selection times and error rates [19, 20].

**Bend.** Moving beyond input techniques using rigid pens, Fellion et al. modified the stylus' design to allow flexible input [15]. As far as we know, this is the only study about bend as an input modality for styluses. FlexStylus measured both absolute and rotational deformation of a stylus and proposed grip-based, menu-based, and in-air interactions techniques. In evaluating the accuracy of bend as a variable input, they conclude that flexible input can perform similarly to pressure input for brushstroke width manipulation. However, their study did not include X-Y movement. In our work, we move knowledge forward in this domain by comparing the performance of brushstroke width manipulation while simultaneously moving in a direction for pressure and bend.

**Combining Inputs.** Controlling multiple auxiliary inputs, in addition to the position, can offer many benefits for pen mode switching, tasks with sequential steps, and multi-parametric selection and manipulation, [19, 49]. Xin et al. found the combination of pressure and azimuth input was best suited for multi-parametric control for writing and drawing tasks due to their loose correlation [49]. Zliding found that pressure input in combination with pen X-Y position, supports higher accuracy and performance for zooming and sliding tasks [35].

## 2.2 Pen-Based Menus

Most pen-based applications display their menus and tools around the edges of the screen, which can be disruptive to users workflow when interacting with, accumulating time and error [27, 28]. A *Marking Menu* is a circular contextual menu that enables users to perform selection tasks by using pen gestures and strokes in place of point-click interaction [25]. Styluses benefit from marking menus speed, efficiency, and easy learning curve for novices to become experts [27, 28]. The disadvantage is that accuracy is restricted by the number of items within the marking menu, where performance starts to decrease with more than 8 items within a level [18, 22, 43, 51]. *Tilt Menu* explored a radial menu technique using tilt input and evaluated users' performance of item location [43]. They found that items occluded by the hand resulted in poor accuracy. We used a radial menu technique with bend input similar to Tilt Menu's experiment design to explore the influence of flexural stiffness on users' performance.

## 2.3 Deformable Interfaces

Researchers have looked towards deformable user interfaces (DUI) as input tools to provide users with a more tactile and intuitive feeling when compared to rigid interfaces [30, 33]. Rigid interfaces also present physical constraints and limitations on how we can interact with them [45]. DUIs are often made up of soft materials that are capable of sensing physical deformation and change in shape as an input technique [7]. Utilizing objects that have the ability to twist, squeeze, rotate, or bend, introduces novel interactions that rigid interfaces cannot accomplish [7, 45]. DUIs have made its statements in gaming [14, 37, 39], accessibility [8, 13], electronic reading [46], music [17, 44], drawing [37], and mobile handheld devices [14, 16, 29, 31, 37, 41, 45] that aspire to enhance intuitiveness, expressiveness, and either augment or replace rigid interfaces.

There is to our knowledge only one existing work about a flexible stylus [15]. However, the authors did not address all research questions arising from this modality. Our work addresses the need to explore flexible styluses as a creative and expressive tool for digital painting and drawing. We further the research area of bendable stylus research by assessing how HyperBrush can be a tool to support creativity, expressiveness, and enjoyment for digital artists. We bring forth the intuitive feeling of using a physical paintbrush to the digital workflow for painting and drawing.

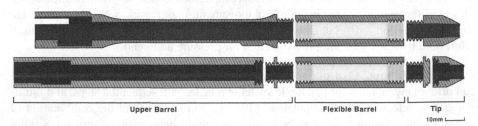

| Upper Barrel | Flexible Barrel | Tip |
| | | 10mm |

**Fig. 2.** Cross section model of both experiments stylus designs. Experiment 1 design (top), with a concave *upper barrel* and pseudo button that suggests orientation of the users' grip. Experiment 2 & 3 design (bottom) features inner screws, improving durability and modularity.

# 3  Apparatus Construction and Design Process

Artists rarely work with only one pen or brush. They rather have a collection of tools, which allow them to produce different stroke size, shape, intensity, colour or effects. In this idea, we were interested in the idea that 1) different flexural stiffnesses could provide artists with substantial benefits in terms of possibilities, 2) input modalities such as flexural stiffness and pressure are complementary. Therefore, we designed HyperBrush, a flexible stylus that features interchangeable components to vary flexural stiffness. We decided to have a modular design and separated our stylus into three main components that attach the *upper barrel*, *flexible barrel*, and *tip* (Fig. 2). Our pen design enabled swapping the flexible section, interchangeable with different stiffnesses. We discuss our construction design and how it differs from previous flexible stylus designs.

## 3.1  Construction Design

We used Stereolithography (SLA) printing to print at a higher quality and durability when compared to Fused Filament Fabrication (FFF) printing, which exhibited tearing and snapping while being bent. We printed both flexible/non-flexible materials using a FormLabs Form 2 [23] printer with photopolymer elastic (Elastic 50A Resin) and rigid resin (Rigid Black/Blue Resin). SLA printing made it easier to design a cavity for our bend sensor and prototype styluses for testing.

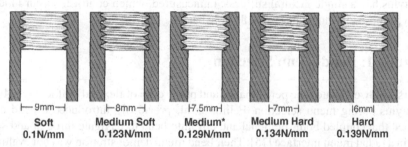

**Fig. 3.** Front cross section of the five flexible barrels, omitting the flexible sensor inside, with flexural stiffness measurement. Medium* flexibility was only used for studies 2 & 3.

**Flexible Barrel.** We varied stiffness by manipulating the inner wall thickness of the flexible barrel (Fig. 3) to maintain a uniform outside diameter of 11.2 mm. Given the photopolymer elastic material, we found that an inner diameter greater than 9 mm would reduce the durability, and less than 6 mm would not yield enough clearance for the sensor to fit. Our method supported a consistent physical outside diameter and an indistinguishable physical touch and visual difference between each barrel. We classified each flexibility as a ratio of amount of force applied per unit of deflection, known as the flexural stiffness. We calculated the flexural stiffness similarly to how a hollowed cylinder cantilever beam test is executed in engineering design [38]. The cantilever test simulated the technique of a user bending the stylus prototype during use. To vary flexibility, we recommend future prototyping to manipulate the inner wall thickness of the flexible barrel as it does not compromise any exterior design.

**Top Barrel & Pen Tip.** As bend gestures are directional, we choose to add a pseudo button on the upper barrel that indicated placement of the index finger to maintain a consistent roll position and reduce incidental rolling. We noticed it helped participants to maintain their grip better and reduce the amount of accidental rolling (Fig. 2). Our pen tip posed as the anchor point for our device during bending. We integrated a permeable rubber nib and attached a conductive wire that was threaded through the barrel of the pen carrying the electrical capacitance from the user's hand to enable X-Y input.

**Two Axis Bend Sensor.** We used a soft angular displacement bend sensor by BendLabs Inc. that offered high precision while rejecting most strain and noise [5]. Their sensor consisted of two capacitive flexible sensors positioned perpendicularly to one other measuring bend input from two orthogonal planes. We coupled the angle measurements to the X-Y position of our bend cursor in our bend menu study. We used an Arduino Mega [1] to communicate data from the sensor to the tablet, a Microsoft Surface [32].

### 3.2 Comparing HyperBrush with Previous Designs

Fellion et al.'s original sensing technique had four hand-made fibre-optic sensors to detect bend in two directions simultaneously [15]. We used a commercial capacitive bend sensor that provided more reliability, robustness, and precision as explained above. FlexStylus had a single flexural stiffness, unmeasured, which contrasts to our modular design purposed to interchange five flexible barrels.

## 4  Study 1: Bend Menu Selection

Our first study evaluated the performance and preference of flexural stiffness on a bendable stylus during menu selection. Fellion et al. previously introduced a bend menu interface that coupled both rotational and absolute bend to navigate through and select items in a radial menu interface [15]. Their bend menu demonstration was not evaluated, therefore we decided to use their menu interface as a medium to explore the influence of different flexibilities.

### 4.1  Methodology

Similar to Tilt Menu's experiment [43], we evaluated menu selection for three menu sizes with each item distributed by 90° (small), 45° (medium), and 35° (large) as well as a constant radius of 2.5 cm. We developed our testing application using Unity Engine and coupled rotational and absolute bend input to control the on-screen cursor. We programmed the absolute bend range from [0°, 45°] and rotational bend range from [0°, 360°]. Based on a pilot study, we proceeded with a Control-Display (CD) gain of 1.5.

- **Neutral Zone.** On initial touch with the screen, the menu's origin is located directly underneath the pen cursor and the state of the pen is in the neutral zone indicated as white; no current items are selected (Fig. 4.1).

- **Selection Zone.** Once the cursor enters the unbounded selection zone, the item underneath the cursor will highlight in red indicating that it is currently being selected (Fig. 4.2 & 4.3).
- **Confirmation Zone.** Items are confirmed once the user exits the selection zone by moving the cursor past the outer diameter of the desired item (Fig. 4.4).

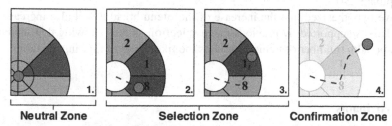

**Neutral Zone**          **Selection Zone**          **Confirmation Zone**

**Fig. 4.** Menu selection process of the cursor (pink circle) to target (green item) shown in the medium size menu. 1. Cursor starting in neutral zone. 2. Moving into selection zone (highlighted in red). 3. Navigating to target item in green. 4. Exiting on the outside radius of the target item to confirm selection (Color figure online).

## 4.2 Study Protocol

We began the experiment with a demographic's questionnaire including their experience with using digital and non-digital pens. We briefed them with a tutorial and explanation of the experiment, to allow time for training and gain familiarity with the device. The tutorial presented a random target to select, mimicking the actual experiment setup, with no repetitions involved.

We recorded participants selection time and error rate. We informed participants that we are more concerned with their performance rather than speed of task completion. Participants started the selection time by moving the cursor into the selection zone and then stopped when an item has been selected. We calculated participants error rate by dividing their total missed targets by their total overall targets. We recorded a missed target when the target item was not successfully selected by the user.

Our experiment followed a within-subject design where participants used 4 flexible pens for each of the 3 menu sizes. Each task was repeated 6 times for a total of 576 selection tasks, 4 flexibility (soft, medium soft, medium hard, hard) × (4 + 8 + 12) menu sizes (small, medium, large menus) × 6 repetitions = 576. We randomized the flexibility type, menu size and menu items to counterbalance learning effects. Study sessions lasted approximately 45 min.

Between each flexibility condition, we asked participants to fill a 5-point Likert scale questionnaire regarding the styluses perceived movement, responsiveness, and accuracy. At this time, we also encouraged participants to take a short break. We ended the experiment with a post questionnaire asking about their experience using a flexible stylus for menu selection and to rank their most to least preferred flexibility input type.

## 4.3 Hypothesis

- **H1.** We hypothesized that an increase in flexural stiffness will result an increase in error rate. Stiffer devices may take more physical exertion to bend, which could make selection tasks more difficult [24].
- **H2.** We hypothesized that the hard stylus will be the least preferred flexibility, as Kildal et al. found that users preferred softer materials as they required less effort to manipulate [24].
- **H3.** We hypothesized that the increase of the menu breadth will also increase error rate. This is supported by previous menu selection studies showing that increase in menu breadth (number of items) increases the likelihood of missing the target [4, 43, 51].

## 4.4 Participants

We recruited participants through email and posters. We had a total of 18 participants: 8 men, 10 women; 15 right-handed, 3 left-handed. Most participants were university students, their average age was 23 years old. None of the participants were experienced with using a bendable device. Participants received a $15 compensation for their time. The Carleton University Research Ethics Board approved this study (CUREB #111345).

## 4.5 Results

We first report the effects of repetition, menu size, and flexibility on selection time and following, we report the effects of the latter on error rate. We were also interested in studying the influence on item location within each menu size. Following, we discuss participants preference results and discuss findings upon their feedback.

**Selection Time and Error Rate.** We conducted a multi-way ANOVA across *repetition* × *flexibility* × *menu size* on selection time. Sphericity was assumed for repetition, flexibility, and was adjusted for menu size ($p < 0.01$) using Greenhouse-Geisser correction. We found a significant effect of *repetition* ($F(5, 90) = 11.7$, $p < 0.01$, $\eta_p^2 = 0.36$) and *menu size* ($F(2, 36) = 124.79$, $p < 0.01$, $n_p^2 = 0.87$) however, did not find any interaction effects. The same multi-way ANOVA across on error rate revealed a significant effect of *repetition* ($F(5, 90) = 3$, $p = 0.02$, $\eta_p^2 = 0.14$) and *menu size* ($F(2, 36) = 32.29$, $p < 0.01$, $n_p^2 = 0.65$) however, no interaction effects were found.

For *menu size*, our pairwise comparison using the Bonferroni adjustment on selection time revealed a significant difference where $p < 0.01$ for each pair. This suggested that the increase in items within a menu also increased the overall selection time for participants (small: 0.88 s, medium: 1.22 s and large: 1.54 s). We found these results to be on par with Tilt Menu and other studies which evaluated a ranking of menu sizes [42]. Our pairwise comparison for menu size on error rate found a significant difference for each menu pair where $p < 0.01$ which suggested that an increase in items within a menu also increases error rate (small: 2.2%, medium: 9.1% and large: 15.1%).

Our hypothesis (H1) assumed that an increase in flexural stiffness will yield in a decrease user's performance. However, we did not find any effects of flexibility type for

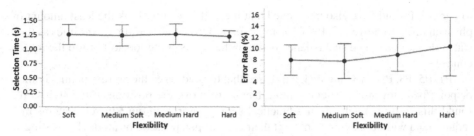

**Fig. 5.** Average selection time (Left) and error rate (Right) with 95% CI for the four flexibility conditions.

both selection time and error rate (Fig. 5). This was interesting for us, furthermore, we discussed this factor in depth alongside with our flexibility preference results.

**Item Location.** We were also interested in comparing each item's selection time within its respected menu. We evaluated the right-handed participants only (n = 15) to mitigate the possibility of left-hand/right-hand occlusion, similarly done by Tilt Menu [43]. Our ANOVA investigated the influence of item location on selection time and found significant differences for all three menu types: small $(F(2, 27) = 10.8, p < 0.01, \eta_p^2 = 0.44)$, medium $(F(3.3, 46) = 2.7, p = 0.05, \eta_p^2 = 0.16)$, and large $(F(4, 51) = 4.5, p < 0.01, \eta_p^2 = 0.24)$. Across all three menu sizes, items located within the south-west region yielded the lowest selection times with relatively low error rates. Comparatively, items located south-east were more difficult to select resulting in relatively high selection times and error rates. We speculate this reasoning due to items being occluded by the user's hand in the south-east region.

Participants filled out a preference questionnaire that asked them to rank the flexibilities from most preferred to least. We had a total of *n = 13* rankings as we neglected 4 participants who misunderstood the question and only provided their most preferred flexibility. We performed a Wilcoxon Signed Rank Test on the rankings and found no significant differences. Figure 6 indicates that most people ranked the *medium soft* (*n* = 8) and *medium hard* (N = 7) flexibilities as their 1st or 2nd preferred flexibility while the *hard* and *soft* flexibilities had the most ranked 4th place (*n = 5* for both).

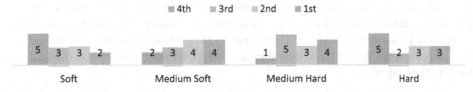

**Fig. 6.** Total participants ranking from most (1st) to least (4th) preferred flexibility input type.

P2, P3, P11, and P14, favoured the harder flexibilities commenting that they felt they had more accuracy, which led to fewer unintentional movements. They also stated that the soft flexibility was too difficult to be precise when making small movements. Opposingly, P1, P6, P8, and P10, argued that the soft flexibilities were more responsive and easier to control. P6 and P10, also mentioned that the soft flexibility took the least amount of physical effort to move. P5, P9, P13, and P16, preferred the medium flexibilities as they stated that it was the perfect balance between the stylus being too soft or too flexible to control.

P1, P5, P8, P9, P13, and P14, expressed that they admired the ability to quickly flick or point/bend towards an item without having to move the position of the stylus. We found this feature beneficial in a practical setting, users can quickly select items in a radial menu without having to disrupt their current pen position or mode. Interestingly, this was also found to be a feature of Tilt Menu where the user tilted the pen towards an item without having to lift off or move the stylus tip from its current position [42].

### 4.6 Discussion

We hypothesized that an increase of flexural stiffness may result in higher error rates (H1). We also theorized that the stiffer materials, medium hard, and hard will be the least favoured (H2). Our subjective rankings did show that many people did not prefer the hard flexibility type (n = 5), moreover there was an equal amount that disliked the soft flexibility type (n = 5). Being there no distinct preferred flexibility type from our analysis, we could not conclude that users favoured the softer conditions for our HyperBrush device. This means every flexural stiffness is relevant, depending on users' preference. Participants' feedback revealed that the type of task may have an influence on what flexibility users favour. Many who preferred a stiffer HyperBrush, reasoned that they felt more control over executing fine and precise movements. While others who preferred a softer HyperBrush, stated that it did not require a lot of physical strength to move and being more comfortable to use.

We hypothesized that with an increase of items within a menu will also increase error rate (H3). From our analysis, we found this was correct for error rate and selection time as well. P7, P8, P10, P14, and P17, mentioned that it was difficult to select items that were located directly underneath their hand (south-east area). We advocate that menu tools of higher importance should be mapped to items located in areas that are not occluded by the users' hand to yield in best efficiency. This is also supported with prior research on radial pen-based menus [26, 42, 50].

We point out limitations of the study. Bending our device does not require a lot of force, however, when consecutive repetitions occur, it can lead to hand strain or fatigue. We did not measure any effects of fatigue on accuracy although, it was evident from participants criticism (P1, P2, P11, and P12). We emphasize that this should be considered during the protocol planning and longer breaks between tasks should be further encouraged.

## 5   Study 2: Brushstroke Width Manipulation Task

Our first study explored the usability of our HyperBrush did not incorporate pen movement. Previous work compared stationary bend and pressure input for brushstroke width manipulation [15]. Our goal in the second study was to compare the ability to simultaneously control pen movement with bend or pressure input. Specifically, we measured the performance (width and movement accuracy) of controlling bend and pressure input while moving on an X-Y plane simultaneously and compared it with the Microsoft (MS) Surface Pen, which includes pressure input. Carrying on from our previous study, we also incorporate measuring the influence of flexural stiffness. For this study, we combined the medium-soft and medium-hard conditions due to our results showing no distinct differences in performance or preference.

## 5.1 Methodology

We investigated the influence of manipulating the brushstroke width by evaluating the user's performance on matching two target patterns: *static* and *dynamic* while moving in the given direction: North, South, East, West (Fig. 7). This additional factor of moving in a direction goes beyond previous work [15], to provide a more comprehensive analysis of real brushstroke patterns, which are not always left to right (i.e., east). Our intention for using two target patterns was to measure performances for holding bend position and varying the position by repetitively increasing and decreasing bend.

- **Static Target Pattern.** User moves in given direction and immediately alternates between holding the maximum width (4 cm) and the minimum width (0.5 cm).
- **Dynamic Target Pattern.** User moves in given direction and gradually alternates increasing towards the maximum width (4 cm) and decreasing towards the minimum width (0.5 cm).

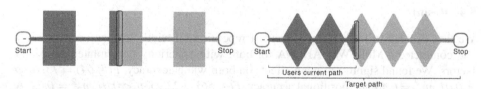

**Fig. 7.** Brushstroke width manipulation task with the static (left) and dynamic (right) target patterns. Illustration of a user matching their path (dark blue) to the target path (light blue), moving east. The cursor (black rectangle) indicates the current position and width size (Color figure online).

Before we start each task, we display the *start* and *stop* indicators outlined in green and red (Fig. 7). We begin the task when the user places the stylus tip within the area of the *start* indicator. We end the task when the user enters the area of the *stop* indicator and then repeats displaying the next task.

We assigned each X-Y position on the path and a brushstroke width value that essentially displayed the target path. We measured the positional accuracy by calculating the mean Euclidian Distance between the target's points and the user's points, known as Proportional Shape Matching [2, 25]. Similarly, we calculated the width accuracy as a measurement of the absolute difference from the target and user widths.

We followed a within-subject design where participants used 4 *inputs* (soft, medium, hard flexibilities, and pressure) × 4 *directions* (north, south, east, west) × 2 *target patterns* (static and dynamic) × 5 *repetitions* = 160 trials that were randomized. Between inputs, participants filled a Likert scale questionnaire regarding the input type.

## 5.2 Hypothesis

- **H1.** We hypothesized that the *soft* flexibility would perform better in *width accuracy* as opposed to the other flexibility conditions.
- **H2.** We suspected that when decreasing in brushstroke width, our HyperBrush would perform better than the pressure stylus in *width accuracy*.

## 5.3 Participants

We recruited participants through email, social media, and posters. The majority were university students with no prior experience with using flexible styluses. None participated in the first study. We had 18 participants, 10 men and 8 women: 17 right-handed and 1 left-handed. These participants conducted Study 2 and 3 in a single session (1 h total), starting with the task in study 3, a creative drawing task, where they drew two illustrations, one with HyperBrush and one with a pressure pen. We chose to present them in a different order in this paper, choose to present the studies that evaluated effects of flexural stiffness sequentially (study 1 and 2) and following, discuss the creative drawing task (study 3). The study was approved by our institution's research ethics board and we provided each participant $15 compensation.

## 5.4 Results

We first decided to remove any effects of repetition on width & positional accuracy and conducted a Multi-Way ANOVA for both with Sphericity not violated across all factors. We found significant main effects on both width accuracy, $F(4, 64) = 13.40$, $p < 0.01$, $\eta_p^2 = 0.46$ and positional accuracy, $F(4, 56) = 22.95$, $p < 0.01$, $\eta_p^2 = 0.62$. A pairwise comparison with Bonferroni adjustment found a significant higher difference in accuracy from the 1st to all other repetitions for width accuracy and 5th to all other repetitions for positional accuracy, both at $p < 0.01$. Based on this result, we proceeded to disregard both the first and last (1st and 5th) repetitions for the following analyses as we were focusing on the learning effects of this study.

**Positional and Width Accuracy.** We conducted a multi-way ANOVA across *input type* × *direction* × *target type* on *positional accuracy*. We found a significant effect of *input type* ($F(3, 39) = 5.6$, $p = 0.03$, $\eta_p^2 = 0.29$) and *target type* ($F(1, 13) = 6.0$, $p < 0.01$, $\eta_p^2 = 0.68$) (Fig. 8). We did not find any interaction effects. We follow up with the pairwise comparison results below.

Our pairwise comparison using Lowest Significant Difference (LSD) adjustment found that the Soft flexibility was significantly lower than the Medium flexibility, $p = 0.04$. The baseline MS pressure pen condition was also significantly lower than the Medium, $p < 0.01$ as well as the Hard, $p < 0.01$ flexibility types. Being that the soft flexibility also yielded in the lowest average distance as opposed to the other flexibilities,

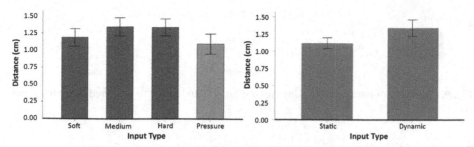

**Fig. 8.** Participants average X-Y distance from the target position for our three flexibilities and the baseline pressure condition (Left) and target type (Right).

this could suggest that the soft flexibility is easier to control than the other flexibility types.

We conducted a pairwise comparison using LSD adjustment and found that the Static target averaged a lower distance and was significantly lower than the Dynamic target, $p < 0.01$. This could assume that users are more accurate with controlling the styluses X-Y position when not consistently changing the bending position of the device.

We conducted a multi-way ANOVA across *input type × direction × target type* on *width accuracy*. We did not find any main effects or interaction effects on any of the above factors on width accuracy.

**Completion Time.** We conducted a multi-way ANOVA for *completion time* and found a significant effect of *direction (F(3, 45) = 3.8, p = 0.02, $\eta_p^2$ = 0.34)* (Sphericity assumed) with no further interaction effects. We followed with pairwise comparison test using Bonferroni adjustment and revealed that moving in the east direction (31 s) yielded in significantly lower average completion time than moving in the west direction (37 s), *p = 0.04*. We also found that moving towards the north direction (32 s) was also significantly lower than moving in the south (35 s) and west (37 s) directions where *p = 0.04 and 0.01* respectively.

**Flexibility Preference Results.** Similar to the first study, our analysis on flexibility preference did not yield significant results. Results showed the medium flexibility with the lowest preferred mean score of 1.7 while the soft and hard flexibilities were 2.3 and 2.0, respectively (Fig. 9).

We further discuss participants feedback and rationale behind their rankings and preferences. P8, P11, and P18, preferred the soft flexibility articulated that it was the easiest to bend because it required less physical effort consequently improving their ability to control the device. Opposingly, P1, P3, P7, and P10 argued that the hard flexibility was the easiest to control and more precise. P3 explained that the soft flexibility allowed for too much bend to be applied thus it was easier to make mistakes and overshoot targets. P6 who preferred the medium flexibility, rationed that it was the perfect medium between the two where it combined the easiness of flexing without compromising too much responsiveness.

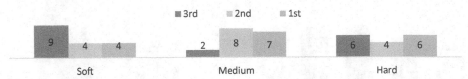

**Fig. 9.** Summary of participant rankings from most (1st) to least (3rd) preferred flexibility input type.

## 5.5 Discussion

We hypothesized that the soft flexibility would perform better in width accuracy than the other flexibility types (H1), yet we did not find any significant differences between flexibility type for width accuracy. From looking at how users perceived the performances for each flexibility, it may also be inconclusive to approximate a dominant flexibility type. Looking back at our bend menu study, we also did not find any effects from flexibility. We found these results interesting as we speculated that flexibility could depend on user's personal preference. With HyperBrush, users have the ability to interchange components to their preferred flexibility or depending on the task.

We found that participants preferred stiffer materials for tasks that require precision, such as writing. As for a softer material, drawing or sketching might be valuable here. As for drawing or sketching, we speculate that the softer material might be of value for these scenarios that require quick gestures and strokes. Commercial versions of HyperBrush could either be a set of several stiffnesses brushes, or a single brush with interchangeable parts of different flexibilities, including a rigid one.

We suspected that when decreasing in brushstroke width our HyperBrush would perform better than the pressure stylus in width accuracy (H2). Our analysis did not find any significant differences between the two input types. These results are aligned with those found in FlexStylus' study [15]. Interestingly, a few participants mentioned that the visual feedback from the curvature of our bent HyperBrush assisted with their control and accuracy during increasing and decreasing brushstroke width.

We point out the limitations of this study. Our HyperBrush had a larger pen tip surface area (28.00 mm$^2$) as opposed to the Microsoft Surface pressure pen (0.80 mm$^2$), which made it difficult for users to make very fine (small) brushstrokes. Additionally, HyperBrush's tip was made from a rubberized compressible material opposed to the matte plastic texture from the MS pen, therefore making it difficult to compare the feeling produced when drawing. We chose a larger pen tip to provide a sufficient amount of frictional force to avoid accidental slippage when bending the device. The MS pen being a commercial product, its manufacturing is precise and robust, and its pressure transfer function is thoroughly calibrated. Therefore, the comparable results of a research prototype such as HyperBrush are encouraging.

We explored a range of flexural stiffnesses for our HyperBrush, from 0.1 N/mm to 0.139 N/mm yet neither study found any influence on users' performance. Considering only that a total range difference of 0.039 N/mm (4 g/mm) could potentially be too narrow to yield any significant differences. While it would have been ideal to explore a larger range of stiffnesses, we were constrained by the thickness of the inner wall without compromising robustness of the device and fitting a sensor within its cavity. We also consider that participants also had prior exposure with using the medium flexibility during study 3 which may have an additional learning effect.

## 6  Study 3: Creative Digital Drawing Task

In this study, we sought to assess how our HyperBrush can be a supportive tool for users' creativity. We were also interested on how it performs compared to a commercially available pressure sensitive stylus, the Microsoft Surface Pen.

### 6.1  Methodology

We developed our own free form digital drawing application that supported input from both stylus types. We programmed our application using Unity Engine and coupled both absolute bend and pressure input to vary the width of the brushstroke. For instance, a larger bend or pressure input resulted in a larger brushstroke width. For the flexible input, we chose to use a single flexibility, the medium condition (0.129 N/mm), being the combination of both hard and soft extremes. This provided participant equal training between the flexible and pressure pen, while fitting within an hour-long study session.

   We followed a study design similar to Aslan et al. that instructed participants to draw an illustration for both input types [3]. We instructed participants to draw two illustrations (cityscape and landscape), one per input type (bend and pressure), in which the order was reversed per participant. We gave participants 10 min for each illustration and was also encouraged to think aloud. We hypothesize that our participants would perceive HyperBrush to support creativity more than a pressure stylus (**H1**). To address H1, we had participants fill out a Creative Support Index (CSI) questionnaire that examined their subjective perception of how each stylus type can support the five dimensions of creativity (Enjoyment, Expressiveness, Exploration, Results Worth Effort, and Immersion) [11]. The 18 participants in Study 3 also completed study 2. They are described in Sect. 5.3.

### 6.2  Results

Figure 10 illustrates P1, P2, P4, and P9 drawings from both input and illustration types. Overall, most illustrations produced by our HyperBrush exhibited larger brushstrokes that was ideal for drawing large patches of land, grass, and sky. There was also a trend of participants drawing skies with colourful sunsets taking advantage of the gradient tool. On the other hand, the MS pressure stylus revealed drawings of smaller strokes detailing thin outlines, birds, small bits of grass, and windows.

   P1, P2, P12, P17, and P18 expressed that the HyperBrush acted similarly to a paint-brush. We believe that this is because the flexible barrel bends in the same fashion to how the bristles on a paintbrush bends, it curves as the tool is dragged on the surface. P5, P14, and P16 also mentioned that the visual affordance from our HyperBrush helped them control the amount of bend due to being able to see the curvature as well feeling the resistive feedback from the flexible barrel.

   P12 commented on how they enjoyed performing a circular motion technique with both styluses, in which the gradient effect added colour depth to objects such as clouds

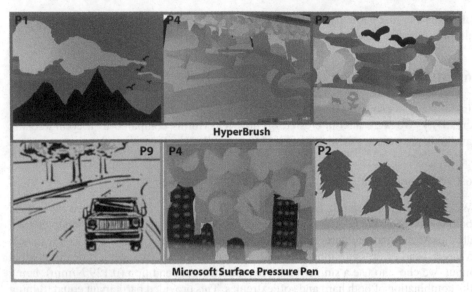

**Fig. 10.** Collage of participants' drawings of a landscape or cityscape from using both styluses.

**Fig. 11.** Example of P12 drawing colourful gradient clouds with using repetitive circular motions while bending and rotating the HyperBrush.

and treetops (Fig. 11). P12 explained that they bent the device while directionally pointing it in a rotational fashion creating colourful gradients and visually appealing cloud like figures. P4 and others have done a similar technique while drawing their own clouds as well as treetops.

We observed that participants held the HyperBrush low on the shaft with the intention to prevent any unintentional bending and continue to use it as a regular stylus. P5 emphasized that it felt unusual gripping the HyperBrush directly over the flexible point as it felt too soft compromising a sturdy grip.

P2 and P16 expressed concerns with the difficulty of changing directions while maintaining bend input. P2 also argued that this could be a feature like painting Chinese calligraphy where directional changes can add a unique style to the size of the brushstroke width. In this case, with some experience and learning, directional changes can be used to the user's advantage to produce smooth, intentional, and artistic, variants in brushstroke width.

We calculated the CSI scores for both our HyperBrush (44.8) and the MS Pressure Pen (46.0) and yielded in similar results. We conducted a Wilcoxon Signed Rank Test for each dimension of creativity and the overall CSI score and did not find any significant differences between our HyperBrush and the MS Pressure Pen.

### 6.3 Discussion

We hypothesized that users would perceive HyperBrush to be a greater tool to support creativity as compared to the pressure stylus (H1). Although we did not find any differences in supporting creativity between our HyperBrush and the pressure stylus, most participants preferred our HyperBrush (n = 13) over the pressure pen (n = 5) as they specified that it was more enjoyable to use. We speculate the reasoning behind this is that many participants referred to our HyperBrush similar to using a digitalized paint brush. Several participants commented that the curve created from bending was almost resembling the bristles of a paintbrush being dragged against the surface. This remark motivated our choice for the name HyperBrush. However, it does not mean that our intent was to specifically replicate a brush. Users can grip the device in different ways, which offers different interaction styles, similarly to FlexStylus [15]. From our results, we found that participants performed larger and expressive brushstrokes for clouds, tree-tops, and skylines. As opposed to the pressure stylus, participants often performed thin strokes for outlines, windows, and birds.

The main limitation of this study is that our participants were recruited from the general population, few considering themselves as artists or experienced using digital stylus interfaces. Although we obtained valuable feedback and exceptional illustrations, a study targeted at digital artists could obtain richer feedback and results.

## 7  Conclusion

We presented HyperBrush, a digital stylus capable of utilizing bendable input as an additional degree of freedom for pen-based applications. We designed HyperBrush to have interchangeable flexible components so that the stiffness of the device can be accommodated to the user's preference and task. We conducted three studies to evaluate HyperBrush, one assessing the performance on a menu technique, a second comparing bend and pressure when controlling brushstroke width while moving the pen, and a third with a more complex creative task.

We observed how HyperBrush can perform similarly to a commercial MS pressure pen when it came to supporting users' creativity and controlling brushstroke width while moving. While we did not find any influence of flexural stiffness on users' performance, feedback exhibited that stiffness could be a result of personal preference. We believe that HyperBrush's variety of flexibility is analogous to having a wide selection of paint-brushes available for an artist, where each flexible brush provides their own distinct advantages and style to the artist. This is, however, still to be validated with a user study involving artists. Regarding our study about menu selection, participants found that quickly bending/flicking towards an item was a fast and effective method of interaction.

For future prototyping of a flexible sensing stylus, we recommend exploring different pen tip sizes and materials. We think that a smaller pen tip size that does not compromise the ability and control of bending could potentially expand this research field into other applications such as digital writing or object manipulation that demands precision of the pen tip. We look forward to an in-the-wild, longitudinal study with digital creative artists or designers to understand how HyperBrush could be a tool to better support their creative applications and workflow, with a comprehensive set of HyperBrush prototypes ready to go similarly to a different pencil type in a pencil case.

**Acknowledgements.** This work was supported and funded by the National Sciences and Engineering Research Council of Canada (NSERC) through the Collaborative Learning in Usability Experiences CREATE grant (2015-465639) and a Discovery grant (2017-06300).

# References

1. Arduino Mega: (2020). https://store.arduino.cc/usa/mega-2560-r3
2. Andersen, T.H., Zhai, S.: Writing with music. ACM Trans. Appl. Percept. **7**(3), 1–24 (2010). https://doi.org/10.1145/1773965.1773968
3. Aslan, I., et al.: Creativity support and multimodal pen-based interaction. In: 2019 International Conference on Multimodal Interaction, pp. 135–144. ACM, New York (2019). https://doi.org/10.1145/3340555.3353738
4. Bailly, G., et al.: Flower menus. In: Proceedings of the Working Conference on Advanced Visual Interfaces - AVI 2008, p. 15. ACM Press, New York (2008). https://doi.org/10.1145/1385569.1385575
5. Bend Labs: BendLabs Inc. https://www.bendlabs.com/
6. Bi, X., et al.: An exploration of pen rolling for pen-based interaction. In: Proceedings of the 21st Annual ACM Symposium on User Interface Software and Technology - UIST 2008, p. 191. ACM Press, New York (2008). https://doi.org/10.1145/1449715.1449745
7. Boem, A., Troiano, G.M.: Non-Rigid HCI: a review of deformable interfaces and input. In: Proceedings of the 2019 ACM Designing Interactive Systems Conference - DIS 2019, pp. 885–906. ACM, New York (2019). https://doi.org/10.1145/3322276.3322347
8. Briotto Faustino, D., Girouard, A.: Bend Passwords on BendyPass: a user authentication method for people with vision impairment. In: ACM SIGACCESS Conference on Computers and Accessibility, p. (to appear) (2018)
9. Buxton, W., et al.: A comparison of pressure and tilt input techniques for cursor control. Conf. Hum. Fact. Comput. Syst. - Proc. E **92-D**(9), 801–804 (2005). https://doi.org/10.1587/transinf.E92.D.1683
10. Buxton, W., et al.: Issues and techniques in touch-sensitive tablet input. Comput. Graph. **19**(3), 215–224 (1985). https://doi.org/10.1145/325165.325239
11. Cherry, E., Latulipe, C.: Quantifying the creativity support of digital tools through the creativity support index. ACM Trans. Comput. Interact. **21**(4), 1–25 (2014). https://doi.org/10.1145/2617588
12. Cho, Y., et al.: RealPen: providing realism in handwriting tasks on touch surfaces using auditory-tactile feedback. In: Proceedings of the 29th Annual Symposium on User Interface Software and Technology - UIST 2016, pp. 195–205 (2016). https://doi.org/10.1145/2984511.2984550

13. Ernst, M.: Bending Blindly: Exploring the Learnability and Usability of Bend Gestures for the Visually Impaired. Carleton University, Ottawa (2015)
14. Fares, E., et al.: Effects of bend gesture training on learnability and memorability in a mobile game. In: Proceedings of the 2017 ACM International Conference on Interactive Surfaces and Spaces - ISS 2017, pp. 240–245 (2017). https://doi.org/10.1145/3132272.3134142
15. Fellion, N., et al.: FlexStylus: leveraging bend input for pen interaction. In: Proceedings of the 30th Annual ACM Symposium on User Interface Software and Technology - UIST 2017, pp. 375–385. ACM, New York (2017). https://doi.org/10.1145/3126594.3126597
16. Girouard, A., et al.: One-handed bend interactions with deformable smartphones. In: Proceedings of the ACM CHI 2015: CHI Conference on Human Factors in Computing Systems, vol. 1, pp. 1509–1518 (2015). https://doi.org/10.1145/2702123.2702513
17. Grierson, M., Kiefer, C.: NoiseBear: a wireless malleable multiparametric controller for use in assistive technology contexts. In: Proceedings of the SIGCHI Conference on Human Factors in Computing Systems - CHI 2013, April 2013, pp. 2923–2926 (2013). https://doi.org/10.1145/2468356.2479575
18. Grossman, T., et al.: Hover widgets. In: Proceedings of the SIGCHI Conference on Human Factors in Computing Systems - CHI 2006, p. 861. ACM Press, New York (2006). https://doi.org/10.1145/1124772.1124898
19. Hasan, K., et al.: A-coord input. In: Proceedings of the 2012 ACM Annual Conference on Human Factors in Computing Systems - CHI 2012, p. 805. ACM Press, New York (2012). https://doi.org/10.1145/2207676.2208519
20. Hinckley, K., et al.: Motion and context sensing techniques for pen computing. In: Proceedings of Graphics Interface Conference - GI 2013, pp. 71–78 (2013)
21. Hinckley, K., et al.: Pen + touch = new tools. In: Proceedings of the 23rd Annual ACM Symposium on User Interface Software and Technology - UIST 2010, p. 27. ACM Press, New York (2010). https://doi.org/10.1145/1866029.1866036
22. Huot, S., et al.: PushMenu: Extending Marking Menus for Pressure-Enabled Input Devices (2008)
23. Inc., F.: Formlabs Form 2 Printer. https://formlabs.com/3d-printers/form-2/
24. Kildal, J., Wilson, G.: Feeling it: the roles of stiffness, deformation range and feedback in the control of deformable UI. In: Proceedings of the 14th ACM international conference on Multimodal interaction - ICMI 2012, p. 393. ACM Press, New York (2012). https://doi.org/10.1145/2388676.2388766
25. Kristensson, P., Zhai, S.: SHARK 2. In: Proceedings of the 17th Annual ACM Symposium on User Interface Software and Technology - UIST 2004, p. 43. ACM Press, New York (2004). https://doi.org/10.1145/1029632.1029640
26. Kurtenbach, G., Buxton, W.: Limits of expert performance using hierarchic marking menus. In: Proceedings of the CHI Conference on Human Factors in Computing Systems, pp. 482–487 (1993). https://doi.org/10.1145/169059.169426
27. Kurtenbach, G., Buxton, W.: The limits of expert performance using hierarchic marking menus. In: Proceedings of the CHI Conference on Human Factors in Computing Systems, pp. 482–487 (1993). https://doi.org/10.1145/169059.169426
28. Kurtenbach, G., Buxton, W.: User learning and performance with marking menus. In: Proceedings of the SIGCHI Conference on Human Factors in Computing Systems Celebrating Interdependence - CHI 1994, pp. 258–264. ACM Press, New York (1994). https://doi.org/10.1145/191666.191759
29. Lahey, B., et al.: PaperPhone: understanding the use of bend gestures in mobile devices with flexible electronic paper displays. In: Proceedings of the CHI, Vancouver, pp. 1303–1312 (2011). https://doi.org/10.1145/1978942.1979136
30. Lo, J., Girouard, A.: Fabricating bendy: design and development of deformable prototypes. IEEE Pervas. Comput. 13(3), 40–46 (2014). https://doi.org/10.1109/MPRV.2014.47

31. Martín-Gutiérrez, J., Contero, M.: FlexRemote: exploring the effectiveness of deformable user interface as an input device for TV. In: Stephanidis, C. (ed.) HCI 2011. CCIS, vol. 174. Springer, Heidelberg (2011). https://doi.org/10.1007/978-3-642-22095-1

32. Microsoft: Microsoft Surface Pro. https://www.microsoft.com/en-ca/p/surface-pro-7/8n17j0 m5zzqs?activetab=overview

33. Murakami, T., et al.: DO-IT: deformable objects as input tools. In: Conference Companion on Human Factors in Computing Systems - CHI 1995, pp. 87–88. ACM Press, New York (1995). https://doi.org/10.1145/223355.223442

34. Ramos, G., et al.: Pressure widgets. In: Proceedings of the 2004 Conference on Human Factors in Computing Systems - CHI 2004, pp. 487–494. ACM Press, New York (2004). https://doi.org/10.1145/985692.985754

35. Ramos, G., Balakrishnan, R.: Zliding. In: Proceedings of the 18th Annual ACM Symposium on User Interface Software and Technology - UIST 2005, p. 143. ACM Press, New York (2005). https://doi.org/10.1145/1095034.1095059

36. Ramos, G.A., Balakrishnan, R.: Pressure marks. In: Conference on Human Factors in Computing Systems, pp. 1375–1384 (2007). https://doi.org/10.1145/1240624.1240834

37. Schmitz, M., et al.: Flexibles: deformation-aware 3D-printed tangibles for capacitive touch-screens. In: Conference on Human Factors in Computing Systems, May 2017, pp. 1001–1014 (2017). https://doi.org/10.1145/3025453.3025663

38. Senturia, S.: Microsystem Design. Kluwer Academic Publishers, Boston (2002). https://doi.org/10.1007/b117574

39. Shorey, P., Girouard, A.: Bendtroller: an exploration of in-game action mappings with a deformable game controller. In: SIGCHI Conference on Human Factors in Computing Systems, pp. 1447–1458. ACM, New York (2017)

40. Song, H., et al.: Grips and gestures on a multi-touch pen. In: Proceedings of the 2011 Annual Conference on Human Factors in Computing Systems - CHI 2011, p. 1323. ACM Press, New York (2011). https://doi.org/10.1145/1978942.1979138

41. Strohmeier, P., et al.: ReFlex: a flexible smartphone with active haptic feedback for bend input. In: Proceedings of the 10th Anniversary Conference on Tangible Embedded and Embodied Interaction - TEI 2016, pp. 185–192. ACM Press, New York (2016). https://doi.org/10.1145/2839462.2839494

42. Tian, F., et al.: Tilt menu: using the 3D orientation information of pen devices to extend the selection capability of pen-based user interfaces. In: Proceedings of the Conference on Human Factors in Computing Systems, pp. 1371–1380 (2008). https://doi.org/10.1145/1357054.1357269

43. Tian, F., et al.: Tilt menu. In: Proceeding of the Twenty-Sixth Annual CHI Conference on Human Factors in Computing Systems - CHI 2008, p. 1371. ACM, New York (2008). https://doi.org/10.1145/1357054.1357269

44. Troiano, G.M., et al.: Deformable interfaces for performing music. In: Proceedings of the 33rd Annual ACM Conference on Human Factors in Computing Systems - CHI 2015, pp. 377–386. ACM Press, New York (2015). https://doi.org/10.1145/2702123.2702492

45. Watanabe, C., et al.: Generic method for crafting deformable interfaces to physically augment smartphones. In: Proceedings of the Extended Abstracts of the 32nd Annual ACM Conference on Human Factors in Computing Systems - CHI EA 2014, pp. 1309–1314. ACM Press, New York (2014). https://doi.org/10.1145/2559206.2581307

46. Wightman, D., et al.: TouchMark: flexible document navigation and bookmarking techniques for E-book readers. In: Proceedings of the Graphics Interface 2010, Canadian Information Processing Society, pp. 241–244 (2010)

47. Xin, Y., et al.: Acquiring and pointing. In: Proceedings of the 2011 Annual Conference on Human Factors in Computing Systems - CHI 2011, p. 849. ACM Press, New York (2011). https://doi.org/10.1145/1978942.1979066

48. Xin, Y., et al.: Natural use profiles for the pen: an empirical exploration of pressure, tilt, and azimuth. In: Proceedings of the Conference on Human Factors in Computing Systems, pp. 801–804 (2012). https://doi.org/10.1145/2207676.2208518
49. Xin, Y., et al.: Natural use profiles for the pen. In: Proceedings of the 2012 ACM Annual Conference on Human Factors in Computing Systems - CHI 2012, p. 801. ACM Press, New York (2012). https://doi.org/10.1145/2207676.2208518
50. Zhao, S., et al.: Zone and polygon menus: using relative position to increase the breadth of multi-stroke marking menus. In: Proceedings of the Conference on Human Factors in Computing Systems, vol. 2, pp. 1077–1086 (2006)
51. Zhao, S., et al.: Zone and polygon menus. In: Proceedings of the SIGCHI Conference on Human Factors in Computing Systems - CHI 2006, p. 1077. ACM Press, New York (2006). https://doi.org/10.1145/1124772.1124933
52. Zhou, X., Ren, X.: A comparison of pressure and tilt input techniques for cursor control. IEICE Trans. Inf. Syst. E **92-D**(9), 1683–1691 (2009). https://doi.org/10.1587/transinf.E92.D.1683.

# Leveraging CD Gain for Precise Barehand Video Timeline Browsing on Smart Displays

Futian Zhang[1]([envelope]), Sachi Mizobuchi[2], Wei Zhou[2], Taslim Arefin Khan[2], Wei Li[2], and Edward Lank[1]

[1] Cheriton School of Computer Science, University of Waterloo, Waterloo, Canada
futian.zhang@uwaterloo.ca
[2] Human-Machine Interaction Lab, Huawei, Toronto, Canada

**Abstract.** One common task when controlling smart displays is the manipulation of video timelines. Given current examples of smart displays that support distant bare hand control, in this paper we explore CD Gain functions to support both seeking and scrubbing tasks. Through a series of experiments, we demonstrate that a linear CD Gain function provides performance advantages when compared to either a constant function or generalised logistic function (GLF). In particular, linear gain is faster than a GLF and has lower error rate than Constant gain. Furthermore, Linear and GLF gains' average temporal error when targeting a one second interval on a two hour timeline ($\pm 5\,\mathrm{s}$) is less than one third the error of a Constant gain.

**Keywords:** CD Gain · Gesture control · Smart TV · Video browsing

## 1 Introduction

Many modern televisions are considered *Smart TVs*, primarily due to the addition of wireless internet (WiFi) connectivity and a set of apps to connect to a variety of on-line services. One of the primary use-cases of these Smart TVs is to consume video, typically through access to various video streaming services such as those offered by Netflix, Amazon, Disney, HBO, Hulu, and others. While a basic use-case for streamed video would be to watch the video stream from start to finish, there are also occasions where users wish to navigate within a video stream using video timelines to rewatch a portion, to return to a location due to interrupted viewing, or even to skip forward through advertisements, credits, or uninteresting scenes.

Video timeline control comprises two distinct tasks: seeking and scrubbing. The seeking task involves acquiring a specific location along the timeline, typically a specific elapsed time within the video. The scrubbing task, in contrast, requires a user to traverse the video in a controlled way, monitoring keyframes, to locate a specific scene whose timing they may not know. In the seeking task, one

© IFIP International Federation for Information Processing 2021
Published by Springer Nature Switzerland AG 2021
C. Ardito et al. (Eds.): INTERACT 2021, LNCS 12935, pp. 72–91, 2021.
https://doi.org/10.1007/978-3-030-85610-6_5

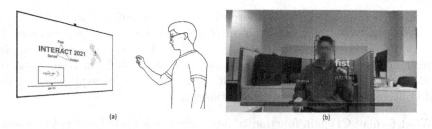

**Fig. 1.** Video timeline control for smart TVs. (a) The usage in a real world task. (b) The view of the camera on the smart TV when the user is navigating.

challenge is that, with limited clutching, we must provide users with sufficient precision to target a specific portion of the video. In a two-hour video (7200 s), one-second-level precision would be ideal, but, on a 4K display, second-level precision requires sub-pixel targeting. Conversely, in the scrubbing task, users must be able maintain an intermediate speed such that they can effectively identify and home-in on a desired scene. Because of the need to support selectable time periods within video with high precision, a variety of researchers have proposed solutions to simplify precise seeking and scrubbing [4, 5, 10, 12, 22]. Despite these innovations, performing seeking and scrubbing tasks on video timelines remains challenging, particularly considering the (frequently limited) input affordances of modern Smart TV remotes.

One feature that has been recently added to Smart TVs is the ability to control the display at a distance using barehand gestures (see, for example, Huawei's X65, Hisense U7, and Samsung F-series displays). Users of these displays typically hold their hand up in front of their body and perform gestures and movements to control the display. Using optical or infrared images, cameras track the users hand position and recognize gestures and movement to support barehand input.

While one can imagine various pointing enhancements to support the selection of sparse on-screen targets (a bubble cursor, various forms of object pointing, target manipulations [7, 8, 17]), as Balakrishnan [1] notes, cursor or target based pointing facilitation techniques assume significant whitespace on the display. However, input along the timeline is continuous. To map barehand movement onto timeline manipulation, we must either replace the timeline (with attendant disadvantages of changing the fundamental video interaction that users are familiar with), or we must choose an appropriate Control-to-Display Gain (CD Gain) function [19] to effectively support range of movement (from beginning to end of the timeline), precision of movement (to enable second or near-second level selection along the timeline), and control of speed (to support key frame monitoring during scrubbing along the timeline). In this paper, we explore this question of the impact of well-chosen CD Gain functions on barehand video timeline manipulation.

An open question that we faced was what would constitute a good CD Gain function, and, indeed, whether it was even possible to identify a good CD Gain function given the above conflicting requirements [19]. Naively, we assumed that the literature would identify an appropriate CD gain function for both seeking and scrubbing tasks, but, based on our reading of the literature, this was not the case. There are numerous instances of research that explore the mapping of freehand movement onto cursor movement [2] and significant recent research in selecting CD gain functions [19], but, even after careful exploration of this related literature, we are left with questions, including:

1. What form of CD gain function is most effective for barehand video timeline control? Should it be a constant CD Gain, similar to direct manipulation, or should some form of cursor acceleration/non-constant gain be used?
2. How well do different variants of CD Gain functions work for both seeking and scrubbing tasks? Is there one CD Gain function that can balance the needs of seeking and scrubbing, or must we prioritize one over the other?

To the best of our knowledge, for the domain of barehand video timeline control, it is not possible to glean from the current research literature answers to these questions.

To probe these questions, in this paper we present a controlled experiment that explores CD Gain functions for barehand video timeline control. We design three primary experimental tasks: interval targeting, where a user acquires a specific spatial region on the timeline with a given tolerance i.e. a time interval selection; scene seeking, where a user moves through the timeline with the goal of identifying a specific scene (via keyframes) that they wish to view; and precise time targeting, where a user moves through the timeline to acquire as accurately as possible a specific 1 unit interval (i.e. one second) in an 7200 unit (i.e. two hour) timeline. Overall, we find that pointer acceleration – whether linear or non-linear – significantly outperforms constant CD Gain, and that a Linear CD Gain function presents overall advantages in throughput.

## 2   Related Work

### 2.1   Video Timeline Control

Even ignoring the problem of barehand video timeline control, the manipulation of video timelines is a recognized problem in HCI research. One common approach to video control is to leverage various forms of content analysis to create sensical representation of the video during forwarding. For example, the SmartPlayer system [4] and Pongnumkul et al.'s [22] content-aware timelines both perform basic analysis of the video scene to modify representations of the video so users can better analyze content during seeking tasks. Alternatively, but still in the domain of content analysis, there exist systems that perform basic analysis of video content so that users can directly manipulate an item in the video image to control video playback to precisely select an individual frame [5,10,12,14].

One alternative approach to controlling video is to replace the video time-line with another structure, for example with hierarchies of keyframes or other structured representations. While a full review of alternative browsing mechanisms is outside the scope of this related work, the interested reader can refer to Schoeffmann et al.'s survey of video manipulation techniques [23].

## 2.2 Mid-Air Pointing

Koutsabasis et al. [13] provided a systematic review on mid-air interaction. Due to the inaccuracy of mid-air pointing, a significant body of work in this area focuses on increasing pointing precision. For example, Nancel et al. [20] provided a coarse and precise strategy for 2D pointing at ultra large wall displays. They also point out the limitations of the human visual and motor system in perceiving and acquiring content. Mayer et al. [16] proposed using a model to compensate for the inaccuracy of direct pointing with an offset. Many other systems have leveraged bi-moded input to support targeting (e.g. variants of hybrid pointing [6]) by alternating between direct or constant CD Gain and indirect manipulation.

Alongside barehand input, a significant body of work uses smartwatches or smartphones [11, 21, 24] to perform mid-air pointing on large displays, including the incorporation of linear or discontinuous CD Gain functions [11]. Finally, techniques such as Multiray [15] employed multiple fingers to raycast on large displays and the system creates patterns for different actions.

## 2.3 CD Gain

In the Windows/Icons/Menus/Pointer (WIMP) paradigm of Graphical User Interface (GUI) input, a CD Gain function maps the movement of a physical input device (the computer mouse, the finger on a touchpad, the hand in the air) onto on-screen pointer movement. CD Gain can either be constant, where speed and/or displacement of the input is multiplied by a fixed scalar value to control on-screen movement, or it can be a dynamic function where the CD Gain function dynamically increases as input speed increases. Constant CD Gain is frequently used in touch-screen based interfaces, primarily because the one-to-one mapping of finger position to on-screen position must be preserved. However, any time there exist spatial offset between the input device and the representation of position, i.e., the on-screen pointer, CD Gain need not be constant. Instead, it can be some form of dynamic function.

The term *pointer acceleration* refers to the use of a dynamic CD Gain function. While commercial systems have included pointer acceleration via dynamic CD Gain functions for at least two decades, Casiez et al. [3] were the first to demonstrate, in 2008, the benefits of dynamic CD Gain for high precision pointing during Fitts's Law tasks in interfaces; prior to this, some thought pointer acceleration could not provide benefits in pointing performance due to the fundamental characteristics of Fitts's Law [9].

Given the seminal work of Casiez et al. in the analysis of the effects of pointing precision, a significant body of recent work exists in analyzing and selecting appropriate dynamic CD Gain functions to support optimal pointer acceleration. One example of this work is work by Casiez and Roussel [2], who introduced a toolkit that allows examination of different real-world pointer acceleration functions by contrasting the movement characteristics of the input device (mouse, touchpad) and the on-screen displacement that results from input device movement. In selection of CD Gain functions, Nancel et al. [19] present an analysis of how best to implement pointer acceleration given the distance needed for pointing and the precision needed for pointing (i.e. function specification given the maximum gain needed for distant targeting and the minimum gain needed for sufficient precision).

While the above work on pointer acceleration demonstrates that pointer acceleration aids in Fitts-style targeting tasks and provides guidance on how to identify the minimum and maximum gain necessary for precision and range, respectively, the literature – to the best of our knowledge – is relatively silent on the mid-range of the acceleration function beyond noting the differences in form across operating systems [2]. However, in video timeline control, alongside precision (e.g. targeting to the second across a two hour movie) and range (e.g. targeting the entire range of a two hour timeline), a common task of users is scrubbing, where, in a controlled movement, users traverse the video scanning keyframes for desired scenes. We are aware of no work that specifically explores these mid-range tasks. As well, for barehand control of video timelines, it is unclear whether the user would perceive this task as a direct manipulation task such that a 1:1 or constant mapping would be desirable, or whether some form of pointer acceleration would prove beneficial. Given this lack of related work, we now describe the design of a study to assess acceleration functions for seeking and scrubbing in video timeline control.

## 3   Barehand Input to Smart Displays

As we note in our introduction, manufacturers of Smart TVs are increasingly incorporating barehand, freespace gestures as a mechanism for controlling the display. While several options for gesture capture present themselves, Huawei, Hisense, and Samsung currently use camera-based solution to capture barehand gestures. In this section, we describe the architecture of our gesture capture system. While the gesture capture system is not the focus of this paper, we include the details to support replicability of our results.

Our gesture capture and recognition system leverages a computer vision application running on HiSilicon's Kirin 990 processors. For experimental set-up, we deployed our test application on a Huawei Mate 30 Pro running Android 9 (API level 28). We used the Mate 30 Pro's front-facing camera to capture movement; by default, the camera captures 1080p video at 30fps.

Our gesture capture system is a four-step process, given an input video frame. Our application first detects the user's face from the image captured by the front-facing camera and generates a virtual gesture activation area just below the user's face. We begin with face detection because face detection is a mature technology, common in modern digital cameras and smartphones. Public domain algorithms are included in open source computer vision toolkits such as OpenCV. We use face position to then identify a gesture activation region. Figure 1b shows a user of our system with the user's face outlined in red and the user's hand outlined in blue. A larger blue shaded rectangle in the figure represents the gesture activation area. The size of this gesture activation area is a function of the size of the user's face during face detection (5 face-widths wide by 3 face-widths high).

Next, our algorithm specifies a rectangular gesture input area below the face (see Fig. 1). Hand tracking and gesture input must start within the gesture activation area. By restricting initial tracking to within the activation area, it is possible to significantly reduce false positives in complex backgrounds. It also makes it easier to associate a hand to a face belonging to the same person. For each detected hand, a hand classification and gesture recognition algorithm is run; this gesture algorithm can detect two hand states, pinch open and pinch close, as shown in Fig. 2. These two gestures allow a simple three-state input model supporting the equivalent of 1) no movement (hand not in frame), 2) mouse move (pinch open with hand moving in activation area) and 3) mouse drag (pinch close with hand moving in activation area) states, analogous to similar states in a computer mouse. From pinch open, a close-open action represents a "click". From pinch close, a pinch open stops a dragging operation. Clutching, as with a computer mouse, is supported during dragging via a pinch-open, move hand, pinch-close action.

(a)                    (b)

**Fig. 2.** The (a) Pinch-open gesture, and (b) pinch-close gestures.

To understand how hand movement is mapped onto screen movement for video timeline control via a CD Gain function, Eq. 1 shows the relationship between on-screen translation, $\Delta T$, and in-air movement of the hand, $\Delta x$.

$$\Delta T = \Delta x \cdot cdgain \qquad (1)$$

The CD Gain function can be constant or it can vary with the movement speed of the user's hand.

One challenge with a camera-based solution is to determine movement distance of the hand. Users can sit closer or farther from the display and they may hold their hand at different distances in front of their body while performing input, which results in changes in the perceived size of the movement in the camera view. To create a distance-invariant movement range, we measure movement in units of the user's hand width ($HW$).

In practice, the above approach works well for supporting barehand timeline manipulation. The algorithm is sufficiently reliable to function across a range of lighting conditions and can easily be deployed in-the-wild for distributed data collection.

# 4 Evaluating CD Gain for Barehand Timeline Control

As we note in the introduction, given the need to support range of motion along a timeline, precision of selection within a timeline, and control of speed to monitor keyframes, it is unclear how best to design a mapping function that maps barehand movement onto timeline manipulation, i.e. an appropriate CD Gain function for timeline manipulation. In this section, we describe an experiment to test three different CD Gain functions (Constant, Linear, and a higher order polynomial function) for three video timeline manipulation tasks.

## 4.1 Participants

Twelve participants aged from 21 to 28 (Mean = 24.5, SD = 1.55) were recruited (four identified as male) from a local university. Each participant received 50 local currency units for their participation in the experiment.

## 4.2 Apparatus and Interaction

To maintain social distancing guidelines[1], experiments were conducted in participants' homes using disinfected equipment provided by the researchers. The experimental equipment consisted of a Huawei Mate 30 Pro smartphone running our experimental software, a 15 in. portable, freestanding display controlled via USB-c, and a USB-c cable. User hand movement was captured by the front-facing camera on the Mate 30 Pro smartphone, while visual output of the program was displayed on the 15-in. display.

To control the timeline, participants were asked to perform a "pinch open" gesture (Fig. 2) with either left or right hand in the activation area in front of their chest to enable the timeline. When the program recognised the "Pinch-open" gesture, a scaled slider bar (0 to 7200 s, with a scale every 600 s) appeared on the bottom of the screen showing the current position of a cursor with a white circle. To manipulate the cursor, the participant brings their index finger and thumb together, i.e. the "pinch-close" gesture (Fig. 2). When the "pinch-close" gesture was recognised, the cursor changed to a blue rectangle with a tick sound to indicate the cursor was ready to drag. The program gave a tick sound for every 10 s-equivalent of movement of the cursor on the 7200 s-equivalent timeline. To select a desired time interval, the participant performed the "pinch open" gesture, releasing the blue rectangle within the desired region. Each trial ended either when the "pinch-open" gesture was recognised while the cursor was in the target range or after 10 s from trial start. In both cases, a audible confirmation sound was played and the trial ended.

## 4.3 Experiment Design

We used a within participant design for the experiment. Participants performed three different tasks for each of the three CD Gain conditions. CD Gain conditions were fully counterbalanced. Tasks were partially counterbalanced across

---

[1] The experiments were conducted during the Covid-19 pandemic.

participant (Tasks 1 and 2 were fully counter-balanced; task 3 was always the final task performed).

**CD Gain Conditions.** One challenge in identifying appropriate CD Gain functions is that a large number of functions have been used in past research (see [3] for a review). As well, some past research has used non-continuous functions as CD Gain functions. For example Muller [18] used a minimum CD Gain of 3.0 for mouse speed up to 10 cm/s (i.e. constant gain); a maximum gain of 5.0 for mouse speed above 30 cm/s (i.e. a second constant gain), and a linear function for mouse speed between 10 and 30 cm/s. Our goal was to avoid complex, piecewise, discontinuous functions while probing CD gain functions that are consistent with the research literature and with modern operating systems.

To accomplish this goal, we used a constant gain function as a control condition, and two accelerated gain conditions: a Linear gain function and a non-linear gain function. We hand tuned the form and parameters for our three gain functions through pilot studies involving members of the research team and colleagues (i.e. *person-down-the-hall testing*).

- For our constant CD Gain condition, we chose a CD Gain value equal to 1 timeline width to five $HW$. In this way, a displacement of five $HW$ of the participant's hand would move the cursor from the beginning to the end of the timeline.
- We implemented our linear CD Gain function as a simple linear function. In the Linear acceleration condition, cdgain was defined as $0.2 \cdot x$ where $x$ is tracked hand speed. Hand movement was calculated in $HW$, speed in $HW/s$; on-screen units were calculated in reference to the timeline width, as with constant CD Gain.
- Finally, for our non-linear acceleration condition, a generalised logistic function (GLF) was used to define the gain (Eq. 2). In this study, we set A = 0, K = 7, B = 0.2, V = 0.05, Q = 0.1, C = 1, M = 5.5. Again, dimensions mimicked constant gain.

$$[h]Y(x) = A + \frac{K - A}{(C + Qe^{-B(x-M)})^{\frac{1}{v}}} \tag{2}$$

Our choice of a generalised logistic function was influenced by pointer acceleration curves used in modern desktop operating systems [2] and by recent research in pointer acceleration dynamics [18]. The GLF both replicates very closely the form of commercial CD Gain functions and serves as an elegant, continuous approximation of Muller's [18] piecewise function. We posit that the CD Gain functions we select have significant benefits in terms of reproducibility. As Casiez and Roussel note, commercial CD Gain functions are difficult to reproduce exactly [2], whereas ours can easily be replicated using the above information. It is possible that a piecewise function with linear range and max-min discontinuities [18] may serve some performance benefit over our GLF, but, if so, this benefit is not apparent to us as our GLF function can closely approximate

Muller's discontinuous, piecewise constant/linear function. Figure 3 visualises CD gain by hand speed in each CD gain condition.

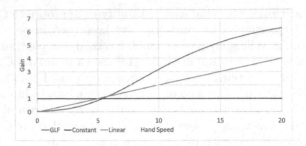

**Fig. 3.** CD gain conditions

**Tasks.** As noted above, there were three tasks: seeking, scrubbing, and a third precise target task. The first two tasks, seeking and scrubbing were counterbalanced; precise time value selection was always the final task. For the first two tasks, seeking (move the timeline cursor to a specific location highlighted on the timeline) and scrubbing (find a hidden along the timeline using simulated keyframes), there were 6 blocks of 9 trials each. The 9 trials consisted of 3 tolerances for the desired timeline location and 3 distances between starting point and desired timeline location. Distances along the timeline were 1200, 2400 and 4800 (out of 7200 maximum units); tolerances were ± 15, 30 and 60 units (out of 7200 along the timeline).

The third task consisted of only one block with 9 trials. The participant attempted to target an exact 1-unit (1 s) point on a timeline with 7200 divisions (analogous to 1 s targeting in a two-hour video).

*Seeking:* Our seeking task is designed to simulate a user jumping to a specific known location on the video timeline. In this task, target range was shown in green on the timeline, and the participants were instructed to move the cursor within the target range as quickly and as accurately as possible (Fig. 4a).

*Task 2: Scrubbing:* This task assumes a user browses video frames to find a specific scene. In this task, a green square was displayed on the screen (above the timeline) while the cursor was in the particular target range. Unlike the first task, the target range was not indicated on the timeline, so that the participants had to "scrub" the bar until they found this green target. As with the previous task, there was a tolerance for the desired location. Participants were instructed to stop the cursor at the position where green square was displayed. To help participants locate the target, a yellow square was shown before and after the target range (Fig. 4b) (at double tolerance). The analog to finding a particular scene in a video is as follows: we often know the context around a desired scene, so we seek proximal key frames (yellow) before homing in on the specific scene (green) we wish to acquire when manipulating a timeline.

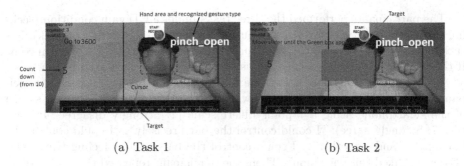

(a) Task 1                                    (b) Task 2

**Fig. 4.** Experimental conditions. (Color figure online)

*Precise Timeline Selection:* Our final task was designed to observe the limits of precision regarding participants' control of the timeline. In this task, participants were instructed to move the cursor to an exact number on the timeline. The number indicating the current cursor position was shown near the cursor above the timeline; the exact number of acquire was given to participants prior to the start of the trial.

## 4.4 Procedure

Participants completed the study individually in their own home. Once participants volunteered for the study, the experimenter fixed a meeting location and provided the participants with a disinfected, reusable bag containing the disinfected smartphone, disinfected monitor, and a disinfected usb-c to hdmi cable. Participants took the equipment to their home and connected with the experimenter via a video call.

After obtaining consent, the experimenter explained the goal of the research, assisted the participant with set-up, and demonstrated the gestures ("pinch-open" "pinch-close") and allowed participants to practice move and drag via barehand input using the gestures. This ensured participants were comfortable with providing input to the system and verified that our system was working effectively, important because of the varied environments in which the study was run.

For set-up, participants were asked to place the monitor on a table (preferably a table of standard dining table height) with the smartphone propped against it pointing toward the user. The monitor was to be placed 1–1.5 m from the edge of the table, with the smartphone propped against the display oriented in landscape mode with the front facing camera pointed forward. Participants then sat in a chair at the edge of the table with their body positioned 0.3 m = 0.5 m from the table edge. Participants were asked to perform gestures in the space between their face and the display to simplify tracking. Participants were permitted to rest their elbow on the table if they became tired. We also asked participants to preference a plain background behind them to ensure optimal tracking (as a preventative measure to ensure good data collection, though our algorithm seems highly stable regardless of background).

The participants performed the three tasks under a CD gain condition (seeking then scrubbing or vice versa, concluding with the precise selection task). For each task, a trial ended either with successful selection or after a 10 s timeout. If the trial timed out, it was marked as an error and the next trial began.

After finishing all trials under one CD gain condition (117 trials), participants were asked to answer the following three questions on the touch screen of the smartphone using a 7 point Likert scale (1: Strongly disagree, 4: Neutral, 7: Strongly agree); "I could control the bar precisely", "I could control the bar quickly and smoothly", "I could control the bar without feeling tired" and "Overall, I liked this condition". Then, the participant repeated the same procedure with a different CD gain condition until they completed all three CD gain conditions.

The participant and experimenter remained in a video call until the end of the experiment. The average time to complete all tasks (351 trials) was approximately 1 h, and the experimenter encouraged the participants to take breaks between blocks to avoid fatigue. At the end of the session, the experimenter collected general feedback and then set up a meeting to collect the experimental equipment from the participants in a physically distanced manner.

## 4.5   Data Collection

Considering all factors above, each participant completed 351 trials: ((3 distances × 3 tolerances × 6 blocks × 2 tasks × 3 CD gain conditions) + (9 trials × 1 task × 3 CD gain conditions)) in total. For 12 participants, we collected 4212 data points for analysis.

Our program recorded time for successful positioning and an error when positioning time exceeded 10 s. Likert question data was stored on the smartphone and downloaded after each participant.

## 5   Results

The primary goal of our study is comparative, i.e. to understand whether a constant versus non-constant CD Gain function can enhance barehand control during seeking and scrubbing video timeline tasks. Because this goal is formative, not summative, we have no hypotheses about which CD Gain function is best. Therefore, we present a statistical analysis of our results comparing our control condition, a constant gain, to linear and non-linear (generalized logistic regression) CD Gain functions organized by task.

### 5.1   Seeking

**Accuracy.** Figure 5 (left) shows the error rate (the proportion of trials participants could not acquire the target within 10 s) of the seeking task. The result of repeated measures ANOVA showed significant main effects of CD gain ($F_{2,22} = 4.49$, p < .05), Target distance ($F_{2,22} = 4.28$, p < .05), and target width

($F_{2,22} = 6.89$, $p < .001$), and a significant interaction between target distance and width ($F_{4,44} = 2.70$. $p < .05$). The result of post-hoc tests (using Holm's correction) showed that error rate in the Constant CD gain condition was higher than that in the Linear condition ($t_{11} = 2.81$, $p = .051$, borderline but with significant RM-Anova for CD Gain).

**Speed.** Figure 5 (right) shows the median task completion time (TCT) of the seeking task for successful trials. The result of repeated measures ANOVA showed significant main effects of CD gain ($F_{2,22} = 9.27$, $p = .001$), Target distance ($F_{2,22} = 36.11$, $p < .001$), and target width ($F_{2,22} = 78.96$, $p < .001$), and a significant interaction between CD gain condition and target distance ($F_{4,44} = 2.72$. $p < .05$). The result of post-hoc test (using Holm's correction) showed that median TCT in the GLF CD gain condition was significantly longer than that in the Linear condition ($t_{11} = 4.11$, $p < .01$) and Constant condition ($t_{11} = -3.24$, $p < .05$).

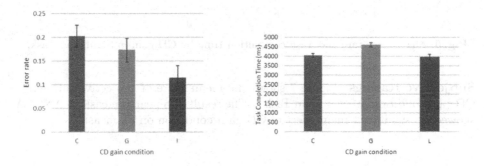

**Fig. 5.** Mean error rate and Task completion time by CD gain in Seeking Task

## 5.2   Scrubbing

**Accuracy.** Figure 6 (left) shows the error rate of scrubbing task. The result of repeated measures ANOVA showed significant main effects of CD gain ($F_{2,22} = 4.99$, $p < .05$), Target distance ($F = 15.52$, $p < .001$), and target width ($F_{2,22} = 33.73$, $p < .001$), and a significant interaction between target distance and width ($F_{4,44} = 6.02$ $p < .001$). The result of post-hoc test (using Holm's correction) showed that error rate in the Constant CD gain condition was higher than that in the GLF CD gain condition ($t_{11} = 2.97$, $p < .05$) and in the Linear condition ($t_{11} = 2.44$, $p = .066$, borderline).

**Speed.** Figure 6 (right) shows the median task completion time (TCT) of the scrubbing task. The result of repeated measures ANOVA showed significant main effects of Target distance ($F_{2,22} = 44.43$, $p < .001$) and target width ($F = 100.31$, $p < .001$), but not CD gain. We also observed significant interactions between

CD gain condition and target width ($F_{4,44} = 3.16$. $p < .05$), between target distance and width ($3.65$, $p < .05$), and a three-way interaction among CD gain, Target distance and target width ($F_{8,88} = 4.02$, $p < .001$). The result of post-hoc test (using Holm's correction) showed that median TCT in the GLF CD gain condition was significantly longer than that in the Linear condition ($t_{11} = 4.11$, $p < .01$) and in the Constant condition ($t_{11} = -3.24$, $p < .05$).

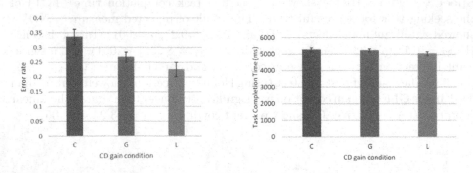

**Fig. 6.** Mean error rate and Task completion time by CD gain in Scrubbing Task.

**Subjective Ratings.** Figure 7 shows the mean score of subjective ratings by CD gain condition in Task 1 and Task 2. The result of repeated measures ANOVA showed no significant main effect of CD gain condition on all measures.

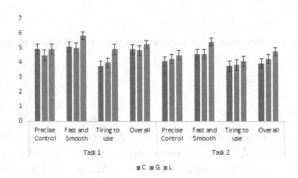

**Fig. 7.** Mean subjective ratings on CD gain conditions with standard errors

### 5.3    Precise Time Selection

Recall that the goal of our third task was to select, as accurately as possible and within a ten-second timeout, an exact value on a timeline with 7200 divisions (i.e. to attempt to select a specific one second location in a two hour timeline within 10 s). We note that, because this involves sub-pixel selection on a 4K resolution display, it is an exceedingly difficult task. Selecting a 1-s interval on a two-hour movie is challenging with a computer mouse on a computer display, so we expect a high error rate. To assess performance on this task, we use two measures: accuracy (i.e. how frequently did participants select the exact second) and average gap (i.e. how far, on average, were participants from the 1s interval when the task completed).

**Accuracy.** Mean accuracy in Task 3 was 0.03 (SD = 0.05), i.e. 97% error rate, in the Constant CD gain condition, 0.31 (SD = 0.21) in the GLF CD gain, and 0.31 (SD = 0.16) in the Linear CD gain condition. In other words, participants had only a 3% success rate selecting a 1s interval with Constant CD gain, whereas their accuracy was more than 10 times higher (31%) with pointer acceleration.

**Average Gap to Target.** Selecting an individual second in a two-hour video – with an attendant 31% success rate – may not be necessary. Perhaps selection within two or even three seconds is acceptable – especially given that selecting a 1-s interval using a mouse along a timeline is also exceedingly difficult. A more important question is *how closely* a 1-s interval can be targeted using barehand, in-air input with an appropriately-chosen CD Gain.

To analyze this, we examined the distance – the gap – between the target one second interval and the actual position selected when a trial finished as a measure of precision in task 3. For those trials which were successful, the gap was 0. To calculate this value, we first calculated median gap in the nine trials of each participant under the same target condition (distance and width), then calculated the mean of all 12 participants. The mean gap in the Constant CD gain condition was 5.92 (SD = 3.01), in the GLF CD gain condition it was 1.33 (SD = 1.11) and in Linear CD gain condition was 1.50 (SD = 1.50). The result of repeated measures ANOVA showed a significant main effect of the CD gain condition ($F_{2,22} = 28.83$, $p < .001$), where the gap to the target in the Constant CD gain condition was significantly larger than that in Linear condition ($t_{11} = 4.78$, $p < 001$) and GLF condition ($t_{11} = 6.44$, $p < .001$).

# 6    Discussion

In our introduction, we posed two primary questions: 1) What CD Gain function is most effective in bare-hand control? and 2) How well do each of these different variants of CD Gain functions work for both seeking and scrubbing tasks? Considering the first question, it is reasonable to ask whether mapping of hand movement onto on-screen movement is more analogous to direct manipulation – with its attendant 1-to-1 mapping or constant gain – or mouse manipulation – where pointer acceleration, i.e. a non-constant gain function, can provide targeting benefits [3]. Furthermore, in the absence of data it is also unclear whether practical gain functions exist to support pointing tasks given potential requirements for precision (e.g. sub-pixel accuracy on a 4K display) and range [19]; in the absence of data it is also unclear whether seeking and scrubbing tasks can be optimally supported by a similar CD Gain function.

Synthesising our results, and considering the performance of various CD Gain functions, we note the following. First, linear CD Gain exhibits lower error rate than constant gain for both seeking and scrubbing during timeline access. Second, a Linear Gain function was faster than a GLF gain for seeking tasks. Finally, our results argue that both Linear and GLF Gain functions allowed higher-precision targeting of a 1-second-sized interval than constant gain. Median average precision for constant gain was 1/10th the precision of Linear or GLF gain. Together, these results indicate an advantage of non-constant CD Gain for both seeking and scrubbing tasks. For example, for both seeking and scrubbing, Linear Gain has better error rate than Constant gain and lower task completion time (higher speed) than GLF gain.

While the overall goal of our studies was timeline manipulation, we note that timeline manipulation is only one of a number of potential targeting and input tasks in smart display/Smart TV input. Video playback requires support for a number of commands (play/pause, volume control) alongside timeline manipulation. The results of our experiments can apply to, for example, volume manipulation, which has similar characteristics to timeline manipulation; however, volume ranges are typically less granular than are timeline manipulations (50 or 100 levels vs thousands of seconds).

Our results may also be applicable to targeting in general on Smart TVs. However, on-screen widget targeting is much more permissive than timeline manipulation. Consider, for example, a Smart TV display with a number of on-screen widgets that a user would like to target. While the amplitude of movements on the display (the distance of movements) are of the same scale as timeline manipulations, it is not typical that on-screen widgets require pixel level (or even sub-pixel level) targeting, i.e. precision requirements are more relaxed because widgets typically span multiple pixels. As well, widget targeting can often benefit from pointing facilitation techniques [1,7,17] that can leverage inter-widget whitespace to increase the effective size of widgets or the cursor, but timeline controls have no inter-target whitespace because every element along the timeline, up to even the sub-pixel level in our experiment, is an allowable target. We would argue that timeline manipulation is among the more challenging targeting tasks to support. We would argue, however, that the ability of barehand manipulations to support near pixel-level targeting (median error rate for precise selection/task 3 is at the pixel-level for both Linear and GLF gain functions) provides evidence that barehand point-and-click style targeting is one effective option for smart TV control across a variety of tasks, even those requiring very high precision.

The caveat to point-and-click style targeting for Smart TVs is that it is unclear if smart TVs should use point-and-click style targeting in all interactions. As one example, video-on-demand streaming services use directional navigation plus object pointing to support elegant scrolling, and it may be that this represents a more effective, controllable interaction for access to multiple pages (both vertical and horizontal) of content. Menuing systems on smart TVs may benefit from gesture-style input (e.g. marking menus) rather than multiple layers of point-and-click widgets. Even non-timeline video playback may benefit from more simplified gesture input rather than requiring the user to target different on-screen widgets.

However, despite these factors, video timeline control is a common task. As we note earlier, because of the complexity of this task with respect to precision, and because of the confound between seeking and scrubbing, researchers continue to seek enhanced ways to balance range and precision. Our work provides important support to this domain by highlighting the potential of effectively designed CD Gain to support barehand gestural dragging as a mechanism to effectively manipulate video timelines.

## 6.1   Limitations and Study Design Factors

As with any study, there exist limitations to this study.

Some limitations are debatable. As one example, one can pose the question of how representative our experimental tasks are of real-world tasks. Our initial seeking task asks participants to acquire a specific range which is highlighted on the timeline; our scrubbing task uses only a green rectangle on the display rather than a full scene; and our 1-second-level precise targeting task on a 7200 s-equivalent timeline is perhaps more precise than a user would require. We made these choices consciously. We varied the tolerance of our first seeking task because we recognise that users vary in their needed precision. We used a green square to indicate desired scene when scrubbing to eliminate visual perception confounds associated with scene recognition. Finally, we use a second-level precision attempt to truly test the limits of different CD Gain functions. Our goal with each of these decisions was to balance experimental and ecological validity, but these choices are debatable.

The experiment design, itself, also has limitations. As a simple example, our display, provided to participants, is both smaller and closer than a typical television. Our goal in providing equipment was to increase control and to limit risk to participants of installing software on their own personal devices (ethics review at our institution is reluctant to allow installation of software on participants' personal devices due to privacy and/or security risks). This drove the need to provide our own hardware to participants in a responsible manner given the context of a global pandemic. However, this fixed hardware represents a risk to generalizability. Specifically, we specified distances for our study to accommodate for the smaller (than typical smart tv) portable display size with closer distance. A 15-in. display at 1 to 1.5 m distance, 0.25 rad of visual arc, is similar in visual arc to a 32 in. at 2 to 3 m or a 65-in. at 4 to 6 m. However, small and or close displays may alter aspects of user behaviour in unanticipated ways, even if the displays appear visually similar in scale.

Another potential limitation is latency. Via an optical camera capturing both user movement and the 15" display, end-to-end latency in our experimental setup was measured at 136 ms. Approximately 2/3 of this latency (90 ms) is from image processing and movement mapping in Android, 20 ms is due to USB-C communication, monitor response (4 ms) and refresh (60 Hz), and the remainder is due to camera capture latency from the Mate30 Pro front camera (30 fps). Latency could represent a risk to validity, especially if camera-equipped commercial smart tvs have lower or higher latency.

Finally, our participant population is a limitation. Our participants were younger and were drawn from a highly educated, relatively affluent demographic. This was not by design, but may have been a result of recruitment challenges and trepidation of older/less healthy individuals, both of which can be attributed to the Covid-19 pandemic concurrent with this study. Older participants may struggle more significantly with issues of precision and reach, which might impact time and/or errors.

**Remote Experiments: Advantages and Disadvantages.** The remote nature of this experiment presents both advantages and disadvantages. From the perspective of advantages, we believe that conducting an experiment in a home-based environment for home-based technologies (e.g. Smart TVs) increases ecological validity versus a laboratory environment. Also, while not availed of in our study, remote experimentation can increase access to studies and increase the demographic heterogeneity of participants because participants who may otherwise not have access to laboratory-based settings may still be able to participate.

On the other hand, there are disadvantages, particularly in logistics and replicability. Logistically, diagnosing problems in remote settings is challenging. If code or tracking performs poorly, it can be difficult to ascertain if it is due to participants' positioning, back lighting, front lighting, or some other factor. We experienced this in our own testing configurations: as one example, side lighting was too bright in one author's desk area, requiring him to close the blinds. This made the environment too dark, which he solved by placing a bright white background on his display screen to increase front lighting. Asking participants to reposition experimental equipment or furniture, change angles, and perform other corrections represents a challenge for those participants. We were fortunate that our participants were able and willing to assist us in configuring their environment during the experiment.

Replicability costs are also increased, both for us and more generally for the research community. In laboratory environments, one can assume optimal experimental conditions. This means that, if another researcher wishes to use a lab-based data set, then they can assume optimality. If their proposed intervention performs better than the lab-based dataset, this represents with high likelihood a real improvement. Our measured dependent variables are likely suboptimal compared to a laboratory setting, meaning that direct numerical comparison to our data must be performed cautiously. This does not impact the internal validity of our results – factors are constant across conditions in our study – but it means that experiments wishing to contrast with ours may need to fully replicate the study rather than relying on an open data set. Essentially, experimental contrasts may be dependent on a repeated measures design to control both participant and environmental variability simultaneously when running experiments. We would argue that this is generally true of remote experiments, and if between subjects contrasts are desired in remote experimentation, it may be necessary to ensure a very high number of participants to obtain sufficient statistical power.

Overall, our goal during remote experimentation was to attempt to replicate as closely as possible a controlled environment despite the varied locations (hence the set-up constraints, equipment exchange, and video-based presence of a member of the research team). It is unclear how much this differs from a lab context (versus in-the-wild). We do identify statistical differences via appropriate analyses, and we believe these differences would hold in-lab. Whether the differences would remain as significant in a less constrained in-home environment with poor lighting, messy rooms, multiple people on camera, oblique angles, varied postures, etc. is unclear.

# 7   Conclusion

Motivated by the introduction of barehand control for Smart TV displays, this paper examines the effectiveness of pointer acceleration in barehand, distant, video timeline control. We evaluate three CD gain variants: a constant function (no pointer acceleration, analogous to direct manipulation) and two different gain functions implementing pointer acceleration, a continuous linear function and a generalised logistic regression function. We find overall benefits to non-constant CD Gain in speed, error, and precision, particularly for our linear CD Gain function.

**Acknowledgements.** We thank participants and our Office of Research Ethics for valuable assistance during the design of our remote study. This research was funded by a grant from Waterloo-Huawei Joint Innovation Laboratory.

# References

1. Balakrishnan, R.: "Beating" Fitts' law: virtual enhancements for pointing facilitation. Int. J. Hum.-Comput. Stud. **61**(6), 857–874 (2004). https://doi.org/10.1016/j.ijhcs.2004.09.002. http://www.sciencedirect.com/science/article/pii/S107158190400103X. Fitts' law 50 years later: applications and contributions from human-computer interaction
2. Casiez, G., Roussel, N.: No more bricolage! methods and tools to characterize, replicate and compare pointing transfer functions. In: Proceedings of the 24th Annual ACM Symposium on User Interface Software and Technology, UIST 2011, pp. 603–614. Association for Computing Machinery, New York (2011). https://doi.org/10.1145/2047196.2047276
3. Casiez, G., Vogel, D., Balakrishnan, R., Cockburn, A.: The impact of control-display gain on user performance in pointing tasks. Hum.-Comput. Interact. **23**(3), 215–250 (2008). https://doi.org/10.1080/07370020802278163. https://www.tandfonline.com/doi/abs/10.1080/07370020802278163

4. Cheng, K.Y., Luo, S.J., Chen, B.Y., Chu, H.H.: Smartplayer: user-centric video fast-forwarding. In: Proceedings of the SIGCHI Conference on Human Factors in Computing Systems, CHI 2009, pp. 789–798. Association for Computing Machinery, New York (2009). https://doi.org/10.1145/1518701.1518823

5. Dragicevic, P., Ramos, G., Bibliowitcz, J., Nowrouzezahrai, D., Balakrishnan, R., Singh, K.: Video browsing by direct manipulation. In: Proceedings of the SIGCHI Conference on Human Factors in Computing Systems, CHI 2008, pp. 237–246. Association for Computing Machinery, New York (2008). https://doi.org/10.1145/1357054.1357096

6. Forlines, C., Vogel, D., Balakrishnan, R.: Hybridpointing: fluid switching between absolute and relative pointing with a direct input device. In: Proceedings of the 19th Annual ACM Symposium on User Interface Software and Technology, UIST 2006, pp. 211–220. Association for Computing Machinery, New York (2006). https://doi.org/10.1145/1166253.1166286

7. Grossman, T., Balakrishnan, R.: The bubble cursor: enhancing target acquisition by dynamic resizing of the cursor's activation area. In: Proceedings of the SIGCHI Conference on Human Factors in Computing Systems, CHI 2005, pp. 281–290. Association for Computing Machinery, New York (2005). https://doi.org/10.1145/1054972.1055012

8. Guiard, Y., Blanch, R., Beaudouin-Lafon, M.: Object pointing: a complement to bitmap pointing in GUIs. In: Proceedings of Graphics Interface 2004, pp. 9–16. Citeseer (2004)

9. Jellinek, H.D., Card, S.K.: Powermice and user performance. In: Proceedings of the SIGCHI Conference on Human Factors in Computing Systems, CHI 1990, pp. 213–220. Association for Computing Machinery, New York (1990). https://doi.org/10.1145/97243.97276

10. Karrer, T., Weiss, M., Lee, E., Borchers, J.: Dragon: a direct manipulation interface for frame-accurate in-scene video navigation. In: Proceedings of the SIGCHI Conference on Human Factors in Computing Systems, CHI 2008, pp. 247–250. Association for Computing Machinery, New York (2008). https://doi.org/10.1145/1357054.1357097

11. Katsuragawa, K., Pietroszek, K., Wallace, J.R., Lank, E.: Watchpoint: freehand pointing with a smartwatch in a ubiquitous display environment. In: Proceedings of the International Working Conference on Advanced Visual Interfaces, pp. 128–135 (2016)

12. Kimber, D., Dunnigan, T., Girgensohn, A., Shipman, F., Turner, T., Yang, T.: Trailblazing: video playback control by direct object manipulation. In: 2007 IEEE International Conference on Multimedia and Expo, pp. 1015–1018 (2007)

13. Koutsabasis, P., Vogiatzidakis, P.: Empirical research in mid-air interaction: a systematic review. Int. J. Hum.-Comput. Interact. 35(18), 1747–1768 (2019)

14. Matejka, J., Grossman, T., Fitzmaurice, G.: Swifter: Improved Online Video Scrubbing, pp. 1159–1168. Association for Computing Machinery, New York (2013). https://doi.org/10.1145/2470654.2466149

15. Matulic, F., Vogel, D.: Multiray: multi-finger raycasting for large displays. In: Proceedings of the 2018 CHI Conference on Human Factors in Computing Systems, pp. 1–13 (2018)

16. Mayer, S., Schwind, V., Schweigert, R., Henze, N.: The effect of offset correction and cursor on mid-air pointing in real and virtual environments. In: Proceedings of the 2018 CHI Conference on Human Factors in Computing Systems, pp. 1–13 (2018)

17. McGuffin, M., Balakrishnan, R.: Acquisition of expanding targets. In: Proceedings of the SIGCHI Conference on Human Factors in Computing Systems, CHI 2002, pp. 57–64. Association for Computing Machinery, New York (2002). https://doi.org/10.1145/503376.503388

18. Müller, J.: Dynamics of pointing with pointer acceleration. In: Bernhaupt, R., Dalvi, G., Joshi, A., Balkrishan, D.K., O'Neill, J., Winckler, M. (eds.) INTERACT 2017. LNCS, vol. 10515, pp. 475–495. Springer, Cham (2017). https://doi.org/10.1007/978-3-319-67687-6_33

19. Nancel, M., Chapuis, O., Pietriga, E., Yang, X.D., Irani, P.P., Beaudouin-Lafon, M.: High-precision pointing on large wall displays using small handheld devices. In: Proceedings of the SIGCHI Conference on Human Factors in Computing Systems, CHI 2013, pp. 831–840. Association for Computing Machinery, New York (2013). https://doi.org/10.1145/2470654.2470773

20. Nancel, M., Pietriga, E., Chapuis, O., Beaudouin-Lafon, M.: Mid-air pointing on ultra-walls. ACM Trans. Comput.-Hum. Interact. (TOCHI) 22(5), 1–62 (2015)

21. Pietroszek, K., Tahai, L., Wallace, J.R., Lank, E.: Watchcasting: freehand 3D interaction with off-the-shelf smartwatch. In: 2017 IEEE Symposium on 3D User Interfaces (3DUI), pp. 172–175. IEEE (2017)

22. Pongnumkul, S., Wang, J., Ramos, G., Cohen, M.: Content-aware dynamic timeline for video browsing. In: Proceedings of the 23nd Annual ACM Symposium on User Interface Software and Technology, UIST 2010, pp. 139–142. Association for Computing Machinery, New York (2010). https://doi.org/10.1145/1866029.1866053

23. Schoeffmann, K., Hudelist, M.A., Huber, J.: Video interaction tools: a survey of recent work. ACM Comput. Surv. 48(1) (2015). https://doi.org/10.1145/2808796

24. Siddhpuria, S., Malacria, S., Nancel, M., Lank, E.: Pointing at a distance with everyday smart devices. In: Proceedings of the 2018 CHI Conference on Human Factors in Computing Systems, pp. 1–11 (2018)

# Seasons: Exploring the Dynamic Thermochromic Smart Textile Applications for Intangible Cultural Heritage Revitalization

Qi Wang[1], Ying Ye[1], Martijn ten Bhömer[2], Mengqi Jiang[3], and Xiaohua Sun[1(✉)]

[1] Tongji University, Shanghai, China
{qiwangdesign,xsun}@tongji.edu.cn
[2] University of Nottingham Ningbo China, Zhejiang, China
Martijn.Ten.Bhomer@nottingham.edu.cn
[3] Xi'an Jiaotong Liverpool University, Jiangsu, China
mengqi.jiang@xjtlu.edu.cn

**Abstract.** Smart textiles have attracted great attention from Human-Computer Interaction and this study explored how dynamic thermochromic textiles may contribute to the transmission and revitalization of textile Intangible Cultural Heritage (ICH). We proposed Seasons which is an interactive cheongsam developed as a novel exploration in traditional craftsmanship of Shanghai-style cheongsam and smart textiles. Seasons consists of animated visual patterns including 4 stages, new leaves sprout and flowers from buds to full bloom as demonstrations of spring and summer, while leaves turn yellow in autumn and snow comes in winter. Subsequently, we presented the implementation process, feedback from the inheritors of ICH and visitors in the exhibition. In conclusion, we explored how computational thermochromic patterns may enhance the aesthetic and expression in traditional clothing. There is a great design space for thermal-activated smart textiles and this paper is believed to contribute to the future development of smart textile applications for ICH.

**Keywords:** Smart textiles · Thermochromic · Intangible cultural heritage

## 1 Introduction

Craftsmanship is one of the key elements of Intangible Cultural heritage (ICH) [1], and the traditional craftsmanship of Shanghai-style cheongsam has been listed as one of the representative projects of the National ICH in China [2]. Cheongsam is known as the treasure and "living" carrier of the Chinese clothing culture and cherished by people all over the world. However, as many other ICH, it is still facing challenges of keeping relevant and being welcomed by the younger generation. One direction is the

**Electronic supplementary material** The online version of this chapter (https://doi.org/10.1007/978-3-030-85610-6_6) contains supplementary material, which is available to authorized users.

revitalization through integration in modern products, previous research reviewed how craftsmanship of embroidery, weaving, blue dyeing included in textile ICH can benefit the modern design. While emerging developments within HCI have shown even more potential for solving the challenges, for example the use of immersive reality technologies to offer users new experiences of visualizing and studying the ICH [3]. While another way is the live protection and transmission by connecting ICH to people's life and novel creation based on the traditional craftsmanship. Smart textiles could offer interesting possibilities in relation to textiles crafts in ICH.

Smart textiles and flexible wearable technology are developing rapidly, and they have broad application potentials in future textiles and smart clothing. Current smart textiles have been widely explored as input mediums, such as gesture interfaces [4] and sensors applied in sports and rehabilitation [5], and as output modalities in the interactive systems, for example, thermochromic display [6], embroidered speaker and smart textile-enabled actuators.

Cheongsam displayed unique artistic charm, inspired by the decorative patterns by hand painting or embroidery techniques which are the important embodiment of oriental artistic aesthetics, we explored how thermochromic may enhance the traditional pattern expression, bringing novel interactive experiences and even extending the market by achieving computational color-changing patterns.

This research focuses on the innovative development of textile ICH in Shanghai, adopting cheongsam as a carrier to explore the intersections between textile color-changing technology and traditional craftsmanship in terms of materials, textile structure, production processes, and finally serve as a living inheritance of traditional ICH textiles. Instead of preserving the original craftsmanship of cheongsam, we explored how to revitalize the traditional cheongsam in case of interactive artefacts.

We proposed Seasons, which is an interactive cheongsam with different areas of the decorative patterns which can be activated and show dynamic color-changing effects. With this exploration, we hope to find new methods of promoting the innovative development of textile ICH from the dimensions of intelligence, personalization, dynamics, and fashion which may create novel experience and motivating users to initiate the culture inheritance.

## 2 Related Work

Color-changing materials are mainly divided into photosensitive, thermochromic, and electro-sensitive types. Thermochromic dyes can change color with temperature changes, while wearable thermochromic technology is programmable so that it has great potential in the application of textiles and smart clothing. Conductive fabric or threads in a particular pattern are often applied as the thermal layer instead of rigid heating elements to keep the textile more flexible.

For example, Social Textiles [7] provided color-changing feedback by the multi-layer structure, which produced icebreaking interaction opportunities among unacquainted, collocated members. Muhammad Umair et al. explored the feasibility of smart materials for developing novel color-changing textile displays for real time visualization of affective data. Chromoskin [8] and Animskin [9] are two cases of thin-film multi-layer structures which can be applied directly on the skin and can emit dynamic color animations. Other explorations seamlessly coated the conductive yarns with thermochromic pigments. For example, Devendorf et al. explored the effect of dynamic textile display through the design prototypes of seven crochet products [6].

Regarding the traditional crafts-enabled innovation, digital technologies have contributed to the transmission of skills embedded in ICH's, which can secure the protection of traditional textiles craftsmanship. For example, inspired by the traditional craftsmanship of lace making, Kuusk et al. developed a lace structure with active perception and intelligent color-changing textiles [10]. Hsin-Liu Kao et al. [11] proposed a fabric interface with perception and color-changing functions based on traditional weaving techniques.

## 3   Seasons

### 3.1   Mechanism

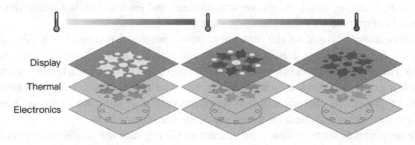

**Fig. 1.** Three layers structure of the conductive textile-based thermochromic mechanisms.

To achieve the dynamic animation, we adopted the multi-layer structure as shown in Fig. 1. The top layer is the display module where the thermochromic pigments are applied following the graphic patterns. Following is the thermal module where the conductive fabrics or conductive threads are located to heat up the display layer and activate the color-changing patterns. Lastly, the wearable electronics modules which includes sensors and microcontrollers can be embedded or integrated in the normal fabric, to control the activation area and color-changing time.

### 3.2   Design

The interactive cheongsam called *Seasons* (see Fig. 2), is a new attempt to apply color-changing visual feedback textile in Chinese traditional cheongsam, by using the multi-layer structure to provide dynamic and interactive properties for static clothing.

Traditional flower patterns are widely applied in cheongsam design, of which the magnolia is a popular variety and season is also a classical topic in traditional Chinese paintings. To expand the novel experience, we explored how computationally changing thermochromic patterns may enhance the aesthetics and expressive capabilities of the dress. We designed the magnolia pattern and divided the pattern into 4 groups of different areas mapped to the appearance of the flower during the four seasons. Each group can be controlled individually by a custom developed sewable microcontroller to create animated visual patterns (see Fig. 3). The groups are activated sequentially (each of them needs around 5-s fade-in, 10-s on and 20-s fade-out) and the four sections light up accordingly to display the animated patterns. In spring and summer, new leaves sprout and flowers from buds to full bloom, leaves turn yellow in autumn and snow comes in winter.

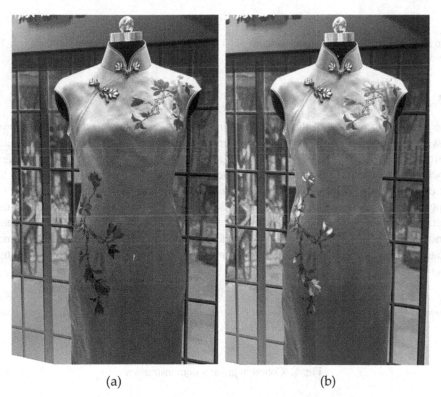

(a)                                                    (b)

**Fig. 2.** Interactive cheongsam, a) thermochromics pattern are not activated; b) thermochromics pattern are activated.

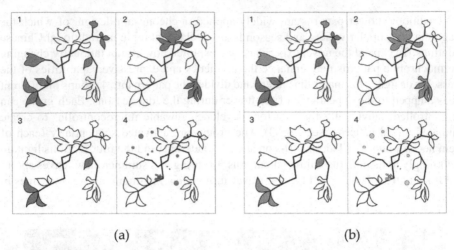

|     |     |     |
| :-: | :-: | :-: |
| (a) | | (b) |

**Fig. 3.** Animated thermochromic patterns in 4 stages. a) Heating up areas in 4 stages; b) Thermochromic pattern in 4 stages.

### 3.3 Implementation

The developing process of the color-changing cheongsam followed a co-creation process in collaboration with expert craftspeople who are responsible of the traditional craftsmanship of Shanghai-style cheongsam. We try to introduce the technology of thermochromic textiles into the traditional production process at the right time. For example, we created the thermochromic pattern by hand-drawing on the silk fabric pieces cut by experts before dress making. After the basic parts of the cheongsam were made, the heating layer was laid out corresponding to the pattern, and a series of tests have been conducted to achieve smooth animation by identification of the suitable voltage and time. Finally, the cheongsam internal lining was made as a heat insulation layer to embed the circuit layout as well (Fig. 4).

**Fig. 4.** Codesign process demonstration.

In details, the interactive cheongsam prototype is developed through multi-layer structure consisting of three layers:

1) For the display layer we mixed the thermochromic pigment (activation temperature is 31C) with normal pigments to enrich the color richness and used hand drawing on the silk to preserve the impression of brushstrokes in a Chinese painting;
2) The thermal layer sticks to the display layer, and is based on the EeonTex High-Conductivity Heater Fabric with a resistance of 20 ohms per square inch. The fabric

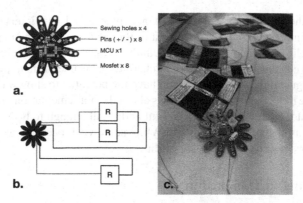

**Fig. 5.** a) Details of the customized sewable microcontroller board; b) circuit illustration; c) thermal textiles embedded in the dress.

was clipped into the same shape as the pattern (demonstrated in Fig. 3) and the heater fabric is programmable based on the connections to the customized sewable microcontroller. Figure 5a demonstrates the details of the microcontroller and Fig. 5b demonstrates the parallel circuit;

3)  Finally, the lining is applied as an insulation layer next to the thermal layer to weaken the thermal stimulations on the skin.

## 4  Study

Semi-structured interviews were carried out to identify the experts and audience attitudes and acceptance of the interactive cheongsam.

We interviewed 2 experts (PE) of traditional craftsmanship and 8 visitors (PV) when the prototype was displayed in the intangible cultural heritage exhibition area of the second China International Import Expo. Among them, expert interviews were mainly focused on exploring the influence of the combination of wearable technology and traditional handicrafts on its inheritance, innovation and its potential for this application. User interviews were mainly focused on the acceptance and preference of thermochromic cheongsam. After the interviews were conducted, notes were transcribed and a thematic analysis has been performed to analyze the results.

Both experts thought that the combination of crafts and technology is novel and interesting, and they agreed that integration of wearable thermochromic technology and ICH is conducive to the inheritance and innovation of traditional textile craftsmanship. *"Whenever I mention intangible cultural heritage, everyone may feel that it is very old and historical. The integration of color-changing elements is novel and can help attract more young generation's attention…" -(PE 1). "This approach is not a concept demonstration, the protection of traditional culture is inherited in an activating and innovative way" -(PE2).* At the same time, they expressed their approval and appreciation for keeping the original materials while new techniques are applied, they mentioned the importance of retaining the materials and techniques used in traditional crafts in the future design and production process.

Regarding the audience's attitude and acceptance, all the interviewed visitors expressed their interest in *Seasons*, and most of the visitors expressed their willingness to wear thermochromic cheongsam in their daily lives. Visitors to the exhibition were surprised by the elegant dynamic pattern of cheongsam. Some of them even mentioned *Seasons* may augment their personality and have the potential to show various information. At the same time, they were also curious about the implementation mechanism, and they thought that the circuit board is beautiful and small enough to be acceptable, even exposed on the surface of the cheongsam. While some visitors expressed their concern about power consumption and unsustainability.

## 5  Discussion and Conclusion

With the aim of providing a dynamic perspective of textile artefact of ICH, we explored how thermochromic smart textile may revitalize the traditional clothing by enhancing the aesthetic and expression. Subsequently, we found that how to design the color-change pattern and implement the animated patterns is challenging as technology and tradition need to bring out the best in each other. Compared with photochromic materials and electrochromic materials, thermochromic materials are more programmable and designable. Thermochromic patterns have great potential for color-changing visual feedback, which can better adapt to different clothing styles and are more acceptable for daily wear because of the non-emissive properties. When using the thermal effects caused by the electrical current to drive the color change, it is necessary to limit the voltage and current within the wearable safety range. The energy consumption of the *Seasons* is large due to the large heating area, while the size and weight of the battery will greatly affect wearability. In the design process, designers should also consider energy consumption to avoid the excessive heating areas.

The cheongsam is a traditional Chinese dress, whose craftsmanship is also listed as an intangible cultural heritage. Combining smart textile technology with traditional manufacturing processes, is not only an attempt of thermal augmented textile in the application of fashion glamor but also an exploration of intangible cultural heritage activation and innovation through enabling technology, the development of textile ICH is an important part of traditional culture. Future work will further explore the integration of thermal-activated smart textiles in interactive clothing and textile products in various applications.

In conclusion, there is a potential design space for thermal-activated smart textiles. Smart textile-enabled dynamic thermochromic mechanisms may enhance the programming ability and pattern creating ability which may contribute to increasing the ability to control the interactivity and aesthetics of textile ICH products.

## References

1. Convention for the Safeguarding of the Intangible Cultural Heritage. http://unesdoc.unesco.org/images/0013/001325/132540e.pdf. Accessed 10 Apr 2021
2. China Intangible Cultural Heritage Protection Center. Craftsmanship of Chinese style clothing (craftsmanship of cheongsam). http://www.ihchina.cn/Article/Index/detail?id=14710. Accessed 10 Apr 2021

3. Alivizatou-Barakou, M.: Intangible cultural heritage and new technologies: challenges and opportunities for cultural preservation and development. In: Ioannides, M., Magnenat-Thalmann, N., Papagiannakis, G. (eds.) Mixed Reality and Gamification for Cultural Heritage, pp. 129–158. Springer Cham. https://doi.org/10.1007/978-3-319-49607-8_5

4. Goudswaard, M., Abraham, A., da Rocha, B.G., Andersen, K., Liang, R.-H.: FabriClick: interweaving pushbuttons into fabrics using 3D printing and digital embroidery. In: Proceedings of the Designing Interactive Systems Conference, Eindhoven, pp. 379–393. ACM (2020)

5. Wang, Q., Markopoulos, P., Yu, B., Chen, W., Timmermans, A.: Interactive wearable systems for upper body rehabilitation: a systematic review. J. NeuroEng. Rehabil. **14**, 20 (2017)

6. Devendorf, L., et al.: I don't want to wear a screen: probing perceptions of and possibilities for dynamic displays on clothing. In: Proceeding s of the CHI Conference on Human Factors in Computing Systems, San Jose, pp. 6028–6039. ACM (2016)

7. Kan, V., Fujii, K., Amores, J., Jin, C.L.Z., Maes, P., Ishii, H.: Social textiles: social affordances and icebreaking interactions through wearable social messaging. In: Proceedings of the Ninth International Conference on Tangible, Embedded, and Embodied Interaction, California, pp. 619–624. ACM (2015)

8. Kao, H.-L. (Cindy), Mohan, M., Schmandt, C., Paradiso, J.A., Vega, K.: ChromoSkin: towards interactive cosmetics using thermochromic pigments. In: Proceedings of the CHI Conference Extended Abstracts on Human Factors in Computing Systems, San Jose, pp. 3703–3706. ACM (2016)

9. Mival, O., et al.: AnimSkin: fabricating epidermis with interactive, functional and aesthetic color animation. In: Proceedings of the Designing Interactive Systems Conference, Edinburgh, pp. 397–401. ACM (2017)

10. Kuusk, K., Kooroshnia, M., Mikkonen, J.: Crafting butterfly lace: conductive multi-color sensor-actuator structure. In: Adjunct Proceedings of the 2015 ACM International Joint Conference on Pervasive and Ubiquitous Computing and Proceedings of the 2015 ACM International Symposium on Wearable Computers, Osaka, pp 595–600. ACM (2015)

11. Sun, R., Onose, R., Dunne, M., Ling, A., Denham, A., Kao, H.-L. (Cindy): Weaving a second skin: exploring opportunities for crafting on-skin interfaces through weaving. In: Proceedings of the Designing Interactive Systems Conference, Eindhoven, pp. 365–377. ACM (2020)

# Time-Penalty Impact on Effective Index of Difficulty and Throughputs in Pointing Tasks

Shota Yamanaka[1]([⊠]), Keisuke Yokota[2], and Takanori Komatsu[2]

[1] Yahoo Japan Corporation, Tokyo, Japan
syamanak@yahoo-corp.jp
[2] Meiji University, Tokyo, Japan

**Abstract.** In realistic graphical user interfaces, clicking outside a target would require recovery time from an error, e.g., selecting an unintended hyperlink requires reloading the previous webpage. Several studies on target-pointing tasks have examined the effects of a "penalty time" for mis-clicks on movement time and error rate, but the effects on throughput (i.e., a unified metric on pointing performance) have not been thoroughly investigated. We conducted a crowdsourcing study with 127 workers and a lab-based controlled study with 30 university students. The penalty times varied from 0 to 10 s, and the results consistently indicated that the throughput differences were less than 5%, although the error rates were remarkably different when the penalty time was 0 s. This demonstrated the potential of normalization capability of the effective width method of Fitts' law, and the throughput is considered a valid metric when researchers would like to compare several task conditions in realistic user interfaces in which error operations induce different recovery times. However, because the model fitness using the effective width method was comparatively low when the penalty time was 0 s, comparing throughputs for different conditions is not recommended. We also discussed potential issues related to the effective width method of Fitts' law, such as endpoints not following a linear relationship to the given target width only under the zero-penalty condition.

**Keywords:** Performance modeling · Fitts' law · Crowdsourcing

## 1 Introduction

We investigated the effects of imposing a penalty time for an operation detected as incorrect on user performance in target-pointing tasks. In typical pointing tasks, clicking on a target is considered a success, and missing it is considered an error. In the latter case, participants would be asked to click on the target again until success (e.g., [44]) or the experimental system ends the current trial and proceeds to the next (e.g., [6]). However, in realistic graphical user interfaces

© IFIP International Federation for Information Processing 2021
Published by Springer Nature Switzerland AG 2021
C. Ardito et al. (Eds.): INTERACT 2021, LNCS 12935, pp. 100–121, 2021.
https://doi.org/10.1007/978-3-030-85610-6_7

(GUIs), if users miss a target, they would have to perform additional operations to recover from the error. For example, if a user misses an intended hyperlink and the neighboring link is clicked, they must go back to the previous webpage, wait for the page to reload, then try to click the intended link again.

Such a recovery time from an error changes depending on the networking status, applications, and so on. It may take 3–5 s to recover after clicking on an unintended link, while clicking on the surrounding empty space incur no additional recovery time (i.e., only a retry is needed). For menu selection, e.g., in Microsoft Paint, mis-clicking on the top-level items (File/Home/View) incurs no recovery time, but if users mis-click the final item in "File → Save as → Export → JPEG picture," a longer retry time is incurred and additional effort is needed. In these realistic tasks, mis-operations and the resulting fatigue will affect user performance. As a more serious case, if users accidentally click on the "Pay" button on the PayPal site, or click the "Buy now with 1-Click" button on the Amazon site, a cancelling email has to be sent or the credit card company must be told to stop the payment, which may take several minutes.

To investigate the effects of such a recovery time on user performance, imposing a penalty time for mis-clicking in target pointing tasks has been examined [3,15,41]. For example, in Banovic et al.'s study, the participants had to wait for a certain time before the task could be resumed [3]. They theoretically and empirically determined that the error rate decreases and the cursor-movement time increases as the penalty time is increased in a mouse-pointing task [3]. This is intuitive because participants would obviously try to point to the target more carefully in a longer penalty time to shorten the overall task-completion time.

However, Banovic et al. reported three separate indicators of user performance: the time for the first click, time for task completion including the penalty, and error rate. For target-pointing studies, it is known that reporting a unified metric called *throughput*, which is used to measure user performance after normalizing the error rate, is needed to compare devices and techniques [23,26,31,35,43]. To compare two or more experimental conditions, such as comparing input devices (e.g., [9]) or user groups (e.g., children vs. older adults [32]), the trade-off between speed and accuracy typically differs under each condition, thus normalizing the error rates if needed. Therefore, when researchers would like to determine if, e.g., "there is no significant difference in user performance for 1- and 10-s penalty times," using the throughputs is preferred.

In this paper, we empirically explore how the penalty time affects throughputs from two viewpoints. First, it has never been studied if the effective width method of Fitts' law [11] holds for pointing tasks with penalty time. Because the throughput is valid if the task is modeled with this method, we have to examine the model fitness. Second, the normalization capability of throughput is unclear. Theoretically, even if participants are biased towards either speed or accuracy, throughputs should not change [28]. In our case, even when we change the penalty time from 0 to 10 s, while the first click time and the error rate could change, the throughputs should not significantly differ. If we confirm these two facts (Fitts' law holds and throughputs are not significantly different), researchers and designers will be able to compare different devices and user groups in realistic GUIs requiring recovery times, which contributes to future human-computer interaction (HCI) studies and GUI design.

We conducted two user experiments: crowdsourcing involving 127 workers and a conventional lab-based study involving 30 university students. Because Fitts' law and the effective width method are for modeling the central tendency of user performance [35], crowdsourcing is useful for recruiting many participants. However, there are issues with crowdsourcing GUI experiments, e.g., some workers may not follow given instructions [12]. Therefore, we were concerned if some of the workers performed the pointing task but ignored the instruction of "Minimize the whole task-completion time including the pointing time and penalty time." Hence, we also conducted the lab-based experiment, which was a self-replication study. Because these two experiments had different advantages, we do not need to compare the results directly; for example, a comparison such as "Crowdworkers were significantly faster than lab-based participants ($p < 0.05$)" is not necessary. Our main findings are as follows:

- For the effective width method of Fitts' law, the model fitness under the zero-penalty condition was remarkably low ($R^2 = 0.232$ and 0.601 for the crowdsourcing and lab-based experiments, respectively), while the other penalty conditions showed $R^2 > 0.9$. This low fit under the zero-penalty condition is consistent with previous studies [37,44]. This questions the reliability of throughput data under the zero-penalty condition.
- The throughputs for the 11 penalty time conditions were close: within 3 and 4% for the crowdsourcing and lab-based experiments, respectively, while the error rates more clearly differed depending on the penalty times. This demonstrated the normalization capability of throughput.

## 2  Related Work

### 2.1  Fitts' Law and the Effective Width Method

According to Fitts' law, the time for the first click, or movement time $MT$, to point to a target relates to the index of difficulty $ID$ in bits [13]:

$$MT = a + b \cdot ID, \tag{1}$$

where $a$ and $b$ are empirical regression constants. The Shannon formulation of $ID$ [26] is widely used in HCI:

$$ID_n = \log_2 (A/W + 1), \tag{2}$$

where the target distance (or amplitude) is $A$ and its width is $W$. This $ID$ is the *nominal* value using nominal $A$ and $W$ drawn on the display.

Typically, participants are asked to point to a target as quickly and accurately as possible [35], but some participants tend to show short $MT$s and high error rates ($ER$s), while others show long $MT$s and low $ER$s [44]. Thus, when researchers compare the performances of several devices or several user groups, normalizing *ER*s is necessary. Using Crossman's post-hoc correction for $W$ [11] is recommended in HCI [35] and the ISO standard [23].

$$W_e = 4.133 \cdot SD_x,\tag{3}$$

where $W_e$ is the effective width and $SD_x$ is the standard deviation of the actual click positions (or *endpoints*) along the movement axis. We then obtain the effective index of difficulty $ID_e$ by replacing the $W$ in Eq. 2 with $W_e$.

Researchers can use a unified measure of user performance called throughput [bits/sec] that integrates the speed $(MT)$ and $ID_e$ [35]:

$$\text{Throughput} = \frac{1}{|A| \times |W|} \sum_{i=1}^{|A| \times |W|} \left( \frac{ID_{e_i}}{MT_i} \right),\tag{4}$$

where $i$ indicates the $i$-th condition among $|A| \times |W|$. We calculate the throughput for a participant then compute the grand throughput by averaging all participants' throughputs [35][1].

The basis of this adjustment is that a spread of hits follows a normal distribution over a target. Using this method, $W_e$ is adjusted so that 3.88% (~4%) of clicks fall outside the target; thus, we can compare the throughputs, e.g., from different user groups. Although the effective width method has issues particularly with its theoretical bases [16], its empirical benefits have been recognized [44].

## 2.2 Penalty-Time Paradigm

**Previous Work on Target-Pointing Task.** It has been demonstrated that, regardless of whether a participant's priority biases towards speed or accuracy, Fitts' law using $ID_n$ holds [14,44]. While these biases have been controlled by monetary incentive/penalty [14] or by oral instruction [44], Banovic et al. determined that the bias is affected by the risk associated with the penalty time (0–20 s) for target misses [3]. Gillan et al. compared 0- and 30-s penalty conditions with a mouse [15], and the latter showed longer *MT* and lower *ER*, which was consistent with Banovic et al.'s report.

These studies consistently reported that, if the penalty time for a target miss was long (e.g., 10 s), the participants would attempt to more carefully point to the target. While this strategy lengthens the *MT* for a single click, the overall task-completion time should be shorter than if the participant performs the task quickly and inaccurately. When the penalty time is short (e.g., 1 s), the risk of the overall task-completion time being lengthened is not serious, even if a participant rapidly aims for the target and misses it in several trials. This strategy may reduce the *MT* per click, so the overall task-completion time would be shorter than with the slow-and-careful strategy. Thus, participants implicitly balance (optimize) the speed-accuracy trade-off for a given penalty time [3].

---

[1] Olafsdottir et al. listed 20 approaches to compute throughput [31]. We used Soukoreff and MacKenzie's method [35].

However, as Banovic et al. found, while a longer penalty time monotonically increases the single-task-completion time, the effect quickly plateaus (see Fig. 4 in [3]).

Banovic et al. showed that the difference in single-task-completion times under 3- and 30-s penalty conditions was less than 0.1 s, regardless of the Fitts' law difficulty. Moreover, the ERs for 3.33- and 6.67-s penalties were not significantly different, whereas they were significantly worse for a 0-s penalty. Since the effects of penalty time on task completion times are assumed to level off quickly, using an extremely long penalty time, such as 30 s, was unnecessary in our experiments, although it would occur in realistic GUIs, as discussed in the Introduction.

Inspired by the work of Banovic et al., Yamanaka evaluated the effects of penalty times (0–4 s) in touch-pointing tasks with 2D square targets on tablets [39]. The results indicated that the task-completion time was not significantly affected by penalty time, whereas ER significantly decreased as penalty time increased. This partially reproduced Banovic et al.'s findings [3]. Furthermore, Yamanaka et al. had crowdworkers perform almost the same task with 1D and 2D targets [41], but the penalty time was fixed at 3 s.

**Unexplored Space for Penalty-Time Paradigm in Pointing Task.** In summary of the previous studies on penalty time, the speed-accuracy trade-off can be controlled by changing the penalty time [3,15,39], which have been confirmed in lab-based experiments. A limitation in these studies is that they reported the results on times and errors separately; thus, the effect of penalty time on throughput remains unclear. Our study bridges the gap between previous studies on penalty time [3,15,39] and the standardized methodology of Fitts' law that unifies the speed ($MT$) and accuracy ($SD_x$) into a single throughput [23,35].

### 2.3 Crowdsourcing User Studies Compared with Lab-Based Ones

Research fields other than HCI have found high internal validity of crowdsourced data in, for example, political science [4] and behavioral economics [21] experiments. For user experiments on GUI operations such as target pointing and menu selection, Komarov et al. concluded that crowdsourcing can be used for conducting performance evaluations of GUIs and that it is a complementary approach to lab-based experiments, with greater diversity of participants and less effort for recruitment [25].

In contrast, by using more powerful statistical analysis methods and recruiting many more participants for lab-based experiments, Findlater et al. showed that crowdworkers have significantly shorter $MT$s and higher $ER$s both in mouse- and touch-pointing tasks [12]. They reported a good model fitness of Fitts' law ($r = 0.926$ using mice). In addition, Schwab et al. showed that a crowdsourcing scrolling task on a desktop environment resulted in a Fitts' law fitness of $R^2 = 0.983$ [33]. These results of good Fitts' law fitness motivated us to conduct an experiment for model fitness and performance evaluation on a crowdsourcing platform.

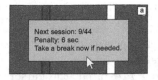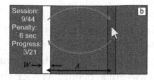

**Fig. 1.** Abstracted image of the experimental system. (a) The penalty time is shown before each session. (b) Serial-target-pointing task in which a worker attempts to click alternating red targets. (c) If a worker misses the target, the target turns yellow, and the cursor cannot be moved for the specified penalty time. (Color figure online)

| session | (*PT*, *W*) | | session | (*PT*, *W*) | | | session | (*PT*, *W*) |
|---------|-------------|---|---------|-------------|---|---|---------|-------------|
| 1 | (7, 40) | | 5 | (9, 20) | | | 41 | (1, 10) |
| 2 | (7, 10) | ⇨ | 6 | (9, 30) | ⇨ | ⋯ ⇨ | 42 | (1, 40) |
| 3 | (7, 30) | | 7 | (9, 40) | | | 43 | (1, 20) |
| 4 | (7, 20) | | 8 | (9, 10) | | | 44 | (1, 30) |

**Fig. 2.** Example case of 44 sessions and the random order of *PT* and *W*

## 3  Experiment 1: Crowdsourcing User Study

We conducted a 1D serial-target-pointing experiment (Fig. 1) on the *Yahoo! Crowdsourcing* platform (https://crowdsourcing.yahoo.co.jp) from September 9 to 11, 2020. The task was offered only in Japan. The study was approved through our company's IRB-equivalent research ethics team. They raised no specific concerns or requested any changes.

### 3.1  Task and Procedure

The experimental system was developed with the `Processing` language (version 3.5.4). The crowdworkers downloaded the executable file from a given URL and ran it. They first completed a questionnaire on their age (numeric), gender (free form to allow for a non-binary or arbitrary answer), handedness (left or right), input device (free form), and history of PC use (numeric in years). The system then proceeded to the pointing-task phase.

There were 11 penalty times (*PT*s) and 4 *W*s. They were fully crossed with each other, so each worker completed 44 *sessions* in total (see Fig. 2). Each session consisted of 21 cyclic clicks back and forth between the left and right targets. Before the next session began, the number out of the 44 sessions and *PT* were displayed, along with a message about taking a break (see Fig. 1a). Clicking on the message area initiated the session.

In the pointing-task phase, the workers were asked to click on the red vertical bar. If the worker clicked on the bar, the colors of target and non-target bars (red and white, respectively) changed, as shown in Fig. 1b. If the worker pressed the mouse button when the cursor was outside the target, we call this "a mis-clicked position." In this case, the target bar's color turned yellow, and the worker could not move the cursor from the mis-clicked position until the $PT$ expired (Fig. 1c). Technically, the system moved the cursor to the mis-clicked position every frame (60 fps by default) by using the `java.awt.Robot.mouseMove` function, and the target did not sense the mouse-click event. When the $PT$ expired, the cursor began moving from the mis-clicked position; i.e., not retrying a new trial.

While Banovic et al. stopped the display of the cursor during the $PT$ [3], we were concerned that some workers might think that there was a bug in the program if the cursor disappeared, so we continued displaying it. Because we could not be sure that all the workers would be able to hear sounds during the task, we did not give auditory feedback for success or failure. The remaining $PT$ was displayed as a countdown timer.

## 3.2   Design

The experiment was an $11 \times 4$ within-subjects design with the following independent variables and levels: $PT = 0$ to $10\,\mathrm{s}$ in 1-s steps and $W = 10, 20, 30,$ and 40 pixels. While Banovic et al. tested $PT = 0, 3.33, 6.67, 10,$ and $20\,\mathrm{s}$, they confirmed that the effects of $PT$ on task-completion times and $ER$s quickly plateau [3], and thus we prioritized testing a shorter range of $PT$s precisely with 1-s steps. Because error-recovery times vary even for a single application or website, we decided to use a within-subjects design for $PT$. The choice of $W$ is independent from the throughput analysis [28,35] but affects $ER$ [13]; thus, we used somewhat narrow targets. We denote the levels with subscripts, e.g., "$W_{20}$."

In each session, the first target was on the left side. To measure the central tendency of each worker's performance under each $PT \times W$ condition, requiring 15 to 25 clicks is recommended [35], so we considered the first 5 clicks to be practice and used the remaining 16 clicks (8 clicks for each side) for data collection. In each session, $PT$ and $W$ were fixed. For four successive sessions, $PT$ was fixed, and the order of the four $W$ conditions was randomized (Fig. 2).

The $ER$ for target pointing is assumed to depend solely on $W$; the target distance $A$ is not an important factor because it does not strongly affect the click-point distribution [5,22,44]. Hence, we fixed $A$ and varied $PT$ widely and precisely, which was the focus of this study. Using a single $A$ is common for studies on measuring throughput [28,31], and since Fitts' law analysis applies even if only the target size changes (e.g., [11,20]), $A$ was fixed at 600 pixels. We recorded a total of $11_{PT} \times 4_W \times 16_{\mathrm{repetitions}} \times 127_{\mathrm{workers}} = 89{,}408$ data points.

## 3.3   Participants

A total of 127 workers completed the task. Their demographics were as follows. Age: ranging from 23 to 64 years, $M = 43.1$ and $SD = 8.39$. Gender: 104 were male and 23 were female. Handedness: 6 were left-handed and 121 were right-handed. Input devices: 6 used a touchpad, 1 a trackball, 1 a trackpoint, 1 a pen tablet (whether direct or indirect stylus input is unknown), and 118 a mouse. PC usage history: from 5 to 40 years, $M = 21.0$ and $SD = 6.49$.

We recruited workers who used Windows (Vista or a later version) because our system runs in only those environments. No other qualifications, such as the worker's skills, were required. Once workers accepted the task, they were asked to read the online instructions explaining the task. The instructions stated that they should complete the task in as a short a time as possible including the $PT$ [3,38,39,41]. They also explained that a $PT$ would be imposed if they missed the target. Because we wanted them to understand how the cursor would remain fixed if they missed a target, we asked them to watch a short video in which one of the authors had performed the task and missed the target.

After a worker finished all 44 sessions, the log data, which included the questionnaire data, clicked positions, and timestamps, were exported to a csv file. The workers uploaded the file to a server to receive payment. The task typically took 20 min, and the payment was JPY 100 (~USD 0.96), so the effective hourly payment was about JPY 300. This amount was determined after a discussion with the platform's advisor; although it was less than that on other platforms such as Amazon Mechanical Turk, it was common for that platform. Previous work has shown that the payment affects workers' motivation [7], and thus our conclusion could change if we set a much higher payment.

## 3.4 Results

**Screening Outlier Data.** For Fitts' law tasks, there are two types of trial-level outliers: spatial and temporal. In addition, there are participant-level outliers in the temporal results: data for workers who performed extremely slowly or rapidly were removed from the analysis. These outliers are described as follows.

A spatial outlier was a position clicked more than $3\sigma$ from the mean clicked position. A temporal outlier was a trial in which the time taken to make the first click, i.e., $MT$, was more than $3\sigma$ from the mean $MT$. These trial-level outlier calculations were run for each session for each worker. This $3\sigma$ criterion was used by MacKenzie and colleagues [27,29,35].

For the participant-level outliers, we calculated the mean $MT$ across all 44 conditions ($11_{PT} \times 4_W$) for each participant. The data for workers whose mean $MT$ was more than $3\sigma$ from the average $MT$ across all workers were removed as outliers. We detected the trial- and participant-level outliers independently.

There are various other approaches to detecting outliers, such as the Smirnov-Grubbs' test and inter-quartile range method, as well as the Fitts' law-specific method, i.e., a cursor's movement distance was less than $A/2$ or the clicked position was more than $2W$ from the target center [3,12]. Although investigating a more robust data-screening method is an important topic in crowdsourcing research, discussing this point by analyzing the data with several criteria is clearly beyond the scope of this study. Hence, in our data analysis, we used a single method (the $3\sigma$ criterion).

We found 55 spatial and 378 temporal trial-level outliers (0.5% of the data). Two participant-level outlier workers were eliminated due to longer $MT$s than the mean. Notably, while the average $MT$ was approximately 1 s, one of the outlier workers had a $MT$ longer than 10 s twice (60 and 307 s), which indicates an obvious lack of concentration. Integrating the trial- and participant-level outliers led to the removal of 2.02% of the data points, which is close to the rate in a previous study [12].

**Analyses of Dependent Variables.** After the outliers were removed, 87,602 data points (98.0%) were analyzed. As with typical pointing studies using the effective width method, the dependent variables were $MT$, $ER$, and throughput. $MT$ data are typically distributed normally, but the Shapiro-Wilk test ($\alpha = 0.05$) showed that 31 of the 44 conditions violated the normality assumption, so we log-transformed the data before applying repeated-measures ANOVA with Bonferroni's $p$-value adjustment method for pairwise comparisons. $ER$s are nonparametric data, so we used ANOVAs with *Aligned Rank Transform* [36] and Tukey's $p$-value adjustment method for pairwise comparisons. Because throughput depends on both $MT$ and click point distribution ($SD_x$), we cannot interpret this as parametric data, so we again used ANOVAs with Aligned Rank Transform. Because the throughput merged the four $W$s (Eq. 4), the only independent variable was $PT$.

To simplify the result statements, we mainly report on the effects of $PT$ and briefly report those of $W$ on the dependent variables. For example, we avoid reporting the results for all combinations of significantly different $PT$ pairs in the $PT \times W$ interaction among the 220 possible pairs ($_{11}C_2 \times {}_4C_1$).

**Movement Time.** For the $F$ statistic, the degrees of freedom for the main effects of $PT$ and $W$, as well as the interaction of $PT \times W$, were corrected using the Greenhouse-Geisser method because Mauchly's sphericity assumption was violated ($\alpha = 0.05$). We found significant main effects of $PT$ ($F_{3.784,469.2} = 9.897$, $p < 0.001$, $\eta_p^2 = 0.74$) and $W$ ($F_{1.441,180.2} = 2280$, $p < 0.001$, $\eta_p^2 = 0.95$). The interaction of $PT \times W$ was significant ($F_{20.12,2495} = 1.544$, $p < 0.001$, $\eta_p^2 = 0.57$). As expected, the $MT$s decreased as $W$ increased ($p < 0.001$ for all pairs). The mean $MT$s for $W_{10}$ to $W_{40}$ were 1.31, 1.05, 0.939, and 0.874 s, respectively.

The mean $MT$s tended to increase as $PT$ increased, as shown in Fig. 3a, which means that the workers became more careful. Although there was a number of significantly different pairs, the mean $MT$s ranged from 1.00 to 1.06 s. This slight effect of $PT$ on $MT$ can also be confirmed with a linear regression. A model of $MT = a + b \cdot ID_n + c \cdot PT$ yields adjusted $R^2 = 0.988$ and $c = 0.00439$ (with $p < 0.0001$). This means that even when $PT$ increases from 0 to 10 s, $MT$ is assumed to increase by only 0.04 s.

**Error Rate.** We found significant main effects of $PT$ ($F_{10,1240} = 25.87$, $p < 0.001$, $\eta_p^2 = 0.17$) and $W$ ($F_{3,372} = 156.7$, $p < 0.001$, $\eta_p^2 = 0.56$). The interaction of $PT \times W$ was significant ($F_{30,3720} = 13.59$, $p < 0.001$, $\eta_p^2 = 0.099$). As expected, the $ER$ decreased as $W$ increased ($p < 0.001$ for all pairs). The mean $ER$s for $W_{10}$ to $W_{40}$ were 2.96, 2.25, 1.91, and 1.40%, respectively.

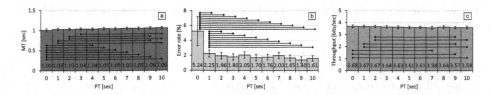

**Fig. 3.** Main effects of $PT$ on (a) $MT$ without log-transformation, (b) $ER$, and (c) throughput in Experiment 1. Error bars show 95% CIs across all 125 non-outlier workers, and horizontal lines indicate significantly different pairs (at least $p < 0.05$).

**Table 1.** Model fitness in Experiment 1. The yellow cell shows the lowest fit using $ID_e$. The pink cell indicates an insignificant ($p > 0.05$) contributor of $ID_e$ to predict $MT$s. The blue cells indicate that there were significant differences in fits using $ID_n$ and $ID_e$.

| $PT$ | Nominal ($ID_n$) | | | | Effective ($ID_e$) | | | | Difference | | |
|---|---|---|---|---|---|---|---|---|---|---|---|
| [sec] | $R^2$ | $p$ value | $AIC$ | $BIC$ | $R^2$ | $p$ value | $AIC$ | $BIC$ | $R^2$ | $AIC$ | $BIC$ |
| 0 | 0.996 | 0.00203 | −21.7 | −22.9 | 0.232 | 0.518 | −0.715 | −1.94 | 0.764 | −21.0 | −21.0 |
| 1 | 0.984 | 0.00796 | −15.6 | −16.8 | 0.920 | 0.0410 | −9.09 | −10.3 | 0.0641 | −6.49 | −6.51 |
| 2 | 0.994 | 0.00284 | −20.0 | −21.2 | 0.993 | 0.00358 | −19.1 | −20.3 | 0.00132 | −0.904 | −0.932 |
| 3 | 0.988 | 0.00598 | −16.7 | −17.9 | 0.975 | 0.0125 | −13.7 | −15.0 | 0.0131 | −2.97 | −2.90 |
| 4 | 0.990 | 0.00493 | −17.5 | −18.7 | 0.998 | 0.00116 | −23.3 | −24.5 | −0.00784 | 5.81 | 5.78 |
| 5 | 0.987 | 0.00652 | −16.1 | −17.4 | 0.980 | 0.0103 | −14.3 | −15.6 | 0.00700 | −1.85 | −1.77 |
| 6 | 0.992 | 0.00400 | −18.3 | −19.5 | 0.981 | 0.00932 | −14.9 | −16.1 | 0.0110 | −3.37 | −3.40 |
| 7 | 0.989 | 0.00553 | −16.9 | −18.1 | 0.980 | 0.00990 | −14.6 | −15.8 | 0.00896 | −2.28 | −2.31 |
| 8 | 0.993 | 0.00343 | −18.9 | −20.1 | 0.943 | 0.0291 | −10.4 | −11.6 | 0.0502 | −8.47 | −8.50 |
| 9 | 0.993 | 0.00355 | −18.9 | −20.1 | 0.998 | 0.00103 | −23.8 | −25.1 | −0.00508 | 4.91 | 4.98 |
| 10 | 0.989 | 0.00560 | −16.3 | −17.5 | 0.973 | 0.0134 | −12.8 | −14.1 | 0.0158 | −3.52 | −3.45 |

The $ER$ for $PT_0$ was remarkably high, as shown in Fig. 3b. The $ER$ for $PT_1$ was nevertheless significantly different from those of $PT \geq 2$ s. Finally, there were no significant differences between any pair for $PT \geq 2$ s.

**Throughput and Fitts' Law Fitness.** We found a significant main effect of $PT$ ($F_{10,1240} = 4.221$, $p < 0.001$, $\eta_p^2 = 0.033$). Pairwise comparisons showed that the throughputs tended to decrease as $PT$ increased, as shown in Fig. 3c. The highest throughput was observed for $PT_0$, and the lowest was for $PT_9$. However, the difference was only $3.68 - 3.57 = 0.11$ bits/s (i.e., 3% of the baseline condition, $PT_0$).

This indicates that throughput performance is not strongly affected by $PT$, which is also supported by the small effect size of $PT$ ($\eta_p^2 = 0.033$). However, Fig. 3c is somewhat misleading. According to the Fitts' law fitness using $ID_e$, the correlation for $PT_0$ was remarkably low ($R^2 = 0.232$, see the yellow cell in Table 1) while it was $> 0.9$ under the other $PT$ conditions. Because judging model fitness on the basis of only the absolute $R^2$ is problematic [17], we argue that Fitts' law cannot capture the $PT_0$ condition on the basis of the $p$ value

**Table 2.** Results of Experiment 1. The blue cells indicate a violation of Fitts' law's assumption that $W$ and $SD_x$ are linearly related.

| $PT$ | $MT$ [sec] | | | | $W_e$ [pixels] | | | | $R^2$ | $ER$ | Throughput |
|---|---|---|---|---|---|---|---|---|---|---|---|
| [sec] | $W_{10}$ | $W_{20}$ | $W_{30}$ | $W_{40}$ | $W_{10}$ | $W_{20}$ | $W_{30}$ | $W_{40}$ | $(W, SD_x)$ | [%] | [bits/sec] |
| 0 | 1.25 | 1.03 | 0.910 | 0.857 | 78.5 | 66.5 | 86.9 | 91.0 | 0.477 | 5.24 | 3.68 |
| 1 | 1.30 | 1.02 | 0.928 | 0.865 | 32.1 | 46.7 | 75.2 | 89.7 | 0.981 | 2.25 | 3.67 |
| 2 | 1.28 | 1.04 | 0.929 | 0.866 | 24.1 | 46.6 | 68.5 | 89.8 | 1.000 | 1.96 | 3.67 |
| 3 | 1.32 | 1.04 | 0.942 | 0.879 | 32.0 | 52.9 | 67.7 | 89.6 | 0.995 | 1.80 | 3.64 |
| 4 | 1.30 | 1.04 | 0.932 | 0.869 | 24.1 | 52.1 | 76.3 | 96.9 | 0.995 | 2.05 | 3.63 |
| 5 | 1.33 | 1.05 | 0.943 | 0.884 | 32.7 | 53.3 | 75.2 | 90.4 | 0.995 | 1.70 | 3.61 |
| 6 | 1.31 | 1.05 | 0.951 | 0.870 | 23.6 | 46.6 | 76.9 | 89.6 | 0.978 | 1.76 | 3.61 |
| 7 | 1.32 | 1.05 | 0.943 | 0.883 | 32.2 | 54.9 | 75.4 | 97.4 | 1.000 | 2.00 | 3.58 |
| 8 | 1.32 | 1.06 | 0.959 | 0.877 | 30.5 | 44.9 | 68.4 | 88.3 | 0.992 | 1.65 | 3.64 |
| 9 | 1.32 | 1.07 | 0.954 | 0.892 | 30.4 | 54.6 | 74.6 | 89.4 | 0.989 | 1.40 | 3.57 |
| 10 | 1.36 | 1.06 | 0.957 | 0.882 | 23.3 | 45.3 | 68.0 | 98.7 | 0.993 | 1.61 | 3.58 |

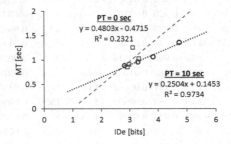

**Fig. 4.** Fitts' law fitness using $ID_e$ for $PT_0$ (red) and $PT_{10}$ (blue). (Color figure online)

for $ID_e$. As shown with the pink cell in Table 1, $ID_e$ was not a significant contributor to explain the $MT$ only for $PT_0$ ($p = 0.518 > 0.05$). Thus, predicting worker performance under the zero-penalty condition on the basis of throughput is not reliable because throughput is an indicator of performance only when the operation can be modeled by Fitts' law. To the best of our knowledge, this finding, i.e., that Fitts' law fitness using the effective width method is notably low ($R^2 = 0.232$) for crowdsourced data, is a novel empirical finding that cautions against measuring worker performance on the basis of only throughput.

In contrast, using $ID_n$ showed $R^2 > 0.98$. To statistically compare the model-fitness difference, we used $AIC$ [2] and $BIC$ [24]. For simplicity, we consider an $AIC$ difference greater than 10 to be significant [8]. This was also applied to $BIC$ [24]. The results indicate that, only under the $PT_0$ condition, the model fitness using $ID_e$ is significantly inferior to $ID_n$ (see blue cells in Table 1). This comparatively low model fitness using $ID_e$ is consistent with previous studies [37,44]. This result again supports the low reliability of throughput analysis under the $PT_0$ condition, while predicting $MT$ using $ID_n$ is not problematic.

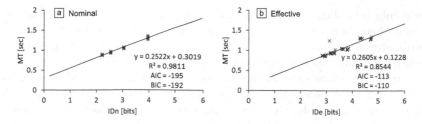

**Fig. 5.** Model fitness using (a) $ID_n$ and (b) $ID_e$ for 44 data points in Experiment 1.eps

We examine this low fitness only for $PT_0$ using $ID_e$ in more detail by visualizing the fits. As example cases, we plot the data for $PT_0$ and $PT_{10}$ in Fig. 4. While the four data points for $PT_{10}$ are close to the regression line, those for $PT_0$ are not. More critically, the spread of the data points on the x-axis for $PT_0$ is narrower than that for $PT_{10}$. This is because the distributions of the click positions ($SD_x$ values) fell in a narrow range. In particular, for $W_{10}$, $W_e = 4.133 \cdot SD_x$ was greater than that for $W_{20}$ (see blue cells in Table 2). This clearly shows that, for $W_{10}$, $W_e$ under the $PT_0$ condition was large compared with the other $PT$ conditions. This was likely due to workers "giving up" pointing to the smallest target accurately on the first attempt, as there was no penalty for mis-clicks. This is supported by the highest $ER$ (8.05%) observed under the $PT_0 \times W_{10}$ condition.

This result violates the assumption of Fitts' law, especially for the effective width method, because this method is based on the fact that the endpoint variability is linearly (or proportionally) related to the given $W$: $SD_x = a + b \cdot W$ [5,11,26,35]. The results from the conditions other than $PT_0$ validate this assumption, with $R^2$ between $W$ and $SD_x$ being over 0.97 (see Table 2). More specifically, for $PT_0$, the larger $W_e$ for $W_{10}$ than that for $W_{20}$ results in smaller $ID_e$ for $W_{10}$ than that for $W_{20}$, meaning "pointing to a narrower target is easier," which is obviously incorrect.

**Normalization Capability of the Effective Width Method.** Even if $ER$s differ under several task conditions (here, the 11 $PT$s), using $ID_e$ normalizes the $ER$s; thus, the Fitts' law fitness without separating the task conditions would show a higher fit compared with $ID_n$. This benefit was empirically demonstrated by Zhai et al. [44]. However, as shown in Fig. 5, we did not confirm such a capability. Because the change in $MT$ due to the 11 $PT$s was small (0.06 s at most), we did not see the benefit of using $ID_e$ for comparing different conditions.

## 4   Experiment 2: Lab-Based User Study

This experiment was conducted in a silent room of our university from December 3 to 16, 2020. We followed our university's compliance policy for in-person user experiments regarding Covid-19. In particular, there should be no more than two individuals in a room at the same time: in our study there were always an experimenter and a participant. We also followed the other requirements, e.g., air ventilation, sanitation of equipment, and mask mandate.

We used the same experimental system with the same task design as in Experiment 1. The procedure, e.g., watching the instruction video and filling the questionnaire, was also the same. The only difference was that we asked the participants to use the apparatus we prepared.

### 4.1  Apparatus

The PC that we used was a Microsoft Surface Laptop 3 (AMD Ryzen 7 3780U, 2.30 GHz, 4 cores; 16-GB RAM; Windows 10). The display had $2496 \times 1664$ pixels (201 ppi resolution), and the refresh rate was set 60 Hz. The mouse was manufactured by Buffalo Inc., (model: BSMBU300, 1600 dpi). We used a standard-sized mousepad ($21\,\mathrm{cm} \times 17\,\mathrm{cm}$).

The cursor speed was set as the default in the OS, i.e., the control-display gain was set at the middle of the slider in the Control Panel configuration. The pointer acceleration (or *Enhance pointer precision* setting in Windows 10) was enabled to allow the participants to perform mouse operations with higher ecological validity [10]. Fitts' law holds even when the pointer acceleration is turned on [1,40].

### 4.2  Participants

Thirty unpaid students were collected from a local university (18 females and 12 males; ages: 18 to 26 years, $M = 22.2$, $SD = 1.59$). All belonged to a computer science department and were good at mouse operations. All had normal or corrected-to-normal vision. Twenty-six were right-handed and the remaining four were left-handed. PC usage history ranged from 0 (i.e., less than one year) to 19 years, $M = 7.63$, $SD = 5.31$.

### 4.3  Results

We recorded a total of $11_{PT} \times 4_W \times 16_{\mathrm{repetitions}} \times 30_{\mathrm{participants}} = 21{,}120$ data points. We applied the same criteria on outlier detection used in Experiment 1. There were no participant-level outliers and 70 trial-level outliers (0.33%); thus, we analyzed the remaining 21,050 data points.

**Movement Time.** The Shapiro-Wilk test showed that 40 of the 44 conditions violated the normality assumption, so we log-transformed the data. We found significant main effects of $PT$ ($F_{5.696,165.198} = 4.393$, $p < 0.001$, $\eta_p^2 = 0.13$) and $W$ ($F_{1.725,50.024} = 910.0$, $p < 0.001$, $\eta_p^2 = 0.97$). The interaction of $PT \times W$ was not significant ($F_{12.982,376.475} = 1.310$, $p = 0.124$, $\eta_p^2 = 0.043$). Possibly due to the small sample size compared with the crowdsourcing study, there were

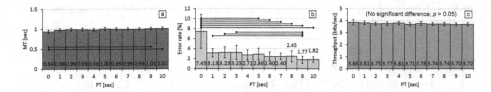

**Fig. 6.** Main effects of $PT$ on (a) $MT$ without log-transformation, (b) $ER$, and (c) throughput in Experiment 2. Error bars show 95% CIs, and horizontal lines indicate significantly different pairs (at least $p < 0.05$).

**Table 3.** Model fitness in Experiment 2. The yellow cell shows the lowest fit using $ID_e$. The pink cell indicates an insignificant ($p > 0.05$) contributor of $ID_e$ to predict $MT$s. Blue cells indicate that there were significant differences in model fitness.

| $PT$ | Nominal | | | | Effective | | | | Difference | | |
|---|---|---|---|---|---|---|---|---|---|---|---|
| [sec] | $R^2$ | $p$ value | $AIC$ | $BIC$ | $R^2$ | $p$ value | $AIC$ | $BIC$ | $R^2$ | $AIC$ | $BIC$ |
| 0 | 0.999 | 0.000619 | −28.0 | −29.2 | 0.159 | 0.601 | −1.90 | −3.13 | 0.840 | −26.1 | −26.1 |
| 1 | 0.987 | 0.00669 | −18.0 | −19.2 | 0.981 | 0.00943 | −16.6 | −17.8 | 0.00566 | −1.38 | −1.40 |
| 2 | 0.986 | 0.00682 | −17.1 | −18.4 | 0.984 | 0.00819 | −16.4 | −17.6 | 0.00240 | −0.735 | −0.763 |
| 3 | 0.981 | 0.00976 | −15.9 | −17.1 | 0.986 | 0.00714 | −17.2 | −18.4 | −0.00543 | 1.28 | 1.26 |
| 4 | 0.996 | 0.00214 | −22.0 | −23.2 | 0.995 | 0.00272 | −21.0 | −22.3 | 0.000726 | −0.991 | −0.918 |
| 5 | 0.998 | 0.000799 | −26.5 | −27.7 | 0.995 | 0.00264 | −21.7 | −22.9 | 0.00340 | −4.78 | −4.81 |
| 6 | 0.986 | 0.00704 | −17.1 | −18.4 | 0.976 | 0.0122 | −15.0 | −16.2 | 0.00996 | −2.15 | −2.18 |
| 7 | 0.982 | 0.00917 | −15.6 | −16.9 | 0.978 | 0.0108 | −15.0 | −16.2 | 0.00374 | −0.641 | −0.669 |
| 8 | 0.991 | 0.00454 | −18.6 | −19.8 | 0.983 | 0.00878 | −15.9 | −17.2 | 0.00793 | −2.68 | −2.60 |
| 9 | 0.993 | 0.00353 | −19.6 | −20.8 | 0.989 | 0.00527 | −18.0 | −19.2 | 0.00395 | −1.56 | −1.58 |
| 10 | 0.997 | 0.00146 | −23.4 | −24.6 | 0.990 | 0.00503 | −18.4 | −19.7 | 0.00709 | −4.99 | −4.92 |

only two pairs showing significant differences affected by $PT$ (Fig. 6a). A linear regression model of $MT = a + b \cdot ID_n + c \cdot PT$ yields adjusted $R^2 = 0.981$ and $c = 0.00458$ (with $p < 0.0001$).

**Error Rate.** We found significant main effects of $PT$ ($F_{10,290} = 7.664$, $p < 0.001$, $\eta_p^2 = 0.20$) and $W$ ($F_{3,87} = 9.939$, $p < 0.001$, $\eta_p^2 = 0.26$). The interaction of $PT \times W$ was significant ($F_{30,870} = 1.567$, $p < 0.05$, $\eta_p^2 = 0.051$). Similarly to Experiment 1, the $ER$ for $PT_0$ was remarkably high, as shown in Fig. 6b. There were no significant differences between any pair for $PT \geq 4$ s. The mean $ER$s for $W_{10}$ to $W_{40}$ were 3.71, 2.82, 3.37, and 2.25%, respectively, and we found three pairs that showed significant differences ($p < 0.05$) for ($W_{10}$, $W_{20}$), ($W_{10}$, $W_{40}$), and ($W_{30}$, $W_{40}$).

**Throughput and Fitts' Law Fitness.** We found a significant main effect of $PT$ ($F_{10,290} = 1.949$, $p < 0.05$, $\eta_p^2 = 0.063$). There were no significant differences in any pair ($p > 0.05$, Fig. 6c)[2]. The maximum difference was $3.86 - 3.70 = 0.16$

---

[2] It is possible for ANOVA that a main effect is significant but the pairwise tests show no significant differences.

**Table 4.** Results of Experiment 2. Blue cells indicate a violation of Fitts' law's assumption that $W$ and $SD_x$ are linearly related.

| $PT$ [sec] | $MT$ [sec] | | | | $W_e$ [pixels] | | | | $R^2$ $(W, SD_x)$ | $ER$ [%] | Throughput [bits/sec] |
|---|---|---|---|---|---|---|---|---|---|---|---|
| | $W_{10}$ | $W_{20}$ | $W_{30}$ | $W_{40}$ | $W_{10}$ | $W_{20}$ | $W_{30}$ | $W_{40}$ | | | |
| 0 | 1.13 | 0.954 | 0.869 | 0.794 | 74.8 | 76.2 | 67.1 | 93.7 | 0.300 | 5.24 | 3.68 |
| 1 | 1.20 | 0.981 | 0.887 | 0.850 | 23.7 | 45.2 | 69.6 | 90.4 | 0.999 | 2.25 | 3.67 |
| 2 | 1.23 | 0.986 | 0.904 | 0.842 | 24.6 | 46.7 | 70.2 | 87.7 | 0.997 | 1.96 | 3.67 |
| 3 | 1.22 | 0.985 | 0.883 | 0.852 | 23.9 | 48.0 | 68.8 | 88.6 | 0.998 | 1.80 | 3.64 |
| 4 | 1.21 | 0.991 | 0.904 | 0.829 | 23.7 | 46.5 | 69.4 | 89.8 | 0.999 | 2.05 | 3.63 |
| 5 | 1.21 | 1.01 | 0.922 | 0.850 | 24.2 | 45.7 | 68.6 | 92.8 | 0.999 | 1.70 | 3.61 |
| 6 | 1.22 | 0.981 | 0.916 | 0.828 | 23.7 | 44.7 | 68.9 | 86.9 | 0.997 | 1.76 | 3.61 |
| 7 | 1.24 | 0.982 | 0.901 | 0.840 | 24.2 | 46.4 | 69.9 | 89.1 | 0.998 | 2.00 | 3.58 |
| 8 | 1.23 | 1.02 | 0.883 | 0.846 | 24.1 | 46.2 | 66.7 | 91.7 | 0.998 | 1.65 | 3.64 |
| 9 | 1.26 | 1.02 | 0.925 | 0.854 | 23.0 | 45.4 | 68.1 | 91.6 | 1 | 1.40 | 3.57 |
| 10 | 1.24 | 1.02 | 0.914 | 0.851 | 23.3 | 44.1 | 67.0 | 91.2 | 0.999 | 1.61 | 3.58 |

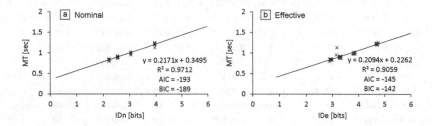

**Fig. 7.** Model fitness using (a) $ID_n$ and (b) $ID_e$ for 44 data points in Experiment 2.

bits/sec (i.e., 4% of the baseline condition, $PT_0$). In comparison, in Experiment 1, the maximum difference was 0.11 bits/sec (3%), but there were several significantly different pairs (see Fig. 3c). The results of this lab-based experiment again supported that throughput performance is not strongly affected by $PT$.

We found the same issues related to the effective width method as in Experiment 1. First, as shown in Table 3, the Fitts' law fitness using $ID_e$ was remarkably low under the $PT_0$ condition ($R^2 = 0.159$, yellow cell), and $ID_e$ was not a significant contributor ($p = 0.601$, pink cell). Second, the $AIC$ and $BIC$ differences between the $ID_n$ and $ID_e$ were significant only under the $PT_0$ condition (blue cells). Third, the correlation between $W$ and $SD_x$ was low only under the $PT_0$ condition ($R^2 = 0.300$), while the other $PT$ conditions showed $R^2 > 0.99$ (Table 4). It seems that the $W_e$s for $W_{10}$ and $W_{20}$ were high for $PT_0$ compared with the other $PT$s.

Overall, the results obtained in Experiment 1 were reproduced in this lab-based experiment. This result rejected our assumption that the remarkably low Fitts' law fitness using $ID_e$ for $PT_0$ was due to the issues related to the crowd-sourcing experiment such as instruction incompliance. It would be common that the endpoint distribution for small target widens than expected with the effective width method of Fitts' law if there is no $PT$. We again did not confirm the benefit to using $ID_e$ for comparing different conditions as Fig. 7 shows the lower model fitness for all 44 data points using $ID_e$.

## 5   Discussion

### 5.1   Effects of Time Penalty on Throughput, Model Fitness, and Endpoint Distributions

Our results indicate that crowdworkers and lab-based participants adjusted their strategy for pointing (speed and accuracy) in accordance with the given $PT$. The results indicate that, overall, a shorter $PT$ is better for $MT$, although a too short $PT$ negatively affects $ER$. The unified performance metric, throughput, was also higher for a shorter $PT$ in Experiment 1 (Fig. 3c), but there were no significant differences in Experiment 2 (Fig. 6c). The throughputs fell within 3% in Experiment 1 and up to 4% in Experiment 2. Thus, the significant differences found in Experiment 1 were due to the larger sample size ($N = 125$ valid workers). We conclude that the normalization capability of throughput was partially demonstrated.

However, there is an issue related to the significantly low model fitness using $ID_e$ under the zero-penalty condition. This was likely because the $ER$ under the $PT_0$ condition was significantly higher, particularly for narrow targets, and the endpoint distribution $SD_x$ (thus $W_e$) was widened. Because the effective width method is based on the assumption that $SD_x$ widens accordingly to the nominal $W$, such a violation was harmful for Fitts' law fitness using $ID_e$.

Inconsistent with previous studies on the effective width method [37, 44], when we regressed all 44 data points ($11_{PT} \times 4_W$), the model fitness using $ID_n$ was significantly better than $ID_e$ in both experiments. This may be due to this lack of regularity between $SD_x$ and $W$. Because there was a small effect of $PT$ on $MT$ ($MT$ changed up to 7% from the baseline), using $ID_n$ was sufficient for predicting $MT$ regardless of $PT$. This is convenient for researchers and designers; when we arrange a new button/icon on a GUI, the only known parameter of the target is the nominal $W$; thus, we can use only the $ID_n$. This point has been mentioned in previous studies [37, 44], and we found that, for the penalty time paradigm, we can use $ID_n$ for predicting $MT$ even if there are several different $PT$s.

In comparison, if researchers would like to compare several input devices and user groups, we should use the accuracy-normalized model, but $ID_e$ showed significantly worse fitness when regressing the 44 data points. This prevents us from recommending using $ID_e$, although it is recommended by the ISO standard [23]. One choice is to analyze the data separately under zero-penalty and non-zero penalty conditions. Because the zero-penalty condition has been used in previous studies and the ISO standard, comparing user groups for the zero-penalty data is not problematic. When we regressed the remaining 40 data points ($PT_1$ to $PT_{10}$) using $ID_e$, the $R^2$ for Experiments 1 and 2 were 0.979 and 0.938, respectively, which were worse than using $ID_n$ but not considerably low. However, in realistic GUIs, there exist both zero-penalty empty space and time-consuming objects of mis-clicked like hyperlinks; thus, this separate analysis is not convenient for practitioners. More sophisticated methods need to be investigated for our future work.

## 5.2 Exception for Zero-Penalty Condition

We found that the $PT_0$ condition resulted in remarkably different results, which is in line with the findings of Banovic et al. [3]. For example, in Banovic et al.'s $MT$ prediction model, the prediction accuracy under all $PT$ conditions showed $R^2 = 0.85$, but the data without $PT_0$ showed $R^2 = 0.98$ (see Fig. 11 in [3]). Banovic et al.'s $MT$ prediction model is based on the effective width method with which the endpoints follow a normal distribution and the $SD_x$ increases accordingly to the given $W$. Thus, if this assumption is violated, the resultant $MT$ prediction does not work well.

Because Banovic et al. did not report the endpoint distributions, we cannot discuss if this assumption is true for their data. However, the violation on $SD_x$ was robustly found in both Experiments 1 and 2, and Banovic et al. reported that the $ER$ for $PT_0$ was remarkably high (i.e., more endpoints fell outside the target). Therefore, we reasonably assume that this violation occurred and negatively affected Banovic et al.'s model fitness. Analyzing the resultant user behavior (here, $SD_x$) enables us to discuss the user strategy and corresponding high/low model fitness, which will lead to future model refinements.

## 5.3 Limitations and Future Work

Our findings are somewhat limited by the experimental conditions, e.g., we did not vary the target distance $A$ and used a 1D target-pointing task. These conditions reflect our main focus, which was to observe the effects of $PT$ on user performance measured as throughput. We chose this because throughput is independent of the choice of $A$ and $W$ [26,35]. However, these limitations restrict the effective range of $PT$. For example, a single trial can be finished in 1 s on average, but other GUI-operation tasks that take a longer time, such as navigation in hierarchical menus and webpage navigation, would likely result in different effects of $PT$ on $MT$ and $ER$.

Regarding the range of $PT$s (0 to 10 s), real GUIs would have much longer $PT$s, as mentioned in Sect. 1, and thus the external validity is limited. This range was designed with reference to [3], which showed the effects of $PT$ on $MT$ and $ER$ quickly plateau, and our experiments were internally valid. The ecological validity is also limited. For example, when an unintended hyperlink is clicked, we assume a recovery time is needed. In real GUIs, however, typically there is a margin between links; clicking this area induces no $PT$. Still, our contribution is bridging the gap between tested conditions and real GUIs, which was inadequate in previous studies using only $PT_0$ conditions.

It is known that devices [9], handedness [19], and ages [18] affect pointing performance. We assumed that evaluating these factors did not strengthen our novelty and contribution, and thus we did not analyze them. However, our tested platform utilizes comparatively older workers than (e.g.) Amazon MTurk: the former has 20% of <30-year-old people, while the latter has 30% [30,34]. Testing the generalizability of our findings to other countries' platforms will be included in our future work.

In particular for the $PT = 0$ s condition, clicking repeatedly around the target could result in finishing the task more quickly. For crowdworkers, such a strategy is effective to maximize payment per time, which might affect the results. Also, we mainly discussed the quantitative data, but a qualitative analysis based on interviews related to subjective strategies would uncover the reasons behind the differences in results.

We found that the model fitness using $ID_n$ and $ID_e$ for non-zero penalties was not significantly different in accordance with $AIC$ and $BIC$. Also, when we analyzed the 44 data points in a mixed manner, the fit for $ID_n$ was better than $ID_e$. These findings are inconsistent with previous studies on the effective width method [37,44], but this might be because we used only one $A$ and a limited number of $W$s. While it is assumed with the effective width method that the $SD_x$ is not affected by $A$ [26,35], it is slightly affected by the nominal $A$ [42,44]. Therefore, we cannot conclude that using $ID_e$ shows comparable model fitness with $ID_n$ if there are several target distances. This informs possible future work that examining if the same findings can be observed.

# 6   Conclusion

We explored the effects of penalty time $PT$ on user performance in terms of the throughput of target-pointing tasks. The throughputs decreased as $PT$ increased in the crowdsourcing experiment, while it was not significantly affected in the lab-based experiment. Because the throughput difference was up to 3 and 4% in these experiments, respectively, we partially found the normalization capability of the effective width method of Fitts' law [23,28,35]. However, we also found that using a 0-s $PT$ resulted in different outcomes under the other conditions, particularly when a high error rate was observed and Fitts' law fitness using $ID_e$ was low, which makes estimating throughput performance difficult. This would make it difficult to model the movement time and error rate as Banovic et al. found [3], because participants behave differently only under the zero-penalty condition. This difficulty probably comes from the fact that the endpoint variability $SD_x$ violates the assumed linear relationship to the nominal $W$, which was consistently found in the both experiments.

Our results filled the gap between the standardized methodology of pointing performance [23,35] and the penalty-time paradigm for realistic GUIs [3,39]. Particularly, the data obtained in our experiments contributed to our better understanding of user behavior in GUIs that would induce time penalty. Thus, this work is a necessary step towards refining current performance prediction models, which may be helpful to researchers and designers in the future. Last, if we look at only the $PT_0$ condition, using $ID_n$ yields $R^2 = 0.996$ and $0.999$ in the two experiments, but using $ID_e$ yields significantly lower fits; this is consistent with previous studies. Comparing $PT_0$ with the other $PT_s$ highlighted the unsuitability of using $PT_0$, but we note that there were also consistencies with previous studies.

# References

1. Accot, J., Zhai, S.: Refining Fitts' law models for bivariate pointing. In: Proceedings of the SIGCHI Conference on Human Factors in Computing Systems, CHI 2003, pp. 193–200. ACM, New York (2003). https://doi.org/10.1145/642611.642646. http://doi.acm.org/10.1145/642611.642646
2. Akaike, H.: A new look at the statistical model identification. IEEE Trans. Autom. Control **19**(6), 716–723 (1974). https://doi.org/10.1109/TAC.1974.1100705
3. Banovic, N., Grossman, T., Fitzmaurice, G.: The effect of time-based cost of error in target-directed pointing tasks. In: Proceedings of the SIGCHI Conference on Human Factors in Computing Systems, CHI 2013, pp. 1373–1382. ACM, New York (2013). https://doi.org/10.1145/2470654.2466181. http://doi.acm.org/10.1145/2470654.2466181
4. Berinsky, A.J., Huber, G.A., Lenz, G.S.: Evaluating online labor markets for experimental research: Amazon.com's mechanical turk. Polit. Anal. **20**(3), 351–368 (2012). https://doi.org/10.1093/pan/mpr057
5. Bi, X., Li, Y., Zhai, S.: Ffitts law: modeling finger touch with Fitts' law. In: Proceedings of the SIGCHI Conference on Human Factors in Computing Systems, CHI 2013, pp. 1363–1372. ACM, New York (2013). https://doi.org/10.1145/2470654.2466180. http://doi.acm.org/10.1145/2470654.2466180
6. Bi, X., Zhai, S.: Bayesian touch: a statistical criterion of target selection with finger touch. In: Proceedings of the ACM Symposium on User Interface Software and Technology (UIST 2013), pp. 51–60 (2013). https://doi.org/10.1145/2501988.2502058
7. Buhrmester, M., Kwang, T., Gosling, S.D.: Amazon's mechanical turk: a new source of inexpensive, yet high-quality, data? Perspect. Psychol. Sci. **6**(1), 3–5 (2011). https://doi.org/10.1177/1745691610393980
8. Burnham, K.P., Anderson, D.R.: Model Selection and Multimodel Inference: A Practical Information-Theoretic Approach. Springer, New York (2003). https://doi.org/10.1007/b97636
9. Card, S.K., English, W.K., Burr, B.J.: Evaluation of mouse, rate-controlled isometric joystick, step keys, and text keys for text selection on a CRT. Ergonomics **21**(8), 601–613 (1978). https://doi.org/10.1080/00140137808931762
10. Casiez, G., Roussel, N.: No more bricolage!: methods and tools to characterize, replicate and compare pointing transfer functions. In: Proceedings of the 24th Annual ACM Symposium on User Interface Software and Technology, UIST 2011, pp. 603–614. ACM, New York (2011). https://doi.org/10.1145/2047196.2047276. http://doi.acm.org/10.1145/2047196.2047276
11. Crossman, E.R.: The speed and accuracy of simple hand movements. Ph.D. thesis, University of Birmingham (1956)

12. Findlater, L., Zhang, J., Froehlich, J.E., Moffatt, K.: Differences in crowdsourced vs. lab-based mobile and desktop input performance data. In: Proceedings of the 2017 CHI Conference on Human Factors in Computing Systems, CHI 2017, pp. 6813–6824. ACM, New York (2017). https://doi.org/10.1145/3025453.3025820. http://doi.acm.org/10.1145/3025453.3025820

13. Fitts, P.M.: The information capacity of the human motor system in controlling the amplitude of movement. J. Exp. Psychol. **47**(6), 381–391 (1954). https://doi.org/10.1037/h0055392

14. Fitts, P.M., Radford, B.K.: Information capacity of discrete motor responses under different cognitive sets. J. Exp. Psychol. **71**(4), 475–482 (1966). https://doi.org/10.1037/h0022970

15. Gillan, D.J., Bias, R.G.: Fitting motivation to Fitts' law: effect of a penalty contingency on controlled movement. In: Proceedings of the Human Factors and Ergonomics Society Annual Meeting, vol. 62, no. 1, pp. 265–269 (2018). https://doi.org/10.1177/1541931218621061

16. Gori, J., Rioul, O., Guiard, Y.: Speed-accuracy tradeoff: a formal information-theoretic transmission scheme (Fitts). ACM Trans. Comput.-Hum. Interact. **25**(5), 27:1–27:33 (2018). https://doi.org/10.1145/3231595. http://doi.acm.org/10.1145/3231595

17. Gori, J., Rioul, O., Guiard, Y., Beaudouin-Lafon, M.: The perils of confounding factors: how Fitts' law experiments can lead to false conclusions. In: Proceedings of the 2018 CHI Conference on Human Factors in Computing Systems, CHI 2018. Association for Computing Machinery, New York (2018). https://doi.org/10.1145/3173574.3173770

18. Hertzum, M., Hornbæk, K.: How age affects pointing with mouse and touchpad: a comparison of young, adult, and elderly users. Int. J. Hum.-Comput. Interact. **26**(7), 703–734 (2010). https://doi.org/10.1080/10447318.2010.487198

19. Hoffmann, E.R.: Movement time of right- and left-handers using their preferred and non-preferred hands. Int. J. Ind. Ergon. **19**(1), 49–57 (1997). https://doi.org/10.1016/0169-8141(95)00092-5

20. Hoffmann, E.R., Sheikh, I.H.: Effect of varying target height in a Fitts' movement task. Ergonomics **37**(6), 1071–1088 (1994). https://doi.org/10.1080/00140139408963719

21. Horton, J.J., Rand, D.G., Zeckhauser, R.J.: The online laboratory: conducting experiments in a real labor market. Exp. Econo. **14**(3), 399–425 (2011). https://doi.org/10.1007/s10683-011-9273-9

22. Huang, J., Tian, F., Fan, X., Zhang, X.L., Zhai, S.: Understanding the uncertainty in 1D unidirectional moving target selection. In: Proceedings of the 2018 CHI Conference on Human Factors in Computing Systems, CHI 2018. Association for Computing Machinery, New York (2018). https://doi.org/10.1145/3173574.3173811

23. ISO: ISO 9241-9. International standard: ergonomic requirements for office work with visual display terminals (VDTS)-part 9: requirements for non-keyboard input devices, international organization for standardization (2000)

24. Kass, R.E., Raftery, A.E.: Bayes factors. J. Am. Stat. Assoc. **90**(430), 773–795 (1995). https://doi.org/10.1080/01621459.1995.10476572

25. Komarov, S., Reinecke, K., Gajos, K.Z.: Crowdsourcing performance evaluations of user interfaces. In: Proceedings of the SIGCHI Conference on Human Factors in Computing Systems, CHI 2013, pp. 207–216. ACM, New York (2013). https://doi.org/10.1145/2470654.2470684. http://doi.acm.org/10.1145/2470654.2470684

26. MacKenzie, I.S.: Fitts' law as a research and design tool in human-computer interaction. Hum.-Comput. Interact. **7**(1), 91–139 (1992). https://doi.org/10.1207/s15327051hci0701_3

27. MacKenzie, I.S., Buxton, W.: Extending Fitts' law to two-dimensional tasks. In: Proceedings of the SIGCHI Conference on Human Factors in Computing Systems, CHI 1992, pp. 219–226. Association for Computing Machinery, New York (1992). https://doi.org/10.1145/142750.142794

28. MacKenzie, I.S., Isokoski, P.: Fitts' throughput and the speed-accuracy tradeoff. In: Proceedings of the SIGCHI Conference on Human Factors in Computing Systems, CHI 2008, pp. 1633–1636. ACM, New York (2008). https://doi.org/10.1145/1357054.1357308

29. MacKenzie, I.S., Sellen, A., Buxton, W.A.S.: A comparison of input devices in element pointing and dragging tasks. In: Proceedings of the SIGCHI Conference on Human Factors in Computing Systems, CHI 1991, pp. 161–166. Association for Computing Machinery, New York (1991). https://doi.org/10.1145/108844.108868

30. Moss, A.: Demographics of people on amazon mechanical turk (2020). https://www.cloudresearch.com/resources/blog/who-uses-amazon-mturk-2020-demographics/. Accessed 4 Apr 2021

31. Olafsdottir, H.B., Guiard, Y., Rioul, O., Perrault, S.T.: A new test of throughput invariance in Fitts' law: role of the intercept and of Jensen's inequality. In: Proceedings of the 26th Annual BCS Interaction Specialist Group Conference on People and Computers, pp. 119–126 (2012)

32. Ren, X., Zhou, X.: An investigation of the usability of the stylus pen for various age groups on personal digital assistants. Behav. Inf. Technol. **30**(6), 709–726 (2011). https://doi.org/10.1080/01449290903205437

33. Schwab, M., Hao, S., Vitek, O., Tompkin, J., Huang, J., Borkin, M.A.: Evaluating pan and zoom timelines and sliders. In: Proceedings of the 2019 CHI Conference on Human Factors in Computing Systems, CHI 2019, pp. 1–12. Association for Computing Machinery, New York (2019). https://doi.org/10.1145/3290605.3300786

34. Shimizu, N., Nakagawa, M.: Crowdsourcing: current status and potential: 2. current trends and issues in microtask-based crowdsourcing. IPSJ Mag. **56**(9), 886–890 (2015)

35. Soukoreff, R.W., MacKenzie, I.S.: Towards a standard for pointing device evaluation, perspectives on 27 years of Fitts' law research in HCI. Int. J. Hum. Comput. Stud. **61**(6), 751–789 (2004). https://doi.org/10.1016/j.ijhcs.2004.09.001

36. Wobbrock, J.O., Findlater, L., Gergle, D., Higgins, J.J.: The aligned rank transform for nonparametric factorial analyses using only anova procedures. In: Proceedings of the SIGCHI Conference on Human Factors in Computing Systems, CHI 2011, pp. 143–146. ACM, New York (2011). https://doi.org/10.1145/1978942.1978963. http://doi.acm.org/10.1145/1978942.1978963

37. Wright, C.E., Lee, F.: Issues related to HCI application of Fitts's law. Hum.-Comput. Interact. **28**(6), 548–578 (2013). https://doi.org/10.1080/07370024.2013.803873

38. Yamanaka, S.: Effect of gaps with penal distractors imposing time penalty in touch-pointing tasks. In: Proceedings of the 20th International Conference on Human-Computer Interaction with Mobile Devices and Services, MobileHCI 2018. ACM, New York (2018). https://doi.org/10.1145/3229434.3229435

39. Yamanaka, S.: Risk effects of surrounding distractors imposing time penalty in touch-pointing tasks. In: Proceedings of the 2018 ACM International Conference on Interactive Surfaces and Spaces, ISS 2018, pp. 129–135. ACM, New York (2018). https://doi.org/10.1145/3279778.3279781. http://doi.acm.org/10.1145/3279778.3279781

40. Yamanaka, S.: Evaluating temporal delays and spatial gaps in overshoot-avoiding mouse-pointing operations. In: Proceedings of Graphics Interface 2020, GI 2020, pp. 440–451 (2020). https://doi.org/10.20380/GI2020.44

41. Yamanaka, S., Shimono, H., Miyashita, H.: Towards more practical spacing for smartphone touch GUI objects accompanied by distractors. In: Proceedings of the 2019 ACM International Conference on Interactive Surfaces and Spaces, ISS 2019, pp. 157–169. Association for Computing Machinery, New York (2019). https://doi.org/10.1145/3343055.3359698

42. Yamanaka, S., Usuba, H.: Rethinking the dual gaussian distribution model for predicting touch accuracy in on-screen-start pointing tasks. Proc. ACM Hum.-Comput. Interact. **4**(ISS) (2020). https://doi.org/10.1145/3427333

43. Zhai, S.: Characterizing computer input with Fitts' law parameters - the information and non-information aspects of pointing. Int. J. Hum.-Comput. Stud. **61**(6), 791–809 (2004). https://doi.org/10.1016/j.ijhcs.2004.09.006. Fitts' law 50 years later: applications and contributions from human-computer interaction

44. Zhai, S., Kong, J., Ren, X.: Speed-accuracy tradeoff in Fitts' law tasks: on the equivalency of actual and nominal pointing precision. Int. J. Hum. Comput. Stud. **61**(6), 823–856 (2004). https://doi.org/10.1016/j.ijhcs.2004.09.007

# Towards Multi-device Digital Self-control Tools

Alberto Monge Roffarello[✉] and Luigi De Russis

Politecnico di Torino, Corso Duca degli Abruzzi 24, 10129 Torino, Italy
{alberto.monge,luigi.derussis}@polito.it

**Abstract.** Users can nowadays take advantage of Digital-Self Control Tools (DSCT) to self-regulate their usage of applications and websites by means of interventions like timers and lockout mechanisms. However, DSCTs mainly focus on the interaction between users and a single device at a time, while people typically use more than one device, and in a concurrent way. This motivates the need of exploring tools that can adapt to multi-device settings. We present *FeelHabits*, a DSCT that allows users to set up, through a novel approach, multi-device intentions, i.e., contextual time and launch limits for the simultaneous and/or alternating use of the PC and the smartphone. Stemming from the defined intentions, *FeelHabits* employs different levels of severity to warn the user about a reached limit on the currently used device. A preliminary study on 7 participants suggests that *FeelHabits* might be effective for reducing some multi-device behaviors, and opens the way for further research.

**Keywords:** Digital wellbeing · Multi device · Technology overuse

## 1 Introduction

Nowadays, users interact with a plethora of "smart" devices every day, ranging from personal computers to smartwatches. In this context, a large number of people feel conflicted about the amount of time they spend with digital technologies [17], and researchers now agree that overusing digital devices, e.g., smartphones [7], can lead to negative outcomes, including stress [20] and mental health problems [14]. In response, tech industries and researchers are designing and creating mobile apps and browser extensions for achieving what Google calls "digital wellbeing [4]." Users can take advantage of such Digital-Self Control Tools (DSCTs) to self-regulate their technology-related behaviors. The majority of DSCTs, either commercial or developed as a research artifact, provide users with self-tracking statistics and interventions like access blockers, timers, and launches limits [18], and they mainly targets single devices at a time, e.g., smartphones [21]. As called for by recent work [16,22], however, this single-device conceptualization may fail in capturing all the nuances of people's digital wellbeing, and more effort should be put into designing multi-device and cross-device interactions to enhance digital wellbeing.

© IFIP International Federation for Information Processing 2021
Published by Springer Nature Switzerland AG 2021
C. Ardito et al. (Eds.): INTERACT 2021, LNCS 12935, pp. 122–131, 2021.
https://doi.org/10.1007/978-3-030-85610-6_8

In this paper, we present *FeelHabits*, a DSCT that allows users to set up novel interventions that can adapt to different devices in different contextual situations. Such interventions, in particular, are specified by means of user's *intentions*. In the Digital Behavior Change Intervention (DBCI) research area, intentions are defined as concrete if-then behavioral-related goals that are linked to a specific contexts. Recent work [23] describes intentions as one of the most promising strategy for assisting users in changing their behavior through technological support. Such a strategy, in particular, can bridge the intention-behavior gap [25]: through repetition, relevant implementation intentions can become impulses, moving from deliberative processes into automatic processes [9]. In our work, we define an intention as a temporal and/or launch limit for the simultaneous and/or alternate usage of different devices that should be respected in a given contextual situation.

In an initial implementation of *FeelHabits*, composed of a mobile app and a Google Chrome extension, a user can define these intentions by targeting her PC and her smartphone (Fig. 1(a)). Intentions can be defined for the overall multi-device usage of the user (*device-level* intentions), or they can be restricted to the usage of specific services available both on the PC and on the smartphone (*app-level* intentions), e.g., a social network that can be accessed through the browser and a dedicated mobile app. Furthermore, intentions can be linked to specific temporal contexts, e.g., the time of the day. *FeelHabits* then monitors the multi-device usage of the user, and it can use different level of severity when intentions are not respected, from simple notifications alerting the user of a reached limit on a given device (Fig. 1(b)) to app-blockers (Fig. 1(c)).

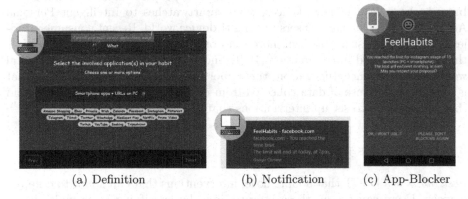

(a) Definition              (b) Notification          (c) App-Blocker

**Fig. 1.** *FeelHabits* is a multi-device DSCT targeting PCs and smartphones. Through a dedicated Google Chrome extension (a), the user can define an *intention*, i.e., a temporal and/or launch limit, for her different devices. When intentions are not respected, *FeelHabits* can send notifications on the device that is currently in use (b), or it can block the access to specific websites or apps (c).

## 2    Related Work

A growing amount of public [8] and research [15] discussion demonstrates that users may experience negative feelings and severe breakdowns of self-regulation due to an excessive use of technology. Recent topics like digital wellbeing [21] and intentional non-use of technology [24] fostered the development of DSCTs both in the academia and as off-the-shelf products [18]. Kovacs et al. [13], for instance, developed HabitLab, a Google Chrome extension that aims to help people achieve their goals online, e.g., waste less time on Facebook. In the smart-phone context, Hiniker et al. [10] proposed MyTime, an app to support people in achieving goals related to smartphone non-use. More complex interventions have been investigated through Lock n' LoL [11] and NUGU [12], two mobile apps leveraging social support to help students focusing on their group activities. Recently, even Google and Apple announced their commitment in designing tech-nology truly helpful for everyone, with the introduction in their mobile operating systems of tools for monitoring, understanding, and limiting technology use [4,5]. Our work stems from the recent need of "designing for self-control," and aims at investigating how to effectively design a DSCT for multi-device scenarios.

Recent reviews on DSCTs [18,21], indeed, highlight that the majority of tools for digital self-control, either commercial or developed as a research artifact, are designed to target single devices at a time, only, e.g., through a mobile app for smartphones [21] *or* a web browser extension for PCs [18]. Contextually, existing literature that can be related to the digital wellbeing context considers (nearly always) one technological source at a time [16], be it a social network [19] or a single device like a smartphone [17]. Such a single-source conceptualization is clearly not sufficient to capture all the nuances of people's digital wellbeing [16]. Indeed, the spread of new devices, from smartwatches to Intelligent Personal Assistants, is now engaging users in a multi-device world. Recent consumer stud-ies reveal that most people own more than one device [2], with multiple devices that are often used in conjunction [1]. To move towards a "multi-device digital wellbeing [22]" conceptualization, this paper presents *FeelHabits*, a DSCT that is able to make sense of data collected from different technological sources, and that allows users to set up interventions that can adapt to them.

## 3    FeelHabits

*FeelHabits* is a DSCT that adopts novel interventions that can adapt to different devices. Users can set up these interventions by specifying their multi-device *intentions*, i.e., contextual temporal and/or launch limits for the simultaneous and/or alternate usage of the user's devices that define how much time the user would like to spend on her devices in different contexts.

We implemented a first prototype of *FeelHabits* by targeting computers and smartphones, only. As shown in Fig. 2, the system is composed of three main components, i.e., a Google Chrome extension (a), an Android app (b), and a Node.js[1] server hosted on Firebase[2] (c).

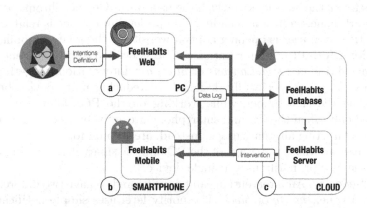

**Fig. 2.** The architecture of the *FeelHabits* prototype.

Both the smartphone and the PC silently collect usage information like used apps and visited web sites, and update the *FeelHabits* server in real time (*Data Log*). The server analyzes the usage data, and, stemming from the defined *intentions*, it selectively triggers adaptable *interventions* on the user's devices. Intentions can be specified through the dedicated Google Chrome extension (Fig. 1(a)). They can be of two different types:

**Device-Level Intention.** Device-Level intentions refer to the overall multi-device usage of the PC and the smartphone, independently of the visited websites or used mobile apps.

**App-Level Intention.** App-level intentions refer to a specific service that can be easily accessed both on the PC and on the smartphone. Examples include social networks, e.g., Facebook and Instagram, that are available both as a website on the PC browser and as a dedicated mobile app on the smartphone. The full list of services presented to the user have been extracted by analyzing the most visited websites and used apps in Italy, i.e., the country in which we conducted the preliminary evaluation of *FeelHabits* (see Sect. 4).

Intentions can be associated to two different temporal contexts, i.e., time of the day (*morning, afternoon, evening*, or *night*) and period (*working days* or *holidays*). Furthermore, an intention is associated to an *intervention*, composed of the following characteristics:

**Intervention Target.** An intervention can be defined as a *temporal* or a *launch* limit. For device-level intentions, a temporal limit aggregates the overall time

---

[1] https://nodejs.org/en/, last visited on October 29, 2020.
[2] https://firebase.google.com/, last visited on October 29, 2020.

spent on Google Chrome and on the smartphone, respectively, while for app-level intentions such a limit involves the selected service, only, independently of the adopted device. Similarly, a launch limit in device-level intentions counts for all the occasions in which the user opens Google Chrome or unlocks her smartphone, while a launch limit in app-level intentions is related to how many times the user is opening a given website or the related mobile app.

**Interaction Modality.** A intervention can be associated to two different interaction modalities, i.e., *simultaneous* or *alternate*. Interventions targeting simultaneous usage are specifically designed for reducing multi-device behaviors like using the smartphone while working on the PC. They are therefore enabled only when the PC and smartphone are actively used together. Interventions targeting alternate usage, instead, are account for situations in which a) the user alternate the usage of the PC and the smartphone during the day, or b) the user primarily uses a single device.

**Level of Severity.** An intervention can be configured to have two different levels of severity, i.e., *notify* or *block*. The notify level uses simple notifications to alert the user of a reached limit, either temporal or launch-based (see Fig. 1(b) for an example of a notification on the PC). When a limit is reached, in particular, a notification is sent to the device that is currently in use. The block level is more restrictive: when a limit is reached, *FeelHabits* blocks the usage of a device or a specific service (see Fig. 1(c) for an example of an app-level block on the smartphone).

## 4   Preliminary Evaluation

We conducted a user study to evaluate *FeelHabits* in a real-world setting. We preliminary investigated how participants defined their intentions, e.g., which type of intentions they preferred, and how they customized the associated interventions. Furthermore, we analyzed the effectiveness of the implemented interventions, by analyzing both quantitative data and qualitative feedback. We recruited 7 participants through convenience and snowball sampling, by sending private messages to our social circles. Participants who accepted to take part in the study (4 male and 3 female) were on average 26 years old ($SD = 4.55$). Four of them were M.S. students, while the remaining 3 were office workers. All the participants declared to regularly use at least an Android smartphone and a laptop or a desktop computer. Before starting the in-the-wild test, we asked them to use the Google Chrome web browser throughout the duration of the study. At the beginning of the study, we sent to the participants an initial questionnaire to collect their demographic data, as well as a consent form to participate in the research study. Then, we sent to them a file with the instructions to install the Android app and the Google Chrome extension, respectively. The file also contained a brief tutorial explaining how to define an intention with the Google Chrome extension. From that moment on, participants were free to use *FeelHabits* for 14 days, without any constraints or restrictions. During the study, we collected data in an anonymous form thanks to the *FeelHabits* database hosted on Firebase. We collected usage data related to participants' smartphone and web browser usage sessions, including the associated contextual information, i.e., time of the day and period. In addition, we kept track of the intentions defined by the participants. In this way, we were able to measure how many times the associated limits were reached, and how many times the interventions were respected or not. At the end of the study, we conducted a debriefing session with each participant to collect their qualitative feedback on their experience with *FeelHabits*. Due to the Covid-19 pandemic [3], interviews were conducted remotely via Zoom [6].

## 4.1 Results

**Intentions Overview.** During the study, participants defined a total of 28 intentions associated to different temporal contexts, with a preference towards morning and afternoon intentions during working days, and night intentions during holidays. Each participant, in particular, defined 4 intentions on average ($SD = 1.07$). Table 1 reports an overview of the defined intentions and the associated interventions. Results clearly highlight a preference towards app-level intentions: 26 intentions out of 28 (92.86%) were defined to target a specific service, while only 2 intentions were defined at device-level. The most common categories for the targeted services include social networks (e.g., Facebook and Instagram, 46%), communication (e.g., WhatsApp and Telegram, 22%) and video (e.g., YouTube and Amazon Prime Video, 18%). For what concerns the associated interventions, most of them were defined as a time limit (25, 89.29%), while only 3 participants defined a launch limit for specific services, e.g., Netflix and Facebook. Participants defined interventions to mitigate both their simultaneous (12, 42.86%) and alternate (16, 57.14%) interactions with their PCs and smartphones. Furthermore, they selected different level of severity for their interventions, by defining 14 notifications and 14 blockers, respectively.

**Table 1.** An overview of the 28 intentions, including the associated interventions, defined in the study.

| Intentions | Type | Device-Level | 2 |
|---|---|---|---|
| | | App-Level | 26 |
| Interventions | **Intervention Target** | Time | 25 |
| | | Launch | 3 |
| | **Interaction Modality** | Simultaneous | 12 |
| | | Alternate | 16 |
| | **Level of Severity** | Notify | 14 |
| | | Block | 14 |

**Intentions Effectiveness.** Table 2 is an overview of the effectiveness of the 28 intentions defined during the study. Overall, the intentions generated 125 notifications and 113 blocks, respectively. Participants respected their intention to stop using a given service or device 40 times after receiving a notification (32%). Intentions with a "notify" level of severity were instead not effective in 85 cases (68%). Blocks, instead, were respected 76 times out of 113 (67.26%), while they were ignored in the remaining 37 cases (32.74%). On average, we did not found an influence of the device on which notifications and blockers were delivered and their effectiveness.

By further analyzing the data collected during the study, we found several differences about the relationship between participants and their defined intentions. Some participants, in particular, defined limits that were almost always reached in the associated contexts. The intentions defined by P1, for instance, triggered an intervention, be it a notification or a block, in 75% of cases, while the intentions of P4 triggered an intervention in 80% of cases. Other participants, instead, defined less restrictive limits that were reached a few times, only. Differences also emerged with respect to the users' acceptance of their own intentions. This was particularly evident for intentions with a "block" level of severity. Also in this case, some participants tended to respect block interventions, while others ignored them most of the time. The intentions of P1, for instance, triggered an average of 7 blocks per day that were respected in 92% of cases. On the contrary, P4 skipped 19 out of the 20 blocks she experienced during the study.

**Table 2.** An overview of the effectiveness of the 28 defined intentions.

|               | Generated | Respected | Not respected |
|---------------|-----------|-----------|---------------|
| Notifications | 125       | 40        | 85            |
| Blocks        | 113       | 76        | 37            |

**Qualitative Feedback.** In the final debriefing session, all the participants shared positive opinions about *FeelHabits*, since it was able to capture the different aspects of their multi-device usage sessions (P4 and P6) and it assisted them in defining their own self-control goals (P3 and P7). *FeelHabits* was described as a particular effective solution for reducing app-related digital interactions. Such a feedback reflects the quantitative data collected during the study. P1, for instance, liked the possibility of defining interventions that reflected her typical usage of a given service on her different devices. To reduce her Netflix usage during working days, in particular, she defined an alternate time limit and a simultaneous launch limit, with 2 separate blockers. P1 stated that the first block was intended to avoid watching films and TV series during lunch, either with her laptop or her smartphone, while the second block was defined to mitigate her frequent behavior of interrupting her work on the PC with a video on the smartphone. Two other participants indicated that *FeelHabits* was particularly useful to control behaviors involving the usage of the smartphone *while* using the PC.

Besides the positive aspects, some participants highlighted the need of having some statistics about their usage of their different devices, e.g., to understand whether their define intentions have a positive effect on their own behaviors. Providing users with statistics about their multi-device use would be also important to assist them in defining appropriate intentions. In line with previous work analyzing "single-device" DSCTs [13], indeed, some users defined limits that were either too strict or too weak, therefore not reflecting their actual interaction with their personal devices.

## 5    Conclusions and Future Directions

This paper presented a first attempt to design a novel multi-device DSCT able to make sense of data coming from different technological sources and adapting interventions to different devices and services. Our *FeelHabits* prototype, in particular, allows users to set up their own intentions, i.e., temporal and/or launch limit for the simultaneous and/or alternate usage of the PC and the smartphone. Intentions can be defined at device or app level, and they can be linked to specific temporal contexts. *FeelHabits* monitors the multi-device usage of the user, and it adopts different levels of severity, from simple notifications to access blockers, to warn the user about a reached limit on the device that is currently in use.

Our work opens the way for future research exploring multi-device and cross-device interactions in the field of digital wellbeing [16]. The preliminary in-the-wild study, in particular, suggests that *FeelHabits* could be effective for reducing some multi-device behaviors, but also highlights several opportunities that need to be explored and further studied. First of all, our evaluation involved a small sample of 7 participants of roughly the same age, and it lasted 2 weeks, only. Longer studies with larger and diverse populations might be needed. That being said, our work only scraped the surface of how interventions in DSCTs could adapt to multi-device scenarios. Our study, for instance, showed that blockers were respected more often than simple notifications, and that participants liked the possibility of adapting interventions to specific services, e.g., social networks, independently of the used device. We argue that such an adaptability of interventions is one of the most important and interesting challenges to be explored in the field of multi-device digital wellbeing. Future works could explore how to adapt the level of severity of an intervention to the target device, either automatically or through user-defined preferences. Finally, we only considered 2 devices in our prototype: the spread of new devices further increases the possibility of investigating multi-device DSCTs from different perspectives [22].

**Acknowledgment.** The authors wish to thank all the anonymous participants of our study, and the MSc student Elia Bravo for developing the FeelHabits prototype.

# References

1. Latest mobile trends show how people use their devices (2016). https://www.thinkwithgoogle.com/advertising-channels/mobile-marketing/device-use-marketer-tips/. Accessed 17 Jul 2020
2. Connected consumer survey 2017 (2017). https://www.thinkwithgoogle.com/intl/en-145/perspectives/local-articles/connected-consumer-survey-2017/. Accessed 17 Jul 2020
3. Coronavirus disease (Covid-19) pandemic (2020). https://www.who.int/emergencies/diseases/novel-coronavirus-2019. Accessed 17 Jul 2020
4. Our commitment to digital wellbeing (2020). https://wellbeing.google/. Accessed 17 Jul 2020
5. Use screen time on your iphone, ipad, or ipod touch (2020). https://support.apple.com/en-us/HT208982. Accessed 17 Jul 2020
6. Zoom meetings & chat (2020). https://zoom.us/. Accessed 17 Jul 2020
7. Ames, M.G.: Managing mobile multitasking: the culture of iphones on stanford campus. In: Proceedings of the 2013 Conference on Computer Supported Cooperative Work, CSCW 2013, pp. 1487–1498. Association for Computing Machinery, NewYork, NY, USA (2013). https://doi.org/10.1145/2441776.2441945
8. Cellan-Jones, R.: Confessions of a smartphone addict (2018). https://www.bbc.com/news/technology-44972913. Accessed 17 Jul 2020
9. Einstein, G., Mcdaniel, M.: Prospective memory: multiple retrieval processes. Curr. Direct. Psychol. Sci. **14**, 286–290 (2005). https://doi.org/10.1111/j.0963-7214.2005.00382.x
10. Hiniker, A., Hong, S.R., Kohno, T., Kientz, J.A.: Mytime: designing and evaluating an intervention for smartphone non-use. In: Proceedings of the 2016 CHI Conference on Human Factors in Computing Systems, CHI 2016, pp. 4746–4757. ACM, New York (2016). https://doi.org/10.1145/2858036.2858403
11. Ko, M., Choi, S., Yatani, K., Lee, U.: Lock n' lol: group-based limiting assistance app to mitigate smartphone distractions in group activities. In: Proceedings of the 2016 CHI Conference on Human Factors in Computing Systems,CHI 2016, pp. 998–1010. ACM, New York (2016). https://doi.org/10.1145/2858036.2858568
12. Ko, M., et al.: Nugu: a group-based intervention app for improving self-regulation of limiting smartphone use. In: Proceedings of the 18th ACM Conference on Computer Supported Cooperative Work & Social Computing, CSCW 2015, pp. 1235–1245. ACM, New York (2015). https://doi.org/10.1145/2675133.2675244
13. Kovacs, G., Wu, Z., Bernstein, M.S.: Rotating online behavior change interventions increases effectiveness but also increases attrition. In: Proceedings of ACM Human-Computer Interaction 2(CSCW), November 2018. https://doi.org/10.1145/3274364
14. Lanaj, K., Johnson, R.E., Barnes, C.M.: Beginning the workday yet already depleted? Consequences of late-night smartphone use and sleep. Organ. Behav. Hum. Decis. Process. **124**(1), 11–23 (2014). https://doi.org/10.1016/j.obhdp.2014.01.001
15. Lanette, S., Chua, P.K., Hayes, G., Mazmanian, M.: How much is 'too much'?: The role of a smartphone addiction narrative in individuals' experience of use. In: Proceedings of the ACM on Human-Computer Interaction 2(CSCW), pp. 101:1–101:22, November 2018. https://doi.org/10.1145/3274370
16. Lascau, L., Wong, P.N.Y., Brumby, D.P., Cox, A.L.: Why are cross-device interactions important when it comes to digital wellbeing? (2019)

17. Lee, U., et al.: Hooked on smartphones: an exploratory study on smartphone overuse among college students. In: Proceedings of the 32Nd Annual ACM Conference on Human Factors in Computing Systems, CHI 2014, pp. 2327–2336. ACM, New York (2014). https://doi.org/10.1145/2556288.2557366

18. Lyngs, U., et al.: Self-control in cyberspace: applying dual systems theory to a review of digital self-control tools. In: Proceedings of the 2019 CHI Conference on Human Factors in Computing Systems, CHI 2019, pp. 131:1–131:18. ACM, New York (2019). https://doi.org/10.1145/3290605.3300361

19. Marino, C., Gini, G., Vieno, A., Spada, M.M.: A comprehensive meta-analysis on problematic facebook use. Comput. Hum. Behav. **83**, 262 – 277 (2018). https://doi.org/10.1016/j.chb.2018.02.009. http://www.sciencedirect.com/science/article/pii/S0747563218300670

20. Mark, G., Wang, Y., Niiya, M.: Stress and multitasking in everyday college life: an empirical study of online activity. In: Proceedings of the SIGCHI Conference on Human Factors in Computing Systems, CHI 2014, pp. 41–50. ACM, New York (2014). https://doi.org/10.1145/2556288.2557361

21. Monge Roffarello, A., De Russis, L.: The race towards digital wellbeing: issues and opportunities. In: Proceedings of the 2019 CHI Conference on Human Factors in Computing Systems, CHI 2019, pp. 386:1–386:14. ACM, New York (2019). https://doi.org/10.1145/3290605.3300616

22. Monge Roarello, A., De Russis, L.: Coping with digital wellbeing in a multi-device world. In: Proceedings of the 2021 CHI Conference on Human Factors in Computing Systems. Association for Computing Machinery, New York (2021). https://doi.org/10.1145/3411764.3445076

23. Pinder, C., Vermeulen, J., Cowan, B.R., Beale, R.: Digital behaviour change interventions to break and form habits. ACM Trans. Comput. Hum. Interact. **25**(3) (2018). https://doi.org/10.1145/3196830

24. Satchell, C., Dourish, P.: Beyond the user: use and non-use in HCI. In: Proceedings of the 21st Annual Conference of the Australian Computer-Human Interaction Special Interest Group: Design: Open 24/7, OZCHI 2009, pp. 9–16. ACM, New York (2009). https://doi.org/10.1145/1738826.1738829

25. Webb, T., Sheeran, P.: Does changing behavioral intentions engender behavior change? A meta-analysis of the experimental evidence. Psychol. Bull. **132**, 249–268 (2006). https://doi.org/10.1037/0033-2909.132.2.249

# Typing on Midair Virtual Keyboards: Exploring Visual Designs and Interaction Styles

Jiban Adhikary[✉] and Keith Vertanen

Michigan Technological University, Houghton, Michigan, USA
{jiban,vertanen}@mtu.edu

**Abstract.** We investigate typing on a QWERTY keyboard rendered in virtual reality. Our system tracks users' hands in the virtual environment via a Leap Motion mounted on the front of a head mounted display. This allows typing on an auto-correcting midair keyboard without the need for auxiliary input devices such as gloves or handheld controllers. It supports input via the index fingers of one or both hands. We compare two keyboard designs: a normal QWERTY layout and a split layout. We found users typed at around 16 words-per-minute using one or both index fingers on the normal layout, and about 15 words-per-minute using both index fingers on the split layout. Users had a corrected error rate below 2% in all cases. To explore midair typing with limited or no visual feedback, we had users type on an invisible keyboard. Users typed on this keyboard at 11 words-per-minute at an error rate of 3.3% despite the keyboard providing almost no visual feedback.

**Keywords:** Text entry · Virtual reality · Head mounted display (HMD)

## 1   Introduction

Virtual reality (VR) and augmented reality (AR) head-mounted displays (HMDs) offer the promise of rich, three-dimensional, interactive user experiences. As technology advances, HMDs will become more capable, portable, and fashionable. As this starts to occur, we believe users will shift to VR and AR devices to perform many of the activities currently supported by smartphones or other portable touchscreen devices. One of the core interaction primitives on touchscreen devices is text input. Similar to the situation with mobile devices, users will likely not want to carry an additional input device to support text input (e.g. a wireless keyboard). Further, using auxiliary devices can be troublesome in VR and AR scenarios where a user may be standing or moving around. Ideally, input would be possible relying solely on the HMD. While HMDs typically have a microphone, speech input can present social or privacy concerns. Moreover, correcting speech recognition errors can be time consuming, especially for text

---

**Electronic supplementary material** The online version of this chapter (https://doi.org/10.1007/978-3-030-85610-6_9) contains supplementary material, which is available to authorized users.

C. Ardito et al. (Eds.): INTERACT 2021, LNCS 12935, pp. 132–151, 2021.
https://doi.org/10.1007/978-3-030-85610-6_9

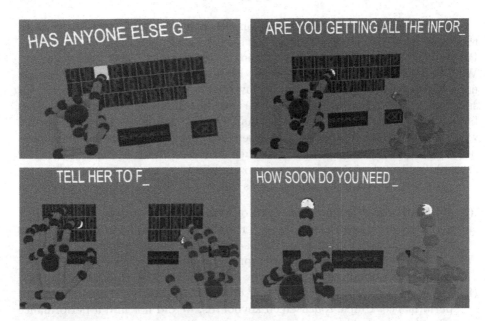

**Fig. 1.** Entering text using the normal keyboard with one hand (top left), the normal keyboard with two hands (top right), the split keyboard with two hands (bottom left), and the invisible keyboard (bottom right).

containing uncommon words [1]. HMDs increasingly feature a front-facing camera that can track the location and pose of a user's hands. Our work explores text input in VR using such hand tracking.

For new or infrequent users of text input in VR or AR, we think a familiar input method leveraging users' experience with auto-correcting touchscreen keyboards may be preferable. Thus we explore text entry by having users tap on a midair virtual keyboard. This keyboard is located directly in front of the user. This position allows an ergonomic front-facing head position, visual guidance of hands to the keys, and positions a user's hands in the tracker's field of view. Our work also provides a walk-up-and-use interface to enter text. While much of the previous work in midair text entry needs training of an hour or more [9,17–19,31,33], our system requires almost no training.

Our focus is on the visual design of the keyboard and the impact of typing with one or both hands. Our system tracks a user's hands via a Leap Motion depth camera mounted on a VR HMD. In the virtual environment, users see a rendering of their hands as well as a virtual keyboard (Fig. 1). In a user study, we compare user performance and preference for typing with the index finger of one or both hands. We also compare typing with both hands on a normal layout versus a split layout. To our knowledge, we are the first to study bimanual typing on a midair auto-correcting virtual keyboard. Despite users seeing only a virtual version of their hands, and without tactile feedback or word predictions, users typed at 16 words-per-minute (wpm) at an error rate below 1% on the normal layout. We found the normal layout was superior to the split layout.

After our main study, participants completed an exploratory session in which they first defined a midair keyboard in a size and location of their own choosing. Participants then typed sentences in midair with no visual keyboard reference. We found typing on an invisible midair keyboard can be surprisingly effective; users entered 71% of sentences on an invisible keyboard with zero errors. This suggests midair keyboard input may be possible even when visual feedback is limited, for example HMDs with a small display area for users with normal vision, or a normal display area for users who are low vision. In some cases, people may also need to input text when visual feedback is non-existent, for example audio-only AR or for users who are blind.

Our contributions in this work are as follows:

(i) With little practice, novices typed on a midair keyboard with autocorrect and achieved acceptable walk-up performance; 16 words-per-minute at less than 1% character error rate. This is likely sufficient for applications requiring only modest amounts of text input. Our approach does not require user training or specialized input devices (as required by much existing work).

(ii) We provide the first comparison of one- and two-handed midair keyboard performance. Unlike touchscreen keyboards, we did not find a performance advantage to typing with two fingers in a walk-up-and-use scenario.

## 2   Related Work

In this section, we review existing work related to text entry in virtual reality. For a detailed overview of the techniques by classification, strengths, limitations, and performance, see Dube and Arif [8].

**AR Keyboards.** ARKB [16] exploited depth information obtained via a stereo camera attached to an HMD. A user's fingers were marked with colored markers. The stereo camera tracked the markers and detected collision with an augmented reality QWERTY keyboard. No user trial results were reported. PalmType [28] allowed text input for smartglasses using a QWERTY keyboard interface on a user's palm. In a user study, users wrote at 8 wpm on an optimized PalmType QWERTY keyboard with Vicon tracking system. Using a wrist-worn infrared sensor and a touchpad, users wrote at 5 wpm.

Our keyboard is similar to VISAR [9], an AR midair auto-correcting keyboard. VISAR uses the same VelociTap [26] decoder for auto-correction as we use here. VelociTap takes a series of keyboard touch locations and outputs the most likely text. Using a Microsoft HoloLens HMD, VISAR tracked a user's hand location and employed a fixed spatial offset to approximate the location of a user's index finger. On a virtualized midair input surface users wrote at 6 wpm. With the help of word predictions and two hours of practice, the entry rate improved to 18 wpm. Compared to VISAR, our system tracks users' fingertips as opposed to users' hands. We add new knowledge regarding bimanual typing performance and compare a normal QWERTY layout versus a split layout. We also explore input in VR rather than AR.

HoldBoard [2] used a smartwatch to enter text on smartglasses. Users selected a character on the smartwatch's screen using a combination of thumb position and index finger tapping. The result was displayed on the smartglasses. Users entered text at 10 wpm after eight sessions. Yu et al. [32] also explored touch-based smartglass text input. Using a Google Glass HMD, users wrote at 9 wpm using one-dimensional touch input coupled with auto-correction.

**Finger Tracking Using Leap Motion.** ATK [30] allowed two-handed touch typing on a midair keyboard using a Leap Motion sensor to track a user's fingers. It provided visual feedback on a desktop display. The sensor was stationary and placed horizontally on a table under a user's hands. ATK inferred text based on 3D fingertip kinematics. After practice, users entered text at 29 wpm. ATK's reliance on ten-finger typing may make it difficult for non-touch-typists. Also ATK used a stationary tracker which could be challenging in standing or mobile use scenarios. While ATK is potentially a fast midair input method that enables 10 finger input, it differs from our work in that: 1) ATK displayed the keyboard on a monitor, 2) the Leap Motion was stationary, and 3) users did not interact with virtual hands in an immersive virtual environment.

Sridhar et al. [23] and Feit et al. [10] used a Leap Motion to track users' fingers. In both works, users entered text in midair by learning specific multi-finger gestures. In contrast to their approaches, we allowed input using just the index fingers. Our approach is intuitive, does not require learning any gestures, and users can easily transfer their experience typing on auto-correcting touchscreen keyboards.

Adhikary and Vertanen [1] investigated text input in VR using speech and a midair keyboard. They also used a Leap Motion sensor to track a user's fingers. A user could enter text with or without speech. When using speech input, a midair keyboard provided a fallback mechanism for correcting speech recognition errors. The midair keyboard supported word prediction. In a study with 18 participants, users entered phrases where half of the phrases contained an uncommon word. Users wrote at 28 wpm with speech versus 11 wpm without speech.

**Auxiliary Input Devices.** Various work has investigated VR input using auxiliary devices. Yu et al. [31] investigated gesture typing using an HMD and a gamepad controller. Head rotation was used to control a pointer on a virtual keyboard. The fastest entry rate was achieved using a word-gesture keyboard [34] at 25 wpm after an hour of practice. PizzaText [33] presented a circular keyboard layout in VR. Using the dual thumbsticks of a hand-held controller, novices wrote at 9 wpm while experts wrote at 16 wpm after two hours of practice.

McGill et al. [19] showed that injecting real-word video in VR significantly improved typing on a physical keyboard in VR. Walker et al. [27] presented a system that assists HMD users in typing on a visually occluded physical keyboard. With the help of auto-correction and visual feedback after each key press, users typed at 40 wpm.

Grubert et al. [12] showed that desktop and touchscreen keyboards can be used as text entry devices in VR. By simply rendering a user's fingers in VR, they showed users retain 60% of their typing speed on a desktop keyboard with no significant learning effects. In another study, Grubert et al. [11] studied hand representations in VR while typing using a standard physical keyboard. Users wrote at 34 wpm with no hand visualization, 36 wpm with fingertip visualization, and 39 wpm with video see-through of their hands.

Knierim et al. [14] also investigated hand visualization in VR while typing on a physical keyboard. They compared user performance on hand visualization, semi-transparent hands, and no hands. Results revealed that expert typists benefited from seeing their hands whereas novice users benefited from semi-transparent hands. To aid typing with a midair VR keyboard, Gupta et al. [13] investigated the utility of tactile feedback. They compared audio-visual only feedback with three different on-finger and on-wrist vibrotactile feedback. While the speed and accuracy across different feedback conditions were comparable, users preferred the tactile feedback conditions.

Markussen et al. [17] analyzed one-handed text input in midair using three selection-based techniques. The location of a user's index finger was sensed via a tracked glove. A large high-resolution displayed a keyboard and a dot representing a user's fingertip. Users typed the fastest at 13 wpm using a QWERTY keyboard after four hours of practice. Speicher et al. [22] investigated text entry techniques using an HMD, hand-held controllers, and visualization of hands sensed via a Leap Motion. Users wrote at 15 wpm with a low error rate of 1% by pointing using hand-held controllers. Using the hand visualization users wrote at 10 wpm with a much larger error rate of 7.6%. We used a similar hand visualization technique in our study. Vulture [18] allowed users to wear gloves and let users write on a word-gesture keyboard in midair. After five hours of practice, users wrote at 20 wpm.

**Bimanual Text Entry.** Bimanual text entry have been investigated for touchscreens [6,20,24,29] and game controllers [21]. Bi et al. [6] and Truong et al. [24] found bimanual gesture typing on touchscreens yielded better performance than unimanual input. Oulasvirta et al. [20] explored a bimanual split keyboard called KALQ. However, they did not compare unimanual and bimanual input. Using two hands, users typed at 37 wpm after one hour of practice. Sandnes et al. [21] showed bimanual game controller input on a QWERTY keyboard had an entry rate of 7 wpm.

Aschim et al. [4] studied one- and two-handed typing performance on a split touchscreen tablet keyboard. Similar to their finding, we found that a split keyboard does not provide better midair typing performance compared to a normal QWERTY layout. Alamdar et al. [3] proposed a new split keyboard layout for improving text entry rate by optimizing different split keyboard layouts and key dimensions. They reported between 7% to 18% improvement in the text entry rate over the other split keyboards. While the past work has investigated bimanual user interaction with touchscreen keyboards, in this paper we conduct the first study comparing unimanual and bimanual input on a midair virtual keyboard.

**Key Aspects of our Work.** Compared with past work, we focus on designing an input method that does not require user or system training, and does not require hand-held devices, gloves, or expensive tracking infrastructure. We also investigate reducing the visual occlusion of the keyboard by splitting the keyboard to allow better perception of the central visual area, and by eliminating almost all visual keyboard elements.

# 3   Interface Design

**Midair QWERTY Keyboard Layouts.** Given the widespread familiarity with QWERTY desktop and touchscreen keyboards, this layout was a clear choice for providing walk-up-and-use functionality. Our system renders a QWERTY keyboard 40 cm in front of the user (Fig. 1). Our system either displays a normal keyboard or a split keyboard. The normal keyboard is 20 cm × 7.5 cm. Each half of the split keyboard is 10 cm × 7.5 cm separated by 10 cm. We divided keys between the two halves based on Apple's iPad split keyboard. We chose the distance between the split halves keeping two things in mind: 1) the halves are positioned such that they are comfortably within the reach of a user's hands when extended, and 2) the user does not have to rotate their head when switching attention between the two halves. These design choices are further supported by Bachynskyi et al. [5] who suggested splitting the input space for the right hand and the left hand when making pointing gestures.

**Vertical Keyboard Orientation.** We placed the keyboard vertically in front of the user. This allowed users to see the keyboard and their input with minimal head movement. We opted not to use a horizontal keyboard orientation. As our depth sensor was mounted on the HMD, a horizontal keyboard would require a user to bend their neck which could be strenuous. Also in many use scenarios, e.g. messaging in a game, users may want to visually attend to things in front of them while also visually guiding their fingers over the keyboard.

**Hand Tracking and Midair Tapping.** We rendered a user's hands via the default visualization in the Leap Motion Orion Beta SDK v3.2. Possible alternatives to a Leap Motion sensor such as a Vicon tracking array may be more accurate, but are expensive, not very portable, and may require wearing special clothing or markers. We wanted to use a tracker that was inexpensive, walk-up-and-use, and portable. The Leap Motion meets all these requirements.

We opted to design our interface around the familiar interaction of tapping visual objects. This provides an easy-to-understand interaction primitive for users, namely making their (virtual) hands contact an object in three-dimensional space. Compared to an approach based on continuous gestures, we thought the tapping primitive would be more robust to tracker inaccuracies and also eliminate the need to train users on how to start or stop gestures.

We displayed the keyboard and rendered a user's hands in the virtual environment. A key was registered and a click sound was played whenever a user's index finger crossed the keyboard plane. Tapping a key caused the nearest key to light up for as long as the finger remained through the keyboard plane. The letter on the key nearest to a tap was added in the text area above the keyboard.

**Input Using Index Fingers.** While we can detect any finger crossing the keyboard plane, we limited our interface to detecting just index fingers. On touchscreens, users usually type with index fingers or thumbs. We choose to use index fingers as thumbs are less precise and unconventional based on prior midair interaction work. In piloting, we found the use of index fingers was indeed the most usable option. While users might switch fingers on a tablet, on a tablet users know when any finger accidentally contacts the touchscreen. In midair, there is no such tactile feedback. This could result in extra key presses due to the sympathetic motion of all of a hand's fingers. We found these extra key presses were surprising to users and difficult to avoid in the heat of text entry.

**Backspace and Space Key.** We expected users would occasionally trigger the wrong key due to inaccuracies in the hand tracking, the virtual hand visualization, or the virtual keyboard visualization. A backspace key in the lower right of the keyboard deleted previous taps from the pending taps. After typing all the letters of a word, users pressed a space key. The split keyboard had a space key on both sides allowing whatever hand was convenient to tap space. This is also consistent with Apple iPad's split keyboard design.

Pressing space sent the location of the pending taps for auto-correction (to be discussed shortly). The location of a tap was the two-dimensional coordinate on the keyboard plane where the tip of a user's index finger crossed the plane. After pressing space, the nearest key text for the pending taps was replaced with the best recognition result. Immediately after recognition, pressing the backspace key deleted the entire previous recognition result rather than backspacing individual characters. This allowed users to quickly delete recognition errors.

**Auto-Correction.** Given the tracking and visualization challenges, as well as the lack of tactile feedback, the only hope of reasonably fast midair keyboard typing is to allow noisy user input but provide a strong auto-correction capability. We used the VelociTap decoder [26] for auto-correction. VelociTap takes the noisy tap locations as input and searches for the most likely word based on a probabilistic keyboard model, a character language model, and a word language model. It assumes tap locations follow a two-dimensional Gaussian distribution centered at each key. Each key is assumed to have the same distribution. The distribution's variance in the horizontal and vertical axes are independently controlled by two decoder parameters. For each tap, VelociTap calculates the likelihood of each key under the keyboard model. This likelihood is added to the probabilities from the decoder's character and word language models. The contribution of each language model is controlled by two additional parameters. The decoder also has two penalties allowing taps to be deleted, and characters to be inserted without a tap. We optimized the decoder's configurable parameters using data collected by five people who did not participate in our user study.

The decoder used a 12-gram character and a 4-gram word language model with a 100 K vocabulary. We trained the language models on billions of words of data from web forums, social media, and movie subtitles. The character and word language models had 25 M and 13 M n-grams respectively. Recognition used any previous text written for the current sentence as context for the language models. In our study, we opted not to provide other features such as word predictions. We wanted to focus on the performance of unimanual versus bimanual interaction, and on the two keyboard designs.

# 4 User Study

The goal of our main study was to explore unimanual and bimanual midair keyboard input using hand gestures sensed via a commodity sensor. We also wanted to see if we could reduce occlusion in the central visual area by splitting the keyboard. The split keyboard separates keys into two halves, potentially making hand-tracking or recognition by the decoder more accurate.

## 4.1 Participants

We recruited 24 participants via convenience sampling. None had uncorrected vision or motor impairments. Participants were aged 18–44 (mean 26.5, sd 6.8), 17 were male and 7 were female. 22 were right-handed and 2 were left-handed. All were familiar with QWERTY keyboards. 15 participants had used VR previously.

## 4.2 Experimental Design

We designed a within-subject experimental study with three counterbalanced conditions: UNIMANUAL, BIMANUAL, and SPLIT. In UNIMANUAL, we instructed participants to tap with the index finger of their dominant hand. In BIMANUAL and SPLIT, we told participants to tap with the index finger of both hands. SPLIT used the split QWERTY layout while UNIMANUAL and BIMANUAL used the normal layout.

## 4.3 Procedure

Participants first filled out a questionnaire asking demographic questions, and about their experience with text entry and VR. We seated participants at a desk and helped them adjust the HTC Vive HMD. The HMD had a Leap Motion controller mounted on the front. We gave participants a few minutes to become familiar with the virtual environment. During this familiarization period, we had participants move their head, lift both hands, and move their virtual hands.

We first explained to participants how the decoder's auto-correction works. Participants then practiced in each condition. They practiced conditions in the same order they would experience them in the evaluation. In each condition, participants wrote four phrases during practice and 12 during evaluation. We used the mem1-5 phrases from the Enron mobile dataset [25]. Participants never saw the same phrase twice. They had as long as they wanted to memorize phrases. Requiring that participants memorize phrases slightly increases entry rate at the expense of slightly increasing error rate [15]. To motivate participants and help them monitor their performance, we showed the entry and error rate after each phrase. We asked participants to enter phrases "quickly and accurately".

After each condition, participants completed a questionnaire and rated their exertion using the Borg CR10 scale [7]. The study including an exploratory session (to be discussed in Sect. 5) took approximately an hour.

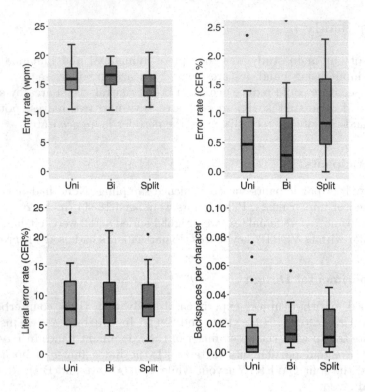

**Fig. 2.** Entry rate, character error rate (after recognition), literal error rate (before recognition), and backspaces per character in the study.

## 4.4    Results

Figure 2 shows our main results. Table 1 gives numeric results and statistical tests. In 10 phrases out of 864, participants left off two or more words at the end of a phrase. Likely this was because they forgot the phrase. We removed these instances from our analysis. This affected at most two phrases from any particular participant in any condition. Unless otherwise stated, we tested for significance using repeated measure analysis of variance (ANOVA). For pairwise comparison, we used paired t-tests and adjusted p-values using Bonferroni correction to guard against overtesting.

**Entry Rate.** We calculated *entry rate* in words-per-minute (wpm). We considered a word to be five characters including space. We measured the duration of entering a phrase as the time between user tapping the first key of the phrase and tapping a done button. The done button was located below and to the right of the keyboard. Participants' mean entry rate was 16.1 wpm (sd 2.9) in UNI-MANUAL, 16.4 wpm (sd 2.3) in BIMANUAL, and 14.7 wpm (sd 2.4) in SPLIT. An ANOVA test was significant (Table 1). Post-hoc tests showed SPLIT was slower than BIMANUAL. Other pairwise comparisons were not significant.

**Table 1.** Results are formatted as: mean ± SD [min, max]. The bottom section of the table shows the repeated measures ANOVA statistical test for each dependent variable. For significant main effects, we show pairwise post-hoc tests (Bonferroni corrected).

| Condition | Entry rate (wpm) | Error rate (CER %) | Literal error rate (CER %) | Backspaces per character |
|---|---|---|---|---|
| UNIMANUAL | 16.1 ± 2.9 [10.7, 21.9] | 0.7 ± 0.9 [0, 3.0] | 8.8 ± 5.4 [1.8, 24.1] | .014 ± .021 [.00, .08] |
| BIMANUAL | 16.4 ± 2.3 [10.5, 19.9] | 0.8 ± 1.2 [0, 4.4] | 9.8 ± 5.6 [3.3, 21.1] | .017 ± .013 [.00, .05] |
| SPLIT | 14.7 ± 2.4 [11.1, 20.5] | 1.4 ± 1.5 [0, 5.9] | 9.0 ± 4.4 [2.3, 20.5] | .017 ± .016 [.00, .05] |
| ANOVA | $F_{2,46} = 5.52, p < 0.01$ | $F_{2,46} = 2.31, p = 0.11$ | $F_{2,46} = 0.45, p = 0.64$ | $F_{2,46} = 0.36, p = 0.7$ |
| Effect size | $\eta_p^2 = 0.19$ | $\eta_p^2 = 0.09$ | $\eta_p^2 = 0.02$ | $\eta_p^2 = 0.015$ |
| Post-hoc | UNI ≈ BI, $p = 1.0$ UNI ≈ SPLIT, $p = 0.079$ SPLIT < BI, $p < 0.05$ | Not applicable | Not applicable | Not applicable |

**Error Rate.** We measured *error rate* using Character Error Rate (CER). CER is the number of character insertions, deletions, and substitutions needed to change the participant's final text into the reference text divided by the total characters in the reference. Error rate was similar and low across all conditions: UNIMANUAL 0.74% (sd 0.9%), BIMANUAL 0.79% (sd 1.2%), and SPLIT 1.41% (sd 1.5%). An ANOVA test was not significant (Table 1). All participants had a CER of 3% or less with many achieving near perfect accuracy (Fig. 3). Error rate was more variable in SPLIT. We conjecture this may be due to the sensor or the user being less accurate away from the keyboard center. We will investigate this further shortly.

We also measured the *literal CER* by comparing the text before auto-correction with the reference. Literal CER was much higher and similar across all conditions: UNIMANUAL 8.8% (sd 5.4%), BIMANUAL 9.8% (sd 5.6%), and SPLIT 9.0% (sd 4.4%). An ANOVA test was not significant (Table 1). The high literal CERs shows the importance of auto-correction for enabling accurate midair typing.

**Interkey Time.** Interkey time was calculated as the time difference between two consecutive taps of letter keys in all the entered words. The interkey time in BIMANUAL was 0.62 s (sd 0.10), in UNIMANUAL was 0.65 s (sd 0.13), and in SPLIT was 0.71 s (sd 0.13). An ANOVA test was significant. In post-hoc tests, we found similar to entry rate, only SPLIT was significantly slower than BIMANUAL (SPLIT < BIMANUAL, p < 0.05; UNIMANUAL ≈ BIMANUAL, p = 0.15; UNIMANUAL ≈ SPLIT, p = 0.10). Thus, locating and tapping keys in SPLIT did seem to contribute to that condition's slower entry rate.

**Correction and Tap Behavior.** Participants rarely used backspace. The backspaces per final output character were: UNIMANUAL 0.014, BIMANUAL 0.0169, and SPLIT 0.0166. An ANOVA test was not significant (Table 1). Recall right after recognition, tapping backspace deleted the recognized word. Word deletions per output word was low in all conditions: UNIMANUAL 0.024, BIMANUAL 0.032, and SPLIT 0.040. Taken together, it seems participants trusted auto-correction and, as evidenced by the low final CER, it delivered acceptable accuracy.

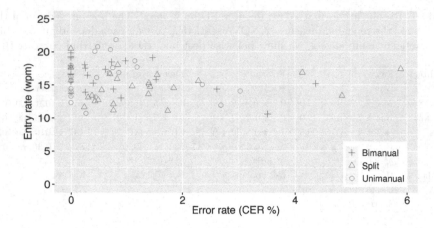

**Fig. 3.** Error rate and entry rate of all participants in each of the three conditions.

We were interested how often participants used their right index finger to tap a key on the left side of the keyboard and vice-versa. Figure 4 shows all taps in the two bimanual conditions. We can see in BIMANUAL, participants frequently typed letters on the left side of the keyboard with their right hand. This even happened in SPLIT, albeit to a lesser extent. In BIMANUAL, despite 53.9% of the reference phrase letters being on the left side of the keyboard, only 50.2% of participants' taps were with their left hand. This shows a tendency for participants (who were almost all right-handed) to favor their dominant hand.

## 4.5   Subjective Feedback

After each condition, participants rated statements on a 5-point Likert scale (1=strongly disagree and 5=strongly agree). The mean rating for "I entered text quickly" was: UNIMANUAL 4.17, BIMANUAL 4.08, and SPLIT 3.75. A Friedman's test was not significant ($\chi^2(2) = 3.96$, p $= 0.14$).

The mean rating for "I entered text accurately" was: UNIMANUAL 3.88, BIMANUAL 3.54, and SPLIT 3.17. A Friedman's test was significant ($\chi^2(2) = 10.27$, p $<$ 0.01). SPLIT was significantly lower than UNIMANUAL (difference $= 18.5$, critical $= 16.6$). Other pairwise differences were not significant (BI-SPLIT 11.5, BI-UNI 7.0). This shows that participants noticed the lower accuracy of SPLIT.

After each condition, we asked participants for a positive and negative aspect of that condition. Table 2 shows a list of such comments. At the end of our study, we asked participants to rank conditions in terms of quickness, accuracy, effort, and overall. The most preferred conditions were as follows:

- Quickness—BIMANUAL 10, UNIMANUAL 8, SPLIT 6
- Accuracy—BIMANUAL 9, UNIMANUAL 9, SPLIT 6
- Effort—UNIMANUAL 11, BIMANUAL 8, SPLIT 5
- Overall—BIMANUAL 10, UNIMANUAL 7, SPLIT 7

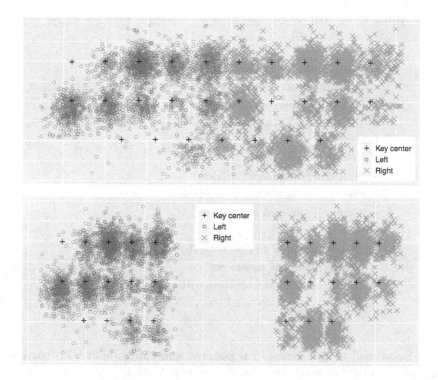

**Fig. 4.** Taps with the left and the right index finger in BIMANUAL (top) and SPLIT (bottom). Center of the keys are shown for better visualization.

Participants rated their exertion on the Borg CR10 scale [7] where 0=no exertion and 10=extremely strenuous. Exertion in all conditions corresponded to "moderate exercise": UNIMANUAL 3.38, BIMANUAL 3.08, and SPLIT 3.04. A Friedman's test was not significant ($\chi^2(2) = 3.27$, p = 0.20). While we had anticipated bimanual input would be more exerting, participants rated it similarly.

Taken in aggregate, the subjective feedback shows participants were varied in their perceptions and preferences about the different visual keyboard layouts (single versus split) and interaction styles (unimanual versus bimanual). This suggests midair virtual keyboards may want to support several layouts and support both one- and two-handed typing.

## 4.6  Further Analysis

Quantitative results (e.g. Fig. 3) show that six participants had an error rate of more than 3.0% in various conditions. This error rate and open comments from participants suggested that some participants experienced occasional hand tracking issues, especially in the SPLIT and BIMANUAL conditions. In our pilot testing with five people prior to the study, we did not encounter tracking issues with the keyboard layouts or interaction styles. In the study, however, four participants in

**Table 2.** Selected positive and negative comments from the study.

UNIMANUAL

---

+ "This felt faster and easier"

+ "I became more comfortable using this system"

- "It's tiring while using only one index finger"

- "At time the virtual fingers would move on their own"

BIMANUAL

---

+ "This felt more natural"

+ "I definitely felt more confident"

- "Seemed to flash when both hands overlapped"

- "Hands got in each other's way"

SPLIT

---

+ "It became easier to play with the keyboard"

+ "It was a learning experience"

- "Had trouble typing accurate with my left hand"

- "I felt my dominant hand was more accurate"

particular seemed to have issues. It is possible something about their particular hand motion or relative distance from the Leap Motion controller made their hands particularly difficult to track.

To investigate this further, we reviewed screen recordings of all the participants' sessions. We flagged 12 of the 854 phrases written in all conditions as having hand tracking issues. Among the flagged phrases, eight were in SPLIT, three were in BIMANUAL, and one was in UNIMANUAL. We removed the flagged phrases from the data and recomputed the entry and error rate in each condition. Removing these phrases and recomputing the entry rate and error rate yielded similar results. Entry rates after filtering were: 16.4 wpm UNIMANUAL, 16.6 wpm BIMANUAL, and 14.7 wpm SPLIT. Character error rates were: 0.7% UNIMANUAL, 0.7% BIMANUAL, and 1.2% SPLIT.

## 5    Design Exploration: Invisible Keyboard

After completing the main study, participants took part in a final design exploration. The focus of this part was to investigate input of small text passages where a visual keyboard may not be possible or desirable. For example, a user may be in an instrumented environment (e.g. car) and need to lookup a contact. To achieve this, the user could trace a rectangle in midair and then type the contact's name in that spatial area. Or in a VR game, a player may want to type a quick message to another player. The player could keep their eyes on their environment while specifying a keyboard off to the side, typing their message using their peripheral vision or motor memory.

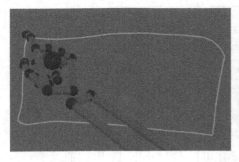

**Fig. 5.** User defining the keyboard geometry (left), and entering text on an invisible keyboard with almost no visual feedback (right).

In addition to the above rationale, this exploration had two additional objectives. First, given the freedom to define a keyboard in the virtual environment, we were interested what keyboard size participants would choose. Second, after the participants had been exposed to unimanual and bimanual midair input in the previous experiment, we wanted to see which method they would choose if they were allowed to use either interaction style.

### 5.1  Procedure

Users first defined the keyboard's size and location by tracing a rectangle with their index finger. A line was displayed as the rectangle was drawn (Fig. 5 left). Users made a thumbs up gesture once they completed their rectangle. The system then drew a keyboard within the rectangle. Users could accept the keyboard geometry or define it again. During input using the invisible keyboard, the only visual feedback was the space key, the backspace key, a key to advance to the next sentence, and the current text (Fig. 5 right).

In this exploratory session, there was no practice period and participants typed 12 phrases. We dropped four participants due to technical issues. We found in 14 phrases out of 240, participants forgot part or all of the target phrase. We removed these phrases from our analysis.

### 5.2  Results

**Entry rate and error rate.** On average, participants wrote at 10.6 wpm (sd 3.0, min 5.5, max 17.4) with an error rate of 3.3% (sd 3.0%, min 0.5%, max 13.1%). As might be expected, input was slower compared to the 15–16 wpm seen in the main study with a visible keyboard. Participants were able to achieve a completely correct input for 71% of their entries.

**Backspaces-Per-Character.** Compared to our main study, we observed a substantial increase in backspacing. The backspace to output character ratio was 0.05 (sd 0.04, min 0.0, max 0.13). The deleted word to final word ratio was 0.15 (sd 0.09, min 0.0, max 0.33).

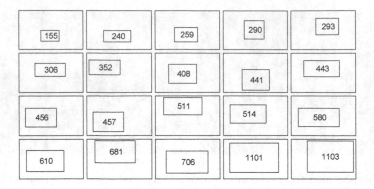

**Fig. 6.** The keyboard rectangles defined by participants in the invisible keyboard. The numeric values are the keyboard areas in square centimeters. Rectangles are arranged in a row-order matrix by ascending area.

**One Versus Two Hands.** We allowed participants to type with one or both hands. We observed 15 out of 20 participants used both hands while the remainder used one hand almost exclusively. For the given reference phrases, 52.1% letters were on the left side of the keyboard and 47.9% letters were on the right side. Participants tapped 36% of keys using their left hand versus 64% using their right hand. Thus it seems that with the invisible keyboard, participants tended to use their dominant hand even more than in the BIMANUAL condition of the main study.

**Keyboard Geometry.** Participants defined their keyboard geometry on average 2.0 times. 11 participants defined the keyboard in a single attempt. Participants defined keyboards of various sizes (Fig. 6). The mean area of the defined rectangles was 495 cm$^2$ (sd 254, min 155, max 1103). The area of the QWERTY normal keyboard rectangle used in the main study was 150 cm$^2$. Thus all participants defined a larger keyboard than the one in the main study. This suggests keyboard developers consider a bigger default geometry or allow users to define their own geometry.

**Subjective Feedback.** At the end of this session, participants rated statements on a 5-point Likert scale (1=strongly disagree and 5=strongly agree). Participants rated the statement "I entered text quickly" at 3.00, and "I entered text accurately" at 2.55. Participants rated the statement "I successfully obtained my desired keyboard size" at 4.20. The mean rating for the statement "I found it easy to enter text without any visual feedback" was 3.05. The mean rating for the statement "I was able to easily understand when and what key I typed" was 3.25. Thus most participants were satisfied with their ability to draw the keyboard as they wanted. However, the ratings on the other statements suggest the invisible keyboard was perceived as slow and not that accurate. Open comments were in general positive (Table 3). Most of the participants remarked that the invisible keyboard was easier than they thought it would be.

**Table 3.** Selected positive and negative comments from exploratory session.

| INVISIBLE |
| --- |
| + "Hitting a close enough key was good enough" |
| + "The adjustable size of the keyboard is good" |
| + "It got easier with practice - when I understood my keyboard" |
| + "It was fun. Easier than I thought it would be" |
| − "The keyboard was too small to use for me" |
| − "Sometimes the fingers were folded" |

# 6  Discussion

We explored how to enable efficient text entry in virtual environments without the use of auxiliary input devices. Our system relied on midair hand gestures. Further, we aimed to design a system that could be used with little or no training. In our study, we focused on how users interact with a familiar virtual keyboard interface. We anticipated bimanual typing would be faster, but our results showed similar entry rates for unimanual and bimanual typing. We think there are a number of possible explanations for this:

1. We conducted a single one-hour session. It is possible users may take more time to become accurate tapping midair targets in VR, especially with their non-dominant hand.
2. Our midair entry rates were also relatively slow at 16 wpm. This speed is consistent with the 18 wpm entry rate reported on an AR midair keyboard [9]. These slow speeds may be because users are struggling to precisely target keys or trigger midair taps. If users are focused on visually guiding their finger or on successfully triggering a tap, they may not be able to effectively plan for their subsequent tap. At least for touchscreen bimanual typing, it has been observed that users employ strategies such as pre-positioning over the next letter [20]. It could be that midair bimanual tapping is too cognitively taxing to allow effective use of such strategies.
3. It could also be that users had to visually guide their finger to each target. Since their hands were in midair, they could not anchor and use motor memory like they can do on small form factor devices like a phone. It would be interesting to investigate typing performance with a higher accuracy hand tracker and with tapping on a rigid surface overlaid with a virtual keyboard.

We found typing on a midair keyboard requires a good auto-correction algorithm. Participants' error rate was around 9% before auto-correction but only around 1% afterwards. The infrequent use of backspaces indicates that participants were largely relying on the system to automatically correct their input.

In our study, users had to tap all of a word's characters. Users tapped the spacebar to send the noisy input sequence to the auto-correct algorithm. Sometimes, the recognized word was different from a user's intended word. This occasionally led to time consuming correction episodes. This issue could be mitigated by adding predictions slots above the keyboard. These slots would allow users to understand what they will get if they tap the spacebar. These slots could also provide alternative options such as word predictions based on the current prefix of a word. If the system needs to support the input of uncommon words such as proper names, a slot providing the literal keys typed may be helpful.

Our study also tested a split keyboard layout. In principle, the split layout forces hand separation which should make tracking easier as it avoids one hand occluding the other. However, we found the error rate before and after correction was similar to the normal layout. The split layout was also slightly slower at 15 wpm compared to the normal layout. We suspect this was because either users had trouble locating which side of the keyboard a letter was on, or it forced more use of a user's non-dominant hand. It may require a longitudinal study to understand if a split layout is a useful design.

Despite the lack of performance advantages to bimanual typing, participant opinions were mixed with some preferring bimanual and some preferring unimanual. We also found participants rated physical exertion similar for bimanual and unimanual tying. Thus it may be worth supporting both input styles on midair keyboards.

We found our invisible keyboard was quite successful in allowing users to enter text without any visual feedback of the keys. Moreover, we found text can be inferred from an invisible keyboard with variable sizes. Whether typing performance depends on a smaller versus larger keyboard size needs further investigation, but our findings suggest that in VR use scenarios where users want to visually attend to other visual content, a user-defined invisible keyboard may be a viable approach.

We think our keyboard designs will be useful in scenarios where users want to send a short message, e.g. while playing a game. It could also be useful in virtual chat rooms or when searching for something in a VR application. We did not look at entering and editing large text passages. We think our current design is best suited for small amounts of text. Supporting efficient entry and editing of large amounts of would require design of features allowing the user to select and change regions of text, and allowing navigation through a passage that might not fit in the HMD's field of view.

One shortcoming of current AR and VR systems is the lack of haptic feedback during interaction with virtual objects. While in our design, we provided audio and visual feedback to signal a keyboard tap, providing additional haptic feedback may be beneficial. This could be done, for example, by aligning the keyboard with a physical surface, or by vibrating a wearable device such as a smartwatch.

# 7    Conclusion

We investigated text entry in virtual environments on a midair virtual keyboard. We compared two keyboard designs: a normal QWERTY layout and a split layout. We investigated the speed, accuracy, ergonomics, and user satisfaction of both these designs. We also compared unimanual versus bimanual interaction on these two different keyboard layouts. We found novice users' performance was similar at around 15–16 words-per-minute with a low error rate of less than 2% for the different visual designs and interaction styles.

Novice users were able to easily learn to use the system and achieved accurate text input despite inaccuracies introduced by the hand tracking, keyboard and hand visualization, and the lack of haptic keyboard feedback. Users were mixed in their preference on typing with one or two index fingers. We found participants reported similar exertion for one- and two-handed interaction.

Finally, we explored a design with only minimal visual feedback. Despite the lack of any visible keyboard or key outlines, users were able to type at 11 words-per-minute at a low 3% error rate. We hope our findings will inform and advance the design of improved text entry methods for use in virtual environments.

**Acknowledgments.** This material is based upon work supported by the NSF under Grant No. IIS-1750193.

# References

1. Adhikary, J., Vertanen, K.: Text entry in virtual environments using speech and a midair keyboard. IEEE Trans. Visual. Comput. Graphics **27**(5), 2648–2658 (2021). https://doi.org/10.1109/TVCG.2021.3067776
2. Ahn, S., Heo, S., Lee, G.: Typing on a smartwatch for smart glasses. In: Proceedings of the 2017 ACM International Conference on Interactive Surfaces and Spaces, ISS 2017, pp. 201–209. ACM, New York (2017). https://doi.org/10.1145/3132272.3134136
3. Alamdar Yazdi, M.A., Negahban, A., Cavuoto, L., Megahed, F.M.: Optimization of split keyboard design for touchscreen devices. Int. J. Hum. Comput. Interact. **35**(6), 468–477 (2019)
4. Aschim, T.B., Gjerstad, J.L., Lien, L.V., Tahsin, R., Sandnes, F.E.: Are split tablet keyboards better? A study of soft keyboard layout and hand posture. In: Lamas, D., Loizides, F., Nacke, L., Petrie, H., Winckler, M., Zaphiris, Panayiotis (eds.) INTERACT 2019. LNCS, vol. 11748, pp. 647–655. Springer, Cham (2019). https://doi.org/10.1007/978-3-030-29387-1_37
5. Bachynskyi, M., Palmas, G., Oulasvirta, A., Weinkauf, T.: Informing the design of novel input methods with muscle coactivation clustering. ACM Trans. Comput. Hum. Interact. **21**(6), 1–25 (2015). https://doi.org/10.1145/2687921
6. Bi, X., Chelba, C., Ouyang, T., Partridge, K., Zhai, S.: Bimanual gesture keyboard. In: Proceedings of the 25th Annual ACM Symposium on User Interface Software and Technology, pp. 137–146. ACM New York (2012)
7. Borg, G.: Borg's Perceived Exertion and Pain Scales. Human Kinetics, Champaign, 07 (1998)

8. Dube, T.J., Arif, A.S.: Text entry in virtual reality: a comprehensive review of the literature. In: Kurosu, M. (ed.) HCII 2019. LNCS, vol. 11567, pp. 419–437. Springer, Cham (2019). https://doi.org/10.1007/978-3-030-22643-5_33
9. Dudley, J.J., Vertanen, K., Kristensson, P.O.: Fast and precise touch-based text entry for head-mounted augmented reality with variable occlusion. ACM Trans. Comput. Hum. Interact. (TOCHI) **25**(6), 1–40 (2018). https://doi.org/10.1145/3232163
10. Feit, A.M., Sridhar, S., Theobalt, C., Oulasvirta, A.: Investigating multi-finger gestures for mid-air text entry. In: ACM womENcourage (2015)
11. Grubert, J., Witzani, L., Ofek, E., Pahud, M., Kranz, M., Kristensson, P.O.: Effects of hand representations for typing in virtual reality. In: 2018 IEEE Conference on Virtual Reality and 3D User Interfaces (VR), pp. 151–158 (2018)
12. Grubert, J., Witzani, L., Ofek, E., Pahud, M., Kranz, M., Kristensson, P.O.: Text entry in immersive head-mounted display-based virtual reality using standard keyboards. In: 2018 IEEE Conference on Virtual Reality and 3D User Interfaces (VR), pp. 159–166 (2018)
13. Gupta, A., Samad, M., Kin, K., Kristensson, P.O., Benko, H.: Investigating remote tactile feedback for mid-air text-entry in virtual reality. In: 2020 IEEE International Symposium on Mixed and Augmented Reality (ISMAR), pp. 350–360. IEEE (2020)
14. Knierim, P., Schwind, V., Feit, A.M., Nieuwenhuizen, F., Henze, N.: Physical keyboards in virtual reality: analysis of typing performance and effects of avatar hands. In: Proceedings of the 2018 CHI Conference on Human Factors in Computing Systems, pp. 1–9 (2018)
15. Kristensson, P.O., Vertanen, K.: Performance comparisons of phrase sets and presentation styles for text entry evaluations. In: Proceedings of the 2012 ACM International Conference on Intelligent User Interfaces, pp. 29–32. IUI 2012, ACM, New York (2012). https://doi.org/10.1145/2166966.2166972
16. Lee, M., Woo, W.: ARKB: 3D vision-based augmented reality keyboard. In: Proceedings of the 13th International Conference on Artificial Reality and Telexistence. ICAT 2013 (2003)
17. Markussen, A., Jakobsen, M.R., Hornbæk, K.: Selection-based mid-air text entry on large displays. In: Kotzé, P., Marsden, G., Lindgaard, G., Wesson, Janet, Winckler, M. (eds.) INTERACT 2013. LNCS, vol. 8117, pp. 401–418. Springer, Heidelberg (2013). https://doi.org/10.1007/978-3-642-40483-2_28
18. Markussen, A., Jakobsen, M.R., Hornbæk, K.: Vulture: A mid-air word-gesture keyboard. In: Proceedings of the 32nd Annual ACM Conference on Human Factors in Computing Systems, pp. 1073–1082. ACM, New York (2014)
19. McGill, M., Boland, D., Murray-Smith, R., Brewster, S.: A dose of reality: overcoming usability challenges in VR head-mounted displays. In: Proceedings of the SIGCHI Conference on Human Factors in Computing Systems, CHI 2015, pp. 2143–2152. ACM, New York (2015). https://doi.org/10.1145/2702123.2702382
20. Oulasvirta, A., et al.: Improving two-thumb text entry on touchscreen devices. In: Proceedings of the SIGCHI Conference on Human Factors in Computing Systems, pp. 2765–2774. ACM New York (2013)
21. Sandnes, F.E., Aubert, A.: Bimanual text entry using game controllers: relying on users' spatial familiarity with QWERTY. Interact. Comput. **19**(2), 140–150 (2006)
22. Speicher, M., Feit, A.M., Ziegler, P., Krüger, A.: Selection-based text entry in virtual reality. In: Proceedings of the 2018 CHI Conference on Human Factors in Computing Systems, pp. 1–13 (2018)

23. Sridhar, S., Feit, A.M., Theobalt, C., Oulasvirta, A.: Investigating the dexterity of multi-finger input for mid-air text entry. In: Proceedings of the 33rd Annual ACM Conference on Human Factors in Computing Systems, pp. 3643–3652. ACM New York (2015)
24. Truong, K., Hirano, S., Hayes, G.R., Moffatt, K.: 2-Thumbs gesture: the design and evaluation of a non-sequential bi-manual gesture based text input for touch tablets. Knowledge Media Design Institute (KMDI), University of Toronto, Canada, Tech. rep. (2013)
25. Vertanen, K., Kristensson, P.O.: A versatile dataset for text entry evaluations based on genuine mobile emails. In: Proceedings of the 13th International Conference on Human Computer Interaction with Mobile Devices & Services, MobileHCI 2011, pp. 295–298. ACM, New York (2011). https://doi.org/10.1145/2037373.2037418
26. Vertanen, K., Memmi, H., Emge, J., Reyal, S., Kristensson, P.O.: VelociTap: investigating fast mobile text entry using sentence-based decoding of touchscreen keyboard input. In: Proceedings of the SIGCHI Conference on Human Factors in Computing Systems, CHI 2015, pp. 659–668. ACM, New York (2015). https://doi.org/10.1145/2702123.2702135
27. Walker, J., Li, B., Vertanen, K., Kuhl, S.: Efficient typing on a visually occluded physical keyboard. In: Proceedings of the 2017 CHI Conference on Human Factors in Computing Systems, pp. 5457–5461. ACM New York (2017)
28. Wang, C.Y., Chu, W.C., Chiu, P.T., Hsiu, M.C., Chiang, Y.H., Chen, M.Y.: PalmType: using palms as keyboards for smart glasses. In: Proceedings of the 17th International Conference on Human-Computer Interaction with Mobile Devices and Services, MobileHCI 2015, pp. 153–160. ACM, New York (2015). https://doi.org/10.1145/2785830.2785886
29. Ye, L., Sandnes, F.E., MacKenzie, I.S.: QB-Gest: QWERTY bimanual gestural input for eyes-free smartphone text input. In: Antona, M., Stephanidis, C. (eds.) HCII 2020. LNCS, vol. 12188, pp. 223–242. Springer, Cham (2020). https://doi.org/10.1007/978-3-030-49282-3_16
30. Yi, X., Yu, C., Zhang, M., Gao, S., Sun, K., Shi, Y.: ATK: enabling ten-finger freehand typing in air based on 3d hand tracking data. In: Proceedings of the 28th Annual ACM Symposium on User Interface Software and Technology, UIST 2015, pp. 539–548. ACM, New York (2015). https://doi.org/10.1145/2807442.2807504
31. Yu, C., Gu, Y., Yang, Z., Yi, X., Luo, H., Shi, Y.: Tap, dwell or gesture?: exploring head-based text entry techniques for HMDs. In: Proceedings of the SIGCHI Conference on Human Factors in Computing Systems, CHI 2017, pp. 4479–4488. ACM, New York (2017). https://doi.org/10.1145/3025453.3025964
32. Yu, C., Sun, K., Zhong, M., Li, X., Zhao, P., Shi, Y.: One-dimensional handwriting: inputting letters and words on smart glasses. In: Proceedings of the SIGCHI Conference on Human factors in Computing Systems, CHI 2016, pp. 71–82. ACM, NewYork (2016)
33. Yu, D., Fan, K., Zhang, H., Monteiro, D., Xu, W., Liang, H.: PizzaText: text entry for virtual reality systems using dual thumbsticks. IEEE Trans. Visual. Comput. Graph. 24(11), 2927–2935 (2018)
34. Zhai, S., Kristensson, P.O.: The word-gesture keyboard: reimagining keyboard interaction. Commun. ACM 55(9), 91–101 (2012). https://doi.org/10.1145/2330667.2330689

# Interaction with Conversational Agents

# "Please Connect Me to a Specialist": Scrutinising 'Recipient Design' in Interaction with an Artificial Conversational Agent

Iuliia Avgustis[1]([✉]) [iD], Aleksandr Shirokov[2] [iD], and Netta Iivari[1] [iD]

[1] University of Oulu, Oulu, Finland
{iuliia.avgustis,netta.iivari}@oulu.fi
[2] Rutgers University, New Brunswick, USA
aleksandr.shirokov@rutgers.edu

**Abstract.** This paper explores how callers formulate information enquiries for an artificial conversational agent in a call centre and compares it with the way enquiries are addressed to human operators of the same call centre. It includes 60 call recordings with human operators and 103 call recordings with the artificial conversational agent, transcribed and analysed using the method of Conversation Analysis. We show that people formulate and reformulate their enquiries differently to an artificial agent, even though the goal in both cases is to get an answer to the same enquiry. When talking to the artificial conversational agent, callers produce short enquiries, similar to web searches. When connected to human operators, callers formulate longer enquiries which include many details. By analysing the differences in the way callers formulate their enquiries to robots and human operators, we show what callers expect artificial conversational agents to process. These expectations affect the way the enquiry is formulated and, as a result, operators and artificial agents encounter different types of problems they have to repair to understand the question correctly and find an answer to it. Our findings have interesting implications for Human Computer Interaction both in terms of "robot-recipient design" and "user-recipient design".

**Keywords:** Conversational agent · Speech interface · Call centre · Conversation analysis · Recipient design

## 1 Introduction

Currently, there is a growing use and continuous development of conversational agents, voice chatbots, voice user interfaces (VUI) and personal assistant devices. They have attracted wide scholarly attention in the field of human-computer interaction (HCI). Recent studies in this field have focused particularly on interaction with advanced conversational agents (Siri, Amazon Echo, Google Home, etc.) in everyday settings, mostly by families in the context of their homes. The studies have emphasized the intricacies involved in embedding the interaction with the agent into the everyday activities and

© IFIP International Federation for Information Processing 2021
Published by Springer Nature Switzerland AG 2021
C. Ardito et al. (Eds.): INTERACT 2021, LNCS 12935, pp. 155–176, 2021.
https://doi.org/10.1007/978-3-030-85610-6_10

conversational settings of the participants (see e.g. [10, 36, 37, 48]). The studies reveal interaction with the agent is being associated with entertainment in many cases, people laughing and being amused [16, 29, 36, 37, 48]. Our study contributes to the stream of research on conversational agents, but directs attention to a different kind of conversational setting: it explores interaction with a conversational agent in a task-oriented institutional setting, in which interaction with the agents differs dramatically from interaction with more advanced conversational agents; the agents follow a very limited, strict set of rules and scenarios of interaction, the task-oriented human participants expecting effectiveness and efficiency above all from the encounters. This kind of less advanced conversational agents are widely used in different kinds of domains such as in survey interviews or service encounters, while they receive clearly less attention in research on interaction with conversational interfaces.

Our study aims to fill in this knowledge gap and investigates features of interaction with less advanced but still human-like conversational agents in task-oriented institutional interaction. The research question of this study is "How formulations and reformulations of enquiries addressed to artificial agents differ from those addressed to human operators?" The element of comparison is important for understanding the specifics of conversations with artificial agents. Therefore, the first section of the analysis is devoted to the comparison of initial formulations, and in the second section we will discuss the difference between the way callers reformulate inquiries to human operators and artificial agents. We consider important to investigate this question, as artificial agents in institutional settings are usually designed based on similar types of interaction with human operators who also follow certain rules. However, people talk differently to non-human agents, they design their enquiries in a different way based on their expectations, and as a result, the input for the agent is different. If we understand how callers talk to artificial agents, we can design artificial agents in institutional setting that will better understand the enquiries. Specifically, we are interested in a caller's initial formulation of a question or an enquiry and its reformulation if the first attempt does not provide the expected answer from an agent. Some differences between the ways people communicate with humans and artificial agents have already been mentioned in the setting of everyday online conversations with chatbots [23]. However, there are still relatively few studies comparing differences between the way people communicate with human operators and voice bots.

This study provides an important opportunity to advance the understanding of the organized structure of interaction with artificial agents (i.e. telephone robots) in telephone enquiry services. It also offers some insights into callers' expectations, reasoning process and challenges that arise during this type of institutional interaction. Telephone robots are now widely used in call centres, as they dramatically reduce human operators' workload. However, callers still often prefer talking to a human operator, as robots cannot always comprehend the enquiry. Understanding features of enquiries formulated for artificial agents can therefore clarify what robots should be able to process. We conclude this study with ideas on how the quality of interaction with artificial agents in institutional calls can be improved.

# 2 Related Research

## 2.1 Interaction with Conversational Agents in Different Settings

Interaction with human-like dialogue systems (systems that aim to imitate human conversation [15]) has become a part of our everyday social life. One can find plenty of HCI research addressing artificial conversational agents and VUIs over the past decades, considering solutions such as search engines, help systems, intelligent personal assistants, or robots. Currently, one can find an increasing HCI interest on conversational agents [3–5, 10, 13, 14, 16, 18, 29, 30, 36, 37, 48], the studies being inspired by the emergence of advanced conversational agents (Siri, Amazon Echo, Google Home, etc.) in everyday settings. These studies examine how families embed artificial conversational agents into the everyday activities of the home, how they are used as resources in interaction, and how the agents are fitted into the sequential organization of the talk, identifying how the agent is addressed and how its responses are handled [16, 29, 36, 37]. Besides home and family use, the studies also explore conversational agents in other entertainment-oriented contexts, such as in museums [4].

We wish to direct attention back to the task-oriented institutional contexts with high requirements for effectiveness and efficiency. Recently, this type of context has received less attention in HCI. However, we maintain research interest is warranted in this type of context, as conversational interfaces have become widely spread and used within. Studies also show interaction problems still prevail in interaction with conversational agents in task-oriented contexts (e.g. [10, 30, 49]). This study focuses on human interaction with an artificial conversational agent in a task-oriented intuitional setting of a call centre. Technology oriented studies addressing call centre or telephone service VUIs or can be found in the computing field [1, 9, 26, 34] as well as studies addressing the user experience and usability of such services and VUIs [28, 43, 46]; however, these studies do not focus in detail on human interaction with a conversational agent or address the influence of the institutional setting.

Calls to telephone helplines and various other telephone services are a type of institutional talk. To understand such talk, we turn to Conversation Analysis, within which it has been shown that the telephone enquiry service, as an institutional setting, imposes certain rules and restrictions on social interaction [21]. This type of interaction has features that distinguish it from ordinary conversation: (a) participants are oriented to specific goals (e.g. obtaining information); (b) the interaction has constraints on what is treated as appropriate contributions to achieving this goal; (c) it is associated with frameworks and procedures that are specific to the institutional context (e.g., digital or paper documentation, etc.) [22]. Human operators in call centres are required to follow written instructions when they introduce themselves, ask clarifying questions and give answers to callers. The rules, however, do not fully determine the practices. They can also be ignored or made explicit and discussed by participants to the communication. Interaction with an artificial agent in a telephone service has a similar structure and it is organized mainly through question-answer adjacent pairs. However, the range of possible response utterances in interaction with an artificial agent is much more limited, and if a caller does not follow the rules, s/he cannot get an answer to her/his enquiry. Human operator can depart from the instructions if necessary, i.e. when communication trouble arises. One could assume it is relatively straightforward to design a well-functional conversational agent in this type of setting, while in this study we will show a lot of trouble may emerge in interaction, showing problems in recipient design and repair. Next, we will elaborate on these concepts.

## 2.2 Conversation with a Conversational Agent

The wide use of various voice technologies makes relevant the debate of the 1990s about the possibility of human-machine conversation [32]. One of the key figures of this debate is Graham Button who stated that only a "simulacrum of conversation" [8], i.e. an imitation as opposed to a real conversation between humans, is possible in interaction with machines. A similar a priori distinction between "human-human" and "human-machine" interaction is found in new research on HCI [38], in which conversation between people is contrasted with intercourse between humans and conversational agents. However, some researchers argue that interaction between a human and a machine can be considered a conversation and analysed as such as long as there are sense-making procedures done by the human [50].

Studies show that conversation with artificial agents differs from conversations with humans. For example, the language in conversations with voice interfaces is found to be command-like and abrupt [19]. Speakers adapt to the system's abilities when they talk to an artificial agent. The concept of recipient design refers to this phenomenon: as a concept used in CA studies, it refers to the tuning of the utterances for different addressees and is performed by people in their everyday interactions [39]. In this paper, we will address its specific category - robot-recipient deign, where the recipient is an artificial agent. Interaction with a non-human recipient raises additional issues for the interlocutor, and we will analyse them in the context of formulations and reformulations of the enquiry in institutional calls. Various aspects of "robot-recipient design" will be identified and discussed throughout the analysis (how callers adapt their initial enquiries when connected to a robot, and how they treat troubles in these conversations). The notion of "robot-recipient design" and its design implications will be more thoroughly addressed in the discussion section.

Prior HCI studies have examined recipient design also from another angle: recipient design has been introduced as a VUI principle in IBM Conversational UX guidelines [16, 33], in which recipient design refers to the adaptation of the artificial agent to the actions of user and her/his knowledge. There is already discussion on request and response design in HCI research along these lines. Studies empirically examine how users formulate requests to an agent and react to its responses [16, 36, 48], the studies also highlighting that designers of artificial agents need to consider what they intend users to say to the agent and how to design resourceful responses for users [10, 16].

Repair has also received attention in HCI research on conversational agents. Different kind of repair strategies have been discussed [3, 37, 48], both from the viewpoint of the agent and the user. The topic of conversation repair has originally been introduced by Schegloff, Jefferson, and Sacks [41], defined as practices that address troubles in speaking, hearing, and understanding. The goal of repair is to maintain or restore intersubjectivity and to move interaction forward [40]. Initially, this phenomenon was described using English-language data, but since then repair has been analysed in various languages [42], including Russian [7]. Repair can be initiated and carried out by one actor, but it can also be initiated by one actor and later be carried out by another actor [27]. Conversation analysts found a structural "preference" for self-repair [41] and a tendency that most often the repair is initiated by the speaker of the "trouble-source" [27]. This highlights one specific problem of interaction with a "simple" call centre agent: even though they can initiate the repair themselves (and thus signal the existence of a problem), they are usually not capable of performing a repair (and thus actually solving the problem). Thus, in such interaction, a significant part of the work of carrying out repair remains with the user.

In this study we address a task-oriented institutional context of a call centre and particularly focus on recipient design and repair in human-agent interaction within: we examine how humans adapt to the agents' assumed abilities when talking with the agent and how the agent has been designed to adapt to users' abilities (or not). We discuss the repair strategies employed in interaction, showing pertinent problems within. It has already been found that repairs are more frequent in task-oriented conversations than in "ordinary" dialogues [12]. A novel angle in this study is comparison of human-agent interaction with human-human interaction in the same setting. This reveals that people talk differently to artificial agents in institutional settings from the beginning of interaction, and therefore, artificial agents should not be designed based on interaction with human operators.

We join the HCI discussion on naturalness of conversation with artificial agents in institutional settings: we show users engaging in 'robotic' interaction with the agent, but also the agent trying to engage to 'human-like' interaction with users. Especially in institutional, task-oriented settings we should be wary of the illusion of natural conversation: the existing literature has already pointed out ([48], see also [5]) that the better the agent works from the users' perspective, the more naturally also the users tend to speak, which increases the risk of trouble in interaction due to giving users an illusion of natural conversation, users remaining or becoming unaware of the agent's limited capabilities. We highlight these concerns as especially acute in task oriented institutional settings.

## 3   Research Design

### 3.1  Data

The data for this study were collected at one major Russian city's call centre that answers citizens' questions considering different administrative issues such as official documents and working hours of public institutions. The artificial conversational agent of this centre was created by this organizations' employees to reduce the workload. It has been programmed to answer every fourth call during a given test period. In calls with the artificial agent, callers are informed that they will talk to a robot (this is the term that we will also use in the paper). The data for this research were provided by the call centre representatives for the analysis and publication purposes. All ethical guidelines were followed.

The collected data include 60 call recordings with humans and 103 call recordings with the artificial agent. Collected audio recordings of naturally occurring conversations with human and robot operators were transcribed and analysed using the method of Conversation Analysis (CA). In this paper, we will present examples of the most frequent types of formulations and reformulations in interaction with artificial agents and human operators, which will allow us to reveal the main differences. In calls with the artificial agent, callers are first informed that they will speak to a robot and then instructed to state the question and speak after the tone. All callers are also informed about the audio recording of the call in this welcome message. After this message the recording, as well as most of the transcripts presented in this paper, start and the caller hears the tone (line 7 in the transcripts presented further).

Human operators in this call centre follow strict instructions and use specified wordings when answering a question. As the artificial operator is representing this institution, and as its answer is considered to be an official response from the governmental structure, it has to follow certain rules of interaction as well. For this reason, its developers have made the decision to create a simple rule-based conversational agent instead of a generative model conversational agent. They gave the robot a set of predefined responses and wrote strict scripts that this robot is supposed to follow. The robot chooses what to say next based on the keywords and connections between these words that it finds in the recognized speech of the caller. For example, if the robot recognizes "readiness" and "social card" in the enquiry of the caller, it asks to indicate the social card application number. The robot's voice is a female voice, and its quality is rather good; however, pauses between some words and phrases are sometimes either too short or too long, and intonations are often inappropriate, so while the voice sounds natural, the speech does not. Despite that, our collection also includes several cases where people confuse the robot with an actual human operator and address it as such. These cases are not presented in this paper due to their infrequency.

Conversations with the robot are ended either by providing information or by transferring the call to a human operator if the robot does not identify relevant keywords or does not have a predefined answer to a particular question. We will provide examples for each of these cases. Both human and robot operators are in the same organization, the same telephone enquiry service, and they both talk to the same type of callers. Therefore, the collected data provides a good opportunity for making a comparison between interaction with an artificial agent and interaction with a human operator.

## 3.2   Method

To analyse the data, we use the method of Conversation Analysis (CA), which was originally established as a method for studying everyday conversation and interaction but was later used to study other forms of interaction, including interaction between humans and machines [20, 44, 45]. CA has already proved to be useful in the field of human-computer interaction and computer-supported cooperative work [2, 11]. It is also often used to study interaction with artificial agents [6, 16, 24, 31, 32, 35, 36].

CA is a qualitative data driven method that draws the researcher's attention to details of naturally occurring interaction. This focused attention allows the researcher to identify methods that members use to accomplish their activities and make these activities accountable to others (e.g. systematic patterns for asking a question or for formulating an enquiry). To analyse the methods of performing actions, a researcher needs to analyse the sequence of actions in one specific conversation. Conversation Analysis does not require analysis of a large number of conversations, but it makes necessary a close attention to the details of interaction in specific situations. The main question therefore is "how" participants carry out a specific social action - instead of "how often" or "why". However, usually conversation analysts investigate more than one case, as the analysis and comparison of different cases may reveal how a specific method works in different situations and what variations of this method exist.

To capture as many details of the interaction as possible, Gail Jefferson's system of transcription [25] is used by conversation analysts. Creating a Jeffersonian transcript is a necessary research step that allows the researcher to see how the conversation actually unfolds. Pauses, changes in speed of talk, intonations and other features of the talk are transcribed to ensure a better understanding of actions accomplished in and by the talk. The following abbreviations are used in the following transcripts: C – caller, R – robot operator, H – human operator. All the personal data (names, application numbers etc.) as well as the name of the service have been changed to preserve anonymity.

We will first focus on methods of formulating an enquiry, and then analyse how initial formulations are repaired by the participants of interaction in various situations.

# 4 Findings

## 4.1 Formulating an Enquiry

If the robot answers the call, the caller hears the welcome message and receives the instruction in one sentence: "please clearly formulate your question and speak after the tone". In interactions with human operators, people are able to produce or formulate a social action and expect that this action will be correctly recognized by the interactional partner. In the interaction with the telephone robot, the caller is faced with the question of what to say and how to say it so that the robot would recognize what has been said [38], i.e. how to design an enquiry for a robot. This is partially due to the fact that the caller has to formulate an enquiry before he or she actually hears the robot and estimates what it is capable of. However, it is also a characteristic of the subsequent interaction, as such interactional agents are not capable of producing actions that simultaneously show what these actions are doing [38].

The instruction – "please clearly formulate your question" does not actually help the caller to understand how to interact with the robot. What does "clearly" mean? Does this imply "in detail" or "briefly" or with respect to articulation? Clearly for whom? The problem of this uncertainty for a caller is indicated by the fact that after the welcome message and the first beep a caller often stays quiet instead of asking a question, as seen in the line 8 in the following example. As we mentioned earlier, all transcripts of interaction with the robot operator start from the line 7, as the caller first hears the introduction message, and only then the audio recording begins, so even though it is the beginning of the interaction for the robot, the caller has previously listened to a short pre-recorded instruction by a human on stating the question after the tone.

Example 1

```
07   R   ((tone))
08       (2.5)
09   C   .hh allo  [mne °by°   ]
         .hh hello [I'd like to]
10   R            [pozhalu-   ]
                  [plea-      ]
11       (2.1)
12   C   .h soedinite menja pozhalujsta so ↑spetsialistom.
         .h please connect me to a ↑specialist.
```

The gap (line 8) is typical only for interaction with a robot operator, and there is no such gap in the interactions with a human operator. After the greeting from a human operator and the question "how can I help you?", a caller immediately begins to speak. We can assume that the initial formulation would be different if the robot would also start with "how can I help you" instead of "please clearly formulate your question and speak after the tone", but this requires a different set of data. Long periods of silence instead of a response are known to be one of the indicators of interactional trouble and they are usually minimized in interaction between humans [40]. In conversation with a robot operator, the average length of a gap is 2.4 s, and it is longer than 1 s in 78% of the cases we have analysed. The robot is programmed to say the phrase "please speak up" (line 10 – here the cut-off) when there is a long gap. Similar straightforward methods are rarely found in communication between humans, even in an institutional context. As can be seen from this transcript, the method itself can lead to an overlap of utterances (lines 9–10), although the robot has been programmed to stop speaking when there is an overlap. This interaction is not successful so far and it is continued by the caller's request to talk to a human operator, who is considered to be a specialist as opposed to the robot (line 12). It is also noteworthy that the caller uses the word of politeness ("please") in this case. These words are rare in this type of interaction, and these enquiries often lead to a transfer to a human operator.

The instruction "clearly formulate your question" can be interpreted in different ways by callers. For example, there are several cases when the caller begins to talk in detail about her/his problem and talks not only about what s/he needs to find out, but also why s/he needs to do so. Often after these requests, the robot uses such replies as "maybe I misunderstood you" or "I'm sorry, I cannot understand" and asks again to "clearly formulate the question". In most of the cases, however, callers make their enquiries short and similar to a web-based search request. In addition, callers often make short pauses after each word and stretch the pronunciation of words (apparently trying to make their speech more understandable for the robot). This "robot-like" speech is one of the aspects of robot-recipient design. Formulating an enquiry as a command similar to a search request leads to successful interaction with the robot, and people quite often make an enquiry this way (Example 2). In the data we have analyzed, 75% of enquiries addressed to a robot operator were formulated this way.

**Example 2**
```
07  R  ((tone))
08     (3.2)
09  C  uznat' o gotovnosti patenta.
       to get information on readiness of a patent.
```

In the second example we also see a long gap, after which an enquiry without any explanations or additional details is provided (line 9 in Example 2). It is further successfully read by the robot, so the caller receives the requested information. This way of formulating a request is specific for interacting with the robot. In cases when a caller is redirected from a robot operator to a human, the same request is formulated quite differently, as seen in the Example 3. The caller first speaks to a robot (lines 8–9 and omitted lines 10–37) and is later connected to the human operator, as interaction with the robot did not lead to the expected by the caller answer.

**Example 3**
```
07  R  ((tone))
08     (2.1)
09  C  xochu uznat' (0.4) zadolzhennost' po kvartplate.
       I'd like to know (0.4) rent arrears.
[...]
38  O  vy pozvonili v tsentr predostavlenija gosuslug Kontakt,
       you called to the service center Kontakt,
39     spetsialist Veselova Ol'ga dobryj den'.
       specialist Veselova Olga good afternoon.
40     (0.7)
41  C  zdravstvujte .hh >podskazhite pozhalujsta<
       hello .hh >please tell me<
42     a ja mogu vot po telefonu uzna:t' summu zadolzhennosti.=
       can I fi:nd out on the phone the amount of debt.=
43     =↑ja tak primerno znaju,
       =↑I know more or less,
44     no vot (1.2) xotela (1.7) ne znaju tam
       but well (1.2) I wanted (1.7) I don't know
45     .hh prosto s sentjabrja my ne platim i .hh a::: °e°,
       .hh it's just that we don't pay since September .hh u::hm °e°,
46     schitat' summu kotoraja mne prixodit na: >nu vot<,
       do I count the sum that comes to: >well<,
47     v pochtovyj ↑jaschik,
       to the ↑mailbox,
48     ili tam kakie-to eschë protsenty byvajut.
       or are there some other penalties.
49     >°ja prosto ne znaju°<
       >°I just don't know°<
```

In this case, even though the robot understands the request stated by the caller, it is unable to provide the caller the necessary information because of the lack of knowledge on the question, so the caller is redirected to a human operator. As seen from this transcript, the same caller formulates the request in a different way depending on the operator: a very short enquiry formulated to a robot (line 9) and a long, detailed enquiry formulated to a human operator (lines 41–49). Note also that the gap after operator's answer (line 40) is much shorter than the gap in interaction with the robot (line 8).

In the second formulation, in addition to the same enquiry, there is a greeting and words of politeness (line 41). Apparently, successful interaction with this artificial agent rarely involves greetings, introductions or other polite forms of conversation. Moreover, in the interaction with a human operator, the caller often gives the circumstances of the call, the reasons for the question to arise or details of the question (lines 45). The question can also be repeated twice during one turn to make it more clear for the human operator (lines 42 & 46–48). All of these elements are rarely present in the case of interaction with the robot operator, and all of them might cause additional problems for the robot. The formulation of a request as a command is a way to successfully interact with the robot and it is the exact way that most people formulate their enquiries.

We can see that the callers orient to the properties of the recipient in their turns-at-talk, and the "recipient design" of initial enquiries is different in the talk with the human and the robot, as the robot is simply introduced as such, and nothing is said about its capabilities. However, although enquiries are different, both the robot and the human operators can rarely answer the question after the first turn of the caller is over. Usually some additional work is needed: either by specifying the request or by clarifying certain details of it. In the next section we will concentrate on repair sequences that people perform to correct their initial enquiry and formulate a question in an adequate form.

## 4.2 Repair Sequences

Repair situations are a useful focus for analysing what we call robot-recipient design. The type of repair solution shows a recipient (and an analyst) how the actor treats the trouble source (as a problem of speaking, hearing, or understanding) and can indicate the actor's assumptions about the recipient. We found a specific pattern of what repair solutions callers tend to propose and accordingly how they tend to interpret trouble sources in interaction with the artificial conversational agent. One of the situations in which a repair sequence typically occurs is when the robot (for an unknown reason) does not recognize speech fully or correctly, as in the following example.

## Example 4

```
07  R   ((tone))
08      (1.5)
09  C   gotova ↑li sotsial'naja karta?
        ↑is the social card ready?
10      (4.1)
11  R   utochnite,
        specify,
12      gotovnost' (.) kakogo dokumenta vas interesuet
        readiness (.) of which document you are interested in
13      (0.7)
14  R   ((tone))=
15  C   =.h SOTSIAL'NA- SOTSIAL'NAJA KARTA
        =.h SOCIA- SOCIAL CARD
```

In line 9, the caller produces an enquiry as a simple question. Even though the enquiry is short and precise, the robot doesn't recognize the name of the document. In lines 11–12, the robot produces a repair initiation, which specifies the document's name/type as the trouble source. Next, there is a 0.7 gap (line 13) and a tone (line 14). The caller doesn't answer immediately but waits for the tone. This shows her orientation to the way the robot works. Right after the tone, the caller produces a repair solution (line 15). She uses the same name for defining the document but pronounces it louder. After this, the robot succeeds in correctly understanding the enquiry and continues to follow its script of actions.

In this case, the caller treats the trouble source as a problem of hearing (or speech recognition) since she doesn't change the document's name. However, the robot didn't specify the type of problem. This could be both a hearing problem and a formulation problem (the document's incorrect name). In such ambiguous situations, callers tend to interpret trouble sources as a problem of hearing. In their repair solution, they don't change the "content" but pronounce it differently, usually louder and with longer pauses between words. This is what we call a robot-like voice. Let us consider one more case in which a robot initiates a repair sequence.

## Example 5

```
11  R   nazovite (.) pozhalujsta
        indicate (.) please
12      nomer zajavlenija na sotsial'nuju kartu
        the social card application number
13      (.)
14  R   govorite posle signala.
        speak after the tone.
```

```
15      (0.4)
16   R  ((tone))
17      (1.3)
18   C  znachit (0.2) PJAT' (0.2) DVA (0.2) ↑SHEST' (0.8) ODIN
        so (0.2) FIVE (0.2) TWO (0.2) ↑SIX (0.8) ONE
19      (0.3) ↓PJAT' (0.8) TRI (0.4) CHETYRE (0.3) DVA.
        (0.3) ↓FIVE (0.8) THREE (0.4) FOUR (0.3) TWO.
20      (4.1)
21   R  vozmozhno ja vas nepravil'no ponjala
        maybe I misunderstood you
22      (.)
23   R  nazovite nomer esche raz po odnoj tsifre
        indicate the number one digit after another
24      (.)
25   R  pozhalujsta govorite posle signala
        please speak after the tone
26      (0.4)
27   R  ((tone))
28      (0.8)
29   C  PJA:T' (0.8) DVA (0.4) SHEST' (0.8) ODIN
        FI:VE (0.8) TWO (0.4) SIX (0.8) ONE (0.6)
30      (0.6) PJAT' (0.5) TRI (0.8) CHETYRE (0.4) DVA.
        (0.6) FIVE (0.5) THREE (0.8) FOUR (0.4) TWO.
```

In lines 11–14, the robot asks for the application number. The caller provides it (lines 18–19), but the robot, for some reason, doesn't accept it. In lines 21–25, the robot initiates a repair by explicating the misunderstanding and giving more detailed instructions. In response, the caller pronounces the same number louder and makes longer pauses between words (lines 29–30). So again, the robot doesn't specify the type of problem, and the caller treats it as a hearing problem.

In the above-mentioned cases, the robot's demand for clarification ignores the fact that the caller has already mentioned all the necessary information. This type of questioning is seen quite often in talks with the robot, but it is rarely seen in interactions with human operators. The latter usually initiate the repair in another way. They propose a repair solution and request confirmation or rejection of the solution. Human operators have instructions they have to follow if the reason for the call is not established after the caller's first turn. To achieve clear understanding of the question, operators are supposed to use following phrases: "You mean that …", "That is, you want …", "So you need …", "You need to clarify …" etc. In most of the cases they also make a guess about the question and ask the caller if they understood them correctly. Here is an example:

Example 6

```
07   C   >dobryj vecher Marina, menja zovut Anna<,
         >good evening Marina, my name is Anna<,
08       ja xotela uznat',
         I want to know,
09       my:: s papoj privatiziruem kvarti:ru,
         me:: and father are privatizing the apa:rtment,
10       mne by interesno bylo uznat' ↑sro:ki
         I am interested in knowing the ↑te:rms
11       .hh vot s momenta kak my ↑podaem
         .hh from the moment we ↑apply
12       vse vot eti ↑dokumenty v ↓portal,
         all these ↑documents to the ↓portal,
13       cherez ↑kakoe vremja ona budet privatizirovana,
         after ↑what time it will be privatized,
         ((the operator starts to type and types until line 17))
14       my prosto ee ↑prodaem,
         we just ↑sell it,
15       poetomu mne by ukazat' etu ↑datu.
         so I would like to indicate the ↑date.
16       (2.8)
17   H   neposredstvenno ↑srok ispolnenija.
         (you mean) ↑document processing time.
18       ↓pravil'no        [°ja vas ponjala°?
         have I ↓correctly [°understood you°?
19   C                     [da >da da<
                           [yes >yes yes<
```

The initial enquiry is formulated through lines 8–15. The caller gives a reason for a call and describes the situation. The operator starts to look for the answer in the data base (line 13) before the caller finishes her turn, which might be the reason why she is able to quickly transform this enquiry to a simple question further. Even though the gap in line 16 is rather long for an interaction with a human operator, the caller as well as the analyst can hear the typing by the operator, which makes her actions accountable. This gap, therefore, is different from those we have seen in interactions with the robot. In lines 17–18, the operator initiates the repair and proposes the repair solution by reformulating the question. As the caller confirms that the enquiry formulated by the operator is correct, she will then get an answer from the operator. In most of the cases, as well as in the one presented here, human operators have to work with the details mentioned in the initial enquiry to help the caller to formulate a question. However, sometimes they also don't get enough details and have to lead the caller towards formulating an enquiry in multiple turns. This is done by phrases such as "yes", "I listen to you", "speak further" etc. In cases, where an operator is not sure about what was said, a guess is also usually made.

Robots are also sometimes faced with an enquiry which is either too detailed or not detailed enough. This could lead to the robot's incorrect (from a caller's point of view) answer as it understands the question by connecting keywords that are recognized during the initial enquiry. In the following example, words in the enquiry were successfully recognized, but not in the way the caller expected the enquiry to be recognized.

Example 7

```
07  R  ((tone))
08     (0.6)
09  C  .h >MFTS Danilovskogo rajona<
       .h >MFC of Danilovskogo district<
10     (4.2)
11  R  tsentr Gosuslug rajona Danilovskij
       the Gosuslug center of the Danilovskij district
12     naxoditsja po ↑adresu
       is located at the ↑address
13     (0.3)
14  C  .tch
15     (0.2)
16  R  ulitsa Xavskaja ↑dom dvadtsat' ↓shest'
       Xavskaja street ↑house twenty ↓six
[...]
29  R  ↑vam povtorit'?
       shall I repeat?
30     (0.6)
31  R  ((tone))
32     (3.5)
33  C  >soedinite pozhalujsta< s MFTS Danilovskogo rajona.
       >please connect< to MFC of Danilovskogo district.
```

Although the formulation of an enquiry in the form of a command assumes a short statement, it must be accurate enough; otherwise, the robot can provide wrong type of information. In the above transcript, the caller learns to formulate the request while interacting with the robot. The first request (line 9) was read by a robot as a request for information about the Multifunctional Centre for Provision of State and Municipal Services (MFC) of a certain area – its location, working hours, etc. (lines 11–16 and omitted lines 17–28). However, as it becomes clear that the robot is going to give this information about the mentioned MFC, the caller produces ".tch" sound which can be interpreted as a sign of discontent. This is something a human operator could orient to and stop, but the robot continues. The caller does not attempt to interrupt the robot either and waits until the end of its turn to add new keywords to the initial enquiry (line 33).

The initial enquiry wouldn't be formulated to the operator in the same way, so it is not possible to make a comparison of a similar trouble source in a conversation with a human. Human operators usually get long and detailed enquiries that often include an account for the enquiry and description of the situation. Even though human operators also need to have an enquiry in a short and simple form to find an answer in their data base, callers tend to transfer this duty to the operator. In case there are not enough details, human operator indicates to the caller that there are not enough details by encouraging the caller to speak further. It is also possible that human operator can misunderstand the question and start to read the answer that is not relevant. In this case, unlike the robot, the human operator can be stopped by the caller, and the enquiry can be reformulated once again before the full answer is given by the operator.

In situations where the robot experiences speech recognition or keyword search failure that eventually leads to the repetition or reformulation of the initial enquiry by the caller, the robot does not use the same methods as human operators use when it needs to make its problem explicit. However, the callers manage to reformulate their enquiries based on their knowledge about how the robot works. In most of the cases, the callers speak either slower or louder or make longer pauses. There are also different combinations of this "voice robotization". Differences in the users' understanding of the reason for interactional trouble can be seen in the way initial enquiries are reformulated. As the robot can only indicate that there was a trouble, the callers tend to treat it as a problem of hearing and repeat their enquiries louder and with longer pauses between words. When talking to human operators, callers rarely encounter troubles in hearing, so a comparison of similar cases is not possible. However, when other problems arise, operators provide a possible solution to the problem (see Example 6).

## 5 Discussion

### 5.1 Summary of the Results

Although the number of artificial conversational agents in institutional settings is constantly growing, there are relatively few studies on how people actually interact with them. Investigating this aspect is important, as it reveals how callers design their utterances for an artificial agent to achieve the goal of institutional interaction. If we understand how people talk to an institutional agent, we can design an agent that will better deal with callers' enquiries, offer smoother and more efficient interaction and ultimately better customer and user experience. In institutional, task-oriented settings, pleasurable customer and user experiences are of utmost importance for continued service or product use and customer and user retention (e.g. [28, 43, 46]). In this paper, we focused on the first step in interaction with an artificial agent in a telephone enquiry service; the formulation of an information enquiry and its repair after the operator's reply.

Even though both human operators and robots follow instructions when talking to callers, they follow them differently, as the robot cannot deviate from the instructions. These differences can especially be seen in how repairs are initiated and carried out. However, as we have shown an initial enquiry is also formulated differently to a robot and a human, and accordingly different types of troubles in interaction arise. In the talk with the human operator, the request includes many details: reason for the call, description of the situation, etc. (see Examples 3, 6). In general, requests to a human operator are longer. Therefore, to repair the caller's enquiry, the human operator shortens it and translates it into the form of a "clearly formulated question" to which the operator can find an answer in a knowledge base (see Example 6). A human operator, therefore, initiates and carries out the repair in most of the cases.

Despite the institutional character of the call which imposes certain rules on the interaction, people formulate and reformulate their enquiries differently to a robot, even though the goal in both cases is to get an answer to the same enquiry (see Example

3). Callers design their utterances based on their knowledge of the recipient, so when talking to a robot they orient to its (in)capabilities. They adapt their responses and perform "robot-recipient design" (as a form of a recipient design). When talking to the robot, people tend to produce simple and unambiguous enquiries (see Examples 2, 3, 4, 7) before giving the details in subsequent answers to robot's questions. In the case of the "robot-recipient design", enquiry is formulated as a command or a search request; hence, the potential difficulties – an incorrectly composed command and the need to reformulate it as a way of carrying out the repair, or a lack of necessary information and the need to add it in the next turn. Repair is usually initiated by the robot in a case of technical or interactional trouble, but the caller is the one who is expected to provide the solution (see Examples 4, 5, 7).

## 5.2  Research and Design Implications

Findings of this study lead to several implications for HCI researchers, designers of conversational user experience, and developers of artificial conversational agents for institutional settings. Our findings have interesting implications both in terms of "robot-recipient design" and "user-recipient design".

This study introduces the notion of robot-recipient design as a novel form of recipient design for HCI research on artificial conversational agents. It highlights that information enquiries are produced differently for human operators and for an artificial agent. Types of repairs are also different in interaction with a human and a robot operator. Overall, this study maintains that humans orient to their assumption about an artificial agent's conversational competence and (in)capabilities, and they adjust their utterances to this knowledge. Our results offer a description of these adjustments.

Robot-recipient design has been acknowledged by HCI research to an extent. The use of a less rich language in interaction with robots has already been noted in previous research [23]. Short pauses after each word and stretch of the pronunciation of words have been found in prior studies on interaction with conversational interfaces [36]. However, this study explicates and makes this form of recipient design more visible, indicating also a new research area for the future: on users' (often implicit) assumptions about the robot-recipients' capabilities – there is a need to study their formation (how they form, when and where, based on what kind of experiences, expectations, bias, pre-knowledge, trajectories) as well as their evolution along people's encounters with different kinds of ever evolving intelligent systems and agents. Such research should determine how the assumptions are enacted in the actual conversation, i.e. in this case their initial enquiries and repairs, in different settings and with different systems. Similarly to the older HCI research stream of mental models, we should start examining what different kinds of people know, expect and assume in relation to artificial conversational agents' capabilities, acknowledging that very likely their understanding is not factual but may well be superstitious, outdated and biased. This, however, should be done based on the analysis of real conversations. We should also follow up the developments in technology and see how people's understanding is evolving and adapting along their encounters with ever more intelligent systems and agents.

We wish to direct HCI attention also to another form of recipient design: "user-recipient design", performed by designers and developers of artificial agents (see also

[10, 16, 33]). Our study indicates that making the robot's capabilities more explicit to the caller might improve and speed up the interaction. This is especially relevant for artificial agents in institutional settings, as their main purpose is getting a task done fast and easy, e.g. through getting enough information to find an answer to an enquiry. In more entertainment-oriented settings people may tolerate or even enjoy more complicated interactions with a lot of reformulation and repair. Our data showed callers tended to formulate their enquiries to human operators in a way that required additional work on the interpretation and reformulation. Both initial requests for an enquiry and requests for its repair should be formulated differently by an artificial agent to avoid the necessity of this additional work. Making explicit what a robot can understand (e.g. by giving callers an input example) will lead to more appropriately formulated information enquires. This will eventually improve the process of parsing, transcribing and processing of an enquiry by the robot. Robot's voice and way of speaking (pauses, intonations, etc.) should correspond to its capabilities, so that callers get a better idea about how they should formulate their enquiries. As we have shown, callers make their speech more robotic (and easier to parse) after they hear a reply from the robot. If the robot introduces itself instead of being introduced in a message pre-recorded by a human, callers can better evaluate robot's capabilities before formulating an initial enquiry. The robot's introduction should be carefully designed to include relevant information on its capabilities. We also suggest that the less natural robot's speech and voice sounds, the less expectations people have, which results in easier formulations for the robots (see also [5, 48]). This hypothesis, however, has to be investigated with a different set of data. Future research could also focus on the comparison of enquiries formulated for the robot by people who interact with it for the first time and by those who have had previous experience of talking to this agent. This could reveal the process of learning to talk to an artificial agent in institutional settings.

Overall, our study leads us to questions about the future of robots in institutional settings as well as in our everyday life: should robots learn to talk like humans (e.g. Google Duplex), or should humans learn to talk like robots; should robots in institutional setting be more natural or should they be more effective; should conversations with robots be merged with our everyday life or should they be recognized as related to technology use? Should our children be taught to human-human as well as human-robot interaction? How should robots introduce themselves to us to make us aware of their nature and capabilities? The HCI research community should be more engaged in reflection on these very broad issues, as human-robot interactions are becoming a prominent part of our everyday life. It is important to remember that not only developers perform "user-recipient design", i.e. design robot's utterances, but users also design their responses, i.e. perform "robot-recipient design". A question for a future study could be on the dynamics between robot-recipient and user-recipient design: "How does robot-recipient design change when the design of the robot changes?" One interesting implication of our study is also that to understand how a human would interact with a robot, it is not sufficient to analyse human interactions of the same type, as it has been done in previous studies [47]. We also wish to point out the significance of emotions and affective computing in relation to human interaction with robots. As we have an interaction-based approach of CA, our focus has been on interactional features and we have not tried to find expressions of emotional stances. However, emotions are an interesting topic for future studies in this context.

This study demonstrates the usefulness of CA in studies on interaction with artificial agents. It has already been known that humans talk to robots differently [17], but CA allows us to see what exactly those differences are [35]. The method focuses on micro level analysis of empirical data and is not strong in generating design implications. Nevertheless, we show CA results can be used as a basis for design implications regarding specific studied phenomena. We acknowledge the idea of robot-recipient design should be developed further through empirical investigations; we have taken only an initial step towards developing this approach. As an initial set of design guidelines, we propose the following: 1) Always consider the target user group(s) and their background knowledge and experiences with conversational agents (of different kind): those will inform their robot-recipient design and should guide the user-recipient design; 2) design the agent so that it makes its (in)capabilities visible for the user as early as possible (consider carefully how natural the interaction should seem for users); 3) design the agent so that it guides the user towards appropriate robot-recipient design (offering help in the formulation of initial enquiries as well as in repair). Naturally, these guidelines need to be developed towards a more practical design approach. Important is also to acknowledge that there are different types of robot-recipient design (e.g. for virtual assistant-recipient design, telephone robot-recipient design, etc.); we have empirically explored only one particular case; future studies are needed in this respect.

## 6   Conclusion

To conclude, in the talk with a robot, callers produce "robot-robot" conversation as they start to produce "robot-like" responses themselves, while in the talk with human operators, callers tend to shift the task of formulating the "clearly formulated question" to the operator. In situations when a repair is necessary, operators also have a bigger role: the robot indicates only the trouble source, while operators also provide a possible solution to the trouble. Interaction with the robot has a particular conversational character, as people constantly orient to their knowledge on robot's (in)capabilities. This raises a question regarding whether robots should be designed based on interaction with humans. There are always discussions in the field of development of conversational agents on how to make a machine speak like a person, but if a robot needs to get an enquiry in a particular form that is easy for him to read and find an answer to it is actually the question of how to make robot more "robot-like" that becomes relevant. It is especially relevant in the design of artificial agents for institutional settings, as the main goal of these agents is to understand an enquiry and provide a relevant response effectively and efficiently. Having a more "robot-like" agent will decrease callers' expectations regarding robots' capabilities and lead to an easier to parse enquiry, which will be correctly interpreted by the robot. This will eventually lead to the relevant response and satisfactory experience for people who use the service.

**Acknowledgements.** Iuliia Avgustis received financial support from the research project "Smart Communication" (2018–2022, Eudaimonia Institute, University of Oulu). We would like to thank members of the EMCA_Ru Research Group (A. Korbut, A. Maximova, K. Popova, A. Reiniuk, N. Belov) in collaboration with whom data for this research were collected and transcribed and who provided valuable insights during data sessions. Special thanks should be given to Florence Oloff for constructive comments and useful critiques, as well as to Gary David and Stuart Reeves for their insightful feedback.

# References

1. Acomb, K., et al.: Technical support dialog systems: issues, problems, and solutions. In: Proceedings of the Workshop on Bridging the Gap: Academic and Industrial Research in Dialog Technologies, pp. 25–31. Association for Computational Linguistics, Stroudsburg (2007)
2. Albert, S., Housley, W., Stokoe, E.: In case of emergency, order pizza: an urgent case of action formation and recognition. Presented at the Proceedings of the 1st International Conference on Conversational User Interfaces, August 22 (2019). https://doi.org/10.1145/3342775.334 2800
3. Ashktorab, Z., Jain, M., Liao, Q.V., Weisz, J.D.: Resilient chatbots: repair strategy preferences for conversational breakdowns. In: Proceedings of the 2019 CHI Conference on Human Factors in Computing Systems, pp. 1–12. Association for Computing Machinery, New York (2019). https://doi.org/10.1145/3290605.3300484
4. Barth, F., Candello, H., Cavalin, P., Pinhanez, C.: Intentions, meanings, and whys: designing content for voice-based conversational museum guides. In: Proceedings of the 2nd Conference on Conversational User Interfaces, pp. 1–8. Association for Computing Machinery, New York (2020). https://doi.org/10.1145/3405755.3406128
5. Barzilai, G., Rampino, L.: Just a natural talk? The rise of intelligent personal assistants and the (hidden) legacy of ubiquitous computing. In: Marcus, A., Rosenzweig, E. (eds.) HCII 2020. LNCS, vol. 12201, pp. 18–39. Springer, Cham (2020). https://doi.org/10.1007/978-3-030-49760-6_2
6. Bennett, G.A.: Conversational style: beyond the nuts and bolts of conversation. In: Moore, R.J., Szymanski, M.H., Arar, R., Ren, G.-J. (eds.) Studies in Conversational UX Design. HIS, pp. 161–180. Springer, Cham (2018). https://doi.org/10.1007/978-3-319-95579-7_8
7. Bolden, G.B.: Negotiating understanding in "intercultural moments" in immigrant family interactions. Commun. Monogr. **81**, 208–238 (2014). https://doi.org/10.1080/03637751.2014.902983
8. Button, G.: Going up a blind alley: conflating conversation analysis and computational modelling. In: Computers and Conversation, pp. 67–90. Academic Press, Cambridge (1990)
9. Cena, F., Torre, I.: Increasing performances and personalization in the interaction with a call center system. In: Proceedings of the 9th International Conference on Intelligent User Interfaces, pp. 226–228. Association for Computing Machinery, New York (2004). https://doi.org/10.1145/964442.964487
10. Clark, L., et al.: What makes a good conversation? Challenges in designing truly conversational agents. In: Proceedings of the 2019 CHI Conference on Human Factors in Computing Systems, pp. 1–12. Association for Computing Machinery, New York (2019). https://doi.org/10.1145/3290605.3300705
11. Clinkenbeard, M.: Multimodal conversation analysis and usability studies: exploring human-technology interactions in multiparty contexts. Commun. Des. Q. **6**, 103–113 (2018). https://doi.org/10.1145/3282665.3282675
12. Colman, M., Healey, P.: The distribution of repair in dialogue. In: Proceedings of the Annual Meeting of the Cognitive Science Society, vol. 33 (2011)

13. Dev, J., Camp, L.J.: User engagement with chatbots: a discursive psychology approach. In: Proceedings of the 2nd Conference on Conversational User Interfaces, pp. 1–4. Association for Computing Machinery, New York (2020). https://doi.org/10.1145/3405755.3406165

14. Dubiel, M., Cervone, A., Riccardi, G.: Inquisitive mind: a conversational news companion. Presented at the Proceedings of the 1st International Conference on Conversational User Interfaces, August 22 (2019). https://doi.org/10.1145/3342775.3342802

15. Edlund, J., Gustafson, J., Heldner, M., Hjalmarsson, A.: Towards human-like spoken dialogue systems. Speech Commun. **50**, 630–645 (2008). https://doi.org/10.1016/j.specom.2008.04.002

16. Fischer, J.E., Reeves, S., Porcheron, M., Sikveland, R.O.: Progressivity for voice interface design. Presented at the Proceedings of the 1st International Conference on Conversational User Interfaces, August 22 (2019). https://doi.org/10.1145/3342775.3342788

17. Fischer, K.: How people talk to computers, robots, and other artificial communication partners. In: Proceedings of the Workshop Hansewissenschaftskolleg, Delmenhorst, 21–23 April (2006)

18. Følstad, A., Skjuve, M.: Chatbots for customer service: user experience and motivation. Presented at the Proceedings of the 1st International Conference on Conversational User Interfaces, August 22 (2019). https://doi.org/10.1145/3342775.3342784

19. Harris, R.A.: Voice Interaction Design: Crafting the New Conversational Speech Systems. Elsevier, Amsterdam (2005)

20. Heath, C., Luff, P.: Technology in Action. Cambridge University Press, Cambridge (2000)

21. Heritage, J.: Conversation analysis and institutional talk. In: Handbook of Language and Social Interaction. Lawrence Erlbaum Associates, Inc., Mahwah (2005)

22. Heritage, J., Clayman, S.: Talk in Action: Interactions, Identities, and Institutions. Wiley-Blackwell, New York (2010)

23. Hill, J., Ford, W.R., Farreras, I.G.: Real conversations with artificial intelligence: a comparison between human–human online conversations and human–chatbot conversations. Comput. Hum. Behav. **49**, 245–250 (2015)

24. Hutchby, I.: Conversation and Technology: From the Telephone to Internet. Polity (2001)

25. Jefferson, G.: Glossary of transcript symbols with an introduction. In: Lerner, G.H. (ed.) Conversation Analysis: Studies from the First Generation, pp. 13–34. John Benjamins Publishing Company, Amsterdam (2004)

26. Jung, H., Kim, H., Ha, J.-W.: Understanding differences between heavy users and light users in difficulties with voice user interfaces. In: Proceedings of the 2nd Conference on Conversational User Interfaces, pp. 1–4. Association for Computing Machinery, New York (2020). https://doi.org/10.1145/3405755.3406170

27. Kitzinger, C.: Repair. In: The Handbook of Conversation Analysis. Wiley-Blackwell, New York (2013)

28. Koca, A., Brombacher, A.C.: Extracting "broken expectations" from call center records: *why* and *how*. In: CHI 2008 Extended Abstracts on Human Factors in Computing Systems, pp. 2985–2990. Association for Computing Machinery, New York (2008). https://doi.org/10.1145/1358628.1358795

29. Lahoual, D., Frejus, M.: When users assist the voice assistants: from supervision to failure resolution. In: Extended Abstracts of the 2019 CHI Conference on Human Factors in Computing Systems, pp. 1–8. Association for Computing Machinery, New York (2019). https://doi.org/10.1145/3290607.3299053

30. Li, T.J.-J., Chen, J., Xia, H., Mitchell, T.M., Myers, B.A.: Multi-modal repairs of conversational breakdowns in task-oriented dialogs. In: Proceedings of the 33rd Annual ACM Symposium on User Interface Software and Technology, pp. 1094–1107. Association for Computing Machinery, New York (2020). https://doi.org/10.1145/3379337.3415820

31. Li, T.-J., Labutov, I., Myers, B.A., Azaria, A., Rudnicky, A.I., Mitchell, T.M.: Teaching agents when they fail: end user development in goal-oriented conversational agents. In: Moore, R.J., Szymanski, M.H., Arar, R., Ren, G.-J. (eds.) Studies in Conversational UX Design. HIS, pp. 119–137. Springer, Cham (2018). https://doi.org/10.1007/978-3-319-95579-7_6

32. Luff, P., Gilbert, N., Frohlich, D. (eds.): Computers and Conversation. Academic Press, Bodmin, Cornwall (1990)

33. Moore, B., Arar, R.: Talk Meets Technology: Conversation Design Guidelines. https://conversational-ux.mybluemix.net/design/conversational-ux/

34. Patel, N., Chittamuru, D., Jain, A., Dave, P., Parikh, T.S.: Avaaj Otalo: a field study of an interactive voice forum for small farmers in rural India. In: Proceedings of the SIGCHI Conference on Human Factors in Computing Systems, pp. 733–742. Association for Computing Machinery, New York (2010)

35. Pelikan, H.R.M., Broth, M.: Why that Nao?: How humans adapt to a conventional humanoid robot in taking turns-at-talk. In: Proceedings of the 2016 CHI Conference on Human Factors in Computing Systems, pp. 4921–4932. ACM, New York (2016). https://doi.org/10.1145/2858036.2858478

36. Porcheron, M., Fischer, J.E., Reeves, S., Sharples, S.: Voice interfaces in everyday life. In: Proceedings of the 2018 CHI Conference on Human Factors in Computing Systems, pp. 640:1-640:12. ACM, New York (2018). https://doi.org/10.1145/3173574.3174214

37. Porcheron, M., Fischer, J.E., Sharples, S.: "Do animals have accents?": Talking with agents in multi-party conversation. In: Proceedings of the 2017 ACM Conference on Computer Supported Cooperative Work and Social Computing, pp. 207–219. Association for Computing Machinery, New York (2017). https://doi.org/10.1145/2998181.2998298

38. Reeves, S.: Some conversational challenges of talking with machines. Presented at the Talking with Conversational Agents in Collaborative Action, Workshop at the 20th ACM conference on Computer-Supported Cooperative Work and Social Computing (CSCW 2017), Portland, Oregon, USA, February 25 (2017)

39. Sacks, H., Schegloff, E.A., Jefferson, G.: A simplest systematics for the organization of turn-taking for conversation. Language 50, 696–735 (1974). https://doi.org/10.2307/412243

40. Schegloff, E.A.: Sequence Organization in Interaction: A Primer in Conversation Analysis. Cambridge University Press, New York (2007)

41. Schegloff, E.A., Jefferson, G., Sacks, H.: The preference for self-correction in the organization of repair in conversation. Language 53, 361–382 (1977). https://doi.org/10.2307/413107

42. Sidnell, J.: Comparative studies in conversation analysis. Annu. Rev. Anthropol. 36, 229–244 (2007). https://doi.org/10.1146/annurev.anthro.36.081406.094313

43. Sporka, A., Franc, J., Riccardi, G.: Can machines call people? User experience while answering telephone calls initiated by machine. In: CHI Extended Abstracts (2009). https://doi.org/10.1145/1520340.1520545

44. Suchman, L.A.: Plans and Situated Actions: The Problem of Human-Machine Communication. Cambridge University Press, New York (1987)

45. Suchman, L.A.: Human-Machine Reconfigurations: Plans and Situated Actions. Cambridge University Press, New York (2007)

46. Suhm, B., Peterson, P.: Call browser: a system to improve the caller experience by analyzing live calls end-to-end. In: Proceedings of the SIGCHI Conference on Human Factors in Computing Systems, pp. 1313–1322. Association for Computing Machinery, New York (2009). https://doi.org/10.1145/1518701.1518899

47. Szymanski, M.H., Moore, R.J.: Adapting to customer initiative: insights from human service encounters. In: Moore, R.J., Szymanski, M.H., Arar, R., Ren, G.-J. (eds.) Studies in Conversational UX Design. HIS, pp. 19–32. Springer, Cham (2018). https://doi.org/10.1007/978-3-319-95579-7_2

48. Velkovska, J., Zouinar, M.: The illusion of natural conversation: interacting with smart assistants in home settings. Presented at the Proceedings of the 2018 CHI Conference on Human Factors in Computing Systems (CHI 2018), Montreal, Canada (2018)
49. Vtyurina, A., Savenkov, D., Agichtein, E., Clarke, C.L.A.: Exploring conversational search with humans, assistants, and wizards. In: Proceedings of the 2017 CHI Conference Extended Abstracts on Human Factors in Computing Systems, pp. 2187–2193. Association for Computing Machinery, New York (2017). https://doi.org/10.1145/3027063.3053175
50. Wooffitt, R., Fraser, N.M., Gilbert, N., McGlashan, S.: Humans, Computers and Wizards: Analysing Human (Simulated) Computer Interaction. Routledge, London (2013)

# An Interactive Paradigm for the End-User Development of Chatbots for Data Exploration

Ludovica Piro[1], Giuseppe Desolda[2], Maristella Matera[1(✉)], Rosa Lanzilotti[2], Sara Mosca[2], and Emanuele Pucci[3]

[1] DEIB, Politecnico di Milano, Milan, Italy
ludovica.piro@mail.polimi.it, maristella.matera@polimi.it
[2] Computer Science Department, University of Bari Aldo Moro, Bari, Italy
{giuseppe.desolda,rosa.lanzilotti}@uniba.it,
s.mosca3@studenti.uniba.it
[3] Awhy Srl, Florence, Italy
emanuele.pucci@awhy.it

**Abstract.** This paper presents an interaction paradigm for the design of chatbots. Its novelty is the completion of conversational patterns that progressively guide the design activity and provide an interactive, immediate representation of the conversation under construction. Thanks to the automatic generation of code, the paradigm facilitates the rapid prototyping of the conversational UI, thus it empowers non-programmers to master the design process. The paper also illustrates some preliminary user studies and discusses some lessons learned for the definition of interactive paradigms for the design of conversational UIs.

**Keywords:** End-User Development · Chatbot design · Conversational UIs

## 1 Introduction

Chatbots for data exploration support conversations that let the user progressively discover and interactively retrieve data from known data sources [8]. Given the multiple advantages that the literature recognizes to the conversational paradigm for data access, and its current diffusion through different applications, the literature is now posing emphasis on methodologies for chatbot design [10, 21, 26]. A diffused opinion is that domain experts are critical in the development of chatbots; but it also emerges that engaging them in chatbot development is difficult due to their lack of technical competencies. To overcome this drawback, this paper presents an interactive paradigm for the End-User Development (EUD) of chatbots for data exploration.

**Electronic supplementary material** The online version of this chapter (https://doi.org/10.1007/978-3-030-85610-6_11) contains supplementary material, which is available to authorized users.

© IFIP International Federation for Information Processing 2021
Published by Springer Nature Switzerland AG 2021
C. Ardito et al. (Eds.): INTERACT 2021, LNCS 12935, pp. 177–186, 2021.
https://doi.org/10.1007/978-3-030-85610-6_11

The new interactive paradigm has been developed on top of CHATIDEA, a methodology for the rapid prototyping of chatbots that is also complemented by a software framework [8]. The paradigm is based on a visual front end that enables non-programmers to complete conversation patterns that mimic the interaction between users and the chatbot under construction. It, therefore, masks the need for technical specifications and allows the designers to manipulate directly the elements of the conversation, also providing immediate feedback on the designed conversation. This modus operandi helps overcome some complexity factors that, more in general, characterize the design of AI-based systems [26], such as the difficulty of identifying the functionality that the system can afford, as well as the possible output that the system can produce. The proposed paradigm also facilitates sketching and rapid prototyping of the conversational UI, two fundamental activities in interaction design, which allow designers to understand what the technology is and can do, engage in creative thinking, and assess and improve on their designs [10, 26].

After discussing some related works (Sect. 2), this paper illustrates the interactive paradigm for the EUD of chatbots (Sect. 3) and the user-centered process adopted to assess the adequateness of the paradigm with respect to the expectations of both chatbot developers and non-expert programmers (Sect. 4). The paper then ends by discussing some lessons learned (Sect. 5) and by outlining our future work (Sect. 6).

## 2  Rationale and Background

The idea of computers behaving like humans dates back to 1950, when Alan Turing proposed his famous test [23]. However, it is from the 90s that several applications benefitted from the advancements in artificial intelligence, natural language processing and speech recognition: the applications became more and more intelligent, capable of better understanding various conversations and performing more complex tasks. With the smartphone era, the technology witnessed an explosion of commercial applications: some examples are IBM Watson [14], Siri [3], WeChat [24], Alexa [1]. If we want to classify those applications from a high-level perspective, we can distinguish between *task-oriented* and *conversational chatbots* [9], the former being oriented toward a resolution of a specific task and the latter designed to carry on a general conversation.

Together with the technology, tools and frameworks to support the creation of conversational interfaces evolved themselves. Such frameworks and tools target both experienced and non-experienced users, trying to ease the process of chatbot creation. The majority of those tools help the user in two fundamental operations: *intent matching* (understanding the action the user wants to perform and match it with an appropriate response) and *entity extraction* (the ability to extract key elements from an utterance). The evolution of the tools, however, has not changed the underlying mechanism of a chatbot creation: either the designer or the developer has to handle from scratch all the questions and answers. Also, it seems to be missing a general approach to develop data-driven chatbots. Even though some tools let the user retrieve information from spreadsheets [6] or the internet thanks to webhooks, mapping intents and entities and developing conversational interfaces using a database as a source is still scarcely explored.

Researchers have been interested in using natural language to access large databases long before chatbots. The use of natural language can help users without formal knowledge of a query language access and perform actions on a structured database [2]. LUNAR, developed in 1972, was one of the first examples of natural language interfaces created to access information structured in a database [25]. One more recent example is NaLIR [16]: it takes complex sentences from the user and generates a query in a technical language following a "human-in-the-loop" approach that asks the user to check the results of the intermediate generation steps. There are not many examples of explorative chatbots used to access databases yet: one of the few we found is Intellibot, a dialogue-based chatbot for the insurance industry [20]. However, Intellibot is still a custom-made chatbot, developed for a domain-specific conversation.

This paper addresses the gap by proposing a visual paradigm that facilitates the design of conversational interfaces for database exploration. The paradigm falls in the category of the End-User Development (EUD) tools [17], which empower non-technical users, e.g., domain experts, to achieve goals for which computing knowledge is needed. Some chatbot frameworks included similar environments that help the user define flow charts or configure the interaction through specific graphic user interfaces (e.g., Dialogflow [11] and Motion AI [13]). However, our approach differs from the previous because it adopts a dynamic interactive paradigm, which is made possible by the capability of the framework to automatically generate the conversation.

## 3   An Interactive Paradigm for the EUD of Chatbots

The contribution of this paper is a new interactive paradigm for the EUD of chatbots for data exploration. The resulting solution is a Web front end built on top of CHATIDEA, a software framework for the rapid prototyping of chatbots for data exploration [8]. The following sections provide details on the CHATIDEA modeling abstractions and the new EUD paradigm.

### 3.1   Modeling Abstractions

CHATIDEA automatically generates a chatbot starting from a dump of a relational database (DB) and a JSON descriptor file. The dump provides the data that can be explored by the users by means of the resulting chatbot, and the definition of the schema for the organization of data. The descriptor contains a set of *annotations* identifying key data elements and properties of the DB, which are relevant for managing conversations for data exploration. By combining the DB dump and the annotation descriptor, CHATIDEA automatically generates the chatbot dialog system, according to conversational patterns that progressively guide the users to explore the data.

One fundamental annotation refers to the *table role*, which can be Primary, Secondary, or Crossable. *Primary tables* represent data that can be queried directly in the chatbot. *Secondary tables* store data dependent on other entities, which are interesting for the conversation only when reached from other (primary) tables. *Crossable tables* represent many-to-many relationships; within the chatbot, they are represented as links to navigate between different entities - while no direct or deferred search is allowed on them. Among others, some annotations can rename tables and attributes by using *names and aliases* that are simpler and more understandable during the conversation. It is possible to specify which attributes can be used in user utterances to *filter the table instances*, which *display attributes* have to be shown when instances are retrieved by the chatbot, which attributes can be used *to categorize primary table instances and display aggregated visualizations.* Lack of space prevents us from fully describing the annotations; a detailed description of the whole set of annotations needed to automatically generate a chatbot with CHATIDEA is reported in [8]. An example of annotations expressed in JSON format is available at https://bit.ly/3x7N6ov.

## 3.2 The Interactive Design Paradigm

Even if the CHATIDEA software framework makes it possible to create chatbots without programming, the designers are still required to manually write descriptor files using technical specification languages (e.g., JSON); this activity is time-consuming, error-prone, and requires complete knowledge of the technical syntax.

The new interactive paradigm, which is the main contribution of this article, aims to enable even people without expertise in programming and/or chatbot development to *visually complete* conversation patterns related to the interaction between users and the chatbot under construction. The chatbot designer is guided through the process by means of text prompts modeled on a hypothetical conversation that the final user may have with the chatbot. The text prompts are skeletons of training phrases to be completed with keywords and data taken from the database. This helps designers implicitly create the annotation schema, i.e., map DB data elements on conversational elements, within the context of a sample conversation based on patterns for DB navigation.

The visual front end enabling this paradigm consists of two main areas. After uploading a DB dump, in the first area (Fig. 1a) the designer can skim the DB by operating on a graph-based visualization of tables and relationships. In a sidebar editor, the designer assigns table roles (primary, secondary and crossable, represented through different colors), and edits table and attribute names if needed to improve the conversation design. Moving to the next area, for each primary and secondary table tagged in the previous section, the designer completes some conversation patterns. For example, for the table *Person,* Fig. 1b illustrates the pattern *"Categorize query results based on <a table attribute>"*. Its completion consists in selecting a categorical attribute, among the ones included in the selected table, which will be used to produce a visualization that categorizes the table data. The *"Research area"* part of the sentence is initially empty; when the designer clicks the empty label, a pop-up window asks to select the categorical attribute. In this example, the designer has selected *Research area.*

A characterizing feature is that a live-preview in the right-hand panel shows the effect of any design choice on a sample of instances retrieved from the DB. In the example, the designer can see that the response to the configured utterance is a pie chart that categorizes the Person instances according to four different research areas. The designers can thus control the outcome of their design decisions. A video demonstrating the visual paradigm is available at: https://youtu.be/hP9lDyJnRG4.

# 4   Evaluation

Two qualitative formative studies were conducted to enhance the quality of some initial, high-fidelity prototypes of the visual front end. A user study was then carried out on an advanced Web-based prototype, to investigate the usability and the perceived workload. Due to the COVID-19 pandemic, the studies were carried out online, using Skype or WebEx, depending on the users' familiarity with these teleconferencing platforms. Each session was video-recorded. Each participant was introduced to the study purpose, informed on what to do, and signed a consent form.

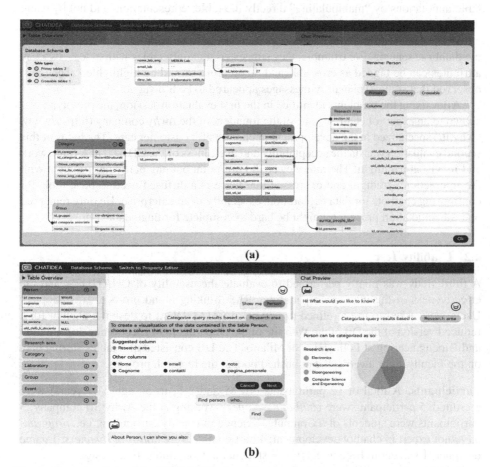

(a)

(b)

**Fig. 1.** Two snapshots of the CHATIDEA visual front end: a) the area for annotating table roles; b) the area for completing conversation patterns.

## 4.1   Preliminary Evaluation: Validity and Usefulness

A first formative study was organized to receive feedback on the validity of the interaction paradigm from users who had already performed annotation-related tasks with

CHATIDEA using the JSON syntax. A first prototype was evaluated by interviewing 4 users who had participated in the development of the CHATIDEA software framework, being former students in Computer Science and Engineering who had worked on CHATIDEA for their master theses. After an initial demonstration of the prototype by one of the researchers moderating the interview, a discussion followed to gather the developers' opinions. They found the UI complete with respect to the design capabilities offered by the software framework, and considered the interaction paradigm clear and effective. They also helped identify some improvements that were mainly related to the table tagging mechanisms on the first page. For example, they thought of expressing table annotations by "manipulating" directly the table representation, and not by using the right-hand panel. They also observed that the system could take some initiatives and guide the design through recommendations that could be derived from an analysis of the database schema. For example, they suggested that only tables with at least two key attributes can be tagged as crossable and this feature should be highlighted. They also observed that some explanatory messages appeared to be too vague.

After fixing the problems identified in the first evaluation session, the prototype was shown to an expert of chatbots, one of the founders of the *Awhy* company (https://www. awhy.it/) specialized in the development of chatbots for customer care. The focus of this second evaluation was on the acceptability and usefulness of the CHATIDEA framework and its visual paradigm. The interviewee did not point out any particular problem with the interaction paradigm and expressed that there is a diffused need to have tools for configuring chatbots for data exploration, especially in an enterprise. He only remarked that the annotation procedure might be hard to complete for huge databases.

## 4.2 Usability Test

A third study was finally performed to evaluate the usability of CHATIDEA and the effectiveness of the interaction paradigm. The thinking aloud protocol was adopted. Users were asked to use a refined prototype of CHATIDEA, to design a chatbot for a reduced version of the DB of the Web site of the Department of Electronics, Information and Bioengineering at Politecnico di Milano. The DB consisted of 8 tables storing data on the faculty, their awards, the published books, the research projects.

**Participants.** A total of 12 participants (10 M and 2 F; mean age 24.5 years) were recruited. 5 participants were *chatbot developers* working at the Awhy Srl company; 3 participants were students of a Computer Science university curriculum, i.e., *programmers* not expert in chatbot development; 4 participants were *non-programmers*: 1 game designer, 1 student in Bioengineering, 2 students in Communication Design.

**Procedure.** During the video call, every user was asked to activate the webcam and share the screen to let the observer identify facial expressions that could reveal spontaneous feelings and see the actions performed to complete the assigned tasks. Each session was video-recorded. Each user was asked to read a brief description of the functionality supported by the visual front end, in the form of a scenario providing information about a possible context of use. The description did not include details on the underlying software framework and its modeling abstractions. The general organization of the front end was explained in a short demo. The user was then provided with a sheet reporting 7 tasks and started the execution of each task. The first two tasks were related to table tagging, while the remaining five tasks covered each of the other annotation concepts. At the end of all the tasks, the participant filled in an online form with the SUS [5, 15] and NASA-TLX [12] questionnaires to be answered one after the other.

**Results.** Quantitative and qualitative data were collected. For quantitative data, the SUS and NASA-TLX scores were computed. SUS estimated the *system usability perceived by users*, as resulting from two factors, *System Learnability* (statements #4 and #10) and *System Usability* (the other 8 statements) [15]. The average SUS score was $\bar{x} = 74.2$, SD $= 15.0$; the System Usability score was $\bar{x} = 76.3$, SD $= 14.8$; the System Learnability score was $\bar{x} = 68.8$, SD $= 17.3$. Due to the limited number of participants, it was not possible to compute inferential statistics for the comparison of the three user groups, but the means and the standard deviations were very similar (*chatbot developers:* $\bar{x} = 74.4$, SD $= 15.2$; *programmers:* $\bar{x} = 73.8$, SD $= 14.5$; *non-programmers:* $\bar{x} = 74.4$, SD $= 19.5$).

NASA-TLX was used to measure the *perceived workload* on a scale from 0 to 100, where 0 equals to low effort, 100 to excessive effort from the user. The average score was $\bar{x} = 38.1$, SD $= 13.3$. On average, the highest score, and therefore the poorer performance, was recorded for the *Mental Demand dimension* ($\bar{x} = 54.2$, SD $= 17.3$), followed by *Effort* ($\bar{x} = 44.2$, SD $= 20.7$), *Performance* ($\bar{x} = 37.5$, SD $= 16.6$), *Temporal Demand* ($\bar{x} = 31.7$, SD $= 24.8$), and *Physical Demand* ($\bar{x} = 23.3$, SD $= 19.7$). In this case as well, the score means for the three groups are very similar (*chatbot developers:* $\bar{x} = 39.6$, SD $= 13.3$; *programmers:* $\bar{x} = 39.6$, SD $= 6$; *non-programmers:* $\bar{x} = 35.6$, SD $= 19.1$), with a lower cognitive load for non-programmers.

The qualitative analysis was performed on the participants' comments [4]. Few themes, not reported here for brevity, were related to very specific problems with few visual elements (e.g., expressiveness of tooltips). The three themes reported in the following, instead, convey more general reflections on the interactive paradigm.

*Theme 1: Conflicts between System Architecture and User Assumptions.* In relation to the annotations on the database schema, users agreed that knowing basic concepts of relational databases helps complete correctly the tasks ("The design is for sure aided by the system, but requires knowledge of the subject [database domain] and a bit of technical knowledge [relational database concepts]"). These concerns did not emerge, however, during the completion of conversation patterns.

*Theme 2: Perceived Ease of Use.* Despite their difficulties in executing some tasks, most participants reported the ease of use of setting and modifying conversation patterns, and noted that the workload is not overwhelming ("Very usable, [the tasks] flow well"). As also highlighted by the questionnaires, this perception was not influenced by the user programming skills, as the scores were comparable among all the three groups.

*Theme 3: Generating Chatbots from Databases.* Participants appreciated the flexibility offered by the prototype through table tagging ("It is particularly powerful that the designer has control on what tables to include and what relationships to use"), and the opportunity to configure user queries easily ("It is nice to design database queries through natural language"). Chatbot experts also asked for advanced features to be invoked on-demand, even by coding, for a deeper customization of the intents.

## 5  Discussion

Besides highlighting usability problems, the insights gained through the user studies brought to light general key points, which are in line with previous findings on EUD, but add interesting perspectives on interactive paradigms for conversation design.

*Closeness of Mapping.* For the effectiveness of an EUD paradigm, it is important to adopt a representation of possible design choices that abstracts from the technical details, also giving immediate feedback on the results [7, 19]. As highlighted by Theme 2, directly manipulating utterances helped the designers understand the conversation patterns that the system can manage, and their effect on the conversation flow [10, 26]. Theme 1 and 3 in a sense confirm this assumption, as they suggest that, even if the users did not mind selecting entities by operating on database tables, they felt more comfortable when manipulating the utterance structure.

*Control on the Conversation Context.* Theme 2 suggests that having a preview on how the sentences will appear during conversation and how they relate to one another, being able to always modify previous annotations and see the consequent effect, were key features for the ease of the interactive paradigm. This is also in line with the results of previous works that studied the effect of immediate representations of the design choices [7, 19]. Looking at the general class of AI-based interactive systems, this feature can give the designer control over the outcome of AI models, and provides a lens for understanding AI's challenges in the design of interactive systems [10].

*Assistance on Intent and Entity Identification.* Theme 3 suggests that, despite the difficulties in dealing with database concepts, the users appreciated having at their disposal tables to represent the entities that could be covered by the conversation, and the flexibility of filtering the most relevant ones. A similar observation applies to the configuration of intents, as designers operate on a set of intents suggested by the system as representative of classes of queries for data exploration. This guidance can help conceptualize the dialogue system capabilities and choreograph the interactions [10, 26].

*Accommodating Different Levels of Control.* Some facets of Theme 3 suggest that it is also important to enable the most skilled designers to extend and personalize the predefined patterns, to ensure a "gentle slope of difficulty" [18]. The designers could be enabled to act also on the modeling abstractions, for example by defining new annotations with impact on the underlying model for dialog generation. These mechanisms can be considered further ingredients to give designers control on AI models.

# 6  Conclusions and Future Work

This paper has presented a new interactive paradigm for the design of chatbots for data exploration. The preliminary evaluation conducted so far has some limitations (e.g., the limited number of users, lack of comparison with other design paradigms, limited number of DB tables in comparison to realistic scenarios). However, it highlights that the paradigm has some potential to bring conversation design within the reach of domain experts who don't have programming knowledge, and also to fasten chatbot development for programmers. However, as also evident from the problems identified through the user studies, some aspects still remain open; our future work will focus on them. At a more general level, an important aspect concerns the control that designers should have on Human-Centered AI [22]. In this respect, our future work will focus on generalizing our research to consider the changing role of humans in the design of AI-based systems and foster a discussion on design practices for human-AI interaction [10].

**Acknowledgment.** This work is partially supported by the Italian Ministry of University and Research (MIUR) under grant PRIN 2017 "EMPATHY: EMpowering People in deAling with internet of THings ecosYstems".

# References

1. Amazon: Amazon Alexa. https://www.amazon.it/b?ie=UTF8&node=15752736031. Accessed 10 Apr 2021
2. Androutsopoulos, I., Ritchie, G.D., Thanisch, P.: Natural language interfaces to databases – an introduction. Nat. Lang. Eng. **1**(1), 29–81 (1995)
3. Apple: Apple Siri. https://www.apple.com/it/siri/. Accessed 10 Apr 2021
4. Braun, V., Clarke, V.: Using thematic analysis psychology. Qual. Res. Psychol. **3**(2), 77–101 (2006)
5. Brooke, J.: SUS-A quick and dirty usability scale. Usab. Eval. Ind. **189**(194), 4–7 (1996)
6. Canh, N.T.: Turn your database into a chatbot. https://medium.com/botfuel/turn-your-dat abase-into-a-chatbot-10dae003b97d. Accessed 10 Apr 2021
7. Cappiello, C., Matera, M., Picozzi, M.: A UI-centric approach for the end-user development of multidevice mashups. ACM Trans. Web **9**(3), 1–40 (2015)
8. Castaldo, N., Daniel, F., Matera, M., Zaccaria, V.: Conversational data exploration. In: Bakaev, M., Frasincar, F., Ko, I.-Y. (eds.) ICWE 2019. LNCS, vol. 11496, pp. 490–497. Springer, Cham (2019). https://doi.org/10.1007/978-3-030-19274-7_34
9. Chen, H., Liu, X., Yin, D., Tang, J.: A survey on dialogue systems: recent advances and new frontiers. ACM SIGKDD Expl. Newsl. **19**(2), 25–35 (2017)
10. Feine, J., Morana, S., Maedche, A.: Designing interactive chatbot development systems. In: Proceedings of the Making Digital Inclusive: Blending the Local and the Globa (ICIS 2020) (2020)
11. Google: Dialogflow. https://dialogflow.com/. Accessed 14 Mar 2021
12. Hart, S.G., Staveland, L.E.: Development of NASA-TLX (Task Load Index): results of empirical and theoretical research. Adv. Psychol. **52**, 139–183 (1988)
13. HubSpot: motion.ai. https://www.motion.ai/. Accessed 14 Mar 2021
14. IBM: IBM Watson. https://www.ibm.com/watson/how-to-build-a-chatbot. Accessed 10 Apr 2021

15. Lewis, J.R., Sauro, J.: The factor structure of the system usability scale. In: Kurosu, M. (ed.) HCD 2009. LNCS, vol. 5619, pp. 94–103. Springer, Heidelberg (2009). https://doi.org/10.1007/978-3-642-02806-9_12

16. Li, F., Jagadish, H.V.: NaLIR: an interactive natural language interface for querying relational databases. In: Proceedings of the International Conference on Management of Data (SIGMOD 2014), pp. 709–712. Association for Computing Machinery, New York (2014)

17. Lieberman, H., Paternò, F., Klann, M., Wulf, V.: End-user development: an emerging paradigm. In: Lieberman, H., Paternò, F., Wulf, V. (eds.) End User Development. Human-Computer Interaction Series, vol. 9, pp. 1–8. Springer Netherlands, Dordrecht (2006). https://doi.org/10.1007/1-4020-5386-X_1

18. Lieberman, H., Paternò, F., Wulf, V. (eds.): End User Development. Springer Netherlands, Dordrecht (2006)

19. Namoun, A., Nestler, T., De Angeli, A.: Conceptual and usability issues in the composable web of software services. In: Daniel, F., Facca, F.M. (eds.) ICWE 2010. LNCS, vol. 6385, pp. 396–407. Springer, Heidelberg (2010). https://doi.org/10.1007/978-3-642-16985-4_35

20. Nuruzzaman, M., Hussain, O.K.: IntelliBot: a dialogue-based chatbot for the insurance industry. Knowl.-Based Syst. 196, 105810 (2020)

21. Ruane, E., Young, R., Ventresque, A.: Training a chatbot with Microsoft LUIS: effect of intent imbalance on prediction accuracy. In: Proceedings of the Conference on Intelligent User Interfaces Companion (IUI 2020), pp. 63–64. Association for Computing Machinery, New York (2020)

22. Shneiderman, B.: Human-centered artificial intelligence: reliable, safe & trustworthy. Int. J. Hum.-Comput. Interact. 36(6), 495–504 (2020)

23. Turing, A.M.: Computing machinery and intelligence. In: Epstein, R., Roberts, G., Beber, G. (eds.) Parsing the Turing Test, pp. 23–65. Springer, Dordrecht (2009). https://doi.org/10.1007/978-1-4020-6710-5_3

24. WeChat: WeChat. https://www.wechat.com/it/. Accessed 10 Apr 2021

25. Woods, W., Kaplan, R., Nash-Webber, B.: The Lunar Sciences Natural Language Information System, Cambridge, MA (1974)

26. Yang, Q., Steinfeld, A., Rosé, C., Zimmerman, J.: Re-examining whether, why, and how human-AI interaction is uniquely difficult to design. In: Proceedings of the Conference on Human Factors in Computing Systems (CHI 2020), pp. 1–13. Association for Computing Machinery, New York (2020)

# ReflectPal: Exploring Self-Reflection on Collaborative Activities Using Voice Assistants

Eleftherios Papachristos$^{(\boxtimes)}$ ⓘ, Dorte P. Meldgaard, Iben R. Thomsen, and Mikael B. Skov ⓘ

Aalborg University, Selma Lagerlöfsvej 300, Aalborg, Denmark
{papachristos,dubois}@cs.aau.dk

**Abstract.** Voice Assistants (VAs) present promising opportunities for the development of applications for the work domain. While previous research is primarily focused on aiding groups and individuals to be more productive, studies exploring the use of VAs to train and develop collaboration skills are rather limited. In this paper, we examine whether VAs can be used to help individuals improve their collaboration skills through self-reflection. We developed ReflectPal, a Google Assistant application designed to facilitate reflection sessions regarding collaboration challenges. First, we identified a list of frequently occurring challenges in a specific collaboration work environment. Then we designed ReflectPal to address a subset of those challenges and tested it in a two-week in-situ deployment with 19 participants. We found that participants benefited from the structure that the practice provided, leading to deeper and more meaningful reflections than before. However, the study also highlighted the need to design applications that take motivational aspects into account to encourage frequent engagement in self-reflection for skill development. Reflecting on insights from our study, we discuss future design directions of VAs for facilitating self-reflection in a collaborative work context.

**Keywords:** Voice Assistants · Conversational agents · Digital assistants · Workplace · Collaboration · Reflection

## 1 Introduction

There is a long tradition of developing technology to support productivity in the work environment, while tools focusing on wellbeing in collaborative activities have received only a little attention [2,25]. Although previous studies have explored reflection as a tool to increase wellbeing among employees [20,25], few have explored designs to facilitate reflection through self-assessment [3,44]. This study explores how reflection can be used to overcome challenges related to group collaboration without applying measures that focus on visible feedback and concrete end results. This motivation stems from a concern expressed by Baumer et al. [3] who states that most studies treat reflection as a means to

© IFIP International Federation for Information Processing 2021
Published by Springer Nature Switzerland AG 2021
C. Ardito et al. (Eds.): INTERACT 2021, LNCS 12935, pp. 187–208, 2021.
https://doi.org/10.1007/978-3-030-85610-6_12

an end by measuring outcomes related to reflection and not the act of reflection itself. Contrary to the goal-oriented paradigm of measuring outcomes of reflection, this study focuses on the act of reflection itself. If through reflection, people can reach the desired outcome (e.g., performance, behavioral change, or goal-reaching), it should only be viewed as a personal achievement and not a means to an end. To conceptualize reflection in this paper, we utilize Schön's [48] definition of *reflection-on-action*, a retrospective act, where the practitioner reflects on an event that already has occurred while reconsidering the situation and what needs changing in the future [48].

We explore the potential of using Voice Assistants (VA) to enable reflection in a group collaboration context. According to recent research, VAs can support both behavior change and wellbeing through the act of reflection [26]. The technology supports natural ways of communicating and has proven beneficial in individuals' willingness to disclose and self-assess [33,51]. In some situations, people can feel less vulnerable, and experience less fear of judgment when interacting with machines compared to other humans [33]. Moreover, VA technology can be advantageous in several contexts because it can support hands-free use and provide accessibility for people with visual impairments [33,43]. The capabilities of VAs have evolved considerably over recent years, especially regarding speech-recognition [38] and in the adoption of human-like features [13,42]. Simultaneously, problems concerning the technology have also been identified, such as usability issues and a gulf between user expectation and technical capabilities [34,42]. Although research has highlighted problems concerning VAs, the rapid improvement of the technology over the past years gives reasons to believe that shortcomings will be addressed and gradually resolved [38].

We developed ReflectPal, an application for Google Assistant, to examine whether VAs can guide and support individual reflection concerning behavioral patterns in collaborative activities. To gain a comprehensive understanding of challenges that occur in collaborative activities, we first examined related literature. We subsequently conducted thematic analysis on 126 student reports concerning university students' self-assessments of their collaborative group activities. We identified common challenges related to behavioral dynamics through the thematic analysis, such as opposing values and personality traits, underlying hierarchical structures, and unequal participation. We designed ReflectPal to address a subset of these challenges and tested it in a two-week in-situ deployment with 19 university students.

This work's contributions are: 1) A collection of challenges concerning group collaboration and activities. 2) The design of ReflectPal, an application in Google Assistant that guides and supports individual reflection on collaborative activities. 3) Findings from an in-situ deployment showing that VAs are capable of aiding reflection and that structured reflection patterns have the potential to lead to deeper and more conscious reflection. However, results also indicated that participants sometimes needed to rely on textual input, highlighting that the technology still needs improvement. Lastly, findings show that VAs supporting reflection is a promising research area that could benefit from more examination by the Human-Computer Interaction (HCI) community.

## 2 Related Work

A variety of technologies to support collaborative activities have been explored over the years in HCI research. Also, as quoted by Licklider in 1960: "*[...] there is a continuing interest in the idea of talking with computing machines.*" [31], which recently has started to become a viable alternative to traditional visual interfaces. Recent developments in VAs give reason to believe that voice interfaces could be the future of many key services [34].

### 2.1 Collaborative Activities and Technology

In collaborative activities, the concept of feedback has been used to increase individual and team performance. DiMicco et al. [12] developed a tool to indicate appropriate group behavior standards to support individual reflection. The study examined how a shared display could impact individuals' behavior in groups during collaborative tasks. Findings revealed that behavior in the extremes was affected by the presence of the display. To detect social interactions, promote behavioral change, and provide feedback to enhance group collaboration, Kim et al. [24] developed the Meeting Mediator. The aim was to bridge the gap amongst distributed groups by detecting, communicating, and visualizing social signals on group members' mobile phones [24]. Tausczik et al. [50] examined a real-time feedback system to monitor communication patterns among students in co-located groups. The results showed that the system improved group performance, but only in the groups that were dysfunctional [50]. Leshed et al. [29] aimed to stimulate reflection on language use and collaborative behavior. For this objective, they developed a chat-based system to present visual feedback to group members. Findings revealed that feedback in collaborative work settings affected social interactions and caused people to alter their communication patterns. The examples above highlight how technology can be used to support feedback in collaborative activities. However, findings also suggest that feedback alone may not be sufficient to make a difference [44]. Hence, a growing number of studies investigate whether the development of systems that encourage open-ended reflection could be more effective in creating meaningful change [21,39,41].

### 2.2 Supporting Reflection with Technology

Positive behavior changes can be triggered when individuals assess their own experiences to reach new understandings and appreciations [4,26]. Reflection is a core mechanism to translate experience into learning and support personal growth has been explored in various contexts and domains (e.g., education, health, and work [26,36]). Several technologies have been developed to inform design on reflection for everyday practices and personal informatics, for example, through self-tracking [46], lifelogging [6], and digital diaries [32]. Isaacs et al. [22] developed Echo, an Android application designed for users to record and systematically reflect on their daily activities. Findings showed that Echo produced improvement in participants' wellbeing after only using the application for a month. Kocielnick et al. [28] developed Reflection Companion, a mobile conversational system that supported reflection on personal sensor data, specifically physical activity data collected with fitness trackers. Their findings suggested that mini-dialogues successfully triggered reflection and led to increased motivation, empowerment, and behavioral change. When designing for reflection, Baumer et al. [3] state: *"[...] sometimes the goal of reflection is not only to increase self-knowledge but to take action based on this increased awareness. Systems of reflection vary as to the extent that they support taking such action."*. Therefore, it is important to design systems that acknowledge reflection as an ongoing process, thus supporting an increase in self-knowledge and granting room for taking action based on the increased awareness.

## 2.3  Voice Assistants

Cho et al. [8] argue that speech-based agents need to support more core values rather than just entertainment. Today VAs are gaining popularity, and it is clear that the technology offers new and innovative opportunities for engagement in collaborative activities [38]. However, it is not entirely clear how this technology can be used to deal with challenges in collaborative work environments. In the work domain, there has been an emphasis on using agents or chatbots for personal organization, administrative tasks, or management of to-do lists [26]. Cranshaw et al. [10] presented a digital assistant that provided fast and efficient scheduling through structured workflows. Liao et al. [30] conducted a field study with a personal agent designed to help employees detect work-related information. Their findings revealed individual differences in preferences towards humanized social interactions, concluding that variability in user needs have to be considered during agent design. McGregor et al. [35] demonstrated how agents could be used to monitor spoken dialogue in group settings, and proactively detect useful actions, and carry those out without any specific commands. These examples show that speech-based technology has made its entry into the work domain by assisting workers in organizational and structural assignments. Few studies have examined how VAs can be used to support workers in processes related to personal wellbeing. Kimani et al. [25] developed Amber, a conversational agent in support of goal achievement, aiming to explore the potential of using conversational agents to improve workplace productivity and wellbeing. Findings indicated that participants enjoyed Amber's work-related suggestions. Workers became more mindful about their practices to the point where they would make changes to increase productivity and become healthier. Kocielnik et al. [26] developed an agent with chat-based communication through a personal device to examine how voice-based and chat-based interaction affected workers' reflection and supported self-learning. Their findings indicated that voice interaction might enable users to step back and reflect on their work.

# 3   Identification of Group Collaboration Challenges

The first step in our analysis was to identify a list of frequently occurring challenges in group collaborations. Our goal was to detect specific problems in which self-reflection could be an appropriate method to improve teamwork skills. For this purpose, we launched an in-depth investigation of frequently occurring collaboration problems in a specific context. The context we chose to investigate was student group projects at Aalborg University. This University utilizes the Problem-Based Learning (PBL) model, which involves a high degree of group work and collaboration among students [14] in their semester projects. Students work together in small groups of four to seven members attempting to solve problems relevant to their interests and learning goals. At the end of the semester, students have to write a report describing their process, summarize their findings, and provide reflections about the quality of their group collaboration. We used these reports as input data in a thematic analysis to identify challenges students encounter when participating in these collaborative activities. Choosing to conduct thematic analysis on university student reports allowed us to focus on a group of individuals with similar and well-defined requirements for group work, who still encounter a variety of collaboration challenges. These challenges were subsequently used to inform our application's design, as it helped us understand what problems it should be able to address to be relevant in this specific context.

## 3.1   Thematic Analysis: Procedure and Findings

We conducted a thematic analysis on 126 reports authored by students at Aalborg University from a variety of educations. These reports are publicly accessible and included a description, analysis, and evaluation of the collaboration and work processes within the group, as well as collaboration with external partners and supervisors. These reports were selected after an in-depth search at the Universities digital project repository. The selection criteria for reports to be included in our final analysis was that they should be authored from 2015 to 2019 and contain subject headings such as 'group work', 'work processes', and 'group collaboration'. The reports that fulfilled the selection criteria were analyzed through a subsequent thematic analysis inspired by [5]. The analysis was conducted in four steps. First, two of the authors read all the reports for the first time to identify initial patterns in the data and to note explicit mentions of collaboration challenges. Second, both authors started generating individual inspection lists after reading and re-reading the reports while taking notes about potential codes. The inspection lists captured all identified instances related to collaborative problems mentioned in the reports that contributed to an initial low-level code. Third, the two inspection lists were merged after an agreement between the two authors, followed by a discussion about potential themes. We identified 17 themes that were checked in relation to the coded extracts in the inspections lists and were organized into thematic maps based on their interrelationship. These themes represent commonly occurring collaboration challenges based on the reflective self-assessment of the students. Lastly, we generated definitions and names for each theme, and we calculated the frequency of mentions in our dataset of each challenge.

**Table 1.** Findings from thematic analysis: identified challenges.

| Challenges | Number of mentions |
|---|---|
| Insufficient time management | 53 |
| Insufficient discussion management | 44 |
| Insufficient decision-making | 44 |
| Non-work related discussions | 44 |
| Unequal participation in discussions | 43 |
| Insufficient use of ICT-tools | 30 |
| Insufficient project management | 29 |
| Missing work ethics | 28 |
| Insufficient agenda management | 26 |
| Insufficient meetings management | 26 |
| Failing to match expectations in advance | 25 |
| Insufficient conflict management | 20 |
| Insufficient break management | 19 |
| Failing to meet as scheduled | 17 |
| Insufficient management of interruption | 16 |
| Domination and hierarchy issues | 15 |
| Written agreements not complied with | 10 |

The thematic analysis revealed collaboration challenges consistent with findings from related literature (e.g., [12,24,42,49]) and some unique to the specific context of project work at this University. This analysis provided a well-grounded collection of collaboration challenges relevant to the particular context we were investigating, which can be seen in Table 1. From this list, we selected challenges addressing group dynamics issues rather than practical or productivity problems such as time management or usage of appropriate collaboration software. We chose four challenges after a discussion among the authors about which of those we considered could be addressed better by personal rather than group reflection sessions. The four selected challenges are (1) Unequal participation in discussions, (2) Domination and hierarchy issues, (3) Insufficient decision-making, and (4) Non-work-related discussions. We used those four challenges to guide our design process but also the evaluation of the Voice Assistant application ReflectPal that we will present in the next section.

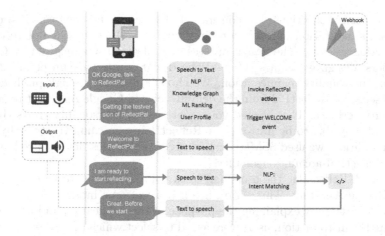

**Fig. 1.** Visualization of ReflectPal's system architecture.

# 4 ReflectPal: An Application for Reflection

Following the thematic analysis, we started the process of designing ReflectPal to address the challenges we identified. Our objective was to develop an application that would support reflection on an individual's behavior in collaborative activities. Inspired by previous research that has demonstrated the benefits of using conversational agents in the context of facilitating reflection in the work environment [26] we developed ReflectPal as a third-party application (Action) for the Google Assistant. Our goals for developing ReflectPal were threefold: (1) provide users with questions to facilitate reflection through a guided dialogue, (2) address the four collaborative challenges identified through the thematic analysis, (3) allow interaction with multiple modalities (e.g. voice, text).

## 4.1 Design and Development

ReflectPal was developed using Google Actions and Dialogflow. This allowed us to use a variety of well-established tools such as Googles Speech to Text (STT), Natural Language Processing (NLP), and Text to Speech (TTS) technologies [1]. The core logic and the conversation structure were implemented in Dialogflow, and we used a webhook service to integrate with Firebase to store application data. We also used the Speech Synthesis Markup Language (SSML) to improve speech intelligibility by modifying TTS responses. The core architecture of ReflectPal can be seen in Fig. 1.

We intended to deploy ReflectPal on devices with an embedded Google Assistant, for example, mobile devices and smart speakers. User inputs are registered through voice or text with a microphone or keyboard, and outputs are generated as audio on a speaker or text on a screen. Although we used Firebase to store basic user information, we decided that ReflectPal should not record and store users' reflections. We considered that we would remove some of our participants' hesitation to disclose their thoughts and feelings by not recording the reflection sessions. The design process of ReflectPal was inspired by Google Developers' design guidelines [11] and the design guide by Kim et al. [23] for consistent personality manifestation. We chose a medium-to-high pitched male voice to separate ReflectPal from the default voice in Google Assistant regarding voice characteristics. The selected voice matched the personality traits that we considered desirable to be mirrored by ReflectPal (e.g., calm, trustworthy, neutral). In addition, we used SSML to make speech responses slower-paced, aiming to give ReflectPal a calm personality.

To launch ReflectPal, the users had to say aloud or type *"talk to ReflectPal"* to the Google Assistant. This action invoked a welcome intent that introduced users to ReflectPal by explaining the purpose of the application and its benefits. Following the introduction, users were asked to select which topic they would like to focus on out of 5 predefined choices. Four out of the five topics referred to the challenges derived from the thematic analysis, while the fifth was a generic one that could be used to reflect on any challenge the user may have encountered. We included a generic topic to make ReflectPal more flexible, enabling reflection on a broader range of challenges. Although our choice of topics for reflection did not encompass challenges related to group management and productivity issues, the self-chosen topic still allowed users to reflect on these matters if they choose to do so. The five reflection topics users could select were the following: (1) Better your contribution to group discussions; (2) Decrease your domination in group work; (3) Get better at decision-making; (4) Get better at not engaging in small-talk during group activities; (5) Pick your own topic. Once users had picked a focus for the session, they were guided through six stages. The stages were explicitly designed to promote reflection. After having gone through the six stages and before ending the session, users were presented with a closing remark, a quote about reflection, and prompted to occasionally take a step back to reflect on their actions and feelings, aiming to encourage reflection in their everyday lives. Time is an essential condition for enabling reflection [28]. This was also taken into account when designing the flow of how users should interact with ReflectPal. Users were provided with the time they needed to reflect and move on whenever they felt ready. This was considered significant for the flow of the conversation to create a pleasurable and unrushed interaction.

## 4.2   Conversation Design to Enable Reflection

ReflectPal's conversation design was based on a theoretical framework, aiming to encourage reflection and guide users through a developmental process [18,28]. The conversation structure was guided by Gibbs's reflective cycle, which proposes a design approach for reflection-on-action based on six reflective stages [18]. The six stages related to (1) Description, promoting to recall what happened in the experience; (2) Feelings, identification of thoughts and feelings; (3) Evaluation, evaluating whether the experience could be deemed good or bad; (4)

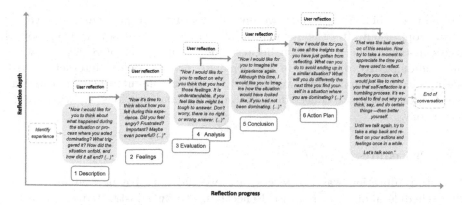

**Fig. 2.** Sample dialogue from ReflectPal related to the reflection point 'decrease your domination on group work', visualizing the connection between reflection levels and conversation structure.

Analysis, relating to what sense could be made from the experience; (5) Conclusion, relating to which actions could have been better to take; and (6) Action Plan, prompting to identify what to do in a similar experience in the future [18]. Figure 2 shows an example of how the reflection levels are related to the dialogue in ReflectPal. Additionally, we directed our focus on ways to design and phrase questions to support reflection. Here, we applied Moon's levels of learning [37], which entailed a comprehensive collection of tools for how to support reflection.

## 5   Field Deployment

To examine whether ReflectPal could support individuals in reflecting on their behavior in collaborative activities, we tested the application in a two-week in-situ deployment [47]. The purpose of the field deployment was to evaluate ReflectPal and assess the feasibility of using Voice Assistant to facilitate self-reflection on a regular basis.

### 5.1   Participants

We recruited 19 participants (M=9, F=10) through Aalborg University's social media pages and email list. Our participants were students from various departments and educations, and all of them had practical and theoretical experience working in student groups that varied in group size, scope, and purpose. They were between 19 to 30 years old, with an average age of 25.2 years. All of them reported high competence in command of the English language. Demographic data also showed that most of our participants (N=13) considered themselves experienced with technology in general but novices regarding VAs (N=15). After agreeing to participate, we provided information about the study, instructions about interacting with ReflectPal, and step-by-step installation guides for iOS and Android. Even though we initially recruited 26 participants, seven of them dropped out after the installation phase. Out of those seven, two reported issues installing the application because they owned older iOS devices, while the remaining five dropped out for personal reasons. Before interacting with the application, participants were asked to sign a consent declaration and fill out a questionnaire to collect demographic data and previous experience with technology.

## 5.2 Procedure

The study duration was two weeks, and we did not give participants a specific schedule about when to use ReflectPal. We only instructed them to use it a minimum of two times per week whenever they felt like it. The reason for not forcing a more frequent use upon the participants was based on prior studies showing that reflection is a time-consuming process that does not necessarily happen all at once [2]. We, therefore, wanted to allow our participants to use ReflectPal at their own pace. Immediately after the two weeks deployment period, we invited our participants for a debriefing study. The study included a post-deployment questionnaire and an interview, which aimed to gather feedback from the participants' experiences when interacting with the application. The questionnaire contained nine questions seeking to assess user perceptions about ReflectPal regarding interaction, usability, and overall usefulness (see Table 2). Participants provided ratings using a 7-point Likert scale with the anchors "I totally disagree" to "I totally agree". The questionnaire was formulated with inspiration from agent rating scales presented by Kimani et al. [25], and Olafsson et al. [40], as these studies had a similar goal of encapsulating user feedback based on VA interactions. Similarly to these studies, we aimed to explore dimensions of usability, user enjoyment, trustworthiness, and whether the application supported the primary purpose of aiding participants in reflecting. After handing in the questionnaire, we conducted a semi-structured interview focused on participants' experiences using ReflectPal, how it affected their reflection patterns, their perception of strengths and weaknesses of the application, and their intention of future use.

## 6    Results

In this section, we will present the findings of our post-deployment data analysis. First, we analyzed data from the questionnaire data by calculating mean scores and standard deviation for each of the items. Overall results from the questionnaire indicate general satisfaction with ReflectPal. Participant both liked (M = 4.32, SD = 1.64) and trusted (M = 4.74, SD = 1.6) the application. They also gave relatively high scores to all three usability related questions (ranging from 4.43 to 5.58). However, although participants perceived the interaction with ReflectPal to be comfortable (M = 5.0, SD = 1.53), they gave a considerably lower score on how natural it felt (M = 3.53, SD = 1.84), showing that there is

**Table 2.** Post-deployment questionnaire items and responses.

| Items | Mean (SD) |
|---|---|
| *Usefulness* | |
| ReflectPal helped me reflect | 4.58 (1.68) |
| I would like to continue reflecting with ReflectPal | 1.68 (1.53) |
| *Perceptions about ReflectPal* | |
| I like ReflectPal | 4.32 (1.64) |
| I trust ReflectPal | 4.74 (1.6) |
| *Perceptions about interaction* | |
| I felt the interaction with ReflectPal was comfortable | 5.0 (1.53) |
| I felt the interaction with ReflectPal was natural | 3.53 (1,84) |
| *Usability* | |
| ReflectPal offered help about how to interact with it | 4.43 (1.58) |
| It was easy to interact with ReflectPal | 5.27 (1.64) |
| It was clear for me how to interact with ReflectPal | 5.58 (1.61) |

still room for improvement in this regard. Arguably the most interesting finding from the post-deployment questionnaire concerns the usefulness of ReflectPal. Based on the results, participants perceived the application useful in helping them reflect (M = 5.0, SD = 1.53), but at the same time, they would probably not continue using it (M = 1.68, SD = 1.53). This could indicate that users did not like to reflect on collaboration challenges in general or that the motivational design of ReflectPal has to be improved. We used this finding during the interview data analysis to uncover reasons and explanations that could provide answers to the discrepancy between usefulness and intention to use.

We then analyzed our qualitative data set from the interview. The interviews had an average duration of 20 min and were audio-recorded and fully transcribed manually by two authors to familiarize themselves with the data. Afterwards, the transcribed text was analyzed through thematic analysis inspired by [9]. We followed an inductive approach [7] by interpreting the raw data and abstracting common themes since no predefined themes were identified before the analysis. The analysis was conducted in three steps. First, two of the authors read through the transcribed text and gained an initial understanding of the data, followed by an initial coding phase. Secondly, the two authors compared and combined their coding schemes and categorized quotes into themes over several iterations. Lastly, the authors finalized the categorization of codes into themes using NVivo. Four themes emerged from our analysis: Overall Experience with ReflectPal, VA's in the context of reflection, Effect on reflection practice, and Suggestions for future usage.

## 6.1 Qualitative Findings

Our qualitative analysis showed that ReflectPal supported individual reflection on collaborative activities. The participants generally reflected more during this period, not only about collaborative activities but also about other life issues. We will present results from the thematic analysis based on the four identified themes in the following sections.

**Overall Experience with ReflectPal.** For all participants, ReflectPal managed to invoke reflection in one way or another. Most participants reported that the application supported them in reflecting on their behavior in collaborative activities. Also, many of them stated that they experienced a substantial increase in how frequently they would reflect and that the sessions led to additional reflection on other parts of their lives. Since we prioritized removing usage barriers, we did not record reflection sessions or collected usage data. However, from the interview, it becomes clear that the usage of ReflectPal varied considerably regarding what participants chose to reflect on. Some reflected on past experiences from several years ago, while others would reflect on more recent collaborative group activities. Also, the choice time for reflection sessions varied considerably among participants. Some reported that they used ReflectPal directly after a collaborative activity; others used it as an intermediate activity between different work tasks, while others used it at the end of the day as a way of debriefing. Finally, one participant reported using ReflectPal before meetings to identify how she could improve her actions compared to the previous meetings. A general finding was that the convenience of natural interaction motivated the participants to reflect more. Even though most provided positive remarks regarding ReflectPal, a few participants were reluctant to continue using it. Those comments and suggestions participants provided to make the application relevant in the long term are provided in the following sections.

**VA's in the Context of Reflection.** Several participants made comments on the context of use with the VA technology. We were particularly interested in those comments considering that most participants did not have extensive previous exposure to VA's. Some mentioned that the interaction with a VA was considerably different from any other type of technology they had encountered before and attitudes towards VA technology varied noticeably. Four participants were extremely positive, three were negative, while the rest were either neutral or had mixed feeling. On the positive side, comments revolved around how easy, fun, and joyful it was to interact with the application using voice. Some mentioned that the interaction felt more natural because there was no screen and that compared to talking to humans, the VA was perceived as more neutral. Because it felt more similar to talking to a person instead of reading text, it made them feel more guided and inclined to reflect more. Also, the act of saying thinks out loud increased the motivation of some to reflect at a deeper level:

> **P19**: *"[...] I talked a bit more with it, and maybe that made me reflect more because I was forced to say it out loud instead of just thinking it."*

Negative comments concerned a general unease with voice technologies and awkwardness talking to a machine about personal feelings. Even though the VA did not instruct participants to say anything aloud, some participants felt that talking to a machine ruined the intimacy of reflecting. Some also thought that the interaction was too rigid and not flexible to their particular needs. Interestingly, this was mentioned more often by participants with none or only a little experience with VAs. Participants with some experience were more moderate about their expectations. One participant said:

> **P1**: *"[...] I feel like it is a joyful experience to talk to it in general. It is a system, and it is not that smart, and some people have made a lot of thoughts about what it will say next and how it will react to what I am saying"*

The majority of participants with mixed feelings mentioned technical issues or misunderstanding of commands. This was particularly visible in the beginning but improved over time. Many noted that talking to a machine felt different and weird initially, but they become accustomed and more comfortable after using it a few times. Finally, the ability to interact both via text and speech was well-received, and many considered it one of the core strengths of ReflectPal. It is noteworthy that quite a few reported difficulties finding a private space to feel comfortable talking out loud to a VA due to their living conditions.

**Effect on Reflection Practice.** The most frequent comment in the interviews was that it provided good structure and guidance during reflection. This was mentioned even by participants who were negative about ReflectPal. Moving gradually from superficial to deep reflection, was perceived by many as a novel way of reflecting, which generally led to a deeper and more conscious reflection than usual.

> **P1**: *"[...]ReflectPal helped me reflect in an organized way, so with Reflect-Pal, I went deeper and deeper into the specific situation [...] usually when I reflect, I am not that organized about it."*

Apart from the depth of reflection, many mentioned that ReflectPal helped them widen their breadth regarding reflect topics. This was evident by comments sowing surprise that one could get something out of reflecting about their own behavior in collaborative activities. A participant, for example, said:

> **P15**: *"[...]normally I think I reflect on other people's behavior in the group, and it is a little bit more difficult to look inwards. But I think that Reflect-Pal really initiates that reflection on your own behavior."*

Out of the 19 participants, only three of them reported that ReflectPal did not support their reflection on collaborative activities in a profound way. One participant already had a reflection routine and did not feel that ReflectPal was creating additional value, and the other two felt that using technology to reflect was too artificial. However, even these participants still reported that they experienced a change in their reflection patterns. Exposure to ReflectPal's structured approach made them evaluate their own way of reflecting from a meta-perspective and adopting some aspects of it into their daily lives. This was mentioned by multiple times during the interviews, indicating a common pattern among participants.

**Suggestions for Future Usage.** Our interview data also illustrated why some participants would probably not use ReflectPal in the future, even though they rated it as highly useful in the questionnaire. The comments about this focused mainly on relevance and personalization. Some participants perceived the application as a learning tool that would lose its usefulness after understanding the lesson it tries to teach them. They mentioned that they had identified the pattern behind the reflection structure ReflectPal suggests, and they already tried to apply it to other aspects of their lives. Therefore, they did not see any value in continuous usage after some time of interaction. But other participants saw value in continued usage of ReflectPal as a stable guide in their reflection practice, but they stressed the need for more personalization. Some mentioned that the reflection topics were not relevant for them and their current situation and that they would use ReflectPal in the future if the topics would cover their needs:

> **P16**: *"[...]I would like more topics because, for example, this semester, we were having some problems in my group, but none of those problems were there."*

Some participants also mentioned that they would appreciate some guidance or suggestions about appropriate action plans after reflecting on a group activity. Even though they understood that the purpose of ReflectPal was not to give them prescriptive advice about collaboration issues, they felt that challenges were left unresolved at the end of the sessions:

> **P17**: *"[...]I know I need to reflect myself and to think about it by myself, but maybe more tips I would have liked. [...] Guide me, but also give me solutions."*

Also, some participants mentioned that they did not enjoy the fact that ReflectPal mainly focused on past negative experiences. As the reflection topics originated from common collaborative challenges that we identified in students' reports, the sessions with ReflectPal were primarily focused on problematic situations. Those participants raised the valid point that reflection about collaborative work's positive aspects would also be beneficial.

> **P19**: *"[...]my experience with the questions was that they kind of had a negative outlook from the start. [...] of course, I understand that reflecting is to make yourself better, but I felt that 'oh, I have done something wrong, so now I need to reflect on it,' and it is only when I have done something wrong that I can reflect on it."*

Finally, three participants pointed out that they would like to see whether ReflectPal could be used be used in a group meeting setting. They understood the value of self-reflecting and focusing on their own behavior, but they could also see clear value in having ReflectPal guide some of their group meetings in the future.

# 7  Discussion

The field deployment results have provided insights into university students' reflection on their behavior in collaborative group activities using a VA. The majority of our participants could see the benefits of using a VA to facilitate reflection sessions mainly because it offered support and structure. At the same time, the conversational interaction felt easy and convenient. In the next sections, we will reflect on our findings and discuss implications for design and future research directions for VA-facilitated self-reflection.

## 7.1  Reflection in a Collaborative Context

Previous research has shown that VA applications can support goal-oriented interactions and interventions to help users achieve goals through self-assessment [26,49]. Our aim was not to examine if the reflection could lead to the desired outcome but to promote the act of reflection itself as a practice that could help develop collaboration skills. Results showed that our VA application was relatively successful in facilitating individual reflection sessions about collaborative activities. However, we also found that it would probably be challenging to regularly motivate users to initiate reflection sessions about collaborative activities.

A variety of approaches could be explored to improve the motivational design of ReflectPal, and here, we only mention some based on participant feedback. To begin with, the application could explicitly communicate the benefits of frequent reflection and provide resources to allow users to understand the possible gains of this activity. We also found that some participants would appreciate support and suggestions about how to act in future scenarios after recognizing aspects of their behavior that could be improved. Another request was to make usage data more visible as a motivational feature to use the application more often. This would be consistent with results outlined by Zhou et al. [52], which describes visible feedback as one of the most useful and effective features for users to achieve goals and maintain motivation by comparing past performances to current ones. Finally, some participants mentioned that reminders or notifications would help them remember to use the application. It could be argued that some of the improvements the participants suggested are counter to the overarching goals of our research, which was to facilitate reflection that is self-initiated and triggered by intrinsic motivations for self-improvement. However, it also becomes clear from our study results that some elements of the motivational design have to be implemented in future versions to increase the possibility of people using ReflectPal for an extended period.

Although this study has focused on individual reflection, there is no doubt that group-based reflection also plays a significant role in collaborative environments. Individual Reflection was described as beneficial for most participants, yet some also expressed an interest in applying the structured reflection plenary with their group members. We see a potential in leveraging both individual and group-based reflection in collaborative contexts to accommodate a larger area of collaborative challenges. It would also be interesting to examine how ReflectPal could fit into existing collaborative practices and group meetings and how this could affect motivation to use. In continuation, it could be relevant to explore the dimension of reflecting with VAs in collaborative activities in groups compared to individual reflection.

## 7.2    VA-Facilitated Reflection

For most participants, using a VA was a new experience, and therefore, we were able to collect feedback showing both advantages and shortcomings of the technology. In particular, the conversational design of ReflectPal was praised for successfully guiding the participants and showing them a new structured way of reflecting. By presenting only small chunks of information at a time, we allowed them to reflect on specific aspects of a challenge, thus enabling a more in-depth reflection before moving on to the next stage. Some participants suggested that the whole experience could be further enhanced if the six stages were split up into several simple questions that would resemble a more natural conversation.

Findings also showed that participant opinions varied regarding using voice as the primary mode of interaction. Some felt that it provided added value to the experience, while some were more reluctant. It is also important to mention that issues with speech recognition were discussed repeatedly during the interview. While developing ReflectPal, we made a proactive choice of accommodating both voice-based and text-based inputs because we knew that our participants would not be native English speakers. Some participants reported that the speech recognition improved over time, while others switched to text-based input. Giving participants the option to switch between voice-based and text-based inputs proved beneficial in lessening frustration with the VA and providing alternative ways to interact. Our results reconfirmed what has been shown multiple times in previous work, that in terms of speech recognition, VAs are still in their infancy [34, 42]. A seamless, purely voice-based interaction appears to be an ambitious but not impossible objective considering how much commercially available devices have been improved in recent years. More than half of our participants indicated that their living conditions made it difficult for them to reflect using voice due to privacy reasons. This illustrates the need for considerations of the target group demographic characteristics while designing for VAs.

Despite technical shortcomings, voice interaction may still be more advantageous over other modalities in facilitating self-reflection in the work context. Even though we focused on individual self-reflection in future studies, we intend to explore the use of VAs to facilitate group reflections. Shared ownership and neutrality of the VA could prove valuable characteristics to facilitate group reflection sessions. Besides, we intend to develop ReflectPal further to be able to facilitate both individual as well as group reflection sessions. We want to explore a process in which individual members anonymously suggest reflection topics that will be used first in individual sessions, followed by a subsequent group session with all members.

## 7.3    Generality Versus Specificity

ReflectPal addressed only four collaboration challenges that were identified in the thematic analysis. This resulted in some participants not being able to relate to the topics presented in the application. We created an option for participants to choose a generic self-chosen topic to cover challenges that ReflectPal did not already support. Participants that mainly used the generic topic felt that Reflect-Pal was a learning tool that would be useful only for a limited number of times. However, it was also observed that the generic guide triggered reflection on other aspects of life that were not constrained to the work environment in contrast to the specific guides that only granted room to reflect on the one selected challenge. Designing ReflectPal to be very specific could provide a better experience but at the same time make the application too rigid. In contrast, designing it too generic could make it more useful to some and irrelevant to other participants. Our goal was to balance generality and specificity in our application's design. This has been difficult due to the participants' subjective opinions and preferences in how they preferred to facilitate their reflections sessions. What becomes apparent from the study is that to support continuous usage of the application, relevance has to be considered. This can be achieved either by including more reflection topics or by providing room for customization and flexibility. It is reasonable to believe that some domains would benefit from a generic design that supports a broader reflection, while other domains would benefit from a more specific design. We suggest that when designing for reflection, both the domain-specific and user perspectives are taken into consideration.

## 7.4    Reflecting on How to Reflect

Throughout this study, it became increasingly evident that the type of Reflection that ReflectPal supported was not only limited to the intended usage regarding reflection-on-action in collaborative experiences. We found that some participants started reflecting on their ways of reflecting and implementing the stepwise and conscious reflection into their daily lives. This use of ReflectPal we refer to as meta-reflection. This type of reflection-on-reflection was overall mentioned by several participants throughout the interviews and was an unanticipated outcome of this study. It became apparent that the meta-reflection occurred, as the sequence of the questions that followed Gibb's six stages of reflection helped some of our participants to gain more skills in personal development. For these participants, ReflectPal served as a learning tool to increase their awareness of how they reflect on their actions. The fact that VAs appear adequate to be introduced as a learning tool to meta-reflection creates several additional questions about how to design VAs to support this purpose. As for now, the field of meta-reflection is an underexplored area within the HCI field, as the body of research covering design guides for this is very limited. Research has focused on related areas such as meta-cognition [16,17], self-reflection [19,27], or reflective practice [15,45]. Although overlaps are present between these research areas and meta-reflection, none of the mentioned areas entirely covers the specific act of reflecting on one's own reflection and accustoming to deeper and more structured reflection patterns. We see potential in further exploration of meta-reflection, as this study has indicated that this could lead to a more meaningful reflection by monitoring, assessing, and adjusting the act of reflection itself.

## 8    Limitations and Future Work

This study has some limitations that have to be noted. First, the relatively small sample size (N=19) and the limited amount of time participants interacted with ReflectPal (two weeks) may limit our results as well as the conclusion that can be drawn from our findings. However, this initial exploratory study aimed to investigate the feasibility of using VAs to facilitate reflection about collaborative activities. In future work, a more extended deployment period and a larger and more varied sample have to be considered to investigate the long-term effects of VA facilitated reflection. Also, our work solely focused on challenges with collaborative activities that occur in a specific university context. Even though we see many parallels between this university's problem-based learning context and many industry practices, the relevance has to be explored in future work. Moreover, efforts should be made to uncover if similar applications as the one presented in this study are relevant and applicable to other domains (e.g., everyday life) in which collaboration is important.

## 9    Conclusions

This study aimed to explore whether VAs could be used to facilitate reflections in the context of group collaboration. Our results show the promise of voice interaction technologies in this area, demonstrating that our VA application was more than sufficient to enable structured reflection among our participants. We developed ReflectPal to provide initial insights about how to design VAs for individual reflection on collaborative activities. We identified a collection of frequently occurring challenges in a specific collaborative context that were used to drive the design process of ReflectPal. Results from two-week in-situ deployment showed that participants generally appreciated being introduced to a structured way of reflecting on their own behavior in collaborative activities and that structured reflection in some cases led to meta-reflection. Moreover, we found that purely voice-based interaction still faces some limitations in its current state, highlighting the importance of providing text-based input as a fallback for VA applications. An important goal in sharing our findings has been to highlight trade-offs, encourage conversation about VA capabilities, and call attention to certain aspects of VAs for reflection that could benefit from further research.

# References

1. Ali, M., Hassan, A.M.: Developing applications for voice enabled IoT devices to improve classroom activities. In: 2018 21st International Conference of Computer and Information Technology (ICCIT), pp. 1–4. IEEE (2018). https://doi.org/10.1109/ICCITECHN.2018.8631906
2. Baumer, E.P.: Reflective informatics: Conceptual dimensions for designing technologies of reflection. In: Proceedings of the 33rd Annual ACM Conference on Human Factors in Computing Systems, CHI 2015, pp. 585–594. Association for Computing Machinery, New York (2015). https://doi.org/10.1145/2702123.2702234
3. Baumer, E.P., Khovanskaya, V., Matthews, M., Reynolds, L., Schwanda Sosik, V., Gay, G.: Reviewing reflection: on the use of reflection in interactive system design. In: Proceedings of the 2014 Conference on Designing Interactive Systems, DIS 2014, pp. 93–102. Association for Computing Machinery, New York (2014). https://doi.org/10.1145/2598510.2598598
4. Boud, D., Keogh, R., Walker, D.: Reflection: Turning Experience into Learning (1985)
5. Braun, V., Clarke, V.: Using thematic analysis in psychology. Qual. Res. Psychol. **3**(2), 77–101 (2006)
6. Byrne, D., Kelliher, A., Jones, G.J.: Life editing: third-party Perspectives on lifelog content. In: CHI 2011, pp. 1501–1510. Association for Computing Machinery, New York (2011). https://doi.org/10.1145/1978942.1979162
7. Chandra, Y., Shang, L.: Qualitative Research Using R: A Systematic Approach. Springer, Singapore (2019). https://doi.org/10.1007/978-981-13-3170-1
8. Cho, M., Lee, S.s., Lee, K.P.: Once a kind friend is now a thing: understanding how conversational agents at home are forgotten. In: DIS 2019, pp. 1557–1569. Association for Computing Machinery, New York (2019). https://doi.org/10.1145/3322276.3322332
9. Clarke, V., Braun, V., Hayfield, N.: Thematic Analysis. Qualitative Psychology: A Practical Guide to Research Methods, pp. 222–248 (2015)
10. Cranshaw, J., et al.: Calendar.help: designing a workflow-based scheduling agent with humans in the loop. In: CHI 2017, pp. 2382–2393. Association for Computing Machinery, New York (2017). https://doi.org/10.1145/3025453.3025780
11. Developers, G.: Conversation Design, July 2019. https://developers.google.com/assistant/actions/design
12. DiMicco, J.M., Pandolfo, A., Bender, W.: Influencing group participation with a shared display. In: CSCW 2004, pp. 614–623. Association for Computing Machinery, New York (2004). https://doi.org/10.1145/1031607.1031713
13. Doyle, P.R., Edwards, J., Dumbleton, O., Clark, L., Cowan, B.R.: Mapping perceptions of humanness in intelligent personal assistant interaction. In: Association for Computing Machinery, New York (2019). https://doi.org/10.1145/3338286.3340116
14. Fink, F.K.: Integration of engineering practice into curriculum-25 years of experience with problem based learning. In: FIE 1999 Frontiers in Education, vol. 1, pp. 11A2-7. IEEE (1999). https://doi.org/10.1109/fie.1999.839084
15. Finlay, L.: Reflecting on Reflective Practice (2008)
16. Flavell, J.H.: Metacognition and cognitive monitoring: a new area of cognitive-developmental inquiry. Am. Psychol. **34**(10), 906 (1979). https://doi.org/10.1037/0003-066X.34.10.906

17. Gama, C.: Helping students to help themselves: a pilot experiment on the ways of increasing metacognitive awareness in problem solving (2001)
18. Gibbs, G.: Learning by Doing: A Guide to Teaching and Learning Methods. Oxford Centre for Staff and Learning Development, Headington (1988)
19. Grant, A.M., Franklin, J., Langford, P.: The self-reflection and insight scale: a new measure of private self-consciousness. Soc. Behav. Pers. Imt. J. **30**(8), 821–835 (2002). https://doi.org/10.2224/sbp.2002.30.8.821
20. Grover, T., Rowan, K., Suh, J., McDuff, D., Czerwinski, M.: Design and evaluation of intelligent agent prototypes for assistance with focus and productivity at work. In: Proceedings of the 25th International Conference on Intelligent User Interfaces, IUI 2020, pp. 390–400. Association for Computing Machinery, New York (2020). https://doi.org/10.1145/3377325.3377507
21. Halttu, K., Oinas-Kukkonen, H.: Persuading to reflect: role of reflection and insight in persuasive systems design for physical health. Hum. Comput. Interact. **32**(5–6), 381–412 (2017). https://doi.org/10.1080/07370024.2017.1283227
22. Isaacs, E., Konrad, A., Walendowski, A., Lennig, T., Hollis, V., Whittaker, S.: Echoes from the past: how technology mediated reflection improves well-being. In: CHI 2013, pp. 1071–1080. Association for Computing Machinery, New York (2013). https://doi.org/10.1145/2470654.2466137
23. Kim, H., Koh, D.Y., Lee, G., Park, J.M., Lim, Y.K.: Developing a design guide for consistent manifestation of conversational agent personalities, pp. 1–17. Manchester Metropolitan University, Manchester (2019)
24. Kim, T., Chang, A., Holland, L., Pentland, A.S.: Meeting mediator: enhancing group collaboration using sociometric feedback. In: CSCW 2008, pp. 457–466. Association for Computing Machinery, New York (2008). https://doi.org/10.1145/1460563.1460636
25. Kimani, E., Rowan, K., McDuff, D., Czerwinski, M., Mark, G.: A conversational agent in support of productivity and wellbeing at work, pp. 1–7. IEEE (2019). https://doi.org/10.1109/ACII.2019.8925488
26. Kocielnik, R., Avrahami, D., Marlow, J., Lu, D., Hsieh, G.: Designing for workplace reflection: a chat and voice-based conversational agent. In: DIS 2018, pp. 881–894. Association for Computing Machinery, New York (2018). https://doi.org/10.1145/3196709.3196784
27. Kocielnik, R., Maggi, F.M., Sidorova, N.: Enabling self-reflection with lifelogexplorer: generating simple views from complex data, pp. 184–191. IEEE (2013). https://doi.org/10.4108/icst.pervasivehealth.2013.251934
28. Kocielnik, R., Xiao, L., Avrahami, D., Hsieh, G.: Reflection companion: a conversational system for engaging users in reflection on physical activity. Proc. ACM Interact. Mob. Wearable Ubiquit. Technol. **2**(2), 1–26 (2018). https://doi.org/10.1145/3214273
29. Leshed, G., et al.: Visualizing real-time language-based feedback on teamwork behavior in computer-mediated groups. In: Proceedings of the SIGCHI Conference on Human Factors in Computing Systems, CHI 2009, pp. 537–546. Association for Computing Machinery, New York (2009). https://doi.org/10.1145/1518701.1518784
30. Liao, Q.V., Davis, M., Geyer, W., Muller, M., Shami, N.S.: What can you do? studying social-agent orientation and agent proactive interactions with an agent for employees. In: Proceedings of the 2016 ACM Conference on Designing Interactive Systems, DIS 2016, pp. 264–275. Association for Computing Machinery, New York(2016). https://doi.org/10.1145/2901790.2901842

31. Licklider, J.C.: Man-computer symbiosis. IRE Trans. Hum. Factors Electron. **1**, 4–11 (1960). https://doi.org/10.1109/THFE2.1960.4503259
32. Lindström, M., et al.: Affective diary: designing for bodily expressiveness and self-reflection. In: CHI 2006 Extended Abstracts on Human Factors in Computing Systems, CHI EA 2006, pp. 1037–1042. Association for Computing Machinery, New York (2006). https://doi.org/10.1145/1125451.1125649
33. Lucas, G.M., Gratch, J., King, A., Morency, L.P.: It's only a computer: virtual humans increase willingness to disclose. Comput. Hum. Behav. **37**, 94–100 (2014). https://doi.org/10.1016/j.chb.2014.04.043
34. Luger, E., Sellen, A.: Like having a really bad pa: the gulf between user expectation and experience of conversational agents. In: Proceedings of the 2016 CHI Conference on Human Factors in Computing Systems, CHI 2016, pp. 5286–5297. Association for Computing Machinery, New York (2016). https://doi.org/10.1145/2858036.2858288
35. McGregor, M., Tang, J.C.: More to meetings: challenges in using speech-based technology to support meetings. In: CSCW 2017, pp. 2208–2220. Association for Computing Machinery, New York (2017). https://doi.org/10.1145/2998181.2998335
36. Mols, I., van den Hoven, E., Eggen, B.: Informing design for reflection: an overview of current everyday practices. In: NordiCHI 2016, Association for Computing Machinery, New York (2016). https://doi.org/10.1145/2971485.2971494
37. Moon, J.A.: Reflection in Learning and Professional Development: Theory and Practice. Routledge, London (2013). https://doi.org/10.4324/9780203822296
38. Moore, R.K.: Is Spoken Language All-or-Nothing? Implications for Future Speech-Based Human-Machine Interaction, pp. 281–291. Springer, Singapore (2017). https://doi.org/10.1007/978-981-10-2585-3-22
39. Oinas-Kukkonen, H.: A foundation for the study of behavior change support systems. Pers. Ubiquit. Comput. **17**(6), 1223–1235 (2013). https://doi.org/10.1007/s00779-012-0591-5
40. Olafsson, S., O'Leary, T., Bickmore, T.: Coerced change-talk with conversational agents promotes confidence in behavior change. In: PervasiveHealth 2019, pp. 31–40. Association for Computing Machinery, New York (2019). https://doi.org/10.1145/3329189.3329202
41. Ploderer, B., Reitberger, W., Harri Oinas-Kukkonen, H., van Gemert-Pijnen, J.: Social interaction and reflection for behaviour change. Pers. Ubiquit. Comput. **18**(7), 1667–1676 (2014)
42. Porcheron, M., et al.: Talking with conversational agents in collaborative action. In: Companion of the 2017 ACM Conference on Computer Supported Cooperative Work and Social Computing, CSCW 2017, pp. 431–436. Companion, Association for Computing Machinery, New York (2017). https://doi.org/10.1145/3022198.3022666
43. Porcheron, M., Fischer, J.E., Reeves, S., Sharples, S.: Voice interfaces in everyday life. In: Proceedings of the 2018 CHI Conference on Human Factors in Computing Systems, CHI 2018, pp. 1–12. Association for Computing Machinery, New York (2018). https://doi.org/10.1145/3173574.3174214
44. Prins, F.J., Sluijsmans, D.M., Kirschner, P.A.: Feedback for general practitioners in training: quality, styles, and preferences. Adv. Health Sci. Educ. **11**(3), 289 (2006). https://doi.org/10.1007/s10459-005-3250-z
45. Prior, J., Ferguson, S., Leaney, J.: Reflection is hard: teaching and learning reflective practice in a software studio. In: Association for Computing Machinery, New York (2016). https://doi.org/10.1145/2843043.2843346

46. Rivera-Pelayo, V., Fessl, A., Müller, L., Pammer, V.: Introducing mood self-tracking at work: empirical insights from call centers. ACM Trans. Comput. Hum. Interact. (TOCHI) **24**, 1 (2017). https://doi.org/10.1145/3014058

47. Rogers, Y., et al.: Why it's worth the hassle: the value of in-situ studies when designing ubicomp. In: Krumm, J., Abowd, G.D., Seneviratne, A., Strang, T. (eds.) UbiComp 2007: Ubiquitous Computing, pp. 336–353. Springer, Heidelberg (2007)

48. Schon, D.A.: The Reflective Practitioner: How Professionals Think in Action, vol. 5126. Basic books, New York (1984)

49. Shamekhi, A., Liao, Q.V., Wang, D., Bellamy, R.K.E., Erickson, T.: Face value? exploring the effects of embodiment for a group facilitation agent. In: Proceedings of the 2018 CHI Conference on Human Factors in Computing Systems, CHI 2018, pp. 1–13. Association for Computing Machinery, New York (2018). https://doi.org/10.1145/3173574.3173965

50. Tausczik, Y.R., Pennebaker, J.W.: Improving teamwork using real-time language feedback. In: Proceedings of the SIGCHI Conference on Human Factors in Computing Systems, CHI 2013, pp. 459–468. Association for Computing Machinery, New York (2013). https://doi.org/10.1145/2470654.2470720

51. Zalake, M., Lok, B.: Non-responsive virtual humans for self-report assessments. In: Proceedings of the 18th International Conference on Intelligent Virtual Agents, IVA 2018, pp. 347–348. Association for Computing Machinery, New York (2018). https://doi.org/10.1145/3267851.3267893

52. Zhou, M., et al.: NIH Public Access: Personalizing mobile fitness apps using reinforcement learning. In: CEUR Workshop Proceedings, vol. 2068, pp. 2–21 (2018)

# Interaction with Mobile Devices

# Exploring How a Digitized Program Can Support Parents to Improve Their Children's Nutritional Habits

Diogo Branco[1]([✉]), Ana C. Pires[1], Hugo Simão[1], Ana Gomes[2], Ana Pereira[2], Joana Sousa[3], Luísa Barros[2], and Tiago Guerreiro[1]

[1] LASIGE, University of Lisbon, Lisbon, Portugal
{djbranco,cdpires,hasimao,tjguerreiro}@fc.ul.pt
[2] Faculty of Psychology, University of Lisbon, Lisbon, Portugal
{ana.fernandes.gomes,aipereira,lbarros}@psicologia.ulisboa.pt
[3] Faculty of Medicine, University of Lisbon, Lisbon, Portugal
joanamsousa@medicina.ulisboa.pt

**Abstract.** Poor eating habits are one of today's significant menaces to public health. Child obesity is increasing, is a concerning reality, and needs to be appropriately addressed. However, most behavior change programs do not consider the needs of parents and their children, their profiles, and environments in the design of this type of intervention. We present the results of a workshop with dietists and clinical psychologists, professionals that deal with different parents and their children's dietary problems, to understand parents' profiles, attitudes, and perceptions. The main contributions of this study are a set of personas, daily scenarios, and design considerations regarding behavior change programs that can be used to guide the creation of new digital programs. This formative contribution is of interest to researchers and practitioners designing digitized behavior change programs targeted at parents to improve their children's habits.

**Keywords:** Behavior change · Nutrition · Children · Parents · Feeding practices

## 1 Introduction

Eating patterns are established earlier in life and trigger future eating behavior. Parents play an important role in defining children's eating habits [16]. Children with unhealthy nutritional habits are at a higher risk of developing obesity in adults and several associated diseases [17].

Previous studies about children's food intake focus on parents' direct registration of meals or children's direct usage of sensors on forks and plates [4]. Recently, there are already studies focusing on children's food habits improvement throughout their parents [22].

© IFIP International Federation for Information Processing 2021
Published by Springer Nature Switzerland AG 2021
C. Ardito et al. (Eds.): INTERACT 2021, LNCS 12935, pp. 211–220, 2021.
https://doi.org/10.1007/978-3-030-85610-6_13

A program able to effectively change parents feeding and eating behaviors should include more information or strategies besides nutritional ones or meal monitorization. Especially, parents and children's needs should be taken into consideration for improving adherence and engagement [22]. To this end, we need to target users' behavior and analyze their daily routine, motivation to change, and possible obstacles.

In this study, we seek to identify how, why, and when users would adhere to a digital program to change their children's feeding habits. To this end, we considered the need to identify users' charactcristics, draw scenarios of their daily lives, and identify possible problems in interacting with a digitized program. For that purpose, we performed a workshop with dietists and clinical psychologists, since they have contact with different parents and children's ecosystems, to understand the following:

1. What impact parents' mental models, motivations and goals have in their willingness to change children's nutritional habits?
2. What influence may parents' daily routines, priorities and barriers have when changing their children's nutritional habits?
3. How and when can a digital platform leverage parents to successfully change their children's habits?

## 2    Related Work

A diet low in fruits and vegetables is one of the challenges facing Western societies today due to its association with increased cardiovascular risk, and certain types of cancer [14]. Simultaneously, we can observe a health improvement and reduce heart problems by reducing saturated fat, and added sugars [5,14].

Children's food intake happens regularly in a home setting [23], with parents being the main responsibles for children eating habits [11]. Therefore, parents are targeted in previous studies as effective agents in positively influencing children's food intake [7]. Nevertheless, the primary constraints are the lack of consistency and permanent engagement in these strategies [6]. As an alternative, studies are positioned on the children's side, providing several ways of feedback to maintain engagement as the usage of lights, music, and photos [2,3,12,13]. However, these approaches might bring unwanted distractions during mealtimes and have questionable efficacy in long-term [10] as they draw too much attention away from the meal itself [10,18].

To aid in surpassing this disengagement, gamified digital health apps to report food intake are common. In App stores (e.g., Google Play Store or Apple Store), we find a range of applications categorized as Nutritional Behavior Change Apps, which encourage people to control food intake. These apps allow the person's education and training maximization to make more conscious food decisions [6].

Therefore, this work presents Lessons Learned based on information gathered with nutrition experts and psychologists regarding parent's profiles and personalization that supplement theory-based approaches to help predict behavior changes through a proactively planned implementation to control the outcomes adequately.

# 3    Workshop with Psychologists and Dietists

Using a participatory design approach with psychologists and dietists from Portugal, we performed an in person workshop to identify the possible barriers and facilitators to motivate parents to change their children's (from 2 to 6 years old) food habits. We aimed to capture the field experts' vision and extrapolate possible influences for the design process.

## 3.1    Participants

Adding to our research team members (3 clinical psychologists and 1 dietist) we recruited additional participants: 1 dietist, 1 psychologist in public health, and 2 clinical psychologists with experience in behavior change, particularly in nutrition, and in working with parents. We divided participants into four groups of two. Each research team member was matched with an outside participant.

## 3.2    Procedure

The entire session had a duration of 2h30. At the beginning, we gave a brief explanation of the session. We divided the workshop into three activities with limited time: *personas*, scenarios, and storyboards. Given the Stakeholders' background, we asked them to characterize patients they have and their difficulties in following an eating behavior change program, either in paper and pencil or digital. In the end, we had a final session debriefing.

***Persona*'s Activity.** The aim was to characterise possible users' profiles (i.e. parents) and their children (i.e. the specific target behaviors). We gave each team cards with possible topics (goals, attitude, priorities, obstacles, motivations, feelings) to aid them in describing each persona. **Scenarios' Activity.** To further characterize these *personas*, we challenge each group to describe each *persona*'s day in detail. This activity could show the difficulties and obstacles to establish a healthy diet and behavioral change. Besides, it enables to envision the toxic habits or barriers families could have in persecuting their goals. It may help to identify the strategies and attitudes of the parents when children fail their expectations. Besides, these scenarios could help extract crucial aspects of parents' relationship, whether they were or not divorced, and grandparents' inclusion in the child's routine.

**Storyboards' Activity.** We asked participants to draw a storyboard considering the *personas* and scenarios just created. The activity included a hypothetical platform (digitized program) to change children's diet and habit behaviors. We used this technique to motivate participants to explore and identify the interactions between *personas*, their scenarios, and the hypothetical platform.

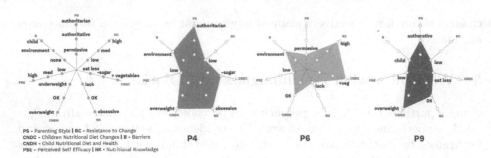

**Fig. 1.** Illustration of the results for *personas* P4, P6 and P9.

This activity could help to highlight relevant aspects that deserve attention for designing: the user experience, believes, and daily routines; possible difficulties and opportunities; trigger events and the solutions to them.

### 3.3 Analyses

We started by looking at the personas created by the participants. Furthermore, we also considered participants' additional notes and the scenarios created to extract prominent themes using open coding. Afterwards, we added to the analysis the storyboards and generated our affinity diagram. Our study generated 10 personas, 9 scenarios, and 10 storyboards which allowed us to identify the heterogeneities of families with children and how their environment influenced children's diet.

## 4    Findings

Throughout the sessions, stakeholders exposed parenting styles, nutritional knowledge, barriers, parent's beliefs and confidence and children's characteristics. Results are illustrated in Fig. 1.

### 4.1    Parenting Styles

Parenting styles are strongly related to parent's adherence to health programs and the responsiveness of their children [21]. We have identified in our results three parenting styles: authoritarian, authoritative, and indulgent or permissive. Authoritarian parents are those with low responsiveness but high demand to their children; their style is rule-based regardless of their child's preferences. *Persona* #4 elucidates this type of attitude; the father is rigid, inflexible, and punishes his son without explaining the reasons beyond it: *"[...] the child asks grandma 200 g of gummies. Afterwards, [the child] has his mouth dirty when he arrives at home and [for that reason] his father punishes him before dinner. Then, they have [a healthy] dinner in silence."*

In the storyboard, P4 brought up challenges to be considered in the design process. P4 seems a little obsessive with a need to control the program as also his environment. This father wants to receive personal notifications with the goals and reflections about the strategies monitored the day before every time he turns his computer ON. This father is a person that likes to be informed; he wants to listen to the contents of each session several times, and for that reason, he prefers to listen to the audio so he could do other things at the same time (e.g., cooking). Besides, as it emerged from the storyboarding and debrief session, this father would constantly need positive reinforcement. The digitized program could include messages and notifications about the achievement of the objectives and activities so far and a progress bar, so the father would be aware of his outcomes and what is missing. So, it is essential to consider such parents who need to receive daily feedback and download materials.

We also identified authoritative parents who try to handle different patterns of behavior and negotiate with the child. This parenting style is related to a high level of demand and rules with high responsiveness to the child in the medium term. They also may exclude going to someplace that could induce some unhealthy temptation to the child, for instance: *"They go to the park and the child asks for an ice cream, and the parents want a cup of coffee, but they do not go to the coffee shop to not expose the child to temptation"* - P9. These parents are already making some efforts to change their children's diet, but they would need guidance to overcome their major obstacle, environmental barriers, as we will refer to later.

Another observed parenting style was indulgent or permissive. This style fosters an environment of acceptance, affection, and dialogue but in contrast with authoritarian, they do not impose rules, and children may have inadequate nutritional habits [21], as in P3: *"[Father] got up at 12h to get prolonged fasting - the son starts school at 13h30. Son woke up at 10 am, eats unhealthy cereals, and watches TV until 12h."*

**Lesson Learned 1: Design Tailored Program Considering Parenting Styles.** The program should provide tailored messages, according to parenting styles, advice, and training on how to change their child's behavior (e.g., setting rules) and increase authoritative parenting practices. This has been targeted as essential for successful interventions, but still, research in this domain are scarce [20].

**Lesson Learned 2: Design Tailored Notifications Considering Parenting Styles.** Give parent's enough options to ease their interaction with the app that supports their parenting style. Parents could select at which time and day and in which device do they want to receive app's notifications, timing between notifications, timing of snoozing, saving data when some disruption happens after x minutes, etc. As our findings indicate some parenting styles would need to receive notifications each day (e.g.: permissive) while others will just need weekly notifications, for instance authoratarian.

## 4.2   Nutritional Knowledge

Nutritional knowledge was another theme from our analyses that may also impact parents willing to change their children's nutritional habits. In this context, nutritional knowledge is the understanding of the health risks and benefits of health practices and the information needed to perform the behavior change. Our results highlighted that parents have different attitudes to follow a program depending on the *children's nutritional diet and health*. Two *personas* had their child facing serious nutritional problems, and children should eat less and better. This simulates what often happens at the doctor, psychologist, or dietist. Some parents are not aware of the risks of having nutritional problems like obesity or/and do not perceive their child as obese (e.g., *P9*). Parental nutrition knowledge also plays a role in the development of child obesity since parents must have a good working knowledge of healthy foods and age-appropriate portion sizes in order to improve food shopping, preparation, and delivery for their children [19].

On the one hand, we identified in our results the recreation of parents with lack of knowledge which is highly correlated with child obesity [19]. For instance, P5 simulates those parents that have an obese child and exhibit a lack of knowledge in two dimensions, consequences of unhealthy food and consequences of obesity. Stakeholders referred that *"P5 consider that the child is healthy and that the pediatrician exaggerates a little. They think the child will learn to choose by himself and will stop eating so much."*

During storyboarding it arose the issue of how to tailor messages/program content for those parents that already have good nutritional knowledge and practice. For instance, the mother recreated in *Persona* 9 already has good nutrition habits and attitudes. So, when participating in sessions to change nutritional behaviour, she will be willing to receive information that perfectly fits her needs, as for instance, strategies to guide the child eating behavior. However, if a session is not related to her current problem, such session would be seen as useless by her and she could quit.

**Lesson Learned 3: Tailor Guided Nutritional Knowledge.** Identify parents' nutritional knowledge and tailor notifications to perfectly fit their needs (e.g. strategies to employ with the children, grandparents, etc.) to avoid boredom or the sensation of lack of personalization.

Identify those parents who misunderstand nutritional habits and consequences in the long term and promote nutritional knowledge: tailored notifications of healthy foods and age-appropriate portion sizes to improve food shopping, preparation, and delivery for their children.

## 4.3   Perceived Self-efficacy

People's confidence in their ability to perform a behavior that leads to an outcome is named perceived self-efficacy [1]. To change the eating behavior, parents first need to identify which behavior needs to be changed and recognize its importance, but also they need to have the confidence and readiness to accomplish it.

Five out of the 10 *personas* represented persons not confident in the treatment success, and 3 of them have the intention and motivation to follow a program to change their children's nutritional habits. The lack of perceived self-efficacy is an important predictor of failure, as indicated in studies with adults to lose weight [8]. However, intention and motivation could moderate this factor.

In the storyboard, several issues related to reduced confidence emerged. For instance, parents would quickly lose interest in the activities and expect results without putting in too much effort. To mitigate this, parents could have a high success rate in the digitized program's activities and several messages with positive reinforcement. Stakeholders referred that parents would need to feel that they have the conditions to do so and that they are in the right way, which can be reinforced by the program.

**Lesson Learned 4: Increase Confidence in Behavioral Change and in Self-efficacy.** To create a positive attitude towards the recommended behavior and increase self-efficacy to perform the behavior, we obtained several insights from our results. For example: a) Display the success rate, progress bar and provide positive reinforcement. b) Refocus on positive outcomes to the detriment of failures. c) Provide suggestions to improve their conditions to behavior change (time and money-saving). d) Provide examples and facts of people that were able to change their children's nutritional behavior.

### 4.4   Barriers

Barriers have an high implication in the perceived self-efficacy of parents and consequently to adherence and program compliance. Specifically, P2, P6, and P9 had a critical barrier that could impede their effort to change the behavior. The family eating *environment* and daily routines could be influencing unhealthy nutrition behaviors. In these three cases, the *grandmother* was responsible for children's school-home transportation and cooking unhealthy meals, which is a persistent barrier. Studies highlight that grandparents may have inappropriate perceptions, knowledge (nutritional facts) and behavior (for e.g. overfeeding, indulging children by excusing children to eat healthy food, and by considering that over weighted children are more healthy, happy and strong [9,15]. For these reasons, the digitized program could guide parents in approaching their family to integrate healthy nutritional habits.

Besides, parents perceived capability also strongly depends on *children characteristics* as temperament, eating traits, and learned behaviors. For instance, parents that attribute the problem to stable child characteristics, as P2 - in which parents have the perception that they have tried everything unsuccessfully and that the child would not change her temperament - would possibly lead to some disbelief about changing their child eating behavior.

**Lesson Learned 5: Awareness of Possible Environmental Barriers.** Help parents identify environmental barriers, such as school eating menus, peers influence, grandparents eating habits). Moreover, guide parents with strategies to overcome such barriers. This could be done by giving specific and tailored messages to communicate with family (e.g., grandparents) and school communities to engage them as part of the change to healthy behaviors, e.g., what to say, printing graphs of progress, goals, and objectives of the weeks.

Help parents understand which characteristics of the children are stable and unchangeable and which are prone to modifications. Give parents strategies to shape children's personalities.

In sum, parents may have great resistance to treatment due to their lack of confidence and self-efficacy in changing their child's eating behavior due to their attribution to their stable characteristics or grandparents' nutritional habits.

## 5    Discussion

Our motivation in this study comes from the need to complement previous interdisciplinary knowledge regarding professionals' information, tailored feedback, and how the parents play a crucial role in influencing child eating behaviors [16,22]. Our work identified specific factors that influence parents' readiness and confidence to participate in these programs for changing their young children eating habits. Our findings highlight the heterogeneity between parents. Furthermore, we elucidate the role different parental styles, goals, motivations, nutritional knowledge, and perceived barriers have when designing digitized programs.

However, our results could be limited because they do not consider parents' and children's perspectives which it would be our next step in the future. Future work should address this topic to increase knowledge and help understand what should be considered when building these application types.

In sum, all the workshop activities helped in abstracting the possible solutions that should be considered when designing applications for improving young children's diets throughout their parents.

## 6    Conclusion

This work contributes to revealing the ecosystem that influences children's food habits and their implications for practitioners and researchers in developing digitized programs to change young children's nutritional habits. Furthermore, this work revealed the need of further explorations with grandparents, parents, and school caregivers to understand the environment that surrounds children profoundly. Hence, there is a need to unfold such complex subjects to develop personalized and tailored programs capable of introducing fundamental changes in the child's eating habits.

**Acknowledgements.** This work was supported by FCT through the project "Food-Parenting: Parentalidade e Alimentação" with the ref. PTDC/PSI-GER/30432/2017 and the LASIGE Research Unit, ref. UID/CEC/00408/2019 . We would like to thank all participants of our study.

# References

1. Bandura, A.: Health promotion by social cognitive means. Health Educ. Behav. **31**(2), 143–164 (2004). https://doi.org/10.1177/1090198104263660, pMID: 15090118
2. Chen, Y.Y., Baljon, K., Tran, B., Rosner, D.K., Hiniker, A.: The stamp plate and the kicking chair: playful productivity for mealtime in preschools. In: Proceedings of the 17th ACM Conference on Interaction Design and Children, IDC 2018, pp. 373–380. Association for Computing Machinery, New York (2018). https://doi.org/10.1145/3202185.3202759
3. Chen, Y.Y., Li, Z., Rosner, D., Hiniker, A.: Understanding parents' perspectives on mealtime technology. Proc. ACM Interact. Mob. Wearable Ubiquit. Technol. **3**(1), 1–19 (2019)
4. Chen, Y.Y., Yip, J., Rosner, D., Hiniker, A.: Lights, music, stamps! evaluating mealtime tangibles for preschoolers. In: Proceedings of the Thirteenth International Conference on Tangible, Embedded, and Embodied Interaction, pp. 127–134 (2019)
5. DiNicolantonio, J.J., Lucan, S.C., O'Keefe, J.H.: The evidence for saturated fat and for sugar related to coronary heart disease. Progr. Cardiovasc. Dis. **58**(5), 464–472 (2016)
6. Golley, R.K., Hendrie, G., Slater, A., Corsini, N.: Interventions that involve parents to improve children's weight-related nutrition intake and activity patterns-what nutrition and activity targets and behaviour change techniques are associated with intervention effectiveness? Obes. Rev. **12**(2), 114–130 (2011)
7. Hendrie, G.A., Lease, H.J., Bowen, J., Baird, D.L., Cox, D.N.: Strategies to increase children's vegetable intake in home and community settings: a systematic review of literature. Matern. Child Nutr. **13**(1), e12276 (2017)
8. Jeffery, R.: How can health behavior theory be made more useful for intervention research? Int. J. Behav. Nutr. Phys. Act. **1**, 10 (2004). https://doi.org/10.1186/1479-5868-1-10
9. Jingxiong, J., Rosenqvist, U., Huishan, W., Greiner, T., Guangli, L., Sarkadi, A.: Influence of grandparents on eating behaviors of young children in chinese three-generation families. Appetite **48**(3), 377 – 383 (2007). https://doi.org/10.1016/j.appet.2006.10.004. http://www.sciencedirect.com/science/article/pii/S0195666306006325
10. Jo, E., Bang, H., Ryu, M., Sung, E.J., Leem, S., Hong, H.: Mamas: supporting parent–child mealtime interactions using automated tracking and speech recognition. In: Proceedings of the ACM on Human-Computer Interaction (CSCW1), vol. 4, pp. 1–32, May 2020. https://doi.org/10.1145/3392876
11. Johnson, B.J., Hendrie, G.A., Golley, R.K.: Reducing discretionary food and beverage intake in early childhood: a systematic review within an ecological framework. Public Health Nutr. **19**(9), 1684–1695 (2016). https://doi.org/10.1017/S1368980015002992
12. Joi, Y.R., et al.: Interactive and connected tableware for promoting children's vegetable-eating and family interaction. In: Proceedings of the The 15th International Conference on Interaction Design and Children, pp. 414–420 (2016)

13. Kadomura, A., Li, C.Y., Chen, Y.C., Chu, H.H., Tsukada, K., Siio, I.: Sensing fork and persuasive game for improving eating behavior. In: Proceedings of the 2013 ACM Conference on Pervasive and Ubiquitous Computing Adjunct Publication, pp. 71–74 (2013)
14. Kushi, L.H., Doyle, C., McCullough, M., Rock, C.L., Demark-Wahnefried, W., Bandera, E.V., Gapstur, S., Patel, A.V., Andrews, K., Gansler, T., et al.: American cancer society guidelines on nutrition and physical activity for cancer prevention: reducing the risk of cancer with healthy food choices and physical activity. CA Cancer J. Clin. **62**(1), 30–67 (2012)
15. Li, B., Adab, P., Cheng, K.K.: The role of grandparents in childhood obesity in China - evidence from a mixed methods study. Int. J. Behav. Nutr. Phys. Act. **91(12)** (2015). https://doi.org/10.1186/s12966-015-0251-z
16. Litchford, A., Roskos, M.R.S., Wengreen, H.: Influence of fathers on the feeding practices and behaviors of children: a systematic review. Appetite **147**, 104558 (2020)
17. Lloyd, L., Langley-Evans, S., McMullen, S.: Childhood obesity and risk of the adult metabolic syndrome: a systematic review. Int. J. Obes. **36**, 1–11 (2012). https://doi.org/10.1038/ijo.2011.186
18. Lo, J.-L., et al.: Playful tray: adopting ubicomp and persuasive techniques into play-based occupational therapy for reducing poor eating behavior in young children. In: Krumm, J., Abowd, G.D., Seneviratne, A., Strang, T. (eds.) UbiComp 2007. LNCS, vol. 4717, pp. 38–55. Springer, Heidelberg (2007). https://doi.org/10.1007/978-3-540-74853-3_3
19. Cluss, P.A., Ewing, L., King, W.C., Reis, E.C., Dodd, J.L., Penner, B.: Nutrition knowledge of low-income parents of obese children. Transl. Behav. Med. **3(2)**, 218–225 (2013). https://doi.org/10.1007/s13142-013-0203-6
20. Raat, H., et al.: Primary prevention of overweight in preschool children, the beeboft study (breastfeeding, breakfast daily, outside playing, few sweet drinks, less tv viewing): design of a cluster randomized controlled trial. BMC Public Health **13**(1), 1–11 (2013)
21. Shloim, N., Edelson, L.R., Martin, N., Hetherington, M.M.: Parenting styles, feeding styles, feeding practices, and weight status in 4–12 year-old children: a systematic review of the literature. Front. Psychol. **6**, 1849 (2015). https://doi.org/10.3389/fpsyg.2015.01849. https://www.frontiersin.org/article/10.3389/fpsyg.2015.01849
22. Zarnowiecki, D., et al.: A systematic evaluation of digital nutrition promotion websites and apps for supporting parents to influence children's nutrition. Int. J. Behav. Nutr. Phys. Act. **17**(1), 17 (2020)
23. Ziauddeen, N., Page, P., Penney, T.L., Nicholson, S., Kirk, S.F., Almiron-Roig, E.: Eating at food outlets and leisure places and "on the go" is associated with less-healthy food choices than eating at home and in school in children: cross-sectional data from the UK National Diet and Nutrition Survey Rolling Program (2008–2014). Am. J. Clin. Nutr. **107**(6), 992–1003 (2018). https://doi.org/10.1093/ajcn/nqy057

# MAWA: A Browser Extension for Mobile Web Augmentation

Iñigo Aldalur(✉), Alain Perez(✉), and Felix Larrinaga(✉)

Faculty of Engineering, Mondragon University, Loramendi 4, Arrasate, Spain
{ialdalur,aperez,flarrinaga}@mondragon.edu

**Abstract.** In recent years, the usage of mobile browsers has experienced an astonishing growth. Nowadays, most citizens use their mobile phones instead of their laptops to surf the Web for immediate availability. Nevertheless, Web design is performed considering laptops screen dimensions and websites are readjusted to mobile screen resolutions using Responsive Web Design. This conversion to smaller screen resolutions causes some drawbacks to mobile navigation. Web Augmentation is an effective methodology that allows end-users to customize third party websites according to their needs. This technique can mitigate the problems caused by small screen resolutions.

This article introduces MAWA, a Firefox mobile browser extension for Web Augmentation designed to remove and move content in any website using a visual programming technique. The article presents the benefits introduced by MAWA in response to the drawbacks arising when websites are adapted from laptop screen resolutions to mobile dimensions. Evaluation is also introduced in this article where end-users with no programming knowledge have adapted four different websites using the extension. Results show that testers claim that drawbacks presented by mobile browsers are mitigated with the utilization of MAWA.

**Keywords:** Human-Computer Interaction · End-user development · Web augmentation · Customization · Mobile browser

## 1 Introduction

In recent decades, there has been an important increase in the use of mobile phones and, as a consequence, a growth in the access to web applications [1]. Several studies predict that the next decade will bring a significant increase in the demand for mobile data [2]. Boehm et al. [3] foresaw in 1995 that in 2005 there would be 55 million of Web practitioners in the U.S. In 2005, Scaffidi et al. [4] estimated 90 million end-users in the U.S by 2012. If we extrapolate this quantity worldwide, we can imagine that nowadays (2020) the real number is uncountable. In fact, today more than half of the Internet traffic is mobile. This increase raises the partaking of end-users in the customization of websites

© IFIP International Federation for Information Processing 2021
Published by Springer Nature Switzerland AG 2021
C. Ardito et al. (Eds.): INTERACT 2021, LNCS 12935, pp. 221–242, 2021.
https://doi.org/10.1007/978-3-030-85610-6_14

to their desires and necessities [5]. The customisation of web pages allows end users to redefine colours, relocate components, remove features or add new elements. In other words, to adapt the functionality, content and design to the user's wishes. The customization process is mainly carried out by users with no programming skills, as most web users around the world are mere consumers with limited programming knowledge. A very popular technique for customizing existing third-party websites is Web Augmentation (WA). This technique has been developed as a method to customize or adapt the features of websites without affecting the server-side code [6]. Furthermore, augmentation is not developed by the website owner but by the website user. There are different approaches to realising WA, but one of the most popular is the use of visual programming techniques [7]. Visual programming can be defined as the use of graphics as the programming language [8].

Lieberman et al. [9] define End-User Development (EUD) as "a set of methods, techniques and tools that allow users of software systems, acting as non-professional software developers, to create, modify or extend a software artefact". End-users are able to start with basic adaptation mechanisms and gradually advance to use more powerful adaptation mechanisms without facing insuperable barriers [10]. WA technique is very appropriate because it can be applied progressively. WA can be applied to any website and it is accomplished by end-users. The same drawbacks experience by desktop users affect mobile users. Problems can even increase since mobile versions are, in many cases, adaptations of desktop versions. Consequently, WA not only can be used for desktop web versions, but mobile web versions can also be customized by end-users. Mobile users need tools and strategies to meet their needs when browsing. This paper investigates WA as a mechanism for customising web pages by end users through a Firefox mobile browser extension for web adaptation.

The remainder of the paper is organized as follows. Section 2 analyses the problem analysis including the issue we want to solve, its causes and its consequences. Section 3 discusses related work in order to give the reader an idea of what has been done in this area from WA perspective. Section 4 describes MAWA[1] (Mobile Application for Web Augmentation), a browser extension that customizes mobile version web pages to adapt them to users requirements. Section 5 presents MAWA evaluation and its results based on different questionnaires (NASA-TLX, SUS and their satisfaction), Sect. 6 shows features we would like to enhance about MAWA and Sect. 7 concludes the paper.

## 2    Problem Analysis

### 2.1    The Problem

Most web designers prepare their initial web configuration for desktop resolution and later think about how to adapt this design to the mobile paradigm [11]. This process is frequently carried out with the Responsive Web Design (RWD).

---

[1] https://addons.mozilla.org/es/firefox/addon/mawa/.

RWD is a design and implementation technique that enables web designers and developers to create websites with a flexible approach to adapt their content and layout to different resolutions on different devices with the same web experience [12]. This web restructuring is not free. It comes with a computational cost as the initial desktop version has to be adapted to the configuration of the mobile browser. Furthermore, this adaptation causes usability problems such as the display of unnecessary content, the reordering important content and, as a consequence, cluttered navigation and scrolling to find the desired information, among others [13]. These usability drawbacks induce a poor web experience for users.

## 2.2 Causes

In the beginning, websites were designed for desktop computers because this was the supported platform for browsing the Web. However, over time, technology has evolved and mobile phones and tablets are common platforms for consuming websites via navigation browsers [14]. Due to this natural evolution, web designers had the habit of designing first for desktops computers where large screen resolutions were required. Later, they would design another website for mobile browsers while maintaining the same style [15]. RWD avoids creating two different versions of the same website and was created for desktop-to-mobile adaptation and not vice versa even though it is common to listen that it should be "mobile first design" [16]. Not only website designs are considered first, but also other aspects, such as the WCAG 2.0 guidelines for desktops, which are created only for desktops and designers have to decide how to proceed for mobile consumption [17]. Desktop version design first causes problems and disadvantages to mobile web browser edition [2] that can be mitigated with our proposal.

## 2.3 Consequences

The negative consequences of the problem previously addressed on users experience are:

- Scroll: scrolling up and down a page without reading the content may be a signal of frustration and lack of confidence, which is a frequent action on mobile browsing [18]. In relation to this, [19] concluded that when users frequently scroll to find irrelevant information in their navigation, they are less satisfied. Furthermore, "the current scrolling method for a mobile device is both time-consuming and fatigue-prone" [20]. So, considering that [21] conducted a study in which they determined that people used the scroll bar on 76% of the pages, and that 22% scrolled to the end regardless of page length. It is extremely important to avoid scrolling in mobile phones.
- Show unnecessary content and hide important content: All mobile web users want to extract the desired information quickly and with minimal mental effort [22]. RWD relocates all content shown in the desktop version hiding some content and maintaining other content visible in the mobile version [12].

Unfortunately, this content may be useless to readers if the desired content is concealed or the user has to scroll to find it.

- Produce cluttered navigation: websites are changed from desktop version to mobile version by adapting the layout and rearranging the content to the size of screen [14]. This step of adapting the website generates different drawbacks such as the obstacle of reading the content correctly from the device [23], which causes more user interaction than for desktop users and consequently the time needed to carry out any task is higher [24]. In addition, it generates more input errors than using the desktop navigation [25].

## 3   Related Work

Bouvin [6] originally coined the term WA in 1999 to describe a tool that "through integration with a Web browser, a HTTP proxy or a Web server adds content or controls not contained within the Web pages themselves to the effect of allowing structure to be added to the Web page directly or indirectly, or to navigate such structure. The purpose of such a tool is to help users organize, associate, or structure information found on the Web. This activity can be performed by a single user or in collaboration with others". Our work focuses on WA and consequently this section analyses the different works accomplished in this concern. On the one hand, an important number of references focus their research in WA for computers. For example WebMakeup [26] is a visual programming Chrome browser extension. End-users can copy different web nodes by clicking on them with the mouse. When using this extension to modify a website, users can insert previously copied nodes from a "Piggybank" by dragging & dropping. WebMakeup permits updating inserted nodes with actual information or not. Additionally, inserted nodes can be collapsed by clicking on certain node defined by the user. MDWA [27] proposes a novel method for designing WA applications based on client-side and server-side components. They propose a model-driven approach that can improve the abstraction level of client-side and server-side development. They provide a set of tools to design the composition of core applications. These applications present new back-end functionality to support WA. The front-end has the main function of augmenting the web page. [28] shows a tool that proposes a data acquisition system capable of capturing the user interaction in web interfaces. Subsequently, these interactions can be reproduced automatically without any human action, which can be a method to reduce the time to perform an activity. Similarly, Excore [29] is designed to add content from repetitive web searches. It detects a keyword on a defined website, automatically carries out the web search on a different website and inserts the desired content on the target site. This automation is defined by an end-user through a visual programmable Chrome browser extension. Chudnoskyy et al. [30] take a step forward in creating web adaptations by assisting users with recommendations and automatic composition. It provides a composition environment for end-users supplied by different elements, which can be placed on the canvas, synchronized with each other and shared with other users. [31]

customize websites depending on the disability a person has (visual, motor, cognitive or hearing impairments) and the attitude towards computers and the Web older people show. [32] introduces a adaptive hypermedia method suitable for adaptive link annotation. This method shows a combination of direct manipulation and automatic linking annotations that allow users to better control the adaptability of the page. This direct control can better support users' attention to information during a task. [33] has design a system in which the webmaster starts with the existing layout and specifies which elements must be modified. Then, touch-based events will be used as implicit input for the adaptive engine, which automatically modifies, rearranges, and re-styles interactive items based on browsing usage. OFIE [34] relies on Programming by Demonstration to define the appropriate native input, which must be executed automatically when the rule is triggered. This method allows end users to define operations simply by performing required native input interactions on the graphical user interface of the application. End-user does not need any necessary programming knowledge or write/edit any code. Trusty et al. [35] developed ALOE, a Firefox browser extension that augments Web pages by translating all selected English words with their translations to defined languages.

On the other hand, research has also been conducted in WA for mobile phones. For example, PageTailor [36] is a Firefox-based browser that runs on Windows Mobile PDAs and is implemented as a Mozilla plugin API. The tool provides a technique for the selection of objects that by dragging a line over the object selects the web node associated. PageTailor permits the customization of traditional websites mainly by increasing the size of important web elements and diminishing the size of irrelevant content. PageTailor does not use Responsive Web Design. Collapse-to-Zoom [37] is a much simpler tool than PageTailor since it only allows expanding and collapsing web elements. It is also designed for modifying traditional websites in PDAs. If the user taps over an element and drags the pen diagonally to the top, the node is expanded. If the movements is towards the bottom, the element is collapsed. MoWA [5] is a mobile browser extension for augmenting existing Web Applications with information that the original web page does not provide. It adapts the website content depending on information obtained from the mobile sensors (GPS, microphone, gyroscope, light...).

Independently on the target aim by these applications (desktop or mobile), their final objective is to enable users in adapting their favourite website to their needs. In our approach, the scope focuses on mobile browsing and the main objective is to ease end users navigation experience by adapting websites to their needs using WA.

## 4   Mobile Websites Web Augmentation

How often do you use your mobile phone browser to look for information on the web? Nowadays it is more common to use mobile phone browsers than desktop browsers[2]. Therefore, it is utmost importance to adapt mobile version websites

---

[2] https://gs.statcounter.com/platform-market-share/desktop-mobile-tablet.

to the needs of users by avoiding or minimizing the consequences presented in Sect. 2. We will illustrate the use of MAWA with some examples with the conference website.

MAWA is a Firefox mobile browser extension for WA designed to remove and move content from any website through a visual programming environment. MAWA abstracts technical details into a visual domain-specific language that facilitates end-user involvement. The goal of this extension is to avoid scrolling, cluttered navigation and the removal of unnecessary content. In MAWA there are two different phases: (1) the editing phase, in which the end-user adapts the website, and (2) the execution phase, in which the system automatically completes the adaption by itself.

## 4.1   Edition Stage

The edition stage begins when the user clicks on the *new* menu button. First, the user browses a website and if they decide that this must be adapted, they double-click on the screen where the menu appears (Fig. 1 left). The user then begins to edit the website just clicking on the node they wish to update. Once the user clicks on a node, its background colour is changed adding an X button to the top right and arrows to its top, bottom, left and right. From this point on, three different actions can be performed, (1) delete the node, (2) relocate the node and (3) select a relative node using the arrows. At the moment the web page modification is completed, the end user double clicks on the screen and the second menu pops up (Fig. 1 middle). When the save button is clicked, the web page is reloaded and the modifications are automatically made visible. To remove the modification or to continue editing the website, the user has to double-click on the screen and the third menu option appears (Fig. 1 right). Note that each menu button has its own color when active and its color never changes, except for deactivated buttons which are shown in gray.

**Remove:** MAWA allows you to remove any node from the web to avoid consuming unnecessary content. Websites may present information that is not relevant to the user. This information may not be annoying on computer screens, however, it is frustrating when consumed on small cell phone screens [24,25]. If the user decides to remove the content of a node, the user must click the X button located in the upper right corner of the node (Fig. 2 left). Once clicked, the node is removed from the web page (Fig. 2 middle). If the user is not interested in some of the conference tracks, they would remove tracks using MAWA and only consume the ones of interest (Fig. 2 right).

**Move:** MAWA also allows you to move nodes from one point on the web page to another. This is done by dragging and dropping the selected node. When the node is dragged, the background colour where the node could be dropped becomes purple. This colour transformation provides the user with information as to what the new location of the node might be. Once the node is dropped, it is inserted into its new locations and removed from the original position. Figure 3 shows at the top left how the user has selected the important dates of

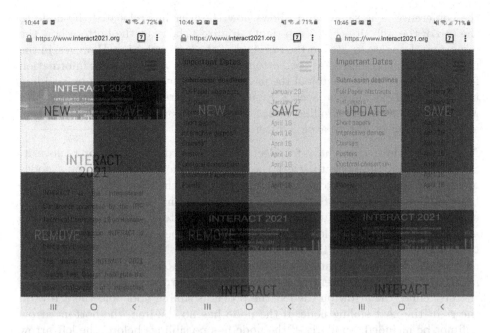

**Fig. 1.** MAWA menus: (left) initial menu, (middle) menu after edition stage, (right) menu after execution stage

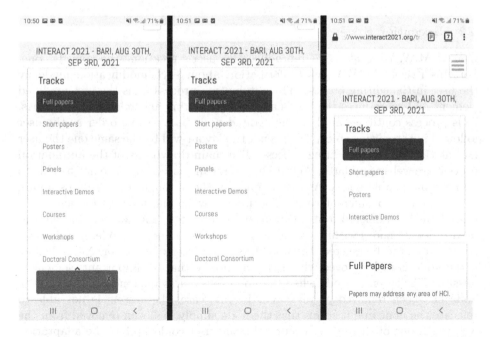

**Fig. 2.** Removing nodes with MAWA: node selection (left), node removal (middle), removing unessential tracks for the user (right)

the conference. The same figure shows how the user has relocated the node to the top of the web site (Fig. 3 top right). Figure 3 shows at the bottom how the important dates are located at the top right of the laptop version. However, in the mobile version it is located at the bottom of the page. All important information for a user should be at the top of the page because it avoids scrolling by avoiding the drawbacks explained in Sect. 2. Figure 3 demonstrates with an example how MAWA helps to avoid scrolling in case essential information is at the bottom and, consequently, also to avoid cluttered navigation.

**Node Selection:** Users have to select a node in order to move or remove it. Simply click on the node to select the desired element. However, some nodes are not so easy to select due to their particular definition. For example, the body of the page is one of these elements. If we want to select the body, it is complicated to click in the upper left edge of the page to select it. Other examples are selecting complete tables or interactive nodes when the user does not want to perform any action on the node. For this reason, MAWA includes an arrow on the top, bottom, left and right of the selected node. If the user clicks the arrow at the top, the parent node is selected, the arrow at the bottom selects the first child, the arrow on the left the previous sibling node and the arrow on the right the next sibling node. If the node has no children, the bottom arrow will not be included. Similarly, if the node has no siblings before, the left arrow will not be included and if the node has no siblings after, the right arrow will not be included.

### 4.2   Execution Stage

One of MAWA's goals is to reproduce the user's creation steps one by one. For this reason, MAWA saves information about each modification made by the user in the editing process. The automation process finds the first modified element and reproduces the user's actions by deleting and relocating all nodes. This process continues until the last edited node in the same order as the user followed in the editing steps. At the end, the layout will be the same one the user had at the end of the editing process. The main drawbacks of the automation process are website updates. Website updates can cause MAWA to not be able to find the modifiable nodes. As a consequence, the automation fails. This failure can occur in two different cases. The first is when the node to be deleted or moved has been deleted from the website or relocated. The locator (mechanism used to locate nodes within a website) is not able to find the node. In this case, if the node is to be deleted, the user does not perceive any error. Nevertheless, if the node is to be moved, the user may notice that an important element is missing. The second case is when the node selected as reference to relocate the node has been removed or relocated. In this case, the system is not able to relocate the node and it seems that the node simply has been removed from the website. If one of these cases occurs, the end user could update the adaptation double-clicking on the screen and selecting update (Fig. 1 right).

**Fig. 3.** Moving nodes with MAWA: selected node before being moved (top left), the node relocated on top of the website (top right), selected node on the laptop version (bottom)

## 4.3  Architecture

MAWA architecture has been designed taking into account the information the system must store during the editing process and the information needed during the execution process. We take advantage of the browser structure to store this information in it. The architecture is illustrated in Fig. 4.

Each adaption registers an ID created exclusively for it and the URL in which the adaptation should be executed. When a web page is loaded, the system checks whether this URL has been used in an adaptation. If this URL is found, the system starts the whole process to perform the complete adaptations. Otherwise, the system waits until another web page is loaded. MAWA allows to have more than one adaptation to the same domain but only one for each subdomain.

Each adaptation has one or more nodes that will be modified in the editing process. All nodes will be identified by an ID. Each node will be populated with its location point on the page and the actions that MAWA should complete when the adaptation is enacted.

The location point is populated with different locators. A Web locator can be defined as a mechanism for uniquely identifying an element in the Document Object Model (DOM) [38]. As explained before, website updates pose a major drawback for WA tools, since nodes might no longer be found. To address this drawback, based on some previous works using multiple locators to extend the life expectancy of locators [39–41], three different locator algorithms have been implemented. These locators are based on Xpath and generate different results when they fail, being able to use another Xpath to try to find the element. If one of them finds the element, we can use the new information to repair the previously broken Xpaths. Over time, the website developers will update the website and, therefore, these three Xpaths will fail. For this reason, an algorithm able to regenerate Xpaths has been implemented. This idea has been extracted from previous works [42–44]. To generate a new Xpath, MAWA stores additional information of each adapted node and all its ancestors. This information is completed with the all their attribute names and all of their values. When previous Xpaths fail, this algorithm is executed. It generates different Xpaths with the stored information until one of them locates a single node inferring that it was the desired node. The evaluation of the algorithm shows that on very few occasions an invalid Xpath is generated.

As a conclusion, this algorithm system improves the life expectancy of the adaptation and the user does not need to re-adapt their augmentations frequently. Some website updates are invisible for users because the website maintains its appearance. However, its structure may have been modified and Xpaths are sensitive to these changes. Website upgrades may create an idea on users that MAWA is of low quality and they might stop using it. Apparently, the website has not been modified but the application does not work properly. This is why it is of utmost importance to implement a robust locator system to improve the quality of the application.

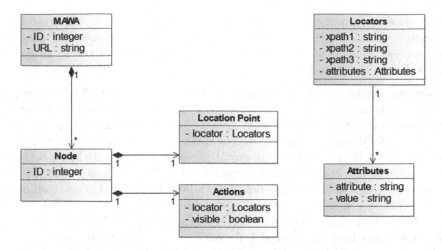

**Fig. 4.** MAWA abstract syntax

# 5 Evaluation

The main objective of MAWA extension is to avoid scrolling, cluttered navigation and removing unnecessary content by adapting your favourite or more visited websites. Allowing users to adapt content to their needs improves usability [45]. In order to validate whether MAWA accomplishes its purpose, we have evaluated MAWA following the NASA-TLX (Task Load Index) and SUS (System Usability Scale) questionnaires. NASA-TLX is "a multi-dimensional scale designed to obtain workload estimates from one or more operator while they are performing a task or immediately afterwards" [46]. SUS is used to quickly evaluate how well people comprehend the usability of a software application they are toiling away [47].

## 5.1 Research Method

**Setting.** The study was conducted at the Mondragon University (Arrasate - Mondragon, Spain). All participants used their own mobile phones on which they had version 61.0 of the Firefox Mobile browser installed. Some of these phones were Samsung Galaxy S8, Samsung Galaxy J2 Core, Xiaomi Mi10, Sony Xperia M2, iPhone SE, OnePlus 6, Huawei P20...

**Procedure.** At the very beginning of the evaluation, participants were informed of the purpose of the study and given a brief description of it. Thereupon, an instance of MAWA was presented to exemplify the main functionality of the application. The example consisted of removing and moving some web elements of the university home page simulating that we were students. Unnecessary content for students was removed and essential content was moved to the top. Next, participants were proposed to adapt in a defined manner the websites of Filmaffinity, Amazon, NBC News and to conclude one of the websites they frequently visit on their phones. Finally, participants were directed to an on-line Google Forms questionnaire[3].

**Subjects.** Sixteen people participated in the evaluation and 62,5% of the participants were male. Regarding their age, all of them were between 18–58 age range and most of them were between 30 and 39 years old. The participants came from Arrasate-Mondragon and the nearby towns. Most of the subjects were married and with a degree from Mondragon University but nobody had a technical knowledge, the aim of the evaluation was to test MAWA with end-users. Most of the subjects were working in different fields when the evaluation was conducted. These fields were finance, construction, teaching, agriculture or sports. 50% of the subjects had never used an editing program such as Photoshop. 87,5% of the participants have installed at least one browser plug-in in their computer with an average of 3,3. In addition, 43,8% of them have installed at least one plug-in in their mobile browser with an average of 1,2. 68,8% of the participants spend less than 30 min a day on the Internet on their laptops and additionally, 56,3% of them are connected to the Internet for between 30 min and 1 h on their mobiles.

**Instrument.** A questionnaire was utilized to gather the users' experience in the evaluation. The questionnaire was composed of four sections; background, their perceived workload (NASA-TLX questionnaire), usability (SUS questionnaire) and satisfaction. Satisfaction was measured by different questions with a 7-point Likert scale (1 = completely disagree, 7 = completely agree).

**Data Analysis.** Descriptive statistics have been used to characterize the sample and evaluate the participants' experience using MAWA.

### 5.2   Results

All users were able to finish the proposed tasks and, at the end of the evaluation, they answered the proposed questionnaire. The modifications made to the Filmaffinity, Amazon and NBC News web pages were guided with a document that included clear images and texts with the actions that users had to complete. Nevertheless, at the end, all subjects were able to modify and additional website, which was one of their favourite web pages on their own. The results of the evaluation are the following.

**NASA-TLX Results:** NASA-TLX results are reported in the Table 1 and summarized in the Fig. 5. NASA-TLX is used to evaluate the perceived workload during a task. The reason for using this questionnaire in this evaluation is to be informed about the subjects' feelings during the exercise. We wanted to be

---

[3] https://docs.google.com/spreadsheets/d/1RKx0xwsZ32-flCtRGUYF1-B0ddfmJ5x yTpqW0gNEEhQ/.

sure that the evaluation was balanced in order to obtain objective results about MAWA. A Likert scale between 0 and 10 was used for the answers.

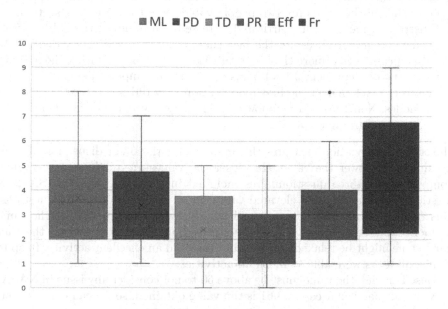

**Fig. 5.** NASA-TLX scores

- Mental Load: is used to determine the subject's mental and perceptual activity during the activity. The results indicate that the mental load was low during the activity due to the fact that the subjects' responses are at an average of 3,69. The highest value was 8 for a person and two other people voted 6. Despite this, the rest voted 5 or less and this is because they did not find the exercise difficult.
- Physical Demand: is closely linked to mental demand. This question is related to the physical activity required during the task. The results are very similar to those for mental demand as users had an average of 3,38 for physical demand and the same 3 people only voted more than 5.
- Temporal Demand: measures the pressure felt by the subject with the tasks accomplished in the evaluation. All subjects voted less than 5 and two of them voted 0, i.e., they did not felt pressure at all. The average is also very low with a value of 2,38.
- Performance: is used to know the degree of success of the subjects in completing the task. In general, all users are confident that they completed the task owing to the fact that they have all voted 5 or less on this item. On average, the subjects are satisfied with their result in the evaluation with a 2,19. This means that, they were able to complete the task completely without any shadow of a doubt from their point of view.

- Effort: evaluates the degree of mental and physical demand of the activity. The subjects in general did not claim that the evaluation was exhausting because the average is 3,38. These results ensure that the evaluation was not at all difficult because only two people voted more than 5 in this section.
- Frustration: measures how irritated, stressed and annoyed the subject feels during the activity. Despite the fact that on average subjects voted a 4,43 only 5 people voted more than 5 on this item. Frustration during the activity was superior than mental load, physical demand, temporal demand or effort due to the fact that in the first modification they did not succeed in moving the nodes. Nonetheless, the following adaptations were easier for them, there is no steep learning curve.

The standard deviation measures the amount of variation or dispersion of a set of values. The lower the value, the closer the values are to the average value. Comparing the three questionnaires included in this evaluation, NASA-TLX questionnaire has the most elevated values in all standard deviation questions. This might indicate that not all users felt the evaluation process in the same manner. Some of them might be more stressed and frustrated and on the contrary, some might be relaxed and feel that they did an excellent activity. In spite of this, all users were able to finish all activities.

Based on [48], the value must be above 60 to not consider any issue in NASA-TLX. In our particular case, 33,61 is the value obtained, so we can consider our results as satisfactory.

**Table 1.** NASA-TLX results (N = 16)

| Feature | AVG | Med | SD | MAX | MIN |
|---|---|---|---|---|---|
| Mental load | 3,69 | 3,5 | 1,96 | 8 | 1 |
| Physical demand | 3,38 | 3 | 1,86 | 7 | 1 |
| Temporal demand | 2,38 | 2 | 1,63 | 5 | 0 |
| Performance | 2,19 | 2 | 1,32 | 5 | 0 |
| Effort | 3,38 | 3 | 1,86 | 8 | 1 |
| Frustration | 4,43 | 4 | 2,61 | 9 | 1 |

**SUS Results:** The SUS results are reported in Table 2 and summarized in the Fig. 6. SUS is used to measure the usability with 10 questions. This usability scale has been used in this evaluation because we wanted to know the overall usability assessment from the user's perspective about MAWA. For the answers, the SUS uses a Likert scale from 1 to 5.

Users considered the overall usability of MAWA to be acceptable. The odd numbered questions have been highly evaluated and even numbered questions have been evaluated with an inferior mark. As expected as a good result in this questionnaire, the odd marks on average have been evaluated with more than 4 and the even ones with less than 2. Regarding the questions directly, people claim that MAWA is easy to use and that most people would learn to use the extension quickly. Moreover, they consider that the system is correctly integrated, that they feel confident using MAWA and finally subjects would use MAWA frequently. On the other hand, questions with the lower score are because subjects found the system complex, they think that they need the support of a technician to use MAWA, there are inconsistencies, the system is cumbersome and they had to learn a large number of thing to use the extension. These questions are the negative usability characteristics that a tool can have. For that reason, the substandard score means that MAWA is usable from the subject's perspective. In general, the standard deviation in all questions is below (with the exception of question S8). This means that users' opinion is very similar in all questions.

[49] estimates that 65 is the minimum value for which the tool is considered to have no usability problems. The result obtained in the SUS evaluation of MAWA is 82,18 thus, users considered the overall usability of the tool to be almost excellent. A result more elevated than 85.5 means that the tool is excellent from the usability point of view.

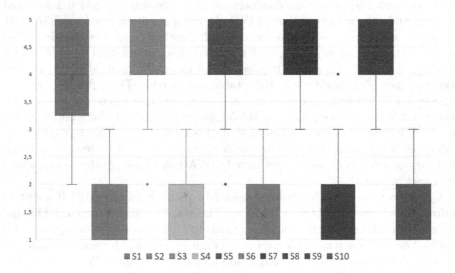

**Fig. 6.** SUS scores

**General Questions:** The results of the general questions are reported in the Table 3 and summarized in the Fig. 7. These questions evaluate the subjects' posture about the consequences of the problem described in Sect. 2. Additionally, we want to know their opinion on whether the actions in MAWA are intuitive or not and their ease of execution. A Likert scale between 1 and 7 was used for the responses.

**Table 2.** SUS results (N = 16)

| Items | AVG | Med | SD | MAX | MIN |
|-------|-----|-----|------|-----|-----|
| S1    | 3,94 | 4   | 0,99 | 5   | 2   |
| S2    | 1,5  | 1   | 0,63 | 3   | 1   |
| S3    | 4,19 | 4   | 0,91 | 5   | 2   |
| S4    | 1,81 | 2   | 0,65 | 3   | 1   |
| S5    | 4,19 | 4   | 0,91 | 5   | 2   |
| S6    | 1,43 | 1   | 0,62 | 3   | 1   |
| S7    | 4,31 | 4   | 0,6  | 5   | 3   |
| S8    | 1,81 | 1,5 | 1,05 | 4   | 1   |
| S9    | 4,31 | 4,5 | 0,79 | 5   | 3   |
| S10   | 1,5  | 1   | 0,63 | 3   | 1   |

Questions 1 to 3 are the most relevant of the article because they would approve whether or not MAWA is suitable for avoiding scrolling, removing unnecessary content and producing comfortable web browsing. Question 1 is about scrolling and subjects claim that MAWA prevents scrolling (mean of 6,37) with a median of 7. Just one person voted 4 and another 5 on this question. This means that, without any shadow of a doubt, users affirm that MAWA avoids scrolling. The second question inquires if the extension facilitates web navigation and they corroborate that this statement is true. The subjects voted on average a 5,94 out of a maximum of 7 and only 4 people voted 5 or less for this question. Finally, question 3 asks if MAWA facilitates to find desired information on a website and they are convinced that this is also true. The average to this statement is 6,12 and this time also only 4 people voted 5 or less. As a result of these questions, we can confirm that MAWA helps to solve the consequences described in Sect. 2.

Question from 4 to 13 can be classified in pairs. First we asked if a certain action is easy and then if this is intuitive. There are 5 different actions. The first one concerns the selection of nodes by simply clicking on a node (questions 4 and 5). For both questions, the results are almost the same because the subjects consider this action to be both simple and intuitive (average 5,75 and 5,81). The next two questions (6 and 7) refer to the selection of nodes using the arrows at the top, bottom or both sides of a selected node. Both questions have obtained similar answers to those of the previous block (average 5,81 and 5,93). In general, we can affirm that node selection is not a drawback in MAWA because it is easy and intuitive to click on the node or if this method is not possible, to use the arrows around the selected node. Questions 8 and 9 concern node removal. These questions have obtained the most elevated score of the questionnaire with an average 6,62 and 6,69 and the median is a 7 for both. The result determines that the way in which users can remove non-essential content from the website is elementary. Questions 10 and 11 enquire how easy and intuitive is node relocation. This time, there is a difference between both results because there is a 0.5 point difference between the two answers (average 6,37 and 5,87). Despite the fact that node removal is intuitive, the subjects feel this action to be more basic than intuitive. Finally, question 12 and 13 refer to the MAWA action menu. The extension designed for the laptop browser provides a menu, which is not possible for mobile version because extension icons are hidden. Double-clicking to show the menu is easy for users and intuitive in spite of the fact that this statement has the lowest mark in the questionnaire (average 5,62 and 5,25). Compared to all previous results, in this occasion, the standard deviation indicates that results have been more distributed (1,31 and 1,23).

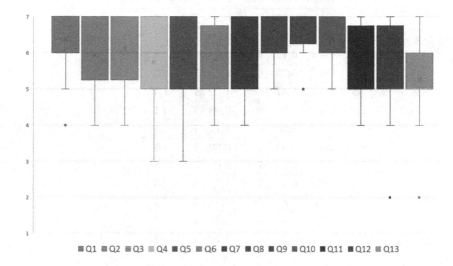

**Fig. 7.** General questions scores

## 6   Future Work

In the future, the first goal is to be capable of adding content from different websites in order to avoid tab switching. The main reason why we would like to include this feature in MAWA is the annoyance caused by the screen resolution. Adding a new tab in the mobile browser needs more actions than computer browsers. Additionally, as presented in this article, looking for information is frustrating. Based on some previous works that have presented tab switching as a drawback in Web navigation [29,50,51], MAWA will include a method to add content from other websites besides the actual actions. Furthermore, in the evaluation we asked about subjects' opinion about web browsing on mobile and laptop and they answered that on a Likert scale of 1 to 7 (average 5,94, median 6) that mobile browser navigation is more cumbersome than laptop browser navigation. Therefore, we feel that this additional feature would help to facilitate mobile web navigation.

On another note, we would like to improve the robustness of the locators due to the fact that we are not the owners of the websites we adapt and when they are updated, locator mechanisms used might fail. Despite the fact that we use different locator mechanisms in MAWA, locators end up failing. This may produce the feeling that the extension is not first-rate and users might uninstall the extension. We would like to develop a locator mechanism capable of adapting to any website upgrade.

**Table 3.** General question results (N = 16)

| Items | AVG | Med | SD | MAX | MIN |
|---|---|---|---|---|---|
| Q1 | 6,37 | 7 | 0,88 | 7 | 4 |
| Q2 | 5,94 | 6 | 0,99 | 7 | 4 |
| Q3 | 6,12 | 6 | 0,95 | 7 | 4 |
| Q4 | 5,75 | 6 | 1,29 | 7 | 3 |
| Q5 | 5,81 | 6 | 1,22 | 7 | 3 |
| Q6 | 5,81 | 6 | 0,98 | 7 | 4 |
| Q7 | 5,93 | 6 | 1,12 | 7 | 4 |
| Q8 | 6,62 | 7 | 0,62 | 7 | 5 |
| Q9 | 6,69 | 7 | 0,6 | 7 | 5 |
| Q10 | 6,37 | 7 | 0,81 | 7 | 5 |
| Q11 | 5,87 | 6 | 0,88 | 7 | 4 |
| Q12 | 5,62 | 6 | 1,31 | 7 | 2 |
| Q13 | 5,25 | 5 | 1,23 | 7 | 2 |

## 7    Conclusions

We have presented MAWA, a Firefox mobile browser extension for WA designed to remove and move content on any website. Users do not need any programming skills to fulfil these actions as these modifications are realized by user actions (click and drag & drop). The purpose of this extension is to mitigate the consequences of adapting websites designed for desktop to mobile browsers, as explained in the Sect. 2. These consequences are scrolling, producing cluttered navigation, displaying unnecessary content and hiding important one. The presented evaluation confirms that MAWA is able to diminish these three drawbacks. Scrolling is avoided by relocating the web content for example, moving some important content from the bottom of the website to the top. In order to shun consuming unnecessary content, the user can remove these nodes from the website by simplifying the web information. The consequence of both actions is to facilitate web navigation and information search. Furthermore, the evaluations validate that MAWA is usable and that the actions that users must carry out to adapt their websites are intuitive and easy to accomplish.

**Acknowledgments.** This work was carried out by the Software and Systems Engineering research group of Mondragon Unibertsitatea (IT1326-19), supported by the Department of Education, Universities and Research of the Basque Government.

# References

1. Nurshuhada, A., Yusop, R.O.M., Azmi, A., Ismail, S.A., Sarkan, H.M., Kama, N.: Enhancing performance aspect in usability guidelines for mobile web application. In: 2019 6th International Conference on Research and Innovation in Information Systems (ICRIIS), pp. 1–6. IEEE (2019)
2. Johnson, T.A., Seeling, P.: Desktop and mobile web page comparison: characteristics, trends, and implications. IEEE Commun. Mag. **52**(9), 144–151 (2014)
3. Boehm, B.W., Clark, B., Horowitz, E., Westland, J.C., Madachy, R.J., Selby, R.W.: Cost models for future software life cycle processes: COCOMO 2.0. Ann. Softw. Eng. **1**, 57–94 (1995). https://doi.org/10.1007/BF02249046
4. Scaffidi, C., Shaw, M., Myers, B.A.: Estimating the numbers of end users and end user programmers. In: IEEE Symposium on Visual Languages and Human-Centric Computing (VL/HCC 2005), Dallas, TX, USA, 21–24 September 2005, pp. 207–214. IEEE Computer Society (2005)
5. Bosetti, G., Firmenich, S., Gordillo, S.E., Rossi, G., Winckler, M.: An end user development approach for mobile web augmentation. Mob. Inf. Syst. **2017**, 2525367:1-2525367:28 (2017)
6. Bouvin, N.O.: Unifying strategies for web augmentation. In: Proceedings of the 10th ACM Conference on Hypertext and Hypermedia: Returning to Our Diverse Roots. HYPERTEXT 1999, Darmstadt, Germany, 21–25 February 1999, pp. 91–100. ACM (1999)
7. Aldalur, I., Winckler, M., Díaz, O., Palanque, P.: Web augmentation as a promising technology for end user development. In: Paternò, F., Wulf, V. (eds.) New Perspectives in End-User Development, pp. 433–459. Springer, Cham (2017). https://doi.org/10.1007/978-3-319-60291-2_17
8. Myers, B.A.: Visual programming, programming by example, and program visualization: a taxonomy. ACM SIGCHI Bull. **17**(4), 59 66 (1986)
9. Lieberman, H., Paternò, F., Wulf, V. (eds.): End User Development. Human-Computer Interaction Series, Springer, Heidelberg (2006). https://doi.org/10.1007/1-4020-5386-X
10. Spahn, M., Dörner, C., Wulf, V.: End user development: approaches towards a flexible software design. In: 2008 16th European Conference on Information Systems. ECIS 2008, Galway, Ireland, pp. 303–314 (2008)
11. Punchoojit, L., Hongwarittorrn, N.: Usability studies on mobile user interface design patterns: a systematic literature review. Adv. Hum.-Comput. Interact. **2017**, 6787504:1-6787504:22 (2017)
12. Marcotte, E.: Responsive Web Design: A Book Apart n 4. Editions Eyrolles (2017)
13. Mahajan, S., Abolhassani, N., McMinn, P., Halfond, W.G.J.: Automated repair of mobile friendly problems in web pages. In: Proceedings of the 40th International Conference on Software Engineering. ICSE 2018, Gothenburg, Sweden, 27 May–03 June 2018, pp. 140–150. ACM (2018)
14. Frain, B.: Responsive Web Design with HTML5 and CSS3. Packt Publishing Ltd., Birmingham (2012)

15. Pinandito, A., Az-zahra, H.M., Fanani, L., Putri, A.V.: Analysis of web content delivery effectiveness and efficiency in responsive web design using material design guidelines and user centered design. In: International Conference on Sustainable Information Engineering and Technology (SIET), pp. 435–441. IEEE (2017)

16. Nebeling, M., Norrie, M.C.: Responsive design and development: methods, technologies and current issues. In: Daniel, F., Dolog, P., Li, Q. (eds.) ICWE 2013. LNCS, vol. 7977, pp. 510–513. Springer, Heidelberg (2013). https://doi.org/10.1007/978-3-642-39200-9_47

17. Tigwell, G.W., Menzies, R., Flatla, D.R.: Designing for situational visual impairments: supporting early-career designers of mobile content. In: Proceedings of the 2018 on Designing Interactive Systems Conference 2018. DIS 2018, Hong Kong, China, 09–13 June 2018, pp. 387–399. ACM (2018)

18. Aula, A., Khan, R.M., Guan, Z.: How does search behavior change as search becomes more difficult? In: Proceedings of the 28th International Conference on Human Factors in Computing Systems. CHI 2010, Atlanta, Georgia, USA, 10–15 April 2010, pp. 35–44. ACM (2010)

19. Lagun, D., Hsieh, C., Webster, D., Navalpakkam, V.: Towards better measurement of attention and satisfaction in mobile search. In: The 37th International ACM SIGIR Conference on Research and Development in Information Retrieval. SIGIR 2014, Gold Coast, QLD, Australia, 06–11 July 2014, pp. 113–122. ACM (2014)

20. Liu, C., Liu, C., Mao, H., Su, W.: Tilt-scrolling: a comparative study of scrolling techniques for mobile devices. In: Huang, D.-S., Huang, Z.-K., Hussain, A. (eds.) ICIC 2019. LNCS (LNAI), vol. 11645, pp. 189–200. Springer, Cham (2019). https://doi.org/10.1007/978-3-030-26766-7_18

21. Radecký, M., Smutný, P.: Evaluating user reaction to user interface element using eye-tracking technology. In: Proceedings of the 2014 15th International Carpathian Control Conference (ICCC), pp. 475–480. IEEE (2014)

22. Setlur, V., Rossoff, S., Gooch, B.: Wish I hadn't clicked that: context based icons for mobile web navigation and directed search tasks. In: Proceedings of the 16th International Conference on Intelligent User Interfaces. IUI 2011, Palo Alto, CA, USA, 13–16 February 2011, pp. 165–174. ACM (2011)

23. Mustonen, T., Olkkonen, M., Häkkinen, J.: Examining mobile phone text legibility while walking. In: Conference on Human Factors in Computing Systems. CHI 2004, Vienna, Austria, 24–29 April 2004, pp. 1243–1246. ACM (2004)

24. Andreadis, I.: Comparison of response times between desktop and smartphone users. In: Mobile Research Methods, p. 63 (2015)

25. Yesilada, Y., Harper, S., Chen, T., Trewin, S.: Small-device users situationally impaired by input. Comput. Hum. Behav. 26(3), 427–435 (2010)

26. Díaz, O., Aldalur, I., Arellano, C., Medina, H., Firmenich, S.: Web mashups with WebMakeup. In: Daniel, F., Pautasso, C. (eds.) RMC 2015. CCIS, vol. 591, pp. 82–97. Springer, Cham (2016). https://doi.org/10.1007/978-3-319-28727-0_6

27. Urbieta, M., Firmenich, S., Bosetti, G., Maglione, P., Rossi, G., Olivero, M.A.: MDWA: a model-driven web augmentation approach - coping with client- and server-side support. Softw. Syst. Model. 19(6), 1541–1566 (2020). https://doi.org/10.1007/s10270-020-00779-5

28. Fernández-García, A.J., Iribarne, L., Corral, A., Criado, J., Wang, J.Z.: A flexible data acquisition system for storing the interactions on mashup user interfaces. Comput. Stand. Interfaces 59, 10–34 (2018)

29. Aldalur, I., Perez, A., Larringa, F.: Customizing websites through automatic web search. In: Lamas, D., Loizides, F., Nacke, L., Petrie, H., Winckler, M., Zaphiris, P.

(eds.) INTERACT 2019. LNCS, vol. 11747, pp. 598–618. Springer, Cham (2019). https://doi.org/10.1007/978-3-030-29384-0_36

30. Chudnovskyy, O., et al.: End-user-oriented telco mashups: the OMELETTE approach. In: Proceedings of the 21st World Wide Web Conference. WWW 2012, Lyon, France, 16–20 April 2012 (Companion Volume), pp. 235–238 (2012)

31. Kurniawan, S.H., King, A., Evans, D.G., Blenkhorn, P.: Personalising web page presentation for older people. Interact. Comput. **18**(3), 457–477 (2006)

32. Tsandilas, T., Schraefel, M.M.C.: User-controlled link adaptation. In: Ashman, H., Brailsford, T.J., Carr, L., Hardman, L. (eds.) HYPERTEXT 2003, Proceedings of the 14th ACM Conference on Hypertext and Hypermedia, Nottingham, UK, 26–30 August 2003, pp. 152–160. ACM (2003)

33. Leiva, L.A.: Restyling website design via touch-based interactions. In: Bylund, M., Juhlin, O., Fernaeus, Y. (eds.) Proceedings of the 13th Conference on Human-Computer Interaction with Mobile Devices and Services, Mobile HCI 2011, Stockholm, Sweden, 30 August–2 September 2011, pp. 599–604. ACM (2011)

34. Bellal, Z., Elouali, N., Benslimane, S.M., Acarturk, C.: Integrating mobile multimodal interactions based on programming by demonstration?. Int. J. Hum.-Comput. Interact. **37**(5), 418–433 (2021)

35. Trusty, A., Truong, K.N.: Augmenting the web for second language vocabulary learning. In: Proceedings of the International Conference on Human Factors in Computing Systems. CHI 2011, Vancouver, BC, Canada, 7–12 May 2011, pp. 3179–3188. ACM (2011)

36. Bila, N., Ronda, T., Mohomed, I., Truong, K.N., de Lara, E.: Pagetailor: reusable end-user customization for the mobile web. In: Proceedings of the 5th International Conference on Mobile Systems, Applications, and Services (MobiSys 2007), San Juan, Puerto Rico, 11–13 June 2007, pp. 16–29. ACM (2007)

37. Baudisch, P., Xie, X., Wang, C., Ma, W.: Collapse-to-zoom: viewing web pages on small screen devices by interactively removing irrelevant content. In: Feiner, S., Landay, J.A. (eds.) Proceedings of the 17th Annual ACM Symposium on User Interface Software and Technology, Santa Fe, NM, USA, 24–27 October 2004, pp. 91–94. ACM (2004)

38. Ricca, F., Leotta, M., Stocco, A., Clerissi, D., Tonella, P.: Web testware evolution. In: 15th IEEE International Symposium on Web Systems Evolution. WSE 2013, Eindhoven, The Netherlands, 27 September 2013, pp. 39–44 (2013)

39. Almendros-Jiménez, J.M., Luna Tedesqui, A., Moreno, G.: Annotating "Fuzzy chance degrees" when debugging XPath queries. In: Rojas, I., Joya, G., Cabestany, J. (eds.) IWANN 2013. LNCS, vol. 7903, pp. 300–311. Springer, Heidelberg (2013). https://doi.org/10.1007/978-3-642-38682-4_33

40. Biagiola, M., Stocco, A., Ricca, F., Tonella, P.: Diversity-based web test generation. In: 27th ACM Joint European Software Engineering Conference and Symposium on the Foundations of Software Engineering ESEC/FSE, Tallinn, Estonia, 26–30 August 2019, pp. 231–242 (2019)

41. Zhang, Y., Pan, Y., Chiu, K.: A parallel XPath engine based on concurrent NFA execution. In: 16th IEEE International Conference on Parallel and Distributed Systems. ICPADS 2010, Shanghai, China, 8–10 December 2010, pp. 314–321 (2010)

42. Kirinuki, H., Tanno, H., Natsukawa, K.: COLOR: correct locator recommender for broken test scripts using various clues in web application. In: 26th IEEE International Conference on Software Analysis, Evolution and Reengineering. SANER 2019, Hangzhou, China, 24–27 February 2019, pp. 310–320 (2019)

43. Song, F., Xu, Z., Xu, F.: An XPath-based approach to reusing test scripts for android applications. In: 14th Web Information Systems and Applications Conference. WISA 2017, Liuzhou, China, 11–12 November 2017, pp. 143–148 (2017)
44. Hammoudi, M., Rothermel, G., Stocco, A.: WATERFALL: an incremental approach for repairing record-replay tests of web applications. In: Proceedings of the 24th ACM SIGSOFT International Symposium on Foundations of Software Engineering. FSE 2016, Seattle, WA, USA, 13–18 November 2016, pp. 751–762 (2016)
45. de Santana, V.F., de Oliveira, R., Almeida, L.D.A., Ito, M.: Firefixia: an accessibility web browser customization toolbar for people with dyslexia. In: International Cross-Disciplinary Conference on Web Accessibility. W4A 2013, Rio de Janeiro, Brazil, 13–15 May 2013, pp. 16:1–16:4 (2013)
46. Hart, S.G.: Nasa-task load index (NASA-TLX); 20 years later. In: Proceedings of the Human Factors and Ergonomics Society Annual Meeting, pp. 904–908. Sage Publications, Los Angeles (2006)
47. Brooke, J.: SUS: a retrospective. J. Usability Stud. **8**(2), 29–40 (2013)
48. Hart, S.G., Staveland, L.E.: Development of NASA-TLX (task load index): results of empirical and theoretical research. In: Advances in Psychology, vol. 52, pp. 139–183. Elsevier (1988)
49. Brooke, J.: Sus: a 'quick and dirty' usability. Usability Eval. Ind. **189**, 4–7 (1996)
50. Díaz, O., Sosa, J.D., Trujillo, S.: Activity fragmentation in the web: empowering users to support their own webflows. In: 24th ACM Conference on Hypertext and Social Media (part of ECRC). HT 2013, Paris, France, 02–04 May 2013, pp. 69–78 (2013)
51. Zhang, H., Zhao, S.: Measuring web page revisitation in tabbed browsing. In: Proceedings of the International Conference on Human Factors in Computing Systems. CHI 2011, Vancouver, BC, Canada, 7–12 May 2011, pp. 1831–1834 (2011)

# *NotificationManager*: Personal Boundary Management on Mobile Devices

Tom Gross[(⊠)] [iD] and Anna-Lena Mueller

Human-Computer Interaction Group, University of Bamberg, 96045 Bamberg, Germany
hci@uni-bamberg.de

**Abstract.** The growing use of mobile devices that are available everywhere can blur the boundaries between life domains work and life. The increasing number of notifications on smartphones leads to interruptions that might be unrelated to the current life domain and task and are therefore disruptive. Despite some tools there is a gap between the preferred and the actual separation of life domains. In this paper we show how concepts from the field of boundary management can be applied for notification management on mobile devices. We present a formal model of the semantic structure of life domains, which is based on the concepts of integration and segmentation from boundary theory. We introduce an app for the management of notifications on Android smartphones that leverages on this formal model. In a field study we evaluated the app with real-life notifications. The results show a significant reduction of the gap between actual and preferred boundary management.

**Keywords:** Boundary management · Notifications · Formal model · Android app

## 1 Introduction

The increasing use of ubiquitous technologies makes the separation of life domains such as work and life more difficult. For instance, smartphones users are constantly reachable for their contacts independent of their personal as well as their contacts' current life domain. Boundary management has become relevant for research in human-computer interaction and computer-supported cooperative work [12, 34, 45, 59]. Current trends contribute to the blurring of boundaries between life domains—for instance, home office, and bring your own device.

Home office work increases the work-related communication outside of the confines of the employer. Employers often provide laptops and mobile devices to their employees allowing them to work from home and be reachable at home. Business smartphones make employees available for work anytime and anyplace. Dual-SIM smartphones can be equipped with private and business SIM cards in one device and make it unnecessary to carry two devices. Sales for dual-SIM smartphones increased by eight percent recently [9].

Bring your own device (BYOD) where employees use their private devices for business purposes is booming. BYOD leads to increased satisfaction and flexibility

© IFIP International Federation for Information Processing 2021
Published by Springer Nature Switzerland AG 2021
C. Ardito et al. (Eds.): INTERACT 2021, LNCS 12935, pp. 243–261, 2021.
https://doi.org/10.1007/978-3-030-85610-6_15

of employees [41, 57]. The development of rules and security standards for the use of employees' private devices is being researched, which will eventually make BYOD possible for more and more employees [4, 56]. Choose your own device (CYOD) is a related concept where the employees can choose the hardware on which they want to work and where the company pays and owns the hardware [7]. Often the employees are allowed to also use the hardware for private purposes.

Such trends bring advantages but also entail challenges. Users are often confronted with different life domains that blur on devices [23]. This makes the separation more difficult.

Overall the number of apps on mobile devices that push notifications to users is increasing. Notifications in general, and notifications from life domains and tasks that are currently not relevant to the respective user, can lead to disruptions and stress [36]. Interruptions and their negative consequences for users have been an important research topic of human-computer interaction [37]. Current research shows that blocking disruptions can have a positive effect on task focus and productivity [35]. However, the total blocking of notifications is often not possible, since it might mean that users might miss important and relevant information and that users might damage social connections [54].

In social science there is a great body of knowledge on boundary management—that is, how humans effectively establish borders between their life domains and how they efficiently organise passages between life domains. It is based on roles and tasks as a basis for structuring and organising life domains [8, 16, 31].

In this paper we show how essential insights of boundary management from social science can be transferred to the design of concepts for managing life domains with a smartphone app. As the literature on boundary management is multifarious domains [8, 16, 31], it is necessary to distil essential insights and to use them as input for requirements for our new concepts. We introduce a formal model on the semantic structure of life domains, which is based on the concept of integration and segmentation from boundary theory [8, 43]. Central building blocks of the formal model are life domains, persons, availability, interruptions, and notifications. The formal model served as the foundation of and Android app. The app was used in a multi-day field study with real users.

## 2 Background and Related Work

Modern technologies are a two-edged sword—they are disrupting and make boundary management necessary, but at the same time they offer support for boundary management [10, 16, 34]. Solutions from notification management reduce the number of disruptions caused by notifications on smartphones or other devices. Still, the boundary management in practice does not always life up to the requirements and needs of users, which can lead to conflicts between life domains, especially between work and life [55].

### 2.1 Notification Management

Notification management follows two paradigms: the automatic detection of opportune moments for the presentation of notifications based on users' current contexts, and the manual specification of user-defined rules for filtering notifications.

The paradigm of automatic detection of opportune moments is based on sensor data to infer on the user's context [20, 30, 61, 65]. Often machine learning is used to carve out the most relevant features from the sensor data in order to detect the user's context [13, 38, 50, 51, 53, 58]. Detecting breakpoints—that is, moments after a user has finished an activity or task and before they start a new one—is promising and has been vastly researched [21, 26, 27, 44, 46–48]. However, their disadvantages are that in general the users do not get any information as to how the system has detected the breakpoints, if and when the system presents notifications. Also, typically users are not in control as to incoming notifications. This reduces the users' acceptability of those systems [40]. Furthermore, these systems only consider measurable sensor data and not the internal state of the users.

The user-centred paradigm requires users to manually specify rules to filter incoming notifications. Users can decide on the relevancy of notifications and the timing and presentation depending on their respective use context and notification contents [3, 14, 29].

The receptivity of notifications for a recipient and therefore the relevance of the message causing the notification strongly depend on the contents of the message as well as the relation between message sender and recipient [11, 39, 40, 52, 60]. In the case of messages from a messenger app, which are the biggest share of daily notifications [52], it is often enough to see the name of the sender in order to infer the relevancy to the current situation [29].

A further factor that influences the personal receptivity of notifications is the relevancy of its contents for the task at hand [1, 18, 22, 62]. For instance, if a message notification is from a working colleague and relevant to the current task, it is more likely that the recipient has a stronger preference to see the notification and the message than for other notifications.

## 2.2 Boundary Management

The research on boundary management has also been dealing with interruptions—especially those caused by technical devices—in different life domains. A life domain is a conceptual category that originates from mental and physical boundaries around persons, things, and a part of the self (e.g., work, or family) [43].

Cross-domain interruptions have an origin outside of a person's current domain, whereas within-domain interruptions originate from within [2].

A person's interruptibility for cross-domain interruptions strongly depends on their boundary management style—that is, whether a person prefers to segment, or integrate life domains [31]. Segmentation refers to an inflexible and impermeable mental and physical boundary [16], and to the lack of a conceptual overlap between the life domains [31]. Integration refers to the opposite with neither clear boundaries between nor clear distinction of life domains' members, thoughts, and intellectual as well as emotional approaches [8]. The boundaries are flexible and permeable [16], conceptually, a continuum connects complete segmentation and complete integration, and humans can be on any position of this continuum.

Boundary work refers to the concrete tactics that a person applies for realising their boundary management style. Those tactics serve the maintenance of boundaries for segmentation, or alternatively the switching between life domains for integration [43].

Technology plays an important role in executing the tactics. For instance, in asynchronous communication tools such as email users can maintain their segmentation by just reading sender names and subjects and decide if the person and contents fits into the current life domain [33].

In our approach, which we present in detail below, we leverage on the user-centred specification of life domains and the automatic adaptation of notifications from notification management. Users can specify of each of their life domain its permeability—that is, its interruptibility preferences for within-domain and cross-domain interruptions. Also it provides a categorisation for each notification, so users can make an easy choice whether to ready and reply to messages immediately or later after switching to a different life domain. Our approach and our implementation contribute a blueprint for a notification management approach that is based on users' interaction with the system and allows exploring users' preferences and behaviour, which is complementary to other approaches that automate the management of notifications.

## 3    Within-Domain and Cross-Domain Interruptibility

The multifarious nature of existing boundary management theories makes it very difficult to transfer the structure of life domains and their components directly into a system. Therefore, we introduce a formal model that distils relevant concepts into components and connections and dependencies that serve as a basis for a future system.

### 3.1    Fundamental Boundary Management Concepts

The main criterion for identifying concepts was their relevancy with respect to the effective management of boundaries and the efficient transitions across boundaries. We put a special focus on the factors that influence the interruptibility for notifications and their mutual connections.

In order to detect the interruptibility with respect to a specific notification it is first of all necessary to identify the life domain of the originator of the notification (mostly the sender of a message behind the notification). Assigning a life domain to a contact is not always unique (e.g., two working colleagues might also share a hobby, and so mutually be in the life domain work, but also leisure). In practice different techniques are used that make it possible to assign a single contact to multiple life domains—for instance, multiple address books [42], but also distinct domain-specific contact channels (e.g., using a contact's private email address in one life domain, and the work email address in another). The more the boundaries between life domains are blurring, the more difficult it gets to assign notifications to specific domains. The use of distinct contact channels has proofed helpful here [34]. Additionally, the interruptibility can depend on the person's current social context—that is, the other persons that are currently with the focal person and their life domain. The role and behaviour of a person as well as the expectations of others towards that person might change according to the current life domain, and so might their interruptibility [31].

## 3.2  Formal Modelling in Human-Computer Interaction

In human-computer interaction formal models have been developed for diverse purposes such as for modelling the problem domain, the interaction, or the system. Formal models provide great benefits when developing concepts and systems: they stimulate the developers to develop a very clear model of the world and force them to clarify all diverse aspects in detail. In discussions among developers they are a great vehicle to foster and focus discussions. As such models are widely used in computer science and mathematics and many other formal areas of research, they aim to provide—also in the HCI domain—a precise documentation of the concepts. They have similar purposes such as other representations (e.g., design patterns), but compared to other representations provide far more precision sometimes at the cost of effortless readability. Overall we belief that besides other models they provide considerable added value and the benefits by far outweigh the cost.

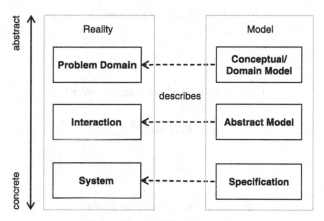

**Fig. 1.** Types of formal models.

Formal models have different levels of abstraction. Abstract formal models describe the problem without any relation to the system that is to be developed (e.g., DSML [28, 63]). Concrete models specify the structure of the systems (e.g., UML [6] or Z [64]). Between those abstract and those concrete models are models that describe the user interaction with the system without details of its implementation (e.g., PiE or TAG [15, 49]). Figure 1 summarises different types of formal models in human-computer interaction and the realms they model.

## 3.3  Formal Models of Interruptibility

In our conceptual model we describe the mental structure of humans concerning a specific domain. We completely separate this step from later interaction and application development. The advantage is that the model is independent and can be used in different systems, no matter how they are implemented or which architectures they use. What we are modelling is a problem domain that is not physically tangible and cannot be observed from outside. It describes a mental concept.

As we want to formally describe our understanding of a specific concept in real world instead of notating the functionality of a system in the first step, we do not use an implementation-related notation. Instead we decided to use simple set theory, basics of first-order logic and n-ary relations. Set theory allows explaining the possible assignment of instances to a set including constraints and particularities of this assignment as well as relations between the instances of objects in a concise manner with only a few simple and short formulas [5, 25]. The advantage of this approach is that we have a clear definition of our assumptions about users' mental concepts concerning their life domains [64].

**Person.** $P$ is the set of all persons in the world. $P$ cannot be empty ($P \neq \emptyset$). Persons have a name and several types of contact information (e.g., email addresses, phone numbers). Other attributes of humans are disregarded in our model. In the model we refer to one focal person who is the interruptee and element of $P^I$. As we only regard one focal person, $P^I$ is a singleton. All other persons, the fellow persons, build the subset $P^F$.

$$P := set\ of\ all\ persons$$

$$P \neq \emptyset$$

$$P \subseteq Name \times \mathfrak{P}(ContactInformation)$$

$$Focal\ Person : P^I \subseteq P$$

$$\#P^I = 1$$

$$Fellow\ Persons : P^F := P - P^I$$

**Domain.** $D$ is the set of all domains. $D$ cannot be empty ($D \neq \emptyset$). A domain consists of the role a focal person has in the domain, the specific behaviours and rules imposed by the domain, its communication channels, its objects, the physical borders given by locations and times, and its channels used for communication. A validity timestamp makes it possible that domains can change over time. The foreground domain is an element of $D$ and is the domain where the focal person is currently situated in. Background domains are all his/her other domains. The relation *owns* specifies which person possesses the domain (i.e., the focal person).

$$D := set\ of\ domains$$

$$D \neq \emptyset$$

$$Time : T = \mathbb{N}$$

$$D \subseteq Role \times \mathfrak{P}(Behaviour) \times \mathfrak{P}(Rule) \times \mathfrak{P}(Channel)$$
$$\times \mathfrak{P}(Object) \times \mathfrak{P}(Location) \times \mathfrak{P}(Time) \times T$$

$$owns \subseteq P^I \times D$$

$$BackgroundDomains : D^B \subseteq D$$

$$ForegroundDomains : D^F \subseteq D$$

$$\#D^F = 1$$

**Assigned Persons.** The relation *isAssignedTo* shows the fellow persons that a focal person assigns to life domains (e.g., one's family members in the domain family). The set $P_{d,p,t}$ is defined as the subset of $P$ containing all persons that are assigned to one domain $d$ belonging to focal person $p$ at time $t$. Figure 2 shows an example on how a graph accompanies our model containing the defined subsets.

$$isAssignedTo \subseteq P^F \times T \times D$$

$$P_{d,p,t} \subseteq P^F$$

$$P_{d,p,t} := \left\{ q \in P^F : owns(p, d) \wedge isAssignedTo(q, t, d) \right\}$$

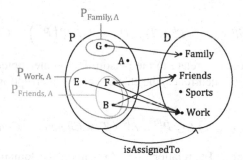

**Fig. 2.** Example of focal person A's life domains and assigned fellow persons at a given moment $t_i$.

**Current Situation.** The relation *situatedIn* shows the relationship between persons and domains depending on time t. At one point in time, persons can be physically situated in one of the focal person's domains. $S_{d,t}$ is defined as the subset of persons that is located in the same domain $d$ at time $t$ (see example in Fig. 3).

$$situatedIn \subseteq P \times T \times D$$

$$\forall p \forall t \forall d \left( \left( p \in P^I \wedge t \in T \wedge d \in D \wedge situatedIn(p, t, d) \right) \rightarrow d \in D^F \right)$$

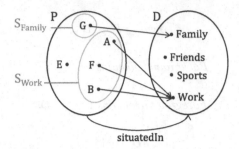

situatedIn

**Fig. 3.** Example of life domains and persons' current situation at a given moment $t_i$.

$$S_{d,t} \subseteq P$$

$$S_{d,t} := \{p \in P : situatedIn(p, t, d)\}$$

**Availability.** Availability is the relation that describes the readiness of the focal person for interruptions by a fellow person. The availability depends on the focal person's preferences, the domain of the interruption, the currently active domain where the focal person is located in, the time, the persons situated in the currently active domain (e.g., availability can differ if the individual in the current domain is alone, together with domain members, or together with domain non-members), and the communication channel of the interruption.

$$Availability : A \subseteq P^I \times D \times D^F \times T \times \mathfrak{P}\left(P^F\right) \times Channel$$

**Interruption.** Interruptions relate to the person that is interrupted, the person that is interrupting, the time of occurrence, the channel of the interruption, and the content of the interruption.

$$Interruption : I \subseteq P^F \times P^I \times T \times Channel \times Content$$

**Interruptions' Domain.** The relation *refersTo* maps cross-domain interruptions to the concerned domain. We assume that for each interruption from a known person, there exists a unique domain the interruption refers to (even if the interrupter and the interruptee share multiple domains), which can be determined using the sender, the channel and the content of the interruption.

$$refersTo \subseteq I \times D$$

$$\forall i \forall p \forall t$$

$$\left( i \in I \wedge p \in P^F \wedge t \in T \wedge \exists! d \, (d \in D \wedge assignedTo(p, t, d) \wedge refersTo(i, d)) \right)$$

**Notification.** According to the availability for a certain domain, the notification of an interruption can differ. The attributes of notifications are the presentation modality (e.g., visual, auditory), the concrete layout of a notification (e.g., type of sound), and the timing (e.g., immediately or diverted to a later point in time).

$$Notification : N \subseteq Modality \times Layout \times Timing$$

Those are the entities we defined in our model. If an interruption appears, we can conclude the focal person's current availability for this interruption and an appropriate notification can be chosen to present to the focal person.

The model is formal and therefore concise—with only a few statements we describe all relevant concepts. The formal model can be used for later system related notations in order to specify the implementation of the entities of the formal model. The structure of the formal model can alternatively be represented in other forms such as UML. However, in UML diverse structural models would be needed for cover all the information of the formal model.

## 4   NotificationManager

We built the *NotificationManager* Android app for managing notifications according to these entities of the formal model. While the formal model was developed thoroughly and based on many years of experience with developing such systems, we still wanted to verify it through the implementation of a real system. Figure 4 depicts how the entities of the formal model were transferred into a UML class diagram and how the classes of the NotificationManager are embedded into the Android operating system.

We decided for Android as the platform, because it enables intercepting and modifying notifications. With notifications we refer to the information snippets shown in the status bar and the notification drawer of Android (esp. version 7).

The app allows users to configure their life domains and the interruptibility in each of them for within-domain and cross-domain interruptions. Furthermore, it provides meta-information on notifications (esp. the life domain of their origin) in order to help users in deciding whether to read a notification immediately or later.

For notifications created by the NotificationManager, the standard behaviour of Android notifications was adapted as much as possible. Notifications are kept in the drawer until the user either accesses the notification or opens the NotificationManager app to see all received notifications in the Notification Log. In the current implementation of the NotificationManager, all notifications are kept persistently in a local database. A clean up mechanism for old notifications after a specific amount of time could be easily integrated.

Users can set up their life domains consisting of a name and an icon and assign contacts, group chats, locations, and times to them. Contacts represent persons and all their information can simply be picked from the smartphone's address book. Communication channels that are currently supported by the NotificationManager are phone calls, SMS, email, messages from messengers (e.g., WhatsApp, Telegram), and social media (e.g., Facebook). Users can either assign a contact with all their communication channels to

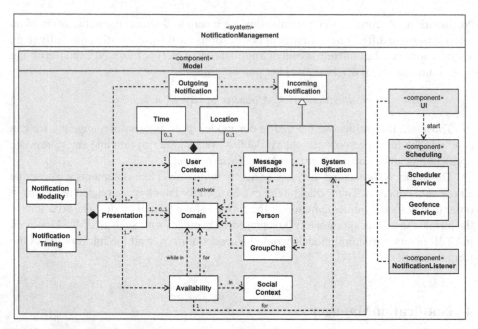

**Fig. 4.** NotificationManager as UML Class Diagram (simplified; without attributes and methods).

one domain, or have more fine-grained assignments with a high degree of segmentation by associating a contact's distinct communication channels to life domains (e.g., one contact's office phone number to work domain and private phone to family domain). Group chats can facilitate the communication with all contacts of a specific life domain. Times can be specified as intervals with a start time and end time for each individual day of the week (e.g., 9–17 h from Monday to Friday for work).

In order to balance the users' wish for fine-grained specifications versus user effort the app supports multiple modes to specify one's interruptibility and presentation of notifications. In the simple mode we distinguish available from not-available. If the user is available, all notifications are shown in the notification drawer. If the user is not-available no notifications are shown in the drawer, but users can open the respective app to see the notifications later. In the advanced mode we distinguish three levels of interruptibility (high, middle, and low) for all with-in and cross-domain notifications. In the app high interruptibility is green, middle is yellow, and low is red (cf. Fig. 5 left side). Users can specify their preferences for the intensity of the presentation of the notifications for each level. All three levels offer default notification intensities that can be changed according to the user's will. When the user first starts the app it does not have life domains, but it already filters according to notifications related to their contacts in the Android address book, notifications from unknown persons, and notifications from the system.

Notifications can be completely suppressed and hidden, or they can be presented in an executive summary that the NotificationManager generates in real-time. Summaries can be compiled according to diverse criteria—both semantics and time. For instance,

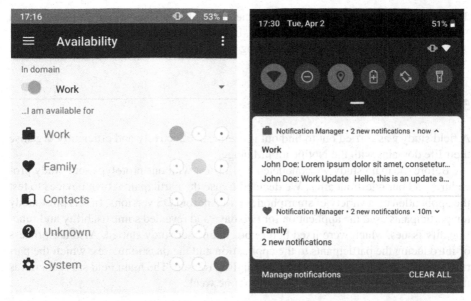

**Fig. 5.** Specification dialog for cross-domain notifications in the domain work (left side); executive summary of notifications according to life domains in the notification drawer (right side).

users can get one summary across all their life domains or a summary for each life domain. Summaries can be presented on an hourly basis, or once a day at a specific time. The NotificationManager suppresses all individual notifications to keep disruption to a minimum. Yet, via the summaries users rest assured that they do not miss notifications. Furthermore, all notifications, those presented and those not presented, are collected in a notification log inside the application, so no information gets lost and the user can browse through the logs and the individual notifications they contain when they please. Logs are ordered by domain and time so previous notifications can easily be found again.

Whereas in standard Android notifications in the drawer carry the icon of the respective app (e.g., WhatsApp), in the NotificationManager they carry the icon of the respective life domain for better priorisation of the user (cf. Fig. 5, right side).

Users can also specify the modality of the presentation (e.g., sound, vibration, LED lights). The number of options and level of detail depends on the hardware capabilities of the respective smartphone (e.g., some smartphones feature LED lights with multiple colours, in which case colours can express semantics, such as life domains).

The NotificationManager provides options for automatically activating a life domain and its interruptibility settings—for instance, when entering a specified location, or during specific time intervals (via the *Google Geofencing API* and the *JobScheduler* in the background). The system then automatically compares the current life domain, checks the interruptibility levels for all other life domains, and adapts the presentations accordingly.

The application was implemented for Android SDK 28 and runs on Android 7.0 or higher. The system configuration as well as the notifications are stored in a SQLite database. For capturing and modifying the original notifications we implemented a Notification Listener Service. It was developed using Android Studio 3.3.1 on MacOS X Version 10.11.6. For testing we used a Samsung Galaxy Note 8 with Android 8 and a Nokia 6 with Android 9.

## 5 Evaluation

A field study was carried out to find out if users can effectively and efficiently organise their life domains with the NotificationManager.

Before the main study we conducted a pilot-test with our prototype, our study procedure, and our questionnaires. We decided to use the participants' own devices to test the application on a variety of smartphones and Android OS versions. In this pilot-study ten participants used the application for two days and revealed some usability and functionality issues, which were fixed before our main user study started. Also the process of introducing the participants to the application and the questionnaires, which the participants had to fill in, were checked and slightly revised. The main field study then was much longer—participants used the app for one week.

### 5.1 Participants

In the main user study 15 participants were invited by personal contact to use the application for one week. From those 15 in the beginning we excluded 4 due to technical issues. The remaining 11 participants were between 23 and 47 years old ($M = 33.55$, $SD = 8.32$). 5 of them were female and 6 male. 8 participants stated to use their smartphone for both private and for work communication, 3 stated that they use it only for private communication. 9 participants were employees, 1 was self-employed, and 1 was student. 2 participants said they use their smartphone 10–25 times a day, 5 participants 26–50 times a day, and 4 participants 50+ times a day.

### 5.2 Procedure

After being briefed and signing a consent form, each participant received a detailed introduction including a video demonstration of the app and individual guidance. We used pre-task and post-task questionnaires, all of which contained questions about both the separation of work from life, and life from work. Before usage, they filled in an online pre-task-questionnaire measuring the users' preferred and actual segmentation and asking for additional demographical data and information about their smartphone usage behaviour. In a post-task questionnaire the users again answered questions concerning actual segmentation to measure changes of behaviour. Additionally, we did post-task interviews via telephone or personal contact to get informal feedback on the participants' boundary management, but also the usability and stability of the app. The participants had only some minor usability issues and reported on small bugs.

The task for the participants was that they could configure and use the Notification-Manager as they liked, but we recommended using a minimum of two domains (work, and life). All participants had at least the two domains work and life. Some participants added also other domains (e.g., for specific hobbies, especially if they involved groups of people and communication with them, such as a sports club, or a big band). The post-task questionnaire was—for comparability reasons—standardised and asked questions about the two core domains work and life.

## 5.3  Measures

Since we were interested in the influence of the app use on the actual boundary management behaviour (eventually even during the week of use in our study), we asked for the actual segmentation before and after the use of the app. We assumed that preferences do not change in such a short time, so we measured preferred segmentation only in the pre-task questionnaire.

We measured preferred boundary management style using Kreiner et al.'s scale for preferred segmentation of the work domain from life domain (PSWL) [32]. As the items only refer to one direction—separating work issues from life—we adapted them for the other direction—separating life issues from work (PSLW). For measuring actual segmentation we used Powell et al.'s scale and again replicated those items in the other direction (ASWL, ASLW) [55].

Finally, we added a specific question about the communication behaviour from Kossek et al. [31]. The participants were asked to rate the statements on a seven-item Likert scale (1 = "strongly disagree", 7 = "strongly agree").

## 5.4  Results

The results show that for participants there is a discrepancy between the preferred segmentation and the actual segmentation of their life domains (cf. Fig. 6). The results confirm that this discrepancy shrank during the use of the NotificationManager. We also found that the participants' segmentations were not symmetrical between their work and life domains.

Starting with the latter we found that preferred segmentation of work from life PSWL was stronger ($M = 6.11$, $SD = 0.95$) that that for life from work (PSLW) ($M = 4.48$, $SD = 1.18$) that is based on a Wilcoxon signed rank test statistically significant ($p < .01$). The actual segmentation of work from life (ASWL) was also stronger ($M = 4.07$, $SD = 1.56$) than that for life from work (ASLW) ($M = 3.66$, $SD = 1.60$), but is based on a Wilcoxon signed rank test not statistically significant ($p = .237$). In the post-task results, the distance between actual segmentation of work from life (ASWL) ($M = 5.25$, $SD = 1.23$) and life from work (ASLW) ($M = 4.57$, $SD = 1.45$) increased, but is based on a Wilcoxon signed rank test not statistically significant ($p = .153$).

We compared preferred and actual segmentation from the pre-task questionnaire using a Wilcoxon signed rank test on the preferred and actual values. The results revealed that there is a statistical difference between PSWL and ASWL in our sample with $p < .01$. In contrast, regarding the other direction, the difference between PSLW and ASLW is smaller and not significant with $p = .185$.

In order to evaluate whether our app improves boundary management we tested if the discrepancy or delta between preferred and actual segmentation decreased throughout

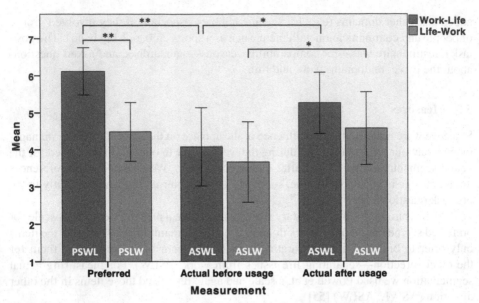

**Fig. 6.** Results of all comparisons of Work-Life (WL) versus Life-Work (LW) for preferred, actual pre-task, and actual post-task segmentation with * for a significance of $p < .05$ and ** for $p < .01$.

the use of our app (i.e., from the pre-task to the post-task). The pre-task delta between preferred and actual segmentation of work from life (PSWL-ASWL) is ($M = 2.05, SD = 1.60$) and more than twice as large as the post-task delta ($M = 0.86, SD = 1.60$) and the results are according to a Wilcoxon test statistically significant ($p < .05$). The pre-task delta between preferred and actual segmentation of life from work (PSLW-ASLW) is ($M = 0.82, SD = 1.86$) disappeared during post-task ($M = -0.09, SD = 1.69$) and the results are according to a Wilcoxon test statistically significant ($p < .05$).

## 5.5  Discussion

The statistical evaluation revealed a significant difference for preferred segmentation between the directions work from life and life from work. This confirms that borders between domains are configured differently depending on the direction of crossing. Such asymmetrical preferences have been found in the boundary management literature before. However, to the best of our knowledge, they have not been shown in the practical use of tools yet. After usage, the distance was greater compared to the pre-task values and thus more asymmetric than before, but not significantly.

Between preferred and actual segmentation, a significant difference could only be found for segmentation of work from life but not for life from work. Thus, our participants seemed to be more satisfied with the separation of life issues from work and need more support in separating work from life. After using our app, the distance between preferred and actual segmentation decreased significantly for both directions. This is an indication that our application successfully supports users to get closer to their boundary management preferences.

# 6 Conclusions

We showed how insights from boundary management literature in social science can be used to reduce the burden of users of smartphones with the increasing number of notifications on their technical devices. In a multi-day field test we could demonstrate that the NotificationManager app helps users to reduce the gap between preferred and actual segmentation of their life domains and to experience fewer disruptions.

The app suppresses and hides notifications, but this was accepted by the users since the configuration mechanisms are transparent and understandable.

In future work the app could be extended. The participants of the study provided some stimuli for further development of functionality for the NotificationManager. The configuration effort could be reduced by repeatedly asking short questions about their preferences and adapting the system behaviour accordingly.

The experience sampling method [17, 19] could be used to better understand the user behaviour and to optimise the default settings of the NotificationManager in order to minimise the configuration effort.

Another possibility is to include the senders of messages—they might add subjects and urgencies to their messages which can be fed into the algorithms for assigning notifications to life domains and forms of presentation [24].

**Acknowledgements.** We thank the participants of the study as well as the members of the Cooperative Media Lab at the University of Bamberg.

# References

1. Addas, S., Pinsonneault, A.: The many faces of information technology interruptions: a taxonomy and preliminary investigation of their performance effects. Inf. Syst. J. **25**(3), 231–273 (2015)
2. Ashforth, B.E., Kreiner, G.E., Fugate, M.: All in a day's work: boundaries and micro role transitions. Acad. Manag. Rev. **25**(3), 472–491 (2000)
3. Auda, J., Weber, D., Voit, A., Schneegass, S.: Understanding user preferences towards rule-based notification deferral. In: Extended Abstracts of the Conference on Human Factors in Computing Systems - CHI 2018, Montreal, Canada, 21–26 April, pp. LBW548:1–6. ACM, New York (2018)
4. Baillette, P., Barlette, Y., Leclercq-Vandelannoitte, A.: Bring your own device in organisations: extending the reversed IT adoption logic to security paradoxes for CEOs and end users. Int. J. Inf. Manag. **43**, 76–84 (2018)
5. Barker-Plummer, D., Barwise, J., Etchemendy, J.: Language, Proof, and Logic. CSLI Publications, Stanford (2011)
6. Booch, G., Rumbaugh, J., Jacobson, I.: The Unified Modelling Language UWSER Guido. Pearson, Englewood Cliffs (2005)
7. Brodin, M.: BYOD vs. CYOD - what is the difference? In: Proceedings of the 9th IADIS International Conference on Information Systems - IS 2016, Vilamoura, Portugal, 9–11 April, pp. 55–62. IADIS Press (2016)
8. Campbell Clark, S.: Work/family border theory: a new theory of work/family balance. Hum. Relat. **53**(6), 747–770 (2000)

9. Canalys: Smartphone Shipment Fall 6.3% in Europe in Q1 2018 (2020). https://www.canalys.com/newsroom/smartphone-shipments-fall-63-europe-q1-2018. Accessed 4 Mar 2020

10. Cecchinato, M.E., Cox, A.L., Bird, J.: Working 9–5? Professional differences in email and boundary management practices. In: Proceedings of the Conference on Human Factors in Computing Systems - CHI 2015, Seoul, Republic of Korea, 18–23 April, pp. 3989–3998. ACM, New York (2015)

11. Chen, K.-Y., Lee, H.-P., Lin, C.-H., Chang, Y.-J.: Who matters: a closer look at interpersonal relationship in mobile interruptibility. In: Adjunct Proceedings of the ACM International Joint Conference on Pervasive and Ubiquitous Computing and Proceedings of the ACM International Symposium on Wearable Computer – UbiComp 2017, Maui, HI, USA, 11–15 September, pp. 910–915. ACM, New York (2017)

12. Ciolfi, L., Lockley, E.: From work to life and back again: examining the digitally-mediated work/life practices of a group of knowledge workers. Comput. Support Coop. Work **27**(3–6), 803–839 (2018)

13. Corno, F., De Russis, L., Montanaro, T.: A context and user aware smart notification system. In: Proceedings of the IEEE 2nd World Forum on Internet of Things - WF-IoT 2015, Milan, Italy, 14–16 December, pp. 645–651. IEEE Computer Society Press, Los Alamitos (2015)

14. De Russis, L., Roffarello, A.M.: On the benefit of adding user preferences to notification delivery. In: Extended Abstracts of the Conference on Human Factors in Computing Systems - CHI 2017, Denver, CO, 6–11 May, pp. 1561–1568. ACM, New York (2017)

15. Dix, A.J.: Formal Methods for Interactive Systems. Academic Press, Chestnut Hill (1991)

16. Duxbury, L., Higgins, C., Smart, R., Stevenson, M.: Mobile technology and boundary permeability. Br. J. Manag. **25**, 570–588 (2014)

17. Fetter, M., Gross, T.: PRIMIExperience: experience sampling via instant messaging. In: Proceedings of the ACM 2011 Conference on Computer-Supported Cooperative Work - CSCW 2011, Hangzhou, China, 19–23 March, pp. 629–632. ACM, New York (2011)

18. Fetter, M., Mueller, A.-L., Vasilyev, P., Barth, L.M., Gross, T.: Towards a better understanding of availability and interruptibility with mobile availability probes. In: Proceedings of the 16th European Conference on Computer-Supported Cooperative Work - Exploratory Papers - ECSCW 2018, Nancy, France, 4–8 June, pp. 14:1–18. Reports of the European Society for Socially Embedded Technologies, EUSSET, Siegen (2018)

19. Fetter, M., Schirmer, M., Gross, T.: CAESSA: visual authoring of context-aware experience sampling studies. In: Extended Abstracts of the Conference on Human Factors in Computing Systems - CHI 2011, Vancouver, Canada, 7–12 May, pp. 2341–2346. ACM, New York (2011)

20. Fetter, M., Seifert, J., Gross, T.: Predicting selective availability for instant messaging. In: Campos, P., Graham, N., Jorge, J., Nunes, N., Palanque, P., Winckler, M. (eds.) INTERACT 2011. LNCS, vol. 6948, pp. 503–520. Springer, Heidelberg (2011). https://doi.org/10.1007/978-3-642-23765-2_35

21. Fischer, J.E., Greenhalgh, C., Benford, S.: Investigating episodes of mobile phone activity as indicators of opportune moments to deliver notifications. In: Proceedings of the 13th International Conference on Human-Computer Interaction with Mobile Devices and Services - MobileHCI 2011, Stockholm, Sweden, August 30–September 2, pp. 181–190. ACM, New York (2011)

22. Fischer, J.E., Yee, N., Bellotti, V., Good, N., Benford, S., Greenhalgh, C.: Effects of content and time of delivery on receptivity of mobile interruptions. In: Proceedings of the 12th International Conference on Human-Computer Interaction with Mobile Devices and Services - MobileHCI 2010, Lisbon, Portugal, 7–10 September, pp. 103–112. ACM, New York (2010)

23. Fleck, R., Cox, A.L., Robinson, R.A.V.: Balancing boundaries: using multiple devices to manage work-life balance. In: Proceedings of the Conference on Human Factors in Computing Systems - CHI 2015, Seoul, Republic of Korea, 18–23 April, pp. 3985–3988. ACM, New York (2015)

24. Grandhi, S.A., Jones, Q.: Knock, knock! who's there? Putting the user in control of managing interruptions. Int. J. Hum. Comput. Stud. **79**, 35–50 (2015)
25. Halmos, P.R.: Naive Set Theory. D. Van Nostrand Company Inc., Princeton (1960)
26. Ho, J., Intille, S.: Using context-aware computing to reduce the perceived burden of interruptions from mobile devices. In: Proceedings of the Conference on Human Factors in Computing Systems - CHI 2005, Portland, OR, 2–7 April, pp. 909–918. ACM, New York (2005)
27. Iqbal, S.T., Bailey, B.P.: Effects of intelligent notification management on users and their tasks. In: Proceedings of the Conference on Human Factors in Computing Systems - CHI 2008, Florence, Italy, 5–10 April, pp. 93–102. ACM, New York (2008)
28. Kelly, S., Tolvanen, J.-P.: Domain-Specific Modelling: Enabling Full Code Generation. Wiley, New York (2008)
29. Kerber, F., Hirtz, C., Gehring, S., Loechtefeld, M., Krueger, A.: Managing smartwatch notifications through filtering and ambient illumination. In: Adjunct Proceedings of the 18th International Conference on Human-Computer Interaction with Mobile Devices and Services - MobileHCI 2016, Florence, Italy, 6–9 September, pp. 918–923. ACM, New York (2016)
30. Kern, N., Schiele, B.: Context-aware notification for wearable computing. In: Proceedings of the Seventh IEEE International Symposium on Wearable Computers - ISWC 2003, White Plains, NY, 21–23 October, pp. 223–230. IEEE Computer Society Press, Los Alamitos (2003)
31. Kossek, E.E., Ruderman, M.N., Braddy, P.W., Hannum, K.M.: Work-nonwork boundary management profiles: a person-centred approach. J. Vocat. Behav. **81**, 112–128 (2012)
32. Kreiner, G.E.: Consequences of work-home segmentation and integration: a person-environment fit perspective. J. Organ. Behav. **27**(4), 485–507 (2006)
33. Kreiner, G.E., Hollensbe, E.C., Sheep, M.L.: Balancing borders and bridges: negotiating the work-home interface via boundary work tactics. Acad. Manag. J. **52**(4), 704–730 (2009)
34. Lim, H., Arawjo, I., Xie, Y., Khojasteh, N., Fussell, S.: Distraction or life saver?: The role of technology in undergraduate students' boundary management strategies. In: Proceedings of the ACM on Human-Computer Interaction, vol. 1, no. 68, pp. 68:1–68:18 (November 2017)
35. Mark, G., Czerwinski, M., Iqbal, S.T.: Effects of individual differences in blocking workplace distractions. In: Proceedings of the Conference on Human Factors in Computing Systems - CHI 2018, Montreal, Canada, 21–26 April, pp. 92:1–12. ACM, New York (2018)
36. Mark, G., Gudith, D., Klocke, U.: The cost of interrupted work: more speed and stress. In: Proceedings of the Conference on Human Factors in Computing Systems - CHI 2008, Florence, Italy, 5–10 April, pp. 107–116. ACM, New York (2008)
37. McFarlane, D.C., Latorella, K.A.: The scope and importance of human interruption in human-computer interaction design. Hum.-Comput. Interact. **17**(1), 1–61 (2002)
38. Mehrotra, A., Hendley, R., Musolesi, M.: PrefMiner: mining user's preferences for intelligent mobile notification management. In: Proceedings of the 2016 ACM International Joint Conference on Pervasive and Ubiquitous Computing - UbiComp 2016, Heidelberg, Germany, 12–16 September, pp. 1223–1234. ACM, New York (2016)
39. Mehrotra, A., Musolesi, M.: Designing content-driven intelligent notification mechanisms for mobile applications. In: Proceedings of the 2015 ACM International Joint Conference on Pervasive and Ubiquitous Computing - UbiComp 2015, Osaka, Japan, 7–11 September, pp. 813–824. ACM, New York (2015)
40. Mehrotra, A., Pejovic, V., Vermeulen, J., Hendley, R., Musolesi, M.: My phone and me: understanding people's receptivity to mobile notifications. In: Proceedings of the Conference on Human Factors in Computing Systems - CHI 2016, San Jose, CA, 7–12 May, pp. 1021–1032. ACM, New York (2016)
41. Niehaves, B., Koeffer, S., Ortbach, K.: The effect of private IT use on work performance - towards an IT consumerisation theory. In: Proceedings of the 11th International Conference on Wirtschaftsinformatik - WI 2013, Leipzig, Germany, 27 February–1 March, pp. 39–53. Merkur Druck- & Kopierzentrum, Leipzig (2013)

42. Nippert-Eng, C.: Calendars and keys: the classification of "home" and "work." Sociol. Forum **11**(3), 563–582 (1996)
43. Nippert-Eng, C.: Home and Work: Negotiating Boundaries through Everyday Life. University of Chicago Press, Chicago (1996)
44. Obuchi, M., Sasaki, W., Okoshi, T., Nakazawa, J., Tokuda, H.: Investigating interruptibility at activity breakpoints using smartphone activity recognition API. In: Adjunct Proceedings of the 2016 ACM International Joint Conference on Pervasive and Ubiquitous Computing - UbiComp 2016, Heidelberg, Germany, 12–16 September, pp. 1602–1607. ACM, New York (2016)
45. Oemig, C., Gross, T.: Impacts of disruption on secondary task knowledge: recovery modes and social nuances. In: Mensch & Computer - 19. Fachuebergreifende Konferenz fuer interaktive und kooperative Medien - M&C 2019, Hamburg, Germany, 8–11 September, pp. 815–818. ACM, New York (2019)
46. Okoshi, T., Nakazawa, J., Tokuda, H.: Attelia: sensing user's attention status on smart phones. In: Adjunct Proceedings of the International Jiont Conference on Pervasive and Ubiquitous Computing – UbiComp 2014, Seattle, WA, 13–17 September, pp. 139–142. ACM, New York (2014)
47. Okoshi, T., Ramos, J., Nozaki, H., Nakazawa, J., Dey, A.K., Tokuda, H.: Reducing users' perceived mental effort due to interruptive notifications in multi-device mobile environments. In: Proceedings of the 2015 ACM International Joint Conference on Pervasive and Ubiquitous Computing - UbiComp 2015, Osaka, Japan, 7–11 September, pp. 475–486. ACM, New York (2015)
48. Park, Y., Jex, S.M.: Work-home boundary management using communication and information technology. Int. J. Stress. Manag. **18**(2), 133–152 (2011)
49. Payne, S.J., Green, T.R.G.: Task-action grammars: a model of the mental representation of task languages. Hum.-Comput. Interact. **2**(2), 93–133 (1986)
50. Pejovic, V., Musolesi, M.: InterruptMe: designing intelligent prompting mechanisms for pervasive applications. In: Proceedings of the International Joint Conference on Pervasive and Ubiquitous Computing – UbiComp 2014, Seattle, WA, 13–17 September, pp. 897–908. ACM, New York (2014)
51. Pielot, M., Cardoso, B., Katevas, K., Serra, J., Matic, A., Oliver, N.: Beyond interruptibility: predicting opportune moments to engage mobile phone users. In: Proceedings of the ACM on Interactive, Mobile, Wearable, and Ubiquitous Technolologies - UbiComp 2017, vol. 1, no. 3, pp. 91:1–91:25 (September 2017)
52. Pielot, M., Church, K., Oliveira Patres, R.: An in-situ study of mobile phone notifications. In: Proceedings of the 16th International Conference on Human-Computer Interaction with Mobile Devices and Services - MobileHCI 2014, Toronto, Canada, 23–26 September, pp. 233–242. ACM, New York (2014)
53. Pielot, M., Dingler, T., San Pedro, J., Oliver, N.: When attention is not scarce - detecting boredom from mobile phone usage. In: Proceedings of the 2015 ACM International Joint Conference on Pervasive and Ubiquitous Computing - UbiComp 2015, Osaka, Japan, 7–11 September, pp. 825–836. ACM, New York (2015)
54. Pielot, M., Rello, L.: Productive, anxious, lonely - 24 hours without push notifications. In: Proceedings of the 19th International Conference on Human-Computer Interaction with Mobile Devices and Services - MobileHCI 2017, Vienna, Austria, 4–7 September, pp. 11:1–11:11. ACM, New York (2017)
55. Powell, G.N., Greenhaus, J.H.: Sex, gender, and the work-to-family interface: exploring negative and positive interdependencies. Acad. Manag. J. **53**(3), 513–534 (2010)
56. Ratchford, M.M.: BYOD: a security policy evaluation model. In: Latifi, S. (ed.) Information Technology – New Generations. AISC, vol. 558, pp. 215–220. Springer, Cham (2018). https://doi.org/10.1007/978-3-319-54978-1_30

57. Romer, H.: Best practices for BYOD security. Comput. Fraud Secur. **1**, 13–15 (2014)
58. Schulze, F., Groh, G.: Conversational context helps improve mobile notification management. In: Proceedings of the 18th International Conference on Human-Computer Interaction with Mobile Devices and Services - MobileHCI 2016, Florence, Italy, 6–9 September, pp. 518–528. ACM, New York (2016)
59. Schuss, M., Gross, T.: Availability and boundary management: an exploratory study. In: Extended Abstracts of the Conference on Human Factors in Computing Systems - CHI 2019, Glasgow, Scotland, UK, 4–9 May, pp. LBW 1215:1–4. ACM, New York (2019)
60. Shirazi, A.S., Henze, N., Dingler, T., Pielot, M., Weber, D., Schmidt, A.: Large-scale assessment of mobile notifications. In: Proceedings of the Conference on Human Factors in Computing Systems - CHI 2014, Toronto, Canada, 26 April–1 May, pp. 3055–3064. ACM, New York (2014)
61. Siewiorek, D., et al.: SenSay: a context-aware mobile phone. In: Proceedings of the Seventh IEEE International Symposium on Wearable Computers - ISWC 2003, White Plains, NY, 21–23 October, pp. 248–249. IEEE Computer Society Press, Los Alamitos (2003)
62. Speier, C., Valacich, J.S., Vessey, I.: The influence of task interruption on individual decision making: an information overload perspective. Decis. Sci. **30**(2), 337–360 (1999)
63. Van Mierlo, S., van Tendeloo, Y., Meyers, B., Vangheluwe, H.: Domain-specific modelling for human-computer interaction. In: Weyers, B., Bowen, J., Dix, A., Palanque, P. (eds.) The Handbook of Formal Methods in Human-Computer Interaction, pp. 435–462. Springer-Verlag, Heidelberg (2017)
64. Woodcock, J., Davies, J.: Using Z: Specification Refinement, and Proof. Prentice Hall, Englewood Cliffs (1996)
65. Yuan, F., Gao, X., Lindqvist, J.: How busy are you? Predicting the interruptibility intensity of mobile users. In: Proceedings of the Conference on Human Factors in Computing Systems - CHI 2017, Denver, CO, 6–11 May, pp. 5346–5360. ACM, New York (2017)

# The Role of Mobile and Virtual Reality Applications to Support Well-Being: An Expert View and Systematic App Review

Nadine Wagener[1]([✉]), Tu Dinh Duong[2], Johannes Schöning[1,3],
Yvonne Rogers[1,2], and Jasmin Niess[1,3]

[1] University of Bremen, Bremen, Germany
nwagener@uni-bremen.de
[2] University College London, London, UK
[3] University of St. Gallen, St. Gallen, Switzerland

**Abstract.** Interactive technologies for autonomous mental health management are on the rise due to limited therapy access and stigma. However, most commercial mental health apps are neither theory-based nor clinically tested, and psychological theories are not easily accessible to app designers. Thus, it remains unclear if current mobile and VR mental health apps meet therapists' expectations. To address this gap, we conducted interviews ($N = 11$) to build an understanding about current therapeutic practices with a focus on emotion regulation and their applicability to mobile apps. We then conducted a systematic app review of 60 mental-health-related mobile and VR apps applying the themes identified in our interviews as an understanding lens. We draw upon the identified discrepancies to pinpoint design implications for better embedding lived therapeutic practice into mental health apps. We contribute by providing a common grounding between therapists and developers on the features and properties of well-being mobile and VR apps.

**Keywords:** Well-being · Mental health · Mobile apps · Virtual reality · Emotions · Feelings · Mood · Therapy

## 1 Introduction and Motivation

Digital technologies such as mobile and virtual reality (VR) applications (apps) supporting autonomous mental health management have now established themselves on the consumer market [13]. Such technologies promise the users opportunities to improve their mental health and foster well-being [59]. While digital therapies might not be able to fully substitute psychotherapeutic treatment [13], they can be a viable alternative in cases in which starting such a treatment is

---

**Electronic supplementary material** The online version of this chapter (https://doi.org/10.1007/978-3-030-85610-6_16) contains supplementary material, which is available to authorized users.

C. Ardito et al. (Eds.): INTERACT 2021, LNCS 12935, pp. 262–283, 2021.
https://doi.org/10.1007/978-3-030-85610-6_16

difficult (e.g. because of stigmatisation [14,40,56,58] or limited availability of services [14]). Thus, many people are instead turning to technological solutions that have the potential to reduce such challenges and support them in their mental health management [40,56,58]. Hence, there is a need to build an understanding of the current mental health technologies available on the consumer market.

Searching for *mental health* or *well-being* apps in the major app stores produces thousands of results for mobile and virtual reality (VR) apps. However, only few of these apps are evaluated through clinical trials [65] and it remains unclear if commercially available apps for mental well-being meet the expectations of mental health experts. Previous work has attempted to understand experts' perspectives on mobile health apps [33,50] and well-being app's content [31,53] separately. Our approach is different as we combine both, using therapists' expectations and attitudes as basis for analysing existing commercial apps. Further, we apply this experts' view on both mobile and VR apps. In contrast to similar studies of the HCI community with a focus on specific topics, e.g. learning [50] and mindfulness [34], we inquire the therapeutic intervention of engaging with feelings (i.e. emotion regulation (ER)). ER is employed in many different therapies (Sect. 2.2). Specifically, our research is guided by the following research questions (RQ):

RQ₁: How should mobile apps and VR apps support and extend the therapeutic process based on current therapeutic practice?

RQ₂: How are mobile apps and VR apps currently supporting mental health and well-being?

To answer these questions, we interviewed 11 therapists about their therapeutic practice. Grounded in the interview findings, we developed themes to systematically analyse 45 mobile and 15 VR commercially available mental health and well-being apps. Since both, mobile and VR apps, are available on the consumer market (e.g. in leading app stores), users interested in improving their well-being could potentially use them separately or together. Thus, it is valuable to analyse the opportunities and limitations of both types of apps together and explore how they can complement each other to support autonomous mental health management.

The contributions of this paper are threefold: (1) By analysing the expectations of therapists, we provide developers and scholars with a clear picture of what is needed to support users' mental self-care. (2) Through analysing different types of apps, we draw a detailed picture of the state-of-the-art features in well-being apps. This can potentially motivate therapists to augment and extend their current therapeutic methods to cater to the needs of patients outside of a therapy room. (3) By interweaving insights from both interviews with therapists and a review of commercial apps, we provide common grounding and shared language between therapists and app developers on the features and properties for well-being apps, which facilitates a productive dialogue among different stakeholders [10].

## 2    Related Work

To provide theoretical context, we first define key terms and discuss the role of feelings for well-being and therapy. We then review existing research of how mobile and VR apps are already used in therapeutic practice.

### 2.1    The Role of Feelings for Well-Being and Therapy

According to the WHO, *mental health* is an integral part of health and forms the foundation for well-being and an effective functioning in society [66]. Yet, *well-being* is an abstract construct that is, for the scope of this paper, best described as *a dynamic optimal state of psychosocial functioning* [11], which is build upon five core pillars, namely positive emotion, engagement, relationships, meaning, and accomplishments [49]. *Emotions* can be classified as a circumplex of two dimensions: valence (negative to positive) and activation (low to high) [45]. Emotions can be triggered by an event or activity [20] and differ from *moods*, which are lower in intensity than emotions, last longer [43] and are often influenced by a range of factors [20]. Emotions and moods are often collectively described as *feelings* [27]. In this paper we primarily focus on apps that are working with emotion regulation (ER). ER is defined as the process by which people modify and regulate their emotions, and how they experience and express them [3,44]. In ER therapy, one key strategy is to become emotionally aware, or using the umbrella term *engaging with feelings* [44]. In our research, we define *engaging with feelings* in regard to digital mental health management as internally *identifying (ID)*, and verbally or visually *expressing (XP)* feelings.

### 2.2    Methods of Emotion Regulation Therapy

ER is a common 'intervention' used in different forms of therapies [24], the most common being cognitive-behavioural therapy (CBT), dialectic-behavioural therapy (DBT), depth psychology or schema therapy. A shared aim of many of these psychotherapies is to provide the support and skills to overcome the difficulty of engaging with feelings. As part of such an ER intervention, generally speaking, patients learn to *identify* their feelings, *understand* the causes, and to consciously *accept* their emotional states [30].

In ER interventions, many different treatment modalities, such as artistic expressions (e.g. art therapy, role-play [48]) and psycho-education are proven to be useful to learn to engage with feelings. *Psycho-education* comprises systemic and didactic psychotherapeutic interventions with the goal to provide information, education and teach therapeutic strategies to improve well-being [52]. We believe that new technologies might offer possibilities to create spaces for therapeutic, artistic expression [9] and individually designed therapeutic environments [25]. Consequently, we strive to explore the potential and challenges of commercially available mobile and VR apps which support autonomous mental health management.

## 2.3   The Potential of Mobile and VR Technologies for Mental Health and Well-Being

Smartphones have become popular for capturing well-being data (e.g. [18]). Past research works on this topic mainly focused on mental health [5], mindfulness [34, 35] and mood [12]. However, the efficacy of well-being interventions is unclear [33, 63]. Further, intervention-driven work has been subject to critique related to its appropriateness, privacy considerations and engagement [42,60].

Similarly, HCI research has started to explore the use of VR for well-being support, given that it has proven to be an affective medium whose immersive virtual environments (IVEs) can evoke emotional states and responses similar to reality [26,32,39,57,62]. Although in the mental health domain VR is mostly used as a method for exposure therapy [40], it has also been explored for other mental health related areas such as mindfulness [41], stress reduction [57,65], role-play [26], journaling [4], and to recreate memories [58].

The interest in commercial mobile and VR well-being systems is steadily increasing. Concurrently, research established guidelines for designing visual content of VR apps used to elicit positive change [29,46] and outlined the design space of VR well-being apps with the means of a systematic literature review [28]. We extend these approaches by analysing commercial well-being mobile and VR apps based on insights derived from expert interviews with a specific focus on ER. In line with Gaggioli et al. [22], we define *commercial well-being apps* as "positive technologies" targeting broad masses through common app stores such as the iOS App Store or Steam.

## 3   Interviews with Therapists

We conducted semi-structured interviews that addressed the therapists' conceptualisation of well-being, which methods for engaging with feelings they use, and how they define the aim of therapy. By conducting interviews with therapists, we gain an in-depth understanding of which therapeutic methods supporting well-being are currently applied in therapeutic practice. Further, we determine what therapists expect from mobile and VR well-being apps (**RQ₁**). The themes deduced from the interviews form the basis for our app analysis (**RQ₂**).

### 3.1   Method

Due to the current COVID-19 pandemic, the whole study was conducted virtually. All participants were contacted via email and interviews were conducted via videoconferencing software.

**Participants.** We conducted interviews with $N = 11$ licensed psychotherapists from Germany ($M = 44.3$ years, $min : 26$, $max : 62$, 11 female). Participants were personally contacted via email obtained from publicly accessible websites. Though education and current occupation vary across the sample (Table 1), all participants are licensed by the state of Germany to practice psychotherapy and have further worked with patients in psychotherapy for at least two years ($M$ = 8.8 years). Six participants majored in psychology (diploma or master degree) and five are educated as alternative practitioners for psychotherapy. Five participants are currently designated as psychological psychotherapists, which means that they continued training for five additional years, three as alternative practitioners for psychotherapy, three specialised in art therapy, two in depth psychology, one in osteopathy, and one works in healthcare. Three participants have a secondary, non-psychological education (P6 and P8 have majored in graphical design, P10 has majored in pedagogy). Our sample encompasses therapists with different educational backgrounds and varying specialisations. Thus, it represents a typical sample of psychotherapists in Germany that use ER in their daily psychotherapeutic work. Regardless of the specialisation, we refer to all participants collectively as "therapists", though some name themselves practitioners or clinicians. In line with most of our interviewees, we refer to people psychotherapists work with as "patients". When we discuss people utilising a mobile or VR app, regardless of their state of well-being, we refer to them as "users".

**Table 1.** All participants are state-approved psychotherapists in Germany and have been working in psychotherapy for at least two years. Psychological/therapeutic education and current occupation within this field differ.

|      | Education | Occupation |
|------|-----------|------------|
| P1   | Alternative practitioner for psychotherapy | Alternative practitioner for psychotherapy |
| P2   | Alternative practitioner for psychotherapy | Alternative practitioner for psychotherapy |
| P3   | Major in psychology | Psychological psychotherapist (focus on depth psychology) |
| P4   | Major in psychology | Psychological psychotherapist, working in healthcare |
| P5   | Major in psychology | Psychological psychotherapist |
| P6   | Alternative practitioner for psychotherapy | Art therapist |
| P7   | Alternative practitioner for psychotherapy | Osteopath |
| P8   | Alternative practitioner for psychotherapy | Art therapist |
| P9   | Major in psychology | Psychological psychotherapist (focus on depth psychology) |
| P10  | Alternative practitioner for psychotherapy | Alternative practitioner for psychotherapy (focus on art therapy) |
| P11  | Major in psychology | Psychological psychotherapist |

**Interview Protocol.** We conducted semi-structured interviews that addressed the therapists' conceptualisation of well-being, which methods for engaging with feelings they use, and how they define the aim of therapy. They further evaluated the benefits of technological aids for (private) therapeutic usage and specified features and properties they think important for both mobile and VR well-being apps. We provided the participants with a short explanation of the well-known use cases of mood tracking mobile apps and anxiety therapy VR apps. The complete interview protocol can be found in the supplementary material.

**Data Analysis.** Interviews were held via videoconferencing software and lasted an average of 42.3 minutes ($min$ : 25, $max$ : 56). Each participant was compensated with 25€. The interviews were audio-recorded, transcribed, and translated into English. For the analysis, we used a six-step process of reflexive thematic analysis with daily feedback cycles between two co-authors [8]. The results are reported using an interpretivist semi-structured approach [6].

## 3.2   Results

Based on our qualitative inquiry, three themes were derived from the data: *From Psychological Theory to Lived Practice, Mental Health as Holistic Concept* and *Offering a Safe Place.* Our findings are described below and illustrated with excerpts from the interviews. Specific topics and features of each theme that will be used for the app review (Fig. 2) are marked in bold font.

**From Psychological Theory to Lived Practice.** The first theme derived from our data focused on how psychotherapists approach the concepts of emotions, feelings and mood in theory versus in practice. Based on psychological theory there is a clear difference between these concepts. One participant explained in more detail: *"[...] in principle we are not aware of the emotions [...]. When they become conscious, then we speak of feelings, that is the 5% that are above the water surface, considering the iceberg model"* (P9). Other participants elaborated on their conceptualisation of mood. For instance, they described mood as a baseline that shapes every emotion to a certain extent or as a *"conglomerate of different emotions"* (P4). Seven participants agreed mood is a longterm concept compared to emotions or feelings. This is further emphasised by the following statement: *"[Mood is] like a weather situation that runs through it, over several hours, over several days, or even through an entire season"* (P3). With these assessments, they agree with widely accepted theories of emotion and mood from related work (Sect. 2.1). However, when specifically asked about the wording they use in practice, 82% state that they do not differentiate between emotions and mood in practice. The majority of participants agreed that it is more meaningful to focus on one illustrative term in their psychotherapeutic work to not confuse their patients. One therapist commented: *"[...] when you work with people it doesn't make sense to differentiate"* (P6). Thus, we follow the terminology of the therapists in this paper and use *feelings* as a generic term for emotions and mood.

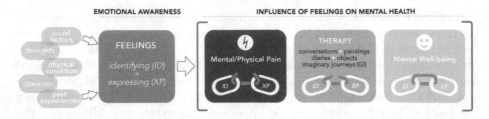

**Fig. 1.** Schematic conceptualisation of the second theme *Mental Health as Holistic Concept* based on the interviews. By using therapeutic methods patients learn to identify (ID) and express (XP) their feelings, which re-establishes their mental well-being.

In line with the approach of focusing on one easily understandable concept (e.g. feelings) to support patients in their psychotherapeutic process, participants further emphasised the importance of responding to individual patients' needs in a flexible manner. Nine therapists elaborated that the specific method that best supports a patient needs to be chosen on an individual basis and may vary as much as using conversations, drawings, diaries, objects, imaginary journeys/guided imagery and many more.

All therapists stressed the importance of **recording** feelings. Even though the majority of therapists mentioned the value of flexibility in interactive technologies when **recording** feelings, seven also imagined utilising **predefined** recording options, using properties like emojis, scales, colours, or labelling words to choose from. However, two therapists stressed not to use intensity scales or graphs, as this could distort the bigger picture of the own well-being and one participant explicitly emphasised not to use smileys: *"They are too vague, an emotion has many layers and is constantly changing"* (P8).

The caution towards **predefined** recording methods is further illustrated by four participants who pictured an **unrestricted** implementation method, like journaling or being able to create own labels for feelings. Further, five therapists suggested **prompts**, meaning that an app urges the user to answer deeper questions, or that an AI suggests how one could feel given a specific situation.

**Mental Health as Holistic Concept.** During our interviews, many participants explained that mental health is a holistic concept. It includes mental, physical and social well-being and is not merely the absence of mental illness. Using the words of one of our participants: *"True healing is about body, mind, and soul"* (P7). Furthermore, therapists explained that thoughts as well as physical conditions influence feelings: *"When I think in a certain way, it affects how I feel. And if I think differently, it may be that my feeling is no longer quite as dramatic"* (P5).

For all therapists, mind, body, and the process of engaging with feelings are directly linked to well-being. Figure 1, composed of the therapists' descriptions, shows the schematic conceptualisation of the role of ER therapy and the influence of feelings on well-being. One therapist highlighted the value and the challenge of being able to connect with and regulate one's emotions: *"Mental health is when emotions are agile and can be contained. When my feelings are frozen, such as with depression, or if my emotions are overflowing and too much and cannot be tamed, [as for example] with borderline patients or self-harming [patients], then that is because the feelings cannot be regulated"* (P1).

Consistent with a holistic approach towards mental health, therapists emphasised that apps should address feelings, thoughts and physical aspects. For seven therapists, the ideal app should **support** the user by offering **teaching & tips**. One therapist stated: *"It's good to know that I feel this way or that way, but it's also good to know how I can feel better, to help people to help themselves"* (P6). To achieve this, five therapists suggested that apps could tutor and guide through exercises. Five others imagined apps offering emotional support, e.g. through affirmative quotes. Therapists also expressed the importance to include some psycho-educational elements to educate and to provide background information about chosen symbols or objects in apps. As an example, P1 imagined that a patient chose a wolf in a VE: *"[. . .] and then you could read two or three sentences about it, and then they [the patients] think about it, 'ah, so I took the wolf, then maybe I feel like this and that'. To have the mirroring aspect again"* (P1). For three participants, another important aspect seemed to be a notification option that support the user to not forget thinking about their own well-being during the day.

Many therapists also thought about the supportive feature of **sharing** data with others. Although three therapists discussed the benefits of sharing thoughts and feelings with other patients via some form of social network, opinions deviated between the productive and destructive nature of social networks. However, four participants approved of sharing content with the therapist. In regard to VR, three participants considered recording and documenting sessions meaningful to revisit later, and to share those with therapists to offer them a better glimpse of their imagination. It was stressed, though, that one of the benefits of VR is to use it in the privacy of your own home: *"[. . .] where nobody sees this but me"* (P3).

**Offering a Safe Place.** Many therapists emphasised that the task of therapy is to support the emotional awareness of the patients by helping to internally *identifying* and externally *expressing* one's feelings, which is in line with related work (Sect. 2.1). This is best highlighted by the following statement: *"Independent of whether it is behavioural therapy, depth psychology, or systemic analysis, it is always about emotions being activated in therapy and this leads to success"* (P9).

By activating emotions and engaging with them, therapy supports patients in processing the past, understanding the present, and developing strategies for the future *"to act appropriately"* (P4). However, therapists stressed that they mostly need to start small. Nearly all, 10 out of 11 participants, elaborated that patients have trouble naming feelings and that therapists spend a lot of time teaching that *"'good', 'bad', and 'I can't get up'"* (P3) are not descriptions of feelings. In Fig. 1, this is expressed by becoming emotionally aware of one's feelings.

Consequently, apps should support the user in identifying and reflecting on one's feelings. For instance, many therapists had some form of psycho-educational training to **reflect** in mind, e.g. to explore the causes of experienced feelings. Seven therapists suggested that apps should prompt the user in linking a feeling with a specific situation to increase the awareness of the causes. That being said, identifying and reflecting on one's feelings can only happen in a space where people feel safe. Therapy is, inter alia, about the possibility to live emotions in a way often inappropriate or suppressed in everyday life. 10 therapists emphasise that it is important in therapy to offer a space *"to just exist with the feelings"* (P1). A quote by one therapist captures this notion: *"It is also very important for the person himself to meet his feelings in a visualised way, to hear or see his loneliness. I provide the framework for him to be angry at times (...). That also has something relieving, because it is just allowed in this specific setting"* (P10). Thus, apps should offer a safe environment to express the own feelings. Therapists assessed VR as an opportunity to offer patients such a safe space.

To illustrate, most therapists saw the benefits of VR apps to **relive** a certain experience or environment that is either similar to own memories or to a desired situation. More precisely, seven participants imagined using **predefined** virtual environments (VEs), e.g. exploring different landscapes or having a walk in a park. Thus, they transferred the therapy method of guided imagery to VR. One participant summarised the positive effect of VR for guided imagery: *"When you take body trips [in real therapy], they have an effect on the body as if you were really there, otherwise you wouldn't do that with the patients. I imagine it to be similar when patients use VR for that, that they really experience this imaginary place as if they were there"* (P6).

Furthermore, eight therapists could also fathom a **partly predefined** implementation. Users would be presented with a simple pre-set VE but were able to create their own *happy place* by enriching it through (pre-set) objects, e.g. choosing animals, the weather, other objects, and colours. One contemplated: *"It [pre-set objects] also takes away a bit of individuality, because I preset something. But for patients who find it difficult to visualise things themselves, this could be really helpful because you give them impetus"* (P4).

Apart from that, five participants thought VR should be *"the freer the better"* (P8), which we call an **unrestricted** implementation. They imagined using abstract forms, colours, or creating avatars representing a specific feeling. Two participants could also envision constructing a VE from scratch. They stated that this would help practice visualisation techniques that are also useful in stressful situations in real life: *"I could also imagine that they [patients] would like it, if they were really angry, that they could simulate a really violent thunderstorm so that the weather and the whole environment would adjust to their mood. For some of them, it would be a great help to accept it [their anger], if they could transform the whole room around them into their feeling"* (P3).

However, six participants were of the opinion, that VR should be rather used to experience positive emotions as they were unsure of the risk of getting re-traumatised. Thus, besides supporting reflection and reliving safe environments, to **relax** is a third important aim of such VEs. Nine participants focused

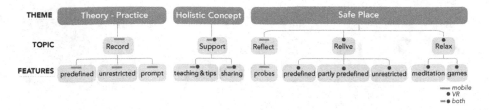

**Fig. 2.** Themes derived from the interviews, including topics and features that form the basis for mobile (orange), VR (dark blue) and both (light blue) app reviews. Specific properties of each feature, e.g. emojis or graphs, are not listed in this figure. (Color figure online)

on releasing stress and further three mentioned that having fun in the process of experiencing a predefined VE or by creating one themselves could already improve one's mood.

## 4    Mobile and VR App Review

To further explore how autonomous mental health management technologies are currently supporting mental health and well-being ($RQ_2$) and to identify possible mismatches between the therapists' recommendations and commercially available apps, we systematically analysed 45 mobile and 15 VR apps that focus on engaging with feelings. We included both mobile and VR apps in our review as users interested in improving their well-being could potentially use them separately or together, since both are available on the consumer market (e.g. in leading app stores). Thus, it is valuable to explore opportunities and limitations of both and how they can complement each other to support autonomous mental health management. Mobile and VR apps were coded using three topics each, which are further divided in several features and properties derived from the interviews (Fig. 2).

### 4.1    Method

Our analysis includes 45 mobile and 15 VR commercial mental health and well-being apps. We inductively coded the features and properties derived from the interview results. Our systematic search process is depicted in Fig. 3.

**Selection Criteria.** Two authors defined several selection criteria in iterative discussion sessions. We selected mobile apps from the iOS App Store and the Google Play Store and VR apps from three major gaming platforms (Steam, Oculus and Viveport). The final search terms encompassed apps that contained *mood, emotion, feeling, wellbeing, well-being,* and *mental health* in either their title or description. We chose these search terms because therapists and patients often use these terms interchangeably (Sect. 3.2), and to take different notation possibilities into account. In addition, we limited the search to the categories of

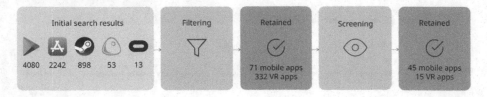

**Fig. 3.** Systematic 3-step process of searching, filtering and screening of mobile and VR apps, resulting in 45 mobile and 15 VR apps.

*Health & Fitness*, *Medical* or *Lifestyle*, which are the same for all app stores. We focused on apps that seem to have relevance for users. As a proxy for this, we used the rating count (i.e. the amount of people that wrote reviews) with a threshold of 100 reviews. Unlike the number of downloads, the rating count is available on iOS App and Google Play Store and is thus comparable. As VR apps tend to have fewer reviews overall, the criterion of a minimum rating was not included. We then screened for duplicates.

The systematic review followed a 3-step process for both mobile and VR (Fig. 3). The initial search rendered 6322 mobile and 964 VR apps. They were then filtered based upon exclusion terms, e.g. *fitness fun* (for a full list see supplementary material), resulting in 71 mobile and 332 VR apps (Viveport does not support exclusion). Finally, the apps were screened manually to ensure their relevance, e.g. horror related VR games were excluded. The final body included 45 mobile and 15 VR apps (collected in September 2020).

**Coding Process.** Based on the interview results, we coded mobile and VR mental health and well-being apps separately (Fig. 2). Two authors initially coded the apps independently. Then, in an iterative process, they discussed the results and coding of features and properties. Any ambiguous case was discussed with the other co-authors. Our final codebook is presented in Fig. 2.

The mobile apps were analysed in-depth by using them at least three times over the course of a week. The VR apps were played at least once[1]. For both, descriptions available on the respective app stores were analysed on the premise of getting insights into important app features that might have been missed while using.

## 4.2 Mobile Apps

**Results Mobile Apps.** Based on the interviews, we analysed 45 mobile apps focusing on the three topics **record**, **support** and **reflect**, and corresponding features (Fig. 2). For a more fine-grained analysis, we also explored the usage of specific properties such as emojis. For a detailed description, please consult the supplementary material.

---

[1] Apart from the App *Prana* [55], which is to date not yet released. Here, we watched demonstration videos and playthroughs on YouTube.

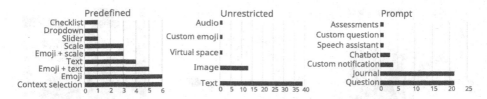

**Fig. 4.** For the topic of *record* the features were categorized by the type of interaction which ranged from *predefined, unrestricted* to *prompt*.

In the topic **record**, we investigated the flexibility of recording one's feelings. The results are depicted in Fig. 4. For the feature *predefined*, emojis and emojis combined with other properties such as text were used most often. For the feature *unrestricted*, a text recording feature was found in 39 apps, surpassing all other properties. We further examined the usage of *prompts*. Using questions as triggers and journals were the most popular form of prompts, found in 23 apps each. Artificially intelligent chatbots that are able to reply dynamically, thus acting more as a therapist than a static journal, were found in three apps.

Mobile apps also offer **support** by providing *teaching & tips* and *sharing* options. To teach, 21 apps used exercises or tasks, 17 apps a form of tip, advice or guide, and eight apps quotes or affirmations. Regarding *sharing* options, 10 apps utilised community based sharing, e.g. with other app users, and four offered private sharing with friends.

The topic **reflect** deals with methods of how apps enable the revisiting of the recorded data to support self-reflection. Some examples for *probes* are shown in Fig. 5. Five apps used statistics, mainly in the form of listed numbers associated to an activity (Fig. 5A). The most common probe used were graphs. Technical graphs (Fig. 5B) were found in 12, and illustrated graphs, using some form of embellishments such as emojis to further support the presentation of data (Fig. 5D,E), were found in eight apps. Two apps used word clouds, virtual spaces and scores (Fig. 5B). Calendars to prompt reflection, not merely as a form to navigate, were found in nine apps (Fig. 5F). The more visual means such as image collection or mood boards were found in two apps (Fig. 5G). As a meta analysis, apps were further rated according to their assistance to reflect upon reasons and causes of feelings, which is called situation analysis. To determine its use, apps were rated as providing low (raw data is presented without guidance), medium (data is presented in context of other data but without direct suggestions about its meaning), or high (direct suggestions and correlations between feelings and causes are presented) levels of situation analysis support. Forty-three apps were rated low, two apps medium and none high.

**Discussion Mobile Apps.** We will now discuss the findings in relation to the insights from the interviews. In line with the requirements of therapists in regard to Sect. 3.2, mobile apps offer a wide range of **recording** possibilities, of which emojis are dominating as predefined properties. We want to emphasise that eight

| A. Statistics | B. Technical Graph and Word Cloud | C. Slider | D. Illustrated Graphs | E. Illustrated Graphs | F. Calendar and Heatmap | G. Image/mood Board |

**Fig. 5.** Examples of *probes* used by apps to **reflect**, ordered with increasing complexity and vividness. Image sources: A [47], B [64], C [54], D [7], E [38], F [37] G [61].

apps combine them with further elements like text or scales, probably to support the learning process of identifying feelings, thus teaching ER skills. A similar reason might also relate to the high usage of text. As a predefined property, it provides labels for feelings, which expedite the recording of data so that it can be captured more regularly, and as an unrestricted property as prompts, it offers individuality, as wished by nine therapists. However, only three apps offer artificially intelligent chatbots, although five therapists mentioned such prompts specifically because of their benefits to teach ER strategies.

Besides offering tips and guides, ten apps provide **support** via *sharing* data with others, although restricted to other users and friends. Based on the therapists' opinions, we emphasise the potential for using apps as a way to also connect with professionals for remote support, which may increase the development of ER strategies.

Whilst recording will already provide some opportunities for reflection, many apps provide further features to explicitly **reflect**. We identified graphs as the most popular probe. This contrasts the findings from our interviews, where two therapists specifically mentioned not to use graphs. We further identified that only two apps support a medium and none a high level of situation analyses, which was addressed by seven therapists. Although some attempt to support a deeper reflection process (e.g. six apps use a labelled photo of a recent activity for context selection), it appears that most apps present raw data without further guidance on how to reflect upon it.

### 4.3   VR Apps

**Results VR Apps.** We analysed 15 VR well-being apps focusing on the three topics **support**, **relive**, and **relax** (Fig. 2). For a detailed description, please consult the supplementary material. The results are shown in Fig. 6.

Fourteen apps provided some form of **support**. Of those, seven offered *teaching & tips* via tutorials and instructions, such as guided meditation sessions (Fig. 7A,B), and two via in-game information, such as psycho-educational elements and affirmative quotes (Fig. 7C). Four apps also offered *sharing* possibilities, either by presenting information about one's game statistics or opportunities for recording and screenshots. One app has what can be interpreted as a link

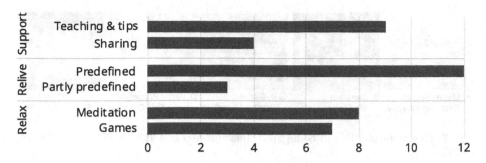

**Fig. 6.** Graph shows the amount of VR well-being apps fitting to the topics *support*, *relive* and *relax*, and its corresponding features.

to professionals, flashing a warning notice and advising professional support if needed [1].

Within the topic **relive**, 12 apps were *predefined*, in which the users are presented with pre-set environments. Users can only choose between different environments or music before they enter an otherwise non-interactable VE. Three apps use a *partly predefined* method, of which two provide some interaction with the VE [16,21] and one offering possibilities to create new (though preset) objects like trees or command the weather (Fig. 7D). None offered an *unrestricted* environment.

Regarding the topic **relax**, eight apps focus solely on meditation exercises. To distinct further, six focus on meditation through preset VEs (e.g. Fig. 7A), while two [17,55] added gamification elements to meditation, e.g. by reviving animals through relaxing one's respiration (Fig. 7B). Further, seven apps offer relaxation through games for enjoyment such as stone skipping or popping balloons.

**Discussion VR Apps.** We will now discuss the findings in relation to the insights from the interviews. To **relax** was the most prominent aim for VR well-being apps, mentioned by nine therapists. Eleven VR apps meet this criterion, consolidating both the participants' opinion and findings from research [51,57, 65]. However, the main focus of the apps is on meditation (six apps of our sample, e.g. Fig. 7A,B). This was surprising as meditation was not once mentioned by therapists. As an explanation, commercial meditating VR apps seem to target mostly non-professionals and are rated as especially helpful and engaging for beginners [19]. This might reflect (and re-influence) the pre-dominant opinion in society, that an average user automatically equates relaxation with meditation, as previously addressed, e.g. by Lukoff et al. [34]. This finding highlights the need to better educate users by including psycho-educational elements, as four therapists emphasised. However, only one app included such psycho-educational in-game information (Fig. 7C).

A. Meditation as     B. Gamified          C. In-Game              D. Partly Predefined    E. Colour-Themed
   Relaxing Exercise    Meditation          Psycho-Education         with Self-Creation      Emotion Worlds

**Fig. 7.** Examples of VR well-being apps. Image sources: A [15], B [55], C [1], D [23], E [21].

Additionally, therapists emphasised the importance of flexible interactive technologies and the possibility to autonomously *create* a VE. Only one [23] included some form of self-creation (Fig. 7D) by allowing the user to grow trees, have butterflies flying around, and changing the weather in an otherwise pre-set VE. This was unanticipated as creating an own VE is already used quite a lot in non-commercial therapeutic apps [4,58]. Thus, we propose that commercial VR well-being apps should enhance the interaction possibilities with the VE to allow users an unrestricted interactable VE to build their own imaginary world, as elaborated in Sect. 3.2.

Additionally, 10 therapists stressed that therapy should offer a space for unbiased emotional exploration and expression. This aspect was only mentioned once in regard to VR, which was surprising because VR is considered an efficient medium for artistic expression [9,29]. Although also switching between virtual settings, e.g. beach and forest, might elicit different feelings, only one app [21] publicly communicates the aim of emotional exploration. It offers coloured emotion worlds to *"discover new emotions"* and to *"explore different kinds of mental states and find your emotional balance"* [21] (Fig. 7E).

Finally, all therapists were sceptical regarding the risks of VR and agreed that digital well-being apps should only be considered as additional tools. Only one app [1] addresses this aspect by adding a note about possible risks. Previous work has shown that meditation, which we found to be the focus in our VR sample, has many potential benefits (e.g. inducing positive emotion [19]). Nevertheless, users should be informed about possibilities and limits of mental health support technology. Thus, based on the recommendations of the therapists we interviewed, we propose that all commercial VR well-being apps should add such a notice.

## 5    Discussion

In this research, we explored current lived therapeutic practice and how commercially available technologies support mental health management. We conducted qualitative interviews with psychotherapists and a systematic mobile and VR app review. We identified several recommendations for digital mental health management **(RQ1)**, including, amongst others, the need for support-ing the user in a holistic way and to offer a safe place in which patients can reflect, relive emotions and relax (Fig. 2). Our mobile and VR app review finds that the implementation of such elements varies to a great extent within each medium **(RQ2)**. We use the themes identified in our qualitative analysis as an outline for our discussion.

### 5.1    From Psychological Theory to Lived Practice

Therapists' opinion about a flexible usage in the wording is met by the apps, as has been demonstrated by the hundreds of results when using the search terms *emotions, feelings, mood, mental health* and *well-being*. However, such labelling is also misleading. To illustrate, based on our initial search, we got presented with a multitude of different mobile apps (e.g. apps to regulate ambient light-ing, to monitor cannabis usage or a violent VR app shooter game). It seems as if the interchangeable use of these terms found in psychological therapy gets transferred to the field of digital technologies, thus, making it hard for users to immediately find an appropriate app. Further, therapists expressed a desire for a flexible framework that does not limit an individual's expression of emotions, feelings or moods, given that most people have trouble understanding or defin-ing such concepts. We propose that apps could provide definitions of terms, e.g. 'feelings' vs. 'emotions', thus offering skill acquisition, but should also allow users to choose their own wording. We also found that apps seldom offer customisable user interfaces and methods to record their feelings, that can be changed accord-ing to the current mood. Effectively, users would need to switch completely to another app in order to individualise their recording experience. However, taking different mobile and VR apps into account, flexibility is quite high: Apps range from being very precise in conveying statistics but being reduced to numbers and graphs (mobile apps), to immersively experiencing feelings but with less information conveyed (VR).

*Recommendation 1: Mobile and VR apps for mental health and well-being could allow users to choose which terms they want to use in their respective app (e.g. feelings vs. emotions).*

### 5.2    Mental Health as Holistic Concept

Therapists envisioned mental health as a holistic concept, stressing that mental well-being is a conglomerate of thoughts, physical and mental health. Regarding the therapists' wish for psycho-educational information (e.g. how to differen-tiate feelings from physical reactions), they, inter alia, imagined the usage of worksheets, quizzes and in-game information. Only few apps reflect the holistic view on mental health. We found a clear lack of psycho-educational features in mobile, and only one VR app included them [1]. This holds also true for affirma-tive quotes, which can strengthen the mindset, which was included in only one VR app [21]. Bakker et al. [5] point out that mobile apps are well positioned to deliver psycho-education by multimedia and audiovisual tools, while [28] highlights the importance of a mind-body-dialogue in VR. Both complement our findings that apps should put more emphasis on teaching and advising mechanisms.

Regarding the physical aspect, it was surprising that although smartphones can easily provide accessible objective data about physical activities like step count [36], only few included such information. One example is *Life Cycle*, which uses Apple Health to import physical activities and sleep data. The developers of the VR app *D.R.I.L.L* [17] were the only ones in our VR examples that acknowledged the physical aspect as part of engaging with one's feelings. Examples such as the iOS Health App [2] and the VR well-being platform DynamixVR, of which D.R.I.L.L. [17] is part of, prove the feasibility of interpreting mental health as a conglomerate of aspects.

*Recommendation 2: Mobile and VR apps for mental health and well-being should approach mental health as a holistic concept, including psycho-educational and sportive elements.*

## 5.3  Offering a Safe Place

In lived practice, therapists offer a safe space for patients to engage with their feelings, to safely reflect upon emotions, to relive (and relieve of) emotions, and to relax. They also stress the importance of digital apps doing the same. Yet, this was one of the most underdeveloped areas of commercial apps. Our study shows that many mobile well-being apps heavily rely on the feature *record*, but the depth and possibilities to *reflect* differs greatly from app to app. An area that is noticeable missing is how apps can scaffold and guide the reflective process, in other words rather than simply displaying data back to a person, apps could explore approaches that provide more guidance on the reflection process. Bakker et al. [5] recommend that apps should report thoughts and feelings by presenting data in regards to the treatment goal. We argue that apps should broaden this aim to provide more guidance on how to interpret the data (reflection).

In both interview and VR app analysis, the VR approach seems to be less focusing on cognitively *identifying* and *reflecting*, than on the topic of *reliving*. Therapists described it as a learning-by-being method, that a) makes users feel automatically calm by visiting predefined VEs, b) can teach them ER strategies, specifically imaginary journeys, that are useful in stressful situations in real life, c) helps in *expressing* emotions by seeing and feeling visualisation techniques, e.g. by adjusting the outer environment to inner feelings (one therapist gave the example of visually expressing anger by a black thunderstorm), and d) can be a gamified process which can relieve users by having fun in the process of creating an own safe place or by adjusting the outer environment according to inner feelings. Research highlights the potential of VR to offer such playful artistic expression [29], which improve one's well-being [28].

However, VR well-being apps should also offer other methods than the learning-by-being approach, such as learning-by-mirroring, e.g. through an avatar. We further assumed more unrestricted environments based on the high demand for individually fitting safe places. Despite literature suggesting that VR (and mobile apps as well) as new technologies could be used as artistic media to individually design therapeutic environments [9,25], we found only one app that at least partly allows for adjusting the environment [23].

*Recommendation 3: Mobile and VR apps should combine cognitive and affective approaches to mental health management (e.g. probes and artistic expression).*

### 5.4   Limitations and Future Work

The interviews revealed interesting distinctions between the envisioned features for mobile and VR well-being apps. Yet, we recognise that the approach used in this paper is prone to certain limitations. As we did not want to influence the participants in any way, we only mentioned the well-known use cases of mood tracking for mobile apps and of anxiety therapy for VR apps. However, as the therapists had very little experience with both mobile and VR well-being apps, we could have used a multiple-choice questionnaire, shown them videos, or have them try out several apps to increase the level of detail with which the therapists answered questions about specific app properties. Future research could identify specific design considerations for mobile and VR apps to make them more attractive for therapists and users. Moreover, future work could take other stakeholders' opinions into account, identifying user and app developer preferences.

## 6   Conclusion

This paper analysed commercially available mobile and VR apps for mental health using lived therapeutic practice as an understanding lens. To that end, we conducted interviews with therapists, developed a coding scheme and analysed 60 mobile and VR apps. We found that there is a mismatch between what therapists envision digital technology to provide and what commercial mobile and VR well-being apps offer. Currently, most mobile and VR well-being apps focus on a specific well-being aspect, cannot be fully customised, lack opportunities for individual expression and should offer more support to users in identifying and reflecting upon their feelings. We hope that our results provide a starting point for future discourse between therapists, scholars and commercial app developers and provide a common grounding and language between different stakeholders.

**Acknowledgements.** We thank all participants for taking part in the study. This work was supported through multiple funding schemes. This research is funded by the German Research Foundation (DFG) under Germanys Excellence Strategy (EXC 2077, University of Bremen) and a Lichtenberg Professorship funded by the Volkswagen Foundation. Also, we acknowledge the support of the Leibniz ScienceCampus Bremen Digital Public Health (lsc-diph.de), which is jointly funded by the Leibniz Association (W4/2018), the Federal State of Bremen and the Leibniz Institute for Prevention Research and Epidemiology—BIPS.

# References

1. Aerolito: Self-knowledge vr (2019). https://store.steampowered.com/app/958680/Selfknowledge_VR/
2. Apple: Your health, from head to toe (2021). https://www.apple.com/am/ios/health/
3. Auszra, L., Herrmann, I.R., Greenberg, L.S.: Emotionsfokussierte Therapie: Ein Praxismanual. Hogrefe Verlag (2017). https://doi.org/10.1026/02425-000
4. Baker, S.J., Waycott, J., Warburton, J., Batchelor, F.: The highway of life: social virtual reality as a reminiscence tool. Innov. Aging **3**(1), 306 (2019). https://doi.org/10.1093/geroni/igz038.1121
5. Bakker, D., Kazantzis, N., Rickwood, D., Rickard, N.: Mental health smartphone apps: review and evidence-based recommendations for future developments. JMIR Ment. Health **3**(1), e7 (2016). https://doi.org/10.2196/mental.4984
6. Blandford, A., Furniss, D., Makri, S.: Qualitative HCI research: going behind the scenes. Synth. Lect. Hum.-Cent. Inform. **9**, 1–115 (2016)
7. Blinky LLC: Perspective, a mindful journal on the app store (2017). https://apps.apple.com/us/app/perspective-a-mindful-journal/id1186753097. Accessed 17 Sep 2020
8. Braun, V., Clarke, V., Hayfield, N., Terry, G.: Thematic Analysis, pp. 843–860. Springer, Singapore (2019). https://doi.org/10.1007/978-981-10-5251-4_103
9. Brown, C., Garner, R.: Serious gaming, virtual, and immersive environments in art therapy, pp. 192–205 (2017)
10. Burrows, A., Gooberman-Hill, R., Coyle, D.: Shared Language and the Design of Home Healthcare Technology, pp. 3584–3594. Association for Computing Machinery, New York (2016). https://doi.org/10.1145/2858036.2858496
11. Butler, J., Kern, M.: The perma-profiler: a brief multidimensional measure of flourishing. Int. J. Wellbeing **6**, 1–48 (2016). https://doi.org/10.5502/ijw.v6i3.526
12. Caldeira, C., Chen, Y., Chan, L., Pham, V., Chen, Y., Zheng, K.: Mobile apps for mood tracking: an analysis of features and user reviews. In: AMIA Annual Symposium Proceedings, vol. 2017, p. 495 (2017)
13. Clay, R.A.: Mental health apps are gaining traction. Monit. Psychol. **52**(1) (2021). http://www.apa.org/monitor/2021/01/trends-mental-health-apps
14. Coyle, D., Doherty, G.: Clinical evaluations and collaborative design: developing new technologies for mental healthcare interventions, pp. 2051–2060 (April 2009). https://doi.org/10.1145/1518701.1519013
15. Cubicle Ninjas: Guided Meditation VR (2016). https://store.steampowered.com/app/397750/Guided_Meditation_VR/. Accessed 17 Sep 2020
16. Devika: Evenness Sensory Space (2018). https://store.steampowered.com/app/973360/Evenness_Sensory_Space/
17. dfree: D.R.I.L.L (2018). https://store.steampowered.com/app/766650/DRILL/
18. Diethei, D., Colley, A., Kalving, M., Salmela, T., Häkkilä, J., Schöning, J.: Medical selfies: emotional impacts and practical challenges. In: 22nd International Conference on Human-Computer Interaction with Mobile Devices and Services, pp. 1–12 (2020)
19. Downey, L.L., Cohen, M.S.: Virtual worlds and well-being: meditating with sanctuarium. Int. J. Virtual Augment. Real. **2**(1), 14–31 (2018). https://doi.org/10.4018/IJVAR.2018010102
20. Ekkekakis, P.: The Measurement of Affect, Mood, and Emotion: A Guide for Health-Behavioral Research, pp. 1–206 (2011). https://doi.org/10.1017/CBO9780511820724

21. Frost Earth Studio: Mind Labyrinth VR Dreams (2018). https://store. steampowered.com/app/856080/Mind_Labyrinth_VR_Dreams/
22. Gaggioli, A., Riva, G., Peters, D., Calvo, R.A.: Positive technology, computing, and design: shaping a future in which technology promotes psychological well-being. In: Jeon, M. (ed.) Emotions and Affect in Human Factors and Human-Computer Interaction, pp. 477–502. Academic Press, San Diego (2017). https://doi.org/10. 1016/B978-0-12-801851-4.00018-5
23. Greenergames: NatureTreks VR (2017). https://www.oculus.com/experiences/ quest/2616537008386430/?locale=de_DE
24. Gross, J.J., Jazaieri, H.: Emotion, emotion regulation, and psychopathology: an affective science perspective. Clin. Psychol. Sci. **2**(4), 387–401 (2014). https://doi. org/10.1177/2167702614536164
25. Hacmun, I., Regev, D., Salomon, R.: The principles of art therapy in virtual reality. Front. Psychol. **9**, 2082 (2018). https://doi.org/10.3389/fpsyg.2018.02082
26. Hadley, W., Houck, C., Brown, L., Spitalnick, J., Ferrer, M., Barker, D.: Moving beyond role-play: evaluating the use of virtual reality to teach emotion regulation for the prevention of adolescent risk behavior within a randomized pilot trial. J. Pediatr. Psychol. **44**, 425–435 (2019). https://doi.org/10.1093/jpepsy/jsy092
27. Jeon, M.: Emotions and Affect in Human Factors and Human–Computer Interaction: Taxonomy, Theories, Approaches, and Methods, pp. 3–26 (2017). https:// doi.org/10.1016/B978-0-12-801851-4.00001-X
28. Kitson, A., Prpa, M., Riecke, B.E.: Immersive interactive technologies for positive change: a scoping review and design considerations. Front. Psychol. **9**, 1354 (2018). https://doi.org/10.3389/fpsyg.2018.01354
29. Kitson, A., Stepanova, E.R., Aguilar, I.A., Wainwright, N., Riecke, B.E.: Designing mind(set) and setting for profound emotional experiences in virtual reality. In: Proceedings of the 2020 ACM Designing Interactive Systems Conference, DIS 2020, pp. 655–668. Association for Computing Machinery, New York (2020). https://doi. org/10.1145/3357236.3395560
30. Lane, R.D., Schwartz, G.E.: Levels of emotional awareness: a cognitive-developmental theory and its application to psychopathology. Am. J. Psychiatry **144**(2), 133–143 (1987). https://doi.org/10.1176/ajp.144.2.133
31. Lau, N., et al.: Android and iPhone mobile apps for psychosocial wellness and stress management: systematic search in app stores and literature review. JMIR Mhealth Uhealth **8**(5), e17798 (2020). https://doi.org/10.2196/17798
32. Lorenzetti, V., et al.: Emotion regulation using virtual environments and real-time FMRI neurofeedback. Front. Neurol. **9**, 390 (2018). https://doi.org/10.3389/fneur. 2018.00390
33. Lui, J., Marcus, D., Barry, C.: Evidence-based apps? A review of mental health mobile applications in a psychotherapy context. Prof. Psychol.: Res. Pract. **48**(3), 199 (2017). https://doi.org/10.1037/pro0000122
34. Lukoff, K., Lyngs, U., Gueorguieva, S., Dillman, E.S., Hiniker, A., Munson, S.A.: From ancient contemplative practice to the app store: designing a digital container for mindfulness. In: Proceedings of the 2020 ACM Designing Interactive Systems Conference, DIS 2020, pp. 1551–1564. Association for Computing Machinery, New York (2020). https://doi.org/10.1145/3357236.3395444
35. Mani, M., Kavanagh, D., Hides, L., Stoyanov, S.: Review and evaluation of mindfulness-based iPhone apps. J. Med. Internet Res. **3**, e4328 (2015). https:// doi.org/10.2196/mhealth.4328

36. Matthews, J., Win, K., Oinas-Kukkonen, H., Freeman, M.: Persuasive technology in mobile applications promoting physical activity: a systematic review. J. Med. Syst. **40**, 72 (2016). https://doi.org/10.1007/s10916-015-0425-x
37. Matzka, C.: Moodistory mood tracker, diary on the app store (2018). https://apps.apple.com/us/app/moodistory-mood-tracker-diary/id1335347860. Accessed 17 Sep 2020
38. Meemo Media Inc.: Bloom: Cbt therapy & self-care on the app store (2019). https://apps.apple.com/us/app/bloom-cbt-therapy-self-care/id1475128511. Accessed 17 Sep 2020
39. Meuleman, B., Rudrauf, D.: Induction and profiling of strong multi-componential emotions in virtual reality. IEEE Trans. Affect. Comput. **007**, 2411–2502 (2018). https://doi.org/10.1109/TAFFC.2018.2864730
40. Meyerbröker, K., Emmelkamp, P.: Virtual reality exposure therapy for anxiety disorders: the state of the art. Adv. Comput. Intell. Paradig. Healthc. 6. Virtual Real. Psychother. Rehabil. Assess. **337**, 47–62 (2011). https://doi.org/10.1007/978-3-642-17824-5_4
41. Navarro Haro, M., et al.: The use of virtual reality to facilitate mindfulness skills training in dialectical behavioral therapy for borderline personality disorder: a case study. Front. Psychol. **7**, 1573 (2016). https://doi.org/10.3389/fpsyg.2016.01573
42. O'Loughlin, K., Neary, M., Adkins, E., Schueller, S.: Reviewing the data security and privacy policies of mobile apps for depression. Internet Interv. **15**, 110–115 (2018). https://doi.org/10.1016/j.invent.2018.12.001
43. Panksepp, J.: Affective Neuroscience: The Foundations of Human and Animal Emotions. Oxford University Press, Oxford (1998)
44. Plate, A., Aldao, A.: Emotion regulation in cognitive behavioral therapy: bridging the gap between treatment studies and laboratory experiments, pp. 107–127 (2017). https://doi.org/10.1016/B978-0-12-803457-6.00005-2
45. Posner, J., Russell, J.A., Peterson, B.S.: The circumplex model of affect: an integrative approach to affective neuroscience, cognitive development, and psychopathology. Dev. Psychopathol. **17**(3), 715–734 (2005). https://doi.org/10.1017/S0954579405050340
46. Quesnel, D., Stepanova, E., Aguilar, I., Pennefather, P., Riecke, B.: Creating awe: artistic and scientific practices in research-based design for exploring a profound immersive installation, pp. 1–207 (2018). https://doi.org/10.1109/GEM.2018.8516463
47. Redwheel Apps: Gratitude plus: Journal (2019). https://apps.apple.com/us/app/gratitude-plus-journal/id1447851477. Accessed 17 Sep 2020
48. Riva, G., Waterworth, J.A.: Being present in a virtual world. In: Mark, G. (ed.) The Oxford Handbook of Virtuality, pp. 205–221. Oxford University Press (2014)
49. Seligman, M.: PERMA and the building blocks of well-being. J. Posit. Psychol. **13**(4), 333–335 (2018). https://doi.org/10.1080/17439760.2018.1437466
50. Slovák, P., Fitzpatrick, G.: Teaching and developing social and emotional skills with technology. ACM Trans. Comput.-Hum. Interact. **22**(4), 1–34 (2015). https://doi.org/10.1145/2744195
51. Soyka, F., Leyrer, M., Smallwood, J., Ferguson, C., Riecke, B.E., Mohler, B.J.: Enhancing stress management techniques using virtual reality. In: Proceedings of the ACM Symposium on Applied Perception, SAP 2016, pp. 85–88. Association for Computing Machinery, New York (2016). https://doi.org/10.1145/2931002.2931017 SAP '16
52. Srivastava, P., Panday, R.: Psychoeducation an effective tool as treatment modality in mental health. Int. J. Indian Psychol. **4**, 123–130 (2017)

53. Stawarz, K., Preist, C., Tallon, D., Wiles, N., Coyle, D.: User experience of cognitive behavioral therapy apps for depression: an analysis of app functionality and user reviews. J. Med. Internet Res. **20**(6), e10120 (2018). https://doi.org/10.2196/10120
54. Success Wizard, Inc.: Happiness (2013). https://apps.apple.com/au/app/happiness-mindfulness-journal/id767467127. Accessed 17 Sep 2020
55. Teo, V.: Prana vr (2017). https://www.youtube.com/watch?v=FnxzUyudh_4. Accessed 17 Sep 2020
56. Thornicroft, G.: Stigma and discrimination limit access to mental health care. Epidemiologia e psichiatria sociale **17**, 14–9 (2008). https://doi.org/10.1017/S1121189X00002621
57. Tichon, J.G., Mavin, T.: Using the experience of evoked emotion in virtual reality to manage workplace stress: affective control theory (act) (2019). https://doi.org/10.4018/978-1-5225-8356-1.ch011
58. Tielman, M.L., Neerincx, M.A., Bidarra, R., Kybartas, B., Brinkman, W.P.: A therapy system for post-traumatic stress disorder using a virtual agent and virtual storytelling to reconstruct traumatic memories. J. Med. Syst. **41**(8), 1–10 (2017). https://doi.org/10.1007/s10916-017-0771-y
59. Torous, J., Myrick, J., Rauseo-Ricupero, N., Firth, J.: Digital mental health and COVID-19: using technology today to accelerate the curve on access and quality tomorrow. JMIR Ment. Health **7**, 18848 (2020). https://doi.org/10.2196/18848
60. Torous, J., Nicholas, J., Larsen, M., Firth, J., Christensen, H.: Clinical review of user engagement with mental health smartphone apps: evidence, theory and improvements. Evid. Based Ment. Health **21**, 116–119 (2018). https://doi.org/10.1136/eb-2018-102891
61. Veraki Inc.: Veraki - personal growth on the app store (2020). https://apps.apple.com/us/app/veraki-personal-growth/id1485751764. Accessed 17 Sep 2020
62. Voigt-Antons, J.N., Spang, R., Kojić, T., Meier, L., Vergari, M., Möller, S.: Don't worry be happy - using virtual environments to induce emotional states measured by subjective scales and heart rate parameters. In: 2021 IEEE Virtual Reality and 3D User Interfaces (VR), pp. 679–686 (2021). https://doi.org/10.1109/VR50410.2021.00094
63. Wang, K., Varma, D., Prosperi, M.: A systematic review of the effectiveness of mobile apps for monitoring and management of mental health symptoms or disorders. J. Psychiatr. Res. **107**, 73–78 (2018). https://doi.org/10.1016/j.jpsychires.2018.10.006
64. Windwer, M.: Moodtrack social diary (2018). https://play.google.com/store/apps/details?id=com.moodtrak.diary&hl=en_GB. Accessed 17 Sep 2020
65. Woodward, K., et al.: Beyond mobile apps: a survey of technologies for mental well-being. IEEE Trans. Affect. Comput. 21 (2020). https://doi.org/10.1109/TAFFC.2020.3015018
66. World Health Organization: Promoting mental health (2004). https://www.who.int/mental_health/evidence/en/promoting_mhh.pdf

# Methods for User Studies

# BRIDGE: Administering Small Anonymous Longitudinal HCI Studies with Snowball-Type Sampling

Frode Eika Sandnes[1,2(✉)] (iD)

[1] Oslo Metropolitan University, 0130 Oslo, Norway
frodes@oslomet.no
[2] Kristiania University College, 0153 Oslo, Norway

**Abstract.** When following participants across multiple sessions one needs a way to link the different session records while protecting the participants' privacy. Privacy is required by recent legislation such as the General Data Protection Regulation (GDPR). Many anonymous linking methods have been proposed, but these involve effort from the participants, involve long IDs, or require all participants to be known a priori. This study presents the BRIDGE procedure for anonymous linking of participant records with dynamically increasing samples. The procedure relies on human intervention to resolve ambiguous cases using manual recognition challenges. Simulation results show that the procedure can successfully map participant names to short and unique anonymous IDs, and that the percentage of human interventions is low. The procedure holds potential for HCI researchers who need to employ simple, flexible, and incremental sampling strategies while protecting participants' privacy.

**Keywords:** Privacy · Longitudinal · GDPR · Record linking · Snowball sampling

## 1 Introduction

Participants' anonymity is a key concern for HCI experimenters. No information should be recorded that directly identifies the participant including their name, phone number, IP-address, voice, photos, video, or information that can indirectly reveal participants' identity such as demographic or geographic patterns. Anonymity is especially essential when recruiting participants with disabilities [1–3]. Anonymity is usually not a challenge when administering experiments that can be conducted in single sessions [4]. However, the challenge arises once the experimenter needs to follow participants over time. For example, pre/post-test experiments [5] may require results from two sessions to be linked to perform pairwise analysis. Longitudinal studies [6–8] follow participants over time

---

**Electronic supplementary material** The online version of this chapter (https://doi.org/10.1007/978-3-030-85610-6_17) contains supplementary material, which is available to authorized users.

© IFIP International Federation for Information Processing 2021
Published by Springer Nature Switzerland AG 2021
C. Ardito et al. (Eds.): INTERACT 2021, LNCS 12935, pp. 287–297, 2021.
https://doi.org/10.1007/978-3-030-85610-6_17

to observe how participants learn a particular interaction mechanism [9, 10]. To analyze the data, the session observations need to be linked.

Obviously, labelling the observations from each session with the participants name is not an option unless strict regimes are in place to protect the data. Traditionally, experimenters employed linking tables where each participant is assigned a unique running number. Observations were labelled with these IDs and the linking table was kept separate and confidential. This allowed observations to be shared or made public while keeping the identity of the participants anonymous. Stakeholders were later able to link data from different sessions without knowing the identity of the participant. However, if the linking table is leaked, the privacy of the participants is compromised. Privacy legislation such as GDPR regulates the storage of personal information. Typically, experimenters need to apply for formal permissions to administer such tables and document that there are convincing safeguards in place and reliable procedures for disposing the tables at the end of the project. Obtaining formal permissions can be time-consuming and daunting for students and HCI researchers who are administering their first experiments. One potential consequence may be that the experimental design is altered so that it can be conducted anonymously in a single session. This is unfortunate if the research question warrants the participants to be followed over time.

Self-generated codes [11] is one approach for overcoming this challenge, where each session starts with the participants answering a questionnaire where the responses are used to generate IDs that are unique to each participant. Unfortunately, self-generated codes divert valuable time and effort away from the experiment. The other approach involves Bloom filters [12] which is a type of hash function that are robust to input errors. The participants' names are applied to a series of Bloom filters and the result is assigned the observations from the session. Bloom filter IDs are typically long (1000 bits) and may be impractical to handle manually (low usability). It has also been shown that the basic Bloom filter approach is vulnerable to systematic attacks [13].

The HIDE procedure [14] attempts to overcome the problem of long IDs, while allowing the IDs to be generated on-the-fly without collisions and intervention from the participants. One key constraint is that HIDE configuration requires all the participants to be known in advance. In practice, an experimenter may have to recruit participants incrementally. For example, snowball sampling is often employed by HCI researchers where the experimenter expands the sample of participants using the network of the already recruited participants. HIDE does not facilitate snowball sampling.

This study therefore proposes the BRIDGE procedure, which allows experiments to be administered with incremental snowball-type sampling while generating short IDs. Names that lead to collisions are resolved manually using recognition challenges. Simulations were used to measure the practical limitations of the procedure.

## 2 Related Work

Strategies for record linkage and related work are summarized in Table 1 with five key characteristics including anonymity, robustness to error, perceived trust, effort from participants and dynamic expansion. The most important characteristic is the capability to protect participants' privacy and maintain anonymity. Robustness to error has also been discussed in the literature [11, 14] as incorrect record linkage may bias the results [15]. Participants' names may for instance be incorrectly transcribed. A linkage procedure that relies on exact matching is therefore vulnerable. Participants' trust in the procedure affects participants' willingness to participate in experiments [16]. Trust and participants' experience with linking procedures have received little attention. Related to participants' trust is also the effort required from the participants. Recruiting participants can be hard and experimenters must balance the size of the tasks against what is realistic to expect given people's general impatience. Clearly, the goal is to prevent diverting attention away from the experiment. Finally, a linkage procedure may be open or closed. An open procedure allows new participants to be added dynamically, while a closed procedure requires all participants to be known a priori.

**Table 1.** Characteristics of record linkage approaches.

| Method | Anonymity | Robust | Trust | Effort | Flexible |
|--------|-----------|--------|-------|--------|----------|
| Direct labelling | None | Yes | None | None | Open |
| Linking table | Risky | Yes | Low | None | Open |
| Participants remember ID | Strong | No | High | Medium | Open |
| Anonymous login | Strong | No | High | High | Open |
| Self-generated ID [17] | Strong | Yes | High | High | Open |
| Auto-generated ID [26] | Weak | No | Low | None | Open |
| Phonetic encoding [27] | Weak | Yes | High | None | Open |
| Ordinary hash [33] | Weak | No | Low | None | Open |
| Bloom filter [5] | Strong | Yes | Low | None | Open |
| Perfect minimal hash | Unknown | No | High | None | Closed |
| HIDE [14] | Strong | Yes | High | None | Closed |

Clearly, labelling data sets with the identity of the participants is straightforward but does not provide anonymity nor contribute to the participants' trust [16]. Linking tables are also simple to administer and do provide anonymity if the linking table is kept private, but participants' privacy is compromised if the linking table is lost.

Another approach is to randomly generate IDs and ask participants to remember their own ID. When the participant attends a session, they must produce their unique ID. This approach is simple and provides anonymity, but there is a risk that they unintentionally or intentionally report an incorrect ID. More importantly, participants may forget their ID, or if they write it down, lose the note. Sometimes it may be possible for participants to identify themselves using some third-party login credentials (such as national authentication schemes, social media accounts, etc.). However, such schemes require that participants have access to credentials, are willing to use their credentials, remember their credentials, or are willing to create an account if they do not have one.

To reduce the participants' memory load various procedures for self-generated codes have been proposed [17–23]. A self-generated code is generated by combining the answers to a questionnaire, for example the third letter of the name of the participant's mother, the number of siblings, the month of birth, etc. Each session is typically started by generating the code using the questionnaire. Clearly, this diverts valuable effort and time away from the experiment itself. Moreover, the questions should result in consistent responses. Self-generated codes have been found to be problematic in certain situations [24], vulnerable to errors [11] and vulnerable to attacks [25].

Other methods involve generating IDs using information about the participants, typically their name, birthdate, gender, or other available information [26]. Early work employed phonetic simplifications of the participants' names using Soundex [27–30], whereby the spelling of a name is converted to brief phonetic codes. The advantage of such schemes is that they are robust to certain types of errors, i.e., vowels and double letters are discarded, and consonants are assigned into coarse grained categories of similar sounding sounds such as $b, f, p$ and $v$. Matching is possible even if a consonant is substituted for a similar sounding consonant. Although phonetic coding are lossy processes, they do not provide anonymity, unless specific mechanisms are employed such as adding fake records [31]. Phonetic methods are also known for resulting in high false positive rates [32]. Hashing is another method for generating unique IDs [33] and phonetic methods have been extended to improve anonymity [34, 35]. Although it is not possible to identify the person from a hash the identity can be discovered if searching for the ID using a list of names (phonebook attack). Hashes are therefore not anonymous. In fact, hashes can be used to confirm that a person participated in an experiment.

Much of the literature published during the last decade has evolved around various Bloom filter approaches [12, 36]. A Bloom filter employs a series of different hash functions to the bigrams (pairs of letters) making up the participants' names. These hash functions set certain bits in a bit vector. Matches are performed by comparing these bit vectors, and degrees of similarity is related to the number of matching bits. The strength of Bloom filters is their robustness to input errors and their flexible deployment at a large scale. They are therefore used in the domain of automatic record linkage. However, Bloom filters have been identified as being vulnerable to attacks [37–40]. Bloom filters generate long IDs, typically 1000 bits, or 250 hex characters. Hash sequences of 250 characters may seem overwhelming compared to running numbers which typically comprise two or three digits. The concept of mapping a set of names to running numbers is analogous to what is achieved with minimal perfect hash functions [41, 42]. However, minimal perfect hashing requires all records to be known a priori and a hash table needs to be stored. Research has shown that the average hash table entry is short (less than 2 bits) [41, 42]. However, to the best of our knowledge, perfect minimal hash functions have not been applied to record linking. Inspired by minimal perfect hash functions the HIDE procedure generates close to running numbers [14]. Instead of running numbers, the range of numbers is expanded with the benefit of not needing a hash table. This procedure first alphabetically sorts the part of the participants' names (first, middle and family name) and then phonetically encodes the name using Soundex, making the procedure robust to many types of input errors. A salt, i.e., a random text, is added to the phonetic representation and the result is hashed. The ID is obtained by truncating the hash. This truncation step provides anonymity in that different names will yield the same

ID. The initialization step of HIDE searches for a salt that provides minimum length unique IDs for a list of names.

The goal of this proposal was to reap the benefits of HIDE while facilitating dynamic inclusion of participants. This study focuses on small experiments with less than 100 participants as HCI experiments typically are small (often just 12 participants) [44].

## 3   The BRIDGE Procedure

The procedure proposed herein builds on the HIDE procedure [14]. First, the participant's name is sanitized for non-alphabetical symbols (hyphens, dots, etc.) and then split into first name, middle name, and family name. These parts are sorted alphabetically (tolerant to different name orderings). Next, the name is phonetically coded using Soundex, but without the four-symbol limit. The Soundex representation is then hashed (using djb2). Finally, the resulting hash is truncated by retaining the $d$ last digits. These $d$ digits comprise the participant's ID. An encoding example is shown in Fig. 1.

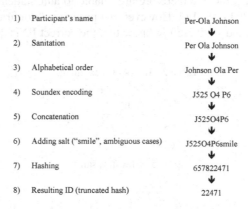

**Fig. 1.** BRIDGE encoding steps.

We assume that the experimenter knows if they encounter a new or a returning participant. Each time a new participant is added the resulting ID is stored in a list of IDs. If the ID already exists, the collision needs to be resolved. This is achieved by searching for a salt that results in an ID that is not already occupied. The salt is a simple text string (based on a list of common English words) that is added to the Soundex representation prior to hashing (see Fig. 1). The identified salt is then associated with the original ID. The experimenter and/or participant is asked to remember that they will be challenged with this word (the salt) in the future.

The IDs of returning participants are looked up as follows. First, the ID is encoded using the procedure above. If there is no salt associated with the resulting ID $A$ there is no collision, and the correct ID has been identified as $A$. If there is a salt identified with the ID, the procedure first attempts to resolve the ambiguity automatically. If the IDs $B$, $C$, $D$, etc., obtained by encoding the participants name with the salts listed, does not match any IDs on the list we can be certain that the original ID $A$ belongs to the participant.

However, if one of the salts leads to a match, we cannot be certain which ID is correct, and the experimenter needs to be consulted. The experimenter is then confronted with the salts, and the experimenter and/or participant must determine if they previously were given the task of remembering any of these salts. If this participant were not asked to remember the salt, we know that the original ID *A* is correct. Otherwise, if the participant recognizes one of the salts (if there are more than one), the ID is given by resulting ID *B*, *C*, *D*, etc., resulting from applying the recognized salt.

Table 2 shows an example ID table with two salts (three collisions). Imagine we want to find the ID of "Per-Ola Johnson". We first computed the ID which is 22471. The table shows that there are no salts listed for this ID, and we have a unique match. Next, imagine we want to find the ID of "Lena Hansson". We first computed the ID 99175. This ID is associated with two salts. We then compute the IDs of "Lena Hansson" with the two salts and get 82023 and 61955, respectively. As none of these IDs are listed, we have identified the unique ID of "Lena Hansson" as being 99175.

Next, imagine we look up the ID of "Gunnar Green" in another session and find that the corresponding ID 99175 has two salts. We find that when applying the salt "sand" we get the valid ID 26294. We therefore are unable to automatically determine if the participants ID is 26294 or 99175. However, the participant confirms that she was told to remember "sand", and we therefore know that the correct ID is 26294.

**Table 2.** ID lookup example.

| ID | Salts |
| --- | --- |
| 22471 | |
| 26294 | |
| 99175 | Elevator, sand |
| 32512 | |

## 4  Method

To assess the proposed procedure a simulation was conducted as this allowed many cases to be evaluated. The lists of names used in [14] derived from [44] were chosen as base populations of which random samples could be drawn. A few errors in the lists were removed and the resulting list comprised 103,472 unique names.

Sample sizes were varied from 5 to 95 in increments of 5 participants, and the ID lengths were varied from 1 to 7 digits. Clearly, the simulations were not performed for sample sizes above 10 with one digit as it is not possible to uniquely map more than 10 participants using one decimal digit. For each configuration, the simulation was repeated 10,000 times, each time with a random draw of participants. The goal of the simulation was to determine the success rate of the BRIDGE procedure, the manual intervention rate, and how many ambiguous cases that could occur at once. The simulations were written in Java.

## 5  Results

The simulation results show the BRIDGE procedure was able to successfully resolve all
IDs (100% success rate). This simulation assumed that the experimenter and participant
responded correctly to the challenges.

Figure 2 shows the probability of having to manually intervene with BRIDGE under
different conditions. A log-linear plot was chosen to emphasize the small probabilities.
The probability of having to manually intervene increased linearly with the sample size.
Moreover, the rate of increase was strongly related to the length of the ID. With IDs
comprising 1 or 2 digits the probability of manually having to resolve ambiguities was
relatively high (more than 20% with more than 20 participants). With IDs comprising
3 digits, the probability of less than 14% with 95 participants, and less than 1% with
20 participants or fewer. With 4 digits the probability of manual intervention did not
exceed 0.4%, and with 5 digits this probability did not exceed 0.05%. The reductions in
the probability for manual intervention is marginal with 6 and 7 digits.

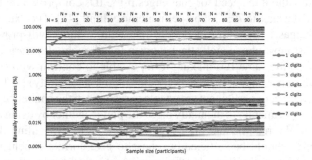

**Fig. 2.** Log-linear plot of manual resolution percentages with BRIDGE for different ID lengths
(10,000 trials, zero values for 6- and 7-digit lines are not shown in the log-plot).

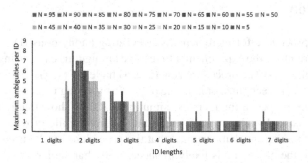

**Fig. 3.** Maximum number of ambiguities per ID as a function of ID length and sample size (10,000
trials).

Figure 3 shows the maximum number of ambiguities observed for each configuration. Note that 1 ambiguity means there are two items that need to be resolved, with 2
ambiguities there is a set of 3 ambiguous items, etc. The plot shows that the maximum

number of ambiguities is related to the length of the IDs. With a length of 1 digit the maximum number of ambiguities is 4 and 5, and with 2 digits the maximum number of ambiguities ranges from 8 to 2, where the maximum number of ambiguities is higher for larger samples. With 3 digits the max ranged from 2 to 4, while with 4 or more digits the max never exceeded 2. With 5 digits there were mostly a max of one ambiguity.

## 6  Discussion

The simulation results demonstrate that the procedure is successfully capable of establishing a unique mapping between participants and the IDs, and the short ID codes ensure that this mapping is anonymous. The procedure assumes that the experimenter and or participants can resolve the manual challenges. These challenges rely on recognition which is less demanding than recall. It is much easier to recognize a word you have been told to remember than to recall the same word.

However, the simulations show that the procedure in more than 99% of cases can be administered without the need for challenges if the IDs comprise 5 digits. IDs with 5 digits are within the classic $7 \pm 2$ short-term memory limit [45]. The extent of manually resolving challenges is therefore moderate. IDs with 5 digits will provide sufficient protection against most phonebook attacks, given the phonebook is large, since several names will lead to the same IDs making it impossible to confirm with certainty that a given person was a participant in an experiment (high k-anonymity) [46].

If the experimenter or participant are unable to respond to the challenge, it may still be possible for the experimenter to manually piece the parts together by using a combination of timestamps in the records and the experimenter's memory. Failing that, statistical testing procedures should be sufficiently robust to give correct conclusions with two incorrectly linked data points, provided the sample size is sufficiently large. Alternatively, the experimenter may choose to discard such observations from the analysis.

## 7  Conclusion

The BRIDGE procedure for incrementally generating anonymous IDs was presented. The procedure requires the experimenter to resolve ambiguous cases using manual word recognition challenges. The procedure generates a challenge (salt) that the experimenter and/or the participant recognize or not. The phonetic encoding means that the procedure is robust to several types of input errors. Simulation results show that IDs with 5 digits results in less than a 1% chance of manual intervention, while providing a high level of anonymity. Simulations demonstrated that the procedure can be used with up to 95 participants, but the procedure is likely to successfully handle larger sample sizes. An implementation of the procedure is available as a browser-based tool (https://www.cs.osl omet.no/~frodes/BRIDGE/). The source is also available at (https://github.com/frode-sandnes/BRIDGE). Future work involves developing a scheme for resolving collisions automatically.

# References

1. Berget, G., Mulvey, F., Sandnes, F.E.: Is visual content in textual search interfaces beneficial to dyslexic users? Int. J. Hum.-Comput. Stud. **92**, 17–29 (2016)
2. dos Santos, A.D.P., Medola, F.O., Cinelli, M.J., Garcia Ramirez, A.R., Sandnes, F.E.: Are electronic white canes better than traditional canes? A comparative study with blind and blindfolded participants. Univ. Access Inf. Soc. **20**(1), 93–103 (2020). https://doi.org/10.1007/s10209-020-00712-z
3. Sankhi, P., Sandnes, F.E.: A glimpse into smartphone screen reader use among blind teenagers in rural Nepal. Disab. Rehabil. Assist. Technol. (2020)
4. Aschim, T.B., Gjerstad, J.L., Lien, L.V., Tahsin, R., Sandnes, F.E.: Are split tablet keyboards better? A study of soft keyboard layout and hand posture. In: Lamas, D., Loizides, F., Nacke, L., Petrie, H., Winckler, M., Zaphiris, P. (eds.) INTERACT 2019. LNCS, vol. 11748, pp. 647–655. Springer, Cham (2019). https://doi.org/10.1007/978-3-030-29387-1_37
5. Kaushik, H.M., Eika, E., Sandnes, F.E.: Towards universal accessibility on the web: do grammar checking tools improve text readability? In: Antona, M., Stephanidis, C. (eds.) HCII 2020. LNCS, vol. 12188, pp. 272–288. Springer, Cham (2020). https://doi.org/10.1007/978-3-030-49282-3_19
6. Vissers, J., De Bot, L., Zaman, B.: MemoLine: evaluating long-term UX with children. In: Proceedings of the 12th International Conference Interaction Design and Children, pp. 285–288. ACM, New York (2013)
7. Jain, J., Boyce, S.: Case study: longitudinal comparative analysis for analyzing user behavior. In: CHI 2012 Extended Abstracts, pp. 793–800. ACM, New York (2012).
8. Karapanos, E., Zimmerman, J., Forlizzi, J., Martens, J.B.: User experience over time: an initial framework. In: Proceedings of the SIGCHI CHI 2009 Conference, pp. 729–738. ACM, New York (2009)
9. Ye, L., Sandnes, F.E., MacKenzie, I.S.: QB-Gest: qwerty bimanual gestural input for eyes-free smartphone text input. In: Antona, M., Stephanidis, C. (eds.) HCII 2020. LNCS, vol. 12188, pp. 223–242. Springer, Cham (2020). https://doi.org/10.1007/978-3-030-49282-3_16
10. Sandnes, F.E.: Can spatial mnemonics accelerate the learning of text input chords? In: Proceedings of the Working Conference on Advanced Visual Interfaces, pp. 245–249. ACM, New York (2006)
11. Schnell, R., Bachteler, T., Reiher, J.: Improving the use of self-generated identification codes. Eval. Rev. **34**(5), 391–418 (2010)
12. Schnell, R., Bachteler, T., Reiher, J.: Privacy-preserving record linkage using bloom filters. BMC Med. Informat. Decis. Mak. **9**(1) (2009)
13. Christen, P., Schnell, R., Vatsalan, D., Ranbaduge, T.: Efficient cryptanalysis of bloom filters for privacy-preserving record linkage. In: Kim, J., Shim, K., Cao, L., Lee, J.-G., Lin, X., Moon, Y.-S. (eds.) PAKDD 2017. LNCS (LNAI), vol. 10234, pp. 628–640. Springer, Cham (2017). https://doi.org/10.1007/978-3-319-57454-7_49
14. Sandnes, F.E.: HIDE: short IDs for robust and anonymous linking of users across multiple sessions in small HCI experiments. In: CHI 2021 Conference on Human Factors in Computing Systems Extended Abstracts Proceedings. ACM, New York (2021)
15. Harron, K., et al.: Challenges in administrative data linkage for research. Big Data Soc. **4**(2) (2017)
16. Audrey, S., Brown, L., Campbell, R., Boyd, A., Macleod, J.: Young people's views about consenting to data linkage: findings from the PEARL qualitative study. BMC Med. Res. Method. **16**(1) (2016). https://doi.org/10.1186/s12874-016-0132-4
17. Yurek, L.A., Vasey, J., Sullivan Havens, D.: The use of self-generated identification codes in longitudinal research. Eval. Rev. **32**(5), 435–452 (2008)

18. Damrosch, S.P.: Ensuring anonymity by use of subject-generated identification codes. Res. Nurs. Health **9**(1), 61–63 (1986). https://doi.org/10.1002/nur.4770090110
19. DiIorio, C., Soet, J.E., Van Marter, D., Woodring, T.M., Dudley, W.N.: An evaluation of a self-generated identification code. Res. Nurs. Health **23**(2), 167–174 (2000)
20. Grube, J.W., Morgan, M., Kearney, K.A.: Using self-generated identification codes to match questionnaires in panel studies of adolescent substance use. Addict. Behav. **14**(2), 159–171 (1989). https://doi.org/10.1016/0306-4603(89)90044-0
21. Kearney, K.A., Hopkins, R.H., Mauss, A.L., Weisheit, R.A.: Self-generated identification codes for anonymous collection of longitudinal questionnaire data. Public Opin. Q. **48**(1B), 370–378 (1984). https://doi.org/10.1093/poq/48.1B.370
22. Vacek, J., Vonkova, H., Gabrhelík, R.: A successful strategy for linking anonymous data from students' and parents' questionnaires using self-generated identification codes. Prev. Sci. **18**(4), 450–458 (2017). https://doi.org/10.1007/s11121-017-0772-6
23. Lippe, M., Johnson, B., Carter, P.: Protecting student anonymity in research using a subject-generated identification code. J. Prof. Nurs. **35**(2), 120–123 (2019)
24. Galanti, M.R., Siliquini, R., Cuomo, L., Melero, J.C., Panella, M., Faggiano, F.: Testing anonymous link procedures for follow-up of adolescents in a school-based trial: the EU-DAP pilot study. Prevent. Med. **44**(2), 174–177 (2007)
25. McGloin, J., Holcomb, S., Main, D.S.: Matching anonymous pre-posttests using subject-generated information. Eval. Rev. **20**(6), 724–736 (1996)
26. Thoben, W., Appelrath, H. J., Sauer, S.: Record linkage of anonymous data by control numbers. In: From Data to Knowledge, pp. 412–419. Springer, Heidelberg (1996)
27. Friedman, C., Sideli, R.: Tolerating spelling errors during patient validation. Comput. Biomed. Res. **25**(5), 486–509 (1992). https://doi.org/10.1016/0010-4809(92)90005-U
28. Mortimer, J.Y., Salathiel, J.A.: 'Soundex' codes of surnames provide confidentiality and accuracy in a national HIV database. Commun. Dis. Rep. CDR Rev. **5**(12), R183–R186 (1995)
29. Rogers, H.J., Willett, P.: Searching for historical word forms in text databases using spelling-correction methods: reverse error and phonetic coding methods. J. Document. **47**(4), 333–353 (1991). https://doi.org/10.1108/eb026883
30. Holmes, D., McCabe, M.C.: Improving precision and recall for soundex retrieval. In: Proceedings of the International Conference on Information Technology: Coding and Computing, pp. 22–26. IEEE (2002)
31. Karakasidis, A., Verykios, V.S., Christen, P.: Fake injection strategies for private phonetic matching. In: Garcia-Alfaro, J., Navarro-Arribas, G., Cuppens-Boulahia, N., de Capitani di Vimercati, S. (eds.) DPM/SETOP -2011. LNCS, vol. 7122, pp. 9–24. Springer, Heidelberg (2012). https://doi.org/10.1007/978-3-642-28879-1_2
32. Camps, R., Daudé, J.: Improving the efficacy of approximate searching by personal-name. In: Natural Language Processing and Information Systems. Bonn, Germany (2003)
33. Johnson, S.B., Whitney, G., McAuliffe, M., Wang, H., et al.: Using global unique identifiers to link autism collections. J. Am. Med. Inform. Assoc. **17**(6), 689–695 (2010)
34. Bouzelat, H., Quantin, C., Dusserre, L.: Extraction and anonymity protocol of medical file. In: Proceedings of the AMIA Annual Fall Symposium, pp. 323–327. AMIA, Bethesda (1996)
35. Quantin, C., et al.: Decision analysis for the assessment of a record linkage procedure. Methods Inf. Med. **44**(1), 72–79 (2005)
36. Benhamiche, A.M., Faivre, J.: Automatic record hash coding and linkage for epidemiological. Methods Inform. Med. **37**, 271–278 (1998)
37. Durham, E.A., Kantarcioglu, M., Xue, Y., Toth, C., Kuzu, M., Malin, B.: Composite bloom filters for secure record linkage. IEEE Trans. Knowl. Data Eng. **26**(12), 2956–2968 (2013)
38. Kroll, M., Steinmetzer, S.: Automated cryptanalysis of bloom filter encryptions of health records. German Record Linkage Center, Working Papers, No. WP-GRLC-2014-05 (2014)

39. Randall, S.M., Ferrante, A.M., Boyd, J.H., Bauer, J.K., Semmens, J.B.: Privacy-preserving record linkage on large real world datasets. J. Biomed. Inform. **50**, 205–212 (2014)
40. Niedermeyer, F., Steinmetzer, S., Kroll, M., Schnell, R.: Cryptanalysis of basic bloom filters used for privacy preserving record linkage. German Record Linkage Center, Working Paper Series, No. WP-GRLC-2014-04 (2014)
41. Cichelli, R.J.: Minimal perfect hash functions made simple. Commun. ACM **23**(1), 17–19 (1980). https://doi.org/10.1145/358808.358813
42. Sager, T.J.: A polynomial time generator for minimal perfect hash functions. Commun. ACM **28**(5), 523–532 (1985). https://doi.org/10.1145/3532.3538
43. Caine, K.: Local standards for sample size at CHI. In: Proceedings of the 2016 CHI Conference on Human Factors in Computing Systems, pp. 981–992. ACM, New York (2016)
44. Ioannidis, J.P., Baas, J., Klavans, R., Boyack, K.W.: A standardized citation metrics author database annotated for scientific field. PLoS Biol. **17**(8), e3000384 (2019)
45. Miller, G.A.: The magical number seven, plus or minus two: some limits on our capacity for processing information. Psychol. Rev. **63**(2), 81–97 (1956)
46. Sweeney, L.: k-anonymity: a model for protecting privacy. Int. J. Uncert. Fuzz. Knowl.-Based Syst. **10**(05), 557–570 (2002)

# Detecting and Explaining Usability Issues of Consumer Electronic Products

Dario Benvenuti, Emanuele Buda, Francesca Fraioli, Andrea Marrella<sup>(✉)</sup>, and Tiziana Catarci

Sapienza Universitá di Roma, Rome, Italy
{d.benvenuti,marrella,catarci}@diag.uniroma1.it
{buda.1775383,fraioli.1696638}@studenti.uniroma1.it

**Abstract.** Usability of a consumer electronic product (CEP) is one of the most important factors that the users consider in purchasing a CEP as well as functionality, price, etc. This has led many companies to realize new shapes of user interfaces (UIs) and styles of interaction for CEPs, ranging from modern touchscreens to physical controls and displays of any kind. Even if the general feeling is that such increased interactivity may enhance the overall user experience, the side effect is that often a CEP's UI provides too many functions that are difficult to learn and use without referring to the user manual, leading to many usability issues. In this paper, we leverage a case study in the CEPs sector to present a novel log-based evaluation technique in the field of Human-Computer Interaction (HCI). Our technique allows us not only to keep track of the user interactions with a CEP's UI during its daily use, but also to understand what has gone wrong during a user interaction, detecting which user actions have caused usability issues and suggesting explanations for solving them, thus providing a crucial feedback to improve the design of the CEP's UI next version.

**Keywords:** Usability of consumer electronic products (CEPs) · Log study · User interface (UI) Log · Interaction model · Trace alignment · Heuristic evaluation

## 1 Introduction

In the last years, there was a rising interest in the integration of Internet-of-Things (IoT) in connected home devices, giving a new lease of life to Consumer Electronic Products (CEPs), which have now functionalities like sensing, actuation, and control [45]. They are often connected to the manufacturer's network via the internet and can send information about product performance, usage trends, and energy consumption. For example, a smart CEP with IoT capabilities like a washing machine has many sensors across its body. It can transmit log data such as water usage, the health of the appliance, ambient and water temperature to the manufacturer. These data are then used by manufacturer designers and software engineers to predict product malfunction, plan for repairs

© IFIP International Federation for Information Processing 2021
Published by Springer Nature Switzerland AG 2021
C. Ardito et al. (Eds.): INTERACT 2021, LNCS 12935, pp. 298–319, 2021.
https://doi.org/10.1007/978-3-030-85610-6_18

and update the custom software made, improving at the same time the design of the next product. For this reason, today major CEP companies use to employ expert analysts to reveal important insights from log data [8].

A not yet well explored knowledge that is recorded into log data concerns the concrete user interactions with the User Interface (UI) of a CEP, which could be exploited by expert analysts to compute the usability of a CEP's UI during its daily use. In the Human-Computer Interaction (HCI) field, usability is the key feature to capture the quality of an interaction with a UI in terms of measurable parameters such as time taken to (and learn how to) perform relevant tasks and number of errors made [4].

Since usability of a CEP is one of the most important factors that the users consider in purchasing a CEP as well as functionality, price, etc. [26], many companies started to realize new shapes of UIs and styles of interaction for CEPs, ranging from modern touchscreens to physical controls [18]. Even if the general feeling is that such increased interactivity may enhance the overall user experience, the side effect is that often a CEP's UI provides too many functions – often hidden behind many undifferentiated buttons – that are difficult to learn and use without referring to the user manual, leading to several usability issues [13]. As a matter of fact, some functions remain untouched until the end of the CEP's life, and some end users do not even recognize those functions exist [22].

To measure the usability of a UI, the HCI literature proposes several *user evaluation* techniques (the work [10] identified 95 techniques in 2003), which mainly belong to two categories: *lab studies* and *field studies*. In *lab studies*, participants are brought into a laboratory and asked to perform certain tasks of interest. Analysts can learn a lot about how participants interact with a UI, but the observed behavior happens in a controlled and artificial setting and may not be representative of what would be observed "in the wild" [23]. Alternatively, *field studies* collect data from participants conducting their own activities in their natural environments. Data collected in this way tends to be more authentic than in lab studies, but the presence of an evaluator observing what participants are doing may interfere with the natural flow of the interaction [15]. Although a wide variety of lab and field tests have been developed to measure the usability of a CEP [13,22,26], the major obstacle is that the cost and time required to conduct these studies are often too high [11], and delay the time that the CEP is introduced to the market. Note that a late CEP launch in any industry can negatively impact revenues, causing the product to become obsolete faster [43]. Moreover, usability issues can be identified mainly in the "pre-release" stage of the UI, i.e., before the CEP is launched to the market. Consequently, many usability issues remain uncovered or not comprehensively investigated until the "after-release" stage, and companies tend to fix such issues only when they are reported by the end users in form of complaints [12,20,50].

*To mitigate the above limitations, in this paper we present a novel evaluation technique that exploits log data collected during the after-release stage of a CEP to the automated identification of what goes wrong during the user interactions with the CEP's UI, detecting which user actions have caused usability issues and suggesting explanations for solving them.* Our technique is based on the concepts of *UI logs*, *interaction models*, *trace alignment* and *heuristic evaluation.*

- UI logs include the user actions (from clicks on a touchscreen to the pressure of physical buttons) recorded "in situ" as people interact with the UI of a CEP while executing a relevant task with the CEP itself (e.g., *wash laundry* with a washing machine), uninfluenced by external observers;
- Interaction models describe the expected human-computer dialogs required to properly executing relevant tasks on the UI of a CEP;
- Trace alignment verifies whether the user's "observed" behavior, which is recorded in a specific UI log, matches the "intended" behavior represented as a model of the interaction itself. A perfect alignment between the log and the interaction model is not always possible, thus making deviations be highlighted. Such deviations reflect mistakes or slips made by the user during the interaction with the CEP's UI, i.e., potential usability issues;
- A heuristic evaluation, which is conducted in the context of the CEP's relevant tasks that are under observation, is employed to derive explanations to the usability issues identified through trace alignment.

If compared with existing literature studies on log-based evaluation in HCI [8], which are mainly focused on collecting UI logs for a subsequent usability assessment performed "manually" by expert evaluators, our technique is able to automatically detect usability issues and suggest explanations to fix them directly from the analysis of the UI logs, thus not requiring the intervention of any expert in the after-release stage of a CEP. We have evaluated the effectiveness of our technique through a case study in the CEPs sector, in which the usability of a real microwave has been assessed against 44 potential end users.

The rest of the paper is organized as follows. Section 2 analyzes the previous works dealing with the usability evaluation of CEPs and investigates the existing log based studies in HCI. Section 3 introduces the main peculiarities of the case study, based on the testing of a real microwave oven currently present on the market. Section 4, after providing the relevant background to understand the paper, describes our log-based evaluation technique. Section 5 presents a user experiment performed with real users over the case study of Sect. 3, in order to assess the effectiveness of our technique. Finally, Sect. 6 concludes the paper with a critical discussion about the general applicability of the technique.

## 2   Related Work

Usability evaluation is considered an essential procedure in CEP development. However, planning and conducting such an evaluation requires considerations of a number of factors surrounding the evaluation process including the product, the user, and environmental characteristics, which are difficult to be captured with traditional lab and field studies [1,16].

For this reason, in 2001 there was an attempt to propose a novel definition of usability and of its main dimensions that could be applied to the case of

CEPs [13]. Usability was defined as *"satisfying the users in terms of both the performance and the image and impression felt by them"*, and characterized by the fact that both aspects should be treated equally important in understanding the usability of CEPs. Around this definition, in [26] a structured framework to support analysts to conduct the usability evaluation of a CEP was proposed. In 2006, the work [24] identified issues and actors with a relation to usability in the product development of CEPs. Then, in 2008, the work [22] has proposed a methodology for developing a usability index of CEPs, which consists of classifying usability dimensions, developing usability measures, and building usability index models that can be applied to check the usability of prototypes of a CEP, during their pre-release stage. More recently, in 2017, the work [25] identified practitioner-reported barriers to and enablers of usability in the development of CEPs, where barriers/enablers are conditions in the CEP development process, team, or context that negatively or positively influence the usability of a CEP.

While all the above works have had the merit of delivering useful strategies to approach the issue of measuring usability of a CEP, none of them has gone beyond proposing the use of traditional lab and field usability techniques, which can be considered appropriated to capture the usability of a CEP in its pre-release stage. Conversely, in this paper, *the target was to develop a log-based technique that may act as a valid inspection method to automatically identify and explain usability problems found in a CEP's UI during its after-release stage.*

Over the last years, there was considerable work in HCI on log based evaluations as complementary to traditional lab and field tests [8]. While the majority of literature works are targeted to exploit log analysis to profile the end users of an application for marketing purposes [27, 46] or to enable comparisons between two or more UIs (e.g., A/B testing) [29, 47], there are two relevant works [11, 38] that are closer to our technique. On the one hand, in [38] the authors present a method that supports evaluators to detect repeated patterns of user errors within log files of multiple user interactions. On the other hand, the work [11] proposes extending the Google Analytics features for mobile applications to store specific low-level user actions for logging real use after application release and perform dedicated lab usability testing. However, in both [38] and [11], the burden to evaluate the usability of the UI is left to the evaluators in the after-release stage, which can be a time consuming and error prone task in presence of UI logs keeping track of hundreds or thousands real user interactions. Conversely, in this paper we exploit UI logs for a different yet little-explored challenge, namely the *support of expert analysts in the CEP industry to conduct automated usability evaluation of a CEP during its daily use.* Our technique moves any effort of the evaluators (i.e., the definition of the interaction models and the enactment of the heuristic evaluation) in the pre-release stage. In this way, the technique is able to automatically detect usability issues and suggest explanations to fix them directly in the after-release stage, thus not requiring the intervention of any human expert in this phase.

# 3    Case Study

As a case study, we consider the working of a real microwave oven currently available on the market (cf. Fig. 1(a)), and sold by a well-known CEP company.[1] Let us imagine that the company wants to analyze if the control panel of the oven (cf. Fig. 1(b)) has the potential for improvements with regards to its UI design, in view of the realization of a new – more usable – version of the oven.

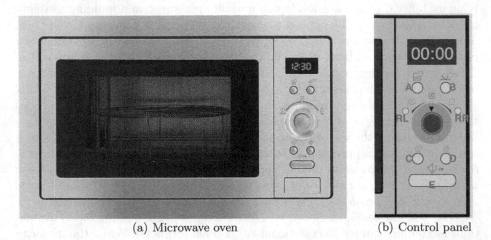

(a) Microwave oven                              (b) Control panel

**Fig. 1.** Screenshots of the microwave oven investigated in the range of case study

The control panel provides: *(i)* a display showing the current settings and time; *(ii)* a door opener mechanism; *(iii)* five clickable buttons and a setting knob, which enable to interact with the different oven's functions, as follows:

- **A** - *Function button.* To choose a specific cooking function of the oven.
- **B** - *Defrost button.* To defrost food by weight or time.
- **C** - *Clock/Timer button.* To set the clock or the timer of the oven.
- **D** - *Stop/Clear button.* To deactivate the appliance or delete the cooking settings.
- **E** - *Start/+30 s button.* To start the appliance or increase the cooking time for 30 s at full power.
- **RR/RL** - *Setting knob.* To increase/decrease the cooking time, weight or to activate the auto cooking programmes.

---

[1] The case study is just an exploration of some possible design issues of a real oven's UI. Since the authors are not affiliated in any way with the CEP company that manufactured the oven, the company name and the oven's model are not disclosed.

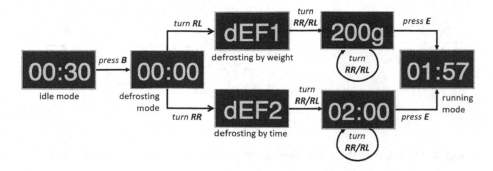

**Fig. 2.** The flow of user actions needed to start defrosting food with the oven

The microwave oven provides different cooking functions to the end users,[2] such as (among the others) the ability to *defrost frozen foods* without cooking them. To use any of the cooking functions, it is required to press the right combination of buttons in the control panel following a specific sequence. For example, as shown in Fig. 2, to defrost a food the user has to: *(i)* press **B** to switch from the "idle mode" (where it is shown the current time in the oven's display) to the "defrosting mode"; *(ii)* turn the setting knob to the left (**RL**) or to the right (**RR**) to enable defrosting by weight or by time, respectively; *(iii)* turn again the setting knob to the left (**RL**) or to the right (**RR**) as many times as it is needed to set the weight of the food to defrost (for weight defrosting the time is set automatically), or the time of defrosting; *(iv)* press **E** to confirm and activate the microwave.

When the microwave is in "running mode", whatever cooking function has been launched, the display will show a countdown timer. When it expires (display shows "00:00"), an alarm will sound to notify that the cooking function has been successfully completed. At any time, the door opener mechanism can be used to pause the microwave when it is in running mode, i.e., opening the door of the oven does not abort the cooking function in progress.

Given the above scenario, in this case study we assume that the analysts of the CEP company want to assess the usability of the oven's UI (i.e., of its control panel) with respect to the task: "*Defrost a food with the oven by weight or by time*", synthetically called DEFROST FOOD. To this end, the common practice would be to employ a lab or a field study, which requires to involve several users that must be observed by external evaluators over an extended period of time during their interaction with the oven. However, both techniques are expensive in terms of the time they require to collect the data, limiting the number of user tests that can be performed and bounding the scope of the testing activity to the pre-release stage of the CEP.

In this paper, we leverage the above case study to present a novel evaluation technique that allows us to reason over the concrete user interactions happened

---

[2] The complete list of cooking functions provided by the microwave oven can be found in the user manual associated to the oven.

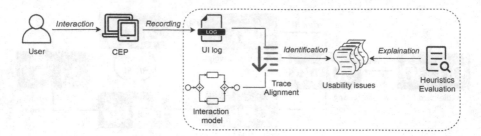

**Fig. 3.** Overview of the main components of the log-based evaluation technique

with the UI of a CEP (in our case, with the control panel of the microwave oven), and recorded into dedicated UI logs, to identify and explain the usability issues found on the CEP's UI directly during the after-release stage of the CEP.

## 4   Log-Based Evaluation Technique

In this section, we describe the key features of our log-based evaluation technique. To be more precise, as shown in Fig. 3, starting from a *UI log* recorded after many interactions with the UI of a CEP, and an *interaction model* representing the expected human-computer dialogue required to properly executing a relevant task on the CEP itself, our evaluation technique leverages *trace alignment* in Process Mining [17,28] and a dedicated *heuristic evaluation* [36] to automatically detect and provide explanations to the usability issues found during the interactions with the CEP. In the following, we describe in detail the above "ingredients" needed to concretely employ our technique.

### 4.1   Collecting User Interface Logs

First, it is necessary to collect a UI log $L$ containing *execution traces* that describe interaction sessions performed by end users during the enactment of a relevant task of interest through the CEP. Such a log can be generated through a massive remote user test, which large companies may periodically conduct with those customers that are known to have purchased the CEP.[3] In fact, nowadays, it is very common that users download a mobile app on their smartphone to register the product ID of the CEP just bought, so that, on the one hand, they can monitor the "health" of the CEP, and – on the other hand – the manufacturer can easily track and contact them if there is a safety alert or CEP recall [21].

To perform a remote evaluation test with a CEP, the end user is instructed via email, or with a notification on the mobile app, to run the CEP in testing mode pushing a special combination of buttons on the CEP's UI (usually the CEP returns a visual or acoustic feedback to inform the user that the testing mode has been activated), and then to perform one (or more) suggested task(s) with

---

[3] Users participating to remote tests are often rewarded with discounts, coupons, etc.

the CEP. In this time frame, a UI log records all the user actions performed on the CEP's UI, until the user decides to exit from the testing mode (this happens using the same special combination of buttons as before). At this point, the UI log is delivered to the manufacturer through the connection with the mobile app, which acts as a proxy between the CEP and the manufacturer servers.

From a technical point of view, a UI log $L$ is a multi-set of *execution traces* $\sigma_1, ..., \sigma_n \in L$. Each trace $\sigma_i \in L$ consists of a sequence of *user actions* $a_1, a_2, ..., a_m \in Z$, such that $\sigma_i = \langle a_1, a_2, ..., a_m \rangle$ is recorded during one user session, i.e., it is related to the *single execution* of a specific relevant task. $Z$ is the universe of user actions included in $L$. In the case study of Sect. 3, we can recognize the set of user actions of interest: $Z = \{A, B, C, D, E, RR, RL\}$. Multiple executions of the same task may consist of the same sequence of actions executed and, hence, result in the same trace. This motivates the definition of a UI log as a multi-set. If we consider our case study, the following $L_1 = [\langle B, RR, RL, E \rangle, \langle B, C, RR, RR \rangle, \langle C, C, C, B, RR, RR \rangle, \langle B, RR, RL, E \rangle,$ $\langle B, B, B, RL, RR, RR, RL, RL, RR, E \rangle]$ is an example of UI log consisting of 5 traces, generated by 5 tests in different user sessions. Within a trace, the concept of time is usually explicitly modeled in a way that user actions in a trace are sorted according to the timestamp of their occurrence.

In this paper, we assume that the user's actions associated to a task executed on the UI are already clustered in execution traces that refer to single enactments of the task itself. This assumption is reasonable, as we envision to collect the user actions performed on a CEP's UI when the CEP is in testing mode, and the user has been asked to perform exactly the task to be tested.

## 4.2   Defining Interaction Models as Petri Nets

Secondly, it is required to formalize the potential dialog between the end user and the CEP by employing dedicated interaction models. An interaction model represents the *expected way* to perform a relevant task on the CEP's UI.

The research literature is rich of notations for expressing human-computer dialogs as interaction models that allow to see at a glance the structure of a user interaction with a UI [1,41]. Existing notations can be categorized in two main classes: *diagrammatic* and *textual*. Diagrammatic notations include (among the others) various forms of state transition networks (STNs) [49], Petri nets [3], Harel state charts [14], flow charts [1], JSD diagrams [44] and ConcurTaskTrees (CTT) [34]. Textual notations include regular expressions [48], Linear Temporal Logic (LTL) [42], Communicating Sequential Processes (CSPs) [7], GOMS [19], modal action logic [5], BNF and production rules [9].

While there are major differences in expressive power between different notations, an increased expressive power is not always desirable as it may suggest a harder to understand description, i.e., the dialog of a UI can become unmanageable [1]. To guarantee a good trade-off between expressive power and understandability of the models, to realize our technique we opted for *Petri nets* (PNs) [35], which have a clear semantics and have proven to be adequate for defining interaction models [1,40,41]. PNs may contain exclusive choices, parallel branches and

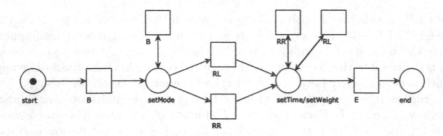

**Fig. 4.** Interaction model of the task DEFROST FOOD represented as a PN

loops, allowing the representation of extremely complex behaviours in a compact
way and with an exact mathematical definition of their execution semantics.

A PN is a directed bipartite graph with two node types: *places* (represented
by circles) and *transitions* (represented by squares) connected via directed arcs.
Technically, a PN is a triple $(P, T, F)$ where $P$ and $T$ are the set of *places* and
*transitions*, respectively, such that $P \cap T = \emptyset$ and $F \subseteq (P \times T) \cup (T \times P)$ is the
flow relation. Figure 4 illustrates the PN used to represent the interaction model
of the task DEFROST FOOD. Transitions are associated with *labels* reflecting
the user actions (e.g., buttons clicked, interactions with the setting knob, etc.)
required to accomplish the task on the UI of the microwave oven.

Given a transition $t \in T$, ${}^\bullet t$ is used to indicate the set of *input places* of $t$,
which are the places $p$ with a directed arc from $p$ to $t$ (i.e., such that $(p, t) \in F$).
Similarly, $t^\bullet$ indicates the set of *output places*, namely the places $p$ with a direct
arc from $t$ to $p$. At any time, a place can contain zero or more *tokens*, drawn
as black dots. Any distribution of tokens over the places, formally represented
by a total mapping $M : P \mapsto \mathbb{N}$, represents a configuration of the net called a
*marking*. The semantics of a PN defines how transitions route tokens through
the net changing the number of tokens in places, i.e., the PN marking, so that
they correspond to a task execution. In any run of a PN, its marking may change
according to the following enablement and firing rules:

- A transition $t$ is *enabled* at a marking $m$ iff each input place contains at least
  one token: $\forall\, p \in {}^\bullet t,\ m(p) > 0$.
- A transition $t$ can *fire* at a marking $m$ iff it is enabled. As result of firing
  a transition $t$, one token is "consumed" from each input place and one is
  "produced" in each output place. Hence, firing a transition $t$ at marking $m$
  leads to a marking $m'$, and this is denoted as $m \xrightarrow{t} m'$.

Figure 5 illustrates the act of firing for various PN configurations. It is
assumed that the firing of a transition is an atomic action that occurs instanta-
neously and can not be interrupted. Within the salient features of PNs is the fact
that several enabled transitions can not fire simultaneously, and that an enabled

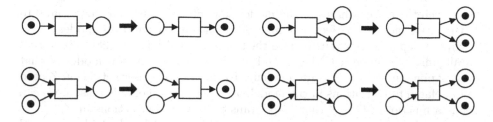

**Fig. 5.** Example of firing for various PN configurations

transition is not forced to fire immediately but can do so at a time of its choosing. In the remainder, given a sequence of transition firing $\delta = \langle t_1, \ldots, t_n \rangle \in T^*$, $m_0 \xrightarrow{\delta} m_n$ is used to indicate $m_0 \xrightarrow{t_1} m_1 \xrightarrow{t_2} \ldots \xrightarrow{t_n} m_n$, i.e., $m_n$ is *reachable* from $m_0$.

Since concrete executions of tasks on a UI have a start and an end, PNs need to be associated with an initial (respectively final) marking, characterized by the presence of one token in at least one of the starting (respectively ending) places of the PN and no tokens in any other place.

All the above features make PNs particularly suitable for modeling concrete interactions with a CEP's UI. Interestingly, an interaction model may allow *different strategies* to perform a relevant task. For example, if we consider the PN in Fig. 4, the number of ways to properly reach the final marking are potentially unbounded (due to the presence of a loop in the model). For instance, the execution traces $[\langle B, RR, RL, E \rangle, \langle D, D, D, RL, RR, RR, RL, RL, RR, E \rangle]$ represent (both) good ways to execute the relevant task underlying the PN in Fig. 4. This basically means that a same task can be completed through different paths of user actions in the UI with equivalent results, as may happen in real UIs. Last but not least, we can define as many interaction models as are the relevant tasks of the CEP to analyze.

In the remainder of this paper, we assume all PNs to be labelled and 1-bounded, also known as *safe*. A PN is 1-bounded if it imposes that the number of tokens in all places is at most 1 in all reachable markings, including the initial one. One-boundness is not a large limitation as the behavior allowed by interaction models can be represented as 1-bounded PNs [1, 40].

## 4.3 Trace Alignment to Detect Usability Issues

Thirdly, given an interaction model of the task of interest and a UI log associated to it, we can construct the *alignment* between any of the traces extracted from the log and the model. Trace alignment [28] is a conformance checking technique within Process Mining that is employed to *replay* the content of any trace of a log against a model represented as a PN, one action at a time. For each trace in the log, the technique identifies the closest corresponding trace that can be parsed by the model, i.e., an *alignment*, together with a *fitness* value, which quantifies how much the trace adheres to the model. The fitness value can vary from 0 to 1 (the latter means a perfect matching between the trace and the model).

In this paper, we have customized the technique developed in [28] to construct an alignment between a UI log $L$ and an PN-based interaction model $N$ that exactly pinpoints where deviations occur. To this aim, the user actions in $Z$ need to be related to transitions in the model, and vice versa. For this reason, we can define a function $\ell(T) \in Z$ that maps transitions with user actions in $Z$.

To establish an alignment between an interaction model and a UI log, we need to relate *moves in the log* to *moves in the model*. However, it may be that some of the moves in the log cannot be mimicked by the model and vice versa. We explicitly denote such "no moves" by $*$. From a formal point of view, *alignment moves* can be defined as follows:

**Definition 1 (Alignment Moves).** *Let $N = (P, T, F)$ be a PN, $L$ a UI log and $Z$ the universe of user actions included in $L$. A legal alignment move for $N$ and $L$ is represented by a pair $(q_L, q_N) \in (Z \cup \{*\} \times T \cup \{*\}) \backslash \{(*, *)\}$ such that:*

- $(q_L, q_N)$ *is a move in log if $q_L \in Z$ and $q_N = *$,*
- $(q_L, q_N)$ *is a move in model if $q_L = *$ and $q_N \in T$,*
- $(q_L, q_N)$ *is a synchronous move if $q_L \in Z$, $q_N \in T$ and $q_L = \ell(q_N)$*

An *alignment* is a sequence of alignment moves:

**Definition 2 (Alignment).** *Let $N = (P, T, F)$ be a PN with an initial marking and a final marking denoted with $m_i$ and $m_f$. Let also $L$ be a UI log. Let $\Gamma_N$ be the universe of all legal alignment moves for $N$ and $L$. Let $\sigma_L \in L$ be a log trace. Sequence $\gamma \in \Gamma_N^*$ is an alignment of $N$ and $\sigma_L$ if, ignoring all occurrences of $*$, the projection on the first element yields $\sigma_L$ and the projection on the second yields a sequence $\delta'' \in T^*$ such that $m_i \xrightarrow{\delta''} m_f$.*

In a nutshell, the alignment activity consists of *replaying* any user action included in a log trace over the interaction model. The output is a pair of aligned traces together with the points of divergence between these two traces. Specifically, a pair shows a trace in the log that does not match exactly a trace in the model, together with the corresponding closest trace produced by the model. For example, Fig. 6 shows a possible alignment for a log trace $\tau_1 = \langle B, C, RR, RR \rangle$ taken by our UI log $L_1$ and the PN of Fig. 4. Note how moves are represented vertically. For example, as shown in Fig. 6, the first move of $\gamma_1$ is (B,B), i.e., a *synchronous move* of B, while the second and fifth move of $\gamma_1$ are a move in log and model, respectively.

$$\gamma_1 = \begin{array}{|c|c|c|c|c|} \hline B & C & RR & RR & * \\ \hline B & * & RR & RR & E \\ \hline \end{array}$$

**Fig. 6.** Alignment of trace $\tau_1 = \langle B, C, RR, RR \rangle$ and the interaction model in Fig. 4.

The presence in an alignment of (non-synchronous) moves in log and model denotes that some actions recorded in the log cannot be matched to any of the actions allowed by the model. As a consequence, the fitness value of $\gamma_1$ is lower than 1. To be more specific, a *deviation* can manifest itself in *skipping* actions that have been executed in the log but are not allowed by the model, (e.g., a user pushing the button $C$ that is not needed to activate the defrosting function of the oven), or in *inserting* actions, namely, some actions that should have been executed (i.e., prescribed by the model) but are not observed in the log, e.g., a user that is not able to complete the task DEFROST FOOD since s/he misses to push button $E$.

If an alignment between a log trace and model contains at least a deviation, it means that the log trace refers to a user interaction that is not compliant with the allowed behavior represented by the model. As a matter of fact, the alignment moves (i.e., skipping or inserting actions) indicate where the interaction is not conforming with the model by pinpointing the deviations that have caused this nonconformity, which is crucial for identifying potential usability issues.

For example, coming back to the alignment in Fig. 6, it is clear that the alignment activity will identify that: *(i)* action $C$ has been executed even if forbidden by the model, and *(ii)* action $E$ is required by the model (even if it does not appear in the trace), and it should have been executed as last action of the trace. The alignment of trace $\tau_1$ with the model will instruct to *skip* action $C$ and *insert* action $E$, i.e., the *repaired trace* is $\hat{\tau}_1 = \langle B, skip(C), RR, RR, add(E) \rangle$. Recovery instructions are labeled with *add* and *skip* to capture those wrong/missing actions that must be skipped/inserted from/into the repaired trace to make it compliant with the model. The analysis of the recovery instructions enables to support an HCI analyst to detect potential usability issues in the UI. For example, considering $\hat{\tau}_1$, it is possible to infer that the user was confused about how to start and conclude the interaction with the oven to activate the desired cooking function, probably due to the lack of visual cues in the control panel of the oven, or could simply not find the feature.

## 4.4 Heuristic Evaluation to Suggest Explanations of Usability Issues

While trace alignment enables the identification of potential usability issues in the range of a user interaction with a UI, the interpretation and repair of such issues is usually let to HCI expert analysts. In this paper, we relax this assumption relying on heuristic evaluations in HCI, to provide possible explanations to the deviations found through trace alignment.

Specifically, the idea is to involve an expert evaluator that, given a specific task to be tested with the CEP, searches for usability violations in the UI design while simulating its execution, judging its compliance with recognized usability principles (i.e., the heuristics). In the proposed case study, we have relied on the well known Jakob Nielsen 10 heuristics [37]: (H1) visibility of system status through appropriate feedback; (H2) match between system and the real world making information appear with concepts familiar to the user; (H3) user control and freedom to leave the unwanted system's states; (H4) usage of consistency and standards; (H5) error prevention; (H6) recognition rather than recall of information; (H7) flexibility and efficiency of use allow users to tailor frequent actions; (H8) aesthetic and minimalist design, filtering out any information that is irrelevant; (H9) help users recognize, diagnose, and recover from errors; (H10) provide help and documentation features.

Thus, for any transition (i.e., user action on the UI) belonging to an interaction model represented as a PN, it is asked to an expert evaluator to motivate the reason why a user should select an action different from the one expected at a certain point of the PN execution, relying on the selected heuristic. The results of this activity, which can be performed in the pre-release stage of the CEP under analysis, thus before collecting UI logs, enable to define a clear mapping between potential usability issues hidden within the CEP's UI and their explanations in terms of violated heuristics. Note that the same heuristic can be violated for many reasons, depending by the specific user actions being performed and by the nature of the task to achieve. At this point, any of the identified heuristic violation can be associated to a precise description of the reason of the violation itself. For example, if we consider our case study in Sect. 3, and specifically the DEFROST FOOD task, the result of the association between the violated heuristics and their explanation in the context of the task is shown in Table 1.

**Table 1.** An example of mapping between explanations and violated heuristics, produced by an expert evaluator for the task DEFROST FOOD.

| Expl. ID | Violated heuristic | Brief description |
|---|---|---|
| E1 | H1 | Users do not have enough feedback about their interaction with the oven |
| E2 | H1 | Users do not know if an interaction with the oven has been successfully completed |
| E3 | H1 | The oven's display does not provide any visual cue to understand which button has been pressed |
| E4 | H2 | The symbol associated to Function button in the oven's control panel is not familiar to the users |
| E5 | H2 | The symbol associated to Stop button in the oven's control panel is not familiar to the users |
| E6 | H2 | The symbol associated to Defrost button in the oven's control panel is not familiar to the users |
| E7 | H2 | Defrost modes as shown on the oven's display have names (dEF1/dEF2) not familiar to the users |
| E8 | H3 | Users find it difficult to undo any cooking function started by mistake |
| E9 | H4 | One of the symbols associated to the Setting Knob is associated also to the Defrost button |
| E10 | H4 | The symbol associated to the Function button does not match well with its intended usage |
| E11 | H4 | The symbol associated to Start/+30 s button does not match well with its intended usage |
| E12 | H4 | The clock symbol associated to the Setting Knob is associated also to the Clock/Timer button |
| E13 | H5 | It is not clear which buttons are useful to activate a cooking function and which are not required |
| E14 | H5 | No confirmation request is asked to the user while pressing any button |
| E15 | H8 | There are too many undifferentiated buttons in the control panel of the oven |
| E16 | H9 | The oven does not show any error message on its display |
| E17 | H10 | The effects of the Function button are not clearly explained in the user manual of the oven |

**Table 2.** Mapping of violated heuristics and explanations related to a wrong execution of the action $B$ in the context of the task DEFROST FOOD.

| Action expected | B | | B | |
|---|---|---|---|---|
| Action executed | A | | RR or RL, C, D, E | |
| Mapping | Explanation ID | Violated heuristic | Explanation ID | Violated heuristic |
| | E6 | H2 | E1 | H1 |
| | E4 | H2 | | |
| | E10 | H4 | E6 | H2 |
| | E17 | H10 | | |

Of course, heuristic evaluation is able to identify potential usability violations, but not to verify if such violations correspond to concrete usability issues in the after-release stage of the CEP. For this reason, it is required to relate heuristic violations found at the outset with deviations detected after the trace alignment step. This can be done by matching the *skip* and *add* actions in an aligned trace with the usability violations found during the heuristic evaluation. For example, given the trace $\tau_2 = \langle C, C, C, B, RR, RR \rangle$ taken by our UI log $L_1$, the aligned trace is $\hat{\tau}_2 = \langle skip(C), skip(C), skip(C), B, RR, RR, add(E) \rangle$. From $\hat{\tau}_2$, it is clear that the correct execution of $B$ is preceded by three wrong occurrences of $C$, which can be interpreted as the violation of the heuristics $H1$ and $H2$ and explained through $E1$ and $E6$, respectively (cf. Table 2). Such explanations are properly described in Table 1 and delivered as an outcome by our technique, together with the deviations (i.e., in this case the *skip* actions) found with the trace alignment activity related to them. Note that similar considerations can be done for *add* actions (i.e., moves in the model) as well.

It is worth to note that the aim of this paper is to validate the effectiveness of the proposed technique for detecting and explaining usability issues, and not the quality of the specific heuristic employed or the clarity of explanations provided by the expert evaluators. In addition, we point out that there is no restriction to analyze the same UI log relying on many different heuristics (and explanations associated with their violation) to obtain different perspectives of a specific set of usability problems.

## 5    User Experiments

To validate the effectiveness of our technique over the case study introduced in Sect. 3, we performed a user experiment involving 44 potential end users (24 females, 20 males) of the microwave oven, selected from a sample of people with an age between 18 and 50 years, that were all familiar (i.e., with a similar level of expertise) with the use of microwaves. Therefore, completely novice users were not considered in the experiment. The users were contacted by broadcasting an email to a large internal university mailing list where we asked them if they wanted to join the experiment and some questions to understand their level of expertise with the use of microwaves. Due to the impossibility of verifying

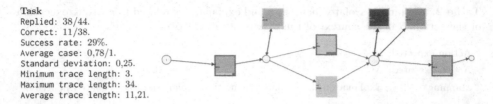

```
Task
Replied: 38/44.
Correct: 11/38.
Success rate: 29%.
Average case: 0,78/1.
Standard deviation: 0,25.
Minimum trace length: 3.
Maximum trace length: 34.
Average trace length: 11,21.
```

**Fig. 7.** Overview of the results of the alignment of the task DEFROST FOOD with its related UI log (Color figure online)

which persons owned the exact version of the oven to be tested, we have implemented a digital clone of the oven using the Processing programming language.[4] The digital clone has been developed relying on the well known Skeuomorphism pattern [39], which is related to the design of UIs that mimic their real-world counterparts in how they appear and/or how the user can interact with them. We notice that the digital clone is not generally requested to make our technique work, as it is thought to be enacted through real-life log data collected using real CEPs. Nonetheless, the presence of the digital clone was required to evaluate the effectiveness of the technique against the case study.

Then, we contacted via email all the users to involve in the experiment asking them to perform the following activities, in this exact sequence:

1. read the user manual of the oven, only the pages related to the tasks to test;
2. try to run some of the cooking functions of the oven with its digital clone;
3. watch a training video that explains the working of the cooking functions of interest for the test, and that emphasizes the potential mistakes that can be encountered during the interaction with the oven;
4. start the user test.

From a technical point of view, the digital clone was hosted in a dedicated web server reachable by any user involved in the experiment. The interaction with the digital clone was possible using any traditional web browser.

The user test consisted of performing four different tasks (in sequence) of increasing complexity with the digital clone of the oven, including the task DEFROST FOOD, which is described in Sect. 3. Of course, a separate PN-based interaction model has been defined for any of the tested tasks:

- *Set the clock* of the oven.
- *Grill food*, which enables to heat and brown food quickly. The complexity of this task is comparable to DEFROST FOOD.
- *Set the auto cooking feature*, which enables to register new pre-programmed cooking times and power level based on the type of food to cook.

For the sake of space, in this paper we have analyzed only the results associated with the task DEFROST FOOD because of its average complexity and since it reflects the most frequent task performed by any end user of a microwave.

---

[4] https://processing.org/.

**Table 3.** Amount of traces in the UI log that violated a specific heuristic in the range of the user action $RL$ within the DEFROST FOOD task.

| Explanation ID | Low Sev. | Medium Sev. | High Sev. | Catastrophic Sev. |
|---|---|---|---|---|
| E1  | 12 | 10 | 1 | 3 |
| E3  | 12 | 10 | 1 | 3 |
| E9  | 4  | 0  | 0 | 0 |
| E11 | 4  | 3  | 0 | 0 |
| E12 | 6  | 6  | 1 | 0 |
| E13 | 12 | 10 | 1 | 3 |
| E14 | 4  | 0  | 0 | 3 |
| E15 | 0  | 0  | 0 | 3 |
| E16 | 9  | 7  | 1 | 3 |
| E17 | 6  | 1  | 0 | 0 |

During the enactment of any user test, we employed a dedicated action logger to collect all the user interactions in form of execution traces recorded into UI logs. Once obtained the UI logs, one per tested task, we ran the trace alignment technique to find deviations between the models and the execution traces in the UI logs. For example, the high-level results concerning the alignment of the task DEFROST FOOD and its associated UI log are described in Fig. 7. Among the various statistics returned, they suggest that 38 out of 44 users tried to perform the task with the oven, but only 11 were able to complete the execution of the task, i.e., to activate the defrosting function. The coloured PN in Fig. 7 can be used to identify which points of the PN were subjected to deviations. Places with the yellow background indicates that at least) a *move in log* deviation occurred before a specific transition, while the green/pink bar placed at the bottom of any transition is used to check the amount of *synchronous moves/moves in the model* found during the alignment.

After having found all the deviations (i.e., potential usability issues), the technique associates them with the heuristic violations identified in the pre-release stage of the CEP (see Sect. 4.4), with the target to relate any deviation to one or more explanations. In Table 3 it is summarized the amount of traces in the UI log that have violated a specific heuristic (and its related explanation) while performing the user action $RL$ in the range of the DEFROST FOOD task. Any violation is classified according to a specific degree of severity: 1-Low (1 violation), 2-Medium (2–3 violations), 3-High (4–5 violations), 4-Catastrophic (6+ violations), which is useful to indicate how many times a specific heuristic has been violated in a single execution trace. For example, as shown in Table 3, it is evident that H1 has been violated six or more times in 12 traces, leading to 12 catastrophic violations of H1. The reasons behind such violations are explained by E1 and E3, whose description is reported in Table 1. Of course, the degree of severity of any violation can be customized by an expert evaluator according to the specific task to analyze.

With this knowledge at hand, extracted from the real interactions with the microwave oven, we have derived the three major usability issues found while users interacted with the control panel of the oven to execute the DEFROST FOOD task. Those can be obtained by looking at the explanations associated to the heuristics violated the most times:

- **Ineffective and confusing UI**, related to *E13*, with too many available buttons if compared with the scarcity of cooking functions provided.
- **Absence of feedback**, related to *E1, E3* and *E16*. In the path towards the activation of a cooking function, the interaction with some of the buttons does not provide any feedback on the oven's display, but changes the status of the interaction. Furthermore, the system does not provide any error message or information about the actions performed previously.
- **Buttons' identifiers are misleading, or too similar between them**, related to *E11* and *E12*. Some of the oven's buttons are associated with symbols that do not help to understand their effects. In addition, some buttons share similar/identical symbols, which make their effect undifferentiated at the eyes of a user.

We have performed the same analysis for any of the other three tested tasks obtaining similar results. The results are also supported by a qualitative evaluation performed after the completion of the user tests. Specifically, we organized a dedicated thinking aloud session by involving 10 further potential end users of the microwave oven (having similar age and characteristics of the users involved in the first test) asking them to execute the four tasks of interest with the digital clone of the microwave, but with an external evaluator observing them. The 10 users were asked to explicitly indicate the usability issues found while interacting with the control panel of the microwave. This allowed us to confirm the validity of the results obtained through our technique, thus certifying it as a valid inspection method to identify and explain usability issues.

## 6    Discussion and Concluding Remarks

The market for smart consumer electronics has expanded over the last few years and is expected to reach approximately USD 1,787 billion in 2024 owing to evolving consumer experiences and changing lifestyle preferences.[5] For this reason, consumer electronics is one of the major industries getting impacted by the IoT revolution [32]. In this direction, today it is becoming common practice to capture the interactions with a UI during daily use and save them into UI log files for later analysis employing dedicated log studies [8]. In fact, UI logs have the benefit of being easy to capture at scale, enabling to observe even small differences that exist between populations, including unusual behaviour that is hard to capture with the other studies. In this direction, in this paper we have presented a novel log-based evaluation technique that can be successfully

---

[5] cf. https://www.zionmarketresearch.com/news/consumer-electronics-market.

employed to automatically detect usability issues of a CEP's UI and suggest useful explanations to support their fixing.

Our technique has been proven to be particularly suitable for evaluating the usability of wizard-based and structured tasks, i.e., with predefined entry and exit points. For this reason, we believe it can be useful for the usability assessment of those categories of CEPs that provide fixed procedures to activate their functions (e.g., domestic appliances, housekeeping tools, etc.). Moreover, the explanations provided to fix the usability issues may support usability experts to realize UIs for next products that are closer to the users' expectations. However, on the other hand, the use of PNs may limit the possibility to model extremely complex behaviours involving many combinations of actions in the context of "less-structured" tasks, such as the ones that are provided by modern audiovisual tools (e.g., smart TVs, game consoles, etc.). This aspect can be potentially mitigated employing less prescriptive modeling notations, such as regular expressions and temporal logics, e.g., see [31].

Another strength of the technique relies on the possibility to be enacted when the user concretely interacts with the CEP in the real user context. Furthermore, for a specific relevant task, different interaction models can be developed to represent the different interaction strategies of novice and experienced users (this can be useful for defining the interactions with less user-friendly CEPs). Finally, the granularity of user actions in interaction models can be customized on the basis of the kind of user logs recorded by the CEPs, i.e., the technique is *scalable*. All these aspects make our technique flexible and customizable for several settings and different types of CEP.

The main limitation of the proposed technique is that the tasks to be tested have to be predetermined and known, since they require to be explicitly modeled through PN-based interaction models. However, although the need to explicitly define interaction models may require some extra modeling effort, we believe that the overhead is compensated by the possibility of detecting the usability issues and their explanations in the after-release stage of the CEP's life-cycle, where it is complex to perform any kind of usability evaluation that is different from the traditional lab and field studies. We think that the above limitation can be mitigated by employing algorithms for PN discovery (cf. [2]), which would allow us to automatically derive the structure of interaction models from the UI logs related to different tasks' executions, thus simplifying the modeling effort.

We note that the proposed technique can be customized with minor modifications to accept in input interaction models defined with other flow-based modeling languages than PNs. In fact, it is undoubtable that there are aspects of the interaction that can not be formalized through PNs, including the objects manipulated by user actions and the representation of the users roles (that can be relevant for certain kinds of CEP). They can certainly be modeled by richer languages, e.g., the standard language CTT (ConcurTaskTrees [34]) for designing interaction sequences. However, in this paper we did not aim at demonstrating that PNs are suitable for modeling human-computer dialogs. In fact, despite their simplicity, it has been already proven that PNs are sufficiently adequate to model the key aspects of an interaction [1,30,40,41]. The same reasoning can be applied to clarify that, for the explanations of the usability issues, different heuristic evaluation methods than the one of Nielsen can be employed without affecting the effectiveness of the technique.

We conclude by emphasizing that our technique takes inspiration from conformance checking techniques in the Process Mining field [6,28]. Such techniques are employed to detect deviations in the execution of real-world business processes, whose structure is more complex than the one of tasks in CEPs [33]. This further emphasizes the practical relevance of our technique in the HCI field.

**Acknowledgments.** This work has been supported by the "Dipartimento di Eccellenza" grant, the H2020 project DataCloud and the Sapienza grant BPbots.

# References

1. Alan, D., Janet, F., Gregory, A., Russell, B.: Human-Computer Interaction. Pearson, London (2004)
2. Augusto, A., et al.: Automated discovery of process models from event logs: review and benchmark. IEEE Trans. Knowl. Data Eng. **31**(4), 686–705 (2018)
3. Bastide, R., Palanque, P., Sy, O., Le, D.-H., Navarre, D.: Petri net based behavioural specification of CORBA systems. In: Donatelli, S., Kleijn, J. (eds.) ICATPN 1999. LNCS, vol. 1639, pp. 66–85. Springer, Heidelberg (1999). https://doi.org/10.1007/3-540-48745-X_5
4. Benyon, D.: Designing Interactive Systems: A Comprehensive Guide to HCI, UX and Interaction Design. Pearson, London (2014)
5. Campos, J.C., Sousa, M., Alves, M.C.B., Harrison, M.D.: Formal verification of a space system's user interface with the IVY workbench. IEEE Trans. Hum.-Mach. Syst. **46**(2), 303–316 (2016)
6. Carmona, J., et al.: Conformance Checking. Springer, Cham (2018). https://doi.org/10.1007/978-3-319-99414-7
7. Dignum, M.: A model for organizational interaction: based on agents, Founded in Logic. Ph.D. thesis, Utrecht University (2004)
8. Dumais, S., Jeffries, R., Russell, D.M., Tang, D., Teevan, J.: Understanding user behavior through log data and analysis. In: Olson, J.S., Kellogg, W.A. (eds.) Ways of Knowing in HCI, pp. 349–372. Springer, New York (2014). https://doi.org/10.1007/978-1-4939-0378-8_14
9. Feary, M.S.: A toolset for supporting iterative human automation: interaction in design. NASA Ames Research Center. Tech. rep. 20100012861 (2010)
10. Ferre, X., Juristo, N., Moreno, A.M.: Improving software engineering practice with HCI aspects. In: Ramamoorthy, C.V., Lee, R., Lee, K.W. (eds.) SERA 2003. LNCS, vol. 3026, pp. 349–363. Springer, Heidelberg (2004). https://doi.org/10.1007/978-3-540-24675-6_27
11. Ferre, X., Villalba, E., Julio, H., Zhu, H.: Extending mobile app analytics for usability test logging. In: Bernhaupt, R., Dalvi, G., Joshi, A., K. Balkrishan, D., O'Neill, J., Winckler, M. (eds.) INTERACT 2017, Part III. LNCS, vol. 10515, pp. 114–131. Springer, Cham (2017). https://doi.org/10.1007/978-3-319-67687-6_9
12. Fu, B., Lin, J., Li, L., Faloutsos, C., Hong, J., Sadeh, N.: Why people hate your app: making sense of user feedback in a mobile app store. In: 19th ACM SIGKDD International Conference on Knowledge Discovery and Data Mining, pp. 1276–1284 (2013)

13. Han, S.H., Yun, M.H., Kwahk, J., Hong, S.W.: Usability of consumer electronic products. Int. J. Ind. Ergon. **28**(3–4), 143–151 (2001)
14. Harel, D.: Statecharts: a visual formalism for complex systems. Sci. Comput. Program. **8**(3), 231–274 (1987)
15. Hartson, H.R., Andre, T.S., Williges, R.C.: Criteria for evaluating usability evaluation methods. Int. J. Hum.-Comput. Interact. **13**(4), 373–410 (2001)
16. Humayoun, S.R., et al.: The WORKPAD user interface and methodology: developing smart and effective mobile applications for emergency operators. In: Stephanidis, C. (ed.) UAHCI 2009, Part III. LNCS, vol. 5616, pp. 343–352. Springer, Heidelberg (2009). https://doi.org/10.1007/978-3-642-02713-0_36
17. Jagadeesh Chandra Bose, R.P., van der Aalst, W.: Trace alignment in process mining: opportunities for process diagnostics. In: Hull, R., Mendling, J., Tai, S. (eds.) Business Process Management. BPM 2010. LNCS, vol. 6336, pp. 227–242. Springer, Heidelberg (2010). https://doi.org/10.1007/978-3-642-15618-2_17
18. Janlert, L.E., Stolterman, E.: Things that Keep us Busy: The Elements of Interaction. MIT Press, Cambridge (2017)
19. John, B.E., Kieras, D.E.: The GOMS family of user interface analysis techniques: comparison and contrast. ACM Trans. Comput.-Hum. Interact. **3**(4), 320–351 (1996)
20. Joung, J., Jung, K., Ko, S., Kim, K.: Customer complaints analysis using text mining and outcome-driven innovation method for market-oriented product development. Sustainability **11**(1), 1–14 (2019)
21. Kao, C.K., Liebovitz, D.M.: Consumer mobile health apps: current state, barriers, and future directions. J. Am. Acad. Phys. Med. Rehabil. **9**(5), 106–115 (2017)
22. Kim, J., Han, S.H.: A methodology for developing a usability index of consumer electronic products. Int. J. Ind. Ergon. **38**(3–4), 333–345 (2008)
23. Kjeldskov, J., Skov, M.B.: Was it worth the hassle?. ten years of mobile HCI research discussions on lab and field evaluations. In: 16th International Conference on Human-Computer Interaction with Mobile Devices & Services (MobileHCI 2014), pp. 43–52. ACM (2014)
24. van Kuijk, J., Christiaans, H., Kanis, H., van Eijk, D.: Usability in the development of consumer electronics: issues and actors. In: 16th World Congress on Ergonomics (IEA 2006) (2006)
25. van Kuijk, J., Kanis, H., Christiaans, H., van Eijk, D.: Barriers to and enablers of usability in electronic consumer product development: a multiple case study. Hum.-Comput. Interact. **32**(1), 1–71 (2017)
26. Kwahk, J., Han, S.H.: A methodology for evaluating the usability of audiovisual consumer electronic products. Appl. Ergon. **33**(5), 419–431 (2002)
27. Lau, T., Horvitz, E.: Patterns of search: analyzing and modeling web query refinement. In: Kay, J. (ed.) UM99 User Modeling. CICMS, vol. 407, pp. 119–128. Springer, Vienna (1999). https://doi.org/10.1007/978-3-7091-2490-1_12
28. de Leoni, M., Marrella, A.: Aligning real process executions and prescriptive process models through automated planning. Expert Syst. Appl. **82**, 162–183 (2017)
29. Lettner, F., Holzmann, C.: Automated and unsupervised user interaction logging as basis for usability evaluation of mobile applications. In: 10th International Conference on Advances in Mobile Computing & Multimedia (MoMM 2012), pp. 118–127. ACM (2012)
30. Marrella, A., Catarci, T.: Measuring the learnability of interactive systems using a petri net based approach. In: Designing Interactive Systems Conference, DIS 2018, pp. 1309–1319 (2018)

31. Marrella, A., Ferro, L.S., Catarci, T.: An approach to identifying what has gone wrong in a user interaction. In: Lamas, D., Loizides, F., Nacke, L., Petrie, H., Winckler, M., Zaphiris, P. (eds.) INTERACT 2019, Part III. LNCS, vol. 11748, pp. 361–370. Springer, Cham (2019). https://doi.org/10.1007/978-3-030-29387-1_20

32. Marrella, A., Mecella, M., Russo, A.: Collaboration on-the-field: suggestions and beyond. In: 8th International Conference on Information Systems for Crisis Response and Management (2011)

33. Marrella, A., Mecella, M., Sardiña, S.: Supporting adaptiveness of cyber-physical processes through action-based formalisms. AI Commun. **31**(1), 47–74 (2018)

34. Mori, G., Paternò, F., Santoro, C.: CTTE: support for developing and analyzing task models for interactive system design. IEEE Trans. Softw. Eng. **28**(8), 797–813 (2002)

35. Murata, T.: Petri nets: properties, analysis and applications. Proc. IEEE **77**(4), 541–580 (1989)

36. Nielsen, J.: Finding usability problems through heuristic evaluation. In: SIGCHI Conference on Human Factors in Computing Systems (CHI 1992), pp. 373–380 (1992)

37. Nielsen, J.: 10 Usability Heuristics for User Interface Design. Nielsen Norman Group (1994). https://www.nngroup.com/articles/ten-usability-heuristics/

38. Okada, H., Asahi, T.: Guitester: a log-based usability testing tool for graphical user interfaces. IEICE Trans. Inf. Syst. **82**(6), 1030–1041 (1999)

39. Page, T.: Skeuomorphism or flat design: future directions in mobile device User Interface (UI) design education. Int. J. Mob. Learn. Organ. **8**(2), 130–142 (2014)

40. Palanque, P.A., Bastide, R.: Petri net based design of user-driven interfaces using the interactive cooperative objects formalism. In: Paternó, F. (ed.) Interactive Systems: Design, Specification, and Verification. Focus on Computer Graphics (Tutorials and Perspectives in Computer Graphics). Springer, Heidelberg (1995). https://doi.org/10.1007/978-3-642-87115-3_23

41. Paterno, F.: Model-Based Design and Evaluation of Interactive Applications, 1st edn. Springer, Heidelberg (1999). https://doi.org/10.1007/978-1-4471-0445-2

42. Pnueli, A.: The temporal logic of programs. In: 18th Annual IEEE Symposium on Foundations of Computer Science. IEEE (1977)

43. Supply & Demand Chain Executive: What Are Late Product Launches Really Costing You? (2017). https://www.sdcexec.com/sourcing-procurement/article/20985884/

44. Sutcliffe, A.G., Wang, I.: Integrating human computer interaction with Jackson system development. Comput. J. **34**(2), 132–142 (1991)

45. Thapliyal, H.: Internet of things-based consumer electronics: reviewing existing consumer electronic devices, systems, and platforms and exploring new research paradigms. IEEE Consum. Electron. Mag. **7**(1), 66–67 (2017)

46. Tyler, S.K., Teevan, J.: Large scale query log analysis of re-finding. In: Third ACM International Conference on Web Search and Data Mining, pp. 191–200 (2010)

47. Valle, T., Prata, W., et al.: Automated usability tests for mobile devices through live emotions logging. In: 17th International Conference on Human-Computer Interaction with Mobile Devices and Services Adjunct (MobileHCI 2015), pp. 636–643. ACM (2015)

48. Van Den Bos, J., Plasmeijer, M.J., Hartel, P.H.: Input-output tools: a language facility for interactive and real-time systems. IEEE Trans. Softw. Eng. **9**(3), 247–259 (1983)

49. Wasserman, A.I.: Extending state transition diagrams for the specification of human-computer interaction. IEEE Trans. Softw. Eng. **8**, 699–713 (1985)

50. Zhang, X., Qiao, Z., Tang, L., Fan, W., Fox, E., Wang, G.: Identifying product defects from user complaints: a probabilistic defect model. In: Decision Support and Analytics (SIGDSA 2016) (2016)

# Introducing Asynchronous Remote Usability Testing in Practice: An Action Research Project

Jonna Helene Holm Pedersen[1], Malene Sørensen[2], Jan Stage[3(✉)],
and Rune Thaarup Høegh[4]

[1] JCD A/S, Systemvej 6, 9200 Aalborg, SV, Denmark
[2] Capgemini Danmark, Skanderborgvej 234, 8260 Viby, Denmark
[3] Department of Computer Science, Aalborg University, 0220 Aalborg East, Denmark
jans@cs.aau.dk
[4] Nykredit, Fredrik Bajers Vej 1, 9220 Aalborg East, Denmark
rh@nykredit.dk

**Abstract.** Asynchronous remote usability testing is a usability evaluation method where users and evaluators are separated both in time and space, and users are directly involved in producing the evaluation results. This paper reports from an action research project on introduction of asynchronous remote usability testing in the IT organization of a bank. The IT organization had extensive experience with traditional usability evaluation but was interested in introducing asynchronous remote usability testing into their repertoire of evaluation methods. The project was initiated with an intensive two-month collaboration followed by a six-month maturation phase. The process of introducing the method and the motivations of the IT organization for introducing the method are described in detail. The findings indicate that the conceptual understanding of usability evaluation and the engagement of the users are crucial for the outcome of the evaluation, and the tool and materials used for the evaluation was an obstacle for high-quality results.

**Keywords:** Methods for HCI · Usability evaluation · Remote asynchronous usability evaluation · Action research

## 1 Introduction

Usability evaluation is an established discipline in modern software development. One of the most commonly proposed evaluation methods is referred to as the user-based think-aloud method, which is usually carried out in a dedicated laboratory. This traditional method has significantly influenced usability evaluation research for several years. In software development practice, there are mixed opinions about the user-based think-aloud method, with the main concern being resource demands, both in terms of calendar time and work hours for the evaluators.

There have been various efforts to meet the demands of industry practice by developing evaluation methods which require less resources. Remote usability testing (RUT) was introduced in 1994 as a less resource-demanding method, e.g. [20, 22]. RUT aims

© IFIP International Federation for Information Processing 2021
Published by Springer Nature Switzerland AG 2021
C. Ardito et al. (Eds.): INTERACT 2021, LNCS 12935, pp. 320–338, 2021.
https://doi.org/10.1007/978-3-030-85610-6_19

to have users and evaluators located in different places, communicating over the internet in a way that is similar to the traditional user-based think-aloud method. The separation in space reduced the logistical challenges; the evaluators and users were not separated in time though. This has later been denoted as synchronous remote usability testing (SRUT) [1].

A related method was suggested a couple of years later. It was originally called critical incident reporting where the users are separated from the evaluator in both time and space, and report the usability problems they experience [6, 21]. The evaluators receive all the critical incident reports from the users and based on that they generate a list of usability problems. This has later been denoted as asynchronous remote usability testing (ARUT) [6].

Some research activities have inquired into the qualities of SRUT and ARUT, and some researchers have also compared the two. SRUT has many qualities in common with the traditional user-based think-aloud method, while ARUT identifies significantly fewer usability problems in comparison to the former two [1]. On the other hand, ARUT is a more cost and time effective approach in comparison to the traditional method and SRUT [5]. This is due to the reduced costs associated with traveling and logistics [3], as well as the scalability of the approach allowing evaluators to add more participants with little added cost [4]. The scalable nature means that the test can be administered to a larger variety and group of participants, as location is not an issue.

A main challenge of ARUT is the quantity of the results, as the method has been found to identify fewer usability problems in comparison to its counterparts [1, 5]. It also lacks the qualitative data that can be collected by evaluators with traditional evaluation and SRUT [14]. In the original form, ARUT is also more time consuming for the users who participate in the tests as they have to report usability problems in addition to working with the system [1, 5, 16]. However, there are more recent forms of ARUT that do not impose this task on the users.

While an increasing body of research inquires into the qualities of remote usability testing methods, the amount of research that focuses on the use of SRUT or ARUT in software development practice is severely limited; for ARUT there are very few exceptions, one being [15]. On a more general level, this illustrates a strong critique of usability research [18]. Practitioners who want to introduce ARUT in an IT organization need advice and experiences to facilitate the process, but the research literature provides very limited support in this respect.

This paper reports from an action research project which explored how ARUT was introduced into an IT organisation that relied on traditional usability evaluation methods. The action research study was carried out in collaboration with the internal IT organisation of a national bank, and focused on activities which were conducted to support the process of introducing ARUT in organisational practice. ARUT was chosen because the IT organisation wanted to explore how far they could go in reducing the evaluator efforts. The aim of this paper is to assist practitioners who intend to go through a similar process.

In the following section we present research literature that relates to our research question. Then we introduce the research method used for the action research study. Next, we present the findings of our study of the introduction of ARUT in the IT organisation, and whether it was successful and can be implemented in the organisation. Lastly, we discuss the results in terms of introducing ARUT in an organisation, unexpected findings and our contribution to current research before concluding on our study by addressing our research question.

## 2  Related Work

There is a limited but increasing body of research on RUT. Some of this is defining various remote methods. A different stream of empirical work demonstrates that RUT is an effective approach [1, 24, 25]. Many of these collected only qualitative data, except [1].

ARUT has been defined and discussed in various contexts. It has been defined and discussed in relation to SRUT, RUT and traditional usability testing [5, 6, 12]. Castillo distinguished between asynchronous and synchronous remote usability testing [6] and clearly defined the different aspects of the two approaches in relation to remote user testing.

Bruun et al. discussed three ARUT methods and compared them to a traditional usability approach; they found that ARUT was more time effective but found fewer usability problems. Martin et al. compared the cost and time spent on traditional lab-based usability testing to ARUT [12]. They conducted testing using both approaches, with the lab-based testing taking place in a university setting. The results indicated that asynchronous remote testing could be considered a comparable alternative to lab-based testing, as it showed that remote testing had used less days of direct evaluator/consultant involvement, resulting in a cheaper cost per problem [12].

Research that compares SRUT and ARUT is much more limited. Andreasen et al. presented the results of a systematic empirical comparison of three remote usability testing methods and a lab-based think-aloud method [1]. The three remote methods consisted of both synchronous and asynchronous methods. The results indicated that synchronous remote testing had produced equivalent results to the lab-based testing. Results from the asynchronous testing condition were less positive with identification offewer usability issues, while spending more time completing the tasks assigned. Andreasen et al. still considers the approach to be worthwhile, as it frees the expert evaluators from a considerable amount of work and enable(s) collection of user data from a large number of participants" [1]. The efforts required by the evaluators per usability problem identified is lowest with ARUT. Thus SRUT identifies more usability problems compared to ARUT, but it also requires more effort both in total and per problem [1, 5].

Varga has also compared SRUT and ARUT but in terms of the qualitative experiences of the test subjects involved. Again, it is concluded that both of the methods have advantages and disadvantages, thus it is not possible to point to one of these methods as being superior to the other [23].

The research of ARUT has been focused on finding strengths and weaknesses of ARUT [5], however, this has all been research-based, in academic settings. There is a distinct research gap regarding the introduction and use of ARUT in industry practices. To our knowledge, there are no empirical studies of the introduction of remote usability testing in a software organisation. According to Wixon, this illustrates a large gape between research and practice [18].

Nørgaard and Hornbæk [19] and Reeves [17] wrote articles examining the practical application of UX practices by industry professionals. Nørgaard and Hornbæk examined how UX professionals conduct and analyse the think aloud method. They found that the industry application differed greatly from the theoretical research, showing that the professionals adjusted the method to fit their specific needs [19]. An article by Reeves presented the results of an ethnomethodological study on how UX practitioners produce findings in usability testing within a design consultancy [17]. The results indicated that usability findings were produced as observers analyse the test while it was still unfolding. It challenged current views of usability findings as something that is "there to be found". The study suggests refinement of the current definition and understanding of usability evaluation to better reflect how usability issues are in practice [17]. These two articles highlight the importance of researching in industry as well as it may differ from the theoretical research.

## 3 Methods

In this section we present the research approach and methods applied in our action research study. We begin by presenting the research approach taken, before describing the collaboration and approach of the usability test (Fig. 1).

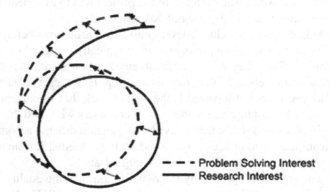

**Fig. 1.** Problem solving interest and research interest [13].

### 3.1 Research Approach

Action Research represents a duality between practice and theory. It is a research approach committed to "the production of new knowledge through the seeking of solutions or improvements to "real-life" practical problem situations" [13]. One of the distinguishing characteristics of action research is the active involvement of the researcher in the study itself [2]. "The action researcher is viewed as a key participant in the research process, working collaboratively with other concerned and/or affected actors to bring about change in the problem context" [13]. This involves having researchers providing new knowledge, while the problem owner has the contextual knowledge required to understand the situation [13]. Action research is partially consisting of the needs and competencies of the people involved, with a key feature being the willingness to share and learn from one another [13].

In this project, we adopted Mckay & Marshall's approach to action research as consisting of two separate cycles "superimposed on each other" [13]. They state that action researchers have a dual purpose of not only having to think of their research interests but also consider the problem-solving interest within the project collaboration [13].

We divided our study accordingly; with our problem solving interest focussing on support to the introduction of ARUT in the IT organization we collaborated with, while the research interest focussed on the exploration of challenges related to the introduction of ARUT in an organisation already relying on traditional usability testing methods.

## 3.2 Research Collaboration

We conducted our action research study in a two-month collaboration with an internal development team in the IT organization of the bank. The development team was using SCRUM and carried out their work in two-week sprints. Their sprint deliveries would typically be additions or changes to graphical user interfaces of the applications for which they were responsible. Their interest in the project was to experience ARUT as a means to improve the quality of these sprint deliveries.

Their development process included developing drawn prototypes before investing in software development. The drawn prototypes were typically designed in collaboration with key end-users. These key end-users involvement often meant that the resulting end product was well received by the broad user group. However, the team sometimes experienced that end-users not involved in the designs, felt that significant needs were not met. This could for instance be feedback from end-users who used the applications for slightly different purposes than the involved key-users. In order to accommodate this problem, the team wanted to utilize ARUT as means to get feedback from a broader set of end-users, possibly even all end-users in their organisation.

They also saw ARUT as opportunity to gradually improve the quality of their prototypes. If significant usability problems were found in the ARUT, the team would improve the design based on the findings, and re-evaluate it in another ARUT similar to the process in the RITE-method [27].

Due to the nature of their agile development approach, the teams perspective was to focus on identifying the most significant usability problems per ARUT iteration, rather than investing in finding all possible usability problems in a more costly traditional usability test. They would also focus their efforts on addressing critical usabillity problems, over minor or cosmetical ones, since they continuously had to prioritize their effort.

The aim of the collaboration was therefore to introduce the organisation to the concept of ARUT while determining the value of the approach in an agile industry practice.

The problem-solving interest of our research focused on conducting an asynchronous remote usability testing of a new internal support application for a national bank. The organisation used this first ARUT as a way to gain insight into, how to further expand the use of ARUT in the organisation.

The usability test was conducted using Preely and focused on the user friendliness and usability of an application by evaluating key use cases in the application. Preely was chosen as tool, since it allows for the use and import of graphical prototypes from the teams typical design tool (Figma), and it supports easy replacements of a frame (a part of the design) as a design is gradually improved. Preely therefore supported the purpose of iteratively testing slightly changed prototypes. Other tools were also considered prior to the selection of Preely, but they were discarded for various reasons ranging from, not having the desired functionality, to failing to live up to the banks security standards regarding data being stored abroad.

Preely was also considered to be the most accessible tool for the end-users, since it did not require the end-users to setup anything on their computers. They would only be required to click an invitation link. Similarly, no video or sound recording would be stored, so the end-users could conduct the ARUT from their desks in the office without being concerned about GDPR-issues.

**Communication.** Due to the outbreak of COVID-19, the collaboration took place using online communication tools such as Skype and Microsoft Teams. This allowed us to conduct meetings with our contact person; conduct walkthroughs of the application, plan testing and share results.

### 3.3 Participants

Three types of participants participated in this study. The internal development team, participants in the ARUT, and the authors of this paper.

The development team consisted of 10 members located in three cities in two countries. It was a full stack development team with members specialising in frontend and backend development, business analysis, UX design and application architecture. Their main focus was development of applications for internal use in the bank. They developed and maintained the application the usability test was conducted on.

Throughout the collaboration, the efforts were coordinated with the team through one specific team member. The results of the collaboration were presented for, and discussed with, the entire team.

For the usability testing, we recruited end-users of the application from within the bank. The test users were 12 members from a support team of mortgage advisers. The support team's role was to help financial advisers, calling in from partner banks, with mortgage lending cases. In this study they helped us collect data related to the usability of the application.

The authors of this paper all participated in the study. Three authors were researchers from the university. They were key participants in the research process, and contributed to the research data by conducting and documenting the application of ARUT within the organisation.

The last author was employed by the bank, and a member of the development team. In the research collaboration, his focus was to align the efforts with the organisation's goal, and to provide access to the organisation. He formulated the user cases based on interviews with the end users, and he was the primary recipient of the usability test result. During the maturation phase, he disseminated the initial results of the collaboration in the organisation, and he used the results of the usability test to redesign areas with significant usability problems.

### 3.4  Procedure and Setting

We divided the procedures between our research and problem-solving interests. For our problem-solving interest we focused on testing the internal application remote and asynchronously. The application had been released as a pilot release to the team of mortgage advisers, and was still being adjusted by the development team according to the feedback given by two pilot users. The research interest covered the application of asynchronous testing as well as the comparison between ARUT and the traditional testing methods usually implemented within the organisation.

The usability test was conducted using an online remote testing platform used for remote users and usability testing, Preely. It allows for the creation of interactive prototypes using screenshots and/or imported prototypes from other prototype development applications. In our case, we developed a clickable prototype using screenshots of the pilot release and a list of key use cases provided to us by the development team.

The prototype was built using Preely's internal prototype builder. It was based on use cases and screenshots provided by the development team, as well as on a walkthrough of the application itself. When completed, it was sent to the development team for feedback and corrections. This resulted in an additional development session in which we made adjustments based on the feedback. After being approved, it was sent to the test users who could then begin testing.

The use cases were constructed by interviewing two end-users about typical scenarios in their daily work. The interviews were also backed up by logged data about support calls. In total, 6 tasks were formulated to represent the use cases. The tasks were set up in Preely and all tasks were presented for the individual end users in the usability test sessions. The tasks can be seen in Table 1.

Besides the usability test, we conducted interviews with test users from both the development and the support team. These were based on Kvale and Brinkmann's interview techniques [10] and addressed their experience with the approach, as well as previous experience with traditional usability testing methods.

### 3.5  Materials

The test users received an email containing a short guide, introducing the test and testing procedure before receiving the test itself. The guide explained how testing would be conducted, as this would be the first time that they had to conduct testing asynchronously.

### 3.6  Data Collection

We collected data in three different areas covering results from the usability test, data on the application of ARUT in the organisation, and data on how usability testing is currently conducted within the organisation.

Testing took place over the course of 2 weeks and resulted in 12 responses. While previous research showed examples of ARUT being conducted over the course of 24 h [15], we would not have been able to replicate this approach. Due to the test user's inexperience with ARUT, which meant they needed more time for testing and familiarizing themselves with the concept, we found that additional time was needed. Other factors influencing the timespan were employee and bank holidays, which cut the actual time spent on testing down to 6 days.

Initially the test included a short guide introducing the test users to the concept of asynchronous usability testing. However, feedback from the users showed the guide to be lacking in its explanation and it was therefore revised to include more information on the approach and on how to identify usability issues within the software prototype. While this provided some discrepancies in the data, it minimised the user's confusion and allowed them to better identify and comment on any usability issues within the application.

Other issues included an initial lack of participation from the users as we only received 4 responses during the first week of testing. We sent out reminders and had the department manager involved to obtain as many responses as possible. This resulted in responses from all 12 department members and enough data to identify the most crucial usability issues within the application.

The end results from the usability test consist of 12 responses from all invited test users. These were collected and analysed through Preely. During the users task solving, Preely recorded the user interactions and recorded the time spent on each task. After each task Preely would prompt the users to rate their experience as well as give them the opportunity to provide additional textual feedback. After each individual tests session, Preely automatically constructed an interactive test report with information about completed tasks, given ratings, click-heat maps, and given feedback.

Aside from data collected through Preely, we conducted follow-up interviews with 2 of the users who had participated in testing.

We documented the development and testing process throughout all phases of the usability test by the diary approach presented by Jepsen et al. [7]. The diary was used to monitor the time spent on developing, conducting and analysing the usability test, as well as to comment on our experience of applying ARUT in the organisation. This allowed for deeper reflection on the approach and on our research goals.

Data covering the application of ARUT in the organisation consisted of 10 diary entries describing and documenting the entirety of the development and testing process, as well as 10-min follow up interviews with 2 test users. The interviews mostly focused on the user's testing experience and suggestions for improvements of the approach.

Lastly, we collected data on how usability testing would usually be conducted within the organisation. This consisted of an interview with a development team member in which we discussed their current testing approach, focusing on the results, time spent on testing, number of users, etc.

## 3.7 Data Analysis

We analysed data in two different ways; content analysis and analysis of metrics. The content analysis was implemented whenever there was textual data that needed to be analysed and sorted. The analysis of metrics was solely based on the usability test and the metrics provided through Preely.

We used content analysis for the interviews and the diary approach. The interview with the development team member was transcribed and sorted based on topics discussed during the interview. This included the tested use cases, time spent on testing, number of users, etc. These categories were later used to compare the current approach and the ARUT approach which we applied.

While we were not able to record the interview conducted with the test users, we based the data on notes taken during the interviews. These were sorted under each interview question and used to support any usability problems, as well as comment on the user experience.

The content analysis of the diary approach was done by categorising the experiences we had chronologically and thematically. We also categories the diary entries based on the development phase. This analysis was then used in the results to describe the application of ARUT and find usability problems of the testing tool.

The analysis of the usability test results was based on metrics provided in the interactive test report generated by Preely. The analysis took place immediately after testing was completed We identified usability problems by analysing the user's ability to reach the end of a task, as well as analysing their interactions while working with the task. We also examined their comments, the time it took to complete a task, and the scores the users gave after having completed a task. The usability problems were assessed based on tasks which had low scoring, a lower than an 80% completion rate, or if negative comments were given. The heat maps and interaction metrics were used to determine if a user would need to explore the prototype a lot in order to complete a task.

The usability test also elucidated certain usability problems that relate to the usability testing tool. This occurred as users often commented on their experience with the tool. These tool related usability problems were found based on the users' comments and our experience with developing the prototype.

## 4    Results

We present the results focusing on the initial introduction and application of ARUT within the organization; How was testing conducted, what data was collected using the approach, what was our experience with ARUT and lastly how did the organization adapt and implement the approach as a part of their existing testing procedures.

### 4.1    ARUT Process

In this section we will present the results of the initial introduction and application of ARUT within the collaborative organisation. These are mostly based on entries made in the diary, as this allowed us to keep track of the time spent on individual tasks, as well as recall and reflect on our experiences with the testing process (Fig. 2).

**Usability Testing.** On average, the test users would spend 13.25 min completing all the tasks. This number was however influenced by one outlier who spent 49 min idle before exiting the test. This inevitably affected the average time spent per user, as it would otherwise have been approximately 8 min per user.

**Follow-up Interviews.** These lasted an average of 10.5 min and discussed their experience testing asynchronously; problems they faced within the prototype, what they believed were the strengths and weaknesses of ARUT and how to improve the approach for future testing. The results were analysed and served as basis for future improvements of the approach, as well as to support any assumptions related to the users experience with asynchronous testing.

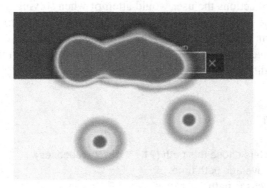

**Fig. 2.** Heatmap.

### 4.2 ARUT Results

By utilising the metrics available through Preely, we had access to plenty of information and statistics related to the users behavior and interaction with the application. This included heatmaps, action statistics, paths and clicks etc. In the following sections we will present the results of our testing, focusing on the value of the available data-collection metrics.

**Heatmaps.** The heatmap provided us with a collected overview of all clicks, swipes and scrolls performed on each screen within the application. It showed areas of the UI

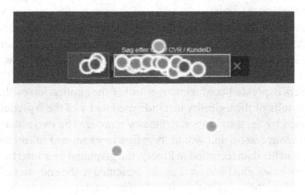

**Fig. 3.** Action overview.

that serve as hotspots for user interaction and was a useful tool when identifying areas that gained unintended attention from users searching to complete a specific task. This helped determine the cause for users not being able to complete a task, as it showed what part of the UI the users were focused on (Fig. 3).

**Action Overview.** While the heatmap served as a collected overview of the user's interactions with the UI, the action overview provided more details in terms of the specific actions and order of actions the user would attempt when solving a task. It allowed us to monitor what the users were clicking on, even when those elements were not programmed to perform any actions within the prototype. This was useful for recognising any mismatch between the users expectation of how the application would work versus its actual functionality and setup (Fig. 4).

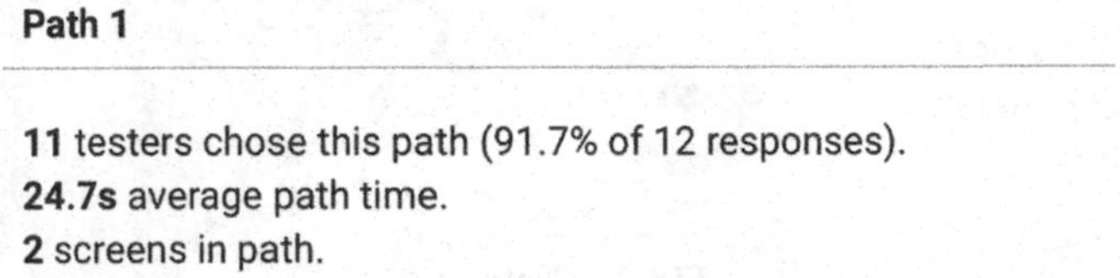

**Path 1**

---

**11** testers chose this path (91.7% of 12 responses).
**24.7s** average path time.
**2** screens in path.

**Fig. 4.** Path overview.

**Paths Overview.** The paths overview showed the different paths the users had taken while completing each task. This was the least useful overview, as the prototype mostly consisted of simple and linear paths that allowed users to find relevant information in a quick and efficient manner. However, while we did not use this overview very much, we recognise the value of this in a more complex application, that would require multiple paths to reach certain information.

**User Experience.** The users' experience was measured through a ten-point scale and comments section included at the end of each task. The ratings and user comments represented how the users felt about the tasks and allowed them to express their thoughts on any issues in their own words.

The average rating of each task (as seen in Table 1) expressed the users experienced solving each task, with examples of comments supporting the average user scores. While most of the tasks received a positive score, some didn't work out as well in an asynchronous setting, with Task 5 & 6 receiving the lowest average scores of 0/10 and 5.5/10. In both cases Users expressed confusion over either the application or the test itself.

The overall results of the usability test indicated that 4 of the 6 predefined use cases could be completed by the users in a satisfactory manner. The two remaining use cases were considered unsuccessful and would therefore be examined in further detail. Based on the feedback, and the data recorded in Preely, the graphical user interface related to the two use cases were redesigned and once again presented to the end-users. These changes were well-received by the users and were therefore implemented in the application, in this research collaboration's maturation period.

**Table 1.** Overview of task ratings.

| Task | Avg. Rating | User Comments |
|---|---|---|
| 1. You are getting a call from a consultant at the bank. The consultant is asking about customer xx (customer number xx). What do you do? | 7.36/ 10 | "We would usually use the customers cpr. number (in the search engine)." "It was easy and accessible" |
| 2. The consultant tells you that the customer has requested to change the payment date. Has the change been registered in the application? | 6.78/10 | *"A little confusing as I could not get down to the last page before I was asked to give feedback"* *"It was easy to figure out, but I did have issues finding where I should say yes or no to the task"* |
| 3. The consultant has asked you to confirm that the customer has received all of the relevant documents for this change | 9/10 | - No User Comments - |
| 4. The customer wants to ensure that the correct price has been used for the payment of the current loan. Which price has the customer been informed of? | 6.6/10 | *"Quite easy to find"* *"Was in doubt if I should click in the task text or on the payment price. The latter gave the result"* |
| 5. You realise that there is a mistake as the user interface and document do not contain the same information. The call is over, and you decide to report the mistake | 0/10 | *"I did not know that we could send an error report directly in the application"* |
| 6. The technical support calls about the same case. The consultant has contacted them as the case has not been approved for release. What is the reason for this? | 5.6/10 | - No User Comments - |

## 4.3  ARUT Experience

Throughout testing, we experienced some different challenges that influenced the initial introduction and application of ARUT within the organisation. In the following section we will present these challenges and discuss how to resolve them in future implementation.

**Test User Training.** The users who partook in testing had no prior training or experience with ARUT before introduced to the concept through our research. While we included a written guide explaining the approach, most users seemed confused and found it difficult to identify usability issues on their own.

The organisation's current testing approach has users conduct usability testing in the presence of a moderator, who can support and guide them. This is not possible with an asynchronous testing approach and users were therefore confused in terms of what to look for and comment on. This issue could however be resolved by training the users and giving them a proper introduction beforehand - either through in-person training or an introduction video. This would require some dedicated time for training but would result in easy asynchronous testing in the future.

**User Engagement.** We initially saw a low engagement from test users to partake in asynchronous testing. This could be due to ARUT not being as committal as traditional usability testing, which requires users to attend testing in person. In our case, users were instructed to do testing in between other tasks, which might have influenced how committed they felt. We did see an increase in responses after the department manager encouraged the users to participate, which then resulted in the 12 responses we ended up receiving.

Another reason could be the timing of testing, as it was conducted during a busy work period, which might have resulted in the users prioritising other work over testing.

**Usability Testing Tool.** We did identify some issues related to the testing tool based on user feedback and our own experience working with it. These issues mostly pertained to some confusing reporting functionalities, lack of input from essential keyboard keys and issues related to the drop-off function of the test. These caused additional confusion for the users, who commented more on issues experienced with the testing tool instead of issues related to the usability of the application and prototype. These issues can however be resolved by working around the tool's weaknesses and by training the users beforehand.

### 4.4 Maturation Phase

The initial collaboration lasted two months, followed by a six month maturation phase. The results from the collaboration phase was considered a success by both the involved team and the organisation. The results contributed to a further investment in a broader introduction of ARUT in the organisation.

In the maturation phase, the organisation has obtained additional licenses for the Preely platform, and invested in training of UX designers and interaction designers in using Preely. Additional agile teams were being introduced to ARUT and a usability test strategy for the use of ARUT was formulated and implemented in the organisation.

Based on the experience from using ARUT on internal applications and with internal users, ARUT was also extended to be used in customer facing applications. The banks' customers are now being invited to participate in ARUT through a user panel.

The front-end team that participated in the study have employed a student worker to help them quickly set up prototypes in Preely, and are now in the process of incorporating asynchronous remote usability evaluations in their agile development process.

# 5  Discussion

In this section we present the unexpected findings which we encountered during the research. We discuss the findings from the organisations perspective and their actions in the maturation phase. We also discuss our findings in the context of current remote usability testing research.

## 5.1  Other Findings

**Experience vs. Prototype.** The test users commented on the experience of the test rather than the prototype of the system. They often provided comments on how they would have worded or designed tasks. They also commented on the usability of the Preely platform, or the material they had been given to guide them in the test. The end-users suggestions include using vocabulary that the users are accustomed to, providing an extensive guide and having a greater understanding of the users and their work tasks.

While all of this feedback is relevant to mature the ARUT process in the organisation, it was also a source of noise in the concrete usability test. In order to improve the "signal to noise"-ratio, we have compiled a list of suggestion for the implementation of ARUT in organisational practice.

**Suggestions for Introduction:**

(1) The users will require a thorough introduction to the approach and tools applied, in order to avoid any confusion. This could come in the shape of either in-person training or an introductional video.
(2) The hypothesis being tested should be short and precise rather than extensive, This allows for more specific feedback on single features.
(3) The diction/language used within the task descriptions should match that of the users, not only to ensure an emulation of realistic use cases, but also to minimise confusion.
(4) The prototype should be pilot-tested with a group that mimics the demographic of the final users. This allows for any rough edges to be smoothed out before the prototype is deployed for full-scale testing.
(5) The users should have access to the development team in order to ask questions throughout testing, to make sure the testing effort is not halted due to technical or practical problems.

These suggestions come out of our action research study which was focussed on ARUT, which is why we only relate them to that approach. However, some of them, may be more generally applicable to remote usability testing in practice.

## 5.2  Introduction of ARUT in the Organisation

In the following, we will discuss the findings related to the introduction of ARUT from the organisations perspective. Again, some of these may be applicable to other approaches than ARUT, but we only have empirical data on ARUT.

**ARUT as a Part of an Agile Process.** The agile development team that participated in the research collaboration, found that the ARUT approach fit their needs. Their goal was to assess whether ARUT would allow for them to gain user feedback about small additions or changes to a graphical user interface in a fast way and with a low investment. The materials used for the test were created with less than two days work. The test was open for 14 days in Preely, but in reality only 6 days were used by the test users. It is further expected the amount of days needed for a test can be reduced even further with additional planning and coordination. Additionally ARUT contributed to finding two use cases that the users could not complete in the application in a satisfactory manner.

With these results in mind, the agile development team has concluded that the ARUT approach qualifies as a testing approach, that will allow for them to get user feedback on a sprint to sprint basis in an agile setting.

**Training of Test Users.** During the follow up interviews with User 1 and User 2, they both stated that they would have preferred more guidance throughout the usability test. They also stated that training the test users beforehand would have been a good idea as well. User 1 stated "introducing us to the testing program before would help". If the department would like to implement this process again, training and offering more support for the usability test would improve the overall experience and results.

Seen from the organisation's perspective, the initial problems of introducing an ARUT approach to internal employees, was manageable. Although the platform itself proved to be an obstacle to the initial users, the obstacle was made smaller by adjusting the instructions. Several of the end-users later said that they saw the benefit of using an ARUT approach, as this approach would allow them to both give feedback on the application they work in on a daily basis, while also being able to fit a 10–15 min test session in between other tasks. They also expressed that while they did have some initial problems with the platform itself, they expected them to be smaller in the future.

Training of the test users is a one time investment for internal users. The bank is also expanding the use of ARUT to external users, such as the bank's customers using various apps, homepages or home banking solutions. In this case, the organisation might not be able to provide similar training to the individual customer. For that reason, the findings related to the instructions, training material and access to support during the test period, is especially relevant, as they otherwise risk customers having a bad experience with the test. This might impact the customers opinion on the bank itself.

### 5.3   Relating Our Results

In this subsection we discuss the contribution of our findings in the context of ARUT research.

This research examines the implementation of ARUT in an IT department to examine its efficiency and efficacy, filling the lack of research regarding the practical application in industry practices. Previous research conducted by Martin et al. [12] and Andreasen et al. [1] discusses the implementation of ARUT in comparison to traditional lab-based usability testing. The findings indicated that ARUT identifies fewer usability problems. While our results supported these findings, we also identified other factors influencing the implementation and results of ARUT in industry practices; The amount of found usability problems is less important than finding the most severe problems in a fast way, the importance of proper user training, having a good understanding of the context of testing and having a high user engagement level.

Nørgaard and Hornbæk found the differences in the theoretical discussion and practical application of the think aloud method. Our research found that several of the strengths and weaknesses of ARUT in theory did not align in practice as UX professionals have different goals when it comes to UX tests. For example, we did find fewer usability problems, but that was also because the test was targeted towards one hypothesis; the purpose of the test was not finding many problems but finding the most significant problems within the 6 use cases. Reeves' study focused on the identification of usability findings in industry practices [17] and described how usability practitioners would work together to locate usability findings during testing. While we were not able to observe users as we conducted ARUT, we were able to analyse individual results as soon as they were submitted. This allowed us to compare results early on and adjust the test as needed.

### 5.4 Action Research Experiences

The research method applied in this paper is action research. The philosophical foundation of action research rise from hermeneutics, existentialism, and phenomenology [26]. There are four criteria for evaluating action research [26].

First, the researchers must intervene into the subject under study. The success of the research depends on engagement rather than detachment, Data are collected with participant observation, and this develops the empathy, the values exchange, and the role reversals that make researchers' knowledge useful and accepted by the subjects. In the research described above, the researchers intervened into the development activities of the IT organization.

Second, the project must be collaborative, and the subjects must be dynamically involved in determining the directions of the project. The researcher's role is not one of prediction in a passive world, but one of making things happen in an interactive world. In the research, the IT organization had a strong say in the design of the research. In particular, the IT organization decided that we should use ARUT and not SRUT, and they decided that we should work with an approach where the focus was on finding a few key problems rather than all usability problems.

Third, the knowledge goals should be interpretive and framed as "understanding" rather than "explanation." Although the theoretical constructs under empirical testing are complex and multivariate, they gain scientific usefulness as the conceptual "point of departure· for intervention in other settings; i.e. the theory must be interpreted and adapted in order to achieve construct validity in each new organizational setting.

Fourth, the action research project must yield a solution to the immediate problem situation. Action research develops learning from experience, which should be disseminated within the organization and published to the scientific community. This learning can lead to further action and major positive effects in diverse organizational settings. In our research, we managed to develop a solution for the IT organization.

# 6 Conclusion

In this article we have presented the results of a two-month collaboration with a national bank in which we introduced and conducted an asynchronous remote usability testing with the aim of determining the value of the approach for usability testing in the IT organisation. We conducted usability testing using a remote testing tool previously described by usability practitioners and implemented user-based work tasks to ensure a realistic testing experience for the test users [14, 8].

We conducted ARUT with 12 users from the internal financial support team. The test was based around 6 use cases supplied by the IT organisation. It had a structured guide for the users and all data was collected and analysed through an ARUT tool, Preely. While we were able to find relevant usability problems related to 2 of the 6 use cases tested, we found that there were several aspects that would have to be changed to maximise the efficiency of the test. This included taking the test users and their experience more into consideration during the development and planning stages. This was evident from the confusion experienced throughout testing, as test results improved when providing more guidance on how to complete individual tasks. However, we conclude that ARUT is a viable addition to the IT organisations repertoire of evaluation methods. This is supported by the fact that the IT organisation has chosen to move forward with further ARUT.

Limitations of this study included the lack of a pilot test before the launch of the actual prototype. Usually prototypes are tested with similar demographics before being tested with the final group. We tested the prototype and the link with a member of the development team, but we did not pre-test with the end-users to ensure the effectiveness of our final usability test. This could have caught any issues with the test before it was sent to the final test user. This research was conducted during the international Covid-19 health crisis, and therefore governmental restrictions also affected this research process. We were not able to meet with the development team or the usability test user in person. This is not required for ARUT testing; however, the follow-up interviews could have been conducted in person and possibly allowed for different insights.

For future research, it would be interesting to conduct an ARUT based usability test within this organisation again, following the steps outlined in the findings. The results from this research would allow for a more effective testing session and could therefore expand on the findings of this research. The implementation of ARUT could also be tested within several organisations, to compare the two workspaces and how easily ARUT can be implemented and how easily employees adapt to a new testing approach. This would allow for broader data on the general implementation of ARUT rather than the specific implementation of ARUT within one organisation.

# References

1. Andreasen, M.S., Nielsen, H.V., Schrøder, S.O., Stage, J.: What happened to remote usability testing? An empirical study of three methods. In: Conference on Human Factors in Computing Systems - Proceedings, pp. 1405–1414 (2007). https://doi.org/10.1145/1240624.1240838
2. Avison, D., Lau, F., Myers, M., Nielsen, P.: Action research. Commun. ACM **42**, 94–97 (1999). https://doi.org/10.1145/291469.291479

3. Bartek, V., Cheatham, D.: Experience remote usability testing, Part 1: examine the benefits and downside of remote usability testing. Developer Works **2**, 1–8 (2003)
4. Bastien, J.M.: Usability testing: a review of some methodological and technical aspects of the method. Int. J. Med. Inform. **79**(4) (2009). https://doi.org/10.1016/j.ijmedinf.2008.12.004
5. Bruun, A., Gull, P., Hofmeister, L., Stage, J.: Let your users do the testing: a comparison of three remote asynchronous usability testing methods. In: Conference on Human Factors in Computing Systems – Proceedings, pp. 1619–1628. ACM Press, New York and NY (2009). https://doi.org/10.1145/1518701.1518948
6. Castillo, J.C., Hartson, H.R., Hix, D.: Remote Usability Evaluation at a Glance (Technical report) (1997). https://doi.org/10.1145/286498.286736
7. Jepsen, L., Mathiassen, L., Nielsen, P.: Back to thinking mode: diaries for the management of information systems development projects. Behav. Inf. Technol. Behav. IT **8**, 207–217 (1989). https://doi.org/10.1080/01449298908914552
8. Jordan, P.W., Thomas, B., McClelland, I.L., Weerdmeester, B.: "Quick and Dirty" usability tests. In: Usability Evaluation in Industry, pp. 107–114 (1996). https://books.google.dk/books?id=ujFRDwAAQBAJ
9. Kjeldskov, J., Skov, M.B., Stage, J.: Instant Data Analysis: Conduction Usability Evaluations in a Day. Department of Computer Science, Aalborg University (2018)
10. Kvale, S., Brinkmann, S.: Part II: Seven Stages of an Interview Investigation. In Interviews: Learning the Craft of Qualitative Research Interviewing, 2nd ed., pp. 97–290. SAGE Publications, Inc., Thousand Oaks (2008)
11. Lewis, J.R.: Usability testing. In: Salvendy, G. (ed.), Handbook of Human Factors and Ergonomics Methods, pp. 1267–1312. John Wiley & Sons (2004). https://doi.org/10.1201/9780203489925
12. Martin, R., Shamari, M., Seliaman, M., Mayhew, P.J.: Remote asynchronous testing: a cost-effective alternative for website usability evaluation. Int. J. Comput. Inf. Technol. 03 (2014)
13. Mckay, J., Marshall, P.: The dual imperatives of action research. Inf. Technol. People. **14**, 46–59 (2001). https://doi.org/10.1108/09593840110384771
14. Pedersen, J.H.H., Sørensen, M.: Asynchronous Remote Usability Testing – Development and State of the Art: A literature review. Department of Computer Science, Aalborg University, Aalborg (2020)
15. Pedersen, J.H.H., Sørensen, M.: Asynchronous Remote Usability Testing in Practice: Exploratory Interviews with IT Professionals. Department of Computer Science, Aalborg University, Aalborg (2020)
16. Thompson, K.E., Rozanski, E.P., Haake, A.R.: Here, There, Anywhere: Remote Usability Testing that Works. In: Sigite 2004 Conference, pp. 132–137. ACM Press, New York (2004)
17. Reeves, S.: How UX practitioners produce findings in usability testing. ACM Trans. Comput.-Hum. Interact. **26**, 1–38 (2019). https://doi.org/10.1145/3299096
18. Wixon, D.: Evaluating usability methods: why the current literature fails the practitioner. Interactions **10**, 28 (2003). https://doi.org/10.1145/838830.838870
19. Nørgaard, M., Hornbæk, K.: What do usability evaluators do in practice? An explorative study of think-aloud testing. In: Proceedings of the Conference on Designing Interactive Systems: Processes, Practices, Methods, and Techniques, DIS, 2006, pp. 209–218 (2006)
20. Hartson, H.R., Castillo, J.C., Kelso, J., Neale, W.C.: Remote evaluation: the network as an extension of the usability laboratory. In: Proceedings of CHI 1996, pp. 228–235. ACM Press (1996)
21. Castillo, J.C., Hartson, H.R., Hix, D.: Remote usability evaluation: can users report their own critical incidents? In: Proceedings of CHI 1998, pp. 253–254. ACM Press (1998)
22. Hammontree, M.L., Weiler, P., Nayak, N.P.: Remote usability testing. Interactions **1**, 21–25 (1994)

23. Varga, E.: An Experiential comparative analysis of two remote usability testing methods. Thesis. Rochester Institute of Technology (2011)
24. McFadden, E., Hager, D.R., Elie, C.J., Blackwell, J.M.: Remote usability evaluation: overview and case studies. Int. J. Hum.-Comput. Interact. 14(3 and 4), 489–502 (2002)
25. Sauer, J., Sonderegger, A., Heyden, K., Biller, J., Klotz, J., Uebelbacher, A.: Extra-laboratorial usability tests: an empirical comparison of remote and classical field testing with lab testing. Appl. Ergon. 74, 85–96 (2019)
26. Susman, G., Evered, R.: An assessment of the scientific merits of action research. Adm. Sci. Q. 23, 582–603 (1978)
27. Medlock, M.C., Wizon, D., Terrano, M. Romero, R., Fulton, B.: Using the RITE method to improve products: a definition and a case study. In: Proceedings of UPA 2002. Usability Professionals Association, Orlando (2002)

# Investigating User Perceptions Towards Wearable Mobile Electromyography

Sarah Prange[1,2]([✉]) [ID], Sven Mayer[2] [ID], Maria-Lena Bittl[2], Mariam Hassib[1], and Florian Alt[1] [ID]

[1] Bundeswehr University Munich, Munich, Germany
{sarah.prange,florian.alt}@unibw.de
[2] LMU Munich, Munich, Germany
info@sven-mayer.com

| (a) Chewing | (b) Gait | (c) Stress |

**Fig. 1.** We conducted a user study (N = 36), investigating users' perceptions of wearable EMG applications. Participants tried out our EMG prototype and watched videos showing several EMG use cases, evolving around (a) Chewing, (b) Gait, and (c) Stress.

**Abstract.** Wearables capture physiological user data, enabling novel user interfaces that can identify users, adapt to the user state, and contribute to the quantified self. At the same time, little is known about users' perception of this new technology. In this paper, we present findings from a user study (N = 36) in which participants used an electromyography (EMG) wearable and a visualization of data collected from EMG wearables. We found that participants are highly unaware of what EMG data can reveal about them. Allowing them to explore their physiological data makes them more reluctant to share this data. We conclude with deriving guidelines, to help designers of physiological data-based user interfaces to (a) protect users' privacy, (b) better inform them, and (c) ultimately support the uptake of this technology.

**Keywords:** Wearable devices · User perceptions · Electromyography · Privacy

**Electronic supplementary material** The online version of this chapter (https://doi.org/10.1007/978-3-030-85610-6_20) contains supplementary material, which is available to authorized users.

C. Ardito et al. (Eds.): INTERACT 2021, LNCS 12935, pp. 339–360, 2021.
https://doi.org/10.1007/978-3-030-85610-6_20

# 1    Introduction

An increasing number of physiological sensors, which can be embedded in wearable devices, are surrounding us today. These allow users' physical, physiological, and even cognitive state to be constantly monitored [64]. With advances in computational power, storage capacity, and network connectivity, large amounts of data gathered through wearable devices can be processed and stored in the cloud. This development allows researchers and commercial applications to build intelligent user interfaces based on physiological data [36, 72]. Furthermore, this also provides insights about users' health and well-being through commercial apps like Google Fit or Fitbit as well as research applications, e.g., [11, 39, 77].

A wide variety of physiological sensors are making their way into consumer electronics, for example, the Apple Watch Series 4 onwards contains an electrocardiogram (ECG) sensor[1]. In this work, we are focusing on electromyography (EMG) as one such sensor. EMG sensors and data are particularly interesting from a research perspective because they can be easily deployed over a long period of time (i.e., several weeks) and on various parts of the body. EMG refers to electrical signals created by the muscles. Sensing the electrical signals allows to track muscle "activity", such as *contraction* or *relaxation* [59]. The signal strongly depends on the anatomical and physiological properties of a muscle and thus can, for instance, serve as a biometric feature [38]. On a higher abstraction level, posture or muscle contraction-specific information can be derived based on an EMG signal and then be classified into control commands using a neuronal network [30] or feature-based classifier [3]. For input purposes even commercial products are available, for example, the Myo wristband enabling advanced gesture input [53]. Moreover, while other sensors, such as ECG, can recognise users being active, EMG data can identify the respective activity (e.g., stepping stairs). As a consequence, EMG can provide more detailed insights into the human's health. For example, research demonstrated how EMG data can be used to gain insights about users' chewing [7, 15], gait [13, 19], and stress [73] behaviour (cf. Fig. 1). At the same time, the underlying data can be used to derive further information, such as users' health and well-being. Thus, this type of sensitive data has to be treated with care [14, 45] – in particular, as Rocher et al. [60] has shown that artificial intelligence (AI) can deanonymize whole data sets.

These developments create a need to investigate users' perception towards collecting, processing and storing physiological data. At the same time, researchers and practitioners should be aware of the risks and users' perception when designing systems involving physiological signals [37]. While users are aware of privacy concerns regarding other sensor data (e.g. GPS [2]), their awareness of risks regarding physiological data, in particular EMG data, is not well understood yet.

To close this gap, we investigate to which degree users are aware of the potential privacy risks posed by EMG data. In a study, we evaluated (1) participants' sharing behaviour in general and for physiological data based on EMG in partic-

---

*All sources last accessed June 8, 2021.*
[1] https://support.apple.com/en-us/HT208955.

ular and (2) assessed participants' opinions towards the privacy of EMG data. We found that participants changed their willingness to share EMG data over the course of the study as they are getting a better understanding of what risks the data entails. Furthermore, we derive a set of guidelines for designers of EMG-based user interfaces, helping them to protect users' privacy, better inform them about the involved risks, and ultimately support the uptake of EMG technology.

## 2    Related Work

To understand users' perception of wearable EMG devices, we first investigate what EMG can reveal about users. Thus, we review work on EMG and describe use cases. We then present state-of-the-art metrics to assess users' perception on personal data and their privacy. Finally, as sensor data is prone to constitute uncertainty, we also review visualization techniques for uncertainty.

### 2.1    EMG-based User Interfaces

Related work shows that EMG and physiological signals provide valuable opportunities for novel user interfaces. As measuring electrical signals from muscle activity offers a new modality for intuitive input, a wide range of applications have emerged. The most prominent area of EMG-based user interfaces is using the signals to classify hand gestures [36,48]. Application areas include scenarios where the hands are occupied, e.g., to support safety during cycling [40], smartwatch interaction [41], or interactive storytelling [23]. In addition, EMG is also used to recognize sign language [1], in human robot collaboration tasks [72], and even fine-grained detection like the pressure applied by a finger [4]. While these prior works placed the EMG electrodes mainly on the arm, a smaller number of research also investigated other muscles. Here, Huang et al. [33] for instance, used facial EMG to help people with disabilities control a mouse cursor. Additionally, Gibert et al. [22] also applied EMG to the face with the goal of providing better facial mimics for virtual reality (VR) avatars.

EMG has also been explored to provide better insights about health and well-being using wearable devices. EMG electrodes on the legs allow motion patterns to be identified, e.g., for distinguishing running from walking [13] or to calculate speed from users' gait [19]. EMG measured at the trapezius muscle (i.e., in the neck) can serve as a stress detector [73]. In daily life self-tracking situations, EMG could support eating reports as it allows detecting chewing [7,15].

From this we learn that EMG sensors can serve a variety of purposes as more detailed activity information – as compared to other sensors – can be revealed. Thus, a large variety of application areas exists for EMG data and we will likely see many novel user interfaces and interaction techniques in the future.

### 2.2    User Perception and Privacy

Privacy is a challenge in ubiquitous computing, due to the properties of novel devices: ubiquity, invisibility, sensing, and memory amplification [42]. Also, collected data can generate knowledge about users which is available to everyone

[50,68]. Calo [12] states "privacy harm as a unique type of injury" [12]. Thus, privacy protection is crucial.

Wearables, one type of ubiquitous devices, are increasingly present in users' daily lives, for example, fitness trackers, or smartwatches. They raise particular privacy concerns as they are continuously tracking sensitive user data (for example, health related). Motti and Cane [49] found several factors influencing users' privacy concerns with wearable devices. They highlight that these concerns depend on the type of device, the nature of data, and on the ability to share or disclose the data. Health tracking is often combined with online sharing, which raises privacy issues [58]. Moreover, Wilkowska and Ziefle [74] highlight privacy aspects to be considered to allow for adoption of medical assistive technologies. At the same time, Rahman et al. [58] showed that fitness trackers, such as Fitbit, are relatively easy to attack.

Privacy issues often arise when health data is being shared. Puussaar et al. [57] show that users' willingness to share fine-grained data is redacted. Gorm and Shklovski [25] showed that, in the workplace, participants got more reluctant to share their counts over time. With regards to mobile app usage, users may perceive privacy being violated in "creepy" ways [67].

To address privacy issues with ubiquitous devices, Langheinrich [42] suggests to preserve privacy by design, for example, by informing subjects about data collection, receiving explicit consent, or by keeping anonymity of tracked subjects. Here, Schaub et al. [63] propose a design space for effectively informing users about a system's data practices. Hoyle et al. [32] suggest in-situ control of privacy for wearable lifelogging cameras. Perez and Zeadally [55] propose mechanisms to control data collection in wearables for privacy protection. They argue that anonymization should be applied even to aggregated data. Lau et al. [43] integrate privacy controls for smart speakers, such as Amazon Alexa. Since the main user concern is potential surveillance via smart speakers, they suggest commands like "Alexa, stop listening" [43]. Paul and Irvine [54] highlight privacy issues when using health monitoring wearables, namely data ownership, classification, and storage.

Related work shows that privacy is a challenge in ubiquitous computing, in particular, when obtaining and potentially sharing users' physiological health state. However, users' perception towards physiological data collection and sharing has not been investigated in depth so far, which is at the focus of our work.

## 2.3    Uncertainity Visualization in Sensor Data

In data visualization, communicating uncertainty [52] is important. This is particularly true for aggregated data, since insights might get lost due to the aggregation, such as weather forecasts [24,27], public transport prediction [35], car range prediction [34], or gene exploration [66]. Moreover, visualizing uncertainty supports making informed decisions [28,62].

Error bars are the most common tool to communicate uncertainty [17,29]. Additionally, uncertainty can be presented by changing the visual properties, e.g., blur [26,29], color, or transparency [16]. To highlight specific data and uncertainty, more complex visual components can be added to the visualization [8,10], such as, for instance, annotations [18]. Results indicate that error bars are suitable for tasks without probability values. We conclude that when visually presenting data, it is important to also represent uncertainty in the visualization to support sense-making. In our work, we use uncertainty visualizations in the form of error bars to support EMG data discovery.

## 3    Hypotheses

EMG sensors are easy to deploy and the data obtained from EMG sensors can not only be used for interaction, but also reveal detailed information about users' activities and well-being. Thus, it is important to foster a better understanding and awareness of personal sensor data. Our research is guided by the following hypotheses:

H1 **Users are concerned about sharing personal EMG data.** Motti and Caine [49] show that wearables are generally of concern for users. As EMG has a rich potential to uncover daily routines, habits, and health status, we hypothesize that users are concerned about recording/sharing their personal EMG data.

H2 **Providing users an understanding of EMG sensor data will change their sharing habits and privacy attitude.** Puussaar et al. [57] show that users' willingness to share fine-grained data is low. We hypothesize demonstrating the richness of EMG data will reduce users' willingness for sharing and recording.

H3 **The degree of detail of data visualization influences participants' opinion on recording and sharing sensor data.** Greis et al. [28] showed that presenting uncertainty information improved users' ability to judge the data. We hypothesize that presenting visualizations (of aggregated data) will result in greater willingness to share, even if content providers may keep fine-grain data.

## 4    Study

To test our hypotheses we conducted a mixed methods user study with 36 participants. We asked participants (Part A) to try a music player prototype which they could control using an EMG device, and (Part B) showed them three videos of activities and the corresponding real EMG data (i.e. chew, gait, and stress – see Fig. 1), and aggregated visualization dashboards.

In Part A, we used prototyping as a research method [61] to convey the experience of using an EMG device. Additionally, we presented users their own real-time EMG feedback. In Part B, we used a low-fidelity prototype [61] of an interactive dashboard with pre-recorded EMG data from three different scenarios and videos showcasing the scenarios. Figure 4 illustrates the two parts of our study and in the following we describe in detail our study design. This research method of presenting videos or images to ask about users' opinions is well established and common in human-computer interaction (HCI) [65,71].

### 4.1    Part A: EMG Music Player Prototype

We implemented a simple EMG application where the user can like or dislike music, using an EMG sensor. We used the Spotify web API[2]. We implemented a genre selection feature as well as play and pause using the mouse. Each song played for 15 s until moving to the next song. Users had the possibility to like or dislike a song by using the thumbs up or down gesture while the system detected the gesture with three dry, passive, non-invasive electrodes placed on the user's forearm (see Fig. 2). The system provided feedback for every EMG like/dislike. Additionally, the users were shown their own EMG signal. Note that the music player was solely meant to showcase what EMG is and how it works in practice, rather than being a privacy-sensitive use case.

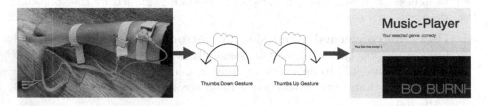

**Fig. 2.** EMG Showcase Music Player: Dry, passive, non-invasive electrodes were mounted on the participants' forearm to receive the thumbs up and down metaphor for like or dislike.

### 4.2    Part B: EMG Use Case Visualizations

In Part B, we follow a mixed-model design with two independent variables: USECASE, and DETAIL. While USECASE was a within-subjects variable with three levels (*Chew, Gait, Stress*), DETAIL was a between-subjects variable with two levels (*Low, High*). We counter-balanced USECASE within DETAIL using a Latin square design [75].

We chose three USECASES, to show participants what information can be extracted from EMG data using video clips which we carefully created in a neutral way (i.e., we generated the videos without highlights, zoom shots, or other special effects to keep them simple, cf. Fig. 1).

(a) *Chewing*: As a more unusual use case, we choose detecting chewing movements from EMG (as shown by Blechert et al. [7]). This is closely related to users' routines, eating behaviour and health state (referring to, for example, eating disorders). In this video, we showed scenes of people eating soft food and hard food as well as drinking water.

(b) *Gait*: Related work showed that gait patterns can be identified from EMG signals [13,19]. In addition, Google SmartLock[3] tracks gait features for on body detection. Moreover, many users keep track of their gait. Thus we assume

---

[2] https://developer.spotify.com/documentation/web-api/.

[3] https://support.google.com/android/answer/9075927.

gait to be an important application case for users of tracking technologies. In this video we showed a short sequence of gait scenes, including walking, running, and stepping stairs.

(c) *Stress*: Tracking productivity is a common use case. At the same time, high workload may result in stress situations for users. Stress can be detected using EMG [73]. The actor of this video was in a relaxed situation first, while showing a stressful exam situation afterwards.

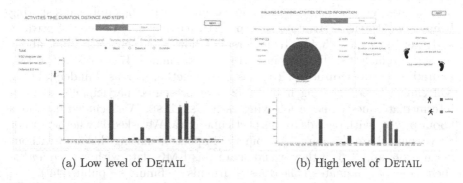

(a) Low level of DETAIL                    (b) High level of DETAIL

**Fig. 3.** EMG Dashboard: We provided insights into fictive EMG data to our USECASES. Participants were randomly assigned to one group of DETAIL: a) *Low* or b) *High*.

We created dashboards to visualize mock EMG data per USECASE. The dashboards were designed similar to other dashboards people use to track their fitness, health state, or analyze their behaviour, e.g., Endomondo[4], Google Fit[5], Apple Health[6], or RunScribe[7]. We evaluated two levels of DETAIL (i.e., *Low* and *High*, cf. Fig. 3), differing in the level of *aggregation*: *Low* presents one bar chart of aggregated data (Fig. 3a), while *High* presents multiple charts and single data values (Fig. 3b). For instance, for the USECASE *Gait*, the dashboard of *low* detail shows the total and average number of steps, distance and duration per day or per week. The *high* level of detail dashboard shows single values for steps, distance and duration as well as information on speed, direction, and movement per foot.

## 4.3 Data Collection

During the study, data was collected by means of questionnaires and interviews (cf. Fig. 4), which we describe in detail below.

**Introductory Interview.** We first conducted a semi-structured interview asking about any use of fitness trackers or other wearables and if so why participants used them. We also asked if they know what electromyography (EMG)

---

[4] https://www.endomondo.com/?language=EN.
[5] https://www.google.com/fit/.
[6] https://www.apple.com/lae/ios/health/.
[7] https://runscribe.com/.

is and explained this if necessary. Further questions included: *"What do you think would be the most likely risks associated with wearable devices?"* and *"What do you think, what role does security and privacy play to health monitoring devices in this respect? Do you think it is important and, if so, why?"*

**Sharing Behaviour & Privacy Questionnaire.** To understand if and how participants generally share personal data (with whom), we designed a questionnaire that synthesizes related work. The questionnaire covered the following topics: social media sharing behaviour [70], how the content type (personal or sensitive, sensational, political, and casual information) influences sharing behaviour [51], the motivation to share [21], participants' opinion of privacy, and their own data [5,47]. To understand how they generally think about privacy, we included the 10-item IUIPC questionnaire [47] (Table 1, Q4–13).

**Intermediate Questionnaire.** To investigate whether increased understanding will change users' sharing habits (H2), we presented participants with an intermediate questionnaire following each USECASE. We included questions about privacy with regards to this particular data. We asked 1) whether or not they would share this data, 2) about the impact of sharing this data without permission, and 3–6) if they would share this EMG data with < *recipient* > (being one of classmates/colleagues — friends — family — public [44]).

**Final Interview.** We conducted a semi-structured interview on possible EMG use cases, what users learned, and their feelings about EMG recording and sharing.

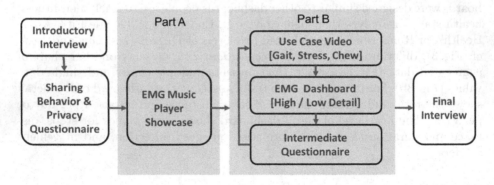

**Fig. 4.** Study procedure. Part A: EMG prototype. Part B: EMG videos/visualizations.

## 4.4   Procedure

The study was conducted in a single room at our institute. The session took 45–60 min per participant. The detailed procedure was as follows (cf. Fig. 4 for an overview):

*(1) Introduction.* We started by welcoming participants, and explaining the purpose of the study. We then asked participants to fill in a consent form, and started with the *introductory interview.* After filling in a demographics questionnaire (including use of social media), we asked participants to fill in the *Sharing Behaviour & Privacy Questionnaire* to understand their behaviour and risk perception prior to the study. We then continued the *introductory interview* as participants by now already thought about possible implications (addressing H1).

*(2) Part A.* Part A started with making all participants familiar with EMG. To close possible knowledge gaps, participants tried our *EMG music player prototype* (around 10–15 min). We attached three electrodes to the participants' forearm (Fig. 2) and showed participants the thumbs up/down gesture to like or dislike songs. The UI showed the current song and genre and, more importantly, visualized the live EMG signal. The visualization enabled participants to explore their own EMG input.

*(3) Part B.* Afterwards, we continued with Part B in which we presented the three different USECASES to participants in counter-balanced order as *videos* (i.e., participants did not try these themselves). Participants were asked to explore the possible insights into the data using our *visualization dashboard.* Participants were randomly assigned to one level of DETAIL to investigate H3. Alongside each USECASE, participants were presented a couple of tasks to solve with the visualization as well as the *intermediate questionnaire* (H2). Tasks were similar to: *"On what day and at what time has the stress level the amount of 12%?"* Additionally, we asked the following three questions for each USECASE: *"What do you find out about the person and the course of the day?"*, *"Can you make any statements about this person's lifestyle?"*, and *"What do you learn about daily habits/routines of this person?"*

*(4) Final Interview.* At the end, we conducted the *final interview* with participants.

## 4.5  Participants

We recruited 36 participants through a university mailing list and social media to take part in the study (24 female, and 12 male). The age range was between 19 and 64 years ($M = 28.6$, $SD = 9.2$). 22 of our participants stated to be students, 12 were employed, 1 was retired and 1 stated to currently be unemployed. We asked participants about their most used social media. Two participants stated they do not use social media. All other used social media. Here, Facebook was stated most often (18 times), followed by Instagram (11 times), and YouTube (4 times). Twitter and Snapchat were named by one participant each. We reimbursed participants with €10.

**Table 1.** Q1 to Q3 are modified questions based on Malhotra et al.'s causal model [47]. Additionally, we asked participants the 10-item IUIPC questionnaire [47] (Q4 – Q13). All reported Likert items are on a 7-point scale (1 = strongly disagree; 7 = strongly agree).

| Question | | M | SD |
|---|---|---|---|
| Q1 | I have been the victim of what I felt was an improper invasion of privacy | 2.2 | 1.7 |
| Q2 | I am very concerned about the privacy of my data | 4.7 | 1.9 |
| Q3 | I always falsify personal information needed to register with some websites | 2.9 | 1.8 |
| Q4 | It usually bothers me when online companies ask me for personal information | 5.7 | 1.5 |
| Q5 | When online companies ask me for personal information, I sometimes think twice before providing it | 5.9 | 1.2 |
| Q6 | It bothers me to give personal information to so many online companies | 6.1 | 1.1 |
| Q7 | I'm concerned that online companies collect too much personal information | 5.5 | 1.4 |
| Q8 | Your online privacy is really a matter of your right to exercise control and autonomy over decisions about how your information is collected, used, and shared | 5.9 | 1.2 |
| Q9 | Your control of your personal information lies at the heart of your privacy | 6.2 | 1 |
| Q10 | I believe that online privacy is invaded when control is lost or unwillingly reduced as a result of a marketing transaction | 5.7 | 1.3 |
| Q11 | Companies seeking information online should disclose the way the data are collected, processed, and used | 6.7 | .6 |
| Q12 | A good consumer online privacy policy should have a clear and conspicuous disclosure | 6.8 | .6 |
| Q13 | It is very important to me that I am aware and knowledgeable about how my personal information will be used | 6.6 | .7 |

## 4.6   Limitations

Our study has few limitations. First, our study sample is biased towards young, female students, and might thus not apply to the general public. Second, we investigated users' perceptions towards wearable physiological sensing by means of one example, that is EMG, and by using use case videos. Future work should investigate if and how our recommendations apply to other physiological sensing technologies as they become more ubiquitous. Lastly, experimenter bias is a known limitation for qualitative experiments. As such, alternative names may be given to themes. However, we believe that this does not impact the resulting discussion and design recommendations.

# 5   Results

We conducted a between subjects study with 36 participants. In the following, we first report on the questionnaires and second on the interview analysis. All reported Likert items are on a 7-point scale (1 = strongly disagree; 7 = strongly agree).

## 5.1   Questionnaire Results

We used a 10-item version of the IUIPC [47]. Using Q4 to Q13 (see *Sharing Behaviour & Privacy Questionnaire*, Table 1) we calculate the following measurements as described by Malhotra et al. [47]. Participants rated their *Awareness* on average with 6.7 (*SD* = .5), *Control* with 5.9 (*SD* = .9), and *Collection* with 5.8 (*SD* = 1.). Thus, overall they were aware of possible concerns (H1).

**Sharing Behaviour (H2).** We conducted Friedman tests for each group over time to understand if the fact that participants needed to explore and understand the data would change their sharing behaviour. We analyzed how likely our participants are to share their EMG data with others over the course of the study (see Fig. 5a). After each of the use cases we asked them the same question (cf. *Intermediate Questionnaire*): "I would share this EMG data with < recipient >", with < recipient > being "public", "classmates/colleagues", "friends", or "family" [44]. Additionally, to see if there is an overall trend in our analysis, we conducted five Friedman tests. Our analysis showed a significant decrease in willingness to share EMG data with the family ($\chi^2(2) = 12.9$, $p < .002$) as well as an overall decrease ($\chi^2(2) = 6.4$, $p < .043$). We found no significant effect for public, classmates/colleagues, and friends ($\chi^2(2) = .743$, $p > .689$; $\chi^2(2) = 2.$, $p > .367$; $\chi^2(2) = 1.882$, $p > .390$; respectively).

**Usage of EMG Wearables (H3).** To understand if DETAIL had an effect on the likelihood that participants want to use EMG wearables in the future, we conducted an analysis of covariance (ANCOVA) based on the initial and final question; see Fig. 5b. Due to the unequal ratings before the study of the two groups, we analyzed the changes resulting from the variable DETAIL. Furthermore, as related work showed an impact of gender on privacy attitudes [20] and technology acceptance [69], we used gender as a covariate. We applied the Aligned Rank Transform (ART) [76] to the Likert items. Our analysis revealed no significant main effects for DETAIL ($F_{1,32} = 1.506$, $p = .228$). We found that participants were very sensitive to their data and had privacy concerns already prior to the study, see Table 1.

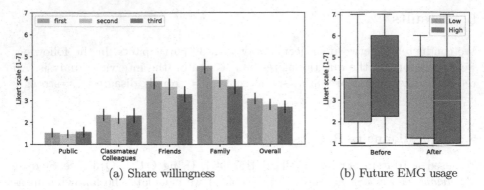

**Fig. 5.** (a) Change in willingness to share EMG data with certain groups over the course of the study. (b) Change in likelihood that a participant wants to use EMG wearables in the future based on the experience in the study independent for DETAIL.

## 5.2   Interview Results

We conducted interviews with 36 participants. We transcribed the interviews literally while not summarizing or transcribing phonetically. This technique is known to offer a subjective experience [6]. A total of three researchers were involved in the interview analysis. First, two researchers independently went through the printed transcripts of three participants and established an initial coding tree. As conflicts were resolved directly, we did not calculate inter-rater reliability. Then, one of them coded the rest of the data in a bottom-up manner and established the final coding tree (i.e., while iterating through the rest of the answers, new themes were defined). Finally, three researchers employed a simplified version of qualitative coding with affinity diagramming [31], which resulted in the themes we discuss below. While participants in our study had the option to express thoughts freely, they did not specifically comment on the use cases and visualization approaches. Rather, we found overarching themes regarding usage of EMG wearables, sharing behavior, personal data perception, and privacy challenges.

We conducted the interviews in our maternal language while only translating single quotes. We cite participants' IDs as well as study groups (*low* or *high* with regards to the variable DETAIL).

**Usage of EMG Wearables.** The interviews revealed details on whether or not and how participants would make use of EMG wearables. Two participants (one of each group low, high) would use it if it is comfortable (in terms of wearing and ease of use). Most participants (12 of group low, 14 of group high) would use EMG only if the purpose would suit them. Specific purposes included sport, health, monitoring stress level, or sleep.

*It must have a purpose and utility. A relief for everyday life. (P19, low)*

*[as an interaction], where it is simply helpful or it facilitates my work. (P3, low)*

On the other hand, participants also named potential risks of usage. Here, four participants named radiation or malfunction of devices.

**Sharing Behaviour** Four participants (two of each group low, high) expressed being aware of the fact that wearable (EMG) devices would collect and potentially share personal data. These concerns are related to concerns of personal data (H1) and sharing habits (H2).

*I know, if I buy such a device, I have to share some of my data and this is okay for me.(P29, low)*

However, most participants expressed to prefer, on one hand, transparency (i.e., knowing that data is been shared) and on the other hand control (i.e., choosing actively to share or not to share their data). Depending on the purpose, participants were willing to share their EMG data.

*If it [sharing the data] has a benefit for me, then I would forego my privacy. (P11, low)*

Specific use cases, for which P11 would share data, include medical studies or personal benefits. 6 participants rated sharing as less critical in case of anonymized EMG data.

Participants described how they would react in case EMG data would be revealed unintendedly. Some participants would actively fight unauthorized data reveallation (i.e., 8 participants would take legal action). Others were more passive (i.e., would not explicitly take action) while still disliking personal EMG data being revealed.

**Personal Data Perception** During the interviews, we discussed how personal participants would perceive their EMG data: less, more, or as privacy sensitive as "other" personal data (e.g., name, birthday).

*If I think about what is possible with this [EMG] data through processing, I think it is important to me to protect this data in the same way as my other personal data. (P24, low)*

This awareness further underlines that users are in fact concerned with sharing their data (H1). Further, participants strongly highlighted the difference between data they were or were not identifiable from (H2).

*You cannot even say who I really am. (P27, low)*

**Privacy Challenges and Threats.** 12 participants were concerned about being tracked and surveyed by the service provider or even the government. 7 participants were worried about being refused for health insurance, in case the insurance would know their EMG data. Privacy plays an important role, but also depends on the context for many participants. Health data was named as particularly concerning (5 participants). Some already mentioned possible attacks (i.e., data leaks) and were concerned about misuse of their data. New threat models may evolve around physiological data and users' health.

### 5.3 Summary

Most participants expressed concerns about sharing their private physiological data. However, only few of them would take any action against undesired sharing. At the same time, anonymous sharing or sharing for a certain purpose would be more acceptable for participants. Hence, we confirm that users are *concerned about their EMG data's privacy* (**H1**). We showed that participants, who were more willing to share personal data prior to the study, were also *more willing to share their EMG data*, which confirms (**H2**). We revealed that working with the dashboard and *getting engaged with EMG data influences the willingness to share data*, thus confirming (**H3**).

## 6   Discussion

Based on our qualitative and quantitative results, we discuss how participants perceived collecting and sharing EMG data. Moreover, we discuss the insights on a more general level with respect to potential risks as well as opportunities for novel, intelligent and mobile interfaces based on physiological sensor data.

### 6.1   User Perceptions of Intelligent Wearables

Participants raised privacy concerns with regards to their personal data already prior to the study. However, they were willing to share their (potential) EMG data with close family and friends, who generally are known to be more trustworthy [9], yet they would only share for certain purposes (e.g., personal benefits or research). Additionally, participants highlighted potential risks connected to physiological sensor data, e.g., if health insurances would get hold of users' physiological data. This leads us to assume that users are generally not reluctant to employ novel, intelligent wearables if they would only fit their need and purpose, which is in line with the privacy calculus theory (i.e., users outweigh their personal benefits over perceived risks, cf. e.g., [46]). However, we can also confirm **H1**: users are concerned about sharing personal EMG data.

## 6.2  Unaware Users

Participants of our study stated that collecting EMG data anonymously would not be critical to them (e.g., referring to P27: *"You can not even say who I really am."*). Thus, they are aware of data type, however, not all are concerned with sharing the data (**H1**) and may not change their behaviour (**H2**). However, preserving anonymity needs special attention as it has been shown that datasets can be de-anonymized [60]. Thus, while physiological sensor data has a great potential to inform user interfaces and users are even fine with the data collection, we argue that users may not be aware of the potential risk and danger their own data bury. Hence, we argue that data should not be hidden from the user, and the user should always be in control of their data being shared and especially the data that is not shared with the public and thus mostly hidden to the user. This may ultimately address users' concerns (**H1**) and change their sharing habits (**H2**).

## 6.3  Enabling an Improved Health Awareness

We found that our participants are open to try EMG-based wearables, especially for use cases that fit their daily needs and habits. They are open to interaction concepts which use EMG as a signal to trigger interactions, like the Myo wristband. More importantly, they are also open to use EMG to foster a better awareness about their own physiological state, for instance, on a dashboard or app. This brings great potential for new quantified self platforms, but also carries responsibility to convey the right data.

In our case, we employed mock visualizations and use case videos showing EMG data in our study. We carefully designed our visualizations to match current dashboards based on physiological data, and our use case videos as neutral as possible. While these may limit our results to connotations we may have communicated unintendedly, we see great potential in future visualizations informed by EMG, supporting various health related use cases, such as informing users about their current state and potentially giving recommendations or advise for health and well-being. This can especially be adopted by people within the "quantified self" movement. Having in mind that users are concerned about their data, it is important to provide them with the necessary information for making informed decisions. This can be achieved by providing users an appropriate level of detail in the data visualization, which may positively impact their opinion on recording and sharing sensor data (**H3**).

# 7  Design Implications

From the insights and results gained through our study, we derived a set of implications for the design of future EMG-based interfaces, which also align well with general physiological sensor-based interfaces. In particular, the relationship between user and provider as well as users' behavior of sharing data with others is not specific to EMG. As participants were generally concerned about (mis)use of their data and wished for transparency and control, we suggest to *educate users*, let them *stay in control*, and *inform* them about data policies. Moreover, as participants were generally more willing to *share data with trusted individuals* and/or for certain purposes with *third parties*, we discuss respective implications.

## 7.1   Educating Users

As participants asked for transparency, we suggest to *not hide data*. In line with related work (e.g., [56]), users wish to be aware of their data being collected. Means to address this include, but are not limited to, providing users means for reviewing all tracked data in detail, e.g., through clear and understandable data visualizations and videos like we did during our study. Other options are to provide indicators at devices when data collection is active (similar to, e.g., webcams) or visualizing spaces of data tracking by means of augmented reality (AR) [56]. Besides showing and describing the collected data, it is important to inform users about potential risks and assess their comprehension. This could be done through questions asked upon the setup of a device that is capable of collecting physiological data. Another possibility is to let users solve tasks similar to the ones used in our study but using their collected data and providing them visualizations. This would not only support understanding, but also internalizing the collected data, which is equally important.

## 7.2   Let Users Stay in Control

We propose to *let users stay in control* of what happens to (which parts of) their data. In particular, users should be able to decide which sensors are actively *tracking*. In addition, users should also stay in control in cases of combining data.

As an example, *combining* physiological data with location data (e.g., obtained from the wearer's smartphone) may create additional insights but at the same time make information even more sensitive. Control is also important in the context of *data storage*. Users should have the possibility to select whether the generated data is stored over longer time periods (e.g., to observe their own behaviour) or if they only allow for real-time assessment of the data (e.g., current stress level). Furthermore, users should be able to choose the level of *aggregation* for their data. Though not apparent from our results, users of future physiological sensing wearables may want to look at the raw data instead of aggregated data visualizations and use it for fine-grained data analysis later themselves. This would also allow for personal interpretation of own data.

## 7.3   Inform Users About Data Storage Aspects

As participants expressed concerns regarding storage and processing of data, we suggest to inform users about all aspects related to *data storage*. This includes where it is stored, to whom it is transferred, and by whom it is processed (in particular for entities beyond the provider of a devices or service). In compliance with data protection laws and regulations such as the General Data Protection Regulation (GDPR), it should also be possible to ask for all data to be deleted at any time, in case the user wishes to do so.

### 7.4 Sharing with Trusted Individuals Vs. Third Parties

Our results show that participants are more willing to *share their data with trusted individuals* than with a general public. Hence, users should have the option to select sharing EMG data with their partner, family, and/or friends. Users should also be able to decide what parts of the data are exactly being shared. Additionally, users should have the option to hide different levels of detail or to share a modified version of the data. The EMG wearable device should allow raw fine-grained data to be accessed first to then decide which level of *aggregation* or which combination of data to share. As an example, for tracked steps it might be that users want to share their achievement, but without the corresponding location data.

Participants also mentioned that they would be willing to *share their data with third parties* for certain purposes. As an example, participants mentioned support of studies (that they may benefit from in the long term). Furthermore, while users might be fine with their service provider having access to their personal data, for third parties they might want data to be anonymized prior to sharing.

A risk index could facilitate users' sharing decisions. Such an index would inform users about risks associated with sharing particular data. As an example, higher gait activity in the EMG data might hint at users currently not being at home.

## 8   Conclusion

In this paper, we investigated users' view on wearable electromyography (EMG). We conducted a user study with 36 participants to evaluate users' perception towards privacy of physiological data obtained from wearable EMG. We found that participants were indeed generally concerned about the privacy of this data. Furthermore, we found that when participants analyzed EMG data, it became less likely that they were willing to share this data with others. Based on our findings, we derive a set of guidelines for designers of future applications based on EMG or other physiological data. Our guidelines are meant to support protecting users' privacy, better inform them about involved risks, and ultimately support the uptake of this technology. We suggest to not hide data from users and enable them to explore the data to asses possible risks. Moreover, we found that it is important to give control to the user on which data to share and with whom.

**Acknowledgements.** The presented work was funded by the German Research Foundation (DFG) under project no. 316457582 and by dtec.bw – Digitalization and Technology Research Center of the Bundeswehr [Voice of Wisdom].

# References

1. Amor, A.B.H., Ghoul, O., Jemni, M.: Toward sign language handshapes recognition using myo armband. In: Proceedings of ICTA 2017, December 2017. https://doi.org/10.1109/ICTA.2017.8336070
2. Barkuus, L., Dey, A.: Location-based services for mobile telephony: a study of users' privacy concerns. In: Proceedings of INTERACT 2003 (2003)
3. Barral, O., et al.: Exploring peripheral physiology as a predictor of perceived relevance in information retrieval. In: Proceedings of IUI 2015 (2015). https://doi.org/10.1145/2678025.2701389
4. Becker, V., Oldrati, P., Barrios, L., Sörös, G.: Touchsense: classifying finger touches and measuring their force with an electromyography armband. In: Proceedings of ISWC 2018 (2018). https://doi.org/10.1145/3267242.3267250
5. Bellekens, X., Nieradzinska, K., Bellekens, A., Seeam, P., Hamilton, A., Seeam, A.: A study on situational awareness security and privacy of wearable health monitoring devices. Int. J. Cyber Situational Awareness (2016). https://doi.org/10.22619/IJCSA.2016.100104
6. Blandford, A., Furniss, D., Makri, S.: Qualitative HCI Research: Going Behind the Scenes. Morgan & Claypool Publishers (2016). https://doi.org/10.2200/S00706ED1V01Y201602HCI034
7. Blechert, J., Liedlgruber, M., Lender, A., Reichenberger, J., Wilhelm, F.: Unobtrusive electromyography-based eating detection in daily life: a new tool to address underreporting? Appetite (2017). https://doi.org/10.1016/j.appet.2017.08.008
8. Bonneau, G.-P., et al.: Overview and state-of-the-art of uncertainty visualization. In: Hansen, C.D., Chen, M., Johnson, C.R., Kaufman, A.E., Hagen, H. (eds.) Scientific Visualization. MV, pp. 3–27. Springer, London (2014). https://doi.org/10.1007/978-1-4471-6497-5_1
9. Brady, E., Morris, M.R., Bigham, J.P.: Gauging receptiveness to social microvolunteering. In: Proceedings of CHI 2015 (2015). https://doi.org/10.1145/2702123.2702329
10. Brodlie, K., Allendes Osorio, R., Lopes, A.: A review of uncertainty in data visualization. Expanding Front. Visual Anal. Visual. (2012). https://doi.org/10.1007/978-1-4471-2804-5_6
11. Buschek, D., Hassib, M., Alt, F.: Personal mobile messaging in context: chat augmentations for expressiveness and awareness. ACM Trans. Comput.-Hum. Interact. (2018). https://doi.org/10.1145/3201404
12. Calo, R.: The boundaries of privacy harm. Indiana Law J. (2011)
13. Cappellini, G., Ivanenko, Y.P., Poppele, R.E., Lacquaniti, F.: Motor patterns in human walking and running. J. Neurophysiol. (2006). https://doi.org/10.1152/jn.00081.2006
14. Chen, D., Zhao, H.: Data security and privacy protection issues in cloud computing, March 2012. https://doi.org/10.1109/ICCSEE.2012.193
15. Chun, K.S., Bhattacharya, S., Thomaz, E.: Detecting eating episodes by tracking jawbone movements with a non-contact wearable sensor. In: Proceedings of the ACM Interaction Mobile Wearable Ubiquitous Technology, March 2018. https://doi.org/10.1145/3191736

16. Collins, C., Carpendale, S., Penn, G.: Visualization of uncertainty in lattices to support decision-making. In: Proceedings of EUROVIS 2007 (2007). https://doi. org/10.2312/VisSym/EuroVis07/051-058
17. Correll, M., Gleicher, M.: Error bars considered harmful: exploring alternate encodings for mean and error. IEEE Trans. Visual Comput. Graphics (2014). https:// doi.org/10.1109/TVCG.2014.2346298
18. Finger, R., Bisantz, A.M.: Utilizing graphical formats to convey uncertainty in a decision-making task. Theor. Issues Ergon. Sci. (2002). https://doi.org/10.1080/ 14639220110110324
19. Gazendam, M.G., Hof, A.L.: Averaged EMG profiles in jogging and running at different speeds. Gait Posture (2007). https://doi.org/10.1016/j.gaitpost.2006.06. 013
20. Gefen, D., Straub, D.W.: Gender differences in the perception and use of e-mail: an extension to the technology acceptance model. MIS Q. (1997). https://doi.org/ 10.2307/249720
21. Ghaisani, A.P., Handayani, P.W., Munajat, Q.: Users' motivation in sharing information on social media. Procedia Comput. Sci. (2017). https://doi.org/10.1016/j. procs.2017.12.186
22. Gibert, G., Pruzinec, M., Schultz, T., Stevens, C.: Enhancement of human computer interaction with facial electromyographic sensors. In: Proceedings of OZCHI 2009 (2009). https://doi.org/10.1145/1738826.1738914
23. Gilroy, S., Porteous, J., Charles, F., Cavazza, M.: Pinter: Interactive storytelling with physiological input. In: Proceedings of IUI 2012 (2012). https://doi.org/10. 1145/2166966.2167039
24. Gneiting, T., Raftery, A.E.: Weather forecasting with ensemble methods. Science (2005). https://doi.org/10.1126/science.1115255
25. Gorm, N., Shklovski, I.: Sharing steps in the workplace: changing privacy concerns over time. In: Proceedings of CHI 2016 (2016). https://doi.org/10.1145/2858036. 2858352
26. Görtler, J., Schulz, C., Weiskopf, D., Deussen, O.: Bubble treemaps for uncertainty visualization. IEEE Trans. Visual Comput. Graphics (2018). https://doi.org/10. 1109/TVCG.2017.2743959
27. Greis, M., Agroudy, P.E., Schuff, H., Machulla, T., Schmidt, A.: Decision-making under uncertainty: how the amount of presented uncertainty influences user behavior. In: Proceedings of NordiCHI 2016 (2016). https://doi.org/10.1145/2971485. 2971535
28. Greis, M., Joshi, A., Singer, K., Schmidt, A., Machulla, T.: Uncertainty visualization influences how humans aggregate discrepant information. In: Proceedings of CHI 2018 (2018). https://doi.org/10.1145/3173574.3174079
29. Gschwandtnei, T., Bögl, M., Federico, P., Miksch, S.: Visual encodings of temporal uncertainty: a comparative user study. IEEE Trans. Visual Comput. Graphics (2016). https://doi.org/10.1109/TVCG.2015.2467752
30. Hakonen, M., Piitulainen, H., Visala, A.: Current state of digital signal processing in myoelectric interfaces and related applications. Biomed. Signal Process. Control (2015). https://doi.org/10.1016/j.bspc.2015.02.009
31. Harboe, G., Huang, E.M.: Real-world affinity diagramming practices: bridging the paper-digital gap. In: Proceedings of CHI 2015 (2015). https://doi.org/10.1145/ 2702123.2702561
32. Hoyle, R., Templeman, R., Armes, S., Anthony, D., Crandall, D., Kapadia, A.: Privacy behaviors of lifeloggers using wearable cameras. In: Proceedings of UbiComp 2014 (2014). https://doi.org/10.1145/2632048.2632079

33. Huang, C.N., Chen, C.H., Chung, H.Y.: Application of facial electromyography in computer mouse access for people with disabilities. Disabil. Rehabil. (2006). https://doi.org/10.1080/09638280500158349
34. Jung, M.F., Sirkin, D., Gür, T.M., Steinert, M.: Displayed uncertainty improves driving experience and behavior: the case of range anxiety in an electric car. In: Proceedings of CHI 2015 (2015). https://doi.org/10.1145/2702123.2702479
35. Kay, M., Kola, T., Hullman, J.R., Munson, S.A.: When (ish) is my bus?: user-centered visualizations of uncertainty in everyday, mobile predictive systems. In: Proceedings of CHI 2016 (2016). https://doi.org/10.1145/2858036.2858558
36. Kerber, F., Puhl, M., Krüger, A.: User-independent real-time hand gesture recognition based on surface electromyography. In: Proceedings of MobileHCI 2017 (2017). https://doi.org/10.1145/3098279.3098553
37. Khamis, M., Alt, F.: Privacy and security in augmentation technologies. In: Dingler, T., Niforatos, E. (eds.) Technology-Augmented Perception and Cognition. HIS, pp. 257–279. Springer, Cham (2021). https://doi.org/10.1007/978-3-030-30457-7_8
38. Kim, J.S., Pan, S.B.: A study on EMG-based biometrics. J. Internet Serv. Inf. Secur. (2017)
39. Kiss, F., et al.: Runmerge: towards enhanced proprioception for advanced amateur runners. In: Proceedings of DIS 2017 Companion (2017). https://doi.org/10.1145/3064857.3079144
40. Kräuter, N., Lösing, S., Bauer, G., Schwering, L., Seuter, M.: Supporting safety in cycling groups using led-augmented gestures. In: Proceedings of UbiComp 2016 (2016). https://doi.org/10.1145/2968219.2968573
41. Kurosawa, H., Sakamoto, D., Ono, T.: Myotilt: a target selection method for smartwatches using the tilting operation and electromyography. In: Proceedings of MobileHCI 2018 (2018). https://doi.org/10.1145/3229434.3229457
42. Langheinrich, M.: Privacy by design – principles of privacy-aware ubiquitous systems. In: Proceedings of UbiComp 2001 (2001)
43. Lau, J., Zimmerman, B., Schaub, F.: Alexa, are you listening?: privacy perceptions, concerns and privacy-seeking behaviors with smart speakers. Proc. ACM Hum.-Comput. Interact. (2018). https://doi.org/10.1145/3274371
44. Lee, L.N., Egelman, S., Lee, J.H., Wagner, D.A.: Risk perceptions for wearable devices. CoRR (2015)
45. Lee, L.M., Gostin, L.O.: Ethical collection, storage, and use of public health data: a proposal for a national privacy protection. JAMA (2009). https://doi.org/10.1001/jama.2009.958
46. Li, H., Wu, J., Gao, Y., Shi, Y.: Examining individuals' adoption of healthcare wearable devices: an empirical study from privacy calculus perspective. Int. J. Med. Informatics (2016). https://doi.org/10.1016/j.ijmedinf.2015.12.010
47. Malhotra, N.K., Kim, S.S., Agarwal, J.: Internet users' information privacy concerns (IUIPC): the construct, the scale, and a causal model. Inf. Syst. Res. (2004). https://doi.org/10.1287/isre.1040.0032
48. McIntosh, J., McNeill, C., Fraser, M., Kerber, F., Löchtefeld, M., Krüger, A.: Empress: practical hand gesture classification with wrist-mounted emg and pressure sensing. In: Proceedings of CHI 2016 (2016). https://doi.org/10.1145/2858036.2858093
49. Motti, V.G., Caine, K.: Users' privacy concerns about wearables. In: Brenner, M., Christin, N., Johnson, B., Rohloff, K. (eds.) FC 2015. LNCS, vol. 8976, pp. 231–244. Springer, Heidelberg (2015). https://doi.org/10.1007/978-3-662-48051-9_17

50. Nissenbaum, H.: Privacy in Context: Technology, Policy, and the Integrity of Social Life. Stanford University Press (2009)
51. Osatuyi, B.: Information sharing on social media sites. Comput. Hum. Behav. (2013). https://doi.org/10.1016/j.chb.2013.07.001
52. Pang, A.T., Wittenbrink, C.M., Lodha, S.K.: Approaches to uncertainty visualization. Vis. Comput. (1997). https://doi.org/10.1007/s003710050111
53. Paudyal, P., Banerjee, A., Gupta, S.K.: SCEPTRE: a pervasive, non-invasive, and programmable gesture recognition technology. In: Proceedings of IUI 2016 (2016). https://doi.org/10.1145/2856767.2856794
54. Paul, G., Irvine, J.: Privacy implications of wearable health devices. In: Proceedings of SIN 2014 (2014). https://doi.org/10.1145/2659651.2659683
55. Perez, A.J., Zeadally, S.: Privacy issues and solutions for consumer wearables. It Professional (2018)
56. Prange, S., Shams, A., Piening, R., Abdelrahman, Y., Alt, F.: Priview- exploring visualisations to support users' privacy awareness. In: Proceedings of CHI 2021 (2021). https://doi.org/10.1145/3411764.3445067
57. Puussaar, A., Clear, A.K., Wright, P.: Enhancing personal informatics through social sensemaking. In: Proceedings of CHI 2017 (2017). https://doi.org/10.1145/3025453.3025804
58. Rahman, M., Carbunar, B., Banik, M.: Fit and vulnerable: attacks and defenses for a health monitoring device. arXiv preprint arXiv:1304.5672 (2013)
59. Reaz, M.B., Hussain, M.S., Mohd-Yasin, F.: Techniques of EMG signal analysis: detection, processing, classification and applications. Biol. Proced. Online (2006). https://doi.org/10.1251/bpo115
60. Rocher, L., Hendrickx, J.M., de Montjoye, Y.A.: Estimating the success of re-identifications in incomplete datasets using generative models. Nat. Commun. (2019). https://doi.org/10.1038/s41467-019-10933-3
61. Rogers, Y., Sharp, H., Preece, J.: Interaction Design: Beyond Human - Computer Interaction, 3rd edn. Wiley Publishing (2011)
62. Sacha, D., Senaratne, H., Kwon, B.C., Ellis, G., Keim, D.A.: The role of uncertainty, awareness, and trust in visual analytics. IEEE Trans. Visual Comput. Graphics (2016). https://doi.org/10.1109/TVCG.2015.2467591
63. Schaub, F., Balebako, R., Durity, A.L., Cranor, L.F.: A design space for effective privacy notices. In: Proceedings of (2015)
64. Schneegass, S., Olsson, T., Mayer, S., van Laerhoven, K.: Mobile interactions augmented by wearable computing: a design space and vision. Int. J. Mob. Hum. Comput. Interact. (2016). https://doi.org/10.4018/IJMHCI.2016100106
65. Schwind, V., Reinhardt, J., Rzayev, R., Henze, N., Wolf, K.: Virtual reality on the go?: A study on social acceptance of VR glasses. In: Proceedings of MobileHCI 2018 (2018). https://doi.org/10.1145/3236112.3236127
66. Shaer, O., et al.: Genomix: a novel interaction tool for self-exploration of personal genomic data. In: Proceedings of CHI 2016 (2016). https://doi.org/10.1145/2858036.2858397
67. Shklovski, I., Mainwaring, S.D., Skúladóttir, H.H., Borgthorsson, H.: Leakiness and creepiness in app space: Perceptions of privacy and mobile app use. In: Proceedings of CHI 2014 (2014). https://doi.org/10.1145/2556288.2557421
68. Solove, D.J.: The Digital Person: Technology and Privacy in the Information Age. NYU Press (2004)

69. Sun, Y., Wang, N., Shen, X.L., Zhang, J.X.: Location information disclosure in location-based social network services: Privacy calculus, benefit structure, and gender differences. Comput. Hum. Behav. (2015). https://doi.org/10.1016/j.chb.2015.06.006

70. Tuunainen, V.K., Pitkänen, O., Hovi, M.: Users' awareness of privacy on online social networking sites - case facebook. BLED (2009)

71. Voit, A., Mayer, S., Schwind, V., Henze, N.: Online, vr, ar, lab, and in-situ: comparison of research methods to evaluate smart artifacts. In: Proceedings of CHI 2019 (2019). https://doi.org/10.1145/3290605.3300737

72. Wang, F., Qi, H., Zhou, X., Wang, J., Zeng, Z., Li, R.: Collaboration robotic compliance grasping based on implicit human - computer interaction. In: Proceedings of CCDC 2018, June 2018D. https://doi.org/10.1109/CCDC.2018.8408109

73. Wijsman, J., Grundlehner, B., Penders, J., Hermens, H.: Trapezius muscle EMG as predictor of mental stress. ACM Trans. Embed. Comput. Syst. (2013). https://doi.org/10.1145/2485984.2485987

74. Wilkowska, W., Ziefle, M.: Perception of privacy and security for acceptance of e-health technologies: exploratory analysis for diverse user groups. In: Proceedings of IEEE (2011)

75. Williams, E.J.: Experimental designs balanced for the estimation of residual effects of treatments. Aust. J. Chem. (1949). https://doi.org/10.1071/CH9490149

76. Wobbrock, J.O., Findlater, L., Gergle, D., Higgins, J.J.: The aligned rank transform for nonparametric factorial analyses using only anova procedures. In: Proceedings of CHI 2011 (2011). https://doi.org/10.1145/1978942.1978963

77. Wozniak, P.W., Colley, A., Häkkilä, J.: Towards increasing bodily awareness during sports with wearable displays. In: Proceedings of UbiComp 2018 (2018). https://doi.org/10.1145/3267305.3267703

# Words, Worlds and Freedom – Insights from School Students in Indonesia and UK

Janet C. Read[1](✉), Eunice Sari[2,3], I. Scott Mackenzie[4], and Josh (Adi) Tedjasaputra[5]

[1] University of Central Lancashire, Preston, UK
jcread@uclan.ac.uk
[2] UX Indonesia, Jakarta, Indonesia
eunice@uxindo.com
[3] Charles Darwin University, Darwin, Australia
[4] York University, Toronto, Canada
mack@cse.yorku.ca
[5] Customer Experience Insight (CX Insight), Perth, Australia
josh@cxinsight.com.au

**Abstract.** As part of a larger project looking at the design of future classrooms, we delivered a survey on technology use to school pupils in the United Kingdom and in Indonesia. Whilst seeking to discover opinions from the pupils in both of these locations, we also had an interest in exploring what the results might also tell us in regard to future design sessions. Over 300 pupils completed the survey, and the results show significant differences and similarities across the two groups. It can be postulated that some of the differences are caused by the students' behaviours around satisficing, and some are a result of experiences. We reflect on implications for the design of design sessions around words, worlds and freedom.

**Keywords:** Cross culture · Future schools · Children · Learning technologies

## 1 Introduction

Ever since Seymour Papert, [1], imagined the classroom of the future, there has been an ongoing debate as to how technology affects both the landscape of, but also the philosophy of, education. In the same way that a building affects its people [2], so the products placed in a school affect the dynamics and the learning [3]. As a result of the COVID-19 pandemic, there is an increased interest in the impacts of, and the possibilities for, digital technologies in classrooms. Many papers are considering the impacts of online education on children's learning and wellbeing whilst seeking to imagine future scenarios where technologies become more ubiquitous in schools and, as a result, where these technologies change learning [4–6].

In our broader work, we are interested in the design of technologies not yet imagined and in empowering children to think about design and imagine their futures. This is part of a large ongoing project in which we have previously engaged in design work with children in Malaysia, Iceland and UAE. This earlier work has surfaced to us some

© IFIP International Federation for Information Processing 2021
Published by Springer Nature Switzerland AG 2021
C. Ardito et al. (Eds.): INTERACT 2021, LNCS 12935, pp. 361–370, 2021.
https://doi.org/10.1007/978-3-030-85610-6_21

problems in such cross-cultural design as we have realized that what might work in one place may not be easily replicable to another. We have noticed that some words need explanation, that we have gaps in our knowledge about children's contexts and we are somewhat ill-equipped to understand the cultural and situational influences on design work. A challenge for us is to articulate these differences and find a framework to help us run better cross-cultural design activities.

It is challenging and expensive in both money and time to explore differences in face-to-face design sessions. For that reason, we were interested to see if we could use a survey method to help us towards a framework for thinking. The work we present here thus explores what can be learned from a survey with children that can help us better situate design with children in an HCI context. We surveyed school-aged children in two quite different countries (Indonesia and the United Kingdom) to answer the following two research questions:

- RQ1: What can be usefully discovered about school with a one size survey for children when applied in quite different contexts?
- RQ2: What can be discovered in a one size survey that can assist in the customization of design activities across different cultures?

## 2   Related Work

### 2.1   Education in Indonesia and the UK, and Technologies in Schools

Education in Indonesia emphasizes knowledge over practice and offers a diverse curriculum of subjects that are quite dense and compulsory for students to participate in, ranging from Indonesian (language), civic education, mathematics, religious education, science, social studies, cultural arts, sports, information technology, and communication (ICT). The curriculum is based on, and has a large emphasis on, the five values of *Pancasila* as described in [7]. Sadly the education system as a whole is considered one of the worst in the world and it is beset with many challenges [8].

In the UK, despite some recent politically motivated efforts, little in education is about national values [9]; the emphasis is on practice and skill development. The standard curriculum includes languages, mathematics, social studies, and science but also extracurricular development in the fields of technology, arts, and sports. The nations of the UK (England, Wales, Scotland and Northern Ireland) each manage their own education provision and each have their own national curriculum, e.g., [10], but the general values are the same with an emphasis on specialization and with externally managed qualifications that have credibility and currency across the world.

UK schools are all imbued with technology. Microsoft has a Microsoft Schools programme[1] within the UK where schools become flagship centres of computer supported learning. Many schools across the world have taken on a BYOD (Bring your own device) approach to learning where pupils bring devices to school. There have been studies of similar approaches in Indonesia for example Supardi, [11], who studied the attitudes

---

[1] https://news.microsoft.com/en-gb/2020/05/04/three-microsoft-showcase-schools-will-help-tea chers-roll-out-remote-learning-across-england/.

of junior high school students, 11–13 years old, living in Yogyakarta and experiencing HTBL (High Technology Based Learning) at school. The results of this research applauded the fun and accessibility of that approach to learning. It is highly likely that in the future all children will have devices in school and that classrooms will be significantly affected by technology.

Software for schools is a huge business. Much of the software used in schools is there to facilitate general learning. Microsoft products are widely used for this purpose across all schools with PowerPoint and Word being extremely commonplace [12–14]. Whilst now being ubiquitous, it has not always been the case that teachers have felt comfortable with these products – as evidenced by a 2007 book on how to use Word in classrooms [15]. The proliferation of Microsoft products into schools is not restricted to the UK - a study in 2018 of education in Iran referred to Microsoft Word as being the most useful educational technology on offer [16] - but there is certainly a lag between the richer and poorer countries. Other Microsoft software like Excel and OneNote is also well used and some products, like Minecraft, have become widely adopted for many uses beyond their immediate remit [17]. Virtual Learning Environments (VLEs) are also very much on the rise in education. Some, like Google Classroom and Doddle are particularly well suited to school use and it is probably fair to say that in most cases the pupil's perception of these will be quite different from the teacher's perception so is valuable to capture.

Software for programming tends to be international in spread, Scratch is an example of a product that is used the world over [18]. Software associated with subjects within curriculums tends to be more localized. One example is MyMaths,[2] which claims to cover the UK curriculum from Key Stage 1 to A Level with interactive lessons, "booster packs" for revision, and assignable homework.

The different shapes and substance of two different educational systems provide a useful backdrop to explore methodological as well as practical solutions to explore education from a pupil's perspective. *Of interest in this paper is – can this be effectively done using a survey? What does such a survey show?*

## 2.2 Child Centred Design of Future Education and HCI4D

HCI4D refers to the application of HCI in areas beyond the USA/UK/European paradigms in an effort to better fit solutions to local cultures – especially those where the countries are developing. Abdelnour-Nocera, [19], writes of the need to take into account diverse cultural and contextual positions in order to make good technology. In this endeavour, the voices of children are critical. In the design of education, where in order to de-colonize any discussion, there is a need to explore how to integrate multiple forms of knowledge; connection with diverse cultures is essential [20].

Human Centered Design is an appropriate approach for the design of future education. One approach can be to ask teachers; in a study of teachers views of technology in Indonesia, Mukminin, [21], describes that the positive belief from the teachers, that technology has a lot of potential to improve students' performance, determines the success of technology adoption in classrooms. This is helpful to know but does not really take into account the children's views.

---

[2] https://www.mymaths.co.uk/.

The HCI community has a long tradition of user engagement in design – this is also found in Child-Computer Interaction where there is a significant emphasis on engaging with children in participatory and co-design activities in order to gather their views, [22, 23]. When carrying out these activities, much emphasis has to be placed on designing appropriate activities to scaffold the children towards design [24]; situating the activity in the local context and asking appropriate questions [25]. In meeting this challenge we strongly believe in the sentiments expressed by Fisher [26, 27] that in order to plan and do design with children we should "*understand the nature of their activities, to understand common strands as well as the differences, particularly as they are affected by factors pertaining to culture, ethnicity and gender in a rapidly changing world.*".

Our work therefore in this study seeks to see *how much we can discover about contexts with a simple survey. How can this be used in the planning of design activities?*

## 3   Study

Our study used a questionnaire to discover pupils' views on their current education and their thoughts for the future. A questionnaire is an effective tool for gathering a large amount of data from a large group in a cost-effective way [28], and it is an easy method for children and young people to interact with as, and, with appropriate questions, it can be low effort to complete [29]. The downside to a survey is that it typically will not give explanations for the observed results. Our survey in this study was intended to gather data about:

- Factual things – do you know this software – do you like it?
- Opinions based on experience – how do you like to learn?
- Opinions based on imagination – what will the future look like?

The survey would be distributed, completed and then considered in regard to its value taking account the two research questions that appear earlier in this paper.

### 3.1   Survey

The Survey asked pupils to record their age and gender and then to reflect on ten software products that have been reported as having been used in schools in the UK and for each one to record a score between 'don't like at all, don't like, like, like a lot. They were then asked about how they liked to learn with a four-point Likert style scale. Finally, they were asked to predict the classroom of the future with a five-point Likert type scale in terms of how likely some scenarios might be in classrooms 20 years from now. The questions and responses are clearly shown in the Figs. 1, 2, 3 and 4.

### 3.2   Procedure and Participants

In the UK, the survey was delivered using Microsoft Teams, in Indonesia, it was distributed by the class teachers. The survey was completed by 164 UK (99 Male, 65 Female) and 189 Indonesian (93 Male and 96 Female) students aged 12 and 13. The UK students were from a single school in England; in Indonesia the students were from 4 schools. All the students participated voluntarily; no incentives were given for participation. No personal data was gathered. Pupils were clear as to the purpose of the survey and told they did not need to submit the survey even after completion.

### 3.3 Results

Figures 1 and 2 refer to the results from the first question which was about software preferences. Figure 1 shows the results from the UK students.

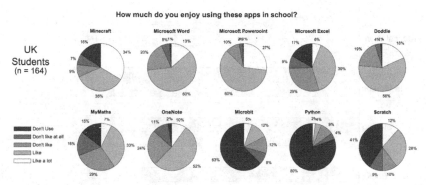

**Fig. 1.** Opinions of software by UK students (Color figure online)

It is immediately clear (from little dark blue) that these students were heavy users of Microsoft Word and Microsoft PowerPoint, as well as Doddle and OneNote. By proportion the most liked product was Minecraft, and the least liked product was MyMaths.

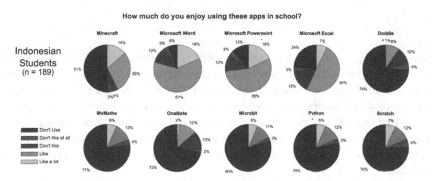

**Fig. 2.** Opinions of software by Indonesian students.

Figure 2 shows the results from the Indonesian students. It is immediately clear that these students were heavy users of Microsoft Word and Microsoft PowerPoint and used Excel and Minecraft. Word and PowerPoint were equally liked. It is interesting to note that in Fig. 2, MyMaths, which is unlikely to be available in Indonesia, had some 'like a lot' scores. On inspection, there were several respondents who chose 'like a lot' for everything on the list. This resonates with research previously by Read [30], that suggests that quite often children will answer very positively for a set of reasons that are not clear but include the desire to please (satisficing).

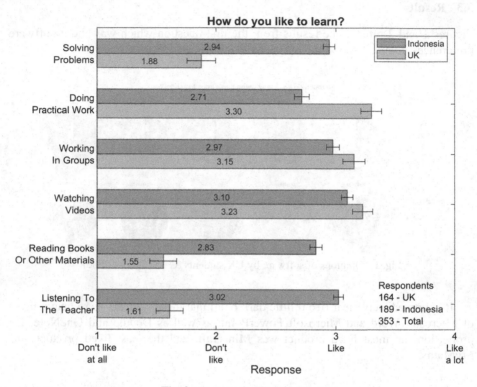

**Fig. 3.** How pupils liked to learn

As seen in Fig. 3, there were noticeable differences but also similarities, in how the pupils from the two countries liked to learn. Indonesian students seemed much more positive overall but were especially more positive than the UK students in terms of what might be called non-technology-based teaching – viz. reading, listening and thinking. It could be that the UK students felt more empowered to critique these approaches than their Indonesian peers (as alluded to in critiques of culture and openness like [31]) or it could be that the Indonesian pupils did indeed have a very positive opinion of these approaches.

The final question in the survey asked the pupils about how they might imagine school in 20 years' time. In almost all cases, the UK students had a stronger belief in the possible suggestions. They were very convinced of the potential for wearables but interestingly still strongly believed, as did the Indonesian students, that the school classroom would remain recognizable.

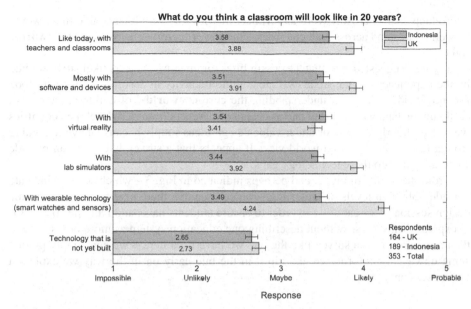

Fig. 4. The school of the future

## 4 Discussion

### 4.1 The Usefulness of Applying a Single Survey Across Two Cultures to Understand Students' Lived Experiences and Ideas Around Education

The single survey was initially designed in the UK. It has helped the UK and Indonesian researchers to have a common ground from the beginning to the end of research process. Despite significant differences between two countries, the single survey provides single uniformity of the types of data collected, which gives consistency when analyzing the large-scale data analysis results. The results showed significance differences, in terms of level of awareness, students' perspectives, and technology adoption between UK and Indonesia.

### 4.2 Implications of the Findings for the Planning and Execution of Design Studies with School Aged Students in Pan-International Studies

Moving from teacher-centred learning to student-centred learning that focuses on problem solving using real practical cases and technology as a platform seems to have become a trend, especially during Covid-19. The use of technology in learning in Indonesia has significantly increased for both teachers and students. As designers, we need to explore different types and levels of learning activities as well as learning tools to develop technology-based classroom design. The survey completed here gave us some facts about what was being seen in the two countries. In a design workshop we could refer to products like Microsoft Word and Minecraft with some confidence that these would be well understood across both countries. The survey therefore helps us get the **'words'** right.

Figure 4 suggested to us that the possibilities for imagination were likely to be limited by the experiences of the students. One common activity in design sessions is to look for 'novel' ideas. Without understanding the current **'worlds'** of children, we cannot easily understand what is novel and as design researchers from rich developed countries we might unfairly dismiss or under value design ideas simply because they are coming from a less technology-rich world view. It appears that a survey like ours can provide some insights into these technology gaps.

From the results in Fig. 2, and perhaps indicated in Fig. 3 – which seem to indicate considerably high levels of satisficing – we can see that there may be a need to frame design sessions very carefully in order to ensure students have, and feel, the **'freedom'** to express themselves. Without describing one education system as more or less liberal than another – from a survey like the one we have used here – we can simply predict some unwanted conformance and nip it in the bud early on in the way we explain a design session.

## 5  Conclusion

A small survey carried out in two countries has shown similarities and differences in the use of technology and the opinions of school pupils. Looking into these differences has allowed us to think about how we can adapt the way we work directly with students in future research settings, specifically in design, and have helped the research team towards a better understanding of the contexts and cultures of the different countries. As a quick and effective method to provide useful understanding we found the survey to be very valuable.

Whilst the main aim of our work is not to examine the survey as a tool for understanding cultures, we did find out useful things about the students' perceptions and experiences and at the same time we were able to distill insights – these answered our research questions.

Future work will further explore technology in school against a lens of children designing future classrooms and will implement the insights from this work into hands on activities with pupils in the two countries.

## References

1. Papert, S.: The Children's Machine: Rethinking School in the Age of the Computer. Basic Books, New York (1993)
2. Ferrari, M., Tinazzi, C., D'Erchia, A.: Imagining the school of the future. In: Torre, S.D., Bocciarelli, M., Daglio, L., Neri, R. (eds.) Buildings for Education. RD, pp. 41–51. Springer, Cham (2020). https://doi.org/10.1007/978-3-030-33687-5_4
3. Courtad, C.A.: Making your classroom smart: universal design for learning and technology. In: Uskov, V.L., Howlett, R.J., Jain, L.C. (eds.) Smart Education and e-Learning 2019, pp. 501–510. Springer, Singapore (2019). https://doi.org/10.1007/978-981-13-8260-4_44

4. Code, J., Ralph, R., Forde, K.: Pandemic designs for the future: perspectives of technology education teachers during COVID-19. Inf. Learn. Sci. (2020)

5. Williamson, B., Eynon, R.: Historical Threads, Missing Links, and Future Directions in AI in Education. Taylor & Francis, Abingdon (2020)

6. Wereley, M., et al.: The day the robots arrived: use of telepresence to support virtual experiential learning in teacher education. In: Society for Information Technology & Teacher Education International Conference. Association for the Advancement of Computing in Education (AACE) (2021)

7. Silalahi, R., Yuwono, U.: The sustainability of Pancasila in Indonesian education system. Res. Soc. Sci. Technol. **3**(2), 58–78 (2018)

8. Agus, C., et al.: Cultural-based education of Tamansiswa as a locomotive of Indonesian education system. In: Leal Filho, W., et al. (eds.) Universities as Living Labs for Sustainable Development. WSUSE, pp. 471–486. Springer, Cham (2020). https://doi.org/10.1007/978-3-030-15604-6_29

9. Elton-Chalcraft, S., et al.: To promote, or not to promote fundamental British values? Teachers' standards, diversity and teacher education. Br. Educ. Res. J. **43**(1), 29–48 (2017)

10. Roberts, N.: The school curriculum in England (2021)

11. Supardi, S., Hasanah, E.: Junior high school students' experiences of high technology based learning in Indonesia. Int. J. Learn. Teach. Educ. Res. **19**(5), 153–166 (2020)

12. Carlson, S.: The net generation goes to college. Chronicle High. Educ. **52**(7), A34 (2005)

13. Parette, H.P., et al.: Teaching word recognition to young children who are at risk using Microsoft® PowerPoint™ coupled with direct instruction. Early Childhood Educ. J. **36**(5), 393–401 (2009)

14. Reedy, G.B.: PowerPoint, interactive whiteboards, and the visual culture of technology in schools. Technol. Pedagogy Educ. **17**(2), 143–162 (2008)

15. Hickerson, A.: Learn & Use Microsoft Word in Your Classroom. Shell Education, Huntington Beach (2007)

16. Soyoof, A.: Iranian teachers' perception of the role of computers in classroom, p. 371 (2018). www.mjltm.com, info@mjltm.org

17. Bourdeau, S., Coulon, T., Petit, M.-C.: Simulation-based training via a "Readymade" virtual world platform: teaching and learning with minecraft education. IT Prof. **23**(2), 33–39 (2021)

18. Zhang, L., Nouri, J.: A systematic review of learning computational thinking through Scratch in K-9. Comput. Educ. **141**, 103607 (2019)

19. Abdelnour-Nocera, J., Rangaswamy, N.: Reflecting on the design-culture connection in HCI and HCI4D. Interactions **25**(5), 8–9 (2018)

20. Wong-Villacres, M., Alvarado Garcia, A., Tibau, J.: Reflections from the classroom and beyond: imagining a decolonized HCI education. In: Extended Abstracts of the 2020 CHI Conference on Human Factors in Computing Systems (2020)

21. Mukminin, A., et al.: Vocational technical high school teachers' beliefs towards ICT for the 21st century education: Indonesian context. Probl. Educ. 21st Century **77**(1), 22 (2019)

22. Frauenberger, C., Foth, M., Fitzpatrick, G.: On scale, dialectics, and affect: pathways for proliferating participatory design. In: Proceedings of the 15th Participatory Design Conference: Full Papers-Volume 1 (2018)

23. Fitton, D., Read, J.C.: Primed design activities: scaffolding young designers during ideation. In: Proceedings of the 9th Nordic Conference on Human-Computer Interaction. ACM (2016)

24. Iversen, O.S., Brodersen, C.: Building a BRIDGE between children and users: a socio-cultural approach to child–computer interaction. Cogn. Technol. Work **10**(2), 83–93 (2008)

25. Lamichhane, D.R., Read, J.C., Fitton, D.: Beneath the Himalayas–exploring design for cultural evenness with Nepalese children (2018)

26. Fisher, K.E., Yefimova, K., Bishop, A.P.: Adapting design thinking and cultural probes to the experiences of immigrant youth: uncovering the roles of visual media and music in ICT wayfaring. In: Proceedings of the 2016 CHI Conference Extended Abstracts on Human Factors in Computing Systems (2016)
27. Fisher, K.E., Yefimova, K., Yafi, E.: Future's butterflies: co-designing ICT wayfaring technology with refugee Syrian youth. In: Proceedings of the 15th International Conference on Interaction Design and Children, pp. 25–36. ACM, Manchester (2016)
28. Maulana, R., Helms-Lorenz, M., van de Grift, W.: Pupils' perceptions of teaching behaviour: evaluation of an instrument and importance for academic motivation in Indonesian secondary education. Int. J. Educ. Res. **69**, 98–112 (2015)
29. Choak, C.: Asking questions. Research and research methods for youth practitioners, p. 90 (2013)
30. Read, J.C.: Validating the Fun Toolkit: an instrument for measuring children's opinions of technology. Cogn. Technol. Work **10**(2), 119–128 (2008)
31. Tan, C.: Comparing High-Performing Education Systems: Understanding Singapore, Shanghai, and Hong Kong. Routledge, Abingdon (2018)

# Personalization and Recommender Systems

# Automated Adaptations for Improving the Accessibility of Public E-Services Based on Annotations

Aritz Sala[✉], Myriam Arrue[✉], J. Eduardo Pérez[✉],
and Sandra M. Espín-Tello[✉]

EGOKITUZ, University of the Basque Country (UPV/EHU), Donostia, Spain
aritz.sala@gmail.com,
{myriam.arrue,juaneduardo.perez,sandramartina.espin}@ehu.eus

**Abstract.** The COVID-19 pandemic has changed the way we interact with public administration, making indispensable the use of online
public services (e-services) to perform required administration procedures. All citizens should be able to interact with public e-services in an
autonomous, satisfactory and easy way. However, these services are not
always accessible to people with disabilities. In this paper, we present
a descriptive model for e-services adaptation based on ontologies, which
contains the e-service annotations, user features and techniques required
for adapting e-services to the needs of people with disabilities. Based on
this model, an automated adaptation system was developed and adapted
versions of three different Spanish public e-services aiming at users with
low vision were obtained as a proof of concept.

**Keywords:** e-Government · Public e-services · Annotation ontology ·
Automated adaptation · Low vision

## 1 Introduction

Last year has been an unusual one due to the COVID-19 pandemic. The impossibility of performing the usual face-to-face administrative tasks has forced many
people to change the way they interact with public administration. The "E-
Government Survey 2020" from the United Nations [22] identified significant
uptakes in digital services in different geographic regions, countries and cities as
well as increased e-participation in relation to the previous surveys.

Public e-services are crucial tools for citizens to guarantee their e-
participation. They are used for different tasks, such as making an appointment
with the public administration, searching for employment and social care, etc.
with online-forms as the predominant style of interaction [14]. However, some
users may experience difficulties when using these services if they are not accessible [5].

C. Ardito et al. (Eds.): INTERACT 2021, LNCS 12935, pp. 373–382, 2021.
https://doi.org/10.1007/978-3-030-85610-6_22

The Web Accessibility Initiative (WAI) has made efforts for ensuring accessibility of websites. The Web Content Accessibility Guidelines (WCAG) are the most well-known and applied for accessibility evaluation. Current version (v2.1) [10], structures the guidelines into four principles: perceivable, operable, understandable, and robust; and includes success criteria for checking the fulfilment of each principle. These guidelines are considered of mandatory conformance for public e-services in many countries and are included in their legislation [4]. Despite this, many people with disabilities experience difficulties when interacting with web interfaces [9]. These difficulties aggravate when referring to public e-services as many of them require the fulfilment of forms that contain complex elements to interact with (e.g., calendars, controls, captcha, etc.) and may present accessibility barriers of more severity than static web pages. Several studies about the experience of accessibility barriers by people with disabilities in governmental websites can be found in the literature [5,21].

The objective of this paper is to present an automated adaptation system for improving the accessibility of e-services as well as to structure the process for the fulfilment of online-forms so more logical and uniform interaction is provided to users. For this, we define a descriptive model through an ontology which contains the required features for e-services annotations as well as the user model and the adaptation techniques to apply. This automated adaptation system was applied to three different Spanish public e-services and adapted interfaces aimed at people with low vision were obtained as a proof of concept.

## 2   Related Work

Ontologies are used as a modeling tool that allows performing designs, establishing relationships, and formulating axioms to infer and deduce information within a specific process in a more personalized and flexible way [7]. Several studies have shown that ontology models are effective in the generation of adaptive web user interfaces at runtime. For example, Catwalk framework [12] that researched how web user interfaces could be dynamically selected, generated, and adapted according to user-aspects such as their profile, the specific task, or goal to be achieved or the location and time characteristics. Unlike our approach, where the adaptation is performed remotely to the e-service, the Catwalk framework was developed to be deployed in the web server, so the web interfaces presented to the user are dynamically adapted as they are requested.

Some of the developed projects using ontologies are aimed to improve web accessibility for people with disabilities, and specifically, for those with visual impairments, such as the one carried out by Bukhari and Kim [3]. They proposed an ontology called "Ontology based on the extraction of information for people with visual disabilities" (HOIEV), composed of 3 layers: interaction with the remote user, extraction of information from the core, and the programming interface (API). This is a comprehensive ontology for obtaining information about users interaction. However, it can not be applied for automated adaptation of e-services at run-time. Another example is the method developed by

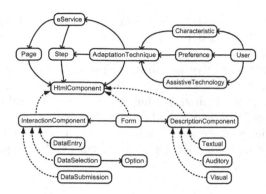

**Fig. 1.** Diagram of the proposed ontology. Continuous lines correspond to 'has' relation type, while dashed lines correspond to 'is a' relation type.

Rosales et al. [18], that proposed a prototype of a semantic platform to enhance web accessibility. This prototype was developed for a specific adaptation as it provides mechanisms for interacting with the interfaces through voice commands. The adaptation system presented in this paper aims at providing a comprehensive adaptation techniques pool for selecting and applying accordingly to different groups of users. The Egoki system [6] deploys a user ontology model to automatically generate user-tailored interfaces in ubiquitous environments. However, the web interfaces were created from models. This approach is not applicable for adapting existing e-services interfaces at run-time.

There are some works aiming at adapting web interfaces at run-time for better fit to the needs of users such as the transcoding systems presented in [1,8]. However, these systems are oriented to specific user needs, based on annotations of single web pages and do not provide a descriptive model applicable to the process of public e-service systems. Another research work worth mentioning is the one shown in [23]. They present a comprehensive web interface adaptation system. However, the adaptation process is individually performed for each web page so it is not applicable for adapting the process of public e-services.

## 3    Basis of Automated Adaptation

To get an automated adaptation system that improves web accessibility of public e-services, we have defined a descriptive model to annotate relationships between the e-service process and components, along with the user features and the adaptation techniques. For this, we have implemented a knowledge base using the Web Ontology Language (OWL) [13] and the ontology editor tool Protégé[1]. Figure 1 shows the class diagram defined in the ontology.

---

[1] http://protege.stanford.edu.

**User Model.** The user model included in our ontology defines the interaction features to consider from each user. Thus, appropriate techniques can be selected to generate the adapted e-service. In particular, three general user groups are included (users with cognitive impairment, physical impairment, and sensory impairment) along with their corresponding features (e.g., colour blindness). This user model can be updated, adding new user groups and features.

In addition, users' preferences and the assistive technology used are also considered in the model, so more specific adaptation techniques may be applied [17], for example, adapting navigation for users of trackballs, adapting components for screen reader users, etc.

**Annotation Model of Public e-Services.** In most cases, accessing public e-services requires the fulfilment of online-forms, which usually include several steps. Therefore, it may be described as a transactional process [15].

Nowadays, public e-services are not uniform and present different fulfilment processes even if their target task is similar. However, it is possible to identify common steps within e-services, as well as similar data to be introduced by users. These common features among public e-services led us to define an annotation model that can be applied to annotate the process in general, the concrete steps of the process, the data required from users, etc. The objective of these annotations is to obtain valuable information in order to automatically apply the selected adaptation techniques depending on user features/preferences in order to obtain more accessible interfaces and enhance the structure of the process by relocating components when necessary.

Figure 1 shows the classes defined in the ontology and the relationships between them. The main classes for the annotation model are the following: eService, Page, Step, and HTMLComponent. One eService may have several Page instances. One Page may have several HTMLComponent instances. The Step class is related to eService, so it is possible to annotate the steps in the process of the eService. In addition, the Step class is also related to HTMLComponent, so it is possible to annotate the information to be required in each step. These relationships make it possible to split one e-service process into several steps assigning the necessary HTML components to each one and automatically creating the necessary interfaces and presenting them in the most adequate order.

There are subclasses for HTMLComponent: InteractionComponent and DescriptionComponent. The former are those HTML components requiring direct data introduction from the user (DataEntry), selecting data from a set of options (DataSelection) and submitting data to the server (DataSubmission). The latter are those HTML components presenting Textual, Auditory or Visual information. This model allows providing alternatives for components, so the most appropriate one is presented to the user. The Form subclass has been also defined as a compound component.

In addition, several properties were added for HTMLComponent class: dimming, stretch, hide and remove. 'Dimming', 'hide' and 'stretch' can be used to hide part of the content of the e-service, such as leaving only part of the instructions to make it simpler and smaller. Finally, 'remove' property is used to remove those elements that can bother the user. For instance, a flashing element is tagged as remove = 'flashing' so it would be removed when the user has photosensitivity. The 'priority' property has been defined for DescriptionComponent class and it can be used to mark the elements as being necessary, reordering them, or selecting the most appropriate for the user. The 'optional' property has been defined for InteractionComponent in order to identify those fields that are not mandatory to fulfil in the process.

**Adaption Techniques.** The knowledge base models the adaption techniques and decides which ones are applicable, but it does not implement them. This approach enables the addition of new adaptation techniques, thus enabling system development to become a continuous process. In the current study, we have defined three groups of adaptation techniques: service adaptations, step adaptations and interaction component adaptations. The definition of these groups is based on a modification of the original classification of Knutov et al. [11]: navigation, content and presentation. In our perspective the navigation adaptations are applied to all the e-service as a whole (e.g., providing orientation components such as breadcrumb of steps, progress information, completed and to-do steps, etc.), content adaptations are mainly applied to each step of the service (e.g., only showing the required fields to fulfil by the users in each step, showing links instead of radio buttons for data selection components, etc.) and presentation adaptations are applied to all (service, steps and components) (e.g., using high contrast colors in forms, visually grouping the mandatory fields, over-sizing interaction components, etc.).

**Table 1.** Features of e-service selected.

| Features | DNI | SPE | SGS |
|---|---|---|---|
| Number of pages | 7 | 3 | 5 |
| DataEntry components | 10 | 6 | 7 |
| DataSelection components | - | 2 | 9 |
| DataSubmission components | 10 | 4 | 5 |
| Mandatory Int. Comp | 9 | 6 | 6 |

## 4    Automated Adaptation System

The architecture of the adaptation system developed is shown in Fig. 2. The Knowledge Base and the e-services annotations are located in a remote machine. The Adaptation engine is implemented as a Web Service whereas a Chrome extension is installed locally on the user computer.

This browser add-on is in charge of starting and completing the adaptation process performed by the system. It gets an e-service to adapt (steps 1 and 2 in Fig. 2) and sends the source code with the user's credentials to the remote Web Service (step 3 in Fig. 2). Then, it presents the adapted version of the e-service returned by the Web Service (step 6 in Fig. 2). The Adaptation engine implements two main functionalities. The first is to query the Knowledge Base about adaptations corresponding to the current user and the e-service (step 4 in Fig. 2). The second is to perform adaptations resolved by the Knowledge Base according to the annotations of the e-service (step 5 in Fig. 2) and return the adapted e-service to the browser add-on (step 6 in Fig. 2). The e-services are adapted using JSON, JQuery, JavaScript and CSS technologies.

**Proof of Concept.** Three different e-services from the Spanish public administration were selected to carry out the proof of concept of the adaptation system: from the Ministry of Home Affairs (DNI[2]), from the Public Service of State Employment (SPE[3]), and from the Social Security (SGS[4]). These e-services had already been tested in an experiment involving people with low vision [19,20], identifying several accessibility barriers. The three e-services offer the same functionality ("make an appointment") but with different features regarding online-forms (e.g., number of pages, data to be inserted, interaction components, etc.). Table 1 shows detailed information about the features of each e-service: number of pages, number of each type of fields implemented in the forms and number of mandatory fields (those dataEntry and DataSelection components users have to interact with).

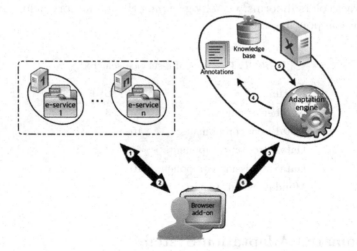

**Fig. 2.** Proposed architecture for the adaptation system.

---

[2] http://www.interior.gob.es/.

[3] https://www.sepe.es/.

[4] http://www.seg-social.es/wps/portal/wss/internet/Inicio.

On the other hand, we identified the following similar steps in the form ful-filment process: providing personal information (UserId), selecting the service (ServSel), selecting the location (LocSel), selecting the date and time (Date-Sel), answering security questions (SecQue). All these steps can be found in the e-services studied, except LocSel in SPE. However, in some cases, the informa-tion related to each step is required in different pages across the e-service. For example, regarding the UserId step, the zip code and the identification (ID) card number is required in the first page of SPE service whereas the name and surname of the user are requested on the second page.

With the objective of providing an automatically adapted version to people with low vision, the three e-services have been annotated using the proposed ontology in the knowledge base. The annotation process was in this way: firstly, a reference to the e-service (for example, DNIeService), is stored as an eSer-vice class. Then, the web pages in the e-service are stored as Page classes and linked with the eService with a property assertion (e.g. 'DNIeService hasPage Page1'). The identified steps are also stored as Step classes and linked with the eService class (e.g. 'DNIeService hasStep UserId'). After that, HTML com-ponents have to be stored which are doubled linked with the Page and Step classes (e.g. 'Page1 hasHtmlComponent Name' and 'UserId hasHtmlComponent Name'). Each HTML component is identified as an interaction or description component and its type is stored accordingly linked with isA subclass relation ('Name isA InteractionComponent' and 'Name isA DataEntry'). The form is a particular HTML component consisted of the HTML components within (e.g., 'Form1 hasHtmlComponent Name'). Some properties are assigned to the compo-nents (e.g. 'PhoneNumber hasProperty optional', 'Advert hasProperty distrac-tor'). Finally, the HTML components are accordingly identified with their name, id or uri. The annotation process is quite tedious as it is necessary to analyse the e-service to define the number of steps and decide the interaction compo-nents it is composed of. In addition, some constraints have to be considered as sometimes the existence of one component may depend on previous user input or the order in which steps are presented to users may be limited by the service program logic which can not be modified.

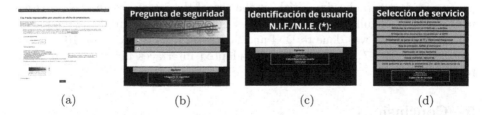

(a)             (b)             (c)             (d)

**Fig. 3.** Examples of original (a) and adapted interfaces (b, c and d) for SPE.

The adaptation techniques applied in this proof of concept are oriented to improve the navigation experience of people with low vision. The selection of techniques to apply was based on a bibliographic revision:

1. Providing uniform style for e-services [15,16]
2. Structuring the process in steps [16]
3. Ordering steps and grouping components in steps [16]
4. Identifying steps and overall progress of the process [14–16]
5. Changing the presentation to high contrast colours [2]
6. Resizing components [2]
7. Replacing the selection components (DataSelection) [19,20]

The rules for the adaptations were specified based on the ontology classes and stored in the knowledge base. For example, adaptation 7 was defined as:
    'HtmlComponent(?el), isInteractionComponent(?el), isDataSelection(?el), 'HtmlComponent((?el) hasOption (?op), $\Rightarrow$ isApplicable(convertToLink, ?el, ?op)

Figure 3(a) shows the original first web page of the SPE e-service. The fields to fill in are: ZIP code, ID card number, selection of the required service (radiobutton with 8 options) and CAPTCHA (with alternative audio and help link). All fields are mandatory and there is one button to send the input data. Based on the descriptive model proposed, these fields are annotated as InteractionComponents: ZIP code, ID card number and CAPTCHA as DataEntry, selection of the service as DataSelection with 8 Option elements and the button as DataSubmission. These fields correspond to different step in the process (UserId, ServSel, DateSel, SecQue) so we annotated the steps of the e-service and each field with the corresponding step: ZIP code and ID card number fields as UserId, CAPTCHA as SecQue and the radiobutton as ServSel. The steps order defined in the adaptation techniques is [SecQue, UserID, ServSel, DateSel]. The components contained in the 4 original web pages of this e-service are relocated according to this order into 8 adapted interfaces. The user input in each field is stored between interfaces and sent to the e-service when it corresponds depending on the program logic. The first three interfaces are shown in Fig. 3 (b, c and d, they correspond to SecQue, UserID, ServSel respectively). The step in the process is identified showing a title at the top of the interfaces and the progress in the process of fulfiling the form is presented at the bottom of the interfaces. The same process was done to DNI and SGS e-services resulting on 10 adapted interfaces for the 7 web pages and 11 adapted interfaces for the 5 web pages respectively.

## 5   Conclusions

The developed automated adaptation system based on annotations may improve the experience of users with low vision when fulfiling forms in the public e-services, as the adaptation techniques applied aim to improve their accessibility. Although for the proof of concept this system was aimed at people with low vision and was only tested in three public e-services, in the short-term, we will also apply it for annotating and adapting other public e-services in order to test if it is useful for a broad range of e-services. Moreover, we plan to add more adaptation techniques applicable to users with diverse kinds of disabilities.

**Acknowledgments.** This research was supported by the Basque Government, Department of Education, Universities and Research under grant IT980-16 and by the University of the Basque Country under grant US20/19. The authors thank all the individuals who participated in the study, as well as to the Begiris and Begisare associations of people with visual impairments for helping with the recruitment of the participants.

# References

1. Akpınar, E., Yeşilada, Y.: Old habits die hard!: eye tracking based experiential transcoding: a study with mobile users. In: Proceedings of the 12th International Web for All Conference. ACM, May 2015. https://doi.org/10.1145/2745555.2746646
2. Allan, J., Kirkpatrick, A., Henry, S.L.: Accessibility requirements for people with low vision, March 2016. https://www.w3.org/TR/low-vision-needs/
3. Bukhari, A.C., Kim, Y.G.: Ontology-assisted automatic precise information extractor for visually impaired inhabitants. Artif. Intell. Rev. **38**(1), 9–24 (2011). https://doi.org/10.1007/s10462-011-9238-6
4. European Commission: the adoption of a directive on the accessibility of the sector bodies' websites and mobile apps, October 2016. https://ec.europa.eu/digital-single-market/en/news/adoption-directive-accessibility-sector-bodies-websites-and-mobile-apps
5. Gambino, O., Pirrone, R., Giorgio, F.D.: Accessibility of the Italian institutional web pages: a survey on the compliance of the Italian public administration web pages to the stanca act and its 22 technical requirements for web accessibility. Univ. Access Inf. Soc. **15**(2), 305–312 (2016). https://doi.org/10.1007/s10209-014-0381-0
6. Gamecho, B., et al.: Automatic generation of tailored accessible user interfaces for ubiquitous services. IEEE Trans. Hum. Mach. Syst. **45**(5), 612–623 (2015). https://doi.org/10.1109/THMS.2014.2384452
7. Gruber, T.R.: A translation approach to portable ontology specifications. Knowl. Acquisit. **5**(2), 199–220 (1993). https://doi.org/10.1006/knac.1993.1008
8. Harper, S., Bechhofer, S.: SADIe: structural semantics for accessibility and device independence. ACM Trans. Comput. Hum. Interact. **14**(2), 10 (2007). https://doi.org/10.1145/1275511.1275516
9. Jaeger, P.T.: Assessing section 508 compliance on federal e-government web sites: a multi-method, user-centered evaluation of accessibility for persons with disabilities. Gov. Inf. Quart. **23**(2), 169–190 (2006). https://doi.org/10.1016/j.giq.2006.03.002
10. Kirkpatrick, A., Connor, J.O., Campbell, A., Cooper, M.: Web content accessibility guidelines (WCAG) 2.1, June 2018. https://www.w3.org/TR/WCAG21/
11. Knutov, E., Bra, P.D., Pechenizkiy, M.: AH 12 years later: a comprehensive survey of adaptive hypermedia methods and techniques. New Rev. Hypermed. Multimed. **15**(1), 5–38 (2009). https://doi.org/10.1080/13614560902801608

12. Lohmann, S., Kaltz, J.W., Ziegler, J.: Model-driven dynamic generation of context-adaptive web user interfaces. In: Models in Software Engineering, pp. 116–125. Springer, Berlin, Heidelberg (2006). https://doi.org/10.1007/978-3-540-69489-2_15

13. McGuinness, D.L., van Harmelen, F.: Owl web ontology language, February 2004. https://www.w3.org/TR/owl-features/

14. Money, A.G., Lines, L., Fernando, S., Elliman, A.D.: e-government online forms: design guidelines for older adults in Europe, vol. 10, pp. 1–16. Universal Access in the Information Society (2010). https://doi.org/10.1007/s10209-010-0191-y

15. Moreno, L., Martínez, P., Muguerza, J., Abascal, J.: Support resource based on standards for accessible e-government transactional services. Comput. Stand. Interfaces **58**, 146–157 (2018). https://doi.org/10.1016/j.csi.2018.01.003

16. Norwegian Ministry of Trade and Industry: Elmer: user interface guidelines for governmental forms on the internet, August 2011. https://brukskvalitet.brreg.no/elmer21/elmer_2_1_english.pdf

17. Pérez, J.E., Arrue, M., Valencia, X., Abascal, J.: Longitudinal study of two virtual cursors for people with motor impairments: a performance and satisfaction analysis on web navigation. IEEE Access **8**, 110381–110396 (2020). https://doi.org/10.1109/ACCESS.2020.3001766

18. Rosales-Huamaní, J., Castillo-Sequera, J., Puente-Mansilla, F., Boza-Quispe, G.: A prototype of a semantic platform with a speech recognition system for visual impaired people. J. Intell. Learn. Syst. Appl. **07**(04), 87–92 (2015). https://doi.org/10.4236/jilsa.2015.74008

19. Sala, A., Arrue, M., Pérez, J.E., Espín-Tello, S.M.: Measuring complexity of e-government services for people with low vision. Presented at the, April 2020. https://doi.org/10.1145/3371300.3383350

20. Sala, A., Arrue, M., Pérez, J.E., Espín-Tello, S.M.: Towards less complex e-government services for people with low vision. ACM SIGACCESS Access. Comput. **1**(128), 1–10 (2020). https://doi.org/10.1145/3441497.3441499

21. Shi, Y.: The accessibility of Chinese local government web sites: an exploratory study. Gov. Inf. Q. **24**(2), 377–403 (2007). https://doi.org/10.1016/j.giq.2006.05.004

22. United Nations, Department of Economic and Social Affairs: un e-government survey 2020, digital government in the decade of action for sustainable development. Technical report, UN (2020). https://publicadministration.un.org/egovkb/Portals/egovkb/Documents/un/2020-Survey/2020UNE-GovernmentSurvey(FullReport).pdf

23. Valencia, X., Pérez, J.E., Arrue, M., Abascal, J., Duarte, C., Moreno, L.: Adapting the web for people with upper body motor impairments using touch screen tablets. Interact. Comput. **29**(6), 794–812 (2017). https://doi.org/10.1093/iwc/iwx013

# Identifying Group-Specific Mental Models of Recommender Systems: A Novel Quantitative Approach

Johannes Kunkel[(✉)], Thao Ngo, Jürgen Ziegler, and Nicole Krämer

University of Duisburg-Essen, 47057 Duisburg, Germany
{johannes.kunkel,thao.ngo,juergen.ziegler,
nicole.kraemer}@uni-duisburg-essen.de

**Abstract.** How users interact with an intelligent system is determined by their subjective *mental model* of the system's inner working. In this paper, we present a novel method based on card sorting to identify such mental models of recommender systems quantitatively. Using this method, we conducted an online study ($N = 170$). Applying hierarchical clustering to the results revealed distinct user groups and their respective mental models. Independent of the recommender system used, some participants held a strict procedural-based, others a concept-based mental model. Additionally, mental models can be characterized as either technical or humanized. While procedural-based mental models were positively related to transparency perception, humanized models might influence the perception of system trust. Based on these findings, we derive three implications for the consideration of user-specific mental models in the design of transparent intelligent systems.

**Keywords:** Mental models · Transparency · Recommender systems · Card sorting · Hierarchical clustering

## 1 Introduction

*Mental models* of intelligent systems are subjective, typically incomplete and flawed understandings of the system's inner working [38,45]. They are shaped through system interaction [38]. Studying mental models can, thus, explain how users perceive a system and how they interact with it, e.g. by identifying superstitions or misconceptions. This is also a crucial prerequisite to explain elements of intelligent systems better and to increase their transparency [13,54].

To investigate subjective mental models, research has focused thus far on qualitative approaches that characterize single mental models in greater detail using small samples (typically smaller than $N = 20$; e.g. [13,34,36]). While such

---

**Electronic supplementary material** The online version of this chapter (https://doi.org/10.1007/978-3-030-85610-6_23) contains supplementary material, which is available to authorized users.

qualitative studies describe single, overarching models and are valuable for a general comprehension of what is included in such a model, they struggle to capture their full *diversity* and lack the ability to reliably identify and systematically compare different mental models that might coexist in large samples. Such comparisons, most importantly, offer systematic insights into relationships between specific mental models and user-centered aspects. We argue that this needs to be addressed through a quantitative approach.

In fact, quantitative methods might reveal individual and reappearing structures of mental models in *large samples* and *across* different systems. Hence, they could allow comparisons of diverse mental models among individuals and groups. Studying mental models quantitatively might also lead to practical implications for the design of user-friendly interfaces. Specific themes and visual perspectives could be designed for certain user groups, commonalities among models could foster general design of transparent systems. However, the application of quantitative methods still poses a serious challenge.

In this work, we aim to close this gap and explore the users' mental models of intelligent systems quantitatively. For this, we applied a novel card sorting setting which captured the entire processing chain of an intelligent system. The card sorting setting provided typical functional steps of intelligent systems (e.g. data acquisition) for users to reconstruct their mental model. The method allows us (1) to identify user groups and characterize their mental models, and (2) to explore the relationship of these user groups and mental models with system perceptions (e.g. transparency).

We applied this novel card sorting setting in the domain of recommender systems (RS) as RS are a mainstay in today's online environment. Furthermore, their decisions are often perceived as subjective which are met with more distrust by users than other systems that make more objective decisions (e.g. route planners) [6]. We asked RS users of a broad sample ($N = 170$) to sort different actions according to how they think the RS works internally. Hence, we aim at answering the following research questions:

*RQ1*: Which different mental models do users hold across RS?
*RQ2*: How do these mental models relate to the perception of RS?
*RQ3*: Based on these findings, which implications can we derive for the design of transparent intelligent systems?

With this work, we contribute to the advancement of research on users' assumptions and knowledge about intelligent systems in three ways: (1) We captured the entire processing chain of an intelligent system (i.e. RS) in a detailed way through a novel card sorting setting. (2) This allowed us to demonstrate and uncover which mental models are prevalent in a broad sample of RS users, thus forming a baseline for future research in this domain. (3) We derive practical implications for system designers regarding how the knowledge of such mental models can be leveraged to increase user-centric qualities of intelligent systems, such as transparency and trustworthiness.

# 2  Background and Related Work

Recommender systems typically appear as *black box* to users, i.e. their internal reasoning and functioning remain hidden. This can affect users negatively, e.g. it can cause feelings of creepiness towards recommendations [47]. Furthermore, users may distrust algorithmic decision making and reject its results [12,40]. This *algorithm aversion* seems to pertain especially to situations of subjective compared to objective decision making [6]. As a result, RS that recommend subjective items (e.g. music or movies) are more affected by distrust than objective systems (e.g. route planners that give directions) [6]. To tackle this potential distrust in subjective decision support systems, transparency appears to be a central factor. Studies indicate that transparency can increase the users' trust in and satisfaction with a system [27,49] and recommendation acceptance [11,20].

A clear understanding of the users' knowledge and interpretation of the system's functioning is a key prerequisite for determining how to improve transparency and which parts of the system to focus on [13,55]. A holistic depiction of such knowledge can be conceptualized as *mental models* [38,39].

## 2.1  Mental Models of Intelligent Systems

Mental models (closely related to *folk theories*[1]) can be defined as cognitive knowledge representations of technological systems that serve users to cognitively simulate system behavior and predict its outcomes [45]. They are subjective in nature, and thus, may be parsimonious and flawed [38]. Mental models are developed through system interaction, especially when confronted with anomalies and unexpected behavior [18]. In other words, mental models represent *what* users know about a system and determine *how* they interact with it.

A field study by Tullio et al. [50] demonstrated that this also holds for intelligent systems. They found that, without prior knowledge about the system, users showed a basic understanding of machine learning methods when confronted with an intelligent agent. In particular users' mental models included decision trees and statistic predictions based on "patterns" and "averages".

Other research has highlighted the impact of mental models on the users' task performance. For example, in a qualitative study Muramatsu and Pratt [34] showed that flaws in mental models of search engines may cause confusion regarding the interpretation of search results. Despite the familiarity and daily use of search engines, many participants did not fully understand how search queries are processed. This is supported by a study of Kulesza et al. [26] which showed that improved soundness of mental models was positively related to the effectiveness of interaction with the system.

Most studies on mental models of intelligent systems focused a single general mental model, e.g. [13,19,36]. Eiband et al. [13] highlighted the importance of identifying one "overarching user mental model" of a target group and indicated that within this model, several group-specific mental models may exist.

---

[1] For a detailed discussion on *folk theories*, e.g. see [15,16].

Indeed, some findings indicate a diverse landscape of mental models. In the domain of RS, Ghori et al. [19] showed that users mostly explain technical concepts, such as collaborative filtering, in their own words. In an interview study, Ngo et al. [36] revealed that mental models of RS might be technical or metaphorical. The study also suggests that users had different views on the importance of themselves in the recommendation process.

To summarize, while the elaboration of an overarching mental model for a system is useful, there is also strong support for the existence of diverse mental models within a population. To find a balance between one overarching mental model and an individual mental model for each user, we therefore argue to identify group-specific mental models. Even though qualitative approaches may provide some insights into the diversity of mental models, a quantitative approach is required to more precisely identify and classify these diverse models.

## 2.2 Methods for Eliciting Mental Models

Few studies have applied a quantitative approach to explore the mental models of intelligent systems. They mostly studied *effects* of mental models on the perception of a system. For instance, Kulesza et al. [26] induced different mental models and captured their "soundness" through multiple-choice questions. Thus, they did not directly investigate the structure and characteristics of mental models but the users' capacity of using them to simulate certain system outputs.

Other studies have used mixed-method approaches: Xie et al. [53] investigated the effects of mental model similarity on web page interaction performance in an experimental study. They combined a card sorting and a path diagram of web navigation and calculated different similarity measures based on these methods. A recent example studied mental models of cooperative AI agents in a game setting [18]. The researchers first applied a think-aloud task to explore the mental models. Then, a large-scale survey was conducted. We encourage such *informed quantitative studies* that exploit insights from former qualitative work.

*Conceptual techniques*, such as the repertory grid, pairwise rating, or card sorting [10,30] can be used to study mental models quantitatively. They are based on an existing body of concepts which needs to be explored before, e.g. through interviews. Thus, they do not rely on direct verbalization [10].

In repertory grid and pairwise rating, users rate different concepts on a certain scale or compare them with one another. This leads to a similarity matrix between the concepts representing the user knowledge. The data can be analyzed through e.g. multidimensional scaling [30]. While both methods have different advantages, they are either time-consuming or are limited in the number of concepts that can be studied. Therefore, Cooke [10] recommends to apply card-sorting techniques, if the number of concepts is higher than 25–30.

In card sorting, users assign certain cards, representing concepts, into categories. The method is often used in usability studies to determine navigation structures [9]. There are different types of settings: In closed card sorting, the content of the cards and the label as well as number of categories are fixed. In open card sorting, participants can label the cards themselves [9]. The method allows for the identification of common themes and differences in samples [44].

**Table 1.** Overview of the four general categories and their associated action cards we used in the card sorting task.

| Acquisition of user data | Comparing items or users |
|---|---|
| [01] Recording my mouse clicks | [10] Comparing items regarding their content |
| [02] Asking me for my age | [11] Matching rating data of items |
| [03] Recording my dwell time on an item's detail page | [12] Calculating a similarity score between items |
| [04] Asking me to explicitly rate items | [13] Calculating a similarity score between users |
| Inference and aggregation | Presenting recommendations |
| [05] Determining my interest in item categories | [14] Suggesting items that are new to me |
| [06] Analyzing my current mood | [15] Showing items, I might like |
| [07] Combining all data about me to an abstract user profile | [16] Presenting items that other users liked in the past |
| [08] Adding additionally item data that users cannot see | |
| [09] Analyzing content of items | |

# 3 Identifying Diversity and Commonalities of Mental Models

We developed a new setting based on card sorting. Card sorting is suitable for large online studies [4], allows open and closed settings [9], and can be used to include a wide range of concepts [10]. Our setting considers the subjectivity of mental models by providing a diverse range of pre-defined cards, and allowing participants to formulate their own thoughts using open cards and as many actions and steps as they find appropriate to describe their mental model.

In our card sorting setting, participants are presented with a set of cards representing typical RS actions and are asked to assign them to up to seven sequential steps. Our method assumes a procedural structure of the inner workings of a RS. This is in line with how these systems typically work and with observations in previous qualitative user studies [36,38,50]. The resulting card sorts of each participant represents their mental model of RS. Through hierarchical clustering, card sorts can be aggregated into groups, allowing us to characterize the differences and commonalities between mental models in a larger sample.

## 3.1 Cards Used as Actions of RS

We carefully created 35 cards for participants to express their mental model:

- 16 *action cards*, represent actions of the recommendation process (Table 1)
- 12 *distractor cards*, represent actions that are not part of the central recommendation process
- 4 *question mark cards*, provide the possibility to express uncertainty
- 3 *open cards*, let users express self formulated actions

The *action cards* correspond to typical paradigms used by RS while still *"speaking the language of the user"*. We extracted concepts of mental models from former qualitative mental model studies [13,19,26,36,50] and contributed our own technical expertise on RS functioning. In particular, we followed the four general categories provided by Ngo et al. [36]: (1) *acquisition of user data*, (2) *inference and aggregation*, (3) *comparing items or users*, and (4) *presentation of recommendations*. For each category, we designed up to five cards (Table 1). We describe the rationale behind the action cards in the following.

**(1) Acquisition of User Data (Cards 01–04):** For any personalized RS, elicitation of user data and their preferences is a necessary prerequisite [42,46]. While these data can take various forms (e.g. ratings, purchases, clicks), the underlying concept appears to be well known by RS users and was mentioned in many in-depth qualitative user studies [13,19,36,50].

**(2) Inference and Aggregation (Cards 05–09):** In almost all cases RS do not perform their recommending on raw user data, but aggregate them or infer further (e.g. situational) data [1,3]. A similar concept can also be found in many user responses of prior interview studies. Users, for instance, mentioned (statistical) inference [50], or construction of a personal interest profile [19].

**(3) Comparing Items or Users (Cards 10–13):** Relating users or items is one of the most common techniques in RS design [25,37]. Such techniques, e.g. the commonly used *collaborative filtering*, are apparently well understood by users. In many prior mental models identified, the similarity between users or items was mentioned or played a central role [19,36].

**(4) Presenting Recommendations (Cards 14–16):** While the form of presenting recommendations seems to play an inferior role in users' mental models [36], it is very relevant for RS research [23,48]. We thus decided to also include three actions for the presentation of RS outcome.

To further diversify answers and to enable analysis of the extent to which the mental models of participants diverge from a *"ground truth"*, we added 12 *distractor cards*. These cards were chosen as misconceptions of RS as well as actions that are not part of the main personalization process. Distractor cards were collected by identifying such actions in results of a previous qualitative user study to which we had access (i.e. [36]). All distractor cards can be found in the supplementary material. Examples are: *"Employees suggest items for me"*, *"Evaluating my satisfaction of recommendations"*, and *"Blocking advertisement"*.

Finally, we added *question mark* and *open cards*. The question mark cards account for uncertainties in participants' mental models, i.e. to indicate that there might be an unknown action performed in a certain step. Open cards account for any missing actions that were not part of the pre-labeled action or distractor cards, but are part of the subjective mental model.

## 4   User Study

Our online study consisted of three parts: instruction, mental model task, and measurement of technical knowledge and perception of RS. At the end, participants

**Fig. 1.** Excerpt of the mental model task with shortened description and examplified for *Discover weekly playlist on Spotify*. For reasons of space efficiency only nine actions and only two steps with three action slots are depicted here.

were debriefed and received 2.76 \$ as compensation. We used Soscisurvey[2] as a survey platform in which we implemented the card sorting setting ourselves. On average participants took 13:39 minutes ($SD = 01{:}55$) to complete the study. This study was approved by the local ethics committee of the University of Duisburg-Essen. We included the complete lists of measures and items in the supplements. This section is organized according to the three parts of the user study.

## 4.1    Instruction

At the beginning, participants were presented with a definition of RS and the term "item", which we defined as all content subject to recommendations, whether it is a product on Amazon, or a person suggested as friend on Facebook. Participants chose a RS they encounter regularly. Eight options were provided: *Top pics for you on Netflix, Video recommendations on YouTube, Discover weekly playlist on Spotify, Recommendations of similar items on Amazon, Friend recommendations on Facebook, Trending hashtags for you on Twitter, Personalized feed on Instagram*, and *Daily news recommendations on Google News*.

Additionally, participants could opt for *"None of the above"*, which resulted in an immediate end of this participant's session. If any of the eight options was chosen, participants were instructed to keep the chosen RS and its items in mind as point of reference for all subsequent questions. As auxiliary reminder, their chosen RS was also explicitly displayed in several texts throughout the survey.

## 4.2    Mental Model Task

Next, participants had to complete the card sorting task described in Sect. 3. They were briefed to use their RS chosen in the previous part as reference while sorting their cards. All 35 cards were displayed on the left and participants were asked to sort as many of them as they deem appropriate via drag-and-drop in

---

[2] https://www.soscisurvey.de.

up to seven steps. The steps were displayed on the right (see Fig. 1). The open and question mark cards were shown at the bottom of the card list. Action and distractor cards were presented in a randomized order.

After the task, participants were asked about the *degree of fidelity* that reflected how well participants were able to express their mental model. We measured this using two self-created items on a 5-point Likert scale (1 ("I strongly disagree") to 5 ("I strongly agree")). The items were: *"I was able to express my ideas through the arrangements of steps and actions very well"* and *"I feel very certain about the arrangement of steps and actions."*, (Cronbach's $\alpha = .725$).

### 4.3   Measures

We asked participants about their perception of RS and technical knowledge: on the one hand, through self-created items on technical or metaphorical perception of RS, and, on the other hand, through standardized scales for social presence, trusting beliefs, transparency, and other user-centric measures of RS.

*Perception of the RS:* To assess whether participants perceived the chosen RS as rather technical or metaphorical, we included a self-created semantic differential consisting of twelve pairs such as *"machinelike"* vs. *"humanlike"* (Cronbach's $\alpha = .809$). Items were assessed on a 5-point Likert scale.

We used the social presence scale from Gefen and Straub [17] consisting of 5 items (e.g. *"There is a sense of human contact in the system."*). Furthermore, we assessed *trusting beliefs* using items from McKnight et al. [32]. Trusting beliefs consist of three dimensions: benevolence, integrity, and competence. For all of these scales, items were rated on a 7-point Likert scale.

We measured *transparency*, *control*, and *perceived usefulness* using the *ResQue* inventory [41], and added *recommendation quality* and *perceived system effectiveness* from Knijnenburg et al. [24]. All items were assessed on a 5-point Likert scale.

*Technical Knowledge of RS:* We assessed the prior *technical knowledge* of participants by using three self-created items, e.g. *"In the past I learned about how recommender systems work"* (Cronbach's $\alpha = .818$). Additionally, we specifically asked for the *confidence* in the capability of learning about RS through one item, (*"I would be capable of understanding the recommendation process, if someone would explain it to me."*). All items were measured on a 5-point Likert scale.

### 4.4   Participants

In total, 170 participants were recruited through the UK-based crowd-working platform *Prolific*[3]. Participants' age ranged from 18 to 67 ($M = 31.42$, $SD = 11.64$). Regarding gender, 71 participants identified as male and 99 as female.

---

[3] https://www.prolific.co/.

The sample was rather educated with 75 participants (44.1 %) holding a bachelor's degree, 55 participants (32.4 %) holding a high school diploma, and 26 (15.3 %) a master's degree. Six participants (3.5 %) held a PhD, while three participants (1.8 %) reported to hold less than a high school diploma. Five participants (2.9 %) indicated other degrees. Participants reported to have a low to moderate technical knowledge on RS ($M=1.87$, $SD = .99$).

Generally, participants were able to express their mental model through the task well: Descriptive analysis revealed a moderate degree of fidelity with a mean score of 3.18 ($SD = 0.90$). Question mark cards were used very rarely (on average participants used $M = 0.03$ ($SD = 0.06$) of them). Only few open cards[4] were used: Participants created 63 cards themselves accounting for 2.32 % of all cards used. Most of them indicated similar ideas as existing action cards, e.g. *"Collecting other data such as gender"*, or were specific to the RS, e.g. *"Monitoring what I watch"*. 25.40 % of them were left blank or were unclear in their meaning.

Overall, participants used $M=15.74$ ($SD = 8.20$) cards and $M=4.90$ ($SD = 1.76$) steps to represent their mental model. When comparing action cards and all other cards, a t-test for paired samples revealed that action cards ($M=9.85$, $SD = 4.15$) were used significantly more often than the others ($M=5.88$, $SD = 4.80$), $t(169) = 14.94$, $p = .001$. The proportion of actions to distractors was at 26.61 % ($SD = 12.70$ %) on average, i.e. for each four action cards that were used in the mental model task, one was a distractor.

# 5   Results

We followed a *data-driven* approach to answer our RQs. Hierarchical clustering on participants' card sorts revealed three distinct user groups in our data. We conducted a descriptive analysis to compare the perceptions of RS of these groups. For the analyses we used SPSS 25 and R 4.0.2.

## 5.1   RQ1: Which Different Mental Models Do Users Hold Across RS?

To determine clusters among the different mental models expressed, we first calculated dissimilarities between card sorts. While card sorts are commonly evaluated this way, we faced two specific challenges in our task setting: (1) The order of steps, the cards were sorted in, was relevant to us, which is not taken into account by typical dissimilarity measures (e.g. *Jaccard Index*). (2) Participants were free to use any number of steps (up to a maximum of 7) and any number of cards (up to a maximum of 35), which resulted in many missing values. To overcome these two challenges, we calculated the dissimilarity between participants as follows:

$$dis(p, u) = 0.7 * d(p, u) + 0.3 * q(p, u)$$

---

[4] Note that a qualitative in-depth analysis of open cards was not within the scope of this work.

**Table 2.** Overview of user groups descriptive statistics. SI values refer to the cluster cut within each group.

| Group | $N$ | No. of cards $M(SD)$ | No. of steps $M(SD)$ | Degree of fidelity $M(SD)$ | No. of clusters | SI |
|---|---|---|---|---|---|---|
| 1 | 66 | 8.53 (2.56) | 4.09 (1.84) | 3.34 (0.88) | 4 | 0.298 |
| 2 | 79 | 16.76 (3.39) | 4.99 (1.42) | 3.46 (0.85) | 2 | 0.238 |
| 3 | 25 | 31.60 (3.20) | 6.76 (0.52) | 2.82 (0.99) | 7 | 0.132 |

This dissimilarity calculation is based on two components. The first one $(d(p, u))$ determines the normalized *Manhattan distance* between any two participants. We interpret each participant's card sort as vector $p \in \mathbb{N}^c$, where $c$ is equal to the number of available cards[5]. Each position of $p$, thus, corresponds to a specific card, while the value indicates the number of the step this participant assigned the card to. The Manhattan distance between these vectors accounts for challenge (1) as it considers the order of steps cards are sorted in. While this could be achieved with other similarity measures (e.g. *Euclidean distance*), the Manhattan distance treats coordinates as discrete, thus matching the discrete steps of our task design. This first component only includes cards that were used by both participants. Therefore, to account for (2), we add a second component $(q(p, u))$ as the difference of how many cards both participants used.

We acknowledged that both components should not equally contribute to the dissimilarity and deemed the step order as more important than the number of cards each participant used. Thus, we assigned different weights to each component and chose a factor of 0.7 for the first, and a factor of 0.3 for the second component. Detailed description of the formulas is included in the supplement.

**Hierarchical Clustering.** Hierarchical clustering can follow a *divisive* or an *agglomerative* clustering algorithm. Divisive clustering follows a top-down pattern, which starts with one cluster containing all items and divides them iteratively until each cluster contains only one single item. Agglomerative clustering takes the opposite approach and starts with each item as an own cluster and iteratively combines them until only one cluster remains [22].

We compared the *clustering coefficients* of divisive and agglomerative variants. This coefficient "describes the strength of the clustering structure" [22]. A coefficient closer to 1 indicates a stronger cluster structure and a better fit with the data. In our case, agglomerative clustering in tandem with the *Ward's* criterion [35,51] resulted in the best performance with a *clustering coefficient* of .949. To determine the number of clusters that fits the data best, we then compared cuts of the hierarchy at 2–7 clusters. For this, we used the respective *average silhouette index* (SI) [43] which reflects the *cohesion* within clusters

---

[5] We ignored open and question mark cards, since they cannot be compared easily.

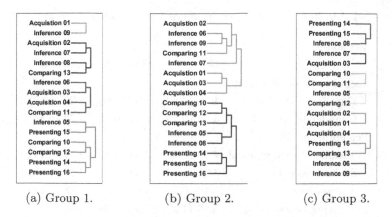

(a) Group 1.          (b) Group 2.          (c) Group 3.

**Fig. 2.** Dendrograms depicting clusters of how cards have been sorted for each identified user group. Clusters and actions within are ordered regarding the median of steps, they have been sorted in.

and *separation* between clusters. The index ranges from −1 to 1. We found the highest SI of .237 when cutting at 3 clusters, and thus, 3 user groups.

Subsequently, we performed hierarchical clustering again. This second clustering was applied to cards within each of the 3 user groups and resulted in 2–7 clusters, depending on the group (Fig. 2 and Table 2). Below we describe the mental models of each user group in detail.

**Group 1: Users with a Parsimonious Concept-Based Mental Model.** This group used the lowest number of cards and steps (Table 2). Participants were convinced of their card sorts (degree of fidelity). Compared to the other groups, they expressed less prior knowledge in RS, but felt confident in understanding them. The group perceived RS as rather rational, planned, and machine-like (Table 3). The dendrogram of this group shows four major clusters (Fig. 2a) and that this group held a rather *concept-based* mental model.

The first major cluster is small and pertains to elicitation and analysis of implicit and less tangible user data ("recording of mouse clicks" (card 01) and "analyzing content of items" (card 09)) which can be considered as a starting point of RS processes. The second major cluster refers to the *inference of a user model* comprising of several processes including processes of data acquisition, inference, and comparison, all regarding the user (card 02, 07, 08, 13).

Following this, the third major cluster (card 05, 10, 12, 14–16) represents the *processing of the user model*. Further user data, e.g. "mood" and "dwell times", are analyzed and recorded. Additionally, the user data is connected to item data. In contrast to this, the fourth major cluster (card 03, 04, 06, 11) focuses clearly on the *processing of items*. It includes different processes, i.e. inference, comparison, and presentation of items.

In sum, this group was parsimonious in their use of cards, i.e. they only used few actions and steps. Participants of this group focused on the concepts of *the user model*, *the user model processing*, and on the *items*. In each cluster,

**Table 3.** Overview of perception of RS for each user group.

| Variables | M(SD) | | |
|---|---|---|---|
| | Group 1 | Group 2 | Group 3 |
| Technical knowledge of RS | | | |
|     Knowledge of RS | 1.56 (0.83) | 1.97 (1.03) | 2.20 (1.10) |
|     Confidence | 4.23 (0.74) | 4.30 (0.65) | 3.72 (0.84) |
| Perception of RS | | | |
|     Technical/ metaphorical | 2.74 (0.48) | 2.65 (0.62) | 3.01 (0.74) |
|     Social presence | 3.11 (1.44) | 3.29 (1.58) | 3.50 (1.62) |
|     Transparency | 3.76 (0.79) | 4.09 (0.75) | 3.88 (0.78) |
|     Trusting beliefs (TB) | 3.85 (1.22) | 4.04 (1.29) | 4.20 (1.38) |
|       TB benevolence | 3.39 (1.42) | 3.44 (1.60) | 3.95 (1.47) |
|       TB integrity | 3.61 (1.36) | 3.66 (1.50) | 4.18 (1.54) |
|       TB competence | 4.45 (1.48) | 4.88 (1.34) | 4.41 (1.57) |

processes are mixed (e.g. acquisition and inferences processes regarding the user model, comparisons, inference, and presentation regarding the items).

**Group 2: Users with a Feasible Procedural Mental Model.** This group could express their mental model through the task well. Their prior knowledge was higher than in group 1, but lower than in group 3 (see Table 3). Like group 1, they perceived RS as rational, planned, machine-like, but as more transparent. The card sorting task resulted in two major clusters (Fig. 2b).

The first major cluster can be divided into two sub-clusters. The first one (card 02, 06, 07, 09, 11) pertains to the inference of a user model using *contextual* user data, such as the "age" or "mood" of the user. The second sub-cluster (card 01, 03, 04) pertains to the acquisition of *interaction* data that is dependent on the use of the RS, e.g. "mouse clicks", "dwell time".

The second major cluster consists of three sub-clusters that represent different processes of RS: comparison of items and users (cards 10, 12, and 13), inferences of the user's interest based on items (card 05, 08), and finally the presentation of recommendations (card 14–16).

In sum, this group showed a procedural mental model that reflected our proposed procedure best (Sect. 3 and Table 1). Only the first major cluster represented a more nuanced understanding of the acquisition of user data which differed from our proposed procedure. Group 2 views the user model as a starting point that is characterized by contextual data, i.e. data that exist prior to the interaction with RS. Thus, they distinguish between contextual and interaction data. The second major cluster represented the last three steps of our proposed procedure accordingly.

This user group seemed to have the most structured comprehension of RS which is indicated by the rather high values for the degree of fidelity, confidence, and transparency.

**Group 3: Users with an Extensive Social-Focused Mental Model.** This group used the highest number of cards and steps (Table 2). The confidence in their card sorts was the lowest, but they expressed a higher knowledge about RS[6]. Group 3 perceived the RS as more empathetic, spontaneous, and human-like. We found this tendency as well when examining the values for social presence and trusting beliefs, which were the highest in this group (Table 3). The dendrogram (Fig. 2c) reveals seven major clusters of action cards.

The first major cluster mainly contains the presentation of recommendations, showing items that are new (card 14) and the user might like (card 05). Based on these presented items, additional, invisible data are considered (card 08). The second major cluster combines user information to an abstract profile (card 07), to which user data (e.g. "dwell time", card 03) are added. The third and fourth major cluster mostly pertain to comparison processes of the items (card 10–12) and determination of user interests (card 05).

The fifth cluster refers to the data acquisition of explicit user data (card 01, 02), while the sixth pertains to items in relation to users (e.g. user ratings of items (card 04), similarity between users (card 13), and presentation of what users liked in the past (card 16)). These processes were mostly assigned to step 3. The last cluster refers to inference processes on the "mood that the user is currently in" (card 06) and "analyzing content of items" (card 09).

This group used nearly all cards and steps, i.e. many distractor, open, and question mark cards were used. We conclude that this user group might have an extensive mental model consisting of many different processes that go beyond the recommendation process described in Sect. 3.

In sum, the mental model of group 3 appears rather unstructured. This is reflected by the high number of clusters (i.e. many small unrelated islands). Like group 1, participants of this group seem to follow a rather concept-based mental model. Yet, they distinctively assigned more human attributes and social presence to the system indicating a higher social focus of their mental models.

## 5.2 RQ2: How Do These Mental Models Relate to the Perception of RS?

Due to the *exploratory* nature of our approach, we analyzed our results descriptively[7]. First, we explored if we find differences for the RS choice in the measures. The descriptive data revealed that confidence intervals (CI) of means of each chosen RS largely overlap for all measures. This indicates that the results are independent of the particular RS a participant had in mind. Instead, we conclude that measured differences resulted from the particular mental model a participant held.

Then, we analyzed the group differences based on 95 % CI of mean differences and effect sizes (using Cohen's $d$ with pooled standard deviation to account for different group sizes). To this end, we first performed a visual analysis of CI of

---

[6] However, the level of knowledge in all groups can be considered as low to moderate.

[7] An overview of all descriptive data can be found in the supplement.

**Table 4.** Overview of descriptive analysis.

| Group comparisons | Cohen's $d$ | 95% CI | Mean diff. | 95% CI |
|---|---|---|---|---|
| Confidence | | | | |
|   Group 1 vs. 3 | −.66 | [−1.13, −0.19] | .51 | [0.10, 0.91] |
|   Group 2 vs. 3 | −.83 | [−1.29, −0.37] | .58 | [0.19, 0.98] |
| Technical/ metaphorical | | | | |
|   Group 1 vs. 3 | .48 | [0.01, 0.95] | −.27 | [−0.60, 0.07] |
|   Group 2 vs. 3 | .55 | [0.10, 1.01] | −.36 | [−0.69, −0.03] |
| Transparency | | | | |
|   Group 1 vs. 2 | .43 | [0.10, 0.76] | −.33 | [−0.64, −0.02] |
| Knowledge of RS | | | | |
|   Group 1 vs. 2 | .43 | [0.10, 0.77] | −.41 | [−0.81, −0.02] |
|   Group 1 vs. 3 | .70 | [0.23, 1.17] | −.64 | [−1.19, −0.09] |

group means for each measure. We only report results with moderate to large effect sizes and CI with little or no overlap (Table 4).

Regarding *confidence*, we found that group 3 was less confident than group 1 and 2. This indicates that users with a social-focused mental model were less confident in their capabilities to understand the RS. The analysis revealed the same pattern regarding *technical vs. metaphorical perception* suggesting that group 3 tended to view RS as more human-like than the other two groups. Concerning *transparency*, we found a difference between group 1 and 2 indicating that the procedural mental model might be associated with higher transparency perception. Finally, regarding *knowledge of RS*, we found that group 1 expressed lower knowledge than group 2 and 3.

The descriptive analysis suggests that the precision of the measures were low. Therefore, the results give first indications of relevant relationships between the structure of mental models and RS perceptions.

# 6    Discussion

This work extends the existing research body on the measurement of mental models through a novel card sorting setting. While it does not investigate single mental models in detail, as fully qualitative methods would, our approach allows for relevant analytical insights. We analyzed *the diversity of mental models* in a large sample. Thus, we envision our card sorting setting as beneficial in a second research stage, after a first general mental model was already revealed.

In line with prior work of Norman [38], who observed the transfer of mental models from one system to another, we found that mental models exist *across systems*. Interestingly, we did not find any relationship between the referenced RS and the perception of RS, i.e. they were independent of another. In fact, differences in users' perceptions of RS were only dependent on users' mental model.

We conclude that mental models appear to be more critical for the perception of RS than the system itself. Hence, for contemporary user-centered design of RS, we suggest a shift from system-focused to mental-model-focused research.

In the following, we discuss the mental models of RS and their relation to the perception of RS. Furthermore, we address RQ3 (*Based on the identified mental models, which implications can be derived from them for the design of transparent intelligent systems?*) and discuss practical implications for the development of more user-friendly, trustworthy, and transparent user interfaces.

## 6.1 Seeing Is Not Understanding

Many participants perceived the referenced RS (e.g. Youtube, Netflix, Spotify) as transparent. However, the transparency perception cannot be ascribed to a factual knowledge about the inner workings of these RS. Firstly, because these systems do not provide any sophisticated explanatory components and, secondly, because participants reported a low to moderate technical expertise of RS. We therefore attribute the transparency perceptions to participants' mental models, which are based on subjective explanations of how the RS work. These explanations, hence, merely form an *impression* of understanding that may not match the actual systems' functioning. In other words, "*seeing*" a system does not necessarily translate to *understanding* it [2]. We argue that such mental models, based on vague information of how the system works, may result in a gap between actual system behavior and users' expectations—a concept known as *gulf of evaluation* [39]. Such gulf was observed to result in false assumptions and erroneous behavior [33,34]. Morris [33] found that social media users can misinterpret the opaque algorithms responsible for composing their news feed. In the case of Morris' observation, this led to the negative public misperception that new mothers post excessively about their newborns when in fact they do not. Muramatsu and Pratt [34] could show that false assumptions and erroneous mental models can be corrected through transparency.

**Practical Implication: Dare to Provide Transparency to Users.** To avoid a false sense of understanding a system, typical straightforward explanatory components might be too shallow to provide "real" transparency in terms of an actual user comprehension. Thus, users' mental models need to be regarded, evaluated, and, if flawed, corrected by providing factually accurate insights into the system's inner working. While we note that such a correction could benefit from knowing the active user's mental model during runtime, it could also be based on a general elicitation of mental models prevalent in a user base. The presented study demonstrates how such elicitation could be performed. Yet, we acknowledge that further research in eliciting mental models and providing transparency of RS is necessary as intelligent systems become increasingly sophisticated.

Previous research has indicated users' interest in more algorithmic transparency, e.g. [15,31]. Our study extends on that: It highlights that there is not only a user *interest*, but also that users feel *confidence* in their ability to understand intelligent systems when appropriate explanations are present. This is especially interesting considering the low technical knowledge of our participants. We, thus, encourage developers to dare to provide sophisticated components of transparency, e.g. in form of explanations [7,21] or visualizations [5,28,29].

## 6.2   Procedural vs. Concept-Based Mental Models

We could uncover three different mental models of RS that coexist in a large sample of RS users. We observed that these models exhibited different structures and perceptions of RS. Concept-based and procedural mental models were the most prevalent models that co-existed in our sample. An extensive and social-focused mental model was held by a minority of the participants.

The mental model of group 2 reflected the procedure, that our method was based on, best. Due to the opacity of RS, we cannot claim this procedure to be a *ground truth* of RS. Yet, it is based on established publications of researchers and practitioners in the field of RS and we deem it—to a certain degree—accurate. In this regard, group 2, interestingly, felt the highest degree of fidelity in expressing their mental model through the card sorting. Based on this, we assume that the mental model of this group was rather well-defined. Therefore, they perceived the highest transparency of RS. The well-defined mental model might also be the cause for the highest competence perception: The RS was perceived as reasonable leading to comprehension of the system and appreciation of its competence. As this group expressed low technical knowledge of RS, we conclude a close connection between a well-defined mental model, understanding the actual system functioning, the transparency and competence perception of the system.

Group 1 and 3 did not strongly adhere to a process-based mental model. It seems that they did not use the steps in a chronological, but in a concept-wise manner. Inspection of the clusters in the dendrogram of group 1 (Fig. 2a) showed that many clusters consisted of actions from different chronological stages. The second cluster, for instance, comprised of four cards (02, 07, 08, 13) of which three cards belong to another chronological stage. Yet, they shared a conceptual focus: the user model. The most frequent and strict concepts in the mental models of group 1 and 3 were *item- vs. user-based recommending*.

**Practical Implication: Increase Transparency Through Procedural Explanations.** We conclude that there are several perspectives on a RS that users can adopt. Delivering different user interfaces to each of these groups might address this issue best. For users adhering to a procedural mental model, explanations that emphasize the chronology of the recommendation process can be useful. To prevent aforementioned false assumptions, we suggest great care that explanations reflect the actual recommendation process as closely as possible.

Users that adhered to a concept-based mental model perceived lower transparency. Hence, we suggest explaining the concepts more clearly to those users, i.e. practitioners could provide clear definitions and examples of explicit and implicit user data and explain their application in RS. Similarly, practitioners can stress clearly whether users or items are compared to generate recommendations. The latter was recently identified to cause confusion for users [36].

However, we acknowledge that treating each user group differently is not always possible, e.g. when no information on the active user is available. While our quantitative approach could be used to correlate mental models to user interaction data (e.g. mouse movements), thus forming a baseline for inferring the user's mental model during runtime, this demands further studies. Yet, in our study, we identified some procedural aspects in all user groups and are thus confident that a procedural perspective could be "imposed" on users with a more concept-wise mental model. Hence, we recommend considering procedural explanations in RS. Apart from matching most user expectations, our findings suggest that this form of explanation also results in a higher perceived transparency.

## 6.3   Technical vs. Humanized RS

While group 1 and 2 held a rather technical understanding of RS (rational, and machinelike), group 3 described them as neutral to metaphorical (empathetic, spontaneous, and humanlike). Thus, group 3 *humanized* the RS more than the other groups, i.e. they ascribed humanlike characteristics to a non-human agent. This humanization acts as a mechanism to combat uncertainty and situations in which a system seems unpredictable [14]. This effect might be at work here: Besides the more humanized mental model compared to the other groups, group 3 expressed low confidence in the ability to learn about the system.

Prior work in autonomous vehicles has indicated a link between humanization and more trust in the non-human agent [52]. Our study shows that this mechanism might also occur in intelligent systems: group 3 perceived higher levels of trusting beliefs. Furthermore, descriptive values indicate a higher social presence for group 3. We ascribe this also to the more metaphorical and humanized mental model of this group. In line with prior work [8,27], this social presence may act as mediator between humanization and trusting beliefs in group 3.

**Practical Implication: Educate Users and Create Social Presence.** Uncertain users might hold an unstructured mental model including metaphorical concepts. As a consequence, such user groups might perceive the system as unpredictable and tend to humanize it. From this, we derive two implications for practitioners: (1) There is a need to educate uncertain users, so that they do not need to develop metaphorical or humanized mental models. As a result the system could be perceived as more predictable and transparent. Yet, we also note that some desirable aspects may arise from a higher social presence of RS and thus, (2), suggest to include social aspects into a user interface. This could, for instance, be realized by adding elements that express metaphors or using a metaphorical language. We, however, note that this is speculative and emphasize the necessity of investigating these aspects in greater depth.

## 6.4   Limitations

We created the cards as carefully as possible and added open cards to formulate new actions. Still, some actions that participants created were redundant with our pre-formulated cards. Therefore, we assume that some participants did not read all cards or did not fully understand them. Thus, we deem 35 cards as maximum in such settings and reconsider wording choices. Another limitation of our study concerns our task setting. While participants were able to express procedural mental models well, this did not necessarily apply to other forms of mental models (although participants managed to express them anyway, see Sect. 6.2). We conclude that the task design could be slightly adjusted to, for instance, express parallel actions or feedback loops. This could, for instance, be achieved through concept networks or flow diagrams. We also acknowledge that we have included only a small fraction of all existing RS in our study and that RS represent only one facet of the full range of intelligent systems. Future work might investigate mental models of additional RS and other intelligent systems.

# 7   Conclusions and Future Work

We introduced a method that enables us to identify mental models quantitatively and to examine their diversity in large samples and across platforms. It poses a substantial extension of prior research on mental models of intelligent systems which relied on qualitative studies with small samples.

We could reveal a relation between mental model structures and user perception of RS: Procedural mental models were positively related to transparency, implying that transparency can be increased through procedural explanations. Such type of explanations could also be imposed on users who hold a concept-based mental model. Additionally, uncertain users might hold social-focused mental models and perceive RS as more humanlike, which leads to ambivalent results: While social-focused mental models might positively relate to trust, they might lead users to be less confident and perceive a system as unpredictable.

Finally, this study highlights that mental models exist *across systems*, i.e. the perception of RS mainly depends on the mental models, and not on the particular system. We consequently emphasize the relevance of mental models for designing user-friendly intelligent systems and advocate a shift from system-focused to mental-model-focused research in that area.

Our method allows to identify mental model in statistically representative user studies, and thus, to make generalizable inferences about the mental models in a target audience and their relations to system perceptions. Moreover, we suggest an analysis of the relationship between user characteristics (e.g. personality traits such as need for cognition) and mental models of intelligent systems. Our method could be used to identify user groups that relate to certain personality profiles. This could contribute to measuring a user's mental model during run-time, enabling presentation of personalized transparency components, tailored towards their mental model and personality. This might be especially useful for system applications that require long-term relation between a user and a system.

# References

1. Adomavicius, G., Tuzhilin, A.: Context-aware recommender systems. In: Ricci, F., Rokach, L., Shapira, B., Kantor, P.B. (eds.) Recommender Systems Handbook, pp. 217–253. Springer, Boston (2011). https://doi.org/10.1007/978-0-387-85820-3_7
2. Ananny, M., Crawford, K.: Seeing without knowing: limitations of the transparency ideal and its application to algorithmic accountability. New Media Soc. **20**(3), 973–989 (2018). https://doi.org/10.1177/1461444816676645
3. Beliakov, G., Calvo, T., James, S.: Aggregation Functions for Recommender Systems. In: Ricci, F., Rokach, L., Shapira, B. (eds.) Recommender Systems Handbook, pp. 777–808. Springer, Boston, MA (2015). https://doi.org/10.1007/978-1-4899-7637-6_23
4. Bussolon, S., Russi, B., Missier, F.D.: Online card sorting: as good as the paper version. In: Proceedings of the 13th Eurpoean Conference on Cognitive Ergonomics: Trust and Control in Complex Socio-Technical Systems. ECCE 2006, New York, NY, USA. ACM (2006). https://doi.org/10.1145/1274892.1274912
5. Cardoso, B., Brusilovsky, P., Verbert, K.: Intersectionexplorer: the flexibility of multiple perspectives. In: Proceedings of the 4th Joint Workshop on Interfaces and Human Decision Making for Recommender Systems. IntRS 2017, CEUR Workshop Proceedings, pp. 16–19 (2017)
6. Castelo, N., Bos, M.W., Lehmann, D.R.: Task-dependent algorithm aversion. J. Mark. Res. **56**(5), 809–825 (2019). https://doi.org/10.1177/0022243719851788
7. Cheng, H.F., et al.: Explaining decision-making algorithms through UI: strategies to help non-expert stakeholders. In: Proceedings of the 2019 Conference on Human Factors in Computing Systems. CHI 2019, New York, NY, USA, pp. 559:1–559:12. ACM (2019). https://doi.org/10.1145/3290605.3300789
8. Choi, J., Lee, H.J., Kim, Y.C.: The influence of social presence on evaluating personalized recommender systems. In: Pacific Asia Conference on Information Systems, p. 49. AISeL (2009)
9. Conrad, L.Y., Tucker, V.M.: Making it tangible: hybrid card sorting within qualitative interviews. J. Doc. **75**(2), 397–416 (2019). https://doi.org/10.1108/JD-06-2018-0091
10. Cooke, N.J.: Varieties of knowledge elicitation techniques. Int. J. Hum.-Comput. Stud. **41**(6), 801–849 (1994). https://doi.org/10.1006/ijhc.1994.1083
11. Cramer, H., et al.: The effects of transparency on trust in and acceptance of a content-based art recommender. User Model. User-Adapted Inter. **18**(5), 455 (2008). https://doi.org/10.1007/s11257-008-9051-3
12. Dietvorst, B.J., Simmons, J.P., Massey, C.: Algorithm aversion: people erroneously avoid algorithms after seeing them err. J. Exp. Psychol. Gen. **144**(1) (2015). https://doi.org/10.1037/xge0000033
13. Eiband, M., Schneider, H., Bilandzic, M., Fazekas-Con, J., Haug, M., Hussmann, H.: Bringing transparency design into practice. In: 23rd International Conference on Intelligent User Interfaces. IUI 2018, pp. 211–223. ACM (2018). https://doi.org/10.1145/3172944.3172961
14. Epley, N., Waytz, A., Cacioppo, J.T.: On seeing human: a three-factor theory of anthropomorphism. Psychol. Rev. **114**(4), 864–886 (2007). https://doi.org/10.1037/0033-295X.114.4.864

15. Eslami, M., Vaccaro, K., Lee, M.K., Elazari Bar On, A., Gilbert, E., Karahalios, K.: User attitudes towards algorithmic opacity and transparency in online reviewing platforms. In: Proc. of the 2019 Conference on Human Factors in Computing Systems. CHI 2019, New York, NY, USA, p. 1–14. ACM (2019). https://doi.org/10.1145/3290605.3300724

16. French, M., Hancock, J.: What's the folk theory? reasoning about cyber-social systems (2017). https://ssrn.com/abstract=2910571, https://doi.org/10.2139/ssrn.2910571

17. Gefen, D., Straub, D.W.: Consumer trust in B2C e-Commerce and the importance of social presence: experiments in e-Products and e-Services. Omega **32**(6), 407–424 (2004). https://doi.org/10.1016/j.omega.2004.01.006

18. Gero, K.I., et al.: Mental models of AI agents in a cooperative game setting. In: Proceedings of the 2020 Conference on Human Factors in Computing Systems, Honolulu HI USA, pp. 1–12. ACM, April 2020. https://doi.org/10.1145/3313831.3376316

19. Ghori, M.F., Dehpanah, A., Gemmell, J., Qahri-Saremi, H., Mobasher, B.: Does the user have a theory of the recommender? A pilot study. In: Proceedings of Joint Workshop on Interfaces and Human Decision Making for Recommender Systems (IntRS 2019), Copenhagen, DK, p. 9. ACM, September 2019

20. Herlocker, J.L., Konstan, J.A., Riedl, J.: Explaining collaborative filtering recommendations. In: Proceedings of the 2000 ACM Conference on Computer Supported Cooperative Work. CSCW 2000, New York, NY, USA, pp. 241–250. ACM (2000). https://doi.org/10.1145/358916.358995

21. Hernandez-Bocanegra, D.C., Donkers, T., Ziegler, J.: Effects of argumentative explanation types on the perception of review-based recommendations. In: Adjunct Publication of the 28th ACM Conference on User Modeling, Adaptation and Personalization, UMAP 20 Adjunct, New York, NY, USA, pp. 219–225. ACM (2020). https://doi.org/10.1145/3386392.3399302

22. Kaufman, L., Rousseeuw, P.J.: Finding Groups in Data: An Introduction to Cluster Analysis. Wiley Series in Probability and Statistics. Wiley, Hoboken (1990). https://cds.cern.ch/record/1254107

23. Knijnenburg, B.P., Willemsen, M.C.: Evaluating recommender systems with user experiments. In: Ricci, F., Rokach, L., Shapira, B. (eds.) Recommender Systems Handbook, pp. 309–352. Springer, Boston, MA (2015). https://doi.org/10.1007/978-1-4899-7637-6_9

24. Knijnenburg, B.P., Willemsen, M.C., Gantner, Z., Soncu, H., Newell, C.: Explaining the user experience of recommender systems. User Model. User-Adap. Inter. **22**(4), 441–504 (2012). https://doi.org/10.1007/s11257-011-9118-4

25. Koren, Y., Bell, R.: Advances in Collaborative Filtering. In: Ricci, F., Rokach, L., Shapira, B. (eds.) Recommender Systems Handbook, pp. 77–118. Springer, Boston, MA (2015). https://doi.org/10.1007/978-1-4899-7637-6_3

26. Kulesza, T., Stumpf, S., Burnett, M., Kwan, I.: Tell me more?: the effects of mental model soundness on personalizing an intelligent agent. In: Proceedings of the 2012 Conference on Human Factors in Computing Systems. CHI 2012, Austin, Texas, USA, pp. 1–10. ACM (2012). https://doi.org/10.1145/2207676.2207678

27. Kunkel, J., Donkers, T., Michael, L., Barbu, C.M., Ziegler, J.: Let me explain: impact of personal and impersonal explanations on trust in recommender systems. In: Proceedings of the 2019 Conference on Human Factors in Computing Systems. CHI 2019, New York, NY, USA, pp. 1–12. ACM (2019). https://doi.org/10.1145/3290605.3300717

28. Kunkel, J., Loepp, B., Ziegler, J.: A 3D item space visualization for presenting and manipulating user preferences in collaborative filtering. In: Proceedings of the 22nd International Conference on Intelligent User Interfaces. IUI 2017, New York, NY, USA, pp. 3–15. ACM (2017). https://doi.org/10.1145/3025171.3025189

29. Kunkel, J., Schwenger, C., Ziegler, J.: Newsviz: depicting and controlling preference profiles using interactive treemaps in news recommender systems. In: Proceedings of the 28th ACM Conference on User Modeling, Adaptation and Personalization. UMAP 2020, New York, NY, USA, pp. 126–135. Association for Computing Machinery (2020). https://doi.org/10.1145/3340631.3394869

30. Langan-Fox, J., Code, S., Langfield-Smith, K.: Team mental models: techniques, methods, and analytic approaches. Hum. Factors 42(2), 242–271 (2000). https://doi.org/10.1518/001872000779656534

31. Lim, B.Y., Dey, A.K.: Assessing demand for intelligibility in context-aware applications. In: Proc. of the 11th International Conference on Ubiquitous Computing. UbiComp 2009, New York, NY, USA, pp. 195–204. ACM (2009). https://doi.org/10.1145/1620545.1620576

32. McKnight, D.H., Choudhury, V., Kacmar, C.: Developing and validating trust measures for e-commerce: an integrative typology. Inf. Syst. Res. 13(3), 334–359 (2002). https://doi.org/10.1287/isre.13.3.334.81

33. Morris, M.R.: Social networking site use by mothers of young children. In: Proceedings of the 17th ACM Conference on Computer Supported Cooperative Work & Social Computing. CSCW 2014, New York, NY, USA, pp. 1272–1282. ACM (2014). https://doi.org/10.1145/2531602.2531603

34. Muramatsu, J., Pratt, W.: Transparent queries: investigation users' mental models of search engines. In: Proceedings of the 24th Annual International Conference on Research and Development in Information Retrieval. SIGIR 2001, New York, NY, USA, pp. 217–224. ACM (2001). https://doi.org/10.1145/383952.383991

35. Murtagh, F., Legendre, P.: Ward's hierarchical agglomerative clustering method: which algorithms implement ward's criterion? J. Classif. 31(3), 274–295 (2014). https://doi.org/10.1007/s00357-014-9161-z

36. Ngo, T., Kunkel, J., Ziegler, J.: Exploring mental models for transparent and controllable recommender systems: a qualitative study. In: Proceedings of the 28th ACM Conference on User Modeling, Adaptation and Personalization, Genoa Italy, pp. 183–191. ACM, July 2020. https://doi.org/10.1145/3340631.3394841

37. Ning, X., Desrosiers, C., Karypis, G.: A comprehensive survey of neighborhood-based recommendation methods. In: Ricci, F., Rokach, L., Shapira, B. (eds.) Recommender Systems Handbook, pp. 37–76. Springer, Boston, MA (2015). https://doi.org/10.1007/978-1-4899-7637-6_2

38. Norman, D.A.: Some Observations on Mental Models. In: Gentner, D., Stevens, A.L. (eds.) Mental Models, pp. 7–14. Psychology Press, New York (1983)

39. Norman, D.A.: The Design of Everyday Things. Basic Books Inc., New York (1988). ISBN 978-0-465-06710-7

40. Prahl, A., van Swol, L.: Understanding algorithm aversion: When is advice from automation discounted? J. Forecast. 36(6), 691–702 (2017). https://doi.org/10.1002/for.2464

41. Pu, P., Chen, L., Hu, R.: A user-centric evaluation framework for recommender systems. In: Proceedings of the fifth ACM Conference on Recommender Systems - RecSys 2011, Chicago, Illinois, USA, p. 157. ACM (2011). https://doi.org/10.1145/2043932.2043962

42. Ricci, F., Rokach, L., Shapira, B.: Recommender systems: introduction and challenges. In: Ricci, F., Rokach, L., Shapira, B. (eds.) Recommender Systems Handbook, pp. 1–34. Springer, Boston, MA (2015). https://doi.org/10.1007/978-1-4899-7637-6_1

43. Rousseeuw, P.J.: Silhouettes: a graphical aid to the interpretation and validation of cluster analysis. J. Comput. Appl. Math. **20**, 53–65 (1987). https://doi.org/10.1016/0377-0427(87)90125-7

44. Rugg, G., McGeorge, P.: The sorting techniques: a tutorial paper on card sorts, picture sorts and item sorts. Expert. Syst. **14**(2), 80–93 (1997). https://doi.org/10.1111/1468-0394.00045

45. Rumelhart, D.E., Norman, D.A.: Representation in Memory. No. 116 in CHIP report, University of California, San Diego (1983)

46. Sparling, E.I., Sen, S.: Rating: how difficult is it? In: Proceedings of the Fifth ACM Conference on Recommender Systems. RecSys 2011, New York, NY, USA, pp. 149–156. ACM (2011). https://doi.org/10.1145/2043932.2043961

47. Torkamaan, H., Barbu, C.M., Ziegler, J.: How can they know that? A study of factors affecting the creepiness of recommendations. In: Proceedings of the 13th ACM Conference on Recommender Systems. RecSys 2019, New York, NY, USA, pp. 423–427. ACM (2019). https://doi.org/10.1145/3298689.3346982

48. Tsai, C.H., Brusilovsky, P.: Beyond the ranked list: User-driven exploration and diversification of social recommendation. In: Proceedings of the 23rd International Conference on Intelligent User Interfaces. IUI 2018, New York, NY, USA, pp. 239–250. ACM (2018). https://doi.org/10.1145/3172944.3172959

49. Tsai, C.H., Brusilovsky, P.: Explaining recommendations in an interactive hybrid social recommender. In: Proceedings of the 24th International Conference on Intelligent User Interfaces. IUI 2019, New York, NY, USA, pp. 391–396. ACM (2019). https://doi.org/10.1145/3301275.3302318

50. Tullio, J., Dey, A.K., Chalecki, J., Fogarty, J.: How it works: a field study of non-technical users interacting with an intelligent system. In: Proceedings of the 2007 Conference on Human Factors in Computing Systems. CHI 2007, New York, NY, USA, pp. 31–40. ACM (2007). https://doi.org/10.1145/1240624.1240630

51. Ward, J.H.: Hierarchical grouping to optimize an objective function. J. Am. Stat. Assoc. **58**(301), 236–244 (1963). https://doi.org/10.1080/01621459.1963.10500845

52. Waytz, A., Heafner, J., Epley, N.: The mind in the machine: anthropomorphism increases trust in an autonomous vehicle. J. Exp. Soc. Psychol. **52**, 113–117 (2014). https://doi.org/10.1016/j.jesp.2014.01.005

53. Xie, B., Zhou, J., Wang, H.: How Influential are mental models on interaction performance? Exploring the gap between users' and designers' mental models through a new quantitative method. Adv. Hum.-Comput. Inter. **2017**, 1–14 (2017). https://doi.org/10.1155/2017/368354

54. Yang, R., Shin, E., Newman, M.W., Ackerman, M.S.: When fitness trackers don't 'fit': End-user difficulties in the assessment of personal tracking device accuracy. In: Proceedings of the 2015 ACM International Joint Conference on Pervasive and Ubiquitous Computing. UbiComp 2015, New York, NY, USA, pp. 623–634. ACM (2015). https://doi.org/10.1145/2750858.2804269

55. Zhou, J., Chen, F.: 2D transparency space—bring domain users and machine learning experts together. In: Zhou, J., Chen, F. (eds.) Human and Machine Learning. HIS, pp. 3–19. Springer, Cham (2018). https://doi.org/10.1007/978-3-319-90403-0_1

# Should I Add Recommendations to My Warning System? The RCRAFT Framework Can Answer This and Other Questions About Supporting the Assessment of Automation Designs

Elodie Bouzekri[1], Célia Martinie[1], Philippe Palanque[1(✉)], Katrina Atwood[2], and Christine Gris[3]

[1] ICS-IRIT, Université Toulouse III-Paul Sabatier, Toulouse, France
{elodie.bouzekri,celia.martinie,philippe.palanque}@irit.fr
[2] University of York, York, UK
[3] Airbus Operations SAS, Blagnac, France
christine.gris@airbus.com

**Abstract.** Automation is widespread in interactive applications, promising multiple benefits to users, including enhancing comfort, safety, security and entertainment. Implicitly or explicitly, automation is now a critical design option for interactive application designers. Unfortunately, despite its long use (especially in safety-critical systems) assessing the benefits and the drawbacks of design alternatives including automation remains a craft activity, unsupported by conceptual frameworks or tools. In order to address this problem, we present the RCRAFT framework. The framework considers five attributes of automation: Resources, Control Transitions, Responsibility, Authority, and System Functions and User Tasks. We show how these attributes support the assessment of designs involving automation. Furthermore, adding the RCRAFT concepts to task models makes it possible to evaluate automation properties such as transparency, congruence and controllability in addition to usability. We demonstrate the utility of our approach in a case study, comparing the design for an existing Flight Warning System currently deployed in Airbus A350 against a redesigned version which incorporates functionality to provide recommendations to pilots handling unusual situations. We demonstrate that the RCRAFT framework helps in highlighting the implications of different design alternatives by making the impact of proposed changes on both users' work and the required properties of automated components explicit.

**Keywords:** Automation · Aircraft cockpits · Properties · Tasks

## 1 Introduction

With different objectives in mind [31], interactive systems designers add autonomous behaviors in most of their designs. Recurring objectives are to increase user performance (e.g. automatic repetitive addition of a letter to a document when pressing a keyboard

© IFIP International Federation for Information Processing 2021
Published by Springer Nature Switzerland AG 2021
C. Ardito et al. (Eds.): INTERACT 2021, LNCS 12935, pp. 405–429, 2021.
https://doi.org/10.1007/978-3-030-85610-6_24

key for a long time), to increase comfort (e.g. adding a conveyor belt in an airport) or to reduce errors (e.g. automatic detection of spelling errors in a word processing application). In the context of safety-critical systems, other objectives may be targeted, such as enhanced safety (e.g. the ABS Anti-lock Braking System in cars that prevents drivers from causing the wheels to lock by pressing the brake excessively) or increased security (e.g. auto-lock systems in most mobile phones to maintain the privacy and integrity of private data).

Such partly-autonomous behaviors may be added to any layer of the architecture of an interactive application [32]. For instance, automation can be added to the presentation part (e.g. automatically snapping a graphical object to a grid), to the dialogue part (e.g. automatic movement of the insertion point in the various text fields of a form) or to the functional core (e.g. autonomous disconnection from a server after too long a period of inactivity). Beyond these engineering considerations, changing automation designs might have a deep impact on operators' work and performance and not always in the expected way. Indeed, as demonstrated by Yerkes and Dodson [49] more automation might reduce operator vigilance (complacency) and prevent operators from reacting promptly to adverse events (loss of situation awareness). Finally, adding automation might also deeply alter the nature of the work itself. This was observed, for example, in the aviation domain [13] where pilots' work changed drastically from flying the aircraft (providing continuous input to the aircraft) to supervising systems of systems (monitoring information and reacting mostly to handle adverse events). Such changes also propagate to the way in which operators are selected, trained and deployed. Indeed, due to automation (and especially to the addition of Flight Management Systems) the standard flying crew in large civil airliners has been reduced from three to two.

These examples demonstrate that design decisions touching automation may have deep consequences, and that designers should clearly understand the scope of the options they are considering and identify their impact both on engineering aspects of the system and on the work context. HCI conceptual frameworks that support the design of inter-active applications provide very limited guidance on automation design. For example, the ISO standard on human-centered design [23] explicitly mentions that it is important to define an appropriate allocation of functions and tasks between the system and the user, but does not provide guidance as to how this could be achieved. Another example is Action Theory [30], which supports the analysis of interactive systems from the per-spective of users trying to reach their goals by perceiving the system's state and acting on it. This can help us to figure out possible misunderstandings when a user evaluates the system's state or errors when a user acts on the system, but it cannot help us compare two different automation designs in terms of their implications for the user's work.

To assess automation, user research (mainly via user testing) is generally performed in a similar way as for any kind of interactive system [2], overlooking the specificities of automation even though some guidelines (focusing on AI systems and not automation) have been proposed to support heuristic evaluations by HCI experts [1].

This paper addresses that problem by providing means for evaluating the benefits and drawbacks of alternative automation designs. The work presented in this paper is part of a research project that aims to propose processes, techniques, methods and tools to take automation into account while engineering interactive systems in the large civil aircraft domain. We propose the RCRAFT framework, which identifies five attributes of automation: Resources, Control Transitions, Responsibility, Authority and System Functions and User Tasks. We show how these attributes support the assessment of automation designs and more precisely how they clarify the effect of different design choices on users' activity. To this end, we extend a task-modelling notation to encompass each of the RCRAFT aspects, and demonstrate that these extended task models support the evaluation of automation-related properties such as transparency, congruence and controllability, as well as usability. These results allow us to answer the questions raised in the paper's title in a systematic way.

In the next section, we present the RCRAFT framework and outline the properties of interactive systems which are directly influenced by automation. We show how these concepts are necessary and sufficient to assess those properties. Section 3 presents the task-modelling notation extended with RCRAFT concepts. Section 4 introduces our avionics case study: the Flight Warning System used in large civil aircraft. We demonstrate the use of the RCRAFT framework on two variants of the Flight Warning System. Section 5 positions RCRAFT with respect to related work, while Sect. 6 concludes the paper with a discussion of the contribution of this work.

## 2 The RCRAFT Conceptual Framework for Automation

Whatever the design objectives are [31], the automation design will influence the underlying properties of the interactive systems. This section presents the RCRAFT conceptual framework, which provides a means to characterize the automation elements of interactive system designs. We demonstrate that the five concepts identified in the RCRAFT framework are sufficient to support the assessment of these properties. The last subsection of this section presents a summary of the relationship between properties of interactive systems (influenced by automations) and the RCRAFT concepts.

### 2.1 Expected Properties for Automation

Automation influences the behavior and the use of the entire interactive system but some properties are more influenced than others are. In this section, we list the main properties of semi-autonomous systems and identify the information required to assess them. Early work from IFIP Working Group 2.7/13.4 [17] introduced the notion of internal and external properties of interactive systems and [14] presented a notation to describe properties and how they are supported (or not supported) by various design options. Automation-related properties constitute a subset of these properties and focus "only" on some design aspects. For each of the selected properties, we propose a definition from the literature and make explicit the prominent concepts related to automation. We only consider here properties that can be assessed by objective measures and thus for which predictive assessment can be made. Indeed, subjective measures require the involvement of users/operators and rely on questionnaires and interviews techniques such as System Usability Scale [7] (to assess user satisfaction) and Attrackdiff [19] (to assess user experience).

**Usability.** Usability is the "extent to which a system, product or service can be used by specified users to achieve specified goals with effectiveness, efficiency and satisfaction in a specified context of use" [22]. Efficiency and effectiveness are two contributing factors to usability that can be measured objectively. Efficiency addresses performance and errors (as cost of recovering from errors) while effectiveness addresses the number of operator tasks that are supported by the interactive system. To analyze effectiveness and efficiency we need to identify:

- the goals and tasks that the user needs to perform and their behavior,
- the functions that are embedded in the interactive system and their behavior,
- the resources (information, knowledge and objects) required to perform the tasks, both on the interactive system side and on the user's side.

**Transparency.** Westin et al. [46] define automation transparency as "the automation's ability to afford **understanding and predictions about its behavior**. It is a measure of the automation's openness in information **communicated, through the interface, to the operator**: *what* the automation is currently doing, *which* **information is being used**, *how* **it is being processed**, and *when* **it is provided**." Predictability and comprehensibility also contribute to transparency. Indeed, McDermott et al. [28] define predictability as "the transparency of future intentions, states, and activities of the automation partner". Cramer et al. [10] define comprehensibility as the extent to which the user understands the meaning of the system feedback. In order to analyze transparency, we need to identify:

- the description of the system behavior and how it displays functions allocated to the system to the operator,
- the resources (information, data, objects) used by the user to perform their tasks and processed by the system,
- which information managed by the system is presented to the user, how it is presented and when,
- the detail of the execution of the functions and especially when functions are made available to the user,
- whether, and when, it is possible for the user and/or the system to interrupt one another, and how behavior is resumed after an interruption has occurred [3].

**Congruence.** Hollnagel [21] defines congruence as a matching between user tasks and system functions: "how the **capabilities of humans and machines should be matched** to achieve the operational system goals over a range of situations". To analyze congruence we need to identify:

- the tasks that are performed by the users and the functions offered by the system,
- the information managed by both entities,
- the requirements of each entity for information and functionality from the other entity, and how assurance will be given that these requirements are satisfied.

**Controllability.** Roy et al. [39] define the controllability of an automated system as "how much **a user is in control of the process**" and "to what extent an **automated result can be manually modified**". To analyze controllability we need to identify:

- which manual and interactive tasks trigger the execution of functions in the system,
- whether or not each system function could be interrupted by some interaction from the user (defined as "full control" in [27]),
- the tasks or functions that have an impact on the resources manipulated by the system or the user.

**Accountability.** Several contributions (e.g. [11, 42]) address the issue of the accountability of automated systems, but they only consider it as a social construct influencing the way the operator performs their activities. Indeed, [42] shows that adding accountability to operators decreases their speed in decision making and might also decrease the quality of their decisions due to the "passing the buck" effect [43] (i.e. postponing decisions or trying to delegate accountability to others). According to the Oxford Dictionary, accountability is "the fact of being **responsible** for your decisions or actions and expected to **explain** them when you are asked". To analyze accountability we need to identify:

- what is the expected result of the work performed (there may be more than one),
- which entity (system or user) is performing which action (function or task),
- which action from an entity influences the expected result of the work.

### 2.2 RCRAFT - Allocation of Functions and Tasks (FT)

The FT part of the RCRAFT conceptual framework deals with the issue of Allocation of Functions and Tasks. The generic term is usually function allocation [47] but RCRAFT differentiates the term function according to the entity that performs it. Activities performed by human operators are called "tasks" while the ones performed by the interactive system are called "functions". Automation designs will thus result in the identification of which activities are carried out by which entity (user or system or both). RCRAFT-based design of automation is thus based on the identification and the complete description of the human-system cooperative work as tasks and functions.

### 2.3 RCRAFT - Allocation of Resources (R)

The "R" part of RCRAFT deals with the identification and representation of resources used by the entities. "Resource" is a generic term used to cover data, information (in the head of the user), physical objects (e.g. a credit card), software objects (information manipulated by the system) and devices (input, output and input/output) required to perform the system functions and the human tasks. As for the "FT" part, automation designs will allocate resources to entities, which may or may not share it with other entities. In [26], the authors have shown that, in order to describe operators' tasks precisely, identification and representation of data related to those tasks are crucial.

## 2.4   RCRAFT - Allocation of Authority (A)

The "A" part of RCRAFT is concerned with identifying the controlling entity (i.e. which entity can influence the situation so that it develops or continues in a way which satisfies its requirements [16]). The entity with authority performs or defines constraints on the tasks and functions that modify the state of a system, an object or the environment to reach a goal. These constraints, tasks or functions affect the resources needed by the user or the system. Automation designs may allocate authority globally (i.e. one entity is a considered as master and the other as slave [50]). This allocation may be static or dynamic/adaptive [48] i.e. changing over time to adapt to changes (context, workload ...).

## 2.5   RCRAFT - Allocation of Control Transition (CT)

The "C" part of RCRAFT deals with the issue of Control Transition, which defines how an entity may takeover control, hand it over or share it with another entity [44]. Automation designs will identify Control Transitions, which describe who can modify the allocation of control. As discussed above, it is possible that the entity that performs a task or a function that initiates a control transition may not have authority. An entity may release control without defining how control is to be allocated going forward, leaving that task to another entity with authority. This justifies the conceptual separation of the two entities.

## 2.6   RCRAFT - Allocation of Responsibility (R)

The second "R" in RCRAFT deals with the issue of Responsibility, which defines which entity can derive a specific outcome on which the user goal depends. This outcome is called the 'result'. Automation designs will identify the list of expected results for the work, and will indicate which activity of which entity influences one of the expected results of the work carried out jointly by the system and the user. The entity that influences one of the expected results will be said to be (at least partly) accountable for the outcome.

## 2.7   RCRAFT – Relationship to Automation Properties

Table 1 summarizes the correspondence between the RCRAFT concepts and the properties of partly-autonomous interactive systems. It is important to note that all of the concepts of RCRAFT are needed to assess the properties identified in Sect. 2.1 and that each property is influenced by at least two RCRAFT concepts.

For transparency, all of the RCRAFT concepts are required, which demonstrates that designing interfaces for partly-autonomous systems necessitates consideration of multiple complex concepts. This fact explains why so much work on the assessment of automation has exhibited bad designs, even in largely distributed systems such as Microsoft Excel [51] and Microsoft Windows [3]. Further, it demonstrates that many of the notable classes of operator errors [33] identified in the context of automation [40] can be explained by this complexity, rather than solely by poorly done design activities.

**Table 1.** Table summarizing the relationship between RCRAFT concepts and the properties.

|                | Resources | Authority | Control transitions | Responsibility | Functions and tasks |
|----------------|-----------|-----------|---------------------|----------------|---------------------|
| Usability      | X         |           |                     |                | X                   |
| Transparency   | X         | X         | X                   | X              | X                   |
| Congruence     | X         |           | X                   |                | X                   |
| Controllability|           | X         | X                   |                | X                   |
| Accountability |           | X         | X                   | X              |                     |

This conceptual framework is based on the work from [2]. In addition to the study of relationships between properties and the main concepts of allocation of automation, the work presented in this paper refines the concept of authority by explicitly highlighting the allocation of control transition. The work presented in this paper also provides a more adapted technique for modelling the allocation of tasks and functions.

It is important to note that this set of properties has only be selected as they are very often put forward by researchers and practitioners in automation e.g. [21] and [3]. As mentioned in the introduction of this section, other properties, such as user experience [38] or trust [29], could have been added, but due to their subjective nature we have not included them in this paper. However, we believe that the constructs inside the RCRAFT framework can be positioned with respect to these properties too, as these concepts constitute the building blocks of automation designs.

## 2.8   RCRAFT – Relationship with UCD Process

Figure 1 indicates where RCRAFT could be used with ISO 9241-part 210 [23]. The blue boxes represent aspects added to the original User Centered Design process. That standard explicitly mentions function allocation in Sect. 6.4.2.2., where it is treated as a sub part of the "Produce design solutions to meet requirements" phase (bottom of Fig. 1). However, the next phase "Evaluate the designs against requirements" does not mention how to evaluate automation designs and how these designs impact user requirements. This is where RCRAFT would be useful in partitioning automation into core concepts that can be designed and assessed independently.

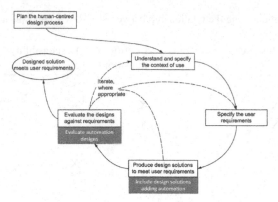

**Fig. 1.** Positioning RCRAFT usage into UCD process (from [23]) (Color figure online)

## 3   Modelling and Analysis of Automation in an Interactive System

As identified in the previous section, the analysis of automation properties requires identification and description of user tasks, system functions, their refinement and their temporal ordering, as well as identification of the data and objects required to perform these tasks and functions. For that purpose, we need a declarative and procedural language, which has the capacity to describe interruptions (such as possible handovers or takeovers).

Task models aim to represent, in a hierarchical and temporally ordered way, the tasks that the user performs to reach a goal. Task models may contain several types of tasks such as user tasks, abstract tasks, interactive tasks and system tasks. Interactive tasks enable us to represent specific interactions with the system, such as an input (e.g. press a button) or an output (e.g. display an alarm). When needed to achieve the user's goal, task models may include pure system functions (called system tasks in CTT [35]) such as data or command processing (e.g. trigger the opening of landing gear). We call this type of task models "integrated task models".

This integrated modeling approach offers a blended view of all the user tasks, their supporting system functions and the temporal ordering between them. However, the models usually focus on describing user activity and leave system description at a higher level of abstraction. A counter example can be found in [24] where both system and operator behaviors are described in a task model. This description makes it possible to assess the benefits of migrating tasks to the automation but it does not scale when tasks are numerous.

### 3.1   Segregated Models and Comparison Process

In order to analyze the automated aspects of the interactive system and, more specifically, the allocation of functions and tasks to each entity, we need to produce a more detailed representation of system functions than that usually provided by integrated task models. Refining system tasks within the same model would greatly increase the complexity of the models and make them difficult to modify and understand. For this reason, we propose to model the system tasks and the operator tasks in two different models that we call the segregated models of tasks and functions. In the same way as user task models are defined for each actor and for each role of that actor, functions models are decomposed into the various roles that the system may play.

This is in line with previous work from Barboni et al. [2], which proposed the use of a combination of a user task model and a system model to assess the consistency and compatibility of user tasks and interactive system behavior. Similarly, Campos et al. [9] have shown that such separation of concerns in different models supports predictive assessment of the effectiveness dimension of usability. However, these previous approaches used different notations for the descriptions of the user tasks and the system ones. Our approach proposes to use the same user tasks-based notation for both.

To compare the two systems, there are 3 activities to carry out:

- First, produce segregated user tasks and system functions for each of the actor roles. They explicitly contain all the resources, tasks and operators describing their temporal relationships. These models encompass the description of the communications between those segregated models.
- Second, integrate each RCRAFT component in the segregated models.
- Third, produce a comparison table of the RCRAFT concepts for both systems under investigation.

### 3.2 Notation for Resources, Authority, Control Transitions, and Responsibility

In order to support the implementation of RCRAFT concepts, a notation needs to be capable of describing both user tasks and system functions, as well as resources that are necessary to perform user tasks and system functions (e.g. information, knowledge, physical or software objects [26]). In addition, tool support needs to be available for the notation, in order to facilitate the description of large numbers of elements, sharing the models between different stakeholders, and amending or reusing models easily. We selected the tool-supported notation HAMSTERS-XL because it fulfills all of these needs. However, in principle, it would be possible to use and extend any other similar notation. We extended HAMSTERS-XL to support the editing of segregated tasks and function models. Furthermore, HAMSTERS-XL and its associated tool HAMSTERS-XLE supports the customization of task types and data types [25] which we exploited to customize task types and to add new resource types needed to model automation aspects (described below).

**Representation of Resources.** HAMSTERS-XL allows us to represent data, objects and devices manipulated by the user and by the system [26]. Resources are represented by labels preceded by the abbreviation of the data type, such as an 'information': , which is data that can be needed or modified by the user. Arcs between tasks (or functions) and data indicates whether the data is needed to perform the task (or function) or is modified by the performance of the task (or function). Required data is indicated by an arrow pointing to the task (or function), and modified data by an arrow pointing to the data. Lines connecting input or output devices to tasks indicate that the devices are required to perform the task.

**Representation of Authority.** The symbol 👑placed on the right-hand side of a task (respectively function) represents the fact that the user (or system) has the authority to perform this task (respectively function) and that this particular task (or function) will affect the resources needed by the user or by the system.

**Representation of Control Transitions.** The symbol 👑 placed on the left-hand side of a task (or function) represents the fact that the user (or system) has the authority to take over on this task (or function).

**Representation of Responsibility.** The symbol ⚖placed on the right-hand side of the task (or function) represents the fact that the user (or system) has the responsibility to perform this task (or function). Two additional elements of the notation - expected results and actual results (which are represented as resources) - allow us to describe the expected result when performing a task (or function). The expected result is indicated by an arrow terminating at the expected result element. Modification of the actual results by a task (or function) is indicated by an arrow terminating at the result.

# 4 Application of the RCRAFT Framework and Process on the Warning System in Commercial Aircraft

In current large civil aircraft, the flying crew is alerted to potential problems with aircraft systems (e.g. engines, air conditioning etc.) via a centralized monitoring and alert system called the Flight Warning System (FWS).

In this section, we present the current FWS of A-350 aircraft cockpit (A350-FWS) and a recommendation-based FWS (REC-FWS). We applied the RCRAFT framework and process to the analysis of the A350-FWS and the REC-FWS. For the purpose of the analysis, we consider each of these systems as an actor with the role of managing the alarms and guiding pilots in resolving them. On the user side, we detail the tasks of the "pilot monitoring" role (PM) who is in charge of managing the systems.

## 4.1 Principles of the Flight Warning System

The Flight Warning System automates some of the tasks previously allocated to the flight engineer, managing system failures by filtering and sorting the alarms triggered by faulty systems. This filtering and sorting process relies on:

- The priority level of the alarm: a **predefined absolute ranking (priority)** of alarms,
- **Inhibition** and **combination rules** (in case of the presence of other alarms),
- The **current flight phase**: some alarms are deferred so as to not disturb the crew (e.g. during take-off when full attention is required).

In addition, the FWS displays different types of information: the procedure corresponding to the alarm, alarm titles and other relevant information about the current context (for example, limitations on the systems) on the Warning Display (WD) of the Electronic Centralized Aircraft Monitoring (ECAM, located in the center of the cockpit as shown in Fig. 2). Finally, FWS triggers attention getters (see the Master Warning and Master Caution visual attention getters in Fig. 4 items numbered 1 and 2).

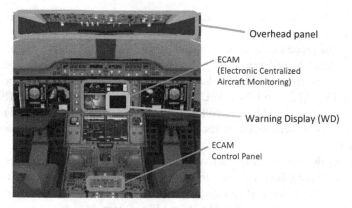

Overhead panel

ECAM
(Electronic Centralized
Aircraft Monitoring)

Warning Display (WD)

ECAM
Control Panel

**Fig. 2.** ECAM in the A350 aircraft cockpit

## 4.2 The A350-FWS User Interface

Figure 3(a) presents a screen shot of the display of a procedure in the Airbus A350. The procedure contains a list of recovery actions to be performed by the pilot to handle an alarm. The procedure here is associated with the alarm "CAB PRESS EXCESS CAB ALT", which states that there is a cabin air pressure problem due to the altitude. The first action tells pilots to use the oxygen masks (line CREW OXY MASKS USE). The "ENG ALL ENGs FLAME OUT" alarm is priority 20 and is raised when both engines are shut down or fail in flight, while the "CAB PRESS EXCESS CAB ALT" alarm is priority 5. If these two alarms are active at the same time, the FWS will display "CAB PRESS EXCESS CAB ALT" before "ENG ALL ENGs FLAME OUT". In this case,

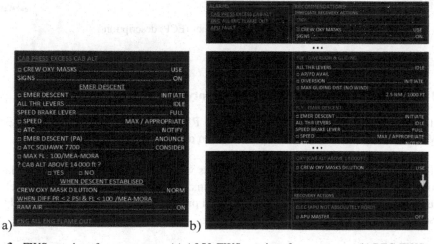

**Fig. 3.** FWS user interface prototypes (a) A350-FWS user interface prototype (b) REC-FWS user interface prototype

only the procedure associated with the alarm "CAB PRESS EXCESS CAB ALT" will be displayed see Fig. 3(a).

To access the procedure associated with the next alarm, the pilots must perform each action line of the displayed procedure and clear this procedure. Completion of a recovery action is either sensed by the FWS or has to be validated (the pilot presses the validation button on the ECAM Control Panel (ECP - located at the bottom of Fig. 1). The pilot can browse the active alarms with the scroll wheel on the ECP (see Fig. 4 item 5). To clear a procedure and its associated alarm, the pilot pushes the CLEAR push button ECP (see Fig. 4 item 3).

Pilots must double-check the active alarm on the ECAM with the overhead panel (top of Fig. 2). If the information is contradictory, the flight crew can declare the alarm to be spurious. The flight crew can discard a cancelable spurious alarm by pressing the EMER CANCEL push button of the ECP (see Fig. 4 item 4).

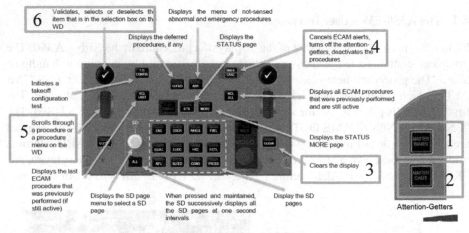

**Fig. 4.** ECAM Control Panel (ECP) description

### 4.3   A Recommendations-Based FWS Prototype

In this section, we present a prototype (called REC-FWS) that differs from the A350-FWS previously presented. There are two main differences:

- Instead of presenting only the procedure associated with the highest priority alarm, the prototype offers a set of recommendations [37] from which the pilots will select.
- Instead of presenting recovery actions as full procedures, procedures are grouped into sets of meaningful recovery actions.

Thanks to this organization, pilots are able to select recovery actions based on the recommendations from the FWS but also on contextual information not available to the FWS, such as the health status of passengers. As in the A350-FWs, the REC-FWS filters the recovery actions. The filtering of recovery actions uses constraints similar to the filtering performed by the A350-FWS. The REC-FWS selects sets of recovery actions associated with the active alarms and sorts them according to a series of rules. There are two levels of criticality for the recommendations: immediate and not immediate. Each recommendation is allocated a level of criticality, which is used to group them on the screen (see Fig. 3.b). In Fig. 3.b, the REC-FWS proposes two recommendations for the FLY goal: "divert and glide" or "emergency descent". Based on the knowledge of the flight crew about the proximity of the nearest airport, the flight crew may choose one or the other.

The ECP scroll wheel allows pilots to select a recommendation and validate when a recovery action has been performed. When all of the actions have been performed, the pilots clear the recommendation using the CLEAR button. The EMER CANCEL button allows pilots to discard spurious recommendations.

## 4.4   Segregated Models of the Pilot Monitoring and A350-FWS

Figure 5 presents the segregated tasks model describing the tasks allocated to the pilot monitoring (PM) in order to resolve alarms. The main goal "Resolve active alarms" is decomposed into a sequence (">>" operator) of several subroutines. A subroutine is a task that points out to another task model, in order to support the structuring and reuse of models [31].

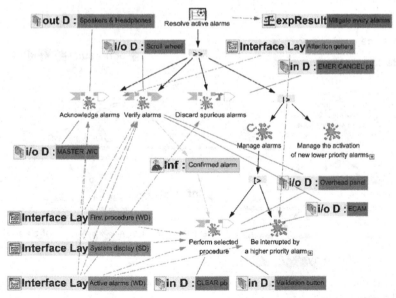

**Fig. 5.** PM-Resolve active alarms with A350-FWS: segregated tasks model of the "pilot monitoring" role to resolve active alarms with the former warning system

418     E. Bouzekri et al.

The main goal is connected to the expected result "Mitigate every alarm" because it is an expected result when performing tasks to reach this goal. The first subroutine "Acknowledge alarms" describes the tasks to perceive, understand and silence the alarms with the Master W/C push button. This is captured in Fig. 5 by the arc between this subroutine and the input/output device "MASTER W/C" and the interface layer "Attention getters". The second subroutine describes the tasks of the PM to verify the alarms. The PM checks that the alarm is not spurious. S/he compares the system display (SD) with the system states displayed on the overhead panel. Third, the PM can discard a spurious alarm by pressing the EMER CANCEL push button. Then, to manage all the active alarms the PM performs the procedure selected by the FWS. When the PM has finished all the recovery actions in the procedure, s/he clears it to be able to perform the next one. This subroutine can be interrupted by a higher priority alarm ("[>" operator). If the priority of the incoming alarm is lower than the alarm associated with the current procedure, the PM can resume her task ("[>" operator).

The following resources are accessible to the PM:

- The system states (through the interface layer: "System Display (SD)", output device "ECAM" and input/output device "Overhead panel"),
- The active alarms (through the interface layer: "Active Alarms (WD)" and "Attention getters" and output device "Master W/C", "ECAM" and "Speakers & Headphones"),
- The procedure (through the interface layer: "First procedure (WD)" and output device "ECAM"): selected set of recovery actions.

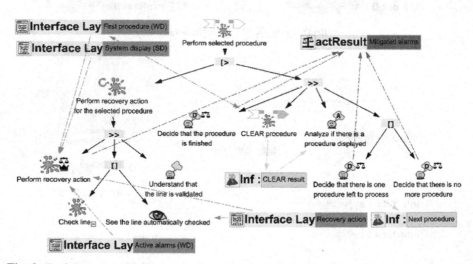

**Fig. 6.** Perform selected procedure: subroutine of the "pilot monitoring" role to perform the selected procedure

Figure 6 presents the subroutine "Perform selected procedure". The PM has the authority to perform the recovery actions (the "Perform recovery action" abstract task). The PM does not have the authority to define the recovery action (i.e. content and execution order) but the PM performs it manually. The PM has the responsibility to perform the recovery actions and to decide whether there are still procedures to perform. If the PM makes an error on these tasks, it will have an impact on the actual result (mitigated alarms). For example, if the PM forgets to perform a procedure, an alarm will remain active.

Figure 7 presents the functions model describing the functions allocated to the A350-FWS. First, the A350-FWS receives, filters and sorts the alarms as described in Sect. 4.2. Second, the A350-FWS displays alarms and the selected procedure. This subroutine is described in Fig. 8. Third, the A350-FWS supports the acknowledgement of the alarms by cutting the attention getters. Fourth, the A350-FWS supports the suppression of spurious alarms if necessary. Then, the FWS-A350 supports the execution of the procedure by the PM until it receives a new alarm. If the new alarm has a higher priority than the alarm associated the current procedure, the A350-FWS initiates a control transition, which interrupts the support to the operator for the execution of the procedure.

The A350-FWS shares resources with the PM:

- The system states (through the interface layer: "System Display (SD)", output device "ECAM" and input/output device "Overhead panel")
- The active alarms (through the interface layer: "Active Alarms (WD)" and "Attention getters" and output device "Master W/C", "ECAM" and "Speakers & Headphones")
- The procedure (through the interface layer: "First procedure (WD)" and output device "ECAM"): selected set of recovery actions.

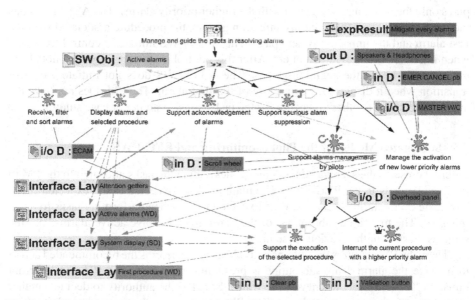

**Fig. 7.** A350-FWS-Manage alarms and guide the pilots in resolving alarms: the model of functions of the A350-FWS role to manage alarms and guide the PM in resolving alarms

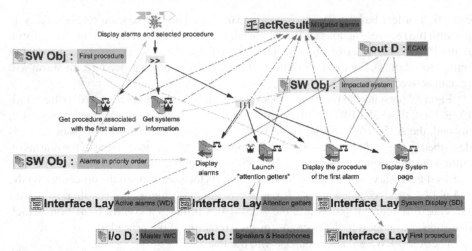

**Fig. 8.** A350-FWS-Display alarms and selected procedure: subroutine of the A350-FWS role to display alarms and selected procedure

The A350-FWS has the authority and the responsibility to get the procedure associated with the first alarm and the system information to display. The A350-FWS defines a set of recovery actions to perform and the order of execution of these recovery actions through a procedure. The A350-FWS adds another constraint on the alarm resolution task by masking the other procedures associated with alarms of lower priorities (it displays only the procedure associated with the higher priority alarm). The A350-FWS has the responsibility to display alarms, attention getters, the procedure associated with the first alarm and the impacted system page. The A350-FWS initiates a control transition when it launches the attention getters. After this control transition, only the pilots have the authority to cut the attention getters. The A350-FWS does not initiate a control transition when it displays the procedure of the first alarm. The PM does not have the authority to select another procedure for the tasks considered in our case study.

### 4.5   Segregated Models of the Pilot Monitoring and REC-FWS

Figure 9 presents the segregated tasks model describing the tasks allocated to the PM to resolve alarms with the REC-FWS. The main goal is connected to the expected result "Mitigate every alarm" because it is an expected result when performing tasks to reach this goal. The first three subroutines of the main goal "Resolve active alarms" are the same as those with the previous system.

Then, the PM analyzes the options and selects and performs the recommended action to manage the alarm. This subroutine is presented in Fig. 11. The PM can interrupt himself ("[>" operator) whenever s/he wants. S/he has the authority to decide whether to perform another recommendation. The PM suspends the "manage alarms" iterative task when s/he needs to manage the activation of a new alarm. Once the new alarms have been acknowledged and verified, s/he can resume her task. The following resources are accessible to the PM:

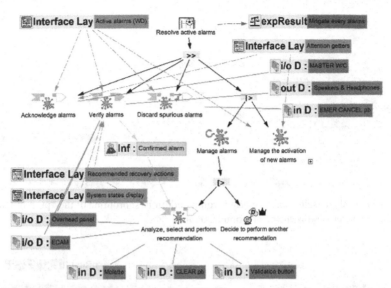

**Fig. 9.** PM-Resolve active alarms with REC-FWS: segregated tasks model of the "pilot monitoring" role to resolve alarms with the REC-FWS

- The system states (through the interface layer: "System states display", output device "ECAM" and input/output device "Overhead panel"),
- The active alarms (through the interface layer: "Active Alarms (WD)" and "Attention getters" and output device "Master W/C", "ECAM" and "Speakers & Headphones"),
- The recovery actions (through the interface layer: "recommended recovery actions" and output device "ECAM"): all recovery actions associated with active alarms.

Figure 10 presents the PM's subroutine "analyze, select and perform recommendation". First, the PM analyzes and selects a recommendation. S/he perceives the recommended recovery actions through the interface layer "Recommended recovery actions". Then, the PM has the authority and the responsibility to decide on the recommendation to be selected and to select this recommendation. The PM defines which recovery actions to perform and the order of execution of these sets of recovery actions. An error on these tasks can cause a derivation of the expected result "Mitigate every alarm". The next tasks of this subroutine are the same as those presented in Fig. 6. (entitled PM-Perform selected procedure with the A350-FWS).

Figure 11 presents the functions model describing the functions allocated to the REC-FWS. Contrary to the A350-FWS functions, the REC-FWS displays alarms and recommended recovery actions. In addition, the REC-FWS manages the activation of new alarms and supports the execution of the selected recommendation concurrently ("|||" operator).

The REC-FWS shares resources with the PM:

- The system states (through the interface layer: "System states display", output device "ECAM" and input/output device "Overhead panel"),

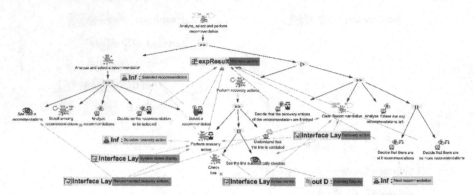

**Fig. 10.** PM-Analyze, select and perform recommendation: subroutine of the "pilot monitoring" role to choose, select and perform a recommendation

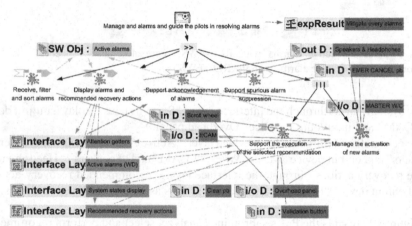

**Fig. 11.** REC-FWS-Manage alarms and guide the pilots in resolving alarms: model of functions of the REC-FWS role to manage alarms and guide the pilots in resolving alarms

- The active alarms (through the interface layer: "Active Alarms (WD)" and "Attention getters" and output device "Master W/C", "ECAM" and "Speakers & Headphones"),
- The recovery actions (through the interface layer: "recommended recovery actions" and output device "ECAM"): all recovery actions associated with active alarms.

Figure 12 presents the subroutine describing the functions allocated to the A350-FWS to display alarms and recommended recovery actions. The REC-FWS has the authority and the responsibility to group recovery actions by user goals and to order recommendations. The REC-FWS defines sets of recovery actions and the execution order of the recovery actions within these sets (i.e. the recommendations). The REC-FWS defines an order of presentation for the recommendations. The REC-FWS initiates a control transition when it displays recommendations. After this control transition, the PM has the authority to select a recommendation and to define a different execution order from the one propose by the REC-FWS. The other functions of the REC-FWS are the same as those presented in Fig. 8: A350-FWS-Displays alarms and selected procedure.

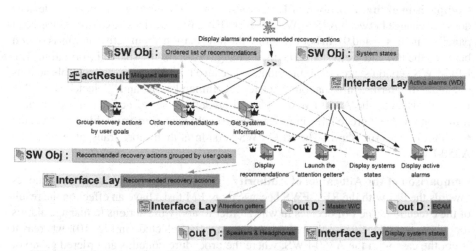

**Fig. 12.** Subroutine of the REC-FWS role to display recommended recovery actions

## 4.6   Comparison of Both Versions of the Warning Systems Using RCRAFT

**Comparison of the Allocation of Functions and Tasks.** The high-level hierarchy of allocation of PM tasks does not change. In the same way, the high-level hierarchy of allo-cation of functions to the flight warning system does not change between the A350-FWS and REC-FWS versions. The main modification in task/function allocation con-cerns the tasks that deal with the actions performed to manage alarms: subroutine "Per-form selected procedure" (in Fig. 5 and Fig. 6) and subroutine "Analyze, select and perform recommendation" (in Figs. 9 and 10). Specifically, the main modification concerns the functions that deal with supporting the execution of the selected procedure: subroutine "Display alarms and selected procedure" (in Fig. 7 and Fig. 8) and subroutine "Display alarms and selected recommendations" (in Fig. 11 and Fig. 12). For the REC-FWS, the number of PM tasks increases, with mainly cognitive tasks, as the PM has to analyze and select actions to perform to manage the alarms (Fig. 10). In particular, the PM has to browse recommendations as well as analyzing each of them, and to decide which to select. This is not the case with A350-FWS which proposes a procedure, a set of actions to perform to deal with an alarm, to the PM. The changes in function allocation between the A350-FWS and the REC-FWS concerns the system functions to prepare recom-mended actions ("Group recovery actions by user goals", "Order recommendations", in Fig. 12). For both versions of the system, the PM tasks match the system tasks, i.e. each system input function matches a user motoric task, and each user perceptive task matches a system output function. For example, the "Display recommendations" system output function in Fig. 12 matches the "See visible recommendations" perceptive task in Fig. 10. The congruence properties are then met for each version of the system. The predictive cognitive load of the user is higher with the REC-FWS, which may have a negative effect on usability.

**Comparison of the Allocation of Resources.** The allocation of interactive devices does not change between A350-FWS and REC-FWS (e.g. devices "ECAM", "Overhead panel"… in Figs. 5 and 9). In both versions, the information about active alarms is shared between the PM and the system. The main change concerns the shared information. The REC-FWS version shares more information because it displays several possible actions to handle the alarms (information "Selected recommendation" and "Selected action" in Fig. 10), whereas the A350-FWS displays a predefined set of actions in a procedure (information "Next procedure" in **Erreur! Source du renvoi introuvable.**) to target the solving of a specific alarm. The REC-FWS version is then more transparent than the A350-FWS.

**Comparison of the Allocation of Authority.** The allocation of authority moves towards the PM with the REC-FWS because more PM tasks have an effect on the result of the execution. The PM decides in which order to apply the actions to manage alarms (cognitive task "Decide on the recommendation to be selected" in Fig. 10), whereas it is not the case with the A350-FWS, where the procedure contains an ordered group of actions to perform. The REC-FWS version better fulfills the controllability property.

**Comparison of the Allocation of Control Transitions.** The A350-FWS can interrupt the PM and take over by displaying a new procedure (task "interrupt the current procedure with a higher priority alarm" in Fig. 7) while the PM is handling a procedure, if a higher priority alarm is incoming. The REC-FWS hand over to the PM and releases control when it recommends actions to the PM (there is no interruption from the system on the task "analysis, select and perform recommendation" in Fig. 9). Controllability is higher with REC-FWS than with A350-FWS.

**Comparison of the Allocation of Responsibility.** The expected results of the PM tasks and system functions are to mitigate every alarm (expected result "Mitigate every alarm" in Figs. 5 and 9). The A350-FWS functions have an impact on the actual mitigation of the alarms (actual result "mitigated alarms" modified by functions in the subroutine "Display alarms and selected procedures" in Fig. 8). The system will then be accountable in case of any mitigation issues. Whereas it is the contrary with REC-FWS: in this case, the PM tasks have an impact on the actual result (actual result "mitigated alarms" modified by tasks in the subroutine "Analyze, select and perform recommendations" in Fig. 10).

# 5   Related Work Addressing RCRAFT

Boy [**Erreur! Source du renvoi introuvable.**] proposed a method to identify functions that could be performed by the system and tasks that could be performed by the user. Dearden et al. [12] refined the way in which the allocation of tasks is determined and by refining the types of functions and tasks. They proposed the IDA-S framework to support engineers in making early decisions about the requirements for automation. It identifies four types of tasks and functions (Information, Decision, Action and Supervision), allowing for finely-tuned allocations and a clearer understanding of how the allocations relate to taxonomies of levels of automation such as Parasuraman et al. [34]. This IDA-S framework has also been associated with UML notations to facilitate the description of allocations [18]. Beyond the analysis of task/function allocation, Boy [6] proposed a conceptual model to support the analysis of how authority is shared between humans and systems. This model comprises concepts that can support the understanding of allocation of authority when comparing several automation designs, however it does not provide explicit guidance for the analysis, and focuses only on authority. Heer [20] proposed recommendations for integrating AI based automation in interactive systems, which address many of the concepts we consider in RCRAFT. They do not provide explicit support for the analysis of the allocation in design solutions, as RCRAFT does. Pritchett et al. [36] proposed the WMC (Work Model that Computes) simulation framework for analyzing the allocation of functions, authority and responsibility. This framework explicitly aims to take functions, tasks, authority and responsibility into account together. However, it is a computational approach to the analysis of automation. Tasks and functions are described programmatically so that a simulator produces the possible sequences of tasks and functions. The analysis has to be done "manually" using these sequences, with no explicit support for the analysis of the concepts of authority and responsibility. These existing approaches demonstrate that there is a need to take the RCRAFT properties into account. The approach presented in this paper takes them into account and in an integrated way.

Beyond the analysis of automation design, Wehrmeister et al. [45] proposed a model-driven approach for the implementation of automation systems. This approach aims to address non-functional requirements about automation and to generate the embedded software to carry out the automated functions. However, it does not explicitly consider the RCRAFT concepts.

## 6  Conclusion and Perspectives

While designing automated functions is known to be a complex and error prone activity, no methods or tools are provided to support this task. The Human Factors community has provided high-level concepts to help understand automation and its impact on the work of operators, such as automation levels [34], metaphors [15] or frameworks [8]. More recent work has focused on the impact of automation designs on workload and as a consequence on its potential for reducing crew size [41].

This paper has presented a complementary, more pragmatic contribution to the assessment of automation designs. First, we proposed a decomposition of automation into five complementary concepts that must be considered while designing automations. We then showed how these concepts can be integrated into a task-modelling notation to represent both system and user behaviors and how these models can be analyzed to understand automation. We demonstrated the usefulness of the approach on a real case study in the domain of civil aviation by comparing the current A350 Flight Warning System with a revised prototype design, which exploits the principles of action recommendation outlined in the early parts of the paper. Using the approach, we have demonstrated that the FWS with recommendations gives more authority and more responsibility to the pilot than the current Airbus A350 FWS does on some specific tasks. In addition, the FWS with recommendations never takes over control from the pilot. Finally, the FWS with recommendations has a higher transparency (less filtering than the A350 FWS). It is important to note that higher transparency does not mean higher usability, as more information presented requires more scanning time and this might reduce task performance.

Even though the paper presents the application of the RCRAFT framework on a case study in the avionics domain, the framework integrates generic automation concepts and is thus applicable to other domains. For instance these concepts have recently been applied to analyze the differences between SAE J3016 levels of automation in the automotive application domain [5] and the levels of automation coming from the air traffic management domain [34].

This work is part of a more ambitious work in the area of command and control systems, targeting at providing notation and tools to support systematic approaches to the design and evaluation of automation, as well as to support the development and implementation of automation-rich interactive systems in their operational contexts [4].

**Acknowledgement.** The authors are deeply indebted with the shepherd of INTERACT 2021 program committee who suggested and made significant improvements in the preparation of the final version of this paper.

# References

1. Amershi, S., et al.: Guidelines for human-AI interaction. In: Proceedings of the 2019 CHI Conference on Human Factors in Computing Systems (CHI 2019), Paper 3, pp. 1–13. Association for Computing Machinery, New York (2019)
2. Barboni, B., Ladry, J.-F., Navarre, D., Palanque, P., Winckler, M.: Beyond modelling: an integrated environment supporting co-execution of tasks and systems models. In: ACM SIGCHI Symposium on Engineering Interactive Computing Systems (EICS 2010), pp. 165–174. ACM (2010)
3. Bernhaupt, R., Cronel, M., Manciet, F., Martinie, C., Palanque, P.: Transparent automation for assessing and designing better interactions between operators and partly-autonomous interactive systems. In: 5th International Conference on Application and Theory of Automation in Command and Control Systems (ATACCS 2015), pp. 129–139. ACM (2015)
4. Bouzekri, E., et al.: Engineering issues related to the development of a recommender system in a critical context: application to interactive cockpits. Int. J. Hum.-Comput. Stud. **121**, 122–141 (2019)
5. Bouzekri, E., Martinie, C., Palanque, P.: A-RCRAFT framework for analysing automation: application to SAE J3016 levels of driving automation. In: Olaverri-Monreal, C., García-Fernández, F., Rossetti, R.J.F. (eds.) Human Factors in Intelligent Vehicles. River Publishers (2020). 9788770222037
6. Boy, G.A.: Orchestrating situation awareness and authority in complex socio-technical systems. In: Aiguier, M., et al. (eds.) Complex Systems Design and Management, pp. 285–296. Springer, Heidelberg (2013). https://doi.org/10.1007/978-3-642-34404-6_19
7. Brooke, J.: System Usability Scale (SUS): A Quick-and-Dirty Method of System Evaluation User Information, vol. 43. Digital Equipment Co. Ltd., Reading (1986)

8. Bye, A., Hollnagel, E., Brendeford, T.S.: Human–machine function allocation: a functional modelling approach. Reliab. Eng. Syst. Saf. **64**(2), 291–300 (1999)
9. Campos, J.C., Fayollas, C., Martinie, C., Navarre, D., Palanque, P., Pinto, M.: Systematic automation of scenario-based testing of user interfaces. In: 8th ACM SIGCHI Symposium on Engineering Interactive Computing Systems (EICS 2016), pp. 138–148. ACM (2016)
10. Cramer, S., Kaup, I., Siedersberger, K.: Comprehensibility and perceptibility of vehicle pitch motions as feedback for the driver during partially automated driving. IEEE Trans. Intell. Veh. **4**(1), 3–13 (2019)
11. Cummings, M.L.: Automation and accountability in decision support system interface design. J. Technol. Stud. **32**(1), 23–31 (2006)
12. Dearden, A., Harrison, M.D., Wright, P.C.: Allocation of function: scenarios, context and the economics of effort. Int. J. Hum.-Comput. Stud. **52**(2), 289–318 (2000)
13. Drogoul, F., Palanque, P.: How to make automation a good solution to the current problems in ATM? Hermes Air Transportation organization, April R19-PP/05, 7p (2019). http://hermes.aero/wp-content/uploads/2019/06/R19-PP_05-EUROCONTROL.pdf
14. Fayollas, C., Martinie, C., Palanque, P., Ait-Ameur, Y.: QBP notation for explicit representation of properties, their refinement and their potential conflicts: application to interactive systems. In: Clemmensen, T., Rajamanickam, V., Dannenmann, P., Petrie, H., Winckler, M. (eds.) INTERACT 2017. LNCS, vol. 10774, pp. 91–105. Springer, Cham (2018). https://doi.org/10.1007/978-3-319-92081-8_9
15. Flemisch, F., Adams, C.A., Conway, S.R., Goodrich, K.H., Palmer, M.T., Schutte, P.C.: The H-Metaphor as a guideline for vehicle automation and interaction. NASA Technical report (2005). https://ntrs.nasa.gov/archive/nasa/casi.ntrs.nasa.gov/20040031835.pdf
16. Flemisch, F., Heesen, M., Hesse, T., Kelsch, J., Schieben, A., Beller, J.: Towards a dynamic balance between humans and automation: authority, ability, responsibility and control in shared and cooperative control situations. Cogn. Tech. Work **14**, 3–18 (2012). https://doi.org/10.1007/s10111-011-0191-6
17. Gram, C., Cockton, G.: Internal properties: the software developer's perspective. In: Gram, C., Cockton, G. (eds.) Design Principles for Interactive Software. ITIFIP, pp. 53–89. Springer, Boston (1996). https://doi.org/10.1007/978-0-387-34912-1_3
18. Harrison, M.D., Johnson, P.D., Wright, P.C.: Relating the automation of functions in multi-agent control systems to a system engineering representation. In: Handbook of Cognitive Task Design, pp. 503–524 (2003)
19. Hassenzahl, M.: The effect of perceived hedonic quality on product appealingness. Int. J. Hum.-Comput. Interact. **13**, 481–499 (2001)
20. Heer, J.: Agency plus automation: designing artificial intelligence into interactive systems. PNAS **116**(6), 1844–1850 (2019). https://doi.org/10.1073/pnas.1807184115
21. Hollnagel, E.: From function allocation to function congruence. In: Dekker, S., Hollnagel, E. (eds.) Coping with Computers in the Cockpit. Ashgate, Aldershot (1999)
22. International Organization for Standardization. Ergonomics of human-system interaction—Part 11: Usability: Definitions and concepts, ISO 9241-11:2018(E). ISO (2018)
23. ISO. "ISO 9241-210:2019". ISO. International Organization for Standardization. https://www.iso.org/standard/77520.html. Accessed 17 Feb 2020
24. Martinie, C., Palanque, P., Barboni, E., Ragosta, M.: Task-model based assessment of automation levels: application to space ground segments. In: 2011 IEEE International Conference on Systems, Man, and Cybernetics, pp. 3267–3273 (2011)
25. Martinie, C., Palanque, P., Bouzekri, E., Cockburn, A., Canny, A., Barboni, E.: Analysing and demonstrating tool-supported customizable task notations. PACM on Hum. Comput. Interact. **3**(EICS), 26 (2019). Article ID 12

26. Martinie, C., Palanque, P., Ragosta, M., Fahssi, R.: Extending procedural task models by systematic explicit integration of objects, knowledge and information. In: 31st European Conference on Cognitive Ergonomics (ECCE 2013), Article ID 23, pp. 1–10. ACM (2013)
27. Maudoux, G., Pecheur, C., Combéfis, S.: Learning safe interactions and full-control. In: Weyers, B., Bowen, J., Dix, A., Palanque, P. (eds.) The Handbook of Formal Methods in Human-Computer Interaction. HIS, pp. 297–317. Springer, Cham (2017). https://doi.org/10.1007/978-3-319-51838-1_11
28. McDermott, P., Dominguez, C., Kasdaglis, N., Ryan, M., Trhan, I., Nelson, A.: Human Machine Teaming Systems Engineering Guide, MP180941. The MITRE Corporation, McLean (2018)
29. Mirnig, A., et al.: Control transition interfaces in semiautonomous vehicles: a categorization framework and literature analysis. In: 9th International Conference on Automotive User Interfaces and Interactive Vehicular Applications (AutomotiveUI 2017), pp. 209–220. ACM (2017)
30. Norman, D.A.: The Design of Everyday Things. Basic Book, New York (1988)
31. Palanque, P.: Ten objectives and ten rules for designing automations in interaction techniques, user interfaces and interactive systems. In: Proceedings of the International Conference on Advanced Visual Interfaces (AVI 2020), Article ID 2, pp. 1–10. ACM (2020)
32. Palanque, P.: Engineering automations: from a human factor perspective to design, implementation and validation challenges. In: ACM SIGCHI Symposium on Engineering Interactive Computing Systems (EICS 2018), Article ID 2, pp. 1–2. ACM (2018)
33. Palmer, E.: Oops, it didn't arm - a case study of two automation surprises. In: 8th International Symposium on Aviation Psychology, Columbus, OH, pp. 227–232 (1995)
34. Parasuraman, R., Sheridan, T.B., Wickens, C.D.: A model for types and levels of human interaction with automation. IEEE Trans. Syst. Man Cybern. – Part A: Syst. Hum. $30$(3), 286–297 (2000)
35. Paternò, F., Mancini, C., Meniconi, S.: ConcurTaskTree: a diagrammatic notation for specifying task models. In: IFIP TC 13 International Conference on Human-Computer Interaction (INTERACT 1997), pp. 362–369. Chapman & Hall (1997)
36. Pritchett, A.R., Kim, S.Y., Feigh, K.: Modeling human–automation function allocation. J. Cogn. Eng. Decis. Mak. $8$(1), 33–51 (2014). https://doi.org/10.1177/1555343413490944
37. Ricci, F., Rokach, L., Shapira, B.: Introduction to recommender systems handbook. In: Ricci, F., Rokach, L., Shapira, B., Kantor, P.B. (eds.) Recommender Systems Handbook, pp. 1–35. Springer, Boston (2011). https://doi.org/10.1007/978-0-387-85820-3_1
38. Roto, V., Palanque, P., Karvonen, H.: Engaging automation at work – a literature review. In: Barricelli, B.R., et al. (eds.) HWID 2018. IAICT, vol. 544, pp. 158–172. Springer, Cham (2019). https://doi.org/10.1007/978-3-030-05297-3_11
39. Roy, Q., Zhang, F., Vogel, D.: Automation accuracy is good, but high controllability may be better. In: Proceedings of the 2019 CHI Conference on Human Factors in Computing Systems (CHI 2019), Paper 520, pp. 1–8. ACM (2019)
40. Sarter, N., Woods, D., Billings, C.E.: Automation surprises. Handb. Hum. Factors Ergon. $2$, 1926–1943 (1997)
41. Schmid, D., Korn, B., Stanton, N.A.: Evaluating the reduced flight deck crew concept using cognitive work analysis and social network analysis: comparing normal and data-link outage scenarios. Cogn. Technol. Work $22$, 109–124 (2020)
42. Skitka, L.J., Mosier, K., Burdick, M.D.: Accountability and automation bias. Int. J. Hum.-Comput. Stud. $52$(4), 701–717 (2000)
43. Steffel, M., Williams, E.F., Perrmann-Graham, J.: Passing the buck: delegating choices to others to avoid responsibility and blame. Org. Behav. Hum. Decis. Process. $135$, 32–44 (2016). https://doi.org/10.1016/j.obhdp.2016.04.006

44. Tan, D., Chen, W., Wang, H., Gao, Z.: Shared control for lane departure prevention based on the safe envelope of steering wheel angle. Control Eng. Pract. **64**, 15–26 (2017)
45. Wehrmeister, M.A., Pereira, C.E., Rammig, F.J.: Aspect-oriented model-driven engineering for embedded systems applied to automation systems. IEEE Trans. Ind. Inform. **9**(4), 2373–2386 (2013). https://doi.org/10.1109/TII.2013.2240308
46. Westin, C., Borst, C., Hilburn, B.: Automation transparency and personalized decision support: air traffic controller interaction with a resolution advisory system. IFAC-PapersOnLine **49**(19), 201–206 (2016)
47. Wright, P., Fields, R., Harrison, M.: Analyzing human-computer interaction as distributed cognition: the resources model. Hum. Comput. Interact. **15**(1), 1–41 (2000)
48. Wu, Y., Wei, H., Chen, X., Xu, J., Rahul, S.: Adaptive authority allocation of human-automation shared control for autonomous vehicle. Int. J. Automot. Technol. **21**, 541–553 (2020)
49. Yerkes, R.M., Dodson, J.D.: The relation of strength of stimulus to rapidity of habit-formation. J. Comp. Neurol. Psychol. **18**, 459–482 (1908)
50. Zhang, Z., Zhao, D.: Master-slave control strategy of tele-manipulator. In: International Conference on Robotics and Biomimetics (ROBIO 2009), pp. 2063–2067. IEEE Press (2009)
51. Ziemann, M., Eren, Y., El-Osta, A.: Gene name errors are widespread in the scientific literature. Genome Biol. **17**, 177 (2016). https://doi.org/10.1186/s13059-016-1044-7

# Social Networks and Social Media

# Improving the Debate: Interface Elements that Enhance Civility and Relevance in Online News Comments

Emilie Bossens(✉) ⓘ, Elias Storms ⓘ, and David Geerts ⓘ

Meaningful Interactions Lab, Mintlab – KU Leuven, Leuven, Belgium
{emilie.bossens,elias.storms,david.geerts}@kuleuven.be

**Abstract.** Online news websites face an increasing amount of hateful reactions of readers, and reactive attempts at enabling more civil discourse, such as moderation, do not prove sufficient. In this study, we propose a proactive approach to counter anti-social behavior by redesigning the comment section's interface. We conducted an exploratory online experiment with 255 participants to determine the impact of including a discussion statement related to the news article's topic in combination with two types of opinion elements. Results reveal a significant positive effect of the novel interfaces on civility and relevance, compared to a traditional comment section (control group). Users evaluated the pragmatic qualities of the traditional comment section significantly more positive compared to the interface with a discussion statement and the continuous opinion element.

**Keywords:** User interfaces · Commenting · Online news

## 1 Introduction

Comments posted on news platforms do not always live up to the ideals of rational reasoning and civility [7]. Often, contributions are irrelevant, uncivil or misleading [13, 18]. Consequently, many journalistic outlets resort in reactive approaches to counter those unwelcome low-quality comments, such as deleting comments, blocking commenters or, more drastically, closing comment sections. Although moderation interventions do have an impact, doing it properly is highly challenging, resource-intense and the results are not always satisfactory [38]. Alternatively, a proactive approach attempts to counter anti-social behavior by supporting civil and respectful discourse in the comment section itself.

In this contribution we explore the potential of such a proactive approach by redesigning the comment section's interface to stimulate healthy conversations. First, we address framing and negativity bias by narrowing down the focus of the debate and proposing a well-defined frame. Therefore, we include a conversational prompt in the interface, namely a specific statement to comment on, to nudge or encourage users to leave more constructive comments and to discourage users to expand on controversial details. Second, to guide participants through their commenting process, we add an opinion element

C. Ardito et al. (Eds.): INTERACT 2021, LNCS 12935, pp. 433–450, 2021.
https://doi.org/10.1007/978-3-030-85610-6_25

below the statement which serves as an anchor from which subjects can start writing. In this research, we explore how the presence of a statement, whether or not combined with an anchor, can influence argumentation, civility, relevance, orthography and length of participants' comments.

Our exploratory online experiment with 255 participants found evidence for a positive impact of the novel interface elements on civility and relevance. More specifically, when a comment section's interface contains a discussion statement, with or without an opinion element, users tend to be more civil and stick more to the central topic compared to users facing a traditional comment section.

This study contributes to research on online discussions and user interfaces in a news environment in two ways. (1) Based on empirical investigation, we reveal insights about how specific interface elements impact the quality of online news comments below controversial news articles in terms of argumentation, civility, relevance, orthography and length. (2) This work opens up new directions in enhancing the quality of the online debate of news outlets by proposing novel interface elements that can be incorporated in a comment section. Such interface designs could assist newsrooms that maintain comment sections and other forms of reader engagement, and contribute to the ideal of online discussion as a space for public deliberation.

## 2   Background and Related Work

### 2.1   Online Discourse in a News Environment

With the advent of 'Web 2.0', our online world has turned into a 'participatory web' [8]. Such nomenclature refers to, among other things, a broad participation in discussions in online spaces. Audiences became more than mere spectators, but could contribute insights and voice opinions. These developments had an impact on news media and the relationship with their readership, as many journalistic outlets attempted to invite contributions from readers via polls, message boards and comment sections [33].

As news media play a crucial role in fostering a constructive debate, these new tools for discussion with and among journalists and their audience can be seen as part of an attempt to create a new public sphere. On a broader level, then, the integration of commenting platforms directly below news stories are an attempt to contribute to the 'deliberative potential' of rational and civil discussion in a digital public sphere [42]. Besides these lofty moral ideals, commenting sections and other forms of audience participation provide journalistic opportunities to engage with the audience [40] or can simply serve as features that draw and retain audiences to news websites. As it stands, however, comment sections seem unable to realize either of these goals. While different themes and newspapers result in variations in the tone of the debate, reader comments on newspaper websites are often uncivil or outright hateful [58]. The general toxicity in such discussion spaces means that maintaining comment sections quickly becomes frustrating and labor intensive. Especially reactive interventions, such as content moderation, take up a substantial number of human resources. As a result, many newspapers have decided to close down their comment sections.

While maintaining a comment section involves considerable effort, research suggests that fighting against toxic participation can benefit of a double win: it increases the overall debate quality and lightens the burden of subsequent moderation. In this context, Fredheim [23] refers to an 'inverse' broken window effect in online comment sections. An overall increase of comment quality (and thus a metaphorical repair of broken windows) stimulates positive behavioral change in other users. An increase in comment quality can spur a virtuous circle. In other words: increasing comment quality could have effect beyond the comments themselves.

## 2.2 Cognitive Biases and Debiasing Strategies to Overcome Them

One type of psychological mechanisms that stand in the way of higher quality comments are cognitive biases. While interpreting information, for example reading news articles, our mind tries to simplify information processing by using 'rules of thumb' to make judgements and decisions with relative speed [71]. In the case of writing online comments, people decide what to write not just based on rational information but also on mental shortcuts, feelings and emotions [1]. Although such heuristics can mostly prove effective, when people blindly rely on filtered information or are not receptive to update their opinion in light of new evidence, these shortcuts can lead to suboptimal decisions, in the sense that important information is also filtered out [71].

One common bias related to news environments is framing bias. Framing refers to the way information is presented which in turn influences how people orient their thinking about an issue. Even subtle changes in the rhetorical frame of the information presentation, such as prioritizing particular interpretations, can significantly influence people's responses [34, 59].

Another bias especially prominent when reading news is the negativity bias or the tendency to pay more attention or to react more strongly to negative stimuli than to positive stimuli [4, 5, 53]. Research has also shown that people perceive negative information as more salient and identify those stimuli with greater ease [53]. That said, it is not surprising that negativity is considered as one of the news values in journalistic agenda setting [25, 39].

A way to reduce the negative effects of cognitive biases is by deploying debiasing techniques. Using certain strategies, individuals could change their thinking to be less susceptible to biases, debias themselves and consequently become more open, constructive and tolerant [15, 44]. Prior research explored various debiasing approaches [12] ranging from simply mitigating the undesired effect of a bias (such as blind reviews) to putting external constraints to force people to detect and correct potential biases in reasoning. Here, Correia [14] refers to the notion of 'choice architecture' of Sunstein and Thaler [68], a model that seeks to promote rational reasoning by setting external constraints on the contexts so that individuals are less likely to make decision errors. A concept closely related to this approach is nudging. Hence, debiasing can take equally subtle forms in the context of online comments, guiding participants' attention in a specific direction [20].

In computer-mediated environments, debiasing or nudging can be achieved by intentionally designing interfaces with the goal of changing a person's attitude or behavior in a certain way [22]. In the context of online discussions, a series of studies found evidence for strategies that can positively affect the commentary such as altering the structure of the comment section [52, 67], applying a specific rhetorical frame [34, 53,

59, 67], providing a short summary to highlight relevant facts or to present contrasting information [52], showing visualizations [34], exposure to CAPTCHA's that prime positive emotions [62], using conversational prompts such as posing questions [16, 49, 69], or through word count anchors and partitioned text fields [48].

More specifically, Peacock [52] found that presenting news readers arguments in favor of and opposed to a statement at the top of the comment section, rather than offering some facts, increased both the quantity and quality of the comments. Another recent experiment [48] reports that a word count anchor below a text field, showing the length of the comment, had a significant positive impact on the number of arguments and respect towards or engagement with others' arguments.

Although several studies were successful in debiasing in the context of online news comments, other results were mixed or inconclusive [3, 14, 44, 48]. For example, based on a quasi-experiment, Stroud [66] suggests that when posing concrete questions in comment sections on Facebook incivility may decrease, but also other forms of engagement such as asking genuine questions and providing evidence may be reduced. The author also implied that prompting participants to make yes- or no-judgements may lead to less substantive discussion. In contrast, inviting people to leave comments without a question, such as 'Tell us your thoughts', was related to increased incivility and reduced chances of offering evidence. Because these effects were only marginally significant, the researchers called for additional investigations.

## 2.3 Defining Comment Quality

Beyond studying the underlying mechanisms leading to low-quality contributions and the techniques to overcome them, a challenging question arises: What exactly describes a high-quality comment? In other words, the challenge lies in finding agreement on what separates a high-quality comment from a low-quality one [7]. In literature, the quality of online discourse has been approached as a multifaceted and complex construct, and various efforts have been undertaken to formulate a definition and a set of normative criteria [9, 18, 20].

Literature often builds on theories of deliberation and group norms to define comment quality. Stroud [66] for example defined the quality of news comments based on incivility, provision of evidence, relevance, and asking genuine questions. More recently, Beckert [19] used two indices, one reflecting deliberativeness (including number of arguments, level of elaboration, information value and comment length) and the other one reflecting (in)civility (including disrespectful language, polarization, simplification and humor). Fredheim [23] measured discourse quality by the use of offensive language, length, the number of proper names (reflecting personalization of the debate) and the comments' orthography and structure. Other attributes of comment quality found in literature are meta-talk [13, 30], engagement with others [7, 9, 13, 20] and additional perspectives [30].

One paper approached the challenging question by studying professionally curated comments: "the NYT Picks" [18]. Based on interviews with moderators, the researchers reported five criteria considered when identifying high-quality comments on a news site: (1) overall quality (spelling, grammar, argumentation, literary value), (2) diversity of perspectives, (3) constructive dialogue with others, (4) short, funny or unusual comments, and (5) relevant personal stories and experiences. The moderators emphasized that these five criteria apply to different situations and that there is no one-size-fits-all model.

For further guidance on which dimensions are critical for identifying qualitative comments posted in response to news stories, we reviewed the comment policies of five local online newspapers that have a comment section for their readers. We found that each of these five news outlets defined guidelines with regard to reasoning, civility, relevance and orthography (such as punctuation, words in all capitals, language). Three newspapers included recommendations about comment length.

These criteria for comment quality correspond with the studies mentioned above. In the following paragraphs, we turn to literature to further reflect on these dimensions. These dimensions will then serve as criteria that allow us to code the comments in our experiment, thus enabling more detailed analysis.

**Argumentation.** One key characteristic of qualitative commenting is reasoned discussion or supporting one's claim with explanations and evidence [24, 52, 65, 70, 73]. Simply expressing an opinion or making an assertion without any kind of validation needs to be distinguished from a justified claim [29, 37, 72]. In addition, the source of validation can vary in legitimacy, ranging from non-sensical rhetorical argumentation to substantiated argumentation [70, 72, 75]. Furthermore, argumentation is often considered as an element of deliberative quality [6, 21, 52, 65], a concept that relates to Habermas' framework of the deliberative public sphere [24]. According to Engelke [20], users value deliberative elements such as rational arguments in comment sections, ensuring the quality of the online discourse. Another study shows that when participants in a political discussion focused on carefully structuring a valid argument, their contributions were more civil [50]. When we consider the local newspapers' commenting policies, the guidelines highlight that claims should be supported with (correct) facts, experiences, expertise, examples, etc.

**(In)civility.** A second criterion that has been proposed as relevant when describing comment quality is the level of (in)civility. Incivility is a complex construct since uncivil speech can take different forms and so-called uncivil language can be perceived differently depending on individual and group characteristics and on the context [10, 13]. Despite the relativeness of the concept, several scholars have attempted to offer some theoretical clarity. Coe [13] for example describes incivility as "features of discussion that convey an unnecessarily disrespectful tone toward the discussion forum, its participants, or its topics". Similarly, Ksiazek [42] identifies uncivil comments as "intentionally designed to attack someone or something and, in doing so, incite anger or exasperation through the use of name-calling, character assassination, offensive language, profanity, and/or insulting language". Uncivil comments on online platforms can increase polarization [2], reduce the willingness of others to participate in the conversation [31] or encourage others to leave uncivil responses as well [10]. Civility, on the other hand, is usually defined as the mere absence of hostility [42, 58], but Herbst [32] offers a more elaborate definition, namely "constructive engagement with others through argument, deliberation and discourse". Based on the review of the newspapers' policies, each of them clearly addresses the issue of respectful commenting, reflecting the elements discussed in literature such as no hate, racism, personal attacks, name-calling, offensive language, etc.

**Relevance.** Third, quality comments are relevant and address the topic at hand [7, 30, 65, 70]. The link between a comment's relevance to the news article and the editor's selection of high-quality posts has been confirmed in a study [18] that shows that comments that are more on-topic are significantly more likely to be selected by an editor as "most interesting and thoughtful comments" ("NYT Picks"). Accordingly, the newspapers' policies we reviewed call for comments that do not stray from the central theme of the respective article. Comments addressing spelling errors, the functioning of the media outlet or irrelevant topics are not desired.

**Orthography.** A dimension associated with civility is the degree to which the comment's orthography is clear and correct. In computer-mediated communication, using provocative punctuation and capitalization of words, for example, are considered yelling [10, 17, 63]. This type of discourse functions as a strategy to evoke the sound and intonation of spoken words and is widely used in hostile and uncivil interactions [10, 17, 26]. Qualitative comments, by contrast, are characterized by correct spelling, grammar and punctuation and are easy to read [51]. This dimension is also reflected in the newspapers' policies, requesting readers to use clear and correct language, and to avoid words in all capitals or excessive punctuation.

**Comment Length.** Expressing a compelling, deliberative argument is assumed to require some space and longer messages can represent more (complex) ideas [9, 10, 22, 29]. Therefore, comment length is final dimension worth taking into account. Prior research has found that longer comments are more likely to contain evidence or legitimate questions, but also to be more uncivil, compared to more concise ones [10]. On the other hand, based on the reviewed policies, newspapers ask their users to remain concise and to not write excessively long comments.

## 3 Research Question

In the current paper we explore a proactive approach to comment quality based on debiasing and nudging theory, whereby we try to subtly encourage participants to engage in debate in a more constructive manner via the implementation of specific interface elements. To translate this goal into a specific interface element, the effects of which we can test, our research focus is two-fold.

First, we address framing and negativity bias by narrowing down the focus of the debate and proposing a well-defined frame. We argue that since a journalist often makes multiple statements in a news article, it might be hard for commenters to agree or disagree with the full article. Therefore, we expect that narrowing down the focus of the discussion using a conversational prompt, i.e. request users to comment on a specific question or statement, can encourage users to comment more constructively. More specifically, we present a concrete discussion statement related to the news article's topic on which users can comment. Since research has shown that relevant commenting is related to higher civility and reasoning, we expect that including a discussion statement has a positive impact on the comment quality variables.

Second, to nudge commenters to take a stance and justify their opinion with arguments, the discussion statement will be expanded with an opinion element that acts as a reference point or anchor [71]. Given that prior information can serve as a reference point from which people make later decisions [71], we combine the statement with two other interface elements: (1) a way for commenters to indicate their opinion, using either two opinion buttons or an opinion scale, and (2) a text box prompting participants to clarify their opinion. As such, the anchor point guides users in the interaction in the sense that participants can set a reference point for themselves, that is the degree to which they agree or disagree with the statement, from which they can start clarifying their opinion with arguments.

In order to evaluate the quality of the posted comments, we take into account the five quality dimensions which we earlier discussed in the literature review and to which we come back in the measurements section. More specifically, this paper focuses on how the design of the comment section in an online news environment can influence the quality of the comments in terms of argumentation, civility, relevance, orthography and comment length. This leads to the following research question: *What is the impact of the presence of a statement, whether or not combined with a way to indicate an opinion, on the quality of the comments posted?*

## 4 Experimental Design and Method

### 4.1 Data Collection and Participants

To examine our research question, we conducted an online experiment using Qualtrics and asked participants to comment on a news article. Subjects were recruited through paid social media posts, a call in the comment section of a local news website and an item in the newsletter of a research platform. A total of 258 subjects participated in the study. Three participants left a comment containing only 'yes' or a punctuation mark and were therefore omitted from the analysis. The remaining sample consisted of 255 participants (108 males, 113 females and 34 did not disclose their gender) between 16 and 84 years old ($M = 47.33$, $SD = 20.09$). Gender, age and education were evenly distributed across the conditions. As an incentive, participants had a chance to win one of the ten gift vouchers of 15 euros. The study was approved by the local Social and Societal Ethics Committee.

### 4.2 Experimental Stimulus

To assess whether the novel interfaces have an impact on the quality of participants' comments, a suitable stimulus, more specifically a news article, was needed. First of all, to limit survey time and to ensure the stimulus was comprehensible for a wide audience, the text had to be short and easy to read. Second, with the aim of having a base level of hateful debate, the content of the news article had to deal with a topic that elicited a high level of heated and polarized reactions. Finally, it was important that the article was published recently so that participants could more easily formulate an opinion with regards to the topic.

The stimulus selected was an article about a local far-right federal MP, Dries Van Langenhove, caught attending a 'lockdown party'. Van Langenhove is the founder of an ultra-conservative student organization and has been a fierce critic of the government's coronavirus policies. Earlier during the Covid-19 lockdown, Van Langenhove publicly criticized citizens going to lockdown parties in a Twitter post, which was included in the article. Consequently, the news article provoked a high number of uncivil comments on social media.

To simulate a real discussion and thus increase ecological validity, we included three comments below the article. These comments were based on Facebook comments and modified to match realistic language and not violate privacy. They varied in tone, quality and language, and were presented on behalf of fictive as well as anonymous user names. In the experimental conditions, the statement presented below the news article and comments was articulated as follows: "A politician must also privately behave according to his or her exemplary role."

### 4.3 Experimental Setup

At the start of the experiment, respondents in all conditions were instructed to read the news article and comments on the next screen, and to leave a spontaneous comment of their own. With the goal of emulating a real online discussion, participants were led to believe that other people would be able to read their comment too and that these other people might in turn react on their comment. Before heading to the next screen to start the writing task, participants had to fill in their (nick)name or choose the option 'anonymous'[1].

Next, participants were randomly assigned to one of the four conditions. All respondents were shown the same news article including three prior comments, but the interface differed according to the condition. The four conditions were: (1) control condition, the news article and comments were followed by the text 'Leave your comment below' and a text box, comparable to a traditional comment section; (2) STATopen, under the article and comments a discussion statement was presented, followed by the text 'Leave your comment about the statement below' and a text box; (3) STATbuttons, the same statement was shown including two buttons 'agree' and 'disagree', followed by the text 'Why do you agree or disagree?' and a text box; and (4) STATscale, instead of two buttons a scale was included with at the left side 'disagree' and at the right 'agree' The scale was followed by 'Why do you agree or disagree?' and a text box (see Fig. 1).

A pilot-study with a similar set-up revealed that the comment section's layout was a fair representation of commenting on a real news site, that users had the feeling that other participants would read their comments and that they had commented almost the same way as they would do otherwise.

---

[1] The choice to request participants' name was relevant with the goal of making the experiment as realistic as possible, since many online platforms do not allow anonymous comments. However, during the first days of the pilot study, many respondents left the questionnaire at this stage. Based upon this finding, an 'anonymous' option was added, and consequently, the completion rate of the pilot survey increased.

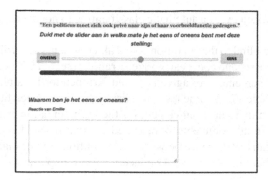

**Fig. 1.** Condition STATscale

## 4.4 Questionnaire

After submitting their comments, participants completed a series of extra questions. First, with the aim of capturing participants' impression of the comment section, the short version of the User Experience Questionnaire [60] was included. This validated questionnaire contains eight items representing the meta-dimensions pragmatic quality and hedonic quality of the original UEQ [21]. Each dimension consists of four pairs of terms with opposite meanings and participants rate each pair on a scale from 1 (if the alternative on the extreme left is marked) to 7 (if the alternative on the extreme right is marked). The four pairs of pragmatic quality are confusing vs. clear, inefficient vs. efficient, complicated vs. easy, and obstructive vs. supportive. The four pairs of hedonic quality are boring vs. exciting, not interesting vs. interesting, conventional vs. inventive, and usual vs. leading edge. A reliability test showed that both the pragmatic and hedonic quality subscales had high reliabilities, with a Cronbach's alpha of respectively .802 and .749.

Following the UEQ, participants were asked to share how frequently they read, write and vote on comments on online platforms, and to provide basic social and demographic characteristics. Since this study involved the use of deception, an elaborate debriefing was included at the end of the questionnaire.

## 4.5 Operationalization and Measurement

To study variations in the quality of the comments, we carefully constructed a classification system to provide a valid and reliable measurement of comment quality, as suggested by Riffe [54]. As discussed in related work, several schemes for classifying online discourse have been developed by researchers, with both manual and automatic approaches. Since we did not find a coding scheme in existing literature that reflects all relevant aspects for assessing the quality of an individual comment in an online news environment, we developed a new codebook for rating news comments based on a review of multiple prior studies [7, 9, 10, 13, 29, 30, 37, 42, 51, 58, 70, 76]. As this literature discusses a wide range of quality criteria, we narrowed down the relevant dimensions based on the comment policies of five local online newspapers. We deliberately chose a manual coding approach over an automatic classification to not overlook textual nuances in comments [64].

One coder being blind to the condition coded all comments according to five criteria. To assess reliability, a second coder categorized a random set of 20% of all comments. For each variable, both percentage of agreement and Krippendorff's alpha were computed and reported (see Table 1). The true level of reliability falls between those two measures [54]. As can be seen in Table 1, agreement for the argumentation criteria is rather low [41]. However, since all comments were coded by one researcher and since we are interested in the relative difference between the conditions rather than absolute scores, we are convinced that this is not a major concern for our exploratory study.

**Argumentation.** Argumentation was measured based on the Assertion, Reasoning and Evidence model [35, 46]. The three steps include "0" = assertion or expressing a simple opinion ("*If you don't set an example as a politician, you're doing a bad job*"[2]), "1" = reasoning that supports the assertion, or the 'because' part of an argument, whether simple or complex ("*That's not something you do. Rules are rules and you follow them. After all, it is for everyone's safety*"), and "2" = evidence that supports the reasoning, whether valid or not, such as referring to an example, expert, personal story, news facts, etc. ("*(...) On the other hand, all Corona measures violate our fundamental rights "treaty of human rights". We live in a rule of law, which means that the measures are invalid. (...)*").

**Civility.** For measuring civility, we drew from past research [57, 58]. Civility was coded on three levels: "0" = explicitly offensive, disrespectful, threatening, vulgar or hateful language or a personal attack ("*Fuck him*"), "1" = implicitly unrespectful, forceful or crude comment, or expression of scorn, ridicule, derision or disapproval, without resorting to hateful language or personal attacks ("*They should put him in strict quarantine for 2 weeks*"), and "2" = none of the uncivil elements and free of any insults ("*Anyone can make mistakes.*").

**Relevance.** All comments were reviewed to assess whether they were related to the news article's topic or not. In line with previous research [30, 52, 65, 66], when (the majority of) a comment was not related to the central theme of the article or when the comment was only one word long (e.g. "*hypocrisy*"), it was coded as "0". Comments that were relevant to the news article's topic were coded as "1" ("*It is a pity that he actually does not stick to the rules himself while he profiles himself that way on Twitter ...*").

**Orthography.** A comments' orthography was measured on a dichotomous scale with code "0" for comments that were not clear, difficult to read, contained at least 2 spelling errors, no or excessive punctuation (e.g. !!! or ???) or words in all capitals. Comments that were clear, easy to read and (largely) correctly written obtained code "1".

**Comment Length.** To quantify comment length, we calculated the number of words per comment and compared this to the overall median. Comments with less than 25

---

[2] Original comments were translated into English.

words were given score "0", whereas comments with 25 or more words were given score "1".

**Table 1.** Intercoder reliability coefficients

| Coding category | Percentage of agreement | Krippendorff's alpha |
|---|---|---|
| Argumentation | 66.67 | .573 |
| Civility | 82.35 | .775 |
| Relevance | 94.12 | .768 |
| Orthography | 92.16 | .77 |

## 5   Data Analysis and Results

Participants in our study are already active in online discussions. More than three out of four respondents (78%) reported reading comments on social platforms at least several times a week. 28.1% of participants stated that they regularly write online comments and 41.5% indicated that they frequently engage in voting such as liking, upvoting or downvoting comments.

Before starting the writing task, 71.4% of participants filled in their (nick)name, whereas 28.6% continued anonymously[3]. Across all conditions, comments averaged 31 words and varied between 1 ("hypocrisy") and 181 words in length. In the following paragraphs, we will first look at the impact of the interface on comment quality, after which we will present the results of the user experience questionnaire.

### 5.1   Comment Quality

We used IBM SPSS software to perform statistical analyses. Since the presumption of normal distribution of observed variables was not justified, we used non-parametric tests. See Table 2 for a complete overview of means and standard deviations by condition for the comment quality variables and Table 3 for the results of the post-hoc tests.

Results of a Kruskal-Wallis test (with a Bonferroni-adjusted significance level of .01 at a 95% confidence level) showed a significant difference between the four conditions for degree of civility ($H(3) = 26.453$, $p < .001$) and degree of relevance ($H(3) = 14.048$, $p < .01$). When it comes to degree of argumentation, strength of argumentation and sentence quality, no significant differences emerged.

Subsequent post-hoc pairwise comparisons (with a Bonferroni-adjusted significance level of .017 at a 95% confidence level) revealed that the mean levels of degree of civility and degree of relevance were significantly higher in each of the three experimental

---

[3] We found no significant impact of anonymity on the comment quality variables.

conditions compared to the control group. Again, these findings indicate that presenting a discussion statement, whether or not combined with one of the two opinion elements, had a positive impact on civility and topic relevance when commenting in an online news environment. When comparing each of the two interfaces including an opinion element (STATbuttons and STATscale) with the statement-only condition (STATopen), no significant differences emerged. Both opinion elements do not have a significant impact on top of the discussion statement regarding the single comment quality criteria. We discuss the implications of these results in the next section.

**Table 2.** Means and standard deviations (in parentheses) for comment quality variables

| Condition | Argumentation | Civility | Relevance | Orthography | Length |
|---|---|---|---|---|---|
| Control | .42 (.731) | 1.05 (.789) | .63 (.487) | .72 (.453) | .46 (.503) |
| STATopen | .63 (.698) | 1.46 (.683) | .84 (.371) | .79 (.411) | .53 (.504) |
| STATbuttons | .67 (.746) | 1.63 (.540) | .88 (.331) | .77 (.426) | .47 (.502) |
| STATscale | .65 (.664) | 1.65 (.593) | .84 (.371) | .78 (.418) | .50 (.504) |

**Table 3.** Post-hoc pairwise comparisons

| Condition | Civility | Relevance |
|---|---|---|
| Control vs. STATopen | U = 1168, z = − 2.795, p < .01 | U = 1264.5, z = − 2.489, p < .05 |
| Control vs. STATbuttons | U = 1244, z = − 4.337, p < .001 | U = 1570.5, z = − 3.279, p < .01 |
| Control vs. STATscale | U = 1132, z = − 4.429, p < .001 | U = 1537, z = − 2.626, p < .01 |

## 5.2  User Experience

Across all conditions, the mean score for pragmatic quality or task-oriented aspects ranged between .77 and 1.32, which is a slightly positive evaluation. On the other hand, the mean score for hedonic quality or non-task-oriented aspects ranged between −.28 and −.19, which represents a rather neutral evaluation [60].

A Kruskal-Wallis test compared users' reported experience and revealed a significant difference between the four groups with regard to pragmatic quality (H(3) = 7.902, p < .05). When it comes to hedonic quality, we observed no significant differences (H(3) = .069, p > .05).

Post-hoc pairwise comparisons with a Bonferroni-correction tested which groups differed from the control group in terms of evaluation of pragmatic qualities and showed a significant difference between the control condition and the condition STATscale (U =

1016, z = −2.442, p < .05). More specifically, participants evaluated the task-oriented aspects significantly more positive in the control condition (M = 1.3207, SD = 1.1434) compared to participants in the STATscale condition (M = .8156, SD = 1.1105). This suggests that, despite the positive evaluation of pragmatic aspects across all conditions, the novel interface with the discussion statement and opinion scale was seen as less clear, efficient, easy and supportive compared to the traditional design. With respect to the conditions STATopen (M = 1, SD = 1.1134) and STATbuttons (M = .7667, SD = 1.3050), pragmatic evaluation did not significantly differ from the control group.

## 6  Discussion and Conclusion

The aim of this study was to explore the effectiveness of debiasing in a news environment by presenting commenters a discussion statement related to the news article's topic, alone or combined with an opinion element. We expected that narrowing down the focus of the discussion using a conversational prompt, i.e. a statement, encourages users to overcome negativity bias and, hence, comment more qualitatively. With the goal of providing users an anchor that guides them through the interaction, the statement was expanded with an opinion element.

First, the results revealed that the three novel interfaces – a discussion statement, a discussion statement with an 'agree' and 'disagree' button and a discussion statement with an opinion scale – produced significant positive effects on civility and relevance of participants' comments compared to a traditional interface. This suggests that when readers have a specific statement to comment on, in particular in the context of controversial news, they are more likely to behave civil and stay on-topic than when the focus of the comment section is more open. This finding is in line with prior research arguing that using conversational prompts may increase the quality of the commentary [16, 49, 69].

Second, although our results clearly illustrate that the statement has a positive impact on civility and relevance, we found no influence on argumentation, comment length and orthography. As we prompted participants to clarify whether they agreed or not with the statement, it was reasonable to expect that participants provided more and stronger arguments compared to the more open instruction of 'Leave your comment below' in the control condition. While research suggests that civility and using evidence go hand in hand [50], we noticed only an increased civility and relevance. In that respect, scholars found mixed evidence about the association between civility and the use of evidence. Coe and colleagues [13] for example concluded that uncivil commenters are slightly more likely to support their claims with evidence, especially with numbers. Chen [10] on the other hand argued that deliberation and mild incivility can overlap, stating that "communication that is too polite or too nasty has no potential for deliberation".

Third, we found no added value of combining the discussion statement with an opinion element. When the discussion statement was combined with one of the two opinion elements, comment quality was still higher compared to the control group, but not higher compared to the statement-only condition. Our experimental design does not allow us to make inferences about the opinion element itself.

Fourth, across all conditions, participants rated the pragmatic and hedonic qualities of the writing task as positive and neutral respectively. Compared to the control group, the mere addition of a statement in the statement-only condition did not significantly influence users' experience. This suggests that they did not felt restricted by the statement to exert an opinion. However, the interface with the discussion statement and the opinion scale received a significantly lower evaluation in terms of pragmatic qualities compared to the traditional interface. In other words, participants perceived the novel design as less clear, efficient, easy and supportive. This could be the result of the higher degree of interaction required from the participant to move the slider, compared to writing a traditional comment.

Finally, we discuss some potential limitations of our study and formulate directions for future research. A first limitation of our experimental design is that we combined two interface elements in one condition, that is the statement and two opinion elements. Although we compared the impact of those interfaces with both the impact of the control and statement-only groups, we were not able to provide insights about the impact of an opinion element in itself. Further research could use a 2 (no statement – statement) × 3 (open commenting – opinion buttons - opinion scale) design to get a clearer view on how an opinion element affects comment quality.

A second limitation is that it is not yet clear to which extent the results can be generalized to other news topics as well as to a real comment section. In our experiment we pursued a high ecological validity, for example by including actual comments reflecting various views and by letting participants believe that others would see and respond to their comments. However, despite the fact that its validity was confirmed in a pilot study and that prior experimental research [30] used the same platform to gather participants' comments, the survey environment was not a real comment section which could have affected the quality of the comments. For instance, it was not possible to react on other comments, and all participants were required to leave a comment. In a real-life setting, readers have their own motivations for engaging in a debate, or they can simply choose not to react. Moreover, enabling constructive conversations implies that only users that have something to say should be encouraged to comment, in order to increase the topical focus of the discussion and to avoid irrelevant posts.

To conclude, this paper demonstrated that particular interface elements can have an impact on the quality of online comments and therefore can bring about a more constructive debate on online news platforms and social media. This finding is a single contribution to the growing field of research, especially in the context of polarizing news, and is a possible approach to pro-actively encourage respectful dialogue in the comment section itself, which in turn can also decrease moderation efforts. Future research opportunities lie in conducting follow-up experiments with other stimuli and on existing platforms within real comment sections.

# References

1. Acquisti, A., et al.: Nudges for privacy and security: understanding and assisting users' choices online. ACM Comput. Surv. **50**(3), 1–41 (2017). https://doi.org/10.1145/3054926
2. Anderson, A.A., et al.: The "nasty effect:" online incivility and risk perceptions of emerging technologies: crude comments and concern. J. Comput.-Mediat. Commun. **19**(3), 373–387 (2014). https://doi.org/10.1111/jcc4.12009
3. Arkes, H.R.: Costs and benefits of judgment errors. Psychol. Bull. **110**(3), 486–498 (1991)

4. Bachleda, S., et al.: Individual-level differences in negativity biases in news selection. Pers. Individ. Differ. **155**, 109675 (2020). https://doi.org/10.1016/j.paid.2019.109675
5. Baumeister, R.F., et al.: Bad is stronger than good. Rev. Gen. Psychol. **5**(4), 323–370 (2001). https://doi.org/10.1037/1089-2680.5.4.323
6. Beckert, J., Ziegele, M.: The effects of personality traits and situational factors on the deliberativeness and civility of user comments on news websites. Int. J. Commun. (Online) **3924**, 22 (2020)
7. Berg, J.: The impact of anonymity and issue controversiality on the quality of online discussion. J. Inf. Technol. Polit. **13**(1), 37–51 (2016). https://doi.org/10.1080/19331681.2015.113 1654
8. Blank, G., Reisdorf, B.C.: The participatory web: a user perspective on Web 2.0. Inf. Commun. Soc. **15**(4), 537–554 (2012)
9. Brückner, L., Schweiger, W.: Facebook discussions of journalistic news: investigating article objectivity, topic, and media brand as influencing factors. SCM **6**(4), 365–394 (2017). https://doi.org/10.5771/2192-4007-2017-4-365
10. Chen, G.M.: Online Incivility and Public Debate. Springer, Cham (2017). https://doi.org/10.1007/978-3-319-56273-5
11. Chen, M., et al.: We should not get rid of incivility online. Soc. Media Soc. **5**(3), 1–5 (2019)
12. Cheng, F.-F., Wu, C.-S.: Debiasing the framing effect: the effect of warning and involvement. Decis. Support Syst. **49**(3), 328–334 (2010)
13. Coe, K., et al.: Online and uncivil? Patterns and determinants of incivility in newspaper website comments. J. Commun. **64**(4), 658–679 (2014). https://doi.org/10.1111/jcom.12104
14. Correia, V.: Contextual debiasing and critical thinking: reasons for optimism. Topoi **37**(1), 103–111 (2016). https://doi.org/10.1007/s11245-016-9388-x
15. Croskerry, P., et al.: Cognitive debiasing 2: impediments to and strategies for change. BMJ Qual. Saf. **22**(2), ii65–ii72 (2013). https://doi.org/10.1136/bmjqs-2012-001713
16. Curran, J., et al.: Media system, public knowledge and democracy: a comparative study. Eur. J. Commun. **24**(1), 5–26 (2009). https://doi.org/10.1177/0267323108098943
17. Darics, E.: Politeness in computer-mediated discourse of a virtual team. J. Politeness Res. Lang. Behav. Cult. **6**(1), 129–150 (2010)
18. Diakopoulos, N., Naaman, M.: Towards quality discourse in online news comments. In: Proceedings of the ACM 2011 Conference on Computer Supported Cooperative Work, pp. 133–142. Association for Computing Machinery, New York (2011)
19. Diakopoulos, N.A.: The editor's eye: curation and comment relevance on the New York times. In: Proceedings of the 18th ACM Conference on Computer Supported Cooperative Work & Social Computing, CSCW 2015, pp. 1153–1157. ACM Press, Vancouver (2015). https://doi.org/10.1145/2675133.2675160
20. Engelke, K.M.: Enriching the conversation: audience perspectives on the deliberative nature and potential of user comments for news media. Digit. J. **8**(4), 447–466 (2020)
21. Esau, K., Friess, D., Eilders, C.: Design matters! An empirical analysis of online deliberation on different news platforms. Policy Internet **9**(3), 321–342 (2017)
22. Fogg, B.J.: Persuasive Technology: Using Computers to Change What We Think and Do. Morgan Kaufmann Publishers, Amsterdam (2003)
23. Fredheim, R., et al.: Anonymity and online commenting: the broken windows effect and the end of drive-by commenting. In: Proceedings of the ACM Web Science Conference on ZZZ, WebSci 2015, pp. 1–8. ACM Press, Oxford (2015). https://doi.org/10.1145/2786451.2786459
24. Friess, D., Eilders, C.: A systematic review of online deliberation research. Policy Internet **7**(3), 319–339 (2015)
25. Galtung, J., Ruge, M.H.: The structure of foreign news: the presentation of the Congo, Cuba and Cyprus crises in four Norwegian newspapers. J. Peace Res. **2**(1), 64–90 (1965). https://doi.org/10.1177/002234336500200104

26. Gervais, B.T.: Incivility online: affective and behavioral reactions to uncivil political posts in a web-based experiment. J. Inf. Technol. Polit. **12**(2), 167–185 (2015). https://doi.org/10.1080/19331681.2014.997416
27. Godi, M.: Beyond nudging: debiasing consumers through mixed framing. Yale Law J. **128**(7), 2034–2086 (2019)
28. Graf, J., et al.: The role of civility and anonymity on perceptions of online comments. Mass Commun. Soc. **20**(4), 526–549 (2017). https://doi.org/10.1080/15205436.2016.1274763
29. Halpern, D., Gibbs, J.: Social media as a catalyst for online deliberation? Exploring the affordances of Facebook and YouTube for political expression. Comput. Hum. Behav. **29**(3), 1159–1168 (2013). https://doi.org/10.1016/j.chb.2012.10.008
30. Han, S.-H., et al.: Is civility contagious? Examining the impact of modeling in online political discussions. Soc. Media Soc. **4**(3) (2018). https://doi.org/10.1177/2056305118793404
31. Han, S.-H., Brazeal, L.M.: Playing nice: modeling civility in online political discussions. Commun. Res. Rep. **32**(1), 20–28 (2015). https://doi.org/10.1080/08824096.2014.989971
32. Herbst, S.: Rude Democracy: Civility and Incivility in American Politics. Temple University Press, Philadelpia (2010)
33. Hermida, A., Thurman, N.: A clash of cultures: the integration of user-generated content within professional journalistic frameworks at British newspaper websites. J. Pract. **2**(3), 343–356 (2008)
34. Hullman, J., Diakopoulos, N.: Visualization rhetoric: framing effects in narrative visualization. IEEE Trans. Vis. Comput. Graph. **17**(12), 2231–2240 (2011). https://doi.org/10.1109/TVCG.2011.255
35. Hung, H.T., Yeh, H.C., Chou, C.H.: An investigation into English language learners' argumentative writing performance and perceptions. In: Wu, T.T., Gennari, R., Huang, Y.M., Xie, H., Cao, Y. (eds.) SETE 2016. LNCS, vol. 10108, pp. 712–720. Springer, Cham (2016). https://doi.org/10.1007/978-3-319-52836-6_76
36. Jang, S.M., Oh, Y.W.: Getting attention online in election coverage: audience selectivity in the 2012 US presidential election. New Media Soc. **18**(10), 2271–2286 (2016)
37. Jensen, J.L.: Public spheres on the Internet: anarchic or government-sponsored - a comparison. Scand. Pol. Stud. **26**(4), 349–374 (2003). https://doi.org/10.1111/j.1467-9477.2003.00093.x
38. Kirman, B., Lineham, C., Lawson, S.: Exploring mischief and mayhem in social computing or how we learned to stop worrying and love the trolls. In: CHI 2012 Extended Abstracts on Human Factors in Computing Systems (CHI EA 2012), pp. 121–130. ACM, New York (2012)
39. Knobloch-Westerwick, S., et al.: Confirmation bias, ingroup bias, and negativity bias in selective exposure to political information. Commun. Res. **47**(1), 104–124 (2020). https://doi.org/10.1177/0093650217719596
40. Kramp, L., Loosen, W.: The transformation of journalism: from changing newsroom cultures to a new communicative orientation? In: Hepp, A., Breiter, A., Hasebrink, U. (eds.) Communicative Figurations. TCSCR, pp. 205–239. Springer, Cham (2018). https://doi.org/10.1007/978-3-319-65584-0_9
41. Krippendorff, K.: Content Analysis: An Introduction to Its Methodology, 2nd edn. Sage, Thousand Oaks (2004)
42. Ksiazek, T.B., Springer, N.: User Comments and Moderation in Digital Journalism: Disruptive Engagement. Routledge, London (2020)
43. Laugwitz, B., Held, T., Schrepp, M.: Construction and evaluation of a user experience questionnaire. In: Holzinger, A. (ed.) USAB 2008. LNCS, vol. 5298, pp. 63–76. Springer, Heidelberg (2008). https://doi.org/10.1007/978-3-540-89350-9_6
44. Lilienfeld, S.O., et al.: Giving debiasing away: can psychological research on correcting cognitive errors promote human welfare? Perspect. Psychol. Sci. **4**(4), 390–398 (2009). https://doi.org/10.1111/j.1745-6924.2009.01144.x

45. Masullo Chen, G., et al.: We should not get rid of incivility online. Soc. Media Soc. **5**(3) (2019). https://doi.org/10.1177/2056305119862641
46. Meany, J., Shuster, K.: On that Point!: An Introduction to Parliamentary Debate. International Debate Education Association, New York (2003)
47. Meffert, M.F., et al.: The effects of negativity and motivated information processing during a political campaign. J. Commun. **56**(1), 27–51 (2006). https://doi.org/10.1111/j.1460-2466. 2006.00003.x
48. Menon, S., et al.: Nudge for deliberativeness: how interface features influence online discourse. In: Proceedings of the 2020 CHI Conference on Human Factors in Computing Systems, pp. 1–13. ACM, Honolulu (2020). https://doi.org/10.1145/3313831.3376646
49. Noveck, B.S.: Wiki Government: How Technology Can Make Government Better, Democracy Stronger, and Citizens More Powerful. Brookings Institution Press, Washington, D.C. (2009)
50. Papacharissi, Z.: Democracy online: civility, politeness, and the democratic potential of online political discussion groups. New Media Soc. **6**(2), 259–283 (2004)
51. Park, D., et al.: Supporting comment moderators in identifying high quality online news comments. In: Proceedings of the 2016 CHI Conference on Human Factors in Computing Systems, pp. 1114–1125. ACM, San Jose (2016). https://doi.org/10.1145/2858036.2858389
52. Peacock, C., et al.: The deliberative influence of comment section structure. Journalism **20**(6), 752–771 (2019). https://doi.org/10.1177/1464884917711791
53. Pingree, R.J., et al.: Effects of postdebate coverage on spontaneous policy reasoning. J. Commun. **62**(4), 643–658 (2012). https://doi.org/10.1111/j.1460-2466.2012.01656.x
54. Riffe, D., et al.: Analyzing Media Messages. Routledge, New York (2006)
55. Risch, J., Krestel, R.: Deep Learning-Based Approaches for Sentiment Analysis. Springer, Singapore (2020)
56. Rozin, P., Royzman, E.B.: Negativity bias, negativity dominance, and contagion. Pers. Soc. Psychol. Rev. **5**(4), 296–320 (2001). https://doi.org/10.1207/S15327957PSPR0504_2
57. Santana, A.D.: Virtuous or Vitriolic: The effect of anonymity on civility in online newspaper reader comment boards. J. Pract. **8**(1), 18–33 (2014)
58. Santana, A.D.: Incivility dominates online comments on immigration. Newspaper Res. J. **36**(1), 92–107 (2015). https://doi.org/10.1177/0739532915580317
59. Saris, W.E., Sniderman, P.M.: Studies in Public Opinion: Attitudes, Nonattitudes, Measurement Error, and Change. Princeton University Press, Princeton (2004)
60. Schrepp, M., et al.: Design and evaluation of a short version of the user experience questionnaire (UEQ-S). IJIMAI **4**(6), 103 (2017). https://doi.org/10.9781/ijimai.2017.09.001
61. Schrepp, M.: User Experience Questionnaire Handbook (2015). https://doi.org/10.13140/RG. 2.1.2815.0245
62. Seering, J., et al.: Designing user interface elements to improve the quality and civility of discourse in online commenting behaviors. In: Proceedings of the 2019 CHI Conference on Human Factors in Computing Systems, pp. 1–14 (2019)
63. Sobieraj, S., Berry, J.M.: From incivility to outrage: political discourse in blogs, talk radio, and cable news. Polit. Commun. **28**(1), 19–41 (2011). https://doi.org/10.1080/10584609.2010. 542360
64. Stoll, A., Ziegele, M., Quiring, O.: Detecting impoliteness and incivility in online discussions: classification approaches for German user comments. Comput. Commun. Res. **2**(1), 109–134 (2020)
65. Stromer-Galley, J.: Measuring deliberation's content: a coding scheme. J. Deliberative Democracy **3**(1), 12 (2007). https://doi.org/10.16997/jdd.50
66. Stroud, N.J., et al.: Changing deliberative norms on news organizations' Facebook sites. J. Comput.-Mediat. Commun. **20**(2), 188–203 (2015). https://doi.org/10.1111/jcc4.12104
67. Sui, M., Pingree, R.J.: In search of reason-centered discussion on China's Twitter: the effects of initiating post and discussion format on reasoning. Int. J. Commun. **10**(1), 416–431 (2016)

68. Sunstein, C.R., Thaler, R.H.: Nudge: Improving Decisions About Health. Wealth and Happiness. Yale University Press, New Haven (2008)
69. Towne, W.B., Herbsleb, J.D.: Design considerations for online deliberation systems. J. Inf. Technol. Polit. **9**(1), 97–115 (2012). https://doi.org/10.1080/19331681.2011.637711
70. Trénel, M.: Measuring the deliberativeness of online discussions. Coding Scheme 2.4. Report. Social Science Research Centrex, Berlin (2004)
71. Tversky, A., Kahneman, D.: Judgment under uncertainty: heuristics and biases. In: Kahneman, D., et al. (eds.) Judgment under Uncertainty, pp. 3–20. Cambridge University Press (1982). https://doi.org/10.1017/CBO9780511809477.002
72. Wales, C., et al.: The structural features and the deliberative quality of online discussions. In: Presented at the Political Studies Association Conference, Edinburgh (2010)
73. Wessler, H.: Investigating deliberativeness comparatively. Polit. Commun. **25**(1), 1–22 (2008)
74. Wilhelm, A.G.: Virtual sounding boards: how deliberative is on-line political discussion? Inf. Commun. Soc. **1**(3), 313–338 (1998)
75. Zhang, W., et al.: The structural features and the deliberative quality of online discussions. Telematics Inform. **30**(2), 74–86 (2013)
76. Ziegele, M., Quiring, O.: Conceptualizing online discussion value: a multidimensional framework for analyzing user comments on mass-media websites. Ann. Int. Commun. Assoc. **37**(1), 125–153 (2013)

# Quantifying the Effects of Age-Related Stereotypes on Online Social Conformity

Senuri Wijenayake[✉], Jolan Hu, Vassilis Kostakos, and Jorge Goncalves

The University of Melbourne, Melbourne, Australia
{swijenayake,jolan}@student.unimelb.edu.au,
{vassilis.kostakos,jorge.goncalves}@unimelb.edu.au

**Abstract.** Social conformity is the act of individuals adjusting personal judgements to conform to expectations of opposing majorities in group settings. While conformity has been studied in online groups with emphasis on its contextual determinants (*e.g.*, group size, social presence, task objectivity), the effect of age – of both the individual and the members of the opposing majority group – is yet to be thoroughly investigated. This study investigates differences in conformity behaviour in young adults (Generation Z) and middle-aged adults (Generation X) attempting an online group quiz containing stereotypically age-biased questions, when their personal responses are challenged by older and younger peers. Our results indicate the influence of age-related stereotypes on participants' conformity behaviour with both young and middle-aged adults stereotypically perceiving the competency of their peers based on peer age. Specifically, participants were more inclined to conform to older majorities and younger majorities in quiz questions each age group was stereotypically perceived to be more knowledgeable about (1980's history and social media & latest technology respectively). We discuss how our findings highlight the need to re-evaluate popular online user representations, to mitigate undesirable effects of age-related stereotypical perceptions leading to conformity.

**Keywords:** Social conformity · Peer age · Age stereotypes · User cues · Bots

## 1 Introduction

Social conformity is a powerful social influence that encourages individuals to change their personal judgements when challenged by an opposing group majority [3,4]. Researchers explain that individuals conform either because they perceive information supported by the majority to be 'correct' (*informational* conformity), or as they attempt to 'fit in' with a group to ensure their membership (*normative* conformity) [23,77–79]. While preliminary studies of social conformity were initially based on face-to-face groups [3,4,9,23,37], as a significant proportion of

© IFIP International Federation for Information Processing 2021
Published by Springer Nature Switzerland AG 2021
C. Ardito et al. (Eds.): INTERACT 2021, LNCS 12935, pp. 451–475, 2021.
https://doi.org/10.1007/978-3-030-85610-6_26

human societal interactions are now taking place through diverse online group settings (*e.g.*, social networks, online chatrooms, discussion forums) [5,15,28,29,51, 60,73], understanding repercussions of social conformity on online group interactions is of growing interest to the HCI research community.

Recent literature has studied conformity behaviour across a wide variety of online groups such as social media [19,52,53,80,81], learning platforms [8,77–79], news websites [69], and support groups [65]. However, the majority of these studies have focused on quantifying online social conformity in terms of its contextual determinants such as majority group size [61,78,80], social presence [45,79] and task objectivity [45,61,78,79]. Conversely, less emphasis has been placed on determining how more personal factors - that have been shown to elicit stereotypical perceptions in online communities (*e.g.*, age [2,13], gender [16,49,77], culture [17], race [20]) - influence online conformity behaviour.

In particular, age of an individual has been recognised as a vital determinant of one's susceptibility to conformity influences in offline groups [22,41–43,74]. Prior work indicate a non-linear relationship between an individual's age and their conformity behaviour, where susceptibility to conformity is seen to increase with age till adolescence, after which it gradually declines [22,74]. Furthermore, studies investigating age differences among adults observe higher conformity behaviour in older adults, than in their younger counterparts [41–43]. These studies rationalise that conformity behaviour runs parallel with socialisation processes that individuals follow to integrate themselves in the community (*e.g.* young children rely on peers to determine their behaviour in groups - leading to higher conformity, whereas by early adulthood they tend to be more confident of their own actions - reducing susceptibility to conformity influences [22]). However, it is unclear if these observations would hold in online groups where social processes may not be obvious or equally strong due to inherently lower social presence and higher anonymity [54]. Moreover, there is evidence in literature that individuals tend to stereotypically perceive competency and trustworthiness of online peers based on peer age [30,57]. Other conformity studies also indicate that similar stereotypical perceptions of peer competency (triggered based on peer gender) can exacerbate online conformity behaviour and lead to incorrect judgements [49,77]. However, such effects are yet to be investigated with regard to age-related stereotypes in online groups.

Therefore, this study takes an initial step towards quantifying effects of age and related stereotypes on online social conformity. We investigate potential differences in conformity behaviour among two distinct age generations - young adults (Generation Z) and middle-aged adults (Generation X) - when completing an online quiz delivered through an Instant Messaging (IM) platform, in small groups. We intend to understand whether and how people infer age of their online peers, and use this information to determine their conforming or non-conforming behaviour against younger/older peers who support a contradicting judgement. This understanding is critical to design future online group platforms that account for possible detrimental effects of age-related stereotypes (*e.g.* unfair treatment of older adults who are perceived as less reliable and trustworthy than their younger counterparts [30,34,57]), to ensure positive societal interactions.

# 2 Related Work

Despite the enhanced anonymity and reduced social presence offered by online platforms [54], individuals are susceptible to both *informational* and *normative* conformity influences in online groups settings [8,19,48,52,53,65,78,81,82]. For example, students completing group quizzes in online learning platforms have been seen to conform to the majority's responses, in an attempt to obtain more 'correct' answers [8,78,79]. Recent work has also shown that Facebook users tend to accept the majority's negative or positive perception of a news article's trustworthiness (inferred through user comments posted underneath the article) as a benchmark to differentiate between fake and real news articles shared on the platform [19,80]. The above studies emphasise the significance of *informational* influences (or the need to be 'right') [23] in prompting conformity behaviour in online group settings. On the other hand, Zhu et al. [82] observe that individuals tend to align their online choices with those of the opposing majority's - even when required to make choices based on personal preference - indicating the presence of *normative* conformity influences (or the need to be 'liked') [23]. Similarly, *normative* conformity has been observed in online support groups, where users tend to conform to community-accepted conventions of behaviour and linguistic norms, with the intention of receiving better support and feedback from other community members [65].

Moreover, prior work investigating implications of online social conformity suggests the potential for both negative and positive effects [8,35,69,77]. For instance, a recent study examining the effect of social information on the accuracy of a visual judgement task highlights that conforming to biased and incorrect responses from peers led to more errors among Mechanical Turk users [35]. Similar observations were noted in students who wrongly assumed the majority to be 'correct' when attempting online quizzes (*informational* conformity), and obtained more incorrect answers than those who attempted the quiz independently [8,77,78]. Conversely, *normative* conformity is considered useful to encourage users of online news websites to follow accepted norms of the community and contribute high quality and 'thoughtful' content [69].

Therefore, it is critical to understand what contextual and personal factors affect susceptibility of individuals to online conformity influences, in order to minimise its detrimental effects on online societal interactions (*e.g.* undue pressure to conform to majority's incorrect judgements). However, the majority of prior studies focus on contextual determinants of online conformity *i.e.*, majority group size, task objectivity (subjective or objective nature of a task) and social presence (sense of being connected with others in the group [66]) [8,45,61,78,79]. In brief, these studies indicate that participants are more likely to conform when challenged by larger majorities, as they attempt objective tasks (with a specific correct answer), and in online settings with higher perceived social presence.

Moreover, several studies investigating personal determinants of conformity indicate effects of users' self-confidence and gender [49,61,77–80]. These studies unanimously note that participants with higher confidence on personal decisions are significantly less likely to conform when challenged by opposing majorities [77–80]. Furthermore, while no significant differences in conformity behaviour is observed among men and women in online groups [61, 78, 79], prior work note that both men and women are more inclined to conform when challenged by male-dominant and female-dominant majorities, in stereotypically masculine and feminine tasks respectively [49, 77]. Findings from these studies imply that when competency of online peers is not explicitly known, users tend to stereotypically perceive peer competency based on available user cues (*i.e.* in this case, user gender derived from their first name or stereotypically gendered avatar) - especially in the presence of stereotypical tasks. These observations emphasise the need to investigate implications of other user cues (such as age) that can trigger similar stereotypical conformity behaviour in online groups.

However, online conformity literature is yet to systematically investigate effects of age on social conformity - despite age being identified as a critical conformity determinant in offline conformity literature [41–43, 74]. Therefore, this study intends to take an initial step towards identifying the effects of age on online conformity behaviour. Next, we summarise the offline conformity literature investigating effects of age on social conformity, which informed the design of our study.

## 2.1   Conformity as a Function of Age

The majority of offline conformity studies investigating effects of age on conformity behaviour have focused on identifying differences in conformity between young adults (18–22 years) and older adults (>55 years) [41–43]. These studies unanimously indicate that on perceptual tasks, older adults conform significantly more often than young adults. For instance, in a study that compared conformity behaviour in young and older adults attempting a series of visual judgement tasks, author observed that older participants were more susceptible to conformity influences than their younger counterparts [41]. Similar observations were noted by Klein and Birren [42], where older participants conformed more often than younger participants in an auditory signal detection task. On the other hand, prior studies investigating determinants of online conformity do not indicate significant effects from participant age [8, 45–47, 49, 61, 78, 79]. However, as most of these studies primarily recruited young adults, it is likely that the age distribution of the recruited participants was not sufficient to reveal significant effects from participants' age on their conformity behaviour. Therefore, in this study we intend to recruit participants in two distinct age generations - Generation Z (young adults between 18–23 years) and Generation X (middle-aged adults between 40–55 years) [24] - to investigate potential age differences in participants' susceptibility to online conformity influences.

Furthermore, literature also indicates that an individual's decision to conform or not, depends on their perceived self-competency in an experimental task, in comparison to the perceived competency of the opposing majority (or peers) [21]. In other words, as a result of *informational* influences (or the need to be 'right') individuals tend to conform to majorities they perceive as more competent or knowledgeable than they are, in a given situation. On that note, we highlight that competency of peers has been often stereotypically inferred through their age in both offline and online groups, subsequently affecting how users interact with their peers [14,25,43]. For instance in offline contexts, school children have been observed to assume peer competency based on peer age, and more often imitate peers they perceive as more competent than themselves [14]. Furthermore, such age-biased perceptions of peer competency have also been noted to trigger stereotypical conformity in offline groups [41–43]. For instance, Klein and Birren [43] observed that both young and older adults stereotypically assumed older peers to be less competent and reliable in visual judgement tasks (due to the perceptual nature of the activity), consequently encouraging older participants to conform more to their younger counterparts, whereas younger participants were seen less inclined to conform to their older peers. Authors also emphasised that when stereotypical perceptions regarding perceived self-competency were controlled so that young and older adults had similar perceptions of their task competency, previously observed differences in conformity diminished.

Similarly, despite the absence of face-to-face interactions, peer age has often been used to gauge peer competency and trustworthiness in online groups [30,50,57]. For instance, in a recent study investigating the impact of borrowers' personal features (e.g., age, gender, physical attractiveness) on online peer-to-peer lending decisions, authors indicate that users actively inferred age of peers through their photographs, and considered assumed age a reliable indicator of peer competency to repay the loan [30]. Similarly, Pak et al. [57] observed that users of an online health management application assumed peers represented using younger anthropomorphic (human-like) avatars as more reliable and trustworthy than peers represented using older avatars. The authors further explained that the above differences in preference could be due to negative stereotypes associated with older adults [59].

However, effects of peer age and related stereotypes on conformity behaviour is yet to be systematically investigated in online groups. Hence, in addition to age differences in conformity behaviour, the present study will also explore how stereotypical perceptions related to peer age and competency may impact conformity behaviour among young (Generation Z) and middle-aged adults (Generation X), as they attempt tasks that are stereotypically age-biased and perceived to be more familiar to either young or middle-aged adults.

## 3   Method

We aim to investigate the impact of three aspects of age on social conformity in an online group setting using a 2 (participants' age: young adults vs. middle-aged adults) × 2 (majority's age group composition: all young/middle-aged, mixed) × 3 (stereotypically perceived question type: young, middle-aged, neutral) mixed design, where participant's age and majority's age group composition are manipulated between subjects (resulting in four experimental conditions). The study was deployed as a group quiz containing multiple-choice questions (MCQ) on Slack (www.slack.com) - an online instant messaging platform - which allowed us to expose participants to stereotypically age-biased questions, in the presence of diverse age group compositions in a realistic online group environment. The decision to use a MCQ quiz for the study was inspired by recent literature which uses quizzes to investigate conformity in online group settings [8, 45, 61, 77–79].

## 3.1   The Quiz

The quiz contained 30 objective MCQs which were equally distributed among topics that young adults (or Generation Z) are perceived to be better at (*i.e.* social media & latest technology), middle-aged adults (or Generation X) are perceived to be better at (*i.e.* 1980's history), and topics that are neutral or timeless (*i.e.* general knowledge). On that note, we emphasise that this study intentionally focused on Generations X and Z, with an entire age generation (Generation Y) separating the two age groups, to avoid potential overlaps in age-related stereotypical perceptions. Moreover, prior work has indicated that there are clearly established age-related stereotypes attached to Generations X and Z, that the aforementioned question topics have been seen to successfully trigger [13, 24, 36, 40, 70]. Furthermore, we chose general knowledge topics to represent neutral questions, as recent work has shown no age differences in conformity for general knowledge questions [45, 61, 77–79].

After determining topics for each question type, we created a question repository by extracting objective MCQs related to the selected topics. The neutral questions were extracted from recent online conformity literature (*i.e.,* [77–79]), whereas questions that are stereotypically perceived as age-biased were extracted from popular online questions repositories *i.e.,* Britannica, Sporcle, and Washington Times quizzes. In order to determine a final list of quiz questions that could trigger age-related stereotypical perceptions, we then followed a filtering mechanism that has been frequently used in recent studies investigating effects of stereotypes on conformity behaviour [46, 47, 49, 77]. Two of the paper's authors (one from Generation Z and another from Generation X) independently rated the stereotypically age-biased questions on their familiarity to young (Generation Z) and middle-aged (Generation X) adults, each on a 10-point Likert scale (1 – Gen Z/X is not at all likely to be familiar to 10 – Gen Z/X is extremely likely to be familiar). The familiarity score for Generation X was then reverse-coded and added to the Generation Z score, to arrive at a final score for each stereotypical question. Similarly, authors rated the neutral questions for their likelihood to trigger an age-related stereotypical perception (1 – Not at all likely to trigger age-related stereotypical perceptions to 10 – Extremely likely to trigger age-related stereotypical perceptions). We computed the weighted kappa (kw) to assess the inter-coder reliability of the two raters, to note kw = 0.81 (95% CI, 0.72 to 0.90, $p < 0.001$) - which indicates excellent agreement beyond chance [26] - further validating the categorisation of the quiz questions. We then selected the top 10 questions from each topic (*i.e.,* topics familiar to Generation Z or young adults, topics familiar to Generation X or middle-aged adults, and topics related to general knowledge) to be included in the quiz. By exposing individuals in groups to different questions types (stereotypically age-biased and otherwise), we intend to determine whether they would consider age as a factor of peer competency when deciding whether to conform or not, especially in topics that are stereotypically perceived to favour a certain age group. We list several questions used in the quiz representative of each question type in Table 1.

**Table 1.** Example questions used in the quiz. Correct answer for each question is in bold.

| Question type | Example quiz question | Answer options |
|---|---|---|
| General knowledge | What is the largest country in the world (by area)? | Canada, USA, China, **Russia** |
| | What is the capital of Bulgaria? | Tirana, **Sofia**, Berlin, Riga |
| Social media & technology | A game based on which animated franchise propelled AR into the mainstream in recent years? | **Pokémon**, Super Mario, Legend of Zelda, Sonic |
| | Which song by "Psy" has been viewed over 2 billion times on YouTube? | Gentleman, Daddy, Hangover, **Gangnam Style** |
| 1980's history | Which Michael Jackson album released in 1982 featured the single "Beat It"? | Invincible, Dangerous, **Thriller**, Bad |
| | What was the top grossing movie of the 1980s? | Star Wars VI, **E.T**, Ghostbusters, Raiders of Lost Ark |

The quiz was conducted in a Slack channel (an online chatroom). We used a pre-programmed Slack bot named "SupportBot" to conduct the quiz without any involvement from the researchers in order to reduce potential experimenter effects and mimic a realistic online environment as suggested in prior work [72, 76, 78].

During the quiz, the SupportBot guides the user through the steps shown in Fig. 1. First, the bot displays a MCQ with four answer options, requesting the user to attempt the question by themselves (Step 1). Upon submitting their personal answer, the bot asks the user to rate how confident they are of the chosen answer from a scale of 1–5, with higher values indicating higher confidence (Step 2). After the user indicates their initial confidence level, the bot displays a list of group answers claiming to display how two 'peers' have answered the same question (Step 3). However, in reality there was only one real user in a single session and the 'peers' were simulated by two confederates of the research team, who provided answers to the quiz questions based on a predetermined script to ensure that one answer always secured a clear majority of votes, while also placing the user's initial answer in the majority as well as in the minority to avoid suspicion. We note that the notion of using confederates to maintain control over the majority–minority group formation was based on prior conformity literature [3, 4, 8, 45, 79]. Following the display of group answers, the bot requests the users to attempt the question again and indicate their confidence on the new answer (Steps 4 and 5), before moving to the next question (Step 6). The above process was repeated for all questions in the quiz, which allowed us to capture how the group feedback influenced users' decision to change or not change their initial answers.

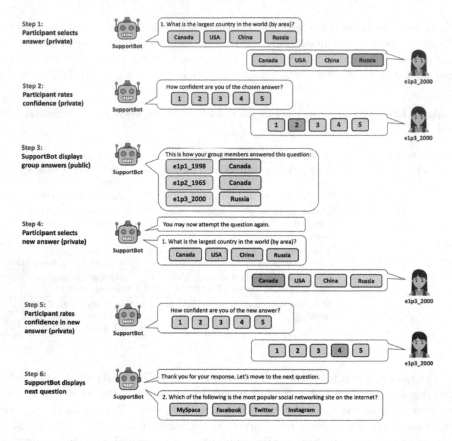

**Fig. 1.** Steps followed by a participant when answering the quiz questions.

## 3.2   Age Group Compositions

We decided to use an overall group size of three, which is the minimum group size required to simulate a clear majority against a minority of one (the user). Moreover, a group size of three has been established as sufficient to elicit conformity behaviour in prior studies [3,4,11,27,63], which was appropriate for this experiment as our focus is not to determine the effect of group size on conformity behaviour.

As per the objectives of the experiment, to determine the effect of the opposing majority's age group composition on participants' conformity behaviour in stereotypically age-biased questions, we exposed users to the following age group compositions. We were interested in the group compositions where the user is challenged by an opposing majority that included at least one peer who does not belong to the same age group as the user as illustrated in Fig. 2.

(a) Young user challenged by two middle-aged peers.
(b) Young user challenged by one middle-aged peer and one young peer.
(c) Middle-aged user challenged by two young peers.
(d) Middle-aged user challenged by one young peer and one middle-aged peer.

| Young user challenged by two middle-aged peers | Young user challenged by one middle-aged peer and one young peer | Middle-aged user challenged by two young peers | Middle-aged user challenged by one young peer and one middle-aged peer |
| :---: | :---: | :---: | :---: |
| (a) | (b) | (c) | (d) |

**Fig. 2.** Overview of age group compositions investigated in the study. The real participant/user is on the left and the simulated 'peers' are to the right. Black and grey avatars represent young users/peers and middle-aged users/peers respectively.

### 3.3 Age Cues

Determining how to indicate peer age to users realistically was a critical decision of this study. We decided against using real photographs of users, as photographs are rich in user cues other than age, and have been seen to elicit stereotypical perceptions of user gender, personality, and even their trustworthiness in online settings subsequently affecting their conformity behaviour [32,62,75,77]. Instead, we chose to represent users using textual usernames that included a unique user ID and their birth year (e.g. e1p3_2000 as shown in Fig. 1), to imply the age group users belonged to. Our decision was motivated by prior work that shows that users tend to include their birth year in online usernames in Twitter and other gaming platforms [44,56]. Furthermore, we chose the mode and median birth years of the young (1998 and 2000 respectively) and middle-aged (1965 and 1976 respectively) users recruited for the study, to be displayed alongside the 'peer' answers during the quiz (see Fig. 1 Step 3). Our intention behind this decision was to ensure that the fake peers represent the age distribution of the user cohort recruited for the study.

### 3.4 Participants and Procedure

We recruited participants using our university's online notice board where individuals willing to volunteer for the study were requested to complete a simple form providing their name, email address, self-described gender and birth year. We described that the study aims to investigate how individuals perform in online group quizzes, as the true purpose of the study could not be disclosed prior to the experiment as expected in conformity studies [67]. Next, we shortlisted potential participants based on their age group (young adults and middle-aged adults only), and contacted them through email to describe the experimental task and obtain their written consent. Out of the individuals who responded with their consent, we recruited a final sample ($N = 32$) that consisted of 16 middle-aged adults (Generation X; born between 1965–1980 as per [24]; $M = 46.63$, $SD = 5.84$) and 16 young adults (Generation Z; born between 1997–2002 as per [24]; $M = 20.5$, $SD = 1.84$), with an equal number of men and women from each age group. Moreover, our participants came from different educational and occupational backgrounds including

Arts, Engineering, Science, Commerce, Physiotherapy, Nursing, Education and Public Health. Participants were then randomly assigned to the eligible experimental conditions (*i.e.* young adults were equally assigned to experimental conditions illustrated in Fig. 2 (a) and (b), and middle-aged adults were equally assigned to experimental conditions illustrated in Fig. 2 (c) and (d)), with an equal number of men and women to each experimental condition. Each participant was assigned to only one experimental condition.

The study was conducted entirely online, using Slack channels for each group session under the supervision of a researcher. Before the quiz, all participants received a link to join the designated Slack channel, using their unique username. Upon joining the Slack channel, the bot welcomed the participants, described the objective of the study and the experimental task, and informed the participants that they are connected with two 'peers' (simulated by confederates) to complete the quiz as a group. The bot also described that all participants are referred to using their usernames during the quiz, highlighting that the username is composed of a unique participant ID and the corresponding participant's birth year. Participants were then prompted to type "@SupportBot ready" once they have completed reading the instructions, upon which the quiz was initiated.

After completing the steps illustrated in Fig. 1 for each quiz question, the SupportBot automatically directed the participants to complete a post-test survey with three questions:

1. Did you experience an urge to change your initial answer after seeing the group answers? If yes, what factors influenced this behaviour?
2. How did you use the feedback received to answer the quiz questions?
3. Did you notice the age distribution of the group? If yes, how did this information affect your final answer?

After participants submitted brief, textual responses to the above questions, the bot thanked them, and explained the true objective of the study and the use of confederates to simulate peers. Participants were then given the opportunity to withdraw their participation and data collected during the study, if desired. No participant chose to do so.

On a different note, we emphasise that the research team includes members from Generation X and Z (age groups considered for participant recruitment) as well as from Generation Y (the age group in between the two age groups investigated in the study). Moreover, the experimental design was approved by the Ethics Committee of our university. The experiment lasted for approximately 30–40 min per participant, including briefing, completing the quiz, and the final post-test survey.

## 3.5   Analysis of Survey Responses

Two of the paper's authors individually coded the survey data following an inductive thematic analysis approach [12]. The emerging themes were then combined in an online spreadsheet before further discussion. These themes indicated perceived pressure from majority, a relationship between confidence in answer and conformity, and how inferring peer age through usernames led to age-stereotypical perceptions of peer competency. Next, the two authors virtually discussed and collaboratively agreed on the final themes: effectiveness of the manipulations used in the study to trigger age-related stereotypes (usernames and questions stereotypically perceived as age-biased), how participants' age, opposing majority's age group composition and perceived question type affected participants' conformity behaviour, and the effect of confidence in initial answer on subsequent conformity behaviour. Next, we present the main findings of our analysis.

**Age Cues and Stereotypical Question Types:** During the quiz, participants were addressed using usernames which included a unique user ID and their birth year (*e.g.* e1p1_1972). The SupportBot also informed that the same naming convention is used to refer to their peers during the quiz (especially when displaying peer answers next to their usernames as shown in Fig. 1, Step 3). In the post-test survey, all participants described that they actively inferred peer age and the age group their peers belonged to (young vs. middle-aged adults), using usernames of peers. Hence, embedding birth years in usernames of the supposed peers was sufficient to trigger awareness of peer age; *"I noticed that each of us is from quite different generations. One of them was born in 1965, another in 1976 and myself in 2000. My peers knew many other things in their era that I did not know, and vice versa"* (P16, Gen Z).

Moreover, participants stereotypically categorised quiz questions as better known by young (*i.e.* social media & latest technology) and middle-aged (*i.c.* 1980's history) adults, indicating that the question types we used in the quiz to trigger age-biased stereotypical perceptions were effective; *"I trusted the older guy (born in 60s) when answering questions from his era (like the movie from the 80's), while I trusted the guy born in 1998 when answering questions like the most popular social media website"* (P23, Gen Z).

**Age-Related Stereotypes:** We further note that the awareness of peer age and assumptions of stereotypical question types significantly encouraged participants to stereotypically perceive peer competency in different questions. The majority of the participants described that they actively linked peer age with the stereotypically assumed era of the question, when deciding whether to trust peer answers or not; *"Some questions are too new like social networking, technology and gaming. I think only young people would know these. But there were also questions that are old (1980s), for which I don't believe the younger generation would know the correct answer"* (P10, Gen X) and *"I will consider peer answers more if the question is something related to events or things of their generation"* (P02, Gen Z).

Moreover, participants also highlighted how such (stereotypical) perceptions impacted their conformity behaviour. As noted by P25 - a middle-aged participant - they were more inclined to conform to younger majorities in questions perceived to be better known by younger generations; *"A lot of the questions" were based around technology and recent things. I thought younger people would know more about these topics, and if I didn't know the answer, I thought they would know better and I trusted them"* (P25, Gen X). Similarly, young participants also claimed to prefer majorities with middle-aged peers for questions that they perceived to be familiar to older generations. Alternatively, for questions they perceived to be familiar to their own age group, they were less inclined to change their personal answer; *"When the question is about history or requires knowledge related to many years ago, I preferred to change my answers so that they can be consistent with the older people's answer"* (P05, Gen Z) and *"The age distribution only affected my decisions in questions that might have been popular in the past as I was the youngest among the group"* (P03, Gen Z).

Our data also provide evidence as to why participants felt encouraged to follow aforementioned stereotypically age-biased perceptions when deciding whether to conform or not. Participants rationalised that following the answers of the age group that is perceived to be more familiar of the question content, improved their chances of reaching the correct answer to the quiz questions - indicating the presence of *informational* conformity influences; *"When the questions were related to an older time, for instance, 1980's popular film, it makes sense to have a higher bet on a person from that era than someone younger. So age did convince me to believe that they might have chosen the right answer"* (P24, Gen Z) and *"I used the 90's person's answers for gaming questions, and if the 60's person had the same answer as me [a middle-aged participant] for history questions, I felt a little more confident that my answer may be correct"* (P31, Gen X).

**Initial Confidence:** Our qualitative analysis also indicate that participants were more susceptible to conformity influences when they were unsure of their personal answers, whereas they were less likely to conform when they trusted their personal answers; *"If I was not very confident in my answer, I would look at what the other two posted. If they both agreed on something different from me, I was likely to change to what they said. If I was reasonably confident, but others gave a different answer, I generally stuck to my answer, but my confidence was less"* (P27, Gen X). Moreover, participants reiterated that the peer feedback was useful when they were unsure of their initial choice, to reach the correct answer to the quiz question (*informational* conformity); *"For some questions I was really only guessing the answers, so answers from my teammates provided me with an answer which I hoped was more likely to be correct than my guess"* (P27, Gen X).

## 4   Results

All 32 participants answered 30 multiple-choice questions (equally distributed among topics covering general knowledge, social media & technology, and 1980's history) which resulted in a total of 960 responses. Moreover, simulated peer answers placed participants in minorities (peer answers unanimously challenged participant's answer) as well as in majorities (one or more peer answers supported the participant's answer) to avoid suspicion. As a result, participants found themselves in the group majority in 618 questions, and in a minority for the rest of the 342 questions. On that note, we emphasise that aim of this study is not to compare results between majority and minority groups, but rather to investigate the impact of opposing majority's age group composition on conformity behaviour, when answering stereotypically age-biased questions.

Upon seeing the group's answers for a question, participants indicated their final answer and confidence level, where they could:

(a) Change both their initial answer and confidence level.
(b) Change only their initial answer.
(c) Change only their confidence in answer.
(d) Make no change to either their initial answer or confidence level.

We note that all participants changed their opinion, confidence level, or both at least once during the study, resulting in a total of 481 changed responses (in majority = 263, in minority = 218) with an average of 15.03 changes ($SD = 5.62$) per participant. Figure 3 illustrates the distribution of the final responses (post-feedback), grouped by whether the participants' initial answer to the question placed them in a minority (minority responses), or a majority (majority responses). When placed in minorities, participants changed their initial answer with or without a change in confidence in 46.4% of the responses, changed only their confidence in 17.3% of the responses ($M = -0.31$ and $SD = 1.44$ per response, indicating an overall reduction in confidence) and made no change to their initial answer or confidence in the remaining 36.3% of the responses. Conversely, when participants found themselves in the group's majority they made either no change to their initial response or changed only their confidence level in the initial answer ($M = 1.14$ and $SD = 1.03$ per response, indicating an overall increase in confidence) in approximately 95.4% of the responses. Hence, our preliminary analysis indicates that participants were aware of their position in the group, and changed their answers post feedback, not randomly but due to the influence of the predictors we considered, confirming the validity of our results.

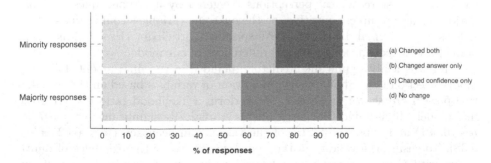

**Fig. 3.** Distribution of minority and majority responses across the four response types.

## 4.1   Model Construction

For the purposes of this study, we consider changing the initial answer option (with or without a change in initial confidence level) to that of the majority, as conformity behaviour. Our results show that 29 (out of 32) participants conformed at least once to the majority, resulting in a total of 97 conformity responses (conformity rate $= 28.36\%$), with an average of 3.03 ($SD = 2.13$) conformity responses per participant. We observe similar conformity rates in prior online conformity literature [45, 77, 79].

We then investigated the impact of the following variables on the conformity behaviour of our participants. The predictor variables were chosen based on the study's objective of determining the effects of participant age, opposing majority's age group composition, and stereotypical question type on online conformity behaviour. For the statistical model we only considered the responses of participants when placed in a minority, as the dependent variable was determining conformity behaviour.

- **PAge**: Participant's age group. Values: Middle-aged (Generation X), Young (Generation Z).
- **MajAgeGroup**: Majority's age group. Values: Middle-aged (majority of two middle-aged peers), Young (majority of two young peers), Mixed (majority of one young and one middle-aged peer).
- **QType**: Stereotypically perceived question type. Values: Neutral (general knowledge), Young (social media & latest technology) and Middle-Aged (1980's history).
- **Initial confidence**: Participant's initial confidence in their answer. Range: 1–5.
- **Gender**: Participant's self-disclosed gender. Values: Man, Woman.
- **User ID**: An unique identifier assigned to a given user during the quiz.

We used the R package *lme4* [6] to perform a generalised linear mixed-effects model (GLMM) analysis of the relationship between the aforementioned variables and participant conformity behaviour (binary variable: conformed or not). A GLMM (family $=$ binomial, link $=$ logit) supports the study's objective to identify potential main and/or interaction effects from multiple personal determinants of offline conformity (*i.e.*, age, gender, self-confidence), in addition to the impact of stereotypical perceptions triggered by age-typed questions and majority's age group composition, on the outcome variable - conformity - which follows a non-normal distribution. We specified participant (User ID) as a random effect to account for individual differences in our model.

All statistically significant predictors included in the final model (following model selection through incremental addition of variables based on their predictive power) are shown in Table 2. We perform a likelihood ratio test with the null model [10] and find that our model is statistically significant ($\chi^2 = 107.56$, $p < 0.001$) and explains 38.21% of the variance in accuracy ($\mathbb{R} = 0.62$, $\mathbb{R}^2 = 0.38$). To ensure the validity of the model, we check for the existence of multicollinearity. Our predictors report a variance inflation factor between 1.16 and 2.71, well below the often-used threshold of 5 to detect multicollinearity [33].

We observe a statistically significant interaction effect between participant's age group, opposing majority's age group composition and stereotypical question type, on participants' conformity behaviour ($p < 0.05$). The model also notes that participants' confidence on initial answer indicates a statistically significant main effect on their conformity behaviour ($p < 0.001$). Our results do not indicate any other main or interaction effects from the variables considered. Next, we describe the above significant predictors in detail.

**Table 2.** Effect of predictors on participant conformity. Statistically significant main effects and interactions ($p < 0.05$) are in bold. The effect sizes are presented as Cohen's $d$ values derived based on relevant log odds ratio [58]. The sign of the effect size or $d$ ($\pm$) denotes the direction of the relationship between the predictor and conformity behaviour. The absolute size of $d$ indicates the magnitude of the effect; d = 0.2 (small), d = 0.5 (medium) and d = 0.8 (large) [18].

| Predictor | Log OR | P-value | Effect size (d) |
|---|---|---|---|
| **Initial confidence** | **−0.65** | **<0.001** | **−0.359** |
| **PAge (Middle-aged) : QType (Young) : MajAgeGroup (Young)** | **2.70** | **<0.001** | **1.503** |
| **PAge (Middle-aged) : QType (Middle-aged) : MajAgeGroup (Young)** | **1.91** | **0.04** | **1.072** |
| PAge (Middle-aged) : QType (Neutral) : MajAgeGroup (Young) | 1.61 | 0.07 | 0.904 |
| **PAge (Young) : QType (Middle-aged) : MajAgeGroup (Middle-aged)** | **1.70** | **0.03** | **0.952** |
| PAge (Young) : QType (Young) : MajAgeGroup (Middle-aged) | 1.57 | 0.11 | 0.884 |
| PAge (Young) : QType (Neutral) · MajAgeGroup (Middle-aged) | 0.97 | 0.31 | 0.551 |
| PAge (Middle-aged) : QType (Middle-aged) : MajAgeGroup (Mixed) | −0.75 | 0.39 | −0.406 |
| PAge (Middle-aged) : QType (Young) : MajAgeGroup (Mixed) | 0.42 | 0.59 | 0.238 |
| PAge (Middle-aged) : QType (Neutral) : MajAgeGroup (Mixed) | −0.87 | 0.27 | 0.473 |
| PAge (Young) : QType (Middle-aged) : MajAgeGroup (Mixed) | −0.33 | 0.66 | −0.181 |
| PAge (Young) : QType (Neutral) : MajAgeGroup (Mixed) | −0.77 | 0.30 | −0.418 |

## 4.2   Participant's Age Group, Opposing Majority's Age Group Composition and Stereotypical Question Type

We note that participants' tendency to conform to the group majority, was significantly influenced by their age group, opposing majority's age group composition and the stereotypically perceived question type as illustrated in Fig. 4 (a) and (b). The two plots visualise the density of the likelihood of conformity (y-axis) for young & middle-aged participants, when challenged by middle-aged and young majorities respectively (x-axis), across the three question types. We calculated the likelihood of conformity for each participant in each of the three question types, as the ratio between the number of conformity responses and the total number of minority responses in the relevant question type.

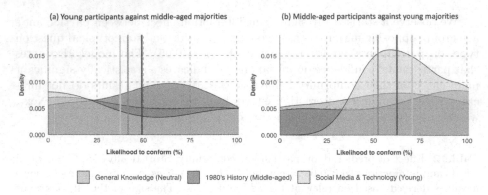

**Fig. 4.** (a) Likelihood of young participants conforming to middle-aged majorities in different question types, and (b) Likelihood of middle-aged participants conforming to young majorities in different question types. The three curves relate to the three question types. Vertical lines indicate average conformity rates for each question type.

Figure 4(a) indicates that young participants were significantly more inclined to conform to majorities with all middle-aged peers for questions stereotypically perceived to be well-known by middle-aged adults (1980's history) than in other question types ($d = 0.952$, large effect size), with their average conformity rates are at 49.17%, 41.67% and 37.50% for 1980's history (middle-aged), general knowledge (neutral) and social media & technology (young) questions respectively. On the other hand, middle-aged participants were seen to conform to majorities with all-young peers, in questions which are stereotypically age-biased in comparison neutral questions. This behaviour was more dominant in questions which are sterotypically perceived to be well-known by young adults ($d = 1.503$, large effect size), than in questions which are stereotypically perceived to be well-known by middle-aged adults ($d = 1.072$, large effect size). This interaction effect is illustrated in Fig. 4(b), which marks the average conformity rates of middle-aged participants at 70.83%, 62.50% and 52.38% for social media & technology (young), 1980's history (middle-aged) and general knowledge (neutral) questions respectively. Moreover, conformity behaviour of both young and middle-aged participants were not significantly affected by mixed majorities, in any of the question types.

## 4.3   Initial Confidence

The statistically significant main effect from participants' initial confidence on their subsequent conformity behaviour ($p < 0.001$) implies that all participants were less likely to conform to the majority, when they were confident of their initial answer - regardless the majority's age group composition or the stereotypically perceived question type ($d = -0.359$, small to medium effect size). We illustrate this in Fig. 5, where we analysed participants' self-reported initial confidence levels across both non-conforming and conforming responses using boxplots. We note that while the range of self-reported confidence levels for both response types range from 1–5, the median values for non-conforming and conforming responses are at 3 ($M = 2.89$, $SD = 1.31$) and 2 ($M = 2.08$, $SD = 1.09$) respectively, reiterating that lower initial confidence values are more likely to result in conforming behaviour.

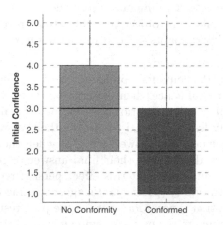

**Fig. 5.** Participants' initial confidence across non-conforming and conforming minority responses.

## 5    Discussion

Currently, our understanding of online social conformity is primarily based on its contextual determinants - *i.e.*, group size [39,61,77,78], social presence [45, 79], and task objectivity [45,61,78,79]. However, as online group platforms are becoming increasingly personal (*e.g.*, social media, online support groups [5,7,15, 28,51,60,73]), it is vital to quantify implications of personal factors such as age and gender on social conformity. Moreover, such personal factors have also been seen to trigger stereotypical perceptions of peer competency among individuals in offline groups, further increasing their susceptibility to stereotypical conformity influences [14,25,43]. However, it is unclear if the above observations would prevail in online groups that lack direct face-to-face interactions, and operate with minimum user cues [54]. Hence, this study takes an initial step towards investigating effects of one such personal factor - age - on online social conformity across three aspects: age group of the participant, age group composition of the opposing group majority, and stereotypically perceived question type.

### 5.1    Online Social Conformity

We note an overall conformity rate of 28.36% - which is similar to conformity rates observed in prior work that investigated effects of contextual conformity determinants [45,77,79]. Furthermore, our results indicate a statistically significant main effect of participants' initial confidence in personal answer, and an interaction effect from the three aspects of age considered in the study, on the conformity behaviour of our participants. Hence, by controlling for contextual determinants such as majority group size (majority was always two), social presence (low social presence, with minimum users cues and interactivity) and task objectivity (all questions were objective), this study revealed implications of personal conformity determinants - which we discuss next.

**Initial Confidence:** Participants' confidence on initial judgements has been previously reported to influence their susceptibility to conformity in online groups [8,47,49,77-79]. Similar to prior observations, we also show that participants are significantly less motivated to change their answer to the majority's when confident of their personal answer, whereas when they are unsure of their initial selection they readily change their final answer to reflect the majority's selection. We further emphasise that this effect persist, regardless of the other factors considered in the study (participant's age, opposing majority's age group composition, and question type). Moreover, in the post-test survey participants described that conforming to the majority when unsure of the their initial answer was a mechanism employed to 'correctly' answer the quiz questions - confirming the existence of *informational* influences as implied in prior studies [77-80].

**Age and Related Stereotypes:** While our results did not indicate main effects from the three aspects of age included in the study, we note that participants' age group (young adult or Generation Z vs. middle-aged adult or Generation X) interacted with the opposing majority's age group composition (all young peers, all middle-aged peers, or a mix of young and middle-aged peers) and the stereotypically perceived question type (social media & latest technology favouring Generation Z, 1980's history favouring Generation X, and general knowledge that do not favour an age group), in determining their conformity behaviour. More specifically, young adults were swayed by an opposing majority with all middle-aged peers, strictly in questions stereotypically perceived to be better known to middle-aged adults (1980's history), whereas middle-aged adults readily conformed to opposing majorities that included all young peers, in questions stereotypically perceived to be well known to young adults (social media & latest technology).

Therefore, while our study did not replicate observations of offline literature where older adults are portrayed as more susceptible to conformity influences than their younger counterparts [41-43], our findings show that stereotypical perceptions that participants derived with regard to peer competency using peer age as an indicator, substantially influenced their online conformity behaviour. Our qualitative analysis confirms that the above perceptions of peer competency were based on popular stereotypes that portray young adults (or the Generation Z) as "digital natives" [24,71], and middle-aged adults (or the Generation X) to possess more "practical knowledge and life experience" [13,36,40,70].

Consequently, participants believed that following the age group that is stereo-typically perceived to be more knowledgeable about certain age-biased topics, improved their chances of being 'correct' - reiterating effects of *informational* influences that have been previously observed with regard to gender stereotypical perceptions of peer competency [49,77]. Moreover, the fact that both young and middle-aged participants showed no motivation to conform to mixed majorities in any of the question types, suggests that participants were not concerned about being singled out against a unanimous majority, and hence were not as susceptible to *normative* conformity influences.

Furthermore, we highlight that prior work that investigated young people's actual use of technology do not identify them as expert users in the matter [64]. Moreover, literature also note that other factors such as education level of young people significantly affect their expertise in technology [1]. Therefore, stereotypical conformity observed in this study, where young adults were stereo-typed as more competent in social media & technology entirely based on their assumed age, is not always reliable and is unlikely to result in 'correct' answers as expected. Furthermore, other studies also indicate that age-biased stereotypes often disadvantage older adults who are perceived as less reliable and trustworthy than their younger counterparts, in online group settings [30,34,57]. Therefore, our findings coupled with prior evidence in literature, urge the re-evaluation of online group platform design, to mitigate undesirable effects of age-stereotypical online conformity behaviour *i.e.*, conforming to incorrect majorities and preju-dice against people from different age generations.

## 5.2   Design Implications

This study presents interesting findings with regard to the use of user cues in online groups. We note that despite its minimalist nature, textual usernames that indicated the birth year of the corresponding peer were sufficient to trigger stereotypical perceptions of peer competency, in both young and middle aged participants - which also subsequently determined their conformity behaviour. Hence, our findings imply that individuals are receptive to the simplest user cues in online groups and often use them to derive stereotypical perceptions of their online peers.

Moreover, it is likely that the effects of age and related stereotypes observed in this study would be further heightened in real online group settings that use richer user representations such as real photographs (*e.g.*, social media, online forums [55,68]) and highly anthropomorphic (human-like) avatars (*e.g.*, gaming platforms, virtual worlds [34,50]). Therefore, we urge designers of online group platforms to reconsider if including user cues is of value to the core purpose of the platform to minimise susceptibility of users to unwanted social pressures. For instance, user age holds important information in online dating websites or social media, but may not be useful in an e-commerce platform. Thus, age-related user cues should only be embedded in platform design only if they are considered value-adding.

Furthermore, we encourage the use of online user representations that are devoid of explicit age-related information - *i.e.*, site specific avatars used by Slack, animal avatars used by Google, identicons used by GitHub etc. - especially in contexts where age stereotypical perceptions of peer competency could trigger conformity behaviour as observed in this study. We argue that using age-neutral user representations in platform design can minimise the occurrence of age-stereotypes that have been observed to trigger prejudice against certain age groups in prior work [30,34,57].

Alternatively, we encourage future studies to explore the possibility of mitigating detrimental effects of age-related stereotypes through alternative user representations, and by displaying user competency through platform specific indicators (*e.g.*, skill assessment tests in LinkedIn [38], badges used in Stack Overflow [31]) - thereby minimising opportunity for stereotypical perceptions of user competency to manifest.

## 5.3   Limitations

We note the following limitations of our study. First, our findings on the effects of age and related stereotypes on online conformity behaviour are specifically with regard to young and middle-aged adults. Hence, further work is required to investigate how age and related stereotypes impact conformity behaviour in other age groups (such as adolescents and older adults). Furthermore, while the sample size used for the study was sufficient to elicit statistically significant effects from age-stereotypical perceptions on online conformity behaviour, further work is required to replicate our findings in larger sample sizes. Moreover, as the study's primary focus was on understanding the impact of personal determinants such as user age and their susceptibility to stereotypes on online conformity behaviour, we did not investigate how the above personal factors manifest alongside popular contextual determinants such as group size, task objectivity and social presence. Therefore, we note that our work is an initial step towards quantifying effects of personal determinants on online conformity, and that future work can extend this work to investigate combined effects of both personal and contextual determinants on online conformity behaviour.

## 6   Conclusion

While age has been identified as a critical conformity determinant in offline groups, its effects on online conformity remained unclear. Hence, this study investigates effects of age and related stereotypes on susceptibility to conformity influences in young and middle-aged adults, as they complete stereotypically age-biased tasks in an online chatroom. Our results indicate that in the absence of explicit information of peer competency, both young and middle-aged adults stereotypically perceived competency of their online peers based on assumed peer age (indicated through usernames of peers) - establishing the existence of age stereotypes in online groups. Furthermore, such stereotypical perceptions were also seen to influence the conformity behaviour of our participants. We note that both young and middle-aged participants conformed to their older or younger counterparts, when attempting tasks that are stereotypically perceived to be well known to the respective age group. Our qualitative data provides further evidence that in the presence of user cues that indicate peer age, the effect of traditional *informational* influences on online conformity was further heightened by age-related stereotypical perceptions. We discuss how our findings encourage designers of online group settings to carefully reconsider if embedding user cues in platform design is value-adding from the perspective of the users as well as the platform. Furthermore, we promote the use of online user representations that are devoid of age cues (*e.g.*, identicons or site-specific age-neutral avatars instead of anthropomorphic (human-like) avatars or real photographs of users) - especially in contexts where age cues could trigger age-stereotypical perceptions of peer competency. In conclusion, our results highlight the need for exploring alternative online user representations and platform specific indicators of peer competency to minimise detrimental implications of stereotypical conformity in online groups.

# References

1. Akçayır, M., Dündar, H., Akçayır, G.: What makes you a digital native? Is it enough to be born after 1980? Comput. Hum. Behav. **60**, 435–440 (2016)
2. Araújo, C.S., Meira, W., Almeida, V.: Identifying stereotypes in the online perception of physical attractiveness. In: Spiro, E., Ahn, Y.-Y. (eds.) SocInfo 2016. LNCS, vol. 10046, pp. 419–437. Springer, Cham (2016). https://doi.org/10.1007/978-3-319-47880-7_26
3. Asch, S.E.: Effects of group pressure upon the modification and distortion of judgements. In: Groups, Leadership and Men, pp. 177–190. Carnegie Press, Oxford, England (1951)
4. Asch, S.E.: Opinions and social pressure. Sci. Am. **193**(5), 31–35 (1955)
5. Barkhuus, L., Tashiro, J.: Student socialization in the age of facebook. In: Proceedings of the SIGCHI Conference on Human Factors in Computing Systems, CHI 2010, New York, NY, USA, pp. 133–142. ACM (2010)
6. Bates, D., Mächler, M., Bolker, B., Walker, S.: Fitting linear mixed-effects models using LME4. J. Stat. Softw. **67**(1), 1–48 (2015)
7. Baym, N.K.: Personal Connections in the Digital Age. Wiley, Hoboken (2015)
8. Beran, T., Drefs, M., Kaba, A., Al Baz, N., Al Harbi, N.: Conformity of responses among graduate students in an online environment. Internet High. Educ. **25**, 63–69 (2015)
9. Blake, R.R., Helson, H., Mouton, J.S.: The generality of conformity behavior as a function of factual anchorage. Difficulty of task, and amount of social pressure. J. Pers. **25**(3), 294–305 (1957)
10. Bolker, B.M., et al.: Generalized linear mixed models: a practical guide for ecology and evolution. Trends Ecol. Evol. **24**(3), 127–135 (2009)
11. Bond, R.: Group size and conformity. Group Process. Intergroup Relat. **8**(4), 331–354 (2005)
12. Braun, V., Clarke, V.: Using thematic analysis in psychology. Qual. Res. Psychol. **3**(2), 77–101 (2006)

13. Broady, T., Chan, A., Caputi, P.: Comparison of older and younger adults' attitudes towards and abilities with computers: implications for training and learning. Br. J. Edu. Technol. **41**(3), 473–485 (2010)
14. Brody, G.H., Stoneman, Z.: Peer imitation: an examination of status and competence hypotheses. J. Genet. Psychol. **146**(2), 161–170 (1985)
15. Brzozowski, M.J., Adams, P., Chi, E.H.: Google+ communities as plazas and topic boards. In: Proceedings of the 33rd Annual ACM Conference on Human Factors in Computing Systems, CHI 2015, New York, NY, USA, pp. 3779–3788. ACM (2015)
16. Christofides, E., Islam, T., Desmarais, S.: Gender stereotyping over instant messenger: the effects of gender and context. Comput. Hum. Behav. **25**(4), 897–901 (2009)
17. Cinnirella, M., Green, B.: Does 'cyber-conformity' vary cross-culturally? Exploring the effect of culture and communication medium on social conformity. Comput. Hum. Behav. **23**(4), 2011–2025 (2007)
18. Cohen, J.: Statistical Power Analysis for the Behavioral Sciences. Lawrence Erlbaum Associates, Hillsdale (1988)
19. Colliander, J.: This is fake news: investigating the role of conformity to other users' views when commenting on and spreading disinformation in social media. Comput. Hum. Behav. **97**, 202–215 (2019)
20. Conaway, W., Bethune, S.: Implicit bias and first name stereotypes: what are the implications for online instruction? Online Learn. **19**(3), 162–178 (2015)
21. Costanzo, P.R., Reitan, H.T., Shaw, M.E.: Conformity as a function of experimentally induced minority and majority competence. Psychon. Sci. **10**(10), 329–330 (1968)
22. Costanzo, P.R., Shaw, M.E.: Conformity as a function of age level. Child Dev. **37**, 967–975 (1966)
23. Deutsch, M., Gerard, H.B.: A study of normative and informational social influences upon individual judgment. Psychol. Sci. Public Interest **51**(3), 629–636 (1955)
24. Dimock, M.: Defining generations: where millennials end and generation z begins. Pew Res. Center **17**(1), 1–7 (2019)
25. Fiske, S.T.: Stereotyping, prejudice, and discrimination. Handb. Soc. Psychol. **2**(4), 357–411 (1998)
26. Fleiss, J.L., Levin, B., Paik, M.C.: Statistical Methods for Rates and Proportions. Wiley, Hoboken (2013)
27. Gerard, H.B., Wilhelmy, R.A., Conolley, E.S.: Conformity and group size. J. Pers. Soc. Psychol. **8**(1, Pt.1), 79–82 (1968)
28. Goncalves, J., Kostakos, V., Venkatanathan, J.: Narrowcasting in social media: effects and perceptions. In: 2013 IEEE/ACM International Conference on Advances in Social Networks Analysis and Mining (ASONAM 2013), pp. 502–509. IEEE (2013)
29. Goncalves, J., Liu, Y., Xiao, B., Chaudhry, S., Hosio, S., Kostakos, V.: Increasing the reach of government social media: a case study in modeling government-citizen interaction on Facebook. Policy Internet **7**(1), 80–102 (2015)
30. Gonzalez, L., Loureiro, Y.K.: When can a photo increase credit? The impact of lender and borrower profiles on online peer-to-peer loans. J. Behav. Exp. Financ. **2**, 44–58 (2014)
31. Gwosdz, M.M.: Stack overflow badges explained, April 2021. https://stackoverflow.blog/2021/04/12/stack-overflow-badges-explained. Accessed 29 May 2021

32. Haferkamp, N., Eimler, S.C., Papadakis, A.M., Kruck, J.V.: Men are from mars, women are from venus? Examining gender differences in self-presentation on social networking sites. Cyberpsychol. Behav. Soc. Netw. **15**(2), 91–98 (2012)

33. Hair, J.F., Black, W.C., Babin, B.J., Anderson, R.E., Tatham, R.: Multivariate Data Analysis. Pearson, New Jersey (2010)

34. Hasler, B.S., Tuchman, P., Friedman, D.: Virtual research assistants: replacing human interviewers by automated avatars in virtual worlds. Comput. Hum. Behav. **29**(4), 1608–1616 (2013)

35. Hullman, J., Adar, E., Shah, P.: The impact of social information on visual judgments. In: Proceedings of the SIGCHI Conference on Human Factors in Computing Systems, CHI 2011, New York, NY, USA, pp. 1461–1470. ACM (2011)

36. Hummert, M.L., Garstka, T.A., Shaner, J.L., Strahm, S.: Stereotypes of the elderly held by young, middle-aged, and elderly adults. J. Gerontol. **49**(5), P240–P249 (1994)

37. Insko, C.A., Smith, R.H., Alicke, M.D., Wade, J., Taylor, S.: Conformity and group size: the concern with being right and the concern with being liked. Pers. Soc. Psychol. Bull. **11**(1), 41–50 (1985)

38. Jersin, J.: Announcing skill assessments to help you showcase your skills, September 2019. https://blog.linkedin.com/2019/september/17/announcing-skill-assessments-to-help-you-showcase-your-skills. Accessed 29 May 2021

39. Joinson, A.N.: Looking at, looking up or keeping up with people?: motives and use of Facebook. In: Proceedings of the SIGCHI Conference on Human Factors in Computing Systems, CHI 2008, New York, NY, USA, pp. 1027–1036. ACM (2008)

40. Kessler, E.M., Rakoczy, K., Staudinger, U.M.: The portrayal of older people in prime time television series: the match with gerontological evidence. Ageing Soc. **24**(4), 531–552 (2004)

41. Klein, R.L.: Age, sex, and task difficulty as predictors of social conformity. J. Gerontol. **27**(2), 229–236 (1972)

42. Klein, R.L., Birren, J.E.: Age differences in social conformity on a task of auditory signal detection. In: Proceedings of the Annual Convention of the American Psychological Association. American Psychological Association (1972)

43. Klein, R.L., Birren, J.E.: Age, perceived self-competence and conformity: a partial explanation. In: Proceedings of the Annual Convention of the American Psychological Association. American Psychological Association (1973)

44. Kokkinakis, A.V., Lin, J., Pavlas, D., Wade, A.R.: What's in a name? Ages and names predict the valence of social interactions in a massive online game. Comput. Hum. Behav. **55**, 605–613 (2016)

45. Laporte, L., van Nimwegen, C., Uyttendaele, A.J.: Do people say what they think: social conformity behavior in varying degrees of online social presence. In: Proceedings of the 6th Nordic Conference on Human-Computer Interaction: Extending Boundaries, NordiCHI 2010, New York, NY, USA, pp. 305–314. ACM (2010)

46. Lee, E.J.: Effects of 'gender' of the computer on informational social influence: the moderating role of task type. Int. J. Hum Comput Stud. **58**(4), 347–362 (2003)

47. Lee, E.J.: Effects of gendered character representation on person perception and informational social influence in computer-mediated communication. Comput. Hum. Behav. **20**(6), 779–799 (2004)

48. Lee, E.J.: When and how does depersonalization increase conformity to group norms in computer-mediated communication? Commun. Res. **33**(6), 423–447 (2006)

49. Lee, E.J.: Wired for gender: experientiality and gender-stereotyping in computer-mediated communication. Media Psychol. **10**(2), 182–210 (2007)

50. Lee, Y.H., Xiao, M., Wells, R.H.: The effects of avatars' age on older adults' self-disclosure and trust. Cyberpsychol. Behav. Soc. Netw. **21**(3), 173–178 (2018)
51. Liu, Y., Venkatanathan, J., Goncalves, J., Karapanos, E., Kostakos, V.: Modeling what friendship patterns on Facebook reveal about personality and social capital. ACM Trans. Comput. Hum. Interact. (TOCHI) **21**(3), 1–20 (2014)
52. Maruyama, M., Robertson, S.P., Douglas, S., Raine, R., Semaan, B.: Social watching a civic broadcast: understanding the effects of positive feedback and other users' opinions. In: Proceedings of the 2017 ACM Conference on Computer Supported Cooperative Work and Social Computing, pp. 794–807 (2017)
53. Maruyama, M.T., Robertson, S.P., Douglas, S.K., Semaan, B.C., Faucett, H.A.: Hybrid media consumption: how tweeting during a televised political debate influences the vote decision. In: Proceedings of the 17th ACM Conference on Computer Supported Cooperative Work & Social Computing, pp. 1422–1432 (2014)
54. McKenna, K.Y., Green, A.S.: Virtual group dynamics. Group Dyn. Theory Res. Pract. **6**(1), 116–127 (2002)
55. Nosko, A., Wood, E., Molema, S.: All about me: disclosure in online social networking profiles: the case of Facebook. Comput. Hum. Behav. **26**(3), 406–418 (2010)
56. Olivier, J.: Twitter usernames: exploring the nature of online South African nicknames. Nomina Africana **28**(2), 51–74 (2014)
57. Pak, R., McLaughlin, A.C., Bass, B.: A multi-level analysis of the effects of age and gender stereotypes on trust in anthropomorphic technology by younger and older adults. Ergonomics **57**(9), 1277–1289 (2014)
58. Polanin, J.R., Snilstveit, B.: Converting between effect sizes. Campbell Syst. Rev. **12**(1), 1–13 (2016)
59. Posthuma, R.A., Campion, M.A.: Age stereotypes in the workplace: common stereotypes, moderators, and future research directions. J. Manag. **35**(1), 158–188 (2009)
60. Reynolds, B., Venkatanathan, J., Gonçalves, J., Kostakos, V.: Sharing ephemeral information in online social networks: privacy perceptions and behaviours. In: Campos, P., Graham, N., Jorge, J., Nunes, N., Palanque, P., Winckler, M. (eds.) INTERACT 2011. LNCS, vol. 6948, pp. 204–215. Springer, Heidelberg (2011). https://doi.org/10.1007/978-3-642-23765-2_14
61. Rosander, M., Eriksson, O.: Conformity on the internet-the role of task difficulty and gender differences. Comput. Hum. Behav. **28**(5), 1587–1595 (2012)
62. Rose, J., Mackey-Kallis, S., Shyles, L., Barry, K., Biagini, D., Hart, C., Jack, L.: Face it: the impact of gender on social media images. Commun. Q. **60**(5), 588–607 (2012)
63. Rosenberg, L.: Group size, prior experience, and conformity. Psychol. Sci. Public Interest **63**(2), 436–437 (1961)
64. Selwyn, N.: The digital native–myth and reality. ASLIB Proc. New Inf. Perspect. **61**(4), 364–379 (2009)
65. Sharma, E., De Choudhury, M.: Mental health support and its relationship to linguistic accommodation in online communities. In: Proceedings of the 2018 CHI conference on Human Factors in Computing Systems, pp. 1–13 (2018)
66. Short, J., Williams, E., Christie, B.: The Social Psychology of Telecommunications. Wiley, Hoboken (1976)
67. Stang, D.J.: Ineffective deception in conformity research: some causes and consequences. Eur. J. Soc. Psychol. **6**(3), 353–367 (1976)
68. Strano, M.M.: User descriptions and interpretations of self-presentation through Facebook profile images. Cyberpsychol. J. Psychosoc. Res. Cyberspace **2**(2) (2008)

69. Sukumaran, A., Vezich, S., McHugh, M., Nass, C.: Normative influences on thoughtful online participation. In: Proceedings of the SIGCHI Conference on Human Factors in Computing Systems, pp. 3401–3410 (2011)
70. Thomas, M.: Deconstructing Digital Natives: Young People, Technology, and the New Literacies. Taylor & Francis, Routledge (2011)
71. Turner, A.: Generation z: technology and social interest. J. Ind. Psychol. **71**(2), 103–113 (2015)
72. Van Berkel, N., Goncalves, J., Hettiachchi, D., Wijenayake, S., Kelly, R.M., Kostakos, V.: Crowdsourcing perceptions of fair predictors for machine learning: a recidivism case study. Proc. ACM Hum. Comput. Interact. **3**(CSCW), 1–21 (2019)
73. Venkatanathan, J., Karapanos, E., Kostakos, V., Gonçalves, J.: Network, personality and social capital. In: Proceedings of the 4th Annual ACM Web Science Conference, pp. 326–329 (2012)
74. Walker, M.B., Andrade, M.G.: Conformity in the Asch task as a function of age. J. Soc. Psychol. **136**(3), 367–372 (1996)
75. Walker, M., Vetter, T.: Changing the personality of a face: perceived big two and big five personality factors modeled in real photographs. J. Pers. Soc. Psychol. **110**(4), 609–624 (2016)
76. Wijenayake, S., van Berkel, N., Goncalves, J.: Bots for research: minimising the experimenter effect. In: International Workshop on Detection and Design for Cognitive Biases in People and Computing Systems, CHI 2020 Workshop, ACM (2020)
77. Wijenayake, S., van Berkel, N., Kostakos, V., Goncalves, J.: Measuring the effects of gender on online social conformity. Proc. ACM Hum. Comput. Interact. **3**(CSCW), 1–24 (2019)
78. Wijenayake, S., van Berkel, N., Kostakos, V., Goncalves, J.: Impact of contextual and personal determinants on online social conformity. Comput. Hum. Behav. **108**(106302), 1–11 (2020)
79. Wijenayake, S., van Berkel, N., Kostakos, V., Goncalves, J.: Quantifying the effect of social presence on online social conformity. Proc. ACM Hum. Comput. Interact. **4**(CSCW1), 1–22 (2020)
80. Wijenayake, S., Hettiachchi, D., Hosio, S., Kostakos, V., Goncalves, J.: Effect of conformity on perceived trustworthiness of news in social media. IEEE Internet Comput. **25**(1), 12–19 (2021)
81. Winter, S., Brückner, C., Krämer, N.C.: They came, they liked, they commented: social influence on Facebook news channels. Cyberpsychol. Behav. Soc. Netw. **18**(8), 431–436 (2015)
82. Zhu, H., Huberman, B., Luon, Y.: To switch or not to switch: Understanding social influence in online choices. In: Proceedings of the SIGCHI Conference on Human Factors in Computing Systems, CHI 2012, New York, NY, USA, pp. 2257–2266. ACM (2012)

# Us Vs. Them – Understanding the Impact of Homophily in Political Discussions on Twitter

Danula Hettiachchi[(✉)] [iD], Tanay Arora, and Jorge Goncalves[iD]

School of Computing and Information Systems, The University of Melbourne,
Melbourne, Australia
contact@danulahettiachchi.com

**Abstract.** Analysing homophily, i.e. people's tendency to associate with others with similar social attributes, can help us unravel and better understand user behaviour in social media. In our work, we analyse the impact of homophily in discussions regarding the Citizenship Amendment Act (CAA) on Twitter. The Indian Government enacted CAA to provide relaxation in the citizenship process to religious minorities in three neighbouring countries. While it was lauded by many, it also fuelled backlash amongst some Indian citizens, resulting in the emergence of two distinctive political dispositions regarding this matter. We collected 78,004 Tweets, including 11,794 original Tweets during a period of two weeks shortly after the ruling, and examined ways of potentially reducing homophily and therefore minimise the presence of *echo chambers*. In particular, we investigated users' political dispositions and expressed sentiment, and how these two social attributes influence homophilic social ties and interactions. Further, we discuss how our findings can be used in social networks to allow people with diverse viewpoints and emotional attitudes to interact with each other in a positive and constructive manner.

**Keywords:** Social media · Homophily · Twitter · Political discussion

## 1 Introduction

People tend to make connections and interact more with people who are similar to themselves in social characteristics such as demographics, occupation and political affiliations. This general social phenomenon, known as homophily, implies that distinction in social characteristics renders network distance, i.e. the number of connections through which any piece of information must travel to connect two individuals [59]. Homophily is also pervasive within online social networks and influences information propagation characteristics [22], which has broader implications on how people seek to form social ties [26], interact with online content [23], and develop common interests over social media channels [46].

© IFIP International Federation for Information Processing 2021
Published by Springer Nature Switzerland AG 2021
C. Ardito et al. (Eds.): INTERACT 2021, LNCS 12935, pp. 476–497, 2021.
https://doi.org/10.1007/978-3-030-85610-6_27

While prior work has investigated homophily in social networks, there is limited understanding on prospects of reducing homophily in networks and promoting the positive interactions between users with different views and emotional attitudes, particularly in the Global South. Thus, we analyse homophily based on the network ties and the content generated over Twitter amidst an Indian political scenario, in which polarity among two-parties led to violent protests.

The Citizenship Amendment Act (CAA), was enacted by the Government of India on 11th December 2019 to grant citizenship to illegal migrants of Hindu, Sikh, Buddhist, Jain, Parsi, and Christian religious minorities, who escaped persecution from Pakistan, Bangladesh and Afghanistan before December 2014 or feared persecution in those countries [47]. The Act relaxed the residence requirement for naturalisation to such persecuted minorities. While it witnessed widespread support within the country, there was a backlash too. It was criticised as discriminatory based on religion since Muslims, in particular, were left out of the scope of the citizenship eligibility criterion in the Act [17,63]. The Act gave rise to two polarising mass movements, one in the support for the Act, and one entirely protesting against it. During these events, Twitter became an active channel for disseminating information regarding the implications of the Act and fostered widespread discussions within and across communities.

Twitter is an open information network and an active platform for social and political engagement and discussions among politicians, social activists and the general public alike [2,6,25,27,66,70]. In the past, despite facilitating many popular online movements like #MeToo [57,80], #BlackLivesMatter [46], or against police brutalities via #NYPD [51], Twitter and other social media channels have been under a critical lens of social activists, journalist as well as academics. They have actively voiced their concerns over social media networks playing a significant role in polarising people and placing them in their own ideological bubbles, popularly coined as 'echo-chambers' [72] or 'filter-bubbles' [65]. Although there is empirical evidence in academia that suggests that homophilic attitudes give rise to the creation of polarised communities or 'echo-chambers' [32,65,72,79], other studies contradict such claims [5,12,49].

Although there are broader studies on the effect of homophily along the party lines [52], few studies examine the impact of political dispositions on homophily in online spaces [20]. Moreover, the role of sentimental attitudes in examining homophilic behaviour in online spaces has not been studied together with political dispositions [38]. Only a few studies have drawn a comparison between the two social attributes [15]. Further, there is no consensus on whether content similarity is a driving factor for homophilic ties [1,19,31]. In this study, we analyse homophily based on political disposition and sentiments expressed over Twitter encircling the public discourse on Twitter over CAA and draw a comparison over the role of each attribute in giving rise to political homophily within the network. We collected Twitter data with the keyword #CAA for a period of two weeks shortly after the ruling using the Twitter Standard API. Initially, we classified all users based on political orientation and sentiment polarity. Our approach has been adapted from the works of Caetano et al. [15] who studied homophily in the context of 2016 US presidential elections. Then for each user group, we aim to uncover homophily. We also examine how the use of common hashtags and similar topical interests impact homophily.

Our findings reveal that political disposition was prevalent in how people formed social ties. A high magnitude of homophilic behaviour was observed in terms of interactions, engagement, again majorly due to the users' political disposition. Informed by our findings, we reflect on several design recommendations and future directions which can separate users from their ideological bubbles and expose them to more different views over social media channels to foster inclusiveness, a cornerstone of democracy.

## 2  Related Work

### 2.1  Political Homophily

Political homophily remains a common research area for sociologists, political psychologists, scientists and scholars in social computing alike. According to Pew Research, in the past two decades, the number of Americans with mixed ideologies has seen a significant decline and political dispositions have become distinctively liberal or conservatives [67]. For instance, in 1960, approximately 5% of Americans felt displeased with their children marrying outside the party lines, whereas by 2010 the numbers shot up to 50% for Republicans and 30% for Democrats [49]. The implications of political homophily are also quite significant in the corridors of public administration. Past research in the US [29] and South Korea [49] provide empirical evidence that similar political ideologies increase the likelihood of inter-organisational coordination and reduce the transactional cost in the collective effort of decision making. In another study concerning public life, Iyengar and Westwood [50] demonstrate the effects of political partisanship in a survey-based experiment in which individuals were asked to evaluate candidates' profiles for high-school scholarships. They found partisans were more biased towards their fellow partisans in granting the scholarships.

Nonetheless, political homophily has likely implications when it comes to our interpersonal preferences. Huber and Malhotra [42] reveal that people are more likely to engage with or show interest in profiles which are more politically compatible to them when selecting a dating partner in contemporary times. Interestingly, in the past, political similarity has taken precedence over other influential factors like ethnicity or education. In the US, it has been alleged that the Democrats and Republicans are more likely to move to neighbourhoods which they deem more politically harmonious [67], popularly coined as 'partisan sorting' [8]. However, experimental and survey-based studies [30,61] report that although politically harmonious communities may be more desirable or highly rated by individuals [44], it does not take precedence over other factors, such as affordability.

## 2.2   Role of Social Media

Prior work highlight different social or cultural factors that are dominant in sorting people in their ideological cocoons. Within these decades, while other social, cultural, legal developments remain a driver for the mass polarisation across societies [67], one of the reasons which academics attribute to growing political homophily is selective exposure or confirmation bias over social media channels and news portals. Lewicka [53] describes confirmation bias as a 'survival equipment' for humans, as humans we have a tendency to automate our routines in a way to obtain preferential results free from futile deliberations in order to keep our mind space centered around more important life decisions. For example, investigating the preferences for media consumption, Iyengar and Hahn [48] reported that Republicans preferred Fox News as their preferred media source and avoided news from CNN and NPR, whereas the Democrats displayed the exact opposite behaviour.

In the context of social media, selective exposure has been studied on the basis of structurality of the network as well on the content with which people interact. Within a social network, users are treated as nodes, and edges are treated as relationships among users. Himelboim et al. [39] developed a structure-based cluster analysis method to discover patterns of selective exposure among conservatives and liberals over the U.S. President's State of the Union speech in 2012. The analysis demonstrated distinctive clusters consisting of only self-identified conservative users, while the liberal clusters illustrated a mix of self-identified liberals and mainstream media organisations. Additionally, it can be inferred from the findings that the conservative users are less likely to form links with the traditional media houses, a pattern also observed in other work [40]. In another study over Twitter, Williams et al. [79] reveal a high presence of communities with strong attitudes (activists or sceptics) with very minimal presence of moderate communities over the debate on climate change. A similar observation has been highlighted in other studies [4,19] which have showcased strong structural connections among ideologically similar users.

On the other hand, studies have suggested that social media conversations around controversial topics tend to exhibit a high level of emotions corresponding to political views or opinions [31]. Additionally, it also has been observed that public discourse around political issues comprises highly negative emotions [3], while on the contrary some studies suggest that political discussions are dominated by positive expressions [84]. Therefore, it can be expected that people may take up similar political dispositions based on the sentiments expressed during a public debate over a political issue, given the relationship between attitudes and political behaviour have been longitudinally studied in the past [43]. Moreover, the role of content on social media in diffusing selective exposure cannot be underestimated. Although content over Twitter can take many forms, this study focuses on tweet text, hashtags and user replies. Researches in the past have shown that the aggregated hashtags facilitate engagement where conversations around particular key issues or events happen [13,14]. Hashtags may encourage similar users to use similar hashtags while other users might be left out of the discussion. Goncalves et al. [31] were able to predict users' political leaning using natural language processing techniques and discovered latent semantic layers by aggregating their hashtag usage. Previous work also suggests that users using a mixed of ideological hashtags were able to produce more inter-ideological interactions than those who mostly use partisan hashtags [20]. On the contrary, although in the context of a cause related marketing campaign, Xu et al. [81] suggest that use of common hashtags increases the likelihood of like-minded people interacting more and at the same time alienating other users. Therefore, it becomes important to analyse whether usage of common hashtags causes people to segregate themselves into distinctive communities.

When it comes to evaluating content similarity, researchers have made use of machine learning techniques to explore semantic similarity between tweet texts. Unsupervised machine learning algorithms such as Latent Dirichlet Allocation (LDA) [9] have been useful in discovering users' topical interests across tweet texts. Wang et al. [78] present strong evidence by employing multiple community detection algorithms over follower topology of the network and demonstrate that the structure-based communities generate common interests among the community members. Kang and Lerman [52] investigated topical interests of users by using lists, lists on Twitter are like groups curated by users on Facebook. The research demonstrated that users who were more topically similar were more likely to be linked with a follower relationship than others who were less topically similar. However, a multi platform study in a wider context Bisgin et al. [7] found that the friendship ties were only 1% similar in their topical interests and over 95% of the friendship ties were less than 50% similar. Given such variations in the previous studies and the nature of the discourse, we are also interested in evaluating to what extent does topic similarity influence user connections and interactions within the network.

## 3   Methods

### 3.1   Dataset

In India, a large number of citizens engage with Twitter, and it has recorded a user base of 18.9 million active users as of 2020[1]. On Twitter, you can engage with other users by *following* a user, *retweeting* a tweet from another user, or *mentioning* the user in your own tweet. These engagements could be either unidirectional or reciprocal (*e.g.,* two users mentioning each other in their tweets). Users may also tag their tweets with a hashtag, usually with a '#' followed by the hashtag name. This functionality enables users to search tweets easily belonging to a certain category of hashtags. During the public discourse over the Citizenship Amendment Act (CAA), *#CAA* was a common trending hashtags frequently used by users on both sides of the discourse. However, there were various

---

[1] https://www.statista.com/statistics/242606/number-of-active-twitter-users-in-selected-countries.

hashtags used in different contexts during the discourse. *#ISupportCAA*, *#IndiaSupportsCAA* emerged as trending hashtags in support of CAA and *#IndiaDoesNotSupportCAA*, *#IndiaAgainstCAA* against CAA. In conversations both for and against the protest *#CAAProtest*, *#CAANRCProtest*, *#ShaheenBagh* (site of a major protest) seemed to be trending. However, post the riots in Delhi, *#DelhiViolence*, *#DelhiRiots2020*, *#DelhiBurning*, *#DelhiGenocide* were some of the common hashtags observed in the conversations pertaining to the violence in Delhi.

**Data Collection.** The data was collected on Twitter social network from 16th February 2020 to 1st March 2020 using the keyword #CAA through the official Twitter standard sandbox API. The mentioned duration is important due to two major geopolitical events; Delhi Riots, 2020 and President Trump's visit to India during the mentioned time period, when extensive discussions happened over Twitter regarding #CAA. We retrieved a total of 78,004 tweets with the majority being retweets (66,210) and the remaining 11,794 being original tweets posted by individuals.

As the focus of the study was on individual behaviour, we excluded all the tweets posted by media houses. However, tweets from political party handles were included, primarily because they can influence masses' opinion. Additionally, we excluded 215 tweets (1.8%) that were labelled as 'unsure' during the political analysis. The final dataset comprised a total of 9,072 original tweets posted by a total of 5,940 users. Regarding connections, the dataset contained 63,065 (reciprocal) and 145,163 (unidirectional) follow connections, 298 (reciprocal) and 1746 (unidirectional) retweet connections, and 108 (reciprocal) and 2610 (unidirectional) mention connections.

## 3.2   User Classification

All the users were classified based on their political standing (Pro-CAA, Anti-CAA, Neutral-CAA) and the sentiments derived post sentiment analysis (positive, negative) over their tweets. Consequently, 6 classes of users were obtained with the different combinations of the categorisations mentioned above.

**Political Analysis.** In this step, we manually labelled and categorised users into three political classes such as Pro-CAA, Anti-CAA and Neutral-CAA. Previous work has highlighted how analysing message content can help understand the behaviour of advocates of political campaigns [69]. Similarly, users' engagement within the community can also be identified based on the usage of hashtags [51]. For example, we categorised a user tweeting with *#IndiaSupportsCAA* as 'Pro-CAA', and similarly a user tweeting with *#IndiaAgainstCAA* as 'Anti-CAA'. However, hashtags like *#CAAProtests*, *#ShaheenBagh* or *#DelhiRiots2020* were common across all types of users.

In order to further understand the nature of the overall discourse over CAA and Delhi riots, we referred to popular knowledge available in the media [41,74] to formulate the classification criteria given in Table 1. Based on this criteria, we performed a semantic analysis over the tweets. Additionally, user profile attributes, such as profile description, were analysed to help classify each user's political orientation. We conducted the classification where two authors come from the Indian subcontinent, and one author is an Indian national and a proficient speaker of the two main languages of India. Furthermore, Hindi (the main language in India) and Urdu (predominantly spoken by Muslims, disadvantaged by the proposed act) are mutually intelligible languages. During this process, we excluded 215 tweets for which we could not determine the political class. This included tweets in languages such as Tamil, Telugu and Malayalam that are not directly related to the main parties involved in the CAA debate.

**Table 1.** Political classification criteria

| Political orientation | Description |
|---|---|
| Pro CAA | In support of Government, BJP or party leaders, or criticising the opposition |
| | Criticising the protests or people who support the protests |
| | Affiliated with BJP |
| | Maligning Muslims |
| Anti CAA | Criticising Government, BJP or party leaders, or supporting the opposition |
| | Supporting the protests or people who support the protests |
| | Affiliation with opposition parties |
| | Maligning Hindus |
| Neutral CAA | Quoting News Articles or Ground Reports |
| | Quoting |
| | Speaking in the interest of peace and harmony |
| | Condemning violence from a neutral standpoint |

**Sentiment Analysis.** Sentiment Analysis or opinion mining is a sub-branch of Natural Language Processing used to computationally extract sentiments, opinions, attitudes from a given text, based on the subjectivity of the text. In this study, we used VADER [45], a lexicon and rule based sentiment analysis approach especially designed to analyse social media text. We opted to use VADER because it derives sentiments from a text, based on syntactical and grammatical relationships among the words in a text. VADER considers the polarity and the intensity of the sentiments expressed by incorporating the order of the words used within the text.

Additionally, VADER's judgement is sensitive to emoticons, sentiment related acronyms and common slang words. Before applying sentiment analysis over tweet text, we removed hyperlinks, special characters such as '&amp',

'/', other characters such as user mentions (@), hashtags (#), single quotes ('), and extra in line spacing.

The VADER sentiment analysis outputs four types of sentiment polarity scores i.e. positive, negative, neutral, and compound scores pertaining to the subjectivity of the text. The first three types of scores above signify the proportion of the text which lies under the three sentiment categories. We used the compound score, which provides a metric by summing all the valence scores across the three categories and then normalising the score between -1 (most extreme negative) and 1 (most extreme positive) [38]. To evaluate the sentiment polarity of all 5940 users, a mean of the compound score for all posts of a user was obtained. Using the mean compound score and a suitable threshold, we then classified the user profiles as positive (score $\geq 0.05$), negative (score $\leq -0.05$) or neutral (otherwise).

## 3.3  Homophily Analysis

In this study, the phenomenon of homophily is analysed under two categories: the structurality of the network i.e. follower, retweet and user mentions relationships; and on the basis of content generated within the network.

**Structural Analysis.** Our dataset contained 208,228 follow, 2,044 retweet, and 2,718 mention connections. Using Eq. (1) [19], homophily was calculated for different user groups considering the user class (*e.g.*, Pro-CAA, positive) and type of connection (unidirectional and reciprocal).

$$H_i = S_i/(S_i + D_i) \tag{1}$$

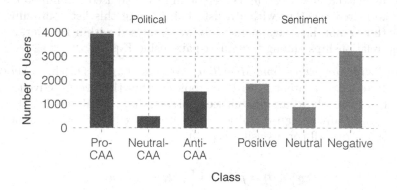

**Fig. 1.** Total count vs type of users

$H_i$ is the homophily index for each user group where $i$, $S_i$ represents the number of homogenous connections and $D_i$ represents the number of heterogeneous connections. As observed in Fig. 1, the overall dataset is predominantly biased towards Pro-CAA users and Negative users. In order to eliminate this bias, Currarini et al. [21] recommends the inbreeding homophily index developed by Coleman [18], which we calculate using Eq. 2.

$$IH_i = H_i - W_i/1 - W_i \qquad (2)$$

Here $IH_i$ is the normalised homophily index for each user group $i$ and $W_i$ is the probability of finding a user of group $i$ within the network i.e. we obtain $W_i$ by dividing group size of $i$ by the total number of users within the network. The higher the value of $IH_i$, greater the tendency of users of group $i$ to form stronger connections with the similar users.

**Content Analysis.** Next, we describe how we analysed tweets using hashtags and topic similarity.

*Hashtag Analysis:* Prior research shows how Twitter users leverage hashtags to disseminate ideas and opinions around social and political issues [83]. Additionally, hashtags streamline user navigation and help identify relevant conversation topics, leading to increased awareness and social media debates around the concerned issue [11,55]. Therefore, we argue that analysing structural ties among people who use common hashtags will help uncover homophily. Specifically, we want to know if people get influenced by their structural ties and contribute to conversations similar to their connections over a public discourse. In this hashtag analysis, we have excluded #CAA as it was the initial search criteria for collecting the overall dataset.

We used three steps to analyse homophily based on common usage of hashtags. First, all the hashtags $HT(u_i)$ used by each user $u_i$ were pooled into a user-hashtag matrix. Second, each user $u_i$ is compared with all the other users within the matrix, and if two users were found to have used a common hashtag, they were paired together within a list. Third, using this list containing user-pairs with common hashtags, homophily was analysed within follower, retweet, mention relationships among these user-pairs using Eqs. 1 & 2.

*Feature Extraction with Topic-Modelling:* We used Latent Dirichlet Allocation (LDA) [9] to extract latent features or topics within the tweets. Given a set of documents, LDA follows a probabilistic approach that postulates that the words used in each document can be subjected to a mixture of hidden or latent topics present in the overall corpus using Eq. (3)

$$p(\theta, z, w | \alpha, \beta) = p(\theta | \alpha) \prod_{n=1}^{N} p(z_n | \theta) \times p(w_n | z_n, \beta) \qquad (3)$$

In Eq. (3), $\theta$ represents topic distribution for document $\theta$, $w$ represents the per-topic distribution, i.e. a list of words contained within a topic along with the probability of the words occurring within the topics, $z$ represents per-document per-word topic word assignments. However, in this analysis only $\theta$ is of relevance as the goal is to identify relevant latent topics for each document.

Additionally, prior to creating the model there are several parameters to be supplied to the model i.e. the number of topics $K$ to be formulated and also hyper-parameters $\alpha$ and $\beta$ which control document-topic and word-topic distribution respectively. A higher value $\alpha$ results in distinctive topics, whereas a higher value results in a uniform distribution across topics, hence topics being more similar to each other. Similarly, a higher value of $\beta$ indicates that topics are likely to made of mix of words, with less weight on dominant terms, whereas lower values of $\beta$ result in topics made of specific terms with more weight on dominant terms.

In order to choose the appropriate number of topics, the value of $\alpha$ was set to 0.1 as we were interested in identifying distinctive topics which the tweets were composed of. Furthermore, model evaluation measures such as coherence score and perplexity were used to determine the values of $K$ and $\beta$ respectively. Coherence score is defined as the degree to which high probability words appearing in a word are semantically similar, perplexity is defined as the log-likelihood of how well the corpus fits the model. After a series of experimentation with $K = [2, 8, 14, 20, ....., 98]$ and $\beta = [0.01, 0.05, 0.1, 0.5, 1]$, the value of $K = 14$ and $\beta = 0.01$ were chosen.

Although, short tweet text pose serious implications to the performance of the topics model, previous work has shown that aggregating all tweets of users into a author-tweet matrix gives better performance than non-pooled corpus [60]. Additionally, since LDA is a bag of words model, prior to performing topic modelling the tweet texts were tokenized; stop words, URLs, special characters were removed, bigrams were created and further lemmatized into their root form. Finally, the resulting corpus was used to train the LDA model using the Python gensim implementation[2].

*Topic Similarity:* To measure the similarity between two users, we calculated the distance between the topical distribution of the users using Jensen-Shannon distance metric [24].

$$JSD(P||Q) = \sqrt{(0.5(D(P||M) + D(Q||M)))} \qquad (4)$$

Equation 4 shows Jensen Shannon distance (JSD) where $P$ and $Q$ are probabilistic distributions and $M = 0.5(P + Q)$. JSD is a smoothed version of the Kullback-Leibler divergence $(D)$ [24]. Topic similarity is $1 - JSD$ where an output of 1 indicates user pairs with most similar topics.

# 4    Results

## 4.1    Structural Analysis

Figure 2 shows the tendency of forming homophilic connections among various types of users within the political and sentiment polarity classes.

---

[2] https://radimrehurek.com/gensim/.

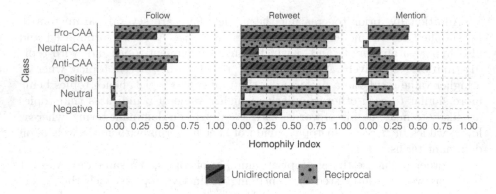

**Fig. 2.** Homophily-Index ($IH_i$) in Follow, Retweet and Mention Connections

**Follow Connections.** Within the political class as observed in Fig. 2 (left), pro-CAA and anti-CAA users both show high levels of inbreeding homophily, which means the presence of users with varied ideologies within the network does not affect the tendency to form follow-relationships. Moreover, the tendency to form homophilic ties is higher in reciprocal relationships than in unidirectional relationships among both pro and anti CAA users. In contrast, neutral-CAA users almost show baseline homophily, which suggests that they tend to follow pro-CAA users and anti-CAA users both by chance and not on the basis of personal preference [59].

Within the sentiment polarity class, we observe that positive and neutral sentiment users show almost baseline homophily, although negative sentiment users show marginal levels of homophily in both unidirectional and reciprocal ties.

**Retweet Connections.** Figure 2 (middle) shows homophily analysis results among both classes of users. Unlike the follow-relationships, similar political ideology as well as similar sentiment polarity drive users to mutually retweet their similar peers.

Within the political class, it can be observed that except for neutral-CAA users in unidirectional retweet-connections, the retweeting behaviour exhibited by pro-CAA, anti-CAA, neutral-CAA users is highly preferential towards their similar peers. These findings corroborate with the findings of prior work [20,79] suggesting that the retweeting behaviour of users is highly partisan during the discourse over a political issue.

On the other hand, within the sentiment polarity class, it is interesting to see that similarity in sentiments elicits more mutual retweet interactions than in unidirectional retweet connections. Although our results show that the users with negative sentiments do indeed show homophily in unidirectional connections, users were more likely to mutually retweet other users who resonated with their own emotional state. Therefore, sentiments in this scenario can be associated with a preference to retweet other users with similar sentiments, a behaviour also revealed in previous work by Stieglitz et al. [71] and Tsugawa and Ohsaki [75].

**Mention Connections.** In Fig. 2 (right), we observe that the mentions network appears to be less segregated than the follow and retweet networks.

Anti-CAA users display the highest level of homophily within unidirectional and lower levels of homophily within reciprocal connections. This behaviour indicates that the mutual interactions of anti-CAA users were more cross-ideological than in other unidirectional connections. Nonetheless, within reciprocal interactions, pro-CAA users appeared to be more organised among themselves than any other group, suggesting they indulged more in mutual discussions over the topic with other pro-CAA users. The neutral-CAA users display marginal levels of homophily within unidirectional and almost baseline homophily within reciprocal mention-connections. Hence, neutral-CAA users were interacting with pro and anti CAA users quite frequently.

Within the sentiment polarity class, generally all users exhibited similar modest levels of homophily in reciprocal mention-connections, indicating that users' sentiments did in fact elicit similar sentiments within the responses received by the users. However, only negative users showcase homophily in the unidirectional interactions, whereas positive users showcase heterophily and neutral users show almost baseline homophily. This behaviour suggests that posts containing negative sentiments tend to attract more attention from positive and neutral sentiment users.

## 4.2   Content Analysis

**Hashtag Analysis.** We present a bi-modal analysis of usage of common hashtags i.e. in terms of formed connections and the interactions between users with common usage of hashtags.

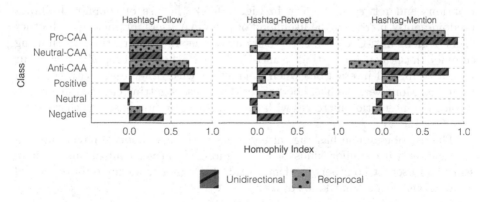

**Fig. 3.** Homophily-Index ($IH_i$) - Common Hashtag usage with Follow, Retweet and Mention Connections

*Follow Connections:* Figure 3 (left) shows that users who had follow-connections were more likely to use common hashtags across the political class. However, such behaviour is extreme among pro and anti CAA users than neutral-CAA users, which implies that in a political debate on Twitter, users get influenced by their followers or followee, and may contribute to a political debate with similar hashtags as their follower or followee.

In contrast, as seen in Fig. 3 (left), users who discuss CAA with positive and neutral sentiments were less likely to get influenced by their follower or followee, and contributed to the discussions with a variety of hashtags. Users with negative sentiments showed a certain level of homophily with their hashtag usage, influenced by their follow-connections, and more likely to occur in unidirectional than in reciprocal connections.

*Retweets:* As seen in Fig. 3 (middle), pro-CAA users who use common hashtags were highly likely to retweet each other and other users who used the same hashtags as them. Hence, the common usage of hashtags increased the likelihood of a pro-CAA user retweeting another pro-CAA user. On the other hand, there were no anti-CAA users who used common hashtags and retweeted each other in the dataset. However, they were highly likely to retweet another anti-CAA user if the other user used the same hashtag as them. Neutral-CAA users show low levels of homophily in unidirectional and low heterophily in reciprocal retweet connections, which means that they were more likely to get exposed to hashtags used by both pro and anti-CAA users.

Within the sentiment polarity class, users with negative and positive sentiments showed some level of homophily when they retweeted other users who used the same hashtags as them, although the likelihood of it remained low in comparison with political attitudes of users. Additionally, users with neutral sentiments in some cases did mutually retweeted other users with neutral attitudes, while their engagement in unidirectional relationships remained close to baseline homophily.

*Mentions:* Pro-CAA users showcase similar homophily behaviour in terms of mentions and retweets. As seen in Fig. 3 (left), the use of common hashtags predominantly increased the likelihood of pro-CAA users interacting with other users. Among anti-CAA users, there are more one-sided interactions when using common hashtags. Interestingly, anti-CAA users show heterophilic behaviour within reciprocal interactions when interacting with other users with common hashtags. Moreover, the likelihood of anti-CAA users getting engaged in a cross-ideological interaction increases with the usage of common hashtags than otherwise (see Fig. 2).

The use of common hashtags also decreased the likelihood of having mutual interactions with similar kinds of users among negative, neutral and positive sentiment users, who otherwise demonstrated a higher tendency to have mutual interactions with similar kinds of users.

**Topic Similarity and Link Percentage.** In this section, we evaluate the likelihood of topically similar users connecting or interacting directly with each other. We calculated the topic similarity for each user pair based on Jensen-Shannon distance as detailed in Sect. 3.3. The number of links between users is binned within the intervals of 0.2 Jensen-Shannon distance units, and the percentage of links in each bin was calculated.

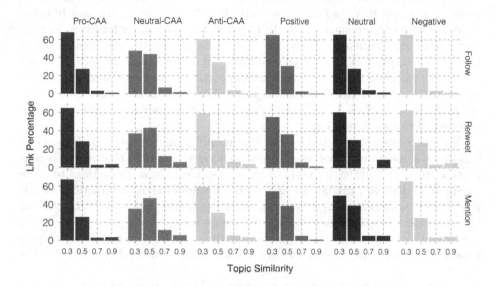

**Fig. 4.** Topic-similarity vs link-percentage

The results are consistent across all forms of ties i.e. follow, retweet and mention connections, see Fig. 4. Approximately 90% of the users across all kinds of connection were less than 60% similar in their topical interests. Based on these results, we show that similar topical interests do not influence how users seek ties or engage in discussions in a political debate over twitter.

## 5   Discussion

In this paper, we analyse homophily based on the structural ties and the user content on Twitter. We draw a comparison over two distinct social media user attributes, political ideology and sentiments, and further explore the significance of each attribute in the homophilic behaviour over a public discourse in India. In this section, we discuss our key findings and their practical and design implications, which may inspire future studies or implementations that aim to counter homophily in social networks.

### 5.1   Political Dispositions, Sentiments and Homophily

From the analysis of following and retweeting behaviour of users, more specifically within the political class, users seemed to follow and retweet their similar peers more often than dissimilar peers, a phenomenon also observed in other political debates on Twitter [19,31,79]. One potential cause of this homophilic behaviour in social media are personalised algorithms. Pariser [65] states that the personalisation of algorithms deployed to customise user experience exposes users to similar individuals and information repeatedly, more likely providing users easy access to information they are likely to resonate with and limiting exposure to cross-cutting content. In other words, without a feedback loop or user control on information feeds, the algorithms dictate the user experience of information consumption on social media [33,68]. From a social behaviour standpoint, Mason [58] pointed out that partisan sorting is no longer limited to one's stance on the current issues in contemporary times. It engulfs other dimensions of one's identity, which lead us to socially sort ourselves from others who form different identities or opinions.

We also observed that the extent of homophily among users' political class was lower in mention connections. Consequently, we can infer that mention connections provide a bridge for users to have cross-ideological interactions to some extent [79]. However, we did not explore the nature of those interactions in our analysis. It is difficult to argue whether the cross-ideological interactions diluted the diversified users or made them feel more strongly about their dispositions. The social identity theory [73] suggests that the propensity to negatively engage outside the community is another way of confirming membership within a community.

Furthermore, the role of sentiments expressed by users cannot be understated when users chose to retweet. As shown in our findings, users who mainly tweeted with similar sentiments were more likely to retweet each other. This finding corroborates with prior work [16,36] that suggests users' emotional attitudes or state influence the type of content a user may interact with. Moreover, individuals' mutual retweet behaviour in the sentiment polarity class indicates the formation of potential 'echo chambers'. We observed that users preferred to get exposed to tweets that primarily resonated with their sentimental attitudes over the discourse [40].

Overall, we conclude that political ideology was a more significant driving factor for homophilic ties over the discourse around CAA. The political ideology largely dictated with whom users preferred to form connections, retweeted or interacted with. Users' sentiments also influenced how the information was disseminated over the network. As observed in the previous research, Twitter communities grow around prominent opinion leaders who may be popular individuals, organisations, celebrities [35]. For example, in different contexts, journalists and media houses [13] and organisations [82] have emerged as influential opinion leaders during public discourses. A longitudinal study is needed to examine opinion leaders' role vs the impact of personalisation in creating homophilic ties or interactions.

Similarly, we observed that in a follow relationship, more specifically within the political class, users were more likely to use the hashtags common with their follow connections. They were also were more likely to retweet tweets of users with whom they have common hashtag usage. In other words, they were selectively exposed to hashtags that were popular in their social network, leading to selective exposure of information coming from users within the political class [4]. Additionally, this indicates that the usage of common hashtags remains a strong indicator of users segregating themselves into communities to express and also promote their ideological positions [51]. Interestingly, we noticed different behaviours across the mention connections. Pro-CAA users had more cross-ideological interactions when they did not use common hashtags as other users. However, they were highly likely to interact with other pro-CAA users whenever they used a common hashtag. In other words, their interactions became more selective with the use of common hashtags. On the contrary, when anti-CAA users used common hashtags, they were more likely to interact with users outside their ideological group. Hence, in this case, the usage of common hashtags diluted the homophily among anti-CAA users. This aried behaviour among users could also be due to the selectivity in using specific hashtags. According to Blevins et al. [10], the nature of the hashtags can be ideological (something that expresses viewpoints, positions) or conceptual (personal stories or interpretation of an event). Future studies can explore categorising hashtags further into ideological or conceptual to better understand the varied effects of homophily when using common hashtags.

Finally, based on prior research [7,78], we analysed the likelihood of users with high topic similarity to having a follow, retweet or mention relationship. Our results indicate that topically similar users are less likely to be connected. Interestingly, on the one hand, our findings suggest that connections or engagement among users could be driven by other factors such as social reputation [56], affinity [28], social capital [54,76], empathy [77], etc. and not topical interests. On the other hand, some topics may have attracted people with diverse ideologies and sentimental attitudes, exposing people to diverse views.

## 5.2   Towards Breaking the Ideological Barrier

We discuss several generalisable approaches to reduce homophily informed by our findings. In our work, political stance was the dominant factor in placing users into their ideological bubbles. Among politically engaged users, the connections and network interactions were centred around politically similar individuals. As a result, exposure to the content via hashtags also remained very selective. All these findings point towards extremely choice-based homophily [59]. Prior research has attempted addressing filter bubbles. Studying political behaviour, Nyhan and Reifler [64] indicate that direct exposure to counter opinions has mostly resulted in a phenomenon called the 'back-fire' effect [64], where people do not seem to value diversity. Hence, the recommendation systems in social media need to recommend opposing views indirectly. Some inspiration can be drawn from the work by Nagulendra and Vassileva [62] which proposed an interactive tool that visualise users' filter bubbles. The tool provides control over the algorithm by allowing users to see which topics and their connections are within their filter bubbles. Users can then choose to either stay or escape from the filter bubble. However, they only evaluated this design from a usability perspective, with less focus on the human-behaviour.

Such design suggestions seem relevant for our use case where politically engaged users were more connected with other similar users. Future research could gauge user behaviour when examining their filter bubbles containing their current connections and the users who share common topical interests but placed outside their filter bubbles. Additionally, future studies could explore whether and how people with similar topical interests get connected and continue to interact. Findings can lead to useful tools and features that can help reduce undesired homophily in social networks. We also note that in some instances, common hashtags can encourage cross-ideological interactions in politically engaged users. Hashtags can provide indirect exposure to opposing views. Tools such as the word cloud visualisation can help provide exposure to opposing views without angering users [34].

### 5.3    Limitations

We note several limitations in our work. First, we manually labelled the political disposition of users based on common knowledge in the media. While we assumed manual annotation is more reliable due to limited resources available around the topic, we acknowledge the potential for bias. Future research could extend our classification criteria and process. For instance, they can also utilise crowd wisdom in labelling users' political dispositions [37].

Second, our analysis was limited to tweet texts, replies and hashtags included in a tweet. Analysing the dissemination of tweets containing external URLs or links to news articles can provide further insights on selective content exposure. Mainly, understanding the trends in disseminating news articles from selected or varied sources and shared by friends within the network can provide deeper insight into users' propensity to diversify themselves or indulge in the process of 'self-brainwashing'.

Third, our final dataset was limited to 9,072 tweets across two weeks, which is not ideal for analysing and comparing topical interests. Future studies could perform topic-modelling on a larger corpus spanning over a longer duration. A broader dataset on politically sensitive issues can help discover more latent topics and the evolution of topics through temporal analysis.

## 6    Conclusion

This paper presents a homophily analysis using a Twitter dataset that includes a highly divisive public discourse in India. Our results indicate that the users' political dispositions predominantly dictate with whom users connect or interact with. Additionally, users also mutually retweet other users who resonate with their emotional states. However, user mentions provide scope for cross-ideological interactions, although the nature of such interactions require further investigation. With the use of common hashtags, the effect of homophily increases within follow and retweet relationships. Nevertheless, the usage of common hashtags with user mentions exhibit mixed outcomes. Pro-CAA users showed a preference to interact with other pro-CAA users. In contrast, anti-CAA users show the opposite behaviour. Hence, common usage of hashtags provides an opportunity for people with diverse points of views and emotional attitudes to interact with each other. Finally, we also show that users with congruent topical interests were less likely to connect or interact with each other, suggesting that topical similarity can bridge the users with different political dispositions or sentimental attitudes. Finally, we discuss how our findings can inform future research and implementations that aim to foster interactions among social media users with divergent viewpoints.

# References

1. Aiello, L.M., Barrat, A., Schifanella, R., Cattuto, C., Markines, B., Menczer, F.: Friendship prediction and homophily in social media. ACM Trans. Web (2012). https://doi.org/10.1145/2180861.2180866
2. Ausserhofer, J., Maireder, A.: National politics on Twitter. Inf. Commun. Soc. **16**(3), 291–314 (2013). https://doi.org/10.1080/1369118X.2012.756050
3. Baek, Y.M., Wojcieszak, M., Delli Carpini, M.X.: Online versus face-to-face deliberation: who? Why? What? With what effects? New Media Soc. (2012). https://doi.org/10.1177/1461444811413191
4. Barbera, P.: Birds of the same feather tweet together. Bayesian ideal point estimation using Twitter data. SSRN Electron. J. (2013). https://doi.org/10.2139/ssrn.2108098
5. Barberá, P.: How Social media reduces mass political polarization. Evidence from Germany, Spain, and the U.S. LXXIII Congress of the Midwest Political Science Association (2014)
6. Bekafigo, M.A., McBride, A.: Who tweets about politics? Soc. Sci. Comput. Rev. **31**(5), 625–643 (2013). https://doi.org/10.1177/0894439313490405
7. Bisgin, H., Agarwal, N., Xu, X.: A study of homophily on social media. World Wide Web (2012). https://doi.org/10.1007/s11280-011-0143-3
8. Bishop, B., Cushing, R.G.: The Big Sort: Why the Clustering of Like-Minded America is Tearing Us Apart. Mariner Books (2009)
9. Blei, D.M.: Probabilistic topic models. Commun. ACM (2012). https://doi.org/10.1145/2133806.2133826
10. Blevins, J.L., Lee, J.J., McCabe, E.E., Edgerton, E.: Tweeting for social justice in #Ferguson: affective discourse in Twitter hashtags. New Media Soc. (2019). https://doi.org/10.1177/1461444819827030
11. Bonilla, Y., Rosa, J.: #Ferguson: digital protest, hashtag ethnography, and the racial politics of social media in the United States. Am. Ethnol. (2015). https://doi.org/10.1111/amet.12112
12. Boxell, L., Gentzkow, M., Shapiro, J.: Is the internet causing political polarization? Evidence from demographics. Nat. Bureau Econ. Res. (2017). https://doi.org/10.3386/w23258
13. Bruns, A., Burgess, J.: The use of twitter hashtags in the formation of ad hoc publics. In: European Consortium for Political Research Conference, Reykjavík, 25–27 August 2011 (2011)

14. Bruns, A., Moon, B., Paul, A., Münch, F.: Towards a typology of hashtag publics: a large-scale comparative study of user engagement across trending topics. Commun. Res. Pract. (2016). https://doi.org/10.1080/22041451.2016.1155328
15. Caetano, J.A., Lima, H.S., Santos, M.F., Marques-Neto, H.T.: Using sentiment analysis to define twitter political users' classes and their homophily during the 2016 American presidential election. J. Internet Serv. Appl. (2018). https://doi.org/10.1186/s13174-018-0089-0
16. Chen, J., Liu, Y., Zou, M.: User emotion for modeling retweeting behaviors. Neural Netw. (2017). https://doi.org/10.1016/j.neunet.2017.08.006
17. CNN: Citizenship Amendment Bill explained: India's controversial bill that excludes Muslims. https://edition.cnn.com/2019/12/11/asia/india-citizenship-amendment-bill-intl-hnk/index.html
18. Coleman, J.: Relational analysis: the study of social organizations with survey methods. Human Organization (1958). https://doi.org/10.17730/humo.17.4.q5604m676260q8n7
19. Colleoni, E., Rozza, A., Arvidsson, A.: Echo chamber or public sphere? predicting political orientation and measuring political homophily in Twitter using big data. J. Commun. (2014). https://doi.org/10.1111/jcom.12084
20. Conover, M., Ratkiewicz, J., Francisco, M.: Political polarization on Twitter. ICWSM (2011). https://doi.org/10.1021/ja202932e
21. Currarini, S., Jackson, M.O., Pin, P.: An economic model of friendship: homophily, minorities, and segregation. Econometrica 77(4), 1003–1045 (2009). https://doi.org/10.3982/ECTA7528
22. De Choudhury, M., Sundaram, H., John, A., Seligmann, D.D., Kelliher, A.: "Birds of a Feather": does user homophily impact information diffusion in social media? (2010). http://arxiv.org/abs/1006.1702
23. De Salve, A., Guidi, B., Ricci, L., Mori, P.: Discovering homophily in online social networks. Mob. Netw. Appl. 23(6), 1715–1726 (12 (2018). https://doi.org/10.1007/s11036-018-1067-2
24. Endres, D.M., Schindelin, J.E.: A new metric for probability distributions (2003). https://doi.org/10.1109/TIT.2003.813506
25. Enli, G.S., Skogerbø, E.: Personalized campaigns in party-centred politics. Inf. Commun. Soc. 16(5), 757–774 (6 (2013). https://doi.org/10.1080/1369118X.2013.782330
26. Fiore, A.T., Donath, J.S.: Homophily in online dating: when do you like someone like yourself? In: Conference on Human Factors in Computing Systems - Proceedings (2005). https://doi.org/10.1145/1056808.1056919
27. Fraisier, O., Cabanac, G., Pitarch, Y., Besançon, R., Boughanem, M.: Uncovering like-minded political communities on Twitter. In: ICTIR 2017 - Proceedings of the 2017 ACM SIGIR International Conference on the Theory of Information Retrieval (2017). https://doi.org/10.1145/3121050.3121091
28. Gerbaudo, P.: Social media and populism: an elective affinity? Media Cult. Soc. 40(5), 745–753 (2018). https://doi.org/10.1177/0163443718772192
29. Gerber, E.R., Henry, A.D., Lubell, M.: Political homophily and collaboration in regional planning networks. Am. J. Polit. Sci. (2013). https://doi.org/10.1111/ajps.12011
30. Gimpel, J.G., Hui, I.S.: Seeking politically compatible neighbors? The role of neighborhood partisan composition in residential sorting. Polit. Geogr. (2015). https://doi.org/10.1016/j.polgeo.2014.11.003

31. Gonçalves, B., Perra, N., Vespignani, A.: Modeling users' activity on Twitter networks: validation of Dunbar's number. PLoS ONE (2011). https://doi.org/10.1371/journal.pone.0022656

32. Goncalves, J., Kostakos, V., Venkatanathan, J.: Narrowcasting in social media: effects and perceptions. In: IEEE/ACM International Conference on Advances in Social Networks Analysis and Mining, ASONAM 2013 (2013). https://doi.org/10.1145/2492517.2492570

33. Goncalves, J., Liu, Y., Xiao, B., Chaudhry, S., Hosio, S., Kostakos, V.: Increasing the reach of government social media: A case study in modeling government-citizen interaction on Facebook. Policy Internet (2015). https://doi.org/10.1002/poi3.81

34. Graells-Garrido, E., Lalmas, M., Quercia, D.: Data portraits: connecting people of opposing views (2013). https://arxiv.org/abs/1311.4658

35. Gruzd, A., Wellman, B., Takhteyev, Y.: Imagining Twitter as an imagined community. Am. Behav. Sci. (2011). https://doi.org/10.1177/0002764211409378

36. Guerra, P.C., Souza, R.C., Assunção, R.M., Meira, W.: Antagonism also flows through retweets: the impact of out-of-context quotes in opinion polarization analysis. In: Proceedings of the 11th International Conference on Web and Social Media, ICWSM 2017 (2017)

37. Hettiachchi, D., Goncalves, J.: Towards effective crowd-powered online content moderation. In: Proceedings of the 31st Australian Conference on Human-Computer-Interaction, pp. 342–346. ACM (2019). https://doi.org/10.1145/3369457.3369491

38. Himelboim, I., Cameron, K., Sweetser, K.D., Danelo, M., West, K.: Valence-based homophily on Twitter: network analysis of emotions and political talk in the 2012 presidential election. New Media Soc. (2016). https://doi.org/10.1177/1461444814555096

39. Himelboim, I., Mccreery, S., Smith, M.: Birds of a feather tweet together: integrating network and content analyses to examine cross-ideology exposure on Twitter. J. Comput. Mediat. Commun. (2013). https://doi.org/10.1111/jcc4.12001

40. Himelboim, I., Smith, M., Shneiderman, B.: Tweeting apart: applying network analysis to detect selective exposure clusters in Twitter. Commun. Methods Meas. (2013). https://doi.org/10.1080/19312458.2013.813922

41. Hindustan Times: #IndiaDoesNotSupportCAA takes Twitter by storm. https://www.hindustantimes.com/india-news/indiadoesnotsupportcaa-takes-twitter-by-storm/story-SwRmAoj4tEh2DY9OUK0mBJ.html

42. Huber, G.A., Malhotra, N.: Political homophily in social relationships: evidence from online dating behavior. J. Polit. (2017). https://doi.org/10.1086/687533

43. Huckfeldt, R.R., Sprague, J.: Citizens, politics and social. Communication (1995). https://doi.org/10.1017/cbo9780511664113

44. Hui, I.: Who is your preferred neighbor? Partisan residential preferences and neighborhood satisfaction. Am. Politics Res. (2013). https://doi.org/10.1177/1532673X13482573

45. Hutto, C.J., Gilbert, E.: VADER: a parsimonious rule-based model for sentiment analysis of social media text. In: Proceedings of the 8th International Conference on Weblogs and Social Media, ICWSM 2014 (2014)

46. Ince, J., Rojas, F., Davis, C.A.: The social media response to Black Lives Matter: how Twitter users interact with Black Lives Matter through hashtag use. Ethn. Racial Stud. (2017). https://doi.org/10.1080/01419870.2017.1334931

47. India Today: Everything you wanted to know about the CAA and NRC. https://www.indiatoday.in/india-today-insight/story/everything-you-wanted-to-know-about-the-caa-and-nrc-1630771-2019-12-23

48. Iyengar, S., Hahn, K.S.: Red media, blue media: evidence of ideological selectivity in media use. J. Commun. (2009). https://doi.org/10.1111/j.1460-2466.2008.01402.x
49. Iyengar, S., Sood, G., Lelkes, Y.: Affect, not ideology: a social identity perspective on polarization (2012). https://doi.org/10.1093/poq/nfs038
50. Iyengar, S., Westwood, S.J.: Fear and loathing across party lines: new evidence on group polarization. Am. J. Polit. Sci. (2015). https://doi.org/10.1111/ajps.12152
51. Jackson, S.J., Foucault Welles, B.: Hijacking #myNYPD: social media dissent and networked Counterpublics. J. Commun. (2015). https://doi.org/10.1111/jcom.12185
52. Kang, J.H., Lerman, K.: Using lists to measure homophily on twitter. In: AAAI Workshop - Technical Report (2012)
53. Lewicka, M.: Confirmation bias. In: Kofta, M., Weary, G., Sedek, G. (eds.) Personal Control in Action, pp. 233–258. Springer, Boston (1998). https://doi.org/10.1007/978-1-4757-2901-6_9
54. Liu, Y., Venkatanathan, J., Goncalves, J., Karapanos, E., Kostakos, V.: Modeling what friendship patterns on Facebook reveal about personality and social capital. ACM Trans. Comput. Hum. Interact. **21**(3),(2014). https://doi.org/10.1145/2617572
55. Lovejoy, K., Waters, R.D., Saxton, G.D.: Engaging stakeholders through Twitter: how nonprofit organizations are getting more out of 140 characters or less. Public Relat. Rev. (2012). https://doi.org/10.1016/j.pubrev.2012.01.005
56. Madden, M., Smith, A.: Reputation management and social media (2010)
57. Manikonda, L., Beigi, G., Liu, H., Kambhampati, S.: Twitter for sparking a movement, reddit for sharing the moment: #Metoo through the lens of social media (2018)
58. Mason, L.: Uncivil Agreement: How Politics Became Our Identity. University of Chicago Press (2018)
59. McPherson, M., Smith-Lovin, L., Cook, J.M.: Birds of a feather: homophily in social networks. Ann. Rev. Sociol. (2001). https://doi.org/10.1146/annurev.soc.27.1.415
60. Mehrotra, R., Sanner, S., Buntine, W., Xie, L.: Improving LDA topic models for microblogs via tweet pooling and automatic labeling. In: Proceedings of the 36th International ACM SIGIR Conference on Research and Development in Information Retrieval (2013). https://doi.org/10.1145/2484028.2484166
61. Mummolo, J., Nall, C.: Why partisans do not sort: the constraints on political segregation. J. Polit. (2017). https://doi.org/10.1086/687569
62. Nagulendra, S., Vassileva, J.: Understanding and controlling the filter bubble through interactive visualization: a user study. In: HT 2014 - Proceedings of the 25th ACM Conference on Hypertext and Social Media (2014). https://doi.org/10.1145/2631775.2631811
63. NPR: India Passes Controversial Citizenship Bill That Would Exclude Muslims. https://www.npr.org/2019/12/11/787220640/india-passes-controversial-citizenship-bill-that-would-exclude-muslims
64. Nyhan, B., Reifler, J.: When corrections fail: the persistence of political misperceptions. Polit. Behav. (2010). https://doi.org/10.1007/s11109-010-9112-2
65. Pariser, E.: Filter Bubble (2012). https://doi.org/10.3139/9783446431164
66. Park, C.S.: Does Twitter motivate involvement in politics? Tweeting, opinion leadership, and political engagement. Comput. Hum. Behav. (2013). https://doi.org/10.1016/j.chb.2013.01.044
67. Pew Research Center: The Partisan Divide on Political Values Grows Even Wider. Technical report (2017)

68. Rader, E., Gray, R.: Understanding user beliefs about algorithmic curation in the Facebook news feed. In: Conference on Human Factors in Computing Systems - Proceedings (2015). https://doi.org/10.1145/2702123.2702174
69. Ranganath, S., Hu, X., Tang, J., Liu, H.: Understanding and identifying advocates for political campaigns on social media. In: WSDM 2016 - Proceedings of the 9th ACM International Conference on Web Search and Data Mining (2016). https://doi.org/10.1145/2835776.2835807
70. Small, T.A.: What the hashtag? Inf. Commun. Soc. **14**(6), 872–895 (2011). https://doi.org/10.1080/1369118X.2011.554572
71. Stieglitz, S., Dang-Xuan, L.: Emotions and information diffusion in social media - sentiment of microblogs and sharing behavior. J. Manag. Inf. Syst. (2013). https://doi.org/10.2753/MIS0742-1222290408
72. Sunstein, C.R.: Republic.com 2.0 (2009). https://doi.org/10.5860/choice.45-5264
73. Tajfel, H., Turner, J.: An Integrative Theory of Inter-group Conflict. In: The social psychology of intergroup relations. Oxford University Press (1979)
74. The Financial Express: 'India Supports CAA' : PM Modi launches Twitter campaign to support Citizenship Act. https://www.financialexpress.com/india-news/india-supports-caa-pm-modi-launches-twitter-campaign-to-support-citizenship-act/1807380/
75. Tsugawa, S., Ohsaki, H.: On the relation between message sentiment and its virality on social media. Soc. Netw. Anal. Min. (2017). https://doi.org/10.1007/s13278-017-0439-0
76. Venkatanathan, J., Karapanos, E., Kostakos, V., Gonçalves, J.: Network, personality and social capital. In: ACM Web Science Conference, WebSci 2012, pp. 326–329. ACM (2012). https://doi.org/10.1145/2380718.2380760
77. Venkatanathan, J., Karapanos, E., Kostakos, V., Gonçalves, J.: A network science approach to modelling and predicting empathy. In: IEEE/ACM International Conference on Advances in Social Networks Analysis and Mining, ASONAM 2013, pp. 1395–1400. ACM (2013). https://doi.org/10.1145/2492517.2500295
78. Wang, F., Orton, K., Wagenseller, P., Xu, K.: Towards understanding community interests with topic modeling. IEEE Access (2018). https://doi.org/10.1109/ACCESS.2018.2815904
79. Williams, H.T., McMurray, J.R., Kurz, T., Hugo Lambert, F.: Network analysis reveals open forums and echo chambers in social media discussions of climate change. Glob. Environ. Chang. (2015). https://doi.org/10.1016/j.gloenvcha.2015.03.006
80. Xiong, Y., Cho, M., Boatwright, B.: Hashtag activism and message frames among social movement organizations: semantic network analysis and thematic analysis of Twitter during the #MeToo movement. Public Relat. Rev. (2019). https://doi.org/10.1016/j.pubrev.2018.10.014
81. Xu, S., Zhou, A.: Hashtag homophily in twitter network: examining a controversial cause-related marketing campaign. Comput. Hum. Behav. (2020). https://doi.org/10.1016/j.chb.2019.08.006
82. Xu, W.W., Sang, Y., Blasiola, S., Park, H.W.: Predicting opinion leaders in Twitter activism networks: the case of the Wisconsin recall election. Am. Behav. Sci. (2014). https://doi.org/10.1177/0002764214527091
83. Yang, G.: Narrative agency in hashtag activism: the case of #blacklivesmatter (2016). https://doi.org/10.17645/mac.v4i4.692
84. Yu, B., Kaufmann, S., Diermeier, D.: Exploring the characteristics of opinion expressions for political opinion classification. In: Proceedings of the 2008 International Conference on Digital Government Research (2008)

# Tangible Interaction

# A Lens-Based Extension of Raycasting for Accurate Selection in Dense 3D Environments

Carole Plasson[1](✉), Dominique Cunin[2](✉), Yann Laurillau[1](✉),
and Laurence Nigay[1](✉)

[1] Univ. Grenoble Alpes, CNRS, Grenoble INP, LIG, 38000 Grenoble, France
{Carole.Plasson,Yann.Laurillau,Laurence.Nigay}@univ-grenoble-alpes.fr
[2] Ecole Superieure d'Art et Design Grenoble-Valence, 26000 Valence, France
dominique.cunin@esad-gv.fr

**Abstract.** In mixed environments, the selection of distant 3D objects is commonly based on raycasting. To address the limitations of raycasting for selecting small targets in dense environments, we present *RayLens* an extended raycasting technique. *RayLens* is a bimanual selection technique, which combines raycasting with a virtual 2D magnification lens that can be remotely moved in 3D space using the non-dominant hand. We experimentally compared *RayLens* with a standard raycasting technique as well as with *RaySlider* an extension of raycasting based on a target expansion mechanism whose design is akin to *RayLens*. *RayLens* is considerably more accurate and more than 1.3× faster than raycasting for selecting small targets. Furthermore, *RayLens* is more than 1.6× faster than *RaySlider* in dense environments. Qualitatively, *RayLens* is easy-to-learn and the preferred technique making it a good candidate technique for general public usage.

**Keywords:** Augmented Reality · HMD · Pointing technique · Lens

## 1 Introduction

Tabletop Augmented Reality (AR) systems, combining a tangible physical surface and virtual objects, support a variety of applications such as architecture and urban design [14,42,43] (Fig. 1) as well as cultural heritage, visualization systems, and 3D modeling [14,46]. When interacting in tabletop AR, most objects are not directly reachable by hand due to the size of the table [6]. In 3D virtual and augmented environments, the selection of such distant objects is largely based on the raycasting metaphor. Raycasting techniques implement a ray generally held by the users to point at distant objects. However, raycasting techniques suffer from several limitations, especially in dense environments. Due to hand

**Electronic supplementary material** The online version of this chapter (https://doi.org/10.1007/978-3-030-85610-6_28) contains supplementary material, which is available to authorized users.

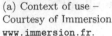

(a) Context of use –
Courtesy of Immersion
www.immersion.fr.

(b) Implemented augmented map of the district of a city. The targeted house is hidden behind another building (left); This house
is selected with *RayLens* (right). The pointed house turns yellow.

**Fig. 1.** Examples of augmented maps. (Color figure online)

tremors and human pointing accuracy, the selection of small objects can be difficult and longer distances to the objects amplify this difficulty. Besides, using
a standard implementation of raycasting, the first object intersecting the ray is
selected, making the selection of occluded objects difficult. Dense environments
with partially occluded objects are frequent in various applications of tabletop
AR as illustrated in the following scenario:

*A property developer presents to two purchasers a district of a city where
several houses are for sale. A 3D virtual model of this district is placed on the
table (Fig. 1a) and allows the purchasers to visualize the buildings, the streets,
and the surrounding shops. The property developer presents the houses for sale
in this district by selecting them on the 3D virtual maps. Some houses are distant
and therefore small. Moreover, as the building sizes are different, several houses
are hidden behind buildings (see the house for sale in red in Fig. 1b).*

This scenario illustrates the importance of overcoming the limitations of ray-
casting. A variety of techniques implement extensions of raycasting to improve
its performance in dense environments [4,11,22,27,47]. For occluded objects,
bendable rays [38] or rays with adjustable sizes [18,47,56] are two approaches.
For precision limitation, pointing facilitation mechanisms initially developed for
cursor-based 2D selection such as target expansion mechanisms [20] are applied
to extend raycasting [4,33]. However, such pointing facilitation is impacted by
the density of the environment and especially the proximity of distractors (i.e.
selectable objects which are not the current target) around a targeted object.

An alternative to facilitate object selection is to use zooming techniques [25].
For instance, a magnification effect can be done to enlarge objects located in
a specific area. In contrast to target expansion mechanisms, zooming is target-
agnostic and does not depend on the immediate surrounding of the targeted
object. Zooming is then "especially relevant on dense populations of targets" [12].
Lens-based selection techniques [53] using magnification are mainly developed
for 2D environments [1,37,39,40]. Very few AR/VR studies have used them for
selection tasks in 3D environments. Also, no study has considered magnification
lenses as a pointing facilitation mechanism for accurate 3D selection in dense
environments.

We propose a new bimanual technique *RayLens* for accurate 3D virtual object
selection which combines a ray held in the dominant hand, with a magnification

lens controlled by the other hand. As a standard magnification lens will enlarge the objects of an area but "lead to the same visual output" [53], the occlusion problem remains. To pass through obstacles and reach an occluded area, the lens can be remotely and freely moved in 3D space (see the metaphor of the "eyeball-in-hand" [51,52]). Once the lens is placed in the scene, the lens is occluded by the objects placed in front of it. To remove this occlusion, we apply a transparency filter on the obstacles placed between the users and the lens. Finally, the selection of an object is performed by pointing to the 2D projection of the magnified object displayed on the distant lens using raycasting.

We compare *RayLens* with a standard raycasting technique as well as with *RaySlider*, a technique extending raycasting with the widely-used target expansion mechanism as a pointing facilitation mechanism. As *RayLens*, *RaySlider* is bimanual: users move the ray using the dominant hand and operate a physical slider to move the cursor along the ray using the non-dominant hand. To facilitate the selection, the cursor always selects the nearest object (such as *Bubble Cursor* [17]). Moreover, the same transparency filter as *RayLens* is applied between the users and the cursor to reduce the occlusion of the area of interest.

In this paper, we first review related work on extended raycasting and lens-based techniques. We then present the design rationale of *RayLens* and also describe *RaySlider* inspired by the design of *RayLens*. We then report an experiment comparing *RayLens*, *RaySlider* and the baseline technique raycasting. We conclude with a discussion of our results and directions for future work.

## 2    Related Work

We build on previous work on pointing facilitation mechanisms that can extend raycasting as well as on lens-based techniques in 3D environments.

### 2.1    Extending Raycasting: Pointing Facilitation Mechanisms

Raycasting selection techniques perform poorly with small distant objects and when the targeted object is occluded by other objects (i.e. dense environments). To overcome these limitations, a variety of techniques implement extensions of raycasting. In the following, we opposed the target-aware techniques (a priori knowledge on potential targets) from the target-agnostic ones [12].

Several target-aware techniques have been proposed for facilitating 2D selection [12] and have been applied to 3D selections. One intensively studied approach, namely target expansion, is to enlarge the effective size of the target. Guillon et al. [20] classify target expansion techniques according to their "underlying visual feedforward mechanisms" and distinguish *target-based* from *cursor-based* visual feedforward. *RayCursor* [4] extends raycasting with a target expansion mechanism: the closest object from the 3D cursor placed on the ray is highlighted. The position of the cursor along the ray is adjusted by forward-backward displacements on the touchpad of a Vive Controller. This technique provides a *target-based* visual feedforward as it always highlights the closest target from the cursor. Other target expansion techniques provide a *cursor-based* visual feedforward by displaying the activation area of the cursor [17,28]. For instance, for 2D selection *Bubble Cursor* [17] displays a bubble with an adaptive size that encompasses the nearest object. Vanacken et al. [56] proposed *3DBubble*, an extension of *Bubble Cursor* for 3D environments. *3DBubble* uses a 3D cursor moved with the virtual hand metaphor and displays a sphere around the 3D cursor that includes the closest object. All targets within 4 cm of the cursor become semi-transparent to reduce the occlusion of objects close to the cursor. Lu et al. [33] propose to display a 2D disc instead of a sphere around the cursor. The technique also includes a bendable ray to connect the ray and the closest target (the closest target being the target with the minimal angular distance with the ray). Another technique proposed by Vickers [58] uses a "sensitive cube" to enlarge the activation area of a 3D cursor manipulated by a wand: when an object enters the cube, the cursor automatically jumps to this object.

One alternative to these target-aware approaches includes multiple-step techniques by manual refinement. The first step selects a subset of objects in the 3D scene. One or several following steps are required to disambiguate the selection. We classify these approaches into two groups: (1) the techniques which select several or all objects along the ray during the first step; and (2) the techniques which use a volume instead of the ray to select objects during the first step.

Grossman and Balakrishnan proposed extensions of raycasting for occluded object selections on 3D volumetric displays [18]. For instance, *DepthRay* highlights all objects intersected by the ray. A cursor on the ray allows users to select one object among the highlighted objects. Instead of moving a cursor along the ray, another approach, *FlowerRay*, displays the selected objects in a marking menu.

Other techniques consider a volume (e.g., a sphere, a cone) instead of a ray. For instance, the technique *SQUAD* [2,27] uses a sphere-casting metaphor to select objects around the raycasting pointer. These objects are then rearranged into a quad-menu: a targeted object is selected by pointing repeatedly the part of the quadrant containing this object. In contrast to the progressive refinement induces by a menu, Cashion et al. [11] proposed to rearrange all selectable objects into a semi-transparent grid displayed in front of the user. With this two-step technique users partially maintain the context of the scene because they can always perceive the scene through the grid.

Our target-agnostic approach also includes two steps by considering magnifying lenses. The first step consists of positioning a magnifying lens and the second step consists of directly selecting the targeted object displayed on the lens by raycasting. In contrast to previous techniques based on space rearrangement methods [2,11,27], magnifying lenses keep the relative positions of the objects (which is essential for some usage contexts such as in augmented maps as presented in the scenario of Sect. 1). Also, lenses implement the concept of *focus+context* [13] by contrast to a standard zoom technique. Thus, users can simultaneously visualize the global scene and the magnified projection of the zone of interest. Magnifying lenses have been largely used for facilitating 2D selection such as *Magic Lens*, [7] *Shift* [60], *Pointing Lenses* [44], *Widgetslens* [1], *Fisheyes* [21], and *Sigma Lenses* [40]. The following section explores the lens metaphor applied to AR/VR environments.

## 2.2   Lenses in AR/VR Environments

We review studies on lenses in AR/VR environments according to the tasks the lenses support, their shape, and how the users move the lenses. A more detailed review on lenses can be found in the survey of Tominski et al. [53].

**Tasks.** Applied in AR [30,34,54] and VR [36,45] environments, lenses are used for several tasks classified by Tominski et al. [53] into 7 tasks: *Select, Explore, Reconfigure, Encode, Abstract/Elaborate, Filter* and *Connect*. For the last 6 tasks, the lenses can display additional information through them [16,34], remove occlusion [7,29,45,54,55] or magnify a part of the scene [30,41,49,50]. For instance, Bane et al. [5] developed an AR system to give users an X-ray vision (i.e. a virtual lens placed on a wall to display the occluded room behind this wall). Few AR/VR techniques use lenses for facilitating the selection of a 3D object (Task *Select* in [53]). The recent *Slicing-Volume* [35] includes a lens for multi-target selection in an occluded area. Looser et al. [30] also propose to use a lens as a tool for selection in tabletop AR. A raycasting metaphor can be implemented to select "objects targeted by the center of the lens" [31].

In summary, while lenses have been widely used in AR/VR environments for exploration tasks, very few studies have used them for selection tasks. And none of the lens-based techniques have considered magnifying lenses to facilitate the selection by raycasting in dense environments.

**Shapes of the Lenses.** In 3D environments, there are 2 shapes of lenses: volumetric and flat lenses [15,59]. As defined by Schmalstieg et al. [48], the *volumetric lenses* [32,34,36] affect "every object inside the lens region" and the *flat lenses* affect "every object that has a projection falling into the area covered by the magic lens" (Viega et al. called this region *the lens frustum* [59]). The shape of the lens can be predefined but can also be adaptive to the visualized data. The lenses with content-adaptive shapes are not the focus of our work. Volumetric lenses are useful for extracting or filtering a portion of the 3D scene. For example, *Slicing-Volume* is a cube-shape lens [35] to extract and interact with occluded objects in a dense scene.

In our context of pointing facilitation techniques, we use a flat magic lens instead of a volumetric lens, to reduce the difficulty of the pointing task, from a task in 3D space to a task in the 2D space of the lens. For instance, the lens implemented by Looser et al. [30] for the selection of objects in tabletop AR is a flat lens. Moreover in [35] the content of the cube-shape volumetric lens defining a region in the 3D space is then projected on a flat lens for multiple selections.

**Movement of the Lenses.** Lenses can be moved using tangible objects held by the users. For instance, Brown et al. propose a 2D mirror-like prop as a lens [9,10] using Head-Mounted Projective Display technology. In the same way, markers are tracked in [30,34] to display the lens over the markers. In a VR environment, Mota et al. [36] use the controller to move the lens in the 3D scene. Similarly, two controllers held in both hands are used to define the *Slicing-Volume* [35]. Moreover, a physical tablet and stylus are fixed to the controllers for haptic feedback and touch input when selecting objects. Finally, freehand gestures can also be used to activate and move the lens, the lens following the position of the users' hand [45,54]. Several of these approaches make the placement of the lens within an out-of-reach area difficult and tedious. Kluge et al. [26] proposed to move a distant lens by using a proxy placed close to the user's hand. This proxy is manipulated by the virtual hand metaphor and the 3D motion of the proxy is translated into the motion of the distant lens.

By combining design elements (i.e. lens, magnification as opposed to space rearrangement, *focus+context* as opposed to standard zooming and transparency effect) that have been applied in different interaction contexts and for different tasks, we propose *RayLens*, the first lens-based technique extending raycasting for accurate selection in dense 3D environments. The novelty of our technique relies on the synergistic combination of these concepts to overcome the limitations of raycasting. The resulting technique is thus greater than the sum of its constitutive parts. We also compare our target-agnostic extension *RayLens* to a target-aware technique *RaySlider* whose design shares elements from *RayLens* while being inspired by the large amount of research on enlarging the activation area of the 3D cursor.

## 3   RayLens

*RayLens* combines two independent components: a ray and a magnification flat lens. A bimanual version of *RayLens*, where users move the ray in one hand and move the lens with the other hand, is intrinsically a bimanual "asymmetric and dependent" [24] technique. Indeed, this design is consistent with Guiard's theory principles [19]: "the two hands have very different roles to play which depend on each other" [24]. As a consequence, we decided to design *RayLens* as a bimanual technique: users move the ray using the dominant hand and move the lens using the other hand.

The virtual ray extends a physical wand held by the users. Users select with the ray the 2D projection of the magnified object displayed on the distant lens. *RayLens* is an extension of the standard raycasting technique and the lens should be used only when needed. Nevertheless in order to compare *RayLens* with the standard raycasting in our experiment (see Sect. 6), an object can be selected only on the lens: a selection by standard raycasting is then not allowed with *RayLens* in the experiment. In the virtual lens, the 2D projections of objects intersected by the ray are highlighted in yellow. A selection is validated by pressing a button fixed to the physical wand.

**Fig. 2.** *RayLens* walkthrough: (1–4) Bimanual selection of a target (left); Occlusion management of the lens (right).

## 3.1 Virtual Lens

The main component of *RayLens* is the virtual lens measuring 22.5 cm × 17.5 cm (equivalent to the size of a physical tablet), see Fig. 2. This virtual component acts as a physical tablet, adding an interactive virtual screen in the scene and another point of view via a camera fixed to the lens (like the "eyeball-in-hand" metaphor). Thus, the lens allows the user to add a new point of view on the scene which stays fixed regardless of the user's position (in a collaborative context, a fixed point of view allows all the participants to share the same view on the lens). When the lens does not move, the displayed content is stable making the selection of objects easier. The lens also magnifies the content placed behind it (Fig. 2): it enlarges the visual representation of the objects that fall inside the *lens frustum*. As visual feedback, all objects in this area are brighter than others.

Users can move the lens in 3D by using the clicker of the HoloLens, tracked in the 3D space. Once a click event is detected on the clicker, the device behaves as a 3D remote controller: its 3D motion is translated into the motion of the lens (1:3 ratio[1].) until the button is released. This lets users do clutching to reach more distant positions. These distant positions would be unreachable by a user holding a physical tablet without moving around the table. This motion of the lens is essential for users to be able to see and select occluded objects. To do so users move the lens through obstacles. In the current implementation, the lens cannot be rotated. The usage context implies that users are standing in front of the table and that the virtual objects are at most 20° to the left and right of the users: a rotation of the lens is then unnecessary.

## 3.2 Occlusion of the Lens

When moving the lens through the 3D scene, some distractors will appear in front of it. This causes the lens to be hidden from the users, which makes selections on the virtual lens screen difficult. To reduce this occlusion, we apply a filter on all the objects placed between the lens and the user (in contrast to the transparency effect of [56,57] which is applied only on the objects within 4 cm of

---

[1] With the 1:3 ratio, a 30 cm motion of the clicker allows users to move the lens from its initial position (30 cm in front of the scene) to the position of the farthest objects (90 cm from the initial position of the lens).

the cursor). As the user is fixed, standing in front of the table, we approximate the filtering area as the area in front of the lens, see the yellow box in Fig. 2-right. This filter makes all these objects semi-transparent to minimize the "visual occlusion" of the lens. The semi-transparent objects cannot be selected by the ray anymore (the ray passing through them) to reduce the "physical occlusion" of these distractors. Thanks to this filter, users can easily reach the lens screen with the ray as illustrated in Fig 2b.

In summary, the design rationale of *RayLens* is based on two properties:
*Precision.* (1) Without voluntary movements of the lens by users (i.e. press on the clicker), the position of the lens is fixed. This stable magnification lens makes the selection of small targets easier. (2) As the selection of an object is done on the lens and not directly on the 3D object, the distance between the users and the target is reduced. The problem of ray stability is consequently also reduced.
*Occlusion & Density.* The movement of the lens in the 3D scene and the transparency effect enable the selection of occluded targets by passing through obstacles. The lens acts as a "clipping plane" in a similar way as in [15,35]. Users can thus erase the distractors in front of a target to increase its visibility.

## 4    RaySlider

*RaySlider* is another extension of the raycasting metaphor that shares design elements from *RayLens* while implementing a target expansion mechanism (Fig. 3). *RaySlider* uses a cursor that moves along the ray to pass through distractors. As *RayLens*, this technique is bimanual: users move the ray with the dominant hand and move the cursor on the ray with the other hand. Considering a cursor attached to the ray, both hands impact the position of the cursor: a 3DOF movement of the cursor is controlled by the dominant hand (i.e. the ray movement) and a 1DOF movement along the ray is controlled by the non-dominant hand. As the dominant hand already controls the 3D position of the cursor, users do not need to additionally move the cursor on the ray when precision is required. Additionally, simultaneous control with both hands could "increase the load on the participant's motor system" and the task could "become more difficult" as observed in [3]. Thus, with such design, the precision phase should be performed by the dominant hand which holds the ray, and the 1DOF movement of the cursor along the ray should be mainly used during the ballistic phase. As a consequence, we design *RaySlider* to quickly place the cursor in the scene.

As *RayLens*, the virtual ray extends a physical wand held by the users. To obtain an easy and fast motion of the cursor along the ray, the cursor is moved thanks to a tangible 7.3 cm long slider held by users. Thanks to muscle memory, participants can quickly place the cursor close to the target. The minimum value of the slider (its bottom position) corresponds to a cursor placed at the tip of the wand. The maximum value of the slider (its top position) corresponds to a cursor at 3 m away from the tip of the wand. In the setting, the farthest target is at 2 m from the user. The range of the slider values [0–1023] enables the user to comfortably only use the lower part of the slider (2/3 of its length).

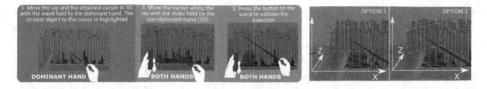

**Fig. 3.** *RaySlider* walkthrough: (1–3) Bimanual selection of a target (left); Two different occlusion managements of the cursor (right).

To facilitate the selection of small targets, the closest object to the cursor is always highlighted (i.e. a *target-based* visual feedforward [20]) and can be selected by pressing the button fixed to the physical wand. To facilitate the selection of occluded objects, we apply a filter making distractors semi-transparent as done with *RayLens* (see the yellow box in Fig. 3-right) to minimize occlusion around the cursor. In a pilot study, we compare 2 possible positions of the filtering box area, see Fig. 3-right: (1) Option 1. The box is placed between the cursor and the user; (2) Option 2. The box is placed along the ray. In this context of scenes with medium sizes (width = 70 cm, depth = 60 cm), participants found no difference between the two implementations. For the conducted comparison experiment, we chose the first option which is similar to the filter of *RayLens*.

## 5    Implementation

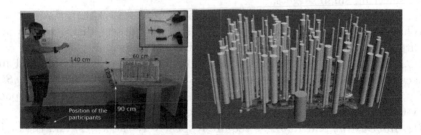

**Fig. 4.** Setup of the experiment (left) and example of a 3D scene (right) with a start target in green, a goal target in red and distractors in grey. (Color figure online)

We use a Microsoft HoloLens 1 to visualize the 3D virtual scene that is created and managed by Unity. This HMD is composed of two HD see-through displays ($FoV = 30 \times 17.5°$) with a frame rate of 60 fps. We also use a tracking system composed of 6 OptiTrack cameras (running at 100 fps). Reflective markers are placed on the wand to track its position and rotation in the 3D space and to be able to extend it with a virtual ray. We fixed a small Arduino button to the wand for the validation of the selection. For *RayLens*, we use the HoloLens clicker to move the virtual lens in the 3D space. We add 4 markers on this clicker to track its 3D position in real-time. For the *RaySlider* technique, users hold a tangible slider. The events of the wand button and the slider are sent via wireless communication (using Arduino radios) to the HoloLens.

To link the OptiTrack system and the Unity Engine, we place an image on the table (which is non-interactive). This image is used as an *Image Target* that Vuforia Engine can detect and track. To optimize the performance of the system, we use Vuforia only at the initialization of the application. Once this image is detected, we create and place a world anchor (see Microsoft MRToolkit) at the bottom left and stop the Vuforia detection. This anchor creates a link between the position of the real objects (e.g., the wand, the clicker, the table) and the position of the virtual objects (e.g., the ray). Figure 4 presents the general setup.

# 6  Comparative Study

In this section, we present the experiment that compares *RayLens* with *RaySlider* and the well-known raycasting to study its efficiency (e.g., performances, users feedback). As several studies such as [4,11] that propose improvements of the virtual pointer metaphor, we choose a standard raycasting technique as a baseline. The *RayCasting* technique is implemented as a ray that selects the first intersected object. Without collision, this ray is infinite. As with the two other techniques, users press the button on the wand to validate a selection.

Our hypotheses are:

- *H1*. *RayLens* and *RaySlider* are faster and more accurate than *RayCasting* for selecting small targets.
- *H2*. With a low density of the environment, *RaySlider* is the fastest technique. When the distance between the target and the closest distractors is large, automatically selecting the closest object is very efficient.
- *H3*. With a high density of the environment, *RayLens* is faster and more accurate than *RaySlider*. Indeed target expansion techniques as *RaySlider* are impacted by the density of distractors [8]. And *RayLens* is little impacted by density thanks to the magnification and the transparency effects.
- *H4*. *RayCasting* and *RayLens* require respectively the lowest and the highest workload. With *RayLens*, switching between the 3D view of the scene and the 2D projected view displayed on the lens may require significant extra cognitive efforts from users.

## 6.1  Tasks

In this experiment, participants have to select 3D cylindrical targets in 3D virtual scenes that visually appear as resting on a table (Fig. 4). Each 3D scene is a set of cylinders, composed of one start target, one goal target, and 120 distractors (Fig. 4). All distractors are gray, the start target is green, and the goal target is red. Pointing at a cylinder changes its color to yellow. The start target is always in front of the participants and of the other cylinders. Before each trial with *RayLens*, the lens is positioned 30 cm in front of the start target. The goal target is randomly positioned but always at a fixed distance of 40 cm from the start target. All the distractors are randomly positioned under the following constraints: they must not intersect nor fully visually occlude the goal target. The diameter size is randomly set between 0.5 cm (small target size) and 3.5 cm (large target size). To ensure similar experimental conditions between the techniques and the participants, we computed a set of unique 3D scenes before the experiment which is shared between all participants and all techniques.

The participants are instructed to stand at 140 cm from the table. The exact location is marked on the ground. The first step of the task is to select the start target. Then, the start target disappears and the participants have to select the goal target. A selection is validated by pressing the button on the wand. A trial ends once the goal target has been successfully selected. The participants are instructed to select the goal target as fast as possible while minimizing the number of selection errors (i.e. number of presses before a successful validation).

## 6.2  Protocol

**Density Spacing.** To control the density of the environment, we rely on a method inspired by [57]. In the 3D scene, we place four additional distractors in the immediate surrounding of the goal target: two are positioned on a line defined by the goal target and the static position of the participant (one in front of and one behind the goal target), and the other two distractors are positioned on a perpendicular line (one on each side of the goal target). To minimize visual occlusion, we set these four distractors with a small diameter size (0.5 cm) and rotate them around the goal target to easily see the target from the participant's position. As in [57], we call *density spacing* the distance between the goal target and these additional distractors. The other 120 distractors are pseudo-randomly placed around these 4 distractors so as not to visually occlude the target.

**Design.** We used a within-subject design with the 3 following independent variables: the technique *TECH* (*RayLens*, *RaySlider* and *RayCasting*), the density spacing *DS* (1 cm for high density, and 5 cm for low density) and the target diameter *SIZE* (0.5 cm, 1.5 cm, and 3.5 cm). To observe a possible learning or tiredness effect, we grouped trials into three blocks per technique. Within each block, the 6 combinations of *DS* × *SIZE* were repeated 3 times in a random order for a total of $3 \times 2 \times 3 = 18$ trials per block. This experimental design results in a total of 54 trials per technique. Before each *TECH* condition, the participants perform a training session to experience each of the *DS* × *SIZE* conditions. Participants can take a break after each technique. The order of the techniques was counterbalanced across participants using a Latin square design. The experiment lasted approximately 75 min per participant.

**Participants.** We recruited 12 unpaid volunteers (2 females, 10 males), ranging from ages 22 to 38 (*mean* = 28.7, *std* = 4.23). All participants were right-handed. None of them was an expert in augmented reality. We applied COVID-19 preventive sanitary measures for the experiment to take place safely.

**Measures.** We consider two objective measures (completion time, number of errors), and two subjective measures (workload, user preference). Completion time refers to the elapsed time between the successful selection of the start target and the successful selection of the goal target. The number of errors refers to the number of error presses (i.e. when a user presses the button while no object or a distractor is selected) before the successful selection of the goal target.

As subjective measures, the participants fill in a questionnaire for each *TECH* condition. It combines questions to rate: the perceived workload based on a shortened version of NASA-TLX (called Raw TLX[2]); the perceived performance (from 1 to 7 points); the perceived usefulness of (from 1 to 7 points): (a) the visual feedback representing the field of view of the lens (*RayLens*); and (b) the transparency filtering effect (*RaySlider* and *RayLens*). The participants also fill in a final questionnaire to determine the least mentally and physically demanding techniques, the most successful, the most accurate, and the fastest techniques. Finally, they rank the techniques in order of preference. The experiment ends with an interview. In particular, the participants were asked about the manipulated techniques, their usage, and the positioning of the lens or of the cursor.

# 7   Results

As the completion times follow a normal distribution (Shapiro-Wilk test), we use ANOVAs and t-tests with Bonferroni adjustment for pairwise comparisons. Means (m) and 95% confidence intervals (CI) are shown in all graphs. For the non-parametric analysis of the number of errors, we apply the aligned rank transformation (ART) [61] with Bonferroni correction for pairwise comparisons.

## 7.1   Objective Measures: Completion Time

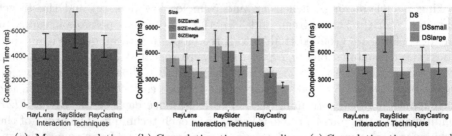

(a) Mean completion times.

(b) Completion times according to the size of the target.

(c) Completion times according to the density spacing.

**Fig. 5.** Completion times of the techniques.

---

[2] According to the survey [23], NASA-TLX and Raw TLX perform equally well.

We do not find a main effect for *TECH* on completion time ($F_{2,22} = 2.51, p = 0.1$), see Fig. 5a. However, we find a main effect for *SIZE* ($F_{2,22} = 103, p < 0.0001, \eta^2_G = 0.31$), and *DS* ($F_{1,11} = 94.8, p < 0.0001, \eta^2_G = 0.12$). The average completion times are 5.9 s for *RaySlider*, 4.6 s for *RayLens* and 4.5 s for *RayCasting*. Also, by comparing performances between blocks, we do not find a learning or tiredness effect.

**Interaction Effect Between *TECH* and *SIZE*.** We observe significant *TECH* × *SIZE* interaction effects ($F_{4,44} = 26.3, p < 0.0001, \eta^2_G = 0.15$), see Fig. 5b. Results show large completion time variations across sizes for *RayCasting* ($RC_{small} = 7.6$ s, $RC_{medium} = 3.7$ s, $RC_{large} = 2.3$ s): the technique is very fast at selecting large targets while it becomes very slow with small targets. Pairwise comparisons show significant differences between small and large targets ($p < 0.0001$) and between medium and large targets ($p = 0.004$). *RaySlider* ($RS_{small} = 6.8$ s, $RS_{medium} = 6.4$ s, $RS_{large} = 4.5$ s) and *RayLens* ($RL_{small} = 5.5$ s, $RL_{medium} = 4.6$ s, $RL_{large} = 3.9$ s) are slightly impacted by the size of the targets. We only find a significant difference between small and large targets ($p = 0.02$ with *RaySlider*, $p = 0.035$ with *RayLens*).

Pairwise comparisons show significant differences between the techniques across sizes. For large targets, *RayCasting* is significantly the fastest selection technique compared to *RayLens* ($p = 0.005$) and *RaySlider* ($p = 0.0003$). For medium targets, *RayCasting* is significantly faster than *RaySlider* ($p = 0.008$). We find no significant difference between *RayCasting* and *RayLens*. For small targets, *RayLens* tends to be the fastest selection technique (1.38× faster than *RayCasting* and 1.24× faster than *RaySlider*). However, we only find a significant difference between *RayLens* and *RayCasting* ($p = 0.038$).

**Interaction Effect Between *TECH* and *DS*.** We observe significant *TECH* × *DS* interaction effects ($F_{2,22} = 35.4, p < 0.0001, \eta^2_G = 0.13$), see Fig. 5c. Pairwise comparisons show a strong effect of *DS* for *RaySlider* ($p = 0.0008$, $RS_{DSsmall} = 7.9$ s, $RS_{DSlarge} = 3.9$ s). We find no significant effect of *DS* for *RayCasting* ($RC_{DSsmall} = 4.8$ s, $RC_{DSlarge} = 4.3$ s) and *RayLens* ($RL_{DSsmall} = 4.7$ s, $RL_{DSlarge} = 4.5$ s).

Pairwise comparisons show no significant difference between the techniques for low density (DS = large). For high density (DS = small), *RaySlider* seems to be the slowest technique (*RayLens* and *RayCasting* are 1.6× faster than *RaySlider* on average) but we do not find a significant difference between *RaySlider* and *RayLens* ($p = 0.06$), and between *RaySlider* and *RayCasting* ($p = 0.08$).

To summarize, *RayCasting* is strongly impacted by *SIZE*, *RaySlider* is strongly impacted by *DS*, and *RayLens* is relatively independent of *SIZE* and *DS*.

## 7.2   Objective Measures: Number of Errors

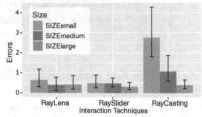
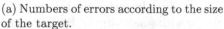
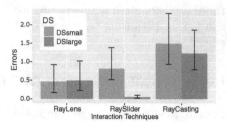

(a) Numbers of errors according to the size of the target.

(b) Numbers of errors according to the density spacing.

**Fig. 6.** Numbers of errors of the techniques.

The number of errors is the number of presses before successful validation of the target. We find a main effect for *TECH* ($F_{2,187} = 46.12$, $p < 0.0001$), *SIZE* ($F_{2,187} = 33.51$, $p < 0.0001$) and *DS* ($F_{1,187} = 14.61$, $p = 0.0002$) on the number of errors. The average number of errors is 0.43 for *RaySlider*, 0.48 for *RayLens* and 1.35 for *RayCasting*. Pairwise comparisons show that *RayCasting* is significantly less accurate than *RaySlider* ($3.1\times$, $p = 0.004$) and *RayLens* ($2.8\times$, $p = 0.001$). We found no significant difference between *RayLens* and *RaySlider*.

**Interaction Effect Between *TECH* and *SIZE*.** We observe significant *TECH* × *SIZE* interaction effects ($F_{4,187} = 23.71$, $p < 0.0001$), see Fig. 6a. Results show large errors variations across sizes for *RayCasting* ($RC_{small} = 2.7$, $RC_{medium} = 1.05$, $RC_{large} = 0.38$): the number of errors with small targets is $7\times$ higher on average than with large targets. Pairwise comparisons show significant differences between small and large targets ($p = 0.0002$), between small and medium targets ($p = 0.016$), and also between medium and large targets ($p = 0.05$). We find no significant difference between sizes for *RayLens* ($RL_{small} = 0.63$, $RL_{medium} = 0.39$, $RL_{large} = 0.40$) and *RaySlider* ($RS_{small} = 0.49$, $RS_{medium} = 0.47$, $RS_{large} = 0.31$).

For small targets, pairwise comparisons show that the number of errors with *RayCasting* is significantly higher than with *RayLens* ($p = 0.001$) and with *RaySlider* ($p = 0.0006$). For medium targets, *RayLens* is significantly more accurate than *RayCasting* ($p = 0.04$). For medium targets, we find no significant difference between *RaySlider* and the other techniques. Finally, for large targets, we find no significant difference between the techniques.

**Interaction Effect Between *TECH* and *DS*.** We observe significant *TECH* × *DS* interaction effects ($F_{2,187} = 11.39$, $p < 0.0001$), see Fig. 6b. Pairwise comparisons show a highly significant difference between densities for *RaySlider*

($RS_{DSsmall}$ = 0.82, $RS_{DSlarge}$ = 0.05, $p$ < 0.0001). We find no significant difference between densities for $RayLens$ ($RL_{DSsmall}$ = 0.47, $RL_{DSlarge}$ = 0.49) and for $RayCasting$ ($RC_{DSsmall}$ = 1.48, $RC_{DSlarge}$ = 1.23).

For high density ($DS = small$), $RayLens$ is significantly the most accurate technique. Pairwise comparisons show significant differences between $RayLens$ and $RayCasting$ ($p$ = 0.009) and between $RayLens$ and $RaySlider$ ($p$ = 0.046) for high density. We find no significant difference between $RayCasting$ and $RaySlider$. For low density ($DS = large$), $RaySlider$ is significantly the most accurate technique. Pairwise comparisons find a significant difference between $RaySlider$ and $RayLens$ ($p$ = 0.006) and between $RaySlider$ and $RayCasting$ ($p$ < 0.0001). We also find that $RayLens$ is more accurate than $RayCasting$ ($p$ = 0.009).

In summary, our results suggest that $RayCasting$ is the least accurate technique, while $RayLens$ and $RaySlider$ present a similar number of errors. The accuracy of $RayLens$ is relatively independent of $SIZE$ and $DS$. By contrast, $RaySlider$ appears very impacted by $DS$ and $RayCasting$ by $SIZE$.

## 7.3   Subjective Measures: Workload and Participants Feedback

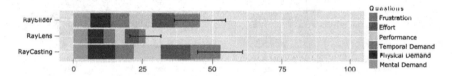

**Fig. 7.** [NASATLX] Total workload between 0 and 100.

**Workload.** $RayLens$ requires the lowest workload by far ($26.16/100 \pm 5.6$), see Fig. 7. The other techniques present similar workloads ($45.6/100 \pm 8.9$ for $RaySlider$ and $52.78/100 \pm 7.9$ for $RayCasting$). Participants find that $RayLens$ is much less frustrating ($\approx 4\times$ less), that it requires less effort ($\approx 2\times$ less), and that they are more successful than with the other techniques ($\approx 2\times$ more).

**Participants Ratings.** The final questionnaire confirms the results of the RTLX questionnaire: 100% of the participants choose $RayLens$ as the least frustrating, the most accurate, and the most successful technique. We thought that moving the lens to find a target in a dense environment would be difficult for the participants. However, they report no difficulty with the motion of the lens for almost all of the trials. $RayLens$ is also chosen as the least physically demanding technique ($RayLens$: 9/12 participants, $RaySlider$: 3/12 participants), and as the technique which demands the least effort ($RayLens$: 9/12 participants, $RaySlider$: 2/12 participants, $RayCasting$: 1/12 participant). Results also show that *RayCasting* is the least mentally demanding technique (*RayCasting*: 8/12 participants, *RaySlider*: 3/12 participants, *RayLens*: 1/12 participants).

The participants unanimously prefer *RayLens* (12/12 participants). They report liking this technique because it is easy to understand, intuitive, and because the selections are easy and stable. *RaySlider* is the least preferred technique for 5/12 participants and *RayCasting* for the 7 remaining participants.

**The Usefulness of the Visual Feedback.** We also ask the participants how useful the visual feedback of *RaySlider* and *RayLens* are. For *RaySlider*, the usefulness of the transparency filter applied on the objects placed in front of the cursor is rated 5/7. For *RayLens*, the usefulness of the transparency filter in front of the lens is rated 5.6/7. The visual feedback representing the field of view of the lens is also found useful by the participants (4.6/7).

## 7.4   Analysis of Lens and Cursor Movement Durations

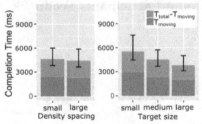
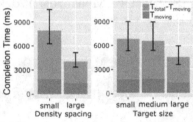

(a) Times spent moving the lens according to *DS* and *SIZE*.

(b) Times spent moving the cursor according to *DS* and *SIZE*.

**Fig. 8.** Times spent moving the lens or the cursor ($T_{moving}$) over total completion times ($T_{total}$).

Figure 8 shows the average time spent to move the lens and the cursor according to the target size and the density spacing. On average, the participants spent $54.9\% \pm 15\%$ of the trial durations moving the lens and only spent $34\% \pm 9\%$ of the trial durations moving the cursor.

For *RayLens*, the time spent moving the lens is slightly impacted by target size ($T_{movingLens} = 2.04$ s for large targets, 2.37 s for medium targets, and 2.91 s for small targets). However, we find no significant effect of *SIZE* nor of *DS* ($T_{movingLens} = 2.36$ s for *DS = large* and 2.46 s for *DS = small*) on this duration, see Fig. 8a. For *RaySlider*, we find no significant effect of *SIZE* ($T_{movingCursor} = 1.37$ s for large targets, 1.82 s for medium targets, and 1.74 s for small targets) nor of *DS* ($T_{movingCursor} = 1.4$ s for *DS = large* and 1.91 s for *DS = small*) on the time spent moving the cursor, see Fig. 8b.

# 8    Discussion

## 8.1    Hypotheses

**Two Extensions Faster and More Accurate than *RayCasting* for Selecting Small Targets.** For the selection of large targets, *RayCasting* remains the best option: it allows users to select large targets faster and with the same accuracy as the two extensions.

*H1* suggested that *RaySlider* and *RayLens* would perform better than *RayCasting* with small targets. This study highlights the limitations of *RayCasting* and clearly shows an advantage of *RayLens* and *RaySlider* in terms of precision for the selection of small targets. Our results also suggest that *RayLens* is faster than *RayCasting*. However, as *RaySlider* is only slightly faster than *RayCasting*, this partially validates *H1*. For medium size targets, *RayCasting* is as fast as *RayLens*: this might reveal the existence of a threshold size below which *RayLens* is more accurate than *RayCasting*.

**_RayLens_ Little Impacted by the Density of the Environment.** This study shows that *RayLens* presents similar completion times and number of errors regardless of density. On the other hand, *RaySlider* is strongly impacted by density. For the case of low environment density (large density spacing), *H2* assumed that *RaySlider* would perform better than *RayLens*. However, all three techniques show similar completion times at low density, so this invalidates *H2*.

For the case of a high density of distractors, the *H3* hypothesis assumed that the performance of *RayLens* would surpass those of *RaySlider*. The results show that *RayLens* is the most precise technique in dense environments. We do not observe a statistically significant difference in terms of completion time, but the results suggest that on average *RayLens* is more than 1.6× faster than *RaySlider* at high density. *H3* is therefore partially validated.

**Higher Workload with *RayCasting* and *RaySlider* than with *RayLens*.** *RayLens* is unanimously the most preferred technique of this study. The RTLX questionnaire reveals that *RayLens* requires the lowest workload. In contrast, *RayCasting* and *RaySlider* show similar results and a much higher workload than *RayLens*. Thus, switching between the 3D view of the scene and the 2D projected view displayed on the lens does not seem to involve additional cognitive efforts as assumed by the *H4* hypothesis: *H4* is therefore invalidated.

## 8.2    Control of the Cursor, the Lens and the Ray

**_RaySlider_: Coupled Control of Cursor and Ray, The Slider Mainly Used During the Ballistic Phase.** The placement of the cursor in the scene with the slider held by the non-dominant hand is reported as fast by some participants (participant 8 reports an "automatic movement with the slider to bring the cursor in the scene"). This technique was designed with the rationale that only the dominant hand is used for the precision phase (the slider being used only for the ballistic phase). This behavior is confirmed by the recorded data. The ratio, *time spent without using the cursor at the end of the task* over the *total time to complete the task*, is 0.48. This ratio shows that the slider is not used during the second half of the total selection time (precision phase).

For the precision phase in dense environments, as we placed 4 distractors around the target, in front, behind, on the left and on the right, participants must be precise not only along the depth axis but also along the left-right axis. The end of the task is thus similar to a task of precisely placing a cursor in 3D, which explains the difficulty of selecting objects in dense environments with *RaySlider*.

**RayLens: Independent Control of Lens and Ray.** *RayLens* is consistent with Guiard's theory principles [19]. As first explained in [24] "such consistency is a good starting point for identifying two-handed usage that seems natural". This is confirmed by our experimental results (Sect. 7, no learning effect) that show a rapid achievement of fast performance with *RayLens*. Moreover, with the bimanual design of *RayLens*, users can refine the position of the lens (e.g., to change the target magnification) and point at the target at the same time without switching between the movement of the lens and the movement of the ray. This possibility has been observed during the study. However, based on the recorded movements of the lens and of the ray we found it difficult to quantify this synergistic use of the two hands because the ray is permanently controlled by the dominant hand (i.e. no specific mode for controlling the ray). However, 5/12 participants asked during the training phase if it was possible to point at and select the target while moving/holding the lens and they reported this feature useful. The synergistic use (e.g., for a relatively easy selection of a target displayed on the lens) is as useful as the sequential use of placing the lens at a fixed position and then selecting on the lens (e.g., for a difficult selection of a small target even after magnification).

### 8.3    Limitations and Advantages of *RayLens*

**Bimanual Technique.** The bimanual design of *RayLens* is reported as useful and intuitive but the use of the two hands can limit its usability in some contexts. In these cases, this technique could be adapted as a unimanual technique; e.g., the lens could be moved along the ray with the dominant hand by using a touchpad placed on the wand. An alternative is to add a button to switch between the movement of the lens and the movement of the ray.

**Physical Objects not Managed.** In an augmented scene, physical objects can be placed on the table and can occlude the target. The current implementation of *RayLens* does not consider these occlusions. A possible extension is to implement an X-ray vision effect [5] of the physical objects placed in front of the lens.

**Good Accuracy.** Results show that the precision of *RayCasting* and *RaySlider* is respectively strongly impacted by the size of the target and the density of the environment. In contrast, *RayLens* presents similar completion times and number of errors, regardless of target size or density. Overall, in dense environments, *RayLens* remains an accurate technique and is 1.7× more accurate than *RaySlider* and almost 3.2× more accurate than *RayCasting*.

Two aspects of *RayLens* can explain these results. First, magnification makes the pointing task easier, especially for small targets. For example, if we consider a lens positioned in the motor space 35 cm from a small target 0.5 cm in diameter, the width of the target projected onto the lens is 2 cm: more than 4 times its initial diameter. Besides, magnification increases in motor space and in visual space the distance between nearby distractors and the target. Finally, the transparency filter applied to the objects placed in front of the lens removes all visual and motor occlusion of the target. Therefore, targets become larger, density and occlusion are decreased, contributing to good accuracy.

**A Facilitated 2D Selection on the Lens.** According to the results obtained in this study, selection tasks with *RayLens* are quick and easy in dense environments and with small targets. The design of this technique may explain these results. First, the selection of an object is done on the lens and not directly on the 3D object. This leads to a shortened pointing distance which also reduces the problem of ray stability. Second, the user points to the 2D plane defined by the lens: the 3D pointing task is facilitated as it becomes a 2D pointing task. Also, the target is enlarged due to the magnification.

**An Easy-to-Learn/Use Technique.** *RayLens* requires the lowest workload and is the preferred technique. As stated in Sect. 8.2, its bimanual design consistent with Guiard's theory principles implies a two-handed usage that seems "natural" [24] and avoids a learning phase (see Sect. 7).

## 9   Conclusion

We presented *RayLens*, a novel bimanual interaction technique extending raycasting for accurate selection in dense environments. It combines a ray with a virtual 2D magnification lens that can be remotely moved in the 3D space using the non-dominant hand. We compared *RayLens* with a standard raycasting and *RaySlider*, a bimanual raycasting that uses a target expansion mechanism.

Our comparative study first confirms that raycasting is fast for the selection of large objects and also highlights its limitations with smaller objects. In the latter case, the two extensions show much higher accuracy than raycasting. However, the performance of *RayLens* and *RaySlider* differs in dense environments. The performance of *RaySlider* is highly impacted by density, while *RayLens* offers very stable performance (both with respect to density and target size) thanks to the magnification effect and the stability of its lens in the 3D space. Qualitative results also show that *RayLens* is the preferred technique, it is easy to understand and requires the lowest workload.

According to our results, we suggest using a 2D magnification lens as an aid for accurate distant selection. While raycasting is controlled with the dominant hand, the *RayLens* extension on the other hand should be used only when needed (i.e. small targets, dense environments). Besides, we evaluate this technique in the context of tabletop AR but *RayLens* is relevant in all the AR and VR applications relying on the widely-used raycasting technique, when the two hands are free. As it is easy-to-learn and intuitive, we also believe that *RayLens* can be used by novice users, for instance in public applications where the users have to rapidly master the technique (e.g., to explore a 3D map of a site to visit).

As future work, we plan to perform an in-depth study of "the temporal overlap in the performance of the two sub-tasks" [24] involved in *RayLens* (lens and ray movements). We also plan to design an adaptive size of the lens for very distant selections (e.g., with the size of the lens increasing proportionally with its distance to the user).

**Acknowledgement.** We gratefully acknowledge the support of the AP2 project ANR-15-CE23-0001.

# References

1. Agarwal, B., Stuerzlinger, W.: Widgetlens: a system for adaptive content magnification of widgets. In: Proceedings of the 27th International BCS Human Computer Interaction Conference. BCS-HCI 2013, Swindon, GBR (2013)
2. Bacim, F., Kopper, R., Bowman, D.A.: Design and evaluation of 3D selection techniques based on progressive refinement. Int. J. Hum.-Comput. Stud. **71**(7–8), 785–802 (2013). https://doi.org/10.1016/j.ijhcs.2013.03.003
3. Balakrishnan, R., Kurtenbach, G.: Exploring bimanual camera control and object-manipulation in 3D graphics interfaces. In: Proceedings of CHI 1999, pp. 56–62. New York, NY, USA (1999). https://doi.org/10.1145/302979.302991
4. Baloup, M., Pietrzak, T., Casiez, G.: Raycursor: A 3D pointing facilitation technique based on raycasting. In: Proceedings of CHI 2019, pp. 1–12. NewYork, NY, USA (2019). https://doi.org/10.1145/3290605.3300331
5. Bane, R., Hollerer, T.: Interactive tools for virtual x-ray vision in mobile augmented reality. In: Proceedings of ISMAR 2004, pp. 231–239. USA (2004). https://doi.org/10.1109/ISMAR.2004.36
6. Banerjee, A., Burstyn, J., Girouard, A., Vertegaal, R.: Pointable: an in-air pointing technique to manipulate out-of-reach targets on tabletops. In: Proceedings of ITS 2011, pp. 11–20. NY, USA (2011). https://doi.org/10.1145/2076354.2076357
7. Bier, E.A., Stone, M.C., Pier, K., Buxton, W., DeRose, T.D.: Toolglass and magic lenses: the see-through interface. In: Proceedings of the 20th Annual Conference on Computer Graphics and Interactive Techniques, pp. 73–80. SIGGRAPH 1993, New York, NY, USA (1993). https://doi.org/10.1145/166117.166126
8. Blanch, R., Ortega, M.: Benchmarking pointing techniques with distractors: adding a density factor to fitts' pointing paradigm. In: Proceedings of CHI 2011, pp. 1629–1638 (2011). https://doi.org/10.1145/1978942.1979180
9. Brown, L.D., Hua, H.: Magic lenses for augmented virtual environments. IEEE Comput. Graph. Appl. **26**(4), 64–73 (2006). https://doi.org/10.1109/MCG.2006.84
10. Brown, L.D., Hua, H., Gao, C.: A widget framework for augmented interaction inscape. In: Proceedings of UIST 2003, pp. 1–10. New York, NY, USA (2003). https://doi.org/10.1145/964696.964697

11. Cashion, J., Wingrave, C., LaViola, J.J., Jr.: Dense and dynamic 3D selection for game-based virtual environments. IEEE TVCG **18**(4), 634–642 (2012). https://doi.org/10.1109/TVCG.2012.40
12. Chapuis, O., Dragicevic, P.: Effects of motor scale, visual scale, andquantization on small target acquisition difficulty. ACM Trans. Comput.-Hum. Interact. **18**(3), 1–32 (2011). https://doi.org/10.1145/1993060.1993063
13. Cockburn, A., Karlson, A., Bederson, B.B.: A review of overview+detail,zooming, and focus+context interfaces. ACM Computing Survey, vol. 41, no. 1 (2009). https://doi.org/10.1145/1456650.1456652
14. Dedual, N.J., Oda, O., Feiner, S.K.: Creating hybrid user interfaces with a 2D multi-touch tabletop and a 3D see-through head-worn display. In: Proceedings of ISMAR 2011, pp. 231–232. USA (2011). https://doi.org/10.1109/ISMAR.2011.6092391
15. Fuhrmann, A., Gröller, E.: Real-time techniques for 3D flow visualization. In: Proceedings of VIS 1998, pp. 305–312. Washington, DC, USA (1998). https://doi.org/10.5555/288216.288296
16. Gasteiger, R., Neugebauer, M., Beuing, O., Preim, B.: The flowlens: afocus-and-context visualization approach for exploration of blood flow incerebral aneurysms. IEEE TVCG, pp. 2183–2192 (2011). https://doi.org/10.1109/TVCG.2011.243
17. Grossman, T., Balakrishnan, R.: The bubble cursor: enhancing target acquisition by dynamic resizing of the cursor's activation area. In: Proceedings of CHI 2005, pp. 281–290. NY, USA (2005). https://doi.org/10.1145/1054972.1055012
18. Grossman, T., Balakrishnan, R.: The design and evaluation of selection techniques for 3D volumetric displays. In: Proceedings of UIST 2006, pp. 3–12. New York, NY, USA (2006). https://doi.org/10.1145/1166253.1166257
19. Guiard, Y.: Asymmetric division of labor in human skilled bimanual action. J. Motor Behav. **19**(4), 486–517 (1987). https://doi.org/10.1080/00222895.1987.10735426, pMID: 15136274
20. Guillon, M., Leitner, F., Nigay, L.: Investigating visual feedforward for target expansion techniques. In: Proceedings of CHI 2015, pp. 2777–2786. NewYork, NY, USA (2015). https://doi.org/10.1145/2702123.2702375
21. Gutwin, C.: Improving focus targeting in interactive fisheye views. In: Proceedings of CHI 2002, pp. 267–274. New York, NY, USA (2002). https://doi.org/10.1145/503376.503424
22. de Haan, G., Koutek, M., Post, F.H.: Intenselect: using dynamic object rating for assisting 3D object selection. In: Proceedings of the 11th Eurographics Conference on Virtual Environments, pp. 201–209. EGVE 2005, Goslar, DEU (2005). https://doi.org/10.5555/2385984.2386013
23. Hart, S.G.: Nasa-task load index (nasa-tlx); 20 years later. In: Proceedings of the Human Factors and Ergonomics Society Annual Meeting, vol. 50, pp. 904–908. Sage publications Sage CA: Los Angeles, CA (2006). https://doi.org/10.1177/154193120605000909
24. Kabbash, P., Buxton, W., Sellen, A.: Two-handed input in a compound task. In: Proceedings of CHI 1994, pp. 417–423. New York, NY, USA (1994). https://doi.org/10.1145/191666.191808
25. Käser, D.P., Agrawala, M., Pauly, M.: Fingerglass: efficient multiscale interaction on multitouch screens. In: Proceedings of CHI 2011, pp. 1601–1610. New York, NY, USA (2011). https://doi.org/10.1145/1978942.1979175
26. Kluge, S., Gladisch, S., Freiherr von Lukas, U., Staadt, O., Tominski, C.: Virtual lenses as embodied tools for immersive analytics. In: GI VR/AR Workshop (2020). https://doi.org/10.18420/vrar2020_8

27. Kopper, R., Bacim, F., Bowman, D.A.: Rapid and accurate 3D selection by progressive refinement. In: Proceedings of 3DUI 2011, pp. 67–74. USA (2011). https://doi.org/10.5555/2013881.2014213

28. Laukkanen, J., Isokoski, P., Räihä, K.J.: The cone and the lazy bubble: two efficient alternatives between the point cursor and the bubble cursor. In: Proceedings of CHI 2008, pp. 309–312. New York, NY, USA (2008). https://doi.org/10.1145/1357054.1357107

29. Lee, J.J., Park, J.M.: 3D mirrored object selection for occluded objects in virtual environments. IEEE Access **8**, 200259–200274 (2020). https://doi.org/10.1109/ACCESS.2020.3035376

30. Looser, J., Billinghurst, M., Cockburn, A.: Through the looking glass: the use of lenses as an interface tool for augmented reality interfaces. In: Proceedings of the 2nd International Conference on Computer Graphics and Interactive Techniques in Australasia and South East Asia, pp. 204–211. GRAPHITE 2004, New York, NY, USA (2004). https://doi.org/10.1145/988834.988870

31. Looser, J., Billinghurst, M., Grasset, R., Cockburn, A.: An evaluation of virtual lenses for object selection in augmented reality. In: Proceedings of the 5th International Conference on Computer Graphics and Interactive Techniques in Australia and Southeast Asia, pp. 203–210. GRAPHITE 2007, New York, NY, USA (2007). https://doi.org/10.1145/1321261.1321297

32. Looser, J., Grasset, R., Billinghurst, M.: A 3D flexible and tangible magiclens in augmented reality. In: Proceedings of ISMAR 2007, pp. 1–4. USA (2007). https://doi.org/10.1109/ISMAR.2007.4538825

33. Lu, Y., Yu, C., Shi, Y.: Investigating bubble mechanism for ray-casting to improve 3D target acquisition in virtual reality. In: Conference on VR and 3D User Interfaces, pp. 35–43. USA (2020). https://doi.org/10.1109/VR46266.2020.00021

34. Mendez, E., Kalkofen, D., Schmalstieg, D.: Interactive context-driven visualization tools for augmented reality. In: Proceedings of ISMAR 2006, pp. 209–218 (2006). https://doi.org/10.1109/ISMAR.2006.297816

35. Montano, R., Nguyen, C., Kazi, R., Subramanian, S., DiVerdi, S., Martinez Plasencia, D.: Slicing-volume: hybrid 3D/2D multi-target selection technique for dense virtual environments, pp. 53–62 (2020). https://doi.org/10.1109/VR46266.2020.1581198507712

36. Mota, R.C.R., Rocha, A., Silva, J.D., Alim, U., Sharlin, E.: 3De interactive lenses for visualization in virtual environments. In: 2018 IEEE Scientific Visualization Conference (Scientific Visualization), pp. 21–25 (2018). https://doi.org/10.1109/SciVis.2018.8823618

37. Mott, M.E., Wobbrock, J.O.: Beating the bubble: using kinematic triggering in the bubble lens for acquiring small, dense targets. In: Proceedings of CHI 2014, pp. 733–742. NY, USA (2014). https://doi.org/10.1145/2556288.2557410

38. Olwal, A., Feiner, S.: The flexible pointer: An interaction technique for augmented and virtual reality (2012)

39. Payne, A.R., Plimmer, B., McDaid, A., Luxton-Reilly, A., Davies, T.C.: Expansion cursor: a zoom lens that can be voluntarily activated by the user at every individual click. In: Proceedings of the 28th Australian Conference on Computer-Human Interaction, pp. 81–90. OzCHI 2016, New York, NY, USA (2016). https://doi.org/10.1145/3010915.3010942

40. Pietriga, E., Appert, C.: Sigma lenses: focus-context transitions combining space, time and translucence. In: Proceedings of CHI 2008, pp. 1343–1352. NewYork, NY, USA (2008). https://doi.org/10.1145/1357054.1357264

41. Pindat, C., Pietriga, E., Chapuis, O., Puech, C.: Drilling into complex 3D models with gimlenses. In: Proceedings of the 19th ACM Symposium on Virtual Reality Software and Technology, pp. 223–230. VRST 2013, New York, NY, USA (2013). https://doi.org/10.1145/2503713.2503714

42. Plasson, C., Cunin, D., Laurillau, Y., Nigay, L.: Tabletop ar with hmd and tablet: a comparative study for 3D selection. In: Proceedings of ISS 2019, pp. 409–414 (2019). https://doi.org/10.1145/3343055.3360760

43. Plasson, C., Cunin, D., Laurillau, Y., Nigay, L.: 3D tabletop ar: a comparison of mid-air, touch and touch+mid-air interaction. In: Proceedings of AVI 2020 (2020). https://doi.org/10.1145/3399715.3399836

44. Ramos, G., Cockburn, A., Balakrishnan, R., Beaudouin-Lafon, M.: Pointing lenses: facilitating stylus input through visual-and motor-space magnification. In: Proceedings of CHI 2007, pp. 757–766. New York, NY, USA (2007). https://doi.org/10.1145/1240624.1240741

45. Ramos Mota, R.C., Cartwright, S., Sharlin, E., Hamdi, H., Costa Sousa, M., Chen, Z.: Exploring immersive interfaces for well placement optimization in reservoir models. In: Proceedings of SUI 2016, pp. 121–130 (2016). https://doi.org/10.1145/2983310.2985762

46. Reipschläger, P., Dachselt, R.: Designar: immersive 3D-modeling combiningaugmented reality with interactive displays. In: Proceedings of ISS 2019, pp. 29–41. New York, NY, USA (2019). https://doi.org/10.1145/3343055.3359718

47. Ro, H., et al.: A dynamic depth-variable ray-casting interface for object manipulation in ar environments and Cybernetics, Man, pp. 2873–2878 (2017). https://doi.org/10.1109/SMC.2017.8123063

48. Schmalstieg, D., Höllerer, T.: Augmented reality: principles and practice. In: 2017 IEEE Virtual Reality (VR), pp. 425–426 (2017). https://doi.org/10.1109/VR.2017.7892358

49. Spindler, M., Dachselt, R.: Paperlens: advanced magic lens interaction above the tabletop. In: Proceedings of ITS 2009. New York, NY, USA (2009). https://doi.org/10.1145/1731903.1731948

50. Spindler, M., Tominski, C., Schumann, H., Dachselt, R.: Tangible views for information visualization. In: Proceedings of ITS 2010, pp. 157–166. NewYork, NY, USA (2010). https://doi.org/10.1145/1936652.1936684

51. Stoev, S., Schmalstieg, D., Straer, W.: Two-handed through-the-lens-techniques for navigation in virtual environments (2001). https://doi.org/10.2312/EGVE/EGVE01/051-060

52. Stoev, S., Schmalstieg, D., Straßer, W.: The through-the-lens metaphor: taxonomy and application, pp. 285–286 (2002). https://doi.org/10.1109/VR.2002.996541

53. Tominski, C., Gladisch, S., Kister, U., Dachselt, R., Schumann, H.: Interactive lenses for visualization: an extended survey. Comput. Graph. Forum 36(6), 173–200 (2017). https://doi.org/10.1111/cgf.12871

54. Tong, X., Li, C., Shen, H.W.: Glyphlens: view-dependent occlusion management in the interactive glyph visualization. IEEE TVCG 23(1), 891–900 (2017). https://doi.org/10.1109/TVCG.2016.2599049

55. Traoré, M., Hurter, C., Telea, A.: Interactive obstruction-free lensing for volumetric data visualization. IEEE TVCG 25(1), 1029–1039 (2019). https://doi.org/10.1109/TVCG.2018.2864690

56. Vanacken, L., Grossman, T., Coninx, K.: Exploring the effects of environment density and target visibility on object selection in 3D virtual environments. In: Proceedings of 3DUI 2007 (2007). https://doi.org/10.1109/3DUI.2007.340783

57. Vanacken, L., Grossman, T., Coninx, K.: Multimodal selection techniques for dense and occluded 3D virtual environments. Int. J. Hum.-Comput. Stud. **67**(3), 37–255 (2009). https://doi.org/10.1016/j.ijhcs.2008.09.001

58. Vickers, D.L.: Sorcerer's Apprentice: Head-Mounted Display and Wand. Ph.D. thesis, vol. 10(5555/906408), aAI7310165 (1972)

59. Viega, J., Conway, M.J., Williams, G., Pausch, R.: 3D magic lenses. In: Proceedings of UIST 1996, pp. 51–58. New York, NY, USA (1996). https://doi.org/10.1145/237091.237098

60. Vogel, D., Baudisch, P.: Shift: a technique for operating pen-based interfaces using touch. In: Proceedings of CHI 2007, pp. 657–666. New York, NY, USA (2007). https://doi.org/10.1145/1240624.1240727

61. Wobbrock, J.O., Findlater, L., Gergle, D., Higgins, J.J.: The aligned rank transform for nonparametric factorial analyses using only anova procedures. Proc. CHI '11, 143–146 (2011). https://doi.org/10.1145/1978942.1978963

# Designing a Tangible Device
# for Re-Framing Unproductivity

Judith Sirera[1]([✉]) and Eduardo Velloso[2]([✉])

[1] KTH Royal Institute of Technology, Kungliga Tekniska Högskolan,
100 44 Stockholm, Sweden
jsip@kth.se
[2] School of Computing and Information Systems,
University of Melbourne, Doug McDonell Building, Melbourne, VIC, Australia
eduardo.velloso@unimelb.edu.au

**Abstract.** We report on the design of a tangible device for encouraging
the acceptance of unproductive time on office workers. We first conducted
interviews for a better understanding of the subjective experience of productivity. We found that while the idea of being productive can evoke
positive feelings of satisfaction, dealing with unproductive time can be
a struggle, negatively affecting people's moods and self-esteem. These
findings guided the design and implementation of RU, a tangible device
for reflecting on self-care time. Our prototype offers a physical representation of the mainstream productivity mindset and plays with the idea
of connecting and charging energy to encourage the user to experience
the time considered unproductive as self-care. In a second study, participants used the device for 5 days and our results suggest that the device
motivates reflection on activities beyond work and increases awareness
of the importance of taking time for self-care.

**Keywords:** Tangible User Interface · TUI · Research through design ·
Productivity · Self-care · Self-awareness · Interaction design · Tools

## 1 Introduction

In an era of hyper-productivity where time is capital, one can identify a deep-
seated mindset that constantly pushes people to be more productive. As society
subscribes increasingly more to this mindset, even children are taught to think
in terms of the productive use of their time [11], and by the time they reach
adulthood, they believe that they should strive to optimise for productivity [26].
Productivity is broadly related to a work-context, and as a consequence, people
struggle with the tension of balancing work and leisure, as what is considered
"unproductive" is de-prioritised [2]. The obsession about avoiding unproductivity results in built-up pressure, leading to stress and anxiety, and potentially
culminating in stress fatigue [32].

Productivity evokes feelings of accomplishment and can work in a positive
reinforcement loop but, if taken to an extreme, it can have damaging health consequences. Setting aside time to breathe and recharge can be deeply beneficial.

© IFIP International Federation for Information Processing 2021
Published by Springer Nature Switzerland AG 2021
C. Ardito et al. (Eds.): INTERACT 2021, LNCS 12935, pp. 525–545, 2021.
https://doi.org/10.1007/978-3-030-85610-6_29

Taking care of one's mental, physical, and emotional health increases wellbeing, and, in turn, contributes to productivity [17,29]. Because productivity and
self-care are two concepts that go hand-in-hand, helping users strike a balance
between both attitudes is an important challenge for interaction designers [34].

While there is a wealth of available tools to support users in self-tracking
for improved productivity [40], we found little research on dealing with the
other side of this coin. Most available solutions consist of tools that track users'
work-related activities at a device or application level, disregarding activities
performed beyond computing devices [16,38,43]. These technologies are characterized by quantification [46], thus reducing the complexity of life to a numeric
representation and ignoring the inherent subjectivity of the lived experience [27].
Instead, in this work, we depart from quantifiable measures, and we tackle the
concept from a subjective experience angle.

The main goal in this work was to explore the potential for re-framing the
negative understanding of unproductivity as an opportunity for self-care through
the design of tangible technology. We consider three different research questions:
(1) around the understanding of the concepts of productivity, unproductivity and
self-care from a subjective experience using qualitative methods; (2) around the
design of tangible technologies, stepping away from digital screen-based devices
and using design as a medium to encourage the acceptance of overlooked aspects
of life, often considered wrong, embarrassing, or taboo, rather than focusing on
aiming to right what is wrong or lacking [4,14]; and (3) around the positive outcomes of making tangible the invisible concepts, and the influence on increasing
awareness on self-care time and acceptance of unproductivity.

We believe that re-framing the concept of unproductivity is the first step for
a better and more positive understanding. Therefore, in this project, we refer as
*self-care* to all activities that fall outside the banner of productivity, but have
a positive potential for wellbeing. This intentional re-naming is to avoid the
dichotomous understanding of one being good and the other being bad.

This paper reports on the design process of RU (see Fig. 1), a device that
motivates users to reflect upon their productivity time, and encourage them to
take time for self-care activities. We named the system RU after the old Swedish
word *ro*, which is pronounced *ru* and means peace and calm. This work consists
of two studies. The first study explores the design space of productivity and its
inherent subjectivity. From the 12 interviews we conducted, we gained a better
understanding of the experience of productivity, and we uncovered problematic
perceptions of unproductivity. Such findings led to the design and implementation of RU, which was deployed in a second study and evaluated in a real-
world setting. Our findings support our design intentions of engaging in self-care
mindset and demonstrate that the device enhances awareness in the benefits and
importance of dedicating time to self-care activities.

We want to state the limitations of this project to research purposes. This
work does not aim for the design of a commercial product nor to implement
an ultimate and definitive device for behavior change. Instead, we use design
practices and qualitative methods to explore the space of productivity, unpro-

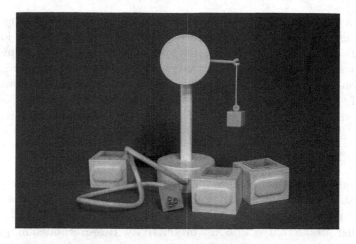

**Fig. 1.** The first working prototype of RU

ductivity, and self-care with the aim of creating new knowledge about these concepts. With this project we want to motivate and inspire other researchers to challenge productivity thinking and insist on the importance of striking an optimal work-life balance. This work also intends to start a discussion around the current hyper-productive era, and offer the reader the opportunity to reflect on their productivity, and self-care time.

## 2   Related Work

### 2.1   Productivity Trackers

Tracking productivity has long been an object of interest to researchers and product developers. The key idea behind it is that by improving self-awareness, one can enhance productivity [29]. When tracking their productivity, the user is given the opportunity to reflect on their behavior, learn from it, and maximise the amount of work they can achieve [8,12,28]. As a result, a variety of self-tracking applications and devices have been developed to support users in boosting their productivity by improving their time management (e.g. RescueTime [38], Toggl [43]) or blocking distracting applications (e.g. Focus [16]). Academic researchers have also proposed frameworks that use computing technologies and data analytics as guidelines for users to track, analyze, and improve their productivity [9,46].

The most common solutions are systems designed for the digital space in the form of screen-based applications that track the activities the user does. The principle behind current systems is that productivity can be quantifiable and time can be classified as productive or unproductive based on data captured as users carry out their activities. While semi-automated approaches minimise user effort [33], the system may define a task as unproductive when, in the eyes of the user, it is perceived as productive. For example, whereas reading the news might be unproductive for an engineer, it is a critical aspect of a journalist's work. This disambiguation is often done a priori, with users labelling different applications and websites as productive or unproductive use of their time. Such automation also misses a valuable opportunity for reflection—solutions that aim to quantify human behavior suppress the user with their option to decide upon their actions and discard the values of personal experience and emotion [36].

## 2.2    The Subjectivity of Productivity

Most research studies focus on productivity in the workplace through a quantitative approach [25], and little is known about personal productivity as a subjective experience that occurs beyond typical office work [27].

Tracking productivity can boost productivity. However, ongoing pressure to be productive leads to stress and anxiety, thereby negatively affecting health outcomes [7,42]. This creates a delicate relationship between wellbeing and productivity—while wellbeing positively contributes to productivity, excessive demands on productivity might hinder wellbeing [17,23]. Therefore, it is crucial to strike an optimal work-life balance [34]: *A state of equilibrium in which the demands of both a person's job and personal life are equal* [47].

The excessive focus on productivity thinking gives birth to a new lifestyle trend that opposes it. *Anti-productivity* challenges productivity thinking, encouraging people to do things that do not yield measurable results, or to do something for the sake of doing it. It also proposes measuring productivity in terms of feelings and emotions rather than on concrete outcomes [13].

In line with this philosophy, the "Anti-ToDo list" [3] method consists of only listing the achievements of the day rather that writing tasks and crossing them out. The user ends their day with a list of all of the things they accomplished rather than a list of things still left to do. As far as we are aware, there is no literature on the concept, yet research suggests that positive feedback induces rewarding feelings, whereas capturing negative behaviors might increase stress levels on the user [28].

At the opposite end of the productivity mindset lies the Chinese concept of *Wu-Wei* [1]. The principle stems from the philosophy of Taoism, which emphasizes living in harmony with the Tao ("The Way"). *Wu Wei* is the balance of the elements both within and outside the body. Although the term translates from Chinese as "do nothing" the actual meaning of the concept is more akin to "effortless action". The mindset embraces the ups and downs of life, accepting them instead of fighting against them. Flow days refer to high-energy days, whereas ebb days refer to low-energy days. Applied in productivity thinking, the Wu-Wei ideal encourages acknowledging the time of not being productive, rather than enforcing productivity at all times.

## 2.3  Designing for the Physical Space

While we found a great number of productivity-related digital tools, few technologies consider tangible interactions within the physical space to design for productivity [10,22,24,35] and self-care.

Physical technologies focused on self-care have resulted in devices that encourage reflection on negative behaviors or situations to gain self-awareness [5]. For example, Nidra [37] targets sleep routines that have been hindered by stress and erratic schedules. The author challenges productivity thinking by encouraging the user to pay more attention to their sleep patterns.

In line with the topic of stress, the Stressball project [39] is a conceptual prototype that explores the emotion of stress from a qualitative perspective. The project not only targets stress but challenges the reductionist nature of self-tracking technologies that quantify the human body down to numbers and diagrams.

So far, we discussed a variety of systems and tools that focus on improving productivity through the design of digital tools that quantify human behavior. While these solutions are mostly based on productivity in a work context, we found literature that suggests productivity to happen anywhere, anytime [27]. These studies use qualitative methods for understanding the inherent subjectivity of productivity. In this research, we also approach productivity from a different perspective. We ground our work on alternatives that explore the design space in the periphery of productivity prioritizing individual values and emotions rather than quantifiable measures. We are also inspired by studies that focus on designing tangible devices that portray abstract concepts, and explore the interactivity and positive outcomes of it. Last, we support all technologies that encourage the acceptance of a rejected attitude. We explore through design the concepts productivity, unproductivity and self-care by making them tangible and interactive. Our research also adds to the knowledge about personal productivity, unproductivity, and self-care, from a subjective perspective.

## 3  Study 1: Understanding Subjective Experiences of Productivity

We began our design process by exploring participants' subjective understanding of productivity, aiming to identify opportunities within the design space of productivity for grounding the design and implementation of prototype.

### 3.1  Study Design

This study consisted of semi-structured interviews about the subjective experience of productivity[1]. Through these conversations, we aimed to learn about

---

[1] We conducted all interviews online via Zoom in either Spanish, Catalan or English as they preferred. All Non-English quotes we report from this study are a translation from the original language.

perceptions and practices in relation to productivity. We covered the following main aspects: conceptualisation of productivity, feelings and emotions of productivity and unproductivity, and tools and methods for boosting productivity.

We recruited 12 participants (7 men and 5 women) for this first study. Our sample was comprised of participants from different backgrounds, nationalities, and ages (23—69) to include a wide range of perspectives. All participants were knowledge workers, either being students or office workers. In this paper, we kept participants' identities anonymous and we refer to them by a numerical identifier (e.g. P9).

We used affinity mapping for synthesizing and concluding the relevant information. We first transcribed all interviews[2] for codification. We identified a collection of different codes that were clustered into more broad themes that portrayed the core findings. Examples of these codes were: mood, motherhood, state of flow, feelings, skills in productivity, productivity standards, acceptance, reward, motivation, locations of productivity, culture, and tools. Some of these codes (e.g. influence of culture, and motherhood, skills in productivity) were rejected as they did not align with our research topic of acceptance of unproductivty. We present the result of the analysis in four main concepts: *the conceptualisation of productivity, the experience of unproductivity*, and *tools and methods*.

## 3.2   Results

**Conceptualisation of Productivity.** Our analysis revealed different conceptualisations of productivity. We derived three themes from participants' responses: *goal achievement, time efficiency, perception of progress.*

The goal achievement approach consisted of defining a set of objectives to accomplish, normally constrained by a time-frame.

*"So for me productivity is achieving whatever goals I set out to do, or achieving small milestones in a project" (P1)*

While this theme is task-driven, participants who focused on using time efficiently were time-driven—meaning participants aimed to seize their time and pursue as much as possible within a given time-frame. Setting the right timing required self-awareness of their own capabilities.

*"It also requires to know what I'm capable of doing in the given time. Of course, my timing has nothing to do with other people's time" (P2)*

On the other hand, participants reported to feel productive when they felt progress in their goals.

*"A productive day is when I set certain goals for the day, and I might not have achieved them, but I feel I made some progress on it." (P5)*

To assess their productivity, the most common parameters were time, tasks, and quality of the outcome. While time and tasks are quantifiable parameters, quality is a more subjective criterion.

---

[2] All interviews were audio-recorded under the participants' consent.

**The Experience of Unproductivity.** All participants used positive adjectives to describe the feeling of productivity, identifying it with success, satisfaction, fulfillment, and relief. These emotions are positive reinforcing and motivating to keep being productive. Participants called this experience as "be in the flow":

> *"The feeling of having finished tasks is what motivates me the most to do more. Once it starts the flow, it's very smooth. [...] Sounds like positive feedback." (P1)*

We found the concept to appear in several interviews. Participants also mentioned to be a state of high concentration in which time flows:

> *"...I'm really in the flow, and I forget the time, and that's very nice" (P7)*

But productivity does not always flow. In these situations, participants felt dejected and struggled with the surge of negative emotions. Unproductivity evoked from guilt to frustration, to uselessness. These feelings might reach a point that negatively impacts mood and, in extreme situations, lowers self-esteem.

> *"When I'm not productive, I'm not in the mood for doing anything. Days I'm unproductive, my self-esteem lowers. I might associate it with my image and things like this. It all builds up, and I start feeling I don't know anything. I feel useless" (P9)*

We collected a wide range of different solutions for fighting unproductivity and getting back on track. Some of these include avoiding distractions, taking breaks, switching to other activities, or changing the environment. In any case, participants who instead accepted being unproductive were able to minimise negative feelings and bring calm and relief.

> *"It can be a very relieving feeling to just put it [the task] aside, for trying out again later. If it doesn't work, then do it another day that you feel with more energy. So it can be good to accept not to be productive." (P7)*

Three interviewees started a discussion about the role of society in personal productivity. All three participants blamed society for imposing high productivity standards, building up pressure and stress. According to them, there is the habit of comparing yourself to others, an attitude that has been amplified by social media. In most cases, such comparison results in negative feelings.

> *"You might feel useless if you're not doing 100 different activities" (P3)*

We found that productivity increases in productive environments. Participants felt more productive when surrounded by other people that seem to be productive. This phenomenon is what we refer to as social influence.

> *"I like the library or any place where other people study. [...] I don't get distracted because I see other people working. Being surrounded by productive people helps me to stay focus." (P6)*

Aside from social influence, we encountered a variety of factors—external and internal— that affect, both positively and negatively, productivity. External factors include weather, and culture, whereas internal factors are intrinsic to the person, such as mood and amount/quality of sleep.

**Tools, Methods and Techniques.** We listed up to 15 different tools and techniques—digital and physical—used by participants in a context of productivity. Participants were interested in tools that induce reflection on their time, and support on mistakes and shortcomings. In one case, the participant was motivated to use systems that enhance their work-life balance, claiming the difficulty of finding the right balance:

> "I would like a system able to monitor all my activities, and determined my productivity in each of my personal areas. I would like to see if I'm in work-life balance." (P4)

### 3.3 Discussion

Our study with 12 participants confirmed the inherent subjectivity of productivity. Although participants shared similar notions of what productivity is—the experience of getting things done within a time-frame—their specific perspectives somewhat differed. In line with previous research [27], productivity was generally related to office work, yet participants included other types of activities (e.g. sports) as well. We identified a pattern among these other activities—they tended to be driven by outcomes, a deadline, or a sense of duty (e.g. cleaning, grocery shopping). Passive activities that required little or no interaction, or lack of a clear purpose (e.g. be on social media, taking a nap) were commonly categorized as "unproductive".

Our findings suggest a need for an improved conceptualisation of productivity, which leads to negative feelings when out of control. Productivity is a dynamic phenomenon, adapting to new situations and environments [27]. Participants also commented on the role of society in the evaluation of productivity. Assessing productivity was, in most cases, also influenced by mainstream productivity thinking. Society setting high standards of productivity and comparing oneself to others results in built-up pressure and stress [42].

All these circumstances might generate frustration in moments of low productivity. Being in a state of flow—highly focused and productive—evokes positive feelings of success, satisfaction, and pride. It works as positive reinforcement and motivation to stay on track. On the contrary, unproductivity can have the opposite effect. The negative feelings might reach a point of impacting mood and even self-esteem. While most participants acknowledged fighting against these situations, those who went through a process of accepting their circumstances were better equipped to cope with negative emotions.

In this first study, we uncovered the need to design for the struggle of dealing with the counter effects of productivity, and enhance the positive consequences of accepting unproductivity. In the current era of hyper-connectivity where digital devices are an extension of the self [6], it is very easy to get carried away in productivity and be deprived from self-care time [19,30]. We consider this an opportunity to create positive impact on people's wellbeing, and to bring knowledge and inspiration to the research community for further research in the topic. The results of this study and previous literature also motivated us to (1) reject the quantification of productivity and use qualitative methods for exploring the experience; (2) challenge mainstream productivity thinking; and (3) explore the potential of designing Tangible User Interfaces (TUIs).

## 4   RU: Design and Implementation

RU is a device for reflecting upon and accepting the time and energy spent on activities that might be considered unproductive, but are essential for maintaining the user's wellbeing. The design of RU is the result of an iterative design process of exploration, sketching, lo-fi prototyping, and role playing. The device is the portrayal of different ideas and themes that departed from symbols of productivity, unproductivity, and self-care (e.g. balance, time, energy) which evolved throughout the design process into the final prototype.

The metaphor that guided the design of RU was that self-care is the energy that allows us to carry the weight of our work life. We designed the system as a device that makes these concepts tangible while giving continuous feedback as an ambient display [45]. As a symbol for the weight of the productivity mindset, the device has an arm that carries a weight. Throughout the day the arm becomes "tired", slowly and almost imperceptibly lowering the weight up to a point where it is dropped.

To prevent the weight from dropping, the user must "charge" the device. This can be achieved by plugging it into one of the sockets in a set of blocks provided to the user (see Fig. 2). Each block represents a self-care activity defined by the user. The user can also set a strength for that activity by turning a knob in the corresponding block, depending on how they conceptualise their contribution to their own self-care. For example, the user might have one socket for the activity "play tennis" set to maximum importance because they feel that is a crucial activity for their wellbeing. Then, every time the user practices the sport, they would connect RU to the socket for charging it.

RU continuously discharges over time. Every 25 min, the arm rotates two degrees clockwise. The movement is small and smooth, making the change only perceptible after a long time. It takes around 16 h for the arm to travel from one end to the other. These are the total of waking hours in a day $(24\,h - 8\,h = 16\,h)$, taking into account that 8 h of sleep is an often recommended amount of sleep time [20].

RU charges when connecting it into a socket. Then, the arm rotates anticlockwise as much as the value given to the socket. This value is proportional to the charge capacity—the bigger the value, the more the charge capacity and the longer is the arm ticking anticlockwise. When charging, the user must push down

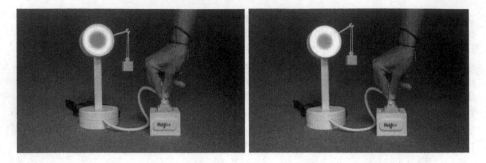

**Fig. 2.** The interaction for charging RU to the socket with the activity "Netflix" assigned to it. Yellow light (left) indicates that is charging. Green light (right) means fully charged (Color figure online)

the plug until fully charged, which can take up to 5 s. Otherwise, the charge is interrupted at half load. This way, we ensure the user does not leave connected the plug with the intention of continuously charging. When connected, RU's face lights up, increasing its brightness as it charges. The light color switches from yellow to green, indicating full charge.

The arm only reaches its highest position when the user has plugged several sockets in a relatively short time. Nevertheless, if the user does not connect RU to any activity for a long time, the arm keeps ticking clockwise to the point of reaching the lower position. This increases the chance that the hanging object drops and fall out the arm. Through this subtle interaction, we notify the user of the need for self-care activities.

RU's aesthetics resembles a scale, thus reflecting the importance of work-life balance. By charging and discharging RU, the user is automatically committing to their self-care. RU demands little effort but continuous use, reminding the user to be consistent with their self-care activities.

### 4.1  Hardware

RU has two different parts: the **main station**, and three **sockets**.

The main station (see Fig. 3, left) consists of the base, at the bottom, and the face, at the top. The stem joins both parts. From the base, a yellow plug comes out from the front. We also added an on/off switch and reset button at the back of the base. The face has a built-in light system and a arm coming out from the right side. From the arm, there is a hanging cube that represents weight. Both the arm and the weight rotate clock- and anticlockwise up to 20° from the balanced position—when the arm is neither tilted upwards nor downwards. When resetting RU, or turning it on for the first time, the arm resets to the balanced position.

The sockets (see Fig. 3, right) are wooden blocks that represent the different self-care activities assigned by the user. Each socket has a whiteboard at the front face for writing down the activities' name. In the back, we added a knob

**Fig. 3.** RU. On the left, the main station. On the right, the three sockets

for the user to indicate the importance of that corresponding box—a higher value means more importance of the activity which translates to more charging capacity.

From a technical perspective, the device consists of four main components: the light, the arm, the plug, and the socket. All of them connect to an Arduino MKR1000 WIFI that controls all the logic of the system. The micro-controller is held in the base of the main station. For the lighting, we used a 24 LEDs NeoPixel Ring that supports different colors and brightness. The arm is attached to a mini servo that rotates clock- and anticlockwise. The servo is limited, with software, to rotate up to an angle of 40° from one end to the other. Last, the plug does not have a standard regulated design, but specific to the device, meaning that only fits to the outlet in the sockets. We recycled the cable and the pins of regular plugs to implement a customized plug with three pins: one for power, the other for ground, and the third is data. The shell was 3D modeled for 3D printing. When plugged to the socket, each pin of the plug connects to the corresponding pin of the potentiometer inside the socket. The potentiometer allows the user to change the value of the socket. The sockets are powerless blocks and when RU is plugged into one, the electronic circuit is powered, and the micro-controller reads the value of the potentiometer resistance. To ensure this connection, we implemented a system made of springs for a better current conduction from the main station to the potentiometer.

Last, the device is powered using a power bank that connects to the black USB port sticking out from the back of the base.

## 5   Study 2: Deployment and Evaluation of RU

The second study focused on the deployment and evaluation of RU in a real-world setting. The objectives were (1) test our design for re-framing unproductivity; (2) get insights on the different interactions with RU; (3) learn about the concept of self-care; and (4) test the device from a technical perspective.

## 5.1   Study Design

We decided for an *in-the-wild* deployment of our research product like a technology probe [21] where participants take the device home and use it without the supervision of a researcher. Each deployment lasted five days. We considered this time-frame to be appropriate for the user to explore RU, and for the research team to identify any changes in the user's experience of unproductivity.

We provided each participant with a complete kit for the use of the system (see Fig. 4). The kit included RU, three sockets, a diary, the instructions of use, one power bank, a whiteboard marker and eraser. We asked participants to complete the diary throughout the study. The diary had four parts: the location, the sockets, the daily report, notes and comments. In the first section, the participant described where they placed RU in their environment. In the second section, we asked the participant to keep track of all the changes regarding sockets and knobs, and the activity assignation process. In the third section, we asked the participant to summarize their feelings of that day, and log in the daily activities used for charging RU.

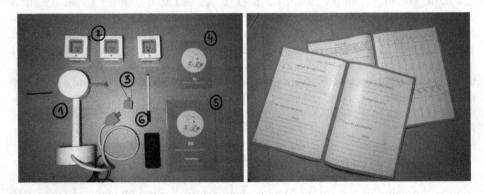

**Fig. 4.** The evaluation kit and diary: (1) RU, (2) three sockets, (3) weight, (4) instructions of use, (5) diary, (6) whiteboard marker and power bank

We recruited five participants (P13—P17) from different backgrounds, ages (25—59), and gender (4 women/1 man) for testing and evaluating RU. Following the same criteria than study 1, we limited the study to knowledge workers.

At the start of the study, we gave participants the details of this research and specific instructions on how the deployment would proceed. We introduced the device and carefully explained how it worked. We also provided the instructions in written form. We emphasized the free nature of certain parts of the study, such as designating activities to the sockets, and the importance given to them, which were left open for participants to assign whichever way they wanted. We explained how to complete the diary, which also contained a written description of each section. Last, we provided them with the contact information of the principal researcher for any problems that might arise during the study. After the evaluation period, we conducted the final interview about their experience using the device.

For data analysis, we followed the same procedure as the first study, using affinity mapping, for synthesizing and structuring all collected data.

## 5.2   Results

**A Tool for Reflection.** Participants described the experience of using RU as positive, helpful, motivating, and innovative. RU helped them to reflect upon activities that fall outside the work environment and contribute to self-care, increasing awareness on the importance of taking time off productive work:

*"It's been a very positive experience. [..] it turned out to be a tool that helped me to take more time for myself."* (P15)

All participants reported the device to be very intuitive and easy to use, and to not feel overwhelmed by the tasks and interactions with RU. They interacted with RU mostly at the end of the day, as it was only possible if they were at home where RU was. Participants opted for a place of high visibility to them, where it could work as a reminder:

*"I chose to put it in my nightstand because it's my 'non-working spot', my place for reflection. Besides, it gives me privacy, and it [RU] won't be exposed to the rest of the family."* (P15)

Not being able to connect RU at any time yield to the opportunity for reflecting on all the activities of the day. One participant elaborated on the idea of productivity is time you invested in others, whereas self-care time is for oneself. Participants translated the interaction of connecting and charging RU to themselves, feeling as if charging their wellbeing:

*"It was like I was doing it to me, as if I was connecting and charging myself."* (P13)

Another participant insisted on how productivity thinking blinds them from self-care activities. The participant used the concept of "generalization" to describe situations of little awareness of good experiences because these are masked in a negative feeling produced by productivity thinking:

*"It helped me to be more aware that I have to take time for myself. Sometimes you feel you only work, but if you stop, you see that there are moments in which we do nothing, and it's good because we need them. Still, we don't stop. [...]"* (P16)

**The Interpretation of Connecting and Charging RU.** Our participants interacted with RU both during weekdays and weekends. In the weekend, participants registered more activities, so RU's arm tended to be tilted upwards and the weight not to fall. One participant mentioned that they managed to keep the device charged at maximum, making the weight fell in the opposite direction. The participant reported this as a very positive experience, rewarding them for spending time on self-care:

> "The day I spent all day with my daughter, [...] and charged to the highest position. That was amazing. It was very positive feedback, and I thought: I achieved it, I reached the top. It was motivating and super satisfying." (P16)

On the other hand, during work days, most of the participants spent a long time without interacting with RU and reported to have less time for self-care activities. For a few participants, not to charge RU in a long period turned out to be inconvenient and frustrating. Yet, all participants were, at different levels, triggered by it and motivated to engage in self-care:

> "I was expecting it [to see the cube on the floor] because I would spend all day at the office. Anyway, it was like a representation that I should spend more time in self-care activities. It was a bit sad [to find it that way], but then I would charge all the activities and think the day wasn't that bad." (P13)

To overcome this situation, participants recommended complementing the system with an app or additional device that allowed them to charge RU anywhere at anytime, allowing interaction with RU throughout the day rather than connecting all the activities at once.

**Assigning Activities to the Sockets.** We found two methods for the use of the sockets: the flexible and fixed approach. The former consists of assigning an activity per socket, having three simultaneously. In case the participant wanted to add a new activity, they would erase the socket's whiteboard and write down the new activity's name. In the fixed approach, the participants gave each socket an importance value—low, medium, or high—and assigned multiple activities to one same socket, based on the level of importance.

For all participants, the importance of the socket was given based on the feeling resulting from the activity. The higher the contribution to self-care, the higher the value of the socket. Participants illustrated the process of giving value with examples:

> "To the activity music, I updated the importance. Maybe at one time, it is of medium importance, and at another moment, I spend the afternoon listening to music, dancing, and singing. Then I'm super happy, so I give it [the socket] a higher value." (P15)

One participant made a distinction between activities and in-activities, requiring the former an active involvement whereas in-activities lack of action. They also reported to be confusing the assignation process, choosing to only register deliberate activities:

*"I didn't add the times I was working and I would check twitter. This was not intentional, I didn't need a break." (P17)*

Participants registered up to 50 entries in the activity registration section of the diary. From all of them, we identified a total of 32 different activities, which we grouped into six categories based on the reasoning for choosing the activity. In some cases, one same activity was experienced differently, thus falling into two different categories. Below, we list the different categories with a short description and examples:

**Relax**: This category covers a wide range of different activities that help the user relax. Participants gave medium and high importance to them. Examples: reading, listening to music, watching TV, playing games, etc.

**Disconnection**: This category covers activities that induced a mental break from productivity thinking and their routines. Hence, most of them had high importance. Examples: reading, going to the beach, hanging out with friends, etc.

**Rest**: This category includes all activities with a passive interaction—the participant's interaction was little or none, and lacked of intended goal. We divided them into two subgroups: sleeping and do-nothing. The former is the time spent sleeping or similar (e.g. taking a nap, snoozing the alarm). The latter includes activities with no clear purpose (e.g. scrolling on the phone). These activities were given medium-low importance.

**Positive Energy**: This category covers activities performed just for the sake of having fun and enjoying the activity. These activities result in a positive change of mood, a feeling described as *"recharging your batteries"* (P13). Hence, participants assigned medium-high importance to all activities. Examples: going out for dinner, watching Netflix, or walking.

**Care**: All activities in this category are related to actions of taking care of themselves or another object/ living being. Participants considered these activities of medium-high importance. Examples: petting your dog, face cleaning, gardening, sport, etc.

**Strengthen Relationships**: This group comprises activities in which what mattered to participants was the social component rather than the activity itself. For these activities, the socket was set to the maximum value. Examples: playing board games, going to the beach with friends, etc.

# 6 Discussion

The use of RU resulted in a novel and positive experience for participants and its design was successful in terms of aesthetics, functionality, and meaning. The device presented a clean, minimal, and creative design that pleased participants.

## 6.1 Using Design for Engaging in Reflection

In our studies we found that RU gave space for reflecting on productive, unproductive, and self-care time, and enhances awareness on the benefits of self-care and the importance of it. The opportunity to focus on the experience of self-care guided participants through an inspiring and positive experience of reflection and self-knowledge. They reflected upon activities commonly understood as unproductive, and instead registered them as self-care activities.

*"Trouble" Design* focuses on designing for acceptance of neglected attitudes and is claimed to create a broader space as a straightforward problem/solution approach [14]. This work took inspiration from trouble design, and rejected all opportunities that aim to make productive the unproductive time. Instead, we used the design of a tangible technology to shift the negative conceptualization of unproductivity towards an opportunity for self-care. Such findings uncover the opportunity for designers of engaging with rejected behaviors, and use alternative design practices that work beyond the design space of fixing problems.

In this research, we used design to create a physical and interactive representation of the concept of productivity. Embodiment of invisible information through tangible forms gives the concepts giving the space and opportunity for the user to interact with them. For example, The Dangling String [45] gives to the invisible computer network a tangible form, providing the users with the opportunity to grasp the idea and reflect on the amount of network traffic of the room. From our findings, we conclude that the physical presence of RU acted as a *Tangible Well-being Reminder* to take time aside form productivity thinking and invest in on self-care activities. The device plays with the idea of "recharging batteries" through the interactions of connecting and charging the device with self-care energy. Participants associated the movement of the arm with personal satisfaction, and triggered a change when the weight fell. Ru demands of effortless but daily use, engaging with the user to find motivation for staying active in their self-care time. The device was designed to embody mainstream productivity thinking, and motivate the user to challenge it.

Our work highlights the valuable of tangible technologies in the context of productivity and self-care. In an era of hyper-productivity where digital technologies fuel productivity [6], we found the need to disconnect from it and find time to focus on oneself, like a "digital detox" [41]. The manual and tangible interaction that RU requires forces the user to create a time and a physical space off productivity for self-care reflection. We open a design space for exploration of different interactions and designs that challenge productivity thinking and encourage a more balanced lifestyle where productivity is not the dominant force.

## 6.2    Productivity, Unproductivity and Self-care

From our findings, we make a clear distinction among the three experiences. Productivity is the state of getting things done. Unproductivity occurs when there is a desire or need to be productive but no success. Our findings revealed several factors that can influence productivity and led to unproductivity. Self-care, however, is strongly related with the contribution to one's wellbeing. However, our results show that a same activity might feel unproductive or self-care based on the interest in being productive. For example, checking out social media is perceived as self-care or distraction according to the productivity goals.

Productivity evokes very contrary feelings, resulting in an imbalanced state of mind. You can be at the top, feeling successful and satisfied, or at the bottom wrapped in negative emotions. Instead, self-care activities always evoke positive emotions. Productivity thinking craves for more production and a busy lifestyle [32], whereas a self-care mindset surrounds people in a calmer and peaceful state of mind. Self-care slows down the high-speed lifestyle. We highlight the importance of finding a balance between the two attitudes to avoid stress fatigue [17,29].

From our studies we conclude that self-care is an abstract concept where feelings prevail. Participants might consider self-care all activities falling off the work environment, or just the time invested in themselves. The conflict aroused when considering active (e.g. sport) and passive activities—or in-active (e.g. lay on the sofa, be on social media). Participants clearly identified the former to self-care, because of the clear contribution to wellbeing, but in some cases, they found it confusing to consider the latter as well. Literature confirms that wellbeing and self-care is a dynamic state that can happen anywhere at anytime [18,31], the same as productivity [27].

These findings emphasize the inherent subjective nature of the three concepts. Our work points out the positive value of offering participants the opportunity to engage in reflection on the concepts and the use of their time. Our approach was to accept this subjectivity and focus on designing a tool to support users in making sense of their behavior [36]. Our findings suggest that this approach was successful, and is something others conducting similar work may be able to learn from.

## 6.3    Further Work

We identified new directions for further research together with design feedback for next iterations of RU. We engage in new research questions with the aim of inpsire other researchers to explore this design space. This paper introduces the idea of re-framing unproductiviy in knowledge office workers. As a result, we uncovered new opportunities to expand this exploration into other scenarios, like the workplace. We are interested in how design can support in embracing unproductivity in a space where productivity is demanded at its best. Similar approaches of bringing acceptance and self-compassion in situations of high levels of stress given in the workplace have been explored in other studies [15]. We also engage in the idea of adding a social component into re-framing unproductivity, as research supports the social influence among people [44], a behavior that we observed in our studies. The same way we found the social component to boost productivity, we are interested in designing and exploring how it can engage in acceptance of unproductiviy and self-care. We also encourage practitioners in critical design to align with this work and use design as a medium to critic the mainstream productivity mindset and bring up questions that challenge the current hyper-productive lifestyle and strike for an more balanced solution where self-care is as important as productivity.

# 7   Conclusion

The main goal in this work was to explore the potential for re-framing the negative understanding of unproductivity as an opportunity for self-care through the design of a tangible technology. Our first research question aimed to gain understanding in the subjective perception of personal productivity. Our findings from 12 interviews with office workers confirm the subjective nature of productivity and reveal insights about the experience. We report on the counter effects of productivity, which are neglected by society. The feeling of being productive is commonly associated with success and satisfaction, whereas unproductivity is considered a failure. However, participants who learned to accept the unproductive time brought relief and calm to their wellbeing. Our second research question focused on the exploration of tangible design for re-framing unproductivity— meaning the acceptance and change of perception from negative to a positive experience. We presented RU, a device that embodies mainstream productivity thinking and plays with the idea of connecting and charging to motivate reflection on unproductive and self-care time. We held a second study with 5 participants for validating our design and evaluating the device in a real-world setting. This leads to the third research question that explored the use of the tangible technology. Our second study confirmed that RU motivated and encouraged reflection on self-care activities, enhanced awareness of the benefits and importance of self-care, and challenged our participants to add the new habit of dedicating time for self-care everyday. In addition, the outcomes of giving a tangible form to these abstract concepts resulted in a enlightening experience that challenges mainstream productivity thinking. This research demonstrates the great potential for using tangible design in shifting the negative conceptualisation of unproductivity towards a positive experience of self-care. Our work is an opportunity for the research community to engage in design explorations of topics that are commonly disregarded and ignored by society. This research also challenges the approaches taken in self-tracking solutions, which reduce human emotions to numeric values, and motivates to integrate qualitative methods for tracking subjective experiences. We also encourage designers to delve into other forms of design, as we explored tangible user interfaces for abstract concepts. In our paper, we tackle an everyday challenge by opening a new design space for productivity, and starting a discussion for raising awareness on the importance of self-care in everyday life.

# References

1. Abowd, G.D., Mynatt, E.D.: Charting past, present, and future research in ubiquitous computing. ACM Trans. Comput.-Hum. Interact. **7**(1), 29–58 (2000). https://doi.org/10.1145/344949.344988
2. Allen, D.: Getting things done: The art of stress-free productivity. Penguin (2015)
3. Andreessen, M.: Guide to personal productivity (2007). https://pmarchive.com/guide_to_personal_productivity.html
4. Bardzell, J., Bardzell, S.: What is "critical" about critical design? In: Proceedings of the SIGCHI Conference on Human Factors in Computing Systems, pp. 3297–3306. CHI '13, Association for Computing Machinery, New York, NY, USA (2013). https://doi.org/10.1145/2470654.2466451
5. Barresi, G.: Tools for connected humans (2018). http://connectedhumans.tools/
6. Belk, R.: Digital consumption and the extended self. J. Mark. Manag. **30**(11-12), 1101–1118 (2014). https://doi.org/10.1080/0267257X.2014.939217
7. Brockner, J.: The relation of trait self-esteem and positive inequity to productivity. J. Pers. **53**(4), 517–529 (1985). https://doi.org/10.1111/j.1467-6494.1985.tb00380.x, https://onlinelibrary.wiley.com/doi/abs/10.1111/j.1467-6494.1985.tb00380.x
8. Cadiz, J.J., Venolia, G., Jancke, G., Gupta, A.: Designing and deploying an information awareness interface. In: Proceedings of the 2002 ACM Conference on Computer Supported Cooperative Work, pp. 314–323. CSCW '02, Association for Computing Machinery, New York, NY, USA (2002). https://doi.org/10.1145/587078.587122
9. Carroll, R.: The Bullet Journal Method: Track the Past, Order the Present, Design the Future. Portfolio (2018). https://bulletjournal.com/pages/book
10. Chan, S.: Bitskit. Master's thesis, OCAD University (2013). https://sallychan.ca/bitskit
11. Chin, C.: Teacher questioning in science classrooms: approaches that stimulate productive thinking. J. Res. Sci. Teach. **44**(6), 815–843 (2007). https://doi.org/10.1002/tea.20171, https://onlinelibrary.wiley.com/doi/abs/10.1002/tea.20171
12. Choe, E.K., Lee, N.B., Lee, B., Pratt, W., Kientz, J.A.: Understanding quantified-selfers' practices in collecting and exploring personal data. In: Proceedings of the SIGCHI Conference on Human Factors in Computing Systems, pp. 1143–1152. CHI '14, Association for Computing Machinery, New York, NY, USA (2014). https://doi.org/10.1145/2556288.2557372
13. Christine Seifert, P.: Do less: Anti-productivity is the new productivity (2019). https://bit.ly/3ly9z8g
14. Devendorf, L., Andersen, K., Kelliher, A.: Making design memoirs: understanding and honoring difficult experiences. In: Proceedings of the 2020 CHI Conference on Human Factors in Computing Systems, pp. 1–12. CHI '20, Association for Computing Machinery, New York, NY, USA (2020). https://doi.org/10.1145/3313831.3376345
15. Devenish-Meares, P.: Call to compassionate self-care: introducing self-compassion into the workplace treatment process. J. Spirituality Mental Health **17**(1), 75–87 (2015). https://doi.org/10.1080/19349637.2015.985579
16. Website blocker and app blocker for mac - focus (2015). https://heyfocus.com/
17. George, H., Dimitrios, B.: The effect of stress and satisfaction on productivity. Int. J. Product. Performance Manag. **59**(5), 415–431 (2010). https://doi.org/10.1108/17410401011052869

18. Godfrey, C.M., Harrison, M.B., Lysaght, R., Lamb, M., Graham, I.D., Oakley, P.: Care of self – care by other – care of other: the meaning of self-care from research, practice, policy and industry perspectives. Int. J. Evid.-Based Healthcare 9(1), 3–24 (2011). https://doi.org/10.1111/j.1744-1609.2010.00196.x, https://onlinelibrary.wiley.com/doi/abs/10.1111/j.1744-1609.2010.00196.x

19. Hair, M., Renaud, K., Ramsay, J.: The influence of self-esteem and locus of control on perceived email-related stress. Comput. Hum. Behav. 23(6), 2791–2803 (2007). https://doi.org/10.1016/j.chb.2006.05.005, https://www.sciencedirect.com/science/article/pii/S0747563206000756

20. Hirshkowitz, M., et al.: National sleep foundation's sleep time duration recommendations: methodology and results summary. Sleep Health 1(1), 40 – 43 (2015). https://doi.org/10.1016/j.sleh.2014.12.010, http://www.sciencedirect.com/science/article/pii/S2352721815000157

21. Hutchinson, H., et al.: Technology probes: inspiring design for and with families. In: Proceedings of the SIGCHI Conference on Human Factors in Computing Systems, pp. 17–24. CHI '03, Association for Computing Machinery, New York, NY, USA (2003). https://doi.org/10.1145/642611.642616

22. Højmose, A.: Daily stack (2010). http://everyoneelse.net/projects/daily-stack/

23. Jeurissen, T., Nyklíček, I.: Testing the vitamin model of job stress in dutch health care workers. Work Stress 15(3), 254–264 (2001). https://doi.org/10.1080/02678370110066607

24. Karlesky, M., Isbister, K.: Designing for the physical margins of digital workspaces: fidget widgets in support of productivity and creativity. In: Proceedings of the 8th International Conference on Tangible, Embedded and Embodied Interaction, pp. 13–20. TEI '14, Association for Computing Machinery, New York, NY, USA (2014). https://doi.org/10.1145/2540930.2540978

25. Kaur, H., Williams, A.C., McDuff, D., Czerwinski, M., Teevan, J., Iqbal, S.T.: Optimizing for Happiness and Productivity: Modeling Opportune Moments for Transitions and Breaks at Work, pp. 1–15. Association for Computing Machinery, New York, NY, USA (2020). https://doi.org/10.1145/3313831.3376817

26. Keinan, A., Kivetz, R.: Productivity mindset and the consumption of collectable experiences. ACR North American Advances (2008)

27. Kim, Y.H., Choe, E.K., Lee, B., Seo, J.: Understanding personal productivity: how knowledge workers define, evaluate, and reflect on their productivity. In: Proceedings of the 2019 CHI Conference on Human Factors in Computing Systems, pp. 1–12. CHI '19, Association for Computing Machinery, New York, NY, USA (2019). https://doi.org/10.1145/3290605.3300845

28. Kim, Y.H., Jeon, J.H., Choe, E.K., Lee, B., Kim, K., Seo, J.: Timeaware: leveraging framing effects to enhance personal productivity. In: Proceedings of the 2016 CHI Conference on Human Factors in Computing Systems, pp. 272–283. CHI '16, Association for Computing Machinery, New York, NY, USA (2016). https://doi.org/10.1145/2858036.2858428

29. Kompier, M., Cooper, C.L.: Preventing Stress, Improving Productivity: European Case Studies in the Workplace. Psychology Press, London (1999)

30. Kushlev, K., Dunn, E.W.: Checking email less frequently reduces stress. Comput. Hum. Behav. 43, 220–228 (2015). https://doi.org/10.1016/j.chb.2014.11.005, https://www.sciencedirect.com/science/article/pii/S0747563214005810

31. Lawton, M.: The varieties of wellbeing. Exp. Aging Res. 9(2), 65–72 (1983). https://doi.org/10.1080/03610738308258427, pMID: 6354725

32. Lazarus, R.S.: Psychological stress in the workplace. Occup. Stress Handb. 1, 3–14 (1995)

33. Li, I., Dey, A., Forlizzi, J.: A stage-based model of personal informatics systems. In: Proceedings of the SIGCHI Conference on Human Factors in Computing Systems, pp. 557–566. CHI '10, Association for Computing Machinery, New York, NY, USA (2010). https://doi.org/10.1145/1753326.1753409

34. Lockwood, N.R.: Work/life balance. Challenges and Solutions, SHRM Research, USA (2003)

35. Projects, S., Software, D.: Bit planner (2013). http://www.bit-planner.com/

36. Purpura, S., Schwanda, V., Williams, K., Stubler, W., Sengers, P.: Fit4life: the design of a persuasive technology promoting healthy behavior and ideal weight. In: Proceedings of the SIGCHI Conference on Human Factors in Computing Systems, pp. 423–432. CHI '11, Association for Computing Machinery, New York, NY, USA (2011). https://doi.org/10.1145/1978942.1979003

37. Raj, V.: Nidra (2020). https://www.varenyaraj.com/project/nidra

38. Rescuetime (2007). http://rescuetime.com/

39. Schramm, S.: Less quantified self-more qualified you//konzepte zu visueller und haptisch erfahrbarer kommunikation von körperdaten. UP 2016 (2016)

40. Snyder, M.: Self-monitoring of expressive behavior. J. Pers. Soc. Psychol. **30**(4), 526 (1974)

41. Syvertsen, T., Enli, G.: Digital detox: media resistance and the promise of authenticity. Convergence **26**(5-6), 1269–1283 (2020). https://doi.org/10.1177/1354856519847325

42. Taylor, H., Fieldman, G., Altman, Y.: E-mail at work: a cause for concern? the implications of the new communication technologies for health, wellbeing and productivity at work. Organisational Transform. Soc. Change **5**, 159–173 (2008). https://doi.org/10.1386/jots.5.2.159_1

43. Free time tracking software (2018). https://toggl.com/

44. Turner, J.C.: Social influence. Thomson Brooks/Cole Publishing Co (1991)

45. Weiser, M., Brown, J.S.: Designing calm technology. PowerGrid J. **1**(1), 75–85 (1996)

46. White, G., Liang, Z., Clarke, S.: A quantified-self framework for exploring and enhancing personal productivity. In: 2019 International Conference on Content-Based Multimedia Indexing (CBMI), pp. 1–6 (2019). https://doi.org/10.1109/CBMI.2019.8877475

47. Work life balance (2012). https://wordspy.com/index.php?word=work-life-balance

# Designing for Inaccessible People and Places

Judy Bowen$^{(\boxtimes)}$ and Annika Hinze

The University of Waikato, Hamilton, New Zealand
{jbowen,hinze}@waikato.ac.nz

**Abstract.** New Zealand forestry has the highest number of accident and fatalities than any other NZ industry. Worker fatigue, work environment and worker demographics all contribute to these high numbers. We have been investigating ways of tackling these problems using wearable and sensor-based technology. Two of the challenges faced by this project are: the personal nature of data collected by wearable technology and the lack of regular access to workers to take part in user-centred design activities. In this paper we describe the use of Lean UX methods with proxy participants and proxy technology to explore key aspects of a proposed technical solution. We show that from these experimental studies we were able to draw appropriate conclusions on which to base the development of a prototype designed to support forestry worker safety.

## 1 Introduction

The forestry industry is one of the most dangerous industries in New Zealand [21]. One of the main contributors to accidents is worker *fatigue* [2] which may be caused by the physical nature of the work as well as the cognitive load required when operating dangerous equipment. It may also be caused by workers taking insufficient breaks due to poor self-evaluation and expected performance [20]. We have been conducting research on the use of wearable technology that can be used to monitor workers for fatigue via personal metrics such as heart-rate variability (HRV) and galvanic skin response (GSR) [4]. Once the data is gathered and analysed, the next step is to investigate how to use this data to inform workers and encourage them to take breaks when they are fatigued. This is challenging due to the demographic of NZ forestry workers – predominantly male (96%) and below the age of 50 (65%) [7]. The work culture means that workers can be described as having a 'staunch kiwi male' attitude, which can lead to a minimising of potential risks and a desire to not appear weak in front of workmates. In addition, the use of personal monitoring in work environments can be controversial due to its invasiveness, without worker buy-in this can lead to deliberate undermining of the technology [1,3]. We have previously undertaken participatory design sessions to determine what types of technology and data collection/use is acceptable to forestry workers. However, time one can spend

© IFIP International Federation for Information Processing 2021
Published by Springer Nature Switzerland AG 2021
C. Ardito et al. (Eds.): INTERACT 2021, LNCS 12935, pp. 546–556, 2021.
https://doi.org/10.1007/978-3-030-85610-6_30

with groups of forestry workers is limited due to: the remote location of forestry work-sites; reluctance of forestry managers to give workers time to take part in research activities; long working days in forestry which makes end-of-day sessions unappealing. As such, we can typically only work with groups of forestry workers for three or four days a year and the rest of the time we have to rely on other design methods.

To report fatigue to workers and encourage them to take breaks, we propose the use of a 'Buddy System' (described below). Given the limited access to workers, we needed to use appropriate methods to investigate the key parts of our proposed buddy system before beginning participatory design which would make use of our limited access to the forestry workers. Taking inspiration from the ideas of Lean HCI and minimal viable product design (MVP) [9] we propose the use of proxies to investigate key attributes of the solution we wish to develop. During design, it is common to use personas as proxies for users to remind the design team of key characteristics of their users [17]. Here, we propose using both proxy participants and proxy technology. *Proxy participants* used in studies are different from the target user group but have characteristics that are relevant for the study. *Proxy technology* is used to investigate a crucial attribute of a system outside of its context (i.e. not in the form it will be implemented). Within our studies we distil the central underlying ideas of the proposed technology to study and use proxy technology within the studies which use proxy participants.

## 2    Background and Related Work

*Fatigue in the Workplace.* A study by Lilley et al. investigated the role that rest and recovery play in accidents and injury of forestry workers [13] and found that 78% of participants reported experiencing fatigue at work at least some of the time. They concluded that impairment due to fatigue constituted a significant risk factor within the industry. To identify fatigue in the workplace, an understanding of physiological markers and how they might be measured using wearable technology is required. Many studies investigated heart-rate and heart-rate variability as indicators of physical and mental stress (see for example [12,15,16]. These have formed the basis for investigations into the use of wearable technologies to detect and manage stress and fatigue in athletes [19], manufacturing operators [22], miners [14] etc. For our work, we combine heart-rate variability and galvanic skin response with contextual factors, such as temperature and terrain, to understand changes which represent the onset of fatigue [2].

*Persuasive Technologies.* Our proposed buddy system is related to persuasive technology and of most relevance for our work are persuasive technologies that focus on health-related behaviour. Halko and Kientz describe eight persuasive strategies that are commonly seen within this research field [10]. Our project is similar to their concept of a "neutral agent, such as a friend or peer to encourage the user to meet their goals" along with co-operative feedback. One of the issues we wish to address is the problem of workers not recognising that they are fatigued, or not responding to prompts to take breaks, because they are not concerned about potential impacts to their own health and safety. This can be seen in the following quote from a forestry workers: "You think you're bulletproof in the forest". Persuasive technology often utilises the ideas of peer support and external motivation. Peer support within technology has been shown to provide positive benefits, for example by motivating healthier lifestyles for people with diabetes [18] or encouraging behaviour change for young offenders [6]. We describe such systems as *'Buddy Systems'* as they build on the practice used in scuba diving where people are paired together for safety and support and monitor each others' well-being throughout the dive. Based on our experiences of working with forestry workers, where a strong team culture is encouraged, it seems likely that such a buddy system would be an appropriate persuasive mechanism for providing fatigue notifications and motivating workers to take breaks. Once wearable technology identifies fatigue, we must notify the worker so that they are aware they need to take a break. If they do not stop working, then their buddy is also notified. However, before we design and develop such a system we need to understand how the workers would feel about their fatigue status being shared with others (their work buddy or buddies) and the use of technology as an intervention.

## 3   Design Exploration with Proxy Participants

With limited access to the forestry workers, we needed to investigate the intrusiveness of our proposed system, and understand the effect on the users before we started developing a prototype for the buddy system. We identified four key features of our proposed buddy system with the potential to make workers feel uncomfortable: public display of fatigue status; technology providing prompts to take a break; notifications to take a rest occurring in a group setting; being prompted by a work buddy to take a break. To evaluate these features outside of a forestry context we followed an approach motivated by Lean UX [8], which uses rapid iterations to explore the experience being designed, rather than the final deliverable. We conducted our experiments with *proxy participants* (not forestry workers) which allowed us to investigate the conceptual aspects of the system separately from the real-world context of use. Proxy participants have been proposed in other contexts, primarily in work where participants may have limited communication abilities, [11]. In these works the proxy participants are closely associated with the target users, medical personnel who work with the end users or parents and teachers [11] and are intended to provide realistic observations about the suitability of the proposed technologies through their understanding of the needs of the end-users. In our experiments, however, rather than trying to use proxies in this way, we instead take the approach of investigating the central concepts of our technology (rather than the technology itself) by understanding its impacts on the general population. We describe each of these experiments next.

## 3.1 Experiment 1: Displaying Emotions Publicly

The buddy system relies on notifications that signal a worker's status (e.g. fatigue) for others to see (i.e. the buddy) to ensure that appropriate action is taken. Our first study was, therefore, designed to investigate how people react when their feelings or health status are made visible and when others comment on this. This was important to explore because people who are uncomfortable with aspects of personal monitoring will find ways to avoid the technology [5]. The study was conducted by a single researcher (R1), the proxy participant, over a four day period. For several hours each day, the researcher would wear one of four different labels describing feelings taped to their back, whilst in a public setting. They noted their own feelings both about this public display and about comments people in the environment made to them. Most of the people they would encounter were people they knew, which replicates the exposing of fatigue status among groups of co-workers. The labels worn by the researcher display emotions rather than a single fatigue status, this was a deliberate decision in order to understand if there were different reactions to *types* of status that was made visible.

At the start of the first day the researcher felt nervous about displaying the labels. They were unsure as to how people would react, and this was unsettling to them. Once the experiment was underway, however, the researcher felt more at ease, but it depended on the label they were displaying. Table 1 details the

**Table 1.** Researcher reactions to each label and reactions

| Emotion label | Reactions to comments | Feelings about the label |
|---|---|---|
| "I am Angry" | I feel annoyed that someone would interject with advice; I like that somebody cares that I am feeling angry; I feel annoyed that they were questioning my anger; | This was a very uncomfortable feeling for me to show because it was like showing them that I was secretly angry. This made me feel unsettled |
| "I am Hungry" | I felt appreciated; I felt cared about; I was frustrated at a lack of empathy; This made me laugh | Overall, I was happy to show this feeling as it was almost nice to hear advice about how to fix my hunger. I was comfortable with all responses |
| "I am Tired" | I felt confused, and slightly exposed; I appreciated the concern; Grateful for a suggestion; I felt belittled | I didn't feel tired, so some responses felt unjustified. I appreciated hearing the concern. It was comfortable to display that I was tired |
| "I am Bored" | This response felt unproductive and lacking empathy; I didn't appreciate the advice given; | I had hoped for more constructive and involved responses, but this feeling was not uncomfortable to display |

observations and reactions to comments made based on different labels. The experiment showed that displaying some feelings was more comfortable than others. For example, displaying anger was unpleasant but broadcasting boredom was emotionally easier to do. As the focus of the buddy system is about displaying fatigue and health status, it was reassuring that reactions to displaying "I am tired" were mostly positive, and the researcher felt comfortable with the display. However, as the researcher self-assigned the labels each day, it was not a true representation of how the worker notifications will function. Therefore, while this first experiment gave some insight into how it might feel when external parties comment on fatigue status, it did not show how it might feel when the display is driven by technology. This led to the second experiment, described next.

### 3.2    Experiment 2: Responding to Technology-Driven Interruptions

The aim of the buddy system is to provide notifications when a worker is fatigued – firstly to the worker, aiming to prompt them to take a break from what they are doing. If they continue working or continue to be identified as fatigued, notifications will be provided to their buddy who should then take action to encourage rest. The second experiment, therefore, investigated how it feels to be interrupted by technology at uncontrolled intervals while engaged in an activity you wish to finish. This experiment was conducted by R1 as well as a second member of the research team, R2.

*Regular Interruptions.* We started with interruptions at fixed intervals to see how the researcher reacted when receiving notifications telling them to rest. The experiment was run while the researcher (R2) worked on their laptop during the day. The Windows Task scheduler was programmed to generate notifications every 30 mins. The researcher took notes about how often they took breaks, the break duration and the emotions felt when told to rest by the notifications. Over an 8 h work day, 15 prompts were made to take breaks. The researcher took 13 breaks (3 to 19 min long), and missed only one notified break. Once, in the afternoon, they wished for a break before being notified, but tried to hold out until the alert. The two longest breaks were 8 and 19 min. The researcher reported spending longer away from their desk than intended, without feelings of frustration. They felt it was easier to spend time taking a break for someone else's sake (i.e. the system) than for their own well-being.

However, they reported that many breaks felt like "token efforts" as they did not feel fatigued. Being told to rest before being aware of fatigue caused frustration, especially when being interrupted from a task that needed concentration. While the researcher felt most noticeably fatigued during the final half-hour of the day, they still did not want to follow the direction to rest but rather wanted to finish the work for the day. Their study diary reports four instances of frustration and annoyance. At the end of the day, the researcher felt both "tired and grumpy". The feelings of frustration about the alerts seemed to accumulate. Potential issues that were identified were: frustrations due to a mismatch between

**Table 2.** Researcher reactions to technology-driven interruptions

| Interruption time | Researcher observations |
|---|---|
| 32 min | I had just finished a mission when this notification came through telling me to stop so it felt almost natural to take a break. The 10-minute break did feel quite long however |
| 34 min | I was in the middle of exploring a new area when this notification came through so that was slightly annoying |
| 31 min | This notification came when I was halfway through an in-game mission. It was annoying to have to stop but once I did, I felt myself being more tired than I had expected. However, I did find myself watching the timer as to when I was able to start playing again |
| 34 min | This notification came at the most annoying time. I was in the middle of a big fight and stopping was the last thing I wanted to do. I really watched the clock as to when I could start playing again. I did not feel that tired, this may have been due to the high intensity of the game play |

not feeling fatigued and the system's interruption (which is likely because fatigue often occurs before it is felt), and discouragement of user initiative and self-management of fatigue. The use of fixed-time intervals provided an interesting finding regarding the potential loss of self-regulating (not paying attention to actual feelings of fatigue). However, it is unclear if this would also be the case with less structured notifications. We therefore also ran a variation of the study under different conditions.

*Random Interruptions.* The researcher (R1) spent a period of three hours playing a video game. During that time an app would schedule a notification some time between 30 and 40 min, advising them to stop and take a break. Once the notification was acknowledged a ten-minute timer started to countdown indicating the length of the break. At each break the researcher recorded their observations about being interrupted, see Table 2 for results. This experiment yielded interesting results. For each of the four interruptions in the experiment the researcher felt differing levels of inconvenience, suggesting that current task may play a part in how willing people are to adhere to such notifications (e.g. forestry workers may respond differently to fatigue notifications depending on what they are doing). For the researcher it was hardest to take a break when they were in the middle of a battle, while a forestry worker might find it hardest to listen to a notification while in the middle of a time-dependent task, such as planting a seedling box that must be completed by the end of the day. However, at the third break, symptoms of fatigue were felt after starting the rest period. This is a promising sign that when taking a recommended break as suggested, a worker may realise they are tired and take the rest they need. This will in turn build trust in the system.

### 3.3    Experiment 3: Notifications Within a Group

For the buddy system there will be multiple workers engaged in both solo and collaborative activities. Our next experiment, therefore, considered the impact of different people being notified to take a break whilst engaged in a collaborative group activity. We recruited six volunteers from a group of University undergraduate students for the experiment, which took place outside on a sports field. They were split into two teams to play a game of 'Rob the Nest'. At random intervals during the game, a participant would receive a phone call or text message from the researcher telling them to slow down to a walking pace. If they did not comply, they would receive another call or message instructing them to stop and sit at the side of the playing field until instructed to rejoin the game. The game was run for eight minutes. The researcher recorded how long it took participants to respond and whether or not they followed instructions given.

It was observed that some of the participants, when told to stop and rest by phone, would argue that they wanted to continue and had to be persuaded to rest. For this experiment, the use of a phone call meant that the researcher could directly respond to the participants creating a dialogue, which enabled them to convince the participants to follow the commands. In a one-way notification system it is possible that users will ignore instructions. For the buddy system to work, the users must either respond to notifications to rest, or be persuaded by their buddy. Our next study, therefore, considered notifications to both the individual concerned as well as to a buddy, in order to understand what impact this might have.

### 3.4    Experiment 4: Prompting by Buddies

This study explored how people react when notified that either they or their buddy needs to rest. We were interested in how people react to their buddy seeing their fatigue status, and how people react when prompted to tell others to rest. We recruited four participants, who were all University undergraduate students, and paired them up. In this study, the system interactions were simulated through a researcher sending text messages. Participants were further able to interact with their buddy by sending and receiving text messages. Possible interactions in this study were: system-generated messages to report on buddy status, check on buddy or respond to check in, and communication between participants which are unprompted. Participants were also encouraged to voluntarily check on their buddy. The researcher observed the time since the last check, and after a pre-defined interval, prompted participants to check on their buddy.

Pairs of participants were designated as each others' buddies, and each participant was instructed to carry out computer-based work for about 1.5 h. This work was required to be something that participants were motivated to complete, such as university work. The participants worked while sitting across from each other at a table, each working on their laptop; the facilitator sat at the head of the same table. The facilitator recorded the participants states as *working* (interacting with their laptop), *slowing down* (distracted, frustrated, or fatigued), or *taking a break* (disengaging from their work). The facilitator used a silent timer for each participant with a random interval between 10 and 20 min (reset after checking in with their buddy). They also collected data on how many prompts each participant acted on. The study was followed by an interview of each pair of participants together. The study and following interview led to a number of observations:

- Shared Information: Participants gave positive feedback and did not find it intrusive that their buddy could see if they were working or resting, or their level of fatigue.
- Fatigue status: Participants showed mixed responses to seeing their buddy's fatigue status. Knowing their buddy was taking a break made them more aware of their own breaks. It was observed (and confirmed by participants) that they did not always truthfully report on their fatigue status.
- Prompts and Interactions: Most participants were willing to act when prompted, even if they felt frustration with the prompt. Participants raised the issue of *prompt fatigue*: wanting to take initiative in checking on their buddy but being prompted so often that they were unable to do this effectively. All participants found the system prompts excessive and reported frustration about the frequency and number of texts.

Frequency of notification and prompts was identified as the key issue. While these caused frustration, participants still checked on their buddy after receiving them.

### 3.5   Summary of Experiments

Analysis of the four experiments yielded a number of insights. In the first experiment, we observed some discomfort about self-disclosure which was somewhat mitigated by positive or caring reactions. However, the disclosure was driven by, and with full knowledge of, the participant. Experiment two looked into interruptions that were driven by technology. We observed frustration about the interruptions as the participant did not feel fatigued, even though they sometimes noticed their fatigue when they took the break. Willingness to take the recommended break depended on the task. It is a concern that the participant felt discouraged to self-regulate and self-manage fatigue and relied on the system. Experiment three explored interaction in a group setting, we encountered again the participant frustration about being interrupted and an unwillingness to rest. Discussion that ensued between participants and the researcher emphasise the importance of the human-human interaction which supports the technology in a buddy system. Experiment four used notifications to both buddies to see if participants could be persuaded to rest. The feeling of annoyance when interrupted (as observed in all studies) seemed to be mitigated by the involvement of a buddy, and the more low-key enquiry (vs claims of fatigue). When being prompted too often, the care turned into prompt fatigue. While participants were not concerned about the information shared (which was high level), some participants tried to hide feelings of fatigue from their buddy. We observed that participants became self-conscious about the breaks they took, and began to self-censor (e.g. by only taking breaks if their partner had a break).

## 4    Discussion and Conclusions

This paper described experiments using proxy participants to investigate key attributes of a proposed buddy system for forestry workers. We found that using both automated notifications to the fatigued person along with human intervention by a buddy was more acceptable to participants than technology alone. This suggests that the choice of a buddy system is the right approach, it's not just about the redundancy of a second prompt when the worker ignores the first one, but more about the human contact. However, we also identify the following dichotomies that need to be explored with the buddy system in situ (forestry workers in their place of work):

- Frustration about frequent prompts vs. reduced self-regulation and engagement
- Disclosure of personal data vs. lying about fatigue
- Interaction with buddy vs. one-upmanship (harder work, less breaks)

For these three identified aspects, we believe that personal preferences should play a role in the final system. We considered whether we can successfully investigate the user impacts of technical solutions without access to the actual workers and work places, using proxy participants in studies. We were interested in how useful these studies would be wrt. proxy participants and proxy technology. We found that our approach provided a workable solution under the constraints of the project. Using proxy participants in situations that would create similar incentives and tensions worked well to expose certain behaviours. However, for the next stages of the project, proxies cannot act as a replacement for user studies with forestry workers in situ. It enabled us, however, to explore design ideas without exhausting the time and good-will of our project partners, not to mention the potential day-long travel to remote forestry locations. Through this method, the design progressed far enough to now be able to develop a working prototype for evaluation in a real-world setting with forestry workers. This will enable us to evaluate further considerations regarding ordering of notifications, escalation and understanding of how the wearer reacts in a real situation.

This paper described a mixed-methods approach to designing software for a real-world context in which access to future users and places was restricted. We hope that our example encourages researchers and software developers to not forgo design explorations for real-world problems with challenging settings, but rather use a method that remains true to the underlying issues without resorting to lab-based design only. This paper contributes to the ongoing discourse about transferring theory to the messy practice of real-world projects.

**Acknowledgements.** Thanks to Daniel Lansdaal, Meleena Radcliffe, James Sheaf-Morrison and all study participants.

# References

1. Botan, C.H., Vorvoreanu, M.: "what are you really saying to me?" electronic surveillance in the workplace. In: Conference of the International Communication Association Conference, Acapulco, Mexico (2000)
2. Bowen, J., Hinze, A., Griffiths, C.: Investigating real-time monitoring of fatigue indicators of New Zealand forestry workers. Accid. Anal. Prev. **126**, 122–141 (2019)
3. Bowen, J., Hinze, A., Griffiths, C., Kumar, V., Bainbridge, D.: Personal data collection in the workplace: ethical and technical challenges. In: British Human Computer Interaction Conference (BHCI), p. 10 (2017)
4. Bowen, J., Hinze, A., König, J., Exton, D.: Supporting safer work practice through the use of wearable technology. In: Ergonomics and Human Factors 2021, vol. 117 (2021)
5. Clawson, J., Pater, J.A., Miller, A.D., Mynatt, E.D., Mamykina, L.: No Longer Wearing: Investigating the Abandonment of Personal Health-Tracking Technologies on Craigslist, pp. 647–658. Association for Computing Machinery, New York (2015).UbiComp '15
6. Fo, W., O'Donnell, C.: The buddy system: effect of community intervention on delinquent offenses. Behav. Ther. **6**(4), 522–524 (1975)
7. Forestry Owners Association and Ministry for Primary Industries NZ: Facts and figures (2018). http://www.nzfoa.org.nz/resources/publications/facts-and-Figures
8. Gothelf, J., Seiden, J.: Lean UX: Applying Lean Principles to Improve User Experience. O'Reilly, Sebastopol (2013)
9. Gothelf, J., Seiden, J.: Lean UX: Designing Great Products with Agile Teams. O'Reilly Media, Inc., Sebastopol (2016)
10. Halko, S., Kientz, J.A.: Personality and persuasive technology: an exploratory study on health-promoting mobile applications. In: Ploug, T., Hasle, P., Oinas-Kukkonen, H. (eds.) PERSUASIVE 2010. LNCS, vol. 6137, pp. 150–161. Springer, Heidelberg (2010). https://doi.org/10.1007/978-3-642-13226-1_16
11. Hamidi, F., Baljko, M., Gómez, I.M.: Using participatory design with proxies with children with limited communication. In: Hurst, A., Findlater, L., Morris, M.R. (eds.) Proceedings of the 19th International ACM SIGACCESS Conference on Computers and Accessibility, ASSETS 2017, Baltimore, MD, USA, 29 October–01 November 2017, pp. 250–259. ACM (2017)
12. Kaur, S., Bhalla, P., Bajaj, S., Sanyal, S., Babbar, R.: Effect of physical and mental stress on heart rate variability in type-a and type-b personalities. Indian J. Appl. Basic Med. Sci. **15**(20), 59–70 (2013)
13. Lilley, R., Feyer, A., Kirk, P., Gander, P.: A survey of forest workers in New Zealand: do hours of work, rest, and recovery play a role in accidents and injury? J. Saf. Res. **33**(1), 53–71 (2002)
14. Mardonova, M., Choi, Y.: Review of wearable device technology and its applications to the mining industry. Energies **11**(3) (2018)
15. Paritala, S.A.: Effects of Physical and Mental Tasks on Heart Rate Variability. Kakatiya University, India (2009).Ph.D. thesis
16. Patel, M., Lal, S., Kavanagh, D., Rossiter, P.: Applying neural network analysis on heart rate variability data to assess driver fatigue. Expert Syst. Appl. **38**(6), 7235–7242 (2011)

17. Pruitt, J., Adlin, T.: The Persona Lifecycle: Keeping People in Mind Throughout Product Design. Morgan Kaufmann Publishers Inc., San Francisco (2005)
18. Rotheram-Borus, M.J., Tomlinson, M., Gwegwe, M., Comulada, W.S., Kaufman, N., Keim, M.: Diabetes buddies: peer support through a mobile phone buddy system. Diab. Educ. **38**(3), 357–365 (2012)
19. Seshadri, D., et al.: Wearable sensors for monitoring the internal and external workload of the athlete. NPJ Digit. Med. **71**(2) (2019)
20. Smith, B., Browne, M., Armstrong, T., Ferguson, S.: The accuracy of subjective measures for assessing fatigue related decrements in multi-stressor environments. Saf. Sci. **86**, 238–244 (2016)
21. Worksafe New Zealand: notifiable incidents: Fatalities (2020). https://data.worksafe.govt.nz/graph/summary/fatalities
22. Zahra, S.M., Mohammad Ali, A.Y., Cavuoto, L., Megahed, F.: A data-driven approach to modelling physical fatigue in the workplace using wearable sensors. Appl. Ergon. **65**, 515–529 (2017)

# Effect of Attention Saturating and Cognitive Load on Tactile Texture Recognition for Mobile Surface

Adnane Guettaf[1]($\boxtimes$), Yosra Rekik[1]($\boxtimes$), and Laurent Grisoni[2]($\boxtimes$)

[1] University of Polytechnique Hauts-de-France, LAMIH, CNRS,
UMR 8201, 59313 Valenciennes, France
{adnane.guettaf,yosra.rekik}@uphf.fr
[2] University of Lille, Lille, Villeneuve d'Ascq, France
laurent.grisoni@univ-lille.fr

**Abstract.** We investigate users ability to recognize tactile textures on mobile surface when performing a primary task that either saturates the attention or is cognitively demanding. Our findings indicate that the attention saturating task decreases performance by 6.98% and increases frustration, mental demand and physical effort compared to a control condition. The recognition task can be done in an eyes-free style while continuing to perform the primary task. While cognitively demanding task demands more time to switch to the texture recognition task but decreases the time needed to recognize the texture without compromising accuracy compared to a control condition. The two tasks are handled sequentially with gaze attention directed to the current performed task. For both primary tasks, the recognition rate stays higher than 82% and the total time does not decrease, suggesting that tactile texture could be effectively recognized and used by users when performing a primary task. Finally, we discuss the implications of our work for tactile feedback based interaction.It is our hope that our findings will contribute toward a better understanding of tactile feedback perception on touchscreen when performing another primary task.

**Keywords:** Tactile texture · Haptic · Primary task · Secondary task · Attention saturating task · Cognitively demanding task

## 1 Introduction

Mobile touchscreens are becoming increasingly important in everyday life, providing different information and services (*e.g.*, communication, social media, gps, travel, education, banking, entertainment, etc.). The growth of mobile applications used in all aspects of life and the easiness of interaction with them through tactile input allow users to interact with touchscreen in many different ways and in different contexts, including situations where interaction complements another, a *primary* task, that either needs full attention (*e.g.*, driving [10]) or

© IFIP International Federation for Information Processing 2021
Published by Springer Nature Switzerland AG 2021
C. Ardito et al. (Eds.): INTERACT 2021, LNCS 12935, pp. 557–579, 2021.
https://doi.org/10.1007/978-3-030-85610-6_31

is cognitively demanding (*e.g.*, receiving a notification when typing a text [9]). Indeed, touchscreen applications most often use visual cues in order to provide feedback, *e.g.*, confirm/verify/response a notification or to guide user finger movements to the correct target item [10], which may in practice induce some perceptual distractions when a user is performing another primary task.

In the same time, touchscreens have been enhanced with tactile feedback that provides users with stimulation when touching the surface [1,3,7,22,24,30,33]. In particular, a rich variety of tactile textures have been proposed that have been shown to be identifiable by users [24,27]. Tactile textures only require user finger exploration on the screen, and can possibly free users from the constraint to get visual feedback; which presents an interesting way to reduce the demand for visual attention to the touchscreen, in the case of secondary interaction task.

There is little existing research concerning the use of tactile textures for secondary tasks. Previous research demonstrated, for standard interaction situations in which no secondary task is involved, the ability for users to accurately recognize tactile textures on touchscreens even when using different finger speeds [27]; or when perceiving simultaneous but different textures [26]; or when the size of the texture is small [19]. However, in all these studies participants have to focus on only the tactile feedback based task. Therefore, it is unclear how the user perception of tactile texture could be impacted by a real-world scenario where participants have to interact with a primary task that can for example, saturates the attention or is cognitively demanding. Among other fundamental questions, one can for instance ask the following: does users perception of textures remain effective when performing another primary task? Does relative position of the tactile surface matter in such setting? How do users handle the two tasks? Do users continue interacting with the primary task when recognizing textures? How do they distribute eye-gaze attention when recognizing textures?

To investigate these specificities, we conducted two experiments to examine users' perception of tactile textures rendered on a mobile touchscreen when performing another primary task on a laptop. In the first experiment, we study the effect of an attention saturating task on textures recognition: the primary task in this experiment is a highly visually demanding task which feature the control of a pseudo-randomly perturbed moving ball, in a manner similar to the approach used in [11]. In the second experiment, we study the effect of a cognitively demanding task on textures recognition: as primary task we consider a text typing task [9]. We also explore the effect of the touchscreen position (on the left, right and forward) relatively to the primary display on the user interaction. For both experiments we refer to a control situation, in which no primary task is involved. Our findings indicate that the attention saturating task decreases performance by 6.98% and increases frustration, mental demand and physical effort, by comparison to the control situation. Different hand postures and strategies to handle and perform the two tasks have been used. In particular, our findings confirm that the recognition task can be done eyes-free while continuing performing the primary task. By contrast, the second experiment shows that cognitively demanding task impacts texture recognition by increasing time to switch to the texture recognition task but also decreases time needed to recognize the texture without compromising accuracy. The primary and secondary tasks are handled sequentially with gaze attention directed to the current performed task (*i.e.*, either the primary display or the touchscreen). For both primary tasks, the recognition rate stays higher than 82% and the total time does not decrease, suggesting that tactile texture could be effectively recognized and used by users when performing a primary task. We also do not find an effect of the touchscreen position on the performances, but indeed on user behaviour.

This paper contributions constitute, to the best of our knowledge, the first empirical investigation of the effectiveness of tactile textures on touchscreen when performing another primary task that either saturates the attention or is cognitively demanding.

## 2    Related Work

In this section, we review previous work on tactile feedback in terms of devices, rendering techniques, textures perception studies and the effect of an attention saturating or cognitively demanding task on tactile feedback interaction.

### 2.1    Tactile Feedback Based Devices

Touch interaction is the primary input modality of many modern mobile devices [24], when enhanced with tactile feedback, it allows to deliver information about touched elements. Vibrotactile stimuli [5,6,8] is the most used tactile feedback. It consists in vibrating a part or the entire touch screen display to induce a physical sensation of vibration. This kind of tactile feedback are more informative then descriptive. Consequently, many researchers investigated the use of physical augmentations on-top of the screen [10,20,28], and of course designed new devices with richer capabilities for tactile feedback [1,7,24,27,30,31]. In particular, two main technologies have emerged to support mobile device-based tactile feedback: (1) electrovibration [3,25,32] which enhance the friction between the finger and the interaction surface and (2) ultrasonic technologies which reduce the friction through the "squeeze film effect" [1,7,24,30]). In the remainder of this paper, we leverage the latter tactile feedback device [30].

### 2.2    Tactile Textures Rendering Techniques

Three main rendering techniques have been proposed in the literature: SHO, SHT and LHT. Surface Haptic Object, or SHO is based on mapping a given texture with a discrete sampling of position and have been used by most existing surface devices (*e.g.*, [1,3,21,24,25]). SHT (Surface Haptic Texture) have been introduced, recently, by Vezzoli et al. [27,30] and relies on real time finger speed. Rekik et al. [27] compared the SHO and SHT techniques. Their findings indicate that SHT leads to the highest level of quality of tactile rendering for dense textures with either fast or moderate velocity; whereas SHO is still more accurate for sparser textures with moderate velocity due to positional shift. Considering these results, Rekik et al. [27] introduced the LHT (Localized Haptic Texture), a new rendering technique [27]. LHT separates the tactile rendering into two different processes: first, the finger position is retrieved from the hardware, and the corresponding texture is selected through a search in a grid of taxels. The taxel texture is then rendered locally by defining only one period of the texture and then repeated in a loop at a rate that depends on the finger's speed. LHT was shown to provide a high-fidelity between the texture and its visual representation. In our work we used the LHT technique.

## 2.3 Tactile Textures Perception

Previous work have examined users perception of tactile textures on touchscreens devices. In [27], the authors investigated the user ability to perceive textures when using different finger speeds. In [19], the authors determined the smallest texture size that user can accurately perceive. Researchers have investigated the users ability to perceive simultaneous but different textures [26], provided the semantic perceptual space of textures [12] and studied the effect of different physically challenging contexts on textures perception [14]. Researchers have also looked at the benefits of tactile feedback to enhance physicality [23], improve pointing techniques [7], help visually impaired people to interact with objects [17] and enhance musical interaction [18]. However, these findings are likely to differ when users are making another primary task that either saturates the attention or is cognitively demanding.

## 2.4 Effect of Attention Saturating and Cognitively Demanding Task on Tactile Feedback Interaction

Harrison et al. [15] investigated the relevance of dynamic buttons displays based on pneumatic actuation when the user is performing simultaneously an attention saturating primary task. They employed the same attention saturating dual task framework than in [4,11] in which users performed a attention-saturating task while simultaneously performing additional tasks on the pneumatic display. As in [4,11] the goal of the attention saturating task was to keep a moving circle centered on a fixed crosshair. The attention needed to perform actions in the secondary task was measured as a drop in performance in the primary one. Results showed that pneumatic displays performs as well as physical buttons with fewer glances towards the surface when performing the primary task. Cockburn et al. [10] investigated users' performances when interacting with a touchscreen covered with a static stencil overlay while driving in a 2D emulator. Their results showed that with tactile feedback, users selected a target quickly and that stencil significantly reduced the visual attention demands on normal touchscreens with shorter eye-glances directed away from the primary task. Rydström et al. [29] used a driving simulator as a primary task while asking participants to interact with a secondary one through a haptic ridges rotary device. Their goal was to investigate whether haptic ridges can facilitate the interaction with the rotary device while driving. Their findings showed that driving performance did not significantly vary between haptic-only and haptic/visual conditions, and that adding haptic ridges to the visual information did not necessarily reduce the

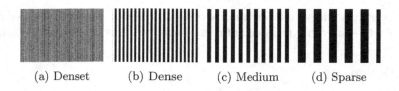

(a) Denset        (b) Dense        (c) Medium        (d) Sparse

**Fig. 1.** The visual representations of the four textures used in the experiment.

gaze-away time from the road. Chen et al. [9] studied the effect of a cognitively demanding primary task, through a typing text, on recognizing spatiotemporal vibrotactile patterns which constitute the secondary task. They found a strong effect of the primary task on recognition rate. However, although the findings there-in are of valuable contribution, users' perception of tactile textures on touchscreen devices and users' mental model and behaviour were not captured. Additionally, we can not blindly apply those results to ultrasonic devices which provide different sensations of tactile feedback [26,30].

## 3    Experiments

We conducted two experiments to investigate the effect of a primary task on tactile textures recognition on a touchscreen. We consider two primary tasks, the first saturates the attention while the second is cognitively demanding. The two primary tasks are described in the corresponding experiment section. The two experiments share many similarities that we describe in this section.

### 3.1    Method

We used *E-vita* [26] as the main device holding our secondary task. *E-vita* is a tactile feedback tablet that support friction reduction using ultrasonic vibrations. It uses the squeeze film effect technique and this by creating an over pressure between the user's finger and the vibrating surface at an ultrasonic frequency [13], this air bearing alter the device's coefficient of friction so that a user can feel different textures thanks to this variation in friction. The *E-vita* [26] tablet supports a sampling frequency 50 Hz thanks to the capacitive sensor included in it's 5-inch LCD display, which guaranties capabilities similar to commercial mobile devices.

We consider four different textures following previous studies [19,26,27,30]. We encode the different textures with respect to different texture densities by considering the following spatial periodicity: *densest* – 1.2 mm; *dense* – 5.1 mm; *medium* – 25.5 mm and *sparse* – 51 mm. In Fig. 1, the tactile textures are shown by alternating black and white bars; high friction is associated with the black color and low friction with the white color. Given that we use the Evita, which, when vibrating, reduces friction, this maps black to off and white to on to create tactile patterns. To render a given texture we used the LHT technique [27].

The primary task was implemented in JavaScript framework using the Node.js runtime and ran on a Dell laptop machine with a 13-inch LCD display screen with a desktop resolution of 1920×1080. Participants' faces were also videotaped.In addition, one author observed each session and took detailed notes, particularly concerning think-aloud data, hand postures, and mental model.

## 3.2   Design

The experiment used a $2 \times 3 \times 4 \times 3$ within-subject design for the factors: *activity, position, texture* and *block*. Activity presents if the participant is doing a primary task or just waiting for the notification that we named here the *control condition*. Consequently, in the first experiment, the activity is either *centering the ball* (i.e., the attention saturating task) on the laptop or the *control condition* and in the second experiment, activity is either the *text-typing* (i.e., cognitively demanding task) or the *control condition*. Position is the position of the surface compared to the laptop and covers three values: right, left and froward. The tactile surface was oriented horizontally (*i.e.*, parallel to the ground). For the right position, the surface was placed 5 cm away diagonally from the bottom-right of the laptop with an orientation of 45°. For the left position, the surface was placed 5 cm away diagonally from the bottom left of the laptop with an orientation of −45°. And for the forward position, the surface was centered and placed 5 cm below the laptop keyboard which in turn was centered in front of participants (Fig. 2). *Texture* covers the four presented textures in the previous section. *Block* covers 3 value (1–3), with the first block serving as a training phase.

## 3.3   Procedure

After asking our participants to seat comfortably on a desk in face to the laptop, participants had to answer a demographic questionnaire, after which, the experiment task was explained along with the additional requirements for both the primary and the secondary tasks. Participants then began the experiment.

The experimental trials were administered as blocks of 12 trials (4 textures × 3 repetitions), each block sharing a primary activity and a tablet position. For each activity, and for each tablet position, participants had to perform three blocks of textures identification . Blocks sharing a tablet position were administered consecutively to minimize physical device displacement; then grouped by primary activity to allow questionnaire assessment. The two primary *activities* were counterbalanced. Inside each *activity*, the three tablet *positions* were also counterbalanced. Inside each *block*, the four *textures* × three repetitions were randomly presented to the participants – a total of 216 (=2 activities × 3 positions × 3 blocks × 4 textures × 3 repetitions) trials per participant. After each block of trials, participants were encouraged to take a break. After each activity, participants completed a NASA-TLX worksheets.

## 3.4   Task

Both experiments required from participants to interact with a primary task on the laptop and to recognize textures on the tablet (secondary task) each time

|       |           |          |
|-------|-----------|----------|
| (a) Left | (b) Forward | (c) Right |

**Fig. 2.** Experiment setup according to the three positions of the haptic table.

they receive a notification. Participants were asked to prioritize the primary task over the secondary one, and were told that their performance was being measured for both tasks.

In the experiment 1, participants had to perform an attention saturating task and a control condition, and in experiment 2, participants performed a cognitively demanding task and the same control condition. In the control condition, participants had only to react to the notifications displayed on the laptop screen to perform the texture recognition task. The rational of adding the control condition, is to better understand the effect of the attention saturating/cognitively demanding primary task on user perception of tactile textures.

For the secondary task, participants were asked to move their index finger on the surface from right to left and inversely to perceive the texture, without a predefined hand or a starting finger position or time restrictions or limited number of clutches or swipes. Participants had the total liberty in choosing how to proceed to explore the whole texture. No visual feedback of the rendered texture was shown on the surface, only tactile feedback was sent to the participants while sensing the texture. In addition, as the Evita device makes noise when alternating high and low frictions, the participants were equipped with noise reduction headphones to avoid any bias. Once the participant recognized the perceived texture, he pressed on the "confirm" button that is positioned on the top of the tactile surface. This location was chosen to be sure to not disturb the texture perception task. A new screen is then displayed, and participants had to select the visual representation of the perceived texture from the four visual representations of the four evaluated textures on the tablet surface and then confirm their choice by pressing again the "confirm" button.

At the experiment phase, participants started interacting with the primary task. And after a random period of time between 2 and 14 s, a notification was shown up in the computer screen and a texture was rendered in the tablet surface. This indicate to the participants that they can start recognizing the rendered texture on the tablet surface. Participants were free to choose the appropriate strategy to handle the primary task and the secondary one while keeping in mind that the primary task should be prioritized. Participants had the total liberty to interact with both tasks at the same time or sequentially by switching from one to another etc. After ending a trial by selecting the visual representation of the perceived texture, our software presented the next notification after a random period of time between 2 and 14 s. Each experiment took around 90 min

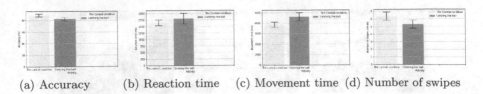

(a) Accuracy    (b) Reaction time    (c) Movement time    (d) Number of swipes

**Fig. 3.** User performances in the first experiment.

to complete. To reduce fatigue, sufficient resting periods were given between conditions and as required by the participants.

## 4    Experiment 1: Effect of an Attention Saturating Task

In this experiment, we investigated the effect of an attention saturating primary task on the recognition of textures. We followed [4,11,15] and used the same primary task that saturates the attention. Our primary attention saturating task featured a circle moving randomly according to a two-dimensional Perlin noise function. Participants were asked to keep the circle centered over a cross-hairs displayed in the center of the square as the best they could, and this by contracting its movement using the arrow keys of the laptop keyboard. Participants were asked to use one hand to perform the primary task while having the total liberty in choosing which hand to use. Participants were free to use the same hand to interact with the secondary task or to use their second hand. Participants were told that keeping the circle centered on the crosshair was the most important task and that their performance was being measured for both the primary and the secondary task. The procedure and task as well as common apparatus are presented in the Experiments section.

Thirteen participants (5 females) volunteered (not paid) to take part into the experiment. Participants ages were between 24 and 36 years (mean = 30.23 years, sd = 4.45years). All participants were right handed.

### 4.1    Results

Results for each of the dependent variables (*reaction time, movement time, total time, accuracy, number of swipes* and *number of clutches*) are presented below. All analyses are using multi-way ANOVA considering the following independent variable: activity, tablet position, texture and block.. Tukey tests are used post-hoc when significant effects are found. We also analyzed subjective responses.

### 4.2    Time Performance

We measured *reaction time, movement time* and *total time. Reaction time* was the interval time between the appearance of a notification on the laptop screen and the first touch on the surface device. It represents the time taken by the participant to react and switch to the secondary task. *Movement time* represents the time taken by the participant to sense and recognize the texture, from the first touch, until pressing the "confirm" button for the first time. *Total time* represents the time taken by a participant all along a trial, from the moment the notification is shown up, until pressing the "confirm" button. It is the sum of reaction and movement times. For time measures, we only considered timing data from correct trials to better account for user performance.

**Total Time.** Repeated-measures ANOVA revealed a significant main effect of *block* ($F_{2,24} = 13.70$, $p < .0001$) on *total time*. Post-hoc tests showed a significant decrease in the time between the first block and the two remaining (p < .05; block1: mean = .6924 ms, s.d = 445 ms, block2: mean = 6174 ms, s.d = 402 ms and block3: 5744 ms, s.d = 383 ms) due to a learning during the first block. As we are concerned with user performance after familiarization, the remaining analysis discards the first block.

There was a significant main effect of *texture* ($F_{3,36} = 15.37$, $p < .0001$) on *total time* with a significant *activity × position × texture* ($F_{6,71.83} = 2.23$, $p = .0498$) interaction. Post-hoc tests revealed that when centering the ball, and having the tablet on the right (respectively, forward), the densest texture is significantly better recognized than both the dense and the medium (respectively, medium) textures ($p < .05$).

**Reaction Time.** There were no significant effects of activity (p = .58), position (p = .36) and texture (p = .82) on reaction time nor interaction (p¿.13), with similar means of 1644 ms (sd = 115 ms) with the control condition, and 1803 ms (sd − 203 ms) when centering the ball (Figure 3b).

**Movement Time.** There was a significant effect of textures ($F_{3,36.23} = 18.26$, $p < .0001$) on movement time. Post-hoc tests revealed that the densest texture (mean = 2619 ms, sd = 376 ms) is recognized faster than the remainder textures (dense: mean = 4513 ms, sd = 445 ms, medium: 5117 ms, sd = 472 ms, sparse: mean = 4684 ms, sd = 411 ms).

### 4.3 Accuracy

Accuracy is defined as the proportion of correct identifications of textures.

There were significant main effects of *activity* ($F_{1,12} = 3.86$, $p = .008$) and *texture* ($F_{3,36} = 3.17$, $p = .0357$) on *accuracy*. Post-hoc tests revealed that the control condition (mean = 88.78%, sd = 2.25%) is significantly more accurate than centering the ball (mean = 82.58%, sd= 2.50%) (Figure 3a). We also, found that the densest texture (mean= 94.44%, sd= 1.42%) is significantly better recognized than the remainder textures. There was no significant interaction ($p > .1951$), suggesting that the drawback of centering the ball activity are consistent across textures and surface positions and the benefits of the densest texture are consistent across different activities and tablet positions.

## 4.4 Number of Swipes and Clutches

**Number of directional swipes** is defined as the number of times the user moves his finger on the surface from left to right or right to left during the movement time. *Number of clutches* is defined as the number of times the user released his finger from the surface and than put it again on the surface from the first touch. We excluded error trials from analyses.

**Number of Swipes.** Analysis of number of swipes shows no significant effect of activity ($F_{1,11.98} = .99$, $p = .33$), with similar means of 6.35 (sd $= .53$) for the control situation and 5.26 (sd $= .52$) for centering the ball (Figure 3d).There was, however, a significant effect of *texture* ($F_{3,36.12} = 10.67$, $p < .0001$) on *number of swipes*. Posthoc tests revealed that the densest texture (mean $=$ 3.42, sd $= .37$) produced significantly less swipe gestures than the remainder textures (dense: : mean $= 6.16$, sd $= .70$, medium: mean $= 7.16$, sd $= .94$ and sparse: mean $= 6.52$, sd $= .76$).

**Number of Clutches.** Similar to number of swipes, when analyzing number of clutches, we found no significant effect of activity ($F_{1,11.98} = 3.27$, $p = .09$) with similar means of .55 (sd $= .09$) for the control condition and .94 (sd $= .14$) for centering the ball ($F_{1,11.98} = 3.27$, $p = .09$). There was a significant effect of *texture* ($F_{3,35.86} = 6.83$, $p = .0009$) on *number of clutches*. Post-hoc tests revealed that the densest texture (mean $= .35$, sd $= .12$) produced significantly less clutches than the remainder textures (dense: : mean $= .78$, sd $= .17$, medium: mean $= .95$, sd $= .20$ and sparse: mean $= .92$, sd $= .17$).

**Table 1.** Mean and s.d questionnaire responses, with 1=very low, and 5 = very high for experiment 1 and experiment 2. The significant tests are highlighted

| | Experiment 1 | | | | | Experiment 2 | | | | |
|---|---|---|---|---|---|---|---|---|---|---|
| | Control | | Centering | | Wilcoxon | Control | | Typing | | Wilcoxon |
| | Mean | S.d | Mean | S.d | Z | Mean | S.d | Mean | S.d | Z |
| Mental demand | 2.38 | .41 | 3.84 | .43 | -3.20 | 2.75 | .68 | 3.41 | .65 | -1.90 |
| Physical demand | 1.84 | .66 | 3.30 | .56 | -2.75 | 1.75 | .42 | 2.75 | .64 | -2.89 |
| Temporal demand | 2.76 | .63 | 3.76 | .32 | -1.96 | 2.25 | .42 | 3.08 | .61 | -2.77 |
| Performance | 4.07 | .34 | 3.92 | .34 | .70 | 3.91 | .44 | 3.58 | .56 | 1.63 |
| Frustration | 1.84 | .53 | 3.23 | .55 | -2.91 | 1.83 | .58 | 2 | .53 | -1.15 |
| Effort | 2.15 | .53 | 4 | .44 | -3.23 | 2.33 | .60 | 2.91 | .61 | -1.86 |

*Note*: Wilcoxon-Signed-Rank tests are reported at $p = .005$ ($^{*}$) significance levels.

## 4.5 Subjective Results and Observations

Our quantitative data were accompanied by considerable qualitative data that capture users' mental models as they handle and perform the primary task and the secondary one.

### 4.5.1 Nasa TLX Results

We recall that our participants were asked to rate the overall task after each activity condition. Overall, questionnaire responses (Table 1) showed that recognizing textures when centering the ball was significantly more demanding mentally and physically while having significantly higher perceived effort and being more frustrated than in the control condition.

We correlate these findings with comments from participants that felt that managing the ball while performing a texture recognition is more difficult than when they had just to identify the texture after receiving a notification. Some quotes:*"for me, doing both tasks simultaneously was difficult"*, *"it is stressful to center the ball and recognize the texture at the same time"*. In addition, one participant felt that *"the overall task demands a lot of effort and is highly frustrating ... I try to quickly identify the texture to not loose time or getting the ball not centred but I felt confident in recognizing the textures"*.

### 4.5.2 Hands Input Posture

We instructed participants to prioritize the primary task (centering the ball) over the secondary one (recognizing the textures) while giving them the total liberty on the number of hands to use and which hand to use to handle and perform the primary and the secondary task. Interestingly, for a given surface position, we observed that once the participant starts the task with a given hands posture, he continues with that posture until finishing all the trials in that position. In the following, we present the different hands postures used to perform the primary and the secondary task once the notification has shown-up:

- **One-handed (dominant hand) – 1H.** Two participants used their dominant hand (here right hand) to perform sequentially the primary and the secondary task during all the experiment and independently on the position of the touch surface (see Fig. 4a).
- **Two-handed directional posture – 2HD.** This hands posture is strongly correlated to the position of the tactile surface and consists of using the hand closed to the tactile surface to perform the secondary task and the other hand to perform the primary one (see Fig. 4b). For the forward position, as to interact with the primary task, participants have to press on the arrow keys which are localized at the extreme right of the keyboard and so the laptop, we then considered the primary task as being more on the right than the secondary one. For 2HD posture, when performing the secondary task, the hand used for the primary task remains on the keyboard arrow keys. While when the secondary task finished (*i.e.*, participants have to only perform the primary task), we were able to observe three postures performed by the hand used for the secondary task: (1) **fingers-above**: the hand fingers are kept above the surface by placing the wrist in a stable position just below the surface (see Fig. 4c), (2) **fingers-closed**: the participants' wrist was placed just below the surface, but the hand was a little bit moved back with a closed fingers (see Fig. 4d), and (3) **hand-moves**: the hand used for the secondary task was putted on the office and maintained in a perimeter around the surface

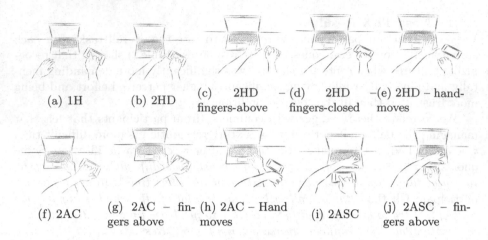

(a) 1H          (b) 2HD          (c)    2HD     – (d)    2HD     –(e) 2HD – hand-
                                 fingers-above      fingers-closed   moves

(f) 2AC         (g)  2AC  –  fin-  (h) 2AC – Hand     (i) 2ASC      (j)  2ASC  –  fin-
                gers above        moves                            gers above

**Fig. 4.** The different hand postures used during the experiment.

(see Fig. 4e). In addition, we observed two participants using the *finger-above* posture often touching the screen of the surface before a notification shows up to anticipate the appearance of this latter. Overall, this hand posture is used by nine participants for the right, eleven for the left and nine for the forward surface position.

–  **Two Arms Crossed – 2AC.** This hand posture is strongly correlated to the task priority and consists of using always the dominant (here right) hand for the primary task and the non-dominant (here left) hand for the secondary task despite the surface is on the right position. Consequently, the participants arms were crossed (see Fig. 4f). Participants kept their dominant hand on the keyboard array keys when performing the secondary task, and when this latter is finished, they used either the *fingers-above* (see Fig. 4g) or the *hand-moves* (see Fig. 4h) for the hand used to interact with the secondary task while keeping the hands crossed. Overall, two participants used this posture for the right surface position.

–  **Two Arms Semi-Crossed – 2ASC.** This posture occurred essentially in the *forward* position, when users used their non-dominant (left) hand to interact with the primary task, and their dominant (right) hand for the secondary task crossing a little their arms to perform both tasks (see Fig. 4i). Here, also participants kept their dominant hand on the keyboard array keys when performing the secondary task, and when this latter is finished, they used the *fingers-above* for the hand used for the secondary task while keeping the hands semi-crossed (see Fig. 4j). Two participants used this posture.

### 4.5.3   Strategies Used to Handle the Primary and the Secondary Task

We noticed different methods or behaviours adopted by our participants to prioritize the primary task (centring the ball) over the secondary task (recognizing the textures), which we grouped into three main strategies that we highlight here-after. Interestingly, we observed that once the participant starts the task with a given strategy, he continues with that strategy until finishing all the trials of the activity independently of the surface position or the hand posture used. We highlight the different strategies and the hand postures used hereafter:

– **Competitive interaction with Exclusive attention to Primary task (CEP).** Five of the thirteen participants kept interacting strongly with the primary task when they were interacting with the secondary one while their gaze attention was mostly conducted toward the laptop screen (*i.e.*, the primary task) with a nearly eyes-free interaction with the tactile surface (*i.e.*, the secondary task). In addition, all of them used to put more visual attention for the tactile surface only when they have to select the texture after perception, as it needs three button selections (confirm the end of perception, selecting a texture and then confirming the selection) with generally glances toward the primary task screen between those three actions. They also, rarely look at the tactile surface before starting perceiving the texture or for locating this latter during the experiment. Two participants using this strategy found that the activity is similar to *"driving"* while *"checking the GPS on the phone"* or *"manipulating their multimedia car radio"*.

  Four of the five participants interacted with the primary task in the same way and with almost the same rhythm during all the experiment *i.e.*, even when they have additionally to identify a texture. While we observed a different behavior for the remaining participant which used to move sequentially the ball from left to right, and from right to left by continuously alternating pressing on the left and the right arrow buttons to *"insure keeping the ball centered"* while performing the texture identification.

  Three hands posture were associated to this strategy. *2-HD* was used by respectively three, five and four participants for the *right, left and forward* surface positions. Two participants used *2AC* for the *right* position and one participant with a *2ASC* for the *forward* position.

– **Reactive Interaction with Shared Attention to Both tasks (RSB)** Three of the thirteen participants interacted principally with the secondary task and reacted to the primary task only when necessary *i.e.*, the ball moves away from the center, while keeping their hand over the arrow keys. Their gaze attention was shared almost equally between the primary and the secondary task when identifying textures, with certain cases where the primary task got more gaze attention then the secondary one. This strategy was used with a *2HD* by three participants for both the *right* and *left* surface positions. Two of them continue using this hand posture for the *forward* position while the latter used a *2ASC*.

– **Divided interaction with Exclusive attention to Secondary task (DES)** Five of the thirteen participants stopped interacting with the primary task and switched to the secondary one until they select a texture. In addition, to insure that the ball will not deviate from the box center, participants perform quick identifications of the rendered textures. And sometimes, when the notification showed up, participants start by making sure to center well the ball before switching to the secondary task. Most of the gaze attention was conducted toward the secondary task with only few glances toward the primary one. Two participants used a *1H* and the three latter used a *2HD* for the three surface positions.

### 4.5.4  Methodologies for Identifying Textures

To better understand how participants were performing, we report hereafter the four different strategies elaborated by participants in order to identify the *textures*; which is the by-product of the discussions that followed each *activity* condition. Four main strategies were identified:

– Visualizing the texture image in the user mental when perceiving the texture.
– Counting the number of all tactile feedback and then match its position with the visual texture.
– Using the densest and the sparse textures as a reference.
– Comparing the distance between two successive feedback and compare it to the user' finger width to determine if the texture is sparse or medium. One participant said: *"for the medium and sparse textures... I had to look to my finger to make the correspondence between the distance between two successive signals and my finger width to determine which texture I am feeling."*.

These findings are correlate to the findings of Rekik et al., [14,26,27]. Interestingly, many participants were able to know that they had made a mistake during the task for a particular texture when they were feeling the next one. With full practice, one may conjecture that the accuracy and the speed should eventually increase. Importantly, our participants used these four main strategies independently on the activity condition.

### 4.6  Discussion

Our key finding is that user's primary task had an impact on recognition rate without compromising the speed. We observed an average decrease of performance of 6.98% (from 88.78% to 82.58%) with an additional mental and physical demands, frustration and effort. These findings are consistent across different surface positions. We also observed different hands postures (one one-handed and three two-handed) and strategies to handle the primary and the secondary task with some participants making the secondary task without the need to see the surface device making the interaction with it eyes-free. Additionally, for the two-handed postures, the hand used for the primary task remains on the keyboard even when performing the secondary task to be ready to react to the primary task. However, interestingly, the hand used for the secondary stays in the surrounding area of the tablet even when the two hands are crossed or semi-crossed.

# 5    Experiment 2: Effect of a Cognitively Demanding Task

In this experiment, we followed [9] and used the same text-typing[1] exercise as our cognitively demanding primary task. We asked our participants to prioritize typing over texture recognition, and told them that their performance was being measured for both the primary and the secondary task. The procedure and task as well as common apparatus are presented in the Experiments section. Twelve new participants (3 females) volunteered (not paid) to take part into this experiment. Participant ages ranged between 22 and 41 years (mean = 30.41years, sd = 6.05 years). All participants were right handed.

## 5.1    Results

We consider the same dependent variables than in experiment 1.

### 5.1.1    Total Time

As in experiment 1, we found a significant main effect of *block* ($F_{2,22} = 9.43$, $p = .0011$) on *total time* with the first block slower than the two remainder ones (block1: mean = 8122 ms, s.d = 872 ms, block2: mean = 8017 ms, s.d = 640 ms and block3: 5744 ms, s.d = 667 ms). Post-hoc comparison confirms these differences ($p < .05$). As we are concerned with user performance after familiarization, the remaining analysis discards the first block.

Analysis of total time shows no significant effect of activity ($F_{1,11.03} = 0.43$, $p < .5251$), with similar means of total time between the control condition (mean= 7761.085   ms,sd= 608.148   ms), and typing (mean= 8421 ms,sd— 726 ms). There was a significant effect of *texture* ($F_{3,33.47} = 9.72$, $p < .0001$) with the densest texture (mean = 6237 ms, sd = 785 ms) being recognized significantly faster than all remainder textures (dense: mean = 8821 ms, sd = 1080 ms, medium: mean = 9163 ms, sd = 1012 ms, sparse: mean = 8210 ms, sd = 814 ms). Importantly, there was no significant interaction ($p > .30$) suggesting that these results are consistent.

### 5.1.2    Reaction Time

There was a significant effect of activity ($F_{1,11.02} = 7.95$, $p = .0166$) on *reaction time*, with the control condition faster (mean = 2065 ms,sd = 208 ms) than typing (mean = 5124.839ms,sd = 661ms) (see Fig. 5b). Post-hoc comparison confirms differences between the control condition and typing ($p < .05$). We correlate this result with user behavior. For instance, contrarily to the control condition where participants started the texture recognition when receiving the notification, in the typing activity, participants continued writing their word/sentence before switching to the recognition task. There was no significant interaction ($p > .35$), suggesting that the drawbacks of typing are consistent across different textures and surface positions.

---

[1] https://www.goodtyping.com/test.php.

### 5.1.3   Movement Time

There was a significant effect of activity ($F_{1,11.02} = 7.47$, $p = .0194$) and *texture* ($F_{3,33.47} = 9.86$, $p < .0001$) on *movement time*. Posthoc texts revealed that typing (mean $= 3296$ ms,sd $= 300$ ms) is significantly faster than the control condition (mean $= 5695$ ms,sd $= 524$ ms)($p < .05$) (Figure 5c). We also found that the densest texture (mean $= 2719$ ms, sd $= 415$ ms) is recognized significantly faster than all remainder textures (dense: mean $= 4968$ ms, sd $= 732$ ms, medium: mean $= 5458$ ms, sd $= 689$ ms, sparse: mean $= 5014$ ms, sd $= 595$ ms). There were no significant interactions ($p > .05$), suggesting that the benefits of typing are consistent across textures and surface position.

### 5.1.4   Accuracy

Analysis of count of trials containing an error shows no significant effect of activity ($F_{1,11} = 1.66$, $p = .2236$) on accuracy, with similar means of 87.15% with the control condition, and 84.95% for typing. There was a significant effect of texture ($F_{3,33.47} = 5.13$, $p = .0051$) with the densest texture (mean$=$ 96.2963%,sd$=$ 1.716964%) being more accurate than the remainder textures (dense: mean $= 96.29\%$,sd $= 1.71\%$, medium: mean$=$ 77.54%,sd $= 4.98\%$, sparse: mean $= 85.41\%$,sd $= 4.15\%$).

### 5.1.5   Number of Swipes

There was a significant main effect of activity ($F_{1,11.02} = 4.57$, $p = .05$) on *number of swipes*. Post-hoc tests revealed that the control condition (mean $=$ 8.33, sd $= .91$) produced significantly more swipe gestures than when typing (mean $= 6.15$, sd $= .85$) ($p < .05$) (Figure 5d). This result is correlated to the movement time that decreases with the typing activity. There was no significant interaction ($p > .12$), suggesting that this finding is consistent across different tablet positions and textures.

### 5.1.6   Number of Clutches

We found no significant effect on number of clutch nor interaction ($p > .05$) (mean $= .81$, sd $= .15$).

### 5.1.7   Subjective Results and Observations

Nasa-TLX responses (Table 1) showed that *typing* was significantly more demanding physically and temporally than the control condition . However, contrarily to experiment 1, in this experiment, only the DES strategy is used to prioritise the handle of both tasks. When participants received a notification, they first finish the word or the sentence they were writing then switch completely to the secondary task. Then-after, they make quick textures identification. The gaze attention was exclusively conducted toward the secondary task *i.e.*, identifying the textures on the tactile surface when interacting with the secondary task, with some rarely glances toward the primary task for the *forward position*.

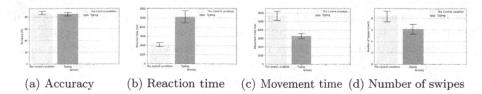

| (a) Accuracy | (b) Reaction time | (c) Movement time | (d) Number of swipes |

**Fig. 5.** User Performances in the second experiment.

The switch from the primary task to the secondary one was accompanied with a switch in the number of used hands: from two hands to one hand. For instance, ten participants used exclusively their dominant hand when interacting with the secondary task, while the two remainder used the closest hand to the tactile surface to identify the texture (*i.e.*, their right hand for *right* and *forward* positions and their left hand for the *left* position). Finally, all our participants used the same methodologies used in experiment 1 for identifying textures.

### 5.2 Discussion

Our key findings is that user's primary task (typing text) had an impact on recognition time and number of swipes and was mentally more demanding than the control condition. We observe an increase in reaction time of 148% (from 2065ms to 5124ms) and a decrease in movement time and number of swipes by respectively 42% (from 5695ms to 3296ms) and 26.17% without compromising total time and accuracy. These findings are consistent across different surface positions. These findings are also correlated to user strategy to handle the two simultaneous tasks while prioritizing the typing task over the texture recognition task. Our participants, first, finished writing the current word or sentence before moving to the textures recognition task. And then-after, our participants made quick interactions with the secondary task, before resuming the primary one.

## 6    Discussion and Implications

In this section, we discuss the implications of our results for attention saturating and cognitively demanding primary task, posture, tactile texture design and eyes-free interaction.

### 6.1    Attention Saturating Primary Task

Our first experiment highlights an effect of the attention saturating primary task on recognition rate: we observed an accuracy drop from 88.78% to 82.58% when participants have to keep the ball centred. However, while at first glance, it may look like using tactile texture with such a primary task is unusable, the recognition accuracy did achieve good rate of 82.58%. Consequently, this suggests that tactile textures could be effectively recognized and used by users on touchscreens when making such primary task. However, researchers interested in validating lab results in more realistic conditions may want to include tasks that saturate the attention as a factor for their experiment. We believe that more attention saturating tasks, in particular when considering a realistic scenario, *e.g.*, driving, would see a higher drop of accuracy.

## 6.2    Cognitively Demanding Primary Task

Our second experiment highlights an effect of the cognitively demanding task (typing) on recognition time: we observed an increase in reaction time from 2065ms to 5124ms and a decrease in movement time from 5695ms to 3296ms without compromising the recognition rate or the total recognition time. However, in the real world, what matters is the total time to convey information, which is why we included the total time to present the stimulus. The differences between the different activities is not significant. Consequently, this suggests that tactile texture could be effectively recognized and used by users when typing-text on laptop. Additionally, we believe that with practice users can cognitively chunk the simultaneous two tasks and greatly reduce their reaction time. The typing activity was as accurate as the control condition, but with shorter movement time to recognize the texture, which requires more concentration. Thus, one may conjecture that the accuracy should eventually increase with practice.

## 6.3    Eyes-Free Interaction Design

Our findings indicate that the perception of tactile textures can be made in an eyes-free interaction when performing at the same time an attention saturating primary task. This suggests that interacting with the tactile surface through textures can permit a user to sense the regions without diverting the eyes from the primary display during visually demanding tasks. Thus, designers should consider tactile texture to create an eyes-free dialog between the surface and the user especially when the user have to interact with another primary task.

## 6.4    Hands Posture During Two Simultaneous Tasks

Different hand postures have been used to handle and perform the primary and the secondary task. In particular, For an attention saturating primary task, our findings indicate that the 2HD posture is the most used posture. This posture is strongly correlated to the position of the surface device (used for the secondary task): the closed hand to the secondary task will perform it. This finding may help designers to choose the appropriate position for the secondary task device dependently on their preferred hand for the primary task.

## 6.5    Tactile Texture Design

Our results showed that the *densest* texture was the easiest and quickest one to identify among the four evaluated textures, and as most participants reported:

*"it's easy to guess the densest texture"*. It also required less effort then the other textures with significantly less swipes and clutches when users had to perform an attention saturating task simultaneously. Those findings suggest that the *densest* texture may be a good choice when designing tactile texture based interactions. Designers can also consider combining the densest texture with the sparse texture to create a large set of textures as our participants felt that *"it's easy to determine the difference"* between those two textures.

### 6.6    Limitations and Next Steps

Like any study, our study presents limitations. For example, in our studies participants were younger than the population average, were right-handed and all are students at the university. Undoubtedly, elder people, children or left-handed would behave differently. These issues are worthy of investigation, but are beyond the scope of the current work.

We observed different strategies to handle and perform the attention saturating task and the texture recognition one, accompanied with either exclusive attention to one task or shared attention to both tasks. However, the current study, do not allow us to determine which strategy is better. Consequently, our upcoming work will compare these different strategies while fixing the gaze attention to examine the effectiveness of tactile textures on touchscreen surfaces in each scenario and to determine its effectiveness when being able to see the tactile surface or not.

Finally, we do not found the same results nor the same behaviour (only one shared strategy to handle both tasks) when changing the primary task in our experiments. We believe that the overall message of this findings is simply that different interaction context produce different performances and behaviour on the texture recognition secondary task for the end user. These differences limit the overall generalization of our findings for other different primary tasks. As other scenarios exist where user can make a primary task while checking his mobile (*e.g.*, a person using his smartphone while being in a meeting or speaking with another person [28] or making a reading comprehension task or a word search [2] or when the attention is fragmented [16]), additional work will be required to explore how best to recognize textures on touchscreen while performing other primary tasks.

## 7    Conclusion

In this paper, we conducted the first investigation on the effect of an attention saturating primary task and a cognitively demanding primary task on tactile textures recognition on ultrasonic haptic tablet. Our findings indicate that for both primary tasks, the recognition rates for tactile textures stays higher than 82% without compromising the total time. However, contrarily to the cognitively demanding task, the attention saturating task increases frustration and mental demand compared to the control condition. We have also gained insight into the mental models of users when handling two simultaneous tasks and have discussed their implications for tactile feedback based interaction. We hope that our findings will prove useful to tactile feedback designers assisting them toward designing novel tactile feedback based techniques that would help users making the secondary tasks without being distracted from the primary task.

# References

1. Amberg, M., Giraud, F., Semail, B., Olivo, P., Casiez, G., Roussel, N.: Stimtac: A tactile input device with programmable friction. In: Proceedings of the 24th Annual ACM Symposium Adjunct on User Interface Software and Technology, pp. 7–8. UIST 2011 Adjunct, ACM, New York, NY, USA (2011). https://doi.org/10. 1145/2046396.2046401
2. Barnard, L., Yi, J.S., Jacko, J.A., Sears, A.: Capturing the effects of context on human performance in mobile computing systems. Personal Ubiquit. Comput. **11**(2), 81–96 (2007). https://doi.org/10.1007/s00779-006-0063-x
3. Bau, O., Poupyrev, I., Israr, A., Harrison, C.: Teslatouch: electrovibration for touch surfaces. In: Proceedings of the 23nd Annual ACM Symposium on User Interface Software and Technology, pp. 283–292. UIST 2010, ACM, New York, NY, USA (2010). https://doi.org/10.1145/1866029.1866074
4. Bragdon, A., Nelson, E., Li, Y., Hinckley, K.: Experimental analysis of touch-screen gesture designs in mobile environments. In: Proceedings of the 2011 annual conference on Human factors in computing systems - CHI 2011. p. 403. ACM Press (2011). https://doi.org/10.1145/1978942.1979000, http://dl.acm.org/citation.cfm?doid=1978942.1979000
5. Brewster, S., Chohan, F., Brown, L.: Tactile feedback for mobile interactions. In: Proceedings of the SIGCHI Conference on Human Factors in Computing Systems - CHI 2007, pp. 159–162. ACM Press (2007). https://doi.org/10.1145/1240624. 1240649, http://dl.acm.org/citation.cfm?doid=1240624.1240649
6. Brown, L.M., Brewster, S.A., Purchase, H.C.: Multidimensional tactons for non-visual information presentation in mobile devices. In: Proceedings of the 8th conference on Human-computer interaction with mobile devices and services - Mobile-HCI 2006, p. 231. ACM Press (2006). https://doi.org/10.1145/1152215.1152265, http://portal.acm.org/citation.cfm?doid=1152215.1152265
7. Casiez, G., Roussel, N., Vanbelleghem, R., Giraud, F.: Surfpad: Riding towards targets on a squeeze film effect. In: Proceedings of the SIGCHI Conference on Human Factors in Computing Systems, p. 2491–2500. CHI 2011, ACM, New York, NY, USA (2011). https://doi.org/10.1145/1978942.1979307
8. Cauchard, J.R., Cheng, J.L., Pietrzak, T., Landay, J.A.: ActiVibe: Design and evaluation of vibrations for progress monitoring. In: Proceedings of the 2016 CHI Conference on Human Factors in Computing Systems, pp. 3261–3271. ACM (2016). https://doi.org/10.1145/2858036.2858046, https://dl.acm.org/doi/10.1145/2858036.2858046
9. Chen, Q., Perrault, S.T., Roy, Q., Wyse, L.: Effect of temporality, physical activity and cognitive load on spatiotemporal vibrotactile pattern recognition. In: Proceedings of the 2018 International Conference on Advanced Visual Interfaces - AVI 2018, pp. 1–9. ACM Press (2018). https://doi.org/10.1145/3206505.3206511, http://dl.acm.org/citation.cfm?doid=3206505.3206511

10. Cockburn, A., Woolley, D., Thai, K.T.P., Clucas, D., Hoermann, S., Gutwin, C.: Reducing the attentional demands of in-vehicle touchscreens with stencil overlays. In: AutomotiveUI 2018, , pp. 33–42. Association for Computing Machinery, New York, NY, USA (2018). https://doi.org/10.1145/3239060.3239061

11. Cuqlock-Knopp, V.G.: Engineering psychology and human performance by Wickens, C., Hollands, J. 508 p. Prentice-hall, Upper Saddle River, NJ (1999). ISBN 0–321–04711–7. Ergon. Des. **8**(4), 37–38 (2000). https://doi.org/10.1177/106480460000800411

12. Dariosecq, M., Plénacoste, P., Berthaut, F., Kaci, A., Giraud, F.: Investigating the semantic perceptual space of synthetic textures on an ultrasonic based haptic tablet. In: HUCAPP 2020, Valletta, Malta, February 2020. https://hal.archives-ouvertes.fr/hal-02434298

13. Giraud, F., Amberg, M., Lemaire-Semail, B., Giraud-Audine, C.: Using an ultrasonic transducer to produce tactile rendering on a touchscreen. In: 2014 Joint IEEE International Symposium on the Applications of Ferroelectric, International Workshop on Acoustic Transduction Materials and Devices & Workshop on Piezoresponse Force Microscopy, pp. 1–4. IEEE (2014). https://doi.org/10.1109/ISAF.2014.6922972, http://ieeexplore.ieee.org/document/6922972/

14. Guettaf, A., Rekik, Y., Grisoni, L.: Effect of physical challenging activity on tactile texture recognition for mobile surface. Proc. ACM Hum.-Comput. Interact. **4**(ISS) (2020). https://doi.org/10.1145/3427318

15. Harrison, C., Hudson, S.E.: Providing dynamically changeable physical buttons on a visual display. In: Proceedings of the 27th International Conference on Human Factors in Computing Systems - CHI 2009, p. 299. ACM Press (2009). https://doi.org/10.1145/1518701.1518749, http://dl.acm.org/citation.cfm?doid=1518701.1518749

16. Harvey, M., Pointon, M.: Searching on the go: the effects of fragmented attention on mobile web search tasks. In: Proceedings of the 40th International ACM SIGIR Conference on Research and Development in Information Retrieval, p. 155–164. SIGIR 2017, Association for Computing Machinery, New York, NY, USA (2017). https://doi.org/10.1145/3077136.3080770

17. Israr, A., Bau, O., Kim, S.C., Poupyrev, I.: Tactile feedback on flat surfaces for the visually impaired. In: CHI 2012 Extended Abstracts on Human Factors in Computing Systems, pp. 1571–1576. CHI EA 2012, ACM, New York, NY, USA (2012). https://doi.org/10.1145/2212776.2223674

18. Kalantari, F., Berthaut, F., Grisoni, L.: Enriching musical interaction on tactile feedback surfaces with programmable friction. In: Aramaki, M., Davies, M.E.P., Kronland-Martinet, R., Ystad, S. (eds.) Music Technology with Swing, Lecture Notes in Computer Science. LNCS, **11265**, 387–401. Springer International Publishing, Heidelberg (2018). https://doi.org/10.1007/978-3-030-01692-0_25, http://link.springer.com/10.1007/978-3-030-01692-0_25

19. Kalantari, F., Grisoni, L., Giraud, F., Rekik, Y.: Finding the minimum perceivable size of a tactile element on an ultrasonic based haptic tablet. In: Proceedings of the 2016 ACM International Conference on Interactive Surfaces and Spaces, pp. 379–384. ISS 2016, ACM, New York, NY, USA (2016). https://doi.org/10.1145/2992154.2996785

20. Kane, S.K., Morris, M.R., Wobbrock, J.O.: Touchplates: low-cost tactile overlays for visually impaired touch screen users. In: Proceedings of the 15th International ACM SIGACCESS Conference on Computers and Accessibility - ASSETS 2013, pp. 1–8. ACM Press (2013). https://doi.org/10.1145/2513383.2513442, http://dl.acm.org/citation.cfm?doid=2513383.2513442

21. Kim, S.C., Israr, A., Poupyrev, I.: Tactile rendering of 3d features on touch surfaces. In: Proceedings of the 26th Annual ACM Symposium on User Interface Software and Technology, pp. 531–538. UIST 2013, ACM, New York, NY, USA (2013). https://doi.org/10.1145/2501988.2502020, http://doi.acm.org/10.1145/2501988.2502020

22. Leigh, D., Forlines, C., Jota, R., Sanders, S., Wigdor, D.: High rate, low-latency multi-touch sensing with simultaneous orthogonal multiplexing. In: Proceedings of UIST, pp. 355–364. ACM (2014). https://doi.org/10.1145/2642918.2647353, http://doi.acm.org/10.1145/2642918.2647353

23. Levesque, V., Oram, L., MacLean, K.: Exploring the design space of programmable friction for scrolling interactions. In: 2012 IEEE Haptics Symposium (HAPTICS), pp. 23–30. IEEE (2012). https://doi.org/10.1109/HAPTIC.2012.6183765, http://ieeexplore.ieee.org/document/6183765/

24. Levesque, V., et al.: Enhancing physicality in touch interaction with programmable friction. In: Proceedings of the SIGCHI Conference on Human Factors in Computing Systems, pp. 2481–2490. CHI 2011, ACM, New York, NY, USA (2011). https://doi.org/10.1145/1978942.1979306

25. Oy, S.: Senseg feelscreen development kit (2016). http://www.senseg.com

26. Rekik, Y., Vezzoli, E., Grisoni, L.: Understanding users' perception of simultaneous tactile textures. In: Proceedings of the 19th International Conference on Human-Computer Interaction with Mobile Devices and Services, pp. 5:1–5:6. MobileHCI 2017, ACM, New York, NY, USA (2017). https://doi.org/10.1145/3098279.3098528, http://doi.acm.org/10.1145/3098279.3098528

27. Rekik, Y., Vezzoli, E., Grisoni, L., Giraud, F.: Localized haptic texture: a rendering technique based on taxels for high density tactile feedback. In: Proceedings of the 2017 CHI Conference on Human Factors in Computing Systems, pp. 5006–5015. ACM (2017). https://doi.org/10.1145/3025453.3026010, https://dl.acm.org/doi/10.1145/3025453.3026010

28. Roudaut, A., Rau, A., Sterz, C., Plauth, M., Lopes, P., Baudisch, P.: Gesture output: Eyes-free output using a force feedback touch surface. In: Proceedings of the SIGCHI Conference on Human Factors in Computing Systems, pp. 2547–2556. CHI 2013, ACM, New York, NY, USA (2013). https://doi.org/10.1145/2470654.2481352, http://doi.acm.org/10.1145/2470654.2481352

29. Rydström, A., Grane, C., Bengtsson, P.: Driver behaviour during haptic and visual secondary tasks. In: Proceedings of the 1st International Conference on Automotive User Interfaces and Interactive Vehicular Applications, pp. 121–127. AutomotiveUI 2009, Association for Computing Machinery, New York, NY, USA (2009). https://doi.org/10.1145/1620509.1620533

30. Vezzoli, E., Sednaoui, T., Amberg, M., Giraud, F., Lemaire-Semail, B.: Texture rendering strategies with a high fidelity - capacitive visual-haptic friction control device. In: Bello, F., Kajimoto, H., Visell, Y. (eds)Proceedings, Part I, of the 10th International Conference on Haptics: Perception, Devices, Control, and Applications, Lecture Notes in Computer science. LNCS, **9774**, 251–260. EuroHaptics 2016, Springer-Verlag, Berlin, Heidelberg (2016). https://doi.org/10.1007/978-3-319-42321-0_23

31. Winfield, L., Glassmire, J., Colgate, J.E., Peshkin, M.: T-PaD: Tactile pattern display through variable friction reduction. In: Second Joint EuroHaptics Conference and Symposium on Haptic Interfaces for Virtual Environment and Teleoperator Systems (WHC 2007), pp. 421–426. IEEE (2007). https://doi.org/10.1109/WHC.2007.105, http://ieeexplore.ieee.org/document/4145211/

32. Xu, C., Israr, A., Poupyrev, I., Bau, O., Harrison, C.: Tactile display for the visually impaired using TeslaTouch. In: Proceedings of the 2011 Annual Conference Extended Abstracts On Human Factors in Computing Systems - CHIEA 2011, p. 317. ACM Press (2011). https://doi.org/10.1145/1979742.1979705, http://portal.acm.org/citation.cfm?doid=1979742.1979705

33. Zhang, Y., Harrison, C.: Quantifying the targeting performance benefit of electrostatic haptic feedback on touchscreens. In: Proceedings of ITS, pp. 43–46. ACM (2015). https://doi.org/10.1145/2817721.2817730, http://doi.acm.org/10.1145/2817721.2817730

# Endless Knob with Programmable Resistive Force Feedback

Yuri De Pra[1], Federico Fontana[1(✉)], and Stefano Papetti[2]

[1] University of Udine, Udine, Italy
federico.fontana@uniud.it
[2] Zurich University of the Arts, Zurich, Switzerland

**Abstract.** Touchscreens today represent the most versatile solution for configuring user interfaces. A toll for this versatility is the intangibility of the displayed virtual controls. The addition of haptic feedback can improve their manipulation by reinforcing or even substituting visual information. While haptic rendering of virtual buttons is advancing, tangible knobs seem yet to come, possibly due to the inherent difficulty to conceptualize rotation as an interaction primitive in absence of a physical control. To address this issue, we propose a hybrid solution consisting in an endless knob with programmable resistance to rotation. Compared to existing related devices, it minimizes costs, encumbrance and power consumption, making its installation also possible on portable equipment. After describing its design and main features, we present a test which assessed how haptic feedback rendered by the knob affects performance in a visual target-matching task: users had to select targets placed on a horizontal slider by dragging its cursor through knob rotation. Results show that haptic augmentation significantly improved target acquisition.

## 1 Introduction

In the last decades, interaction with machines has undergone radical changes. In spite of a long-established design tradition of their physical layouts, typical controls such as buttons, switches and knobs have often been replaced by virtual counterparts finding place on touchscreens and capacitive surfaces. Whenever direct manipulation provides safer and simpler interactions, however, tangible controls are still preferred. In today's cars, for instance, most auxiliary functions are accessible from touchscreens, whereas those which more closely affect driving are still a domain of physical knobs and selectors [16]. Tangible controls in fact provide rich haptic feedback allowing safe eyes-free selection while performing other main tasks such as driving [21]. Furthermore, by distributing part of the cognitive load onto the somatosensory channel, they ensure control accuracy in several everyday contexts and work environments [14].

Even if eyes-free interaction can be partially enabled on touchscreens through advanced vibrotactile feedback [19], electroadhesion [24] and friction modulation [26], on the other hand such augmentations do not guarantee more efficient interactions. For instance, no significant effect on performance was found using

C. Ardito et al. (Eds.): INTERACT 2021, LNCS 12935, pp. 580–589, 2021.
https://doi.org/10.1007/978-3-030-85610-6_32

touchscreens with vibrotactile feedback under demanding conditions (e.g., when dialing a telephone number while driving a car) [14].

In between virtual and physical layouts, tangible digital controls can be provided with variable haptic feedback: programmable buttons [15] and sliders [3] can render different force/displacement curves, whereas haptic knobs can generate multiple effects such as detents, barriers, spring repulsion through variable torque (see Sect. 2). The main downside of devices offering force feedback usually reside in their size, power requirements, and cost which may be several orders of magnitude higher than that of their purely mechanical counterparts. For instance, a mechanical detented knob can cost less than 1 USD, whereas a programmable haptic knob may easily be 100 times as expensive (e.g. [1,5]); moreover, a haptic knob requires electrical power and is usually much larger. These drawbacks typically limit the use of such haptic devices to expensive or safety-critical control panels [27] and to the research laboratory [13].

Here we propose a low-cost, compact knob with programmable resistive force, built around an electromagnetic braking system. Because of the absence of a motor and other active components, power consumption is much lower than that required by similar existing products. The effectiveness of the implemented resistive force effect was tested in a visual target-matching task operated using the knob with or without feedback: the former resulted in higher accuracy and shorter execution time.

## 2  Related Work

Different studies focusing on the manual control of visual tasks, occurring especially during machine operation, have found that the inclusion of context-dependent haptic feedback can improve human performance, particularly when the cognitive load is high and multiple tasks are performed at the same time [6,14,22].

For instance, experiments comparing physical and virtual knobs have shown that tangibility has positive effects on several interaction efficiency measures [21,28]. More in detail, physical knobs decrease error rate and speed up task completion up to 20% as compared to their virtual counterparts. Mainly for this reason, some recent smart gadgets incorporate or offer additional physical knobs: examples include Google Nest [10], an intelligent touchscreen-based thermostat, and the remote multimedia controllers Griffin PowerMate [11] and Microsoft Surface Dial [17].

These evidences suggest that the tangibility of physical knobs is still appealing. At the same time, today it would be desirable to expand their flexibility towards multi-parametric control as currently offered by virtual knobs, which, on the other hand, cannot be operated when visual attention is focused elsewhere (e.g., during teleoperation) [6,20].

One way to make the manipulation of multiple quantities through a single physical knob more intuitive is to provide it with haptic effects simulating various mechanics. However, this comes at the cost of embedding actuators and their

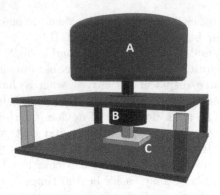

**Fig. 1.** Schematic of the haptic knob: the end effector (A) is connected to an encoder (C) by means of an electromagnetic braking system (B).

relative electronics in the knob, adding cost, complexity, encumbrance and power consumption. As a result, force-feedback rotary controllers are found only where this can be tolerated: car dashboards, piloting systems, professional audio/video editors, robot controls and medical devices. Most such controllers make use of DC motors to generate force feedback [2,12,23]. Hybrid solutions that combine motors and brakes have been proposed as well [5]: while allowing the design of subtle effects, they further increase hardware complexity. Even more expensive and technologically advanced solutions make use of magneto-rheological fluids in which the knob shaft is immersed [1,27]: in this case, magnetic-field variations are used to change the density of such fluids, allowing precise control of the resistive torque.

Finally, programmable haptic feedback is going beyond the mere reproduction of mechanical features like torque and detents, as the idea of branding machine interfaces with a unique haptic "feel" is progressively finding a relevant place in current technology trends [4,13,23,25]. In synergy with rigorous functional design constraints, this idea has nurtured controllers such as the jog wheel aboard the recent Traktor Kontrol S4 DJ console [18]. With this design scenario in mind, we have prototyped an endless knob with programmable resistive force feedback, which is described in what follows.

## 3    Hardware/Software Design

Our knob can be programmed to generate frictional patterns which, by resisting against rotation, induce resistive force-feedback effects. Its main hardware components consist of a rotary encoder coupled with an electromagnetic braking system that is controlled by an Arduino microcontroller through its pulse-width modulation (PWM) output. The details of the hardware have been filed in view of patenting the technology [8], whereas its application as a multimedia production controller has been presented in [9].

Compared to existing haptic knobs, the proposed electromagnetic braking system has advantages and drawbacks. The main advantage is that it can easily couple a standard knob to an encoder (see Fig. 1), resulting in a thin, lightweight and low-cost device. It also needs less power than DC motors [2], hence enabling battery-supplied portable solutions. The main shortcoming is lack of active force, which limits the feedback to changes in torque, and reproduction of detents as well as end-stops. The implemented control algorithm samples the encoder position and estimates its rotation speed during unidirectional shifts; these data are then used to set the magnitude and duration of the resistive force. The current prototype mounts a magnetic encoder with a resolution of 4096 points per revolution, that is, less than 0.1°.

The output voltage of the microcontroller (between 0 and $V_{CC}$) depends on the relative length of the PWM duty cycle, and directly controls the resistive torque of the knob. For example, if the output maintains a constant voltage, then a proportionally constant torque is applied against rotation.

Detents are reproduced as follows: once the encoder detects the position occupied by a detent, the algorithm sets the length of the PWM duty cycle and the value of a counter, depending on the programmed resistance and estimated rotation speed. The counter is decremented at every cycle, and the electromagnetic system operates at a constant PWM value until the counter reaches zero. The harder the detent, the longer the knob resists against motion.

Figure 2a shows the temporal evolution of the mentioned variables for two different haptic effects: in the first event (E1), a soft detent is simulated by applying the highest possible resistance for 50 ms; in the second (E2), the action of the braking system is modulated with short activations so as to generate a lower resistance, slowing down hand movement however without stopping it.

In addition to rotation, the knob can also be pushed as a button. Overall, six different input modes are made available by combining clockwise and counterclockwise rotation with no, short or long push.

## 4    Evaluation

A visual target-matching task was set up to test the effect of resistive feedback while performing an action that was functionally equivalent to a drag-and-drop action.

### 4.1    Procedure

Participants were asked to sit at a desk where a computer screen, keyboard and the knob were placed. The screen displayed a GUI developed in Processing 3.5 (see Fig. 3): using the knob, a red vertical segment representing a cursor could be dragged horizontally along a virtual slider which contained five equally spaced round markers. Two buttons completed the GUI, labeled 'Confirm' and 'Reload': they were operated by the computer keyboard respectively for confirming that

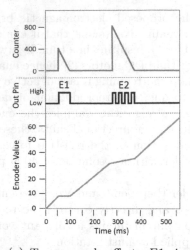 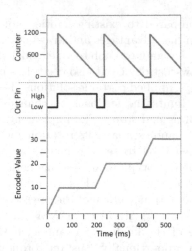

(a) Two example effects: E1 simulates a soft detent by setting the PWM duty cycle to 100% for 50 ms, resulting in a brief rotation stop; E2 simulates a lower constant resistance by repeating several PWM duty cycles at 50%.

(b) Hard detent effect, repeated every ten encoder steps. Hard detents are simulated by almost stopping hand movement. This is achieved by setting the PWM duty cycle to 100% for 150 ms, resulting in a strong resistive force.

**Fig. 2.** Temporal evolution of control variables for various haptic effects: when the encoder position (blue line) reaches a predefined value, resistive force is generated by activating the output signal (black line) until the counter (green line) is decremented to zero. The generated resistive force is proportional to the length of the PWM duty cycle (Color figure online).

a target was successfully matched, thus ending the trial, or for repeating the current trial.

The shift of the cursor had an accuracy equal to 11.4 pixels per degree of rotation; the markers were set 320 pixels apart from each other, corresponding to a rotation by about 28°.

At the beginning of each trial, the cursor was reset to the position marked with 'Home' in Fig. 3, and one of the markers along the slider was surrounded by a red circle, symbolizing the current target. Participants had to select this target by dragging the cursor over it: in order to move the cursor they had to push down the knob and turn it. When they reached the target, they released the knob and chose whether confirming or repeating the trial by pressing the respective button on the keyboard using the other hand. At each trial, haptic feedback was either present or absent; when present, it reproduced a hard detent (see Fig. 2b) in correspondence of a marker. Each factor combination of 5 targets × 2 feedback conditions was repeated 10 times, hence resulting in 100 trials which were randomly balanced for each participant.

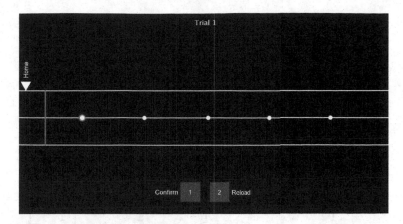

**Fig. 3.** The GUI used in the experiment. A vertical red cursor is controlled by the haptic knob; it moves along a virtual horizontal slider which hosts five round markers. At each trial, one marker is highlighted with the red color, thus becoming the current target. The blue squares are activated by pressing the corresponding buttons on the computer keyboard. (Color figure online)

A repetition was typically invoked when participants released the knob off-target, similarly to what happens when a wrong drag-and-drop action made with the mouse must be undone. If a trial was confirmed, then the time elapsed from the knob initial press to its release was measured, along with the distance of the cursor from the target (called mismatch from now on).

Ten participants (7 males, 3 females) aged between 24 and 57 (M = 39.9, SD = 10.3), all right-handed, took part in the test on a voluntary basis and were not paid. Before the test, participants performed a training session consisting of 10 trials, in which each factor combination was presented once in random order.

## 4.2   Results

Figures 4 and 5 respectively show box plots of the mismatch in pixel and time-to-match in ms, for each factor combination. Tests on the data distributions with the D'Agostino method [7] confirmed no significant deviation from normality.

A two-way ANOVA was conducted to study the influence of the two independent variables (target position, feedback condition) on mismatch. Using a Greenhouse-Geisser correction for insphericity, the main effect for feedback yielded $F(1,9) = 13.4$, $p < .005$, indicating a significant difference between trials in presence of haptic feedback (M = 3.7, SD = 0.31) and without it (M = 4.54, SD = 0.31). The main effect for position instead was not significant with $F(1.5, 13.6) = 0.2$, $p > .05$, and so was the interaction effect: $F(2.5, 22.5) = 2$, $p > .05$. In agreement with previous studies [22], our results show that haptic feedback significantly improved the precision of the action. The smaller mismatch did not come unexpected though, as the increased resistance to rotation occurring while traversing a marker supported participants

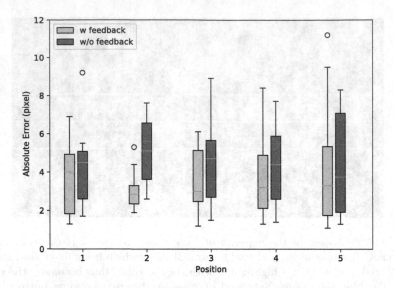

**Fig. 4.** Box plots showing the mismatch for each factor combination.

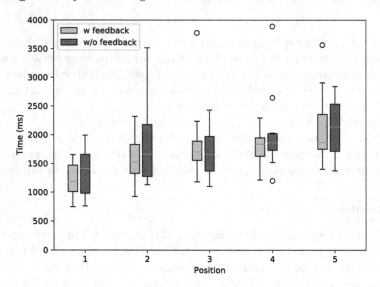

**Fig. 5.** Box plots showing the time-to-match for each factor combination.

to stop the cursor at the right location. A further two-way ANOVA was performed to study the influence of the two independent variables on the time-to-match. After a Greenhouse-Geisser correction for insphericity, the main effect for feedback was not significant with $F(1, 9) = 0.43$, $p > .05$. The main effect for position yielded $F(1.4, 12.8) = 22.3$, $p < .001$, indicating a significant difference between position 1 ($M = 1396$, $SD = 150$), position 2 ($M = 1720$, $SD = 145$), position 3 ($M = 1799$, $SD = 133$), position 4 ($M = 2049$, $SD = 184$) and position 5 (M = 2223, SD = 170). The interaction effect was not significant: $F(1.5, 13.3) = 1.4$, p > .05. The time-to-match depended on the position, with longer time associated to farther targets. While this result may appear obvious at first, one must consider that haptic feedback caused resistance to knob rotation each time a marker had to be traversed, however this had no significant effect on time-to-match. Even further, the time-to-match in presence of haptic feedback was on average generally lower, suggesting that resistive force potentially enables even faster execution of target-matching tasks.

## 5    Conclusions

A low-cost knob controller with programmable resistive feedback was proto-typed.

Its effectiveness was assessed in a visual target-matching test that showed a significant reduction of the positional mismatch when resistive feedback was applied to the knob.

Our study suggests that, even in absence of active forces as those provided by more expensive, bulky and power hungry motorized knobs, resistive feedback has concrete potential to support effective visual browsing of sequential domains such as sliders, top-down menus, and in general all those maps where physical rotary controls can be conveniently employed for the selection of targets.

Future plans include the design of refined haptic effects and the development of a systematic software communication framework operating between the knob and applications able to send/receive control messages belonging to standard protocols.

**Acknowledgments.** This research was partially supported by project HAPTEEV funded by the Swiss National Science Foundation (grant 178972). Yuri De Pra's Ph.D. is funded with a scholarship of The Research Hub by Electrolux Professional SpA.

## References

1. Battlogg, S.: Magnetorheological transmission device, 28 Jul 2015, U.S. Patent 9,091,309
2. Beni, N., Grottoli, M., Ferrise, F., Bordegoni, M.: In: Rapid prototyping of low cost 1 DOF haptic interfaces, pp. 479–483. IEEE (2014)
3. Berdahl, E., Kontogeorgakopoulos, A.: The firefader: Simple, open-source, and reconfigurable haptic force feedback for musicians. Comput. Music J. **37**(1), 23–34 (2013)
4. Bordegoni, M., Ferrise, F., Lizaranzu, J.: Multimodal interaction with a household appliance based on haptic, audio and visualization. In: Proceedings of IDMME-Virtual Concept (2010)

5. Chapuis, D., Michel, X., Gassert, R., Chew, C.M., Burdet, E., Bleuler, H.: A haptic knob with a hybrid ultrasonic motor and powder clutch actuator. In: Joint Euro-Haptics Conference and Symposium on Haptic Interfaces for Virtual Environment and Teleoperator Systems (WHC), pp. 200–205. IEEE (2007)
6. Corujeira, J., Silva, J.L., Ventura, R.: Effects of haptic feedback in dual-task tele-operation of a mobile robot. In: Bernhaupt, R., Dalvi, G., Joshi, A., K. Balkrishan, D., O'Neill, J., Winckler, M. (eds.) Human-Computer Interaction - INTERACT 2017, pp. 267–286. Springer International Publishing, Cham (2017)
7. D'Agostino, R.B.: An omnibus test of normality for moderate and large size samples. Biometrika **58**(2), 341–348 (1971)
8. De Pra, Y., Fontana, F.: Haptic controller with programmable resistive force, vol. I.P.O. n. 102021000009068. Status: Pending (2021)
9. De Pra, Y., Fontana, F., Papetti, S., Simonato, M.: A low-cost endless knob con-troller with programmable resistive force feedback for multimedia production. In: Proceedings of the 17th Sound and Music Computing Conference (SMC 2020), Turin, Italy (2020)
10. Filson, J.B., Daniels, E.B., Mittleman, A., Nelmes, S.L., Matsuoka, Y.: Dynamic distributed-sensor thermostat network for forecasting external events, 31 Dec 2013, U.S. Patent 8,620,841
11. Griffin Technology: PowerMate multimedia control knob. https://www.iclarified.com/i1112/. Accessed 29 Mar 2021
12. Hua, T.P., Fai, Y.C., Yap, R., Ming, E.S.L.: Development of a low cost haptic knob. Int. J. Mech. Aerospace Indust. Mechatron. Manuf. Eng. **5**(10), 1-4 (2011)
13. Kim, L., Han, M., Shin, S.K., Park, S.H.: A haptic dial system for multimodal pro-totyping. In: International Conference on Articial Reality and Telexistence (ICAT) (2008)
14. Lee, J.H., Spence, C.: Assessing the benefits of multimodal feedback on dual-task performance under demanding conditions. People Comput. XXII Cult. Creat. Interact. **22**, 185–192 (2008)
15. Liao, Y.C., Kim, S., Oulasvirta, A.: One button to rule them all: Rendering arbi-trary force-displacement curves. In: The 31st Annual ACM Symposium on User Interface Software and Technology Adjunct Proceedings, pp. 111–113 (2018)
16. Meixner, G., et al.: Retrospective and future automotive infotainment systems–100 years of user interface evolution. In: Automotive user interfaces, Human-Computer Interaction Series, 3–53. Springer, Cham (2017). https://doi.org/10.1007/978-3-319-49448-7_1
17. Microsoft: Surface Dial. https://support.microsoft.com/it-it/help/4036279/surface-meet-surface-dial. Accessed 29 Mar 2021
18. Native Instruments: Traktor Kontrol S4. https://www.native-instruments.com/en/products/traktor/dj-controllers/traktor-kontrol-s4/. Accessed 29 Mar 2021
19. Park, C., Yoon, J., Oh, S., Choi, S.: Augmenting physical buttons with vibrotac-tile feedback for programmable feels. In: Proceedings of the 33rd Annual ACM Symposium on User Interface Software and Technology, pp. 924–937 (2020)
20. Park, W., Kim, L., Cho, H., Park, S.: Dial-based game interface with multi-modal feedback. In: Yang, H.S., Malaka, R., Hoshino, J., Han, J.H. (eds) Entertainment Computing - ICEC 2010. ICEC 2010. Lecture Notes in Computer Science, **6243**, 384-396. Springer, Heidelberg (2010). https://doi.org/10.1007/978-3-642-15399-0_42

21. Pauchet, S., Letondal, C., Vinot, J.L., Causse, M., Cousy, M., Becquet, V., Crouzet, G.:ACM, : Gazeform: dynamic gaze-adaptive touch surface for eyes-free interaction in airliner cockpits. In: Proceedings of the Designing Interactive Systems Conference (DIS), pp. 1193–1205. ACM (2018)

22. Prewett, M.S., et al.: The benefits of multimodal information: a meta-analysis comparing visual and visual-tactile feedback. In: The benefits of multimodal information: a meta-analysis comparing visual and visual-tactile feedback. In: Proceedings of the 8th International Conference on Multimodal Interfaces, pp. 333–338 (2006)

23. Shin, S., et al.: Haptic simulation of refrigerator door. In: IEEE Haptics Symposium (HAPTICS), pp. 147–154. IEEE (2012)

24. Shultz, C.D., Peshkin, M.A., Colgate, J.E.: Surface haptics via electroadhesion: expanding electrovibration with johnsen and rahbek. In: 2015 IEEE World Haptics Conference (WHC), pp. 57–62 (2015). https://doi.org/10.1109/WHC.2015.7177691

25. Spence, C., Gallace, A.: Multisensory design: reaching out to touch the consumer. Psychol. Mark. 28(3), 267–308 (2011)

26. Vezzoli, E., et al.: Friction reduction through ultrasonic vibration part 1: modelling intermittent contact. IEEE Trans. Haptics 10(2), 196–207 (2017)

27. Vitrani, M., Nikitczuk, J., Morel, G., Mavroidis, C., Weinberg, B.: Torque control of electrorheological fluidic resistive actuators for haptic vehicular instrument controls. In: Proceedings of the IEEE International Conference on Robotics & Automation (2006)

28. Voelker, S., Øvergård, K.I., Wacharamanotham, C., Borchers, J.:Knobology revisited: a comparison of user performance between tangible and virtual rotary knobs. In: Proceedings of the International Conference on Interactive Tabletops & Surfaces (ISS), pp. 35–38. ACM (2015)

# *GrouPen*: A Tangible User Interface to Support Remote Collaborative Learning

Yanhong Li[✉], Yu Sun, Tianyang Lu, Thomas Weber, and Heinrich Hußmann

LMU Munich, Frauenlobstr. 7a, 80337 Munich, Germany
{yanhong.li,thomas.weber,hussmann}@ifi.lmu.de,
{Yu.Sun,Tianyang.Lu}@campus.lmu.de
http://www.medien.ifi.lmu.de

**Abstract.** Tangible User Interfaces (TUIs) have been used in many learning contexts. However, its application in the remote collaborative learning area remains relatively unexplored. In this study, we contribute to this use case with *GrouPen*. It is a TUI prototype embedded in a regular pen, thus allowing easy-to-use tangible interaction. We showed how it could be used to enable and enhance collaborative learning and engage students. *GrouPen* uses natural gestures to show statuses in several learning phases. We evaluated the prototype using a survey that yielded positive feedback and supported the hypothesis that TUIs like *GrouPen* could facilitate learning connectedness and engagement.

**Keywords:** Tangible user interface · Tangible learning · Remote collaborative learning · Human-centered design · Ubiquitous computing

## 1 Introduction

Online or distance learning is becoming an important part of formal education, particularly – but not exclusively – during the COVID-19 pandemic. It is often facilitated via video conferencing tools such as Zoom or Microsoft Teams [8]. These tools are convenient for verbal communication, but often fall short in engaging learners to collaborate effectively. Even though direct communication via video is fairly easy, secondary communication via implicit cues is much more challenging, and can quickly cause information overload of the visual and auditory senses. Tangible User Interfaces (TUIs), which provide a physical interface and can help learners interact in a natural way, can alleviate this and thus support remote collaborative learning. Manipulating objects physically and tangibly requires less cognitive effort [7], and provides an embodied way to interact with the world. However, as far as we know, there are few studies about the use of TUIs to facilitate remote collaborative learning. In this paper, we therefore

---

Y. Li, Y. Sun and T. Lu—Equally contributed to this study and were parallel first author

© IFIP International Federation for Information Processing 2021
Published by Springer Nature Switzerland AG 2021
C. Ardito et al. (Eds.): INTERACT 2021, LNCS 12935, pp. 590–598, 2021.
https://doi.org/10.1007/978-3-030-85610-6_33

introduce *GrouPen*, a TUI designed to help learners to be more engaged in collaborative group learning (Sect. 3). It allows students to see their peers' progress, get matched with their peers and also lets teachers get an overview of their students' learning progresses. A first evaluation (Sect. 4) shows *GrouPen* as a TUI can help solve the communication problems that are caused by a spatially asynchronous learning scenario. Our work thus makes a contribution to explore how TUIs can make students more connected and engaged in a remote collaborative learning environment.

## 2    Related Work

### 2.1    Remote Collaborative Learning

Compared with individual learning or competitive learning, collaborative learning was found to be a better learning strategy to develop students' critical thinking skills and make them have a higher achievement [6,10]. With the development of communication technology, collaborative learning happens more often remotely. It is good for making students collaborate and communicate with group members regardless of location. However, engaging all group members and making them feel connected with others is challenging. Except peer-to-peer communication, previous studies found technology and teachers were the most valuable and important factors for students in remote collaborative learning [4,9]. Therefore, a remote collaboration tool should not only consider to facilitate group communication, but also could help teachers understand their students' learning progresses and provide them timely feedback.

### 2.2    TUI for Learning

As a part of Weiser's "ubiquitous computing" [13], technology becomes ubiquitous and embedded in our daily life objects, which can be naturally interacted with, like grabbing. Tangible learning involves gesture, motion or full-body interaction and "emphasizes the use of the body in educational practice" [5]. TUI for learning emphasizes physical activities and manipulation of physical objects for learning [1]. In the field of education, TUI has been applied to multiple projects as well, aiming to help students better understand abstract concepts like mathematical problems or programming. Danli et al. [12] proposed *T-Maze*, a tangible programming environment designed to allow children to build computer programs by manipulating a set of wooden blocks which are interconnected by magnets. By using physical manipulation, learners could benefit more from *T-Maze*. To help students understand abstract probability problems, Bertrand et al. [11] designed and developed an interactive interface for collaborative learning. Students could rearrange physical tokens to see the effects of various constraints on the problem space. However, these TUIs are not embedded in everyday objects and can not be seamlessly integrated into everyday usage and compute ubiquitously. Moreover, current TUIs focus little on remote learning, where students can cooperate with others remotely with TUIs. This is a gap especially in the time of the pandemic. Therefore, we designed and developed *GrouPen* to explore the possibilities of TUI for remote collaborative learning.

# 3   GrouPen

## 3.1   Concept Ideas

To design an idea that is suitable for remote collaborative learning, we were inspired by the ubiquitous physical tools in daily life. TUI would work better if it can be integrated with computing ability. The pen is an essential tool in learning activities, thus it's worth making a pen as a TUI that users can directly interact with. Our target users are students who learn and discuss in a small group with *up to 6 students*. Possible user scenarios could be solving quiz-based group learning tasks, e.g. mathematics and physics, etc. *GrouPen* is equipped with one micro-controller, five sensors, two actuators, and one pen base to hold the pen. Students can use the LED colors on the pen to show their learning progresses, such as finish the quiz, have a question, or get matched with their peers. As shown in Fig. 1, collaborative learning processes are divided into five stages, which are working, having questions, discussing, finished, offline. Correspondingly, it can be identified with five different colors: yellow, red, blue, green, and grey. The color codes are consistent with daily conventions such as red is for urgency, and in our case red is for questioning. This is, of course, adaptable to individual preferences or circumstances.

| Color | | ● | ● | | |
|--------|-------------|--------------------------------------|----------------------------------|----------------------------------------|---------|
| **Status** | In progress | Having questions/ needing help | Discussing with other students | Finished/ available for discussion | Offline |

Fig. 1. *GrouPen*'s color coding concepts

To change the light color, learners can interact with the pen by performing specific gestures: (1) take the pen from the pen base; (2) raise the pen vertically; (3) shake the pen; and (4) put the pen back to the pen base. As the light colors are triggered by gesture interactions, information will be conveyed in a tangible way.

## 3.2   Design Process

We came up with the idea that *GrouPen* should have an embodiment of a real pen, because a pen is the most common tool used in our learning activities. It fits well to some remote learning situations. For example, when it is not convenient to have an audio chat in the online virtual room, because other students are still working. In addition, when the student wants to know the availability of his or her teammates, he or she needs to frequently check the notifications or chats. It is easy to cause information overload. Therefore, we designed a color-changeable pen with LEDs on it to indicate the status of each group member. More specifically, *GrouPen* is attached with LED strips, each of which represents the status of a team member. It avoids students to frequently check notification and be distracted by irrelevant messages. Meanwhile, it is also suitable for remote collaboration without accessing communication device such as laptops. Figure 2 shows how gesture interactions can realise the transition between various states.

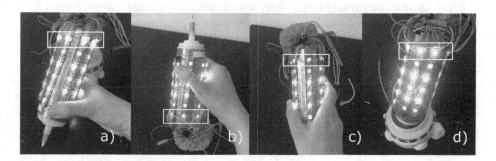

**Fig. 2.** Gesture interactions with *GrouPen*: a) Take the *GrouPen* from pen base; b) Raise it vertically; c) Shake it; d) Put it back to the pen base. The first row represents the user itself, and the other rows represent the team mates.

These gestures are intuitive to understand and have consistency with daily learning habits. There are four main interactions with *GrouPen*: As the pen base is suitable to be designed as the "started" and "finished" trigger, the first interaction is to *take the pen out of the pen base*. In the meantime, the LED, which indicates the users' status, will show a yellow light to convey the working status. The second interaction is to *raise the pen vertically* to switch to a questioning state, which was inspired by raising our hands when we have a question in the face-to-face (F2F) classroom. By *shaking the GrouPen*, students are able to connect with other group members for discussion. The inspiration was from the WeChat[1] "shake to get paired" function for social activity. As it is easy to become a habit, we adopted "shake" as the trigger for matching. After shaking, the system will automatically search for other students who have shaken the pen and are ready for discussion. If there is no one to match, the user will be in the waiting queue until someone else shakes to start a discussion or raise vertically to ask a question. After completing the learning task, students can *put the pen back in the pen base*, their light will thus turn to green, which means they have finished the task and are available for discussion.

Except the functions above, we added the following other four features. **Progress Bar:** While working on a learning task, students might want to see how much time they have spent and how much time they have left, therefore, we decided

---

[1] WeChat is a popular Chinese social media application.

to design a progress bar on the pen base to enable time management. **Focus mode**: students can turn off light status to concentrate on the task without being disturbed. In this context, *GrouPen* becomes an ordinary writing pen. **Show emotion**: A study of Botzer et al. [2] showed that grip force could be thought as a measure in joystick-controlled tasks and the participants who were under higher stress had a significant higher grip force. Therefore, we used grip force as a design element and made *GrouPen* emotion-aware. It has a pressure sensor to perceive how tight the student grip the pen and shows it through the brightness of LEDs. The information of stress level can not only be timely shared with peers and teachers, but also can be stored for the analysis of learning behavior. *GrouPen* can help the teacher in the collaborative learning through: (1) enhance peer-to-peer discussion so that there are fewer students in the waiting queue; (2) let the teacher know if students have questions. *GrouPen* can also be used in a self-organised learning environment without the presence of teachers.

### 3.3   Prototype

For the hardware, all used sensors and actuators are demonstrated in Fig. 3. We used Teensy board as the micro-controller, which was much smaller than Arduino Uno board to fit in the plastic bottle. The LEDs we used were WS2812B strips, which could be cut and soldered to indicate the progress and status of group members. For gesture recognition, a 3-axis gyroscope and a 3-axis accelerometer MPU6050 were used. They could obtain the value of the pen in the $x$-$y$-$z$ axis, determine the orientation of the pen, and recognize the user's gestures. In addition, we used the digital shake sensor SKU:SEN0289. During the function testing, it worked more accurately than MPU6050 to detect users' shaking movement. The light sensor LM393 was placed in the pen base to detect users' behavior of picking up/dropping down the *GrouPen*. The TTP223B digital capacitive touch sensor was implemented on the top of the pen, which was designed to be touched by the students for turning on and off the lights. In order to show the learning emotion, a Force Sensing Resistor (FSR) MD30-60 was implemented to detect students' grip force. The brightness of the LED will then be changed according to the pressure value. Finally, a vibration module is mounted in our prototype for providing tactile feedback to indicate the changes of status or functions. For the software, we used the Teensyduino IDE for programming and testing. A web server was built on an ESP 32 micro-controller to realise communication among group members.

In order to show our proof-of-concept, we need to make it look like a real pen. We used a 300 ml size plastic bottle as the shell of the *GrouPen*. We cut the dip from a pencil with the electric cutter and inserted it into the plastic bottle, so that *GrouPen* can have a replaceable and usable dip for writing.

### 3.4   User Study

In order to test *GrouPen*'s usability, user experience, and willingness to use for remote collaborative learning, we conducted user studies with 7 participants

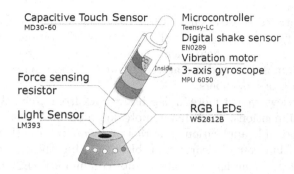

Capacitive Touch Sensor
MD30-60

Microcontroller
Teensy-LC

Digital shake sensor
EN0289

Vibration motor

Force sensing
resistor

3-axis gyroscope
MPU 6050

Inside

Light Sensor
LM393

RGB LEDs
WS2812B

**Fig. 3.** Hardware details in the *GrouPen*

(4 females, 3 males). Their average age was 33 ($M = 24$, $SD = 14.93$). Six of them learn daily in the remote situation, the other one learns weekly in the remote situation.

Our user study was conducted in two forms, online with Zoom platform and F2F, both of which lasted for about 30 min. Online study had four steps: first, participants filled the consent and demographic questionnaire to get their personal information (e.g. age and gender) and remote learning experience and habits. Then, we played the video of the *GrouPen* and had a verbal explanation of its usage and functions. After that, participants were asked to fill the System Usability Scale (SUS) [3] questionnaire (a ten-item attitude Likert scale to understand *GrouPen*'s effectiveness, efficiency, and satisfaction) and rate the user experience of for collaboration (i.e. "Using this *GrouPen* would help me engage in remote collaborative learning", and "Using the *GrouPen* could make me more aware of my group members"). Finally, an interview was conducted to know more about their opinions, for example, what they thought was the biggest problem in remote learning and suggestions to improve *GrouPen*. The interview was audio recorded for interview analysis. The F2F study was conducted in a similar process, except we showed them our physical prototype and demonstrated the features lively. However, participants for online just watched our functional video.

## 4    Findings

From the results of SUS, we found users' overall attitude towards *GrouPen* was 70, which was above average score of 68. According to the general guideline on the interpretation of SUS score [3], a score above 80.3 is excellent, between 68 and 80.3 is good.

According to their responses, *GrouPen* was thought to be more effective than non-physical learning tools to help students engage in collaborative learning. More specifically, users found *GrouPen* was interesting to use and strongly agreed it could help them for remote collaborative learning. All participants agree that it would be a good idea to use *GrouPen* for remote learning, which indicated a high user acceptance of TUI. They also agreed that *GrouPen* could be used as an enhancement and complement to the existing collaboration tool. In addition, their said *GrouPen* could help them be more aware of group members. We also found that most respondents agreed *GrouPen* could make them feel more connected with group members.

In the interview, we got more in-depth feedback from users. We summarized it from three dimensions: (1) What remote learning problems can be solved? (2) What are possible application scenarios of *GrouPen*? (3) How do users feel while using it? Many remote learning problems can be solved by *GrouPen*, such as "mitigate the problem that students can not communicate F2F due to the pandemic", "better understand if my teammates have problems", "*GrouPen* makes the status update easier". Some talked about it from the second dimension: what are the suitable remote learning scenarios that *GrouPen* could be applied to. "suitable for solving mathematical problems". As for personal feelings, we got some feedback such as "the feeling of binding together is increased", "feel more motivated", "want to help him/her actively if the light changed to red" etc.

## 5    Discussion

From the results, we found that users had a positive reception and were willing to use *GrouPen* in the remote learning environment. They thought our prototype was useful to solve their remote collaboration problems, such as convey and receive the progress and availability information. *GrouPen*, as a TUI learning tool, could make the information more noticeable, make students pay more attention to their teammates, and be more aware of their peers' needs. Participants feel more active to take some actions when they saw someone's color has changed. As the information that someone needs help can be conveyed so directly, a more active connection can be made.

Participants were enthusiastic of using TUI, because the current tools they used for remote learning were all non-physical software, such as Zoom or Microsoft Teams. In comparison to digital tools, TUI provides opportunities that students can directly interact with their gestures and get immediate visual and haptic feedback, which facilitates their emotional connections with the teacher and classmates.

A biggest advantage of *GrouPen* is that it only conveys the most basic and essential information to the learners. Therefore, users do not need to use digital devices on a regular basis and feel more simliar like learning in the F2F classroom. However, *GrouPen* also has limitations. For example, it can only support non-verbal and easy communication (i.e. status, availability, and group members' emotions). When it comes to general or discussion situations, audio calls and video conferencing are still needed.

In addition, four suggestions could be considered for future development. Some of these suggestions come from the feedback of the participants in our study, the other derive from our reflections. First, hardware enhancement: it might be better to integrate a function of audio recording, which can make it more independent with computer; Second, writing experience: *GrouPen* could be "thinner, compacter", which could make users have a real writing experience; Third, personalisation: concerns and ideas about force-sensing were expressed in the interview, for example, "the individual baseline for the force of holding pens should be measured before". Thus, future work needs to consider users' diversities and adjust for their differences; Finally, learning habits analysis: *GrouPen* could be a good medium to trace learners' behavior or habits. Like one of our participant mentioned, "the data of force level should be sent to the teacher".

## 6 Conclusion

By combining computing technology and everyday objects into TUIs, like *GrouPen*, we hope to create engagement in scenarios such as remote collaborative learning. This is a particular important learning context but also challenging. Our early prototype in this study is a first step to enhance group connectedness in this situation. Integrating the interaction into everyday objects, which are being used anyway, ensures that overhead is kept to a minimum and allows for a number of natural interactions (as we described in our prototype). Receiving information about the status of group members or tasks via such a TUI should help keep mental load and distraction low. This in turn would benefit students' learning. The positive feedback from our evaluation corroborated this hypothesis, because participants saw the benefits of our interface.

Certainly, even with natural gestures and everyday objects, there will be a learning curve, which needs a larger and long-term study to see the effectiveness. These should particularly take place in real-world learning scenarios with different learners ranging from elementary school to university students. Beyond that, *GrouPen* should also be adapted into new usage scenarios such as project-based learning tasks.

**Acknowledgements.** This research is funded by the Elite Network of Bavaria (K-GS-2012-209).

## References

1. Bakker, S., Antle, A., van den Hoven, E.: Embodied metaphors in tangible interaction design. Personal Ubiquitous Comput. **16**, 433–449 (2011)
2. Botzer, A., Sahar, Y., Wagner, M., Elbaum, T.: Analyzing individuals' grip force over short intervals in a joystick-controlled task with and without a stress manipulation. Behav. Inf. Technol. **40**(5), 476–482 (2021)
3. Brooke, J.: Sus - a Quick and Dirty Usability Scale, pp. 189–194 (1996)
4. Davies, R., Yeung, E., Mori, B., Nixon, S.A.: Virtually present: the perceived impact of remote facilitation on small group learning. Med. Teach. **34**(10), e676–e683 (2012)
5. Eisenberg, M., Pares, N.: Tangible and full-body interfaces in learning, pp. 339–357 (2014)

6. Gokhale, A.A.: Collaborative learning enhances critical thinking (1995)
7. Hallam, J., Zheng, C., Posner, N., Ericson, H., Swarts, M., Do, E.: The light orchard: an immersive display platform for collaborative tangible interaction. pp. 245–248 (2017)
8. Kristóf, Z.: International trends of remote teaching ordered in light of the coronavirus (covid-19) and its most popular video conferencing applications that implement communication. Central Eur. J. Educ. Res. 2(2), 84–92 (2020)
9. Mallon, M., Bernsten, S.: Collaborative learning technologies. Association of College and Research Libraries and American Library Association, USA (2015)
10. Roseth, C.J., Johnson, D.W., Johnson, R.T.: Promoting early adolescents' achievement and peer relationships: the effects of cooperative, competitive, and individualistic goal structures. Psychol. Bull. 134(2), 223 (2008)
11. Schneider, B., Blikstein, P., Mackay, W.: Combinatorix: a tangible user interface that supports colaborative learning of probabilities, pp. 129–132 (2012)
12. Wang, D., Wang, T., Liu, Z.: A tangible programming tool for children to cultivate computational thinking. Sci. World J. 428080(02) (2014)
13. Weiser, M.: The computer for the 21st century. SIGMOBILE Mob. Comput. Commun. Rev. 3(3), 3–11 (1999)

# TactCube: Designing Mobile Interactions with Ambient Intelligence

Pietro Battistoni(iD), Marianna Di Gregorio(iD), Marco Romano(✉)(iD), Monica Sebillo(iD), and Giuliana Vitiello(iD)

Università di Salerno, 84084 Fisciano, SA, Italy
{pbattistoni,madigregorio,marromano,msebillo,gvitiello}@unisa.it

**Abstract.** This paper presents TactCube, a novel tangible user interface based on a cube-shaped device. It is designed to interact with Ambient Intelligence and allows users to give commands and receive rich feedback using only one hand. A guessability user study was conducted involving 60 participants and results were used to map the device interactions onto commands invoked on an Ambient Intelligence system. The study considered three smart devices, properly a smart speaker, a smart bulb, and a smart curtain. For each of the devices, users were asked to propose his/her favorite interaction modality through TactCube, for 12 different commands and a kind of admissible feedback for 8 different states of the ambient intelligence system. The analysis of the responses led us to derive a set of interaction design implications which could be taken into account for any tangible interface inside an intelligent ambient system.

**Keywords:** Tangible interaction · User study · Interactive environment

## 1 Introduction

The Internet of Things has the vision to pervade our daily environment. One of the main characteristics of such environments is the growing amount of smart devices and their complexity. Indeed, due to the weaknesses of existing user interfaces, when interacting with intelligent environments, users are overloaded by the multitude of networked devices [3]. Identifying and activating the right device or service from a huge amount of existing devices to perform a specific task is a challenge for users in these environments. Moreover, devices can disappear in the background and can be invisible to users requiring new forms of interaction [1]. Researchers are dealing with the design of interfaces enabling the interaction through different devices and in different forms depending on the characteristics of the ambient environment [13]. In [1], a systematic review on meta-interfaces to interact with the environment points out that the most relevant unexplored issues are related to the lack of spontaneous discoverability [6] of

Partially supported by MIUR PRIN 2017 grant number 2017JMHK4F004, and MIUR 2019 grant number AIM1872991-2.

The original version of this chapter was revised: The name of the author "Marianna di Gregorio" was incorrect. The correction to this chapter is available at
https://doi.org/10.1007/978-3-030-85610-6_44

C. Ardito et al. (Eds.): INTERACT 2021, LNCS 12935, pp. 599–609, 2021.
https://doi.org/10.1007/978-3-030-85610-6_34

such interfaces and the lack of adequate feedback [5, 11]. When Artificial Intelligence (AI) takes the orchestration of Smart Environment devices, this results into Ambient Intelligence (AmI). AmI should satisfy human requests by piloting the devices in a context-aware manner [4]. The context, in this case, refers to both the environment and user circumstances. For example, a context could depend on smart devices availability, environmental conditions, and user position. Thus, the need to let AmI understand the user context and requirements demands for new interactive Human-Computer Interfaces (HCIs). The idea and architecture of an utterly tactile interface device that interacts with an AmI were already presented in [2]. The proposed device, named TactCube, promotes a tactile-only interface that could allow human interaction with AmI without visual or audio means. Furthermore, an effort was made to design a small wireless cube-shaped hardware device that could be used with one hand only and to be kept in a pocket. This work aims to investigate the modalities of admissible interactions by users with AmI through a tangible mobile interface. The TactCube device was initially introduced to users, and three smart devices (smart bulb, speaker and curtain) were selected to conduct a guessability study. Guessability studies have been widely used to define sets of touch or motion gestures on various types of devices equipped with multitouch screens, both large-screened devices and common smartphones [7, 9]. For each device, the study allowed us to investigate users' preferences among the set of admissible TactCube interactions to be mapped onto a set of device behaviors governed by an AmI system. Finally, the analysis of the responses led us to define a set of design implications that designers should consider when developing tangible mobile interfaces for ambient intelligence systems.

## 2  Interactive Cube

The idea behind TactCube was to design a fully tactile interface, helping users to communicate with AmI avoiding video and audio media. For the sake of brevity, we do not report here all the details on the TactCube prototype implementation, for which we address the reader to [2], and instead focus on what is relevant for the present study. TactCube design aims to offer a non-intrusive tangible interface, which let user communicate with an AmI system his/her contextual needs through simple gestures, just holding the small device in one hand. A users may start the interaction holding the cube with the fingers, as in Fig. 1, and may perform the following 10 gestures: *1. a single tap of index finger on one of cube faces; 2. a double tap of index finger on one of cube face; 3. the forward rotation followed by a single tap; 4. the forward rotation followed by a double tap; 5. the backward rotation followed by a single tap; 6. the backward rotation followed by a double tap; 7. the right rotation (clockwise) followed by a single tap; 8. the right rotation followed by a double tap; 9. the left rotation (anticlockwise) followed by a single tap; 10. left rotation followed by a double tap.*

Besides these ten gestures, five types of haptic feedback are also admissible, namely: *1. one short vibration; 2. two short vibrations; 3. a combination of short and long vibrations 4. a face of the device warming up; 5. a face of the device cooling down.*

TactCube deploys WiFi connectivity with AmI and a Bluetooth Low Energy (BLE) solution that unveils the smart devices in proximity, helping the AmI system to recognize the user position inside the environment. TactCube communicates to the AmI contextual information about the users to pilot the smart devices and support their needs. As an example, if the user is turning the cube forward in a dark room, and AmI is adequately trained, by the context and the position of the user, it may infer that more light is needed and then switch the lamps on. If the same action was made in the proximity of a curtain and the light was already on, given the different context and user's position, the AmI system may infer that the request was related to the desire to open the curtain, instead.

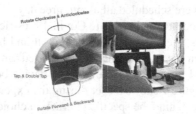

**Fig. 1.** The TactCube prototype and a user interacting with it.

## 3   The User Study

The idea behind TactCube was to design a fully tactile interface, helping users to communicate with AmI avoiding TactCube provides users with multisensorial feedback involving touch, vibrations and temperature changing and a large number of motion and touch interactions to be mapped onto the commands. In our study, we investigate on the one hand which are users' favorite TactCube interactions for precise commands and feedback in a smart environment and, on the other, if such preferences may depend on the kind of smart device under control. To do so, we set up a mixed-design experiment performed with 60 participants equally distributed intro 3 different groups. We considered 2 factors that are respectively: Factor 1 the 12 Tasks as a within-subject variable, and Factor 2 the 3 devices as a between-subject variable. Participants were selected from a group of 130 volunteers IT students who had passed one of the computer science exams dealing with the discipline of human computer interaction, at the authors' university. Based on a short questionnaire, we were able to select the 60 students, who best grasped the goal of the study, all of them being technologically skilled enough to interact with a tangible device like TactCube without distorting the experimental results. The chosen number of subjects was suitable to get preliminary insights and in line with similar experiments present in the scientific literature [9, 10, 12]. We divided our subject participants into three subgroups, properly Gr1, Gr2 and Gr3. To each subgroup we assigned a different device to interact with using TactCube – precisely a smart bulb, a smart speaker and a smart curtain, which are common everyday devices. Table 1 shows 20 guessability tasks for each device, including 12 navigation/action items and 8 feedback items. The tasks are split into three categories, specifically, *Action*, *Navigation* and *Feedback*. The items of each category are distributed into two subcategories: AmI Environmental system and Smart Device. Then, we assign a label to each item depending on its category and subcategory, precisely EA and DA for Action, EN and DN for Navigation, EF and DF for

*Feedback.* The categories are adapted from the work presented in [10] which considers the generic tasks in a smartphone system environment. Apart from the categories *Action* and *Navigation*, we also added the category *Feedback* originally missing in [10] but necessary, as recommended also in [10], considering that also the feedback must be mapped correctly in the system to be interpreted by users. For each task, the participants were required to propose a specific gesture or feedback to associate to the prototype chosen from the 10 basic available gestures and the 5 kinds of feedback. The experiment took place in a controlled environment, that is the usability research lab of the University of XXXX, the participants were scheduled all along three days and only one participant at a time could access the laboratory, also due to Covid-19 restrictions. A workstation was set up for the participants, then, they were asked to sit and hold the TactCube device and interact with it. When the experiment session started, an application running in a computer desktop showed for each task the specific device behavior and asked for an interaction preference. Figure 1 shows a user during the experiment. To better evaluate the potential and rationale behind the specific interaction choices, a "think-aloud" technique was used. Moreover, users were photographed and recorded, in order to allow the researchers a systematic analysis of the experiment. At the end of the experiment, we asked participants to discuss any possible suggestion or issue. Each session lasted on average 30 min. During it, the authors took notes to discuss at the end of the session and of the whole experiment.

**Table 1.** The guessability tasks for the smart bulb, speaker and curtain.

| ID | Interacting with a smart bulb | Interacting with smart speaker | Interacting with a smart Curtain |
|----|----|----|----|
| Action | | | |
| EA1 | Access to the environment | Access to the environment | Access to the environment |
| DA1 | Turn on the light | Turn on the speaker | Turn on the curtain |
| DA2 | Turn off the light | Turn off the speaker | Turn off the curtain |
| DA3 | Stop/play | Stop/play | Stop/play |
| Navigation | | | |
| EN1 | Select the smart bulb | Select the smart speaker | Select the curtain |
| EN2 | Deselect the smart bulb | Deselect the smart speaker | Deselect the curtain |
| DN1 | Increase the intensity of the light | Increase the speaker volume | Increases the amount of light that can filter |
| DN2 | Decrease the intensity of the light | Decrease the speaker volume | Decrease the amount of light that can filter |
| DN3 | Change the color of the light | Change audio preset | Change fissure preset |

*(continued)*

**Table 1.** (*continued*)

| ID | Interacting with a smart bulb | Interacting with smart speaker | Interacting with a smart Curtain |
|---|---|---|---|
| DN4 | Select a behavioural program (The bulb simulates the sunrise, sunset...) | Select playlist type (The speaker plays rock, pop, classic...) | Select a behavioural program (The curtain follows the movement of the sunrise, sunset...) |
| DN5 | Select the switch-on time | Select the switch-on time | Select the switch-on time |
| DN6 | Select the shutdown time | Select the shutdown time | Select the shutdown time |
| Feedback | | | |
| EF1 | Presence of intelligent environment | Presence of intelligent environment | Presence of intelligent environment |
| DF1 | Device announcement | Device announcement | Device announcement |
| DF2 | Device is not ready | Device is not ready | Device is not ready |
| DF3 | Device is on | Device is on | Device is on |
| DF4 | Device is off | Device is off | Device is off |
| DF5 | Device is loading | Device is loading | Device is loading |
| DF6 | Sction successfully accomplished | Action successfully accomplished | Action successfully accomplished |
| DF7 | Device generated an error | Device generated an error | Device generated an error |

## 4   Analysing the Results

In the experiment, we involved 60 participants divided into three distinct groups. We asked each user to propose one interaction on the prototype for 12 tasks and select one kind of feedback from those eligible for further 8 tasks. Each group was also assigned to a distinct scenario in which to execute the tasks with a different smart device, specifically a bulb, a speaker, and a curtain. To evaluate the degree of consensus among participants we adopted the process of calculating an agreement score for each task [12, 13]. An agreement score, $A_t$, reflects in a single number the degree of consensus among participants. Wobbrock [12] provides a mathematical calculation for agreement, where: $A_t = \sum_{P_i} \left( \left| \frac{P_i}{P_t} \right| \right)^2$. In equation, $t$ is a task in the set of all tasks T, $P_t$ is the set of proposed gestures for $t$, and $P_i$ is a subset of identical gestures from $P_t$. The range for $A$ is [0, 1].

**Table 2.** Agreement scores for each item and group

| | EA1 | DA1 | DA2 | DA3 | EN1 | EN2 | DN1 | DN2 | DN3 | DN4 | DN5 | DN6 | EF1 | DF1 | DF2 | DF3 | DF4 | DF5 | DF6 | DF7 |
|---|---|---|---|---|---|---|---|---|---|---|---|---|---|---|---|---|---|---|---|---|
| Smart bulb | 0,55 | 0,49 | 0,50 | 0,40 | 0,63 | 0,31 | 0,22 | 0,26 | 0,11 | 0,14 | 0,15 | 0,60 | 0,52 | 0,52 | 0,38 | 0,46 | 0,75 | 0,66 | 0,50 | 0,91 |
| Smart speaker | 0,41 | 0,42 | 0,46 | 0,47 | 0,44 | 0,30 | 0,29 | 0,33 | 0,19 | 0,26 | 0,14 | 0,68 | 0,58 | 0,50 | 0,46 | 0,51 | 0,66 | 0,61 | 0,51 | 0,74 |
| Smart curtain | 0,49 | 0,36 | 0,36 | 0,43 | 0,42 | 0,34 | 0,20 | 0,19 | 0,12 | 0,16 | 0,19 | 0,40 | 0,55 | 0,55 | 0,28 | 0,46 | 0,74 | 0,59 | 0,50 | 0,82 |

Table 2 shows the agreement score reached by groups for each action and in relation to the specific smart device.

A consideration that can already be made is that in all the proposed tasks a minimum consensus has always been found by all the groups, indeed the agreement score is always greater than 0.1. Anyway, five tasks related to *Actions* and *Navigation* achieved the highest degrees of consensus, which are EA1, DA1, DA2, DA3, EN1 and DN6 in Table 2. Indeed, their degrees of consensus are higher than 0.4. This means that in a group, more than 40% of the proposals were for a given interaction on average. On the other side, the agreement scores for the 8 feedback items are generally higher. In particular, EF1, DF1, DF3, DF4, DF5, DF6 and DF7 are higher or close to 0.5 as shown in Table 2. Figure 2 shows a graphical comparison of the choices made by the three groups for each task in the *Action* and *Navigation* categories. Regarding the first category, EA1 is about taking action to access an intelligent environment. In this case, the proposals by users of all groups focused almost exclusively on two actions, single tap and double tap with a small predominance for the latter. In particular, double tap was selected by all the users 37 times and single tap was selected 20 times. This indicates an almost total consensus among the three groups for actions that involve only the tap, excluding actions that involve rotations of the cube. DA1 concerns the switching on of a smart device. Gr1 and Gr2 had a similar behavior proposing mostly double tap and single tap. On the other hand, although Gr3 participants proposed a certain number of both double and single tap, they slightly preferred the right rotation followed by a single tap. Similarly, for DA2, which is about turning off a smart device, double and single tap are generally predominant preferences, however, Gr3 slightly preferred left rotation followed by a single tap. Some of the users across all groups explained their interaction preference commenting it. Many justified the tap or double tap because they suggest the action of turning an electronic device on using a conventional but-ton, however it should be noted that double tap has often been the predominant choice. A participant from Gr1 explained: *"I chose the double tap because the tap reminds me of the click on the light button, but the double tap gives me the certainty of not pressing it by mistake"*. Some participants from Gr3 chose right or left rotation because this recalls the gesture of turning a crank with which to open or close a shutter or a Venetian blind. This suggests that in order to turn on and off a smart device both tap, and double tap are interactions generally understandable by all the users regardless of the type of device, but certain devices can also suggest a more specific interaction connected to their particular affordance, as in the case of the smart curtain. DA3 is related to the command stop, play or act on a program of a smart device. As in the previous cases, there is a predominance in the use of tap, although this time among the three groups the most common choice was the single tap. However, the predominant choice relative to Gr1 is the forward rotation followed by a single tap. In this case, one participant explained that the rotation suggests the action of starting the car rotating the key, and another that it is linked to the idea of a two-way switch. Regarding the *Navigation* category, only EN1 and DN6 showed significant agreement where recurrent interaction patterns can be appreciated. As regards to the EN1 item, for all the groups, the two most proposed actions are right rotation to the right followed by a single tap, and double tap. The rotation was proposed 34 times and the double tap 21 times. Then, both the rotation and the double tap are interactions considered understandable by the three groups regardless of the target smart device. In choosing this gesture, some users imagined moving through a wheel control on a menu to select the desired device. Participants who used the double tap or the tap stated that they were imagining choosing the device with a *"click"* being close to it. Finally, in DN6, related to the programmed shutdown, the combination of backward rotation and double tap is the main preference, chosen 41 times by all.

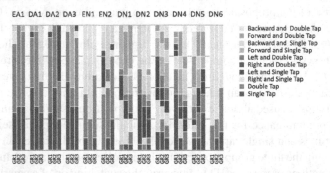

**Fig. 2.** Comparison of preferences in the Action and Navigation categories.

Concerning the tasks involving the preference of the type of feedback, the degree of consensus among the participants of the different groups is particularly high and homogeneous among the 3 groups. Figure 3 shows a comparison of the users' preferences for each item in the *Feedback* category. More specifically, DF7, which is related to the feedback of a device error, received a very high level of consensus among all groups on a combination of short and long vibrations. Indeed, 54 users indicated a sequence of vibrations as it suggests *"a shock"*, *"an impact"* or *"a movement that cannot be completed"*. Regarding the feedback of a successful action (DF6) the participants of the three groups, equally distributed, chose 31 times a short vibration and 29 times two short vibrations. Users explained their choice by associating it with the behavior of their phone. When a task ends, the phone shortly vibrates one or more times or makes a short beep. DF5 is the feedback status *"loading"*. In this case, the choices of the participants were polarized on the face of the cube warming up. One participant said: *"In an electronic device the heating is often a clue that it is working"*. Another added: *"an object that is working may heat up slightly"*. On the other hand, regarding DF4, which is related to a device switching off, a majority of 48 participants proposed the cube face cooling down. Then, a smart device cooling down is perceived by the users as a device that stops working. Similar considerations can be made for DF3, which is the feedback related to the device switching on. The participants' preferences are distributed almost halfway between a short vibration and the face of the cube warming up. Also, in this case the warming suggests to users the idea of a device that gives off heat because it works, while the vibration suggests the correctness of an action or a state, due to previous experiences with mobile phones. Finally, DF1 and EF1, which refer to the feedback connected to the spontaneous discoverability of the smart device and the intelligent ambient, polarize the preferences of all groups around one short vibration or two short vibrations. Moreover, to understand whether the user preferences for each task is directly linked to the device chosen for the scenario, we ran the Kruskal-Wallis one-way ANOVA by ranks [8] on the participants' preferences expressed on each task. This analysis is a non-parametric test used to compare three or more sets of data and can be considered when the samples are independent. The association between two variables is statistically significant if the resulting P-value is less than 0.05. In our experiment, the test was executed in the IBM SPSS Statistics software. Except for DN4 ($\approx$ 0.00), all the P-values calculated by the statistical method are higher than 0.05. Moreover, the DN4 item can be questionable, indeed the users' preferences are variegated. This means that, even if many users' comments suggest a link between the smart device form and the interaction preference, statistically no evidence proves it, and more investigation is needed to understand such potential links.

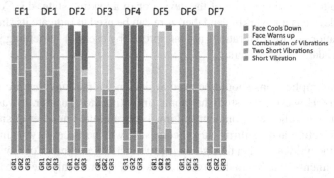

**Fig. 3.** Comparison of preferences in the Feedback category.

## 5    Design Implications and Final Remarks

The guessability study presented here leads to implications that can be useful when designing tangible interfaces for devices interacting with the AmI.

a) **Design the interactions to be meaningful and consistent with everyday life experience of your users.** Even if some preferences are suggested to users by the affordance of the controlled smart device, mainly the preferences are led by other factors such as previous experiences in other contexts such as mobile phones, or common buttons as light switches and the affordance of the device controller. An example is given by the results in the category *Action*: the interactions preferences for tasks such as turning on or off, and play can be related to the form factor of the smart device that suggests specific manipulations, although generally single or double taps are commonly understood by all users for this kind of tasks.

b) **Use the double tap without combination or the single tap if you are combining the tap with other gestures.** In combination with rotation, the single tap is the gesture chosen more frequently, nevertheless, when the gesture is not combined, double-tapping can be preferred as it gives users the certainty of not performing it accidentally.

c) **Use rotations to navigate the device parameters and settings.** In the *Navigation* category the main preferences are given to rotation even if in different directions and in different combinations with the tap, then it is not easy to find a recurrent pattern. Anyway, right rotation appears as a consistent preference for selecting a smart device in the environment, forward rotation can be indicated when increasing a device parameter, and backward rotation for programming shutdown time.

d) **Consider tactile feedback as strongly related to the real world.** In our experiment, the types of possible feedback are transversal to the various smart devices and are linked to behaviors related to the real world. **d1.** As in mobile phones, a short vibration or two short vibrations express something positive, such as the correctness of an action, a functioning state of the device, or also the discovery of a close smart device. **d2.** Heat perception is connected to something running on the device, and therefore to the switching on of the device or to a loading state. **d3.** Cold suggests that the device is not working and therefore can be used to indicate its shutdown. **d4.** Combinations of long vibrations are interpreted by users as something problematic and thus adapt to warn users.

The above implications should be used to design interactions that are truly meaningful to users. However, this study has some limitations to consider. It was developed within a static controlled environment and involving a limited number of smart devices and users. To refine and confirm our outcomes, it will be necessary to introduce the TactCube in the wild through a field study involving a larger number of devices and different environments. Finally, in the present work we explored only the 10 basic gestures provided by the TactCube prototype, while we plan in the future to consider a memorability study to show if a larger set of gestures can benefit or not the user interaction experience with such device.

# References

1. Abdul, A., Vermeulen, J., Wang, D., Lim, B.Y., Kankanhalli, M.: Trends and trajectories for explainable, accountable and intelligible systems: An HCI research agenda. In: Proceedings of the 2018 CHI Conference on Human Factors in Computing Systems, pp. 1–18. CHI 2018, Association for Computing Machinery, New York, NY, USA (2018)
2. Battistoni, P., Sebillo, M.: A tactile user device to interact with smart environments. In: Degen, H., Ntoa, S. (eds.) Artificial Intelligence in HCI: Second International Conference, AI-HCI 2021, Held as Part of the 23rd HCI International Conference, HCII 2021, Virtual Event, July 24–29, 2021, Proceedings, pp. 461–471. Springer International Publishing, Cham (2021). https://doi.org/10.1007/978-3-030-77772-2_30
3. Bilgin, A., Hagras, H., Malibari, A., Alghazzawi, D., Mohammed, J.: A computing with words framework for ambient intelligence. In: 2013 IEEE International Conference on Systems, Man, and Cybernetics, pp. 2887–2892 (2013). https://doi.org/10.1109/SMC.2013.492
4. Cook, D.J., Augusto, J.C., Jakkula, V.R.: Ambient intelligence: technologies, applications, and opportunities. Pervasive Mob. Comput. 5(4), 277–298 (2009)
5. Djajadiningrat, T., Wensveen, S., Frens, J., Overbeeke, K.: Tangible products: re-dressing the balance between appearance and action. Pers. Ubiquit. Comput. 8(5), 294–309 (2004)
6. Gellersen, H., et al.: Supporting device discovery and spontaneous interaction with spatial references. Pers. Ubiquit. Comput. 13(4), 255–264 (2009)

7. Landua, S., Wells, L.: The merging of tactile sensory input and audio data by means of the talking tactile tablet. In: Understanding Touch and Motion Gestures for Blind People on Mobile Devices, vol. 60, pp. 291–297. EuroHaptics (2003)

8. Lazar, J., Feng, J.H., Hochheiser, H.: Research Methods in Human-Computer Interaction. Morgan Kaufmann, New York (2017)

9. Romano, M., Bellucci, A., Aedo, I.: Understanding touch and motion gestures for blind people on mobile devices. In: Abascal, J., Barbosa, S., Fetter, M., Gross, T., Palanque, P., Winckler, M. (eds.) INTERACT 2015. LNCS, vol. 9296, pp. 38–46. Springer, Cham (2015). https://doi.org/10.1007/978-3-319-22701-6_3

10. Ruiz, J., Li, Y., Lank, E.: User-defined motion gestures for mobile interaction. In: Proceedings of the SIGCHI Conference on Human Factors in Computing Systems, pp. 197–206. CHI 2011, Association for Computing Machinery, New York, NY, USA (2011)

11. Wensveen, S., Djajadiningrat, J., Overbeeke, C.: Interaction frogger : a design framework to couple action and function through feedback and feedforward. In: Benyon, D. (ed.) Across the spectrum : designing interactive systems; DIS 2004, Cambridge, Massachusetts, 1–4 August 2004, pp. 177–184. Association for Computing Machinery Inc., United States (2004)

12. Wobbrock, J.O., Aung, H.H., Rothrock, B., Myers, B.A.: Maximizing the guessability of symbolic input. In: CHI 2005 Extended Abstracts on Human Factors in Computing Systems, pp. 1869–1872. CHI EA 2005, Association for Computing Machinery, New York, NY, USA (2005)

13. Wobbrock, J.O., Morris, M.R., Wilson, A.D.: User-defined gestures for surface computing. In: CHI 2009: Proceedings of the SIGCHI Conference on Human Factors in Computing Systems, pp. 1083–1092. CHI 2009. Association for Computing Machinery, New York, NY, USA (2009)

# The Hubs: Design Insights for Walking Meeting Technology

Ida Damen[1,2], Steven Vos[1,2], and Carine Lallemand[1,3(✉)]

[1] Industrial Design Department, Eindhoven University of Technology, Eindhoven, Netherlands
c.e.lallemand@tue.nl
[2] School of Sport Studies, Fontys University of Applied Sciences, Eindhoven, Netherlands
[3] HCI Research Group, University of Luxembourg, Esch-sur-Alzette, Luxembourg

**Abstract.** As an active form of meeting, walking meetings can be beneficial for office workers who often have a sedentary work routine. Despite their substantial benefits in terms of health, social interactions, and creativity, walking meetings are not yet widely adopted. Some key barriers limiting their social acceptance and wider adoption, for instance, the difficulty to present files or take notes, might be addressed by technology. Using the Hubs - a network of stand-up meeting stations - as a design exemplar, we conducted a scenario-based survey (N = 186) to provide insights into how technological solutions can support the practice of walking meetings. Focusing on the size of the group and type of meetings, we identify scenarios of use and discuss design implications for the development of future technologies and service design components to support walking meetings.

**Keywords:** Walking meetings · Office environment · Sedentary behavior · Survey · Physical activity · Work

## 1 Introduction

We are currently on the brink of a fourth industrial revolution, where artificial intelligence as an emerging force is reshaping and disrupting our world. This will transform the way we work by fusing technologies and blurring our physical and digital world. Our offices are becoming more and more "flexible", with remote work and telecommunications on the rise. Be it at the office or from home, knowledge work is characterized by sedentary behavior, with 71% of working hours of office workers spent sitting [12]. This has been further emphasized during the COVID-19 pandemic [39]. Sedentary behavior is however a major public health risk [8]. Physical inactivity is now considered the fourth leading cause of death worldwide, with over 5 million -theoretically preventable- deaths per year [23, 48, 49] as it is associated with a variety of diseases such as type II diabetes, cardiovascular diseases, colon- and breast cancer [6, 19, 33, 47, 48].

Office work is characterized by physically inactive behavior, with office workers spending most of their working hours sitting [12]. To reduce this considerable sedentary time, a myriad of digital tools and interventions have been developed over recent years

© IFIP International Federation for Information Processing 2021
Published by Springer Nature Switzerland AG 2021
C. Ardito et al. (Eds.): INTERACT 2021, LNCS 12935, pp. 610–629, 2021.
https://doi.org/10.1007/978-3-030-85610-6_35

[14, 21], with a focus on mobile applications, smartwatches and prompting software. Most of these products however consider physical activity as a break from work [14], encouraging workers to take more breaks during the day [14]. Very few tools and interventions are based on the underlying principle that physical activity and office work are not mutually exclusive.

Within the field of Human-Computer Interaction (HCI), a few tools or interventions that facilitate physically active ways of working are described. The most common example is a dynamic workstation, as described by Tobiasson [45], Choi [11] and Probst [35]. These designs aim to support the integration of physical activity with work behind a standing desk.

Beyond the individual desk, a promising opportunity for physically active ways of working can be found in the context of meetings. Previous work did research position changes through modular meeting furniture [15] or strongly emphasized the potential of walking meetings [1–3, 13, 16]. Ahtinen et al. [1–3] developed and researched the use of mobile technology to mediate walking meetings, whereas Damen et al. [13, 17] implemented a service design for walking meetings called the WorkWalk [13, 17]. Both research teams gained users insights on the barriers and drivers of walking meetings and provided some design recommendations [1, 17]. What remains however underexplored is how technology can support the practice of walking meetings in order to overcome barriers and strengthen opportunities for users. This is a timely topic that the HCI community can address to contribute to future and healthier ways of working.

In this paper, we build on the work of Damen et al. [16] in order to explore workers' needs during walking meetings with an emphasis on the match between specific tasks or use scenarios and potential technological support. To the best of our knowledge, no previous study did sample a large number of participants in order to understand users' perceptions and needs with regards to walking meetings. Through a scenario-based online survey (N = 186), we explore the most relevant use cases for the design of "walking meetings Hubs", stand-up meeting stations that accommodate different tasks during walking meetings. We purposively used the Hubs as exemplar of a tangible technology situated in a physical work environment, in order to investigate this under-research area (previous work in HCI focusing mostly on mobile-mediated concepts). We discuss the usefulness and relevance of the Hubs concept to overcome the obstacles associated with walking meetings and expand the discussion on how existing and emerging technologies can support efficient walking meeting experiences. We finally emphasize implications for design, relevant for the development of future technologies and service design elements to support walking meetings.

## 2    Related Work

### 2.1    Physically Active Ways of Working

A large and growing body of literature has investigated the role of sedentary behavior in office workers, ranging from the negative health effects [18–20, 23, 29, 33, 42, 44] to how we should design interventions to reduce sitting at work [14, 21, 24, 25, 29, 31, 41]. There is, however, a relatively small body of work that is concerned with physically active ways of working. Especially within the field of human computer interaction, we see very little research on this topic. In 2012, the concept of working "in motion" was introduced to facilitate seamless changes between different work task and work position such as sitting and standing [35]. Probst et al. [35] promote a paradigm shift towards an integrated supportive work environment through active office design, for instance an interactive chair as an ubiquitous input device to control the workplace computer by tilting, rotating, or bouncing [34].

Other examples of designs that facilitate physically active ways of work are active desks or desk applications, like the design "Tap-Kick-Click" of Saunders and Vogel [37]. They present a foot interaction technique to control conventional desktop applications at a standing desk. Similar to this concept is the "Foot-Mouse" concept of Tobiasson [45], that is presented as a physical movement probe for the office in their paper "Still at the Office", together with the concepts "active desk" and "irritating chair". All probes were designed in an attempt to transform the sedentary nature of office work into more physically sustainable work [45]. A final notable example is the work of Nieuweboer et al. [30], a provocative design called "The Office Jungle". With their work on "designing for wildness", they propose to transform the way we work by turning the office environment into an office jungle.

## 2.2 Walking and Walking Meetings

According to the ancient Greek philosopher Hippocrates "walking is a man's best medicine". This old wisdom still holds true according to modern science. Walking is beneficial for several physical and mental health issues [9]. Walking can for instance decrease bodyweight, BMI and bodyfat percentage [7, 27]. It can furthermore increase maximum aerobic capacity, lower blood pressure and decrease resting diastolic blood pressure in previously sedentary adults [27]. Moreover, walking can reduce the risk of cardiovascular diseases [28].

In addition to these physical health parameters, walking can have a positive influence on various mental and emotional outcomes. Thayer et al. [43] found that the amount of daily walking predicted a wide variety of positive psychological conditions. They report a positive correlation between step count and self-rated health, energy, overall mood, happiness and self-esteem. In addition, walking can reduce stress and anxiety [10] and decrease or even prevent depressive symptoms [4].

Walking at work may even enhance work performance of employees. Walking increases blood flow to the brain, which may result in cognitive benefits like increased creativity [32]. It can also counteract the health risks that are associated with prolonged sitting such as an increased risk of anxiety [42] and intermediate levels of psychological distress [22]. Walking could also facilitate psychological processing and promote a collaborative way of working, as is used in therapy settings [26, 36].

Despite all the positive effects that walking can have on a person's health and wellbeing, walking meetings are not a common work practice. Several barriers remain for office workers to engage in this practice. Damen et al. [9] have identified nine, amongst which the most common barriers are unpredictable weather, cultural acceptance, difficulties of integrating walking meetings into daily routines and the lack of possibilities to take notes or give a presentation [17]. In 2016, Ahtinen [3] presented ten design implications for persuasive, mobile walking meetings. One of these implications is that enabling walking meetings to "become an accepted way of work" by designing an "official" tool could support the uptake of this practice.

### 2.3 Walking Meeting and Technology

By designing tools and interventions that enable and facilitate walking meetings at work, walking might become a more natural part of an office day. In contrast to the current intervention strategy to encourage people to take more breaks and interrupt their work, walking meetings can integrate physical activity with work. This may make it feasible to adhere to the expert statement on the growing case for change towards better health and productivity in office work that states that *"Workers should aim to initially progress toward accumulating 2 h per day of standing and light activity, such as light walking during working hours, eventually progressing to a total accumulation of 4 h per day"* [8].

To date, there is a dearth of research on how technology can mediate the practice of walking meetings. We found merely three designs can be found in the field of HCI. Ahtinen developed and studied the use of mobile technology to mediate walking meetings by means of an app [1–3]. The "Brainwolk" and the preceding "walking metro" mobile application provides an introduction to walking meetings at work to increase the social acceptance. The Brainwolk app features a university campus map, suggestions for walking routes, checkpoints with short visual break exercises and motivational thoughts about walking and a reward system [2]. One of the drawbacks of this applications was that "the use of the application caused too much disruption and the users were not able to concentrate on the meeting itself" [1]. According to the authors, researchers and practitioners can encourage physically active ways of work by combination of digital and non-digital discreet persuasion techniques to help motivate sedentary workers to become more active, creative and sociable [1].

Damen et al. [13, 17] developed and studied a service design for walking meetings called the WorkWalk. The WorkWalk consists of a physical route of 1.8 km long, has meeting point signs at all faculty buildings and is integrated in the university's room booking system [13]. Damen et al. [17] used this concept as a design research artefact to study walking meetings and reflect on them during walking interviews with the participants. Their findings suggest five design recommendations for the development of future technologies and service design elements to support walking meetings, such as *"Embedding active ways of working in existing infrastructure and work routines by making it physically visible increases social acceptance"* [17].

In 2020, Damen et al. [16] presented a case study detailing the design and pilot study of The Hubs. Based on previous research addressing the barriers of walking meetings, the Hubs were designed to accommodate different work-related tasks during walking meetings. Damen et al. [16] report on two pilot user tests investigating users' experiences and ideas for improvement. They did not, however, gather insights in how the Hubs could be used in different scenarios and what potential features a Hub should have to accommodate specific meeting types.

## 2.4 The Hubs Concept

This research focusses on how technology can support walking meetings, and more specifically how users envision themselves using the Hubs concept. The Hubs in the present study are used as a research artefact in order to gain broader insights into the support technology could bring to facilitate the adoption of walking meetings. The Hubs network is a series of stand-up meeting stations (Fig. 1) that accommodate different work-related tasks during indoor or outdoor walking meetings [16]. Several Hubs form a route that guide the meeting for a pre-set duration. The Hubs are equipped with touchscreen-controlled laptops, which can be used independently or in a duplicate mode. By scanning an employee card using the RFID scanner on top of the Hub, the user can access a custom-made web environment with their personal files. The Hub is currently controlled by an Arduino and Processing sketch.

**Fig. 1.** Hub, as part of a network of stand-up meeting stations

# 3 Methodology

In order to explore the most relevant use scenarios for walking meetings with technologies such as the Hubs, we designed an online survey combining Likert scales with vignette-like scenarios [5]. The scenarios feature two distinct variables: the number of coworkers involved in a walking meeting, with three conditions (a group of 2–4, a larger group, or by oneself) and the type of meeting, with eight defined meeting types.

## 3.1 Participants

A total of 186 respondents (99 females, 81 males, 6 prefer not to say) filled out the survey, with a mean age of 33.4 (SD = 12.3). Of the 145 respondents (78%) who specified their occupation or background, fifty-four respondents (29%) were students,

18 (9.7%) designers, 20 (10.8%) researchers and 53 (28.5%) categorized as "other". The level of experience with walking meetings was on average M = 1.79 (SD = 1.07, Min = 1, Max = 4) on a scale from 1 'Novice' to 5 'Expert'. The majority (56.5%) of respondents self-described as novices to walking meeting (rating of 1), 21% little experience (rating of 2), 9.7% some experience (rating of 3) and 12.9% leaned to the expert side (rating of 4).

## 3.2  Procedure and Material

The survey was disseminated online during a 6-weeks period early 2020 and advertised on social and professional networks, targeting people involved in sedentary professional activities such as office and knowledge workers (this second category also included students in higher academic institutions). It thus involves a non-probabilistic sample. Ethical approval for the study was obtained from the university's review board. The questionnaire is composed of 4 sections.

**Socio-Demographics and Meeting Routines**
This section included questions about age, gender, job title, as well as the experience with walking meetings (assessed on a 5-points Likert scale from "No experience" to "Expert") and the type of meetings conducted in their professional activity. For this last question, respondents assessed the frequency of 8 categories of meetings (described in Fig. 3) using 5-points Likert from "Never" to "Very often".

**Introductory Scenario and Desired Features**
In this section, we used a storyboard to introduce the Hubs as a network of interactive device designed to support walking meetings. We then asked respondents to assess the importance of nine potential features of the Hub to support their walking meetings using 5-points Likert scales from 1 "Not important" to 5 "Very important". These features were note-taking, presenting, web browsing, sketching, video calling, access to personal files, brainstorming tools, access to email and calendar, printing. In addition, respondents could come up with additional features in an open-ended text field.

**Scenarios Based on the Number of Team Members Involved in the Walking Meeting**
We created three storyboards representing office workers going for a walking meeting using the Hubs (Fig. 2). Following the method used by Walsh et al. [46] the scenarios presented are incomplete: it is up to the respondents to imagine how they will use the Hubs. The scenarios varied in the number of co-workers involved in the meeting, with three alternatives presented, respectively walking (a) with a group of 2–4 (b) with a larger group or (c) by oneself. Using a multiple-choice question, respondents are asked *"Which types of meetings would you most likely have in this scenario?* (potential answer options based on the 8 meetings types described in Fig. 3).

Two subsequent open-ended questions asked, *"In your opinion, what influence can the Hub have on your meeting when (meeting context based on the meeting size)?"*, one being focused on the positive influence, the second on the negative influence in order to counterbalance biases. Both questions suggest an influence and are not neutral in essence, because our aim is not to prove a positive or negative tendency but to act as a trigger for respondents to envision ways such a technology can affect their meetings.

Finally, respondents declared how likely they were to personally go walking meeting in each scenario using 5-points Likert scales from 1 "Very unlikely" to 5 "Very likely".

## Walking Meeting with a group of 2-4

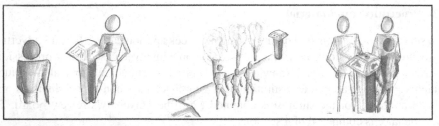

**Step 2:** You meet-up with your colleagues at the starting point, equipped with a Hub.    **Step 3:** You go for a walking meeting by following the network of Hubs.    **Step 4:** You stop at a next Hub.

**Fig. 2.** Example of an incomplete scenario used as a prompt in the walking meeting survey

**Walking Meeting Journey**

The last part of the survey asked respondents to define and describe their own walking meeting journey. First, they picked their preferred group composition and preferred meeting type. Instructions were as follows: "In order to design optimal interactions with the Hub, we need people to imagine themselves in a precise context of use. We will thus ask you to pick a type of meeting and a number of participants (the most suitable meeting situation for you) and then to walk us through the story of this meeting, supported by the use of the Hubs. You can rely on a previous meeting you already had and transpose it to the situation of a walking meeting with a Hub or rely on a future meeting you expect to have at work."

Respondents freely described their actions through the meeting journey, at 3 defined stages: 1/ "You are starting your walking meeting at the starting point, equipped with a Hub, could you describe the actions you would do at the first Hub?" 2/ "After a couple of minutes of walking, you arrive at an intermediate Hub. Could you describe the actions you would do at this intermediate Hub?" 3/ Finally, it is almost time to wrap up this meeting and you go to the last Hub on your path. Could you describe the actions you would do at this last Hub?".

### 3.3  Data Analysis

Qualitative answers were coded and analyzed with MaxQDA 2018 by thematic analysis using an inductive approach. The first and last author independently coded a data sample and made a coding scheme, after which consensus was sought among them to derive a final coding scheme. The survey questions are provided as supplementary material.

# 4   Results

## 4.1   Types of Meetings

To gain insights into the types of (traditional) meetings the respondents generally have in their job, they were asked to rate the occurrence of eight types of meetings from 1 (never) to 5 (very often). Figure 3 shows the distribution of these frequencies and the average ratings. Regular meetings occurred the most (M = 3.75, SD = 1.01), followed by information sharing meetings (M = 3.68, SD = 0.96) and one-on-one meetings (M = 3.39, SD = 1.09). These were closely followed by decision making (M = 3.37, SD = 1.04), problem solving (M = 3.34, SD = 0.95) and brainstorming (M = 3.24, SD = 1.08). Presentation (M = 2.99, SD = 1.05) and training sessions (M = 2.47, SD = 0.99) were the least frequent types.

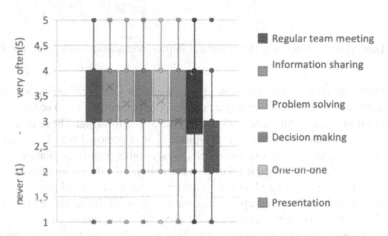

**Fig. 3.** Descriptive statistics of the meeting type frequency, assessed on 5-points Likert scales

## 4.2   Features of the Hubs

Participants were asked to evaluate the importance of potential features of the Hubs, ranging from not important (1) to very important (5). Nine features were evaluated (Fig. 4), of which note taking (M = 3.84, SD = 1.14) was considered the most important, and printing notes or documents (M = 2.19, SD = 1.28) the least important. It was hypothesized that walking meeting experience could affect the rating of features, yet we found no significant difference based on walking meeting experience.

In addition to the Likert scale questions featuring nine predefined potential features of the Hubs, respondents could add additional features they would personally need. The most frequent replies were related to time management and route planning. Seventeen respondents mentioned that the Hubs should help to keep track of time by displaying the time left for the meeting. In addition, eleven people expressed the need for directions or walking route options.

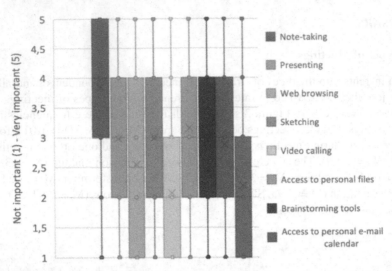

**Fig. 4.** Descriptive statistics of the Hubs features importance assessed on 5-points Likert scales

Another common feature suggested by respondents was voice or video recording, mainly to replace written meeting minutes. Some people would like to see an automatic transcription of their audio recordings at the end of the meeting. These transcriptions should be sent to their email account or uploaded in a personal cloud. An automated generation of written minutes or to-do lists was another recurring feature, yet most respondents mentioned the need to take notes manually. Like the audio recordings, these writings should be easily shared with all participants or send to third parties.

Lastly, a couple of Hubs set-up features were suggested, for instance the adjustable height of the Hubs. The Hubs could also be used "as static meeting points by adding something to lean against while using them. This might be useful when you need some more time with a visual or for people with less mobility that still want to have outdoor meetings". Finally, one person mentioned the use of "inspirational ideation prompts", to make sure people do not linger at one Hub and walk to the next Hub for instance by giving a question to think about while walking to the next Hub.

## 4.3   Expected Positive and Negative Effects

In order to assess how people felt the Hubs would affect their meetings, they were asked to think about the potential positive and negative effects of the Hub network (Table 1). Participants mentioned several positive effects, the meeting structure being the most common. Thirty participants expressed that the Hubs could support meeting structure by giving direction, providing demarcation time or by using the Hubs as distinctive "landmarks" which could "give a marker in space and time". These landmarks could be related to the agenda points, act as a trigger for decision making or transitioning to a new topic. A respondent also expressed that the presence of Hubs could "ensure targeted meetings", since "Hubs are intermediate cells where you can take notes" and can wrap up your meeting by discussing and setting future agenda points.

A considerable number of benefits mentioned did not specifically address the Hubs but were related to the practice of walking meetings. People stated that it could promote health, creativity, camaraderie, social interaction, keep people engaged and stimulate out-of-the-box thinking. The fact that the Hubs could facilitate note taking, presenting and looking up information, made walking meetings more accessible according to the majority of the respondents.

However, several people questioned why they would not use their phone or tablet to do these tasks. This held particularly true for individual walking meetings. In addition, some people felt that the Hubs conflicted with the essence of walking meetings, often being 'low tech' and triggering mind wandering and divergent thinking. Several other drawbacks were mentioned. While lack of recording and note-taking opportunities is a commonly documented barriers to walking meetings [17], which was confirmed through our survey, some people felt that the Hubs provided "too much infrastructure for too little value". In addition, one participant expressed that the Hubs would probably never be there at the exact moment when you need them: "It could disrupt the flow of the meeting". This is aligned with a few participants expressing concerns that one could forget the elements to write down in-between the Hubs. Another potential barrier was that people would stay at the Hub for a long period thus stopping their walk. As one respondent stated, "it then becomes a standing desk outside". According to several respondents, such a practice would nullify the positive effects that walking meetings could have such as out-of-the-box thinking and being physically active.

Another common negative effect was distraction. The Hubs itself could provide distraction according to some, however, most felt that the environment and other people could drive them to distraction during the practice of walking meetings (no matter if technology is involved or not). This was especially true for larger groups, as "it is difficult to let everyone hear the one who is speaking due to surround noise and spatial organization." Several respondents explained that it could lead to people splitting up into groups, staying behind or not participating in the meeting. In addition, not everyone is able to use or view the Hub to take notes or see what is presented. Less common concerns were matters of privacy, such as how to deal with people that could overhear a private conversation. Some people also said it would look weird or feel lonely to stand at a Hub by yourself.

**Table 1.** Summary of the most cited positive and negative effect of Hubs technology

| Potential positive effect | Potential negative effect |
|---|---|
| Structuring the meetings | Conflicting with the perceived "low-tech" and |
| Being landmarks or markers in space and time | unique nature of walking meetings |
| Practical purpose of note taking and presenting | Not being supportive when needed |
| Making walking meetings more accessible | Infrastructure costs might be too high for the added value (as compared to mobile tech) |

### 4.4  Envisioned Use

The likelihood to go for a walking meeting using a Hubs network varied among respondents and depended on the meeting size (aka. number of team members involved) and the level of experience with walking meetings. A walking meeting in a small group (2–4 persons) was most likely to occur (M = 3.84, SD = .91). The individual walking meeting scored between "neutral" and "likely" (M = 3.27, SD = 1.38), whereas the likelihood of people going for a walking meeting in a larger group (over 5 people) was overall considered unlikely (M = 1.85, SD = 0.92).

Consecutively, we asked respondents which types of meetings they would most likely have while walking, dependent on the group size. As shown in Fig. 5, information sharing and brainstorming sessions were considered the most likely types of meetings to do while walking, in both small and larger groups. The likelihood of individual walking meetings was highest for problem solving and brainstorming meetings. Presentations and training sessions were overall least likely to be done while walking.

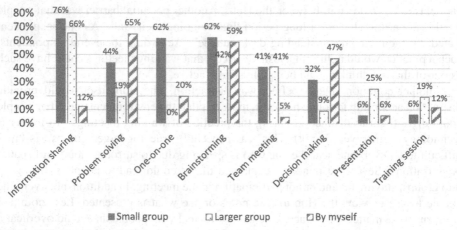

**Fig. 5.**  Likelihood of doing a walking meeting, based on meeting type and group size (N = 186)

To explore the use scenarios, we presented the respondents with an incomplete storyboard to complete. First, they picked their preferred group composition, and preferred meeting type. Twenty participants selected a walking meeting by themselves, five choose the large group meeting, and a vast majority (n = 161) picked the small group composition. A brainstorming meeting was the most popular choice (n = 55), followed by information sharing (n = 42), regular team meetings (n = 31), problem solving (n = 30), decision making (n = 14), and one-on-one meeting (n = 12). 'Training sessions' and 'Presentation meetings' were not chosen by respondents.

A thematic analysis resulted in 29 distinct activities that respondents would undertake at the Hubs. These activities were clustered into nine overarching categories, based on the subdivision of possible features of the Hubs (Table 2). The clusters link to the technological modalities that might be needed to carry out the tasks. For instance, "writing down action points" will probably need similar note taking modalities as "setting meeting objectives", whereas "sharing meeting results" would require different features like emailing or uploading to a shared folder.

**Table 2.** Activities clustered around possible Hubs features

| Cluster | Activities |
|---|---|
| Note taking | Take notes, check notes, document ideas, start audio recording, setting meeting objectives/agenda, write down action points, recap, evaluate/summarize outcomes, make decisions, scope problem |
| Presenting | Discuss case/ideas, present meeting objectives or agenda, present work, logistics (time management, route setting), explain Hub, give update |
| Web browsing | Check info |
| Sketching | Sketch |
| Video calling | (not mentioned within the scenarios) |
| Access to personal files | Log in, check meeting agenda, emails, log out |
| Brainstorming tools & printing | Show artefacts, brainstorming techniques, automated inspirations |
| Access to e-mail and calendar | Send or share results, rephrase ideas |

Based on the different scenarios imagined by the respondents, we created a walking meeting user journey (Fig. 6). This journey presents the most commonly cited meeting activities for each meeting type. Documenting users' goals and needs aim at supporting the development of future walking meeting technologies, which might not necessarily build upon the concept of Hubs stations along a walking meeting path.

In this typical walking meeting journey, note-taking and presenting were the most frequent activities in all meeting type scenarios. Video calling, on the other hand, was not mentioned at all in the stories of the participants (which confirms the results found in Sect. 4.2).

Notable differences between the envisioned activities can be found between the different types of meetings, but also between the first, intermediate and final Hub. For instance, presenting was mostly done at the first and second Hub, whereas access to personal email and calendar was solely mentioned at the final Hub in order to schedule a follow-up meeting or to send notes. Web browsing and access to personal files were mentioned in all meeting types and at all stages of the meeting. Access to personal files was most prominent in the information sharing and presenting meeting type category, and particularly relevant at the beginning of a meeting.

Not surprisingly, sketching was mostly mentioned as an activity during brainstorming meetings, as well as brainstorming tools and printing. Brainstorming tools were not mentioned for regular team meetings, one-on-one meetings and information sharing and presenting meetings.

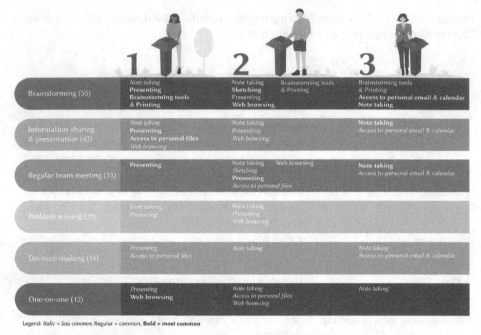

Legend: *Italic = less common*, Regular = common, **Bold = most common**

**Fig. 6.** Walking meeting journeys representing six types of meetings, ranked from the most commonly chosen to the least commonly chosen in the survey

Table 3 displays illustrations of the top three scenarios, inspired by representative participants' quotes about the actions they would typically perform at each stage of their walking meeting.

These typical scenarios feature mostly common work task and corresponding features and are useful to define minimal viable walking meeting products and services. In addition, we also looked at unique or inspiring responses. Original or unique insights (mentioned by only a few participants) can be used as design inspiration for future research and development of innovative tools and technologies [38, 40]. They may open up new perspectives for novel, but also current technologies, that could be used to facilitate physically active ways of working.

Participants for instance mentioned creativity tools to be used while walking to the next Hub, for instance an inspiring ideation prompt (e.g., from the Oblique Strategies technique by Brian Eno) that would be printed out on a receipt using a thermoprinter. This would provide a pleasant surprising effect and trigger curiosity. A second idea was that the Hubs could present different activities to help structure a meeting, such as selecting a brainstorm technique at the first Hub, sorting out ideas at the second Hub and elaborating on it to sketch it at the third Hub. A related idea was that the Hubs would generate automated meeting minutes and action points, based on audio recordings.

Suggestions were also provided regarding logistics. The Hubs could give direction on the route and could adjust the route based on the intended meeting duration or the style/tone of the meeting. Imagine an 'inspiring route' that could be designed around artistic installations or charming points of interest, whereas a decision-making route'

**Table 3.** Illustrative scenario sketch of three meeting types, featuring the most common actions at each stage of the meeting journey

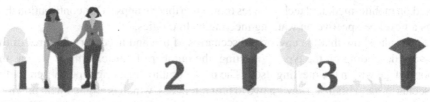

**Brainstorming**

| | | |
|---|---|---|
| *"As a starting point, I would use the Hub to sketch a mind-map or use other brainstorming tools to define the scope of the problem."* | *"After ideating between the two Hubs, I would stop a the second point as a milestone to discuss the ideas and draw them out"* | *"At the last one, I would use tools to visualize all ideas we gathered along the way and select the most promising ones"* |

**Information sharing**

| | | |
|---|---|---|
| *"I would use the first Hub to share some prepared points to be discussed during the meeting. So the agenda points, as well as the documents we need to consult before starting"* | *"Intermediate Hubs can be useful to input relevant information that came up during the walk so that we don't forget it."* | *"I would do the same at the last Hub. In addition I would check if all the agenda points were discussed and schedule a follow-up meeting if necessary"* |

**General team meeting**

| | | |
|---|---|---|
| *"The team should open our shared files/calendar to check the agenda points, and decide on which ones will be discussed while walking"* | *"After a few minutes of walking, the next Hub can be the place to structure the initial discussions, like a formal moment within the less formal walking time"* | *"We would open our shared folders again, talk about what has ot be done and who will be responsible for those action points"* |

would make use of natural landmarks (e.g., a tree alley or crossroads) in order to structure the meeting and push for decision moments. Technology could also be used to advise you to take either an indoor or outdoor walking meeting, depending on the weather, perhaps even displaying the weather forecast as a prompt (e.g., "It won't be raining within the next two hours, it is an ideal weather for a walking meeting"). Finally, more futuristic visions included the possibility to interact with a remote teammate via holographic projection.

## 5  Discussion

The present study set out to provide insights into how technological solutions can support the practice of walking meetings. We conducted an online survey to identify scenarios of use of the Hubs, a network of stand-up meetings stations. The Hubs concept was not the main object of interest per se, but was used as a virtual research artefact intended to trigger reflection in office workers about their needs to conduct walking meeting in an efficient and pleasant way. The use of the Hubs as a design exemplar supporting respondents in envisioning use scenarios was intended at investigating perceived benefits and limitations of stationary artefacts located in the physical work environment. The insights we collected can be confronted to previous work, which is scarce and mostly focused on mobile-mediated technologies (e.g., smartphone apps). Our contribution thus brings a novel perspective on walking meeting technologies.

Our results show that the envisioned scenarios of use and necessary features of the hubs vary depending on the type of meeting, the number of participants as well as the temporal stage within the meeting itself. The most common meeting type chosen for the user scenario was a brainstorm with two to four attendees, which is aligned with previous research on walking meeting practices [17]. This scenario deviated the most from the other meeting type scenarios in terms of envisioned use. Not surprisingly, brainstorming tools and sketching features were more prominent in brainstorming meetings. Presenting features, on the other hand, were emphasized in all user scenarios and mainly considered useful at the start of a meeting. This does not present any major technological challenge, except for the need for robust outdoor screens which are already well spread in the public space for information or advertisement purposes. An original idea would consist of repurposing public screens currently used for interactive advertisement (e.g., on bus stations) or smart city information displays in order to make them punctually available to office workers.

In terms of desired features, we see a link between the rating of features' importance and the envisioned activities at the Hubs. Note taking, for instance, was considered the most important feature, and was also the most mentioned activity in the scenarios. Printing notes or documents and video calling were perceived as least important features and were not often mentioned in the user scenarios. At the end of the meeting, access to personal files, agenda and e-mails were considered key features. These insights could be used to rethink our office environment and how we adapt different areas at and around our workplace to different temporal stages of a meeting. One could for instance envision starting a meeting indoors in a meeting room to show and discuss the agenda, before going outside for the second part of the meeting. This part could be more creative or social, which relates well to the beneficial effects of walking.

While walking meetings are often perceived as less structured and more open than regular meetings [17], a common opinion shared by the respondents was that Hubs could have a beneficial effect on the meeting structure. Several ideas mentioned in the scenario revolved around the fact of using the Hubs as structuring devices, supporting a sequence of activities and tasks. Of the few existing studies on walking meetings, Ahtinen et al. [1–3] report findings from mobile-mediated concepts, which might be considered as the ideal medium - mobile, multifunctional and private - to support walking. While mobile technologies in general might be used to address challenges related to walking meetings, shared interactive products or urban furniture placed in the physical environment present alternative opportunities which are relevant to investigate. They might for instance contribute to overcome known barriers of walking meetings, by providing visible support and giving walking meetings a more official status. As an ecosystem of devices clearly visible in the work environment, technologies similar to the Hubs can constitute an 'official' sign that walking meetings is an accepted way of work in a company. More than the

Workwalk by Damen et al. [13, 17] presented as a dotted path, physical artefacts can support the communication of a modern organizational cultural and the social acceptance of the practice. This official character is emphasized by the physical presence of the devices inside the company's building or outdoor in the vicinity, sponsored by the company or the municipalities. This is in line with one of the design implications of Ahtinen [3] to design an "official tool" to increase acceptance of walking meeting practice.

## 5.1 Implications for Design

As a synthesis of our findings, our walking meeting journey (Fig. 6) presents typical scenarios. These tend to be aligned with current meeting practices, featuring a selection of common work tasks and corresponding features (e.g., presenting, note-taking and scheduling). While not surprising, these synthetic findings can be useful to define minimal viable products and services supporting walking meetings, relying on the most relevant features only. Similarly, quantitative findings about the preferred meeting type and number of coworkers involved provide designers with a precise scope to focus on.

While the overall perceived need for features in our survey was close to the tools used during regular meetings, the question is whether designers can encourage new practices rather than solely supporting existing ones? In our experience, it is a challenging endeavor to disrupt ways of working entirely and technologies such as the Hubs (which support rather typical meeting scenarios) might constitute a first step towards new practices, which designers can encourage.

Walking meeting technology should not be a copy-paste of regular meeting tools. Walking meetings have distinct characteristics, which should be considered to strive for positive, and perhaps innovative, meeting experiences. As reported by Damen et al. [17], walking meetings offer different social dynamics and set-up of meetings. This invites the design field to rethink what is needed to facilitate walking meetings, both in adapting current technologies (e.g., speech-to-text), as well as in inventing new interactive products or services specifically designed for this practice. Some of the original user insights uncovered through our survey can provide inspiration for more disruptive technology use. One can also approach the challenge from a 'technological push' perspective, by considering how current and new technologies developed in other application areas could be applied to walking meeting practices. The Gartner Hype Cycle for the digital workplace (www.gartner.com/smarterwithgartner/6-trends-on-the-gartner-hype-cycle-for-the-digital-workplace-2020) might for instance be a starting point.

Interestingly, the impact of the Covid19 pandemics on workers triggered reflections and questioned the status quo and ways of working in general. In terms of walking meetings, not only can designers think of synchronous face-to-face (or rather side-by-side) meeting types, but also on how to support walking meetings with geographically distributed participants. Gamified processes could be implemented in order to trigger new dynamics, for instance by "forcing" participants to walk a certain distance in order to submit ideas in an online remote brainstorm (one idea every 500 m). GPS technology could be used there in a similar fashion as the app DeepTimeWalk, a narrative experience which requires the users to walk to listen to the story. As mentioned earlier, it might also be interesting for policy makers to look at ways of repurposing the public space to support innovative and healthier working practices. Could urban parks become places where office workers meet, supported by walking meeting technologies?

Yet despite benefits on the practical and social side, one can argue that the downside of technologies for walking meetings such as the Hubs is to remove part of the freedom that characterizes walking meetings. The "freedom from computer" is highlighted by Ahtinen et al. [2] who argue that "without the usual office tools, one gets more space for thinking and concentration to the actual topic". Although technology has the paradoxical effect of being both confining and liberating at the same time, we believe this work can spark new research and development to the under researched field of HCI for active ways of working. Beyond developing more interactive products and services around this practice, a challenge to be addressed by the HCI community will be to find the right balance between the level of support provided by technology and the nature of walking meetings.

## 5.2 Limitations

Our work entails several limitations. First, the example chosen and the method in general might have influenced some of the results of the study, for instance by suggesting a 3-steps meeting structure or using a set of specific scenarios. Our sample is mostly composed of respondents who have little (or no) experience with walking meetings. Their perceptions are thus rather based on envisioned practices, and might differ from the ones of more experienced participants. Although many generic findings align with previous work [1, 17], some user needs are only uncovered in-situ, and further research is thus needed in the field.

One can also question the soundness of an online survey, as compared to field tests using actual devices. However, pilot tests of the hubs, briefly described in the late-breaking work paper by Damen et al. [17] hinted at many variables hard to research experimentally and had a different purpose. The survey allowed respondents to imagine how a technology such as the hubs would suit their needs and made it possible to collect insights on a large and diverse sample of office workers. The insights derived from the hubs as a design exemplar in our survey point towards a broader application and contribute to inform the design of technologies to support walking meetings.

## 5.3 Future Work

Future work includes semi-experiments with office workers to study the experience of walking meeting technologies in-situ. We are particularly interested in investigating the benefits of combining mobile and stationary technologies, and even the ones of including low-tech approaches (e.g., walking meeting routes using traditional signage).

In line with previous work done by industrial designers, we first aim at conducting design-through-research studies on artefacts making use of the physical space to support walking meetings, and to nudge office workers to adopt this practice. Our focus will be on the role of these modular artefacts, their influence on the meeting flow, and the optimization of the location/number of artefacts in a workplace environment. From a UI perspective, many elements are still to be researched. We are also conducting design explorations on interactive walking routes, to indicate the position and availability of walking meeting devices or to suggest personalized paths depending on the meeting type. Finally, a special attention could be paid to the facilitation of walking meetings.

## 6 Conclusion

In this paper, we provide insights into walking meeting scenarios that can serve as input for new technologies to facilitate physically active ways of work. We sampled a large number of participants in order to understand users' perceptions and needs with regards to walking meetings. Through a scenario-based online survey (N = 186), we explored the most relevant use cases for the design of walking meetings Hubs, stand-up meeting stations that accommodate different tasks during walking meetings. We purposively used the Hubs as a design exemplar of a tangible technology situated in a physical work environment, in order to investigate this under-research area (previous work in HCI focusing mostly on mobile-mediated concepts). The insights collected and subsequent discussion points can be used by design researchers and practitioners to rethink the office environment and related working practices, in order to combine productivity and wellbeing at work. We encourage the HCI community to unite around this timely and societally relevant topic.

**Acknowledgements.** This research is part of the project POWEr FITTing enabled by Eindhoven Engine.

## References

1. Ahtinen, A., Andrejeff, E., Harris, C., Väänänen, K.: Let's Walk at Work – Persuasion through the Brainwolk Walking Meeting App Full Paper Towards Physically Active Ways of Work. AcademicMindtrek (2017)
2. Ahtinen, A., Andrejeff, E., Väänänen, K.: Brainwolk – A Mobile Technology Mediated Walking Meeting Concept for Wellbeing and Creativity at Work, pp. 307–309 (2016)
3. Ahtinen, A., Andrejeff, E., Vuolle, M., Väänänen, K.: Walk as you work. In: Proceedings of the 9th Nordic Conference on Human-Computer Interaction - NordiCHI 2016, pp. 1–10 (2016)
4. Artal, M., Sherman, C., Dinubile, N.A.: Exercise against depression. Exer. Against Depress. Phys. Sportsmed. **26**(10), 55–70 (1998)
5. Barter, C., Renold, E.: Issue 25 Summer 1999 The Use of Vignettes in Qualitative Research. 25 (1999)
6. Biddle, S., Nanette, M.: Psychology of physical activity: determinants, well-being, and interventions (2001)
7. Bravata, D.M., et al.: Using pedometers to increase physical activity and improve health. J. Am. Med. Assoc. **298**, 19 (2007)
8. Buckley, J.P., et al.: The sedentary office: an expert statement on the growing case for change towards better health and productivity. Br. J. Sports Med. **49**(21), 1357–1362 (2015)
9. C3 Collaborating for Health: The benefits of regular walking for health, well-being and the environment. The benefits of regular walking for health, well-being and the environment 8, September: 48 (2012)

10. Carmack, C., de Moor, C., Boudreaux, E., Amaral-Melendez, M., Brantley, P.: Aerobic fitness and leisure physical activity as moderators of the stress-illness relation. Ann. Behav. Med. **21**(3), 251–257 (1999). https://doi.org/10.1007/BF02884842

11. Choi, W., Song, A., Edge, D., Fukumoto, M., Lee, U.: Exploring user experiences of active workstations: a case study of under desk elliptical trainers. In: Proceedings of the 2016 ACM International Joint Conference on Pervasive and Ubiquitous Computing - UbiComp 2016, pp. 805–816 (2016)

12. Clemes, S., O'connel, S., Edwardson, C.: Office workers' objectively measured sedentary behavior and physical activity during and outside working hours. J. Occup. Environ. Med. **56**(3), 298–303 (2014)

13. Damen, I., Brankaert, R., Megens, C., van Wesemael, P., Brombacher, A., Vos, S.: Let's walk and talk : a design case to integrate an active lifestyle into daily office life. In: CHI 2018 Extended Abstracts 2012, pp. 1–10 (2018)

14. Damen, I., et al.: A scoping review of digital tools to reduce sedentary behavior or increase physical activity in knowledge workers. Int. J. Environ. Res. Public Health **17**, 2 (2020)

15. Damen, I., Heerkens, L., van den Broek, A., et al.: PositionPeak: stimulating position changes during meetings. In: CHI 2020 Extended Abstracts (2020)

16. Damen, I., Kok, A., Bas, V., Brombacher, H., Vos, S., Lallemand, C.: The hub: facilitating walking meetings through a network of interactive devices. In: DIS 2020 Companion

17. Damen, I., Lallemand, C., Brankaert, R., Brombacher, A.: Understanding walking meetings: drivers and barriers. In: Proceeding of the CHI Conference on Human Factors in Computing Systems, pp. 1–14 (2020)

18. Dempsey, P., Owen, N., Biddle, S., Dunstan, D.: Managing sedentary behavior to reduce the risk of diabetes and cardiovascular disease. Curr. Diabetes Reports **14**(9), 1–11 (2014). https://doi.org/10.1007/s11892-014-0522-0

19. Gibbs, B.B., Hergenroeder, A.L., Katzmarzyk, P.T., Lee, I., Jakicic, J.M.: Definition, Measurement, and Health Risks Associated with Sedentary Behavior. August 2014, pp. 1295–1300 (2015)

20. Healy, G.N., et al.: Objectively measured sedentary time, physical activity, and metabolic risk. Diabetes Care **31**(2), 369–371 (2008)

21. Huang, Y., Benford, S., Blake, H.: Digital interventions to reduce sedentary behaviors of office workers: scoping review. J. Med. Internet Res. **21**(2), e11079 (2019)

22. Kilpatrick, M., Sanderson, K., Blizzard, L., Teale, B., Venn, A.: Cross-sectional associations between sitting at work and psychological distress : reducing sitting time may benefit mental health. Ment. Health Phys. Act. **6**(2), 103–109 (2013)

23. Kohl, H.W., Craig, C.L., Lambert, E.V., et al.: The pandemic of physical inactivity: global action for public health. Lancet **380**(9838), 294–305 (2012)

24. Lewis, B.A., Napolitano, M.A., Buman, M.P., Williams, D.M., Nigg, C.R.: Future directions in physical activity intervention research: expanding our focus to sedentary behaviors, technology, and dissemination. J. Behav. Med. **40**(1), 112–126 (2016). https://doi.org/10.1007/s10865-016-9797-8

25. Martin, A., et al.: Interventions with potential to reduce sedentary time in adults: systematic review and meta-analysis. Br. J. Sports. Med. **49**, 1–10 (2015)

26. McKinney, B.L.: Therapist's perceptions of walk and talk therapy: a grounded study. Dissert. Abst. Int. Sect. A. Hum. Soc. Sci. **73**, 7 (2013)

27. Murphy, M., Nevill, A., Murtagh, E., Holder, R.: The effect of walking on fitness, fatness and resting blood pressure: a meta-analysis of randomised, controlled trials. Preventive Medicine **44**(5), 377–385 (2007). https://doi.org/10.1016/j.ypmed.2006.12.008

28. Murtagh, E.M., Murphy, M.H., Boone-Heinonen, J.: Walking – the first steps in cardiovascular disease prevention. Curr Opin Cardiol. **25**(5), 490–496 (2010)

29. Neuhaus, M., Eakin, E.G., Straker, L., et al.: Reducing occupational sedentary time: a systematic review and meta-analysis of evidence on activity-permissive workstations. Obes. Rev. **15**, 10 (2014)

30. Nieuweboer, I.: The office jungle : a vision for wildness to turn offices into jungles. In: DIS 2020 Companion: Companion Publication of the 2020 ACM Designing Interactive Systems Conference, pp. 341–344 (2020). https://doi.org/10.1145/3393914.3395818

31. Nooijen, C.F.J., Kallings, L.V., Blom, V., Ekblom, Ö., Forsell, Y., Ekblom, M.M.: Common perceived barriers and facilitators for reducing sedentary behaviour among office workers. Int. J. Environ. Res. Public Health **15**, 4 (2018)

32. Oppezzo, M., Schwartz, D.L.: Give your ideas some legs: the positive effect of walking on creative thinking. J. Exp. Psychol. Learn. Memory Cogn. **40**(4), 1142–1152 (2014). https://doi.org/10.1037/a0036577

33. Owen, N., Salmon, J., Koohsari, M.J., Turrell, G., Giles-Corti, B.: Sedentary behaviour and health: mapping environmental and social contexts to underpin chronic disease prevention. Br. J. Sports Med. **48**(3), 174–177 (2014)

34. Probst, K., et al.: Rotating, tilting, bouncing: using an interactive chair to promote activity in office environments. In: CHI 2013 Extended Abstracts on Human Factors in Computing Systems, pp. 79–84. ACM (2013)

35. Probst, K., Perteneder, F., Leitner, J., Haller, M., Schrempf, A., Glöckl, J.: Active office: towards an activity-promoting office workplace design. In: CHI 2012 Extended Abstracts on Human Factors in Computing Systems, pp. 2165–2170. ACM (2012)

36. Revell, S., McLeod, J.: Experiences of therapists who integrate walk and talk into their professional practice. Couns. Psychother. Res. **16**(1), 35–43 (2016)

37. Saunders, W., Vogel, D.: Tap-Kick-Click: Foot Interaction for a Standing Desk, pp. 323–333 (2016)

38. Shah, J.J., Smith, S.M., Vargas-Hernandez, N.: Metrics for measuring ideation effectiveness. Des. Stud. **24**(2), 111–134 (2003). https://doi.org/10.1016/S0142-694X(02)00034-0

39. Smit, S., Tacke, T., Lund, S., Manyika, J., Thiel, L.: The future of work in Europe (2020)

40. So, C., Joo, J.: Does a persona improve creativity? Does a persona improve creativity? Des. J. **20**(4), 459–475 (2017)

41. Stephenson, A., McDonough, S.M., Murphy, M.H., Nugent, C.D., Mair, J.L.: Using computer, mobile and wearable technology enhanced interventions to reduce sedentary behaviour: a systematic review and meta-analysis. Int. J. Behav. Nutr. Phys. Activ. **14**(1), 105 (2017)

42. Teychenne, M., Costigan, S.A., Parker, K.: The association between sedentary behaviour and risk of anxiety : a systematic review. BMC Public. Health. **15**, 1–8 (2015)

43. R. E. Thayer, L. Biakanja, P. O'Hanian, et al. 2005. Amount of daily walking predicts energy, mood, personality, and health. 113th annual conference of the American Psychological Association.

44. Thorp, A., Dunstan, D.W.: Stand Up Australia: Sedentary behaviour in workers, 3–12 August 2009

45. Tobiasson, H., Hedman, A., Sundblad, Y.: Still at the office - designing for physical movement-inclusion during office work. In: IHC 2014, pp. 130–139 (2014)

46. Walsh, T., Petrie, H.: Localization of Storyboards for Cross-Cultural User Studies. Mum, pp. 200–209 (2015)

47. World Health Organisation WHO: Preventing Noncommunicable Diseases in the Workplace through Diet and Physical Activity (2008)

48. World Health Organisation WHO: Global recommendations on Physical activity for health (2010)

49. World Health Organisation WHO: Global recommendations on Physical activity for health (2020). https://doi.org/10.1136/bjsports-2020-102955

# Touch, See and Talk: Tangibles for Engaging Learners into Graph Algorithmic Thinking

Andrea Bonani[1] , Andreas Bollin[2] , and Rosella Gennari[1](✉) 

[1] Free University of Bozen-Bolzano, Bolzano, Italy
andrea.bonani@scuola.alto-adige.it, gennari@inf.unibz.it
[2] Universität Klagenfurt, Klagenfurt, Austria
Andreas.Bollin@aau.at
https://www.unibz.it/en/faculties/computer-science/,
https://aau.at/en/informatics-didactics/

**Abstract.** Algorithmic Thinking (AT) is at the core of Computational Thinking (CT). A number of initiatives target CT, few of them focus on AT and even less deal with Graph Algorithmic Thinking (GAT) with younger learners. This paper reports on tangibles' design for GAT, appealing to different senses so as to engage learners actively. It presents a field study with GAT tangibles and 14–15 years old high-school learners, divided into two groups: one group used tangibles, the other used traditional means, namely, paper and pencils. The study results show that tangibles were more engaging than in the traditional GAT setting, and differences among groups are statistically significant. The paper concludes by discussing the study results and advancing suggestions for future interventions related to engagingly teaching GAT.

**Keywords:** Multimodal · Tangible · Algorithmic thinking · Computational thinking · Children · Teens

## 1 Introduction

### 1.1 Background and Rationale

In parallel with the rapid growth of digital technology and its pervasiveness in everyday life, all citizens must have a range of new Computer Science related skills and competences, which schools need to teach in order to help grow tomorrow's citizens, starting from the early years of primary schools [13,17,41]. A number of educational initiatives have been developed to promote such skills, in various contexts. Among others, *Computational Thinking (CT)* initiatives have gained popularity in different countries, e.g., in Italy, with "Programma il Futuro" [35]. CT represents a universally applicable attitude, and a set of Computer Science skills needed by everyone, not just by computer scientists [55].

C. Ardito et al. (Eds.): INTERACT 2021, LNCS 12935, pp. 630–651, 2021.
https://doi.org/10.1007/978-3-030-85610-6_36

At the core of CT skills are *Algorithmic Thinking (AT)* skills. Strictly related with problem solving, AT is concerned with representing a problem in a suitable abstract manner, and planning its resolution through a step-by-step strategy. This paper stems from research which promotes AT at school in a novel manner: it abandoned frontal lectures or computer screens, and it designed tangibles for AT which promote diverse interaction modalities (briefly, *tangibles*).

Such tangibles are designed primarily for 9–15 years old children. Reference theories for the their design were, mainly, socio-constructivism and multi-modal learning, as explained in the following. Socio-constructivism holds that children actively construct their knowledge through diverse interactive experiences. In line with that, tangibles are designed for different learning scenarios, according to the envisioned learning goal. Moreover, tangibles are designed intentionally screen-less so as to enable social interactions as head-up games do [52]. By leveraging on multi-modal learning, such tangibles aim at appealing to different senses and making immediately perceivable otherwise too abstract reasoning forms for 9–15 years old children [31]. In particular, Moreno and Meyer defined guidelines and recommendations for multi-modal learning, which have been considered in the design of tangibles for AT so as to best combine different sensory stimuli (e.g., audio and tactile) [36].

In summary, the research at the basis of this paper designed AT tangible for fostering an engaging experience, as in multi-modal learning and socio-constructivism.

## 1.2   Focus and Contributions

This paper reports on a field study with tangibles for AT with specific data structure: graphs. Example problems with graphs are found in social networks, computer networks, traffic networks. The formal definition of a graph, subsumed in the rest of the paper, is as follows: a(n undirected) graph is an ordered pair $G = (V, E)$, with $V = \{v_1, ..., v_n\}$ the set of nodes, and $E = \{\{v_i, v_j\} \mid v_i, v_j \in V\}$ the set of edges between pairs of nodes.

The paper deals with *Graph AT* (GAT). GAT is relevant and applicable in different learning contexts; it is possible to find concrete examples taken from real life contexts, and hence to contextualise problems that learners are asked to tackle. Imagine a traffic network context, with islands to connect via bridges. Islands can be modelled as graph nodes, and edges between nodes represent connecting bridges. See a graphical representation of such a situation in Fig. 1, which has four islands (A, B, C, D) and four connecting bridges to construct. Therein, a sequence of connecting bridges from the island A to the island C gives a so-called path, e.g., through the bridges from A to B and then from B to C.

GAT in this context can mean tackling diverse problems: Can an island connect to all the others, and how? Is there a way of connecting all the islands together, so that there is exactly one path from any one island, to any other? And, in case bridges have different costs, is there a way of minimising the total cost? Answering the first question means deciding if the graph is connected. Answering the second means deciding whether there exists a spanning three.

The answer to the third question considers the costs of bridges, and selects those leading to a minimum cost. By referring to Fig. 1, this would be the path with all bridges except the one connecting D and C. That amounts to finding a so-called minimum spanning tree.

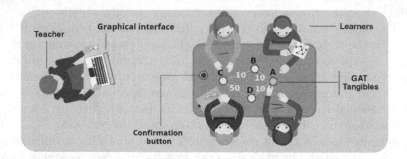

**Fig. 1.** Typical intervention with a graphical representation of islands (A, B, C, D) and connecting bridges with costs (e.g. 10 and 50 cents). The GAT tangibles represent nodes and edges of the graph.

At the same time, GAT is a topic rarely dealt within schools; no children involved in the study of this paper knew of graphs or GAT, which enabled the study to test engagement in GAT through tangibles without children having prior experience of it. Teaching GAT means asking learners to:

1. understand what graphs are,
2. model a problem with graphs,
3. design general strategies to solve the problem and similar problems by relying on graphs,
4. explore general strategies for doing so.

In the study reported in this paper, learners were randomly divided in two groups: one group used GAT tangibles; the other group used pencils and paper. All learners, however, tackled the same scenarios for GAT at school (briefly, *GAT scenarios*), so as to have a comparable GAT experience in terms of learning goals and tasks. Initial scenarios started with goals and tasks at the basis of GAT, that is, understanding graphs and modelling a problem with graphs. Subsequent scenarios gradually moved learners to more advanced goals and through the related tasks, such as exploring the Prim Algorithm for constructing a minimum spanning tree for a given graph.

Data related to learners' engagement in the GAT experience were gathered with different instruments and analysed. The comparison of engagement results shows differences across the two groups in relation to the overall experience with GAT: engagement is statistically significantly higher in the group who worked with tangibles. Further analyses related to the group with tangibles help unveil reasons for the superior engagement results: tangibles seem to engage learners into watching, touching and talking for collaborating around a GAT scenario, thereby soliciting diverse interaction modalities.

## 1.3   Novelty and Outline

Compared to related work, to the best of our knowledge, the study reported in this paper is the first that introduces 14–15 years old children to GAT via tangibles. The study leveraged on a series of past actions, conducted by following an action-research paradigm [12,34]. Notice that past actions concerning GAT tangibles focussed on the usability of the tangibles and the co-creation of preliminary learning scenarios for GAT. The refined tangibles and scenarios, resulting from past research, are employed in the study reported in this paper. The study, reported in this paper, was never described in other publications prior to this. The results of the study pave the way for work related to the design of multi-modal interactive solutions for (G)AT, which stimulate different senses and engage learners.

The paper is organised as follows. Section 2 presents relevant related work. Section 3 describes the field study design. Section 4 presents its results. Section 5 discusses the results of the study, along with reflections related to limitations and future work.

## 2   Related Work

CT is relevant for nowadays' children. Different interventions bring CT into schools, but relatively few activities are related to AT, and even fewer are those that employ tangibles. The next subsection briefly reports on some of them. The goal of the reported study is to explore engagement in a GAT experience with tangibles, which stimulate different senses—visual, tactile, auditory and kinesthetic. The follow-up subsection outlines how engagement in an activity can be defined and assessed.

### 2.1   Computational Thinking and Algorithmic Thinking

The twenty-first century is arguably the century of computing. Computing is increasingly involved in transforming work, commerce, and everyday life: big data, the internet of things, cloud computing, voice, and facial recognition, robotics, and more. Social media are changing how and where people work, collaborate, communicate, shop, travel, receive news and entertainment. Information technology is also transforming and innovating every discipline, becoming an integral and transversal tool for every activity [30].

All that inevitably demands to prepare younger generations to CT to make them able to interpret the world they are in and help shape it [54]. CT initiatives in compulsory education curricula are being undertaken in Europe and various other parts of the world [8]. The New Skills Agenda (European Commission, 2016) explicitly invites the Member States to develop "coding / Computer Science" in education [20]. Indeed, more and more new projects aim at establishing CT, and AT in basic education [39,42].

In the latest decade, the school world has shown a growing interest for introductory activities on basic elements of Computer Science, in many cases carried

out through CT activities. The European Schoolnet published a report survey-
ing the current situation in 20 European countries [21]. In 13 of these countries,
programming has been (or soon will be) introduced in K-9 education. In seven
of these, among them Estonia, England and Greece, programming is included
as a compulsory part of the curriculum [4,53]. In non-European countries (e.g.
Israel, USA, Australia, New Zealand), elements of computer science have been
introduced into the basic school curricula [5,18]. More relevant for this paper
is research by Bollin et al.: they introduced a way to analyse and compare curricula, education standards and competency models, by using a graph-based
representation form and several graph-theoretical metrics [40].

Recent research reflects on the importance of making learners concentrate not
on the technology itself or programming per se, but on core CT skills, and especially AT skills [9]. AT, in particular, is promoted via three main approaches: (1)
without a computer such as CS unplugged [6]; (2) with computers for coding with
specific programming environments for younger learners, such as Scratch [33];
(3) with tangibles. This last approach is the one followed in this study.

Several research studies highlight the benefits that tangibles play in problem solving tasks [50]. Well-known examples gravitating around various tangibles are instructional activities with robotics, and others requiring different
physical computing devices, which have been used in educational settings for
many decades [25]. Specifically, there are several activities which rely on educational robotics [32]. An example is TangibleK, which used robotics and a tangible interface as tools for teaching an engineering design process [7]. Teaching
AT through tangibles or physical objects has received increasing attention in
recent years albeit examples are few [26]. AT has been introduced, for instance,
with a haptic model [14,25]. That turned out to be helpful in different learning
contexts [19]. Another example is a tangible computational drum kit with programmable behaviour, or other tangibles that show how learners can successfully
develop AT [3,43,48,56]. A research highlighted that learners who used physical
manipulation (e.g., through the use of flashcards) were better at strategy design
than learners who did not use physical manipulation [1].

## 2.2  Engagement

Engagement is a debated construct in education, to the point that there is great
variety in the ways engagement is defined and operationalszed [47]. Although the
researchers' interest in engagement has increased in the last years, its distinction
from other constructs such as motivation remains subject to debate [2,15].

Many researchers consider engagement as a meta-construct that includes
other sub-constructs [47]. Fredericks described what have become the three common sub-constructs of engagement in learning, with or without technology [23]:
behavioural, emotional, cognitive engagement. This paper focuses on behavioural
and emotional engagement, so as to assess whether children are engaged in GAT,
with or without tangibles.

In technology-mediated learning experiences, behavioural and emotional
engagement have been measured in different manners. The study in this paper

considers two main instruments for assessing engagement, namely, observations and self-report questionnaires, which are often combined in the design of exploratory and evolving learning technologies [27,28]. The original instruments are explained, separately, in the following.

**Questionnaire.** Non-observable aspects of engagement, such as emotional engagement, are often assessed with self-report questionnaires at the end of an experience [2]. Self-reports have the advantage of representing the most direct way of having insight on people's emotional world [46]. For instance, learners are asked to reflect on the various aspects of their commitment, and select the answer that best describes them [24].

As suggested by Read and MacFarlane, such questionnaires for children need to phrase questions in a language clear for children and have a specific format, adequate to the considered age range [45]. In this research, the again-and-again instrument of the standardised Fun Toolkit by Read and MacFarlane was used to assess participants' engagement in the entire experience. This consists of a single question, asking participant children whether they "would do it again" or whether they would suggest the experience to others. Younger learners answer by choosing one out of usually 3 possible items on a discrete Likert type scale, from "absolutely not", to "absolutely yes". The scale was changed to 5 items with older children, as in the study reported in this paper.

**Observations.** Observations are most reliable when all learners are present in the same location, and when they perform similar tasks, as in the case of the field study reported in this paper with GAT tangibles. Observations can be direct by an observer present in class, or indirect observations such as videos [22]. This study employed videos, which enable for more reliably coding observations. The BROMP observation protocol can be employed in observations so as to detect and code diverse indicators of engagement [38]. Indicators, in general, are markers or descriptive parts inside the target construct [51]. The coding can be later used to perform quantitative or qualitative analyses in relation to engagement, as in the study reported in the remainder. The BROMP indicators are related to tasks with a technology, and can be grouped into two broad categories, as follows:

- behavioural indicators, related to being acting as supposed (e.g., using GAT tangibles to find a spanning tree), or off-task, for a learner who is working neither on his/her own nor interacting with others for the task at hand (e.g., using GAT tangibles to play);
- affective indicators, related to either (1) positive emotional states, such as "delight", for learners who are smiling or otherwise indicating that they are having a pleasurable experience, (2) or negative emotional states, such as "boredom", for learners who appear to find the task dull or tedious.

The field study, reported in this paper, considered them all and slightly revised behavioural indicators to the context of usage of GAT as explained in details in the next section.

# 3   Field Study

The field study, reported in this paper, took place in a technical school in Merano. It involved 14–15 years old learners and their teacher. It took place at the end of the school year.

This study leverages on prior work by Bonani et al., which studied and improved on the usability of tangibles besides on the co-creation of learning scenarios, e.g., [10,11]. Specifically, by following an action research paradigm, actions involved teachers and learners of various age groups, from 9 to 14 years old. Actions led to the co-design of GAT scenarios with teachers. In turn, scenarios with teachers stirred the design of more and more usable tangibles. The final revised tangibles and scenarios are employed in the study reported in this paper.

This section starts with the research questions of the study. Then it reports on the participants and how they were involved in the field study. The section describes the adopted GAT scenarios, each with its own learning goal and related tasks, for all participants in the study. It concludes with an outline of the GAT tangibles and information on the data collection instruments.

## 3.1   Research Questions

The study revolved around two main research questions:

(**RQ1**) Are there differences in the engagement of learners with tangibles, over the engagement of those with traditional paper-and-pencil means?
(**RQ2**) In case so, what could be task-related engagement indicators?

## 3.2   Participants

Before the study, parents or guardians were informed and asked to state their agreement with their child's research participation with a consent form approved by the ethical board of the organising university.

A total of 28 learners participated in the study. Their teacher randomly divided them into two groups. All tackled the same scenarios, as follows:

1. 20 learners tackled GAT scenarios with paper and pencil;
2. 8 learners tackled GAT scenarios with GAT tangibles.

Their participation lasted a total of 6 hours, split across different days.

The division of the groups into 20 and 8 was dictated for operational reasons. The students who worked with tangibles operated in working groups of 4 students. The limited time available due to school organisational constraints, as well space-related constraints imposed by the tangibles did not allow for the creation of additional working groups.

Before the study, all participants already knew the word *algorithm* and knew of CT, in that they had studied the basics of programming using the programming language C#. None of the learners, however, had ever studied algorithms, and they had no knowledge of graphs.

**Fig. 2.** Students with GAT tangibles.

### 3.3   Scenarios

GAT shares several similarities with problem-solving in educational contexts. In the research described in this paper, GAT in educational contexts is supported by GAT scenarios, co-designed with school teachers over time.

GAT scenarios link the contents of learning to learners' everyday life situations, and target the following main GAT skills:

(a) *understanding:* making learners understand certain graphs;
(b) *modelling:* making learners model certain problems with certain graphs;
(c) *designing:* making learners design strategies for solving certain problems with certain graphs;
(d) *exploring:* making learners explore strategies for solving certain problems with certain graphs.

All GAT scenarios follow the same structure. They share characteristics with traditional learning scenarios [16]. They come with a learning goal, which is related to one out of the four aforementioned ones (understanding, modelling, designing or exploring). Moreover, they turn the goal into measurable objectives for teachers, which are related to assessment instruments that teachers can use in class. The scenarios also document the relevant information concerning the environment in which they take place and the used technology, in case any is used. GAT scenarios also share characteristics with scenarios of interaction design, in that they focus on tasks of learners or teachers [44]. The description of is mainly a narration of tasks in GAT, linked to the learning objectives of the scenario and the primary learning goal. An example scenario is in Table 1.

The GAT study, reported in this paper, centred around GAT scenarios listed in Table 3. Based on the main goal to be achieved, scenarios are grouped into three main areas:

**Table 1.** A scenario, related to building simple graphs

| Title: | Simple graphs |
|---|---|
| Participants | 9–15 years old children; their teachers; possibly, a researcher as observer or for technical assistance |
| Goal | To understand simple graphs, and to model problems with simple graphs |
| Objectives: | To understand the properties of a simple graph, namely, (P1) it has no self-loops, and (P2) it has no parallel edges; to model a problem with simple graphs so that P1 and P2 are satisfied |
| Assessment instruments | Question-answering during the activity; post-activity questionnaire |
| Environment | A classroom (with a table for placing GAT tangibles, if present); learners are free to move around and collaborate |
| Description | The teacher introduces a problem which can be modelled as a simple graph, e.g., islands to connect as in Fig. 1. The teacher introduces mistakes on purpose and asks learners to reflect on them (according to the feedback of GAT tangibles, if used). Mistakes are related to properties of simple graphs: (P1) self-loops; (P2) parallel edges |
| | Then, the teacher introduces other similar example problem and asks learners to model them as simple graphs (with GAT tangibles, if present). An example for teachers is in Table 2. The teacher invites learners to reason upon their choices |
| | Finally, the teacher stirs the conversation so as to abstract properties P1 and P2 from the examples, in order to foster the understanding of simple graphs |

- building graphs,
- finding a spanning tree,
- finding a minimum spanning tree.

Each area is preparatory to the next one: a teacher starts from scenarios pertaining to building graphs and gradually moves towards the others. Specifically, a teacher starts asking students to build a graph for real-life situations, e.g., see the simple-graph scenario in Table 1. Next, the teacher asks learners to find first a tree, then a spanning tree and finally a minimum spanning tree, always referring to real-life situations, e.g., how to connect all islands with connecting bridges by minimising the costs of bridges (find a minimum spanning tree). See Fig. 1.

### 3.4   Tangibles

GAT tangibles are physical objects, made interactive and smart through programmable microelectronics. Examples of GAT tangibles of the study are in Fig. 2, whereas a possible educational setting has already been depicted in Fig. 1.

From an architecture viewpoint, GAT tangibles are part of a distributed client-server system, with server and clients communicating through WiFi. The server, usually the teacher's laptop, coordinates clients, displays the interface

**Table 2.** An example for teachers related to the simple graph scenario

| Graph |
|---|
| Desks are located as shown in the image. During the whole year, the teacher recorded the classmates of each learner: |

| *learner* | *classmates during the year* | |
|---|---|---|
| Anna | Paul, Markus | |
| Martina | Hans, Markus | |
| Hans | Martina, Markus | |
| Paul | Anna, Miriam | |
| Miriam | Paul | |
| Markus | Hans, Martina, Anna | |
| Julia | —— | |

(a) Can you represent this situation with a graph?
(b) What do nodes represent? And what do edges stand for?
(c) What are the properties of this graph?

for teachers, verifies graph properties and hence enables for GAT with tangibles, according to what is specified in GAT scenarios. See Fig. 3 for the teacher interface as well as Fig. 1 for the overall setting.

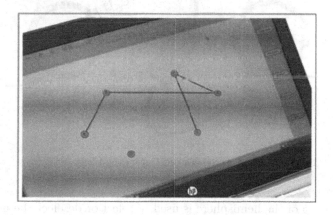

**Fig. 3.** The teacher interface.

GAT tangibles are the clients of the system. See Fig. 4. They are used by learners to construct and reason with graphs and graph algorithms.

GAT tangibles interact with the server and learners through microelectronic components. They represent parts of a graph, such as nodes and edges, and additional components such as the so-called confirmation button. They are explained briefly in the following.

**Nodes.** Nodes of a graph are 3D-printed hemispheres with a Raspberry Pi 3 micro-computer, a PowerBank, several micro-electronic components such as LED coloured strips or simple red LEDs, 4 USB sockets for cables, representing edges.

**Table 3.** List of scenarios

| Scenario | GAT skill |
|---|---|
| Nodes and edges | Understanding a graph, modelling a problem using A graph |
| Simple graph | Understanding a graph, Modelling a problem using a graph |
| Connected graph | Understanding a graph, Modelling a problem using a graph |
| Spanning tree | Understanding a tree, modelling a problem using a tree, Designing a strategy |
| Spanning tree | Understanding a tree, modelling a problem using a tree, Exploring a strategy |
| Minimum spanning tree | Understanding a tree, modelling a problem using a tree, Designing a strategy |
| Minimum spanning tree | Understanding a tree, modelling a problem using a tree, Exploring a strategy |
| Minimum spanning tree | Understanding a tree, modelling a problem using a tree, Exploring a strategy (Prim) |
| Minimum spanning tree | Understanding a tree, modelling a problem using a tree, Exploring a strategy (Prim) |

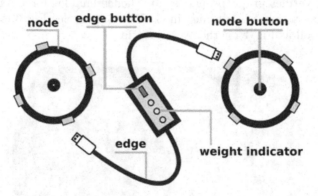

**Fig. 4.** Schema of GAT tangibles.

A button on top of the hemisphere is used to select or deselect the node, e.g., in case learners have to select components of a spanning tree. See Fig. 5.

**Edges.** Edges of a graph are electrical cables ending with USB connectors, terminating in nodes. Similarly to nodes, edges have a button on a small 3D-printed box, positioned halfway through the cable, enabling edge selection or deselection, e.g., when learners are building a spanning tree. Near the button, small LEDs in a small box serve to indicate the edge's weight, e.g., when learners are working with weighted graphs. This small box also contains a Raspberry Pi 0, a lithium-polymer battery and several electronics components. See Fig. 5.

**Confirmation Button.** The confirmation button is a cylinder having on top a large LED blue button, pressed for giving specific feedback, typically for checking whether a task is complete, according to the GAT scenario under consideration.

It consist in a Raspberry Pi 0 with a PowerBank and several electronic components. See Fig. 5.

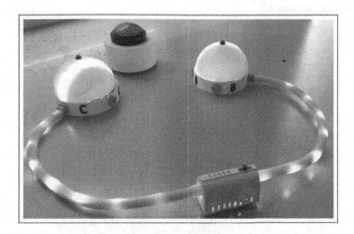

**Fig. 5.** GAT tangibles: two nodes, one edge and its confirmation button.

### 3.5   Data Collection

Data were collected in relation to the main research questions: (RQ1), which investigates differences in engagement between those using tangibles and those using traditional means; (RQ2), which explores task-related engagement with tangibles.

By following a mixed-method approach, data were collected with two instruments, explained in Sect. 2, one per research question. The again-and-again instrument of Read and MacFarlane was used in order to tackle (RQ1). In case of (RQ2), indirect observations (videos) were used, considering engagement indicators of the BROMP protocol with tasks of GAT scenarios.

The again-and-again instrument was administered to learners at the end of the study. It had a single question: *would you suggest the GAT experience to another class?*. Learners answered by choosing one out of 5 possible items on a discrete Likert type scale, from "absolutely not", to "absolutely yes".

The BROMP protocol was employed by researchers trained in coding indicators of engagement in videos, at the end of the study.

## 4   Results

### 4.1   Engagement Differences (R1)

Both the group with tangibles and the group with pencil-and-paper reported about their engagement in GAT via the again-and-again instrument. Their answers were aggregated into: non-positive, indicating lack of engagement, in case of "absolutely not", "probably not" and "neuter"; positive, indicating engagement, in case of "probably yes" and "absolutely yes". Table 4 shows the proportions of answers per item of the scale, divided per group, and the proportions of positive answers.

Table 4. Again-and-again question answers

| Answers | Pencil-and-paper | Tangibles |
|---|---|---|
| *Absolutely not* | 1 | 0 |
| *Maybe not* | 0 | 0 |
| *Neuter* | 10 | 0 |
| *Maybe yes* | 4 | 3 |
| *Absolutely yes* | 0 | 5 |
| **Total** | **15** | **8** |
| **Positive** | **4** | **8** |

Then 95%-Confidence Intervals (95%-CIs) were calculated by using the Adjusted Wald method around proportions of positive answers out of all given answers. Results are different per group:

- 95%-CI[0.1, 0.52] for the pencil-and-paper-group,
- 95%-CI[0.7, 1] for the tangible-group.

Since the CIs of the positive answers between the two groups do not overlap, there is 95% confidence about a significant difference between the two groups' engagement [49].

Given such strong engagement results for the group of learners using GAT tangibles, two researchers analysed the videos of the learners' tasks with GAT tangibles, in order to confirm, or not, the self-report findings, and to explore further opportunities for engaging learners in GAT. How they proceeded and results of the analysis are reported next.

## 4.2    Task-Related Engagement (R2)

Videos were segmented and annotated by considering tasks of GAT scenarios and the BROMP engagement indicators. The usage of BROMP was briefly motivated in Sect. 2. Its usage in the study is explained in details as follows.

An on-task behaviour refers to a student who is doing what he or she is supposed to be doing, whereas an off-task behaviour refers to the opposite case. It is also possible to make other distinctions and those relevant for the study are listed in Table 5. BROMP generally uses a dual coding scheme, which records the behaviour simultaneously, but separately from affect. The affective indicators commonly used are recapped in Table 6.

**Table 5.** BROMP behavioural indicators of (dis)engagement

| On-task | Description |
| --- | --- |
| Conversation | Who is working toward his assignment while having conversation with another learner or teacher about the learning task |
| Help seeking | Who has paused work, but only because she/he is seeking help from another learner/teacher |
| Proactive remediation | Teacher receives information on learner progress and intervenes to work with the learners |
| Off-task | Description |
| Aggression | Who is off task and behaving in a threatening manner towards another learner |
| Passive | Who is off task but not interacting with anybody |
| Social | Who interacting with peers not about the task |

Two researchers, both trained in coding, worked independently on a set of videos of learners, not in the tangible-group, with GAT tangibles. For each learner and task, they coded behavioural and affective indicators, simultaneously but independently.

They compared their results, and agreed on the "work" indicator for a learner interacting directly with the GAT material (e.g., tangibles), or observing other learners doing it. They also merged "conversation", "help seeking" and "proactive remediation" into "conversation", given that they were not easy to distinguish. All other indicators were maintained as in Tables 5 and 6.

**Table 6.** BROMP affective state indicators of (dis)engagement

| Positive | Description |
| --- | --- |
| Engaged concentration | Who is paying focused attention to his/her primary current task |
| Delight | Who is smiling or otherwise indicating that they are having a pleasurable experience |
| Surprise | When posture, facial expressions, or vocal expressions indicate that a previous affective state was interrupted unexpectedly |
| Negative | Description |
| Confusion | Who looks like they are having difficulty understanding the learning material/tasks |
| Boredom | Who appears to find the task dull or tedious |
| Frustration | Who presents feelings of distress or annoyance |

Thereby the two researchers proceeded, independently, to code all videos of the tangible-group of the field study. Finally, they compared their results. Their percentage agreement was calculated (83%) and differences were resolved through discussion with a third researcher. No off-task behaviour or negative affective indicators emerged. All on-task behaviour indicators emerged. As for the affective indicators, "engaged concentration" and "delight" emerged.

Table 7 reports the coding of all tasks with GAT tangibles by means of engagement indicators, behavioural and affective, and the related percentages of occurrence. In particular, 39.17% of tasks were coded as "work". The majority of tasks, namely, 57.50%, were coded specifically as "work with conversation", a novel indicator which emerged with GAT tangibles. This denotes a collaborative conversation-based activity, e.g., a group of learners spontaneously started a discussion on the strategies for creating a spanning tree. Moreover, conversation opportunities were coded in almost all modelling, design or exploration tasks, whereas they did not emerge in understanding tasks, which apparently required more individual reflections.

As for affective indicators, 84.17% of tasks were coded as "engaged concentration", and 15.83% as "delight". Delight indicators were most difficult to trace in videos. However, they emerged mainly when feedback through LEDs was given.

**Table 7.** Indicators for coded tasks with GAT tangibles and occurrence percentages

| Indicator for coded tasks with GAT tangibles | Percentage |
|---|---|
| Work | 39.17% |
| Work with conversation | 57.50% |
| Engaged concentration | 84.17% |
| Delight | 15.83% |

Other interesting observations were traced by researchers in their own notes while coding. In particular, it emerged that, when learners were designing and exploring strategies for building trees, the teacher sometimes had to stop them: the novelty and ease of use of tangibles tended to make learners rush through tasks of scenarios without deeply reflecting on strategies. Moreover, learners were able to see all nodes and edges arranged on tables and, based on this global view, they tended to construct a minimum spanning tree, without reflecting about a step-by-step strategy, unless invited by the teacher to do so.

## 5    Discussion

This section reflects on results of the mixed-method research study, reported above, in relation to the two research questions, gravitating around engagement in GAT: (RQ1) differences in engagement among groups, with either pencil and paper, or tangibles; (RQ2) task-related engagement indicators and what may be reasons for them.

Results concerning engagement in the entire GAT experience and differences among groups (RQ1) were collected through a self-report standardised instrument, asking whether learners would repeat the experience. Statistical analyses show that engagement was different between the pencil-and-paper group and the tangible group. See Table 4. Note that only 4 out of 15 in the pen-and-paper group were positive ("maybe yes"), whereas 8 out 8 of the tangible were positive or very positive ("maybe yes", "absolutely yes"). As remarked by an anonymous reviewer of this paper, it is also interesting that only 1 out of 15 in the pencil-and-paper, and none in the tangible group were absolutely negative ("absolutely no"). Such result suggests that the GAT topic per se was interesting and the usage of tangibles seems to have played a role in engaging learners differently.

In particular, there is a statistically significant difference among the two groups, with positive results for the tangible-group. In other words, GAT turned out to be significantly more engaging with tangibles than with pencil-and-paper, in spite of the period in which it was proposed—the end of the school year, right before the start of a long summer break.

Given such results, videos of the tangible-group were analysed and coded, so as to trace reasons for the superior engagement results and answer the second research question (RQ2). Coding looked for (dis)engagement indicators, both behavioural and affective, recapped in Table. The video analysis of the tangible-group confirmed results about engagement self-reports. It also indicates what might have mostly engaged learners, as discussed in the following.

First of all, the video analysis highlighted that the use of GAT tangibles enabled learners to reflect on the tasks they were carrying out, mainly through conversations with others, in line with socio-constructivism for learning which GAT tangibles refer to. For instance, learners spontaneously started a discussion on the strategies for creating a spanning tree. Moreover, conversations were coded in modelling, design or exploration tasks, whereas they did not emerge in understanding tasks, which apparently relied on individual reflections.

The video analysis also highlighted that learners from the tangible-group were mostly engaged with concentration, and show delight expressions especially when LED or sound feedback was given in response to their actions. However, notes by coders also reveal an aspect which deserves attention in a learning context: when learners were designing and exploring strategies for trees, the teacher sometimes had to stop them, because they tended to rush through scenarios and manipulate tangibles. Such results deserves reflections for the future design of tangibles for GAT, which are presented in the conclusions.

## 6    Conclusions

This paper reports on research related to the usage of tangibles for fostering AT, part of CT, in schools. The research in the paper focuses on AT for graphs, namely, GAT. Grounded on socio-constructivism and soliciting a multi-modal experience, it supports a novel approach to GAT for schools, which requires the usage of GAT tangibles with companion scenarios for different learning goals. It stems from past action-based research, which helped design GAT scenarios and develop GAT tangibles of the study.

The study was conducted with 14–15 years old learners, from the first year of a technical high school, and their teacher. No learners knew of graphs or GAT before participating in the study, albeit they understood the concept of algorithm. All learners performed the same GAT scenarios, which consider different GAT skills, ranging from the understanding of basic graph properties to the exploration of strategies for solving problems with graphs. However, the participant learners were split into two groups, one using GAT tangibles and the other instead using pencil-and-paper material. Data processing adopted a mixed-method research approach so as to investigate the main research question, that is, what learners' engagement in GAT was. Data were processed by means of two different instruments: the standardised again-and-again self-report instrument, asking whether learners would like to repeat the GAT experience; observations in videos of learners in GAT, lately coded by adopting and slightly adapting engagement indicators, standard in the technology-education literature.

Self-reported data were analysed with SPSS and compared between groups, with and without GAT tangibles. Results show differences between groups. The group working with tangibles tended to have higher levels of engagement with the experience than the other group: differences for engagement are statistically significant. Such results were then triangulated with results of the analysis of observations, related to learners' engagement in tasks with GAT tangibles, so as to understand possible reasons for the strongly positive engagement results for GAT with tangibles. It emerged that scenarios with GAT tangibles spontaneously led students to move and engage in conversations, whereas paper-and-pencil based scenarios did not naturally lead students to interact and collaborate. That can partly explain differences in engagement.

The paper concludes acknowledging the limitations of the reported research, related to learners' engagement with GAT, and with lessons for future work related to GAT, both from the education researchers' and practitioners' perspective, and the perspective of Human Computer Interaction (HCI).

## 6.1   Limitations of the Work

The contextual nature of the reported work, and the small number of involved participants affect the generality of its results. However, the intervention at school was described with contextual factors, so as to make it possible to replicate it in other different contexts. Further detailed information on the study protocol, and the data collection instruments are publicly available in a report [12].

Furthermore, the employed tangibles per se might have also placed constraints. The limited number of available tangibles affected the number of learners using them in the study. The use of tangibles, and the time spent every time before using them (e.g., connecting and activating edges) also constrained the time-span of the GAT intervention within the educational context.

However, results of learners with GAT tangibles indicate their strong engagement with respect to results of learners using pencil and paper, advocating for interactive multi-sensory experiences for teaching GAT, as discussed in the remainder of this paper.

## 6.2 Recommendations for Future Work

In view of the results concerning the group using GAT tangibles, in the future, education researchers and teachers could consider collaborative approaches to teaching GAT through tangible artefacts, which stimulate conversations, physical manipulations and movement, as GAT tangibles do. In fact GAT tangibles seem to have played a role in engaging learners in work-related conversations in all tasks which go beyond pure understanding of basic concepts (e.g., graphs and trees), namely, in modelling, designing or exploring (e.g., modelling a problem with a graph and designing a strategy concerning how to find a spanning tree).

HCI researchers could consider the fact that the number of GAT tangibles made learners approach tasks related to (spanning) trees without thinking strategically. Future work may consider adopting a larger number of nodes and edges. Such a choice might induce learners to appreciate the importance of a step-by-step general strategy, as opposed to intuitive choices on an ad-hoc basis.

Although this paper did not focus on learning, learning and engagement are often correlated. For instance, Gennari et al. show that a high level of engagement, related to self-reported affective indicators, significantly correlated to high learning performances, related to the quality of children's products, part of the learning activity [29]. On-going work of authors of this paper is considering learning and engagement results, reported in this study, and studying their correlations.

Last but not least, this paper considered observable indicators of engagement with technology-mediated tasks, part of the the technology education literature. The original indicators were slightly adapted and made evolve, as documented in the paper, by considering the specific context of tangibles for GAT, which is collaborative and relying on physical objects to move. Future work may apply such indicators in similar contexts. Interestingly, as pointed out by an anonymous reviewer of this manuscript, similar engagement indicators were considered in the HCI literature, in the work by Nasir and colleagues [37]. Their results point to at least two distinct multi-modal behavioural patterns which indicate "high learning in constructivist, collaborative activities". Future work can investigate whether their specific patterns are correlated to engagement indicators found across GAT tasks, reported in this paper.

**Acknowledgements.** Authors would like to thank anonymous reviewers, who helped reflect on the paper and improve on it. They are grateful to V. del Fatto, for helping with coding, G. Mahlknecht, the teacher of the school in Merano, who also collaborated on the co-creation of scenarios, besides all participant learners.

# References

1. Aggarwal, A., Gardner-McCune, C., Touretzky, D.S.: Evaluating the effect of using physical manipulatives to foster computational thinking in elementary school. In: Proceedings of the 2017 ACM SIGCSE Technical Symposium on Computer Science Education, SIGCSE 2017, New York, NY, USA, pp. 9–14. ACM (2017). https://doi.org/10.1145/3017680.3017791
2. Appleton, J.J., Christenson, S.L., Kim, D., Reschly, A.L.: Measuring cognitive and psychological engagement: validation of the student engagement instrument. J. School Psychol. 44(5), 427–445 (2006). https://doi.org/10.1016/j.jsp.2006.04.002
3. Athanasiou, L., Topali, P., Mikropoulos, T.A.: The use of robotics in introductory programming for elementary students. In: Alimisis, D., Moro, M., Menegatti, E. (eds.) Edurobotics 2016 2016. AISC, vol. 560, pp. 183–192. Springer, Cham (2017). https://doi.org/10.1007/978-3-319-55553-9_14
4. Barendsen, E., et al.: Concepts in k-9 computer science education. In: Proceedings of the 2015 ITiCSE on Working Group Reports, ITICSE-WGR 2015, New York, NY, USA, pp. 85–116. ACM (2015). https://doi.org/10.1145/2858796.2858800
5. Bargury, I.Z., et al.: Implementing a new computer science curriculum for middle school in Israel. In: 2012 Frontiers in Education Conference (FIE), pp. 1–6. IEEE (2012)
6. Bell, T.A.J., Freeman, I., Grimley, M.: Computer science without computers: new outreach methods from old tricks. In: Proceedings of the 21st Annual Conference of the National Advisory Committee on Computing Qualifications (2008)
7. Bers, M.U.: The Tangiblek robotics program: applied computational thinking for young children. Early Childhood Res. Pract. 12(2), n2 (2010)
8. Bocconi, S., et al.: Developing computational thinking in compulsory education. European Commission, JRC Science for Policy Report (2016). https://doi.org/10.2791/792158
9. Bocconi, S., et al.: Developing computational thinking: approaches and orientations in k-12 education. In: EdMedia: World Conference on Educational Media and Technology, pp. 13–18. Association for the Advancement of Computing in Education (AACE) (2016)
10. Bonani, A., Del Fatto, V., Dodero, G., Gennari, R., Raimato, G.: First steps towards the design of tangibles for graph algorithmic thinking. In: Vittorini, P., et al. (eds.) MIS4TEL 2017. AISC, vol. 617, pp. 110–117. Springer, Cham (2017). https://doi.org/10.1007/978-3-319-60819-8_13
11. Bonani, A., Del Fatto, V., Dodero, G., Gennari, R., Raimato, G.: Participatory design of tangibles for graphs: a small-scale field study with children. In: Mealha, Ó., Divitini, M., Rehm, M. (eds.) SLERD 2017. SIST, vol. 80, pp. 161–168. Springer, Cham (2018). https://doi.org/10.1007/978-3-319-61322-2_16
12. Bonani, A., Del Fatto, V., Gennari, R.: Interactive Objects for the Scaffolding of Graph Algorithmic Thinking at School. https://doi.org/10.13140/RG.2.2.34628.37760. Accessed 14 Jan 2021
13. Brondino, M., et al.: Emotions and inclusion in co-design at school: let's measure them! Adv. Intell. Syst. Comput. 374, 1–8 (2015). https://doi.org/10.1007/978-3-319-19632-9_1
14. Capovilla, D., Krugel, J., Hubwieser, P.: Teaching algorithmic thinking using haptic models for visually impaired students. In: 2013 Learning and Teaching in Computing and Engineering (LaTiCE), pp. 167–171. IEEE (2013)

15. Christenson, S.L., Reschly, A.L., Wylie, C.: Handbook of Research on Student Engagement. Springer, Boston (2012). https://doi.org/10.1007/978-1-4614-2018-7

16. Collaborative Education Lab: Learning scenarios. http://colab.eun.org/learning-scenarios. Accessed 14 Jan 2021

17. Corradini, I., Lodi, M., Nardelli, E.: Conceptions and misconceptions about computational thinking among Italian primary school teachers. In: Proceedings of the 2017 ACM Conference on International Computing Education Research, ICER 2017, New York, NY, USA, pp. 136–144. ACM (2017). https://doi.org/10.1145/3105726.3106194

18. Duncan, C., Bell, T.: A pilot computer science and programming course for primary school students. In: Proceedings of the Workshop in Primary and Secondary Computing Education, pp. 39–48. ACM (2015)

19. Eisenberg, M., Elumeze, N., MacFerrin, M., Buechley, L.: Children's programming, reconsidered: settings, stuff, and surfaces. In: Proceedings of the 8th International Conference on Interaction Design and Children. pp. 1–8. ACM (2009)

20. European Commission: New Skills Agenda for Europe. https://ec.europa.eu/social/main.jsp?catId=1223. Accessed 14 Jan 2021

21. European Schoolnet: Computing our future. European Schoolnet (2015). http://fcl.eun.org/documents/10180/14689/Computing+our+future_final.pdf

22. Figg, C., Jamani, K.J.: Exploring teacher knowledge and actions supporting technology-enhanced teaching in elementary schools: two approaches by pre-service teachers. Austral. J. Educ. Technol. **27**(7) (2011)

23. Fredricks, J.A., Blumenfeld, P.C., Paris, A.H.: School engagement: potential of the concept, state of the evidence. Rev. Educ. Res. **74**(1), 59–109 (2004). https://doi.org/10.3102/00346543074001059

24. Fredricks, J.A., McColskey, W.: The measurement of student engagement: a comparative analysis of various methods and student self-report instruments. In. Christenson, S., Reschly, A., Wylie, C. (eds.) Handbook of Research on Student Engagement, pp. 763–782. Springer, Boston (2012). https://doi.org/10.1007/978-1-4614-2018-7_37

25. Futschek, G., Moschitz, J.: Learning algorithmic thinking with tangible objects eases transition to computer programming. In: Kalaš, I., Mittermeir, R.T. (eds.) ISSEP 2011. LNCS, vol. 7013, pp. 155–164. Springer, Heidelberg (2011). https://doi.org/10.1007/978-3-642-24722-4_14

26. Futschek, G.: Algorithmic thinking: the key for understanding computer science. In: Mittermeir, R.T. (ed.) ISSEP 2006. LNCS, vol. 4226, pp. 159–168. Springer, Heidelberg (2006). https://doi.org/10.1007/11915355_15

27. Gennari, R., Melonio, A., Rizvi, M.: The participatory design process of tangibles for children's socio-emotional learning. In: Barbosa, S., Markopoulos, P., Paternò, F., Stumpf, S., Valtolina, S. (eds.) IS-EUD 2017. LNCS, vol. 10303, pp. 167–182. Springer, Cham (2017). https://doi.org/10.1007/978-3-319-58735-6_12

28. Gennari, R., Melonio, A., Rizvi, M.: From turntalk to classtalk: the emergence of tangibles for class conversations in primary school classrooms. Behav. Inf. Technol. 1–20 (2019)

29. Gennari, R., et al.: Children's emotions and quality of products in participatory game design. Int. J. Hum Comput Stud. **101**, 45–61 (2017)

30. Grover, S., Pea, R.: Computational thinking: A competency whose time has come. Computer Science Education: Perspectives on Teaching and Learning in School, p. 19 (2018)

31. Hourcade, J.P.: Interaction design and children. Found. Trends Hum. Comput. Interact. **1**(4), 277–392 (2008). https://doi.org/10.1561/1100000006

32. Lee, I., et al.: Computational thinking for youth in practice. ACM Inroads **2**(1), 32–37 (2011)
33. Maloney, J., Resnick, M., Rusk, N., Silverman, B., Eastmond, E.: The scratch programming language and environment. ACM Trans. Comput. Educ. (TOCE) **10**(4), 16 (2010)
34. Mascio, T., Gennari, R., Tarantino, L., Vittorini, P.: Designing visualizations of temporal relations for children: action research meets HCI. Multimed. Tools Appl. **76**(4), 4855–4893 (2017). https://doi.org/10.1007/s11042-016-3609-6
35. Miur & CINI: Programma il futuro. https://programmailfuturo.it/chi-siamo. Accessed 14 Jan 2021
36. Moreno, R., Mayer, R.: Interactive multimodal learning environments. Educ. Psychol. Rev. **19**(3), 309–326 (2007). https://doi.org/10.1007/s10648-007-9047-2
37. Nasir, J., Bruno, B., Dillenbourg, P.: Is there one way' of learning? A data-driven approach. In: Companion Publication of the 2020 International Conference on Multimodal Interaction, ICMI 2020 Companion, New York, NY, USA, pp. 388–391. ACM (2020). https://doi.org/10.1145/3395035.3425200
38. Ocumpaugh, J., Baker, R., Rodrigo, M.: Monitoring protocol (BROMP) 2.0 technical & training manual. Teachers college, New York, NY (2015)
39. Parmentier, Y., et al.: PIAF: developing computational and algorithmic thinking in fundamental education. In: EdMedia+ Innovate Learning, pp. 315–322. Association for the Advancement of Computing in Education (AACE) (2020)
40. Pasterk, S., Bollin, A.: Digital literacy or computer science: where do information technology related primary education models focus on? In: 2017 15th International Conference on Emerging eLearning Technologies and Applications (ICETA), pp. 1–7 (2017). https://doi.org/10.1109/ICETA.2017.8102517
41. Pasterk, S., Sabitzer, B., Demarle-Meusel, H., Bollin, A.: Informatics-lab: attracting primary school pupils for computer science. In: Proceedings of LACCEI International Multi-Conference for Engineering, Education, and Technology, San José, Costa Rica (2016)
42. Pawlowski, J., et al.: Computational thinking and acting: an approach for primary school competency development. In: CEUR Workshop Proceedings. RWTH Aachen (2020)
43. Peng, H.: Algo.rhythm: Computational thinking through tangible music device. In: Proceedings of the Sixth International Conference on Tangible, Embedded and Embodied Interaction, TEI 2012, New York, NY, USA, pp. 401–402. ACM (2012). https://doi.org/10.1145/2148131.2148234
44. Preece, J., Sharp, H., Rogers, Y.: Interaction Design: Beyond Human-Computer Interaction. Wiley, Hoboken (2019)
45. Read, J.C., MacFarlane, S.: Using the fun toolkit and other survey methods to gather opinions in child computer interaction. In: Proceedings of the 2006 Conference on Interaction Design and Children, IDC 2006, New York, NY, USA, pp. 81–88. ACM (2006). https://doi.org/10.1145/1139073.1139096
46. Reinhard Pekrun, M.B.: Self-Report Measures of Academic Emotions, chap. 28. Routledge (2014). https://doi.org/10.4324/9780203148211.ch28
47. Reschly, A.L., Christenson, S.L., Jingle, J.: Conceptual Haziness: Evolution and Future Directions of the Engagement Construct, pp. 3–19. Springer, Boston (2012). https://doi.org/10.1007/978-1-4614-2018-7_1
48. Root, E., et al.: Grasping algorithms: exploring toys that teach computational thinking. In: Proceedings of the 16th International Conference on Mobile and Ubiquitous Multimedia, MUM 2017, New York, NY, USA, pp. 387–392. ACM (2017). https://doi.org/10.1145/3152832.3156620

49. Sauro, J., Lewis, J.R.: Quantifying the User Experience: Practical Statistics for User Research. Morgan Kaufmann, Burlington (2016)
50. Schneider, B., Jermann, P., Zufferey, G., Dillenbourg, P.: Benefits of a tangible interface for collaborative learning and interaction. IEEE Trans. Learn. Technol. 4(3), 222–232 (2011). https://doi.org/10.1109/TLT.2010.36
51. Skinner, E.A., Pitzer, J.R.: Developmental Dynamics of Student Engagement, Coping, and Everyday Resilience, pp. 21–44. Springer, Boston (2012). https://doi.org/10.1007/978-1-4614-2018-7_2
52. Soute, I., Markopoulos, P., Magielse, R.: Head up games: combining the best of both worlds by merging traditional and digital play. Pers. Ubiquit. Comput. 14(5), 435–444 (2010). https://doi.org/10.1007/s00779-009-0265-0
53. Sysło, M.M., Kwiatkowska, A.B.: Introducing a new computer science curriculum for all school levels in Poland. In: Brodnik, A., Vahrenhold, J. (eds.) ISSEP 2015. LNCS, vol. 9378, pp. 141–154. Springer, Cham (2015). https://doi.org/10.1007/978-3-319-25396-1_13
54. Wang, D., Wang, T., Liu, Z.: A tangible programming tool for children to cultivate computational thinking. Sci. World J. 2014 (2014). https://doi.org/10.1155/2014/428080
55. Wing, J.M.: Computational thinking. Commun. ACM 49(3), 33–35 (2006)
56. Yu, J., Zheng, C., Tamashiro, M.A., Gonzalez-millan, C., Roque, R.: CodeAttach: engaging children in computational thinking through physical play activities. In: Proceedings of the Fourteenth International Conference on Tangible, Embedded, and Embodied Interaction, pp. 453–459 (2020)

# Usable Security

# An Empirical Study of Picture Password Composition on Smartwatches

Marios Belk[1,2(✉)], Christos Fidas[3], Eleni Katsi[2], Argyris Constantinides[2,4], and Andreas Pitsillides[2]

[1] Cognitive UX GmbH, Heidelberg, Germany
belk@cognitiveux.de
[2] Department of Computer Science, University of Cyprus, Nicosia, Cyprus
{ekatsi03,andreas.pitsillides}@cs.ucy.ac.cy
[3] Department of Electrical and Computer Engineering, University of Patras, Patras, Greece
fidas@upatras.gr
[4] Cognitive UX LTD, Nicosia, Cyprus
argyris@cognitiveux.com

**Abstract.** Recent research works suggest that human cognitive differences affect security and usability of picture passwords within a variety of interaction contexts, such as conventional desktops, smartphones, and extended reality. However, the interplay of human cognition towards users' interaction behavior and security of picture passwords on smartwatch devices has not been investigated so far. In this paper, we report on such a research attempt that embraced a between-subjects in-lab user study ($n = 50$) in which users were classified according to their cognitive processing characteristics (*i.e.*, Field Dependence-Independence cognitive differences), and further composed a picture password on a smartwatch device. Analysis of results reveal that already known effects of human cognition towards interaction behavior and security of picture passwords within conventional interaction contexts, do not necessarily replicate when these are deployed on smartwatch devices. Findings point towards the need to design for diversity and device-aware picture password schemes.

**Keywords:** Graphical authentication · Human cognition · Efficiency · Security

## 1 Introduction

Research on smartwatch user authentication has become a complex endeavor, since it entails a variety of factors that affect human behavior, security and user experience [1–5]. Smartwatch-based user authentication is primarily achieved with Personal Identification Numbers (PIN) and Pattern Lock [1, 6]. User authentication methods on smartwatch devices can be grouped in two broad categories.

*Knowledge-based user authentication approaches* include CirclePin [6], which asks users to enter a PIN through a 10-item color index using the smartwatch crown; Draw-a-Pin [7], which authenticates users by drawing the PIN on the touchscreen; 2GesturePIN

© IFIP International Federation for Information Processing 2021
Published by Springer Nature Switzerland AG 2021
C. Ardito et al. (Eds.): INTERACT 2021, LNCS 12935, pp. 655–664, 2021.
https://doi.org/10.1007/978-3-030-85610-6_37

[8], which requires from users to conduct two gestures through the smartwatch rotating bezel or crown; TapMeIn [9], that allows users to tap a secret and memorable melody on the screen; and Personal Identification Chord [10], a chorded keypad that allows users to enter various tap-based inputs. Studies have also investigated the effectiveness of user authentication methods on smartwatch devices [1, 11].

*Biometric-based user authentication approaches* have been proposed that leverage on device-specific signals (*e.g.*, accelerometer, physiological, heart rate, etc.), including MotionAuth [12], which authenticates users by analyzing their gestures (raising/lowering hand, rotation, circle) utilizing a smartwatch; iAuth [13], which continuously authenticates users by exploiting built-in device sensors; and SoundCraft [14] that authenticates users based on non-vocal hand acoustics.

In this paper, we focus on knowledge-based user authentication schemes and in particular on *picture passwords* [15], which require from users to select regions on a background image that acts as a cue. Picture password authentication already represents an alternative knowledge-based user authentication scheme in conventional interaction contexts (*e.g.*, desktops, smartphones, etc.) [15] and used daily by millions of users [16]. However, picture passwords have not been deployed and investigated within smartwatch-based interaction contexts, despite the fact that they can leverage on the picture superiority effect, suggesting that individuals are effective in recalling visual information [15, 17], and they can be easily adapted for touch interaction [5].

Picture password systems require from users to perceive, represent and recall visual information that is processed on a cognitive level, and researchers have studied the effects of human cognitive differences in information processing on various aspects of user authentication [5, 18–21, 35], which are described next.

## 2 Related Work and Research Motivation

Field Dependence-Independence (FD-I) is considered an accredited theory [22–25], which indicates the users' abilities to extract relevant information in visual scenes. *Field Dependent (FD)* individuals obtain experiences through an integral approach and their perception can be easily affected by the environment. They are not attentive to detail, tend to handle problems in a holistic way and they are not efficient and effective in extracting relevant information from a complex whole [5, 26]. *Field Independent (FI)* individuals can obtain experiences through analysis and their perception is not easily affected by the context. FI users are effective in disembedding information from a complex whole, they prefer to handle it in an analytical way and are able to distinguish pertinent visual information embedded in an image [5, 26].

From a human cognition perspective, prior research has shown FD-I effects on *picture password exploration and composition time* [5, 18], and *password selections* [19] within conventional interaction contexts, *i.e.*, desktops, smartphones, extended reality. For example, the work in [5, 18] revealed that FD users spend more time to explore and compose a picture password on desktop and mixed reality devices compared to FI users. The work in [19, 35] showed that FD users make stronger password selections than FI users during picture password composition on desktop computers.

In this context, we further examine whether such effects continue to hold when picture passwords are deployed on smartwatch devices. Hence, the contribution of this paper is two-fold: *a)* we deploy picture password schemes on smartwatch devices, which is the first attempt so far to the best of our knowledge, and we study users' interaction behavior and security under the light of an accredited human cognition theory (*i.e.*, Witkin's Field Dependence-Independence [22]); and *b)* we provide initial empirical evidence on the effects of human cognition towards users' interaction behavior and security of smartwatch-based picture passwords.

## 3   Method of Study

### 3.1   Null Hypotheses

*H 01.* There are no interaction effects between FD-I users and password selections towards picture password composition efficiency on smartwatch devices.

*H 02 .* There are no significant differences between FD-I users towards picture password security on smartwatch devices.

### 3.2   Research Instruments

**Picture Password System.** A cued-recall-based graphical authentication system (Fig. 1) was designed and developed, following guidelines of Microsoft Windows 10™ Picture Gesture Authentication [29] in which users create selections on a background image that acts as a cue. For representing the users' selections, the system creates a 4x4 grid on the image, and consequently, stores the corresponding segment that was selected. Users are asked to make five click-based selections (repeated selections are allowed) in a specific order aiming to achieve a comparable theoretical key space of PIN-based authentication on the picture password. Specifically, a six-digit PIN yields $10^6$ combinations, with a theoretical entropy of $log_2(10^6) = 19.93$ bits, while a five-click-based selection on a 4x4 image grid yields $16^5$ combinations, with a theoretical entropy of $log_2(16^5) = 20$ bits.

**Smartwatch Device.** The picture password system was deployed on a Fitbit Versa smartwatch (https://www.fitbit.com), which has a 1.34" and 300x300 pixels display.

**Picture Password Image.** We intentionally chose an image that would include Points of Interests (PoI – regions on an image that attract the users' attention) across four quadrants, and including widely applied image semantics (*i.e.*, scenery [33]). Figure 1 illustrates the picture password and background image used in the study, and its corresponding saliency map that indicates the Points of Interests.

**Cognitive Factor Elicitation.** We used Witkin's Group Embedded Figures Test (GEFT) [30], which is an accredited and widely applied paper-and-pencil test [5, 18, 19, 26, 27]. The test measures the user's ability to find common geometric shapes in a larger design. Depending on the users' responses, scores range between 0–18. Using a widely applied cut-off score [5, 18, 19, 26], users that identify less than 12 items are classified as FD, and users that identify 12 items and more are classified as FI.

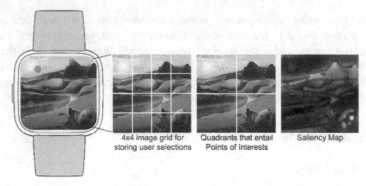

**Fig. 1.** Picture password and background image used in the study, and its corresponding saliency map that indicates the Points of Interests.

### 3.3 Sampling and Procedure

A total of 50 individuals participated in the user study with ages ranging between 21 to 44 years old ($m = 32$; $sd = 5.7$). All individuals participated voluntarily and could opt-out from the study at any time. All participants were familiar with using smartwatches and PIN-based authentication. No participant was familiar with picture passwords. Based on the users' GEFT scores, 21 participants were classified as FD and 29 participants as FI (GEFT scores: $m = 12.34$; $sd = 4.26$; $min = 2$; $max = 18$).

We adopted the University's human research protocol that considers users' privacy, confidentiality and anonymity. Participants were invited and visited the researchers' laboratory at a time convenient for the participants. The user study was conducted with one individual at a time. Participants were informed about the study, and were asked to read, accept and sign a consent form to participate. Once participants accepted and signed the consent form, the GEFT test was administered aiming to highlight the participants' cognitive characteristics (*i.e.*, classify them as FD *vs.* FI). Participants were then instructed to wear the smartwatch on the hand they usually wear one and familiarized themselves with the picture password system on the smartwatch. Aiming to increase ecological validity of the study, we asked participants to compose a picture password that would be used to access individual data on the smartwatch.

### 3.4 Data Metrics

The following data were measured: *i) visual exploration and overall password composition time:* visual exploration time includes the time as soon as the user is shown with the task until the user makes the first password selection, and overall password composition time further includes the time until the user successfully completes the password composition task; and *ii) picture password strength:* we adopted a widely used metric for picture password strength [16, 31] by calculating *password guessability*, which is the number of guesses required to crack the users' passwords. Following prior approaches that consider Points of Interests (PoI) [16, 19, 31, 32], we used a PoI-assisted brute-force attack model [16] starting from segments covering the PoIs, then checking the neighboring segments, and finally checking the rest segments.

# 4  Analysis of Results and Main Findings

## 4.1  Interaction Effects between FD-I Users and Password Selections towards Picture Password Composition Efficiency on Smartwatch Devices ($H_{01}$)

To investigate $H_{01}$, we ran a two-way mixed analysis of variance (ANOVA) with the FD-I group (FD *vs.* FI) and users' password selections (five consecutive selections) as the independent variables, and the time to make each password selection as the dependent variable. There was a statistically significant interaction between the FD-I group and users' password selections on the overall time to compose the picture password, $F(1, 48) = 7.11, p < .01, partial \eta^2 = .129$. Figure 2 depicts the time to make each of the five password selections.

Given the interaction effect, we further examined simple main effects for each password selection. Data are mean ± standard error, unless otherwise stated. The analysis revealed that visual exploration time, *i.e.*, from start until making the first password selection between the two groups, was statistically significant (FD: 3.14 ± .34 s *vs.* FI: 2.21 ± .29 s) with a mean difference of .927 s, $F(1, 48) = 4.161, p = .047, partial \eta^2 = .08$. For the remaining four password selections (selections 2–5), there were no significant differences between the FD and FI group ($p > .05$).

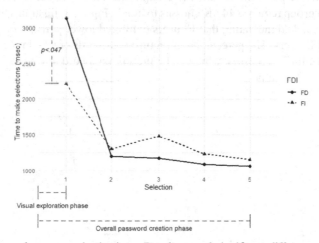

**Fig. 2.** Time to make password selections. Results reveal significant differences between FD-I users in exploration time (*i.e.*, from start until making the first password selection), whereas in the remaining four password selections (selections 2–5), there are no significant differences.

**Main Finding Related to $H_{01}$.** FD users spent significantly more time exploring the image prior making their first selection (visual exploration phase). This can be explained by the fact that FD users (having more trained the global information processing stream) [22–25], spent more time exploring the visual cue since they follow a more holistic and exploratory approach during visual search compared to FI users, who typically focus on specific focal points of an image during interaction.

This finding is in line with prior studies on investigating FD-I effects on password composition time in desktop computers and mixed reality [5, 18]. Hence, existing effects continue to exist when picture passwords are deployed on smartwatch devices. Another interpretation can be based on the fact that FI users might be more efficient in adapting to contextual and field changes (desktop *vs.* smartwatches) than FD users, who need more time to adapt to new interaction design paradigms, further supporting previous findings in the field [5, 18, 26–28]. Furthermore, this study is also in line with previous cognitive studies in a different context [34], which revealed that the holistic and analytic behaviors of FD and FI users are respectively amplified when interacting with mixed reality environments compared to conventional desktops.

## 4.2 Differences between FD-I Users Towards Picture Password Security Aspects on Smartwatch Devices ($H_{02}$)

We ran a Welch t-test to determine whether the two user groups (FD *vs.* FI) generated different password strengths in terms of password guessability, due to the assumption of homogeneity of variances being violated, as assessed by Levene's test for equality of variances ($p = .044$). Results revealed significant differences with a mean difference of 169K guesses (95% CI, −317 K to −20 K), $t(47.633) = -2.289, p = .027$. In particular, user-chosen picture passwords of the FD group required 278 K guesses to crack, while those of the FI group required 447 K guesses to crack. Figure 3 illustrates the percentage of passwords cracked indicating that FI users exhibited lower percentage of passwords cracked than FD users. The percentage of picture passwords cracked reached 100% for both groups within $2^{20}$ guesses, which is the picture password key space. Also, a spike occurred after $2^{18}$ attempts.

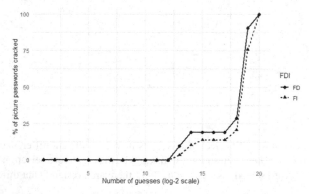

**Fig. 3.** Percentage of picture passwords cracked, as assessed by the PoI-assisted attack model [16]. FI users exhibited lower percentage of picture passwords cracked than FD users.

We further conducted an analysis on the user password segment selections of the picture password. Figure 4 illustrates an intensity map of the frequencies of user password selections on the background image of the picture password system among FD-I groups. Each column illustrates the layout of the image grid, with each cell representing a segment in which a user password selection is made. Cell colors indicate the frequency at which each segment was selected as the first, second, third, fourth or fifth selection (darker colors indicate higher frequencies).

We ran a chi-square goodness-of-fit test to determine whether the selected segments are evenly distributed across the entire image grid for both user groups. For doing so, we further split the image in four even quadrants and calculated the frequencies of user password selections of each quadrant. In the FD group, the number of selected segments are statistically significantly different among the quadrants ($\chi^2(3) = 13.133, p = .004$). In the FI group, the number of selected segments are not statistically significantly different among the quadrants ($\chi^2(3) = 1.78, p = .61$).

Finally, we analyzed the participants' selections with regards to PoI segments. We ran an independent-samples t-test, with the FD-I group as the independent variable, and the proportion of selections falling into PoI segments as the dependent variable. There was homogeneity of variances, as assessed by Levene's test for equality of variances ($p = .07$). There were no significant outliers in the data, as assessed by inspection of boxplots, and data were normally distributed, as assessed by Shapiro-Wilk's test ($p > .05$). The analysis revealed that FD users had a higher proportion of selections that fall into PoI segments ($73.33\% \pm 21.29\%$) than FI users ($60.68\% \pm 18.11\%$), a statistically significant difference of $12.64\% \pm 5.58\%$ (95% CI, 1.4 to 23.87), $t(48) = 2.263, p = .033$.

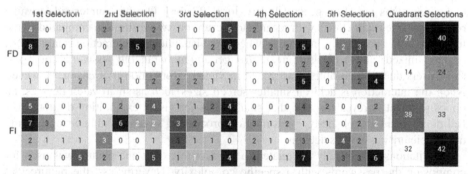

**Fig. 4.** Frequencies of user selections on the image of the picture password system. User choices of FI users are more evenly distributed across the entire grid, compared to FD users.

**Main Finding Related to $H_{02}$.** FI users created significantly stronger picture passwords than FD users. The PoI-assisted brute-force attack required 278K guesses to crack FD passwords, and 447K guesses to crack FI passwords. The intensity map of user selections further revealed that user choices of the FI user group were more evenly distributed across the entire grid, compared to the FD group. Given that user password selections of the FI group entailed more randomness, this can explain the improved security strength compared to the FD group. In addition, FD users had a higher proportion of selections that fall into PoI segments compared to the FI users.

Prior research has shown that FD users create stronger passwords than FI users [19] when composing picture passwords on conventional desktop devices since FI users typically tend to select Points of Interests (PoIs – regions that attract the users' attention and are prone to brute-force attacks) due to their inherent ability to focus on the details. In contrary, in this study we found an opposite main effect, which can be explained by the limited screen size and visual field that might have affected the users' selections towards certain regions that would not take place when the background image would have been deployed on a conventional desktop computer with a larger visual field and clearer attention points. Finally, findings also indicate that users in general tend to make password selections that are based on generic PoI segments, which is in line to recent research [32, 36] that revealed similar observations in desktop interaction contexts.

## 5 Conclusions and Future Work

In this paper we investigate whether deploying picture passwords on smartwatch devices embraces similar effects of human cognition towards users' interaction behavior and picture password security, as shown in previous studies in conventional interaction contexts [5, 18, 19]. For doing so, we adopted an accredited human cognition theory (Witkin's Field Dependence-Independence) and conducted a between-subjects in-lab user study ($n = 50$) in which participants composed a picture password that was deployed on a smartwatch device.

With regards to Points of Interests (PoI) selections and password composition time, results reveal consistent effects with previous studies, *i.e.*, FD users spend more visual exploration and password composition time than FI users [5, 18], and users tend to make selections based on generic PoI regions [32, 36]. On the counter side, results reveal opposite main effects with regards to picture password strength compared to the literature [19]. Specifically, in contexts where the visual field of interaction is larger (*i.e.*, desktop, mixed reality), FD users create stronger and more random passwords compared to FI users due to their holistic approach in visual information processing. However, when the interaction is held on smaller screen sizes such as smartwatch devices, an opposite effect is revealed given that small areas for visual exploration do not allow full deployment of holistic-type information processing streams and decision-making during picture password selection.

Limitations of the study are related to the fact that only one picture was used for composing the passwords with a specific complexity. Nevertheless, the picture was intentionally chosen based on its complexity, which included widely applied image semantics and points of interest (*i.e.*, scenery and real-life objects [33]). Furthermore, the study was run in a controlled in-lab setting, which might have affected the behavior of users. Nonetheless, we aimed to increase ecological validity by applying the picture password composition task in a real task-based scenario in which users created a picture password for accessing individual data on the smartwatch.

**Acknowledgements.** This research has been partially supported by the EU Horizon 2020 Grant 826278 "Securing Medical Data in Smart Patient-Centric Healthcare Systems" (Serums), the Research and Innovation Foundation (Project DiversePass: COMPLEMENTARY/0916/0182), and the European project TRUSTID - Intelligent and Continuous Online Student Identity Management for Improving Security and Trust in European Higher Education Institutions (Grant Agreement No: 2020–1-EL01-KA226-HE-094869), which is funded by the European Commission within the Erasmus+ 2020 Programme and the Greek State Scholarships Foundation I.K.Y.

# References

1. Nguyen, T., Memon, N.: Smartwatches locking methods: a comparative study. In: WAY 2017 Workshop at the Symposium on Usable Privacy and Security, USENIX (2017)
2. Harbach, M., De Luca, A., Egelman, S.: The anatomy of smartphone unlocking: a field study of android lock screens. In: ACM CHI 2016, pp. 4806–4817. ACM Press (2016)
3. Aviv, A., Gibson, K., Mossop, E., Blaze, M., Smith, J.: Smudge attacks on smartphone touch screens. In: USENIX Conference on Offensive Technologies (WOOT 2010), USENIX Association, pp. 1–7 (2010)
4. von Zezschwitz, E., De Luca, A., Janssen, P., Hussmann, H.: Easy to draw, but hard to trace?: On the observability of grid-based (un)lock patterns. In: ACM Conference on Human Factors in Computing Systems (CHI 2015), pp. 2339–2342. ACM Press (2015)
5. Belk M., Fidas, C., Germanakos, P., Samaras, G.: The interplay between humans, technology and user authentication: a cognitive processing perspective. Comput. Hum. Behav. 184–200 (2017)
6. Guerar, M., Verderame, L., Merlo, A., Palmieri, F., Migliardi, M., Vallerini, L.: CirclePIN: a novel authentication mechanism for smartwatches to prevent unauthorized access to IoT devices. ACM Trans. Cyber-Phys. Syst. 4(3), 1–19 (2020). https://doi.org/10.1145/3365995
7. Nguyen, T., Sae-Bae, N., Memon, N.: DRAW-A-PIN: authentication using finger-drawn pin on touch devices. Comput. Secur. 66, 115–128 (2017)
8. Guerar, M., Verderame, L., Migliardi, M., Merlo, A.: 2GesturePIN: securing PIN-based authentication on smartwatches. In: IEEE Conference on Enabling Technologies: Infrastructure for Collaborative Enterprises, pp. 327–333. IEEE (2019)
9. Nguyen, T., Memon, N.: Tap-based user authentication for smartwatches. Comput. Secur. 78, 174–186 (2018)
10. Oakley, I., Huh, J.H., Cho, J., Cho, G., Islam, R., Kim, H.: The personal identification chord: a four button authentication system for smartwatches. In: Asia Conference on Computer and Communications Security (ASIACCS 2018), pp. 75–87. ACM Press (2018)
11. Zhao, Y., Qiu, Z., Yang, Y., Li, W., Fan, M.: An empirical study of touch-based authentication methods on smartwatches. In: ACM Symposium on Wearable Computers (ISWC 2017), pp. 122–125 ACM Press (2017)
12. Yang, J., Li, Y., Xie, M.: MotionAuth: motion-based authentication for wrist worn smart devices. In: IEEE Conference on Pervasive Computing and Communication Workshops (PerCom Workshops 2015), pp. 550–555. IEEE (2015)
13. Lee, W., Lee, R.: Implicit sensor-based authentication of smartphone users with smartwatch. In: ACM Conference on Hardware and Architectural Support for Security and Privacy (HASP 2016), pp. 1–8. ACM Press, article 9 (2016)
14. Han, T., Hasan, K., Nakamura, K., Gomez, R., Irani, P.: SoundCraft: enabling spatial interactions on smartwatches using hand generated acoustics. In: ACM Symposium on User Interface Software and Technology (UIST 2017), pp. 579–591. ACM Press (2017)
15. Biddle, R., Chiasson, S., van Oorschot, P.: Graphical passwords: learning from the first twelve years. ACM Comput. Surv. 44(4), 41 (2012)
16. Zhao, Z., Ahn, G.J., Seo, J.J., Hu, H.: On the security of picture gesture authentication. In: USENIX Security Symposium (USENIX Security 2013), USENIX, pp. 383–398 (2013)
17. Paivio, A., Csapo, K.: Picture superiority in free recall: imagery or dual coding? Cogn. Psychol. 5(2), 176–206 (1973)
18. Fidas, C., Belk, M., Hadjidemetriou, G., Pitsillides, A.: Influences of mixed reality and human cognition on picture passwords: an eye tracking study. In: Lamas, D., Loizides, F., Nacke, L., Petrie, H., Winckler, M., Zaphiris, P. (eds.) INTERACT 2019. LNCS, vol. 11747, pp. 304–313. Springer, Cham (2019). https://doi.org/10.1007/978-3-030-29384-0_19

19. Katsini, C., Fidas, C., Raptis, G., Belk, M., Samaras, G., Avouris, N.: Influences of human cognition and visual behavior on password security during picture password composition. In: ACM Human Factors in Computing Systems (CHI 2018), p. 87. ACM Press (2018)

20. Ma, Y., Feng, J., Kumin, L., Lazar, J.: Investigating user behavior for authentication methods: a comparison between individuals with down syndrome and neurotypical users. ACM Trans. Access. Comput. 4(4), 1–27 (2013). https://doi.org/10.1145/2493171.2493173

21. Grindrod, K., et al.: Evaluating authentication options for mobile health applications in younger and older adults. PLoS ONE 13(1), e0189048 (2018)

22. Witkin, H., Moore, C., Goodenough, D., Cox, P.: Field-dependent and field-independent cognitive styles and their educational implications. Educ. Res. 47(1), 1–64 (1977)

23. Riding, R., Cheema, I.: Cognitive styles - an overview and integration. Educ. Psychol. 11(3–4), 193–215 (1991)

24. Peterson, E., Rayner, S., Armstrong, S.: Researching the psychology of cognitive style and learning style: is there really a future? Learn. Indiv. Differ. 19(4), 518–523 (2009)

25. Kozhevnikov, M.: Cognitive styles in the context of modern psychology: toward an integrated framework of cognitive style. Psychol. Bull. 133(3), 464–481 (2007)

26. Hong, J., Hwang, M., Tam, K., Lai, Y., Liu, L.: Effects of cognitive style on digital jigsaw puzzle performance: a gridware analysis. Comput. Hum. Behav. 28(3), 920–928 (2012)

27. Raptis, G.E., Katsini, C., Belk, M., Fidas, C., Samaras, G., Avouris, N.: Using eye gaze data and visual activities to infer human cognitive styles: method and feasibility studies. In: ACM User Modeling, Adaptation and Personalization (UMAP 2017), pp. 164–173 (2017)

28. Davis, J.: Educational implications of field dependence-independence. In: Field Dependence-Independence: Cognitive Style across the Lifespan, Lawrence Erlbaum, 149–175 (1991)

29. Johnson, J.J., Seixeiro, S., Pace, Z., van der Bogert, G., Gilmour, S., Siebens, L., Tubbs, K.: Picture Gesture Authentication (2014). https://www.google.com/patents/US8910253

30. Witkin, H.A., Oltman, P., Raskin, E., Karp, S.: A Manual for the Embedded Figures Test. Consulting Psychologists Press, Palo Alto, CA (1971)

31. Zhao, Z., Ahn, G., Hu, H.: Picture gesture authentication: empirical analysis, automated attacks, and scheme evaluation. ACM Trans. Inf. Syst. Secur. (TISSEC) 17(4), 1–37 (2015)

32. Constantinides, A., Fidas, C., Belk, M., Pietron, A.M., Han, T., Pitsillides, A.: From hotspots towards experience-spots: leveraging on users' sociocultural experiences to enhance security in cued-recall graphical authentication. Int. J. Hum. Comput. Stud. 149, 102602 (2021). https://doi.org/10.1016/j.ijhcs.2021.102602

33. Dunphy, P., Yan, J.: Do background images improve "Draw a Secret" graphical passwords?. In: Computer and Communications Security (CCS 2007), pp. 36–47. ACM Press (2007)

34. Raptis, G., Fidas, C., Avouris, N.: Effects of mixed-reality on players' behaviour and immersion in a cultural tourism game: a cognitive processing perspective. Int. J. Hum Comput Stud. 114, 69–79 (2018)

35. Katsini, C., Fidas, C., Raptis, G., Belk, M., Samaras, G., Avouris, N.: Eye gaze-driven prediction of cognitive differences during graphical password composition. In: ACM SIGCHI Intelligent User Interfaces (IUI 2018), pp. 147–152. ACM Press (2018)

36. Constantinides, A., Pietron, A., Belk, M., Fidas, C., Han, T., Pitsillides, A.: A cross-cultural perspective for personalizing picture passwords. In: ACM User Modeling Adaptation and Personalization (UMAP 2020), pp. 43–52. ACM Press (2020)

# Communicating Privacy: User Priorities for Privacy Requirements in Home Energy Applications

Lisa Diamond(✉) and Peter Fröhlich

AIT Austrian Institute of Technology, Giefinggasse 2, 1210 Vienna, Austria
lisa.diamond@ait.ac.at

**Abstract.** Perceived privacy plays a crucial role in the acceptance of technologies that rely on sensitive data. To mitigate concerns and build trust, privacy must not only be protected, but this protection should also be successfully communicated. Residential energy consumption data are at the center of applications that facilitate improved energy management and support a more sustainable future, but such data are privacy-sensitive since they have the potential to reveal a great number of details about the daily life of users. Our study contributes to an understanding of how to communicate energy data privacy via user interfaces by looking into the relevancy and accessibility priorities of potential privacy requirements in home energy monitoring, management, and production applications. All investigated requirements showed themselves to be of relevance to users, with control aspects (access, transfer, and deletion of data) being both perceived as most important and receiving the highest accessibility priority ratings, and control of data storage joining them as top access priority requirement. Our results indicate that placing the settings and information emphasized in our results prominently in the user interface, going through extra effort to ensure easy comprehensibility, and communicating them proactively, is likely to go a long way in successfully communicating privacy. Investigation of accessibility priority differences in relation to data storage location provided less clear answers but suggests a higher importance of access to general information on data collection if data are stored centrally and of the ability to view data if stored decentrally.

**Keywords:** Privacy requirements · Usable privacy · Smart grid

## 1 Introduction

Privacy is a sensitive issue for smart services and systems [1], which present a considerably larger risk for misappropriation or illegal access to personal information due to the continuous and often extensive data collection and data exchange between an ever-increasing number of connected devices [2]. Home Energy applications are prime suspects for privacy concerns because the energy usage data at their center can reveal a lot of details about the home life of end-users and can contain further user-related

© IFIP International Federation for Information Processing 2021
Published by Springer Nature Switzerland AG 2021
C. Ardito et al. (Eds.): INTERACT 2021, LNCS 12935, pp. 665–675, 2021.
https://doi.org/10.1007/978-3-030-85610-6_38

information such as name, billing number and account details. If users feel that their privacy is threatened when using a service or a product, they react, and acceptance suffers. This has already affected smart meter introduction negatively, leading to a significantly delayed smart meter roll-out in Denmark [3].

There is a strong awareness of potential privacy and security risks in the smart grid community that has prompted a multitude of work to develop appropriate protection mechanisms [4, 5]. But without successful communication of such protection to end-users the risk of diminished acceptance remains. Only if end-user privacy is not just established, but also successfully communicated and consequently experienced, can adverse emotional and business consequences be avoided, and the related products and services be realized to their full potential.

Research on how to communicate (and enable management of) privacy has covered a wide range of different tools, mechanisms and features including creative user interface design solutions for individual challenges [6], methods to raise disclosure awareness [7–9], and ways to reduce the cognitive load of users [10, 11]. However, to the best of our knowledge, there has not been a user requirements investigation looking at a comprehensive compendium of potential privacy features that could be communicated by a system to its users with regards to their comparative importance to users. Such information is, however, of great value to designers of smart services as it can serve as a guide for decisions such as which privacy features should receive special attention and be placed most prominently in the interface in order to communicate the protection of privacy to its users efficiently and effectively. Since interface space as well as human attention and cognition are limited it is important to make informed choices as to which content and features should be prioritized in terms of placement and active vs. passive communication.

In this paper, we present a questionnaire study that investigates people's preferences about privacy information and features that can be integrated into the user interfaces of home energy monitoring and management applications such as smart meters or smart home technologies and discuss practical implications of the results. Our guiding research questions were: Can all identified requirements be regarded as relevant and which ones are most important (RQ1), to what extent does perceived relevancy match desired accessibility (as in easy to locate) within the interface (RQ2) and are there differences regarding accessibility preferences depending on data storage location (RQ3).

## 2    Background and Literature Review

### 2.1    Privacy and the Smart Grid

The smart grid is heralded as the next generation of the electricity supply network, aiming to strengthen grid reliability, and prepare it for future needs [12]. Consumers are connected to the smart grid via smart meters which record energy usage data in short intervals of typically 15 min to 1 h [13]. Fed back into the grid, these consumption data can facilitate efficient network management, outage detection, mapping and restoration, asset management, load forecasting, and power quality monitoring, as well as open up opportunities of demand-side management through manual or automated load shifting [14].

Within the home of the consumer, the recorded energy usage data enables active end-user participation in several forms. Most directly, it allows home owners to monitor energy usage via smart meter portals, deepening a consumer's understanding of household energy usage patterns and facilitating their adjustment [15]. Other forms of use are within energy management systems or for prosumer technologies [16, 17]. Such uses can enable financial savings and provide an important contribution to a sustainable future - but they rely on the recording and transmission of energy consumption data.

For private consumers connected to the smart grid this means the collection, storage and transmission of vast quantities of personal data containing information on household energy usage. And with the collection of these data comes the risk of their abuse. Presence or absence of household occupants can be revealed and daily device usage and behavioral routines of users such as when somebody in a household ate and showered can be deduced [18, 19]. With sufficiently detailed consumption data and the appropriate comparison patterns it even becomes possible to derive which specific devices can be found in a household and which TV programs are watched [18–20]. Passwords, smart meter IP address, customer name and address, billing information, and bank account number are also at risk [18, 21, 22] and the opportunities for misappropriation of such information are manifold.

## 2.2 Energy Consumer Privacy Concerns and Needs

Not surprisingly, data privacy and security concerns are very much on the mind of users if they are asked to discuss their hopes and concerns around smart meters, their energy data, and applications relying on these data. In a large-scale study conducted by O$_2$ in the UK in 2013, 59% of the participants who did not want smart meters installed named privacy concerns as their most central concern [23] and the Boston Consulting Group reported 41–48% of their study participants to be concerned about privacy, security, and the disclosure of smart meter data to third parties [24]. A closer look at different aspects of such concerns show 49% to be worried about data accuracy, 38% about missing information on and control over data collection, access and use, and 36% about both illegal accessing of their data in order to use gained insights for targeted crimes, as well as the misappropriation of data obtained legally by the provider [25].

In the smart home context, perceived privacy risks are also a prevalent concern. Both Krishnamurti et al. [26] and Balta-Okzan et al. [27] list invasion of privacy and loss of control next to rising costs as the main concerns in the context of smart meters and smart homes. Paetz, Dütschke and Fichtner [16] name protection of privacy in smart homes as the most important concern of study participants independent of age.

Turning towards privacy requirements rather than concerns, being able to control one's energy consumption data oneself appears to be the most prominent requirement with study participants in a number of studies emphasizing the wish to have sole access and control of high granularity data [28], to be able to limit access and prevent the selling of data to third parties (90%), control the use of collected data (88%) and be able to access and potentially correct data (84%) [29]. Döbelt et al. [30] investigated consumer-driven energy data privacy concerns in Austria via an online survey and complementary focus groups and recommend based on their results that consumption data be stored as decentralized as possible, clear statements on which data are collected and how they are used, and the provision of access control mechanisms to consumers.

Consumer Futures [31] developed a "Privacy Charter", a document providing consumers with the most critical information surrounding smart meters with regards to privacy. This charter includes (1) information on what the data will be used for, (2) why these data are needed and how they differ from data currently collected, (3) who will be responsible for obtaining the data and keeping it safe, (4) which choices are available to consumers, (5) which consumer benefits are connected with data collection, and (6) where more information can be found. The study concludes that providing consumers with choices how data are collected and managed is critical, as well as giving context information, information on who can access data and whether consumers have a choice with regards to this. Further, it is important to reassure end-user about data security.

## 3 Methods

Based on the results of the literature research and current data protection guidelines such as the privacy protection guidelines published by the Institute of Standards and Technology (NIST) [22] and the new European General Data Protection Regulation (GDPR), a set of core privacy requirements was compiled. The list was evaluated via a small preliminary questionnaire study [32] and detailed further through a number of interviews with stakeholders from the energy sector and consumer representatives, as well as through end-user feedback collected in a focus group. Through this process we identified 21 distinct requirements (see Table 1 under *4* for the full list).

In order to answer our research questions, we conducted an online questionnaire study with 312 participants recruited via a panel and approximately representative of the Austrian population. It was composed as follows: 51.6% female, 48.4% male (gender); 13.7% 16–29 years, 19.2% 30–39 years, 25.3% 40–49 year, 19.9% 50–65 years, 11.9% 66+ years (age); 9.6% completed compulsory schooling, 43.9% an apprenticeship, 21.2% a technical/trade school, 15.4% high school and 9.9% university (educational level). Participants' technological affinity and general privacy concerns, measured with 3 items each adapted from existing instruments [33, 34] on a 5-point scale, were slightly above scale-average ($m = 3.44$ with $sd = 0.99$ and $m = 3.50$ with $sd = 0.78$, respectively), and they had very positive attitudes towards sustainable energy production and consumption ($m = 4.14$ with $sd = 0.93$) (3 items developed by the authors).

In the first part of the questionnaire, survey participants were introduced to home energy applications and the role of their energy consumption data within them. They were asked to rate the 21 final requirements with regards to their relevance for the communication of data privacy on a 5-point Likert scale ranging from *1 = not at all important* to *5 = very important*. In the second part of the questionnaire the respondents were presented with the task of sorting the previously introduced 21 privacy requirements within 4 prioritization categories concerning accessibility and visibility within the user interface. Category 4 was described as "*High priority: As accessible as possible within the user interface*", category 3 as "*Medium priority: Easily accessible but does not have to be directly visible*", category 2 as "*Low priority: Does not have to be particularly accessible*", and category 1 as "*Not relevant: I don't need this in the user interface at all*".

Participants were asked to sort the requirements twice under 2 different scenarios: Scenario 1 was described as a user interface for a service/product for which collected data would be stored and processed externally on a central server of the organization responsible (example: smart meter web portal). Scenario 2 was described as a user interface for a service/product for which collected data would be stored and processed locally or within a user-associated cloud storage (example: a smart home system with local data storage). Figure 1 shows a screenshot of the online card sorting task. There was no limit to the number of requirements per priority level.

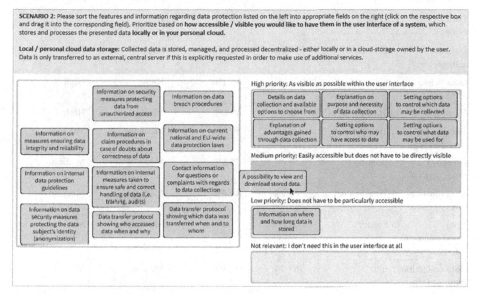

**Fig. 1.** Screenshot of the privacy requirement accessibility prioritization sorting task within online questionnaire; participants were asked to sort the different requirement cards according to desired accessibility in the appropriate field

# 4  Results

To verify internal consistency of the privacy requirements concept, Cronbach's alpha was calculated for the requirement scale and proved to be satisfying at *0.85*. To validate the relevancy of all presented requirements and answer RQ1, the percentage of participants rating a requirement as important with regards to privacy communication (rating 4 or 5 with 5 being "*very important*") was determined. All privacy requirements included in the questionnaire showed average ratings of above 50%. To determine which requirements were most important, the ones displaying a "top relevancy" with over 50% of the participants rating them with the highest score (5), were identified. Such "top requirements" are *Data Access Settings, Data Use Settings, Data Delete Settings,* and *Data Access Transparency.* All requirements showed statistically significant, very weak to weak positive correlations with age (ranging between *0.16* and *0.3, p < .05*) with the ones between age and availability of *Data Storage Settings, Data Delete Settings, Benefit Information, Claim Procedure Info* and *Contact Info* being the strongest at $r = 0.25$ or above. There were no statistically significant sex differences concerning perceived requirement relevancy.

**Table 1.** Privacy requirement relevancies and scenario-dependent accessibility priorities

| Privacy requirement | Requirement type | Relevancy | Top-relevancy | Access priority centr. | Access priority decentr. |
|---|---|---|---|---|---|
| Data access settings | Control | 75.0% | 58.0% | High | High |
| Data use settings | Control | 74.0% | 52.9% | High | High |
| Data delete settings | Control | 71.8% | 55.1% | High | High |
| View data | Transparency | 70.8% | 49.0% | Medium | High |
| Data access transparency | Transparency | 70.5% | 50.0% | Medium | Medium |
| Breach procedure info | Security | 70.2% | 45.5% | Medium | Medium |
| Data transfer transparency | Transparency | 69.9% | 48.4% | Medium | Medium |
| Data anonymization info | Security | 69.6% | 49.0% | Medium | Medium |
| Data collection purpose info | Info | 69.2% | 47.1% | Medium | Medium |
| Data security info | Security | 68.9% | 47.4% | Medium | Medium |
| Data safety and integrity info | Security | 68.3% | 43.9% | Medium | Medium |
| Contact info | Accountability | 66.3% | 43.6% | Medium | Medium |
| Claim procedure info | Accountability | 65.1% | 46.2% | Medium | Medium |
| Data storage settings | Control | 64.1% | 36.2% | High | High |
| Benefit information | Information | 63.8% | 35.9% | Medium | Medium |
| Data storage transparency | Transparency | 63.5% | 40.7% | Medium | Medium |
| Download data | Transparency | 60.3% | 37.5% | Medium | Medium |
| Data protection laws | Accountability | 59.3% | 34.9% | Low | Low |

(*continued*)

**Table 1.** (*continued*)

| Privacy requirement | Requirement type | Relevancy | Top-relevancy | Access priority centr. | Access priority decentr. |
|---|---|---|---|---|---|
| Internal data protection guidelines | Accountability | 55.1% | 31.4% | Low | Low |
| General information on data collection | Information | 54.8% | 34.6% | High | Medium |
| Other data protection measures | Security | 52.2% | 33.0% | Low | Low |

In order to answer RQ2, we looked at the accessibility priorities of each requirement based on the observed median according to the sorting performed by the participants. All presented requirements received medians above 1 in both scenarios (external and local data storage) and are therefore not only perceived as relevant but participants wanted to be able to access them via the system interface. Further, in both scenarios the control-related requirements, which were identified as top requirements via the relevancy ratings, also received top accessibility priority (md = 4). There were 2 noticeable differences: Data Storage Settings, the 4th control-related requirement, which did not receive a top-relevancy rating but was in the lower half of average relevancy ratings, did, however, receive top accessibility priority in both tested scenarios. Second, General Information on Data Collection, which displayed the 2nd-lowest average relevancy, was seen to be of high accessibility priority under centralized data storage conditions and medium priority under decentralized storage conditions. Further, Data Access Transparency was, despite its top relevancy ratings, not a top accessibility priority in either scenario.

Answering RQ3 required a detailed look at rating differences between the 2 storage scenarios. Differences concerning top accessibility priority with regards to storage location were observed in 2 requirements: *General Information on Data Collection* received a top accessibility priority sorting when data was stated as stored centrally but not when it was stated as stored locally. The *View Data* requirement showed the opposite. In a last step, we looked at statistically significant differences concerning top accessibility depending on storage location. Wilcoxon signed rank tests indicated significant sorting differences for 4 requirements (the familywise error rate was controlled with the Bonferroni-Holm correction): *Benefit information* ($Z = -2.61; p = .009$ with *alpha* = *.013*), *Data Transfer Transparency* ($Z = -2.92; p = .003$ with *alpha = 0.017*), *View Data* ($Z = -3.83; p = .000$ with *alpha = 0.05*) and *Download Data* ($Z = -3.41; p = .001$ with *alpha = 0.025*) all were sorted into a higher accessibility priority category more often, when data storage was described as decentralized/local. The detailed results of the findings reported above can be found above in Table 1.

## 5    Discussion and Conclusions

The results of this study give readers an insight into user priorities with regards to privacy features in Internet of Things applications processing energy usage data. Our results provide a systematic and formal confirmation of the relevancy of privacy aspects typically included in privacy protection plans – control, transparency, security, information and accountability – from an end-user perspective. They further show control related requirements to be most important for end-user privacy experience both in terms of perceived relevancy and required accessibility within the interface. To successfully communicate privacy, control-related information and setting options should therefore receive special attention by placing them more prominently in the user interface of energy management applications than is practice nowadays, assuring excellent usability use via user-centered design approaches, and communicating them more proactively.

Looking at the applicability of these findings, our results suggest that user interface designers for home energy management applications consider the following recommendations:

- Place the information and settings that received top accessibility (as in easy to locate) priority ratings – data storage, data access, data use and delete settings, as well as general information on energy data collection and a possibility to view data – in highly visible and accessible spots and stress their existence, e.g. via a privacy-related wizard or other approaches to inform end-users proactively. They should receive special attention during the developmental phase in order to ensure that they are comprehensible to end-users and that their implications are clear. They should be linked to all related spots and potentially proactively provided in relevant moments e.g. via "Just-In-Time-Click-Through Agreements" [47].
- Functions with medium prioritization such as information on security measures or breach procedures do not require quite as prominent spots – they should be easy to access but do not need to be actively "pushed" and, although comprehensibility is still important, do not need as many iterations and feedback-rounds. We would suggest placing them such that they can be easily located through a "further information and settings" link and inform end-users about them proactively once. Regarding transparency related requirements, visual data privacy diagrams [23] that allow access to more detailed information might be an attractive approach.
- Functions with low prioritization such as general and internal data protection guidelines should be accessible but do not need to be promoted to users – they just need to be "there" if someone is actively looking for them. It is also of less importance to optimize their comprehensibility as they are less likely to be perused in detail.

The differences in requirement prioritization between the two presented data storage scenarios were minimal, indicating that data storage location does not greatly affect which privacy requirements are deemed most important regarding accessibility. There does, however, seem to be a somewhat higher interest in transparency-related requirement accessibility under local data storage conditions. We interpreted this as increased interest in the data, potentially motivated through a stronger sense of "ownership" and suggest underlining data ownership through wording and visual cues that add a sense of confirmation in this regard to increase the privacy comfort levels of home owners.

Finally, we want to emphasize the importance of simplicity, efficiency and effort minimization in privacy communication. Our days are full and busy, there is already an overwhelming amount of information to constantly process and control is a "finite resource". Our data are processed everywhere – it is impossible to control all details and there comes a point where control becomes meaningless. We will need to find a middle road – a way to enable users to control their data without overwhelming them to a degree that they click through checkboxes without reading just to cope with the sheer amount of them. Tackling this challenge will be an interesting task for future research in this field and we hope that our findings can provide a contribution by clarifying what needs highlighting and what simply needs to be available if searched for, so that privacy can be communicated sufficiently without taxing end-user attention unnecessarily.

**Acknowledgements.** The work presented in this paper has received funding from the Austrian Research Promotion Agency FFG under grant agreement n° 848811 (RASSA).

# References

1. Hong, J.: The privacy landscape of pervasive computing. IEEE Perv. Comput. **16**, 40–48 (2017)
2. Chow, R.: The last mile for IoT privacy. IEEE Secur. Priv. **15**, 73–76 (2017)
3. Cuijpers, C., Koops, B.-J.: Smart metering and privacy in Europe: lessons from the Dutch case. In: Social Science Research Network, Rochester, NY (2013)
4. Ferrag, M.A., Maglaras, L.A., Janicke, H., Jiang, J., Shu, L.: A systematic review of data protection and privacy preservation schemes for smart grid communications. Sustain. Cities Soc. **38**, 806–835 (2018)
5. Uludag, S., Zeadally, S., Badra, M.: Techniques, taxonomy, and challenges of privacy protection in the smart grid. In: Zeadally, S., Badra, M. (eds.) Privacy in a Digital, Networked World. CCN, pp. 343–390. Springer, Cham (2015). https://doi.org/10.1007/978-3-319-08470-1_15
6. Jackson, C.B., Wang, Y.: Addressing the privacy paradox through personalized privacy notifications. In: Proceedings of the ACM on Interactive, Mobile, Wearable and Ubiquitous Technologies, vol. 2, p. 68 (2018)
7. Acquisti, A., et al.: Nudges for privacy and security: understanding and assisting users' choices online. ACM Comput. Surv. (CSUR) **50**, 44 (2017)
8. Patrick, A.S., Kenny, S.: From privacy legislation to interface design: implementing information privacy in human-computer interactions. In: Dingledine, R. (ed.) PET 2003. LNCS, vol. 2760, pp. 107–124. Springer, Heidelberg (2003). https://doi.org/10.1007/978-3-540-409 56-4_8
9. Raschke, P., Küpper, A., Drozd, O., Kirrane, S.: Designing a GDPR-compliant and usable privacy dashboard. In: Hansen, M., Kosta, E., Nai-Fovino, I., Fischer-Hübner, S. (eds.) Privacy and Identity 2017. IFIP AICT, vol. 526, pp. 221–236. Springer, Cham. (2017). https://doi.org/10.1007/978-3-319-92925-5_14
10. Kelley, P.G., Bresee, J., Cranor, L.F., Reeder, R.W.: A nutrition label for privacy. In: Proceedings of the 5th Symposium on Usable Privacy and Security, p. 4. ACM (2009)
11. Fox, G., Tonge, C., Lynn, T., Mooney, J.: Communicating compliance: developing a GDPR privacy label (2018)

12. Tuballa, M.L., Abundo, M.L.: A review of the development of smart grid technologies. Renew. Sustain. Energy Rev. **59**, 710–725 (2016). https://doi.org/10.1016/j.rser.2016.01.011
13. McKenna, E., Richardson, I., Thomson, M.: Smart meter data: balancing consumer privacy concerns with legitimate applications. Energy Policy **41**, 807–814 (2012). https://doi.org/10.1016/j.enpol.2011.11.049
14. Dütschke, E., Paetz, A.-G.: Dynamic electricity pricing—which programs do consumers prefer? Energy Policy **59**, 226–234 (2013). https://doi.org/10.1016/j.enpol.2013.03.025
15. Karlin, B., Zinger, J.F., Ford, R.: The effects of feedback on energy conservation: a meta-analysis. Psychol. Bull. **141**, 1205–1227 (2015). https://doi.org/10.1037/a0039650
16. Paetz, A.-G., Dütschke, E., Fichtner, W.: Smart homes as a means to sustainable energy consumption: a study of consumer perceptions. J. Consum. Policy **35**, 23–41 (2012)
17. Zafar, R., Mahmood, A., Razzaq, S., Ali, W., Naeem, U., Shehzad, K.: Prosumer based energy management and sharing in smart grid. Renew. Sustain. Energy Rev. **82**, 1675–1684 (2018). https://doi.org/10.1016/j.rser.2017.07.018
18. Cho, H.S., Yamazaki, T., Hahn, M.: AERO: extraction of user's activities from electric power consumption data. IEEE Trans. Consum. Electron. **56**, 2011–2018 (2010). https://doi.org/10.1109/TCE.2010.5606359
19. McDaniel, P., McLaughlin, S.: Security and privacy challenges in the smart grid. IEEE Secur. Privacy **7**, 75–77 (2009). https://doi.org/10.1109/MSP.2009.76
20. Cárdenas, A.A., Safavi-Naini, R.: Security and privacy in the smart grid. In: Handbook on Securing Cyber-Physical Critical Infrastructure, pp. 637–654. Elsevier (2012)
21. Molina-Markham, A., Shenoy, P., Fu, K., Cecchet, E., Irwin, D.: Private memoirs of a smart meter. In: Proceedings of the 2nd ACM Workshop on Embedded Sensing Systems for Energy-Efficiency in Building, pp. 61–66. ACM, New York (2010). https://doi.org/10.1145/1878431.1878446.
22. National Institute of Standards and Technology (NIST), U.S. Department of Commerce: Guidelines for Smart Grid Cyber Security, vol. 2, Privacy and the Smart Grid (NISTIR 7628r1). National Institute of Standard and Technology (NIST), U.S. Department of Commerce (2014)
23. O2: Effectively engaging consumers to ensure smart meter success (2013)
24. Seshadri, P., Barton, C., Manfred, K.: Capturing the value of smart meters (2010).www.bcgperspectives.com
25. Valocchi, M., Juliano, J.: Knowledge is power: driving smarter energy usage through consumer education. IBM Inst. Bus. (2012)
26. Krishnamurti, T., et al.: Preparing for smart grid technologies: a behavioral decision research approach to understanding consumer expectations about smart meters. Energy Policy **41**, 790–797 (2012). https://doi.org/10.1016/j.enpol.2011.11.047
27. Balta-Ozkan, N., Davidson, R., Bicket, M., Whitmarsh, L.: Social barriers to the adoption of smart homes. Energy Policy **63**, 363–374 (2013)
28. Wimberly, J.: Separating smart grid from smart meters? Consumer perceptions and expectations of smart grid. EcoAlign (2010)
29. Lundin, B.V.: Breaking down consumer privacy barriers. http://www.smartgridnews.com/story/breaking-down-consumer-privacy-barriers/2015-03-10. Accessed 14 Mar 2015
30. Döbelt, S., Jung, M., Busch, M., Tscheligi, M.: Consumers' privacy concerns and implications for a privacy preserving smart grid architecture—results of an Austrian study. Energy Res. Soc. Sci. **9**, 137–145 (2015). https://doi.org/10.1016/j.erss.2015.08.022
31. Consumer Futures, R.: Smart and clear. Customer attitudes to communicating rights and choices on energy data privacy and access (2014)
32. Diamond, L., Schrammel, J., Fröhlich, P., Regal, G., Tscheligi, M.: Privacy in the smart grid: end-user concerns and requirements. In: Proceedings of the 20th International Conference on Human-Computer Interaction with Mobile Devices and Services Adjunct, pp. 189–196 (2018)

33. Smith, H.J., Milberg, S.J., Burke, S.J.: Information privacy: measuring individuals' concerns about organizational practices. MIS Q. **20**, 167 (1996). https://doi.org/10.2307/249477
34. Karrer, K., Glaser, C., Clemens, C., Bruder, C.: Technikaffinität erfassen–der Fragebogen TA-EG. Der Mensch im Mittelpunkt technischer Systeme. **8**, 196–201 (2009)

# Designing Parental Monitoring and Control Technology: A Systematic Review

Zainab Iftikhar[✉] , Qutaiba Rohan ul Haq, Osama Younus, Taha Sardar, Hammad Arif, Mobin Javed, and Suleman Shahid

Lahore University of Management Sciences (LUMS), Lahore, Pakistan

**Abstract.** An increasing number of children around the world are spending a significant amount of time online today. Unfiltered access to the Internet exposes them to potential harms, which can have detrimental effects in the crucial stages of their life. Parental control tools play a vital role in empowering parents to regulate their children's Internet usage. In this work, we present a systematic review of literature on the design of these tools from the last decade, synthesize design guidelines proposed so far, identify gaps in the literature, as well as highlight future opportunities for the HCI community.

**Keywords:** Parental control tools · Privacy · HCI · Usable security · ICT4D

## 1 Introduction

As the world moves to digital solutions due to the outbreak of the COVID-19 pandemic [32,43], users including millions of young children are at an increased risk of threats of the online world [10]. As of July 2020, the global Internet penetration rate is 59%, i.e., 4.57 billion people [30]. Approximately 3.6 billion of these users actively use social media today [31]. Children and teenagers form one of the main user groups online, accounting for about one in three Internet users [4]. As the Internet becomes more accessible and affordable, more and more children from various parts of the world are going online, and for longer periods of time.

An estimated 1.5 billion children have access to the digital world today, and participate in a variety of online activities: taking classes online, playing games, and socializing with friends online. The Internet provides great learning and entertainment opportunities for the children, helping them develop an interest in various topics and online social experiences [9]. Children typically access Internet from a variety of devices, including laptops, tablets, gaming consoles, and smartphones. Access to personal devices, especially smartphones, changes when and where children go online, often providing them with a personalized, private, and unsupervised experience [4]. On average, 2 out of 3 children in Europe and Japan own a cellphone with 12 as the average age of acquisition [6]. Similarly, according to one survey conducted in the United States, 95% of the participating teens had access to a smartphone, and 45% of them were online

© IFIP International Federation for Information Processing 2021
Published by Springer Nature Switzerland AG 2021
C. Ardito et al. (Eds.): INTERACT 2021, LNCS 12935, pp. 676–700, 2021.
https://doi.org/10.1007/978-3-030-85610-6_39

'almost constantly'; 92% of them went online daily, and 71% used more than one social networking site [17]. The rate of smartphone usage is also increasing in the developing regions, with teens leading the way in smartphone ownership [71].

Unfortunately, these higher usage numbers also directly lead to higher potential risks ranging from cyberbullying and harassment on social media [1, 16], oversharing of personal information [58], chatting with strangers online, to exposure to inappropriate content online [23]. Parents play a crucial role in the safety of children online, and can employ a variety of strategies to protect their children from these risks [72]. A study involving 1,000 parents in the United States found that 55% monitored their teen's tech usage by limiting when and how they can be online, 39% used parental control tools to block, filter, and monitor their child's online activities on home computers, and 16% used parental tools on their child's mobile phone [15]. Similarly, another study found that half of the participating parents used parental control tools, content filters, or blockers [5]. The relatively moderate use of parental control tools is not surprising given that this technology can be overwhelming to understand, overly restrictive and highly invasive—creating a rift in parent-child relationship, or can be evaded by children without coming into parents knowledge [7, 33, 38].

This work seeks to understand and systematize the existing body of knowledge around the attitudes and perceptions of parents and children towards parental monitoring and control tools, as well as the existing work on the design of these tools. In the remainder of this section, we first provide background and related work, and then lay out our study aims and research questions.

## 1.1 Background and Related Work

Parental control technology is a technical mediation strategy employed by parents and caregivers to monitor, restrict, and filter the content their children can access online. Some solutions are moderate, providing filtering of pornographic content, but some tools take extreme forms, giving parents access to their child's SMS and call logs, which can potentially damage the parent-child relationship. Despite the increasing number of children exposed to online risks today, research on the design and analysis of parental control tools is limited. Below we summarize the existing literature reviewing work in this space.

A study conducted in 2015 by Fuertes et al. analysed some state-of-the-art parental control tools and measured their functionality, efficiency, usability, security, and accuracy, commenting little on the design and development of these tools [36]. Through their results, the authors established that parents do not use tools to safeguard their children from online risks and are unaware of the ways they can block content. However, the study reported these findings through a survey, as opposed to parents' interaction with the investigated tools, which can provide a qualitative view and deeper insights into the usability and user feedback on the design of the tools.

Other works, for instance, Pinter et al.'s review focused their research around the stakeholders, methodologies, and conceptual categories that make up the multidisciplinary field of adolescent online risks and safety [66]. The authors presented a structured review on the topic of adolescent online safety and risks, but did not focus on the existing parental control tools. Similarly, Guerrero et al.'s review on 'Parental Mediation', provided recommendations for parental mediation, such as: careful choice of appropriate content for children, setting time limits on digital media consumption, and constructive use of media instead of passive consumption [44]. Just like [66], the authors analysed the risks and implications of exposure of children to technology but did not review the existing tools and their design.

An overview of the existing adolescent online safety apps, and a study of user reviews of the apps were reported in [77] and [38,42] respectively, but the studies focused on the analysis of user reviews and did not take stock of the literature studying usability of the tools using an in-person research methodology, thereby missing the user participation view in the tools' evaluation. Further, these studies were limited to apps available on the Android Play store and tested on only one mobile device for the usability testing. Lastly, while Altarturi et al.'s bibliometric study on cyber parental control provided insights regarding the most influential research practices and a taxonomy of parental control tools based on the type of risk, parenting style, content, and filtering approach, the study did not incorporate analysis of underlying design frameworks and in-person research design [14].

## 1.2   Study Aims

Although researchers have explored adolescent online risks, children and parental perspectives on online risks and safety, and parental tech mediation, no prior work provides a holistic view of research on parental control tools: the users involved, the frameworks employed in designing them, and user feedback on these tools.

In our work, we systematize the body of knowledge around user perceptions and existing parental control tools, and attempt to understand the challenges and future research directions. In particular, we answer the following research questions:

- What are the user (both parents' and childrens') attitudes towards online risks and parental mediation strategies?
- What are the underlying frameworks and study designs employed in the design of existing parental control tools?
- What parental control tools have been designed in the context of HCI4D? (Human-Computer Interaction for Development (HCI4D) refers to research that focuses on maximising the usability of interactive tools designed specifically for under-served, under-resourced, and under-represented populations [21]).

Based on the above research objectives, we seek to develop an understanding of how parental control tools have been approached in HCI research on children's safety. We synthesize the existing literature and present guidelines on how researchers and designers can conduct their studies and design the emerging parental control tools, while valuing both stakeholders (i.e. parents and children).

We cover both stakeholder's perceptions (i.e. parents and children) in our work to study whether the current practices have been reflective of the needs of both population groups.

## 2   Literature Search Methodology

For the literature search, we followed the process proposed by Webster and Watson [76] (shown in Fig. 1). Our review focused on identifying studies focusing on parental control tools' design, usability, or impact, as well as studies covering behaviors and attitudes towards online/tech parental control, online/tech child safety or online/tech parental mediation.

### 2.1   Systematic Literature Search

Four digital libraries were identified for the search, namely: ACM Digital Library, IEEE Xplore, SpringerLink, and ScienceDirect, since they host a plenitude of interdisciplinary research on human factors in computing and technology, relevant to and reflecting our review scope. Search strings were formed for identifying publications relevant to our domain respective to each database. The following search string was used for the ACM Digital Library; slightly tweaked versions were used for the rest of the libraries respective to their search constraints:

```
(Parent* OR Teen* OR Adolescent* OR Child* OR Family) AND
(Security OR Privacy OR Risk OR Safety OR Usability OR Protection
OR Control OR Value* OR Ethic* OR Monitor* OR Mediate*) AND
(Online OR Internet OR App*)
```

The additional criteria (i.e., including terms on safety and privacy in the search string) was crucial to make the search results correspond to the review scope. Publication dates were limited to Jan 2010 – Jun 2020. This filter was added so that the included studies capture research from the last decade and are reflective of recent trends in this area. Also, the online risks today are paradigmatically similar to risks post-2010 [8,51]. We then proceeded to the next two steps proposed by Webster and Watson [76] for literature search.

### 2.2   Going Backward and Forward

After getting an initial pool of papers by applying the inclusion and exclusion criteria, we checked all the papers cited by the papers in our initial pool. We then identified relevant papers from this set, and added the ones not already present in the initial pool. This cycle was repeated until we stopped encountering newer relevant papers from the cited papers. Once we covered the backward search, we turned to identifying the papers which cited the papers in our initial pool. Here again, we added all the relevant papers which were not in the initial pool. This cycle was similarly repeated until we stopped encountering newer relevant papers.

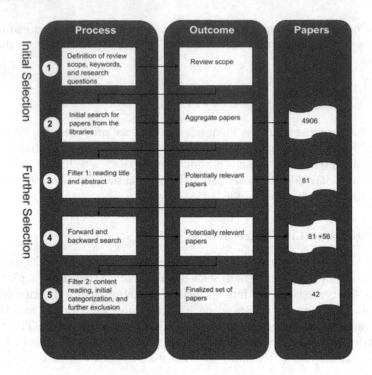

**Fig. 1.** Literature search process

## 2.3   Categorization of Literature

After classifying papers around study aims, methodology, and user groups, we identified a final set of 42 papers for analysis that aimed to inform the community about any aspect of parental control. Papers having common aims were further clustered into the following categories and sub-categories (n below represents the paper count in the respective category):

- Perceptions and attitudes towards online risks and parental control tools (n = 27)
  - What do parents think, want, and do about parental control tools?
  - What do children know, ask, and do about online risks and safety?
  - Predictors and effects of parental tech mediation
- Designing tools for online child safety (n = 15)

Each paper was then coded according to the study's aims, design, methodology, findings, limitations, and implications for the HCI community if any. The papers in the first category were coded by authors 3, 4, and 5 collaboratively, whereas authors 1 and 2 coded the second category. Authors 6 and 7 were consulted if there was any ambiguity in the relevance of the category or the relevance of the publication. The materials were studied in an iterative manner to identify the content of the publications reflective of our categories. After the coding process, the results were summarized in a tabular form.

As the final set of publications (n = 42) is relatively small, we did not perform a quantitative analysis, and instead proceeded with a narrative-based synthesis to systematize the current knowledge and highlight directions for future research.

# 3  Perceptions and Attitudes Towards Online Risks and Parental Control Tools

The literature contains 27 papers that study the perceptions and attitudes of different user groups (parents and children) towards parental control tools, and how they affect the parental mediation employed for online child safety. These papers along with main study characteristics are listed in Table 1. We provide a review of the main findings of these papers, as they provide the background crucial to the design of parental control tools.

## 3.1  What Do Parents Think, Want, and Do About Parental Control?

As parents want to get a view into their children's online activities to keep them safe [56], Ghosh et al. found more than half of the participants in their study used at least some kind of technical mediation on mobile phones of their teens [40]. Badillo et al.'s work corroborated this, and found that parents would rather prefer their child's safety over completely preserving their privacy [18]. Other works suggest that the needs and concerns of parents about their child's online safety are highly influenced by their parenting style [24,82].

A spectrum of parental mediation strategies exist, from active mediation (i.e. parents engaging in discussions with their children about their online activities) to deference (i.e. parents purposefully doing nothing to avoid conflict with their children) [62]. Therefore, 'safety' in the online context is an evolving concept, which requires a nuanced response from the parents to ensure a balance between risk prevention and child autonomy [47,68]. Some parents use restrictive strategies by setting rules for time, frequency, and location of use [46], while others deem open communication as the best strategy to mediate their child's Internet use [47,74]. Parents also feel that content control/monitoring tools are not very effective, as there will remain some part of children's online activities which they might not be able to monitor due to lower tech-literacy in comparison to their children [13,46,80]. Some parents also do not trust these applications as they think children can easily evade them [67,70]. Badillo et al. found that most parents in their interview-based study were also not aware that these solutions exist [18].

## 3.2    What Do Children Know, Ask, and Do About Online Risks And safety?

Parents and children differ in their perceptions, such as on social media, where parents tend to oversimplify teen's online experience, and children tend to hide certain aspects of their online lives from their parents. Studies found that for parents, privacy in the online and physical world was an identical concept; whereas children thought of privacy as different in these two environments [22,33].

According to Goh et al., children prefer that parents do not set up rules regarding the usage of devices; at maximum they would like to ask their parents before they use the devices [75]. While navigating the digital world, children also develop some strategies to manage privacy and security risks, but still like to rely on parents for support. However, per Kumar et al.'s study some parents only employ passive strategies to control their children and fail to adequately address the privacy and security risks [55]. Children also do not feel good when parents use strategies that at times hinder and jeopardize their privacy [81]. They fear privacy invasion more likely from household members, instead of strangers that they encounter on the Internet [81]. This should raise some concerns as Kumar et al. pointed out that children rely heavily on their parents for protection [55]. Children realise the need and significance of independence and parental trust in their online experiences for countering any threats [33]. They prefer applications which provide them with control and a secure, wholesome experience rather than ones that outright give complete control to their parents [19].

## 3.3    Predictors and Effects of Parental Tech Mediation

Low autonomy granting parents are more prone to opt for parental control tools [39]. This happens due to the scarcity of knowledge and expertise among parents to perform active mediation; hence they either go for stern restrictive measures or no measures at all. [65,79] support this notion. Studies emphasize that it is essential to educate parents about the latest applications and the Internet, their inherent risks, as well as proven strategies for online safety, in order to equip them to better handle the posed risks [45,78]. Moreover, studies recommend that restricting and limiting online experience is not the best way to protect children online as it has adverse effects and is less effective [78,79].

Active mediation might be the way forward in order to protect children from these risks [52,78]. Most parental monitoring tools promote the authoritarian parenting style where parents strictly monitor their children [39,78,79]. Authoritarian parenting is a parenting style characterized as low in responsiveness but high in demanding-ness [20]. These parents have exceedingly high expectations of their children and they may monitor almost every aspect of their child's life and behavior [28]. Unlike authoritarian parents, some parents adopt an authoritative parenting style where children are encouraged to explore and navigate their lives in an independent manner [28]. This parenting style is characterized by high in responsiveness and demanding-ness [28]. Studies advise that applications built on the idea of authoritative parenting should replace the current

**Table 1.** Study Design: *User Attitudes and Perceptions* category

| Study | Sample size | Study design | Population | Age | Location |
|---|---|---|---|---|---|
| Yardi et al. [80] | 16 | Interviews | Parents | – | US |
| Broekman et al. [24] | 591 | Survey Interviews | Parents | Mean = 41 | Netherlands |
| Zimmer et al. [82] | 60 | Interviews Questionnaire | Parents | – | Germany |
| Hartikainen et al. [47] | – | Discourses Survey | Parents Children Teachers | – | Finland |
| Symons et al. [74] | 34 | Interviews | Parents | Mean = 44 | Belgium |
| Ghosh et al. [40] | 215 | Survey | Parent-teen pairs | | US |
| Kuzminykh et al. [56] | 10 | Self-reports Semi-structured Interviews | Parents | 32–50 | Canada |
| Nouwen et al. [62] | 20 | Interviews Workshops | Parents Corporate Stakeholders | – | Belgium |
| Hamade et al. [46] | 152 | Questionnaire | Parents | – | Kuwait |
| Alqahtani et al. [13] | 60 | Survey | Parent-child pairs | – | Saudia Arabia |
| Badillo-Urquiola et al. [18] | 29 | Interviews | Parents | – | US |
| Ringland et al. [68] | – | Digital Ethnography Semi-structured interviews | – | – | US |
| Schiano et al. [70] | 472 | Survey Follow Up Interviews | Parents | Median = 41 | US |
| Nouwen et al. [63] | 11 | Interviews | Parents | – | Belgium |
| Prasad et al. [67] | 29 | Interviews Focus Groups | Parents | Parents (31–60) | US |
| Zhang-Kennedy et al. [81] | 14 | Interviews | Parent-Child pairs | Children (8–11) Parents (21 - 50) | Canada |
| Kumar et al. [55] | 18 | Interviews | Parents and children | Children (5–11) | US |
| Cranor et al. [33] | 10 | Semi-structured Interviews | Parents and teenagers | Children (14–18) | US |
| Blackwell [22] | 42 | Semi-structured Interviews | Parent and children | Children (10–17) | US |
| Badillo-Urquiola et al. [19] | 12 | Semi-structured Interviews | Children | Children (7–11) | US |
| Ghosh et al. [39] | 215 | Survey | Parent-Child Pair | Children (13–17) Parents (>25) | US |
| Padilla-Walker et al. [65] | 276 | Interviews | Mother-child pairs | – | US |
| Wisniewski et al. [79] | 12 | Semi-structured interviews | Parent-Child pairs | Children (13–17) | US |
| Wisniewski et al. [78] | 588 | Survey | Parent-Child pairs | Teens (Mean = 15) Parents (Mean = 47) | US |
| Gomez et al. [45] | 39K | Survey | Children | Children (12–17) | Spain |
| Khurana et al. [52] | 629 | Survey | Parents and children | Children (12–17) | US |
| Padilla-Walker et al. [64] | 478 | Interviews Questionnaires | Families | Children (11–15) | US |

apps which cater to the authoritarian style [39, 78, 79]. In fact, these applications might have a far higher user base and would push parents towards using an authoritative parenting style, which brings positive reinforcements in children while being more effective [39, 64].

# 4    Designing Tools for Online Child Safety

A set of fifteen papers propose parental control and monitoring tools or their technical components. We further categorize these into two classes based on whether they include a user study. The first set, i.e., publications with tool design and no user study, shown in Table 2, contains eight papers and suggests that developers tend to focus on direct parental monitoring or automatic content control when developing a tool. Most tools such as   [11, 29, 34, 54, 59, 61] enhance monitored or automatic content control of children's online activities, taking little account of children's agency and perceptions around online threats and parental monitoring. One study mentions incentive based parental control model and suggests blockchain technology to implement it [73]. Another study discovered flaws in the YouTube interface and suggested some features to counter the existing vulnerabilities that allow access to inappropriate content [25].

**Table 2.** Study Characteristics: *Tool Design with No User Study* category

| Author (year) | Study purpose | Tool name | Tool purpose | Target audience | Target threat |
|---|---|---|---|---|---|
| Mugni (2019) | To determine basic information about sites that are most frequently visited by children and implement an internet screening program | DNSBL | Content filtering on social networks | Children | Exposure to inappropriate content |
| Suchaad (2018) | To apply blockchain as a form of disciplining children | - | Encourage good behavior and discourage bad behavior | Children | Online risks and third party privacy issues |
| Fahrnberger (2014) | To propose a framework for protecting children's communication channel for obnoxious sources | SafeChat | Content | Children | Exposure to inappropriate content |
| Noor (2012) | To propose a parental mobile control system for monitoring children's online activities | Parental Mobile Control | Capture, detect and block harmful content | Children | Exposure to inappropriate content |
| Kumar (2016) | To propose a real-time software against pornography by MATLAB and SQL queries | Protection Against Pornography | To protect against pornographic content | Parents | Exposure to pornographic content |
| Majchrowicz (2018) | To demonstrate that it is possible to build a parental control system by rooting a Samsung Smart TV | Prototype | To control a TV remotely and apply parental controls to it | Parents | Children watching TV without permission or viewing inappropriate content |
| Chiu (2019) | To propose a reliable defensive architecture against inappropriate websites | Network Guardian Angels (NGA) | Identify and block inappropriate websites. The tool also puts time limit on internet use | Taiwanese students | Exposure to inappropriate content |
| Buzzi (2011) | To discuss the effectiveness of Youtube user interface for signaling inappropriate content | – | – | Children | Accessing inappropriate content by accident |

The second set of studies includes publications with a tool design and a corresponding user interaction study. We review this sub-category in detail to present a picture of which user populations have been represented in the literature for designing tools and studying their usability. We summarize the user samples and tool characteristics in Table 3, and discuss them below:

**Table 3.** Study Characteristics: *Tool Design with User Study* category

| Author (year) | Study purpose | Sample characteristics | Tool design | Main findings |
|---|---|---|---|---|
| Yasmeen (2014) | To introduce a new approach towards content filtering by involving children and focusing on child involvement and education rather than control | **Sample size:** N = 13 sets of family <br> **Population type:** Parents and children <br> **Age:** Parents of 6–8 year olds <br> **Location:** Canada <br> **Data collection:** In-person research (interviews) <br> **Type of data collected:** Participants impressions of the We Choose prototype <br> **Incentive:** Parents received a $10 gift card and children received a toy | **Tool name:** We-Choose <br> **Purpose:** Facilitates an educational approach to control by involving children in the filtering process <br> **OS:** Android <br> **Accessibility:** Android app <br> **Target population:** 6–8 year old age group <br> **Target threat:** Exposure to inappropriate content <br> **Design Framework:** - | **Usability:** Participants' perspectives: Parents found the collaborative approach as an effective way to engage in conversations with their children. Children were not as vocal as their parents but overall, they enjoyed working with their parents in setting the content control <br> **Design guidelines:** Visual indicators for content types and their appropriateness can help the parents in setting filters. Child friendly representations such as color schemes should also be explored |
| Ghosh (2020) | To design a new approach to mobile online safety and evaluate its strengths and weaknesses | **Sample size:** N = 17 parent-child pairs <br> **Population type:** Parents and children <br> **Age:** Parents of teens 9–17 <br> **Location:** USA <br> **Data collection:** In-person research (interviews), surveys, observational notes <br> **Type of data collected:** Likert scale survey, how parents and children interact with one another and the app <br> **Incentive:** $20 gift card for a pair for stage 1, $30 for stage 2 | **Tool name:** Circle of Trust <br> **Purpose:** Lets parents and children co-mediate the text messaging (i.e., SMS and MMS) activity that takes place via the child's phone <br> **OS:** Android <br> **Accessibility:** Android app <br> **Target population:** Parents and children <br> **Target threat:** Exposure to risky messages and strangers <br> **Design Framework:** Value sensitive design | **Usability:** Participants' perspectives: Parents and children preferred Circle of Trust as compared to baseline app since it was designed for the values of teen privacy, trust and parental control. Participants found the app less privacy invasive and beneficial for parent-child relationship <br> **Design guidelines:** Value sensitive design and Participatory design sessions need to be employed for designing mobile online safety |

(continued)

**Table 3.** (*continued*)

| Author (year) | Study purpose | Sample characteristics | Tool design | Main findings |
|---|---|---|---|---|
| McNally (2018) | To understand children's perceptions by analysing their feedback on an existing parental mobile monitoring application | **Sample size:** N (1) = 12 for tool evaluation, N (2) = 8 for feature design **Population type:** Children **Age:** 7–12 **Location:** University of Maryland's KidsTeam **Data collection:** Co-design sessions: 1. Survey and Feature re-design 2. Paper prototyping **Type of data collected:** The extent to which children find parental tools appropriate and what features do they desire **Incentive:** - | **Tool name:** TeenSafe **Purpose:** Monitor and restrict what children can do on their phones **OS:** - **Accessibility:** - **Target population:** Parents and teenagers **Target threat:** Exposure to harmful places, strangers, inappropriate content **Design Framework:** - | **Usability:** Participants' perspectives: Children accepted some parental controls. Monitoring location was accepted by 84% (10/12) and search history was accepted by 75% (9/12). However, after the second stage of design session, it was showed that while children accept some parental controls, they have a desire of privacy in their digital activities |
| Ko (2015) | To discuss how participatory parental mediation can overcome restrictive and invasive approaches | **Sample size:** N (1) = 4 families for design testing, N (2) = 12 families (17 parents and 18 teenagers) for app evaluation **Population type:** Families **Age:** Parents (40–60), Children (Average: 16.39) **Location:** Korea **Data collection:** Group interview for Stage 1, Within-subject experiment for Stage 2 **Type of data collected:** Usage experience for Stage 1, Changes in parental mediation of smartphone use after introducing FamiLync for Stage 2 **Incentive:** $50 card for Stage 1 | **Tool name:** FamiLync **Purpose:** Considers use-limiting as a family activity and provides a public space for parents and teens to have social awareness and improve self-regulation **OS:** - **Accessibility:** - **Target population:** Families **Target threat:** Excessive usage of smartphones **Design Framework:** Persuasive System Design | **Usability:** Participants' perspectives: Members of the family became aware of their usage patterns with FamiLync's self-monitoring support. Smartphone usage were significantly reduced improving parent-child interactions **Design guidelines:** Study adopts iterative prototyping with field evaluations for their parental control service. Designing for abstraction of content and hiding private details would assist in participatory parenting |

(continued)

**Table 3.** (*continued*)

| Author (year) | Study purpose | Sample characteristics | Tool design | Main findings |
|---|---|---|---|---|
| Hundlani (2017) | To design, develop and explore the feasibility of a parent-child authentication mechanism | **Sample size:** N (1) = 20 for prototype 1, N (2) = 20 for prototype 2, N(3) = 30 for prototype 3 <br> **Population type:** Parents and children <br> **Age:** Children aged 7–11 <br> **Location:** Canada <br> **Data collection:** Pre-test interview, Prototype testing, Post-test interview <br> **Type of data collected:** User feedback on current online practices and their experience with the prototypes <br> **Incentive:** - | **Tool name:** KinderSurf <br> **Purpose:** To allow children to log in to website without requiring a password and enabling parents to authorize the login request <br> **OS:** - <br> **Accessibility:** - <br> **Target population:** Children aged 7–11 <br> **Target threat:** Exposure to non-permissive websites <br> **Design Framework:** Iterative design | **Usability:** Participants' perspectives: Participants thought that such a tool is necessary, however many parents wanted additional parental control features, beyond the scope of an authentication mechanism while others thought that even this mechanism is too invasive for a child's privacy <br> **Design guidelines:** Iterative design can help developers with recognizing and correcting flaws in their prototypes, gather additional requirements making the system more usable. Children are more likely to give feedback on a prototype rather than in an interview |
| Belanger (2011) | To describe the design of an automated tool for protecting children's online privacy | **Sample size:** N = 25 user responses <br> **Population type:** Parents and children <br> **Age:** Parents with children under the age of 13 <br> **Location:** - <br> **Data collection:** Online survey <br> **Type of data collected:** Measures of ease of use, perceived behavioral control, cost benefits <br> **Incentive:** - | **Tool name:** POCKET <br> **Purpose:** Allows parent to control access <br> **OS:** Windows XP <br> **Accessibility:** Microsoft IE <br> **Target population:** Parents, merchant website owners <br> **Target threat:** Exposure of personal information <br> **Design Framework:** Multiple design frameworks researched in Decision Support System | **Usability:** The tool developed after acquiring requirements from parents through focus group was evaluated using white and black box testing. The system was easy to use and met the needs of the parents <br> **Design guidelines:** The study follows the design methodologies from decision science literature, not explicitly naming any |

(continued)

**Table 3.** (*continued*)

| Author (year) | Study purpose | Sample characteristics | Tool design | Main findings |
|---|---|---|---|---|
| Santisarun (2015) | To design and implement a mobile application that will enable parents in monitoring their children's activities on social networks | **Sample size:** N = 20<br>**Population type:** Parents and children<br>**Age:** -<br>**Location:** Thailand<br>**Data collection:** -<br>**Type of data collected:** Application's experiences<br>**Incentive:** - | **Tool name:** -<br>**Purpose:** Helps parents monitor their child's activities on social networks to foresee threats<br>**OS:** Android<br>**Accessibility:** Android app<br>**Target population:** Parents<br>**Target threat:** Inappropriate activity on social media<br>**Design Framework:** - | **Usability:** Participants' perspectives: 18/20 parents were satisfied with the application and its ease of use for generation X and early generation Y |

**User Study Characteristics:** All seven studies involved the end-users in either the design or evaluation of a parental control tool. This involvement was either in the form of in-person research where authors conducted interviews and surveys, or they held design sessions with participants for consistent feedback on prototypes and updated requirements. The studies incorporated value-sensitive design, iterative design, and general feedback to guide the development and/or evaluation of the tool. Out of the 7 studies, 2 were based in Canada, 2 in the USA, 1 in Korea, and 1 in Thailand. Our systematic search revealed only one study that was based in the third world [69]. The participants in all the studies, except for one, involved parents and children whereas McNally et al. [60] conducted their study only with children. All of the studies had a sample of fewer than 100 participants. Six of the studies designed a tool whereas one study evaluated an existing tool. Six studies involved parents and children in their user study whereas one study only included children to guide the design of the tool. One study tested three in-sequence prototypes for their tools.

**Parental Control Features:** Of the 7 studies reviewed, 4 involved tools for participatory mediation between parents and their children suggesting alternative approaches to restrictive parental control whereas 3 studies delegated all monitoring authority to parents. The studies focusing on participatory mediation valued child privacy, trust between parents and their children, education, and self-awareness. 5 out of the 7 papers proposed an Android application for regulating children's Internet usage. One study focused on website login safety. None of the studies catered to the development of a cross-platform tool.

*Features Supporting Parent-Child Collaboration:* Hashish et al. designed an Android application that included children in the design process for giving them more authority in setting content control filters [48]. The application was designed aligning with the Positive Youth Development framework [27] to demonstrate that educating youth about the opportunities, norms, and risks can help them in making good decisions about their safety as compared to restricting them. This is also beneficial for parents as the novel approach encourages healthy communication between parents and children. Through interviewing parents, the authors found out that parents did not employ software-based control solutions, except using passwords, due to their difficulty of use, a finding also supported by Ko et al. [53].

Based on these findings, the authors in [48] designed an application to facilitate an educational parent-child session on the appropriateness of the content, opening opportunities for dialog between the parties. Just as Hashish et al. [48], Ghosh et al. [41] conducted a within-subjects experimental design with parents and children to evaluate their novel approach to online mobile safety. Through the Value Sensitive Design framework – a framework to design systems accounting for human values [35], they aimed for designing an Android application empowering teen privacy, trust, and parental involvement. For keeping their application teen-centric, they employed: (i) less granular activity monitoring, (ii) avoiding features that restrict teens' online behavior, (iii) self-monitoring techniques to increase the self-awareness of teens, and (iv) appraisals for teens and parents to work together towards risk identification and how to respond to them.

Similarly, Ko et al. [53] also centered their application on family values developing a participatory parental control service. By conducting an online survey, they found that 77.14% participants had concerns with their children's smartphone usage which led them to mediate their child's phone (78.10%). Most of these parents relied on restrictive rule-setting to regulate usage. A substantial fraction of parents (27.95%) complained that they found parental controls effective but had difficulties in installation and maintenance. This led the authors to design for self-regulation and goal-based use-limiting, encouraging both populations to understand each other's behaviors. The tool lets family members share their smartphone usage but abstracts the representation of content hiding private details assisting in participatory parenting.

*Features Supporting Parental Authority and Control:* In contrast to the above studies, McNally et al. conducted design sessions with children on an existing app called TeenSafe [60]. Participants surveyed 10 features of this application, of which 7 were based on monitoring while the rest of the 3 were based on restriction. A trend was noticed where children's acceptance decreased as the features became more privacy invasive. Another thing noticed was that the redesigned features by children incorporated active mediation although no surveyed features had any sort of active mediation. Supporting the previous studies' findings, children in this study also wanted the applications to support parent-child communication.

In contrast, Hundlani et al.'s proposed mechanism puts everything in the hands of the parents [49]. Their mechanism takes the burden of creating and managing passwords from children and puts this responsibility upon parents. They offered features such as parents receiving a request to grant approval each time the child decides to log in. It was up to the parents whether they wanted to configure the app in a way where it would automatically perform the action according to the predefined rules or whether they want to approve it manually every time. It also provides parents with the power to register new devices on behalf of their children and manage and register new accounts. Parents also have access to the login history of their children. Additionally, they can set up rules on both per child and per website basis. It is also the choice of parents if they want to create a master password for children.

Another approach along these lines was proposed by Santisarun et al. [69]. They designed an application which gives parents the power to observe and control what children do on social media. They aimed to let parents monitor all the activity, and edit or delete the comments and photographs they did not deem fit to be posted. They built a mock up social media application closely mirroring Facebook's functionalities.

Just as Santisarun et al. [69] and Hundlani et al. [49], Belanger et al. also created an application centered around parental authority [26]. Their tool, POCKET, was created to enforce COPPA (Children's Online Privacy Protection Act) while being easy to use simultaneously, so that parents are able to set up their controls. The app also maintained a log for each website it interacted with. Initially a mock up was designed and then opinion was sought from parents about the design. These opinions were then synthesized to come up with requirements.

**User Acceptability:** Most of the studies reported positive feedback from parents. Findings from Hashish et al. [48] and Ghosh et al. [41] demonstrated that parents like the teen-centric approach for parental control measures as well. They were aware of their children's needs for privacy and trust and encouraged tools that highlighted these values. Hundlani et al. [49] had a similar finding where although most parents wanted monitoring features beyond simple authentication, some thought that even this is too invasive for their teens. Belanger et al.'s [26] designed tool POCKET is the only app which mentions that it was found to be user friendly and this is an important decisive factor for choosing an app when it comes to parents who are not tech savvy. This study also highlighted that designing is as important as the end product.

Children also seemed to like applications designed for online safety with features of monitoring and autonomy. For instance, McNally et al.'s findings revealed that participants acknowledged that they faced risks while being online and accepted that there is a need for involvement of parents [60]. However, they maintained that parents should only be able to control to a certain degree and privacy of children should not be invaded, at least directly. They only found certain kinds of monitoring to be acceptable and argued for the need of privacy to carry out their activities. The findings from all studies highlights that although there are differences between the views of parents regarding how much to control and the ways to control, the demand of children is almost always to acknowledge their need for privacy and adopt strategies which invade their privacy as passively as possible.

## 5   Discussion

### 5.1   Designing Tools for Online Child Safety

Our research resulted in very few studies that have involved users in the design, development, and evaluation of a tool. To the best of our knowledge, this systematic review is the first one to provide an index for existing literature on parental control tools and user perceptions. It also serves as a guide to help with the design, development, and analysis of these tools. This guide is based on an in-depth analysis of design practices and in-person researches described in the included studies.

**Designing for Users:** Children mostly find parental control tools invasive and damaging to their relationship with their parents [12,53].

Authoritative measures also hinder their personal growth and self-resilience. Our findings suggest that although the risks and threats online are immense and dangerous, authoritative and restrictive measures are not the best option for keeping the children safe. Adults will have to strike a balance between trust, involvement, and control. Instead of restricting and stalking their children, they will have to use active measures of educating their child about the security and privacy threats online. This can be achieved by designing tools that strike a balance between self-regulation and parental control. Findings from Hashish et al. [48] and Ghosh et al. [41] demonstrated that parents like the teen-centric approach for parental control measures as well. They were aware of their children's needs for privacy and trust and encouraged tools that highlighted these values. Hundlani et al. had a similar finding where although most parents wanted monitoring features beyond simple authentication, some thought that even this is too invasive for their children [49].

Studies also showed that although parents are aware of these tools, they do not use them, as they find them hard to understand and operate. Through their explanatory study, Hashish et al. showed that although parents are aware of software-assisted control, they seldom use it because of their difficulty in operation and the overhead of configuration [48]. Ko et al. also conducted a survey where they found that parents find it difficult to install and maintain parental control apps on their children's smartphones [53]. This opens room for approaching parental control tools with participatory design by involving all stakeholders.

**Designing for Usability and Effectiveness:** Even though these tools have a low adoption rate and parents seldom use and operate them [15], little to no researchers have opted for usability testing in their studies as guided by a previous systematic review [50]. Almost no information is present on the user experience and effectiveness of these tools. None of the user studies reviewed were conducted in the field, which could have provided more accurate results on the usability and effectiveness of the developed tools.

We recommend that future work needs to be conducted that develops a parental control tool by following certain criteria: (i) user-friendly, i.e., the tool must be easy-to-use for the target population, (ii) usability, i.e., the tool must cater to the needs of the end-users: children (iii) privacy, i.e., the tool should be non-intrusive towards the child's privacy, and (iv) content and functionality, i.e., the tool should explore features of teen self-regulation and awareness. Although we identified studies that dealt with the tool's functionality and content in-depth [11,29,34,54], the studies did not present information about the design framework that was adopted or shed light on user experiences. A testing framework needs to be conducted to provide quantitative data on the usability of the tool.

**Designing for Inclusion:** Our search for relevant tools and user interaction revealed scarce research in low literate countries. The existing literature did not highlight the needs and requirements of a low literate user population group when it comes to designing for teen's online safety. Although Belanger's application, POCKET, was designed for technologically unsophisticated parents, more research is needed in the area of designing and developing parental control tools to cater to the needs of a non-tech savvy and low literate population, which will likely not adopt these tools if they involve configuration and maintenance overheads [26]. In addition to this, tools need to be designed for children in third world countries as well. Statistics show that more and more children, estimated to be around 100 million from Africa and South-East Asia, and 2 million from developing countries worldwide are connecting to the Internet for the first time. Without adequate parental control measures exploring educational and safety approaches for the less literate, the world's most disadvantaged children will face greater risks when exposed to the risks online [4].

## 5.2  Design Implications and Future Research

Another aim of our systematic review was to provide design insights for future parental control tools from the perspectives of both end-users: parents and children. We discovered that parents face multiple but interlinked challenges regarding parental control tools. These ranged from a lack of awareness about these tools [63] to difficulty in keeping up with rapidly changing technological trends [33,70], to lack of ease in using the tools [48], to installation and maintenance problems [53]. Children found these tools are useless, invasive, easy to evade [47], and damage their relationship with their parents. Our literature synthesis helped us identify the following design guidelines that researchers and designers can incorporate to cater to both user populations as one unit of family instead of individuals with different values.

- **Flexibility for Different Parenting Styles, Age, and Context:** Parental control applications need to be flexible and support different styles of parenting so that parents are able to alter the restrictions and strictness according to different factors such as age, context, and parenting styles [39,41,47,53,57].
- **Education of Children about Online Dangers:** Parental control applications need to facilitate the education of children in regards to the risks posed as well as dangerous behaviors which could potentially put them in the harm's way [19,47,48,60,67]. Along these lines, interfaces should be designed to visually emphasize situations of risk so that users may be warned [19].
- **Children as Design and Communication Partners:** Children need to be included in the designing and decision-making process of the applications built for their safety, and parents need to talk to their children and negotiate and discuss the online activities and the restrictions being placed along with the reasons [19,47,48,63,79].
- **Teen Privacy and Self-Regulation:** Parental control applications need to be more respectful of children's privacy and incorporate features that empower teens to self regulate themselves, or the application itself is able to automatically monitor children while parents only get the data which is abstract and does not invade the privacy of children [19,41,47,53,60,67,79].
- **Usability and Education of Parents on Tool Use:** Parental control applications should be built keeping in mind the ease of use and capabilities of parents as well as their desires, and should work towards educating parents

about how to configure these tools as well as about the online risks posed to their children [19, 53, 63, 74, 79].

Future design must take into account the variables for effective parental control tools, which would not disturb the parent-child relationship. However, the present insights are guided by studies conducted in developed world, as shown in Table 3. Our research for existing literature on the design of parental control tools in the low-literate world produced only two studies [36, 69], which implies that even though Internet usage is increasing in these regions [2, 3], little to no studies are focusing on the population's needs for children's safety in the low literate world. The design insights mentioned above might not be applicable to the low literate world where one in four people is unable to read a sentence [37]. Future research should specifically explore the user requirements and needs of this population group. In addition to this, the design insight *Flexibility for Different Parenting Styles, Age, and Context* highlights a contradiction in literature on the design of parental control tools. Despite the current research discouraging the design of tools based on authoritarian parenting style, some studies have advocated for customization of parental controls that can address different parenting styles [39, 57]. Further work needs to be conducted, especially in different cultural contexts, in order to resolve this conflict and identify a concrete guideline for designers.

Our systematic literature search also revealed little to no studies on cross-platform tools designed for online safety. We were unable to find any work that studies or designs a cross-platform tool with a user study. As stated in Table 3, five of the of the seven studies involving user interaction with a parental control proposed an Android application whereas one study designed a mechanism for permission to website login. This opens room for future designers to include end-population as design partners for cross platform tools, as parents tend to manage multiple devices of their children: laptops, smartphones, and gaming consoles.

## 6   Conclusion

In this study, we conducted a systematic review including 42 publications analyzing parents' and children's perceptions, as well as the design of parental control tools. Through our review, we found that the low adoption rate of parental control tools is because parents find these tools difficult to install, use, and maintain. Studies on children's perspective show that they find these tools to be invasive and damaging to the parent-child relationship, and can be evaded if tried. Little to few studies employ any usability framework to quantify their tool's usability. Existing parental control tools focus on automatic content control or direct parental monitoring. Even though studies have confirmed that parents find existing parental control tools hard to operate, hardly any works cater to the needs of the non-tech savvy population, especially in the low literate world. Our review identified such gaps in the literature, and also presented guidelines for future researchers and designers on the design of parental control tools.

# References

1. Cyberbullying statistics. https://internetsafety101.org/cyberbullyingstatistics
2. Ict facts and figures (2017). https://www.itu.int/en/ITU-D/Statistics/Documents/facts/ICTFactsFigures2017.pdf
3. Measuring digital development facts and figures (2019). https://www.itu.int/en/ITU-D/Statistics/Documents/facts/FactsFigures2019.pdf
4. The state of the world's children 2017 children in a digital world. https://www.unicef.org/media/48601/file
5. Children and parents: Media use and attitudes report, November 2017
6. Extent of cellphone usage by children and teens worldwide, November 2017. https://www.tnuda.org.il/en/populations-risk/children-adolescents—introduction/extent-cellphone-usage-children-and-teens
7. 7 out 10 teens want parents to use parental controls, February 2018. https://www.internetmatters.org/hub/esafety-news/revealed-7-10-teens-want-parents-set-filters-protect-online/
8. A decade of digital dependency, May 2019. https://www.ofcom.org.uk/about-ofcom/latest/features-and-news/decade-of-digital-dependency
9. Done right, internet use among children can increase learning opportunities and build digital skills (2019). https://www.unicef.org/press-releases/done-right-internet-use-among-children-can-increase-learning-opportunities-and-build
10. Children at increased risk of harm online during global covid-19 pandemic, September 2020. https://www.unicef.org/press-releases/children-increased-risk-harm-online-during-global-covid-19-pandemic
11. Al Mugni, A., Herdiansah, M.F., Andhika, M.G., Ridwan, M.: DNSBL for internet content filtering utilizing pfsense as the next generation of opensource firewall. In: 2019 6th International Conference on Electrical Engineering, Computer Science and Informatics (EECSI), pp. 117–121 (2019)
12. Alelyani, T., Ghosh, A.K., Moralez, L., Guha, S., Wisniewski, P.: Examining parent versus child reviews of parental control apps on Google Play. In: Meiselwitz, G. (ed.) HCII 2019. LNCS, vol. 11579, pp. 3–21. Springer, Cham (2019). https://doi.org/10.1007/978-3-030-21905-5_1
13. Alqahtani, N., Furnell, S., Atkinson, S., Stengel, I.: Internet risks for children: Parents' perceptions and attitudes: an investigative study of the Saudi context. In: 2017 Internet Technologies and Applications (ITA), pp. 98–103 (2017)
14. Altarturi, H.H., Saadoon, M., Anuar, N.B.: Cyber parental control: a bibliometric study. Child. Youth Serv. Rev. **116**, 105134 (2020)
15. Anderson, M.: Parents, teens and digital monitoring, January 2016. https://www.pewresearch.org/internet/2016/01/07/parents-teens-and-digital-monitoring/
16. Anderson, M.: A majority of teens have experienced some form of cyberbullying, September 2018. https://www.pewresearch.org/internet/2018/09/27/a-majority-of-teens-have-experienced-some-form-of-cyberbullying/
17. Anderson, M., Jiang, J.: Teens, social media and technology 2018, May 2018. https://www.pewresearch.org/internet/2018/05/31/teens-social-media-technology-2018/
18. Badillo-Urquiola, K., Page, X., Wisniewski, P.J.: Risk vs. restriction: the tension between providing a sense of normalcy and keeping foster teens safe online. In: Proceedings of the 2019 CHI Conference on Human Factors in Computing Systems, pp. 1–14. CHI 2019. ACM, New York (2019)

19. Badillo-Urquiola, K., Smriti, D., McNally, B., Golub, E., Bonsignore, E., Wisniewski, P.J.: Stranger danger! social media app features co-designed with children to keep them safe online. In: Proceedings of the 18th ACM International Conference on Interaction Design and Children, pp. 394–406. IDC 2019. ACM, New York (2019)

20. Bi, X., Yang, Y., Li, H., Wang, M., Zhang, W., Deater-Deckard, K.: Parenting styles and parent-adolescent relationships: the mediating roles of behavioral autonomy and parental authority. Front. Psychol. **9**, 2187 (2018)

21. van Biljon, J., Renaud, K.: Human-computer interaction for development (HCI4D): the Southern African landscape. In: Nielsen, P., Kimaro, H.C. (eds.) ICT4D 2019. IAICT, vol. 552, pp. 253–266. Springer, Cham (2019). https://doi.org/10.1007/978-3-030-19115-3_21

22. Blackwell, L., Gardiner, E., Schoenebeck, S.: Managing expectations: technology tensions among parents and teens. In: Proceedings of the 19th ACM Conference on Computer-Supported Cooperative Work and Social Computing, pp. 1390–1401. CSCW 2016. ACM, New York (2016)

23. Bray, R.: Young people online: encounters with inappropriate content, May 2017. http://eprints.lse.ac.uk/79155/

24. Broekman, F.L., Piotrowski, J.T., Beentjes, H.W., Valkenburg, P.M.: A parental perspective on apps for young children. Comput. Hum. Behav. **63**, 142–151 (2016)

25. Buzzi, M.: Children and Youtube: access to safe content. In: Proceedings of the 9th ACM SIGCHI Italian Chapter International Conference on Computer-Human Interaction: Facing Complexity, pp. 125–131. CHItaly. ACM, New York (2011)

26. Bélanger, F., Crossler, R.E., Hiller, J.S., Park, J.M., Hsiao, M.S.: Pocket: a tool for protecting children's privacy online. Decision Support Syst. **54**(2), 1161–1173 (2013)

27. Catalano, R.F., Berglund, M.L., Ryan, J.A.M., Lonczak, H.S., Hawkins, J.D.: Positive youth development in the United States: research findings on evaluations of positive youth development programs. ANNALS Am. Acad. Polit. Soc. Sci. **591**(1), 98–124 (2004)

28. Cherry, K.: What is authoritarian parenting? (2021). https://www.verywellmind.com/what-is-authoritarian-parenting-2794955

29. Chiu, C., Yang, C.: A defense tool to prevent inappropriate website on Internet. In: 2019 International Conference on Intelligent Computing and its Emerging Applications (ICEA), pp. 51–54 (2019)

30. Clement, J.: Digital users worldwide 2020, July 2020. https://www.statista.com/statistics/617136/digital-population-worldwide/

31. Clement, J.: Most used social media platform, August 2020. https://www.statista.com/statistics/272014/global-social-networks-ranked-by-number-of-users/

32. Cohen, J.: Online communication platforms see record rise since quarantine began, April 2020. https://www.pcmag.com/news/online-communication-platforms-see-record-rise-since-quarantine-began

33. Cranor, L.F., Durity, A.L., Marsh, A., Ur, B.: Parents' and teens' perspectives on privacy in a technology-filled world. In: Proceedings of the Tenth USENIX Conference on Usable Privacy and Security, pp. 19–35. SOUPS 2014, USENIX Association, USA (2014)

34. Fahrnberger, G., Nayak, D., Martha, V.S., Ramaswamy, S.: Safechat: A tool to shield children's communication from explicit messages. In: 2014 14th International Conference on Innovations for Community Services (I4CS), pp. 80–86 (2014)

35. Friedman, B., Kahn, P., Borning, A.: Value sensitive design: theory and methods. University of Washington technical report (2–12) (2002)

36. Fuertes, W., Quimbiulco, K., Galárraga, F., García-Dorado, J.L.: On the development of advanced parental control tools. In: 2015 1st International Conference on Software Security and Assurance (ICSSA), pp. 1–6 (2015)
37. GDN: Developing nations face illiteracy crisis, warns UNESCO, February 2014. https://www.scmp.com/lifestyle/family-education/article/1423008/developing-nations-face-illiteracy-crisis-warns-unesco
38. Ghosh, A.K., Badillo-Urquiola, K., Guha, S., LaViola Jr, J.J., Wisniewski, P.J.: Safety vs. surveillance: what children have to say about mobile apps for parental control. In: Proceedings of the 2018 CHI Conference on Human Factors in Computing Systems, pp. 1–14. CHI 2018. ACM, New York (2018)
39. Ghosh, A.K., Badillo-Urquiola, K., Rosson, M.B., Xu, H., Carroll, J.M., Wisniewski, P.J.: A matter of control or safety? Examining parental use of technical monitoring apps on teens' mobile devices. In: Proceedings of the 2018 CHI Conference on Human Factors in Computing Systems, pp. 1–14. CHI 2018. ACM, New York (2018)
40. Ghosh, A.K., Badillo-Urquiola, K.A., Xu, H., Rosson, M.B., Carroll, J.M., Wisniewski, P.: Examining parents' technical mediation of teens' mobile devices. In: Companion of the 2017 ACM Conference on Computer Supported Cooperative Work and Social Computing, pp. 179–182. CSCW 2017 Companion. ACM, New York (2017)
41. Ghosh, A.K., Hughes, C.E., Wisniewski, P.J.: Circle of trust: a new approach to mobile online safety for families. In: Proceedings of the 2020 CHI Conference on Human Factors in Computing Systems, pp. 1–14. CHI 2020. ACM, New York (2020)
42. Ghosh, A.K., Wisniewski, P.: In: Understanding user reviews of adolescent mobile safety apps: a thematic analysis, pp. 417–420. GROUP 2016. ACM, New York (2016)
43. Griffith, E.: Almost two-thirds of us workforce must work from home, many with crap Internet, April 2020. https://www.pcmag.com/news/almost-two-thirds-of-us-workforce-must-work-from-home-many-with-crap-internet
44. Guerrero, M.J.C., Forment, M.A.: Coping with and addressing the risks of children tv and online devices usage: a review and proposal of guidelines for parents. In: Proceedings of the Seventh International Conference on Technological Ecosystems for Enhancing Multiculturality, pp. 891–898. TEEM 2019. ACM, New York (2019)
45. Gómez, P., Harris, S.K., Barreiro, C., Isorna, M., Rial, A.: Profiles of internet use and parental involvement, and rates of online risks and problematic internet use among Spanish adolescents. Comput. Hum. Behav. **75**, 826–833 (2017)
46. Hamade, S.N.: Parental awareness and mediation of children's Internet use in Kuwait. In: 2015 12th International Conference on Information Technology - New Generations, pp. 640–645 (2015)
47. Hartikainen, H., Iivari, N., Kinnula, M.: Should we design for control, trust or involvement? A discourses survey about children's online safety. In: Proceedings of the The 15th International Conference on Interaction Design and Children, pp. 367–378. IDC 2016. ACM, New York (2016)
48. Hashish, Y., Bunt, A., Young, J.E.: Involving children in content control: a collaborative and education-oriented content filtering approach. In: Proceedings of the SIGCHI Conference on Human Factors in Computing Systems, pp. 1797–1806. CHI 2014. ACM, New York (2014)

49. Hundlani, K., Chiasson, S., Hamid, L.: No passwords needed: the iterative design of a parent-child authentication mechanism. In: Proceedings of the 19th International Conference on Human-Computer Interaction with Mobile Devices and Services. MobileHCI 2017. ACM, New York (2017)

50. Isola, S., Fails, J.A.: Family and design in the idc and chi communities. In: Proceedings of the 11th International Conference on Interaction Design and Children, pp. 40–49. IDC 2012. ACM, New York (2012)

51. Jackson, K.: A brief history of the smartphone, July 2018. https://sciencenode. org/feature/Howdidsmartphonesevolve.php

52. Khurana, A., Bleakley, A., Jordan, A.B., Romer, D.: The protective effects of parental monitoring and internet restriction on adolescents' risk of online harassment. J. Youth Adolescence 44(5), 1039–1047 (2015)

53. Ko, M., Choi, S., Yang, S., Lee, J., Lee, U.: Familync: Facilitating participatory parental mediation of adolescents' smartphone use. In: Proceedings of the 2015 ACM International Joint Conference on Pervasive and Ubiquitous Computing, pp. 867–878. UbiComp 2015. ACM, New York (2015)

54. Kumar, M.S., Kumar, P.N., Deepa, R.: Protection against pornography. In: 2016 IEEE International Conference on Engineering and Technology (ICETECH), pp. 837–839 (2016)

55. Kumar, P., Naik, S.M., Devkar, U.R., Chetty, M., Clegg, T.L., Vitak, J.: 'no telling passcodes out because they're private': understanding children's mental models of privacy and security online. Proceedings ACM Human-Computer Interaction 1(CSCW), December 2017

56. Kuzminykh, A., Lank, E.: How much is too much? Understanding the information needs of parents of young children. Proceedings of the ACM on Interactive, Mobile, Wearable and Ubiquitous Technologies, vol. 3, no.2, June 2019

57. Lee, J., Jude, A., Shirazipour, M., Forgeat, J.: "I don't need to see that" seeking, avoiding, and attempting to control video content. In: Extended Abstracts of the 2018 CHI Conference on Human Factors in Computing Systems, pp. 1–6 (2018)

58. Lenhart, A.: Teens, technology and friendships, August 2015. https://www. pewresearch.org/internet/2015/08/06/chapter-4-social-media-and-friendships/

59. Majchrowicz, M., Kapusta, P., Faustryjak, D., Jackowska-Strumillo, L.: System for remote parental control and management of rooted smart TVs. In: 2018 International Interdisciplinary PhD Workshop (IIPhDW), pp. 357–360 (2018)

60. McNally, B., et al.: Co-designing mobile online safety applications with children. In: Proceedings of the 2018 CHI Conference on Human Factors in Computing Systems, pp. 1–9. CHI 2018. ACM, New York (2018)

61. Md Noor, R., Noor Sahila Syed Jamal, S., Zakaria, K.H.: Parental mobile control system for children's internet use. In: International Conference on Information Society (i-Society 2012), pp. 511–513 (2012)

62. Nouwen, M., Van Mechelen, M., Zaman, B.: A value sensitive design approach to parental software for young children. In: Proceedings of the 14th International Conference on Interaction Design and Children, pp. 363–366. IDC 2015. ACM, New York (2015)

63. Nouwen, M., Zaman, B.: Redefining the role of parents in young children's online interactions. a value-sensitive design case study. Int. J. Child-Comput. Interact. Interaction 18, 22–26 (2018)

64. Padilla-Walker, L.M., Coyne, S.M.: "Turn that thing off!" parent and adolescent predictors of proactive media monitoring. J. Adolescence 34(4), 705–715 (2011)

65. Padilla-Walker, L.M., Coyne, S.M., Fraser, A.M., Dyer, W.J., Yorgason, J.B.: Parents and adolescents growing up in the digital age: latent growth curve analysis of proactive media monitoring. J. Adolescence **35**(5), 1153–1165 (2012)

66. Pinter, A.T., Wisniewski, P.J., Xu, H., Rosson, M.B., Caroll, J.M.: Adolescent online safety: Moving beyond formative evaluations to designing solutions for the future. In: Proceedings of the 2017 Conference on Interaction Design and Children, pp. 352–357. IDC 2017. ACM, New York (2017)

67. Prasad, A., Ruiz, R., Stablein, T.: Understanding parents' concerns with smart device usage in the home. In: Moallem, A. (ed.) HCII 2019. LNCS, vol. 11594, pp. 176–190. Springer, Cham (2019). https://doi.org/10.1007/978-3-030-22351-9_12

68. Ringland, K.E., Wolf, C.T., Dombrowski, L., Hayes, G.R.: Making "safe": Community-centered practices in a virtual world dedicated to children with autism. In: Proceedings of the 18th ACM Conference on Computer Supported Cooperative Work and Social Computing, pp. 1788–1800. CSCW 2015. ACM, New York (2015)

69. Santisarun, P., Boonkrong, S.: Social network monitoring application for parents with children under thirteen. In: 2015 7th International Conference on Knowledge and Smart Technology (KST), pp. 75–80 (2015)

70. Schiano, D.J., Burg, C.: Parental controls: oxymoron and design opportunity. In: Stephanidis, C. (ed.) HCI 2017. CCIS, vol. 714, pp. 645–652. Springer, Cham (2017). https://doi.org/10.1007/978-3-319-58753-0_91

71. Silver, L.: Smartphone ownership is growing rapidly around the world, but not always equally, August 2020. https://www.pewresearch.org/global/2019/02/05/smartphone-ownership-is-growing-rapidly-around-the-world-but-not-always-equally/

72. Srl, C., Networks, D.G.f.C., Srl, I., Chancen, S.D., Angeletti, Croll, Vulcano: Benchmarking of parental control tools for the online protection of children : final report, May 2018. https://op.europa.eu/en/publication-detail/-/publication/cbbf9543-58b7-11e8-ab41-01aa75ed71a1/language-en

73. Suchaad, S.A., Mashiko, K., Ismail, N.B., Abidin, M.H.Z.: Blockchain use in home automation for children incentives in parental control. In: Proceedings of the 2018 International Conference on Machine Learning and Machine Intelligence, pp. 50–53. MLMI2018. ACM, New York (2018)

74. Symons, K., Ponnet, K., Walrave, M., Heirman, W.: A qualitative study into parental mediation of adolescents' Internet use. Comput. Hum. Behav. **73**, 423–432 (2017)

75. W. L. Goh, W., Bay, S., Chen, V.H.H.: Young school children's use of digital devices and parental rules. Telematics Inform. **32**(4), 787–795 (2015)

76. Webster, J., Watson, R.T.: Analyzing the past to prepare for the future: writing a literature review. MIS Q. **26**(2), xiii–xxiii (2002)

77. Wisniewski, P., Ghosh, A.K., Xu, H., Rosson, M.B., Carroll, J.M.: Parental control vs. teen self-regulation: is there a middle ground for mobile online safety? In: Proceedings of the 2017 ACM Conference on Computer Supported Cooperative Work and Social Computing, pp. 51–69. CSCW 2017. ACM, New York (2017)

78. Wisniewski, P., Jia, H., Xu, H., Rosson, M.B., Carroll, J.M.: "Preventative" vs. "reactive": How parental mediation influences teens' social media privacy behaviors. In: Proceedings of the 18th ACM Conference on Computer Supported Cooperative Work and Social Computing, pp. 302–316. CSCW 2015. ACM, New York (2015)

79. Wisniewski, P.J., Xu, H., Rosson, M.B., Carroll, J.M.: Adolescent online safety: the "moral" of the story. In: Proceedings of the 17th ACM Conference on Computer Supported Cooperative Work and Social Computing, pp. 1258–1271. CSCW 2014. ACM, New York (2014)

80. Yardi, S., Bruckman, A.: Social and technical challenges in parenting teens' social media use. In: Proceedings of the SIGCHI Conference on Human Factors in Computing Systems, pp. 3237–3246. CHI 2011. ACM, New York (2011)
81. Zhang-Kennedy, L., Mekhail, C., Abdelaziz, Y., Chiasson, S.: From nosy little brothers to stranger-danger: children and parents' perception of mobile threats. In: Proceedings of the 15th International Conference on Interaction Design and Children, pp. 388–399. IDC 2016. ACM, New York (2016)
82. Zimmer, F., Scheibe, K., Henkel, M.: How parents guide the digital media usage of kindergarten children in early childhood. In: Stephanidis, C. (ed.) HCII 2019. CCIS, vol. 1034, pp. 313–320. Springer, Cham (2019). https://doi.org/10.1007/978-3-030-23525-3_41

# Integrating Dark Patterns into the 4Cs of Online Risk in the Context of Young People and Mobile Gaming Apps

Dan Fitton[1]([⊠]) [iD], Beth T. Bell[2] [iD], and Janet C. Read[1] [iD]

[1] ChiCI Research Group, University of Central Lancashire, Preston, UK
{DBFitton,JCRead}@UCLan.ac.uk
[2] School of Psychological and Social Sciences, York St John University, York, UK
b.bell@yorksj.ac.uk

**Abstract.** Mobile technologies potentially expose children and adolescents to increasing online risk. These risks take many forms and are widely categorized using the 4Cs: Content, Conduct, Contact, and Commerce. Commerce is the least developed category and, while it has significant overlap with what is known as Dark Design within the field of UX, amalgamation of Dark Design and the 4Cs has not yet been considered. Within this paper we integrate Dark Design into the 4Cs to provide a set of questions we call RIGA (Risk In Games Assessment) and use RIGA to identify potential risks to children and adolescents in free-to-play mobile gaming apps. The key contribution of this paper is the integration of contemporary understandings of Dark Design into the 4Cs framework, through the RIGA question set, which can support research and practitioner communities in identifying potential risk to young people present in mobile gaming apps.

**Keywords:** Dark patterns · Dark Design · Online risk · Games · Children

## 1 Introduction

Mobile digital technologies are ubiquitous in contemporary society and are increasingly considered to be integral to the daily lives of young people (adolescents and children) [1, 2]. Young people often use their phones as a source of entertainment ([3, 4]) and particularly for mobile gaming. At the time of writing indications [5] are that the Google Play store contains almost 3.2 million apps/games and the Apple iOS app store almost 1.8 million, with tens of thousands being added monthly. Both Apple and Google require that products submitted to their app stores include an age rating to protect adolescents and children from inappropriate content, but each takes different approaches to ensuring compliance. Apple use their own staff for vetting whereas Google provide policies for developers to engage in their own vetting through a self-report process. For example, the Google Play store has a 'Restricted Content' policy [6] that developers are expected to adhere to which references child endangerment, inappropriate content, finance, gambling, illegal activities and user generated content. While Google's approach is scalable,

© IFIP International Federation for Information Processing 2021
Published by Springer Nature Switzerland AG 2021
C. Ardito et al. (Eds.): INTERACT 2021, LNCS 12935, pp. 701–711, 2021.
https://doi.org/10.1007/978-3-030-85610-6_40

the developer-reported content ratings may be applied inaccurately [7, 8] and are only queried when users (typically parents) report inappropriate content. The effectiveness of the approach depends to some extent on developers understanding the wording and nuances of the guidance provided to them. At the time of writing this paper the Google Child Endangerment policy states 'Apps that appeal to children but contain adult themes are not allowed'; this raises questions of how the developer would know what age child is being referred to, or how appeal may differ between age groups, or even how appeal would be measured. It is also the responsibility of the app developer themselves, or users who identify and report breeches of policy, to ensure adherence.

Due to their limited spending power, young people often use free-to-play mobile games where there is no initial cost for download and use. The business model for such apps requires that monetization is included within the gameplay; typically implemented through adverts which the user must watch or in-app purchasing possibilities the player is encouraged to engage in. To encourage such engagement subtle 'Dark' techniques may be employed like coercion to pay or making it deliberately hard to close an advert [9]. As the free-to-play model is used in over 95% of mobile apps, not just those targeted at young people, the implementation of monetization in apps and games is commonly developed by adults for adults. It is unclear whether younger users are considered in the design of these monetization mechanisms, and the effect these mechanisms (along with their associated risk) may have on younger users compared to adults is not well understood.

The key contribution of this work is the integration of Dark Design into the 4Cs framework, achieved in this paper through the creation and application of the RIGA (Risk In Games Assessment) question set. Our work also highlights the importance of an interdisciplinary approach to topics such as technology risk, combining work from the fields of UX and Psychology. The RIGA questions provide a means for identifying potential risk to young people in mobile gaming apps which operationalizes and elucidates the motivations which underpin the guidance provided to app developers. Additionally, RIGA can potentially be used by a range of stakeholders including academics, developers, parents, educators and young people themselves.

## 2  Related Work

Risks of harm in relation to technology use among young/vulnerable users are typically clustered around four Cs; Content, Contact, Conduct and Commerce [10].

**Content** risks refer to those stemming from exposure to potentially harmful digital media content (e.g., self-harm content, appearance ideals, violence [10]). Research has demonstrated how violent media content, particularly in video games, can have negative, yet small, effects on childrens' and adolescents' aggression and mood [11] though these effects are widely debated (e.g., [12]). More recently, content that alludes to self-violence (e.g. self-harm and suicide) in social media spaces has been identified as posing risks to children and young people, triggering distress or possible contagion [13]. Sexualized media content has received considerable attention from researchers with research documenting the negative consequences of accessing both graphic sexual material (e.g., nudes, pornography) and non-graphic sexual material (e.g., revealing images; [14, 15]).

Research has also highlighted how unrealistic body ideals (e.g., surgically enhanced or ultra-thin models) can foster negative body image and encourage unhealthy body-shaping strategies in young people [16], including in mobile games played by girls aged 8–9 years old [17].

**Contact** risks are those that stem from online social interactions/relationships with those who wish to bully/abuse/troll. Contact risks can take many forms, including the experience of unwanted sexual messaging (e.g., sexting), harassment, grooming, cyber-bullying, hate speech, denigration, and other users pretending to be someone who they are not [18]. As contact risks stem from the misappropriation of communication tools by users rather than from the app itself, these risks can be more difficult to regulate than content risks. The Google Play policy specifies that apps that contain or facilitate threats, harassment or bullying are restricted, and app developers are responsible for ensuring that the app, including any user-generated content facilitated by it adhere to this policy [6], although this policy can be difficult to police.

**Conduct** risks stem from a user's own personal conduct within digital spaces. Anti-social behavior is perhaps the most prominent of these conduct risks and encompasses a diverse range of behaviors from bullying to harassment [2]. In addition to causing harm to others (i.e., the victim/receiver of the antisocial behavior), there are important negative consequences for the perpetrator including loss of reputation, criminality and potential legal repercussions e.g., [19]. In mobile gaming, anti-social behavior may be directed at other users (e.g., through in-game contact) or it may be directed at within game characters. Conduct risks can also stem from sharing of personal data, since it potentially exposes users to harms associated with the misuse of this data and/or privacy breaches [20].

**Commerce** risks (also known as commercial risks or cyberscams [10]) refer to risks stemming from the commercial or profit-making aspects of online space, e.g., fraud, accidental spending, perceived pressure to spend, etc. Commerce risks are growing; in 2018, around 17% of 12–15 year-olds in the UK reported that they have accidentally spent money online, up from 9% the previous year [1]. These risks are a late addition to the 4C framework and remain relatively understudied in relation to children and teenagers, in comparison to other types of online risks [10]. According to Ofcom [1], spending pressures in gaming is 'an area of specific and growing concerns among parents of children of all ages'; 39% of parents of children aged 5–15 years old are concerned about pressures to make in-app purchases. These in-app purchases take many forms including access to additional points, tokens or levels, full-app teasers or for game up-grades and add-ons [9], and are integral to revenue generation in free-to-play apps (and games). In-app purchases are regulated, including through opt-in parental controls that moderate spending, such as the "Ask to Buy" system in the app store. In addition to in-app purchasing, advertising is also a way in which users may be exposed to commercial risks within games, resulting in accidental spending, perceived pressure to spend, etc. Perhaps unsurprisingly, advertising is much more salient in free-to-play apps than paid for apps [21] reflecting the integral nature of advertising to current business models.

In the UX and HCI communities there is a small, but growing, body of work explor-ing 'Dark Design' within technologies [9, 22–24]. The notion of Dark Design Patterns initially emerged from the UX practitioner community, defined as 'a user interface carefully crafted to trick users into doing things they might not otherwise do' [25]. A Design Pattern is a proven solution to a general problem which is intended to be reused [26]. Dark Design is driven by economic motivations and emerged from the study of e-commerce web sites where the intention of the designer appeared to be utilizing the design of the web sites to 'trick' shoppers into spending more than they intended or generating other potential income. Twelve original Dark Design patterns were identified [27] which were then explored in a gaming context by Zagal [24] and also studied in more detail by Gray [23]. Fitton [9] brought together existing work on Dark Design and related areas (in-app advertising, in-app purchasing etc.) though a user study involving teenagers to define the ADD (App Dark Design) framework to support the critical consideration of Dark Designs which included six categories containing multiple types of Dark Design: Temporal (Grinding, Play by Appointment, Interstitial Non-app Content), Monetary (Pay for Permanent Enhancements, Pay for Expendable Updates, Pay to Skip/Progress, Pay to Win, Subscriptions, Intermediate Currencies), Social (Impersonation/Friend Spam, Prompts to Share/Review, Social Pyramid Schemes), Disguised Ads (Advergames, Characters Placement), Sneaky Ads (Difficult/Deceptive to Dismiss, Camouflaged Game Items, Notification-based Ads), and Inappropriate (Unsuitable Adverts, Encouraging Anti-Social Behavior, Psychological Manipulation, Persuasive Design, Developmentally Insensitive).

Dark Design is employed heavily in free-to-play mobile apps games for monetization to generate the required revenue for the developers. For those installing a 'free' game on their phone it is unlikely that spending time watching adverts or making in-game purchases in order to play that game would be desirable, and so this provides the motivation for Dark Design. Mechanisms do exist to minimise designers including Dark Design elements in apps. Apple provides guidance to developers submitting their apps for review which states that 'tricking' users is not acceptable [28]. Google Play has a 'Monetization and Ads' policy [29] which contains a 'Deceptive Ads' section; this mentions several basic Dark Design examples which should not be used (Disruptive Ads, Deceptive Ads, Inappropriate Ads) with examples. However, the authors found examples of all three types of these 'Deceptive Ads' in the Android games they evaluated in this work. In 2015 Google Play launched a 'Design for Families' initiative which included a specific 'Family' policy [30] which should be adhered to when developing apps intended for child users. Compliance with the Family policy is specified as requiring age-appropriate advertising, excluding any adult content, adhering to applicable data/privacy laws and more stringent 'Ads and Monetization' guidance [30].

Despite this existing work, Dark Design is often very nuanced and requires a high level of knowledge or experience of design in order for it to be identified and fully understood. There is therefore a need to develop more clear guidance on Dark Design for researchers and practitioners both inside and outside of the field of HCI. Governments are also beginning to take the regulation of apps and games for children more seriously in their policy making. For example, in January 2020 in the UK the Age-Appropriate Design Code [31] was published which primarily controls how data shared by children can be used. This code states 'Do not use nudge techniques to lead or encourage children to provide unnecessary personal data or turn off privacy protections.' which relates directly to the use of Dark Design by app developers. Despite this recent policy work, Dark

Design is not currently part of mainstream approaches to understanding online risks of harm among youth. There is therefore a need to integrate the two together, particularly focusing on Dark Design within Commerce risk.

## 3   Study: Integrating the 4Cs and Dark Design

In order to integrate the 4Cs and Dark Design the approach taken was to develop a set of questions that could be used to identify specific aspects within mobile gaming apps. Bell, a psychologist and expert in the role of digital media and technology in relation to youth mental health, developed a set of questions to identify evidence of the 4Cs of online risk in gaming apps. Fitton, an expert in youth UX, developed a set of questions to identify evidence of Dark Design (based on the ADD framework mentioned previously). The two authors then pooled their question sets and worked together to refine them, ensuring that the questions were simplified as much as was practical with the intention of allowing them to be applied with low levels of ambiguity by those outside the fields of UX and Psychology. This set of questions forms the RIGA (Risk In Games Assessment) question set which is shown later in the paper in Table 2 RIGA included 15 of the 22 Dark Design types in the ADD framework which made small contributions to Content and Conduct but was most useful in defining the Commerce dimension.

### 3.1   Evaluation Procedure

RIGA was subsequently used to evaluate 12 popular free-to-play mobile gaming apps that had been previously identified during a UK STEM event as containing 'interruptions and annoyances' (i.e. potential Dark Design elements [11]). The data was gathered prior to the COVID - 19 pandemic from 120 pupils aged between 7–12 years from two junior schools, and from 90 pupils aged 13–14 from two high schools. The question posed in that study was 'What are the worst apps/games for interruptions or annoyances?'. Responses from the two age groups were collated and totaled. Then apps which were not games, and games with extensive gameplay complexity ('Roblox' and 'Fortnite') were removed to leave a final list of 12 games (See Table 1, games ordered by popularity of response, high-low).

In a heuristic-style evaluation, two of the authors of the paper (the evaluators), who were also the designers of RIGA individually played each game for familiarity and then inspected each with reference to the RIGA questions. In both first and second play episodes the evaluators attempted to 1) Complete on-boarding tasks [32], 2) Complete the first level or other equivalent objective, 3) Gather in-game currency and purchase an in-game upgrade. The ordering in which the games were played (then evaluated) was consistent and followed the ordering shown in Table 1. Games were played until the evaluators were satisfied that they had explored as much of the game as was necessary to form judgements or encountered high levels of repetition. Mean total gameplay time per game was approximately 30 min across both evaluators. The testing was done independently on two identical Android phones. A screen recorder was used for all gameplay to enable review of what was seen by each evaluator in each game if required. A spreadsheet was used for coding containing the RIGA questions with drop-down lists for answers and areas for comments. Individual coding data (yes/no answers to each of the RIGA questions for each game) from each evaluator was then compared (risk totals per-game are shown in Table 1 including initial and final agreed totals out of a possible maximum score of 26). Disagreements were resolved through initial discussion of the reasons underpinning the coding, then revisiting and discussing the screen recordings of gameplay if needed. All incidences of coding disagreement were able to be resolved using this method to give the totals show in the far-right column of Table 1.

**Table 1.** Number of risks identified in mobile gaming apps using RIGA.

| Game | Coder 1 (psychologist) | Coder 2 (UX) | Agreed |
|---|---|---|---|
| Geometry dash | 8 | 8 | 8 |
| Candy crush saga | 8 | 9 | 9 |
| Helix jump | 7 | 7 | 7 |
| Subway surfers | 17 | 15 | 17 |
| Cooking fever | 8 | 8 | 8 |
| Crossy road | 10 | 9 | 10 |
| Knife hit | 14 | 12 | 14 |
| Piano tiles 2™ (don't tap…2) | 16 | 17 | 17 |
| BitLife - life simulator | 8 | 8 | 8 |
| Pick me up™ | 12 | 11 | 12 |
| Episode - choose your story | 15 | 15 | 15 |
| Rider | 11 | 11 | 11 |

## 4   Results

Table 2 shows the results of the evaluation. On the title row for each category we show the number of apps which contained at least one example of that type of risk (e.g. eight contained one or more Contact risk) followed by the results for the specific sub-categories. Nine apps contained some form of **content** risk with the most common content risk was advertising of age-restricted products such as TikTok or Instagram (which are restricted to users aged over 13 years old). Two apps featured unrealistic body imagery (Subway Surfers and Episodes) and two apps featured sexualized content/themes (BitLife and Episodes), with one featuring violent themes, though these were not particularly strong or graphic (Bitlife). Eight apps contained some form of **contact** risk through encouraging users to connect via social media, and of those three incentivized this contact. Two apps (Episodes and Candy Crush Saga) offered bespoke-to-app where users could connect via forums perceptibly over a shared love of the game.

Candy Crush Saga integrated contact between users within the app itself, by allowing users to share in-game 'lives'. Seven apps contained some form of **conduct** risk which often stemmed from the sharing of personal information with the app developers and/or third parties. This conduct risk was incentivized by appearing as a condition of use in three games which is a form of Dark Pattern. For example, Fig. 1 shows screen captures from the data collection agreement when the Helix Jump game is first opened, it appears to the user all three agreements need to be given to 'Start Playing' but only the third one is actually necessary. Two apps facilitated anti-social behavior but in both instances, this was aimed at characters within the game rather than other users. Just one app incentivized antisocial behavior (Episodes). In this game, avatars could be instructed to behave in socially manipulative ways to gain praise from in-game characters.

**Table 2.** RIGA (risk in games assessment) questions and results of coding

| Risk | *n* | % |
|---|---|---|
| **1. Contact** | **8** | **66.67%** |
| 1.1 Does the game facilitate contact between users within the app/bespoke community spaces? | 2 | 16.67% |
| 1.2 Does the game allow facilitate contact between users through social media? | 8 | 66.67% |
| 1.3 Is communication between users incentivized? | 3 | 25.55% |
| **2. Content** | **9** | **75.00%** |
| 2.1 Does the game contain unrealistic body imagery? | 2 | 16.67% |
| 2.2 Does the game contain extreme body-shaping behavior? | 0 | – |
| 2.3 Does the game contain users to nude images/pornography? | 0 | – |
| 2.4 Does the game contain sexualized content/imagery/themes? | 2 | 16.67% |
| 2.5 Does the game contain violence (visuals and themes)? | 1 | 8.33% |
| 2.6 Does the game contain images of self-harm or suicide? | 0 | – |
| 2.7 Does the game include advertising of age-restricted products/services? | 7 | 58.33% |
| **3. Conduct** | **7** | **58.33%** |
| 3.1 Does the app allow the user to engage in high risk conduct? | 6 | 50.00% |
| 3.1.2 Was this incentivized/nudged? | 3 | 25.00% |
| 3.2 Does the game allow users to engage in anti-social behavior? | 2 | 16.67% |
| 3.2.1 Was this incentivized? | 0 | – |
| **4. Commerce** | **12** | **100.00%** |

(*continued*)

**Table 2.** (*continued*)

| Risk | n | % |
|---|---|---|
| Commerce: *compulsive use* | | |
| 4.1.1 Does progression require in-game resources which can be earned through repetitive play? | 7 | 58.33% |
| 4.1.2 Does the game attempt to make its use compulsive or habitual? | 8 | 66.67% |
| Commerce: *in-app purchasing* | | |
| 4.2.1 Can the user pay to gain permanent enhancements to the gameplay experience? | 10 | 83.33% |
| 4.2.2 Can the user pay to gain temporary enhancements to the gameplay experience? | 4 | 33.33% |
| 4.2.3 Can the user pay to progress? | 3 | 25.00% |
| 4.2.4 Can the user make regular payments to the game? | 3 | 25.00% |
| 4.2.5 Does the user need to purchase immediate currency to buy in-game items? | 9 | 75.00% |
| Commerce: *advertising* | | |
| 4.3.1 Does the game include advergames? | 8 | 66.67% |
| 4.3.2 Does the game include advertising which is challenging to dismiss? | 10 | 83.33% |
| 4.3.3 Is there advertising related directly to in-game items? | 1 | 8.33% |
| 4.3.4 Does the game include full-screen content not linked to the game? | 9 | 75.00% |
| 4.3.5 Does the game feature adverts that constrain playing times? | 6 | 50.00% |

All apps contained some form of **commerce** risk linked to in-app purchasing, including the ability to purchase permanent or temporary game enhancements, pay a regular game subscription or to pay to progress within a game. Nine apps had an in-game currency to facilitate in-app purchasing. Ten out of the twelve apps contained some form of risk linked to advertising, including adverts that were difficult to dismiss, full screen adverts advergames, adverts that constrained playing times, and adverts disguised as in-game items. Figure 2 (left) shows an advergame with a clear instruction to interact to play the game, Fig. 2 (right) shows the install page which opened once the user touched the phone screen. Nine apps contained features designed to foster habitual use, including allocating rewards (e.g., in-game currency) for daily log-ins and requiring repetitive play in order to progress.

**Fig. 1.** Helix jump privacy policy          **Fig. 2.** Deceptive advergame

## 5 Conclusion

We have integrated Dark Design research from the UX domain into the broader literature on the 4Cs of online harms from the Psychology domain to create the RIGA question set. The study showed that the RIGA questions proved a useful tool in identifying potential risk of harm in a set of popular Android free-to-play mobile gaming apps used by young people. Despite the existing guidance provided to developers, through using RIGA we found evidence of content, contact and conduct risks, including evidence of Dark Design being used to incentivize this risk. We found - perhaps unsurprisingly given the business models of current free-to-play gaming apps - substantive evidence of commerce risks within the games that we reviewed. It is important to remember that not all risks (or associated harms) are equal and that identification of a risk does not guarantee that an associated harm will occur. However, identification of risks (such as those discussed in this paper) is a crucial first step in understanding and addressing them. While this work is at a relatively early stage it makes a valuable contribution to the growing body of knowledge around Dark Design patterns and shows how understandings of Dark Design can be valuable in other contexts. The RIGA questions are intentionally easy to understand and have potential to be a valuable tool for a range of stakeholders involved in creating, understanding, and safeguarding the use of mobile gaming apps in the context of young people.

## References

1. Ofcom: Children and parents: media use and attitudes report. https://www.ofcom.org.uk/res earch-and-data/media-literacy-research/childrens/children-and-parents-media-use-and-attitu des-report-2018. Accessed 25 Jan 2020
2. Unicef: Global Kids Online Comparative Report. https://www.unicef-irc.org/publications/ 1059-global-kids-online-comparative-report.html. Accessed 25 Jan 2020
3. Mascheroni, G., Ólafsson, K.: The mobile internet: access, use, opportunities and divides among European children. New Media Soc. **18**, 1657–1679 (2016). https://doi.org/10.1177/ 1461444814567986
4. Sudan, M., Olsen, J., Sigsgaard, T., Kheifets, L.: Trends in cell phone use among children in the Danish national birth cohort at ages 7 and 11 years. J. Expo. Sci. Environ. Epidemiol. **26**, 606–612 (2016). https://doi.org/10.1038/jes.2016.17

5. 42Matters: Store Stats for Mobile Apps.https://42matters.com/stats. Accessed 25 Jan 2020
6. Google Play: Restricted Content - Developer Policy Center. https://play.google.com/about/restricted-content/. Accessed 25 Jan 2020
7. Hu, B., Liu, B., Gong, N.Z., Kong, D., Jin, H.: Protecting your children from inappropriate content in mobile apps: an automatic maturity rating framework. In: International Conference on Information and Knowledge Management, Proceedings, pp. 1111–1120. Association for Computing Machinery, New York (2015). https://doi.org/10.1145/2806416.2806579
8. Luo, Q., Liu, J., Wang, J., Tan, Y., Cao, Y., Kato, N.: Automatic content inspection and forensics for children android apps. IEEE Internet Things J. 7, 7123–7134 (2020). https://doi.org/10.1109/jiot.2020.2982248
9. Fitton, D., Read, J.C.: Creating a framework to support the critical consideration of dark design aspects in free-to-play apps. In: Proceedings of the 18th ACM International Conference on Interaction Design and Children, IDC 2019, pp. 407–418. Association for Computing Machinery, Inc. (2019). https://doi.org/10.1145/3311927.3323136
10. El Asam, A., Katz, A.: Vulnerable young people and their experience of online risks. Hum.-Comput. Interact. 33, 281–304 (2018). https://doi.org/10.1080/07370024.2018.1437544
11. Mathur, M.B., VanderWeele, T.J.: Finding common ground in meta-analysis "wars" on violent video games. Perspect. Psychol. Sci. 14, 705–708 (2019). https://doi.org/10.1177/1745691619850104
12. Ferguson, C.J.: Does media violence predict societal violence? It depends on what you look at and when. J. Commun. 65, E1–E22 (2015). https://doi.org/10.1111/jcom.12129
13. Vanderweele, T.J., Mathur, M.B., Chen, Y.: Media portrayals and public health implications for suicide and other behaviors (2019). https://doi.org/10.1001/jamapsychiatry.2019.0842
14. Owens, E.W., Behun, R.J., Manning, J.C., Reid, R.C.: The impact of internet pornography on adolescents: a review of the research (2012). https://doi.org/10.1080/10720162.2012.660431
15. Perse, E.M., Lambe, J.: Media Effects and Society. Routledge, Abingdon (2016). https://doi.org/10.4324/9780203854693
16. Holland, G., Tiggemann, M.: A systematic review of the impact of the use of social networking sites on body image and disordered eating outcomes (2016). https://doi.org/10.1016/j.bodyim.2016.02.008
17. Slater, A., Halliwell, E., Jarman, H., Gaskin, E.: More than just child's play?: an experimental investigation of the impact of an appearance-focused internet game on body image and career aspirations of young girls. J. Youth Adolesc. 46(9), 2047–2059 (2017). https://doi.org/10.1007/s10964-017-0659-7
18. Livingstone, S., Smith, P.K.: Annual research review: harms experienced by child users of online and mobile technologies: the nature, prevalence and management of sexual and aggressive risks in the digital age. J. Child Psychol. Psychiatr. 55, 635–654 (2014). https://doi.org/10.1111/jcpp.12197
19. Goldsmith, A., Wall, D.S.: The seductions of cybercrime: adolescence and the thrills of digital transgression. Eur. J. Criminol. 147737081988730 (2019). https://doi.org/10.1177/1477370819887305
20. Montgomery, K.C., Chester, J., Milosevic, T.: Children's privacy in the big data era: research opportunities. Pediatrics 140, S117–S121 (2017). https://doi.org/10.1542/peds.2016-1758O
21. Meyer, M., Adkins, V., Yuan, N., Weeks, H.M., Chang, Y.-J., Radesky, J.: Advertising in young children's apps: a content analysis. J. Dev. Behav. Pediatr. 40 (2019)
22. Mathur, A., et al.: Dark patterns at scale: findings from a crawl of 11K shopping websites. (2019). https://doi.org/10.1145/3359183
23. Gray, C.M., Kou, Y., Battles, B., Hoggatt, J., Toombs, A.L.: The dark (patterns) side of UX design. In: Proceedings of the 2018 CHI Conference on Human Factors in Computing Systems, p. 534:1–534:14. ACM, New York (2018). https://doi.org/10.1145/3173574.3174108

24. Zagal, J.P., Björk, S., Lewis, C.: Dark patterns in the design of games (2013). http://dblp.uni-trier.de/db/conf/fdg/fdg2013.html#ZagalB013
25. Brignull, H.: Dark patterns: inside the interfaces designed to trick you. https://www.theverge.com/2013/8/29/4640308/dark-patterns-insidethe-interfaces-designed-to-trick-you
26. Alexander, C., Ishikawa, S., Silverstein, M.: A Pattern Language: Towns, Buildings, Construction. Oxford University Press, New York (1977)
27. Brignull, H.: Types of Dark Pattern.https://darkpatterns.org/types-of-dark-pattern. Accessed 25 Mar 2019
28. Apple: App Store Review Guidelines. https://developer.apple.com/app-store/review/guidelines/. Accessed 11 June 2021
29. Google Play: Ads—Monetization and Ads - Developer Policy Center. https://play.google.com/about/monetization-ads/ads/. Accessed 25 Jan 2020
30. Google Play: Families - Developer Policy Center. https://play.google.com/about/families/. Accessed 25 Jan 2020
31. ICO: Age appropriate design: a code of practice for online services (2020)
32. Petersen, F.W., Thomsen, L.E., Mirza-Babaei, P., Drachen, A.: Evaluating the onboarding phase of free-to-play mobile games: a mixed-method approach. In: CHI PLAY 2017 - Proceedings of the Annual Symposium on Computer-Human Interaction in Play, pp. 377–388. Association for Computing Machinery, Inc. (2017).https://doi.org/10.1145/3116595.3125499

# Passphrases Beat Thermal Attacks: Evaluating Text Input Characteristics Against Thermal Attacks on Laptops and Smartphones

Yasmeen Abdrabou[1]([✉]), Reem Hatem[2], Yomna Abdelrahman[1],
Amr Elmougy[2], and Mohamed Khamis[3]

[1] Bundeswehr University Munich, Neubiberg, Germany
yasmeen.essam@unibw.de
[2] German University in Cairo, New Cairo, Egypt
[3] University of Glasgow, Glasgow, UK

**Abstract.** We investigate the effectiveness of thermal attacks against input of text with different characteristics; we study text entry on a smartphone touchscreen and a laptop keyboard. First, we ran a study (N = 25) to collect a dataset of thermal images of short words, websites, complex strings (special characters, numbers, letters), passphrases and words with duplicate characters. Afterwards, 20 different participants visually inspected the thermal images to attempt to identify the text input. We found that long and complex strings are less vulnerable to thermal attacks, that visual inspection of thermal images reveals different parts of the entered text (36% on average and up to 82%) even if the attack is not fully successful, and that entering text on laptops is more vulnerable to thermal attacks than on smartphones. We conclude with three learned lessons and recommendations to resist thermal attacks.

**Keywords:** Thermal imaging · Security · Privacy · Side-channel attack

## 1 Introduction

Recent research has revealed that thermal cameras can be used to infer different types of passwords, such as text passwords [12] and PINs/Patterns [7,8]. This presents a threat to authentication on safes [20], smartphones [7,8], keyboards [8,12], cash machines [16], digital door locks, and payment terminals [19]. Attacks that use thermal cameras are often referred to as "thermal attacks" [7]. They were shown to be feasible using both high-end and low-cost commercial cameras [7,8], and were evaluated under threat models where attackers have access to automated image processing approaches [7,12] and where attackers are non-experts that rely on visually inspecting the thermal images [8,12,20].

Despite the recent work on thermal attacks, it is unclear which characteristics of text strings impact their vulnerability to thermal attacks. To address this gap,

© IFIP International Federation for Information Processing 2021
Published by Springer Nature Switzerland AG 2021
C. Ardito et al. (Eds.): INTERACT 2021, LNCS 12935, pp. 712–721, 2021.
https://doi.org/10.1007/978-3-030-85610-6_41

this paper investigates how successful visual inspection of thermal images taken by an off-the-shelf thermal camera can retrieve text strings entered on laptops and smartphones. We studied different input characteristics such as presence duplicates and special characters and input length. We study attacks by non-expert attackers, which we define in this context as attackers who have access to a thermal camera and can visually inspect the recorded images, but do not have the skills to implement an automated approach as done in some prior research [7,12]. Attacks by such non-experts are more likely as thermal cameras become significantly cheaper (e.g., at the time of writing this paper, a thermal camera can be bought for less than < £200 [1]). Our results show that employing thermal attacks on text input is effective; without training and using visual inspection, our participants were able to infer up to 90% of short text input and almost half short text inputs that contain duplicates. We found that longer text input, such as passphrases, and the inclusion of special characters in text input significantly reduce vulnerability. We conclude with learned lessons on securing text input against thermal attacks.

## 2   Background and Related Work

When a user touches a surface, heat is transferred from the user's fingers to touched surfaces. This generates a temperature difference at the point of contact referred to as heat traces. Thermal cameras allows its users to see heat traces.

Thermal attacks exploit this phenomenon by interpreting the user's input on a user interface based on the heat traces [7,16]. Thermal attacks have an advantage over other types of side-channel attacks, such as shoulder surfing [10] in that they allow determining the order of the entered input; for example the last touched digit in a PIN often has the warmest heat trace. Another advantage for attackers it that thermal attacks are performed after the user had left the device. This gives an advantage over shoulder surfing as attackers no longer need to observe the user while interacting, which makes the attack more covert.

Previous work demonstrated the effectiveness of thermal attacks on PINs on different devices such as safes [20], smartphones [7,8], keyboards [8,12], cash machines [16], digital door locks, and payment terminals [19]. High-end thermal cameras as well as low-cost commercial cameras have been used in different research showing the real threat to users' privacy [7,8,16]. Both automated approaches [7,12] and visual inspection attacks by non-expert human attackers [8,20] were highly successful. Most of the research has investigated thermal attacks on PINs or patterns which are usually short entries. An exception is one work that compared the success of thermal attacks against strong and weak passwords [12] which are relatively longer than PINs and patterns. In their research, Kaczmarek et al. [12] studied attacking weak and strong passwords entered on external keyboards using a commercial thermal camera. They found that a non-expert attacker can recover key presses up to 30 s after entry.

This paper complements previous work by reporting on an in-depth analysis of how well thermal attacks perform on user text input. We study different input characteristics that were not studied before, such as text length, presence of duplicates, and presence of special characters, and investigate their effect on the thermal attack's success. We collect thermal images of inputs entered on a smartphone's touchscreen and a laptop's keyboard. In our threat models, non-expert attackers visually inspect thermal images taken by an off the shelf thermal camera. Our results shed light on how to protect against thermal attacks.

## 3   Evaluation

In this work, we investigate different text input characteristics (length, duplicate letters and special characters, upper and lower case letters) and their influence on the attack success rate (**RQ**). To answer our research question, we ran a lab study consisting of two phases (1) Thermal Images Collection and (2) Thermal Attacks. We implemented a simple website interface for users to enter their input. The interface shows the input text to be typed and a text area for input entry.

### 3.1   Threat Model

In our threat model, the attacker waits until the victim leaves the laptop or a smartphone unattended. This could be the case when the user texts someone, googles something or visits a website and then leaves the device. To ensure optimal but realistic conditions, we assume the user's only interaction was to enter the text. The attacker then captures the thermal image and visually inspects.

### 3.2   Phase 1: Thermal Images Collection

To collect thermal images to be used in the analysis of thermal attacks, we recorded thermal images of a laptop and a smartphone after participants entered text with different characteristics. We studied five categories of text:

**Category 1: Short** average length of $4 \pm 1$ characters and no duplicates.

**Category 2: Duplicates** short words with average length $4 \pm 1$ characters and include duplicates.

**Category 3: Websites** RootDomains (domain name and Top level Domain)[5] with average length $9 \pm 2$. The websites were chosen from the 50 most visited websites [6] and included one duplicate letter.

**Category 4: Complex** medium length inputs with special characters of an average length of 8 characters and no duplicates. We generated those using a password generator [4].

**Category 5: Passphrase** a passphrase is a password in the form of a phrase e.g., aMooseSendsAgoal. The idea behind passphrases is that they are long yet easy to remember by users [18]. The passphrases were chosen from a passphrase generator [3] with an average length of $20 \pm 2$ and includes three duplicate letters.

*Participants, Apparatus, and Setup.* We recruited 25 participants (16 males, 9 females) using a mailing list. Their ages varied between 18 to 23

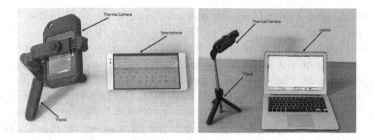

**Fig. 1.** The thermal images collection setup showing the input device, and the thermal camera placed on a tripod placed 30 cm away from the device.

($M = 21.32$, $SD = 1.14$). Only one participant was left-handed and none of the participants had experience with thermal cameras. We used a Flir C2 Camera [2] thermal camera with resolution (80 px × 60 px). The camera was mounted on a 25 cm high tripod placed 30 cm away from the device (see Fig. 1). Input was provided on a Lenovo Tango Phab 2 Pro smartphone with a gorilla glass screen (1440 px × 2560 px) pixels, and a MacBook Air Laptop (1440 px × 900 px).

***Study Procedure.*** After arriving at our lab, participants signed a consent form and provided their demographics data. Participants were asked not to exert physical activity before arriving in the lab including taking the stairs lest it impacts their body temperature. Participants were asked to remove any metal objects in their hand as well as gloves. To let the participants familiarize themselves with the keyboards, they were asked to enter random text 3 times, then the experiment started. Participants provided text input based on a predefined list which covered the 5 aforementioned categories. Our web interface displayed the text input to be entered. Participants were asked to wait one minute in-between each two text entries to make sure heat trackers had decayed, and the thermal image was taken 4 s after entry. These decisions were inspired by prior work on thermal attacks [8]. Each participant entered a total of 40 entries (4 per category, half on the laptop and the other half on the smartphone). The room temperature was kept the same throughout the study 24 °C.

### 3.3 Phase 2: Thermal Attacks

The aim of this phase was to measure the success of thermal attacks by visually inspecting the thermal images collected in the previous phase.

***Study Design and Measures.*** This phase followed a within-subjects design and included two independent variables: the input category and the input device. We measured: 1) Levenshtein distance and 2) successful attack rate. The Levenshtein distance is a metric for measuring the difference between two strings and was used to measure how close the attacker's guess is to the original text. The *success rate* is the percentage of attacks that fully recover the full entered input in the correct order from visually inspecting the thermal image. These metrics are recommended by literature [8,9,11,13–15,21].

***Participants and Procedure.*** We invited 20 participants (9 males, 11 females) to our study. Their ages varied from 15 to 29 ($M = 21.85, SD = 3.297$). None of them had participated in phase 1 nor had experience with thermal cameras.

After arriving at the lab, participants were asked to fill in the consent and demographics forms, then were explained the study. We created a questionnaire that included the thermal images collected from the previous phase, and 3 text fields to allow participants to provide up to 3 guesses. Each participant inspected 20 images, 5 for each input device and two for each input category. The images were randomly chosen from our collected dataset and the order was counterbalanced using a Latin square.

## 4    Results

### 4.1    Levenshtein Distance

Figure 2 (left) shows the mean Levenshtein distance per input category and input device. The Levenshtein distance is "The smallest number of insertions, deletions, and substitutions required to change one string or tree into another" [17]. Overall, participants were more successful in guessing the correct characters and positions on the smartphone than on the laptop (shorter Levenshtein distance). This was also proven statistically: a repeated measures ANOVA showed statistical significant effect of device (laptop ($M = 7.85; SD = 1.18$) and smartphone ($M = 6.70; SD = .71$)) on Levenshtein distance ($F_{1,19} = 46.6875, P < .001$).

Overall the Levenshtein distance was shorter on laptops for short and duplicate inputs than for complex, websites, and passphrase inputs. This was also reflected in a repeated measures ANOVA where it showed a statistically significant effect of the input category on the Levenshtein distance ($F_{4,72} = 264.855, P < .001$). Pairwise comparison showed statistical significance between all input categories, short ($M = .97; SD = 1.33$), duplicates ($M = 2.71; SD = 2.47$), complex ($M = 7.85; SD = .24$), website ($M = 6.5; SD = 1.83$) and passphrases ($M = 15.72; SD = .34$), all $P < .001$.

For the laptop, the Levenshtein distance is shorter for short and duplicate inputs. This was also reflected statistically, where a repeated-measures ANOVA revealed a significant main effect of the input category on the Levenshtein distance ($F_{4,72} = 264.855, P < .001$). Pairwise comparison with Bonferroni correction showed statistical significance between all input categories, short input ($M = .28; SD = .61$), duplicates ($M = 2.71; SD = 2.47$), complex ($M = 7.53; SD = .72$), websites ($M = 10.18; SD = 3.5$), passphrases ($M = 18.71; SD = 1.18$), all $P < .05$.

On the smartphone, the same behavior was noticed where the Levenshtein distance was also shorter for short and duplicates input categories. A repeated-measures ANOVA revealed a significant main effect of the input category on the Levenshtein distance ($F_{4,72} = 409.246, P < .001$). Pairwise comparison with Bonferroni correction showed statistical significance between all input categories, short input ($M = .28; SD = .6$), duplicates ($M = 2.55; SD = 1.73$), complex ($M = 10.25; SD = 3.43$), websites ($M = 7.5; SD = .71$), passphrases ($M =

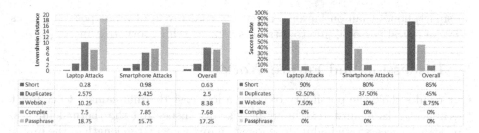

**Fig. 2.** The Levenshtein Distance between the attackers' guesses and the original input (left) – shorter bars represent smaller differences between the guessed and the actual input – and the attack success rate (right). Passphrases and complex input are significantly more secure than short inputs, words with duplicated and websites. Attacks are more successful on the laptop than on the smartphone.

18.72; $SD = 1.16$), all $P < .001$. This means that guesses against short input are significantly closer to the correct input than those against all other categories.

## 4.2   Success Rate

Figure 2 (right) shows the overall success rate of all input categories. As seen, the success rate is higher on laptops than on the smartphone. This was also statistically significant as found by a repeated-measures ANOVA where the input interface (laptop ($M = 30; SD = 11.23$) and smartphone ($M = 22.50; SD = 15.52$)) have a significant effect on the success rate of the attack $F_{1,19} = 7.703, P = .012$. The figure also shows that short and duplicate inputs are the most vulnerable.

Success rate in case of attacks against input on the laptop was the highest for short inputs. A repeated measures ANOVA showed a statistically significant effect of the input category on the success rate of attacks against input on the laptop ($F_{4,72} = 56.410, P < .001$). Pairwise comparison with Bonferroni-correction showed statistical significance for the success rate between all pairs of the following input categories: short ($M = 90; SD = 20.51$), duplicates ($M = 50; SD = 37.28$), website ($M = 7.5; SD = 24.47$), $P < .001$. There was 0% success rate against complex and passphrases inputs.

The same patterns were also found for attacks against input on smartphone, where the attack success rate was higher for short, duplicates and website inputs. A repeated-measures ANOVA revealed a significant main effect of the input category on the attack success rate against input on the smartphone ($F_{4,72} = 33.921, P < .001$). Pairwise comparison showed statistical significance for all pairs of input categories: short input ($M = 80; SD = 29.91$), duplicates ($M = 34.21; SD = 41$), websites ($M = 10; SD = 26.15$), $P < .001$. Attacks against passphrases and complex inputs were never successful (0% success).

The results suggest that attackers can guess many parts of all input categories, but are less likely to guess the entire string. This is particularly clear in attacks against laptops, as the success rate against laptops is higher than against smartphones, but on average the guesses seem to be closer to the original text on smartphones than on laptops. Even a partial reveal of input poses a risk as this can reveal personal info to attackers e.g., search history, text messages, etc.

## 5  Discussion and Future Work

Our results show the possibility of using a low-cost thermal camera to conduct thermal attacks against text input by visually inspecting the thermal images. The attack success rate highly depends on many aspects, the length of the input, the characters entered, and the victim's hand and device temperature.

**Lesson 1: Passphrases and Complex Entries are Less Vulnerable to Thermal Attacks.** We found that attacks were more successful on short words and words with duplicates rather than websites, long sentences and complex combinations of letters. This is likely because the longer length of the input results in longer entry time, which means that by the time the attacker takes a thermal image, the heat traces resulting from entering the first characters will have decayed. In the case of duplicates, the overlapping heat traces made identifying the input more challenging. This can be seen in the successful attack percentage of 53% for duplicates and 90% for short input. For medium input length represented in websites and complex combinations of letters, we found that attacks were significantly more successful against website inputs than against complex input. In case of complex entries, the need to press the shift button first and then select the uppercase, special characters or even a number adds more heat traces that distract the attacker. In case of passwords, this means passwords with special characters or duplicates are less likely to be vulnerable to thermal attacks than those without. This also applies when users choose a passphrase for their password as its length alone sufficiently reduces the thermal attack risk.

Therefore, to protect from thermal attacks, we recommend users to use long passwords and/or complex entries. The fact that these two types of input are resilient to thermal attacks is positive because users are recommended to use them to protect against other types of attacks (e.g., offline dictionary attacks).

**Lesson 2: Text Input on Laptop Keyboards are more Vulnerable to Thermal Attacks than on Smartphones Touchscreens.** We found that thermal attacks against text input were more successful on laptop keyboards than on smartphone touchscreens. Smartphones' screen is directly attached to the processing unit which means that it may heat up due to CPU usage. This may distort heat traces. On the other hand, laptop's processing unit is rather affecting a relatively smaller area of the keyboard, leaving heat traces on the rest of the keyboard unaffected and potentially more visible (see Fig. 3). This correlates with the literature where thermal attacks on passwords entered on external keyboards were 80% successful [12]. Another reason for the ineffectiveness of thermal attacks on smartphone keyboards is that the soft keys are too close to each other, which makes it more likely for the attacker to mix nearby keys.

In a study on thermal attacks against graphical passwords by Abdrabou et al. [8], they found that entering graphical passwords on laptops using their

**Fig. 3.** Thermal images for (Left) Laptop keyboard with visible heat traces. (Right) Touch screen smartphone with less visible heat traces due to device temperature.

touchpads is more secure against visual inspection thermal attacks compared to when entering them on smartphone touchscreens. This attributed to the fact that entering graphical passwords on touchpads requires first navigating to the initial point, which distorts the heat traces. This does not contradict our results. In a nutshell, previous work [8] shows that entering *graphical passwords* is more secure on touchpads of laptops than on smartphones, whereas we show that entering *text* is less secure on laptop keyboards compared to smartphones.

**Lesson 3: Victim and Device Temperature Affects the Success of the Thermal Attack.** We found a statistically significant difference between the temperatures of user's hand the device temperature. This means having colder or warmer hand temperature affects the thermal attack success. This suggests that holding hot or cold objects shortly before typing impacts the user's vulnerability to thermal attacks. For future work, we suggest running an uncontrolled study where thermal images are collected from interfaces after users have interacted in everyday conditions e.g., after exercising, holding hot/cold drinks, etc.

## 6   Conclusion

In this work, we investigated the possibility of attacking user text input on laptop keyboards and touchscreens of smartphones using a thermal camera. We collected a dataset of thermal images of a smartphone's touchscreen and a laptop's keyboard after participants entered different text input categories varying in length and complexity (e.g. some including special characters). In a second study, 20 participants visually inspected the thermal images to infer the input text. We found a significant effect of Input characteristics on vulnerability to thermal attacks. We also found that attacks are more successful on laptop keyboards than smartphone touchscreens due to the high temperature of the smartphone device. We showed that even if the success rate is not high in the case of long and complex input, the Levenshtein distance showed that attackers were still able to detect different parts of the input text but not enough to make the attacks successful. We concluded with three main learned lessons.

**Acknowledgments.** This work was supported by the Royal Society of Edinburgh (RSE award number 65040), and the EPSRC (EP/V008870/1).

# References

1. Affordable thermal camera on amazon. https://www.amazon.co.uk/dp/B07CMD CZGV/. Accessed 13 Apr 2021
2. Flir c2 (2021). http://www.flir.eu/instruments/c2/. Accessed 13 Apr 2021
3. Make me a password. (2021). https://makemeapassword.ligos.net/. Accessed 13 Apr 2021
4. Online password generator (2021). https://passwordsgenerator.net. Accessed 13 Apr 2021
5. Rootdomains (2021). https://moz.com/learn/seo/domain. Accessed 13 Apr 2021
6. Top 50 most visited websites (2021). https://www.alexa.com/topsites. Accessed 13 Apr 2021
7. Abdelrahman, Y., Khamis, M., Schneegass, S., Alt, F.: Stay cool! understanding thermal attacks on mobile-based user authentication, pp. 3751–3763. Association for Computing Machinery, New York (2017). https://doi.org/10.1145/3025453. 3025461
8. Abdrabou, Y., Abdelrahman, Y., Ayman, A., Elmougy, A., Khamis, M.: Are thermal attacks ubiquitous? When non-expert attackers use off the shelf thermal cameras. In: Proceedings of the International Conference on Advanced Visual Interfaces. AVI 2020, Association for Computing Machinery, New York (2020). https:// doi.org/10.1145/3399715.3399819
9. De Luca, A., von Zezschwitz, E., Pichler, L., Hussmann, H.: Using fake cursors to secure on-screen password entry, pp. 2399–2402. Association for Computing Machinery, New York (2013). https://doi.org/10.1145/2470654.2481331
10. Eiband, M., Khamis, M., von Zezschwitz, E., Hussmann, H., Alt, F.: Understanding shoulder surfing in the wild: stories from users and observers, pp. 4254–4265. Association for Computing Machinery, New York (2017). https://doi.org/10.1145/ 3025453.3025636
11. George, C., Khamis, M., Buschek, D., Hussmann, H.: Investigating the third dimension for authentication in immersive virtual reality and in the real world. In: 2019 IEEE Conference on Virtual Reality and 3D User Interfaces (VR), pp. 277–285 (2019). https://doi.org/10.1109/VR.2019.8797862
12. Kaczmarek, T., Ozturk, E., Tsudik, G.: Thermanator: thermal residue-based post factum attacks on keyboard data entry. In: Proceedings of the 2019 ACM Asia Conference on Computer and Communications Security, pp. 586–593. Asia CCS 2019, Association for Computing Machinery, New York (2019). https://doi.org/10. 1145/3321705.3329846
13. Katsini, C., Abdrabou, Y., Raptis, G.E., Khamis, M., Alt, F.: The role of eye gaze in security and privacy applications: survey and future hci research directions. In: Proceedings of the 2020 CHI Conference on Human Factors in Computing Systems, pp. 1–21. CHI 2020, Association for Computing Machinery, New York (2020). https://doi.org/10.1145/3313831.3376840
14. Khamis, M., Alt, F., Hassib, M., von Zezschwitz, E., Hasholzner, R., Bulling, A.: Gazetouchpass: multimodal authentication using gaze and touch on mobile devices. In: Proceedings of the 2016 CHI Conference Extended Abstracts on Human Factors in Computing Systems, pp. 2156–2164. CHI EA 2016, Association for Computing Machinery, New York (2016). https://doi.org/10.1145/2851581.2892314
15. Mathis, F., Williamson, J.H., Vaniea, K., Khamis, M.: Fast and secure authentication in virtual reality using coordinated 3D manipulation and pointing. ACM Trans. Comput.-Hum. Interact. **28**(1) (2021). https://doi.org/10.1145/3428121

16. Mowery, K., Meiklejohn, S., Savage, S.: In: Heat of the moment: characterizing the efficacy of thermal camera-based attacks, p. 6. WOOT 2011. USENIX Association, USA (2011)

17. Navarro, G.: A guided tour to approximate string matching. ACM Comput. Surv. **33**(1), 31–88 (2001). https://doi.org/10.1145/375360.375365

18. Porter, S.N.: A password extension for improved human factors. Comput. Secur. **1**(1), 54–56 (1982)

19. Wodo, W., Hanzlik, L.: Thermal imaging attacks on keypad security systems. In: SECRYPT, pp. 458–464 (2016)

20. Zalewski, M.: Cracking safes with thermal imaging. ser (2005). http://lcamtuf. coredump.cx/tsafe

21. von Zezschwitz, E., De Luca, A., Hussmann, H.: Survival of the shortest: a retrospective analysis of influencing factors on password composition. In: Kotzé, P., Marsden, G., Lindgaard, G., Wesson, J., Winckler, M. (eds.) INTERACT 2013. LNCS, vol. 8119, pp. 460–467. Springer, Heidelberg (2013). https://doi.org/10. 1007/978-3-642-40477-1_28

# Understanding Insider Attacks in Personalized Picture Password Schemes

Argyris Constantinides[1,2(✉)], Marios Belk[1,3], Christos Fidas[4],
and Andreas Pitsillides[1]

[1] Department of Computer Science, University of Cyprus, Nicosia, Cyprus
{aconst12,cspitsil}@cs.ucy.ac.cy
[2] Cognitive UX LTD, Nicosia, Cyprus
argyris@cognitiveux.com
[3] Cognitive UX GmbH, Heidelberg, Germany
belk@cognitiveux.de
[4] Department of Electrical and Computer Engineering, University of Patras, Patras, Greece
fidas@upatras.gr

**Abstract.** Picture passwords, which require users to complete a picture-based task to login, are increasingly being embraced by researchers as they offer a better tradeoff between security and memorability. Recent works proposed the use of personalized familiar pictures, which are bootstrapped to the users' prior socio-cultural activities and experiences. However, such personalized approaches might entail guessing vulnerabilities by people close to the user (*e.g.*, family members, acquaintances) with whom they share common experiences within the depicted familiar sceneries. To shed light on this aspect, we conducted a controlled in-lab eye-tracking user study ($n = 18$) focusing on human attack vulnerabilities among people sharing common sociocultural experiences. Results revealed that insider attackers, who share common experiences with the legitimate users, can easily identify regions of their selected secrets. The extra knowledge possessed by people close to the user was also reflected on their visual behavior during the human attack phase. Such findings can drive the design of assistive security mechanisms within personalized picture password schemes.

**Keywords:** Picture passwords · Security · Eye-tracking · User study

## 1 Introduction

Computer security systems encompass concepts and methods for the protection of sensitive information. In this context, user authentication is an essential security task performed daily by millions of users. Traditional solutions employ text-based passwords, which require users to memorize a sequence of alphanumeric characters. However, memorizing strong text-based passwords results in increased cognitive load and often leads to poor usability and limited security [1]. To offer a better tradeoff between security and

© IFIP International Federation for Information Processing 2021
Published by Springer Nature Switzerland AG 2021
C. Ardito et al. (Eds.): INTERACT 2021, LNCS 12935, pp. 722–731, 2021.
https://doi.org/10.1007/978-3-030-85610-6_42

usability, prior works proposed various picture password schemes [3], which require users to complete a picture-based task to authenticate.

An important interface design factor that affects both the security [4, 5, 7] and usability [9–11, 13] of picture password schemes is the background picture(s) used [4, 5, 15]. Several studies have investigated various picture content types, which can be broadly categorized as *generic* (*i.e.*, not familiar to the users, *e.g.*, stock, landscapes, abstract, etc.) and personal (*i.e.*, highly familiar to the users, *e.g.*, depicting scenes, people, or objects highly familiar to users), and reported their effects on the security and memorability of the user-chosen picture passwords. In particular, the use of generic pictures impacts negatively both the security and memorability of picture passwords [4, 15], while the use of personal pictures impacts negatively the security but leads to increased memorability of picture passwords [15, 16]. In an attempt to achieve a better tradeoff between security and memorability, more recent works investigated and proposed the use of personalized familiar pictures, which are bootstrapped to the users' prior sociocultural activities, experiences and explicit memories [18, 19, 34, 35], revealing a positive impact on the security without hampering the memorability of picture passwords [18, 19]. Nevertheless, such personalized picture delivery approaches might be susceptible to attacks performed by insiders [21, 22] (*i.e.*, people close to the user, such as, family members, acquaintances) with whom they share common experiences within the depicted familiar pictures.

Given that the process of picture password authentication is a visual search task, eye-tracking technology could be used to shed light on how a legitimate user's gaze path relates to an insider attacker's gaze path, and eventually infer whether the person attempting to login is a legitimate user or an insider attacker close to the legitimate user. While attempts have been made towards improving and estimating the security of authentication schemes using eye-tracking technology [15, 23–25, 27, 28], to the best of the authors' knowledge, no research attempts have been made to estimate the legitimacy of the user authenticating in a personalized picture password scheme that leverages on users' prior sociocultural activities, experiences and explicit memories. This work presents the initial findings of applying an eye gaze-driven metric for unobtrusively estimating the legitimacy of the person authenticating in a personalized picture password scheme by analyzing the users' eye gaze behavior during login.

## 2  Related Work

### 2.1  Picture Content in Picture Passwords

Prior works investigated the use of picture semantics and their effects on the security and memorability of user-chosen picture passwords. Pictures can be broadly categorized as generic (*i.e.*, not directly relevant nor familiar to the users, *e.g.*, abstract, nature, landscapes, etc.) or personal (*i.e.*, directly relevant and highly familiar to the users, *e.g.*, depicting people, objects, or scenes highly personal to users). The use of generic picture content has a negative impact on both the security and memorability of the user-chosen passwords. Studies in [4, 15] revealed that various generic pictures are susceptible to hotspots (*i.e.*, certain points on a picture that are more likely to be selected by users), which leads to the creation of predictable passwords that are prone to automated attacks [30]. From the memorability perspective, generic picture content leads to decreased memorability since users experience difficulties in creating strong connections between their episodic memories and the depicted content [16, 31]. The use of personal picture content also impacts the security and memorability of picture passwords. From the security perspective, the use of pictures that are familiar to the user increases the likelihood of certain areas on the picture to be chosen as part of the password [15]. However, from the memorability perspective, the use of personal pictures leads to increased memorability possibly due to familiarity of users with the depicted picture content [16]. More recent works investigated the use of personalized familiar pictures, which are bootstrapped to the users' prior sociocultural activities, experiences and explicit memories, revealing a positive impact on the security without hampering the memorability of picture passwords [18, 19].

## 2.2 Eye Gaze in User Authentication

Eye-tracking technology has been widely used in the context of user authentication. Darrell and Duchowski [23] proposed a rotary interface for gaze-based PIN code entry during user authentication, while Bulling et al. [15] proposed to hide potential picture hotspots using saliency maps. A study conducted by Sluganovic et al. [27] revealed that the reflexive physiological behavior of human eyes can be used to build fast and reliable biometric authentication systems. More recent works employed eye gaze data for predicting image content familiarity in picture password schemes [36], as well as for understanding how individuals make their picture password selections [26]. Moreover, works in [24, 28] proposed eye gaze-driven security metrics for estimating the strength of picture passwords.

## 3 Eye-Tracking Study

Bearing in mind that when using the personalized picture password approach, the password selections are based on the users' existing sociocultural experiences, it is probable that such personalized approaches might be susceptible to attacks performed by insiders [21, 22] (*i.e.*, people close to the user, such as, family members, acquaintances) with whom they share common experiences. In order to shed light on this aspect, we conducted an in-lab eye-tracking human attack study focusing on attacks performed by insiders among people sharing common sociocultural experiences. Each session of the study embraced pairs of participants that were closely related (*e.g.*, friends, couples, relatives, etc.) and who shared common experiences. In each session, both participants were first requested to create a picture password, and then each participant was requested to guess the password selections of the other participant.

### 3.1 Research Question

*RQ.* Is there a significant difference in users' visual behavior between legitimate users and insider attackers when authenticating in a picture password scheme that employs personalized picture content?

**Fig. 1.** A subset of pictures used in the human attack study illustrating sceneries in which participants share common experiences.

### 3.2 Study Instruments and Metrics

**Picture Password Authentication Scheme.** We implemented a Web-based picture password scheme, similar to Windows 10™ PGA [32], in which users can create picture passwords consisting of three gestures (any combination of taps, lines, and circles). The picture is divided in a grid containing 100 segments on the longest side and scaled accordingly on the shortest side. The mechanism allows for a tolerance distance in terms of the coordinates on the grid (36 segments around each initial selected segment are acceptable[1] [13], thus, building a circle of 3 segments radius). This tolerance allows for better accuracy of users' selections during login. However, there is no tolerance regarding ordering, type, and directionality of the gestures.

**Picture Content.** To control participants' sociocultural familiarity with the picture semantics and thus investigate the research question, we adjusted the picture semantics to reflect participants' shared, individual and common sociocultural experiences from their daily life context (*i.e.*, working places in the case of colleagues, café/bars in which couples or close friends usually hang out, etc.), as depicted in Fig. 1. For doing so, prior to the study, we asked each pair of participants to provide a set of pictures from places in which they share common experiences. To avoid bias effects, we did not inform the participants about the reason they were providing us the pictures until the end of the study. The sets of pictures were based on existing research that has shown that users tend to select pictures illustrating sceneries [5, 8, 33].

Considering that the number of hotspots and the picture complexity affect the password strength [6, 13], we chose pictures of similar number of hotspots and complexity. For doing so, we followed a semi-automated approach to detect the hotspots regions through a combination of computer vision techniques for object detection[2,3] and saliency filters [12]. Furthermore, we assessed the equivalence of the two picture sets by calculating the picture complexity using entropy estimators [29].

**Equipment and Eye Gaze Metrics.** An All-in-One HP computer with a 24″ monitor was used (1920 × 1080 pixels, 16:9 aspect ratio). To capture eye movements, we used

---

[1] *Microsoft^{TM} Picture Password blog - bit.ly/2SajCDO.*
[2] *Google Cloud Vision - bit.ly/21xSsUV.*
[3] *Tensorflow - bit.ly/1MWEhkH.*

Gazepoint GP3[4] eye tracker, which captures data at 60 Hz and was calibrated following the manufacturer's guidelines. No equipment was attached to the participants. Following existing approaches for capturing the variability of users' eye movement characteristics within picture password schemes [24, 28], we relied on the gaze transition entropy proposed by Krejtz et al. [14]. In particular, we estimated the stationary entropy $H_s$, which captures the distribution of fixations over the stimulus (*i.e.*, areas of interest (AOIs) in which the eye-tracking metrics are applied). Greater values of $H_s$ occur when the visual attention is distributed more equally among AOIs, while lower values of $H_s$ indicate that fixations tend to be concentrated on certain AOIs. Stationary entropy $H_s$ was conducted using Shannon's entropy equation:

$$H_s(X) = \sum_{i=1}^{N} p_i * log_2\left(\frac{1}{p_i}\right) \tag{1}$$

where $X$ is the set of fixations for each user, $N$ is the number of the available AOIs, and $p$ is the probability of a user to fixate on AOI $i$. Considering that fixation duration correlates with cognitive processing [17, 20], and that users who exhibit longer fixations on AOIs tend to select them [2], the probability $p_i$ is computed as follows:

$$p_i = \frac{d_i}{N}, \sum_{i=1}^{N} = 1 \tag{2}$$

where $d_i$ is the distribution of $p_i$ across $N$, representing the total fixation duration on AOI $i$. By applying Eq. (2) to Eq. (1), the entropy of fixations is computed as follows:

$$H_s(X) = \sum_{i=1}^{N} \frac{d_i}{N} * log_2(N) \tag{3}$$

$N = 3$: the picture is divided into three vertical AOIs [14].

### 3.3 Sampling and Procedure

**Participants.** A total of 18 individuals (9 females) participated in the study, ranging in age between 25–60 years old ($m = 41.43$, $sd = 11.88$). Since the purpose of this study was to understand whether there are differences between legitimate users' and insiders' visual behavior, we intentionally recruited pairs of participants that are close to each other (3 couples, 3 pairs of close friends, 3 pairs of colleagues). To increase the internal validity of the study, we recruited participants that had no prior experience with picture password authentication mechanisms, as assessed by a post-study interview in order to exclude any participants with prior knowledge on picture passwords.

**Experimental Design and Procedure.** Participation in the study was anonymized to ensure privacy compliance according to the EU General Data Protection Regulation. Participants were informed that the collected data will be analyzed for research purposes

---

[4] *GP3 Eye Tracker - bit.ly/3g8rDWq.*

only. Also, we took all the necessary measures against Covid-19 to ensure the participants' safety. The study was conducted in a quiet lab room with only the researcher present and was split in two phases as follows: *i) Phase A – Password Creation:* Each pair of closely related participants (*e.g.*, friends, couples, colleagues, etc.) visited the laboratory in a pre-scheduled time within the Covid-19 safety regulations. First, the eye calibration process started, and then participants were requested independently to create a picture password by drawing 3 gestures on the picture (any combination of taps, lines, circles) in order to access an online service. To avoid bias effects during *Phase B (Human Guessing Attack)*, each participant created a password on a different picture that depicted places in which they share common experiences; *ii) Phase B – Human Guessing Attack:* We switched the picture of the pairs and each participant was requested to guess the other participant's secrets by indicating 3 areas (*i.e.*, 3 (x, y) segments on the grid) on the picture for which they believe that the other participant made their selections around them. Also, we adopted the think-aloud protocol aiming to elicit whether the rationale behind the attacker's selections is related to the shared memories and experiences with the other participant from the same pair. Finally, both participants completed a questionnaire on demographics.

## 3.4  Analysis of Results

**Visual Behavior Differences Between Legitimate Users and Insider Attackers During Login.** To investigate our *RQ*, we ran a paired-samples t-test with the entropy from Eq. (3) as the dependent variable tested under two different conditions (*i.e.*, during legitimate user login and during insider attacker login). The analysis revealed that insider attackers exhibited higher stationary entropy $H_s$ (8.70 ± 2.02 bits) than legitimate users (1.55 ± 0.78 bits), a statistically significant difference of 7.15 ± 1.24 bits (95% CI, 3.35 to 10.94 bits), $t(8) = 4.04$, $p = .001$. Figure 2 shows the stationary entropy $H_s$ of both legitimate users and insider attackers.

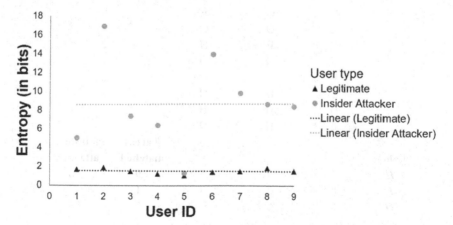

**Fig. 2.** Stationary entropy $H_s$ of both legitimate users and insider attackers.

**Revealing the Insider Attacker's Strategy When Guessing a Picture Password.**
To get further insights about the approach followed by the insider attackers, at the
end of *Phase B (Human Guessing Attack)* we asked each participant to show us the
picture password selections they made on the screen, and we labelled them as either
*H* (Hotspot), *E* (Experience spot; provided by the user), or *O* (Other; non-hotspot,
non-experience spot). In order to understand the similarities in terms of areas correctly
matched on the picture grid between legitimate users' password selections and insider
attackers' guessing selections, we disregarded the order and the type of the gestures and
rather focused on the positions of the password selections as follows: For circles, we
disregarded the radius and the directionality, and kept only the center of the circle as
a (x, y) segment, while for lines, we considered only the (x, y) segment of the starting

**Table 1.** Summarization of the approach followed by the legitimate users and areas correctly
matched by the insider attackers. *H* denotes hotspot selection; *E* denotes experience spot selection;
and *O* denotes other (non-hotspot, non-experience spot) selection. The insider attackers' areas
matched are highlighted in gray color.

| Gesture 1 | Gesture 2 | Gesture 3 | # of insider attacker's areas matched (out of 3) |
|:---:|:---:|:---:|:---:|
| H | E | O | 1 |
| H | O | O | 0 |
| H | O | O | 0 |
| O | O | H | 0 |
| E | H | O | 1 |
| O | H | O | 0 |
| O | O | O | 0 |
| O | O | E | 1 |
| H | H | O | 1 |
| E | H | E | 2 |
| O | O | E | 0 |
| E | O | O | 1 |
| E | E | H | 2 |
| E | O | O | 1 |
| E | E | O | 2 |
| E | H | H | 1 |
| H | H | H | 1 |
| E | H | H | 1 |

| Labels | | | | # areas matched | # insider attackers |
|:---:|:---:|:---:|:---:|:---:|:---:|
| *H* | 5 | 7 | 5 | 0 | 6 |
| *E* | 8 | 3 | 3 | 1 | 9 |
| *O* | 5 | 8 | 10 | 2 | 3 |
| | | | | 3 | 0 |

point of the line. Table 1 summarizes the approach followed by the legitimate users and the areas correctly matched by the insider attackers.

## 4 Conclusions and Future Work

In this work, we conducted a controlled in-lab eye-tracking user study focusing on human attack vulnerabilities among people sharing common sociocultural experiences within personalized picture password schemes. Results revealed that insider attackers who share common experiences with the legitimate users can easily identify regions of their selected secrets, as shown in Table 1. The extra knowledge possessed by people who are close to the legitimate user was also reflected on their visual behavior during the human guessing attack phase. In particular, we found that the insider attackers exhibited higher stationary entropy $H_s$ than the legitimate users. As stated previously, greater values of $H_s$ occur when the visual attention is distributed more equally among AOIs, which might occur in cases of insider attackers who use extra knowledge to guess the user's picture password, while lower values of $H_s$ indicate that fixations tend to be concentrated on certain AOIs, which might occur in cases of legitimate users who know their passwords and make fixations on certain AOIs.

Such findings can be used for the estimation of the legitimacy of the user authenticating in a personalized picture password scheme that leverages on users' prior sociocultural activities, experiences and explicit memories, and drive the design of assistive security mechanisms. We envision that such visual behavior differences in personalized picture password schemes can be used for the creation of multi-class classifiers for predicting the legitimacy of the individual during authentication (*i.e.*, legitimate user, insider attacker, other attacker). Such a classifier will notify the legitimate users about the type of attacker attempting to login to their account, as well as limit the account lockout threshold accordingly (*e.g.*, apply a more strict policy in cases of insider attackers). Expansion of our research will consider the feasibility of building such a multi-class classifier for predicting the legitimacy of the user authenticating, as well as conducting additional user studies to triangulate findings with diverse user communities and sociocultural experiences.

**Acknowledgements.** The work has been partially supported by the EU Horizon 2020 Grant 826278 "Securing Medical Data in Smart Patient-Centric Healthcare Systems" (Serums), the Research and Innovation Foundation (Project DiversePass: COMPLEMENTARY/0916/0182), and the European project TRUSTID - Intelligent and Continuous Online Student Identity Management for Improving Security and Trust in European Higher Education Institutions (Grant Agreement No: 2020-1-EL01-KA226-HE-094869), which is funded by the European Commission within the Erasmus+ 2020 Programme and the Greek State Scholarships Foundation I.K.Y.

## References

1. Sasse, M.A., Brostoff, S., Weirich, D.: Transforming the 'weakest link'—a human/computer interaction approach to usable and effective security. BT Technol. J. **19**(3), 122–131 (2001)

2. Raptis, G.E., Katsini, C., Belk, M., Fidas, C., Samaras, G., Avouris, N.: Using eye gaze data and visual activities to infer human cognitive styles: method and feasibility studies. In: ACM UMAP 2017, pp. 164–173. ACM Press (2017)
3. Biddle, R., Chiasson, S., Van Oorschot, P.C.: Graphical passwords: learning from the first twelve years. ACM Comput. Surv. **44**(4), 41 p. (2012). Article no. 19
4. Thorpe, J., van Oorschot, P.C.: Human-seeded attacks and exploiting hot-spots in graphical passwords. In: USENIX Security Symposium (SS 2007), pp. 1–16 (2007). Article no. 8
5. Alt, F., Schneegass, S., Shirazi, A.S., Hassib, M., Bulling, A.: Graphical passwords in the wild: understanding how users choose pictures and passwords in image-based authentication schemes. In: ACM MobileHCI 2015, pp. 316–322. ACM Press (2015)
6. Wiedenbeck, S., Waters, J., Birget, J.C., Brodskiy, A., Memon, N.: Authentication using graphical passwords: effects of tolerance and image choice. In: Symposium on Usable Privacy and Security (SOUPS 2005), pp. 1–12. ACM Press (2005)
7. Zhao, Z., Ahn, G.J., Seo, J.J., Hu, H.: On the security of picture gesture authentication. In: USENIX Conference on Security (SEC 2013), pp. 383–398 (2013)
8. Zhao, Z., Ahn, G.J., Hu, H.: Picture gesture authentication: empirical analysis, automated attacks, and scheme evaluation. In: ACM TISSEC 2015, vol. 17, no. 4, pp. 1–37 (2015)
9. Mihajlov, M., Jerman-Blažič, B., Ciunova Shuleska, A.: Why that picture? Discovering password properties in recognition-based graphical authentication. Elsevier IJHCS **32**(12), 975–988 (2016)
10. Mihajlov, M., Jerman-Blažič, B.: On designing usable and secure recognition-based graphical authentication mechanisms. Interact. Comput. **23**(6), 582–593 (2011)
11. Everitt, K.M., Bragin, T., Fogarty, J., Kohno, T.: A comprehensive study of frequency, interference, and training of multiple graphical passwords. In: ACM SIGCHI 2009, pp. 889–898. ACM Press (2009)
12. Perazzi, F., Krähenbühl, P., Pritch, Y., Hornung, A.: Saliency filters: contrast based filtering for salient region detection. In: IEEE Conference on Computer Vision and Pattern Recognition, pp. 733–740. IEEE (2012)
13. Katsini, C., Fidas, C., Raptis, G.E., Belk, M., Samaras, G., Avouris, N.: Influences of human cognition and visual behavior on password strength during picture password composition. In: ACM CHI 2018, pp. 1–14. ACM Press (2018). Paper 87
14. Krejtz, K., et al.: Gaze transition entropy. In: ACM TAP 2015, vol. 13, no. 1, pp. 1–20 (2015)
15. Bulling, A., Alt, F., Schmidt, A.: Increasing the security of gaze-based cued-recall graphical passwords using saliency masks. In: ACM SIGCHI 2012, pp. 3011–3020. ACM Press (2012)
16. Tullis, T.S., Tedesco, D.P.: Using personal photos as pictorial passwords. In: ACM CHI EA 2005, pp. 1841–1844. ACM Press (2005)
17. Fidas, C., Belk, M., Hadjidemetriou, G., Pitsillides, A.: Influences of mixed reality and human cognition on picture passwords: an eye tracking study. In: Lamas, D., Loizides, F., Nacke, L., Petrie, H., Winckler, M., Zaphiris, P. (eds.) INTERACT 2019. LNCS, vol. 11747, pp. 304–313. Springer, Cham (2019). https://doi.org/10.1007/978-3-030-29384-0_19
18. Constantinides, A., Fidas, C., Belk, M., Pietron, A., Han, T., Pitsillides, A.: From hot-spots towards experience-spots: leveraging on users' sociocultural experiences to enhance security in cued-recall graphical authentication. Elsevier IJHCS **149** (2021). 102602
19. Constantinides, A., Pietron, A., Belk, M., Fidas, C., Han, T., Pitsillides, A.: A cross-cultural perspective for personalizing picture passwords. In: ACM UMAP 2020, pp. 43–52. ACM Press (2020)
20. Irwin, D.E.: Fixation location and fixation duration as indices of cognitive processing. In: Henderson, J.M., Ferreira, F. (eds.) The Interface of Language, Vision, and Action: Eye Movements and the Visual World, pp. 105–133. Psychology Press, London (2004)

21. Aljahdali, H.M., Poet, R.: Educated guessing attacks on culturally familiar graphical passwords using personal information on social networks. In: ACM SIN 2014, pp. 272–278. ACM Press (2014)
22. Muslukhov, I., Boshmaf, Y., Kuo, C., Lester, J., Beznosov, K.: Know your enemy: the risk of unauthorized access in smartphones by insiders. In: ACM MobileHCI 2013, pp. 271–280. ACM Press (2013)
23. Best, D.S., Duchowski, A.T.: A rotary dial for gaze-based PIN entry. In: ACM ETRA 2016, pp. 69–76. ACM Press (2016)
24. Katsini, C., Raptis, G.E., Fidas, C., Avouris, N.: Towards gaze-based quantification of the security of graphical authentication schemes. In: ACM ETRA 2018, 5 p. ACM Press (2018). Article 17
25. De Luca, A., Denzel, M., Hussmann, H.: Look into my eyes!: can you guess my password?. In: ACM SOUPS 2009, 12 p. ACM Press (2009). Article 7
26. Constantinides, A., Fidas, C., Belk, M., Pitsillides, A.: "I recall this picture": understanding picture password selections based on users' sociocultural experiences. In: IEEE/WIC/ACM WI 2019, pp. 408–412. ACM Press (2019)
27. Sluganovic, I., Roeschlin, M., Rasmussen, K.B., Martinovic, I.: Using reflexive eye movements for fast challenge-response authentication. In: ACM SIGSAC CCS 2016, pp. 1056–1067. ACM Press (2016)
28. Constantinides, A., Belk, M., Fidas, C., Pitsillides, A.: An eye gaze-driven metric for estimating the strength of graphical passwords based on image hotspots. In: ACM IUI 2020, pp. 33–37. ACM Press (2020)
29. Cardaci, M., Di Gesù, V., Petrou, M., Tabacchi, M.E.: A fuzzy approach to the evaluation of image complexity. Fuzzy Sets Syst. 160(10), 1474–1484 (2009)
30. Salehi-Abari, A., Thorpe, J., Van Oorschot, P.C.: On purely automated attacks and click-based graphical passwords. In: IEEE ACSAC 2008, pp. 111–120 (2008)
31. Renaud, K.: On user involvement in production of images used in visual authentication. J. Vis. Lang. Comput. 20(1), 1–15 (2009)
32. Johnson, J.J., et al.: Picture gesture authentication (2014). https://www.google.com/patents/US8910253. Accessed 10 June 2021
33. Dunphy, P., Yan, J.: Do background images improve "draw a secret" graphical passwords?. In: ACM CCS 2007, pp. 36–47. ACM Press (2007)
34. Constantinides, A., Belk, M., Fidas, C., Samaras, G.: On cultural-centered graphical passwords: leveraging on users' cultural experiences for improving password memorability. In: ACM UMAP 2018, pp. 245–249. ACM Press (2018)
35. Constantinides, A., Fidas, C., Belk, M., Samaras, G.: On sociocultural-centered graphical passwords: an initial framework. In: ACM MobileHCI 2018 Adjunct, pp. 277–284. ACM Press (2018)
36. Constantinides, A., Belk, M., Fidas, C., Pitsillides, A.: On the accuracy of eye gaze-driven classifiers for predicting image content familiarity in graphical passwords. In: ACM UMAP 2019, pp. 201–205. ACM Press (2019)

# Visuals Triumph in a Curious Case of Privacy Policy

Shree Nivas, C. J. Gokul[✉], Vijayanand Banahatti, and Sachin Lodha

TCS Research - Tata Consultancy Services, Pune, Maharashtra, India
{shree.nivas,gokul.cj,vijayanand.banahatti,sachin.lodha}@tcs.com

**Abstract.** A privacy policy statement discloses the practices carried out by an organization to gather, use, and share users' data. Previous studies have shown concern of users about understanding the content of privacy policies due to its textual format that has remained an open challenge because of complexity, verbosity, and legal jargon. Video format is proven to have higher impact on engagement and comprehensibility compared to other formats in domains such as education and entertainment. This study focuses on using video as a tool to represent online text-based privacy policies. We created modular animated video-based policies of two different organizations and compared them with their textual counterparts. The results were evaluated in terms of duration and accuracy to comprehend the content of both formats. Our findings suggest that animated video privacy policies have a significant effect on user engagement, delivery of content, and comprehensibility of information.

**Keywords:** Privacy policy · Cyber security · Videos · Security · Communication

## 1 Introduction

Effective communication of online privacy policies has remained an open challenge, primarily due to the fact that they do not convey information in a way understandable to most Internet users. The language used does not communicate information which is easy to understand by most of the end users [29]. Further, the need (or greed) to consume (sometimes apparently free) online services by the end users have resulted in turning a blind eye to the privacy notices. A study conducted by Pew Research in 2014 found that half of the internet users did not know what a privacy policy was [1]. Another experiment using a fictional website with 543 participants was conducted by Michigan State University [22], which showed that over 74% skipped or ignored the privacy policy notices while joining a social network for the first time.

Even those who read privacy policies still struggle to grasp them. Online privacy policies often contain ambiguous language that undermines the purpose and value of

**Electronic supplementary material** The online version of this chapter (https://doi.org/10.1007/978-3-030-85610-6_43) contains supplementary material, which is available to authorized users.

the privacy policies for end users [26]. According to a study [22], in America, if users were to go through all the privacy policies of every site they visit annually, then around 201 h would be spent for reading all the policies. In monetary terms, it would result in a loss of US \$3,534 in revenue per capita for the time spent. It has been noted that the text-based online privacy policy content is much more in comparison to what a user would be willing to read and spend time on [13]. There are more struggles for the end users on the cards as privacy policies are laborious to look at due to text heavy content, time consumption for reading, and difficult to comprehend due to the complex language.

This has now become a more critical issue with the advent of the European Union's much touted General Data Protection Regulation (GDPR) that emphasizes on "privacy by default". While this has forced organizations to reconsider and rewrite their privacy policies, it has been observed that these updated policies contain even more incomplete and ambiguous information flow statements. A recent survey [30] has found that 45% of all pre-GDPR policies and 63% of the post-GDPR policies suffer from this flaw. In addition, the content in both previous and updated versions of privacy policies continue to suffer from "parameter bloating", leading to more verbose text [15]. Studies have shown that post GDPR implementation, there was an average increase in word count of privacy policies of 25.88%. Also, the average change in reading level to comprehend the content increased from 13.6 to 14.1 by 3.68% [27].

Besides that, the language and terms used in the privacy policies obviate the end users from reading large textual content for understanding in context of their requirement. Most policies are written in English at a level suited for college level educated end users, with frequent use of unfamiliar terminologies [3, 10]. For upcoming regions such as India and African countries (for example, Benin, Sierra Leone, Niger, and Mozambique), the rate of Internet penetration has been increasing by more than 20% annually [12, 18]. This includes a vast number of people with only school level education or less. In rural areas, smart phones are becoming the primary means of internet consumption for online services. More and more people are connecting to the internet, but the effectiveness of online privacy documents remains a challenge. Privacy policies often ignore the need for effective design, layout, and visual presentation, leading to decision paralysis [29]. Many studies have stated that reading privacy policies is related to economic proposition and concluded that asymmetric information makes the task of reading them not worthy [2, 28].

Research has been done to convert privacy policy in terms of data visualizations. However, translating a whole privacy statement into a grid that conveyed information using icons did not improve its efficacy [25]. Attempts for creating effective policy through visualizations are still going on using the modeled icons [6] for Privacy, under Creative Commons [5, 8]. CommonTerms tried to resolve this with a standardized view based on review of a large number of available privacy policies and other standardization and iconography work [24]. Iconography and visualizations are not able to convey full information to users. They still require additional access tools such as hover tip for clarifications which further explains what the icon attempts to convey. Kelley et al. [23] were inspired by nutrition labels to design the summary of privacy policies. These privacy labels showed the usage of the users' data on a website in a tabular form. Nutrition labels and privacy icons offered a good starting point, but some questions still remained about their effectiveness. This includes how people would use labels in practice, loss of details while combining multiple categories of policy to make it shorter and prerequisite knowledge of users to interpret icons [21]. These shortcomings motivated us to work on the alternative approach to communicate privacy policy content to end users.

## 2 Our Approach

We selected animation-based video as an alternative for textual privacy policies because of its high engagement and effectiveness in content delivery. Animated video alternative for delivering text-based content raises user motivation, improves communication, and expands potential for deeper understanding of the subject concepts [7]. Cisco's forecast report has stated that videos will soon exceed 80% of the global internet traffic in next few years [11]. As per the reports, countries such as India (with major rural population) are not far behind the leading nations of the world to view online content through videos [12] by means of over the top (OTT) platforms such as YouTube, Netflix and Amazon prime. Videos thus, are a great tool to make content more accessible and inviting to a wider audience. For this study, we analyzed online privacy policies of 15 different organizations as shown in Table 1. These organizations are spread across domains such as e-Commerce, retail, technology, entertainment, banking and finance. We found that majority of the content of these privacy policies can be categorized into distinct sections with similar agendas, and it can be used to create short video assets. Two different privacy policies were selected from retail (Amazon) and Entertainment (Netflix) domains that have more end user interaction, overall popularity, and worldwide recognition.

**Table 1.** Comparative study of privacy policies of different organizations

| Organisation | Domains | Collection of Personal Information | Use of Collected Information | Information Storage and Security | Transparency and Choice | Access Management of Personal Information | Cookies and Other Technologies | Legalities and Disclosure of Information | Third Party Information Sharing | Protection for Children's Data | Changes/Updates to Privacy Policies | Miscellaneous Privacy Related Materials | Contact | Global Operation | Opt in/out of Online Marketing |
|---|---|---|---|---|---|---|---|---|---|---|---|---|---|---|---|
| eBay | eCommerce | ✓ | ✓ | ✓ | ✓ | ✓ | ✓ | ✓ | ✓ | | ✓ | ✓ | ✓ | ✓ | ✓ |
| Netflix | Entertainment | ✓ | ✓ | ✓ | ✓ | ✓ | ✓ | ✓ | ✓ | ✓ | ✓ | ✓ | | | ✓ |
| Amazon | e-Retail | ✓ | ✓ | ✓ | ✓ | ✓ | ✓ | ✓ | ✓ | ✓ | ✓ | ✓ | | | |
| AmEx | Finanacial Services | ✓ | | ✓ | ✓ | ✓ | | | ✓ | | | ✓ | ✓ | ✓ | ✓ |
| CitiBank | Finanacial Services | ✓ | ✓ | ✓ | | ✓ | ✓ | | ✓ | | ✓ | | ✓ | | |
| JP Morgan | Finanacial Services | ✓ | ✓ | ✓ | | ✓ | ✓ | ✓ | ✓ | | ✓ | | | | ✓ |
| Visa | Finanacial Services | ✓ | | | ✓ | ✓ | ✓ | ✓ | ✓ | | | | | | |
| WhatsApp | Messaging | ✓ | ✓ | | | ✓ | ✓ | ✓ | ✓ | | ✓ | | ✓ | ✓ | |
| Walmart | Retail | ✓ | ✓ | ✓ | ✓ | ✓ | | ✓ | | ✓ | ✓ | ✓ | ✓ | ✓ | |
| Facebook | Social Networking | ✓ | ✓ | ✓ | | ✓ | ✓ | ✓ | ✓ | | ✓ | ✓ | | | |
| Instagram | Social Networking | ✓ | ✓ | ✓ | ✓ | ✓ | ✓ | | ✓ | | ✓ | ✓ | | | |
| Twitter | Social Networking | ✓ | ✓ | ✓ | | ✓ | | ✓ | | | ✓ | | | | ✓ |
| Apple Inc | Technology | ✓ | ✓ | ✓ | ✓ | ✓ | ✓ | ✓ | ✓ | ✓ | | ✓ | | | ✓ |
| Google | Technology | ✓ | ✓ | ✓ | ✓ | ✓ | ✓ | ✓ | ✓ | | ✓ | ✓ | ✓ | ✓ | ✓ |
| Microsoft | Technology | ✓ | ✓ | ✓ | ✓ | ✓ | | | | | ✓ | ✓ | | | |

Our approach was to convert each section of Amazon and Netflix privacy policies into individual animated video modules. These modules can then be sequenced according to the textual privacy policies under consideration keeping the content layout similar in both formats. Our video creation process followed the proven guidelines provided in well-established studies [14, 9]. The theme of the videos, including colors, logos and fonts, were kept according to Amazon and Netflix websites' layout to give a familiar impression to the participants while accessing their privacy policies. The flow of the video is similar to that of the text-based privacy policy using animated icons, illustrations, characters, and infographics. For video narration, we selected two people, one male and one female, to do a mixed voice-over. This would help to remove any bias from participants' mind towards the narration and narrow down their focus towards the content. The video is sub-divided into small sections as shown in Table 1. The overall length of Amazon's privacy policy video is 5 min and 14 s and for Netflix, it is 5 min and 46 s. The video covered all the categories of the text-based privacy policy.

Further study involves the comparison of effectiveness of our video-based approach with respect to textual privacy policy. To substantiate the video counterpart, a user study was conducted to compare it with the existing textual privacy policies. The findings are exemplified herein with analysis of correctness and time to answer the survey questions based on the selected privacy policies.

## 3  Comparative Study

For the recruitment of participants, we broadcasted an email within our organization for their voluntary participation. We selected 64 participants from the responses indicating willingness to participate in our study. As stated earlier, most policies are written in English at a level suited for college level educated end users [9]. Therefore, we selected participants with a minimum of post-secondary education where 31.25% were identified having Bachelor's Degree, 59.37% with Master's Degree and 9.37% with PhDs in educational qualification. Participants' ages ranged from 21 to 45 years with 64% identifying as male and the rest as female. These participants were asked to visit our lab for conducting the experiments in a controlled condition. They were divided equally (n = 16 each) into four independent groups, i) Amazon's Text Policy (AT), ii) Amazon's Video Policy (AV), iii) Netflix's Text Policy (NT) and iv) Netflix's Video Policy (NV). We tried to keep the age and gender ratio as similar as possible in each group. All participants were presented with a US $10 gift as an appreciation for their participation.

### 3.1  Data Collection

For our experiment, we created surveys consisting of multiple-choice questions (with more than one correct answer) and pre-post feedback forms. Responses of feedback forms collected from participants were based on Likert scale for psychometric analysis [4]. Following the examination of policy statement language [17, 20] and survey design process [16], questionnaires were created to tap into what the users' value in terms of privacy policies. These questionnaires were reviewed by our policy and legal experts to ensure that it covered all the important aspects of the privacy policy document. The objective of our surveys is twofold, 1) to compare the users' understanding of the content in both text and video-based privacy policies and 2) to evaluate their experience with the two different mediums of delivering privacy policy content. The surveys were divided into four fragments as follows:

- **Part I-Participants' data** *(common for all groups)*. It captured the demographic details of the participants concerning their gender, age group and educational background. We refrained from collecting any Personally Identifiable Information (PII) and kept the participants' data anonymous for a group-level analysis.
- **Part II** *(common for all groups)*. It was a pre-questionnaire feedback form, which consisted of questions with responses based on Likert Scale ratings [4]. It explored the participants' experiences with online privacy notices and policies.
- **Part III.** It consisted of the questionnaire related to all the nine categories mentioned in the Section – *Categorisation of the Contents*. The questions were formed so that each category required a thorough exploration from participants thus making them to go through all the content of privacy policy. It evaluated participants' understanding of the content. Since the length of privacy policy varied across nine sections, there was a difference in total number of questions.

*Questionnaire 1 (Amazon – Participants' Group AT and AV)*: 35 questions in total with an average of 3.88 questions per category.
*Questionnaire 2 (Netflix – Participants' Group NT and NV)*: 30 questions with an average of 3 questions per category.

- **Part IV** *(common for all groups)*. A post-feedback form was provided to capture the experience of participants with the experiment. It also gathered participants' thoughts through comments by asking their opinions on what can be improved in privacy policy document to make it more effective.

For data collection, we chose to opt for printed surveys using pen and paper which would be easier for participants while answering. The text-based policy was provided in printed format whereas a digital screen (laptop) was used for video-based policy under a laboratory setting. Printed survey method was used to eliminate the chances of skipping through the content using search and find. This reduced any possible bias and/or any distractions towards the content.

Time duration for giving responses was measured for analogical inference of the effectiveness of content. Participants could refer back and forth to text or video-based policy while answering the questions. This gave us an overall understanding of the effectiveness of finding information in two different mediums of communication.

### 3.2 Results

Part II of our survey was based on a pre-questionnaire form exploring participants' experiences with online privacy notices and policies. Following were the inferences based on the pre-questionnaire of Part II:

- 62.5% participants have faced the situation at least once where they visited the policy page (directed automatically on the website or clicked by user) but still 87.5% of them skipped reading.
- 73.45% stated that they never read the privacy policy of a website whenever they visited one.

- 81.25% said, they would not read the complete text in case they were presented with a situation to refer to a privacy document.

**Comparison in Terms of Completion Time.** Part III of the survey allowed us to compare the duration and accuracy of the questions answered by the participants with a confidence interval of 95%. The duration of completion of the survey for each participant is measured from the time they receive the questionnaire till they complete and submit the same. Figure 1(a) depicts the comparative analysis of the average time for completing the survey, with error bars.

The average time for completing the questionnaire for full text-based privacy policy of Amazon was 33 min and 8 s. This was reduced to an average of 19 min and 11 s for the video-based survey resulting in around 42.07% reduction from the full text-based policy. For Netflix, average time for completing the questionnaire for full text-based privacy policy was 26 min and 48 s with an average reduction of 32.63% for video-based policy resulting in 18 min and 4 s.

During the study, we provided printed copies of online privacy policy to the participants in text-based policy condition for easy reading, instead of showing it on a digital device. This may have resulted in an increase in completion time for the survey. We can confirm this hypothesis in future studies by providing on-screen (laptop/desktop/mobile) privacy policy for reference instead of printed copy.

**Comparison in Terms of Correctness.** The average correctness score for the Amazon video-based policy (M = 26.062) is increased by 21.57% as compared to textual privacy policy (M = 21.437). A similar trend is observed in case of Netflix with an increase of 22.12% correctness score for video-based version (M = 25.187) to textual policy (M = 20.625). Average scores of the questionnaire based on the privacy document depicted in Fig. 1(b) provided us with positive results for the video-based privacy policy compared to text-based version.

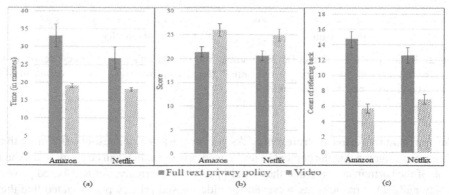

**Fig. 1.** (a) Average time comparison for completing the survey. (b) Average score comparison of text and video survey. (c) Analysis of the count of referring back to text and video. (All error bars at 95% confidence interval)

**Comparison in Terms of Count of Referring Back.** The count of referring back to full-text and video policies while completing the questionnaire was gathered using selective observation technique in a laboratory setting [19]. Analysis of the count for both Amazon and Netflix is shown in Fig. 1(c). For textual version of Amazon's policy document, the count averaged to 14.75 times per participant while for the video it was limited to 6 times per participant resulting in an average reduction of 57.14%. Similarly, for Netflix's textual policy, the average count was 13 times which reduced to 7 times (reduction by 46.15%) for video-based version. This data shows that visual representation of privacy policy content improves comprehensibility with less referring back to the given content.

**Comparison in Terms of Consistency.** The scatter plots shown in Fig. 2(a, b) using Kernel Density Estimation clearly illustrate the fact that the overall responses of participants in the case of video shifted towards the top left part of the graph. This suggests that the participants consumed lesser time, with higher accuracy rate, for answering the questionnaire in case of video-based policies. The plots also show higher dispersion in scores for full-text versions which signifies lower consistency and predictability for full-text privacy policies. The results show that when participants answered the questionnaire using video-based policy, their score increased as compared to text-based policy indicating improved comprehensibility of the content.

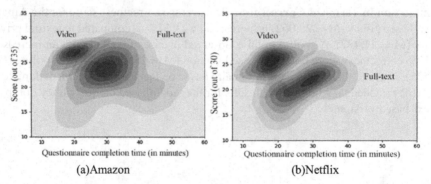

(a)Amazon                    (b)Netflix

**Fig. 2.** Scatter plot using Kernel Density Estimation (a) Amazon's privacy policy: score versus time for full-text and video-based questionnaire (b) Netflix's privacy policy: score versus time for full-text and video-based questionnaire

**Comparison in Terms of Preference.** As per the post survey questionnaire more than 81% people agreed that the content of text-based privacy policy can be shortened. About 97% of the participants said that they would prefer an alternative for text-based privacy policy and all the participants surveyed for video-based privacy policy stated that they would prefer video over text.

**Statistical Analysis.** An independent-samples t-test was conducted to compare time consumed in answering the questionnaire for full-text and video-based policies. Participants who watched the video-based policy (for Amazon M = 19.19, SD = 4.34, for

Netflix M = 18.06, SD = 3.37) compared to the participants who read text-based policy (for Amazon M = 33.12, SD = 7.94, for Netflix M = 26.81, SD = 6.51) consumed significantly lesser time for completing the questionnaire (for Amazon t(23) = 6.15, p = 0.0000014 and for Netflix t(23) = 4.77, p = 0.000041).

Similarly, an independent-samples t-test was conducted to compare score of participants for correctly answering the questionnaire of full-text and video-based policies. Participants who watched the video-based policy (for Amazon M = 26.06, SD = 1.91, for Netflix M = 25, SD = 1.96) compared to the participants who read text-based policy (for Amazon M = 21.44, SD = 4.11, for Netflix M = 20.62, SD = 3.03) demonstrated significantly better scores in the questionnaire (for Amazon t(21) = 4.08, p = 0.00027 and for Netflix t(26) = 4.77, p = 0.000025).

**Comparison in Terms of Accuracy Rate.** In the comparison of video-based policy to text-based policy, we found that greater number of participants scored over 80% in the questionnaire for video policies. Figure 3 depicts distribution of participants' scoring at different levels for both video and text-based policies. For both Amazon and Netflix, the participants' mean percentage scores were higher for video-based policy as compared to textual policy. 87.5% of the participants who were surveyed for video-based policies scored above 70% in the questionnaire. While 66% participants scored below 70% for textual policies. Thus, video policies out-performed text-based policies in terms of percentage scores in the questionnaires.

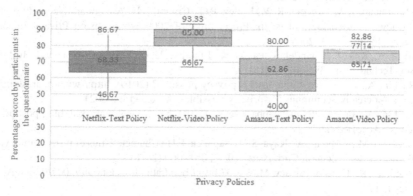

**Fig. 3.** Distribution of participants by percentages scored in different privacy policy formats. Note: percentage scores of participants calculated for Amazon's policy (out of 35 questions) and for Netflix (out of 30 questions)

## 4   Conclusion and Discussion

We studied current textual privacy policies and came up with an alternative way of communicating the privacy policies. Our animated video approach is a step towards visualizing the content of the privacy policy in terms of its comprehensibility, engagement, and reduced time consumption. The data clearly indicates that animated video-based privacy policy influence time consumption and correctness score achieved by participants for answering the questionnaire. This implies higher accuracy and content understanding for video-based policies as compared to textual versions. Animated video privacy policy is not a replacement for the text-based version. Visual representation of the privacy policy acts as an alternative mode of communication to improve the readability of current policies and reduce users' cognitive burden and time for understanding them. Enforcement of GDPR will increase awareness about data rights and privacy education among the internet users. Hence, we need to enhance the efficacy of privacy policy statements and more innovative solutions should be sought to help end users. In future, our aim is to target broader modular design of the video content, which can act as a template for most of the content across multiple privacy statements of different organizations. With reusable assets available from animated video-modules, we can reduce time and efforts for creating new privacy policy videos for different organizations.

# References

1. Smith, A.: Half of online Americans don't know what a privacy policy is; Pew Research Center. http://www.pewresearch.org/fact-tank/2014/12/04/half-of-americans-dont-know-what-a-privacy-policy-is/. Accessed Feb 2021
2. Acquisti, A., Grossklags, J.: Privacy and rationality in individual decision-making. Secur. Privacy Mag. IEEE **3**, 1 (2005)
3. Mc Donald, A.M., Reeder, R.W., Kelley, P.G., Cranor, L.F.: A comparative study of online privacy policies and formats. In: Proceedings of 2009 Workshop on Privacy Enhancing Technologies. ACM (2009)
4. Joshi, A., Kale, S., Chandel, S., Pal, D. K.: Likert scale: explored and explained. Br. J. Appl. Sci. Technol. **7**(4), 396–403 (2015)
5. Raskin, A.: Is creative commons for privacy possible? (2010). http://www.azarask.in/blog/post/is-a-creative-commons-for-privacy-possible/. Accessed Jan 2021
6. Raskin, A.: Privacy Icons: Alpha release (2010).http://www.azarask.in/blog/post/privacy-icons/. Accessed Jan 2021
7. Beheshti, M., Taspolat, A., Kaya, S.O., Sapanca, F.H.: Characteristics of instructional videos. World J. Educ. Technol. Curr. Issues **10**(1), 061–069 (2018)
8. Bendrath, R.: Icons of privacy, May 2007.http://bendrath.blogspot.com/2007/05/icons-of-privacy.html
9. Betrancourt, M., Tversky, B.: Simple animations for organizing diagrams. Int. J. Hum. Comput. Stud. (in press)
10. Jensen, C., Potts, C.: Privacy policies as decision making tools: an evaluation of online privacy notices. In: Proceedings of the SIGCHI Conference on Human Factors in Computing Systems, Vienna, Austria (2004)
11. Cisco Visual Networking Index: Forecasts and Trends (2017–2022). DocID:1543280537836565, https://www.cisco.com/c/en/us/solutions/collateral/service-provider/visual-networking-index-vni/white-paper-c11-741490.html
12. eMarketedu: The Power of Internet and Online in India. https://www.emarketeducation.in/power-internet-penetration-online-india/. Accessed Feb 2021
13. Florian Schaub: Article-nobody reads privacy policies-here's is how to fix that. https://theconversation.com/nobody-reads-privacy-policies-heres-how-to-fix-that-81932. Accessed Jan 2021

14. van der Meij, H., van der Meij, J.: Eight guidelines for the design of instructional videos for software training (2013)
15. Helen, F.: Nissenbaum. Privacy as contextual integrity (2004). https://www.andrew.cmu.edu/user/danupam/bdmn-oakland06.pdf
16. Nunnally, J.: Psychometric Theory. McGraw-Hill, New York (1978)
17. Smith, J., Milberg, S., Burke, S.: Information privacy: measuring individuals' concerns about organizational practices. MIS Q. **20** (1996)
18. Obar, J.A., Oeldorf-Hirsch, A.: The biggest lie on the internet: ignoring the privacy policies and terms of service policies of social networking services. York University, Quello Center, Michigan State University, 7 July 2016
19. Kawulich, B.B.: Participant observation as a data collection method. Forum: Qual. Soc. Res. **6**(2) (2005)
20. Cranor, L., Reagle, J., Ackerman, M.: Beyond concern: understanding net users' attitudes about online privacy. In: Vogelsang, I., Compaine, B.M. (eds.) The Internet Upheaval: Raising Questions, Seeking Answers in Communications Policy. MIT Press, Cambridge (2000)
21. Cranor, L.F.: Necessary but not sufficient: standardized mechanisams for privacy notice and choice. J. Telecommun. High. Technol. Law **10**, 273 (2012)
22. McDonald, A.M., Cranor, L.F.: The cost of reading privacy policies. ISJLP **4**, 543 (2008)
23. Kelley, P.G., Bresee, J., Cranor, L.F., Reeder, R.W.: A "nutrition label" for privacy. In: Proceedings of the 2009 Symposium on Usable Privacy and Security (SOUPS) (2009)
24. Lanner, Pr.: Previewing online terms and conditions: CommonTerms alpha proposal (2012). http://commonterms.net/commontermsalphaproposal.pdf
25. Reeder, R.W., Kelley, P.G. McDonald, A.M., Cranor, L.F.: A user study of the expandable grid applied to P3P privacy policy visualization. In: WPES 2008: Proceedings of the 7th ACM Workshop on Privacy in the Electronic Society, pp. 45–54. ACM (2008)
26. Reidenberg, J.R., Bhatia, J., Breaux, T., Norton, T.: Ambiguity in privacy policies and the impact of regulation (March 22, 2016). J. Legal Stud. Forthcoming; Fordham Law Legal Studies Research Paper No. 2715164. SSRN: https://ssrn.com/abstract=2715164 or https://doi.org/10.2139/ssrn.2715164
27. Sobers, R.: Compliance & regulation. The Average Reading Level of a Privacy Policy.https://www.varonis.com/blog/gdpr-privacy-policy/. Accessed Feb 2021
28. Vila, T., Greenstadt, R., Molnar, D.: Why we cannot be bothered to read privacy policies: models of privacy economics as a lemons market. In: ACM International Conference Proceeding Series 5 (2003)
29. Waldman, A.: Ezra, privacy, notice, and design. Stanford Technol. Law Rev. **47** (2018). https://law.stanford.edu/wp-content/uploads/2018/03/Waldman_Final_031418.pdf. Accessed Feb 2021
30. Shvartzshnaider, Y., Apthorpe, N., Feamster, N., Nissenbaum, H.: Analyzing privacy policies using contextual integrity annotations. arXiv preprint arXiv:1809.02236 (2018)

# Correction to: TactCube: Designing Mobile Interactions with Ambient Intelligence

Pietro Battistoni⊙, Marianna Di Gregorio⊙, Marco Romano⊙,
Monica Sebillo⊙, and Giuliana Vitiello⊙

**Correction to:**
**Chapter "TactCube: Designing Mobile Interactions**
**with Ambient Intelligence" in: C. Ardito et al. (Eds.):**
***Human-Computer Interaction – INTERACT 2021,***
**LNCS 12935, https://doi.org/10.1007/978-3-030-85610-6_34**

In the original version of this book the name of the author "Marianna di Gregorio" was incorrect. This has now been corrected.

---

The updated version of this chapter can be found at
https://doi.org/10.1007/978-3-030-85610-6_34

# Author Index

Abdelrahman, Yomna  712
Abdrabou, Yasmeen  712
Adhikary, Jiban  132
Aldalur, Iñigo  221
Alt, Florian  339
Arif, Hammad  676
Arora, Tanay  476
Arrue, Myriam  373
Atwood, Katrina  405
Avgustis, Iuliia  155
Avouris, Nikolaos  20

Banahatti, Vijayanand  732
Barros, Luísa  211
Battistoni, Pietro  599
Belk, Marios  655, 722
Bell, Beth T.  701
Benvenuti, Dario  298
Bittl, Maria-Lena  339
Bollin, Andreas  630
Bonani, Andrea  630
Bossens, Emilie  433
Bouzekri, Elodie  405
Bowen, Judy  546
Branco, Diogo  211
Buda, Emanuele  298

Catarci, Tiziana  298
Chen, Yuan  29
Constantinides, Argyris  655, 722
Cunin, Dominique  501

Damen, Ida  610
De Pra, Yuri  580
De Russis, Luigi  122
Desolda, Giuseppe  177
Di Gregorio, Marianna  599
Diamond, Lisa  665
Duong, Tu Dinh  262

Elmougy, Amr  712
Espín-Tello, Sandra M.  373

Fidas, Christos  655, 722
Fitton, Dan  701
Fontana, Federico  580
Fraioli, Francesca  298
Fröhlich, Peter  665

Geerts, David  433
Gennari, Rosella  630
Girouard, Audrey  51
Gokul, C. J.  732
Gomes, Ana  211
Goncalves, Jorge  451, 476
Gris, Christine  405
Grisoni, Laurent  557
Gross, Tom  243
Guerreiro, Tiago  211
Guerrero, Alfrancis  51
Guettaf, Adnane  557

Haq, Qutaiba Rohan ul  676
Hassib, Mariam  339
Hatem, Reem  712
Hettiachchi, Danula  476
Hinze, Annika  546
Høegh, Rune Thaarup  320
Hu, Jolan  451
Hußmann, Heinrich  590

Iftikhar, Zainab  676
Iivari, Netta  155
Irani, Pourang  29

Javed, Mobin  676
Jiang, Mengqi  92

Katsi, Eleni  655
Khamis, Mohamed  712
Khan, Taslim Arefin  72
Komatsu, Takanori  100
Koroyasu, Yusuke  3
Kostakos, Vassilis  451
Krämer, Nicole  383
Kunkel, Johannes  383

Lallemand, Carine   610
Lank, Edward   29, 72
Lanzilotti, Rosa   177
Larrinaga, Felix   221
Laurillau, Yann   501
Li, Wei   29, 72
Li, Yanhong   590
Lodha, Sachin   732
Lu, Tianyang   590

Mackenzie, I. Scott   361
Marrella, Andrea   298
Martinie, Célia   405
Matera, Maristella   177
Mayer, Sven   339
Meldgaard, Dorte P.   187
Mizobuchi, Sachi   72
Monge Roffarello, Alberto   122
Mosca, Sara   177
Mueller, Anna-Lena   243

Nagatani, Yoshiki   3
Namikawa, Kosaku   3
Ngo, Thao   383
Niess, Jasmin   262
Nigay, Laurence   501
Nivas, Shree   732

Ochiai, Yoichi   3

Palanque, Philippe   405
Papachristos, Eleftherios   187
Papetti, Stefano   580
Pedersen, Jonna Helene Holm   320
Pereira, Ana   211
Perez, Alain   221
Pérez, J. Eduardo   373
Petsanas, Paraskevas   20
Pietrzak, Thomas   51
Pires, Ana C.   211
Piro, Ludovica   177
Pitsillides, Andreas   655, 722
Plasson, Carole   501
Prange, Sarah   339
Pucci, Emanuele   177

Read, Janet C.   361, 701
Rekik, Yosra   557

Rogers, Yvonne   262
Romano, Marco   599

Sala, Aritz   373
Sandnes, Frode Eika   287
Sardar, Taha   676
Sari, Eunice   361
Schöning, Johannes   262
Sebillo, Monica   599
Shahid, Suleman   676
Shirokov, Aleksandr   155
Simão, Hugo   211
Sintoris, Christos   20
Sirera, Judith   525
Skov, Mikael B.   187
Sørensen, Malene   320
Sousa, Joana   211
Stage, Jan   320
Storms, Elias   433
Sun, Junwei   29
Sun, Xiaohua   92
Sun, Yu   590

Tedjasaputra, Josh (Adi)   361
ten Bhömer, Martijn   92
Thomsen, Iben R.   187

Velloso, Eduardo   525
Vertanen, Keith   132
Vitiello, Giuliana   599
Vos, Steven   610

Wagener, Nadine   262
Wang, Qi   92
Weber, Thomas   590
Wijenayake, Senuri   451

Xu, Qiang   29

Yamanaka, Shota   100
Ye, Ying   92
Yokota, Keisuke   100
Yoshida, Nozomu   3
Younus, Osama   676

Zhang, Futian   72
Zhou, Wei   72
Ziegler, Jürgen   383

Printed in the United States
by Baker & Taylor Publisher Services